THE DOCUMENTARY FILM READER

THE DOCUMENTARY FILM READER

HISTORY, THEORY, CRITICISM

Edited by
JONATHAN KAHANA

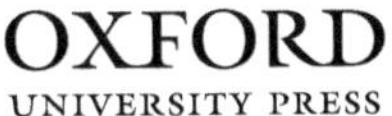

OXFORD
UNIVERSITY PRESS

OXFORD
UNIVERSITY PRESS

Oxford University Press is a department of the University of Oxford. It furthers the University's objective of excellence in research, scholarship, and education by publishing worldwide.

Oxford New York
Auckland Cape Town Dar es Salaam Hong Kong Karachi
Kuala Lumpur Madrid Melbourne Mexico City Nairobi
New Delhi Shanghai Taipei Toronto

With offices in
Argentina Austria Brazil Chile Czech Republic France Greece
Guatemala Hungary Italy Japan Poland Portugal Singapore
South Korea Switzerland Thailand Turkey Ukraine Vietnam

Published in the United States of America by
Oxford University Press
198 Madison Avenue, New York, NY 10016

Library of Congress Cataloging-in-Publication Data
The documentary film reader : history, theory, criticism / edited by Jonathan Kahana.
pages cm
Includes bibliographical references and index.
ISBN 978-0-19-973964-6 (cloth) — ISBN 978-0-19-973965-3 (pbk.) — ISBN 978-0-19-022654-1 (ebook)
1. Documentary films—History and criticism. I. Kahana, Jonathan, 1966—
PN1995.9.D6D5755 2015
070.1′8—dc23
2015013454

CONTENTS

ACKNOWLEDGMENTS

The editorial staff at Oxford University Press who saw this book through from conception to production—Shannon MacLachlan, Stephen Bradley, and, most of all, Brendan O'Neill—have been patient, persistent, and encouraging throughout the process, and I thank them sincerely for their confidence in such a large and complex project. I am also very grateful to Natalie Foster and Jayne Fargnoli for their valuable editorial input at early stages of the project, when it was still looking for a home.

In addition to Oxford University Press, a number of sources provided financial support toward the costs—especially the fees paid to copyright owners, in some cases scandalously high, to reprint previously published works—of producing this volume. For their generosity, I thank the Arts Research Institute in the Division of the Arts at the University of California, Santa Cruz (UCSC); Scott Brandt, Vice Chancellor for Research in the Office of Research at UCSC; the Office of Sponsored Programs at New York University (NYU), through its Research Challenge Fund Emergency Support Program; and the Department of Cinema Studies at NYU, which funded a series of graduate research assistants, including Ian Hetherington, who provided various kinds of help. In the Tamiment Library at NYU, Donna L. Davey and Peter Meyer Filardo provided access to unpublished papers in the Jay Leyda collection.

Among the many scholars, doctoral students, and colleagues who have influenced and contributed to this book, Charlie Musser has my deepest debt of gratitude, for long, formative, and spirited conversations early in the process of forming the table of contents: his impact on my thinking about film history is visible throughout. "Research assistant" is technically correct but too perfunctory a title to fully describe the degree and kind of contributions made to this book by Paul Fileri, who, over several years, suggested, located, reconsidered, and trouble-shot so much of the material collected here that I sometimes thought of him as a co-producer, and equally often as the book's intended user. Blind and non-blind peer reviewers—most thoughtfully, Roger Hallas, Jeffrey Skoller, Charles Wolfe, and several anonymous others—shaped and improved the conception of the book's scope, audience, and function. On various editorial, archival, administrative, and linguistic questions I frequently turned to, and received sage counsel from, colleagues around the office and around the world: Richard Allen, Kees Bakker, Brad Evans, Sandy Flitterman-Lewis, Mick Gidley, Jill Godmilow, Jenny Horne, Dana Polan, Michael Renov, Marita Sturken, Steven Ungar, Tom Waugh, Mark Williams, Tami Williams, Brian Winston, and Arlene Zimmerle. Masha Salazkina spent many hours on the translation of some unpublished Eisenstein notes we decided in the end not to use in this edition. Some of the excellent doctoral students at NYU—including Brady Fletcher, Leo Goldsmith, Anuja Jain, Martin Johnson, Ohad Landesman, Laliv Melamed, Michael Talbott, and Jennifer Zwarich—offered valuable opinions on the material in their particular areas of expertise. Alex Johnston assisted with the selection and production of illustrations. And I am especially grateful to those authors who generously responded to my invitation to rethink sentences originally published years ago. Trust that any cuts we had to make—to those selections, and of the scores of others left on the cutting-room floor—hurt me more than they hurt you.

FOREWORD

In assembling *The Documentary Film Reader: History, Theory, Criticism*, Jonathan Kahana has undertaken an essential but impossible task. Documentary is a dynamic and capacious field that resists easy distillation, and it is hardly surprising that earlier versions of this undertaking had almost twice the number of entries. That Kahana has taken up such a vexing assignment is best understood in light of his previous book-length study, *Intelligence Work: The Politics of American Documentary*. In this impressive investigation, Kahana examined crucial moments in the history of the social issue documentary as a way to interrogate the very nature of documentary itself. He is interested in the process of thinking—of what he calls public intelligence—that is operative both for filmmakers in the making of these documentaries but also by their spectators. As Kahana remarks, "when documentary compels our attention or addresses us in certain ways . . . it evokes forms of public subjectivity and civil interaction that transport viewers beyond the immediate context of viewing."[1] It can impact and destabilize the social imaginary such that "an audience comes to understand itself as an agent of change."[2]

If publics are constructed and addressed by individual films and the critical apparatuses that surround them, more sustained and multi-dimensional publics are often created around groups of documentaries—either cycles of films or specific genres such as the courtroom documentary (from Errol Morris's *The Thin Blue Line* [1988] to, most recently, Alex Gibney's "Death Row Stories" [2014]). Finally, as Kahana has pointed out, the relationship between individual examples and broad generalizations, between individual documentaries and documentary theory, criticism and practice are crucial. Each documentary engages a field of antecedents with varying degrees of originality and transgression. (Errol Morris, for one, has become a proponent of a "fuck you" theory of art, which is certainly evident in his films.[3]) In this regard, *The Documentary Film Reader* performs the critical task of sketching out the ground against which individual films or groups of films can be contextualized and new films measured. With all the necessary qualifications, this collection of essays and documents inevitably proposes a canon of films and texts either as a starting point for further exploration or as a handy reminder of what one figure in this field of study finds particularly significant.

To assemble an anthology such as *The Documentary Film Reader* at this moment, when documentary itself is still absorbing the tremendous impact of the digital revolution, requires a certain audacity. In this regard, Kahana's use of the term "film" in the title is strategic: it limits the reach of his anthology while enabling him to establish many of the contours of American documentary from the early 1900s until almost the present day. Shortly after the debut of projected motion pictures, exhibitors such as E. Burton Holmes began to integrate short films into their illustrated lectures, which displayed a series of lantern slides (projected still photographs). Though they were often labeled travel lectures, these took on a wide range of subjects, as a *Washington Post* review of Holmes's lecture on the Russo-Japanese War, *Port Arthur: Siege and Surrender* (Fall 1905), underscores. Although such programs are certainly in the "documentary tradition," their mode of production and exhibition would make it awkward and ahistorical to label them documentary *sui generis*. Rather, Kahana has gestured towards a long pre-history that in many respects is not a pre-history at all. Indeed, *the documentary tradition* of audio-visual programming goes back to the very origins of the projected moving image in the 1650s and 1660s, when Althanius Kircher and others presented illustrated accounts of the life of Christ. By the second half of the nineteenth century, with the introduction of the stereopticon or optical lantern (a much improved magic lantern that was generally used to show photographic lantern slides), the illustrated lecture had become a rich and respected form of audio-visual communication that required the same kind of intelligence work as later documentaries. The discussion of this mode of programming that quickly incorporated motion pictures gestures towards this longer tradition without having to address it directly.

Correspondingly, *The Documentary Film Reader* effectively concludes with reflections on such American documentaries as Jonathan Caouette's *Tarnation* (2003) and Michael Moore's *Fahrenheit 9/11* (2004). By this period, documentaries were being shot almost exclusively with high definition digital cameras and edited on computers. Nevertheless, a theatrical release still required the transfer from digital to 35mm film. When audiences went to a theater to see a documentary, they were still seeing film even though documentaries were much more likely to be seen on a television screen or projected from VHS or DVD onto a screen in the classroom. Over the last ten years, this practice has disappeared and festivals and theaters now screen digital formats such as Blu-ray, DigiBeta, and DCPs (Digital Cinema Packages). The use of "film" has essentially disappeared, particularly for documentary, but it remains as a term that is deeply embedded in our language. "Film" no longer refers to the physical medium (film stock) but to well-established cultural practices that have been more or less transformed by the possibilities of digital media. The motion picture industry has cleverly introduced the term "digital cinema" to refer to motion pictures designed to be shown in commercial theaters, but the term "digital film" is a contradiction in terms, which practitioners have avoided. Will the term "film" be replaced by some new designation just as the term "documentary" emerged to replace the anachronistic term of "illustrated lecture" some ten to fifteen years after the lecture had been replaced by intertitles? Whatever the future may bring, Kahana's *The Documentary Film Reader* brings us to a point beyond which film *per se* has disappeared.

Documentary as a practice and as a field of scholarly investigation occurs on three levels beyond that of the biographical: the local and regional, the national, and the international. Although grounded in the American tradition, this anthology is global in its reach, and it begins by recognizing that documentary as an emergent formation was an international phenomenon. *Nanook of the North* (1922), which has traditionally been seen as the "first documentary," was made by an American in Canada for French fur company Révillon Frères. Three of documentary's founding members were Europeans who had a major impact in the United States and worldwide: Dziga Vertov (the Soviet Union), Joris Ivens (the Netherlands), John Grierson (Great Britain)

Correspondingly, Robert Flaherty had an international impact, not least of all in the Soviet Union. All four founders are appropriately recognized in these pages.[4]

Of course, if documentary was an international phenomenon, how one has encountered and understood its international presence has always been highly situated. In this respect, this anthology offers a fairly familiar American perspective on what should be included. This documentary tradition from the 1920s to the mid 1960s is overwhelmingly Anglo-American and European. Third World documentary from Cuba and South America began to impact on American practices in the late 1960s. In their search for a transgressive style, the radical Newsreel collectives were inspired by *The Hour of the Furnaces* (1968), made by Argentina filmmakers Octavio Getino and Fernando Solanas, and the short films of Cuban Santiago Alvarez. The fall of the Berlin Wall, the aftermath of the 1989 Tiananmen Square protests and massacre, the death of Ayatollah Khomeini, and the end of the Cold War coincided with an increasing interest in global documentary in the United States. Although this included the important work of Indian filmmaker Anand Patwardhan (*Bombay, Our City*, 1984), Hatian Raoul Peck (*Lumumba: La mort du prophète*, 1990), China's Wu Wenguang (*Bumming in Beijing: The Last Dreamers*, 1990), and Cameroon's Jean-Marie Teno (*Afrique, je te plumerai*, 1992), the interest far exceeded individual auteurs. Courses devoted to Chinese documentary, South Asian documentary and World documentary more generally have become relatively common. In the post–Cold War era, Anglo-Americans' interest in and understanding of documentary practices became fully global in scope, a fact that is made evident by *The Documentary Film Reader*.[5]

Although documentaries shot with Portapaks were occasional being broadcast in the mid-1970s, it was not until the 1990s that the shift to video began to transform the documentary field more broadly.[6] Wu Wenguang's documentaries as well as those of his Chinese colleagues were made possible by camcorders (introduced in the mid-1980s) followed by three-chip video cameras and digital video cameras (introduced around 1995) as well as by video cassettes and later DVDs (ca. 2004) since their films were independently funded and reached Chinese viewers outside formal channels of theatrical exhibition or television broadcast. These innovations did much to make documentary a worldwide, broad-based phenomenon that escaped established gatekeepers whether in Sri Lanka, the Philippines or among indigenous peoples of Peru, Brazil, New Zealand, Canada, and other parts of the world.[7] A reader simply devoted to world documentary after 1989 would be hard-pressed to do the category full justice: Kahana provides us with key signposts for this much larger phenomenon.

Histories of documentary can be—and need to be—constructed on the local and regional level. Celluloid-based film production required labs and a whole series of services from equipment rental houses to mixing studios, and so tended to concentrate documentary production in large metropolitan centers. In some instances, local histories and national histories of documentary have been virtually interchangeable for extended periods—for instance Paris with France, and London with Great Britain. If this sometimes seemed true for New York and the United States, it was for several reasons: New York's place as a cultural capital often posited itself as an alternative to Hollywood commercial imperatives, which documentary also embodied. Not surprisingly, Lewis Jacobs's *The Documentary Tradition: From Nanook to Woodstock* was written from a New York perspective (and the perspective of materials in the Museum of Modern Art's film collection). Los Angeles–area documentary may have flourished in the shadow of Hollywood, but

Hollywood itself gave this mode of filmmaking little attention. One of Kahana's notable achievements has been to avoid these false equations of local with national filmmaking practices; as a result, one must necessarily look elsewhere to understand the ways and reasons for these more localized documentary identities.

As documentary practices have become increasingly robust, local identities have become increasingly important to recognize. Scott MacDonald has devoted a recent book to the Cambridge School of documentary, writing provocatively and insightfully about a community of Boston-area filmmakers who crosses several generations.[8] In this respect, I have found my recent visits to film festivals and local film communities to be particularly illuminating. At the 2014 Big Sky Documentary Film Festival in Missoula, Montana, the American Northwest was admirably represented by an array of strong films such as Anna and Nicholas Hudak's *Where God Likes to Be* (2013) and Suzan Beraza's *Uranium Drive-In* (2013). Amy Benson, president of the Seattle Documentary Film Association who attended the festival, ranked Seattle documentary filmmaking right after New York and Chicago—a view not shared with Scott MacDonald, who places Cambridge firmly in the first position. Regional dynamics are not only an American phenomenon. In the Philippines, the digital era has fostered several localized centers that have situated themselves in opposition to the pervasive Tagalog cinema of greater Manila. Cebuano is the largest language group in the Philippines: digital technologies and emergent film programs at universities in Cebu have played key roles in the renewal and unprecedented vitality of Cebano cinema as evidenced by the 2013 Cebu International Documentary Film Festival. The situation is admittedly complex as Cierlito Tabay's feature *Walay Tumoy na Punterya* (2011), about illegal gunmaking in Cebu, had to be pulled in the midst of an upsurge in local violence while veteran Cebu filmmaker Leonardo Chiu, much of whose earlier work seems to be lost, was only represented by shorts *Voices* and *Vanishing Waste*. In this regard, student work represented the future aspirations of Cebuano documentary. Importantly, Cebuano documentary culture is not only determined by locally-made films. The festival addresses its public through truly global offerings with Asia and Europe represented in its selections far more than North America. In this sense, the festival's programming has consciously reasserted the cosmopolitan nature of Filipino culture in a way that was characteristic of movie-going in that country during the 1910s and before. Its perspective on documentary is very different from what one finds in, say, Thom Powers's DOC NYC festival, or Powers's selections for the documentary program at the Toronto International Film Festival. In the end, all of these festivals remind us of the famous Saul Steinberg *New Yorker* magazine cover "View of the World from Ninth Avenue": our understanding of documentary, its history and styles vary widely depending on the regional orientation of the festival, programmer, writer or teacher.

In his general introduction to this volume, Kahana invites readers to critically engage the collected essays and documents in a process of deconstruction—and so perhaps to reconstruct another selection of texts from it and other sources. One way to think about this challenge is to compare this reader to its most obvious and important predecessor, Jacobs's *The Documentary Tradition* (1971). Certainly there are some interesting and necessary overlaps. Jacob favored post–Second World War New York filmmaking as well as the *cinéma vérité* moment of the 1960s. Kahana has retained some choices, replaced others with updated scholarship, thinned out or dropped other groupings altogether and added important new elements drawn from his own research as well as the state of the field. Of course, Kahana also has had to contend with another 35 to 40 years of documentary history and reflection--essentially a doubling of the time span with which Jacobs contended.[9] One wonders what a documentary film reader will look like some 30 years hence: what will be the creative solutions to an essential but impossible undertaking?

As this book goes to press, the digital has pushed celluloid film as a medium to the most esoteric margins: DuArt (formerly known as DuArt Film & Video), which once processed films for such Academy Award-winning documentaries as *Hearts and Minds* (1974) and *Harlan County, U.S.A.* (1976), has closed its laboratory and has been emptying its film vaults. Eastman Kodak, the world's largest supplier of film stock, went bankrupt early in 2012. High-definition digital filmmaking has changed the nature of documentary, often liberating it in profound ways. The cost of film was always a major impediment to actual filmmaking, for veterans as well as novices. New kinds, indeed all kinds, of documentary have become much more viable. This became particularly evident during the Iraq War when a group of daring, generally young and aspiring filmmakers went to Iraq either to embed with American soldiers or with the civilian population. They produced such documentaries as Michael Tucker's *Gunner Palace* (2004), Garrett Scott and Ian Olds's *Occupation Dreamland* (2005), Andrew Berends's *The Blood of My Brother: A Story of Death in Iraq* (2005) and *When Adnan Came Home* (2006), James Longley's *Iraq in Fragments* (2006), Laura Poitras's *My Country, My Country* (2006), Jon Alpert and Matthew O'Neill's *Baghdad ER* (2006), Petra Epperlein and Michael Tucker's *The Prisoner or: How I Planned to Kill Tony Blair* (2006), and Deborah Scranton's *The War Tapes* (2006).

Those who were making documentaries in the 1970s and 1980s can only find this new world of digital filmmaking to be more efficient and versatile, much cheaper, and emancipatory. The once standard rituals of synching up dailies and coding the picture and sound track are positively antediluvian. No one needs to make title cards or shoot pencil tests on reversal film stock. Gone too are 16mm flatbeds. Hit a few keys using editing programs such as Final Cut Pro and a shot can be slowed down or speeded up, something that used to be done by costly optical houses. The Internet has likewise transformed many aspects of filmmaking: material can be downloaded from YouTube, bypassing the need to go to stock footage houses. Program deliverables have shifted from film to videotape, then DVD and now to Internet services such as Dropbox, Vimeo or Netflix. As a result, students who insist on embracing conventional forms can make documentaries that look like familiar one-hour television programs (at least superficially). Others are much freer to be experimental because the required investment is so much lower. Digital technologies have enabled documentary as a mode to flourish within the university. Harvard now has a Secondary Ph.D. in Critical Media Practice; UC-Santa Cruz has an MA program in Social Documentation; and the MA and MFA programs in documentary filmmaking have proliferated. At my institution, a number of faculty members—besides traditional filmmaking professors—now make documentaries as part of their scholarly profile. So too are graduate students enrolled in Yale's Law School, its School of Forestry and Environmental Studies, the School of Medicine, the School of Public Health and the Graduate School of Arts and Science.

Innovation and rapid growth mean that documentaries have become an ever more important element of traditional film festivals even as festivals devoted exclusively to documentary have proliferated.[10] Likewise, a wide variety of cable channels have ensured that independent documentary has moved beyond the boundaries of PBS. Not only have many more outlets been created through the Internet and iTunes, they have encouraged the art of mini documentaires and webisodes. Funders for social issue documentaries such as the Fledgling Fund have emerged. Interested in funding the process of outreach and community engagement to effect change, these organizations imagine documentaries as one piece of a much larger package of advoacy activities. Simultaneously Kickstarter has provided ways for documentary filmmakers to bypass familiar grant-seeking methods. Meanwhile, the loss of traditional gatekeepers is evident in the vogue for YouTube documentaries that are often "user generated." Conspiracy theory videos such as Peter Joseph's *Zeitgeist: The Movie* (2007) and *Zeitgeist: Moving Forward* (2011) have become among the most successful "documentaries" on the web. Meanwhile, form and format continue to change as William Uricchio and his colleagues at MIT are beginning to experiment with the concept of interactive documentary. Documentary is heading in new directions—and heading there rapidly. But to understand where it is going, we need to understand where it has been. In this respect, Jonathan Kahana's *The Documentary Film Reader: History, Theory, Criticism* will play a crucial role.

Charles Musser
Yale University

NOTES

1. Jonathan Kahana, *Intelligence Work: The Politics of American Documentary* (New York: Columbia University Press, 2008), 23.
2. Ibid., 24.
3. Errol Morris, presentation at Yale School of Art, 17 April 2013; Morris reiterated this theory at the opening of *The Unknown Known*, DOC NYC, 14 November 2013.
4. The Soviet's Esfir Shub, whose groundbreaking historical documentaries (e.g., *The Fall of the Romanov Dynasty*, 1927) reworked surviving footage from newsreels and other sources, was one founder whose contributions failed to reach an international audience until much later.
5. *The Documentary Film Reader* includes an entry by Chris Berry, editor of the recent *The New Chinese Documentary Film Movement: For the Public Record* (Hong Kong: Hong Kong University Press, 2011).
6. Significant examples of American video documentary in the 1970s include Jon Alpert's *Cuba: The People* (Downtown Community TV, 1974) and Alan and Susan Raymond's *The Police Tapes* (1976). See Deirdre Boyle, "A Brief History of American Documentary Video," in Doug Hall, Sally Jo Fifer, David Bolt, *Illuminating Video: An Essential Guide To Video Art* (Aperture, 2005), 36–39.
7. Pamela Wilson and Michelle Stewart, eds. *Global Indigenous Media: Cultures, Poetics, and Politics* (Durham, NC: Duke University Press, 2008).
8. Scott MacDonald, *American Ethnographic Film and Personal Documentary: The Cambridge Turn* (Berkeley and Los Angeles: University of California Press, 2013). Interestingly, MacDonald virtually ignores the two Cambridge-based filmmakers included in the present *Documentary Film Reader* as figures of national renown: Frederick Wiseman and Errol Morris.
9. There have been other collections in the interim, such as Alan Rosenthal's *New Challenges for Documentary* (Berkeley: University of California Press, 1988), but Rosenthal sought to gather together contemporary scholarship with the inevitable result that some essays became classics while others were more forgettable.
10. In the United States, the Margaret Mead Film Festival, started in 1976, is the longest running showcase for international documentary in the US. More recently established documentary film festivals now include Hot Springs Documentary Film Festival (est. 1992), Full Frame Documentary Film Festival (1998), AFI DOCS Documentary Film Festival (2003), the Big Sky Documentary Film Festival (2004) True/False Film Festival (2004), Atlanta International Documentary Film Festival (2006) and DOC NYC (2010). Each receives over a thousand entries every year. There is also a host of more specialized festivals which feature documentaries on the environment, human rights, and so forth.

THE DOCUMENTARY FILM READER

THE DOCUMENTARY FILM READER

History, Theory, Criticism

Editor's general introduction

Documentary is a clumsy description, but let it stand.

—John Grierson, "First Principles of Documentary"

And why not? Has a better, non-hyphenate term been invented? Like the famous Potter Stewart judgment on pornography—it's hard to define, but we know it when we see it—documentary is a notoriously slippery eel, perhaps the oldest and slipperiest concept in the history of cinema's public and commercial modes and genres. From time to time and from place to place, the term "documentary" has refused to mean something consistent, but it has been in continuous use for a hundred years. And we are pretty sure that we know one when we see (and hear) one. Some critics go so far as to insist that, outside of particular historical circumstances—certain perfect storms of public interest, technical development, and politics—the term "documentary" has no meaning.[1] Awkward as it sounds, I prefer the notion that there are "protocols of documentarism," as John Corner puts it, or formal and informal rules for ways of making and using documentary that made a special kind of sense at certain moments, while having lasting value in describing other times, too.[2] Although, come to think of it, if documentary can lead to an *ism*, it must have been a thing in itself to begin with.

So let's back into a definition, over the next thousand pages of critical history.

This anthology integrates historical and theoretical approaches to the study and criticism of documentary film, bringing together writing by scholars, critics, filmmakers and others with an interest in the art, business, and science of documentary, covering the entire history of the form. The essays, lectures, polemics, interviews, reviews, correspondence, and personal reflections collected here present an international perspective on the most significant developments and debates from several decades of critical writing about documentary, from statements by the pioneers of documentary film theory and practice to more recent thinking about the history, aesthetics, industry, and politics of documentary and nonfiction cinema and media. Artifacts from the recent or distant past present the reader with documentary values, methods, and controversies in their moment, decade by decade; and secondary critical literature, drawn from scholarly journals and books, re-examines formative moments of the documentary tradition in the retrospective light of later paradigms, and provides context for judging the merits, pleasures, and problems of individual works of documentary. Readers will be able to trace the development of particular threads in this tradition from earlier to later selections in the anthology, while noting changes and continuities across its span. Any media form that aims to be "useful"—that aspires not only to the intellectual criterion of truth, but also to novelty, to social instruction, to moral conviction or political action, to ethnological originality—has its phases of relevance and urgency as well as its periods of obsolescence and obscurity. To many readers, some of the names in the following texts, starting with the names of their authors, will be unfamiliar. Others have become "classics," because they exercise a timeless fascination, or because the habits of teaching and publication have made them touchstones of critical discourse. Such a historical, geographical, and stylistic variety is intended not only to be a consolation to the editor or publisher of this volume, for whom its multifarious readership is an imaginary community. This book is also designed to surprise and delight its readers.

Included here are many of the kinds of writing you would expect to find in a collection like this, on questions that have kept critics of documentary busy in recent decades: analyses of documentary form, meaning, and rhetoric; semiotic and philosophical approaches to the issues of reality and truth; speculations on the ethics of method and image in social and ethnographic documentary representation. Some of this writing was originally intended for a general public of readers, appearing in the arts and culture, or editorial and opinion, pages of the newspaper or other mainstream outlets. Some of it was designed for more specialist audiences: artists and art critics; cinephiles, filmmakers, and film professors; researchers in the social and the natural sciences. But you will also find here writing on matters that ceased to be of pressing concern many years ago, or which have fallen out of and back into fashion as ways of measuring the cultural, political, or artistic impact of non-fiction film and media: investigations of documentary institutions, audiences, and markets that draw on the methods of media studies and communication studies, anthropology, sociology and political science (including an erstwhile preoccupation in documentary theory, since at least the 1910s, with the concept of propaganda, once an acceptable way to describe impact, and now a term of opprobrium); historical criticism of documentary representations of the past (including the regular appearance and disappearance of the once widespread, then reviled, now avant-gardist uses of historical reenactment); and periodic fluctuations in the meaning of the term "popular" as it might apply to the methods, aims, and audiences of documentary and non-fiction film practice, whether these are encountered on the highest (professional, industrial) or lowest (amateur, personal) scales of capitalization and organization. And reflecting recent developments in the study of non-fiction film history and theory, selections throughout *The Documentary Film Reader* address the shifting boundaries between documentary and other non-fiction practices, sometimes considered too quotidian, too topical, too instrumental or too ephemeral to have a place in the documentary tradition. These occasional practices include: sponsored, industrial, and promotional film; state (or revolutionary) propaganda; newsreels; the travelogue; the film diary and the home movie. Indeed, these taxonomic distinctions have themselves been used to give shape to the history of documentary, as Tom Gunning points out in his essay "Before Documentary: Early Nonfiction Films and the 'View' Aesthetic," where Gunning reflects on John Grierson's famously dismissive accounting of the early decades of documentary cinema. One could just as well raise the same concern about the terms used in more recent decades, where the putative distinction between properly documentary works and "reality-based" art and entertainment has again become a source of worry for some commentators. One basic lesson emerges over and over from the pages of this anthology: the history of documentary is only re-invented.

Along similar lines, one might wonder why this is called a reader in documentary *film*, when another more modern or capacious term—"media," for instance—might better describe the current state of the art, and when so many different media are covered by the writings that follow—among them, film, print and slide photography, analog and digital video, television, recorded sound, prose and poetry, the lecture, and various kinds of performances, sometimes in combination with one another. To the most up-to-date student, considering the topic of documentary in the reflected light of new technologies for producing, storing, circulating, exhibiting, and viewing moving images and sound, "film" might seem a rather limiting, even archaic, way to define the scope of this field. Likewise, some historians of documentary and other media of recorded sound and image might object that insofar as the term "film" implies a certain way of containing and consuming moving images or talking pictures—conventions we often distinguish with the term cinema—the documentary film is a concept of too recent invention to capture the ways in which documentary effects were produced and experienced in pictorial, auditory, and discursive forms for years before (and for many years after) what many critics have, over the years, called the "first" documentary films, Robert Flaherty's feature-length silent movies of the 1920s, *Nanook of the North* (1922) and *Moana: A Romance of the Golden Age* (1926). The work of film historians like Rick Altman, Charles Musser, and Jeffrey Ruoff has been instrumental in helping us see that different modes of non-fictional entertainment, besides the self-contained and self-explanatory moving image text presented to a group of silent viewers massed in a dark room, not only pre-dated by many years the documentary film, but have long co-existed with it, making it that much harder to say what or when, exactly, was the first documentary. (The first section of this anthology is indebted to Musser's research on early modes of non-fiction and documentary cinema.) And even the least historically-minded maker or viewer knows that although films can be transferred to "video," and watched on television or a computer screen, film is not video; nor is film television, even if many viewers, from the most casual viewer of documentary to the most committed student, have never seen a documentary film shot on or projected from celluloid. "Film" is, at best, a euphemism for the experience of moving-image technology and form that many of us have on a regular basis with documentary.

Nonetheless, documentary film seems more suitable as the heading for the writing in this collection than any of the alternatives, even if (or because) "film" now means many things. Film can, for instance, name a moving-image or audiovisual technology, or series of technologies, capable of reproducing visual and auditory images of real (past or present) time and space. Film can also refer to the particular kind of raw materials used in this recording and reproduction process: strips made from one of a number of types of plastic, treated with a compound sensitive to light and taken through a photochemical process that exposes, develops, and fixes the images registered (in negative or positive form) in the emulsion as it passes through the camera. Film can also suggest the field or fields of practice—social, cultural, institutional, professional—one occupies while in the process of making a documentary film, or otherwise becoming expert in works and practices of moving-image social-historical documentation, or "documentary film." If you say you are working in or on (a) documentary (film), you probably mean something quite different than if you say you work in journalism, or in reality television, or in the moving-image branch of a national archive, or in the history or sociology department of a university, or in "Hollywood," or on a radio program, even though all of these might involve working in or on (a) film(s), or working on or with filmed or recorded documents, or working in a documentary style with subjects drawn from real life. Even more confusingly, the term "documentary" can be used in different ways in different countries, as a modifier: for example, broadcasters in some countries are much more likely to refer to a long-form report on a television or radio news program as a "documentary" than are broadcasters in the United States. One can certainly work in or on documentary film without ever finishing, or even making, a film, even though when we say *a* film, we tend to mean a whole, finished work, something constructed and completed, exhibited, and viewed according to principles established by years of producers' and exhibitors' and viewers' rules and expectations; thus, everyone involved in the process of creating and consuming such objects—films—can agree that what they encounter is a complete work, the final outcome of a collective process: something with a look, a sound, and a sensibility different from other kinds of cultural production. And in return for its viewers' attention, the documentary film promises a certain kind of experience with the screen and the world, one no other audiovisual form of edification or amusement can promise.

By the same token, we can and do loosely apply "film" to all sorts of audiovisual moving-image works, as long as they seem to bear the qualities and principles of (a) film: just as we consider a long-form work of historical or social inquiry shot with digital video cameras, edited with computer software, and viewed on a television or a computer screen a "documentary film," we might call a short piece of video we watch on YouTube, or an experimental work that combines scraps of home movies shot with 8mm and 16mm cameras, shown in a theater or on a cell-phone, "a film." Artists and critics working in the 1920s around the Russian editor-director Esfir Shub, as Mikhail Iampolsky observes, advocated a documentary filmmaking practice that would simply gather material in the present for films to be finished in the future, and not necessarily by the same filmmakers whose job it was to gather this "archival" material. According to this logic, the documentary film was an extraordinarily capacious concept, one that could accommodate any number of present and future configurings of its basic materials. Shub predicted the form of the documentary film almost anyone with a computer can practice today.

The reader will, in the following pages, encounter writing that deals with work produced and circulated not only with once-conventional film-based techniques and technologies, but on analog or digital video, shown not in conventional movie theaters, but in classrooms, or in museums and art galleries, or in meeting halls, or on television, or on private screens, watched, perhaps not in one sitting, but over several weeks or months, a little at a time. Did the twelve one-hour episodes of the television series *An American Family* (1973), shot in synchronous sound 16mm film by documentary filmmakers Alan and Susan Raymond in the style then widely known as *cinéma vérité*, and watched by public television viewers over the course of several months, constitute a documentary film? In the article about the series that she wrote for the magazine *TV Guide*, the American anthropologist and filmmaker Margaret Mead argued that it was neither film nor a documentary, even though it showed viewers "the real life of others interpreted by the camera."[3] And what about British filmmaker Peter Watkins's celebrated and controversial short film *The War Game*, made for BBC television in 1965? Depending on the viewer's perspective, Watkins's film can be seen as a conjectural documentary that describes a future thermonuclear war in England, a biting satire of Cold War–era civil-defense instructional media, the deadpan account of actual statements by public officials on the prospects of surviving a nuclear war, or all three at once. (Watkins, who had produced a somewhat more conventional historical film for the BBC prior to making *The War Game*, and would go on to make film, television, and video about war and global conflict, discusses *The War Game* with the American avant-garde filmmaker and critic James Blue, in an interview reprinted here, without once using the term "documentary"; "a newsreel situation" that "looks real," and "organized unorganization," are about as close as Watkins comes. In "Familial Pursuits, Editorial Acts: Documentaries After the Age of Home Video," Marsha Orgeron and Devin Orgeron foreground this problem of names in their analysis of some widely-circulated documentaries whose source material was, in large measure, highly personal "home movies" and amateur video diaries. Despite the panoply of technologies, materials, aesthetics, and conditions of production that went into the making of *Capturing the Friedmans* (dir. Andrew Jarecki, 2003), *Tarnation* (dir. Jonathan Caouette, 2003), or *Grizzly Man* (dir. Werner Herzog, 2005), "film" is still the most flexible term we have to describe the kind of text that their makers construct, their distributors and exhibitors circulate, and their audiences watch. "Film" still captures best how such texts signify to their producers, viewers and critics, despite many good arguments one can make against being comfortable with this designation. Since in these situations and many others represented in this book, "film" seems the least of all terminological evils, let's stick with that name for the central object of the writings gathered here.

Thornier still is the question of what we mean by "documentary." That question *is* within our purview, and the aim of *The Documentary Film Reader* is to pose it as fully and variously as possible, and to allow readers to answer it many different ways. "The documentary film has been a boxing ring for the experts," wrote an American non-fiction film producer in 1947.[4] During the war, he argued, documentary had shown itself to be "instructional," "authoritative," and "vital"; but now documentary threatened to lapse back into the thoughtless capacity of a "moving picture advertisement." And at the same moment, on the other side of the Atlantic, the science-film pioneer Jean Painlevé was lamenting a "glut" of "mediocre documentaries" devoid of the "sincerity" and "inventiveness" that originally inspired true documentary artists, experimenters, and audiences alike. Such dire pronouncements had already been heard for years from producers, promoters, and other documentary film experts, from John Grierson's declaration of "First Principles" in the early 1930s, where he laments the "babblings" of the "peacetime newsreel," to the recent diagnosis of a "postdocumentary"[5] condition signaled by the rise and spread of so-called reality television. But what each of these commentators means by "documentary" might diverge a little or a lot from any other definition. Watching how and where the meanings of this concept change, develop and retreat, in line with or in opposition to definitions coined in other places and at other times, is one way to use this collection: its international and historical range was conceived with an eye to highlighting both continuity and contradiction.

These points of comparison should help us understand why the question "what is a documentary?" has persisted, even if they make it that much more difficult to answer once and for all. One variation on this fundamental question is epistemological. Many writers have concerned themselves with the issue of not only *what* we learn from documentaries, but also *how*. What makes a documentary trustworthy or true as an account of or argument about events, people, or ideas past or present? How does film complement or compete with other ways of observing, reflecting upon, and explaining history, society, nature, culture, or psychology? (Compare the essays by Rick Altman, Kristen Whissel, Hamid Naficy, and Nicholas Reeves for a sample of how some recent scholars ask what the earliest documentaries—even before that was what they were called—added to our knowledge of the world, and our ways of knowing it, in the present or the past.) There are also versions of the question "what is a documentary?" that approach it as a problem of genre or form. What styles of documentary seem more non-fictional than others? How *much* style—how much artifice, how much play and experimentation with the plastic and expressive tools of the medium—do we permit in something we call a documentary or a non-fiction film? These issues were debated vigorously in the 1920s and 1930s by filmmakers and critics in the U.S., Europe, and Russia; examples of these controversies can be found in section II. And the matter of manipulation—the idea that documentary not only involves artifice and craft, but that it exerts ideological or political pressure on its viewers—is a concern of long standing in the question of what documentary is, and is for. The term "propaganda," for example, has a quite different sense before the Second World War, as in the affirmative use of the term in writing by John Grierson or Pare Lorentz, and after, when it takes on a much more negative connotation, as it does for critics assessing or re-assessing the work of state-sponsored filmmakers in the "classic" era (1930s–1960s) of social documentary production in the West. By the same token, the resistance to didacticism that overtakes documentary filmmaking in Western Europe and North America after 1960 doesn't necessarily extend to other parts of the world, where didacticism can still be seen as a creative and progressive quality of documentary method (as, for instance, in Jorge Fraga, Estrella Pantin, and Julio Garcia Espinosa's "Towards a Definition of the Didactic Documentary," an essay the authors presented to a Cuban educational film conference in 1971). And—in addition to these epistemological, aesthetic, and political inflections of the question "what is (or is this) a documentary?"—the reader will find here many examples of critical writing about documentary concerned less with abstract, theoretical problems of documentary content, rhetoric, or form than with specific historical questions about the difference a particular documentary made in the world of its subjects or its viewers, about the reception of a particular film in its time or later, or about how the activity of documentary filmmaking in a particular place and moment reflects on the society that hosts or occasions this work, what one might call documentary chronotopes in broader historical or social forms of inquiry.

From one item in this anthology to another, you might find it difficult to identify particular rules or standards governing critical writing about documentary. Since the materials that make up this collection were originally composed at different times and places, for a variety of audiences and an equal variety of purposes, differences of language, style, and attitude from one text to another will and should be noticeable, especially where different authors deal with a common documentary topic, object, or problem. How were these items chosen from among the many possibilities for representing a particular documentary film, filmmaker, method, period, place, movement, institution, or way of thinking? On the one hand, I searched for materials that would provide the reader with an especially useful or important view of a documentary context, helping to locate particular works in a historical period, a situation of production, or a social, intellectual, or political era. On the other hand, I wanted examples that embodied different times, places, and styles of critical writing, while serving as models for students, instructors, and other readers looking for precise, detail-oriented studies of documentary films. Creating a survey of critical writing that was historically, geographically, and methodologically diverse was an editorial goal always in tension with the aim of being comprehensive in each of these areas. As in any long-lived aesthetic endeavor, the standards of both utility and beauty in critical writing about documentary are highly variable and idiosyncratic. It might help to keep in mind that the pieces gathered here—and, in particular, the balance between primary materials and secondary ones—are meant to be effective for the present task of criticism and to be representative of past ways of thinking, but not always both at once. Editorial justifications notwithstanding, it is hoped and expected that the articles and essays collected here will be read in unpredictable combinations.

Complementing these principles of inclusion are divisions into the larger periods marked by the sections. These might be thought of as seven ages, or seven arts, of documentary film, since they are meant to group critical writing according to both historical and formal distinctions. To be sure, history is not just chronology, and the reader will notice that there is some overlap between the years covered in one section and another. The elasticity of these boundaries is intentional, and is meant to reflect the way that documentary principles and techniques important to one historical era remain in use well after their period of novelty and invention, or fall from fashion and then return, or are remade, many years later. This overlapping set of groupings also underscores the cultural and national diversity of documentary practice: even as movements or technological innovations create what appear to be lasting shifts and changes in the form, the uptake of these changes is not universal, and documentary always contains a variety of stylistic possibilities. In this sense, the division into seven parts should be seen as a convenient way to assign dominant historical qualities to different tendencies that come and go in the long tradition of documentary filmmaking and documentary film criticism.

The first section, "Early Documentary: From the Illustrated Lecture to the Factual Film," deals with the earliest kinds of factual moving images exhibited to a public and the earliest attempts to combine these pictures with historical or scientific commentary; this, paradoxically, is also the period of documentary film history most recently excavated by scholars, and the period least likely to be covered in earlier historical surveys. It takes the reader from the age of the illustrated travel lecture and the historical spectacles put on by showmen like Buffalo Bill to the feature non-fiction cinema of Robert Flaherty, whose 1922 film *Nanook of the North* was traditionally considered the starting point for a history of documentary cinema. Section II, "Modernisms: State, Left, and Avant-Garde Documentary Between the Wars," focuses on international experiments with documentary film in art and politics. Reactionary, reformist, and revolutionary perspectives on the power of machines and of mechanical reproduction to build, capture, and explode our world dominate documentary discourse of this period. The third section, "Documentary Propaganda: World War II and the Post-War Citizen," emphasizes a relatively brief historical development, but one with lasting effects for many of the most important institutions of documentary film in North America, Western Europe, and other parts of the world (including territories where documentary was becoming useful in the cause of national self-determination, a prominent theme in sections four and five). A time of tremendous productivity for non-fiction film industries, the Second World War and its aftermath—which included the re-invention of the nation-state and the citizen for the Cold War—have routinely been dismissed, by filmmakers and historians alike, as the most doctrinaire and least imaginative period for documentary film. The writing in this section corrects that impression.

In sections IV and V, the reader encounters a plethora of perspectives on the conditions, both within documentary filmmaking and without, that produced forms and debates central to what is sometimes called "new documentary." Section IV, "Aesthetics of Liberation: Free, Direct, and *Vérité* Cinemas," maps the widespread attempts to reduce the scale and loosen the frame of documentary production, taking cameras and microphones where they hadn't been before in an effort to show (as Jonas Mekas writes in 1966) "everything, everything." Section V, "Talking Back: Radical Voices and Visions after 1968," follows this enthusiasm through a sharp left turn, as documentary filmmaking inspires and joins social and political struggles against colonialism, imperialism, war, and the domestic ideologies that complement these national and international forms of violence: capitalism and class, sexual difference, racism and heterosexism. Not coincidentally, the 1970s and 1980s is also a time when critics begin writing alternatives to the traditional Euro-American genealogies of documentary, a piecemeal critical program that continues into the periods of sections VI and VII. As is suggested by the title of section VI, "Truth Not Guaranteed: Reflections, Revisions, and Returns," fundamental assumptions about the enterprise of documentary come under concerted attack by filmmakers and critics alike. In this period, the study of documentary film and media gains traction as a discrete branch of academic film and media studies, and core values of documentary work—truth, ethics, historical certainty, authenticity, spontaneity, the public good—are subject to rigorous historical and theoretical examination. This skeptical scholasticism, in turn, finds its way back into documentary practice, where new forms, technologies, venues and audiences coincide in a new culture of experimentation, even as documentary becomes a fully transnational (or, not the same thing, "global") product of the culture industries. Section VII, "Documentary Transformed: Transnational and Transmedial Crossings," considers some aspects of this expanded field, and extends our inquiry toward the field's unstable borders and uncertain horizons.

Each of the following sections has a brief introduction of its own. These opening statements serve as guides to the contents of each section: they note unique and important features of the filmmaking and criticism represented in the section, so that the reader, as she wends her way through the section or the book, can attend to patterns that give a historical period its character, or distinguish one thematic grouping from another; they make a case for defining a historical period, ragged as its ends may be, as the section covers it; and they draw attention to some differences between the way such films were seen at the time and the way we, looking back, see them now. Of course, these directives suggest that, held at any angle, the book and each section of it will reveal logics of history, culture, and form that bind the whole, and the reader may doubt, especially when he notices differences between the view expressed in one place in the book and the view expressed in another, or what seem to him holes and notable absences, that this "logic" is anything other than a convenient fiction. Describing the philosophical method known as deconstruction as a way of teaching and of conducting research, the historian Joan Wallach Scott writes of its "critical engagement with the premises of the endeavor."[6] In this way, the reader might think of this collection as a deconstruction of the history of documentary, one that she is welcome to continue in her own classroom, with her own work, and in her own head.

A note about versions:

In most cases, the chapters in this book republish the most complete version of a text previously published, with only the most minimal adjustments: correcting obvious orthographic or typographic errors in original and/or subsequent printing; conforming variant spelling, punctuation or typesetting of foreign terms and phrases; etc. In some cases, errors, idiosyncrasies, or discrepancies of date, spelling, or punctuation have been retained as they originally appeared, to preserve something interesting about the way documentary discourse is written and circulated, including the changes, mistakes and contradictions that are inherent in the material process of publication. Citation and documentation formats diverge widely across the history of publication represented here, however, and have largely been left in that discrepant state.

Where more significant modifications have been made, the reader will see two kinds of indices. In the regrettable but necessary situation where the length of a text had to be reduced to accommodate it and all its neighbors in such an already overstuffed book, the editor has put an ellipsis in square brackets to show that some sentences or paragraphs have been cut: [. . .]. And in several other instances, cuts were made and/or entirely new words added by the authors themselves, in consultation with the editor. Those versions can be discerned by their asterisked date (1975*) and the corresponding footnote (*Revised 2015) on their first page. A full listing of the sources of every chapter appears at the end of the volume, and serious (or casual) readers are strongly encouraged to consult the full and original versions of any of these substantially modified works.

Any other editorial interventions are the work of an earlier or original editor or translator, as indicated by the signs of an "Ed." or a "Trans." before or after such remarks.

NOTES

1. Martha Rosler and John Tagg make forceful arguments for this extreme position in their writing about the history of documentary photography. See Martha Rosler, "in, around, and afterthoughts (on documentary photography)," in *3 Works* [1981] (Halifax: The Press of the Nova Scotia College of Art and Design, 2006), 61–93, as well as the "Afterword" to the 2006 edition of *3 Works*; and John Tagg, *The Burden of Representation: Essays on Photographies and Histories* (Minneapolis: University of Minnesota Press, 1988).
2. John Corner, "Performing the Real: Documentary Diversions," *Television and New Media* 3, no. 3 (August 2002): 262.
3. Margaret Mead, "As Significant as the Invention of Drama or the Novel," chapter 66 in this volume. See also Susan Murray, " 'I Think We Need a New Name for It': The Meeting of Documentary and Reality TV," in *Reality TV: Remaking Television Culture*, ed. Susan Murray and Laurie Ouellette (New York: New York University Press, 2004), 40–56.
4. Wesley F. Pratzner, "What Has Happened to the Documentary Film?," *The Public Opinion Quarterly* 11, no. 3 (Autumn 1947): 394.
5. Corner, "Performing the Real," 257.
6. Joan Wallach Scott, "Against Eclecticism," *differences: A Journal of Feminist Cultural Studies* 16, no. 3 (Fall 2005), 115–37.

SECTION I

EARLY DOCUMENTARY

From the Illustrated Lecture to the Factual Film

1

JONATHAN KAHANA

INTRODUCTION TO SECTION I

"Early documentary" is a controversial term, not least because no one can seem to agree on what makes early documentary "early," or "documentary." Calling something "early" suggests that it is not yet, or not fully, that thing. At the same time, adding the modifier "early" to "documentary" (or "documentary film") suggests that there might have been a period of documentary film before what we have traditionally regarded as the origin of "mature" documentary film. These seemingly minor lexical worries about what to call the baby steps of an emergent art form open a larger can of worms for film historians and theorists, starting with the nature of documentary itself.

For decades, it has been critical custom to treat the feature-length ethnographic exploration films of Robert Flaherty, starting with his 1922 feature film about "Eskimos," *Nanook of the North*, as the "first" documentaries.[1] (*Nanook* was already Flaherty's second attempt, after a nearly fatal accident in the editing room with the first version, to make such a film; you can read an account of a public screening in Toronto of material from his first version in this section.) During the 1990s, film historians began to occupy themselves with the question of what else there was to learn about the very earliest years of cinema, from the mid-1890s to the first decade of the 1900s, even in the absence of many surviving films from this period. Not surprisingly, the archaeological work done by this group of historians, and the discoveries they made in the areas of film language, culture, and industry, occasioned reflection on the very question of what exactly was "early"—a term that replaced the prejudicial "primitive"—about cinema before 1907 or so. Although some of this cutting-edge research dealt with non-fiction filmmaking, the mainstream of documentary scholarship and criticism remained largely unaffected by it for many years, preoccupied as it was with the effort to establish a properly theoretical study of documentary film, one that would give documentary film the same standing in academic discussions, as an object of rigorous theoretical analysis, that narrative fiction film gained in the 1960s and 1970s. (Some examples of this important work can be found in section VI, "Truth Not Guaranteed: Reflections, Revisions, and Returns.") In this sense, the critical study of documentary film continued to follow the historical model derived from John Grierson and his prescriptive writing of the 1920s and 1930s, which was sometimes dismissive and condescending toward earlier non-fiction films, filmmakers, and audiences.

Take, for example, media historian Erik Barnouw's book *Documentary: A History of the Nonfiction Film*, arguably the most influential English-language treatment of the history of documentary since its initial publication in 1974. Barnouw's first chapter, subtitled "Prophet," establishes a prehistoric period of documentary, one in which visionary filmmakers blazed a trail toward *Nanook*, along lines virtually identical to the principles laid out in Grierson's early essay "First Principles of Documentary." Following Grierson's dictum that documentary tells "the essential story of the location," the mavericks described by Barnouw as proto-documentary filmmakers venture out into the world—that is, away from the stage and the studio—to capture visible evidence of that world. And in line with Grierson's insistence that documentary filmmakers should provide more than the ephemeral excitements of the commercial travelogue or the newsreel, or the didactic instruction of propaganda, Barnouw's prophets pursue knowledge for its own sake, rather than the selfish ends of power or profit.

It is only relatively recently that serious challenges to the idea that documentary starts with *Nanook* have gained traction and begun to change the way we study and write about non-fiction film at the turn of the 19th century. Grierson's writing figures prominently in this section and the next; but around it appear examples of earlier and later writing that discover in the early, experimental decades of the documentary the potential for a kind of experience quite different from the cinema envisioned by Grierson and enshrined in Barnouw. Out of this alternate evidence, arguments can be built for earlier and different starting points for documentary film, ones that need not lead only to the mature, self-contained explanation of a moving image of actuality first realized in the mid-1920s. Indeed, some of the early public displays of real life in far-away lands or times described in this section demonstrate that qualities we might think of as central to the medium of documentary film came less from the big-screen experience of documentary technologies—what Charles Musser calls "life-sized photographs which moved"[2]—than from the producers' claims, the audience's expectations and attitudes, and the viewing (and listening) situation itself. In historical, religious and ethnographic spectacles, in narrated travelogues, and in reports sent home from battle in triumph or despair, early non-fiction producers, promoters, exhibitors, and audiences may together have constructed the "documentary" experience. In press accounts and promotional materials circulated with these scenes of conquest, war, and the violence of "primitive" life, one gleans the various promises made for the medium we would eventually know as documentary film. And in the retrospective accounts and analyses of these productions, we see how the promised capacity to "convey certain information and affect its audience both emotionally and intellectually," as Musser puts it, served ideological, political, and commercial ends, as well as the purer aims of knowledge and universal understanding. Surveying the exploits of popular documentary from this period, we cover terrain—attitudes, as well as places—that can seem to us harsh, strange and manipulative, exploitations in the fullest sense. Some of the landmarks on this tour are excessively familiar to viewers with the slightest knowledge of the history of documentary film; others—like *In the Land of the Head Hunters* (dir. Edward Curtis, 1914), an ethnographic fantasy constructed with native people from the west coast of North America—may be known to specialists and scholars but largely unseen, owing to their scarcity or fragility in the period of their initial release, or since. The section ends with considerations of a film well-positioned by contemporary and retrospective accounts to displace *Nanook* as the first successful popular documentary feature: *Battle of the Somme*. Made by a propaganda agency of the British government in 1916 to document this terrible battle and promote the war, *Battle of the Somme*—still a moving and difficult film to watch—was seen by tens of millions of viewers on both sides of the Atlantic. Publicity, propaganda, exploitation, entertainment, commercial spectacle: these original uses of non-fiction film might now look to us like abuses, blurring the distinction between fiction and non-fiction we hold central to our definition of documentary cinema.

NOTES

1. This custom persists in even recent scholarly writing: in *American Ethnographic Film and Personal Documentary: The Cambridge Turn*, Scott MacDonald begins the "early" period of American documentary film with Robert Flaherty. Scott MacDonald, *American Ethnographic Film and Personal Documentary: The Cambridge Turn* (Berkeley: University of California Press, 2013), 7.
2. Musser's point is that by 1896, the year after the putative invention of cinema, the "life-sized" moving photograph was already losing its power to narrate or explain in a singular fashion. Charles Musser, "The Eden Musée in 1898: The Exhibitor as Creator," *Film and History* 11.4 (December 1981): 74.

2

RICK ALTMAN

FROM LECTURER'S PROP TO INDUSTRIAL PRODUCT

The Early History of Travel Films (2006)

The history of cinema has by and large been configured as a history of films. Understandable in a post-1915 world dominated by feature films, a film-oriented approach to cinema reveals its shortcomings all too rapidly in the field of early cinema. Early moving pictures were in many cases like theatrical props: they gained meaning only to the extent that performers were able to integrate them into their acts. When film entered the American scene, the entertainment arts were heavily dominated by performers. The leading theatrical trade organs of the period—*The Billboard*, the *New York Clipper*, and the *New York Dramatic Mirror*—organized their reporting around acts and the people who performed them, not around products and the people who produced them. Even though the era was hardly without its entertainment products (including sheet music, phonograph records, and moving pictures), a long tradition of covering the stage led the trades to consider these products as little more than props for singers, impersonators, and lecturers. During cinema's formative years, films often existed only to the extent that they could be included in a live performance. Edited or combined to suit the situation, moving pictures long remained subservient to existing forms of entertainment and the performers who provided them.

In order to understand certain aspects of early cinema, we must therefore put aside our firmly entrenched film-oriented approach to cinema in favor of a performer-oriented position. This is especially true for the study of documentary films in general and travel films in particular. For many years, histories of documentary film began with the twenties, lionizing Robert Flaherty and ignoring virtually everything earlier (e.g., Barsam 1973). Even Kristin Thompson and David Bordwell have recently claimed that "before the 1920s, documentary filmmaking had largely been confined to newsreels and scenic shorts" (1994: 202). While this claim might seem to be borne out by production company catalogues, it fails to reckon with the full range of production during cinema's first quarter century. Though it may be possible to base a history of *Hollywood* cinema on studio production, a history of travel films must start elsewhere. Because early cinema was a world not of films but of performers, the history of travel films must begin with those who "performed" them.

In order to discover early travel films, it is useless to search indexes under "films, travel." Instead, we must look under the rubric "lecturer." During cinema's formative years, many different types of lecturers used or accompanied films. Some simply read out loud the film descriptions provided by production companies. Others made up their own commentary on existing films. For the history of travel films, however, the most important lecturers were the performers who traveled the Lyceum and Chautauqua circuits with projector and homemade film in hand (Gaudreault and Lacasse 1996; Lacasse 2000; Musser and Nelson 1991; Altman 2004b). Since the 1830s, when the National American Lyceum grew out of lectures given by Josiah Holbrook in Millbury, Massachusetts, Americans had regularly been regaled by public lectures designed to educate and uplift. Recognizing a widespread hunger for spiritual and intellectual revival, in 1868 James Redpath established a talent bureau to provide lecturers for the many established lyceums spread throughout the country. In 1874 Lewis Miller, a businessman, and John Heyl Vincent, a clergyman, established a summer version of the lyceum on the shores of Lake Chautauqua in western New York. Soon, year-round lyceum lectures (on what was often termed the "platform circuit") would be joined by short-lived chautauqua meetings all over the country. In 1904 these chautauquas were organized into circuits, thus facilitating performer scheduling and travel. The Redpath Lyceum Bureau continued for decades to contract with lecturers for both lyceum and chautauqua performances.[1] Lyceum circuit lecturers typically held forth in the many public buildings that dotted the turn-of-the-century cityscape, especially town halls and public auditoriums, concert halls and opera houses, union halls and churches. At first borrowing the same venues, chautauqua lectures were eventually moved to more easily ventilated tents for the summer season.

For several decades, lecturers remained the featured performers on the lyceum and chautauqua circuits. Moving from town to town, they would typically repeat the same lecture or coordinated course of lectures throughout a season, using the summer slow period to develop a new lecture or course for the following year. Not until around 1915, with the growing popularity of so-called tent chautauquas that filled the summer season, would this familiar pattern be disturbed. During the final quarter of the nineteenth century, this schedule had been followed by many well-known travel lecturers who illustrated their lectures with lantern slides shot in foreign countries, including Edward L. Wilson, the legendary John L. Stoddard, and his successor E. Burton Holmes. Whereas Wilson had begun lecturing before the heyday of the lyceum circuit, Stoddard's career began with lectures on Constantinople as part of the Redpath Lyceum Course at the Boston Music Hall, and on the Rhine and the Alps for the Concord Lyceum in that city's town hall (Barber 1993: 700). Like Wilson, Stoddard illustrated his lectures with lantern slides taken or purchased during his travels. Only the text was included when Wilson's lectures were published, but Stoddard's photographs were reproduced in the immensely popular published versions of his lectures (Wilson 1874–88; Stoddard 1897).

Wilson's and Stoddard's lectures provided Burton Holmes all the education he needed to develop his own illustrated lecture style. Like all other late-nineteenth-century travel lecturers, Holmes practiced the art of what is rightly called the "illustrated lecture." At the heart lies the noun—the lecture itself, the verbal discourse simultaneously assuring temporal and geographical continuity, accompanied by continuous communication with the audience. The illustrations occupy no more than an adjectival role, helping to define and exemplify the words of the lecture. Because Holmes usually took his own photographs (or had them taken to his specifications), he managed to provide greater continuity within his illustrations than many other travel lecturers, who often bought stock slides from catalogues. Even Holmes always subordinated his illustration program to the verbal lecture, however (Holmes 1901; Altman 2004b: chap. 4). Though Wilson, Stoddard, and Holmes each made a career out of showing slides, to their audiences it made no difference whether they shot their own pictures or not.

In 1897 Holmes began to make moving pictures to supplement his lantern slides. Working with his cameraman, Oscar B. Depue, Holmes filmed many of the famous sites that he had previously photographed (Depue 1967: 60–64). In a move that is entirely predictable from his previous practice, and that would presage the next two decades of travel filmmaking, Holmes managed his moving pictures in exactly the same way that he handled his photographs. At first treating his films as a novelty, he located them at the end of his lecture, as he might place a series of unusual photos or trick slides. Then, a few years later, he began to intersperse them within his program, using them like lantern slides to illustrate particular portions of his lecture (Barber 1993: 81–82). When he was working with still photographs, Holmes had never been thought of as a photographer but always as a lecturer. Now that he had begun to make films and to integrate them into his performances, he would continue to be known as a lecturer, not as a filmmaker. Ads for Holmes's performances thus always stressed his name and the term "lecture," consigning his illustrations—even when they included moving pictures—to the small print. A 27 February 1898 *New York World* advertisement, for example, announced Holmes's performances at Daly's in the following manner:

BURTON HOLMES
LECTURES
MAGNIFICENTLY ILLUSTRATED
IN COLOR
accompanied by a series of original
MOTION PICTURES
Tomorrow at 11. Tuesday at
3. Wednesday at 11.

"CYCLING THROUGH CORSICA"
Thursday at 11. Friday at 3. Saturday at 11.

"YELLOWSTONE NATIONAL PARK"
Reserved Seats, $1.50 and $1. Admission, 50¢.

Over the next twenty years, many a travel lecturer would complement his stock of travel slides with motion pictures. In most cases, these films were made by (or under the supervision of) the lecturer himself. A particularly representative example is provided by Edward Burton McDowell (who called himself "Dr." and who around 1907 changed the spelling of his name to MacDowell, perhaps to capitalize on the fame of contemporary American composer Edward MacDowell). Prior to 1902, McDowell offered typical fare for a travel lecturer on the platform circuit: lectures recounting his own trips, "illustrated by lantern slides which were developed by his own hands" (McDowell folder). During the summer of 1902—the platform circuit off-season—McDowell traveled "Through Arizona Canyon and Yosemite to the Glaciers of Alaska," where in addition to his photographs he made the first in a series of annual travel films. Ever since they had become national parks in 1872 and 1890, respectively, Yellowstone and Yosemite had constituted prime targets for travel photographers and lecturers. Now McDowell would complement his lantern slides by motion pictures representing, according to his publicity, such animated subjects as

Feeding Time on Pigeon and Ostrich Ranches in California
Surf Lashing a Rocky Coast
Parades during the Carnival of Roses
Waterfalls of the Enchanted Yosemite Valley
Panorama of the Yosemite Mountains
Yosemite Stage Coach passing through the Mariposa Grove "Tunnel Tree"
Bathers Diving and Tobogganning
Locomotives Laboring Up Steep Mountain Grades
Ocean Steamer in a Storm, Tossing and Plunging through a Heavy Sea
Railway Panorama of the White Pass, Alaska
Klondike Miners Shooting the Perilous White Horse Rapids, etc.

Projection of these films in alternation with lantern slides was facilitated by the design of contemporary projectors, which always combined a lantern slide light source and transport mechanism with an add-on "motion head" permitting the unspooling of motion pictures. Of course McDowell did not himself project his films. Turn-of-the-century platform lecturers always depended on a confederate to handle projection duties while they lectured. When McDowell added films to his arsenal, motion picture projection was thus added to the duties of "Mr. D. C. Denmark, Assistant, Stereoptician and Motion Picture Expert." From a 1909 document in the Redpath Chautauqua Collection we know that the railroad fare for McDowell's projectionist was paid by the Redpath Lyceum Bureau as part of McDowell's lecturing contract (McDowell folder). During the century's first decade, contracts were typically made between the lecturer and the booking company, with the projectionist handled just like the motion picture portion of the projector—as an add-on.

In 1903 McDowell photographed and filmed "Samoa: The Tropical Paradise of the South Pacific." His 1906 publicity doesn't spare the italics to claim that "*his motion picture camera was the first to be operated in either the Samoan or Fiji Islands*; and that his moving pictures of savage life and customs in these remote lands are *today the only ones in existence.*" Though McDowell's films of Samoa are not known to still exist, his description helps us to grasp how he understood his filmmaking activity. McDowell never says that he made a film about Samoa, nor does he advertise that he will show a film about Samoa. Instead he promises "The Story of a Summer Cruise, Illustrated by Original Motion Pictures, and Copyrighted Photographic Slides Colored by a Master Hand." Whenever they are mentioned, "motion pictures" are always subservient to the verbal lecture, and always in the plural. In Samoa, we are told, "Dr. McDowell, with an equipment of three cameras, secured 40 motion pictures and more than 1,000 negatives of still subjects." Designed to replace lantern slides when the lecture calls for illustration of an activity rather than a landscape, building, or still life, McDowell's motion pictures put the accent on motion, including:

Samoan Dance by Twenty Men and Women
Canoe Race
War Dance
Waterfall
Food Offering and Processional March
Samoan Youths Bearing the Roasted Pig
Running Dance of Taupou and Manaia
Depositing the Cocoanuts
Moonlight Dance
Diving Scene by Thirty-five Native Boys
Firing Gun on U.S. Man-of-War
Surf Dashing on a Lava Walled Shore
Remarkable Samoan Children's Dance
Ship at Sea

Just as contemporary catalogues designated and sold individual Passion play scenes as separate entities, for McDowell each of these "subjects" constituted a separate "motion picture" capable of replacing a lantern slide. In a sense, these films were still defined as "views," according to the era's conception of still photographs. They did not yet constitute the stand-alone object that would later be understood by the term "motion picture" (in the singular). In 1904 McDowell returned to the South Pacific in order to film the Fiji Islands. The following year he would join a bevy of filmmakers to record the building of the Panama Canal. His publicity is careful to point out that the motion pictures were "made by Dr. McDowell with his own motion picture camera; and these motion pictures of the canal work are the first and only ones yet made" (McDowell folder).

In 1907 McDowell (having now changed the spelling of his name) took his Goerz-Anschutz camera to Cuba, where he filmed not only well-known tourist and battle sites but also the back country. Whereas his previous film footage had always consisted of separate short "subjects," each appropriate to replace a lantern slide, McDowell's Cuban motion pictures are in large part organized around the story of his own difficulties:

> After feasting his cameras along these beaten paths of travel, and in accordance with his reputation for seeking out of the way places because of his great love for "roughing it," he then answered a "call of the wild" and began to follow the muddy bends of an alligator stream, the only navigable river in Cuba, far up into the interior forests.
>
> Dr. MacDowell there visited Estrada Palma, the recently deposed president of Cuba, who, with his children and grandchildren, has retired to a lonely cattle ranch that he may more easily bury his crushed ambitions and try to forget an ungrateful world.
>
> From the Palma ranch Dr. MacDowell journeyed farther up the river toward the interior to near the head of navigation where there is a little grass hut village, which does not possess a resident who knows a word of English.
>
> A bed among the salt and sugar barrels in the back room of a country store was his resting place for several days.
>
> His story about how he "got out of the wilderness" is most interesting and thrilling.
>
> How the rainy season came on suddenly and how a long forced horseback ride was made through the forests and flooded swamps back to civilization.
>
> How the floods had swept away the bridges and how his horses swam three rivers during the trip are among the strenuous adventures which Dr. MacDowell's motion picture camera has faithfully reproduced.

McDowell's increasing tendency to organize his short motion picture subjects into self-contained stories was shared by several other itinerant lecturer/filmmakers of the period.

As we know from the route slips kept by the Redpath Bureau, late in the first decade of the century McDowell took his illustrated lectures to an extraordinary range of small to medium-size Midwestern towns. From 8 to 23 January 1909, for example, he lectured in the Michigan towns of Adrian, Traverse City, and Muskegon, before dipping down to Covington, Kentucky, on his way to Chillicothe, Columbus, Hebron, and Glenford, Ohio. After four weeks' break, McDowell then moved on to Medina and Lima, Ohio, plus Peru and Warren, Illinois, and, after an excursion to Mankato, Minnesota, the Iowa towns of Toledo, Osage, Manchester, and Thornton. All of this from 22 February to 4 March. In just a month on the road, during the coldest months of the year, McDowell had thus taken the warm climates of Samoa, Fiji, Panama, and Cuba to seventeen towns in six states.

During this period, several other lyceum circuit lecturers took to making their own travel films. Best known for his Passion play lectures, delivered over two thousand times to over two million people, John J. Lewis also delivered travel lectures illustrated with motion pictures (Lewis folder). Like John Stoddard and Burton Holmes, Lewis had not hesitated to provide a travel frame to make his locally shot Passion play pictures appear to have been made in Oberammergau. By prefacing the play itself with scenes on an express train and an Atlantic liner, and footage from Paris, Switzerland, and Munich, Lewis reinforced the impression that his religious tableaux were shot as the culmination of an actual trip to Oberammergau. In other films, Lewis used motion pictures to illustrate everything from the Canadian Rockies and old New England to Vesuvius and the 1900 World's Fair.

Like Edward McDowell, George Earle Raiguel had taken advantage of universal fascination with the building of the Panama Canal to expand his repertory. In subsequent years, he would make motion pictures of Paris, Switzerland, the shores of the Mediterranean, Japan, and China (Raiguel folder). One of the few female filmmaking lecturers, Bernyce Childs, began in 1906 to film the North American West Coast from San Diego as far north as Nome, Alaska. For years her lectures were accompanied by these films, until she eventually sold her negatives to the Charles Besler Company (*Moving Picture News* 1911). By 1910, virtually every corner of the globe had been included in travel films shot by itinerant lecturers. Robert Dyball Scarlett parlayed his time in the Philippines into a series of films that supported his lecturing career for many years (Scarlett folder). In support of his "Travelogues," Clarence Price offered "the most wonderful moving pictures ever exhibited in the United States. These pictures were taken in foreign countries under the personal direction of Mr. Price, with his own photographers and picture machines." Price's films covered the great cities of Europe and the Mediterranean, including Pompeii, Venice, Algiers, Paris, and Copenhagen, as well as Holland, Sweden, Switzerland, Egypt, and China. In addition, his publicity promised "smugglers at work on the France-Italy border" and "scenes in darkest Africa, India, Ceylon, Japan, Russia, Germany, England, and Norway" (Price folder). Though these films have not to my knowledge been preserved, their role in a program of platform lectures is made clear in the lecturer's publicity pamphlets.

Throughout the first and into the second decade of the century, traveling lecturers continued to fill out their programs with moving pictures. When the summer tent chautauqua movement was organized, ever new opportunities were created for lecturers. As Jane Schulz put it: "Residents of Chautauqua communities were searching for inspiration and enlightenment, but they also were looking for stories that took them outside the limited orbit of their experience. Sensing this interest, Chautauqua management made sure that they booked an occasional travel and adventure program for each summer season" (2002: 104–6). With his wife, A. W. Stephens accompanied his performances with moving pictures wherever he lectured in the upper Midwest. The press clippings dossier included in his publicity pamphlet related his triumphs in such towns as Earlville, Iowa; Camargo, Illinois; Peebles, Ohio; and Pardeeville, Wisconsin (Stephens folder). George Earle Raiguel and Frederick Poole featured their films of Europe and China in Philadelphia's Witherspoon Hall, as part of a University Extension Society lecture series (Raiguel folder). Arthur K. Peck offered not only traditional views of the landmarks of European culture and the beauties of American nature in many high-profile East Coast venues as well as Midwest chautauquas but also a series of moving pictures depicting the activities of the coastal lifesaving service—a topic destined to help free travel films from their dependency on accompanying lectures. According to his publicity, Peck "was among the very first to offer moving pictures to his patrons to supplement Travel Lectures when desired" (Peck folder). J. E. Comerford not only projected films in support of his lecture "A Day and a Night with Our Life Savers," his troupe also provided "sensational stage effects," including sound effects of every sort (Comerford folder).

In addition to travel films in the tradition of Stoddard and Holmes, many platform lecturers produced nature films to accompany their lectures. John P. Gilbert shot his own nature study and "microphotography" films (Gilbert folder). Richard E. Follett, director of the Detroit Zoological Society, was a leader in producing wildlife films (Follett folder). In this domain he was joined by the curator of the Bronx Zoological Park, Raymond L. Ditmars, with his 1914 film *The Book of Nature* (Hanson 1988: 89). Other nature films were produced by lecturers Howard Cleaves and Lee Keedick and by Kadow Productions (Cleaves, Keedick, and Kadow folders). Before he perfected his famous camera, Carl Akeley used films shot in Africa to complement his lectures (Akeley folder). The lectures delivered by the naturalist Arthur C. Pillsbury were accompanied by motion pictures made with the help of x-rays.

During the second decade of the century, several developments conspired to break travel films and nature documentaries out of the performance orientation that had previously defined them. Until about 1910, moving pictures were considered by travel lecturers as essential props in their program. Like comedy routines, stage dialogue, and specially confected sets, moving pictures provided necessary differentiation among live performers. For this reason, lecturers carefully protected their films from duplication. When they showed films taken by others, they often claimed authorship of those films in order to promote their own individuality. The growing complexities of film production and the difficulty of balancing a lecturing career with production of moving pictures (along with the development of summer tent chautauquas, which offered lucrative engagements during the very period when lecturers had previously shot their films) eventually combined to change this situation. Increasingly, lecturers collaborated with film production companies to shoot and edit their films. As early as 1907, the veteran journalist Alfred Patek had illustrated his lectures with films of the Panama Canal made in conjunction with a cameraman from the Edison Company (*Moving Picture World* 1907: 137). J. E. Comerford's life-saving films were produced in collaboration with the Kinetograph Company (Comerford folder). Edwin L. Barker developed the first of his so-called industrial photoplays, *Back to the Old Farm*, with the Essanay Company (Barker folder). The professional support of an established production company was much appreciated by lecturers who had a hard enough time meeting a busy lecture schedule.

Once their signature films were widely distributed, however, some of the shine was instantly rubbed off their performances. In many cases, lecturers responded by shifting their focus. Once a renowned monologist, impersonator, and lecturer, in subsequent years Edwin L. Barker would turn his entire attention to filmmaking, as director of "Barker's World Picture Stories," including *The Dawn of Plenty, The Dawn of Power,* and *The Dawn of Commerce* (Barker folder). Another lyceum-circuit lecturer, F. Tennyson Neely, would eventually style himself as "publisher and lecturer," thanks to his "Wonder Pictures." These films, including *The Nations at War, With the German Army, Submarine Warfare, The Bandits of Mexico, Great Italian-Austrian Struggle*, and *Our Country at Peace*, were advertised as having been shot on the battlefields of the Great War (*Exhibitors Herald* 1916; Neely folder). As

Neely put it, he began booking his films "with or without lecturer" (Neely folder). This potential separation of the film from its lecturer-author bespeaks a major change in travel and other documentary films. Once tied ineluctably to a lecturer's performance, films might now be understood as separable and even separate commodities, a potential source of income for any exhibitor, even in the absence of the film's author-lecturer.

This process had been facilitated by two important 1912 film events. In February 1912, Kinemacolor opened its most successful film in New York City. *Durbar in Kinemacolor* showed King George V of Great Britain and Queen Mary participating in the durbar held in Delhi, India. At first presented with Lawrence Grant's lecture, the film was so successful that it took on a life of its own, independent of Kinemacolor's house lecturer (Musser and Nelson 1991: 162ff.). Two months later came the unprecedented success of *Paul J. Rainey's African Hunt*. Originally eight reels long, this record of a high-profile African safari—led by the explorer Paul J. Rainey accompanied by John C. Hemment, a photographer, and a taxidermist from the Smithsonian Institution, Professor Edmund Heller—was edited to five thousand feet for its April 1912 release and subsequently expanded to six reels for a November 1913 re-release. Initially, a lecture by Hemment accompanied the film, but by November 1913 subtitles had been added, thus facilitating distribution of the film "with or without lecturer" (Hanson 1988: 703). In June 1914 a sequel, *Rainey's African Hunt*, opened at New York's Casino Theater (Hanson 1988: 755). Both of these films were extensively covered not only by the trade press but by the popular press as well.

The success of Rainey's films led to a boom in expedition and nature films. Though destined for traditional distribution (usually on a states-rights basis), many of these films were at first presented by a lecturer in a lyceum-like context. When it opened in New York in May 1912, *The Alaska-Siberian Expedition* (Alaskan-Siberian Motion Pictures, 1912) was accompanied by a lecture delivered by the filmmaker, Frank E. Kleinschmidt, himself. In Philadelphia the lecture was presented by another member of the expedition (Hanson 1988: 10). In all likelihood, the competing *Atop of the World in Motion* (Beverly B. Dobbs, 1912) received the same treatment. The photographer Martin Johnson documented life in the South Pacific in the 1913 *Jack London's Adventures in the South Seas*. A year later, Kleinschmidt was back with *Captain F. E. Kleinschmidt's Arctic Hunt* (Arctic Film Co., 1914). The same year, Albert Blinkhorn offered *The Capture of a Sea Elephant and Hunting Wild Game in the South Pacific Islands* (Albert Blinkhorn, 1914); the explorer Vilhjalmur Stefansson produced *Rescue of the Stefansson Arctic Expedition* (Sunset Motion Picture Co., 1914); and J. Campbell Besley produced *The Captain Besley Expedition* (Captain Besley Motion Picture Co., 1914). The following year, Besley would offer a sequel, *In the Amazon Jungles with the Captain Besley Expedition* (Captain Besley Motion Picture Co., 1915). Lady Grace Mackenzie also recorded her safari in *Lady Mackenzie's Big Game Pictures* (Lady Mackenzie Film Co., 1915). Even America participated in this movement, through films like Frank M. Buckland's and J. F. Cleary's *American Game Trails* (Education Films Corp. of America, 1915).

In many ways, these expedition films served to perpetuate the tradition of films made and accompanied by platform lecturers. Always closely identified with a specific explorer, who often made personal appearances and provided lectures in conjunction with film screenings, these films were usually distributed by the explorer himself or herself rather than by one of the era's well-known production companies. A series of films produced by the explorer Edward A. Salisbury helped to break this bondage to a personal appearance aesthetic. In 1915 Salisbury had lectured in San Francisco, New York, and

Chicago to accompany *Wild Life of America in Films* (Edward A. Salisbury, 1915), made in cooperation with government officials (Hanson 1988: 1039), but Salisbury's next film would break free from the filmmaker/explorer-returns-home-as-lecturer approach. Using footage shot on a year-long expedition down the East Coast of the United States, through the Caribbean and the Panama Canal, and up the western coast of Central America, Salisbury produced three films—*On the Spanish Main, Pirate Haunts,* and *The Footsteps of Capt. Kidd.* At first presented by the explorer himself in a traditional lecture-oriented fashion, the films were soon outfitted with titles by the novelist Rex Beach (who had also participated in the exhibition) and shown in March and April 1917, without a lecturer, in New York's prestigious Rialto Theater. Subsequently, these films were distributed by the Grand Feature Film Company.

The rise of newsreels shortly after 1910 further aided in wrenching documentary films out of the live performance lecturing world and establishing them as viable products available for general distribution. Every year would bring additional competition for Pathé's pioneering newsreel, which had begun in August 1911. In February 1912 Gaumont began offering its *Animated Weekly*. On the first day of 1913, the *Mutual Weekly* was introduced. In 1914 Selig teamed up with the Hearst newspapers to produce its own newsreel (Bowser 1990: 185). Before and after the turn of the century, traveling lecturers had regularly built programs around news from the other side of the world. Many lectures on Cuba and the Philippines were spawned by the Spanish-American War; these were often accompanied by moving pictures showing important locations and reconstructing newsworthy events. During the 1904–05 season, both Lyman Howe and E. Burton Holmes showed films presenting aspects of the Russo-Japanese War, with special attention to the siege and capture of Port Arthur (Musser and Nelson 1991: 162ff.). When the building of the Panama Canal was the big news, everyone from Holmes and McDowell to Patek and Raiguel got into the act. Every year, as they struggled to produce or cobble together films to support their routines, lecturers looked to current events as one potential guide. The increasing popularity of newsreels in the new decade put a decided brake on the production of contemporary-event films in support of traveling lecturers. For example, the Mexican Revolution was virtually ignored by lecturing filmmakers but provided material for several feature films, including *Barbarous Mexico* (America's Feature Film Co., 1912), *Mexican War Pictures* (Lubin Mfg. Co., 1913), and *The Life of General Villa* (Mutual Film Corp., 1914). Produced for regular distribution, these films went straight to movie theaters rather than to the lecture circuits.

When war broke out in Europe in 1914, many companies rushed to produce and distribute feature documentaries. While a few of these, like *The Battle and Fall of Przemysl* (American Correspondent Film Co., 1915), were outfitted with lectures meant to be read during screening (Hanson 1988: 48), by far the majority were prepared for commercial theatrical distribution by the inclusion of explanatory intertitles. Within eighteen months of the war's beginning, American exhibitors had been offered such forgotten gems as *On the Belgian Battlefield* (Tribune Company, 1914), *The War of the World* (Lewis Pennant Features, 1914), *The Battles of a Nation* (American Correspondent Film Co., 1915), *The German Side of the War* (Chicago Tribune, 1915), *The History of the World's Greatest War* (Selig Polyscope Co., 1915), *History of the Great European War* (Picture Playhouse Film Co., 1915), *European War Pictures* (Apex Film Co., 1915), *On the Firing Line with the Germans* (Industrial Moving Picture Co., 1915), *Russian Battlefields* (Chicago Tribune,

1915), and *The Warring Millions* (American Correspondent Film Co., 1915).

During the first decade of the century, homemade films about foreign places and events had provided itinerant lecturers with personalized props for their programs. Like other contemporary stage performers, these lecturers used every means at their disposal to individualize and popularize their routines. Moving pictures provided a perfect medium for this process. By the middle of the next decade, however, films about faraway places had earned a new status. Travel and war films had been severed from the live stage, turned instead into commodities expected to stand by themselves. With information previously provided by a lecturer now built into intertitles, these films were able to enter into a new type of commercial configuration, where the films would do the traveling, without the need for a lecturer to accompany them. No longer lecturers' props, these films had now become industrial products.

NOTE

1. This essay relies heavily on the papers of the Redpath Lyceum Bureau, which are deposited in the Department of Special Collections of the University of Iowa Library. The largest existing collection on this topic, the Redpath Chautauqua Collection includes 7,949 publicity brochures, promotional advertisements, and flyers for 4,545 lecturers, teachers, preachers, politicians, actors, singers, concert companies, magicians, whistlers, and other performers who traveled the lyceum and chautauqua circuits at the beginning of the twentieth century. All subsequent mentions of named folders refer to portions of the Redpath Chautauqua Collection. For further information on this collection, see Altman 2004a.

WORKS CITED

Altman, Rick, ed. 1990. *Sound Theory/Sound Practice.* New York: Routledge.

_____. 2004a. "The Redpath Chautauqua Collection." *Cinema & Cie* 3.

_____. 2004b. *Silent Film Sound.* New York: Columbia University Press.

Barber, X. Theodore. 1993. "The Roots of Travel Cinema: John L. Stoddard, E. Burton Holmes and the Nineteenth-Century Illustrated Travel Lecture." *Film History: An International Journal* 5, no. 1: 68–84.

Barsam, Robert Meran. 1973. *Nonfiction Film: A Critical History.* New York: Dutton.

Bowser, Eileen. 1990. *The Transformation of Cinema: 1907–1915.* New York: Charles Scribner's Sons.

Depue, Oscar B. 1967. "My First Fifty Years in Motion Pictures." In *A Technological History of Motion Pictures and Television*, ed. Raymond Fielding, 60–64. Berkeley: University of California Press.

Exhibitors Herald. 1916. 5 February.

Fairweather, Kathleen. 1998. "The Towering Challenge of Everest." *American Cinematographer* 75, no. 5 (May): 8–52.

Gaudreault, André, and Germain Lacasse, eds. 1996. *Le bonimenteur de vues animées/The Moving Picture Lecturer.* Special issue *Iris* 22.

Griffiths, Alison. 1996. "Science and Spectacle: Native American Representation in Early Cinema." In *Dressing in Feathers: The Construction of the Indian in American Popular Culture*, ed. S. Elizabeth Bird, 79–95. Boulder, Colo.: Westview Press.

_____. 2002. *Wondrous Difference: Cinema, Anthropology, and Turn-of-the-Century Visual Culture.* New York: Columbia University Press.

_____.2003. "Medieval Travelogues: Tapestry and Gothic Architecture as Precursors to Imax." Paper presented at the Multi-Media Histories Conference, Exeter University, UK.

_____.2004. "The Largest Picture Ever Executed by Man': Panoramas and the Emergence of Large-Screen and 360 Degree Technologies." In *Screen Culture: History and Textuality*, ed. John Fullerton, 199–200. London: John Libbey Press.

Hanson, Patricia King, ed. 1988. *The American Film Institute Catalog of Motion Pictures Produced in the United States: Feature Films, 1911–1920.* Berkeley: University of California Press.

Holmes, E. Burton. 1901. *The Burton Holmes Lectures, with Illustrations from Photographs by the Author.* 10 volumes. Battle Creek, Mich.: Little-Preston.

_____. 1953. *The World Is Mine.* Culver City, Calif.: Murray and Gee.

Lacasse, Germain. 2000. *Le bonimenteur de vues animées: Le cinéma muet entre tradition et modernité.* Québec: Nota bene; Paris: Méridiens Klincksieck.

Moving Picture News. 1911. "Educational Lectures." 11 March, 9.

Moving Picture World. 1907. 4 May, 137.

Musser, Charles, and Carol Nelson. 1991. *High-Class Moving Pictures: Lyman H. Howe and the Forgotten Era of Traveling Exhibition, 1980–1920.* Princeton, N.J.: Princeton University Press.

Pfefferman, Naomi. 1995. "On Top of the World." *American Cinematographer* 76 (August): 32–34.

Stoddard, John L. 1897. *John L. Stoddard's Lectures: Illustrated and Embellished with Views of the World's Famous Places and People, Being the Identical Discourses Delivered During the Past Eighteen Years Under the Title of the Stoddard Lectures*. 10 volumes. Boston: Balch Bros.

Thompson, Kristen, and David Bordwell. 1994. *Film History: An Introduction*. New York: McGraw-Hill.

Wilson, Edward L. 1874–88. *Wilson's Lantern Journeys: A Series of Descriptions of Journeys at Home and Abroad for Use with Views in the Magic Lantern or the Stereoscope*. 3 volumes. Philadelphia: Benerman and Wilson.

3

ANONYMOUS

BURTON HOLMES PLEASES A LARGE AUDIENCE AT THE COLUMBIA (1905)

To be as near eye-witnesses of the wonderful Japanese campaign against Port Arthur as the ingenuity of human inventiveness could make possible—such was the unique treat enjoyed by a deeply interested audience at the Columbia Theater yesterday afternoon. Burton Holmes' "travelogue" transcended thus the merits of even his other most beautifully illustrated picture-lectures, in that it transported its spectators not merely to far-away scenes, but into the very heart of a thrilling and supremely important war, the echoes of which have scarcely died out in the peace of Portsmouth. The photographer on the field of battle and the moving picture expert, snapshotting the perilous flight and explosion of tremendous death-dealing shells, have brought vividly before the view, as though one were actually on the battlefield, the terrors and mighty enginery of siege and assault. The little "press gallery" of war correspondents and photographers on the hill outside Port Arthur was shown, and those who gazed could have felt almost as though they, too, were sitting there watching the breathlessly momentous conflict. These views—authentic battle pictures and panorama of bursting shells and mines—gave one an overpowering idea of the force of explosives in modern warfare. The monster bombardment of the huge "Osaka babies" (17-ton guns), spitting destruction on the Russian forts, was impressive enough, but the climax came in the canvas-thrown spectacle of the blowing up of the crucial Russian stronghold by a giant undermine of dynamite. Against these remarkable triumphs of motion photography were shown the trials and hard labors of the little Japanese soldiers afield—tugging, a thousand in a line, at the overland-drawn cannons, slowly working as sappeurs with pick and spade in the trenches, carrying out the will of the iron-nerved Gen. Nogi. The Russian himself was shown as a brave fellow, but every heart in the audience responded to the peculiar, emphatic marching, with the steps of conquerors, of the victorious Japs into the fallen citadel of the foe. From the razor-like sweep of the Japanese battleships on sea to the firm tramp, tramp of the inmarching heroes at Port Arthur, the whole "travelogue" was a sort of picture-epic of Japanese heroism and triumph.

A notable feature of the Russian pictures was the presence in one of them of Gen. Trepoff, on whose shoulders the Jewish assassinations of Russia are laid.

4

KRISTEN WHISSEL

PLACING THE SPECTATOR ON THE SCENE OF HISTORY

Modern Warfare and the Battle Reenactment at the Turn of the Century (2008)

In January 1900, after the celebrations of the victory over Spain by the United States had waned and the Philippine-American War and the Boer War were escalating, an article in *Leslie's Weekly* entitled "Pictures That Will Be Historic" announced that "the American Biograph is taking a prominent part in the two wars which are now occupying the center of the world's stage . . . We are promised some vivid, soul-stirring pictures of actual, grewsome war, and the conditions under which the Biograph operators in the Transvaal and the Philippines are working are so favorable that the promise will probably be made good."[1] The much-hoped-for fulfillment of the cinema's promise to provide a technologically mediated view that visually placed the audience on the imperial battlefield echoed speculations about the same promise made by photography in the middle of the nineteenth century. Writing on the eve of the Crimean War and the U.S. Civil War, Oliver Wendell Holmes predicted that "the next European War will send us stereographs of battles. It is asserted that a bursting shell can be photographed. The time is perhaps at hand when a flash of light as sudden and brief as that of lightning which shows a whirling wheel standing stock still, shall preserve the very instant of the shock of contact of the mighty armies that are even now gathering. The lightning from heaven does actually photograph objects on the bodies of those it has just blasted—so we are told by many witnesses. The lightning of clashing sabres and bayonets may be forced to stereotype itself in a stillness as complete as the tumbling tide of Niagara as we see it self-pictured."[2]

At both of these cultural-political moments, new technologies of visual representation promised to transform the shock of modern warfare into consumable spectacles available for mass consumption by civilian spectators eager to *see* history. Holmes's anticipation of instantaneous photography by approximately thirty years allowed him to imagine an ideal form of image making analogous to a bolt of lightning and hence able to match the violence of modern mechanized warfare. He describes a form of photography powerful enough to arrest an otherwise unstoppable motion at the point of irreversibility—the spinning of a wheel, a waterfall, a bursting shell, or clashing armies—and thereby make the historically significant moment of military shock visible while diminishing its capacity to harm the observer. Half a century later, the author of the *Leslie's* article asks the reader to return to Holmes's era and to the Civil War and the Crimean and "imagine the historical value of a moving picture of the charge at Balaclava, or of the advance upon Gettysburg." Like Holmes, this author imagines future military history captured and rendered visible at its most dynamic and incendiary moment when charging armies reach the peak of their momentum and collide. Moreover, the technologies they discuss seem to shape their understanding of history—for in each case to "see history" is to see the "vivid" and the "grewsome," or the "moment of the shock of contact" between clashing forces. In short, technologies of vision promised to satisfy curiosity about (the gruesomeness of) modern warfare and a hence desire to participate visually in the *trauma* of history. Photography and film seemed to offer viewers the opportunity to savor what Alan Trachtenberg calls "that pleasurable fright from the safest of distances: that between one's eyes and a photograph,"[3] or between spectator and screen.

Holmes's expectations and the actual outcome of photographic enterprises during the Civil War in many ways parallel the expectations and outcome of cinema and of American imperial wars at the turn of the last century. As Trachtenberg notes, Holmes's prediction of the imminent photographic recording of military shock was belied by the actual output of Civil War photographs. The camera's technological limitations and long exposure times (from three to twenty seconds) excluded "actual battle" from the kinds of events and scenes that photography might record; hence Matthew Brady's photographers captured only war preparations and the aftermath of battles in images of damaged and dismembered bodies, ruins, and war-torn landscapes.[4] In turn, as Timothy Sweet notes, many of the latter were photographic reenactments of sorts: often the pictured scene was arranged or composed by the photographer to yield ideological meanings about the nature of the war, its inevitable outcome, and the future of the Union.[5] Like their counterparts during the Civil War, moving picture cameramen such as Biograph's Billy Bitzer (who landed with U.S. forces in Cuba) and W. K. L. Dickson (attached to British forces in South Africa), C. Fred Ackerman (who was attached to U.S. forces in the Philippines), and Edison's William Paley (who followed U.S. troops to Cuba only to have to depart because of illness), were frustrated by their attempts to record battles on film. The hypermodern condition of contemporary warfare—its unprecedented mechanization of violence and unpredictable, traumatizing shocks; its unstable visual fields; its surprise attacks and blinding smoke; its dispersal of charging, falling, and dismembered bodies across distant, tropical landscapes—made cinematic recordings of real battles difficult if not impossible. As the *Leslie's* article suggests, the same technology of vision that had produced a surplus of films of camp life and war preparations, new military technologies, victory parades, and military drills had also produced a paucity of "vivid, soul-stirring, pictures of actual, grewsome war." To represent this most modern scene cinematically, companies resorted to reenactments restaged after the fact, and on U.S. soil, by national guardsmen or hired actors.

Hence the battle reenactment film seems to have addressed twinned desires linked to the visual consumption of the nation's military-imperial history: the desire to follow the movements of armed forces, even in battle, and the attendant need to "manage" the inevitable trauma incurred by modern warfare. That such desires were paramount in American culture in the late nineteenth century and the early twentieth is not surprising, for U.S. history had long been inscribed within ideologies of expansion that required the conquest of space by the military, by settlers, and by technologies such as the railway. And [. . .] by the end of the nineteenth century the soldier had become a rather celebrated icon of modern mobility within American culture. In turn, new technologies of war enabled the annihilation of space and time in profound new ways that were calculated to accelerate the momentum of clashing forces, thus making military "shock" an effect of new types of mobilization. Live and film battle reenactments addressed the spectatorial desire to be absorbed visually into paths of military traffic as it moved across distant frontiers and to view the "moment of the shock of contact" between clashing forces. In turn, the reiterative structure of the reenactment—its rehearsal and repetition of violent conflict—seems to have made it a powerful form for mastering the trauma of war. The fact that numerous live and filmed reenactments produced in the United States represented military subjects suggests that the very artificiality of the reenactment provided the pleasurable means of knowing and "seeing" military-imperial history that documentary actualities could not, thereby giving rise to an early film genre that continues to challenge any easy classification as fiction or nonfiction film. Hence the feature of the battle reenactment that I seek to address [. . .] is its imaginary circulation of audiences along with imperial traffic to distant frontiers through spectacularly rendered live performances and moving images that blurred the distinction between representation and the "historical" real and in the process annealed the shocks of warfare.

When discussing the generic liminality of early reenactment films, historians tend to agree that, as Richard Abel notes, "imposing the later distinction between documentary and fictional genres ... is problematic in several respects." As Abel states in his history of early French film, prior to 1908 "the difference between recording a current public event as it was happening and reconstructing a past (or even present) historical event in a studio" was relatively insignificant. More important "was that a representation of the 'historical' differed from a representation of the 'purely fictive' or imaginary—which meant that referential differences mattered more than differences in modes of representation ... In other words, the 'historical scene' was bound to the actualité within an unbroken continuum uniting historical past and present." This historical continuum allowed French filmmakers such as Pathé and Méliès to "exploit the shared 'family resemblance' between historical reconstructions and actualites."[6] Miriam Hansen concurs by noting that "many actualities involved reconstructions ... yet not necessarily with the intent to deceive; as a subgenre, dramatic reenactments of current events were considered legitimate. [While the] boundaries between documentary reality and *mise-en-scène* may have been relative, they seem to have mattered less than the kind of fascination which connects, for instance, the 'realistic imitation' of President McKinley's assassin in the electric chair in *The Execution of Czolgosz* (Porter/Edison 1901) with historical reenactments such as *The Execution of Mary Queen of Scots* (Edison 1895)—or the substitution trick in *Execution by Hanging* (Biograph 1905) with the authentic footage of *Electrocuting an Elephant* (Edison

1903)."[7] For Hansen, then, sensationalist appeal joined to a historical referent helped construct the reenactment's legitimacy in representing "actual" events.

Following on from Abel and Hansen, [. . .] I will turn to the question of *how* or upon what representational, epistemological, and aesthetic grounds the reenactment film achieved legitimacy for articulating the historical real in general and the battle in particular. For while we know that the reenactment film achieved legitimacy as historical discourse, we also know that audiences and reviewers were often able to recognize the (visible) formal and aesthetic differences, as well as the subject matter, that frequently distinguished the two. Though the relationship between the actuality film and the reenactment film tells us much about the reception of the reenactment as a legitimate historical discourse, the significant cultural and aesthetic relationship between the reenactment film and the live reenactment reveals even more. Importantly, the *live* reenactment prepared consumers of urban commercialized leisure for their encounter with film reenactments and, in the process, helped establish what we might call this early film genre's peculiar authenticity. Moreover, like battle reenactment films, live battle reenactments often mobilized audiences to scenes of expansion and spatial conquest while simultaneously addressing the trauma that inevitably resulted from the soldier's—and the spectator's—absorption into this violent form of imperial traffic. In order to demonstrate how it did so, I will analyze the live battle reenactments and military displays featured in Buffalo Bill's Wild West and the particular relations they constructed between "history" and its spectacular simulation, and between the "original" witness of an event and the secondary audience who delighted in its reenactment. After contrasting the mode of address and visual lure of the battle reenactment to that of P. T. Barnum's hoaxes and humbug, I will analyze how many battle reenactment films share the mode of address, spectatorship, and reality effects previously manufactured by the Wild West. Historical evidence suggests that by 1898 the culturally established form of the battle reenactment strongly informed turn-of-the-century notions of what modern warfare would look like to a "witness" on the battlefield. When turn-of-the-century commentators speculated about the appearance of the actuality films of battles, they described texts that featured the point of view, content, and formal features provided by reenactment films. Paradoxically, then, to seem most "real" the turn-of-the-century war actuality had to achieve the "reality effects" that had already been established by the (live and film) battle reenactment.[8]

The Peculiar Authenticity of the Live Reenactment

The reenactment was a prominent and profitable part of live urban commercialized leisure in U.S. culture since the 1880s. John F. Kasson notes that amusement seekers at Coney Island could see spectacular reenactments of famous disasters such as "The Fall of Pompeii" (which simulated the eruption of Mount Vesuvius), another that simulated the eruption of Mount Pelée, and still others that restaged the Johnstown flood of 1889 and the Galveston, Texas, flood of 1900.[9] The reenactment of military campaigns, however, were most popularly incarnated in William F. Cody's traveling entertainment enterprise—Buffalo Bill's Wild West. Between 1883 and 1913 the Wild West appeared before audiences in numerous cities in the United States and Europe, including New York, Atlanta, Manchester, London, Rome, Paris, and also at a number of world's fairs, including Chicago's 1893 World's Columbian Exposition (where it was located just beyond the official grounds) and Buffalo's 1901 Pan-American

Exposition.[10] Wild West reenactments and military displays were often promoted as "object lessons" that demonstrated through visually compelling spectacles the higher ideals characteristic of a fast-receding, nostalgically rendered past. Cody's Wild West represented early stages of continental expansion by the United States through reenactments of Indian battles (including Custer's Last Stand), attacks on pioneer cabins, stagecoach ambushes, buffalo hunts, and catastrophes such as prairie fires, stampedes, and cyclones.[11] These high-tech reenactments synthesized the sensationalism of the dime novel (in which Cody made his first mass-cultural appearance)[12] and the popular stage melodrama with the myth of the frontier that had become so compelling for urban easterners mired in big-city life.[13] The resulting "Drama of Civilization" was produced by Steele McKaye, whose stage melodramas, Nicholas Vardac argues, represent the culmination of the theater's late-nineteenth-century drive toward a realist "pictorial ideal" later actualized in the moving pictures.[14] Played out against a backdrop of massive panoramas and cycloramas and accompanied by live music and a lecturer's narration (but virtually no dialogue), Wild West reenactments featured grand spectacles of the dynamic, violent action of frontiersmen, scouts, and cavalry as they circulated through hostile landscapes and subordinated "villainous" native populations to American "civilization."

Though Cody promoted his Wild West reenactments as factual, Richard Slotkin notes that "the Wild West wrote 'history' by conflating it with mythology. The reenactments were not recreations but reductions of complex events into 'typical scenes.' Cody's 'West' was a mythic space in which past and present, fiction and reality could co-exist; a space in which history, translated as myth, was reenacted as ritual."[15] In turn, the moral of the story rehearsed the American stage melodrama's characteristic conflict between "innocence" (civilization) persecuted by villainy (its savage foe), with the former ultimately defeating the latter. As Linda Williams notes, though the Wild West elaborated scenes of expansion and imperial conquest by the United States, it consistently represented the conquerors as victims whose suffering at the hands of Native Americans needed to be displayed and then avenged, over and over again, in racialized spectacles of power and dynamic action.[16] Cody's profitable articulation of national "history" via the conjoined modes of myth, realist spectacle, sensation, and melodrama was nevertheless championed as an example of progressive education about the nation's recent history of continental expansion.[17] Indeed, as Joy Kasson notes, the Wild West became a compelling force for translating Cody's personal memories into broadly embraced historical memories shared by audiences who participated in his reconstitution of the nation's past.[18]

Sold for ten cents before every show, the extensive program for the Wild West gives insight into the modes of address and forms of spectatorship around which Cody and his partner, Nate Salsbury, constructed their reenactments. The program was purchased by those attending the show as well as by those who could not afford to attend, and hence it was a form of mass cultural entertainment in its own right. It provided detailed discourse on the nature of continental expansion and overseas imperialism by the United States, narrative summaries of the reenacted events, brief biographies of Cody and the other featured "historical characters," as well as reprinted reviews of the Wild West and letters of support from military officials and historians who testified to the exhibition's authenticity. In this respect, the program provided a supplementary discourse that helped shore up the claims that the Wild West made about the historical authenticity of its reenactments. Hence, just as it detailed the historical contexts in which the reenacted events "originally" took place, the program also provided cues regarding the attraction-spectator relation on which the visual pleasure of the reenactment relied. The program even provided audiences with a (perhaps already familiar) vocabulary for thinking about the realism and sense of historical presence that the reenactment evoked, deploying terms such as "actual pictures," "living pictures," and "faithful pictures." As explained in the program text, for example: "Our aim is to make the public acquainted with the manners and customs of the daily life of the dwellers in the far West of the United States through the means of actual and realistic scenes from life. At each performance marked skill and daring are presented. Not only from the standpoint of the spectator, but also from a critical point of view, we assure the auditor that each scene presents a faithful picture of the habits of these folk, down to the smallest detail."[19]

[. . .] To bolster the realism of its reenactments, the program for the Wild West suggested that the (original) Wild West often appeared before the frontiersman "as a picture set up before a subject." Hence, the Wild West program insisted that life on the frontier was characterized by participation in—and the visual consumption of—live spectacles of dynamic action, violent conflict, and astonishing displays of power. Put differently, the program included awed *spectatorship* as a component of life on the frontier and the battlefield. Pomeroy's reprinted review of the Wild West suggests that Cody fulfilled his promise to "illustrate life as it is *witnessed* on the plains." He continued by stating: "Could a man now living have stood on the shore of the Red Sea and witnessed the passage of the children of Israel and the Struggle of Pharaoh and his hosts, what a sight he would have seen, and how interested would be those to whom he related the story. Could the man who stood on the shore to see Washington and his soldiers cross the Delaware have lived till now to tell the story, what crowds he would have to listen. How interesting would be the story of a man, if he were now living, who had witnessed the landing of Columbus on the shores of the New World, or the story of one of the hardy English Puritans who took passage on the 'Mayflower,' and landed on the rock-bound coast of New England. So, too, the angel who has seen the far West become tame and dotted under the advancing civilization as the pioneers fought their way westward into desert and jungle. What a story he can relate as to the making of that history and what a history America has, to be sure!"[20]

As an "angel who has seen the far West become tame," Cody occupies the ideal and unique position of one who was simultaneously and somewhat paradoxically a part of the spectacle he witnessed. The claim that the reenactment's spectacular simulation of an equally spectacular real had been tailored around Cody's privileged point of view loaned support to the reenactment's claim to historical authenticity. As Pomeroy's review explained: "Since the railroad gave its aid to pioneering, America is making history faster than any other country in the world. *Her pioneers are fast passing away.* A few years more and the great struggle for possession will be ended and generations will settle down to enjoy the homes their fathers located and fenced in for them. Then will come the picture maker—he who with pen, pencil, and panel can tell the story as he understands it. The millions will read and look at what the pioneer did and what the historian related, wishing on the whole that they could have been there to have seen the original. These are some of the thoughts that crowd in upon us as we view the great living picture that the Hon. Wm. F. Cody ('Buffalo Bill') gives us at the Wild West Exhibition, which every man, woman and child the world over should see and study as realistic fact."[21]

According to Pomeroy, the urge to see the "original" frontier was an effect of industrialization: the railway had accelerated the pace of history itself and annihilated the past with the same rapidity that it annihilated space. The Wild West reanimated an image of pretechnological movement across the frontier and to ritualize forms of motion and transport displaced by new technologies. Yet the Wild West does not simply represent these protomodern forms of frontier traffic as do books and pictures. Pomeroy contends that literary and painterly representations of the West only intensify the desire to see a no-longer-available "original" Wild West visible to, observed, and known only by those pioneers who began "the great struggle for possession." The gap left between the pioneer and the picture maker, the "original"/historical real and its inadequate representation in literature, written history, and painting is filled by Cody's historical reenactments. Here, the reenactment claims to achieve the status of a "great living picture" appearing as "realistic fact" precisely by reproducing the point of observation from which this unfolding history—taking the shape of dynamic movement across space—was "originally" seen. The power and the pleasure of the Wild West's live reenactments were predicated on the splitting of Cody's own status as the "agent/witness" of history: to reenact spectacular history, he repeated the (violent, dynamic) actions of the historical agent of continental conquest; however, he passed along the (pleasurable) function of the witness-spectator to the audience.

By first establishing the presence of a spectator as an integral part of the original historical event, Cody made such a position available and seemingly authentic when the event was reenacted before a paying audience. Put differently, by placing an "original" spectator on the "scene" of history and then replicating such a position for spectators at its simulation, the Wild West made the reenactment highly pleasurable and in the process supported its claims of authenticity. Yet central to the pleasure of Cody's live reenactments was the trauma, violence, and shock of the historical scenes they repeated. On one hand, the Wild West insisted that the process of westward expansion it reenacted took place in an extremely harsh context characterized by violent conflict and circulation across the vast spaces of the frontier, and it was therefore *by definition* beyond the scope of any "audience" other than the exceptional pioneer. On the other hand, it insisted that the process of moving through the protomodern paths of frontier traffic was so central to American history and identity that it demanded a national—even international—audience. Hence, the particular visual pleasure and peculiar authenticity of Wild West reenactments seems to have derived from their power to endow audiences with an imaginary presence—or presence by visual proxy—at significant and highly sensational moments and movements in history that by definition precluded their attendance. It was precisely the "proximate distance" of the "agent-witness" that the Wild West aimed to reconstruct for its audiences. [. . .]

With their emphasis on dynamic movement across space and strenuous physicality, the Wild West's live reenactments were part of a shift in late-nineteenth-century popular culture away from a mode of intellection central to the "operational aesthetic" typical of P. T. Barnum's hoaxes and humbug and toward more "vigorous" forms of entertainment that, according to John F. Kasson, had previously "existed only on the margins of American life." Such amusements included prize fighting, competitive athletics, moving picture shows, and amusement parks, as well as literature that celebrated "masculine toughness" such as Owen Wister's literary western *The Virginian* (1902) and Jack London's *The Call of the Wild* (1903).[22] This shift is quite important for understanding the cultural history of the popular reenactment and the battle reenactment film's place in that history, for it is tempting to see the reenactment film as a kind of hoax or sham. Indeed, at first glance Cody's Wild West reenactments seem to be in the same vein as Barnum's famous hoaxes. As Barnum had done before him, Cody's Wild

West staged a buffalo hunt, claimed to display "authentic" relics such as the Deadwood stagecoach, and exhibited feats of physical skill (notably Annie Oakley's sharpshooting) so astonishing as to seem impossible and hence the effect of a trick. A closer comparison of the aesthetic and spectator-attraction relation typical of Barnum's and Cody's attractions suggests that Wild West reenactments signaled something of a departure from humbug. However, it is nevertheless worthwhile to think of Barnum's and Cody's audiences alongside one another; for though each audience paid to encounter and engage with simulations, neither seems to have done so naively.

In his study of Barnum's humbug, Neil Harris defines the particular pleasure and the cultural and social conditions involved in nineteenth-century audiences' encounter with, and consumption of, attractions such as the "Feejee mermaid" (a half-monkey, half-fish), a sham buffalo hunt, the display of Santa Anna's wooden leg, or the ostensibly "ancient" slave Joice Heth, which made such hoaxes pleasurable for audiences and profitable to purveyors. According to Harris, humbug thrived in a Jacksonian social and cultural milieu that was insistently egalitarian, rejected "secret learning and private information" in favor of lecture going, embraced widespread common-school education as "a guarantee for the republic's future," and was in the midst of a technological revolution supported by popular enthusiasm for scientific and industrial progress.[23] As technologies such as the railway and telegraph became more diffuse in American culture, so too did mechanical language and a measure of technical know-how. As Harris notes, "machinery was beginning to accustom the public not merely to a belief in the continual appearance of new marvels but to a jargon that concentrated on methods of operation, on aspects of mechanical organization and construction, on horsepower, gears, pulleys, and safety valves."[24] Popular delight in learning and the widespread acquisition of knowledge was accompanied by a widespread skepticism—a tendency to "test" anything and anyone for truthfulness. This combination made the American individual susceptible not to deceit and fraud but to the closely related (and more pleasurable) experience of "humbug" organized around a contest of wits between showman and amusement seeker. As Harris explains: "Experiencing a complicated hoax was pleasurable because of the competition between victim and hoaxer, each seeking to outmanoeuvre the other, to catch him off balance and detect the critical weakness.... Barnum understood that the opportunity to debate the issue of falsity, to discover how deception had been practiced, was even more exciting than the discovery of fraud itself. The manipulation of a prank, after all, was as interesting a technique in its own right as the presentation of genuine curiosities. Therefore, when people paid to see frauds, thinking they were true, they paid again to hear how the frauds were committed."[25] To exploit the popular propensity for skepticism and truth testing as well as critical evaluation and detection, Barnum encouraged his patrons to approach his attractions fully armed with doubt—ready to match wits with the showman and eager to penetrate the surface deception that cloaked the truth of the matter—and thereby provide a solution to the conundrum on display. In such a milieu, the ideal amusement seeker took up the position of the detective who "enjoyed disentangling the true from the false, the spurious from the genuine."[26]

[...] Live reenactments such as the Wild West helped establish a cultural disposition toward the historical reenactment, its mode of address, the kinds of visual pleasure it might provide, and its peculiar authenticity. In this respect, the Wild West and its detailed program helped to prepare audiences for their encounter with the reenactment film. Certainly, there were crucial differences between the live reenactment and that of the film. The live reenactment promised the presence of real "historical characters" and featured authentic relics, such as the Deadwood stagecoach, bearing scars and auratic traces of their past. However, the thick materiality of the Wild

West and its emphasis on authenticity and the physical presence of objects and individuals placed relative limitations (when compared to moving pictures) on its ability to circulate to audiences. And, while its pleasures derived from its power to place its audience on the simulated "scene" of history, its staging in large arenas (such as Madison Square Garden) held the audience at something of a distance from the depicted events and thereby placed limits upon the audience's sensation of immersion or absorption within such scenes. Battle reenactment films, by contrast, rarely featured "historical characters" or authentic relics but instead enlisted the skills of generic substitutes, such as national guardsmen, to reenact battles "originally" fought by the army. To compensate for the absence of live and "real" historical figures and for the filmed image's characteristic "presence of absence," battle reenactment films brought audiences closer to the field of battle, intensifying the sense of the spectator's visual presence on the depicted scene of history by aligning the audience's point of view with that of the camera. Indeed, the point of view provided by battle reenactment films tends to position spectators in the crossfire between enemy combatants as they move through and defend space, making it somewhat comparable to the point of view of those privileged few spectators who rode in the Deadwood stagecoach at the Wild West. And, as we shall see, the battle reenactment film's closer proximity to the historical "scene" of imperial conquest brings into sharper focus one crucial aspect of the cultural "work" done by the reenactment: its tendency to repeat the trauma of history in order to master it. [. . .]

Like Roosevelt's redeployment of the "Rough Rider" motif, the cinema's redeployment of the reenactment to represent violent struggle on this new frontier provided audiences with a familiar and familiarizing format for consuming "authentic" representations of national history as military spectacle. Such films promised audiences the (imaginary) proximate position of an agent-witness on the scene of imperial expansion. For example, in a paragraph introducing the section "War Films"—which includes actualities as well as reenactments of the Spanish-American War—the catalogue of the Edison agent F. M. Prescott promised exhibitors and their audiences precisely the sensation of being present as a witness on the battlefield: "In these superior films can be seen the dead and wounded and the dismantled cannon lying on the field of battle. The men are seen struggling for their lives, and the American flag proudly waves over them and can be plainly seen through the dense smoke. The brave American and Cuban soldiers show their valor and superiority in fighting the hated Spaniards. You think you can hear the huge cannon belch forth their death-dealing missiles, and can really imagine yourself on the field witnessing the actual battle."[27] Within this catalogue, the only films that depict battles or any significant "action" are reenactments and films of military drills. Hence, like the program for the Wild West, the Prescott catalogue suggests that the particular pleasure (and profitability) of reenactment films derived from their capacity to inspire the spectator's fantasy of presence on the scene of history, of finding oneself suddenly "on the field *witnessing* the actual battle" and perceiving the shock and trauma of modern history.

Not surprisingly, then, battle reenactment films shot after the war by the Edison Manufacturing Co. in New Jersey continue the tendency to orient the movement of the Rough Riders' "shock force" toward the camera. For example, *US Infantry Supported by Rough Riders at El Caney* (Edison, 1899) shows "a detachment of infantry, firing, advancing, kneeling and firing, again and again. The advance of the foot soldiers is followed by a troops of Rough Riders, riding like demons, yelling and firing revolvers as they pass out of sight."[28] The camera is placed at an oblique angle to the action, just at the side of the road along which the foot soldiers and Rough Riders advance, such that the soldiers fire at and advance toward it. *Skirmish of Rough Riders* (Edison, 1899) similarly angles its action obliquely toward the camera: the film opens with two marksmen lying behind a "dead" horse at the turn of a road, firing at the unseen enemy. In the background of the frame, the mounted Rough Riders wait. As the catalogue explains, "Suddenly comes the command, 'Forward,' and the riders dash up the road, out of sight, leaving behind them a great cloud of dust and smoke."[29] An alternating pleasure in power and powerlessness lies at the heart of such films: spectators might thrill in their imaginary placement in the path of this shock force—as its object—while knowing all along that they were (nationally, politically) aligned with the agents of this same force. Military shock and cinematic shock thereby intersected in the battle reenactment film to endow the civilian observer with spectatorial fantasies of imperial power, agency, and mobility. In turn, these films also foreground the mythologizing tendency of American battle reenactments: as it turned out, the Rough Riders saw only dismounted action in Cuba and so were the objects of a different kind of military shock. But perhaps the greatest mythologization effected is the visibility and visuality represented within these particular scenes of history; for, as many soldiers and journalists testified, the experience of modern warfare was defined by high-tech battlefield blindness and scenes of erasure. Just as Roosevelt's appropriation of the appellation "Rough Riders" suggests his canny use of the "Wild West" to shape popular perception of the war, it also suggests the degree to which live battle reenactments and military displays had shaped contemporary notions about the experience of "actual" battle. Preparations for the war were highly mediated, and the presence of newspapermen (such as Richard Harding Davis) and cameramen (such as Edison's William Paley) undoubtedly contributed to the sense of the war as something of an intertextual spectacle. In describing the moments immediately preceding the outbreak of fighting on the morning of the Battle of San Juan Hill, Roosevelt recounted: "It was a very lovely morning, the sky of cloudless blue, while the level, shimmering rays from the just-risen sun brought into fine relief the splendid palms which here and there towered above the lower growth. The lofty and beautiful mountains hemmed in the Santiago plain, making it an amphitheatre for the battle."[30] Roosevelt's description of the plain as "an amphitheatre for the battle" suggests his own perception of the contested territory as a stage designed to provide the agent-witness (and, perhaps, the world as audience) with an optimal point of view on the proceedings, replete with a "lofty and beautiful" picturesque backdrop. Yet the ensuing battle sharply undermined this expectation, for the Rough Riders experienced it as a terrifying combination of blindness and perilous visibility arising from the development and deployment of new military technologies—specifically the Krag-Jorgensen and smokeless gunpowder—calculated precisely to increase the "shock force" of the salvo.

According to Wolfgang Schivelbusch, the standard issue of firearms in the eighteenth century made possible the "salvo" or "volley"—the simultaneous, "collective, un-aimed discharge of firearms by the entire unit" from a technologically mediated distance. The perfectly timed salvo first razed as many soldiers as possible, and in doing so it created a vast spectacle of simultaneous casualties that terrified and demoralized those left standing in closed ranks on the battlefield. Schivelbusch notes that the salvo's technologically mediated distance meant that "the force of the clash lost its concrete physical manifestation," thereby changing the soldier's sensory experience of war: now the assault "occurred suddenly, invisibly; it came 'out of nowhere,'" denying the soldier the means of preparing himself for the blow. Hence, in comparing the state of mind of the medieval duelist with that of the modern combatant, Schivelbusch notes that "the intense relationship between the state of duelists may be seen as one of alert expectation. The individual combatants were able to see from exactly which direction the possible wound may be caused: they were, as it were, well prepared for it. From the eighteenth century on, such a state of readiness no longer existed."[31] A passive, psychological-perceptual meaning became grafted onto shock's active, physical-mechanical meaning. The salvo's terrifying invisibility and the soldier's inability to prepare for it resulted in his delayed realization of the wound or "overthrow" that had taken place within his body. As the military historian G. H. Groningen explains, this insensate state resulted "not only because of the rapidity of the damage but rather because of the total exertion of all their psychological powers towards other goals. Every sensation requires a degree of attention, however small."[32]

New military technology further denied the U.S. soldier's required "degree of attention": whereas Spain used smokeless gunpowder and Krag-Jorgensen rifles, the U.S. still used Springfield rifles and black gunpowder. Roosevelt described the effect of the smokeless gunpowder used by Spanish soldiers as "remarkable": "The air seemed full of the rustling sound of the Mauser bullets, for the Spaniards knew the trails by which we were advancing, and opened up heavily on our position. Moreover, as we advanced we were, of course, exposed, and they could see us and fire. But they themselves were entirely invisible. The jungle covered everything, and not the faintest trace of smoke was to be seen in any direction to indicate from whence the bullets came." While smokeless gunpowder and thick tropical vegetation gave Spain the military advantage of invisibility, gunpowder smoke coming from the Americans' weapons revealed their position and further obscured their already blocked vision. As Roosevelt concludes, "It was most bewildering to fight an enemy whom one so rarely saw" whose presence was indicated only by the menacing sound of Mauser bullets "singing through the trees over our heads, making a noise like the humming of telephone wires."[33] The invisibility of the Spanish forces, and the state of blocked vision experienced by the U.S. soldiers, found its way into popular representations of the war. As the catalogue description for the Wild West reenactment of the Battle of San Juan Hill explains: "To add to the horror of the situation, the infernal Spanish guerillas, concealed in the treetops and using smokeless gunpowder, which renders it impossible to locate them, make targets of our wounded and the surgeons and wearers of the Red Cross."[34] In turn, Frederic Remington represented this terrifying battlefield blindness in *Scream of Shrapnel at San Juan Hill, Cuba*—in which soldiers are shown convulsively flailing, ducking, dropping, and fruitlessly looking in every possible direction for the source of a salvo. However, as Alexander Nemerov notes, Remington's direct observation of the battle was prevented by the extreme conditions of modern warfare; he therefore described the famous battle as "the most glorious feat of arms I ever heard of."[35]

[. . .] On the other side of the world, battlefield blindness also afflicted the motion picture camera's mechanical eye. W. K. L. Dickson in *The Biograph in Battle*, his memoirs of his experiences filming British soldiers in the Boer War, described his attempt to film a battle in the valley of the Upper Tugela. Dickson used a telephoto lens and set up the Biograph "not fifty feet from the big guns." Though, as Dickson recounted, "the air was full of bursting shells," and though he could see "the flash of a Boer gun that might just probably miss the naval guns and strike us," the resulting film appears onscreen as nothing more than a panorama of the South African landscape: "The depth and vastness of the scene was so great as to somewhat disqualify it for a biographic view. I fear very few will be able to discern the shells bursting, or the cavalry and artillery below us ... As for the foot soldiers in khaki, it will be quite impossible to see them, as they are always invisible from a distance, being the color of the earth. The exact position of our guns and those of the enemy can be seen by studying the accompanying panoramic sketch ... Every hill and dale and winding of the [valley] is shown, and should one see the Biograph panoramic projection of the valley at the time of the battle he will get a very good idea of the whole thing, even if the distant puffs should be invisible."[36] Khaki-colored uniforms and the battle's massive scale—caused in part by the extended trajectory of modern artillery—conspired to camouflage weapons and soldiers alike, rendering the battle indistinguishable from the surrounding landscape.[37] Hence at precisely the historical moment that the cinema's panoramic perception and documentary capacities held forth the promise of actuality footage of such battles, the moving pictures encountered something of a limit case. The battle reenactment film emerged as a compromise between the at-times-conflicting scopic regimes of early cinema and turn-of-the-century imperial warfare. Like the live reenactments staged by the Wild West, reenactment films of the Spanish-American War and the Philippine-American War transformed the shock, surprise, and contingencies of modern imperial warfare into spectacular displays of military power and progress. In the process, film reenactments carved out the imaginary position of the agent-witness for their audiences by creating the illusion of being "embedded" within imperial traffic, and in so doing they created the pleasurable illusion of presence "on the scene" of history.

Edison's *Advance of the Kansas Volunteers at Caloocan* (Edison, 1899) provides a stunning example of such mediation. Unlike Dickson's failed battle actuality, the landscape in this reenactment film remains subordinated to the action, which in turn remains centered in the frame. The film opens with a line of "Filipino insurgents" firing directly at the camera. Then U.S. troops emerge from behind the camera, firing several rounds as they advance toward the now-retreating Filipinos. The U.S. color-bearer is shot and falls, at which point another soldier picks up the flag and waves it furiously. The U.S. troops disappear into the foliage in the background of the frame, behind a veil of smoke. Nothing in the catalogue description for the film suggests that it was passed off as an actuality to unsuspecting audiences, and the popularity of the live reenactment as a form of commercialized leisure suggests that few would have been easily duped. Indeed, the catalogue description for the film trades upon precisely those formal details that would reveal its generic status to urban, relatively sophisticated turn-of-the-century exhibitors and spectators—the placement of the camera/spectator directly in the crossfire between the Filipinos who shoot directly at the camera and the Americans who charge from behind it: "This is one of the best battle pictures ever made. The firing is first done directly toward the front of the picture, and the advance of the US troops apparently through the screen is very exciting; the gradual disappearance of the fighters sustaining the interest to the end."[38] David Levy notes that the reenactment's perilous point of view led one reviewer to determine such films obvious reenactments.[39] And while such a response provides evidence that some exhibitors might have passed off reenactments as actualities, it also provides evidence that urban spectators were well aware of one of the characteristic features of the battle reenactment: the placement of the audience in an impossible position at the edges of—or in this case in the middle of—military traffic. Indeed, the film provides a mediated sensation of being visible and hence vulnerable to the enemy's frontal assault, yet the camera-endowed disembodied presence in the scene transforms the terror of such a position into the pleasurable satisfaction of curiosity about the shock force of imperial warfare. And unlike the blindness experienced by U.S. troops assaulted by and in search of an elusive enemy, the camera endows spectators with a prosthetic vision that allows them to see the enemy and the source of the salvo, translating the imperial soldier's (and cameraman's) terrifying battlefield blindness into scopic clarity and power. Hence the gunpowder smoke that blinded soldiers on the battlefield here creates an aesthetic effect as the Filipinos retreat from vision, with "the gradual disappearance of the fighters sustaining interest to the end."

Like Cody's reenactments, this film presents military conquest as a spectacle of U.S. power in which soldiers act as agent-witnesses, for the soldiers are revealed to have been "alongside" the spectator, on the other side of the camera, until they charge in front of it to become part of the spectacle—a formal strategy that helps carve out an imaginary presence on the scene of history for the spectator. This illusory placement of the spectator within the circuits of military traffic also entails a positioning vis-à-vis the project of imperialism. The camera's placement has the effect of aligning the audience with the agents of U.S. imperialism, who emerge from behind the camera to protect them from the frontal assault that opens the film. Placing civilian spectators in the line of this frontal assault supported the pro-imperial press's representation of Filipino resistance as an unwarranted, savage attack on the so-called innocent agents of civilization, progress, and uplift. Indeed, reenactments of battles fought against the Filipino resistance consistently begin with Filipinos firing first. For example, both *Capture of the Trenches at Candaba* (Edison, 1899) and *Filipinos Retreat from Trenches* (Edison, 1899) open with the camera in a trench occupied by Filipinos, who fire several rounds at the initially unseen U.S. soldiers who ultimately advance into and take the trench. As with Wild West reenactments, the agents of U.S. imperialism appear as victims who, in the process of defending themselves, aid in territorial expansion as they are seen moving dynamically across the depicted space of a new frontier.

Though battle reenactment films did not show "actual" images of battle, they allowed audiences to "see" ostensible (and highly ideological) "truths" about the overseas expansion by the United States promoted by proimperialists in the popular press that dovetailed with the ideology of manifest destiny. *Capture of the Trenches at Candaba* places the camera/spectator in the trenches via a sidelong view of Filipino soldiers defending their possession of a small strip of land. Initiating the movements of the U.S. troops with an act of "aggression," the insurgents fire several rounds as their color-bearer waves the flag of the Philippine Republic in the middle of the frame. Suddenly they retreat, exiting frame left as U.S. troops advance into the trench from frame right. The camera not only creates an illusory visual presence on the scene but also seems to anticipate the historic moment when possession by the United States takes place. In doing so, the camera and the spectator's anticipatory presence in this space marks the trench as *already* conquered, suggesting the inevitable and even unstoppable movement of the imperial traffic of the United States. *Filipinos Retreat from Trenches* repeats this simple narrative of Filipino aggression, retreat, and "inevitable" incorporation of space into the circuits of the new American empire. Much like Cody's Wild West reenactments, battle reenactment films suggested that imperial conquest was not only the fulfillment of destiny by the agents of "progress" but that this destiny, and its long history, was a traumatic one for the imperial agent. Put differently, the reenactment makes clear that circulation within imperial traffic subjected the modern individual to shocks more violent than those experienced in urban street traffic. This suggests that the reenactment appealed not just to the desire to see "actual, grewsome war," but also, as the review quoted at the beginning of this chapter suggests, to repeat via reenactment the trauma of military history. [. . .]

The Mastery of Trauma: Reenactment, Repetition, and Heroic Femininity

To understand the appeal of reenactment's reiterative structure it is important to note that unlike the actuality film, the remit of the reenactment was not simply to record but, first, to repeat. Moreover, like audiences at Cody's Wild West, as well as those attending later film reenactments such as *The Execution of Czolgosz* (Edison, 1901) and *The Capture of the Biddle Brothers and Mrs. Soffel* (Edison/Porter, 1902), audiences watching battle reenactments would have arrived at the theater knowing the outcome of the conflicts already widely reported in the press. Indeed, most of the reenacted battles were quite bloody and were treated quite sensationally by the press, which also increasingly reported on the high number of civilian casualties suffered by the Filipinos. The tendency to reenact bloody, notorious, or otherwise well-known battles suggests that the visual pleasure of the reenactment was perhaps uncompromised by its status as a "mimic"—for the reenactment's reiterative structure perhaps promoted the sense of mastery that Freud argues results from the repetition of a traumatic event. Indeed, live and film battle reenactments involved showmen, filmmakers, and audiences alike in the act of replaying the historical trauma of warfare.[40]

[. . .] The battle reenactment film provides a unique opportunity to undertake such analysis, for it is precisely an "artistic imitation" "aimed at an audience" that repeated traumatic *historical* events. We might even speculate that such repetition allowed audiences to shift from a passive position vis-à-vis the event ("this is happening to us over there") to a more active position that seemed to place audiences on the battlefield and in the trenches alongside U.S. soldiers (" 'we' must subordinate 'them' "). And, as noted above, live and film battle reenactments revised as they repeated conquest such that each battle begins with an assault on white Americans by a hostile racial foe, followed by a charge/attack that ultimately makes U.S. forces the masters of violent conflict. Hence, reenactments "recollected and worked over" the "most painful experiences" associated with imperial expansion in such a way that made the colonizer both victim (of an apparently unwarranted aggression) and ultimate master (of violent conquest). The very presentation of imperial aggression as trauma is, of course, a mythologization that allowed imperial agents to pose as "innocent" objects of attack even as they engaged in violent conquest. The battle reenactment's placement of the spectator on the "scene" of historical trauma and its mode of repetition provided a cultural form for revealing and mastering the shock of warfare experienced by the soldier on the new frontier and, by extension, the nation as it became an overseas empire. [. . .]

NOTES

1. "Pictures That Will Be Historic," *Leslie's Weekly*, January 6, 1900, 18. Part of this article is quoted in Stephen Bottomore, "'Every Phase of Present-Day Life': *Biograph's Non-Fiction Production*," *Griffithiana* 66-67 (1999-2000): 147–211. My thanks to Giorgio Bertellini for bringing this article to my attention.
2. Oliver Wendell Holmes, "The Stereoscope and the Stereograph," *Atlantic Monthly* 3 (1859): 748.

3. Alan Trachtenberg, "Albums of War: *On Reading Civil War Photographs*," *Representations* 9 (Winter 1985) 6.
4. Ibid.
5. Timothy Sweet, *Traces of War: Poetry, Photography, and the Crisis of the Union* (Baltimore: Johns Hopkins University Press, 1990).
6. Richard Abel, *The Ciné Goes to Town: French Cinema, 1896-1914* (Berkeley: University of California Press, 1998), 92.
7. Hansen, *Babel and Babylon*, 30–31.
8. To trace this cultural history, this chapter focuses on reenactments of land battles and does not consider naval battle reenactments.
9. John F. Kasson, *Amusing the Million: Coney Island at the Turn of the Century* (New York: Hill and Wang, 1978), 71.
10. Sarah Blackstone in *Buckskins, Bullets, and Business*, 26–27, notes that even though Cody's Wild West was set up just outside the gates at the Columbian Exposition, it nevertheless was one of the most popular attractions and grossed one million dollars in summer 1893 alone. Sarah Blackstone, Buckskin, Bullets, and Business: *A History of Buffalo Bill's Wild West* (New York: Greenwood, 1986).
11. For details of features of the Wild West, see Joy S. Kasson, *Buffalo Bill's Wild West: Celebrity, Memory, and Popular History* (New York: Hill and Wang, 2000); Blackstone, *Buckskins, Bullets, and Business*; Paul Reddin, *Wild West Shows* (Urbana: University of Illinois Press, 1999); and Richard Slotkin, *Gunfighter Nation: The Myth of the Frontier in Twentieth-Century America* (Norman: University of Oklahoma Press, 1992), 29–87.
12. Edward Zane Carroll Judson (known by the pen name Ned Buntline) published the first instalment of *Buffalo Bill, King of the Border Men* in the *New York Weekly* in December 1869. See Marcus Klein, *Easterns, Westerns, and Private Eyes: American Matters, 1870–1900* (Madison: University of Wisconsin Press, 1994).
13. For an analysis of the social, cultural, and economic transformations that made the myth of frontier life so compelling to upper-class urban easterners, see G. Edward White, *The Eastern Establishment and the Western Experience* (New Haven: Yale University Press, 1968).
14. A. Nicholas Vardac, *Stage to Screen : Theatrical Origins of Early Film: David Garrick to D. W. Griffith* (New York: Da Capo, 1949), 135–51.
15. Slotkin, *Gunfighter Nation*, 69.
16. Linda Williams, *Playing the Race Card: Melodramas in Black and White from Uncle Tom to O. J. Simpson*, (Princeton: Princeton University Press, 2001) 43–44.
17. In his review Pomeroy noted: "I wish there were more progressive educators in this world like Wm. F. Cody" (quoted in *Buffalo Bill's Wild West: Historical Sketches and Programme*, 11).
18. Kasson, *Buffalo Bill's Wild West*, 5.
19. *Buffalo Bill's Wild West: Historical Sketches and Programme*, 5.
20. Ibid., 11 (my italics).
21. Ibid., 11–12.
22. *Amusing the Million*, 6–7. For Kasson's more recent analyses of Sandow and Houdini, see *Houdini, Tarzan and the Perfect Man: The White Male Body and the Challenge of Modernity* (New York: Hill and Wang, 2001).
23. Neil Harris, *Humbug: The Art of P. T. Barnum* (New York: Little, Brown), 1973, 74.
24. Ibid., 75.
25. Ibid., 77.
26. Ibid., 8.
27. F. M. Prescott, *Catalogue of New Films For Projection and Other Purposes* (New York, 1899), in *Motion Picture Catalogs by American Producers and Distributors, 1894–1908*, edited by Charles Musser (Frederick, MD: University Publications of America, 1985), 22.
28. *Edison Films Catalogue*, no. 94 (March 1900): 11.
29. Ibid., 10–11.
30. Theodore Roosevelt, *The Rough Riders* (New York: G. P. Putnam's Sons, 1900), 117.
31. Wolfgang Schivelbusch, *The Railway Journey: The Industrialization of Space and Time in the Nineteenth Century* (Berkeley: University of California Press, 1977), 155, 156.
32. G. H. Groeningen, *Über den Shock: Eine kritische Studie auf physiologischer Grundlage* (Wiesbaden: J. F. Bergmann, 1885), cited in Schivelbusch, *The Railway Journey*, 157.
33. Roosevelt, *The Rough Riders*, 89.
34. *Buffalo Bill's Wild West: Historical Sketches and Programme* (1900), 34.
35. Alexander Nemerov, *Frederic Remington and Turn-of-the-Century America* (New Haven: Yale University Press, 1996), 86–87.
36. W. K. L. Dickson, *The Biograph in Battle: Its Story in the South African War* (London: Flicks Books, 1995 [1901]), 124–25.
37. Dickson also noted the British soldier's experience of battlefield blindness: "The thing which chiefly demoralized our men . . . was the fact that half the time they had to fire at nothing, so cleverly were the Boers hidden, while the British were being mowed down by [their] Maxim-Nordenfeldt repeating guns, making it quite impossible for our men to escape . . . Our men shudder at the very sound . . . for the accurate shooting accomplished with the murderous weapon is something fearful to see" (*The Biograph in Battle*, 135).
38. *Edison Films Catalogue*, no. 94 (March 1900): 4.
39. David Levy, "Reconstituted Newsreels, Reenactments and the American Narrative Film," in *Cinema 1900/1906: An Analytical Study by the National Film Archive (London) and the International Federation of Film Archives*, edited by Roger Holman (Brussels: Fédération Internationale des Archives du Filme, 1982) 247. Levy does not directly quote the article, which was published in May in the Rochester newspaper the *Democrat and Chronicle*.
40. Sigmund Freud, *Beyond the Pleasure Principle* (New York: W. W. Norton, 1989 [1920]), 14.

5

DAI VAUGHAN

LET THERE BE LUMIÈRE (1999)

To look critically and sympathetically at the beginnings of cinema—at those programmes of one-minute scenes first publicly exhibited in Paris in December 1895, and in London the following February—is like pondering what happened to the universe in the first few microseconds after the big bang.

We need not doubt that, so far as the genesis of film art is concerned, these early shows mounted by the Lumière brothers represent the nearest we will find to a singularity. Before them, notwithstanding such precedents as the photographic analysis of animal movement by Marey and Muybridge, the public projection of animated drawings in Reynaud's Théatre Optique, or anticipations of film narrative methods in comic strip and lantern slide sequence, cinema did not exist. A story so frequently repeated as to have assumed the status of folklore tells how members of the first audience dodged aside as a train steamed toward them into a station. We cannot seriously imagine, though, that these educated people in Paris and London expected the train to emerge from the screen and run them down. It must clearly have been a reaction similar to that which prevents us from stepping with unconcern onto a static escalator, no matter how firmly we may assure ourselves that all it requires is a simple stride on an immobile flat surface. What this legend means is that the particular combination of visual signals present in that film had had no previous existence *other* than as signifying a real train pulling into a real station.

Yet already, in this primitive world, we find structures tantalisingly prophetic of some we know today. Compare the *Workers Leaving the Lumière Factory,* very few of whom return our gaze with even a glance from the screen, with the members disembarking from a riverboat for the *Congress of Photographic Societies at Neuville-sur-Saône,* who greet the camera with much waving and doffing of headgear. Do we not see here that distinction, very much a part of our television experience, between those who wield the power of communication and those who do not: between those granted subjectivity and those held in objectivity by the media?

Perhaps, if we wish to infer a state of cinema anterior to this almost instantaneous spawning of connotatory formations—and it is worth bearing in mind, in this regard, that the photographers arriving at Neuville-sur-Saône did not even know they were confronted with a *ciné*-camera—we should perhaps examine more closely the recorded responses of the earliest viewers. A curious example is offered in Stanley Reed's commentary to the BFI's sound version of the first British Lumière programme. This programme ended with *A Boat Leaving Harbour*; and we are told that visitors came forward after the performance to poke at the screen with their walking sticks, convinced that it must be made of glass and conceal a tank of water. Whilst we may allow this to pass as a measure of the wonderment caused by the first cinematographic projections, it becomes on consideration rather puzzling. How could people have supposed that the screen concealed a tank of water when it would also, by the same supposition, have had to conceal a garden, a railway station, a factory, and various other edifices? Yet I believe that this little story, like the one about the train, is telling us something important.

A Boat Leaving Harbour does, even today, stand out among the early Lumière subjects. (Indeed, an ulterior motive behind this article is my desire to pay tribute to a film I have loved since first encountering it very many years ago.) The action is simple. A rowing boat, with two men at the oars and one at the tiller, is entering boldly from the right foreground; and it proceeds, for fifty-odd seconds, toward the left background. On the tip of the jetty, which juts awkwardly into frame on the right, stand a child or two in frilly white and two portly women in black. Light shimmers on the water, though the sky seems leaden. The swell is not heavy; but as the boat passes beyond the jetty, leaving the protection of the harbour mouth, it is slewed around and caught broadside-on by a succession of waves. The men are in difficulties; and one woman turns her attention from the children to look at them. There it ends. Yet every time I have seen this film I have been overwhelmed by a sense of the *potentiality* of the medium: as if it had just been invented and lay waiting still to be explored.

I do not think it is just the Tennysonian resonances—crossing the bar, and so forth—which invest this episode with nostalgia for cinema's lost beginnings: a nostalgia which one would expect to be prompted equally, if at all, by the other items in the programme. One thing which will be obvious even from the above brief description is that the subject, with its waves glimmering to a distant horizon, could not possibly have been simulated in an indoor tank. So why were those early visitors poking at the screen with their walking sticks? A superficially similar reaction, this time to Edison's "kinetoscope," is quoted in the first volume of Georges Sadoul's *Histoire générale du cinéma*. The kinetoscope was an individual viewing box which ran continuous bands of film, the subjects being photographed by daylight in a blackened studio which could be revolved to face the sun; and in 1894 Henri de Parville wrote of it in *Les Annales politiques et littéraires*: "Tous les acteurs sont en mouvement. Leurs moindres actes sont si naturellement reproduits qu'on se demande s'il y a illusion." What he presumably meant by "illusion" was some system whereby the images of live actors might have been brought by mirrors under the eyepiece of the machine. But it is clear that the relevance of this lies not in similarity but in contrast: for there was no way that the image of a French harbour could have been reflected by mirrors into the auditorium of the Regent Street Polytechnic. The gentlemen with their walking sticks were not trying to discover how the trick worked. Their concern was not that they might have been the victims of an illusion, but that they had experienced something which transcended the cosy world of illusionism altogether.

We need look no further than Sadoul's standard *Histoire générale* for ample evidence of the fact that what most impressed the early audiences were what would now be considered the incidentals of scenes: smoke from a forge, steam from a locomotive, brick dust from a demolished wall. Georges Méliès, a guest at the first Paris performance (who was soon to become a pioneer of trick filming), made particular mention of the rustling of leaves in the background of *Le Déjeuner de bébé*—a detail which, as Sadoul himself observes, would scarcely be remarked today. It is worth asking why this should be so—and why, by implication, we consider Lumière cinema and Edison not: for surely, it might be argued, what mattered was the photographic rendering of movement, regardless of what moved. Sadoul entitles his chapter on Lumière "La Nature même prise sur le fait"; and Stanley Reed points out that audiences had hitherto been familiar only with the painted backdrops of the theatre. But to put it this way round is to understate the most revealing aspect of it: that people were startled not so much by the phenomenon of the moving photograph, which its inventors had struggled long to achieve, as by the ability of this to portray spontaneities of which the theatre was not capable. The movements of photographed people were accepted without demur because they were perceived as performance, as simply a new mode of self-projection; but that the inanimate should participate in self-projection was astonishing.

Most of the people in the Lumière show either are performing for the camera—whether knocking down walls or feeding babies—or are engaged in such neutral activities as leaving the factory or alighting from a train. What is different about *A Boat Leaving Harbour* is that, when the boat is threatened by the waves, the men must apply their efforts to controlling it; and, by responding to the challenge of the spontaneous moment, they become integrated into its spontaneity. The unpredictable has not only emerged from the background to occupy the greater proportion of the frame; it has also taken sway over the protagonists. Man, no longer the mountebank self-presenter, has become equal with the leaves and the brick dust—and as miraculous.

But such an invasion of the spontaneous into the human arts, being unprecedented, must have assumed the character of a threat not only to the "performers" but to the whole idea of controlled, willed, obedient communication. And conversely, since the idea of communication had in the past been inseparable from the assumption of willed control, this invasion must have seemed a veritable doubling-back of the world into its own imagery, a denial of the order of a coded system: an escape of the represented from the representational act. Thus what the early audiences suspected was not the presence of a water tank but the presence, in some metaphysical sense, of the sea itself: a sea liberated from the laboriousness of painted highlights and the drudgeries of metaphor. And their prodding of the screen was comparable with our own compulsion to reach out and "touch" a hologram.

Yet if this helps to explain why, in 1896, a representation of the sea should have caused greater bemusement than that of a factory or railway station, it does not explain why *A Boat Leaving Harbour* should have retained its fascination for a hundred years. To understand this, we must turn the other way: not toward a notional first moment but towards the future already latent in Lumière. The earliest programme contained an episode, *L'Arroseur arrosé*, which is generally considered to mark the initiation of screen narrative. A man is watering a garden; a boy puts his foot on the hose and stops the jet; the gardener peers into the nozzle; and the boy removes his foot so that the gardener is squirted in the face. But is this a fiction film or simply a filmed fiction?

One answer would be that the fiction film comes into being only when the articulations of camera movement and editing form an inalienable component of the narration. Another, slightly more sophisticated, would be that the distinction is meaningless at this primitive level of organisation, and that *L'Arroseur arrosé* may be said to be filmed fiction and fiction film at once. But let us consider the question from the point of view of what seemed at the time the essential triumph of Lumière: the harnessing of spontaneity. It is clear how this applies to the men rowing the boat out of the harbour; but it is far from clear how it applies to the *Arroseur* episode.

At first it may seem that there are two simple alternatives: either this was an event observed in passing, perhaps with a concealed camera; or it was a scene staged by the filmmaker with the complicity of both parties. Furthermore, the gaucheness of the performances suffices to resolve any doubt in favour of the latter, thus perhaps leading us—our definition swallowing its tail—to say that what we see is an *attempt* at fiction film which, insofar as it is *perceived* only as an attempt, reverts to the spontaneous. But it is not so easy. Suppose, for example, that the camera had been set up only to record the garden-watering, and that the boy had played his trick unprompted; or that the boy and the cameraman had been in collusion to trick the unsuspecting gardener; or the boy and the gardener in collusion to surprise the cameraman.... Spontaneity begins to seem, in human affairs, a matter less of behaviour than of motivations—and of transactions in which the part of the mountebank *behind* the camera cannot long be excluded from question. "Spontaneity," that is to say, comes down to what is not predictable by—and not under the control of—the filmmaker. As for the gaucherie, it is arguable that flawless performances would have given us not true fiction but mendacious actuality.

Fiction film arises at precisely the point where people tire of these riddles. As audiences settle for appearances, according film's images the status of dream or fantasy whose links with a prior world are assumed to have been severed if they ever existed, film falls into place as a signifying system whose articulations may grow ever more complex. True, the movement of leaves remains unpredictable; but we know that, with the endless possibility of retakes open to the filmmaker, what was unplanned is nevertheless what has been chosen: and the spontaneous is subsumed into the enunciated. Even in documentary, which seeks to respect the provenance of its images, they are bent inexorably to foreign purpose. The "big bang" leaves only a murmur of background radiation, detectable whenever someone decides that a film will gain in realism by being shot on "real" locations or where the verisimilitude of a Western is enhanced, momentarily, by the unscripted whinny of a horse.

A Boat Leaving Harbour begins without purpose and ends without conclusion, its actors drawn into the contingency of events. Successive viewings serve only to stress its pathetic brevity as a fragment of human experience. It survives as a reminder of that moment when the question of spontaneity was posed and not yet found to be insoluble: when cinema seemed free, not only of its proper connotations, but of the threat of its absorption into meanings beyond it. Here is the secret of its beauty. The promise of this film remains untarnished because it is a promise which can never be kept: a promise whose every fulfilment is also its betrayal.

6

BOLESLAS MATUSZEWSKI

A NEW SOURCE OF HISTORY (1898)

Paris, March 25, 1898

Sir,

Allow me to call your attention to a project, an outline of which follows, which is ready to be executed and in which I hope to interest you. It is a question of giving a location of general interest to a collection of cinematographic documents, collected under very particular circumstances, which have been most favourably received in the select circles in which I had the opportunity to show them.

I would be very grateful if you would communicate to me, through your newspaper or otherwise, any criticisms or new suggestions that this project might suggest to you, and I am at your disposal with any supplementary information that you may desire.

B.M.

Place of Animated Photography among the Sources of History

It is wrong to believe that all the various kinds of *illustrated documents* that come to the aid of History have a place in Museums and Libraries. Next to prints, medals, figured pottery, sculpture, etc., etc., which are collected and classified, photography, for example, does not have a special department. Truly, the documents furnished by photography are only rarely of noteworthy historical interest, and above all *there are too many of them*! Someday, however, portraits of men who have had a marked influence on their times will be classed by series. But this will be only a backward move, because from this point it is a question of moving even further in this direction; and, in official spheres, the idea has been welcomed to create in Paris a *Cinematographic Museum* or *Depository*.

This collection, of necessity restricted in the beginning, will expand more and more, in the measure that cinematographic photographers' curiosity moves from merely entertaining or whimsical scenes to actions and spectacles of a documentary interest, and from *humorous slices of life* to *slices of public and national life*. From simple pastime, animated photography will thus become an agreeable method for studying the past; or rather, since it will give a direct view of the past, it will eliminate, at least on certain points of some importance, the necessity of investigation and study.

Moreover, animated photography could become a singularly efficacious teaching process. How many lines of vague description in books intended for young people will be rendered unnecessary, the day we unroll in front of a classroom in a precise, moving picture the more or less agitated aspect of a deliberative assembly; the meeting of Heads of State about to ratify an alliance; a departure of troops or squadrons; or even the changing, mobile physiognomy of the city! But necessarily a good deal of time must pass before we can have recourse to this resource for teaching History. In order to unfold graphic, external history before the eyes of those who did not witness it, it is necessary first to store it.

One difficulty might briefly give us pause: namely, that a historical event does not always appear where one expects it. It is far from the case that History is composed solely of scheduled solemnities, organized in advance and ready to pose in front of the lenses. It is the beginnings, initial movements, unattended facts that avoid capture by the photographic camera . . . just as they escape inquiry.

Without doubt historical effects are always easier to seize than causes. But the two shed light upon each other; these effects brought into the broad daylight of cinematography will cast bright flashes of light upon causes lying in their shadow. And to secure not all there is, but all that can be secured, is already an excellent result for any type of inquiry, scientific or historical. Even oral accounts and written documents do not deliver to us all the class of facts to which they correspond, and nevertheless History exists, true after all in its broad outlines, even if its details are distorted. And then, the cinematographic photographer is indiscreet by profession; always lying in wait, his instinct very often enables him to divine where those events will pass that will become historical causes. It is necessary more often to check his excesses of zeal than to deplore his timidity! Sometimes the natural curiosity of the human spirit, sometimes the lure of profit, often the two sentiments combined make him inventive and daring. Authorized in somewhat official circumstances, he will contrive to slip unauthorized into others, and most often will know how to find the occasions and places where the history of tomorrow is unfolding. A popular movement, the start of a riot does not scare him, and even in a war one can well imagine him aiming his lens in the same way a soldier does his gun, and seizing at least a piece of the battle. Everywhere a ray of light gleams, the photographer goes as well . . . If, for the First Empire and the Revolution, for example, we only had reproductions of scenes that animated photography could easily bring to life, imagine what useless torrents of ink could have been saved with regard to questions that, though perhaps secondary, are nevertheless interesting, even thrilling!

Thus the cinematographic print, in which a thousand negatives make up a scene, and which, unrolled between a light source and a white sheet, makes the dead and gone get up and walk, this simple ribbon of imprinted celluloid constitutes not only a historic document, but a piece of history, a history that has not vanished and needs no genie to resuscitate it. It is there, scarcely sleeping, and—like those elementary organisms that, living in a latent state, revive after years given a bit of heat and moisture—it only requires, to reawaken it and relive those hours of the past, a little light passing through a lens in the darkness!

Particular Character of the Cinematographic Document

Perhaps the cinematograph does not give history in its entirety, but at least what it does deliver is incontestable and of an absolute truth. Ordinary photography admits of *retouching*, to the point of transformation. But try to retouch, in an identical way for each figure, these thousand or twelve hundred, almost microscopic negatives . . . !

One could say that animated photography has a character of authenticity, accuracy, and precision that belongs to it alone. It is the ocular evidence that is truthful and infallible *par excellence*. It can verify oral tradition, and, if human witnesses contradict each other on some matter, it can bring them to accord, shutting the mouth of whoever would dispute it. Suppose a discussion began about a military or naval manoeuvre whose steps had been recorded by the cinematograph; it would soon be settled . . . It can give with mathematical exactitude the distance between points in the scenes it has fixed. Most often it attests with very clear signs the time of day, season, and climactic conditions in which the event took place. Even what escapes the eyes—the imperceptible progress of moving objects—the lens seizes, from their distant beginnings on the horizon to the point closest to the fore-plane of the screen. In short, one wishes that other historic documents had the same degree of certitude and clarity.

Establishment of the Depository of Historical Cinematography

We need to accord this perhaps privileged source of History the same authority, the same official existence, the same access that already established archives have. This is a concern in the highest spheres of the State, and moreover the ways and means do not seem hard to find. It would suffice to assign to cinematographic prints that have a historical character a section of the Museum, a shelf in the Library, a cabinet in the Archives. The official depository would be installed either at the Bibliothèque Nationale or that of the Institut [National], in the keeping of one of the Academies concerned with History, or at the Archives, or, again, at the Museé de Versailles. We will choose among these and decide. Once the foundation is established, consignments will not fail to arrive, as free donations or even from interested parties. The price of the cinematographic camera, like that of film stock, very high in the early days, decreases rapidly and will tend to come within the reach of simple amateur photographers. Many among them, not including professionals, will begin to take an interest in the cinematographic application of this art and would like nothing better than to contribute to the making of History. Those who do not supply their collections now will gladly make a bequest of them. A competent committee will accept or discard the proposed documents after having appraised their historic value. The rolls of negatives that are accepted will be sealed in cases, labelled and catalogued; these will be the *standards* that will remain untouched. The same committee will determine the conditions under which the *positives* will be presented and will place in reserve those which, for certain reasons of propriety, cannot be released until after a certain number of years have elapsed. The same is done at other archives. A curator from the chosen establishment will care for this new collection, small to begin with, and a future institution will be founded. Paris will have its *Depository of Historical Cinematography*.

First Bases of the Projected foundation

This is an establishment that is absolutely essential, and it will take place sooner or later in some large European city. I would like to contribute to its endowment in this city where I have been received with such good grace. And here I ask modestly to enter the picture.

As photographer to the Emperor of Russia, I was able, on the express orders of His Majesty himself, to capture with the cinematograph as they happened, among other curious views, important scenes and intimate events of the visit to Petersburg by the President of the French Republic in September 1897.[1]

These negatives, which an initiative from on high gave me permission to take, were projected for his eyes; after which I was able, in some sixty consecutive sessions, to offer the same spectacle to soldiers in the Paris barracks. I was surprised and charmed by the effect produced upon these simple souls, to whom I gave the opportunity to learn about the physiognomy of a foreign people and country, about the organization of official events so new to them, and finally about a great national spectacle.

I propose this uncommon first series of cinematographic negatives as the base for the establishment of the new Museum. I was fortunate to win to my point of view some persons of considerable authority, and, with their influence, I may soon be able to see this new kind of archive founded in Paris.

I have stated why I predict an easy and rapid development for these archives. I will contribute to them myself. Other than the scenes I have mentioned, I already have by my account many more to offer, relating to the coronation of HM Nicholas II, the travels in Russia of two other emperors, the Jubilee of the Queen of England. In recent times I have been able to capture portions of events in Paris that were most unexpected and breathtaking. I intend to gather throughout Europe and send to the future Depository reproductions of all scenes that seem to me to be of historical interest.

My example will be imitated ... if you would like to encourage this very simple but novel idea, suggest it to others who will carry it through, and above all liberally give the publicity necessary for it to be lively and fruitful.

NOTE

1. The projection of one of these films was found indisputably to refute a false assertion from abroad, touching on a misconduct that was supposedly perpetrated during that juncture. Doubtless the event has its little importance, but ultimately it is only an example of the services that animated photography can render to the truth, verifying human testimony. This is a whole anecdotal side of History that until now has escaped the imagination of narrators.

7

TOM GUNNING

BEFORE DOCUMENTARY

Early Nonfiction Films and the "View" Aesthetic (1997)

A Deferred Discovery

The recent re-evaluation of early cinema springs from a determination to approach the films of cinema's first decades on their own terms. While recognizing that a historiographic project which attempts to fully reproduce the past "as it really was" is doomed to a naive historicism, nonetheless, a responsible historian must try to recreate the original horizon of expectation in which films were produced and received. The recent revision of early film history dates from the 1978 FIAF conference at Brighton, England which inaugurated a new era in the study of early cinema by collecting together a larger number of films from the period 1900–1906 than had been gathered previously. This "Brighton project" arranged for scholars to view and discuss these films, rather than relying on canonical descriptions and accounts of cinema's evolution contained in traditional histories. A series of presentations at Brighton and later a number of published essays re-evaluated these films, making use of contemporary narrative theory and formal analysis. Since Brighton a broader project of placing early cinema in a social and economic context has begun. While many unanswered questions remain, the work undertaken by historians in many countries to establish the modes of production, the range of cinematic styles and genres, and the means of exhibition in early cinema continues to make strong headway, emerging from (and in some ways surpassing) the simple principle formulated at Brighton of a close and fresh examination of the texts themselves.

But, as is always true, decisions in the initial gathering of material ended up shaping a corpus in ways which had unforeseen consequences. Two principles which governed the selection of the films shown at Brighton in 1978 contributed to a general neglect of nonfiction film in the re-evaluation of early cinema.[1] Both of these decisions, as I understand it, were of a practical rather than polemic bent, and neglect was simply a by-product rather than intent. The first was the decision to focus on a period beginning at 1900, some years after the most commonly agreed upon dates of cinema's debut. The motive for this decision came from a desire to avoid the controversies over rival claims of invention which had so often dominated the study of early cinema, sidetracking it into often bitter quarrels between advocates of competing inventors, spurred on by personal or national loyalty. The second decision was to concentrate on fiction filmmaking, leaving nonfiction to the side. The motive for this decision seems to be less the avoiding of controversies than a reasonable reluctance to wade into a great unexplored territory, a space left blank on all charts. The mass of nonfiction films were difficult to date, trace or identify. Wisdom seemed to dictate restricting this initial foray in the revision of early film history to the more containable area of fiction films.

The consequence of these eminently rational decisions was that nonfiction cinema had to wait for a reconsideration of its role in early cinema. This delay contained some irony, since it is during the period of early cinema that nonfiction film could claim its greatest hegemony. During the initial years of film history (and hence the effect of the decision to begin the re-evaluation of early cinema at Brighton with 1900) nonfiction production greatly outnumbered the production of fiction films. Clearly the recent focus of the 1994 Domitor conference of these first five years of production (including extensive screenings), the workshop of nonfiction cinema from the 1910s at the Nederlands Filmmuseum at Amsterdam, and the large-scale screenings at the Cinema Ritrovato at Bologna and the Giornate del Cinema Muto in Pordenone[2] indicate that the tide has turned. The place of nonfiction filmmaking in early cinema has at least been acknowledged and has begun to be theorized and investigated.

Discoveries of Differences: Actualities versus Documentaries

What are the issues that face us in task? I must stress that I feel we are at the beginning of this investigation. But, as at Brighton nearly two decades ago, it is important to make some preliminary observations, even if they can only serve as tentative hypotheses, early surveys and probes that provide starting points to further study, theses to be further demonstrated or perhaps discredited. A new conception of early nonfiction film must begin from a starting point similar to that of much of the work on early fiction film: an acknowledgement of a basic difference between early nonfiction film and later documentary filmmaking. This is not to deny any continuity between the two forms or the possibility of some continuous tradition. However, even if such continuity could be established and a tradition fashioned from it, I believe we must confront a gaping abyss that separates the earlier and later modes of nonfiction filmmaking. I propose that we use the already existing terms for these different periods in nonfiction filmmaking: "actuality" referring to this practice before World War I and "documentary" reserved for the practice that begins with the later period of the war. The dates for this periodization are certainly provisional, an area which calls for further discussion. However, I believe that the First World War itself plays an important role in the transformation of nonfiction filmmaking.

When John Grierson introduced the term "documentary," primarily to describe the work of Robert Flaherty,[3] he did not intend the term to cover all nonfiction filmmaking. In fact, Grierson wished to differentiate through this term a new approach to nonfiction films. He distinguished the documentary from other films made from "natural material," such as newsreels or scientific or educational films. For Grierson the move from these earlier nonfiction forms to the documentary proper represented a transformation "from the plain (or fancy) descriptions of natural material, to arrangements, rearrangements, and creative shapings of it."[4] I will return to the concept of creative shaping and arrangement later, but for now I want to stress Grierson's understanding of this earlier mode as "descriptive." As Charles Wolfe points out, this differentiation continued to be discussed during the thirties, with a retrospective arranged by the highly influential Film Department at the Museum of Modern Art in New York City in 1939, taking as its title "The Nonfiction Film: From Uninterpreted Fact to Documentary." As Wolfe states, this "drew what for many was a crucial distinction between the simply 'descriptive' function of earlier forms of nonfiction and the 'interpretive' ambitions of true documentary."[5] The term "documentary," then, announced an historical fissure in film criticism and filmmaking, separating a new and valorized practice from an earlier approach which was now condemned to a sort of prehistory. With this act of polemic periodization Grierson and others set a pattern followed by most historians of nonfiction filmmaking. After ceremonial nods to the Lumière brothers, the enormously rich period of nonfiction filmmaking before Flaherty basically remains undiscussed, as if shrouded by a collective amnesia. However irresponsible it may be for contemporary historians to maintain this attitude, it does function as an important historic signpost. The documentary as conceived by Grierson did differ from earlier nonfiction filmmaking practice in significant ways.

If the documentary in the Griersonian sense needs to be theorized and analyzed from the viewpoint of its "arrangements, rearrangements and creative shapings," what defines the formal and pragmatic impulses of the actuality film and, therefore, structures its history? In fact, the history of the actuality film from the viewpoint of its formal development challenges the methods of historians of early film, as a characteristically observant point made by Ben Brewster at the 1994 Amsterdam Workshop demonstrates. Brewster observed that many nonfiction films from the 1910s, most especially travelogues, look surprisingly similar stylistically to nonfiction films from earlier periods. This apparently largely static evolution of nonfiction cinema from, say, 1903 to 1917 contrasts sharply with the dynamic evolution of fiction cinema in that period, not only in the development of editing, but in the clarification of narrative form and character delineation. No film historian would confuse a fiction film from 1906 with one from 1912. In the case of nonfiction, however, the stylistic traits show considerable less differentiation over the same period. As Brewster put it at the workshop, nonfiction films "don't seem to exist in the regime of stylistic pressure that was clearly there for fiction filmmakers."[6]

Of course, tracing stylistic developments entails learning where to look for transformations. Viewing a larger number of early actuality films does alert us to a number of formal/technical transformations during this period. The growth of multi-shot films certainly differentiates the actuality films of the early 1900s from those of the 1890s, which were restricted to single shots. The development of editing in actuality film, while not as programmatic as in the fiction film, nonetheless displays concerns for clarity and logic in the presentation of information, as in the "process film" in which one sees the successive stages of industrial or handicraft manufacturing (which I discuss later in this essay). Some editing practices change rather early. For instance, the earliest actuality films, from the Lumières on, made strong use of camera stoppages (moments when the camera has stopped filming, then resumes shooting from the same position but with an ellipsis of action); viewers today often don't notice this important tool in early actuality filmmaking, or they attribute the visible jump in action to a splice in the film.[7] Around 1905 (or possibly earlier) these stoppages became rare and 'jumps' within shots were replaced by actual cuts to different shots. Likewise the increased use of intertitles in actuality films after 1905 or so reflects not only a change in presentational strategy (possibly as a result of a gradual abandonment of the lecturer), but also a desire to make actuality filmmaking more self-sufficient in its organizational strategies.

However, a certain consistent series of strategies and thematics in early actualities remains, making such stylistic transformations seem more like technical refinements than the equivalent to the radical transformations in fiction films of the first two decades. Accounting for this apparent lack of radical transformations should not lead us to think of the nonfiction film as somehow stagnant or, worse yet, retarded in relation to fiction film. Models of necessary stylistic progress distort our sense of film history. The radical development of film style in the fiction film during the early 1910s derives from the need to develop characters and establish clear patterns of temporality as these films took on new, more complex models of storytelling and attempted to achieve an autonomous mode of comprehensibility. One could attribute the relative lack of development in the nonfiction film to the fact that the existent modes of film style remained entirely *effective* for the genres then practised. In other words, I feel that the aims and purposes for nonfiction filmmaking during the early 1910s (and therefore the formal models for nonfiction films) had changed very little since about 1906. Since the available and familiar forms served these purposes quite effectively, there was little motivation for transformation.[8]

The "View" Aesthetic

What, then, was the model for nonfiction filmmaking which I am claiming was relatively consistent from around 1906 or so until World War I and which the fairly straightforward descriptive style of filming served so well? While there are certainly many different sorts of nonfiction films during this period, I would maintain that a particular aesthetic subtends or could embrace most of this diversity. This *Urform* of early nonfiction film I propose to call the "view." With this term, frequently used by contemporaries to describe early actuality films (as well as, before film, photographs of places or events of interest), I mean to highlight the way early actuality films were structured around presenting something visually, capturing and preserving a look or vantage point. In this respect the "view" clearly forms part of what I have called the "cinema of attractions," the emphasis found in early cinema upon the act of display and the satisfying of visual curiosity.[9] As an actuality a "view" makes a greater claim to recording an event of natural or social history, while attractions include artificially arranged scenes enacted precisely to arouse and sate the spectator's curiosity. However, a differentiation between the arranged and the simply recorded is so difficult to maintain or demonstrate that I do not wish to draw this line too firmly. "Views" tend to carry the claim that the subject filmed either pre-existed the act of filming (a landscape, a social custom, a method of work) or would have taken place even if the camera had not been there (a sporting event, a funeral, a coronation), thus claiming to capture a view of something that maintains a large degree of independence from the act of filming it. Clearly there are degrees of independence and borderline cases that blur such distinctions. But I feel that the "view" as opposed to the "act" or "scene" delineates a perceived distinction between actuality and staged films during the early era of film history. Needless to say, both "views" and "acts" could function as attractions.

To my mind the most characteristic quality of a "view" lies in the way it mimes the act of looking and observing. In other words, we don't just experience a "view" film as a presentation of a place, an event or a process, but also as the mimesis of the act of observing. The camera literally acts as a tourist, spectator or investigator, and the pleasure in the film lies in this surrogate of looking. The primary indication of this mode of observation lies in the clear acknowledgement of the camera's presence. People filmed respond to the camera, either through looks or gestures directed towards it, or through the way they present their actions to it, demonstrating a work process or custom. Likewise the camera's placement tends to take the best view possible of the action, and one senses its placement as being far from casual. In a "view" the world is presented to the camera, and therefore to the spectator.

While my description of "views" may sound simple to the point of tautology—a film showing something—the films themselves are far from simplistic. As I hope to demonstrate by contrasting them with later documentaries, these films do take on a certain quality partly through the things they *don't* do. In addition, the forms of showing and observing in these films are quite varied and their apparent simple styles are well adapted to a variety of tasks. Two large genres of "view" films are evident in a survey of early nonfiction films (although there are others). These genres allowed "views" to become more than single shots and organized a number of single views within a larger, multi-shot logic of exposition. First, there are the films which tour and present locations, an organization based on space and place presented as a series of views. Secondly, there are the films dedicated to activities and processes, views strung together with a temporal, rather than a spatial, organization and with a more determinate sequential logic of transformation.

"View" Genres: Place and Process

Unlike the single shot films typical of the turn of the century, the "place films" from at least 1906 on edit together a series of shots in order to provide a rich and varied sense of locale. These films include scenes of cities, rural areas or even a tour of a foreign country. While the imagery may capture either natural landscapes, man-made structures or a combination of both, the selection of shots serves to develop a variety of sights—much like a tourist album—and to articulate an aesthetic that would remain remarkably consistent in travelogue films of future decades. The view of the tourist is recorded here, placing natural or cultural sites on display, but also miming the act of visual appropriation, the natural and cultural consumed as *sights*. Perhaps nowhere is the dramatizing of the act of visual appropriation more palpable than in the many "phantom ride" films of this era, films shot from moving vehicles (primarily trains, but also autos and boats) moving through a landscape or urban environment. These films, still visually powerful today, place on view the unfolding visual horizon, the sense of an eye moving through space, clearly featuring the act of seeing as much as the sight to be seen. In phantom rides, place and act of seeing become dynamically interrelated through the creation of a view in motion, foregrounding the unique appetites of the film medium for both the visual and the mobile.

The longevity of the phantom ride genre stands as another indication of the basic coherence of the "view" aesthetic for nearly two decades of film history. At the same time, I sense some transformation in the genre, a transfer from an earlier form which emphasized both landscape and the novelty of the mobile gaze cutting through space, to a later form which primarily stressed the unfolding landscape and directed attention away from the technology of the movie camera and mode of transport. These later phantom rides seem more contemplative, less attuned to the thrills of fast locomotives, sudden curves and looming tunnels than to the natural panorama spread before the viewer. For instance, *Burnham Beeches*[10] passes by the natural forms of a grove of trees, creating a leisurely pace conveyed by a smooth, jarless movement, a reflective rhythm of contemplation further guaranteed by the soft dissolves that link shots. One not only loses oneself in this natural imagery, one has no sense of whether one is transported by train or car or other means. The mobile means, once the centre of such phantom rides, is now only the vehicle for a communion with nature. This contrasts sharply with the modes of reception of early train films, with their emphasis on speed, danger and sensation.[11] The modality of the "view" is open to a variety of approaches.

The spatial unfolding and linking that forms the structure of these 'place films' gives way to temporal strategies in the films which offer a view of a process, whether the production of a consumer good through a complex industrial process, the creation of an object through traditional craft, or the detailing of a local custom or festival. While such films also make use of a spatial logic, as the films present a variety of viewpoints on an action (especially in films of industrial processes, which partly function as factory tours), their dominant organization principle is temporal, detailing the stages of a process in a logical order. Clearly many films combine these two orders of logic, both spatial exploration and temporal explication, showing that the structure of viewing and construction of "view" actualities can indeed be complex. While both these forms rely primarily on structures of succession, devices such as cut-ins to closer views or to details allow a degree of editing sophistication, especially after 1906 or so.

The increased temporality of the process films brings them closer to narrative form, though clearly lacking the consistent diegesis and creation of character that the fiction film of this period strove to achieve (and which produced the "regime of stylistic pressure" that Brewster speaks of). While rooted still in a descriptive approach, recurring narrative patterns are evident in many of these films. The most fully developed narrative pattern is the transformation of raw material into consumable goods. In many of these films the narrative process moves from opening scenes of raw material through the various stages of production to culminate in a scene of delighted consumption.

Films such as the *Manufacture of Walking Sticks*[12] and *Messrs. Barlow and Jones Ltd., Manchester and Bolton*,[13] both shown at the 1995 Pordenone film festival, begin with unloading of raw materials (sticks, cotton) at factories. Similarly such process films as *Making Christmas Crackers*,[14] *A Day In The Life of an English Coal Miner*,[15] or *Culture Et Récolte Des Pommes À Washington*,[16] shown at the same festival, end with scenes of pleasurable consumption of the manufactured good within a comfortable or even glamorous bourgeois interior.

This trajectory from raw material to consumable product enacts a basic narrative of industrial capitalism, already sketched by Prince Albert in his plan for the displays in the 1851 Crystal Palace relating raw material to finished products,[17] and rehearsed in world fairs and school text books for decades. Work not only transforms, it mediates between nature and culture, for the benefit of the comfortable classes. The class basis (and bias) of this narrative is especially clear in *A Day in the Life of an English Coal Miner*, which opens with a miner leaving his cottage and family for work. The penultimate shot shows him returning home, but the final interior shot brings us, not into the miner's home, but presents a comfortable middle class family gathered around the hearth and warmed by the coal he mined. Perhaps the most dramatic tracing of this trajectory comes in *D'ou Viennent Les Faux Cheveux*,[18] which begins with a series of pans around a small Breton town square and market in which women have gathered to have their long hair cut off (a gathering of raw material detailed in medium close up). The process of cutting, gathering, sorting, carding, and finally sewing this hair into wigs and hair pieces is detailed, leading to the last shot which shows a glamorous bourgeois woman in medium close up taking off her hat, then removing false hair pieces, and smiling fetchingly at camera.

Uncovering the Look

As Grierson indicated, the primary mode of these early films was descriptive. While clearly they cannot claim to present an untouched raw reality (however mythical such a concept might be), their "interference" with reality, the means by which they shape it, centre on the act of looking and describing. Actions and people may be arranged so that the camera can get a better look at them, but this arrangement is for the most part fully evident in the manner in which people acknowledge the camera or display their talents, costumes or physical characteristics to it. I believe that Grierson was right in declaring that this style of filmmaking was quite different from the creative shaping of the material which he felt defined the documentary film.

As complex ideologically as these process and place films may be, rehearsing as well as shaped by narratives of colonialism and consumer culture, nonetheless they remain rooted in the "view" aesthetic. The ultimate act of consumption in these films is the audience's act of viewing; and everything—people, places, and things—is offered to our view. Recurringly this is marked by the returned look of people within the film, the gaze directed out at camera and viewer which transfixes the act of looking as central to the descriptive mode, the act of display as the primary act of the filmmaker. These films often show a range of these returned looks (from the shy laughter of the women about to have their hair cut to the coquettish gaze of the woman removing her hair pieces in *D'ou Viennent Les Faux Cheveux*), and even incorporate scenes where such looks are avoided (the staged sequences of the miner leaving and returning to his cottage in *A Day in the Life of an English Coal Miner*, in which he avoids looking at the camera, contrasting sharply with the shot in the same film, introduced with the intertitle "Belles of the Black Diamond Field," in which women workers smile at a voyeuristic panning camera). However, in the construction of the films the primacy of the view affirms itself. If these images find their place within ideological narratives, this place is as much a *sight* as a site, and not a diegetic story incident or part of an articulated social or political argument. The social attitudes here are pre-existent, rather than argued, and the images hardly serve as evidence.

While many actuality films exemplify this aesthetic of the "view," with travelogues and process films being perhaps the clearest examples, the desire evident in these films to provide a nearly endless and (ideally) exhaustive catalogue of views of the world reached a climax in the films shot for Albert Kahn and his utopian project of "*Les archives de la planète,*" in the 1910s and 1920s. Although this fascinating phenomenon calls for more in-depth research than I have yet undertaken, the films that have been made available from this archive on video reveal a fascinating archaeology of the non-fiction films through a peerless demonstration and an encyclopedic collection of the "view" aesthetic.

Kahn was a rich Parisian banker of the early twentieth century, who supplemented his other philanthropic cultural and social endowments with the project of collecting on film a series of motion picture images from around the world, seizing, as he put it, life where it exists. These films consist predominantly not of edited documentaries explicating social customs or political events, but rather simply of views of daily life around the world: modes of dress, city streets, national "types," native festivals, religious customs, processes of agriculture and handicraft. Taken collectively the films construct an exotic panorama of the planet on display, the ultimate cinematic World Exposition. Perhaps the most extraordinary of these short films is a shot of an Indochinese woman, filmed (apparently for modesty's sake) out of focus as she undresses for the camera, revealing both the layers of native clothing and her body.[19] The sense of voyeurism as a source of the desire for knowledge (of the Other, of the body) is so boldly demonstrated by this film that it stands as a sort of confession of the drives behind the 'view' aesthetic.

As this film reveals, even these simple unedited films are hardly bereft of ideology (a whole vocabulary of colonial and sexist gazes is unfurled here), but it is an ideology contained within the fascinating subterfuges and revelations of the look. One is always aware—and I believe this is true of all the early actuality films I am describing here—of a drama staged between camera and subject, the observer and the observed, and ultimately, the "view" and the audience. These "views" represent a sort of primal exchange and encounter contained in the act of looking with all its possible scenarios of dominance, curiosity, seduction, objectification and even identification.

For Grierson the documentary went beyond this primary encounter. However, just as I have maintained that the aesthetic of attractions persists in a less obvious form within later fictional films, the staging of the look certainly subtends much of later documentary practice, including, even, much of *Nanook the North*. But the documentary moves beyond (and obscures or, perhaps, camouflages) this primal act of looking through its creative reshaping and dramatizing of "natural material." Undoubtedly editing plays a key role in the restructuring of material that defines the advent of the documentary. I would claim that even though actuality films make often sophisticated use of editing, the "view" privileges the relation between camera and subject. Editing basically plays the role of providing a succession of views, whether spatially (as in the travelogue) or temporally (as in the films of process). This editing can be quite elegant, including cut-ins to closer views or a truly creative sense of juxtaposing different points of view (such as certain phantom ride films which vary the angle from which the passing landscape is seen) with grace or sensational effects. But the editing does not possess the same drive toward dramatizing and rhythm that can be found in fiction films of this period, where articulation between different shots increasingly becomes an expressive mode of narration and ideological comment.

War and the Argument of Images

Although it is always a perilous task to try to demarcate historical periods in aesthetic practice and locate a transformation in style with precision, I believe from my viewing of the films from the 1910s shown at the 1994

Amsterdam Workshop that one can locate the transformation from the "view" to the documentary in a period somewhat earlier than *Nanook of the North*. Let me restate in semiotic terms Grierson's idea of the documentary as the reshaping of natural material. We could describe this transformation from "view" to documentary as a move from films conceived as a look to a film form which embedded its images in a larger argument and used those images as evidence to substantiate or intensify its discourse. Not surprisingly, this transformation becomes extremely visible in the films that are made during World War I as propaganda for one side or the other.

Although there were undoubtedly a large number of such films made, some of the films at the Amsterdam Workshop stand out for their strongly discursive arrangement of image and text in order to present arguments about the course of the Great War. These films include *Londen in Oorlogstijd*,[20] *Vernietiging Britse Schepen*,[21] and *Der Zeppelin-Angriff Auf England*.[22] As Charles Musser pointed out, the first two of these titles are government films which tried to establish or deny claims of damage inflicted on the enemy, and thus foreground their "evidentiary function."[23] They employ film images in order to prove a thesis whose main claims are carried in an accompanying verbal discourse, usually embodied in the films' intertitles. In LONDEN IN OORLOGSTIJD this verbal discourse is even embodied in some of the shots themselves, such as those in which a man stands in a number of prominent sites in metropolitan London holding a placard which bears the date "Sept. 26 1917."[24] The date thus inscribed into this view makes an evidentiary claim in an argument about the extent of destruction caused in London by German bombing attacks before this date. As Nicholas Hiley demonstrated at this workshop, such images can even be arranged to make an argument which in fact is contradicted by the images themselves, provided a viewer has certain knowledge (for instance, in *Der Zeppelin-Angriff Auf England* Hiley could identity the Zeppelin footage as showing prewar flights and the images of destruction in England as showing the result of naval raids rather than air attacks).[25]

Certainly it would be an oversimplification to claim that the earlier "view" films are entirely innocent of larger discourses. To pick and critique the terms of the Museum of Modern Art nonfiction retrospective from 1939, in cinema there is no such thing as the "uninterpreted fact." No image is innocent of ideological assumptions and the syntax of the look exchanged between camera and subject or screen and spectator can be quite complex. Further, as Charles Musser would be the first to point out, early nonfiction films were the genre of early productions most likely to be accompanied by a lecture which could place these views in a variety of discursive contexts. Finally, audiences would undoubtedly receive an image in terms of preconceived discursive contexts (such as the narratives of production and consumption embedded in the process films discussed earlier) and tend to fit them into already learned discourses. But the contrast that the Museum of Modern Art wished to draw remains significant in its differentiation, even if naive in its attitude toward representation. A difference in the degree, methods and purposes of interpretation and argument separate "view" films and documentaries. I believe that the birth of the documentary appears, as Grierson puts it, when the filmic material has been rearranged, has been placed into an explicit discursive context through editing and intertitles. Rather than a succession of views, the documentary fashions from its images an articulated argument, as in the wartime films discussed, or a dramatic structure based on the basic vocabulary of continuity editing and the creation of characters borrowed from fiction filmmaking, as in *Nanook*.

Therefore, I contrast the *view*, a descriptive mode based on the act of looking and display, with the *documentary*, which is a more rhetorical and discursive form inserting images into a broader argument or dramatic form. The "view" relies more on individual shots, while the documentary creates a larger, closer structured context for these images. In the documentary individual shots lose much of their independence as separate "views" and become instances of evidence or illustration within an argument or story. Such structures depend on a closer weave of edited relations (including a greater use of the codes of continuity editing in the films which create characters or stories), and a greater reliance on intertitles to explain or interpret the images. Issues of accuracy and evidence become foregrounded in the documentary, largely because the authenticity of the image becomes part of the argument (and therefore issues of faking evidence, as the Zeppelin film). Specific claims of accuracy are much looser in the "view," which permits manipulations of the image for their spectacular effects (such as the magical trick effect appearance of Santa Claus in the bourgeois parlour at the end of *Making Christmas Crackers*) and which therefore don't undermine any truth claim.

Looking Both Ways: The Ambiguity of the "View"

I want to emphasize again that this contrast does not absolve "view" films from any expression of ideology. However, I do feel that the enormous—and neglected—fascination of these early 'view' films lies in their thorough and often complex exploration of the look in a manner outside of the creation of a fictional space, dramatic structure or character development. These films present for us a new conception of vision, which technological revolutions in photography and in transportation made possible, and whereby all the sights in the world and its people were made subject to a new roving form of vision and representation. Following in the footsteps of the stereoscope and magic lantern views, actuality filmmaking developed and exploited a new form of visual curiosity. The addition of motion photography not only added a temporal dimension to these earlier view forms, but allowed the drama of the look to develop a more dialogic relation to its filmed subjects, whose faces and gestures gained a further expressiveness and independence as they were filmed in time. Both the movement through the landscape available in phantom rides and the expressiveness of a darting glance or a mobile countenance show the new forms of experience and knowledge available through the motion picture view. A view which could be mobile and a form which could record the mobility of filmed subjects opened up a new realm of visualization, picturing new phenomena for the curious observer, as well as recording instances of resistance to the dominance of the touristic or colonial gaze.[26]

The aesthetic of the "view" in early actuality filmmaking has been neglected by a film history which has generally followed the contours of cinema's main mode of economic development, the fiction film. But, more scandalously, it has also been radically repressed by the official history of documentary film (certainly no history of narrative film could consider passing over the decades from the 1890s to the 1920s with the same silence that the canonical histories of documentary display as they skip blithely from Lumière to Flaherty). It would seem that the documentary needs (or has needed) somehow to disavow this intensely rich earlier tradition (just as the "fly-on-the-wall" aesthetic of American cinéma vérité seemed to disavow the dynamic power of the camera's gaze in cinema). The motivation for this repression must be carefully examined, and I don't want to rush into conspiratorial scenarios. However, it seems to me that the most frequently given reason for this neglect, the belief that this early material remained too raw, too close to reality and bereft of artistic or conceptual shaping (compared to the more "cooked" documentary), doesn't take us very far. I believe, rather, that "view" films made the fashioners of the documentary tradition uncomfortable, because they reveal the ambiguous power relations of the look so nakedly. The voyeurism implicit in the tourist, the colonialist, the filmmaker and the spectator is laid bare in these films, without the naturalization of dramatic structure or political argument. These "views" stage for us the impulse towards "just looking" so important to our modern era; and we have learned in the work on visual culture over the last decades that "just looking" is never *just* about looking.

The mass of actuality films from the first decades of film history in our archives around the world are ripe for rediscovery and re-examination. They constitute a neglected and, indeed, repressed aspect of film history. They present an incredibly rich reserve of information about the foundation of our modern culture, not only for the vast variety of things displayed as audiences and filmmakers sought to slake a seeming inexhaustible visual appetite, but also as demonstrations of this modern visual curiosity itself. From these films we gain access to a viewing practice which was one of the foundations of our modern world. And from them we can also rethink and reformulate the tradition of documentary, a tradition filled with both beauties and terrors, scenarios of power and resistance, turning on the act of looking and the creation of the view.

***

This essay is an expanded and revised version of the essay "Vor der Dokumentarfilm: früher nonfiction Filme und die Ästhetik der 'Ansicht,'" published in *Anfänge des dokumentarischen Films* (Basle: Stroemfeld / Frankfurt am Main: Roter Stern, 1995), pp. 111–123, KINtop, 4. I wish to thank the bold and imaginative archivists of the Nederlands Filmmuseum in Amsterdam for their staging of the Workshop, which allowed me to see these films and develop my ideas, as well as the other members of the workshop whose insights helped shape mine. I also want to thank the organizers of the third Domitor conference at the Museum of Modern Art (especially, as always, Eileen Bowser), Roland Cosandey for his exhibitions of nonfiction films from the Joye collection, and Jeanne Beausoleil for alerting me to the Albert Kahn archive.

NOTES

1. This neglect has been relative, of course. In the recent rediscovery of early cinema, the study of actuality filmmaking has had a number of powerful advocates. The work of Roland Cosandey, Stephen Bottomore, Charles Musser and others has made a vital contribution to exploring and defining the issues of early nonfiction cinema. But even with these contributions, I believe these authors would agree that nonfiction filmmaking remains not only less thoroughly studied than early fiction filmmaking, but also less theorized.
2. The third Domitor conference, "Cinema turns 100," held in New York in 1994, focused on cinema before 1900. The 1994 Amsterdam Workshop at the Nederlands Filmmuseum focused on nonfiction from the teens, which is also the title of the book published from its discussions. Both Bologna and Pordenone staged festivals in 1995 focusing on silent nonfiction films.
3. The *locus classicus* for the term "documentary" in relation to film is usually given as Grierson's review of Flaherty's *Moana*, which appeared in *The New York Sun* in February of 1926. This review is reprinted in Lewis Jacobs, *The Documentary Tradition: from* Nanook *to* Woodstock (New York: Hopkinson and Blake, 1971), pp.25–26, where Jacobs notes that "for the first time he gave currency to the term 'documentary' in English." However, Charles Wolfe in "The Poetics and Politics of Nonfiction: Documentary Film," a chapter in Tino Balio, *Grand Design: Hollywood as a Modern Business Enterprise, 1930–1939* (New York: Charles Scribner's Sons, 1993), points out that this early use of the term by Grierson was "unexceptional" and only became a defined concept in his essays in the early thirties.
4. "First Principles of Documentary," in Forsyth Hardy (ed.), *Grierson on Documentary* (New York: Harcourt, Brace and Co., 1947), p. 100. This section is culled from an article originally published in 1932 in *Cinema Quarterly*.
5. Charles Wolfe, *op. cit.*, p. 353.
6. Brewster's comment appears on p. 32 of Daan Hertogs & Nico de Klerk (eds.), *Nonfiction From the Teens: The 1994 Amsterdam Workshop* (Amsterdam: Nederlands Filmmuseum, 1994).

7. See André Gaudreault, "De quelques figures de montage dans la production Lumière," a paper delivered to the *Congrès Lumière* at the Universitè Lumière-Lyon 2 (7–10 June, 1995), for a description of this practice in Lumière films.
8. The recondite English scholar of early documentary films Stephen Bottomore made a similar point at the Amsterdam Workshop, pointing out early documentary's strong inheritance of visual forms from the magic lantern lecture preceding film. See Hertogs & de Klerk, *op. cit.*, p. 33.
9. "The Cinema of Attractions: Early Film, Its Spectator and the Avant-Garde" in Thomas Elsaesser (ed.), *Early Cinema: Space, Frame, Narrative* (London: British Film Institute, 1990), pp. 56–63.
10. *Burnham Beeches*, United Kingdom (Hepworth) 1909. NFTVA print, London.
11. See my " 'The Whole World within Reach': Travel Images without Borders" in Roland Cosandey & François Albera (eds.), *Cinéma sans frontières 1896–1918 Images without Borders. Aspects de l'internationalité dans le cinéma mondial: représentations, marché, influences et réception / Internationality in World Cinema: Representations, Markets, Influences and Reception* (Lausanne: Payot / Quebec: Nuit Blanche, 1995), pp. 21–36.
12. *The Manufacture of Walking Sticks*, United Kingdom (Heron) 1912. NFTVA print, London.
13. *Messrs. Barlow and Jones Ltd., Manchester and Bolton*, United Kingdom, 1919. NFTVA print, London.
14. *Making Christmas Crackers*, United Kingdom (Cricks and Martin) 1910. NFTVA print, London.
15. *A Day in the Life of an English Coal Miner*, United Kingdom (Kineto) 1910. NFTVA print, London.
16. *Culture Et Récolte Des Pommes À Washington* [United States (American Kin), 1915]. Print from Lobster Film.
17. See: Thomas Richards, *The Commodity Culture of Victorian Britain: Advertising and Spectacle 1851–1914* (Stanford: Stanford University Press, 1990), p. 28.
18. *D'ou Viennent Les Faux Cheveux*, France (Pathé) 1909. CNC print, Bois d'Arcy.
19. My knowledge of the films commissioned by Albert Kahn, which are preserved by the Musée Albert Kahn in Paris, comes from the videotape *La Planete Albert Kahn*, which includes the film I describe. I thank Jeanne Beausoleil, the director of the Musée, for making it available to me.
20. *Londen in Oorlogstijd / Wartime London* / ?, United Kingdom, 1917. NFM print.
21. *Vernietiging Britse Schepen / Destruction British Ships* / ?, Germany [1916]. NFM print.
22. *Der Zeppelin-Angriff Auf England / Zeppelin Attack On England / Der Zeppelin-Angriff Auf England*, Germany (E. Hubert) 1915. NFM print.
23. Mussers's comments are contained in Hertogs & de Klerk, *op. cit.*, p. 30.
24. A photogram of this image is reproduced in Hertogs & de Klerk, p. 32.
25. See Hiley's comments in Hertogs & de Klerk, p. 42.
26. Miriam Hansen made a related point about resistance in her discussion of *De Avonturen Van Martin Johnson Onder De Kannibalen Op De Zuidzee-Eilanden / Martin Johnson's Adventures Among The Cannibals of The South Sea Islands / Among The Cannibal Isles of The South Pacific*, (United States, 1918; NFM print) at the Amsterdam Workshop. See Hertogs & de Klerk, p. 58.

8

EDWARD S. CURTIS ET AL.

THE CONTINENTAL FILM COMPANY (1912)

Associated with several of Seattle's leading business men, Mr. Edward S. Curtis has formed a small company for the making of commercial motion pictures of the Indian and the Indian life.

Through his remarkable knowledge of this subject, Mr. Curtis will be able to make pictures which could be secured in no other way, and owing to his international standing as one associated with the Indian, the marketing of such pictures will be comparatively easy, and the demand a large one.

The profits to be had from such pictures are quite large, and exceptionally substantial dividends can be depended upon.

In forming a company for this purpose, Mr. Curtis feels that he is giving his friends an opportunity to participate in the advantage of the standing he has built up through many years of hard and careful work, and at the same time the capital furnished by such a corporation will make it possible for him to take advantage of the present world-wide demand for such pictures as he is so logically qualified to make.

During the last two years Mr. Curtis had made a careful study of the motion picture subject and the marketing of the product, in the course of which investigation he has fortunately had the confidence and received the advice of the foremost men in the field. Also he has consulted with many of the country's leading scientists and educators, and they are most enthusiastic in regard to the making of such a series of pictures. There is no question that every educational institution in the land will be interested in its success.

For the present the more important activities of the company will be the making of a complete series of motion pictures of Indians and Indian life. All this work is to be done by or under the immediate supervision of Mr. Curtis, who is so well known in association with his great pictorial work dealing with all tribes of Indians.

A series of pictures such as Mr. Curtis proposes to make will be of the greatest national importance—something of permanent educational and historical value. More than that, it should be exceptionally profitable. The production of motion pictures is a most profitable undertaking, and great as is the business today, it is but in its infancy. Genuine Indian pictures will be far more valuable than regular dramatic subjects. The reason for this is that the regular motion pictures have a life of but a few months, usually six. At the end of that time they go to the junk pile. The Indian pictures, owing to their historical and ethnological importance, will remain in existence for all time: rather than being junk in six months, they will become of increasing value, paying a dividend on the cost for years to come.

It is Mr. Curtis' purpose and desire to include in the series all the tribes of America, both North and South. These pictures, while made to meet the demands of the scientist and students, will at the same time be so rendered that they will possess the interest needed to make the tastes of the masses or those who are looking for amusement only. Mr. Curtis' experience as a lecturer fits him to grasp the wants of the amusement-seeking public.

In the making of this series of motion pictures of Indian life, there is a great work which Mr. Curtis can do as no other man can. He is backed by a lifetime of experience with this subject, and has the peculiar ability to handle the primitive people in a way which means success.

The questions might be raised as to whether the documentary material would not lack the thrilling interest of the fake picture. It is the opinion of Mr. Curtis that the real life of the Indian contains the parallel emotions to furnish all necessary plots and give the pictures all the heart interest needed. In this respect it is as important that we take into consideration the Indian's mental processes as it is to picture his unique costume.

To do the work in a way creditable to the subject and to the nation would require a vigorously conducted campaign covering a period of five to fifteen years, this presumably to include Central and South America. All pictures made should be classed among the educational, and should be preserved as a part of the documentary material of the country. It is needless to say that such a collection of material would be an important national asset, and would from the beginning have the encouragement of every educational institution.

In making such pictures, the greatest care must be exercised that the thought conveyed be true to the subject, that the ceremony be correctly rendered, and above all, that the costumes be correct. It must be admitted that the making of such a series of pictures would be the most difficult thing attempted in motion photography, but it can be done, and will be one of the most valuable documentary works which can be taken up at this time.

The Indians and the Indian life do now and will for all time furnish an important part of the literature, art, and drama of our country.

As to motion pictures and their bearing on the subject, it is safe to say that properly produced under proper and permanent arrangement, they can be made of more importance than books or printed illustrations.

The market for motion pictures is very large. This will be particularly so with those made by one with a world-wide reputation. Not only would there be a market in the United States and Canada, but in Europe and South America as well. The commercial advantage of the motion picture producing business is that the market is world-wide, with but a trifle taken from any one. It is, in fact, but a small tax upon the people of the world. Those who have not kept in touch with motion picture matters can have but a slight idea of the magnitude of the business. Many millions of people daily visit the motion picture theatres in the United States. There are more than 25,000 motion picture theatres in the country, and if these averaged but 2,000 admissions in a day it gives an almost unbelievable total. The fact of such a very large attendance means that the greatest single influence in our country today is the motion picture. Likewise, no other business reaches so great a number of people.

Mr. John Collier, of the National Board of Censorship of motion pictures, says: "A new kind of book has been produced and is being read by millions of people daily. The motion picture is a book, and an acted play, and a scenic wonderworld in one. It is more popular today than our public libraries, and it should concern the educational and religious agencies more than the printed book for the reason that motion pictures, being a form of drama, nearly always have a moral or immoral lesson to convey. Whether it be sermons, or educational lectures, or temptations to wrong-doing, each and all of these things can be conveyed more vividly through motion pictures than through printed books."

To sum it all up, the subject treated is one of the most interesting, the business is one of the most profitable of the day, the market world-wide, the man doing the work personally known to you and of international reputation.

The plans for the present are that all pictures made will be special feature subjects of from three to six reels in length. As to the marketing, there are two feasible methods. The first is to sell them by the state rights plan. By this method each subject should pay a profit of $25,000 to $50,000 within a year of its production, and two pictures a year should be produced. The second and best plan is to make pictures of six reels in length, make the strongest and most important production possible, and then booking the picture to be played in first class theatres throughout the United States. In fact, tentative arrangements have been made for so marketing the Indian pictures made by Mr. Curtis. This plan means putting on the road from ten to twenty sets of the film, and playing in each city a week or more with a return engagement ninety days later. Such booking of the pictures will be made through one corporation in New York, to cover the United States, and on a percentage basis. A moderately successful picture should pay a minimum profit the first year of $100,000, and one that proved particularly successful a profit of many times that. As an illustration, with a minimum of ten pictures playing at a profit of $100 a night from each picture, it is easy to see what the profit would be, and such an estimate is less than half what could rightly be expected.

9

W. STEPHEN BUSH

REVIEW OF *IN THE LAND OF THE HEAD HUNTERS* (1914)

Remarkable Motion Picture Produced by Edward R. Curtis, Famous Authority on North American Indians

***

If I were asked to point to some particular film illustrating the educational value of the motion picture I would unhesitatingly mention this production. As a drama it may be a mere curiosity though even as a drama it has a singularly compelling charm. As a gem of the motion picture art it has never been surpassed. As I saw it at the Casino, New York City, with suitable music the picture is overwhelmingly beautiful and impressive. You get the impression of having feasted on one of the world's great picture galleries and there follows that most delightful of sensations, a new perception of pleasure in which the eye and the brain take special shares.

I remember many efforts to make the life of remote countries and strange tribes live on the screen. I remember how the attempt was made to get the natives into a moving picture scenario and thus render the film more acceptable. It is not a pleasing recollection by any means because all these efforts were strikingly futile. Mr. Curtis has found the short cut of genius and he eminently succeeds where others have dismally failed. It is said that Mr. Curtis is a profound student of Indian lore. This is evident enough from the films, but it does not at all explain his success with this subject on the screen. The cause of that must be sought in an extraordinary perception of artistic and dramatic values, in an uncommon skill of selection and in a sort of second sight with the camera. I confess that I learned a good deal looking at this picture. It has brought before my eyes a new vista of camera miracles. The low flight of the birds over the waters tinted and burnished by the setting sun is a veritable revelation of motion picture art. I am loath to confine myself to this one example when the recollection of others equal in beauty and power still linger hauntingly in my mind, but here I can do no more than allude to one or two beside: the capture of the whale, the scenes of the sea-lions, the dances, the wedding ceremonies, the vigil of the hero. The direction of this play entitles Mr. Curtis to high rank in that difficult profession, but it is after all only one of the lesser merits.

Mr. Curtis conceived this wonderful study in ethnology as an epic. It fully deserves the name. Indeed, it seemed to me that there was a most striking resemblance all through the films between the musical epics of Richard Wagner and the theme and treatment of this Indian epic. The fire-dance, the vigil journey with its command of silence and chastity, the whole character of the hero were most strangely reminiscent of Parsifal and the Ring of the Nibelungs. I have indicated but a few general outlines, any one can pursue the likeness in all its details to his heart's content.

Mr. Curtis has extracted from his vast materials nothing but the choicest and nothing but that which will please the eye and stir the thoughts of an intelligent white audience. All the actors are full-blooded Indians. The Indian mind is, I believe, constitutionally incapable of acting; it cannot even grasp the meaning of acting as we understand it. Probably nobody understands this fact better than Mr. Curtis. The pictures speak volumes for the producer's intimacy with the Indians and his great power over them. They are natural in every move; the grace, the weirdness and the humor of their dances have never been brought home to us like this before.

I cannot say enough for the scenic beauty of this film. Beauty does not describe that aspect of the film as fully as I would want to explain it. There is a natural beauty which simply soothes and flatters such as a pretty sunset, a fine river view, a bold rock or a beautiful shore. In this film the scenic portions have character, we feel instinctively that a virgin wilderness is conjured up before us and that the conjurer is a master craftsman, a wizard with the camera. The very solitude is there on the screen and the stern moods of Nature, the frowns no less than the smiles.

I speak advisedly when I say that this production sets a new mark in artistic handling of films in which educational values mingle with dramatic interest. Even the scenes showing the head-hunters is redeemed from the gruesome by the exceeding skill which characterizes the production as a whole. "In the Land of the Head Hunters" is a title which does not begin to describe all the film contains. It is not a feature for the nickelodeon or the cheap house, but it ought to be welcomed by the better class of houses that are looking for an occasional departure from the regular attractions and that want to give their patrons a special treat.

10

CATHERINE RUSSELL

PLAYING PRIMITIVE (1999)

The Indian thereby driven back into the ghetto, into the glass coffin of virgin forest, becomes the simulation model for all conceivable Indians *before* ethnology. The latter thus allows itself the luxury of being incarnate beyond itself, in the "brute" reality of those Indians it has entirely reinvented—savages who are indebted to ethnology for still being Savage: what a turn of events, what a triumph for this science which seemed dedicated to their destruction!

—JEAN BAUDRILLARD, "The Precession of Simulacra"

In the archives of film history, traces and fragments of disappearing films occasionally surface in "restored" versions. If experimental ethnography relies "on the use of past texts as sounding boards"[1] for a revision of ethnographic method, the restoration and recovery of "lost" films provides a particularly rich site of analysis. In this chapter, one particular film from 1914 will be analyzed as an instance of retrospective ethnographic history. *In the Land of the War Canoes* is an authentically inauthentic text, a restoration of one of the earliest ethnographic films, a film that observes very few principles of objectivity or reliable fieldwork. It is a rare example of a premodern ethnographic film that anticipates many of the elements of postmodern ethnography. To return to it as an experimental film, rather than as an anthropological film, is to trace the effects of fragmentation and historical distance on the representation of culture.

Nonfiction films of the second decade of the twentieth century are in many ways a caesura in film history. Neither actualities within the aesthetic framework of the cinema of attractions, nor "documentaries" in the style initiated by Flaherty in 1922, they constitute a wealth of cultural documentation that has only recently begun to be recognized by scholars and archivists. The 1994 Amsterdam Workshop was devoted to this material, and in the published record of the discussion of a program of "Fictional Anthropology," the participants were struck by the way that native peoples appear to "perform" themselves for the camera.[2] With the development of cinema, culture immediately becomes a representation, in which people participate with different degrees of complicity. Performances for the camera can occasionally be read as forms of cultural resistance,[3] especially once this cinema has become an archival text, and the tensions between the body and the machine become tangible. *In the Land of the War Canoes* exemplifies the role of performance in documentaries of this period, although in its particular combination of anthropology and Hollywood melodrama, it is an anomaly of film history.

In 1914, Edward Curtis, in close collaboration with the Kwakiutl Indians on Vancouver Island, attempted to make a "photoplay," or narrative drama, that would be both entertaining and educational. An enormous failure on both counts, the film quickly disappeared. In 1973 two anthropologists, Bill Holm and George Quimby, restored the film in collaboration again with the Kwakiutl, adding a soundtrack and changing the title from Curtis's original *In the Land of the Headhunters* to *In the Land of the War Canoes*. We really have two films under consideration, the first of which, *Headhunters*, is virtually unknown and unseen.[4] Its theatrical run was extremely brief,[5] and by the time the film came to be restored, neglect and fire damage had destroyed entire scenes and numerous frames.[6] My remarks on the original are somewhat hypothetical, based on the fragmentary glimpses made available in the "restored" film. They are also made with a view toward a redemptive form of ethnography inspired by the virtual reappropriation of *Headhunters* by the Kwakiutl people. The 1973 version of the film features a soundtrack of Kwakiutl dialogue, chanting, and singing—none of it subtitled—as well as drumming and natural sound effects of birds and water. Made in consultation with fifty surviving cast members, the "restored film" functions as a kind of prism through which the 1914 film might be glimpsed in fragmentary form.

War Canoes is on one level a kind of repossession of *Headhunters* by and for those whom it was ostensibly "about." However, Holm and Quimby's restoration of the film also destroys the narrative flow of Curtis's original, replacing all of his intertitles with their own, reducing the total from forty-seven to eighteen.[7] Brad Evans, one of the few people to have viewed Curtis's original footage, argues that the reediting of the film destroys its sense of storytelling, "leaving us much more with a 'cinema of attractions' than Curtis ever imagined."[8] The result is a curious hybrid of a "photoplay drama" and primitive cinema, in which the anthropologists have reproduced an earlier cinematic language in the remnants of Curtis's experiments with narrativity. Although Curtis's original film may have had a narrative coherence comparable to the fiction filmmaking of the early teens, in Holm and Quimby's restoration, *War Canoes* still retains the traces of early (pre-1907) cinema.

Curtis's inspiration was the huge success of the Indian film genre, which was most popular between 1908 and 1913.[9] He intended his film to be commercially competitive with the Hollywood-produced Indian film because it would be more authentic, featuring actual Indian actors and real props, customs, dances, and activities. The vehicle of this authenticity, however, was a convoluted narrative of romance, intrigue, and adventure, which Curtis wrote and had the Kwakiutl act out. In *War Canoes*, the anthropologists have added intertitles that are elliptical and highly condensed, making the story absolutely impossible to follow.[10] The plot has become an odd supplement to the images, which bear little resemblance to the narrative events announced in the titles. It is possible that in the 1970s the Hollywood photoplay was felt to be an inappropriate vehicle for ethnographic documentation, and so in the interests of social science, the narrativity of the original was dismantled. The effect is a radical separation of the text of the performers and the text of the author-filmmaker. The Kwakiutl, now dubbed in on the un-translated soundtrack, seem to have one film, and the anthropologist and non-Kwakiutl spectator have quite another.

In the attempt to provide an "authoritative" text of visual evidence, the anthropologists may have been less interested in narrative continuity than in preserving images of Kwakiutl culture, and yet they actually reshot one spectacular death scene in which a dummy body is thrown off a cliff after a dramatic struggle (echoes of *The Great Train Robbery*).[11] With very little cutting within scenes, and infrequent close-ups, most of the action unfolds uninterrupted in front of single static camera setups. Besides many instances of mismatched screen directions, *War Canoes* includes a vision scene, a popular convention of early cinema. Small camera movements are occasionally used to reframe action, but the frame serves for the most part as a static proscenium with little depth of field. The restored film includes Curtis's still portraits of the lead actors in costume as a means of introducing the characters, but these were not used in the original, and there are few close-ups to maintain character identification. All of these characteristics of *War Canoes* link it to the period that Noël Burch calls "primitive," before the fall of cinematic language to the limited conventions of narrative realism.

The 1973 version is designed to show off as much ethnographic data as possible about Kwakiutl life, and it is very much a process of "showing and telling," which André Gaudreault has identified as the privileged narrational form of early cinema. In the absence of Curtis's dialogue titles, the native actors lose a great deal of their characterization and become objects to be seen.[12] If for Curtis the all-native cast was a sign of the film's authenticity, in the restoration, the anthropologists have stamped the film with a different sign of authenticity. A long string of credits notes all of the institutional and museum personnel involved, as well as all the native informants and cast members. They have also privileged the canoes as the centerpiece of the film, in order to downplay the savagery implied in Curtis's original title.

"Vanishing Races" and the Performance of Culture

The exploitation of "head-hunting" in Curtis's title and story line aligns even the original film to some extent with the cinema of attractions. Among the actualities of early cinema, one can find a whole range of "Indian pictures" with titles such as *Teasing the Snakes* (Edison, 1901) and *Circle Dance* (1898) in which exotic images of Native Americans were exploited for white audiences. Curtis's early motion picture footage entered mainstream circulation in this manner, as an extension of his pursuits in commercial photography.[13] Despite Curtis's ambitions for a theatrical release for *Headhunters*, its narrative interruptions of ceremonial dances and displays, along with the other traits of early cinema, suggest that it combined the "attraction" of the spectacle of otherness with dramatic narrativity. The incorporation of a museological gaze may help to explain the film's failure at the box office.

In all his various photography, film, and research activities, Curtis took it upon himself to document the native cultures that he saw as dying, and he perceived his work as an urgent task. His photography of Native Americans is consistently tinged with a romantic sense of loss, but that sense of inevitable decay is significantly absent from

Headhunters, although to make the film, he undertook a massive recovery project of traditional Kwakiutl culture. All of the architecture, totem poles, masks, and costumes were prepared specially for the film. All signs of nonnative culture were carefully eliminated from the *mise en scène* to create the impression of an untainted Indian culture.

The collecting of trophy heads in war had not been practiced by the Kwakiutl for several generations, but within this version of the salvage paradigm, the Indians were depicted as full-fledged savages. Not only do they triumphantly wave fake trophy heads around, but a couple of scenes also feature human skulls decoratively arranged in the lair of an evil "sorcerer." Given the theatricality of these scenes, in terms of both performance and *mise en scène*, the head-hunting can be perceived as a narrative device, a practice performed only allegorically by the Kwakiutl descendants of ancient warriors. And it is in terms of allegory, in the way that the Kwakiutl perform their culture and their traditions, that the film constitutes a resistance to ethnographic authority. Underscoring the savage violence is a violence of representation that challenges the colonialist mandate of the film. *Headhunters* is not a text of mourning, but a text of the triumph of good over evil, in which the repressed violence of Curtis's noble savage photography is unleashed.

The inauthenticity of the film's ethnography is not simply due to the incorporation of script, performance, and props. Curtis freely invented names and mixed elements of different rituals and ceremonies together.[14] He spent four years preparing for the film and from his fieldwork produced one volume of his mega-opus, *The North American Indian*, on the Kwakiutl. He did make an effort to reproduce all of the masks, totem poles, canoes, and other objects of Kwakiutl life quite faithfully, and yet the requirements of the photoplay demanded an imposition of a foreign narrative form and a blatant disregard of the subtleties of Kwakiutl culture. The difference between Curtis's meticulous research and his carelessness in film production is indicative of a faith in cinematic representation as a transparency—based partially in the aesthetics of the actuality and partially in those of the new narrative realism. It was presumably enough that the Indians were played by Indians and that the props were made by them for the film to be "authentic."

In 1912 Curtis had assembled his photographs and early motion picture footage together as an illustrated lecture that he toured with orchestra, under the title "The Vanishing Race."[15] Curtis's ethnography was produced on the margins of academic anthropology, as a sideshow informed equally by the entertainment market for exploitation curiosities and by a serious sense of commitment to cultural documentation. Curtis was notorious for supplying costumes and props to create a noble savage effect for native peoples long since separated from their ancestral heritage.[16] The sense of urgency behind Curtis's project was produced within a romantic sensibility that entitled him to take artistic license of some scope in what he called his photographic art-science. To his credit, at least he represented an embodied culture and linked native peoples with the signs of their ethnicity, even if his pictures are inflected with a melancholy sense of loss. Only seven years after *Headhunters* was released, the Kwakiutl potlatch ceremonies, outlawed since 1885, began to be raided, and the ceremonial artifacts confiscated by the National Museum in Ottawa.

Curtis's own description of his intentions in *The North American Indian* is telling. His twenty-volume photographic record "represents the result of personal study of a people who are rapidly losing the traces of their aboriginal character and who are destined ultimately to become assimilated with the 'superior race.'"[17] The last two words may be in quotation marks, but Curtis's fascination with native peoples was firmly based in the racist presumption that cross-cultural encounter was necessarily a contest subject to evolutionary laws of survival. By insisting on the otherness of native peoples in his photographs, he cultivated a mystique of Indianness that could only contribute to the racist preclusion of cultural diversity. Otherness could only be valued in its specificity on the verge of its extinction. The exotic value of Indian pictures was in direct proportion to the elimination of lived native cultures. In the frame, on the page, and on the screen, Native Americans were made safe, a process that Edward Curtis, with the benevolent support of Theodore Roosevelt, was instrumental in aestheticizing.

The Northwest Coast native peoples played an important role in the ideology of "vanishing races."[18] Curtis was not alone in being attracted to a culture that, in the early twentieth century, was still quite isolated from European society and had retained many indigenous arts and customs.[19] The Kwakiutl figured prominently in Franz Boas's anthropology, a body of work that was far more significant than Curtis's in altering racist views of native peoples. Curtis acknowledges Boas in his introduction to his own Kwakiutl ethnography, but the more important link between these men is their mutual "informant," George Hunt.

The son of an Englishman and Tlingit Indian, Hunt was trained as a field-worker by Boas and guided both men through the Kwakiutl culture and language in which he grew up. Jeanne Cannizzo has argued that "George Hunt is one of the most important originators of our current view of 'traditional' Kwakiutl society; he is a primary contributor to the invention of the Kwakiutl as an ethnographic entity."[20] Hunt played an instrumental role in the production of *Headhunters*. Not only were most of the actors Hunt's own relatives, but photographs of the shoot suggest that he was Curtis's assistant director, holding a megaphone and instructing the performers.[21] This figure of the informant as assistant director may be an instance of what Trinh Minh-ha calls the "Inappropriate Other,"[22] or what James Clifford describes as an exemplary cultural traveler.[23] Unlike the ethnographers Curtis and Boas, Hunt is neither insider nor outsider, but a slippage between positions that unfixes them both. As assistant director, his role as translator and interpreter is revealed as one of anthropological creation and, literally, direction.

Both Boas and Curtis were engaged in totalizing, exhaustive documentation enterprises that were necessarily doomed to incompletion. Curtis's work was explicitly framed as art-science but fell in between both camps, into the realm of popular culture.[24] Boas's work was equally problematic as a "science," though. James Clifford notes that while Boas may not have subscribed to the "vanishing race" theory of cultural evolutionism, his conception of culture was nevertheless one in which "culture is enduring, traditional, . . . a process of ordering, not of disruption. . . . It does not normally 'survive' abrupt alterations."[25] Like Curtis, Boas "wrote out" of his account all signs of Kwakiutl adaptation to European culture, attending only to the pure elements of traditional life.

Boas introduced methods of fieldwork that were designed to be "as free as possible from the certain self-contamination of the data by the ethnographer himself." To understand culture on its own terms, to "present Kwakiutl culture as it appears to the Indian himself,"[26] one can do little more than transform it into "data." Helen Cordere notes that "Boas has been charged with being indifferent or hostile to the proper scientific goal of formulating scientific laws . . . that his ethnography is an arid accumulation of fact upon fact."[27] Boas himself filmed the Kwakiutl in 1930 but never edited the footage. Rosalind Morris has suggested that the "raw footage" was in fact more in keeping with Boas's ethnographic method: "For much of Boas's written ethnography reads like the footage for [a film]: numerous sequences of detailed images strung together one after the other with only minimal theorization. Moreover, while he occasionally discussed anthropological uses for the footage, these did not include the production of an edited 'film.' "[28]

To make "a film" from raw footage necessarily implies a narrative structure or form, which Boas may have been reluctant to impose.[29] Curtis, on the other hand, by using the narrative model closest at hand, that of the Hollywood photoplay, forces the natives into the twentieth century. Boas's ethnography may have been an important step toward the eradication of scientific racism, and yet in objectifying culture, it leaves little room for the subjective space of native peoples. It is a far cry, in other words, from "how culture appears to the Indian himself." Boas's contribution to ethnography was instrumental in transforming the stereotype of the primitive, and yet Curtis's profoundly primitive attempt to dramatize Kwakiutl culture represents on some level a recognition of native subjectivity.

The myth that Curtis devised for *Headhunters* is composed of Oedipal desires, repressions, conflicts, and triumphs. In the original scenario of the film, the hero, Motana, transgresses a "divine" law by dreaming of a woman when he is supposed to be fasting; a rival suitor steals a lock of Motana's hair, but Motana fights the magic spell and beheads the evil sorcerer to win the maiden, Naida (Figure 10.1). After a series of adventures, battles, kidnappings, and rescues, Motana triumphs over evil and takes the place of Naida's father, the chief.[30] Instead of a monotonous collection of "data" that was the downfall of the contemporary travelogue, Curtis positioned the natives within a discourse of desire. Clearly modeled on the contemporary photoplay scenario, which might be considered a powerful mythology of middle-class America, the story nevertheless, in principle, allows the native character to assume the Oedipal role.

In the film as it has come to us via *War Canoes*, an allegorical subjectivity is produced through a multilayered performance style. Curtis says that he was attracted to the Northwest Coast Indians because "their ceremonies are developed to a point which fully justifies the use of the term

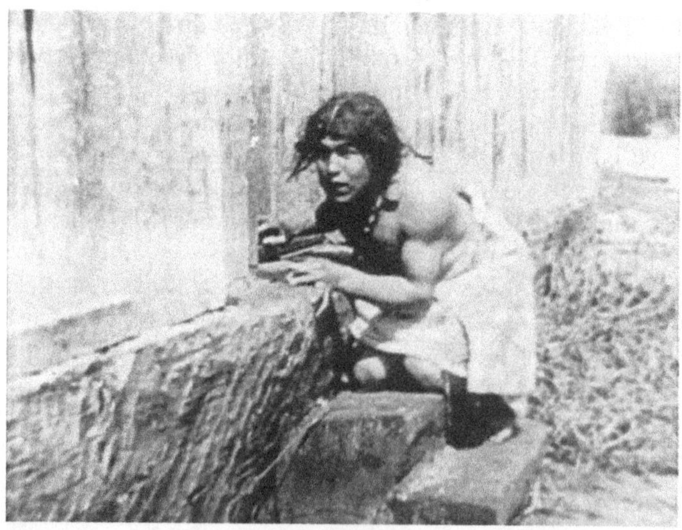

FIGURE 10.1 Edward Curtis's *In The Land of the War Canoes* (1914): Motana, the hero, sneaks into the enemy's home to rescue the princess, Naida. Still capture from DVD.

dramatic."[31] The Kwakiutl had a whole range of dances and roles that individuals and families exchanged ceremonially. The potlatch system involves the distribution of wealth, and this economic structure is closely bound up with a dramatic structure of mythologically based costumes, masks, songs, dances, roles, and even dialogue. The winter ceremonial that occurs toward the end of *Headhunters* is an annual event that Boas describes as a "great impressive ceremony of sanctifying the tribe." He also notes that the Kwakiutl name for the ceremony, *ts!e'ts!equa*, means "to be fraudulent, to cheat."[32]

The Kwakiutl, in other words, were experienced actors, which may explain the ease with which they were able to follow directions without having seen a motion picture themselves. The acting in the film ranges from naturalistic performances of activities such as canoeing and clam digging to melodramatic hysteria and, given the prevalence of long shots, can be readily compared to primitive cinema's reliance on gesture, costume, and setting for characterization. Curtis had all the actors wear wigs and costumes, which enabled them to pose as their ancestors rather than themselves, even when performing the nonceremonial activities such as hunting and paddling. The actors do not completely fill their assigned roles, partly because the characters are so clearly foreign to their culture, and partly because of their histrionic performance style. The integration of their own ceremonial dances, in which people are dressed as animals and birds complete with masks, furs, and feathers, only enhances this sense of the doubleness of the performance style.

If allegory is one of the principal means of inverting the salvage paradigm that informs conventional ethnographic praxis, performative doubling is a valuable cinematic technique. Realist aesthetics demand a disappearance of the social actor into his or her "role" in the film; the veracity of the aesthetic precludes any indices of "acting." Performative strategies that enable social actors some distance from their "image" are means of pointing to another reality outside and beyond the discourse of visual knowledge. The Kwakiutl performances in *War Canoes/Headhunters* constitute a rare display of the allegorical structure of native performance and might be described as a form of postcolonial translation, as proposed by Homi Bhabha: "The power of the postcolonial translation of modernity rests in its *performative, deconstructive* structure that does not simply revalue the contents of a cultural tradition, or transpose values 'cross-culturally.' . . . It is to introduce another locus of inscription and intervention, another hybrid, 'inappropriate' enunciative site, through that temporal split—or time-lag . . . for the signification of postcolonial agency."[33] *Headhunters* (as seen through the prism of *War Canoes*) challenges the purist implications of primitivism because it is designed so clearly as a spectacle of the primitive. Its allegorical fantasy of otherness seems to be modeled on nothing less fantastic than *Voyage dans la lune*.

Ethnography and Silent Film History

Within the history of film, the allegorical style of *Headhunters* needs to be recognized as being somewhere between Georges Méliès's *Voyage dans la lune*, made twelve years earlier, and Fritz Lang's Niebelungen films, made ten years later. The proscenium-framed ceremonial sequences and the crowding of the frame by rows of agitated, costumed people are reminiscent of the opening shots of *Voyage dans la lune*, and the prominence of skulls and trophy heads as decor and fetishes also echoes Méliès's over decorated and prop-laden *mise en scènes*. The primitivism of Curtis's visual style translates Kwakiutl exoticism into the language of magic and adventure initiated by Méliès, and as we have seen, Méliès's science fiction is itself an ethnographic cross-cultural fantasy articulated in the language of colonialism and tribalism.

The parallel with *Siegfried* (1924) and *Kriemhild's Revenge* (1925) is a little more oblique, and I certainly do not want to suggest that Lang may have in any way been influenced by Curtis's film. Lang was immersed in the European modernist discovery of primitivism and incorporated many tropes of African art into the expressionist sets and costumes of these films. Although he uses far more close-ups, Lang's characters are just as completely enveloped in costumes, wigs, and headdresses as are the Kwakiutl in *Headhunters*. Both Lang's and Curtis's films feature monumental proscenium-framed sets, and the action is often staged either in front of stylized architectural facades or in pastoral nature settings. The Niebelungen films are also about romance, power struggles between families, revenge aided by magical powers, marriage ceremonies, savage tribes (the Huns in *Kriemhild*), and tests for the hero to undergo.[34] The parallels are testimony to Curtis's imposition of European culture onto the Kwakiutl, but at the same time, they indicate the strength of the "primitivist" analogy in experimental film praxis.

Whereas comparing *Headhunters* to the work of Méliès and Lang is an important means of indicating the ethnographic discourse latent in the history of experimental fiction filmmaking, comparing it to Flaherty demonstrates the subversive potential of experimental ethnography. In 1915 Robert and Frances Flaherty met Curtis in Toronto and had a private screening of *Headhunters*. Flaherty also screened his 1914 footage of the Inuit, his first motion picture attempt that was destroyed by fire before *Nanook of the North* was made. In Frances's comparison of the two films in her diary, she says that Flaherty's images "in all their crudity . . . stood out human, real, convincing and big in contrast to the spectacular artificiality of Curtis's. . . . As Mr. C. himself said of our pictures, there was an intimacy about them; but he also criticized them as monotonous."[35] In 1914 Flaherty's footage was shot and assembled in the travelogue mode popularized by expedition films such as Herbert Ponting's 1911 film of the South Pole, *The Great White Silence*, although even Flaherty's first Inuit footage featured a single protagonist and his family.[36] From Curtis, Flaherty learned the importance of narrative and the commercial doors it might open as a means of financing ethnographic filmmaking. Frances Flaherty also notes that Curtis was having trouble marketing his film because it was regarded as too "highbrow." Ironically enough, by replacing Curtis's "photoplay" melodrama with an existential drama of human survival, Flaherty was able to reach the audience that Curtis himself missed.

The difference between *Nanook* and *Headhunters* lies not only in the kind of story but more crucially in the narrative form in which the story is told. The vehicle of Flaherty's humanist intimacy is a tightly edited narrative in which close-ups individualize the natives as characters, and extreme long shots locate these characters in the picturesque and radically foreign Arctic setting. A careful integration of titles and images naturalizes the narrative and cloaks the colonialist perspective with a tone of familiarity. In the full-fledged "institutional mode" of the narrator system, or interiorized film lecturer,[37] Nanook's story appears to tell itself. It may well have been progressive in comparison with the "curio" approach of contemporary travelogues such as those of Martin and Osa Johnson, and indeed Flaherty was quite conscious of wanting to create a more "intimate" portrait than had been done in any other ethnographic motion picture.[38] The subjectivity that Flaherty creates for his characters is, however, extremely limited. The simplicity of the raw struggle between man and nature in *Nanook* imputes an existential simplicity to the performers, who are identified completely with the roles they were asked to play.

Both Curtis and Flaherty chose to depict their respective native communities in the eternal present tense of the ethnographic "salvage paradigm." Flaherty was perhaps motivated less by an ethnographic concern to document the ways of a "vanishing race" than by a concern for dramatic content. The early scenes in the film that juxtapose the Inuit with the white man's world of gramophones and cod-liver oil do more to primitivize the Inuit than any of Curtis's head-hunting, precisely because of the heightened realism of Flaherty's visual style. It is *because* of Flaherty's naturalized narrative realism, created through his "mastery" of film language, that he could be charged with faking scenes, a charge that only authenticizes the realist context of the staging. This realism is promoted by the performances of the Inuit, as well as the drama of everyday life that they were asked to enact.

With the removal of all signs of acting and theater, *Nanook* could be more fully accommodated into the aesthetic realm of cinematic realism and, through John Grierson's endorsement, become instrumental in the development of documentary codes of authoritative authenticity. Flaherty's still photographs of the Inuit are in much the same style as Curtis's Indian photography, but that romantic stylization is more acceptable as realism when the still pose is animated in "moving pictures." *Nanook* is in a sense the cinematic equivalent to Curtis's photographic romanticism in its stylized aestheticization of native life. It completely fulfills the modernist predicament of recognizing the cultural purity and integrity of the ethnographic other while keeping that culture at a safe distance. The distance is made safe by representing native culture as outside of history, stuck in an eternally present tense. Both *Nanook* and *Headhunters* blur the distinction between the native performers and their ancestors, and yet the failure of *Headhunters* as narrative realism invites that historical difference to be read back into the film.

Headhunters is a film that forces ethnography into a wider discussion of film history. The theatrical aspect of *Headhunters* supplements narrativity with a discourse of the ethnic body ("tribalism") that can be traced to many other films of the first thirty-five years of film history, including the Hollywood Indian pictures that were Curtis's inspiration.[39] *Nanook* has become a privileged instance of art cinema precisely because its universal humanism subjugates the ethnic subject to the authority of realism. In *Headhunters* the stereotype of the primitive redeems the ethnic subject in a discourse of specificity and historicity. Its peculiar mix of art and science needs to be recognized as a prototypical experimental film with a complex spectatorial address.

Ethnographic Spectatorship

The Kwakiutl dances and ceremonies in *Headhunters*, like Curtis's earlier actuality footage of Navajo and Hopi Indians, are shot from a single camera setup with no editing within continuous actions. Compared to the actualities, the Kwakiutl are much more exhibitionist in their presentation of their culture. This theatricality, both in their performances of Curtis's melodramatic characters and in their own mythical characters, is what makes the film such a different form of ethnography. The address to the spectator is thus somewhat different.

The sets where the ceremonial dances are staged are designed as proscenium-framed platforms, with totem poles on each side and a curtain behind the performers. In one scene, the curtain drops to reveal another row of costumed dancers. In another, a front row of dancers face the camera, a second row have their backs to the camera, and behind them a row of painted boards are raised and waved about. Holm and Quimby say that these boards "represent a supernatural being, and are described as being dangerous to look at."[40] Their explanation is surprising because the film lacks any sense of supernatural or mystical forces. The presentational aspect of these ceremonies and their indication of the theatricality of Kwakiutl culture suggest that they were designed precisely "to be looked at," but not by the camera, or by the white ethnographer and his audience. Curtis's single wide-angle lens cannot even represent the depth of field necessary for the full effect of the spectacle. Again, the image is an allegorical one, slightly distanced from the "magic," precisely because of the structure of the "attraction" that keeps spectacle and spectator very separate. The sacred aspect of the ritual is essentially protected from filmic appropriation.[41]

Curtis claims that he had to enter into intensive negotiations in order to cast the film, as it had to be determined that each actor and actress was "entitled" to play his or her designated part.[42] In the end, Motana was played by George Hunt's son; three different women played the female lead, Naida; and one actor played two of the principal male leads. When Holm and Quimby screened the unedited remains of Curtis's film in the 1960s, some Kwakiutl spectators who recognized actors and actresses could not follow the story line, which arbitrarily identified individuals as characters. They likewise saw locations as familiar places rather than as the places named in intertitles.[43] Insofar as the Kwakiutl spectators read the images indexically rather than symbolically, theirs is a resistant reading, against the metaphoric grain of the text.

Instead of a "photoplay," Kwakiutl audiences may well see a documentary of their performance in a white man's movie. The film constitutes a living memory of both the traditional practices and the colonial containment activated by the rigorous framing and "photoplay" conventions. As a text of cultural memory, the film is formally allegorical, enacting several layers of representation. The contact between the 1914 performers and the 1972 soundtrack is in itself a vibrant historical correspondence, an inscription of the distance between generations, and the echoing sense of community between them. The peculiar mix of fiction and documentary that is *War Canoes* invites a broad spectrum of readings and meanings. The fictional aspect enables the documentary to be read differently, to be "displaced" and made ambiguous, giving the viewer more control. Dai Vaughan argues that once the boundary between fiction and documentary is perceived as being more fluid, ethnographic film style can and should be wide open: "Superficially reasonable demands that our films be comprehensible are often in effect demands that the viewer be browbeaten into sharing *our* understanding of them. Documentary's images are, ideally, not illustrative but constitutive. They are constitutive of the viewer's meanings, since it is the viewer who constitutes them as documentary."[44]

It is only recently that *Headhunters* became a documentary through its second life as *War Canoes*. Originally, it was apprehended as a fiction, constituted by quite a different audience than that of the anthropology and native communities. In *Moving Picture World* in 1914, Stephen Bush enthusiastically described the film as "a gem of the motion picture art." He praised its epic quality and compared it to Wagnerian opera.[45] Film theorist Vachel Lindsay described the representation of the Indians as "figures in bronze."[46] These critics confirm the affinities of ethnological primitivism and modern art that were so prevalent during this period, but they also point to the highly allegorical nature of the film. Even for these viewers, the actors represent their own nobility, savagery, and spirituality without becoming fully identified with the primitivism they enact.

Nanook of the North has also lent itself to reappropriation by the Inuit community. Zacharias Kunuk's *Quaggiq* (1989), a videotape made for the Inuit Broadcasting Corporation, is a kind of remaking of *Nanook* by and for Inuit actors. The community television aesthetic and amateur acting retains exactly the sense of doubleness conveyed by the histrionic performance style of *Headhunters*. Claude Massot's documentary *Nanook Revisited* (1990) features contemporary Inuit audiences laughing at and critiquing *Nanook*, but also exhibiting a certain fascination with its romanticism. The apparent persistence of *Nanook* in Inuit culture as a site of re-viewing, remaking, and rereading suggests that while the salvage paradigm is an ethnographic allegory of colonialism, it may also preserve a utopian form of memory of some historic value to native communities.

War Canoes and *Nanook* represent exceptional moments in film history because they are already so highly intertextual, representing the salvage paradigm as a form of narrative desire. The ideal of cultural autonomy and integrity is represented in these films as an ideal, and on some level, they do answer to the narcissism of film spectatorship, to see oneself or one's ethnic group on-screen, occupying the space of a privileged subjectivity. Despite the imperialist paradigms in which these silent ethnographic films were made, native viewers need to be credited with the ability to read against the grain of colonialism. In the attempts of native communities to maintain cultural identity through traditional languages and activities, the films offer a unique image of the previous generation's attempt to do exactly the same thing.

Interviewed in *Box of Treasures* (Chuck Olin, 1983), Gloria Cranmer Webster, a Kwakiutl museum curator, points to the monumental canoes in motion as the most valuable aspect of the film, which to her is otherwise "hokey." Obviously, we cannot impute readings or viewings to native audiences, and the playfulness that for me raises the film far above the hypocrisy of so much scientific and aesthetic ethnography may ultimately be just another academic argument. And yet Webster's explanation for why the Kwakiutl so eagerly took part in Curtis's film is that it was, quite simply, a lot of fun. If the film can teach us anything about postmodern ethnography, it might be in the very perversity of the "photoplay" intertext of entertainment and the "primitive" cinema of attractions. As an antirealist discourse, it frees ethnography from the burden of authority and from the weight of a historiography of loss. War *Canoes* is a many-layered film about a vibrant, living, native community with strong ties to both its colonial and precolonial past. The film, in its many layers and fragmentary survival, is a unique example of a postmodern document of cultural memory. Instead of representing a dying culture, Curtis's film inscribes death into the reenactment of a culture whose cinematic documentation becomes a form of redemption.

Primitive Cinema and "Free Play"

Within the history of ethnographic film, *Headhunters* may be the primitive moment, the primal ethnographic style that is so politically incorrect that it is perfectly legible as an allegory of colonialist practice. The beauty of the film is in its perverse inauthenticity, its stylized artifice and theatricality. Its allegorical structure points to that which cannot be represented, that which lies outside the domain of the white man's camera. Curtis's artistic aspirations were far more commercial than those of the avant-garde that came to identify with early cinema, and yet it was his artistic license that enabled him to challenge the fiction and travelogue conventions of his day. Especially in its contemporary form, as an archival text, the film can be aligned with the avant-garde and its rereading of primitive cinema. However, *In the Land of the Headhunters* is best situated somewhere between Buffalo Bill's Wild West Show and Josephine Baker in its attempt to capitalize on Curtis's ethnography by means of Hollywood film conventions. In the sheer perversity of the project, the film may provide a model for a postcolonial, postmodern form of ethnographic representation.

The affinities between the American avant-garde and early cinema lie in the discovery and rediscovery of film as a language of representation. From the perspective of gender relations, Judith Mayne has suggested that the alterity of "primitive" cinema has been a rich source of inspiration for feminist film practice. She points out that "the inquiry into 'primitivism' is very much connected, not to the dismantling or bracketing of narrative, but to its reconceptualization."[47] In the case of primitive ethnography, we have a similar opportunity that might restore the utopian thrust of primitivism to a postcolonial narrative. Although Curtis's original film may have moved beyond the forms of early cinema and included some of the devices of continuity editing associated with the nascent codification of narrative realism, the "restored" version of the film interrupts that narrativity and displays it as an archival series of fragments. Despite the different terms of authenticity informing the original and the remake, the Kwakiutl survive their cinematic (mis)treatment as performers. If Curtis's still photography preserved native people in a perpetual perspective of disappearance, this disappearance, his turn to melodrama repositions the native in the role of agency and desiring subjectivity. In its present state, as a film that is neither a documentary (because it is so inauthentic) nor a fiction (because the narrative is so incomprehensible), *Headhunters/War Canoes* is a key instance of the survival of a "cinema of attractions" beyond the parameters of early cinema. The imbrication of cinematic and ethnographic primitivism ultimately produces an excessive discourse of native subjectivity.

NOTES

1. Marc Manganaro, "Textual Play, Power, and Cultural Critique: An Orientation to Modernist Anthropology," in *Modernist Anthropology: From Fieldwork to Text*, ed. Marc Manganaro (Princeton, N.J.: Princeton University Press), 12.
2. Daan Hertogs and Nico de Klerk, eds., *Nonfiction from the Teens: The 1994 Amsterdam Workshop* (Amsterdam and London: Nederlands Filmmuseum and the British Film Institute, 1994), 58–66.
3. Miriam Hansen, discussion at 1994 Amsterdam Workshop, *Nonfiction from the Teens*, 62.
4. In an earlier version of this chapter, published in *Visual Anthropology* 8, nos. 55–77 (1996), I described the 1914 *Headhunters* as a lost film. Since then, Brad Evans has found Curtis's original footage, apparently intact, at Chicago's Field Museum. His comments are published as a response to my article in *Visual Anthropology* 11, no. 3 (1998): 221–41. I have modified my original article somewhat in light of his findings, and my response to his "discovery" can be found in the same issue of *Visual Anthropology*.
5. *Headhunters* opened in New York and Seattle in 1914 and ran in "theaters around the country" until 1915. It was hand tinted and accompanied by full orchestra. Curtis financed the film through his own production company, the Continental Film Company, which never recovered the production costs. The huge investment was justified by Curtis's expectation that "the Indian Pictures, owing to their historical and ethnological importance, will remain in existence for all time: rather than being junk in six months, they will become of increasing value, paying a dividend on the cost for years to come." Quoted in Bill Holm and George Irving Quimby, *Edward S. Curtis in the Land of the War Canoes: A Pioneer Cinematographer in the Pacific Northwest* (Vancouver: Douglas and McIntyre, 1990), 113.
6. Evans's description of the extant film would seem to contradict this claim by Holm and Quimby, although many of the shots included in their remake are evidently damaged.
7. Brad Evans, "Commentary: Catherine Russell's Recovery of the Head-Hunters," *Visual Anthropology* 11, no. 3 (1998).
8. Ibid., 4.
9. D. W. Griffith alone had made at least eighteen films featuring Indians played by white actors. Although some films pictured Indians as rampaging savages, a good many portrayed individual Indians as sympathetic characters abused by whites, and some romantic melodramas were set entirely in Indian communities with no "white" characters at all. Eileen Bowser, *The Transformation of Cinema, 1907–1915* (Berkeley: University of California Press,

1990), 173–77. The Library of Congress Paper Print Collection offers plot descriptions of many "Indian pictures." In addition to the Griffith films, there are a number of others worth mentioning: *The Indian*, by Klaw and Erlanger (1914), a three-reeler featuring 250 Indian extras; and *The Tourists*, by Mack Sennett (1912), in which Mabel Normand accidentally seduces an Indian chief.

10. One intertitle early in the film reads: "Motana again builds his fire on the heights where he fasts and dances, still seeking spirit power. The sorcerer's daughter resolves to spare him and win his love, but he spurns her, and she returns to her father with Motana's hair and neck-ring."
11. Holm and Quimby, *Edward S. Curtis*, 26.
12. Evans, "Commentary," 6.
13. *The Shadow Catcher: Edward S. Curtis and the North American Indians* (T. C. McLuhan, 1974) includes early *actualité* footage shot by Curtis of both Hopi and Navajo ceremonies.
14. Examples offered by Holm and Quimby include the fact that Motana, the ostensible hero of the film, is seen to hunt both sea lions and a whale as part of a "test." The Kwakiutl have never hunted whales, and killing sea lions was a part of everyday life, not a test of manhood (66). In one of the ceremonial scenes, a huge number of costumed dancers appear, but the various mythological figures represented would never normally appear together. In another instance, a dance is performed in a circle, and the participants remember Curtis drawing a circle on the floor, "apparently to guide the dancers to stay in camera range" (102).
15. Holm and Quimby, *Edward S. Curtis*, 27.
16. Christopher M. Lyman, *The Vanishing Race and Other Illusions: Photographs of Indians by Edward S. Curtis* (Washington, D.C.: Smithsonian Institution Press, 1982).
17. Edward Curtis, *The North American Indian: Being a Series of Volumes Picturing and Describing the Indians of the United States and Alaska*, vol. 1, ed. Frederick Webb Hodge (Cambridge: Harvard University Press, 1907–1930), xiii.
18. Gloria Cranmer Webster, former curator of the U'Mista Cultural Society, the Kwakiutl-run museum that now houses the treasures stolen by the Canadian government, says of the Kwakiutl, "We are the most highly anthropologized group of people in the world" (*Box of Treasures* [Chuck Olin, 1983]).
19. Pierre Stevens of the Canadian National Archives has estimated that "more than 200 films about Northwest Coast natives were made prior to 1940." Like Webster's remark, this of course begs the question of the relation of the Kwakiutl to the many other native groups in the area, a problem that has preoccupied many anthropologists of the Northwest Coast. Rosalind C. Morris, *New Worlds from Fragments: Film, Ethnography, and the Representation of Northwest Coast Cultures* (Boulder: Westview Press, 1994), 13.
20. Jeanne Cannizzo, "George Hunt and the Invention of Kwakiutl Culture," *Canadian Review of Sociology and Anthropology* 20, no. 1 (1983): 45.
21. Holm and Quimby, *Edward S. Curtis*, 57; Cannizzo, "George Hunt," 45.
22. Trinh T. Minh-ha, *When the Moon Waxes Red: Representation, Gender, and Cultural Politics* (New York: Routledge, 1991), 75.
23. James Clifford, "Traveling Cultures," in *Cultural Studies*, ed. Lawrence Grossberg, Cary Nelson, and Paula Treichler (New York: Routledge, 1992), 97.
24. Lyman explains how Curtis's work was appreciated neither in art-photography circles nor in ethnographic circles. His photography, however, was a huge commercial success, at least until about the time of *Headhunters* (*Vanishing Race*, 39–43, 78).
25. James Clifford, *The Predicament of Culture: Twentieth Century Ethnography, Literature, and Art* (Cambridge: Harvard University Press, 1988).
26. Helen Cordere, introduction to *Kwakiutl Ethnography*, by Franz Boas (Chicago: University of Chicago Press, 1966), xv.
27. Ibid., xvii.
28. Morris, *New Worlds*, 43.
29. It is not clear why exactly Boas did not edit his footage. Although he believed it to be lost, it was compiled, posthumously, by Bill Holm in 1973 as *The Kwakiutl of British Columbia* (Morris, *New Worlds*, 43).
30. Holm and Quimby, *Edward S. Curtis*, 42.
31. Ibid., 31.
32. Franz Boas, *Kwakiutl Ethnography* (Chicago: University of Chicago Press, 1966), 172.
33. Homi Bhabha, *The Location of Culture* (London: Routledge, 1994), 241–42.
34. Lang's films in the German context constitute a radical de-Wagnerization of the Teutonic myth. Instead of passion, Sturm und Drang, he offered an allegory of opera, the characters frozen in gothic, silent tableaux, and he played up the ethnic representation of Aryans and vaguely Semitic "others" to the extent that it became a Nazi favorite. A key image in *Siegfried* is the skull that appears as a kind of vision to Kriemhild in a premonition of her husband's death. In Lang's antirealist mise-en-scène, this "death's head" becomes the emblem of his thoroughly allegorical style. Its symbolism is effectively drained by its heavy-handed use. If Lang's skull, in symbolizing fate, announces the textuality of the film, the skulls in *Headhunters* likewise symbolize "savagery" in such a stylized way that they can be said to free the natives from documentary.
35. Frances Flaherty, quoted in Jay Ruby, " 'The Aggie Will Come First': The Demystification of Robert Flaherty," in *Robert Flaherty, Photographer/ Filmmaker: The Inuit, 1910–1922*, exhibition catalog (Vancouver, B.C.: Vancouver Art Gallery, 1980), 456 n.
36. Ibid., 60.
37. See Tom Gunning, *D. W. Griffith and the Origins of American Narrative Film: The Early Years at Biograph* (Urbana: University of Illinois Press, 1991).

38. Ruby, "The Aggie Will Come First," 68.
39. Bowser notes that one of the attractions of the Indian picture was the near naked bodies of white men playing natives. Charles Inslee became most well known for his portrayal of noble savages (*The Transformation of Cinema*, 176).
40. Holm and Quimby, *Edward S. Curtis*, 85.
41. In one of Curtis's earlier *actualités* of a Navajo dance, the dancers reputedly performed the dance backward to secularize it for the film camera. The "mistake" was identified by contemporary Navajo viewers of *Shadowcatchers* (Lyman, *Vanishing Race*, 69).
42. Curtis, quoted in "Filming the Headhunters: How the Vanishing Race Is Being Preserved in Moving Pictures," *Strand Magazine*, American ed., August 1915; (reprinted in Holm and Quimby, *Edward S. Curtis*, 122). Holm and Quimby note the unreliability of this article, and indeed the piece is full of exaggerations and misrepresentations designed to exoticize the production as an anthropological adventure.
43. Holm and Quimby, *Edward S. Curtis*, 59.
44. Dai Vaughan, "The Aesthetics of Ambiguity," in *Film as Ethnography*, ed. Peter Ian Crawford and David Turton (Manchester: Manchester University Press, 1992), 114.
45. Stephen Bush, "*In the Land of the Head Hunters:* Remarkable Motion Picture Produced by Edward S. Curtis, Famous Authority on North American Indians," *Moving Picture World* 22 (1914): 1685.
46. Vachel Lindsay, *The Art of the Moving Picture* (New York: Macmillan, 1915), 114.
47. Judith Mayne, *The Woman at the Keyhole* (Bloomington: Indiana University Press, 1990), 183.

11

ANONYMOUS

MOVIES OF ESKIMO LIFE WIN MUCH APPRECIATION (1915)

Probably the most remarkable "movies" ever shown in Toronto and surely the first of their kind ever shown in Canada were those put on at Convocation Hall last night. It was the pictures of Eskimo life in Baffin Land secured and exhibited by Mr. Robert J. Flaherty, head of the Sir William Mackenzie Arctic Expeditions. Every scene brought applause from the large audience of scientists, archaeologists and laymen to whom the pictures were a source of wonder and instruction.

As well as the motion pictures there were many views showing the simple arts of the Eskimo in engravings and drawings. Mr. Flaherty explained each picture.

The motion pictures series started with the picture of the family rising in the morning in their snow huts. It went on to show them eating their breakfast of raw meat. Following this came the pictures showing the Eskimo building the hut, including the cutting of the snow blocks and the putting of them together. It also showed the oil lamps, the only source of heat and light that the Eskimo knows.

Other intensely interesting pictures showed the hunting of seals, The Eskimo finding the seal breathing place in the ice and waiting until the animal appeared and then the actual harpooning. It also showed the pulling out of the large animal and then the cutting up process and the feast that followed the success.

Another interesting feature was the motion pictures of the dances and festive occasions of the Eskimo. The dances, if such they may be called, were not unlike the sun and other dances of the North American Indian.

A decidedly human touch and one that the audience appreciated was the Eskimo flirtation, which was a decidedly rough affair, winding up with the lady in the case wielding a stick rather handily.

12

ANONYMOUS

REVIEW OF *NANOOK OF THE NORTH* (1922)

Nanook of the North, produced by Robert J. Flaherty, F. R. G. S., for Revillon Freres; "My Country," one of Robert C. Bruce's "Wilderness Tales." Held for a second week. At the Capitol.

***

If a man goes among a strange people whose life is reduced to an elemental struggle for existence, if he has the disposition to photograph these people sympathetically, and the discernment to select his particular subjects so that their life in its relation to their opposed environment is illumined, the motion picture which he brings back may be called "non-dramatic" only by the acceptance of the trade's arbitrary use of the term. Such a picture has the true dramatic essentials—and such a picture is Robert J. Flaherty's "Nanook of the North," which is at the Capitol this week.

Beside this film the usual photoplay, the so-called "dramatic" work of the screen, becomes as thin and blank as the celluloid on which it is printed. And the photoplay cannot avoid the comparison that exposes its lack of substance. It is just as literal as the "travel" picture. Its settings, whether the backgrounds of nature or the constructions of a studio, merely duplicate the settings of ordinary human experience—or try to. And its people try to persuade spectators that they are just ordinary people, ordinary, that is, for the environment in which they happen to be placed. So the whole purpose of the photoplay, as a rule, is to reproduce life literally. And this is the purpose of the travel film. But the average photoplay does not reproduce life. Through the obvious artificialities of its treatment, through the unconcealed mechanics of its operation, through its reflection of a distorted or incomplete conception of life, rather than of life itself, it usually fails to be true to any aspect of human existence. It is not realistic in any sense. It remains fiction, something fabricated. It never achieves the illusion of reality.

But "Nanook of the North," also seeking to give an impression of reality, is real on the screen. Its people, as they appear to the spectator, are not acting, but living. The struggles they have are real struggles. There is no make-believe about the conflict between them and the ice and snow and wind and water that surround them. When Nanook, the master hunter and a real Eskimo, matches himself against the walrus there is no pretense about the contest. Nanook's life depends upon his killing the walrus, and it is by no means certain that he will kill him. Some day he may not. And then Nanook will die. So the spectator watches Nanook as a man engaged in a real life-and-death struggle. And how much more thrilling the sight is than that of a "battle" between two well-paid actors firing blank cartridges at each other!

And people want character in their hero, courage and strength, quick and sure resourcefulness and, for them, a friendly disposition. They have all these things in Nanook when he faces a Northern blizzard, when he harpoons a giant seal, when he builds an igloo, when he stands on a peak of ice directing the movements of his followers. He is emphatically a leader, a man, who does things, a man who wins, but who, at any moment, may lose. He is a genuine hero then, one who is watched with alert interest and suspense and far-reaching imagination. What "dramatic" photoplay can show such a one!

Nor is he alone. His family, his wife, his children, his dogs, and the paraphernalia of his life are around him. So he is not isolated. The picture of his life is filled out, humanized, touched with the humor and other high points of a recognizably human existence. Thus there is body, as well as dramatic vitality, to Nanook's story. And it is therefore far more interesting, far more compelling purely as entertainment, than any except the rare exceptions among photoplays. No matter how intelligent a spectator may be, no matter how stubbornly he may refuse to make concessions to the screen because its pictures are "only the movies," he can enjoy "Nanook of the North."

And this is because of the intelligence and skill and patience with which Mr. Flaherty has made his motion picture. It took more than just a man with a camera to make "Nanook of the North." Mr. Flaherty had to wait for his light, he had to select his shots, he had to compose his scenes, he had to direct his people, in order that Nanook's story might develop its full force of realism and drama on the screen. So it is due to Mr. Flaherty that Nanook, who lives his life by Hudson Bay, also lives it at the Capitol.

Also at the Capitol, held over for a second week and well deserving the distinction, is the third of Robert C. Bruce's "Wilderness Tales," entitled "My Country." Mr. Bruce's country is the Far Northwest, and as he revels in it many will envy him his possession of it.

13

JOHN GRIERSON

FLAHERTY'S POETIC *MOANA* (1926)

The golden beauty of primitive beings, of a South Sea Island that is an earthly paradise, is caught and imprisoned in Robert J. Flaherty's *Moana* which is being shown at the Rialto this week. The film is unquestionably a great one, a poetic record of Polynesian tribal life, its ease and beauty and its salvation through a painful rite. *Moana* deserves to rank with those few works of the screen that have a right to last, to live. It could only have been produced by a man with an artistic conscience and an intense poetic feeling which, in this case, finds an outlet through nature worship.

Of course, *Moana* being a visual account of events in the daily life of a Polynesian youth and his family, has documentary value. But that, I believe, is secondary to its value as a soft breath from a sunlit island washed by a marvelous sea as warm as the balmy air. *Moana* is first of all beautiful as nature is beautiful. It is beautiful for the reason that the movements of the youth Moana and the other Polynesians are beautiful, and for the reason that trees and spraying surf, soft billowy clouds and distant horizons are beautiful.

And, therefore, I think *Moana* achieves greatness primarily through its poetic feeling for natural elements. It should be placed on the idyllic shelf that includes all those poems which sing of the loveliness of sea and land and air—and of man when he is a part of beautiful surroundings, a figment of nature, an innocent primitive rather than a so-called intelligent being cooped up in the mire of so-called intelligent civilizations.

Surely the writer was not the only member of the crowd that jammed the Rialto to the bursting point yesterday afternoon who, as *Moana* shed its mellow, soft overtones, grew impatient with the grime of modern civilization and longed for a South Sea island on the leafy shores of which to fritter away a life in what "civilized" people would consider childish pursuits.

Moana, which was photographed over a period of some twenty months, reveals a far greater mastery of cinema technique than Mr. Flaherty's previous photoplay, *Nanook of the North*. In the first place, it follows a better natural outline—that of Moana's daily pursuits, which culminate in the tattooing episode, and, in the second, its camera angles, its composition, the design of almost every scene, are superb. The new panchromatic film used gives tonal values, lights and shadings that have not been equaled.

The film traces pictorially the capture of a wild boar by the youth Moana and his family, the capture of a giant turtle, surf ridings, the preparation of a native meal (made fascinating by clever cinema technique), and finally winds into the already talked of tattooing episode. Here, as a tribal dance proceeds, a fantastic design is pricked by a needle onto Moana's glossy epidermis. It is a period of intense pain for him, but as the sweat pours off his face he bravely bears it, for, as the subtitle has it, "the deepest wisdom of his race has decreed that manhood shall be won through pain."

Possibly I should become pedantic about this symbolizing of the attainment of manhood. Perhaps I should draw diagrams in an effort to prove that it is simply another tribal manifestation of the coming of age? It is not necessary, for the episode is in itself a dramatic, truthful thing. And if we regard the tattooing as a cruel procedure to which the Polynesians subject their young men—before they may take their place beside manhood—then let us reflect that perhaps it summons a bravery that is healthful for the race.

The film time and again induces a philosophic attitude on the part of the spectator. It is real, that is why. The people, these easy, natural, childlike primitives are enjoying themselves or suffering as the case may be before the camera. Moana, whom we begin to like during the first reel, is really tortured and it affects us as no acting could. Moana's life is dramatic in its primitive simplicity, its innocent pleasure, and its equally innocent pain.

Lacking in the film is the pictorial transcription of the sex life of these people. It is barely referred to. Its absence mars its completeness.

The most beautiful scenes that Mr. Flaherty conjures up are (1) Moana's little brother in the act of climbing a tall bending tree flung across a clear sky; (2) the vista showing the natives returning after the boar hunt; (3) Moana dancing the Siva; (4) all the surf and underwater scenes; and (5) the tribal dance.

I should not, perhaps, say that any group of scenes is any more beautiful than any other; for all are beautiful—and true.

Moana is lovely beyond compare.

14

JOHN GRIERSON

FLAHERTY (1931–32)

A happy fortune has at last brought Robert Flaherty to England. Flaherty was the director of *Nanook* and *Moana*, the originator of *White Shadows of the South Seas*, the co-director, with Murnau, of *Tabu*. He was the initiator of the naturalist tradition in cinema, and is still the high-priest of the spontaneities. The happy fortune lies in the fact that of all distinguished foreign directors he is the one whose sympathies are most nearly English. Technically, he is American, but the major part of his life has been spent exploring or filming within the British Empire.

This long association, together with his explorer's hatred of Hollywood artificialities, makes him the one director whose cinematic persuasion is most likely to benefit our present England. He comes to London for the first time with an eye for its authority in the world, which adds fantasy to the most familiar. He has seen Eskimos travel a thousand miles to buy an English blanket which would last them a lifetime, when the shoddy article of more recent commercial tradition was at their igloo doors. He has eaten out an Arctic winter on the superior construction of English bully-beef tins, which refused to rust with foreign competitors. He has blessed the name of England ten thousand miles away for the one glue in the world which the tropics could not melt.

I knew Flaherty in New York, and he was the only man I knew there whom Babel did not enthral. This seemed to me a most perverse feat of the mind at the time, but in these later days I would more sensibly describe it as a feat of most necessary simplicity. It is only now apparent how the Blazonry of American ballyhoo was selling a generation into slavery. Flaherty used to say: "They are a tribe of sharks preying on the weakness of their neighbours. This is their way of being ferocious." He contrasted the public decency of Polynesians. Economics, of which he professes nothing, have most strangely found him right. I know not how many millions the American people will have to pay their irresponsible exploiters when prosperity comes again; for goods consumed.

Now in London I find Flaherty's eye for things as fascinating as before. He tells me that wholesomeness went out of American humour when Mark Twain died, and that behind all the flashing wit of American cross-talk is an essential unkindliness. He tells me that England is dirty and scrambled, that its humor is simple, but that this original human wholesomeness remains to it. He tells me that English faces retain an individuality which stands up to the buildings as American faces cannot. He contrasts the manicured landscape of the Continent with the informality and intimacy of the Chilterns. He praises, most unfashionably, craftsmanship.

These hints and emphases are very close to the problem we have to solve in our English cinema, for we are more than ever in search of the national certainties we are to proclaim. We have not yet evolved a *style*. We imitate Hollywood, and occasionally we imitate Neubabelsburg and Moscow. There is some original lack of affection for our own English worth, a lack of knowledge of it, a lack of bravery in it which prevents our bringing beauty, and convincing beauty, out of the films we make.

It is, I know only too well, difficult to be sure of one's attitudes in a decade like this. Can we heroicize our men when we know them to be exploited? Can we romanticize our industrial scene when we know that our men work brutally and starve ignobly in it? Can we praise it—and in art there must be praise—when the most blatant fact of our time is the bankruptcy of our national management? Our confidence is sapped, our beliefs are troubled, our eye for beauty is most plainly disturbed: and the more so in cinema than in any other art. For we have to build on the actual. Our capital comes from those whose only interest is in the actual. The medium itself insists on the actual. There we must build or be damned.

Flaherty's most considerable contribution to the problem is, as always, his insistence on the beauty of the natural. It is not everything, for it does not in the last resort isolate and define the purposes which must, consciously or unconsciously, inform our craftsmanship. But it does ensure that the raw material from which we work is the raw material most proper to the screen. The camera-eye is in effect a magical instrument. It can see a thousand things in a thousand places at different times, and the cunning cutter can string them together for a review of the world. Or he can piece them together—a more difficult task—for a review of a subject or situation more intricate and more intimate than any mortal eye can hope to match. But its magic is even more than this. It lies also in the manner of its observation, in the strange innocence with which, in a mind-tangled world, it sees things for what they are. This is not simply to say that the camera, on its single observations, is free from the trammels of the subjective, for it is patent that it will not follow the director in his enthusiasms any more than it will follow him in the wide-angled vision of his eyes. The magical fact of the camera is that it picks out what the director does not see at all, that it gives emphasis where he did not think emphasis existed.

The camera is in a measure both the discoverer of an unknown world and the re-discoverer of a lost one. There are, as everyone knows, strange moments of beauty that leap out of most ordinary news reels. It may be some accidental pose of character or some spontaneous gesture which radiates simply because it is spontaneous. It may be some high angle of a ship, or a crane, or a chimney stack, or a statue, adding some element of the heroic by a new-found emphasis. It may be some mere fore-shortening of a bollard and a rope that ties a ship to a quay in spirit as well as in fact. It may be the flap of a hatch cover which translates a gale. It may be the bright revelation of rhythms that time has worn smooth: the hand movement of a potter, the wrist movement of a native priest, or the muscle play of a dancer or a boxer or a runner. All of them seem to achieve a special virtue in the oblong of the screen.

So much Flaherty has taught us all. If we add to it such instruction as we have taken from Griffith and the Russians, of how to mass movement and create suspense, of how to keep an eye open for attendant circumstance and subconscious effect, we have in sum a most formidable equipment as craftsmen. But the major problem remains, the problem I have mentioned, the problem the critics do not worry their heads over, though creators must: what final honours and final dishonours we shall reveal in this English life of ours: what heroism we shall set against what villainy. The field of cinema is not only a field for creators but also for prophets.

The method followed by Flaherty in his own film-making might give us a most valuable lead. He took a year to make his study of the Eskimos and this after ten years' exploration in the Eskimo country of Labrador and Baffin Land. He took two years to make his study of Samoan life, and only now, after three more years in the South Seas, feels he could do justice to it. He soaked himself in his material, lived with it to the point of intimacy and beyond that to the point of belief, before he gave it form. This is a long method, and may be an expensive one; and it is altogether alien in a cinema world which insists on forcing a pre-conceived shape (one of half a dozen rubber-stamped dramatic shapes) on all material together. Its chief claim to our regard, however, is that it is necessary, and particularly necessary in England. We know our England glibly as an industrial country, as a beautiful country of this epic quality and that; we know it by rote as a maker of Empire and as a manipulator of world-wide services. But we do not know it in our everyday observation as such. Our literature is divorced from the actual: it is written as often as not in the south of France. Our culture is divorced from the actual: it is practised almost exclusively in the rarefied atmosphere of country colleges and country retreats. Our gentlemen explore the native haunts and investigate the native customs of Tanganyika and Timbuctoo, but do not travel dangerously into the jungles of Middlesbrough and the Clyde. Their hunger for English reality is satisfied briefly and sentimentally over a country hedge.

We might make an English cinema, as we might make English art again, if we could only send our creators back to fact. Not only to the old fact of the countryside which our poets have already honoured, but to the new fact of industry and commerce and plenty and poverty which no poet has honoured at all. Every week I hear men ask for films of industry. They want it praised and proclaimed to the world, and I would like to see their money used and their purposes fulfilled. But what advice can I give them? We can produce them the usual slick rubbish, some slicker, some less slick; but who of us knows an industry well enough to bring it alive for what it is? And what statescraft is willing to send a creator into an industry, so to know it: for a year, for two years perhaps, for the length of a hundred thousand feet of film and possibly more. Our businessmen expect a work of art to schedule, as the housewife expects her daily groceries. They expect it of a new medium. They expect it from raw material which they in their own hearts despise.

Flaherty, as an individual artist, cannot answer the whole problem. He knows his primitives and will do a job for them out of the strength of his affection. He could do a job for English craftsmanship and for the tradition of quality in English work, and for the native solidity in English institutions, and English criticism and character; but he is of a persuasion that does not easily come to grips with the more modern factors of civilization. In his heart he prefers a sailing barge to a snub-nosed funnel-after, and a scythe to a mechanical reaper. He will say that there is well-being associated with the first and none with the second, and in a manner he is right: right in his emphasis on well-being. But how otherwise than by coming to industry, even as it is, and forcing beauty from it, and bringing people to see beauty in it, can one, in turn, inspire man to create and find well-being? For this surely is the secret of our particular well-being, that men must accept the environment in which they live, with its smoke and its steel and its mechanical aids, even with its rain. It may not be so easily pleasant as the halcyon environment of Tahiti, but this is beside the point.

I think in this other matter one may turn to the Russians for guidance rather than to Flaherty. Their problem, of course, is different from ours. The industrial backwardness of the country, the illiteracy of their people, and the special factors of Russian psychology make for a rhetoric in their cinema which we cannot blindly imitate. Apart from this national difference, which is in effect their *style*, there is an ardour of experiment in their treatment of industrial and social material. They have built up rhythms from their machinery; they have made their work exciting and noble. They have made society on the move the subject-matter of art. Their sense of rhythm is not necessarily our sense of rhythm. Their sense of nobility and sense of social direction need not be identical with ours. The essential point, however, is that they have built up this rhythm and nobility and purpose of theirs by facing up to the new material. They have done it out of the necessity of their social situation. No one will say that our own necessity is less than theirs.

When I spoke with Flaherty on the Aran Islands he was full of the possibilities of the British documentary cinema. If on these islands—only so many hours from London—there was this story of romantic life ready to the camera, how many more must there be! He mentioned the Hebrides and the Highlands, and sketched out a film of Indian village life. He spoke of the tales of fine craftsmanship which must be tucked away in the Black Country. But first, he emphasized, there must be the process of discovery and freedom in discovery: to live with the people long enough to know them. He talked with a certain rising fury of the mental attitude of the studio-bred producer who hangs a slicked-out story of triangles against a background of countryside or industry. Rather must the approach be to take the story from out the location, finding it essentially there: with patience and intimacy of knowledge as the first virtues always in a director. He referred to a quotation I once wrote for him in New York, when his seemingly tardy method of production was first an issue in the studios. It was Plato's description of his metaphysics where he says that no fire can leap up or light kindle till there is "long intercourse with the thing itself, and it has been lived with." No doubt the studios, with their slick ten- or fifteen-day productions of nothing-in-particular, still disagree with Flaherty and Plato profoundly. His idea of production is to reconnoitre for months without turning a foot, and then, in months more perhaps, slowly to shape the film on the screen: using his camera first to sketch his material and find his people, then using his screen, as Chaplin uses it, to tell him at every turn where the path of drama lies.

No director has the same respect as Flaherty for the camera; indeed very few of them even trouble to look through the camera while it is shooting their scenes. Flaherty, in contrast, is always his own "first cameraman." He spoke almost mystically of the camera's capacity for seeing beyond mortal eye to the inner qualities of things. With Fairbanks he agrees that children and animals are the finest of all movie actors, because they are spontaneous, but talks also of the movements in peasants and craftsmen and hunters and priests as having a special magic on the screen because time or tradition has worn them smooth. He might also add—though he would not—that his own capacity for moving the camera in appreciation of these movements is an essential part of the magic. No man of cameras, to my knowledge, can pan so curiously, or so bewilderingly anticipate a fine gesture or expression.

Flaherty's ideal in the new medium is a selective documentation of sound similar at all points to his selective documentation of movement and expression in the silent film. He would use the microphone, like the camera, as an intimate attendant on the action: recording the accompanying sounds and whispers and cries most expressive of it. He says the language does not matter at all, not even the words, if the spirit of the thing is plain. In this point as in others, Flaherty's cinema is as far removed from the theatrical tradition as it can possibly be. His screen is not a stage to which the action of a story is brought, but rather a magical opening in the theatre wall, through which one may look out to the wide world: overseeing and overhearing the intimate things of common life which only the camera and microphone of the film artist can reveal.

15

HAMID NAFICY

LURED BY THE EAST

Ethnographic and Expedition Films about Nomadic Tribes; The Case of *Grass* (2006)

Expedition and ethnographic films encode the nations' ideologies and collective longings for form—expressed in socially acceptable, aesthetically pleasing, and commercially successful generic and narrative schemas—and the psychology and desires of individual filmmakers. As a result, it is important to deal not only with overarching ideologies, such as colonialism, Orientalism, nationalism, and imperialism that shape the thinking and imagination of nations but also with filmmakers' personal histories, politics, and imperatives that help to form both them and their films. One topic in which early traveling filmmakers from the West showed great interest was the Eastern nomads. United States explorers and filmmakers were attracted to such nomadic tribes for personal and national reasons, among them wanderlust; manifest destiny, consisting of national expansionism, exceptionalism, and triumphalism that characterized both American pioneers of past centuries and global explorers of the twentieth century; a desire for authentic experiences and modernist primitivism found in the struggle against harsh nature; and a racialist nostalgia for origins.

As a case study of this complex attraction, this essay examines the seminal film *Grass: A Nation's Battle for Life,* about the semiannual migration of the Baba Ahmadi tribe in Iran.[1] It examines both the film's text and its context—the personal, political, ideological, and cultural forces that informed its genealogy, filming, intertitling, publicity, theatrical exhibition, nontheatrical touring, and reception by diverse audiences and critics both in the United States and in Iran. Recognized as a classic of documentary, ethnographic, and expedition films, it was made by three Americans, Merian C. Cooper, Ernest B. Schoedsack, and Marguerite E. Harrison—intrepid explorers, anti-Soviet adventurers, members of the U.S. military or intelligence services, journalists, and filmmakers.

By the early 1920s, interest in the East and the Orient was keen and Orientalist conceptions were circulating widely in fiction films such as in Cecil B. DeMille's *The Arab* (1915), Louis Gasnier's *Kismet* (1920), and Rex Ingram's *The Arab* (1924). Iran, a subject of many documentaries by Western travelers (Naficy 1984, 1995), is not Arab but a non-Semitic and overwhelmingly Muslim country, located in the Middle East where most of the Arabs and a high percentage of the world's Muslims live. As a result, its cinematic representations have conformed to many of the Orientalist discourses about Arabs and Muslims and posed problems for them. In many ways, *Grass* played into these discourses and problematized them.

The Filmmakers and Their Triumphalist Wanderlust

Grass is a silent, 35mm, black-and-white, seventy-minute film that deals with the trio of American explorers traveling through Turkey, Syria, Iraq, and Iran in search of a "forgotten" Asiatic tribe. Having "found" them in Iran and identified them, the explorers follow their transhumance migration from hot, dry regions to cool, green pastures. Cooper is the film's producer, Schoedsack the cameraman, and Harrison the on-camera personality.

Ernest Beaumont Schoedsack (1893–1979) had been a cameraman for the Mack Sennett Studio and for the United States Signal Corps; and he was perhaps the first airborne combat photographer. He devised a way of filming through the machine-gun openings that synchronized the camera shutter's motion with the airplane's propeller (Wiley 1981). After World War I, he joined the Red Cross relief mission, driving ambulances, helping Polish refugees to escape from Soviet occupied lands, and filming "unparalleled" newsreel footage of the Polish fighters' incursion into Russia (Goldner and Turner 1975: 25). At least two Red Cross films about these events, *To the Aid of Poland* (1919) and *The Fall of Kiev* (1919), contain Schoedsack's footage. He also made at least two films for the Red Cross Travel Film series: *'Neath Poland's Harvest Skies* (1920) and *Shepherds of Tatra* (1921). These were upbeat in tone, emphasizing the quaint and exotic life of the peasants in a devastated Europe (Veeder 1990: 61). As a freelance cameraman, Schoedsack also filmed newsreels for the U. S. government as well as for commercial newsreel companies. Among these were scenes of the Versailles Treaty deliberations in Paris and the brutal Greek-Turkish war of 1921–22 that resulted in an independent Turkey under Mustapha Kemal Pasha (Ataturk), which sparked Schoedsack's interest in the Near East.[2]

Merian Coldwell Cooper (1895–1973) worked as a journalist in several U. S. cities and served in General Pershing's army in Mexico, chasing Pancho Villa. In 1917 he was flying low over the western front as a tactical aerial observer when he was shot down over the Argonne. Badly burned, he became for a time a prisoner of the Germans. Like Schoedsack, he viewed the Bolsheviks as a potential enemy, and at the outbreak of the Polish-Russian War, he formed with Major Cedric E. Fauntleroy the Kosciusko Aerial Squadron to fight the Bolsheviks. Again, he was shot down and this time he became a prisoner of the Red Army in Wladykino Prison, near Moscow. For months he assumed the identity of Corporal Frank R. Mosher, the name that was stenciled on the secondhand underwear that the Red Cross had given him. He was certain that if the Soviets discovered his true identity, he would be executed. During this time, Marguerite Harrison, who was spying for the U. S. military in the Soviet Union, smuggled food, blankets, tobacco, books, and money to him. Because of this, Cooper acknowledged that he owed his life to her (Brownlow 1979: 516; Goldner and Turner 1975: 24). Subsequently, in a daring and successful attempt, he escaped to freedom.

In 1922 Schoedsack, who had met Cooper earlier in Warsaw, joined him on a filmic expedition with Captain Edward A. Salisbury, an explorer and conservationist, on his ship *Wisdom II*. This collaboration resulted in a short film, *Golden Prince*, about Ras Tafari—then prince regent of the Abyssinian Empire, later crowned Emperor Haile Selassie of Ethiopia—and some newsreel footage of Muslims on their *hajj* pilgrimage in Jedda, Saudi Arabia. However, an accidental fire by a crewman that burned much of their footage caused Cooper and Schoedsack to adopt an idea they had abandoned earlier: making an epic film about a nomadic tribe's struggle against nature.

As a precocious child who began talking at eight months, Marguerite Harrison (born Marguerite Elton Baker, 1879–1967) had traveled to Europe extensively, thanks to her father, a wealthy transatlantic shipping magnate (Harrison 1935: 8; Olds 1985: 158–59). As an adult, she satisfied her insatiable urge for travel and adventure by becoming a reporter for various papers, including the *Baltimore Sun*, and by contacting the U.S. Army Military Intelligence Division (MID), offering to become a spy. After preliminary interviews, MID signed her on and sent her to Europe to report on the social climate and psychological conditions of the Germans in the wake of their defeat in the Great War. She worked hard and in a disciplined fashion, chasing leads and regularly filing interesting and accurate reports with her military superiors about the Germans' postwar attitudes, including reactions to the cost of the severe terms of the peace treaty and the emergence of anti-Semitism (Olds 1985: 170). Some of these reports were also printed in the *Baltimore Sun*. Although the Versailles peace treaty brought an end to Harrison's spying in Europe, she soon obtained another intelligence assignment, spying in the Soviet Union. After some success there she was caught and spent ten nightmarish months in the notorious Lubianka Prison and, later, in Novinsky Prison—the first American woman to become a prisoner of the Bolsheviks. It was from Novinsky that a grateful Cooper had planned to rescue Harrison. That became unnecessary, however, as she was released through the intervention of the American Relief Administration, which offered food for famine-starved Russians in exchange for freedom for all American prisoners (Olds 1985: 181–83).

Cooper and Harrison had first met years earlier in Warsaw at a Red Cross ball, an acquaintance that grew once Harrison returned to the United States in the early 1920s. However, she was restless and her powerful wanderlust uncontainable. Her autobiography testifies:

> I knew that I should have been content to live with my boy in New York where I had made hosts of friends, but I could not settle down. During the late spring nights I lay awake listening to the sirens of the ocean liners that were leaving for distant ports. They were truly sirens to me, urging, enticing, irresistible. Finally, I could stand it no longer. I made up my mind that I would have to go somewhere before the summer was over. (1935: 565)

That "somewhere" was nowhere else but the Middle East and Iran, where she went to make *Grass*.

The wanderlust of all three was driven not only by their personal desires for elsewhere and for other times but also by the Great War, which had shaken many people out of their routines, leaving them at a loss, dissatisfied with their own societies, and curious about other places. Modernity and improvements in communication and transportation had made literal travel and virtual travel (by means of film and photography) possible and within reach of ordinary people. The trio's sense of exceptionalism, expansionism, and triumphalism was fueled not only by the victory of the Americans and their European allies over their Western and Eastern foes but also by the emergence of the United States from the Great War as a new global power. It was perhaps also driven by the exceptionalism, expansionism, and triumphalism of the U.S. film industry, emblematized by Hollywood's dominance of the world's screens since that war. Political and cinematic supremacy facilitated the emergence of an American travel cinema.

The film's budget was small at ten thousand dollars, at least half of which was supplied by Harrison (Harrison 1935: 566) and the rest by Cooper and Schoedsack (Brownlow 1979: 516, Wiley 1981: 1), with the latter also contributing his lightweight, hand-cranked French Debrie camera, mounted on a tripod and equipped with a 400-foot film magazine. Although Schoedsack was opposed to taking a woman on a dangerous expedition, he agreed to an equal partnership, according to which all three would share the film's profit in equal parts.

Struggle against Nature and Filmic Conditions

Grass contains two overarching plots of struggles: the filmmakers' search for the "Forgotten People" and the tribes' migration with thousands of animals over rough terrain. The first plot opens the film and lasts the first third of its length, while the latter plot takes up the rest of the film. Schoedsack and Cooper had originally planned to film the migration of Kurdish tribes in Turkey because they had the "most interesting costumes and customs" and lived in a "wildly photogenic country" (Schoedsack 1983: 43).

Indeed, the film begins like an early theatrical feature by introducing the intrepid travelers, much like cast members: in close-up portrait shots, filmed behind Paramount's Astoria Studios, looking at each other or at the camera (Figure 15.1). After this opening, Harrison is the only expedition member on camera. Such self-referentiality enhanced the film's documentary claims at the same time that, through the artifice of the search for the tribe and Harrison's on-camera presence, it provided Western audiences with a pleasurable narrative world and a figure of identification.

The newly independent Turkey, formed out of the rubble of the Ottoman Empire, suspicious of foreigners, made the explorers' forays into Kurdish region unsafe. During the weeks of waiting for travel and filming permits, Schoedsack filmed some newsreel and travelogue footage to support the team financially. A few of these sequences made it into *Grass*, such as the scene of the dancing bear and village children. As they became convinced that permits were not forthcoming, they evaded police surveillance and, following ancient caravan routes, trekked southwest from Istanbul to Angora (Ankara) in search of a new Forgotten People. They spent a memorable night in an old caravansary, sharing a hot meal cooked over an open fire with Turkoman travelers. Using flares, Schoedsack filmed this scene dramatically, which was cut into the film. Weeks later they entered the Anatolian desert during a bitter winter, but this did not deter them from fulfilling one of the requirements of desert travelogues—a sandstorm. They re-created it by having porters shovel bran out of bags just outside Schoedsack's camera frame while Harrison and her carriage driver drove straight into the wind. The result on film was highly realistic, as waves of bran came at them, covering them from head to foot, entering their hair, noses, and teeth—Harrison having to remove bran from her long hair for days.

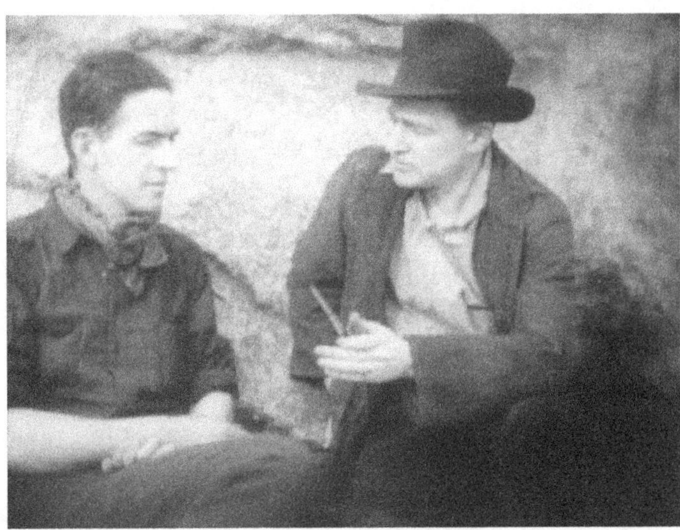

FIGURE 15.1 Ernest Schoedsack (left) and Merian Cooper being introducded to the audience (Paramount back lot, Astoria, NY), in *Grass* (1925). Still capture from DVD.

Continuing their search, the trio headed into the Taurus Mountains toward Syria (Figure 15.2). In the midst of a blinding snowstorm, with snow coming up to the bellies of their horses, they encountered hospitable natives, among them a local hunter named Halil Effendi, who provided them with another re-created episode. Using a specially built portable canvas screen as camouflage, with three holes in it for eyes and the gun muzzle, Effendi stalked wild mountain goats, shooting and killing one. However, since the shooting occurred off camera, they re-created it by propping the carcass high on a cliff. When Schoedsack was ready, Halil took a shot and someone pulled a cord that caused the carcass to tumble over the mountainside for the filming. Harrison justified the fakery in the way many documentarists have justified re-creations: "It was merely a repetition before the camera of what had actually happened" (1935: 586).

Disappointed in not finding their picturesque and heroic Forgotten People in Turkey, Syria, or Iraq, the filmmakers finally chose the Bakhtiari tribes in Iran. In this choice they were advised by the British politician Sir Arnold Wilson, chairman of the board of the Anglo-Persian Oil Company, and by the chief of British intelligence for Iraq, Gertrude Bell. The Bakhtiaris' semiannual migration in search of pasturage was massive and dramatic, and their route highly picturesque; it was to begin in April 1924, a schedule the filmmakers could readily accommodate; and their area of migration was within the jurisdiction of the giant oil company's operation, where the filmmakers could benefit from its influence and protection. Sir Arnold's introductory letter, urging local and tribal officials' cooperation, opened many doors to them, including their audience with the Il-Khani, the chief of all the Bakhtiari tribes, and with his cousin and second in command, the Il-Begi, Amir Jang.[3] The older Il-Khani was puzzled by the idea of foreigners accompanying tribal migration for filming, but he was won over by the younger Il-Begi, who had been to the movies in Tehran and had liked them. The filmmakers' desire to follow a tribe whose route was through the wild mountains, not on the gravel road that the British had built, resulted in their joining the Baba Ahmadi subtribe, headed by Haidar Khan.

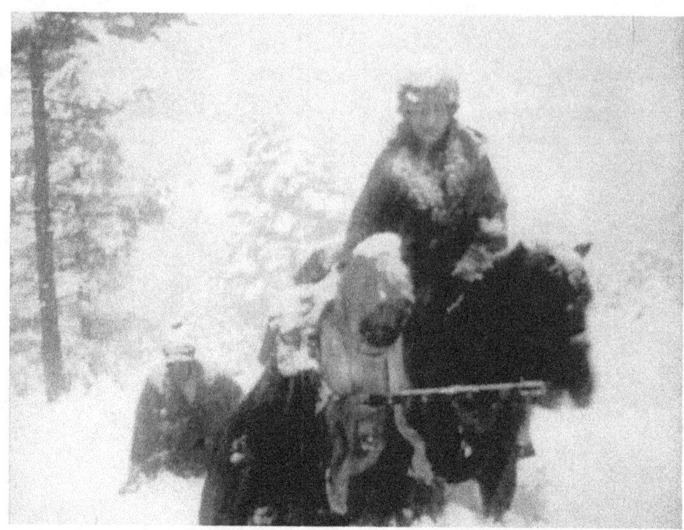

FIGURE 15.2 Marguerite Harrison and local attendants in a snowstorm in the Taurus Mountains (Turkey) in *Grass*. Still capture from DVD.

At this juncture, the filmmakers were justifiably delighted about finally locating the site of the Forgotten People—a delight that is enacted in *Grass* in the drama of discovery, a characteristic of the expedition genre—which is marked on a map of Asia Minor and Persia (now Iran) on which a large caption identifies the Forgotten People's location and the trio's route to find them. As part of this drama of discovery, viewers are treated to the only scenes of nonmigratory aspects of the tribes' life in the film: the tribal black tents in the valleys and women who are spinning cotton, dancing with a handkerchief, feeding a baby, and milking a goat while men perform the stick dance.

From this point on, the film's first plot—the filmmakers' struggle to find their subjects—joins its second plot—the struggle of the Baba Ahmadi tribe numbering some five thousand people and fifty thousand animals to migrate from their southwest winter region near the Persian Gulf to the cooler summer pastures near Isfahan. This massive movement began on 17 April 1924, and lasted forty-eight days, during which Schoedsack and Cooper generally slept on the ground, while Harrison slept in a small tent. As Schoedsack explains in a tape letter, "We ate the food they gave us—we had no supplies of our own—and it was very good. They'd bring us their food every night. We'd stretch out on our bedroll, and they'd give us barley, which they stored in goatskin sacks, and every few days they'd have a shish Kebab—and always plenty of yogurt" (Schoedsack 1971). Cooper, too, loved the outdoors life with the Bakhtiari, considering it, according to his wife Dorothy Cooper, as "one of the happiest periods in his life" (D. Cooper 1984).

Schoedsack filmed by hand-cranking his Debrie camera at the silent speed of 16 fps, exposing some 20,000 feet of black-and-white negative. Tribespeople did not have a problem with being filmed, perhaps because they had developed a good rapport with Schoedsack and trusted him and because they were too busy with their migration to pay attention to the camera. Harrison often slept with the precious film cans and the trio's moneybags in her tent to safeguard them. As the only Westerner with sustained on-camera presence, she stands out among the tribespeople with her white horse, her light-colored Western safari suit, her pith helmet held on her head with a scarf, and her fashionably made-up face. She took care to apply make up for each shot and she washed her clothes regularly to make herself "presentable" (Harrison 1935: 626–27). Schoedsack's shot compositions, which centered her, also contributed to her visibility.

The filmmakers turned the two massive and dramatic obstacles of the migration into the film's narrative complications. One involved thousands of tribespeople and animals crossing the torrential and icy rapids of the Karun River, which was a half-mile wide and without a bridge in the vicinity. In this process, human lives and livestock were inevitably lost annually. Schoedsack, who had gone ahead to secure a position to film the tribes' arrival at the river, sent a note to Cooper, saying: "Coop! I hate to say it before we start shooting, but this is what we have been traveling months to see. Better be here before sunrise tomorrow. This is it!" (M. Cooper 1925: 218–19). The lengthy sequence he filmed shows in graphic detail the way tribesmen inflate goatskins and tie them together to form rafts, which carry their wives, children, small animals, and belongings, while the men swim across the turbulent waters simultaneously herding thousands of sheep, donkeys, cows, and horses. Later, when he had confronted the river and witnessed the Baba Ahmadi's efforts to cross it, Cooper wrote: "It was a show, all right. For five days Schoedsack and I, rushing about with the cameras, watched the greatest piece of continuous action I have ever seen" (1925: 233). The documentary historian Erik Barnouw offered a similar assessment of Schoedsack's filming: "One of the most spectacular sequences ever put on film" (1993: 48).

The other obstacle and narrative complication involved the barefoot tribespeople, dressed in light clothing, carving a narrow zigzag trail into the snow-covered side of Zardeh Kuh up to its vertical 15,000-foot summit. Filming such a massive and moving target posed major logistical and aesthetic problems, one of which was the impossibility of rehearsals or retakes. Another was that, to avoid the intense daytime heat, the tribe generally broke camp in complete darkness, depriving the crew of any nighttime scenes or ethnographic footage of tribal socializing. The blinding early morning sun, and the often bright background, also made it impossible to film the lightly dressed tribespeople. However, Schoedsack learned to cope with these problems admirably. His cinematography is crisp, dramatic, and breathtaking, particularly where humans are framed against massive mountains, vast valleys, or torrential waters. Kevin Brownlow calls one of these scenes "the most unforgettably epic shot of documentary history" (1979: 526). Apparently based on a painting of Napoleon crossing the Alps, which Cooper had seen in Paris, it pictures the zigzagging multitude of tribespeople flattened against the far valley like thousands of flies (Figure 15.3). Schoedsack's intimate shots are also dramatic, showing women carrying babies in wooden cradles on their backs, a young girl climbing the rocky path with a lamb on her shoulders, and pack animals creating a traffic jam on the zigzag trail.

The filming of *Grass* itself was also a heroic struggle and achievement, given the weight and bulkiness of the 35mm equipment and film stock and the exigencies of tribal migration, which demanded mobility, spontaneity, and great stamina. In such circumstances, planning was nearly impossible. Schoedsack did well on that account as well, for by the end of the seven-week migration, he had exactly eighty feet of film left with which to record the tribes' triumphal arrival in what the film intertitles call "the land of milk and honey—the land of Grass"

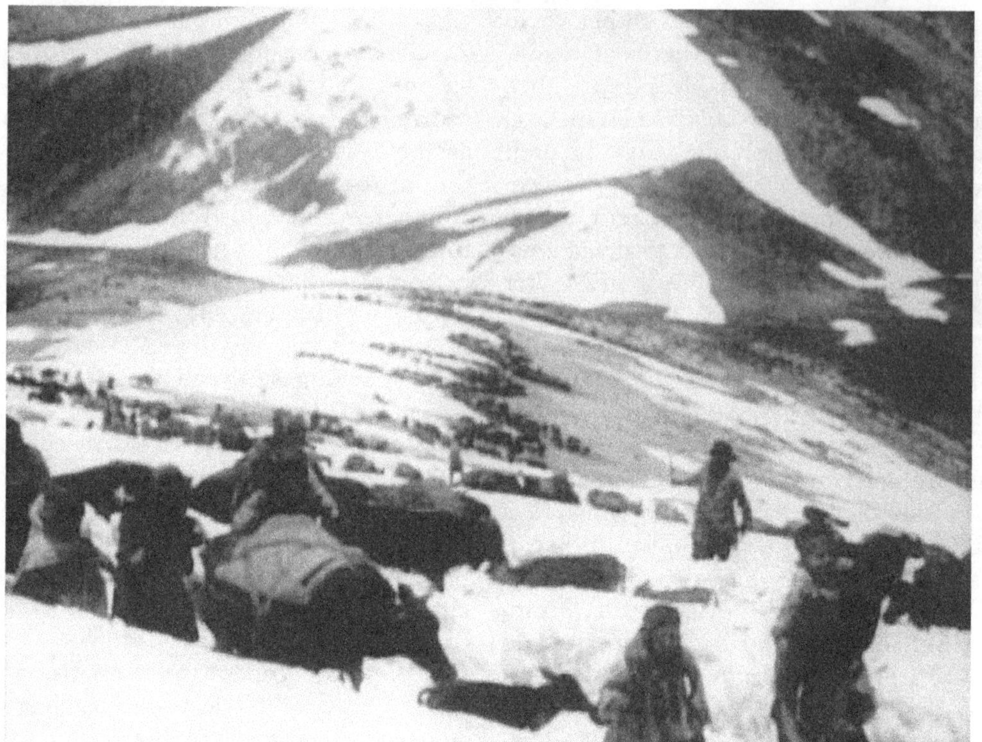

FIGURE 15.3 5,000 tribespeople and 50,000 animals on the zigzag trail up the Zadeh Kuh (Iran) in *Grass*. Still capture from DVD.

(Schoedsack 1971). This is why that scene is so brief and contrived.

The U.S. travelers' search for the Forgotten People and the two key river and mountain crossings are driven not only by wanderlust and desire to escape to elsewhere but also by the theme of the tribes' nomadic life as an elemental struggle for survival against violent nature. Robert Flaherty's *Nanook of the North* (1922) had memorably depicted this theme in the Inuit's efforts to survive in the Canadian tundra. Cooper wanted to achieve a similar effect, for he hypothesized that "when man fights for his life, all the world looks on. And where does man have to fight harder than when he finds his opponent the unrelenting and stern forces of Nature? . . . We decided to attempt to throw on the screen the actual struggle for life of a migratory people" (1925: x).

By the time filming was over, however, Cooper and Schoedsack had grown to regard their film as "half a picture" and a "great missed chance" (Brownlow 1979: 528–29). While their footage was impressive in scale and grandeur, it lacked human intimacy and personality. Their plan to complete the film by raising funds to film the tribes' autumn return migration and Haidar's family life with his two wives and son did not materialize. In their preparation to leave Iran, all three stayed in Tehran for a while, where they had two fateful engagements, with significant impact both on their film's fate in Iran and on the politics of Iran-U.S. relations. Cooper and Schoedsack stayed at the home of U.S. Vice Consul Robert Imbrie, who notarized a testimonial letter for them, written by tribal chiefs, that offered proof of their expedition. Within months, Imbrie would be murdered by a fanatical mob in Tehran. In the meantime, Harrison gained an audience with Reza Khan, minister of war *and* prime minister, who used Imbrie's murder to consolidate his hold on power and become the shah (see below).

Editing and Intertitling the Film

Cooper and Schoedsack took the exposed footage to Paris for development and, later, edited it into a 7-reel film in New York City (about seventy minutes). It was during a private screening of this version that Jesse Lasky (of Famous Players-Lasky Corporation) liked what he saw and decided to complete the film for theatrical distribution—not wanting to repeat his mistake of passing up the opportunity to distribute *Nanook of the North* seven months earlier.

To that end the studio made several major changes and additions to the film, copyrighting it on 21 June 1924. The portraits of the three explorers were added to the start of the film. The tribal chiefs' testimonial letter was inserted at the film's end. Dated 28 June 1924, written in Persian and English by Haidar Khan and Amir Jang, and notarized by Major Robert W. Imbrie, it confirms that Cooper, Schoedsack, and Harrison were "the first foreigners who have crossed the Zardeh Kuh pass and the first to have made the forty-eight day migration with the tribes" (in the Persian version, it is forty-six days).[4] In addition, the film was turned into feature length (ten reels) by padding it with outtakes, which angered Schoedsack in particular (Brownlow 1981: 2). Finally, innumerable intertitles were inserted (some 174 in the version that Milestone is currently distributing). The final ignominy was that the credit for editing the film did not go to Cooper and Schoedsack, but to Terry Ramsaye and Richard P. Carver, who also had a major hand in writing the intertitles.

Famous Players-Lasky may have felt they needed dramatic and snappy titles to make what they feared would be a dreary documentary entertaining. In the late silent era, all films employed title writers, whose job was "to make subtitles entertaining," and by 1925 some of them had succeeded too well, eliciting "howls of laughter from delighted audiences" (Brownlow 1981: 1). Of the filmmaking trio, Harrison disliked the intertitles the most. After viewing *Grass* once on the public screens, she could not "bear to see it" again because she "loathed" the artificiality and theatricality of the intertitles (1935: 648).

Taken together, the film's visuals and intertitles create a dichotomous, "split" text. While the visuals by and large document, authenticate, and celebrate the reality, bravery, stamina, and resourcefulness of the tribe, the intertitles are often ethnocentric, Orientalist, narratively manipulative, and overly dramatic. This textual split may be a result of the division of labor, with the filmmakers, experienced about the migration and sympathetic to the tribe, in charge of the visuals, and the studio writers, ignorant of the tribes' way of life, supplying the intertitles.[5] However, this division was not that hard, for Cooper admitted to having written some of the titles himself (Brownlow 1981: 1). That the intertitles in the next Cooper-Schoedsack documentary, *Chang* (1927), and the captions for the numerous stills of the migration in Cooper's book about *Grass* suffer from similar problems underscores Cooper's ethnocentric view of non-Western people.

The film is also a "hybrid" text in the way it borrows from fiction cinema and contributes to an emerging nonfiction cinema. It borrows from the silent fiction films the scenario of search, the filmmakers' "discovery," and the way the intertitles dramatize, narrativize, entertain, characterize, stereotype, and visualize. On the other hand, the documentary footage of the expedition and migration, the film's self-reflexivity, and the way the intertitles and maps provide context, diegetic and extradiegetic information, and framing give evidence of the codes of the as yet unnamed documentary form.

Racialist Nostalgia for Origins

Another theme that attracted the early Western travelers to the tribes was that focusing on tribes allowed them to establish continuity and hierarchy in the chain of human evolution, with non-Western tribes residing in the earlier stages and Western societies occupying the pinnacle of evolutionary developments. There is a marked difference, however, between the manner in which traveling filmmakers, such as Martin and Osa Johnson, represented African blacks around the same time in such films as *Simba* (1928), *Congorilla* (1932), and *Baboona* (1935) and the way that the makers of *Grass* represented the Iranian nomads. In representing the African blacks, and sometimes Arabs, the traveling filmmakers imbued the social Darwinism paradigm with latent and manifest racism, both of which posited the Africans as inherently different, separate, unequal, and inferior to the whites. They were stereotyped, ridiculed, infantilized, and reduced to the level of subhuman. However, the use of this racialist paradigm was more complicated and more favorable to the Iranian tribes. It was more complicated because the representation of the Baba Ahmadi by Harrison and Cooper in their memoirs differs markedly from that in the film, undermining a unified ideological vision of the tribe. Harrison writes that there was "nothing particularly glamorous about their struggle for existence," as the tribe was terribly poor and existed on a totally inadequate diet (1935: 617). Cooper, too, speaks of the Bakhtiari often in uncomplimentary fashion as "wild nomads" (1925: 9) and "barbarian hordes" (3), and he quotes past observers of Iran who describe the tribes as "a race of robbers" and "bloodthirsty" people (151). Both Harrison and Cooper note that their chief, Haidar Khan, was gorilla-like, brutal, a wife beater, an opium smoker, and a horse thief, who loafed about while his people did the work. Despite these very negative appraisals, both also praise the Baba Ahmadi tribe and its chief for their valor, endurance, and ingenuity.

The film does not visualize the team's negative private observations and prejudices, perhaps because it would have countered the projection of the tribespeople as noble savages, which was its overarching theme. Instead, *Grass* emphasizes the positive public display of tribal bravery and stamina, in support of which it marshals ample documentary evidence. This ideological split between the private and public views of the tribe can be detected in the film's other textual split discussed earlier, between complimentary visuals and condescending intertitles. The racialist depiction of Iranian tribes was more favorable compared to that of Arabs and Africans, because these tribes were construed to be white, non-Semitic, and Aryan, a fact that both the film's intertitles and the filmmakers' writings point up. Like Harrison, Cooper invokes the common racial bond between the tribes and white Americans, musing that "it may well be that the migratory life which we are going to live with them is that of our own Aryan forefathers of many thousands of years ago" (1925: 143). *Grass*'s opening intertitles also reiterate this theme.

Such a racialist differentiation between Iranian "primitives" and African "primitives" is also evident in an unpublished exchange between Brownlow and Schoedsack. At one point, Schoedsack states that he took still portrait shots of the Baba Ahmadi, which they liked very much in general; their only complaint was that they were only head-and-shoulder shots. Brownlow then reminds Schoedsack of Martin and Osa Johnson's expeditions in Africa during which they showed the natives still pictures of themselves and discovered that the natives could not make sense of them. Brownlow asks Schoedsack if he encountered the same problem with the Iranian tribe. This is Schoedsack's response: "These aren't low down stupid thick old coloured, you know. These are very intelligent white folk. They knew what pictures were, and they had a lot of old stone carvings on graves and things like that" (Brownlow 1969–70: 9).

Because of these racial and hierarchical conceptions, the Bakhtiari tribes are included in the line of human progress but are kept safely sealed in their time capsule in the earlier evolutionary stages. They came to represent a bygone era of simplicity and authenticity, and their way of life a prelapsarian world of before—before civilization and modernity separated humans from their Edenic origin. Thus a return to and recovery of such a world, in the form of the search and discovery of the Forgotten People, became alluring prospects. Of course, the tribespeople were neither forgotten nor unknown to themselves or to the Iranians, a great percentage of whom were then—and are still—tribal or have tribal roots. But it was necessary to create this fiction of loss and amnesia in order to feed the fiction of the documentary: the discovery of the forgotten tribe by Western filmmakers.

The film's play of the gazes replicates a series of binary power relations: between East and West, ethnographer and subject, and male and female. It contains only one instance of diegetic eye contact and eye-line cutting; significantly, that is in the film's opening between the two male filmmakers, who form a small exclusive club among equals. Harrison, on the other hand, is shown in the opening in a single shot by herself, looking at the camera without any exchange of looks between her and them. And in the rest of the film, where she is on camera, her personal point of view is rarely shown. As a result, both Harrison and the tribespeople are excluded from the process of signification; they are objectified and looked at. However, they are objectified differently. As a white mediator, even though a woman, Harrison has a higher status than the tribes, since she is also a diegetic subject from whose narrative perspective the audience sees the migrating tribe and the trio's expedition. The natives, on the other hand, are objectified thrice: first as the subject of Harrison's regard, then as the subject of the camera's gaze, and finally with their muteness, since the intertitles rarely quote any actual native dialogue.

The film's self-congratulatory attitude also bolsters the Western filmmakers' power position.[6] The tribal leader's letter at the film's end must be seen in this light, for it testifies to, and dramatizes, their accomplishment in braving the tribes' primitive world. Barnouw thought the film's final emphasis was not on the endurance of the tribe but on "the brash display of egoism—on the heroic accomplishment of the film makers" (1993: 48).

On the Lecture Circuit: Commercial Exhibition and Reception in the United States

After the film's completion, Cooper and Harrison went on the lecture circuit, extensively screening *Grass* while providing live narration about their experiences of traveling and filming. Cooper acquired an agent who booked his film tours at clubs, scientific societies, and colleges, particularly in the Midwest. The National Geographic Society in Washington, D.C., invited him to lecture with the film, and among the distinguished audience was the president of the United States. His average net profit from each lecture was about two hundred dollars, which he split equally with his two partners. He also wrote a series of illustrated articles about the filming for *Asia Magazine* and published a book about that experience, containing Schoedsack's dramatic photographs (M. Cooper 1925), which was subsequently serialized in newspapers and translated into Persian (M. Cooper [1934] 1955). His publisher also arranged for a one-hour radio appearance sponsored by the Goodyear Tire and Rubber Company, for which Cooper received the high sum of one thousand dollars.

Harrison, too, traveled widely with the film, talked on the radio, and lectured with it, particularly to women's clubs and societies. One example of her public lecturing is her presentation on 13 December 1938, at UCLA'S giant Royce Hall Auditorium for the university's "lifelong learning" program. The printed flyer boasts that she was lecturing with "the only complete copy of *Grass* available for public presentation." An organist, Harry Q. Mills, was on hand to provide live musical accompaniment. That the event was scheduled in a hall that could seat over one thousand spectators indicates the size of the expected audience. Although, as she admits, she had "acquired a reputation for unreliability" because of her "incurable habit of going off on trips" and missing her appointments, she secured enough speaking engagements with the film to remain financially afloat (Harrison 1935: 648). Like Cooper, she also wrote a book—narratively more engaging than Cooper's—in which, among her other life stories, she recounts the threesome's experience of the filming of *Grass* (1935).

In those days, women travelers, explorers, and filmmakers were not taken seriously, and the mass media were often more interested in their love affairs with exotic foreigners than in their explorations and accomplishments. Harrison complained that all the reporters wanted to know was "if I had become enamoured of a sheik!" (1935: 650). Cooper and Schoedsack, too, did not sufficiently acknowledge her contribution to the film—although Cooper in his memoir applauded her linguistic facility and her paramedical abilities. Schoedsack was downright hostile, calling her involvement in the film "a sore spot" and "a bad idea." Nonetheless, he acquiesced, since having a "white woman" on camera was a "cute" idea, and he felt "honor bound" to "make a shot" of her every so often. He also asserted that there was nothing romantic between the men and Harrison and that Cooper brought her along to repay her for saving him from starvation in the Soviet prisons (Brownlow 1969–70: 9; Brownlow 1979: 528). His antagonism may have stemmed not only from his sexism but also from his professional jealousy of a woman who considered herself the film's heroine and co-producer. Power was also a factor (see below). Although this hitherto unpublished account of the hostile undercurrent of the relationship among the expedition members was kept private, soon after *Grass*'s first theatrical run, the partnership dissolved. Cooper and Schoedsack, however, joined forces on several subsequent productions, which in some ways replayed, echoed, and signified on *Grass*, notably *Chang* and *King Kong* (1933).

These diverse forms of publishing, publicizing, lecturing, touring, broadcasting, and film screening before general and specialized audiences were part of the cross-fertilizing culture industry infrastructures that were coming together for both fiction films and documentary films. The wide dissemination of such ideologically loaded projections of non-Western people would ensure that these ideologies would become part of the political unconscious of Westerners, helping, in the words of Edward Said, to ideologically "produce" the "East," or the "Orient" (1979).

Famous Players-Lasky produced *Grass*, while Paramount released it commercially. A variety of film archives, independent film libraries, university film libraries, and independent distributors handled its nontheatrical distribution. In 1991 Milestone

Film and Video acquired the rights to the film from the Museum of Modern Art in New York City and re-released the most complete version of it on videocassette, laser disk, and DVD, with an added Persian musical score.[7]

Grass performed well at the box office, particularly in major cities. It remained on the screen at the Criterion Theater in New York City for three months (April-June 1926), earning $85,346, and it earned in its first run in Philadelphia, Chicago, and Los Angeles a total of $37,400 (Dannenberg 1927: 253). It did not do as well in smaller cities, perhaps because it was so remote from the lives of ordinary Americans and because there were "no pretty girls in it, no love scenes" (Harrison 1935: 648–49). With this income, the three partners paid their expenses, recouped their investment, and earned several thousand dollars each in royalties.

The film did surprisingly well in terms of critical response, as well (Gerhard 1925; Hall 1925; Lawrence 1925; Johnson 1982). In the United States, nationwide film reviewers voted *Grass* one of the best pictures of 1925. Many reviewers ranked it among the ten best films, and overall they ranked it number twelve, a high ranking given that it was a documentary in the company of luminary feature films such as F. W. Murnau's *The Last Laugh* (ranked number two), John Ford's *The Iron Horse* (number four), Erich von Stroheim's *Greed* (number five), Charles Chaplin's *The Gold Rush* (number seventeen), and Raoul Walsh's *Thief of Baghdad* (number twenty-two). In addition, the National Board of Review ranked it fifteen in a list of forty best pictures of 1925 (Dannenberg 1927: 417–26). In 1926 *Grass* was selected among four hundred films "suitable for children" (Kann 1927: 471–73). Geographers and ethnologists "hailed it as a substantial contribution to human knowledge" (Harrison 1935: 648), and historians recognized it as a "classic" of documentary cinema, rating it second only to *Nanook of the North* (Brownlow 1979: 529).

Sociopolitical Reception in Iran

Apparently, *Grass* was not screened in Iranian public cinemas for about two decades, for several reasons. For one, it showed armed nomadic tribesmen freely moving about at the time that the government was forcibly pacifying all tribes. Showing the film publicly would have countered that national policy, spearheaded by the autocratic prime minister Reza Khan, with grave consequences. Its depiction of Iran as a "primitive" and pastoral country would also have falsified his modernist projection of Persia (whose name he changed to Iran in 1935). That he was aware of the film is almost certain, for Harrison met with him in Tehran after filming in 1924. However, there is no evidence that he had viewed and banned the film.

The film's screening may also have been hampered by a foreign-policy crisis that occurred immediately after filming. This was the tragic murder of the signer of the testimonial letter for *Grass*, U.S. Vice Consul Robert Imbrie, by a Tehran mob angry at his photographing a religious shrine and procession, which became the first of several major rifts in Iran-U.S. relations in modern times. The Iranian government apologized for the incident, paid for the indemnity of Imbrie's widow, underwrote the cost of the warship *Trenton* to repatriate the body, and hanged three culprits. Significantly, Reza Khan used Imbrie's brutal murder to consolidate his power by declaring martial law, arresting his political opponents, muzzling the opposition press, and curbing the clergy. A year later, he dissolved the Qajar dynasty and declared himself the shah of the new Pahlavi dynasty. The United States government, which had publicly taken a hardline approach with the Iranian government to save face, implicitly encouraged his assumption of dictatorial power as a "price that had to be paid for satisfactory settlement of the Imbrie dispute." For the Americans, the lesson from this incident reverberated for decades, for as late as the 1950s, the U.S. embassy in Tehran routinely warned Americans against photographing religious events in Iran by invoking Imbrie's unfortunate fate (Zirinsky 1986: 283–88).

When *Grass* was eventually shown after the Allied Powers had occupied Iran and forced Reza Shah into exile in 1941, it was not the feature-length, silent American film. Rather, it was a forty-minute sound version (perhaps produced by the BBC), with Nikolay Rimsky-Korsakov's *Scheherazade* (1888) as the sound track and a Persian-language voiceover narration. The well-known scholar Mojtaba Minovi wrote and read the narration himself, which provided a sympathetic and nationalistic counterdiscourse to the original ethnocentric intertitles. The British Council distributed the film nationally to movie theaters and to cultural and educational institutions as late as the mid-1970s.

According to the filmmaker Mohammad Ali Issari, this version was highly popular with Iranians because seeing themselves on the screen for the first time and in a generally positive light "satisfied their sense of national pride" (1982). The French sociologist Edgar Morin also noted that many grown Bakhtiari men, who on seeing the film recognized themselves as children, were delighted about what they saw. The Persian-language narration must have indigenized the film, increased its attractiveness, and enhanced what Morin calls the "pleasure of auto-identification" of cinema (1977: 109). Issari's auto-identification by means of *Grass* had a lasting effect on him, initiating his lifelong commitment to documentary filmmaking.

At the same time, however, like a Lacanian mirror, the film's wider circulation produced contradictory reactions, causing not only self-identification but also self-alienation. The writer Ali Javaherkalam, who viewed the film in 1931 in a cinema in Abadan operated by the Anglo-Persian Oil Company, relates that during the screening, some oil workers became so agitated by the perceived negative depiction of Iran that they loudly objected to the film and walked out of the theater. The next day, however, a high-ranking Iranian official of the company admonished them for their defensive anger at a film that he thought had honestly documented Iranian reality (Rahimian 1988: 61). Bakhtiari tribal leaders also expressed mixed reactions about it to me. Amir Bahman Samsam confirmed that he had seen both versions, that the migration was depicted "realistically and without errors," and that the Baba Ahmadi's route was their normal route (Samsam 1984). This latter statement, coupled with similar comments below, dispenses once and for all with the notion put forward by some scholars (Sadoul 1965: 105; Barsam 1992: 55) that the tribe had taken an unusually picturesque and difficult route to accommodate the desire of the filmmakers for dramatic footage. Hamid Khan Bakhtiari, the son of the Il-Khani who had facilitated the filmmakers' migration with the tribe, had also viewed the British Council's version as a young governor of the region. He corroborated the accuracy and truthfulness of the film. However, his emotional reaction was mixed: "I was made proud of the defiance of the men and women of the tribe but very saddened by their poverty, ignorance, and illiteracy" (Bakhtiari 1984).

Grass captured the imagination of not only Issari but also other filmmakers, inside and outside Iran, some of whom attempted to reproduce and update that primordial vision of humankind by examining tribal life—with mixed results. *Grass* continues to be screened in documentary film, Middle Eastern history, and visual anthropology courses in the United States and elsewhere. One barometer of its longevity is the statistic from the Museum of Modern Art in

New York City, which reported some fifty "circulations" a year as late as the 1980s, about 80 percent of which went to colleges and the remainder to cultural institutions (Sloan 1982). The availability of the film on video in the 1990s bolstered its circulation enormously, as Milestone Film and Video reports sales of over five thousand videocassettes and DVDs in one decade since it began distributing the film (Doros 2003). This sudden surge may owe partly to the presence of over half a million Iranians in the United States, the largest population outside Iran, who are interested in their cultural heritage.

Attempted Color and Sound Remake in 1956

Aware of some of *Grass*'s shortcomings, Cooper attempted another version in Technicolor and sound, but against Schoedsack's advice (Schoedsack 1983: 114). He assembled a large fifteen-person, Hollywood-style crew consisting of technical personnel, guards, and actors along with half a dozen muleteers and some forty-three mules, who carried their gear, tents, cameras, vodka, orange juice (imported from the United States), canned food (corned beef and hash), and sleeping bags. Most would not eat the tribes' food (Sadeqi 1984). Lowell Farrell was to direct the film for C. V. Whitney Productions, with Cooper as executive producer and Winton Hock as director of photography. This was a far cry from the nimble, three-member crew of *Grass*, who slept in the open or in a pup tent and ate what the tribespeople ate.

Their filming approach, guided by first-time director Farrell, was also Hollywood inspired in that it was based on scripted narrative films, unsuitable for spontaneous filming of a massive migratory tribe. Under government supervision, they managed to film scenes of Bakhtiari daily life, migration, river crossing, and city life, but they ran out of time, money, and steam. This footage was edited into a forty-minute "demo" film that was accompanied by a musical track and a verbose voice-over narration designed to raise funds to finance yet another trip to complete the film (which did not happen). This footage, which I have viewed, lacks the scale and drama of the original, a lack that is particularly noticeable in its mundane river- and mountain-crossing sequences. Having been filmed like a scripted documentary, it also lacks curiosity and the sense of wonder and discovery about the profilmic world that distinguished *Grass*, which remains an unsurpassed expedition documentary of one of humanity's vanishing ways of life.

NOTES

1. I would like to thank the following people who over the many years of my research on *Grass* agreed to be interviewed; corresponded with me; and put at my disposal documents, photographs, reviews, and other personal items related to the works of the Cooper-Schoedsack-Harrison team. They are Jalal Asghar (Schoedsack's friend), Kevin Brownlow (film historian), Dorothy Cooper (Cooper's wife), Robert Dickson (filmmaker), Dennis Doros (Milestone Films and Video), Dr. John Gilmore (Schoedsack's optometrist), Shusha Guppy (writer and folk singer), Khosrow Zolqadr Sadeghi (Schoedsack's friend), Peter Schoedsack (Schoedsack's son), Maxine Swanson (former Maxine Logan, Maxine Howard, and Maxine Butcher, nurse and caretaker of Schoedsack in his last years), Gerry Veeder (film scholar), and Ken Wiley (Schoedsack's friend). Not all of these sources are cited here. Jeff Fegley helped with scanning the stills. This research was partially funded by a National Endowment for Humanities Travel to Collections grant.
2. By the mid-1960s, Schoedsack had lost his sight due to a detached retina, glaucoma, and bullous keratitis (Gilmore 1983). He became a bitter, cantankerous, and paranoid man who demanded narcotics for his pain and sometimes hallucinated about fighting the Iranian tribes (Swanson 1984). He communicated with distant friends by audiotapes. I have a copy of his tape letter narrating the complete story of the making of *Grass* (Schoedsack 1971).
3. At the time, the Il-Khani was Gholamhosain Khan Sardar Mohtasham and the Il-Begi was Mohammad Taqi Khan Amir Jang. There were two Baba Ahmadi

tribes, Baba Ahmadi-ye Kashki and Baba Ahmadi-ye Sarajeddin. The U.S. filmmakers were attached to the Kashki branch (Samsam 1984).

4. The version of this letter reproduced in Cooper's book (1925: 13) is markedly different, supplying more information about the route taken. Dated 5 June 1924, it states that Cooper, Schoedsack, and Harrison are "the first foreigners who have made the 46-day migration with the Baba Ahmadi tribe of the Bakhtyari, over the Zardeh Kuh trail from the Jungari district in Arabistan to the Chahar Mahal valley in Ehleck."
5. The low regard of the title writer, Terry Ramsaye, for the tribes and his instrumentalist view of intertitles come through in his letter in *Atlantic Monthly* in response to a review of *Grass* that the periodical had published. He states: "The fact is that the Bakhtyari are shown merely driving their cows over a mountain to pastures. They do it twice a year. It is a chore, not an epic, even if I did utter considerable typographical excitement on the screen about it." Reacting to the reviewer's admission of enjoying the "wealth of details," he notes that "she may have enjoyed it, but she did not see it. It was not in the pictorial negative. That beautiful detail was Barnumed into words calculated to speed the spectator past the camera's omissions" (1926: 142–43).
6. Even the catalogue of Kodascope Library, which circulated *Grass*, bore such an attitude: "In all the world, only three white people have ever seen this marvelous depiction of elemental life and mighty courage" (*Descriptive Catalogue of Kodascope Library* 1932: 193).
7. Milestone has the rights to *Grass* until 2015, when the copyright runs out (Doros 2000). The musical score is by Gholamhosain Janati-Ataie, Kavous Shirzadian, and Amirali Vahabzadegan.

WORKS CITED

Bakhtiari, Hamid Khan. 1984. Correspondence with Hamid Naficy. July 27.

Barnouw, Erik. 1993. *Documentary: A History of the Non-Fiction Film.* Rev. ed. New York: Oxford University Press.

Barsam, Robert Meran. 1973. *Nonfiction Film: A Critical History.* New York: Dutton.

———. 1992. *Non-Fiction Film: A Critical History.* Rev. and exp. ed. Bloomington: Indiana University Press.

Brownlow, Kevin. 1969–70. Interview with Ernest B. Schoedsack.

———. 1979. *The War, the West and the Wilderness.* New York: Alfred A. Knopf.

———. 1985. Correspondence with Hamid Naficy. 7 March.

Cooper, Dorothy. 1984. Interview with Hamid Naficy. Coronado, Calif. July 21.

Cooper, Merian C. 1925. *Grass.* New York: G. P. Putnam's Sons.

———. 1955. *Safari beh Sarzamin-e Delavaran* (Journey to the Land of the Brave). *Grass*, trans. Amir Hosain Zafar. Tehran: Franklin Books.

Dannenberg, Joseph, ed. 1927. *Film Year Book, 1926.* Hollywood: Film Daily.

Descriptive Catalogue of Kodascope Library. 5th ed. 1932. New York: Eastman Kodak.

Doros, Dennis (Milestone Film and Video). 2000. E-mail message to Hamid Naficy. 23 October.

———. 2003. E-mail message to Hamid Naficy. 9 January.

Gerhard, George. 1925. "Reel Reviews." *New York Evening World.* 3 March, n.p.

Gilmore, John. 1983. Interview with Hamid Naficy. Santa Monica, Calif. 20 January.

Goldner, Orville, and George E. Turner. 1975. *The Making of: The Story behind a Film Classic.* South Brunswick, N.J.: A. S. Barnes.

Hall, Mordaunt. 1925. "A Persian Epic." *New York Times.* 31 March, n.p.

Harrison, Marguerite. 1935. *There's Always Tomorrow: The Story of a Checkered Life.* New York: Farrar and Rinehart.

Issari, Mohammed Ali. 1982. Interview with Hamid Naficy. Los Angeles, 25 August.

Johnson, Timothy W. 1982. *Grass: A Nation's Battle for Life.* In *Magill's Survey of Cinema, Silent Films*, vol. 2, ed. Frank N. Magill, 502–4. Englewood Cliffs, N.J.: Salem Press.

Kann, Maurice, ed. 1927. *Film Year Book, 1927.* New York: Film Daily.

Lawrence, Florence. 1925. "'Grass' Thrilling Film Innovation with Big Appeal." *Los Angeles Times.* 21 May, n.p.

Naficy, Hamid. 1984. *Iran Media Index.* Westport, Conn.: Greenwood Press.

———. 1995. "Mediating the Other: American Pop Culture Representation of Postrevolutionary Iran." In *The U.S. Media and the Middle East: Image and Perception*, ed. Yahya R. Kamalipour, 73–90. Westport, Conn.: Greenwood Press.

———. 2001. *An Accented Cinema: Exilic and Diasporic Filmmaking.* Princeton, N.J.: Princeton University Press.

Olds, Elizabeth Fagg. 1985. *Women of the Four Winds.* Boston: Houghton Mifflin.

Rahimian, Behzad. 1988. "Mazi-ye Naqli." *Mahnameh-ye Sinemai-ye Film* 63 (April-May 1988): 60–61.

Ramsaye, Terry. 1926. Letter to the Editor. *Atlantic Monthly.* January: 142–43.

Sadeqi, Khosrow Zolqadr. 1984. Interview with Hamid Naficy. Monterey, Calif. December 2.

Sadoul, Georges. 1965. *Dictionnaire des films.* Paris: Éditions du Seuil.

Samsam, Amir Bahman Khan. 1984. Correspondence with Hamid Naficy. July 31.

Schoedsack, Ernest B. 1971. Tape letter to Arnold Goldner, Chico State College, Chico, Calif., September.

———. 1983. "*Grass*: The Making of an Epic." *American Cinematographer.* February: 41–44, 109–14.

Sloan, William. 1982. Correspondence with Hamid Naficy. May 12.
Swanson, Maxine (Maxine Logan, Maxine Howard). 1984. Interview with Hamid Naficy. Delta, Colo. August 12.
Veeder, Gerry, K. 1990. "The Red Cross Bureau of Pictures, 1917–1921: World War I, the Russian Revolution and the Sultan of Turkey's Harem." *Historical Journal of Film, Radio, and Television* 10, no. 1: 47–70.
Wiley, Ken. 1981. Correspondence with Hamid Naficy. September 6.
Zirinsky, Michael. 1986. "Blood, Power, and Hypocrisy: The Murder of Robert Imbrie and American Relations with Pahlavi Iran." *International Journal of Middle Eastern Studies* 18: 275–92.

16

BÉLA BALÁZS

COMPULSIVE CAMERAMEN (1925)

The posthumous film of the South Pole explorer Robert Falcon Scott, who filmed his own death as if he were screaming his death cry into a phonograph, was the second film of its kind. In the previous year, the film of Ernest Henry Shackleton's journey to the South Pole had showed far more dramatically, even though Shackleton escaped with his life, the struggles of a man who in his campaign of conquest transcended his own physical limitations. What is particularly remarkable about these films is not their images of hand-to-hand combat with murderous nature, nor their depiction of bravery, determination, and heroic solidarity—a good director could have invented all these scenes and staged them far more effectively. Nor is it that these are actual events—we have had numerous reports of men capable of staring death calmly in the eye well before these English seamen and geographers. What is unusual and new is that these men looked at death through the lens of the movie camera.

That is the new, objectified form of human self-awareness. As long as these men did not lose consciousness, they did not take their hand off the crank of their camera. Shackleton's ship is broken to bits by massive slabs of ice. It was filmed. Their last dog dies. It was filmed. The way back to normal life was blocked, there was no hope. It was filmed. They drift on an ice floe, and the ice floe melts beneath their feet. It was filmed. Captain Scott sets up his last tent and with his comrades goes inside as though into a tomb to wait for death. It was filmed. Just as the ship captain on the bridge and the telegraph operator at his Marconi apparatus are to stay at their posts, the cameraman stayed at his and filmed until his hand froze to the handle.

This was a new kind of self-examination. These men thought about themselves in that they filmed themselves. The interior process of accounting for themselves shifted to the outside. Their self-observation was mechanically preserved up to the last minute of their lives. The film of self-control that heretofore consciousness had unreeled inside their heads wound up on the spool of the camera, and conscience, which previously mirrored itself only for itself, relegated this function to a machine, which preserved that mirror image for others to see as well. In this way subjective mentality is transformed into a social one.

Of course the camera has the advantages of not having nerves and of being harder to confuse than the conscience. And the psychological process reverses itself. One doesn't film as long as one remains conscious; one remains conscious as long as one films. It is as though mental acuity is buttressed from without. Presence of mind becomes the presence of the camera. And in that presence one behaves as in the presence of a stranger, more disciplined than when alone. That is the mystery of *self-possession,* of which the Anglo-Saxons have given us so many imposing examples. Since they lose consciousness with such difficulty, they know nothing of the attendant ecstasy. But also nothing of panic.

A young woman behind us in the cinema asked her companion, Why did these men have to die? A level-headed and intelligent person, she was enraged. What was the point of all their effort, their suffering? Who profited from it? It was a pointless struggle, senseless heroism, energy wasted on nothing at all, she felt, and she was much too clever to believe in the exalted scientific goals with which her companion tried to excuse the poor English captain, and which, though they are indeed a factor, have no bearing on the sacrifices involved. One would have to explain the meaning of such senselessness to this rational little woman with different, even wholly irrational arguments. One could have said, for example, that through such foolhardy and impractical exertions man reveals his true humanity. All else is but a more sophisticated manifestation of the survival instinct, which in no way distinguishes man from the beasts. The human soul reveals itself most clearly and in its purest form in such follies, and that is why these films are so gripping and so splendid despite their ludicrous senselessness.

One might also have assured the young Viennese woman that these Englishmen were true earth dwellers. They have a conscious *feeling for the earth,* in the same way that one is said to have feeling for one's country, for example, one that implies a definite sense of responsibility: a person has to know where he is. They do not live in Vienna or London; they inhabit the globe, and they explore all the cellars and attics of their ancestral property. A person is never truly at home in any place until he has fully explored it. Also, one could have reminded the young, middle-class wife that, at the sight of this white infinity, where the polar night merges with the blackness of space, all of human civilization, with its great metropolises, suddenly strikes one as hopelessly provincial, like the Podunk of the planet. Is it not understandable, then, that a man who is aware of this greater truth but lives in the oppressive constriction of Berlin, Paris, London, or New York develops a yearning for the strenuous life that relegates the petty life of ordinary men to the shadows?

As for the pointlessness of such displays of energy, it must be said that a man is never aware of his goals from the outset, so that he might subsequently develop the strength for them. It is his new ability that sets new goals, and his increasing strength expands the boundaries of what is imagined impossible. The fire has to be burning before we can begin to see what can be illuminated.

That is the meaning of every human fire, even if its immediate purpose is not instantly clear to us. The pointless heroism of these English seamen was perhaps nothing more than an exercise demonstrating man's moral force. A person has to know what he is capable of; when worse comes to worst such a yardstick is crucial.

17

ANONYMOUS

NEW FILMS MAKE WAR SEEM MORE PERSONAL (1916)

The all-absorbing idea which takes possession of the mind as one watches the "Battle of the Somme" on the screen is "Keep us out of the war at any cost." Heaps of mutilated bodies lying in grotesque attitudes once were men—the same men which wound in a long trail for miles and miles across the horizon. Laughing and carefree they came and went, brave in kilties or khaki, on their way to meet with a smile "the greatest adventure in life." The pictures make the war personal. One feels acquainted with the soldiers and realizes that vast as the armies of the war are they are made up of individuals, each with a world of his own.

It is apparent in the films that individually the Allies and the Germans do not regard each other as enemies, for the kindliest feeling is displayed.

All the literature in the world could never give one so clear an idea of the war as is obtained by a view of these pictures. The films were shown privately yesterday. They will be released at the Strand Theatre next week.

18

NICHOLAS REEVES

CINEMA, SPECTATORSHIP, AND PROPAGANDA

Battle of the Somme (1916) and Its Contemporary Audience (1997)

[...]

The Historiography of *Battle of the Somme*

In the historiography of *Battle of the Somme,* judgements about the film's apparent impact on its audience abound, not least because the very nature of the film demands some speculation as to the extent to which it was able to achieve its propaganda goals and it is immediately clear that this has not led to any scholarly consensus—indeed, much of this writing reveals radically different views of the film. Most detailed and most damning is the earliest scholarly analysis of the film, Stephen Badsey's 1983 *Historical Journal of Film, Radio and Television* article, in which it is argued that the opportunity to construct a powerful propaganda film was "simply missed"—"through haste and poor control the British propaganda organisations had combined to produce something which was not, strictly speaking, a propaganda film." And Badsey reached this judgement because the film failed to represent "the missing leadership, enemy and pattern that the Somme offensive possessed." In other words, the total absence of any focus on the commanders of the British armies denies the audience any sense that this battle was the result of advance planning and that the fighting itself was directed by senior officers. Even more striking, however, was another absence for, in Badsey's view, "the film has no enemy": because the film was shot entirely in the British lines, enemy soldiers who are seen in large numbers are *only* seen as prisoners of war—wounded, broken, tired, even harmless. The formidable, dangerous and barbaric "Hun," so prominent in unofficial wartime propaganda is totally absent. And, finally, Badsey argues, the film made no attempt to explain to its audience the military logic of what was being attempted on those early days on the Somme—the film "produces a battle which is patternless and at last bewildering"; the exclusive focus on the very early days of the offensive seriously distorts the reality of the battle as a whole. To be fair, Badsey does emphasise the film's remarkable popularity and at one point he describes the film as "a haunting masterpiece," concluding that the film's "ghostly soldiers and monstrous guns are by far the most familiar image of the First World War today." But given the root and branch criticisms developed in the main body of the article, the reader is left in no doubt about Badsey's overall and essentially negative assessment of the film.[1]

Subsequent assessments of *Battle of the Somme* have been more mixed. Modris Eksteins' important re-examination of the First World War's role in cultural history, locating "the birth of the modern age" within the experience of the war, identified one strand of that modernity in the novel character of so much wartime propaganda:

> All the belligerents were involved in the creation of myth and the distortion of reality. Reality, a sense of proportion, and reason—these were the major casualties of the war. The war became a figment of imagination rather than imagination being a figment of the world.[2]

And if wartime propaganda in general developed this "modern" approach to "truth," then film was to become "the most appropriate medium of this fractured age" with its unique ability to blur distinctions between fact and fiction in constructing a peculiarly naturalistic form of narrative.[3] And, according to Eksteins, *Battle of the Somme* was an important early example of film's ability to do just that. He reached such a conclusion

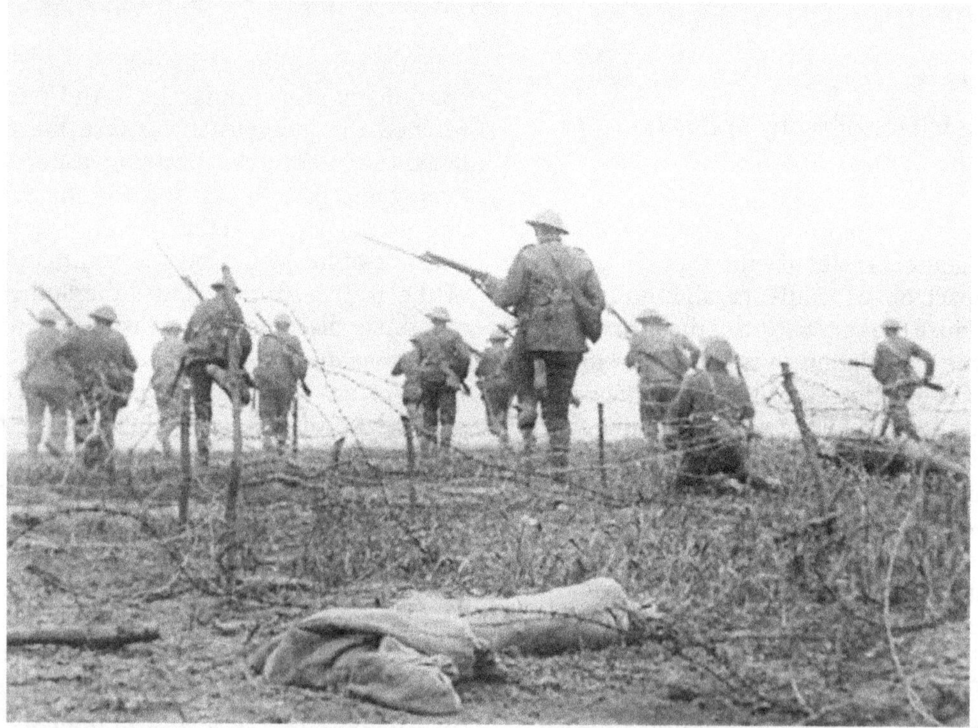

FIGURE 18.1 British troops going "over the top" in *Battle of the Somme* (1916). Still capture from DVD.

by focusing attention on those sequences in the film which are believed to have been faked, notably the famous sequence at the start of Part III in which troops scramble out of a trench, "over the top" and into battle—two fall before they leave the trench and two more are shot as they walk towards the enemy. Working from the assumption that the sequence was faked, Eksteins concludes:

> Most films made during the war trivialized the war by presenting it as melodrama or adventure. Here was a rare film that purported to tell the truth; and still the key sequence in this important film was faked, and there was no attempt to point this out. On the contrary, everybody was left believing the battle sequence was real. Documentary and fiction, news and story-telling, blur in our century.[4]

Unlike Badsey, Eksteins has little doubt that the film made a very considerable impact—"most of the film's viewers found it a gripping document, some of whose images would not leave them . . ."[5]—but in placing so much emphasis on the combination of staged and actuality footage, he is concerned above all else to draw attention to the way in which that audience was in effect deceived by the film.[6]

Roger Smither has looked in very much more detail at the issue of faking in *Battle of the Somme,* but his rigorous analysis reaches a rather different conclusion:

> . . . excessive zeal in crying "fake" does an undeserved discourtesy to the original makers of the film and, in obscuring a very real achievement in pioneering the battlefield documentary, a serious disservice to the modern viewer.[7]

Like almost every so-called documentary film, *Battle of the Somme* does include faked or "improved" sequences, but focusing attention on these few sequences at the expense of the authentic footage which constitutes the overwhelming majority of the film seriously misrepresents its character. That said, Smither has real reservations about its quality—although it "holds the interest . . . it scarcely overflows with dramatic incidents . . . the film overall does not convey the impression of great sophistication."[8] His reference to its "pioneering" character does, in a sense, damn the film with faint praise.

Nicholas Hiley, on the other hand, sees the film rather differently, not least because of a determined attempt to confront the intractable problem of the size of the original audience. Working from the rather limited and inconclusive contemporary data, he was able to make some startling "guesstimates": by his calculations, 1 million Londoners saw the film during its initial run and during the first six weeks of its nationwide release, more than 19 million people saw the film. Moreover, as it continued in circulation for many months thereafter, it may well have reached the majority of the domestic population. Hiley is thus in no doubt that this was a "staggering response from the British cinema audience" and that the film provided the public with "its most enduring images of the battle" which "had the power to shock." In contrast to Badsey, he argues that the film had "a tight dramatic structure" and that this "strong narrative" was an important factor in its huge success. Powerful as the film was, however, he is quite clear that it was "the ability of the cinema audience to control the meaning of the images on the screen" that ultimately explains why it was so successful. Audiences were actively involved in the production of meaning in the film and it was this reason above all others which explained why the film was able to appeal to such an enormous and disparate audience.[9]

The two most recent discussions of the film share an even more positive view of the nature of its success. Rainer Rother's discussion of *Bei unseren Helden an der Somme* (*With our Heroes at the Somme*), the German equivalent to *Battle of the Somme*, emphasises again and again the enormous success of the British film in comparison to its German counterpart. Moreover, he demonstrates that it was precisely because the German authorities recognised the extent of the success of the British film, that they commissioned their own film in response; *Battle of the Somme* serves as "an explicit model" for the German film. Rother is equally clear that other, earlier views of the film were misplaced. Thus in contrast to Badsey, he has no doubt that *Battle of the Somme* was a propaganda film, evidenced above all else by the way in which it conceals the extent of British losses. In contrast to Eksteins, he emphasises the factual character of the film: late twentieth-century audiences may be struck by the mixture of actuality and staged footage, contemporaries were struck above all by its veracity:

> It was the first time that a film had been made which, at least in some scenes, showed the horror of the war. Possibly the perceptual difference between fictional film for viewers is made clear here for the first time . . .[10]

Finally, in a brief discussion of the historiography of the film, David Culbert takes issue with Badsey, Smither, and myself: endorsing Rother's view, he is clear that this is indeed a propaganda film, arguing that it is a "brilliant achievement, *the* great propaganda film of World War I."[11]

My own position is in fact rather different. I first viewed *Battle of the Somme* on an editing table in the Imperial War Museum Film Archive in the early 1970s and even at that very first viewing on the small editing screen, it made an enormous impact. Perhaps because I had already had occasion to view some of the earlier official films, it was the extent to which the film revealed some of the brutal realities of war on the Western front that seemed so especially remarkable. Indeed, so startling were some of the sequences at that first viewing, that I had to run them again to be sure that my eyes had not deceived me. Moreover, it was precisely the film's lack of that kind of special pleading which seems an inescapable quality of most propaganda films which gave it its extraordinary power. The lack of a sophisticated structure, the roughness of some of the editing, the sparse, factual character of the intertitles, coupled with its remarkable cinematography, are at the very heart of its unique appeal. In short, many of the characteristics used by Badsey to explain the film's weaknesses, seem to me to constitute its very special strength: the images make such an impact *because* they are presented in such an unpolished form. And what do those images record? What was it about the nature of the war on the Western front in the summer of 1916 that the official cameramen were able to share with their audiences? Notwithstanding the many and powerful images of military hardware in the opening sections, it is above all else the ordinary soldier who is at the heart of this film. The battle was being fought by hundreds of thousands of ordinary working men and this is their film. Not only is the absence of footage of their commanders not a weakness, it would in fact have been quite out of place in this film record of the soldiers' war. It is *their* faces which confront us on the screen—jokey and smiling as they "perform" for the camera *en route* to the front: fixed and immobile, staring through and past the camera as they wait to go "over the top"; exhausted, shattered, staring again as they return from the battle. These are ordinary men enduring the unendurable, men who in the face of apparently impossible odds retain their dignity, their self-respect, even their humanity. This is the nature of the war on the Western front to which *Battle of the Somme* gives the audience today (at the end of the twentieth century) direct access and it does so to an extent scarcely paralleled in any other single cultural product of the period. Moreover, that access is so direct precisely because the film is, in so many ways, so apparently simple, so apparently unsophisticated, so apparently "naive." For a generation which has grown weary with the manipulative skills of the accomplished documentary film-maker, it is the very rawness of *Battle of the Somme* that makes it such a special film.

Of course it does not tell the whole story—above all else, as Rother quite properly emphasises, it makes no attempt to give its audience any sense of the catastrophic scale of the casualties which the British suffered on these early days at the Somme. However, for an official propaganda film, its extended sequences of the physical devastation of war, the battlefield landscape, the prisoners of war, the wounded, and, above all else, the footage of the dead construct a remarkable and remarkably powerful representation of war on the Western front. Moreover, this is not just my own personal view of the film. Over the last ten years I have had the opportunity to screen the film to undergraduate audiences and time and again I have been startled at its ability to move them, even when, as in the early years, the absence of a print with a soundtrack meant that they viewed the film in the wholly artificial environment of silence. Thus for me and for many of my students, there was nothing remarkable about the fact that film made such an impact on contemporary audiences—it retains the ability to make that impact today on audiences whose sensibilities have long been deadened by regular exposure to unprecedented levels of film and television violence. It is indeed "*the* great propaganda film of World War I," more than capable of standing alongside other, apparently more complex, more sophisticated propaganda films of later generations.

Battle of the Somme and Its Audience

The only way to resolve the questions posed by the contested historiography of the film is to look once again and with new rigour at the surviving evidence of its contemporary reception[12] and in embarking on such an investigation, there is much to be said for starting with the general claims made for official wartime propaganda by Geoffrey Malins, the most famous of that small group of official film-makers who worked on the Western front in the months after November 1915. Malins had no doubts at all about what he had achieved and he wrote at the conclusion of his own, very distinctive account of his wartime service:

> In all the pictures that it has been my good fortune to take during the two and a half years that I have been kept at work on the great European battlefield, I have always tried to remember that it was through the eye of the camera, directed by my own sense of observation, that the millions of people at home would gain their only first-hand knowledge of what was happening at the front.[13]

It was a very large claim to make and, given the nature of Malins' book, many readers must have concluded that this was simply the most overblown of a series of exaggerated claims that he had made about his wartime career as an official British cameramen. And yet, for all his talent for hyperbole, is his claim quite as exaggerated as it appears at first sight? Did "the millions of people at home" see *Battle of the Somme* and, if so, did the film give them a "first-hand knowledge of what was happening at the front"? The answers to these questions will not only help to resolve the problems posed by the contested historiography of the film, they will also enable us to understand a little more about the nature of the domestic experience of the war. For while that experience was of course shaped in large measure by the myriad changes in the social, economic and personal circumstances brought about by the war, another important element in the situation was that "knowledge" of the war which was constructed for the mass of the people by that small minority whose access to the traditional media of communication had now been supplemented by access to the new media of mass communication. Nor were they slow to take advantage of the special opportunities which war presented. A plethora of words and images confronted the people at every turn as journalists and painters, advertisers and politicians, churchmen and poets, constructed and communicated their own particular images of the war. And of course within that mass of information were those moving images of the war which had been constructed by Malins and a handful of other official cameramen who had filmed the war on the Western front.

While cinema was a comparatively recent phenomenon in British society,[14] it had quickly established itself as the major force in British popular culture. With a pricing policy which undercut the theatres and the music hall,[15] it was already at the outbreak of the war the dominant form of popular entertainment, with more money being spent on cinema tickets each week than the combined receipts of all other forms of commercial entertainment put together—indeed, by the summer of 1916, twenty million tickets were being sold each week.[16] So, the millions to whom Malins referred were going to the cinema. But it was not official, factual, war films that they were going to see. The heart of the cinema programme consisted of a variety of fiction films, in which drama and comedy, romance and adventure, reinforced by an increasingly important star system, persuaded ordinary people to spend some of their hard-earned cash on the two hours or so of entertainment which a typical programme provided.

Official film propaganda, on the other hand, was firmly wedded to the factual, non-fiction film. Both the cinema trade and the government's own propagandists had been convinced that this was the only appropriate form for official wartime film propaganda to take and it was this very approach that had delayed the launch of the official films until the end of 1915. For, of course, factual war films, films of the army or navy, required the agreement of the service departments—and securing that agreement proved to be a long and difficult process. Not only did those advocating official film propaganda have to overcome the usual military and naval concerns with secrecy and security, they had to win the consent of people who were almost entirely ignorant of the new mass medium, who regarded it as a distasteful form of commercial, working-class entertainment, a medium which therefore, by definition, could play no proper part in the deadly serious business of prosecuting the war.[17] Thus, it took over a year to overcome this opposition and it was not until the very end of 1915 that the first official film reached British cinema screens.[18] Malins himself, as one of the first two official cameramen to be sent to the Western front, did not arrive in France until November 1915 and the first British footage from France was not publicly exhibited until the following January.

Six series of short films drawing on this Western front footage were released to British cinemas in the first six months of 1916 and while their novelty did attract some attention and certainly ensured a wider distribution than comparable factual films would normally have achieved, nothing in these early months of official film propaganda substantiates Malins' grandiose claims.[19] All that changed, however and changed dramatically with the release of

Battle of the Somme in August 1916. For here at last was a film which really caught the popular imagination and its release inaugurated a brief period of immense success for the official films. *Battle of the Somme* was followed in October 1916 by *The King Visits His Armies in the Great Advance*, and a trio of popular films was completed with *Battle of the Ancre and the Advance of the Tanks*, released in January 1917. That said, the release of *Battle of the Ancre* already revealed the first signs of some wavering in public interest in the films[20] and by the time the third "battle" film (*The German Retreat and the Battle of Arras*) was released in June 1917, official film propaganda had passed its peak. Indeed, from the early summer of 1917 until the end of the war, the official propagandists were engaged in an (ultimately fruitless) attempt to try to win back the audiences they had lost.[21] Thus, at best, Malins' claim can only apply to a very short period of the war: it was not until the late summer of 1916 that the vast majority of British cinema-goers saw the official films and by the following spring they had lost interest in them.

The fact that the films did not sustain their popularity over a long period of time does not in itself deny them their value; what matters is how many people saw them and what sense they made of what they saw. In exploring these issues, this analysis will concentrate entirely on the first of these popular official films, *Battle of the Somme*, not least because the film attracted far and away the most contemporary discussion and thus gives us a unique opportunity to probe the way in which contemporary audiences responded to the film. Indeed, few if any films in the history of British cinema have been discussed so widely: the trade press lavished fulsome attention on the film, but at a time when cinema was still largely ignored by much of the press, this film was also discussed in every major national daily paper and large numbers of regional and local papers as well. Moreover, a wide cross-section of other publications discussed the film, ranging from the Anglican *English Churchman* and the free church *British Journal*, to service journals such as the *Regiment* and the *Army and Navy Gazette* to less specialised journals such as the *Illustrated London News*, the *Sphere* and the *Spectator*.

The film recorded events in the very early days in the series of campaigns fought in the Somme Valley in northern France in the summer and autumn of 1916 which became known in Britain almost at once as the Battle of the Somme.[22] The objective was to force the Germans back from their strongly fortified position, thereby relieving German pressure on Verdun and, more generally, weakening the fighting capacity of the Germany army. The advance itself was to be preceded by a colossal preliminary bombardment which would both destroy the German front line defences and kill or demoralise their inhabitants; the infantry would then advance, take the German positions and prepare themselves for any German counterattack. The key to success lay in that preliminary bombardment and accordingly on 24 June the British guns opened fire. In all, just over 1.5 million shells fell on the German positions before the guns fell silent in the early hours of the morning of 1 July. Then at 7.30 a.m., on the assumption that the German lines had been destroyed, nearly 100,000 men climbed out of their trenches and walked steadily across no man's land, towards the enemy line. The artillery barrage had made a real impact on the German lines, but it had not effected the total destruction on which success depended. German machine gunners re-established their positions and the advancing British troops presented the easiest of targets. By the end of the day, they had sustained 57,000 casualties, of whom no less than 20,000 were dead. It was without question the most bleak day in British military history and as such has quite properly been the subject of the most detailed historical investigation.[23] And yet, notwithstanding the events of 1 July, the British commanders determined to press ahead with their strategy and in the days and weeks that followed some limited progress was made until heavy autumn rains turned the battlefield into an impenetrable quagmire of mud. The men were literally bogged down and the battle finally came to an end on 18 November, by which time the British had lost over 400,000 men.[24]

The film, *Battle of the Somme*, concentrates entirely on the opening days of the offensive. It draws on footage shot by two official cameramen, Geoffrey Malins and J.B. McDowell. Malins started filming on 25 June 1916 and on 29 June he was joined by McDowell, and they continued to film the preliminaries, including the massive artillery bombardment.[25] Then on 1 July they were in position at two different locations with Rawlinson's Fourth Army to film the opening day of the Battle of the Somme. They continued to film on the Somme until, on 10 July, they left the front; two days later, the first rushes of their footage were seen in London by the trade committee which supervised their work. The committee was so impressed with what it saw that, whereas up until then it had released short films (the longest ran just under twelve minutes), the decision was taken to release the Somme footage in one consolidated film. Over the next fortnight it was edited by Charles Urban[26] and Geoffrey Malins and was then subjected to censorship, both at the War Office in London and at GHQ in France. By 28 July the film was back in London: minor changes in the intertitles arising from the censorship were made and it was then ready for exhibition. In its finished form, *Battle of the Somme*[27] ran for seventy-five minutes and followed a broadly chronological structure. It is divided into five separate parts, in which Parts I and II record the preliminaries—moving troops to the front, stockpiling supplies and, most spectacular of all, the preliminary artillery bombardment of the German positions. Part III briefly records action in the front line, including probably the most famous sequence in the film (a group of men climbing out of their trench and advancing across the barbed wire of no man's land), but thereafter quickly shifts its focus to the consequences of the attack—the wounded, German prisoners of war, and so on. Indeed, the remainder of the film continues to concentrate on the consequences of war, with yet more footage of the wounded and German prisoners, together with repeated images of the physical devastation of war and the landscape of battle; Part IV ends with a singularly powerful sequence made up entirely of images of the dead.

While such a structure presented a chronologically coherent narrative, it suffered from one major potential disadvantage, namely that the climax came in the middle and what followed might have been seen as anticlimax or even perhaps as subversive of the patriotic message of the film. In any event, this was the film that had its first trade showing on 7 August 1916 and three days later at a second screening for a specially invited audience, an enthusiastic message of support for the film from Lloyd George (the recently appointed Secretary of State for War) was read to the audience and the film was extensively reported in the national press the following day. Three weeks later it received the most prestigious endorsement of all for, following a private screening at Windsor, the king urged people to see it and this too was widely reported. This initial publicity was complemented by extensive advertising in the trade press and a number of additional trade showings. All this vigorous promotion clearly paid off, for when *Battle of the Somme* went on public exhibition in London on 21 August, it opened at no less than thirty-four cinemas simultaneously; a week later it went on national release, a hundred prints being distributed nationwide.

The film did extraordinarily good business wherever it was shown. The opening week in London proved enormously popular, with numerous cinemas reporting that they were simply unable to cope with the scale of demand[28] and the London experience of screening the film simultaneously at a number of different cinemas (a most unusual practice at the time) was repeated in most of the major centres of population. Thus, the film was screened at twenty cinemas in Birmingham, most adopting the equally unusual strategy of showing the film all week (where normally programmes changed mid-week);[29] in Dublin's Theatre Royal, no less than 10,000 people saw the film in the first half of the week in which it was shown.[30] In Leeds the film was screened simultaneously at the Picture House, the Assembly Rooms and the Harehills Picture House[31] and the distributor reported that "never has a war picture been so much in demand."[32] In Glasgow and Edinburgh, the film opened simultaneously in at least a dozen cinemas, playing to full houses throughout the week, from 11 a.m. to 10 p.m.[33] In Cardiff, six cinemas ran the film simultaneously, while at Swansea huge crowds were reported and special morning performances had to be arranged to meet the demand.[34] In west London, the two Ealing cinemas shared the film between them, each launching it with a special performance attended by local dignitaries—both cinemas were sold out for the whole week, with police being required to control the crowds outside the Kinema in West Ealing,[35] while outside the Walpole in Ealing Broadway there were queues five deep all along the road between 4 p.m. and 9 p.m. every evening.[36]

Queuing was a common experience for people wanting to see the film and the fact that the trade press saw it as newsworthy is evidence in itself of how unusual it was.[37] In all, cinemas simply could not keep up with the scale of popular demand and there are frequent references to people being turned away from cinemas that were full.[38] The film proved especially popular with children and an investigation into the film preferences of children in two schools in London (one in Holborn and the other in St Pancras) revealed that war films were the second most popular category among both boys and girls and when asked to list their five favourite films, a majority ranked *Battle of the Somme* and *Battle of the Ancre* at the top of their list.[39] A subsequent, larger study of the film preferences of nearly 7000 children found that such films ranked fourth in popularity out of eight categories of films, but that still put them ahead of "crook films," serials, "love films" and educational films.[40] Nor was it just a question of numbers. The film succeeded in attracting middle-class customers, many of whom may never have been to a cinema before. Thus, one correspondent commented that the audience which he saw in the Southport Palladium included "several of the leading citizens in the district who are more usually to be found at performances of legitimate drama of the 'intellectual' type"[41] and the larger of the two studies of the film preferences of children cited above found that such films were more popular with children in "good districts" than with children in "poor districts."[42] In all, *Battle of the Somme* proved immensely popular wherever it was shown: cinema after cinema played the film to full houses, often having to turn would-be patrons away. And although no national box-office statistics for the film were collected, as we have seen, Nicholas Hiley has calculated that the film probably achieved twenty million attendances in its first six weeks and may eventually have been seen by a majority of the domestic population.[43] While these claims may perhaps be a little exaggerated, the film was clearly an extraordinary box-office phenomenon, quite without precedent in the history of the British cinema. And it means of course that Malins' claim about the size of the audience, at least in respect of *Battle of the Somme*, was not exaggerated; the "millions of people at home" did see this film.

The Contemporary Construction of Meaning in *Battle of the Somme*

But what of the second question: millions of people may have seen the film, but what did it mean to them? In exploring that second question, the most obvious point to make is that the film received universally favourable reviews, in marked contrast to reviews of the earlier Western front films which had been distinctly mixed,[44] with the trade press often openly hostile.[45] This time the trade press was unanimously enthusiastic in its view—*Kine Weekly*, for example, wrote

> Speaking for ourselves, we never remember in all our long experience, to have seen any picture which, for power of appeal and intense gripping interest comes within measurable distance of this wonderful kinematograph record ... The film record of "The Battle of the Somme" is the greatest five-reel drama that will ever be shown in this or any land ...[46]

Bioscope claimed that no other medium, literary or visual, could "hope to convey to the man at home the reality of modern warfare, with the force and conviction shown in the marvellous pictures taken by the British Topical Committee for War films,"[47] while for the *Cinema* it was quite simply "the greatest war picture ever shown."[48] This fulsome praise was echoed right across the national press, with the *Daily Express* arguing that "for sheer realism, there has perhaps never been anything to excel this wonderful film,"[49] while for the *Daily Mirror* it was "a glorious tribute to British valour ... [which] should be shown in every British and neutral picture theatre the world over."[50] The *Daily Telegraph* argued that "nothing like the new series of war films has hitherto been seen, nothing so vivid, so detailed and so consecutive"[51] and *The Times* claimed that when in the future historians would "wish to know the conditions under which the great offensive was launched, they will only have to send for these films."[52] The local and provincial press was equally enthusiastic: for the *Leeds Mercury* the film was a "great war picture [that] depicts in a most realistic fashion the grim and glorious incidents connected with this episode of the war,"[53] while the *Yorkshire Evening Press* commented that "never before has such a production been screened ... it is all so real."[54] The *Birmingham Gazette* asserted that it was "very thrilling, very intimate, and very touching,"[55] while for the *Glasgow Citizen* it was "a great picture and one that cannot fail to grip and hold the attention."[56]

There is a certain irony in this emphasis on the "realism" of the film, for while it consisted largely of footage filmed at the time and place claimed for it in the film, it does include a number of sequences where the presence of the camera clearly influenced the events that were being filmed. This does not in itself distinguish it from most other factual film-making, but what is different here is that these sequences are shot and edited in such a way that the intervention of the cameraman is rather more apparent.[57] On the other hand, as we have already noted, there is an important sequence in the film which apparently shows men climbing out of a trench, going "over the top" into battle and here the charge against the film-makers is much more serious. This twenty-one second sequence, which attracted so much attention at the time was, in all probability, faked.[58] The evidence is not absolutely conclusive, but even if we assume for the moment that it was, it is quite clear that, in the main, the contemporary audience was quite unaware of this possibility. For the vast majority, this was, as the *Manchester Guardian* put it, "the real thing at last";[59] overwhelmingly the contemporary audience accepted at face value the authenticity of the Somme footage presented to them.[60]

A number of particular characteristics of the film were singled out in the public discussion of the film. The "over the top" sequence won particular praise, described variously as "perhaps the most striking part of the picture,"[61] "an amazing scene"[62] and "a thrilling and inspiring sight."[63] Moreover, it was the fact that it apparently showed men being killed that gave it its power—as the *Spectator* put it

> It would indeed be a cold heart that could resist the thrill of the battle that rushes upon one from the shivering screen. In the right-hand corner of the picture, one of the brown clad, helmeted men, just as he tops the parapet, instead of going over, slides back flattened out with arms extended against the wall of the trench—the first life sacrificed in the assault. It is a wonderful example of how reality—remember this is no arranged piece of play acting but a record taken in the agony of battle—transcends fiction.[64]

The *Bath and Wiltshire Chronicle* made a similar point in contrasting the film's "vivid pictures" with "how little cold print conveys,"[65] and the *Daily Express* argued that "For sheer realism, there has perhaps never been anything to excel this wonderful film. You are in the battle and of it."[66] Thus, it was the film's ability to construct realistic images of the war which was emphasised again and again. The *Daily Mirror* saw the film as "a visualisation of the hell that is war. It is a true picture, and is therefore stark and realistic."[67] The *Morning Post* described the film as "extraordinarily realistic" showing "all the grim horrors of war,"[68] and the *Daily Sketch* wrote simply "It is war, grim, red war; the real thing."[69] The *Manchester Guardian* made the point even more clearly: "The film casts no glamour over war. It leaves out many terrors that we know to exist; but on the whole, it reveals war in its true aspect—as a grimly destructive and infernal thing."[70] And that sentiment was echoed by *Bioscope*'s Leeds correspondent who argued that "whereas the battle pictures of the past have incited to war and tried to show the 'glory' of war, these Somme pictures teach what war really means."[71] A journalist who had visited both the British and French fronts claimed that "it was not until I saw these pictures the other night that I seemed to grasp this great thing."[72]

Moreover, these claims about the film's realism can also be found in journals written for a service audience. An emotional piece by the editor of the *Regiment*, reiterates a common view in journals of this kind that civilians were woefully ignorant of the reality of war, but argues that this film might perhaps shake them out of their complacency, claiming it would teach "millions ... the true meaning of war."[73] Lyn Macdonald describes a front-line screening at which the men watched "rapt and attentive."[74] That said, some soldiers emphasised the limits of its realism—one, asked whether the film was "like the real thing" replied, "Yes ... about as like as a silhouette is like a real person, or as a dream is like a waking experience. There is so much left out—the stupefying din, the stinks, the excitement, the fighting at close quarters."[75] However, such comments (which derive of course from serving soldiers, not civilians) are extremely rare and the overwhelming picture presented by the surviving evidence suggests that Malins was right in believing that the film offered the audience at home a degree of access to the war that was quite outside their experience.

Perhaps the most striking evidence of audience response to the film is revealed in the intense debate which its screening provoked. For while people shared a common view that the film was realistic and powerful, this very realism led them to disagree passionately about whether or not it should be shown. Even before its public release, J.A. Farrar had written to the editor of the *Manchester Guardian* protesting that the film included scenes

> . . . so gruesome in their realism as to be hardly bearable; nor will a public view make them more so. Is it tolerable that our brave soldiers cannot go through the ordeal of their self-sacrifice without the details of their manifold sufferings being turned into a spectacle for the pleasure of those who like to gloat, in perfect safety themselves, over the agonies of others?[76]

And four days later, James Douglas in the *Star* reported that

> There is no doubt that the Somme pictures have stirred London more passionately than anything has stirred it since the war. Everybody is talking about them. Everybody is discussing them. Everybody is discussing the question whether they are too painful for public exhibition. It is evident that they have brought the war closer to us than it has ever been brought by the written word or by the photograph.[77]

The shape of the debate was given a sharper focus at the beginning of September with the publication of another letter in the *Manchester Guardian* arguing that the film "merely satisfied the morbid or idle curiosity of the people"[78] and two further letters in *The Times*, the first of which, from Hensley Henson (the Dean of Durham), protested that

> . . . crowds of Londoners feel no scruple at feasting their eyes on pictures which present the passion and death of British soldiers in the Battle of the Somme . . . a "film" of war's hideous tragedy is welcomed. I beg leave respectfully to enter a protest against an entertainment which wounds the heart and violates the very sanctities of bereavement.[79]

Two days later, his protest was supported by Professor Ray Lankester, the eminent zoologist, who was "surprised and disappointed" that so many people could "find pleasure in experiencing the thrills of horror . . . which such exhibitions provide"; after all, people had long since stopped "witnessing the hangings at Newgate and the floggings of the mad-men at Bedlam."[80] These two letters provoked a vigorous response in *The Times'* letter columns over the next six days, all of which rejected Henson's and Lankester's claims—indeed, such was the size of the correspondence that it prompted an editorial giving the film an enthusiastic endorsement.[81]

Nor was the debate about the morality of screening footage of this kind limited to *The Times*. Even before the publication of Henson's letter, the evangelical journal, the *English Churchman*, had argued that "many have been deeply distressed" by the film[82] and the following week a second editorial quoted Henson's letter with approval, arguing the case even more powerfully:

> The matter is one of proper feeling, and the feelings of the bereaved should not be harrowed by the knowledge that the loved forms of their sons and brothers who fell in that awful battle are now on show to

> gratify the jaded and degraded taste of sight-seers.[83]

This provoked the Anglican *Guardian* to respond that it was "highly desirable . . . that the realities of war should be made clear to those who stay at home"[84] and further responses to Henson's criticism can be found right across the national, provincial, and local press—a *Daily Sketch* columnist, for example, berated "Durham's doleful Dean" on the grounds that such an eminent person "ought to know better."[85] Even the service press joined in, with the *Army and Navy Gazette*[86] attacking Henson's views, citing (like many others) the king's approval of the film in its defence.[87] On the other hand, another service journal reported that a screening of the film attended by a group of serving soldiers (some of whom had been wounded in action) had provoked vigorous debate. Some argued that "civilians want waking up! They should know what the horrors of war are and nine-tenths of the horrors are not seen at all in these pictures." But others took a wholly opposed position, claiming that the film was

> . . . too poignantly tragic for the eyes of women and children. Almost every woman has someone out there; or, worse still, has lost son, husband, or sweetheart. These pictures would stab them to the heart. These pictures of the huddled dead, too, would create an indelible impression of horror in the minds of children, of whom there were many in the theatre.[88]

Thus, once again, it was the film's unprecedented realism that was so striking to so many in the domestic audience and this led many to argue that the film gave them an entirely new understanding of the nature of the war. Thus, one of *The Times*' correspondents wrote "I have already lost two near relatives, yet I never understood their sacrifice until I had seen this film";[89] another explained

> I have lost a son in battle, and I have seen the Somme films twice. I am going to see them again. I want to know what was the life, and the life-in-death, that our dear ones endured, and to be with them again in their great adventure. . . . If the Dean had lost what I have lost, he would know that his objections are squeamish and sentimental.[90]

Perhaps even more remarkable, after a private viewing of the film, Frances Stevenson (Lloyd George's secretary and mistress) wrote in her diary in very much the same terms about the film's ability to enable her to understand her brother's death. Her words have often been quoted, but both because of her very particular personal and professional position and for the eloquence of the words themselves, they surely deserve repetition.

> We went on Wednesday night to a private view of the "Somme films" i.e. the pictures taken during the recent fighting. To say that one enjoyed them would be untrue; but I am glad I went. I am glad I have seen the sort of thing our men have to go through, even to the sortie from the trench, and the falling in the barbed wire. There were pictures too of the battlefield after the fight, & of our gallant men lying all crumpled up & helpless. There were pictures of men mortally wounded being carried out of the communication trenches, with the look of agony on their faces. It reminded me of what Paul's [her brother's] last hours were: I have often tried to imagine myself what

> he went through, but now I *know*: "and I shall never forget. It was like going through a tragedy. I felt something of what the Greeks must have felt when they went in their crowds to witness those grand old plays—to be purged in their minds through pity and terror.[91]

Many of these correspondents also argue that the audiences with whom they saw the film had responded in much the same way. Thus, James Cooper asserted that:

> It is, in my opinion, as untrue as it is uncharitable to say that crowds of Londoners feast their eyes on pictures representing the passion and death of British soldiers. The tears in many people's eyes and the silence which prevailed when I saw the films showed that every heart was full of love and sympathy for our soldiers . . .[92]

Another wrote: "I have been twice to see these films and was profoundly struck by the emotion, and almost reverence with which they were followed."[93] The women's correspondent in the free church *British Weekly* reported that the audience with whom she saw the film was "as quiet as worshippers in a cathedral,"[94] a view echoed by the *Star*'s columnist who wrote of "a depth of reverence as profound and pure as any ever evoked in the Cathedral aisle."[95] *Kine Weekly*'s Manchester correspondent wrote of "the 'tenseness' of the atmosphere while the film was running,"[96] while a Birmingham trade paper described the intensely emotional response of the audience—"Strong men found unexpected lumps in their throats, and were thankful for the 'dim religious light' of the theatre. Women audibly sighed."[97] The *Spectator* argued that "there was nothing but the deepest sense of respect for a brave soldier shown by the audience when the present writer saw the film"[98] and the *Army and Navy Gazette* commented both on the silence in which the films were viewed and the "sympathy for our soldiers which they evoke."[99] For the *Birmingham Daily Mail* "the tense silence with which scenes of the dead were received were significant of the emotions which stirred the audiences"[100] while the *Nation*'s London diarist noted that "women wept when the wounded came in."[101]

These comments provide a rare insight into the way in which contemporary audiences responded to *Battle of the Somme*, and this evidence is all the more striking because at that time audiences did not watch films in respectful silence; rather they responded actively to what they saw on the screen in a vocal and often rowdy manner.[102] And at least some of the evidence suggests that not every audience responded in the deferential, almost religious tone suggested thus far. One account draws attention to the fact that what the writer called "the marching and lighter scenes," were met with vigorous cheers;[103] at the original London trade show, the famous sequence of a soldier carrying a wounded comrade over his shoulders, evoked "a thunderous cheer."[104] And some footage provoked even more distinctive responses. Thus, one cinema-goer's response to the whole film was apparently summed up in the words "Praise God, from whom all blessing flow, A few more Germans gone below."[105] German prisoners, who played an important part in the film,[106] were described variously as "nerve-wracked and cowed,"[107] "staggering along 'like drunken men,' "[108] "demented"[109] and, most commonly, following the film's own intertitles, "nerve-shattered";[110] indeed, one Leeds audience laughed at the images of German prisoners.[111] But even that audience was moved by that part of the film

> . . . which shows the dead . . . Here is the meaning of war. It is Death.
>
> At last the hardened picturegoer is moved. It is war in all the stark nakedness of the "thriller" to which he is accustomed. Dead bodies with upturned faces, and the grave ready. They are German dead, but here the dullest imagination is stirred into activity . . . This is why, in the end, we all leave the building chastened and silent.[112]

We are back with the clear, central conclusion which emerges from this wealth of evidence. The film made an immense emotional impact on audiences who were stunned by the apparent realism of what they saw. Very many would surely have endorsed Malins' claim that this was indeed "their only first-hand knowledge of what was happening at the front."

There remains what is in a sense, the most important matter of all. Millions of people saw *Battle of the Somme* and they were clearly powerfully moved by what they saw—but what conclusions did they draw from viewing the film? What did it tell them about the nature of war? Did it lead any to question their commitment to the continued prosecution of the war? In the politics of the situation these were crucial questions, and the evidence makes it clear that there was no single, unambiguous response. In endorsing the film in the first place, Lloyd George had argued that it would reinforce popular commitment to the war and, in particular, encourage munitions workers to work even harder[113] and clearly part of the audience responded to the film in just these terms. Thus, the *Army and Navy Gazette* suggested that in enabling civilians better to understand the nature of the war, it would make them even more determined "that the nation must be utterly crushed that has brought so dreadful a war upon mankind,"[114] and this notion of shaking complacent civilians into a proper recognition of the sacrifices that were being made on their behalf is echoed in a number of other reviews.[115] James Douglas in the *Star* went so far as to assert that the film was "the only substitute for invasion," demonstrating "the power of the moving picture to carry the war to British soil."[116] Probably the most direct expression of a straightforward, patriotic response to the film came from those whose viewing of the film prompted them to write to the press. A correspondent in the *Manchester Guardian* argued that

> Anything that takes us from our smug security and gives us an insight into the horrors and discomforts our troops are suffering must awaken in us a sense of admiration for their bravery and inspire us with a desire to do all we can for them whilst on the field of battle, and on their return home.[117]

Another wrote

> I came away feeling humiliated and ashamed, for at last I was able to realise what Britain's soldiers were doing for her. If my turn comes, I hope that the memory of that film will stay with me to keep me as brave and smiling as they are.[118]

Yet another, who had three sons serving in the army, argued that the film "if possible, increased my admiration and sympathy for them and their fellows and their cause."[119]

On the other hand, this was not the only conclusion which audiences drew from the film. In reporting on Leeds audiences' response to the film, *Bioscope*'s correspondent argued that they formed a rather different conclusion:

> . . . these Somme pictures teach what war really means. They will do more to preserve the peace of the world

> than a hundred peace societies and thousands of sermons.[120]

In writing in the film's defence in *The Times*, James Cooper argued that "no better means could be found of making English men and women determined to stop the repetition of such a war as the present one"[121] and the *Manchester Guardian* editorial concluded that

> As for the horror of them [the Somme pictures], no good can come of gilding war into a romance. The more of its trappings that are stripped from it, the more will men see its waste, its madness and its cruelty, as well as its glory, and the more earnestly will they cleave to peace.[122]

None of this discussion goes the further step of arguing that, on the basis of the evidence of the film, war is so terrible that a way should be found of bringing it to an immediate end, but the more cautious conclusion that the film demonstrated the need to avoid any repetition of the war could perhaps be seen as a step in that direction.

And this of course makes sense in the context of the period in which the film was shown. British public opinion in the late summer and autumn of 1916 (when most people saw *Battle of the Somme*) was still broadly committed to the war effort, even though that clear shift in public opinion which eventually found its most direct expression in the resurgence of widespread industrial unrest the following spring, took place over the coming winter. It is possible that the exhibition of the film may have played a part in this and it is at the very least intriguing that, after the exhibition of the *Battle of the Ancre* at the start of 1917, no subsequent official British film included graphic and detailed images of the dead and wounded.[123] Certainly the surviving evidence makes it clear that some audiences *outside* Britain drew much more radical conclusions from the exhibition of the film[124] and it may be that the propagandists did have evidence to suggest that some in the domestic audience responded in the same way. [. . .]

Conclusion

[. . .] In discussing the problem of spectatorship in early cinema, proper account must be taken of the surviving data about the nature of audience responses at the time the film was first shown. The fact that the film text survives must not deceive us into thinking that our view of the film will necessarily accord with the views of those first audiences—indeed, in this particular case, it is all too clear that it does not. The millions of men, women, and children who made up the domestic cinema audience in the summer of 1916 believed that in viewing *Battle of the Somme* they had seen the face of modern war for the very first time. We concentrate on the extent of faking in the film; contemporaries were struck by its honesty, by its realism, by its truthfulness. And they saw the film like this because their wider cultural context was so dominated by dishonest, unrealistic, mendacious images of war. In posters, in cartoons, in speeches, in newspaper stories, the war was characterised as a titanic but exhilarating struggle between good and evil—honourable British Tommies resisting and defeating barbaric Huns, who broke all the rules of war and revelled in committing the most frightful atrocities. Set in that context, there is nothing at all surprising about the fact that contemporary audiences saw the film as offering them their first real glimpse of the reality of war on the Western front. Indeed, this powerful sense of novelty was clearly reinforced by the form of the film itself—a feature-length factual film, in which the restrained, dispassionate style of the cinematography, the editing, and the intertitles was so strikingly at odds with the overblown words and images of so much unofficial wartime propaganda. Indeed, the very fact that this was an official film, explicitly approved by the War Office, served in the prevailing climate of 1916 to reinforce further that sense of truthfulness—a fact which, in itself, demonstrates all too clearly the extent of the gulf which separates us from those wartime audiences.

Having said all of that, however, we must be careful not to overstate the power of this single film. When attitudes to the war changed during the winter of 1916–1917, attitudes towards the official films changed as well and audiences who had been so eager to see *Battle of the Somme* only months before, quickly tired of the feature-length battle film. We must be careful, therefore, not to draw long-term conclusions about the impact of film propaganda on the home front from the success of a single film.[125] However, we can and must give proper recognition to the fact that, at the time of its initial screening, this one film did give its audience a sense that they had seen the true face of modern war. It may have been short-lived, but in the months when *Battle of the Somme* was screened, millions of cinema-goers throughout the country were persuaded that the official factual film was indeed an appropriate medium in which to visualise the nature of the battle front. And the importance of that achievement is demonstrated most clearly perhaps by the enormous success enjoyed by films like *Desert Victory* or *The True Glory* during the Second World War, official factual films which in almost all important respects built directly on the foundations laid down by Malins and his colleagues in the First World War. In short, *Battle of the Somme* represented both something very new and very important in the history of spectatorship in the early cinema and also something very new and very important in the history of the factual film. It was, by any criteria, a truly remarkable achievement.

NOTES

1. S.D. Badsey, "*Battle of the Somme*: British war propaganda," *Historical Journal of Film, Radio and Television*, 3 (1983), p. 108.
2. Modris Eksteins, *Rites of Spring. The Great War and the Birth of the Modern Age* (London, 1989), p. 318.
3. Modris Eksteins, "Harvests of Violence: The Great War and Culture," an address to the *XVth Conference of the International Association for Media and History*, Amsterdam, 10 July 1993, p. 21.
4. Ibid., p. 8.
5. Ibid., p. 17.
6. For a fuller discussion of Eksteins' assessment of the film see Nicholas Reeves, "The real thing at last": The film *Battle of the Somme* and the domestic cinema audience of 1916, *The Historian*, No. 51 (Autumn 1996), pp. 4–8.
7. Roger Smither, "A wonderful idea of the fighting": the question of fakes in "The *Battle of the Somme*," *Historical Journal of Film, Radio and Television*, 13 (1993), p. 160.
8. Ibid., pp. 159 and 160.
9. Nicholas Hiley, "The *Battle of the Somme* and the British news media," a paper presented at a conference held at the Centre de Recherche de l'Historial de la Grande Guerre, in Péronne on 21 July 1992, pp. 10–11.
10. Rainer Rother, *Bei unseren Helden an der Somme* (1917): the creation of a "social event," *Historical Journal of Film, Radio and Television*, Vol. 15 (1995), p. 527.
11. David Culbert, review essay. "The Imperial War Museum: World War I film catalogue and The *Battle of the Somme* (video)," *Historical Journal of Film, Radio and Television*, 15 (1995), p. 578.
12. I was prompted to do this in the first instance by the request to present a paper to a conference on the First World War held in Leeds in 1994. The theme of the conference was the *experience* of the First World War and in re-examining the role of film within the war, I looked much more closely at the (abundant) evidence of the way in which contemporaries responded to the film, attempting thereby to reconstruct the way in which the domestic audience "experienced" the war on the Western front through film. The analysis which follows formed the basis of the paper I presented to that conference, subsequently reprinted in Hugh Cecil & Peter Liddle (eds), *Facing Armageddon*,

The First World War Experiences (London, 1996), pp. 780–800. I am most grateful to the editors for permission to use much of that material again here.

13. Geoffrey H. Malins (edited by Low Warren), *How I Filmed the War* (London, 1920), pp. 303–304. In 1993, Malins' memoir was republished by the Imperial War Museum with an introduction by Nicholas Hiley.
14. The first public demonstration of the new technology had taken place early in 1896.
15. Prices ranged from 1d. to 1s. with a majority of seats being sold for 4d. or less.
16. For a fuller discussion of the nature of the contemporary cinema audience see Nicholas Hiley, "A proletarian public sphere. The British cinema auditorium in the First World War," a paper presented to the *International IAMHIST Conference Film and the First World War*, Amsterdam July 1993, pp. 1–3.
17. For a fuller discussion of problems encountered in winning the approval of the Service Departments and the way in which they were overcome see Nicholas Reeves, *Official British Film Propaganda* (London, 1986), pp. 45–56. Hereafter Reeves (1986).
18. *Britain Prepared*, premièred on 29 December 1915—for a further discussion see Reeves (1986), pp. 222–223.
19. For a fuller discussion of these early films and their reception see Reeves (1986), pp. 145–157 and 238.
20. The Scottish section of the trade journal *Bioscope* reported that while the film did good business for the first 2 days, thereafter attendances fell off so badly that some cinemas took the film off for the last 2 days of the week, *Bioscope*, 15 February 1917, p. 737.
21. For a fuller discussion of the limited success of official film propaganda see Nicholas Reeves, "The power of film propaganda—myth or reality?," *Historical Journal of Film, Radio and Television*, 13 (1993), pp. 181–201. Hereafter Reeves (1993).
22. The literature on the Battle of the Somme is extensive. For an excellent brief introduction to both the battle and its historiography see J. M. Bourne, *Britain and the Great War 1914–1918* (London, 1989), pp. 51–52 and 59–67.
23. See, for example, Martin Middlebrook, *The First Day on the Somme* (London, 1971).
24. The debate over whether there is any sense in which the battle can be seen to have succeeded has raged ever since. However, even if it can be argued that Haig's strategic objectives were achieved, as John Bourne observes, that success is "seen as irrelevant. British perceptions of the battle have been transfixed by its human costs. . . . No amount of revisionist historical scholarship, however exacting or eloquent, will ever change this verdict," John Bourne, *op. cit.*, p. 67.
25. For a more detailed discussion of the circumstances in which the cameramen worked and the production of the film see Reeves (1986), pp. 94–113; S.D. Badsey, "*Battle of the Somme*: British war-propaganda," *Historical Journal of Film, Radio and Television*, 3 (1983), pp. 99–115; Nicholas Hiley's introduction to Malins' *How I Filmed the War* (London, 1993), pp. xxiii–xxvi. The remainder of this paragraph is drawn from these three sources.
26. An experienced film producer who represented his company (Kineto Limited) on the trade committee which supervised the official cameramen.
27. An excellent video print of *Battle of the Somme* (coupled with a print of the 1916 official film *Battle of the Ancre*) is available from the Imperial War Museum, London; a short introduction to the films titled, *The Battles of the Somme and Ancre*, edited by Roger Smither, is available from the same source.
28. "War film crowds," *Evening News*, London, 22 August 1916, p. 3.
29. "Birmingham notes," *The Cinema News and Property Gazette* (hereafter *Cinema*), 14 September 1916, p. 78.
30. Irish times in *Cinema*, 21 September 1916, p. 69.
31. "Provincial Film Centres. Leeds," *Bioscope*, 31 August 1916, p. 852.
32. "Provincial Film Centres. Leeds," *Bioscope*, 14 September 1916, p. 1053.
33. "Scottish section," *Bioscope*, 7 September 1916, p. 943.
34. Ibid., p. 68.
35. *Ealing Gazette*, 26 August 1916, pp. 3 and 6; 2 September 1916, pp. 2 and 3.
36. "Our visit to the London shows," *The Kinematograph and Lantern Weekly* (hereafter *Kine Weekly*), 21 September 1916, p. 109.
37. See, for example, "Northern notes" by "gossip" in *Kine Weekly*, 7 September 1916, p. 118.
38. For example, a friend of the *Bioscope*'s Manchester columnist reported that after trying repeatedly to gain admission to one of the many cinemas that was showing the film, he eventually gave up in disgust, *Bioscope*, 14 September 1916, p. 1051.
39. *The Cinema. Its Present Position and Future Responsibilities. Being the Report and Chief Evidence of an Enquiry Instituted by the National Council of Public Morals* (London, 1917), pp. 259–260.
40. Ibid., pp. 272–275.
41. See, for example, "With the exhibitors, Southport," *Bioscope*, 28 September 1916, Supplement, p. v.
42. The findings of this study of 6701 school children carried out by Dr C.W. Kimmins were published in *The Cinema* (London, 1917), *op. cit.*, pp. 272–275.
43. Hiley (1992) *op. cit.*
44. See, for example, contrasting reviews in *The Times* and the *Star*, Reeves (1986), p. 238.
45. See, for example, "Done again!," *Cinema*, 17 January 1916, p. 2.
46. "Film that will make history," *Kine Weekly*, 10 August 1916, p. 7.
47. "*Battle of the Somme*. The reality of war," *Bioscope*, 10 August 1916, p. 476.
48. "Editorial: the cinema and 'the big push,' " *Cinema*, 10 August 1916, p. 2.

49. "Somme Battle on the film. Thrilling pictures of the 'big push,' " *Daily Express*, 11 August 1916.
50. "This morning's gossip by 'The Rambler,' " *Daily Mirror*, 11 August 1916, p. 10.
51. "Somme Battle films," *Daily Telegraph*, 11 August 1916, p. 9.
52. "War history on the cinema. The British offensive," *The Times*, 11 August 1916, p. 3.
53. "Amusements. War pictures in Leeds," *Leeds Mercury*, 29 August 1916, p. 4.
54. "Amusements in York. The picture house," *Yorkshire Evening Press*, 29 August 1916, p. 3.
55. "The Somme Battle. Great film pictures in Birmingham," *Birmingham Gazette*, 5 September 1916, p. 3.
56. "City and round about," *Glasgow Citizen*, 29 August 1916, p. 2.
57. Thus, for example, in a sequence in Part IV of the film where we see post from home being distributed to soldiers at the front, it is clear that the participants wait for a signal (presumably from the cameramen) before they start to give out the parcels and letters, *Battle of the Somme*, Part IV, 690' to 734'.
58. The extent of faking in the film has been explored with immense rigour and intelligence by Roger Smither in "A wonderful idea of the fighting": the question of fakes in "The Battle of the Somme," *Historical Journal of Film, Radio and Television*, 13, 1993, pp. 149–168.
59. "Film pictures from the Somme. The official record of the advance," *Manchester Guardian*, 11 August 1916, p. 4.
60. There is just one public comment at the time which refers to the issue, although only to argue that the footage is in fact genuine ("The Somme films and the men who have taken them," *Sphere*, 23 September 1916, p. 263). Furthermore, some of the publicity for *Battle of the Ancre* asserts explicitly that "nothing in the nature of a 'fake'" has been allowed to be shown (Smither, *op. cit.*, p. 151). There is just one reference to the issue in the surviving papers of the propagandists themselves; in February 1917 Beaverbrook claimed a statement had been "systematically circulated with intent to do damage, that portions of the last Official films are of a faked description," although of course at the time of writing, "the last Official films" would have been *Battle of the Ancre* (House of Lords Record Office, Beaverbrook Papers, Series E, Vol. 14, File "Cinema General January, February, March 1917 3–2," Beaverbrook to Secretary War Office, 16 February 1917).
61. "Amusements. War pictures in Leeds," *Leeds Mercury*, 29 August 1916, p. 4.
62. "Third leader, 'The *Battle of the Somme*,' " *Evening Times*, Glasgow, 29 August 1916, p. 2.
63. "Somme Battle on the film. Thrilling pictures of the 'big push,' " *Daily Express*, 11 August 1916, p. 5.
64. "News of the week," *Spectator*, 26 August 1916, p. 227.
65. "The Battle of the Somme. What our soldier boys are enduring. Vivid pictures in Bath this week," *Bath and Wilts Chronicle*, 11 September 1916, p. 3.
66. "Somme Battle on the film," *Daily Express*, *op. cit.*
67. "The morning's gossip by 'The Rambler,' " *Daily Mirror*, 11 August 1916, p. 10.
68. "Somme Battle pictures. Mr. Lloyd George's appeal," *Morning Post*, 11 August 1916, p. 6.
69. "Somme Battle on the films. Pictures taken in the fighting line, which show war as it really is," *Daily Sketch*, 11 August 1916, p. 12.
70. "Kinema pictures of the Somme Battles," *Manchester Guardian*, 16 August 1916, p. 4.
71. "Leeds," *Bioscope*, 7 September 1916, p. 957.
72. "Ought we to see the pictures, by 'Alpha of the Plough,' " *Star*, 6 September 1916, p. 2.
73. "Quite between ourselves," *Regiment*, 2 September 1916, p. 219.
74. Lyn Macdonald, *Somme* (Harmondsworth, 1993), p. 256.
75. "A correspondent," *Manchester Guardian*, 1 September 1916, p. 3.
76. J.A. Farrar to the editor, *Manchester Guardian*, 15 August 1916, p. 10.
77. James Douglas, "The Somme pictures. Are they too painful for public exhibition?," *Star*, 25 August 1916, p. 2.
78. Frank E. Marshall to the editor, *Manchester Guardian*, 1 September 1916, p. 3.
79. H. Hensley Henson to the editor, *The Times*, 1 September 1916, p. 7.
80. E. Ray Lankester to the editor, *The Times*, 4 September 1916, p. 11.
81. "The Somme films," in *The Times*, 5 September 1916, p. 9.
82. "Editorial," *The English Churchman and St James's Chronicle*, 31 August 1916, p. 447.
83. "Editorial," *The English Churchman and St James's Chronicle*, 7 September 1916, p. 459.
84. "The week," *Guardian. The Church Newspaper*, 7 September 1916, p. 749.
85. "Echoes of the town," *Daily Sketch*, 5 September 1916, p. 5.
86. The journal of the reserve and territorial forces.
87. "Army notes. The Somme films," *Army and Navy Gazette*, 9 September 1916, p. 582.
88. "Heard in the army. News and views by 'Khaki,' " *Regiment*, 9 September 1916, p. 249.
89. "Forty-six" to the editor, *The Times*, 2 September 1916, p. 3.
90. "Orbatus" to the editor, *The Times*, 2 September 1916, p. 3.
91. A.J.P. Taylor (Ed.), *Lloyd George: a Diary by Frances Stevenson* (London, 1971), p. 112.
92. James Cooper to the editor, *The Times*, 2 September 1916, p. 3.
93. "70" to the editor, *The Times*, 5 September 1916, p. 6.
94. "The woman's world by 'Lorna,' " in *British Weekly. A Journal of Social and Christian Progress*, 7 September 1916.
95. "Ought we to see the pictures, by 'Alpha of the Plough,' " *Star*, 6 September 1916, p. 2.
96. "Northern notes by 'The Gossip,' " *Kine Weekly*, 7 September 1916, p. 118.
97. "History in a nation's eyes. 'The *Battle of the Somme*,' " *Films. The Cinema Trade Journal*, 24 August 1916, p. 12.

98. "News of the week," *Spectator*, 26 August 1916, p. 227.
99. "Army notes. The Somme films," *Army and Navy Gazette*, 9 September 1916, p. 582.
100. "Battle of the Somme. Official pictures shown in Birmingham," *The Birmingham Daily Mail*, 4 September 1916, p. 5.
101. "A London diary by 'A wayfarer,' " *Nation*, 26 August 1916, p. 654.
102. For a fuller discussion of this see Nicholas Hiley, "A proletarian public sphere. The British cinema auditorium in the First World War," a paper presented to the *International IAMHIST Conference Film and the First World War*, Amsterdam July 1993, pp. 1–3.
103. Lucy Clifford to the editor, *The Times*, 6 September 1916, p. 11.
104. W. G. Faulkner, "The greatest picture in the world," *Evening News*, 11 August 1916, p. 2.
105. "In cinemaland," *Yorkshire Evening News*, 19 August 1916, p. 2.
106. It occupied just over 10% of the whole film.
107. "Somme Battle pictures. Mr Lloyd George's appeal," *Morning Post*, 11 August 1916, p. 6.
108. J.A. Farrar to the editor, *Manchester Guardian*, 15 August 1916, p. 10.
109. James Douglas, *op. cit.*
110. See, for example, "The Somme Battle. Great film pictures in Birmingham," *Birmingham Gazette*, 5 September 1916, p. 3.
111. "The battle film as seen by one of the crowd. Thoughts in a Yorkshire picture theatre," *Yorkshire Evening Post*, 29 August 1916, p. 5.
112. Ibid.
113. "War history on the cinema. The British offensive," *The Times*, 11 August 1916, p. 3.
114. "Army notes. The Somme films," *Army and Navy Gazette*, 9 September 1916, p. 582.
115. See, for example, "The woman's world by 'Lorna.' Impression of the war films," *op. cit.*
116. James Douglas, *op. cit.*
117. Robert Heatley to the editor, *Manchester Guardian*, 2 September 1916, p. 4.
118. "Forty-six" to the editor, *The Times*, 2 September 1916, p. 3.
119. Jas Walmsley to the editor, *The Times*, 4 September 1916, p. 11.
120. *Bioscope*, 7 September 1916, p. 957.
121. James A. Cooper to the editor, *The Times*, 2 September 1916.
122. "The pictures on the Somme," *Manchester Guardian*, 21 August 1916, p. 4.
123. For further discussion of this decision see Reeves (1986), pp. 167–168.
124. Ibid., pp. 245–246.
125. For a more detailed discussion of the broader problem of the success or failure of wartime film propaganda as a whole see Reeves (1993), *op. cit.*

SECTION II

MODERNISMS

State, Left, and Avant-Garde Documentary between the Wars

19

JONATHAN KAHANA

INTRODUCTION TO SECTION II

In his essay in this section, "Straight Shots and Crooked Plots: Social Documentary and the Avant-Garde in the 1930s"—an excellent place to start, for the reader who wants an overview of this international epoch before grappling with any handful of its fragments—Charles Wolfe remarks on the challenge posed to our received idea of documentary film by the actual history of the form in the 1920s and 1930s. How can the same period that gave rise to the notion of documentary as a vehicle for social reform, concerned with the common people and with modern, institutional solutions to their problems—a genre that needed to be simple and direct to be effective—was also a time of great experimentation and artistic invention, of filmmaking that could be abstract, intellectual, beautiful, and difficult? Modernism, the name historians have given to certain tendencies within this period in the arts, is a discourse of conflict and contradiction, so it should come as no surprise that it isn't easy to make the various facets of this movement (or period, or style), line up with each other. This section includes a dizzying variety of statements on the use in documentary of modern, modernist, and modernizing ways of thinking. It is a cross-section, to borrow the thoroughly modern term Siegfried Kracauer uses to describe the "city symphony" genre popular in this period, of roughly two decades of experiments with filmed reality that have retained the capacity to startle, instruct, and puzzle viewers of all kinds.

The word *modern* comes from a Latin word meaning "just now," and we recognize in it also a word we use for "fashion," or being current. And although we often think of modernity and modernism as forward-looking, futuristic dispositions, concerned with the next new thing, they are just as much about the fragile nature of the time we call the present. One way to distinguish the "early" period of documentary from the period discussed here is by the stark difference between the two in their forms of time-consciousness: rather than the recent or distant past, the filmmakers in this section concerned themselves with the problem of *now*, of capturing the present and presenting the moment to come. From this perspective, the figure featured in the first section as the origin of the mature documentary film, Robert Flaherty, looks positively old-fashioned, not only in his fascination with traditional societies before the arrival of modern man and his technologies, but also in his special contributions to the art of documentary: the use of linear narrative and character-based storytelling; the documentary film as complete picture and organic whole; the vision of human society as a story capable of telling itself. (That these were not outdated beliefs beyond which documentary evolved so much as a position that some of its partisans took, the aesthetic ideology of Romanticism, is suggested by the historical conundrum in which Flaherty's first complete feature debuted *after* the earliest examples of documentary modernism discussed in this section.) For the films and filmmakers of documentary modernism, however, the problems of the present are not just themes or topics, ideas the viewer takes in as discourse: as basic problems of film itself, they were central to these filmmakers' concept of documentary form, and thus central to their viewers' fragmentary, distorted, or unstable experience of the modern world as it appeared in the films.

The modern world, as seen and imagined in modernist documentary, was also a world that was in the process of modernizing—of changing, many hoped, for the better. New systems of manufacturing, communication, and transportation, and new collective forms of social and political activity might all stand for the progress that modernization could bring. Of greatest interest to documentary filmmakers were those innovations that would harness the energies of the new masses and working classes, whether the harness was a greatly expanded governmental apparatus, or one of the national and transnational revolutionary movements that gained steam in the era. Equally important to documentary film, however, was the idea of *aesthetic* progress, the argument that modernization—enhanced by cinema—entailed an improved and expanded capacity to depict and perceive reality as the world became bigger, denser, and faster. And in the hands of filmmakers trying to link these technical and social changes to new models of consciousness, the mechanical capacities of documentary cinema and cinematic perception—image and sound recording, and editing, or montage, in particular—could serve as an expressive sign of how new truths and new states of being were thought, felt, and experienced by the modern subject. To some, film was a *symptom* of these problems. To many of the artists and writers collected in this section, it was not only a way to express the effects of these transformations, but an appropriate way to respond, whether in the interest of speeding change or retarding it.

These responses go by a variety of names, among them some well-known movements and ideologies that each had its own use for documentary film: constructivism, communism, futurism, surrealism, socialism, progressivism, welfare-statism, fascism. . . . The imprint of all of these *isms* can be found in this section, frequently in combination or opposition. Many filmmakers and critics in the period saw documentary as a way to advance a cause or movement; some, true to the modernist idea of the individual as "subjectivity," shifted from one position to another as circumstances demanded. John Grierson—whose famous phrase "the creative treatment of actuality" appears here in its original setting, the short essay "The Documentary Producer"—constructs his polemical "First Principles" of documentary around the differences between progressive and regressive forms of modernism, relegating the hero of his earlier writing, Robert Flaherty, to the role of a bad example of the latter. Two of the magisterial figures of the era, Joris Ivens and Dziga Vertov, embodied radical inconsistency, trying on a number of different modernisms in their filmmaking and their writing. Ivens, an international legend of left-wing filmmaking, makes a compelling argument in "Reflections on the Avant-Garde Documentary" for industrially-sponsored filmmaking as the most experimental and liberating structure for the filmmaker committed to the struggle against capitalism and for artistic individuality. Writing about his short film *Rain* (1929), Ivens describes the making of the film as a perfect modernist system, one with the ludic goal of organizing cultural labor on the unpredictable schedule of the natural elements. Vertov, too, is seen here from different angles: the faithful Marxist who served the Soviet revolution by chronicling its daily life in newsreels; the "epistemologist" and the heterodoxical "magician" (as the title of Annette Michelson's landmark essay puts it). We are used to thinking of Vertov as the counterpoint to his great antagonist Sergei Eisenstein, who dismissed Vertov's non-fiction work as indulgent and superficial, in terms echoed by Grierson and by the German film critic Siegfried Kracauer, in his study of montage as an avant-garde documentary technique. Less well-known are the conflicts *within* Soviet documentary, described in Jay Leyda's "Bridge" and Mikhail Iampolsky's "Reality at Second Hand," where Vertov's urgent practice of montage was challenged by the archival ethos of Esfir Shub and her supporters, who asked whether documentary needed to involve shooting, or completing, films at all, endlessly deferring the "now" of the present to a future moment of assemblage.

The history of modernism in the arts has often been told as a story in which in the central drama is that of the individual: drifting in a world blown apart by violent change, modern consciousness struggles to piece together a coherent representation of this world from the pieces of its wreckage. Critics and historians of documentary have given perhaps too much credit to this narrative, and the period has frequently been explained—sometimes by these characters themselves, who weren't shy about writing their own myths—as the encounter between strong-willed figures like Vertov, Grierson, Lorentz, or Riefenstahl and the modern forces of state, technology, bureaucracy, and "the people" that dwarfed them. Without discounting the importance of these characters and their roles in the development of some of the period's most forceful and lasting images of society, we can revise the history of documentary modernism, putting the drama of individual consciousness in the proper perspective. Reviewed as studies of bodies, machines, and movements, in both the physical and the political senses, documentary modernism looks less like a requiem for the individual than a series of games, experiments, pranks, or celebrations, trying out alternatives to a society of the self. In this light, the struggles among members of the American radicals of the Workers Film and Photo League, who began the 1930s serving the international cause of communism, and ended it serving a variety of state and corporate institutions, look less like pitched personal battles and more like an experiment in dialectical thinking, trying to get the most artistic mileage of out conflicts. And Luis Buñuel's hilarious *Land Without Bread*—a film that confounded commentators of its time and one of the most misunderstood documentaries of this or any period—seems less a document of individuals' suffering than the posing of a question about the principles of collective life, and about the place of documentary media in mass modernity.

20

ROBERT ALLERTON PARKER

THE ART OF THE CAMERA

An Experimental "Movie" (1921)

A few weeks ago the Rialto exhibited a short series of motion picures of New York. These motion pictures were the work of Charles Sheeler and Paul Strand, two American artists. Sheeler is well-known as one of our modern painters whose works are in the collections of discriminating connoisseurs and galleries. He is also a photographer of great distinction—an artist in photography. Strand is likewise a master in photography, an experimenter and a pioneer in this youngest of the arts. In entering the field of the motion picture, Sheeler and Strand sought to apply the technical knowledge gained from their experiments and achievements in "still" photography to the more complex problem of the motion picture—"to register through conscious selection and space-filling those elements which are expressive of the spirit of New York, of its power and beauty and movement."

The results have fully justified this daring adventure in a new art. Short as this film was in the showing, it suggested all sorts of glorious possibilities in the development of the movies. It was not merely artistically satisfying. It was a great stimulus to thought. At a time when our motion picture critics are shouting the praises of "Dr. Caligari" and the rest of the German importations, it is strange that they should neglect such a significant achievement as this one of two American artists. But perhaps these critical gentlemen can register only the merits of imported art and of the demerits of domestic.

In spite of this critical apathy, the Sheeler-Strand pictures mark a turning point in the development of the art of the camera. The direct, expressive, unashamed photography, the salient selection and discrimination by which these "camera men" managed, with the most effective economy, to capture the very spirit of lower Manhattan, the eloquent silence of these brief "shots," all lead one to claim that in the hands of such craftsmen the camera becomes truly an instrument of great art.

Such pictures possess that uncanny power of awakening and kindling our interest in that neglected beauty that crowds in upon us from all sides, and through which too many Americans walk with blind and unseeing eyes. It is always the exalted function of the true artist to make us see things through his eye, to reveal beauties undiscovered. In the fulfillment of this mission, he legitimatizes the means at his disposal. And so the camera of Sheeler and Strand dramatizes such a commonplace routine event as the entrance of a Staten Island ferryboat into the South Ferry slip, with its crowd of commuters suddenly released into the streets of lower Manhattan. The docking of the *Aquitania*, surrounded by those busy Lilliputian tugs; the pencil-like office buildings stretching upwards for a place in the sun—"High growths of iron, slender, strong, splendidly uprising toward clear skies." They give us the vision of Whitman in plastic poetry, viewed always from unsuspected points of vantage: the restless crowds of lower Broadway, for instance; view from balustrades hundreds of feet above; plumes of silvery smoke and steam; curious geometry of massive shadows and sharp sunlight; the molten silver of surging waters at dusk; all that dynamic power and restless energy of the metropolis. All of these were captured in the motion photography of the American artists.

There was no heroine, no villain, no plot. Yet it was all thrilling, exciting, dramatic—but dramatic in the language of plasticity. It was honestly, gloriously photographic, devoid of trickery and imitation. They used no artifice of diffusion. They did not resort to the aid of the soft-focus lens. They did not attempt to make pictures that looked like paintings. They did not "retouch" to produce the effect of a spurious etching. Always were they vigorously, rigorously, photographic. These artists avoided the well-known "points of interest." Instead, they gave us, by a brilliant emphasis of its own way of speaking, the spirit of Manhattan itself, Whitman's "city of the world," Whitman's "proud and passionate city." The city, they discovered, reveals itself most eloquently in the terms of line, mass, volume, movement. Its language is plastic. Thus it expresses its only true individuality.

How does this experiment, this glorious adventure, differ from the ordinary movie? It emphasizes anew the art of the camera. Properly understood and used intelligently, the motion picture camera, like the ordinary camera, becomes an invaluable instrument, registering the vision of the creative artist. With it he is endowed with a new power of capturing on the wing, as it were, all that fleeting and evanescent beauty of places and people. At last the artist can register those strange accidental moments when light, lines, form, and movement seem by chance to combine into an unearthly divine beauty, transmuting every-day objects into plastic poetry.

Of course, there are complex difficulties, obstacles almost impossible to overcome. But to dismiss the camera as a mere "machine," to deny it a place in the realm of legitimate art, is to cast away forever the possibility of discovering its latent potentialities and secrets. But to accept it, as these American artists have, with respect and reverence, to use it as an instrument of art, is to acquire the key to a vast and unexplored treasure house of expression. A comparison with another art may illuminate this point. Both for the creation and the interpretation of great music we accept without question the legitimacy of the musical instrument. The piano of a Chopin, the 'cello of a Casals, the violin of a Kreisler, are never considered as "music machines." In the hands of a Sheeler the camera should likewise be accepted as an instrument of art, objectifying the creative vision of the artist. The difference between the camera and the musical instrument is a difference in degree, not in kind.

Photography still remains the Cinderella of arts. Once its legitimacy is recognized, once we awaken to the urgent duty of developing its latent potentialities, it may become an essential in any adequate art-education. Perhaps the time is far distant when photography may be taught in the schools, or schools of photography as an art established and endowed. Mr. Eastman, we read, has endowed a music school in Rochester. Might he not, with singular appropriateness, likewise establish a school of photography through which the art of the camera might be elevated to its legitimate place among the arts?

The Sheeler-Strand experiment brings up another question. Is there no place in the motion picture world, as organized at present, for such pioneering experiments? At least two answers to this question have been offered.

The first is that there should be a "little movie" movement, paralleling the so-called "little theatre" movement, which has a beneficial influence upon native American drama, releasing new talents, and demonstrating that the public will support worthy plays. In the field of the motion picture, such a movement might take the form of a small producing group of directors, scenarists, actors, and photographers. The "release" of a film produced in this manner might be effected through the regular exhibitors. Or it might be shown in theatres especially rented for that purpose. In either case the expense would be enormous and the profits small. In view of the uncertainty of results, the almost insuperable obstacles in the way of any widespread exhibition, this plan is hardly feasible. In an art in which the studio and laboratory costs are so high, it is to be doubted whether the experimenter could ever attain even the technical excellence of the professional producers. And without this excellence the experiment would fail.

The second suggestion is the organization by the most firmly established and reputable producers of a research or experimental department, in which true artists of the camera would be free to carry out their adventures and experiments. Occasionally, perhaps often, they would attain results that might be used with the greatest artistic benefit in the regular productions. In this way the art of the motion picture would be developed from within. A great variety of methods might be attained. And instead of submitting every scenario to one cut-and-dried method, each picture would be screened in a highly individual and novel manner. It might then be interpreted in a manner best suited to the realization of its values. Such a research department would eventually do away with the hit-and-miss methods at present employed. It would in time prevent the enormous waste of effort, the conspicuous expenditure on non-essentials, of which the press-agents now, for some strange reason, actually boast. All the inherent powers of the motion picture camera might thus be developed into eloquent expression, and the motion picture industry would be assured of continuous novelty and artistic vitality. The lamentable evidences of repetition, imitation, and conventionalization would disappear.

If it be objected that such a suggestion is wildly idealistic and "highbrow," we need in reply only point to the example set by other highly successful industries and commercial organizations. Professor Soddy, the great English authority on radio-activity, recently declared that the department of scientific research established by the General Electric Company was doing more for pure science than the majority of British universities. Such a department, based on far-sighted commercial policy, is recognized as essential to the health and growth of the electrical industries. A similar department, we are informed, is supported by the Bell Telephone system. In the more immediate field of the industrial art, we may point to the eminent example of one of our foremost manufacturers of American silks. The Cheney Brothers Company have long supported an experimental studio, in which a staff of artists, designers, and weavers are given the freedom to pursue unhindered their artistic adventures in the realm of design. There are no directions, no prohibitions, no insistence upon turning out work that may be immediately gauged in terms of dollars and cents. In this fashion the art standards are upheld and the public is assured of the artistic quality of the finished product.

An insane passion for immediate profit in any industry may in the long run become the most unprofitable of policies. And it is precisely this mad passion that has worked to the detriment of the motion picture. The geese that lay the golden eggs are beginning to rebel. Millions have been spent, often unwisely and without appreciable result. The "camera men," who really hold the strategic key to the situation, are only beginning to be recognized. Few directors have the "camera" sense. Light too often is used merely as a necessary evil, when it should be used to enhance and vitalize the movement. When the producers awaken to the fact that the "camera men" must be artists of intelligence and discrimination, educated and efficient in their craft, the art of the motion picture will attain its maturity.

Without this co-operation of science and art, no permanent progress in the field of the motion picture can ever be effected. A far-sighted policy, looking not merely to immediate profits, nor resting on the miraculous success of the past, must recognize and protect the new art of the camera. Once this Cinderella of the arts is recognized by our Princes of the Celluloid, the latter may discover the only true way in which motion pictures may become not merely more artistic, but more popular and profitable as well.

21

SIEGFRIED KRACAUER

MONTAGE (1947)

In the grip of the existing paralysis, the German film-makers cultivated a species of films presenting a cross section of some sphere of reality. These films were even more characteristic of the stabilized period than the Pabst films, for their neutrality was the logical result of the cross-section principle itself. They would have upset their own rules if they had sided with any of the pros and cons they surveyed. They were the purest expression of New Objectivity on the screen. Their such-is-life mood overwhelmed whatever socialist sentiments played about in them.

The first German film of that kind was *Die Abenteuer eines Zehnmarkscheins* (*The Adventures of a Ten-Mark Note,* 1926), produced by Karl Freund for Fox Europe. Béla Balázs wrote the original script; he himself called the film a "cross section."[1] This picture of Berlin during the inflation consists of a number of episodes which record the capricious travels of a ten-mark note continually changing hands. Guided by it, the film meanders through the maze of those years, picking up otherwise unrelated characters, and glancing over such locales as a factory, a night café, a pawn-shop, the music room of a profiteer, an employment agency, a rag-picker's den and a hospital. According to Balázs, it is as if the plot "followed a thread that, connecting the dramatic junctions of the ways of Fate, leads across the texture of life."[2]

However, Balázs was not yet sufficiently bold, or indifferent, to substantiate his idea to the full. The documentary character of the cross-section pattern is blurred by its combination with a sentimental Berlin local drama concerning a worker and a factory girl. Like the Polish lovers in Griffith's *Isn't Life Wonderful?*, these two finally achieve one of those wooden cabins that spread all over the outskirts of Berlin, and, to complete their happiness, the ten-mark note returns to them. Its vagabondage not only serves to familiarize the audience with the infinite "texture of life," but also assumes the function of rounding out the local drama. That is, the succession of episodes results from two divergent tendencies, only one of which conforms to the cross-section principle, while the other obstructs it. This ambiguity of meaning explains why the allegedly purposeless adventures of the ten-mark note often give the impression of being concocted artificially. As if to reinforce the cross-section tendency, Berthold Viertel's staging imbues street life with especial significance. "There is a fascinating shot of the villain sitting in the window of a café. Trams, buses and passers-by are reflected in the plate-glass. The city is intent on doing something."[3] The thread intersecting various regions of social life is bound to lead through the street.

Street scenes predominate in the prototype of all true German cross-section films: *Berlin, die Symphonie einer Grossstadt* (*Berlin, the Symphony of a Great City*, 1927). This most important film, a quota production of Fox Europe, was devised by Carl Mayer. About the time he stigmatized hypocrisy in his *Tartuffe*, Mayer recognized that the moment had come for him to turn from the externalization of inner processes to the rendering of externals, from freely constructed plots to plots discovered in the given material. Paul Rotha, a close friend of Mayer until the latter's death, reports on this symptomatic change of attitude: "Mayer was tiring of the restriction and artificiality of the studios. All these films had been wholly studio-made. Mayer lost interest in 'fictional invention' and wanted his stories to 'grow from reality.' In 1925, standing amid the whirling traffic of the Ufa Palast am Zoo, he conceived the idea of a City Symphony. He saw 'a melody of pictures' and began to write the treatment of *Berlin*."[4] It does not lessen Mayer's profound originality that under the influence of the spirit of Locarno this idea asserted itself in France as well. Cavalcanti's documentary film of Paris, *Rien Que Les Heures*, was released a few months before *Berlin*.[5]

Like Mayer, the cameraman Karl Freund was tired of the studio and its artifices, so he enthusiastically espoused Mayer's project and set out to shoot Berlin scenes with the voracious appetite of a man starved for reality. "I wanted to show everything," he himself relates in a revealing interview in 1939. "Men getting up to go to work, eating breakfast, boarding trams or walking. My characters were drawn from all the walks of life. From the lowest laborer to the bank president."[6] Freund knew that to such ends he would have to rely on candid-camera work. Craftsman that he was, he hypersensitized the stock film which was then on the market, so as to cope with poor lighting conditions, and moreover invented several contrivances to hide the camera while shooting.[7] He would drive in a half-enclosed truck with slots in the sides for the lens or he would walk about with the camera in a box that looked like an innocent suitcase. No one ever suspected that he was taking pictures. Asked at the end of the above-mentioned interview whether he considered candid photography an art, Freund answered, glowing with zeal: "It is the only type of photography that is really art. Why? Because with it one is able to portray *life*. These big negatives, now, where people smirk and grimace and pose.... Bah! That's not photography. But a very fast lens. Shooting life. Realism. Ah, that is photography in its purest form...."[8]

Walter Ruttmann, who up to then had excelled in abstract films, edited the immense amount of material assembled by Freund and several other photographers. His sense of optical music made Ruttmann seem the right man to produce "a melody of pictures." He worked in close collaboration with the young composer Edmund Meisel, known for his interesting score for *Potemkin*. Meisel dreamed of synchronizing Ruttmann's visual symphony with a symphonic composition which might even be performed independently of the film. The role he reserved for the music was bound to strengthen the formal tendency of the editing.[9]

Ruttmann's *Berlin* is a cross section of a Berlin working day in late spring. Its opening sequence pictures the city at dawn: a night express arrives, and streets still void of human life seem the very counterpart of that limbo which the mind traverses between sleep and consciousness. Then the city awakens and stirs. Scores of workers set out for their factories; wheels begin to turn; telephone receivers are lifted off. The passage devoted to the morning hours is filled with glimpses of window-dressings and typical street incidents. Noon: the poor, the wealthy and the animals in the zoo are seen eating their lunch and enjoying a short respite. Work is resumed, and a bright afternoon sun shines over crowded café terraces, newspaper vendors, a woman drowning herself. Life resembles a roller coaster. As the day fades, the machine wheels stop, and the business of relaxation begins. A kaleidoscopic arrangement of shots surveys all kinds of sports, a fashion show, and a few instances of boys meeting girls or trying to meet them. The last sequence amounts to a pleasure drive through nocturnal Berlin, luminous with ruthless neon lights. An orchestra plays Beethoven; the legs of girl dancers perform; Chaplin's legs stumble across a screen; two lovers, or rather two pairs of legs, make for the nearest hotel; and finally a true pandemonium of legs breaks loose: the six-day race going on and on without interruption.

"The film as Ruttmann made it," Rotha reports, "was far from Mayer's conception. Its surface approach was what Mayer had tried to avoid. He and Ruttmann agreed to differ."[10] This accounts for Mayer's early withdrawal from the production of *Berlin.* (His next enterprise—years before the appearance of river films in America and France—was a script narrating the story of the Danube. But this script was never produced.)

When Mayer criticized *Berlin* for its "surface approach," he may well have had in mind Ruttmann's method of editing. This method is tantamount to a "surface approach," inasmuch as it relies on the formal qualities of the objects rather than on their meanings. Ruttmann emphasizes pure patterns of movement.[11] Machine parts in motion are shot and cut in such a manner that they turn into dynamic displays of an almost abstract character. These may symbolize what has been called the "tempo" of Berlin; but they are no longer related to machines and their functions. The editing also resorts to striking analogies between movements or forms.[12] Human legs walking on the pavement are followed by the legs of cows; a sleeping man on a bench is associated with a sleeping elephant. In those cases in which Ruttmann furthers the pictorial development through specific content, he inclines to feature social contrasts. One picture unit connects a cavalcade in the Tiergarten with a group of women beating carpets; another juxtaposes hungry children in the street and opulent dishes in some restaurant. Yet these contrasts are not so much social protests as formal expedients. Like visual analogies, they serve to build up the cross section, and their structural function overshadows whatever significance they may convey.

In his use of "montage," Ruttmann seems to have been influenced by the Russians—to be more precise, by the Russian film director Dziga Vertov and his "Kino-eye" group.[13] Vertov, infatuated with every expression of real life, produced weekly newsreels of a special kind from the close of the Civil War on, and in about 1926 began to make feature-length films which still preserved a definite newsreel character. His intentions and Ruttmann's are much the same. Like Ruttmann, Vertov deems it essential to surprise life with the movie camera—the "Kino-eye." Like Ruttmann, he cuts his candid shots on the rhythmic movements inherent in them. Like Ruttmann, he is interested not in divulging news items, but in composing "optical music." His *Man with the Movie Camera* (1929) can be considered a lyric documentary.[14]

Notwithstanding such an identity of artistic intentions, Ruttmann's *Berlin* carries a meaning that differs basically from the message Vertov's productions impart. This difference originates in a difference of given conditions: the two artists apply similar aesthetic principles to the rendering of dissimilar worlds. Vertov endeavors to live up to Lenin's early demand that "the production of new films, permeated with communist ideas, reflecting Soviet actuality, must begin with newsreels."[15] He is the son of a victorious revolution, and the life his camera surprises is Soviet life—a reality quivering with revolutionary energies that penetrate its every element. This reality has a significant shape of its own. Ruttmann, on his part, focuses upon a society which has managed to evade revolution and now, under the stabilized Republic, is nothing but an unsubstantial conglomeration of parties and ideals. It is a shapeless reality, one that seems to be abandoned by all vital energies.

Ruttmann's film reflects this reality. The innumerable streets of *Berlin* resemble the studio-built thoroughfare of Grune's *The Street* in yielding an impression of chaos. Symbols of chaos that first emerged in the postwar films are here resumed and supplemented by other pertinent symbols. Conspicuous in this respect is a unit of successive shots combining a roller coaster, a rotating spiral in a shop window, and a revolving door. The many prostitutes among the passers-by also indicate that society has lost its balance. But no one any longer reacts vigorously against its chaotic condition. Another old motif called upon betrays the same lack of concern: the policeman who stops the traffic to guide a child safely across the street. Like the shots denoting chaos, this motif, which in earlier films served to emphasize authority as a redemption, is now simply part of the record—a fact among facts.

The excitement has gone. Indifference remains. That everybody is indifferent to his fellow men can be inferred from the formalization of social contrasts as well as from the repeated insertion of window-dressings with their monotonous rows of dolls and dummies. It is not as if these dummies were humanized; rather, human beings are forced into the sphere of the inanimate. They seem molecules in a stream of matter. In the Ufa brochure on contemporary *Kulturfilme*, one finds the following description of industrial documentaries: "Blast furnaces ... emit ... fire vapors, ... white-hot iron pours into molds, material is torn, material is compressed, material is milled, material is polished, material becomes an expression of our time."[16] People in *Berlin* assume the character of material not even polished. Used-up material is thrown away. To impress this sort of doom upon the audience, gutters and garbage cans appear in close-up, and as in *The Street* waste paper is seen littering the pavement. The life of society is a harsh, mechanical process.

Only here can the difference between Ruttmann and Vertov be fully grasped: it is a difference of attitude. Vertov's continued survey of everyday life rests upon his unqualified acceptance of Soviet actuality. He himself is part of a revolutionary process which arouses passions and hopes. In his lyric enthusiasm, Vertov stresses formal rhythms but without seeming indifferent to content. His cross sections are "permeated with communist ideas" even when they picture only the beauty of abstract movements.

Had Ruttmann been prompted by Vertov's revolutionary convictions, he would have had to indict the inherent anarchy of Berlin life. He would have been forced to emphasize content rather than rhythm. His penchant for rhythmic "montage" reveals that he actually tends to avoid any critical comment on the reality with which he is faced. Vertov implies content; Ruttmann shuns it. This reluctance to appraise content is entirely consistent with his obvious delight in the "tempo" of Berlin and the *marche des machines*.[17] Tempo is a formal quality, and the socialist optimism that may manifest itself in the machine cult is nothing more than a vague "reformist illusion." Here is why Mayer called *Berlin* a "surface approach." He did not object to formal editing as such; what he condemned was Ruttmann's formal attitude towards a reality that cried out for criticism, for interpretation. To be sure, Mayer was no revolutionary like Vertov; but he had a pronounced sense of the humane. It is hardly imaginable that he would have misused social contrasts as pictorial transitions, or recorded increasing mechanization without objectifying his horror of it.

Ruttmann's rhythmic "montage" is symptomatic of a withdrawal from basic decisions into ambiguous neutrality. This explains the difference between *Berlin* and the street films. Whereas *Berlin* refrains from idealizing the street, such films as *Asphalt* and *Tragedy of the Street* praise it as the refuge of true love and justified rebellion. These films are like dreams called forth by the paralyzed authoritarian dispositions for which no direct outlet is left. *Berlin* is the product of the paralysis itself.

A few contemporary critics identified it as such. In 1928, I stated in *Frankfurter Zeitung*: "Ruttmann, instead of penetrating his immense subject-matter with a true understanding of its social, economic and political structure . . ., records thousands of details without connecting them, or at best connects them through fictitious transitions which are void of content. His film may be based upon the idea of Berlin as the city of tempo and work; but this is a formal idea which does not imply content either and perhaps for that very reason intoxicates the German petty bourgeoisie in real life and literature. This symphony fails to point out anything, because it does not uncover a single significant context."[18]

Berlin inaugurated the vogue of cross-section, or "montage," films.[19] They could be produced at low cost; and they offered a gratifying opportunity of showing much and revealing nothing. Several films of that kind utilized stock material. One of them summarized the career of Henny Porten (1928); a second, similarly produced by Ufa, extracted love episodes from old movies (*Rund um die Liebe*, 1929); a third was the *Kulturfilm Die Wunder der Welt* (*Miracles of the Universe*, 1929), a patchwork of various explorer films.[20]

Of greater interest were two cross-section films which, after the manner of *Berlin*, reported actual life through an assemblage of documentary shots. In *Markt am Wittenbergplatz* (*Street Markets in Berlin*, 1929), Wilfried Basse used the stop-motion camera to condense the lengthy procedure of erecting tents and stands to a few seconds. It was neat and unpretentious pictorial reportage, a pleasing succession of such characteristic details as bargaining housewives, stout market women, glittering grapes, flower displays, horses, lazy onlookers, and scattered debris. The whole amounted to a pointless statement on colorful surface phenomena. Its inherent neutrality is corroborated by Basse's indifference to the change of political atmosphere under Hitler. In 1934, as if nothing had happened, he released *Deutschland von Gestern und Heute*, a cross-section film of German cultural life which also refused "to penetrate beneath the skin."[21]

Shortly after this market film, another more important bit of reportage appeared: *Menschen am Sonntag* (*People on Sunday*). Eugen Shuftan, Robert Siodmak, Edgar Ullmer, Billy Wilder, Fred Zinnemann, and Moritz Seeler collaborated in the production of this late silent film. Its success may have been due to the convincing way it pictured a province of life rarely noticed until then. A salesgirl, a traveling salesman, an extra, and a chauffeur are the film's main characters. On Sunday, they leave their dreary homes for one of the lakes near Berlin, and there are seen bathing, cooking, lying about on the beach, making futile contacts with each other and people like them. This is about all. But it is significant inasmuch as all the characters involved are lesser employees. At that time, the white-collar workers had turned into a political factor. They were wooed by the Nazis as well as the Social

Democrats, and the whole domestic situation depended upon whether they would cling to their middle-class prejudices or acknowledge their common interests with the working class.

People on Sunday is one of the first films to draw attention to the plight of the "little man." In one sequence, a beach photographer is busy taking pictures which then appear within the film itself. They are inserted in such a way that it is as if the individuals photographed suddenly became motionless in the middle of an action.[22] As long as they move they are just average individuals; having come to a standstill, they appear to be ludicrous products of mere chance. While the stills in Dovzhenko's films serve to disclose the significance of some face or inanimate object, these snapshots seem designed to demonstrate how little substance is left to lower middle-class people. Along with shots of deserted Berlin streets and houses, they corroborate what has been said above of the spiritual vacuum in which the mass of employees actually lived.[23] However, this is the sole revelation to be elicited from a film which on the whole proves as noncommittal as the other cross-section films. Kraszna-Krausz states of it: "Melancholic observation. Not less, not more."[24] And Béla Balázs points out the "fanaticism for facts" animating *People on Sunday* and its like, and then comes to the conclusion: "They bury their meaning in an abundance of facts."[25]

NOTES

1. Balázs, "Der Film sucht seinen Stoff," *Die Abenteuer eines Zehnmarkscheins*, and Balázs, *Der Geist des Films*, p. 86.
2. Balázs, "Der Film sucht seinen Stoff," *Die Abenteuer eines Zehnmarkscheins*.
3. Quoted from Blakeston, "The Adventures of a Ten-Mark Note," *Close Up*, Nov. 1928, pp. 59–60.
4. Rotha, "It's in the Script," *World Film News*, Sept. 1938, p. 205.
5. Cf. Rotha, *Documentary Film*, pp. 87–88; *Film Society Programme*, March 4, 1928.
6. Evans, "Karl Freund, Candid Cinematographer," *Popular Photography*, Feb. 1939, p. 51.
7. Evans, ibid., pp. 51, 88–89; Blakeston, "Interview with Carl Freund," *Close Up*, Jan. 1929, pp. 60–61.
8. Evans, ibid., p. 89.
9. *Film Society Programme*, March 4, 1928; Meisel, "Wie schreibt man Filmmusik," *Ufa-Magazin*, April 1–7, 1927. For Ruttmann's other films during that period, see *Film Society Programme*, May 8, 1927.
10. Rotha, "It's in the Script," *World Film News*, Sept. 1938, p. 205.
11. Cf. *Film Society Programme*, Jan. 18, 1929.
12. Balázs, *Der Geist des Films*, p. 59. For other devices in *Berlin*, see Arnheim, *Film als Kunst*, p. 98, and Rotha, *Film Till Now*, p. 295.
13. Rotha, *Documentary Film*, p. 89; Potamkin, "The Rise and Fall of the German Film," *Cinema*, April 1980, p. 25.
14. Vertov, "Dziga Vertov on Film Technique," prefaced by Moussinac, "Introduction," *Filmfront*, Jan. 28, 1985, pp. 7–9. For Vertov and "montage" in Russian films and in *Berlin*, see Pudovkin, *Film Technique*, pp. 188–89; Richter, "Ur-Kino," *Neue Zürcher Zeitung*, April 2, 1940; Balázs, *Der Geist des Films*, pp. 57–58, 89, 94–95; Brody, "Paris hears Eisenstein," *Close Up*, April 1930, pp. 283–89.
15. Quoted from Leyda, *Program Notes*, Series VII, program 2.
16. Cf. p. 142, and also "30 Kulturfilme," *Ufa-Leih*.
17. Rotha, *Film Till Now*, p. 283.
18. Kracauer, "Der heutige Film und sein Publikum," *Frankfurter Zeitung*, Dec. 1, 1928, Rotha, *Documentary Film*, p. 161, comments on *Berlin* in about the same way.
19. Cf. Potamkin, "The Rise and Fall of the German Film," *Cinema*, April 1930, p. 25.
20. Cf. Kraszna-Krausz, "The Querschnitt film," *Close Up*, Nov. 1928, p. 27; "Rund um die Liebe," *Film-Magazin*, Jan. 27, 1929; Stenhouse, "The World on Film," *Close Up*, May 1930, pp. 417–18.
21. Quoted from Rotha, *Documentary Film*, p. 121. For *Street Markets in Berlin*, see *Film Society Programme*, May 4, 1930; Arnheim, *Film als Kunst*, p. 123; Balázs, *Der Geist des Films*, pp. 106–7.
22. Arnheim, *Film als Kunst*, p. 140.
23. Cf. p. 131 f.
24. Kraszna-Krausz, "Production, Construction, Hobby," *Close Up*, April 1930, p. 318.
25. Balázs, *Der Geist des Films*, p. 202.

22

ANNETTE MICHELSON

THE MAN WITH THE MOVIE CAMERA

From Magician to Epistemologist (1972)

This introductory essay on the cinema of Dziga Vertov, one of four intended as a section in a critical reconsideration of Soviet cinema between 1920 and the death of Eisenstein, is offered in grateful and affectionate tribute to P. Adams Sitnev, whose intelligence, energy, and wit have been a constant stimulation during my past three years of intensive involvement with the subject. The convergence and divergences of our thinking make for a complementarity of approach I especially value. I think, in particular, of the manner in which his own preoccupation with and knowledge of classical rhetoric, far exceeding my own, have—in the form of conversation, lectures, and in essays yet unpublished—sharpened, confirmed, or corrected, views only embryonically my own at the time.

I should like to thank both Mr. Sitney and Jonas Mekas, as directors of the Anthology Film Archives, for the courtesy of special screenings which helped in the preparation of this particular essay.

The Film Department of the Museum of Modem Art has, for these past three years, made it possible to teach Soviet film in the pleasantest of circumstances and to use their rich archive. For this opportunity and for the patient cooperation of Mr. Arthur Steiger, their projectionist, I am grateful.

***

We are in Moscow, in January, 1935. A dozen men, suspending for a moment the contradictions and rivalries which oppose them in polemical cross fire and tactical maneuver, are poised in the uneasy amity of a command performance. They are in fact the Class of 1925 and sit, surrounded by their juniors, for a portrait; the All-Union Creative Conference of Workers in Soviet Cinematography[1] recomposes in the attitudes of official concord for the still photographer.

The photograph will instruct us of the general contours of an heroic era, projecting the topography of a culture which engendered that which we now know to

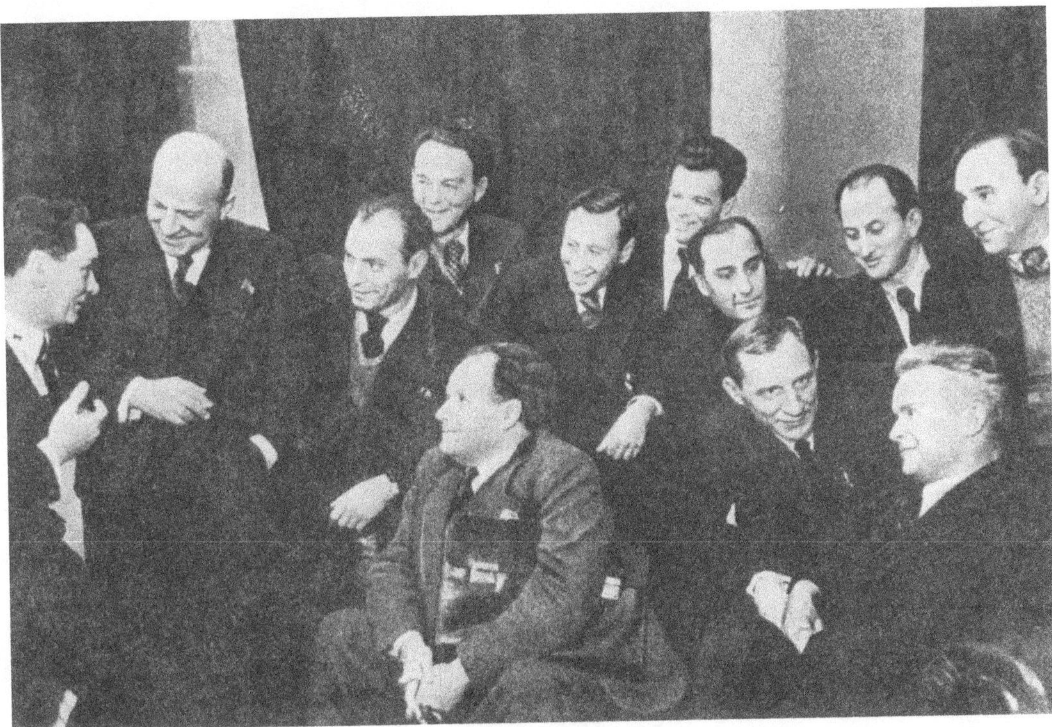

FIGURE 22.1 The All-Union Conference of Workers in Soviet Cinematography, 1935.

be, in more than any vaguely metaphorical sense, a "language of cinema." The placing of these men, their attitudes, the trajectories of glances offered, exchanged, deflected, describe the interplay of character and sensibility which articulates a grand collective aspiration. This picture is an historic text; it demands a reading, in every which way: across, up, down, around, all the way through.

In the first row, subtending as it were, the presence and efforts of men such as Raisman, Trauberg, Romm, Donskoi, Yutkevitch, Beck-Nazarov, who form a second rank, are four elder masters: Pudovkin, Eisenstein, Tissé, Dovjenko—prime animators of revolutionary cinema's first dozen years or so. The man peering at top left over the heads of his intermediary colleagues and just coming into view, smiling—as well he might—is Vassiliev who, together with his brother, has produced the film whose easy narrative flow and psychological inflection of a revolutionary hagiography has taken that year's honors and the most general official assent. Its success, and his, hover premonitorily in the air of this assembly, thickening it almost irrespirably with ironies and ambiguities.

Eisenstein, the session's embattled Chairman, known to friends in the authority of his achievement and international reputation—and the dignity of his thirty-seven years—as "The Old Man," sits in the center of the first row. He's clutching a briefcase containing, one would think, the elaborate notes and bibliography for an opening address whose brilliance, irony, and controlled intellectual pathos were to bring his listeners to a pitch of fury, releasing from these talented and pressured men, a massive and concerted lynching. He is for this moment, however, alive with a characteristic smile of generous delight in a colleague's success, attending wholly to the man standing at the left and half turned from us in an attitude of entirely graceful vivacity. This man is Pudovkin, and like the gifted and disciplined actor we know him in the widest range of film roles to be, he is at work charming and diverting the assembly.

The lean and elegant creature on Eisenstein's other side, bending toward us, poised and concentrated, is Tissé, the great cameraman and Eisenstein's lifelong friend and co-worker. His gaze slants to the right beyond the scene action past the camera, through rather than towards things. It "pierces," as we say. Then, at an angle almost perpendicular to that gaze, as if far to the left, but, so far as one can see, looking at nothing in particular, travels another glance. It is Dovjenko's. He is, as in all his pictures, beautiful; he rests, slightly slouched in an abandon of meditation, his person half-encircled by the sweep of Tissé's arm. Tissé's pure focused gaze and Dovjenko's stare would seem—if this were possible—to cross but nowhere to meet. And this might be because indeed one is a stare, the other a gaze. Tissé's eyes, looking out upon the world, embrace another virtual scene somewhere between our space and his. Dovjenko's look seems recollected back into itself. He smiles slightly—again as if to himself.

The juniors are involved in a general contraposto of body and focus whose traces will produce a tangle that must drive a reader to distraction—or to pedantry. Eisenstein's eyes, though fixed upon the moving object, must see Pudovkin, his old adversary who has been, in fact, addressing himself just slightly past him to that tangle of the general assembly. . . .

Two men, however, are missing from this dialectical icon. Kuleshov, the pioneer of montage and once the teenage teacher of these men, is nowhere to be seen. We do nevertheless know him to have spoken from the floor in a splendidly candid and courageous defense of Eisenstein.[2] The arena of public honor and debate, contracting in the Stalinist climate, was precipitating conflicts and realignments by the second; pressures falsified positions. We must suppose that by this time Kuleshov was somewhat removed from the public scene, and with him that one artist most problematic in his radicalism for even the greatest of his peers: Dziga Vertov. Vertov could have, as we shall see, no place in this picture.

We do, of course, have pictures of him, and the really speaking likeness is one which has him arrested in mid-air, leaping or pirouetting, delivering him to us as a body in violent movement, immobilized in what the stilled presence of motion suggests might be a "frame." It projects the preoccupation spelled out in the pseudonym which replaced, at the very threshold of his working life, the family name of Denis Kaufman. Dziga Vertov, translated, is "Spinning Top." That photograph, taken in maturity, is of course the late image of these early thoughts:

> Nineteen-eighteen. I moved to Gnezdnikovsky No. 7.
>
> Did a risky jump for a slow-motion camera.
>
> Didn't recognize my face on the screen.
>
> My thoughts were revealed on my face—irresolution, vacillation and firmness (a struggle within myself), and again the joy of victory.
>
> First thought of the Kino-Eye as a world perceived without a mask, as a world of naked truth (that cannot be hidden).[3]

That "world of naked truth" is, in fact, the space upon which epistemological inquiry and the cinematic consciousness converge in dialectical mimesis. And Vertov is its great discoverer. His work is paradoxically concrete, the original and paradigmatic instance of "an attempt to film, in slow motion, that which has been, owing to the manner in which it is perceived in natural speed, not absolutely unseen but missed by sight, subject to oversight. An attempt to approach slowly and calmly that original intensity which is not given in appearance, but from which things and processes have none the less in turn derived."[4]

The evolution of his work, and of the master work with which I'm now concerned, renders insistently concrete, as in another dialectical icon, that philosophical phantasm of the reflexive consciousness, the eye seeing, apprehending itself through its constitution of the world's visibility.

We are dealing certainly with a very special case, a film with a forty-year history of the most generally distrustful and hostile reception and of systematic critical neglect. The hostility and distrust are not, of course, unique, but the sustained neglect, the shared distrust and bewilderment of some generally perceptive and qualified spectators, the totally evasive and inadequate literature on *The Man with the Movie Camera* give us pause. Soviet film is, after all, one of the most elaborately and swiftly documented and consecrated areas in the history of the medium. It's true, of course, that much remains to be done and to be redone, to be rescued from the damaging mold of piety, but the absence of close and serious attention makes this film something of a very special case. Shoved hastily and distractedly into the ashcan of film history, it has been left to tick away, through four decades, like a time bomb.

Here is one contemporary judgment of the film, published in the December, 1931, issue of *Close-Up*, two years after the initial release in the Soviet Union. Offered by Jay Leyda as a focus for the film's presentation in *Kino*, it is an excellent index of general reaction.

> Theorists mostly love their theories more than a father loves an only child. . . . Vertov also has waged fierce, vehement and desperate battles with his material and his instruments (reality and the film camera) to give practical proofs of his ideas. In this he has failed. He had failed already in the era of the silent film by showing hundreds of examples of most cunning artistry in turning acrobatic masterpieces of poetic jigsaw, brilliant *conjuring* (italics mine) of filmic association—but never a rounded work, never a clear, proceeding line. His great efforts of strength in relation to detail did not leave him breath for the whole. His arabesques totally covered the ground plan, his fugues destroyed every melody.[5]

This rhetoric and imagery, though interesting, are not my immediate concern. The judgment most significantly echoes that of Eisenstein, and in a manner which induces reflection on one of the most interesting and knotty critical issues in Soviet film history and esthetics: the relation between Eisenstein and Vertov. For Eisenstein, *The Man with the Movie Camera* is a compendium of "formalist jackstraws and unmotivated camera mischief," and its use of slow motion is unfavorably compared with Jean Epstein's in *The Fall of the House of Usher*. It's compared, rather, with that which had been reported of Epstein's film in the press, since Eisenstein admits, in what must have been an impatient afterthought, that he had not yet seen the film! Attempting to account for the naked and disingenuous belligerency of those remarks,[6] one recalls Eisenstein's late strictures on his own first mature work, the film closest in style and tone to Vertov's. *Strike* he professed to see, from the vantage point of maturity, as infected with "the childhood disease of leftism," a metaphor for esthetic formalism borrowed from Leninist polemical literature.

But here is a third view, that of Leyda himself, our senior and in every way exemplary scholar of the period, advanced with a characteristic scrupulousness: "My memory of *The Man with the Movie Camera* is not reliable; I have not seen it since it happened to be, in 1930, the first Soviet film I saw. It was such a dazzling experience that it took two or three other Soviet films with normal 'stories' to convince me that all Soviet films were not compounded of such intricate camera pyrotechnics. But I hope to be forgiven for not bringing away any very clear critical idea as I reeled out of the Eighth Street Playhouse—I was even too stunned to sit through it again. The apparent purpose of the film was to show the breadth and precision of the camera's recording ability. But Vertov and his cameraman-brother, Mikhail Kaufman, were not content to show any simple vocabulary of film practice; the cameraman is made an heroic participant in the currents of Soviet life. He and his methods are treated by Vertov in his most fluid montage style, establishing large patterns of sequences: the structure resembles that of *Kino-Eye*, with a succession of 'themes'—the audience, the working day, marriage, birth, death, recreation—each with a whirling galloping climax; but the execution of the two films, separated by less than five years, are worlds apart. The camera observation in *Kino-Eye* was alert, surprising, but never eccentric. Things and actions were 'caught,' but less for the catching's sake than for the close observation of the things themselves. In *The Man with the Movie Camera* all the stunts that can be performed by a cameraman armed with Debrie or hand-camera and by a film-cutter armed with the boldness of Vertov and Svilova can be found in this full-to-bursting film, recognized abroad for what it really is, an avant-garde film, though produced by VUFKU, a State trust."[7] And Leyda's later viewing at the Parisian Cinemathèque confirms his initial impressions of brilliance.

Now all these texts deserve a closer reading than I shall give them: they raise problems directly or implicitly of all sorts: historiographic, stylistic, esthetic, political. Leyda's estimation of the nature of Vertov's development from *Kino-Eye* on, the precise similarities and differences of style between earlier and later films demand revision, but the films demand a finer, closer reading than anyone could at that time give. *The Man with the Movie Camera* was simply unavailable for study within the Eastern zone. Yet here is a film, available for rental in this country from a major distributor of 16 millimeter work, and obviously, for all practical critical purposes, just as "unavailable." That double circumstance tells us that its author does indeed inhabit another space: it is an index of its strangeness as a filmic object.

Thinking again of Eisenstein, one is led to inquire whether Vertov's masterwork does not constitute a redefinition of that "intellectual cinema" which had so haunted Eisenstein's imagination. We know that his career produced not only an oeuvre, but that shadow oeuvre of unrealized projects, its poles defined by the projected filmic versions of *Capital* and of Joyce's *Ulysses*. One might, in fact, see them as positing a shift from the articulation of a comprehensive and dialectical view of the world to the exploration of the terrain of consciousness itself. I will suggest that it is Vertov who effects that shift, and who maps that terrain in *The Man with the Movie Camera*. Suggesting that, I then suppose that only a shock of recognition, a shudder of remembrance and perhaps of reawakened aspiration long repressed, could elicit this bitter triviality from the intellectually powerful and generous man we've watched beaming so disarmingly at Pudovkin, his old antagonist.

Vertov begins his career in 1919 with a death verdict pronounced on all motion pictures made until then. He is making no exceptions and redefines cinema as capturing "the feel of the world" through the substitution of the camera, that "perfectible eye," for the human eye, that "imperfectible one." For Vertov, then, the distinction or conflict between what was known as the "art film" and any other kind of cinema then being made was totally without meaning. He relocated the frontier between mimesis and "the feel of the world," recalling to us Shklovsky's command: "We must recover the world; we live as if coated with rubber." So too, in the preparation of *Enthusiasm*, his first sound film, he entirely redefined the problems and possibilities created by the new parameter, shifting the focus of research from the borderline separating synchronous and asynchronous sound to that which distinguishes the fictive from the evidential, the composed from the concrete.

Vertov's disdain of the mimetic, his concern with technique and process, with their extensions and revelation, stamp him as a member of the Constructivist generation. The shared ideological concern with the role of his art as the agent of human perfectibility, of a social transformation which issues in a transformation of consciousness in the most complete and intimate sense, the certainty of accession to that "world of naked truth" are grounded in the acceptance, the affirmation of, the radically synthetic quality of film-making in the stylistics of montage.

> *Kino-Eye* is a victory against time. It is a visual link between phenomena separated from one another in time. *Kino-Eye* gives a condensation of time, and also its decomposition.
>
> ... *Kino-Eye* avails itself of all the current means of recording ultra-rapid motion, microcinematography, reverse motion, multiple exposure, foreshortening, etc., and does not consider these as tricks, but as normal processes of which wide use must be made.
>
> *Kino-Eye* makes use of all the resources of montage, drawing together and linking the various points of the universe in a chronological or anachronistic order as one wills, by breaking, if necessary, with the laws and customs of the construction of cine-thing.
>
> In introducing itself into the apparent chaos of life, the *Kino-Eye* tries to find in life itself an answer to the question it poses; to find the correct and necessary line among the millions of phenomena which relate to the theme.[8]

The montage style, a refinement and extension of the heritage of Griffith and Kuleshov, was original in the intensity of its refinement and in the imaginative power of that extension to every parameter of the cinema. For Vertov, as for Eisenstein—inheritors, as well, of the last great philosophical system of the West—the responsibilities implicit in this double birthright were felt as weighty and imperious. As Bazin was later to hypostasize his ontology of film into an ontology of existential freedom (rejecting, as he did so, the "tricks" of montage), so for the prime theorists of Soviet cinema, montage thinking became "inseparable from dialectical thinking as a whole." The process of intellection elicited in the experience of the montage unit is thus hypostasized into the triadic rehearsal of the dialectic.

To survey or somewhat more concretely to grasp the sense in which Vertov shares the concerns and strategies of Constructivism, one does best, I think, to defer thinking about his employment of Gans and Rodchenko as collaborators and to consider rather—initially, at least—the possible relation of this particular filmic object to another object of the period, as strange and bewildering in its time, as controversial—though not, of course, as universally condemned. This is Tatlin's model for *The Monument for the Third International* made, as Shklovsky remarked, of "iron, glass and revolution."

I have, in quite another context, discussed the manner in which Tatlin, caught in the dialectic of the "esthetic" and the "functional," moves into the real space of function while preserving the esthetic character of sculpture, thereby initiating a movement of transgression, bewildering in the extreme to its beholders and manifest in contradictions and ambiguities of the contemporary debate over the nature and qualities of the *Monument.*[9] Confronting this work, those beholders produced a map of intellectual life in the Soviet Union of the early '20s: Punin sees it as functional, as an "organic synthesis of the principles of architecture, sculpture, and painting"; Ehrenberg, as an expression of the dynamic tomorrow, surrounded by the poverty of the present. For Trotsky, it is a nonfunctional intrusion, a luxury in the devastated city of the immediately postrevolutionary period, and for Shklovsky, of course, a formal structure with its own immanent logic, its own semantics.

This triadic structure, multifunctional in design, turning at three different and simultaneous speeds (encompassing the full temporal scale of day, month, and year), receiving and emitting information, bulletins and manifestos, projecting film from a screen and writing weather forecasts in light upon the heavens, is "based," as Malevich remarked, "upon the Cubist formula" as much as *The Man with the Movie Camera* is grounded in the technique of montage.[10] Both structures propose an hyperbolic intensification of those techniques, insisting upon the materiality of the object and upon its architectonics as the core of interest. It is for these reasons and perhaps insofar as both structures do, in their polyvalence and circularity, more literally revolve about a core, that they seem—in a common movement of transgression—to converge upon the definition of a style, a program, a "semantics" of construction. And here is Vertov's adumbration of a "culture of materials":

> To make a montage is to organize pieces of film, which we call the frames, into a cine-thing. It means to write something cinematic with the recorded shots. It does not mean to select pieces, to make "scenes" (deviations of a theatrical character), nor does it mean to arrange pieces according to subtitles (deviations of a literary character).
>
> Every Kino-Eye production is mounted on the very day that the subject (theme) is chosen, and this work ends only with the launching of the film into circulation in its definitive form. In other words, montage takes place from the beginning to the end of production.[11]

Vertov then proceeds, in this second lecture on *Kino-Eye*, to articulate the stages of montage production involved in "Evaluation of Documents," "directly or indirectly related to the chosen theme (manuscripts, various objects, film clippings, photographs, newspaper clippings, books), the plan of shots which is the focus of Montage Synthesis, and General Montage, the synthesis of the observations noted on the film under the direction of the machine-eye. Proceeding to the discussion of composition through organization of "intervals," upon the movement between frames and the proportions of these pieces as they relate to one another, taking into account relations of planes (small and large), relations of foreshortenings, relations of movements within the frame of each piece, relations of lights and shades, relations of speeds of recording. This theory, which has been called the "theory of intervals" was launched by the *kinoks* in their manifesto *WE*, written as early as 1919. In practice, this theory was most brilliantly illustrated in *The Eleventh Year* and especially in *The Man with the Movie Camera*."[12]

And

> All who love their art seek the essence of technique to show that the eye does not see—to show truth, the microscope and telescope of time, the negative of time, the possibility of seeing without frontiers or distances; the tele-eye, sight in spontaneity, a kind of *Communist decoding of reality*. Almost all art film workers were enemies of the Kinoks. This was normal;

> it meant they would have to reconsider their *métier*. *Kino-Pravda* was made with materials as a house is built with bricks.

In 1924, Vertov made the film we know as *Kino-Glaz* or *Kino-Eye*, the first of a projected series. The *Kino-Pravda* series, his first major work, had involved him for some years in the production of short documents or newsreels on the widest variety of themes. *Kino-Glaz* is a didactic work, centered on episodes which articulate major preoccupations of the young Soviet regime: it deals with the manufacture and distribution of bread, the processing and distribution of meat, celebrates the constructions of youth camps, and discusses the problem of alcoholism.

Kino-Glaz is going to interest us especially (my own first viewing of it came some years after I had come to know some of Vertov's mature work, much after my sense of the dynamics at work in *The Man with the Movie Camera*, so that my experience of it was primarily as a stage in the evolution of those dynamics as of something fitting, as with a final click, into place). It introduces Vertov's formal adoption of the articulation of filmmaking technique as his subject. It begins, as well, to suggest what we may understand by "the negative of time" as a key "to the Communist decoding of reality." Looking for the negative of time, we find it in the use of reverse motion as analytic strategy.

It is near the beginning of *Kino-Glaz* that we first see a peasant woman on her way to the market to buy meat. We next see her, walking backwards, propelled by the reversal of that sequence, whence she came. The processing and distribution of meats is then recapitulated in reverse, as well.

Here are the numbered intertitles of that:

23. Kino-Eye pushes time backwards
24. Only to meat market and freezer
25. Beef 20 seconds ago
26. Beef gets its intestines back
27. Skin is returned to him
28. Resurrection of the bull

And later in the film, from a Pioneer's diary, title 64: "If time went backwards the bread would return to the bakery." And the film then continues with a recapitulation of bread distribution and manufacture.

It is, however, essential that we note the sequence separating these two recapitulations in reverse action: it is entirely devoted to the presentation of a magician, and its intertitles read as follows:

56. Film Eye about a Chinese magician
57. Gui Yuan works for his bread
58. Behold
59. Observe, observe, the whole hand
60. Observe the hand, observe the hole
61. Nothing—nothing
62. Now, make one live mouse

The transition, then, between the two reversals of action is the image of the magician. Vertov is presenting him, of course, as a worker, someone who earns his bread by the creation of illusion, that worker whose prestidigitation is perhaps closest in effect to that of the filmmaker. We shall meet with the magician once again in the paradigmatically reflexive film in which the processes of filmmaking, editing, and projection will be revealed and assimilated, through constant and elaborate parallel montage, to the processes and functions of labor. If the filmmaker is, like the magician, a manufacturer of illusions, he can, unlike the prestidigitator and in the interests of instruction of a heightening of consciousness, destroy illusion by that other transcendentally magical procedure, the reversal of time by the inversion of action. He can develop as it were, "the negative of time" for "the Communist decoding of reality." This thematic interplay of magic, illusion, labor, filmic techniques, and strategy, articulating a theory of film as epistemological inquiry is the complex central core around which Vertov's greatest work develops. I want, therefore, to suggest that *Kino-Glaz* directly articulates in a remarkably subtle and complex manner a polemical statement made the very same year. Extracted from the stenographic record of his speech made during a colloquium on Art and Everyday Life, it was published for the first time in Moscow in 1966.

> We raise our protest against the collusion of the director as enchanter with the public submissive to enchantment.
>
> Only consciousness can fight the sway of magic.
>
> Only consciousness can form a man of firm opinion and solid conviction.
>
> We need conscious men, not an unconscious mass submissive to any passing suggestion.
>
> Long live the class consciousness of healthy men with eyes and ears to see and hear with.
>
> Away with the perfumed veil of kisses, murder, doves and prestidigitation.
>
> Long live the class vision.
>
> Long live the cinema eye.

Reverse motion, first used in *Kino-Glaz* to illuminate process, will come to occupy a privileged place in a work dedicated to the creation of a dialectically inflected consciousness. It will, in fact, develop into the most personally characteristic and central visual tropes of Vertov's mature work, the formal pivot of his epistemological discourse. That development is, in its complexity and coherence, unique within the history of film. Turning, for some analogous example of the strength and organicity with which that central trope will infuse his mature work, one reaches for the complex image clusters which articulate the later plays of Shakespeare.

The notion of film as language, the concern with the linguistic aspects and analogues of film structure, is, as we know, one of the dominant characteristics of Soviet filmmakers and theoreticians of the heroic period. The hyperbolic intensification and growth of montage style with its attendant metaphoric thrust, the manner in which film after film—from *Strike* through Trauberg's *China Express*—tends towards the elaboration of a central metaphoric cluster, testifies to the importance and the depth of a concern natural in men living close to the sources of modern linguistics and of formalist criticism, close to the work of Shklovsky, Brik, Jakobson. And it is, of course, a sure sign of the times that Eisenstein's sustained concern with these problems, his attempt to extend and refine upon earlier formulations in the light of recent anthropological studies, should have triggered the fury of the Conference of 1935.

The Man with the Movie Camera is, among other things, a massive testimonial to this concern, sharing, hyperbolizing the use of metaphor, simile, synecdoche, rhyming images, parataxis and incurring, above all, the reproach of gramatical inconsistency, one might better term a strategic use of anacolutha.

The trope developed in *Kino-Glaz*, quintessential in the evolution of Vertov's style, flowering in the film of 1929, is the cinematic embodiment through reversal technique of the figure of speech known in classical rhetoric as hysteron proteron, that figure by which what should come last is put first, positioning or arranging things in the reverse of their natural or rational order. (An example, extracted from the *Oxford Shorter Dictionary* and therefore properly biblical, is: "Take ye, eat ye, this is my body": the injunction to eat preceding the presentation of the substance, its condition. Another would be Enobarbus' description in Act III, scene 8, of *Antony and Cleopatra*: "Th'Antoniad, the Egyptian admiral, with all their sixty, fly, and turn the rudder.") Action reversed, then, "the negative of time" will function as a prime agent of Vertov's structural and conceptual projects. We shall be seeing its consummate development in the admitted dazzlement of *The Man with the Movie Camera*.

Something of great moment was, however, to occur between the making of the two films. Vertov saw in April of 1926, the first film of the young René Clair, *Paris Qui Dort* (known in this country as *The Crazy Ray*), and the experience was upsetting. He records in his journal the mixed feelings it elicited, the sense of delight mixed with the exasperation felt upon encountering the work one wanted—one had indeed planned—to make one's self.

Paris Qui Dort is a film about a rather amiably mad scientist who immobilizes all of Paris in a trance of sleep with a magical paralyzing ray machine. Only the handsome young guard of the Eiffel Tower and his guests—an airplane pilot and four passengers—and the scientist's pretty daughter are exempt, through the altitude of the tower to which the ray cannot penetrate. The last quarter of this charming work is animated by the series of variations played, in a shower of gentle gags, upon the basic techniques of stop-motion, acceleration, deceleration, animation. The sustained climax, involving the subjection of an entire city to the erratic control of the ray is extraordinary. A sort of electric charge or thrill is produced by the instants of freeze and of release. This, of course, is the aspect of filmic experience most characteristic of moviola or editing-machine experience of film, and one most stubbornly resistant to the effort of verbal description. It is in so far as Clair and Vertov are engaged in the direct manipulation of filmic process that their finest work resists description. To describe a movement is difficult; to describe the instant of arrest and of release reversal, of movement, is something else again; it is to confront that thrill on the deepest level of filmic enterprise, to recognize the privileged character of the medium as being in itself the promise of an incomparable, an unhoped for, grasp upon the nature of causality.

These instants of complex magic—Clair's arrest of boats in their slow cruising on the Seine (slow to the point of being rendered visibly in motion *through* that arrest), the paralysis and vivification of whole city crowds, the resuscitation of figures frozen, unsupported in a slouch of sleep—all deserve their Ode, must have, in any case, an essay of their own....

Remarkable in *Paris Qui Dort* are the quality and aspect of the Parisian streets, intimately reminiscent of the photographs Atget would continue to make until his death in 1927 and of which Walter Benjamin remarked:

> It has quite justly been said of [Atget] that he photographed [the streets of Paris] like scenes of crime. The scene of a crime, too, is deserted; it is photographed for the purpose of establishing evidence. With Atget, photographs become standard evidence for historical occurrences and acquire a hidden political significance. They demand a specific kind of approach; free-floating contemplation is not appropriate to them. They stir the viewer; he feels challenged by them in a new way. At the same time picture magazines begin to put up signposts for him, right ones or wrong ones, no matter. For the first time, captions have become obligatory. And it is clear that they have an altogether different character than the title of a painting. The directives which the captions give to those looking at pictures in illustrated magazines soon become even more explicit and more imperative in the film, where the meaning of each single

> picture appears to be prescribed by the sequence of all preceding ones.[13]

Those deserted streets will reappear in the opening section of *The Man with the Movie Camera*, the greatest of the "city documentaries," the silent film from which Vertov resolutely excluded titles. Atget's concern with the space of places and of objects and with the virtual spaces and images of reflection will also reappear in Vertov's shops and their display windows. And the window pane will be the plane on and through which, in reflection, the space outside, of city landscape and its figures will be confounded with the space inside and its mannequins. Vertov will carry the conceit of the glass as both camera and projector to its dazzling extreme in a sequence in which the glass of a revolving door will project, in its swing of 180 degrees, its panning image of the neighborhood surrounding it.

Vertov had planned to make a film of *Moscow Asleep* two years prior to his encounter with the Clair film, and of course that general idea is rendered in the opening shots of Odessa, her streets empty, her shutters and blinds opening, her machinery set in motion as her people stir to life again in the morning. Both Vertov and Clair do build to a finale through a coda of Rossini-like acceleration. Clair's scientist, however, with his endearingly simple, freaky-looking little machine, irresistibly suggests to us, as well he might to Vertov, a metaphor for the movie maker and his camera, an invention roughly the contemporary of both the tower itself and that other dream machine, the aeroplane. It remained, then, for Vertov to draw the conclusion of which that metaphor is a sort of premise, to work out, as it were, the consequences of that insight.

Supposing this, I will suppose as well that the encounter with *Paris Qui Dort* was more than frustrating; it was catalytic, sharpening and confirming Vertov's epistemological orientation stimulating the more systematic deployment of the filmic techniques and strategies. The multiple themes of *The Man with the Movie Camera*—the life of man from birth through marriage and death, the progress of a day, the making and projection of a film—will be articulated not only through the use of metaphor, synecdoche, simile, comparison, rhyming images, but through the freeze-frame, acceleration, split-frame, superimposition, all the "anomalies" of his own inventory, and many more.

The result, articulated most powerfully through the presentation of the filmmaking editing and projection process, is a revelation, an exposure of the terms and dynamics of cinematic illusionism. And this it is—and not the speed, complexity, formal virtuosity, "obscurity,"—that produced the shock, the scandal, the bewilderment in its beholders. It is the manner in which Vertov questions the most immediately powerful and sacred aspect of cinematic experience, disrupting systematically the process of identification and participation, generating at each moment of the film's experience, a *crisis of belief.* In a sense most subtle and complex, he was, Bazin to the contrary, one of those directors "who put their faith in the image"; that faith was, however, accorded to the image seen, recognized as *an image* and the condition of that faith or recognition, the consciousness, the subversion *through* consciousness, of cinematic illusionism.

Thirty years after the invention of the medium, four years after Eisenstein's inaugural master-work of the Revolutionary period,[14] Vertov had produced a film which, taking cinematic consciousness as its theme, defined in a stroke the outermost limits of his art, that art par excellence of this century and its revolution. How many bold and innovative filmic enterprises by gifted and energetic men might not look somewhat conservative, if not regressive, in comparison? Vertov had thus produced an impossible situation, a situation hardly to be borne. Or to be borne only in the rigidity of shock, dealt with through the reflex of exclusion, the cri du coeur which speaks the idiom of invective.

We now want, however, a closer view of Vertov's work, some knowledge of his strategies. Here is a brief and partial inventory:

1. *The continual reminder of the presence of the screen as a surface.* As in the repeated, simultaneous movement into the depth of its illusionist projection and out towards the spectator of the trams, a kind of push-and-pull which coexist in a virtual stasis, and neutralizing one another, tend to pull one's eye back to the screen's surface, their point of encounter.

2. *The intrusion of animation techniques into the action.* Our magician appears once more, but suddenly, as if conjured up by another magician, another magic. This apparition is followed by another, that of carrousel horses quickly coming into view on the carrousel which has been presented without them. We then see a trick of magic performed by animation of inanimate objects. The magician's appurtenances are animated by the filmmaker, who has taken the magician's place or function. After this, the layout of a poster, performed by animation magic, once again, and we focus on the poster, whose image of an athlete leads us into the slow motion of the sport sequence.

3. *The alternation within one large sequence of slow and "normal" speeds.* In the sports sequences we see athletes performing, in slow motion, sometimes arrested, and in normal speed as well. We also see spectators watching (them) in intercut sequences. They are, it would seem, looking at what we see. There is, at least, as in all montage sequences of this sort, the implication of a spectacle shared by filmed spectator and spectator of the film. They are seen, however, in a setting which implies as well an integral space which contains them and the athletes, and their activity of looking is shot at normal speed, while we see the athletes performing in slower speed. The implication of shared spectacle is therefore subverted, and one is made conscious of this disjunction.

4. *The subversion and restoration of filmic illusion acting to distend and contract the filmic image.* As in the penultimate sequence in which we are constantly alternating between the image of the cyclist racing and the image of the theater auditorium containing the stage containing the screen upon which the image is projected. The oscillation between illusion experienced and illusion revealed accelerates in the final coda of the film.

5. *The subversion of the cinematic illusion, through processes of distortion and/or abstraction.* These involve the use of the split screen which will multiply images in repetitive patterns (as with the trams), impose the abstraction of visual gags (the image of the athlete exercising with dumbbells, converted into a trunkless, many-limbed monster) and, most importantly, arrest—through a process of multiplication or opposition or superimposition of spaces—of the temporal flow which generates the illusion. This is involved, most interestingly, in the technique of superimposition and deserves some particular study, though I would propose the work of Stan Brakhage as an evidently richer field for this particular investigation.

6. *The process of intellection so constantly solicited by the complex structure, the entire texture of this most assertively edited film.* This is the most constantly used distancing technique.

It is, however, the reversal of order and of action, the hysteron proteron which, as the pivot of Vertov's strategy, most strongly solicits our attention. One thing is plain: the manner in which the use of that trope has evolved since the making of *Kino-Glaz*. In the earlier film it is employed straightforwardly, for directly didactic purposes: simple reverse motion sends the peasant woman backwards through the streets, the bull back through dismemberment to resurrection, as though by magic. In *The Man with the Movie Camera*, the figure is employed in a manner far more complex, refined, varied, heightened. Applied very seldom in the manner of *Kino-Glaz* (an exception would be the reordering of a chess set back to its initial position on the board), it is sometimes even difficult to detect—as in the sequence of a locomotive moving either so quickly or so slowly that we deduce its inversion from other elements in the image—from the movement of human figures at the periphery of the screen. It is used metaphorically, as in the swift and somewhat humorously reversed orientation of the telephoto lens which intervenes between sequences showing marriage and divorce bureaus—as if to intimate that marriage is another process, and therefore, reversible. Here, though, are other instances:

The film contains, as we know, an image of the life cycle—in which mourning (the image of a mother grieving, weeping over a tomb) proceeds the funeral procession of the young hero.

One sees the railway train roaring towards one, and later the cameraman and the camera on the track, the level from which that shot was filmed. Or one sees, emerging from a mine shaft, a worker steering a coal wagon, shot at a tilt. He passes, and one sees the cameraman prone on the ground, filming him.

The shot of an elevator moving up, then down, is followed by the shot of the cameraman on the ground filming. This second shot, filmed from the elevator cage in motion, causes the cameraman, standing stationary on the landing, to appear in vertical motion.

It is above all in the detailed elaboration of the processes of filming and of editing, projection and viewing that Vertov has seized upon the trope as a master strategy, elevating it to the function of a radical innovation. These sequences, initiated about halfway through the film, begin with the summer promenade of elegant ladies from a peasant market in a carriage followed by the cameraman who is cranking madly away as they chatter, laugh, observe, and mimic. Their horse gallops to a sudden stop, hooves poised in mid-air, as Vertov freezes all the life and elegance into an interval that fills the screen with what one might call the *evidence* of life. He then contracts that image into the strip manipulated by the editor's skill. We have seen some minutes ago a young peasant woman in the market. We see her now as a series of single frames composing a strip to be organized into the film we are watching, the segment we've just seen. As if to intensify the subversion of illusion involved in the contraction and multiplication of the image, Vertov swivels the image about so that the strip lies on its side. We have been confronted with an Eleatic paradox in which confusion as to the anteriority of the woman's existence to her presence as an image is compounded by confusion as to the anteriority of the film strip to the projected illusion.

Another, ultimate variation on this theme presents the strip of frames which record the faces of children, and it is only much later in the film that we see, we recognize, these children in movement—alive within the illusion of the film. They are the magician's enchanted and enchanting children, brought to life by a "conjurer," that conjurer who has in turn animated the magician. For behind every image of the cameraman is another cameraman, and behind the magician.... We have, then, a loop which runs as in a Möbius strip, from twisting from "live" to "fictive" and back again.

Pushing beyond the disclosure of filmmaking techniques, Vertov has abandoned the didactic for the maieutic, rendering causality visible. Now, it is the most general characteristic of adult logic as distinguished from that of children, to be reversible. The logico-mathematical operations characteristic of adults are, as we know, interiorized actions, reversible in that each operation involves a

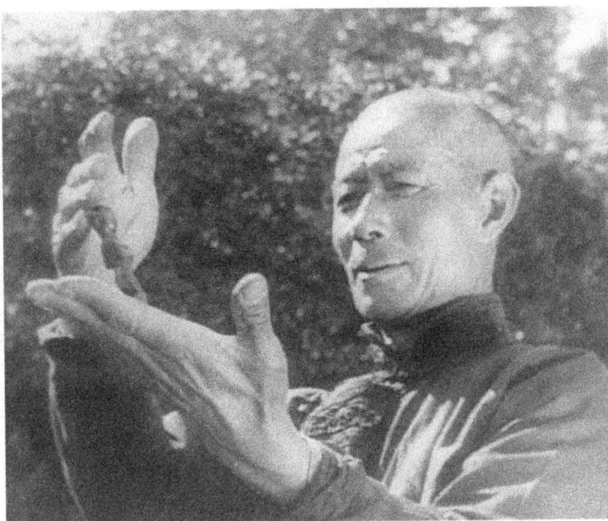

FIGURE 22.2 Magician, in *The Man With the Movie Camera* (1929). Still capture from DVD.

counteroperation—as in addition and subtraction.[15] We must, then, looking at *The Man with the Movie Camera*, see, in that eye reflected by the camera lens, Vertov as defining—through the systematic subversion of the certitudes of illusion—a threshold in the development of consciousness. "Rendering uncertainty more certain," he invited the camera to come of age, transforming with a grand cartesian gesture, *The Man with the Movie Camera* from a Magician into an Epistemologist.

NOTES

1. An account of this conference, called in celebration of the 15th anniversary of the Soviet film industry and from which Eisenstein emerged with a humiliating fourth-class award, is presented in Marie Seton's *Eisenstein: A Biography*, New York, n.d., pp. 330–50.
2. Ibid., p. 339.
3. From *The Notebooks of Dziga Vertov*, trans. Val Telberg, from *Iskusstvo Kino*, 3, 1957, and reprinted in Harry M. Geduld, *Film Makers on Film Making*, Indiana, 1967.
4. The metaphor of this formulation, by Gérard Granel, of the phenomenological project and method is discussed in my previous essay, "Toward Snow," *Artforum*, June, 1971. For Granel's text, presented here in my own translation, see *Le Sens du Temps et de la Perception chez Husserl*, Paris, 1968, p. 108.
5. Jay Leyda, *Kino: A History of the Russian and Soviet Film*, London, 1960, p. 251.
6. They occur in Eisenstein's important theoretical essay "The Cinematographic Principle and the Ideogram" written in 1929. Discussing the style of the Kabuki theater and its "unprecedented slowing down of all movement," he goes on to say,

   > here we see disintegration of the process of movement, viz., slow motion. I have heard of only one example of a thorough application of this method, using the technical possibility of the film with a compositionally reasoned plan. It is usually employed with some purely pictorial aim, such as the 'sub-marine kingdom' in *The Thief of Bagdad*, or to represent a dream as in *Zvenigora* (Dovjenko's first film). Or, more often, it is used simply for formalist jackstraws and unmotivated camera mischief as in Vertov's *The Man with the Movie Camera*. The more commendable example appears to be in Jean Epstein's *La Chute de la Maison Usher*—at least according to the press reports. In this film, normally acted emotions filmed with a speeded-up camera are said to give unusual emotional pressure by their unrealistic slowness on the screen. If it be borne in mind that the effect of an actor's performance on the audience is based on its identification by each spectator, it will be easy to relate both examples (the Kabuki play and the Epstein film) to an identical causal explanation. The intensity of perception increases as the didactic process of identification proceeds more easily along a disintegrated action.
   >
   > Even instruction in handling a rifle can be hammered into the lightest motor-mentality among a group of raw recruits if the instructor uses a 'break-down' method.

   Eisenstein, Film Form, Essays in Film Theory, ed. and trans. Jay Leyda, Cleveland, Ohio, pp. 43–44.

7. Leyda, *Kino*, pp. 251–52. Leyda has, quite understandably, exaggerated the film's reputation abroad.
8. Dziga Vertov, *Kino-Eye: Lecture II*, in Geduld, *Film Makers*, p. 102.
9. Annette Michelson, Robert Morris. *An Aesthetics of Transgression*, for the Corcoran Gallery of Art, Washington, D.C., 1969, pp. 71–75.
10. The Malevich text, pertinent to this discussion and quoted in extenso on page 73 of Michelson's *Robert Morris* catalogue is exacted from Kasimir S. Malevich, *Essays on Art:* 1915–1928, trans. Xenia Glowacki, Copenhagen, 1968, p. 77.
11. See Vertov, *Kino-Eye: Lecture II*, in Geduld, p. 102.
12. Ibid., pp. 103–105.
13. See Benjamin's celebrated essay, "The Work of Art in the Era of Mechanical Reproduction," in *Illuminations*, ed. Hannah Arendt, trans. Harry Zohn, New York, 1969. I reserve discussion of Benjamin's views on photography and upon cinema for another essay, pointing out on this occasion his view that the "resources of (the camera's) lowerings and liftings, its interruptions and isolations, its extensions and accelerations, its enlargements and reductions introduce us to unconscious optics as does psychoanalysis to unconscious impulses."
14. *Strike* was made in 1925.
15. For a presentation of this notion, central to Jean Piaget's theory of developmental epistemology, see his *Six Etudes de Psychologie*, Geneva, 1964. For previous discussion within a specifically cinematic context, see Annette Michelson, "Bodies in Space: Film as Carnal Knowledge," *Artforum*, February, 1969.

23

SETH FELDMAN

CINEMA WEEKLY AND *CINEMA TRUTH*

Dziga Vertov and the Leninist Proportion (1973)

It has become increasingly apparent to those concerned with Soviet cinema that previously accepted explanations of the birth of the "golden age" of the 1920s are no longer adequate. It is simply foolish, for instance, to explain Russian montage as the result either of a shortage of raw stock or of Kuleshov's study of Griffith. A third theory, linking the films of the 1920s with activities in other Soviet arts, fails to take into account the special status given to film by the newly victorious Bolshevik government. Of all the arts practised in Russia, film was chosen by Lenin to play the greatest role in consolidating the power of the new regime. It was not, however, the conventional film of 1917 that Lenin had in mind. In a memo dictated some time after his original pronouncement on cinema, Lenin added the proviso that the Soviet film industry ought to devote 75 per cent of its resources to the factual film—a genre which, by the time of the Revolution, had fallen into worldwide neglect.

The Soviet cineaste who most staunchly advocated adherence to the "Leninist proportion" was Dziga Vertov. That Dziga Vertov discovered the basics of Soviet montage simultaneously with Kuleshov, and that he developed the technique with an intensity far surpassing that of his contemporaries, would in itself justify the attention he is now receiving from historians and film-makers. What makes Vertov's work even more interesting is that he accomplished his ends not by virtue of an abstract aesthetic, but rather by attempting to meet the needs of post-Revolutionary Russia with uniquely ingenious applications of the potentials of film.

Vertov's earliest works show this awareness of how to create films in response to social realities. The *Kinonedelia* ("Cinema Weekly") and *Kinopravda* ("Cinema Truth") newsreel series were, respectively, his first work in film and his first attempt to go beyond the limitations of a time when, as Vertov remembered it, "filming was being conducted under battle conditions on all fronts."[1] *Kinonedelia* demonstrated how effective a newsreel could be as a tool for social change. *Kinopravda* expanded the scope of the newsreel to include analytic interpretations of non-immediate subject matter. In all, *Kinonedelia* consisted of 43 issues released in 1918 and 1919. Twenty-three issues of *Kinopravda* were produced between 1922 and 1925.

Vertov's introduction to cinema, according to Alexandre Lemberg's account of it,[2] was typical of his generation's accidental discoveries. Some time during the Kerensky period, Lemberg, a newsreel cameraman just back from the front, met Vertov, a would-be Futurist poet, at what Lemberg refers to only as a "poets' café." Like a Russian Jules and Jim, the two men struck up an immediate friendship. Vertov frequented Lemberg's home and experimented with the equipment owned by Lemberg and his cameraman father. By the time the October Revolution came to Moscow, he was convinced he had found his calling.

The immediate results of the Revolution were not encouraging to any would-be film-maker. As neither film stock nor film equipment had ever been produced in Russia, the Bolsheviks, in the face of a trade embargo, could make no promises of supplies. What little stock and equipment remained in the country was largely in the hands of those hostile to the new regime. But on March 4, 1918, some five months after the Revolution, the first step was taken to provide the Government with an agency for cinema production. On that date, the Praesidium of the Soviet of Workers', Soldiers' and Peasants' Deputies of the City of Moscow decreed that an inventory be made of all cinema equipment in the city and forbade further hoarding of equipment and stock. Two weeks later NARKOMPROS, the People's Commissariat of Education, took control of the resources of the Skobelev Committee, the State film production unit under Kerensky. But it would not be for another two months that the equipment so taken would be allocated to the only group within NARKOMPROS with any idea for its use, the self-proclaimed Moscow Kino Committee.

Handed their equipment on May 26, the Committee, under the direction of Mikhail Koltsov, was able to release *Kinonedelia No. 1* one week later. Whatever part Vertov, as the Committee's secretary, played in this first production was probably eclipsed by the skills of the cameramen Lemberg, A. A. Levitskii, P. K. Novitskii, G. B. Giber, Eduard Tisse, P. V. Ermlov, and others. While these men went out in search of news, Vertov watched how the fragments of what they shot were pieced together by his future wife and editing assistant, Elizabeta Svilova.

By the time Koltsov was called to the front in the summer of 1918, Vertov had gained the acumen to take over the entire operation.

The primary task he inherited from Koltsov was to emphasise the establishment of Bolshevik authority throughout the expanses of what was to become the USSR. Amid interventionist invasions and the emerging forces of the Civil War, the most important message *Kinonedelia* had to deliver was that the new govemment was continuing to function and was establishing roots deeper than those of the ephemeral regime that had so recently fallen. To achieve this end, *Kinonedelia* relied on conventional newsreel images whose power can only be appreciated if they are seen in the context of their times. Item one in *Kinonedelia No. 1* consists of nothing more than the dedication of a monument to Marx in Moscow. We see speakers standing at the base of a large bust of Marx, and later a parade. But what we are also seeing is the opening of a new set of eyes, the first images that Soviet film was able to produce of the achievement of Communism in Russia. The simple item is a dedication to the future of *Kinonedelia*, its purpose and its audience. It is also a self-congratulatory proclamation by those who, only fifteen months before, had been ruled by a medieval monarchy.

Approximately one-third of the items in *Kinonedelia* deal with this theme of the establishment of the Soviet State. They range from shots of children on a peasant commune to the meeting of the VI Extraordinary All-Russian Congress of Soviets. In some cases, it can be assumed, the presentation of these items was primarily informative, telling people about new and unfamiliar institutions. In other cases, depending on how well informed a particular audience was, such items could have the equally useful function of reinforcing previously publicised information by the addition of photographic "proof."

Complementing the items on new institutions are film portraits which served to introduce the new leaders of the Soviet Government and armed forces, lending an air of reality to figures who had been publicised by other media. In two instances, however, the images of leaders take on a more important function. In *Kinonedelia No. 22*, shots of Lenin recovering from wounds are inserted as a reassurance to those concerned about him after Dora Kaplan's assassination attempt. A similar item, contradicting rumours of the death of E. K. Breshko-Breshovskaya, also recognises and reacts to a specific question in the mind of a potential audience.

Soviet leaders were not the only political figures presented to the public by *Kinonedelia*. Film portraits of enemies appeared with some frequency; and the device of portraying the enemy among items concerning the new regime was consistent with the theme of conflict that runs through the newsreel series. As the Civil War intensified, the juxtaposition of images of pro- and anti-Soviet leaders was complemented by a growing number of items concerning battles and trials of anti-govemment figures.

As the number of items concerning conflict increased, so did the sophistication and intensity of montage with which these conflicts were presented. Early news stories about the Civil War are placed almost haphazardly. An item entitled "Workers Appeal for the Defence of the Socialist Nation" (in *No. 4*) can almost be mistaken for another "human interest" story, sandwiched as it is between an item on the Kazan Station in Moscow and a part of the regular "Petrograd in These Days" series. But a vastly improved presentation of war news can be seen in *Kinonedelia No. 19*. In item four, we are shown a sequence which begins with shots of a dead sailor, continues with shots of the interventionist arms used to kill him, and ends with a pan around newly captured territory. The sailor, the mute evidence of the invaders, and the long shot of the captured land together achieve a montage effect, creating a motif present in no single image. It is only because the three images are put together the way they are that we know a battle has taken place.

The montage structure of *Kinonedelia No. 19* does not end with item four. Item five is a series of shots of the Ukrainian Nationalist leader Skoropadskii leading public prayers against the Soviets. Item six, announcing the execution of an enemy, follows as if to predict the fate of anti-Soviet figures such as Skoropadskii. Item seven is then presented with a dual effect. While it too announces the death of an enemy leader (Bochkareva, the commander of the reactionary Women's Fighting Battalion), it leaves as the final image of the entire newsreel shots of Bochkareva at a moment of power. By using these old shots of Bochkareva, Vertov achieves a montage collision between images of the counter-revolutionary in action and the news transmitted by the title. The net effect is to reiterate the overriding theme of these last four items: the Revolution's inevitable triumph over its enemies.

A third kind of montage that Vertov began to develop in *Kinonedelia* was the more formal cutting between images which was later to become his trademark. In *Kinonedelia*

No. 30, one can all but feel Vertov's exhilaration when, for the first time, he cuts purely on motion. The shots are taken from the front of a train as it goes round bends in a snow-covered, mountainous area. As the cars begin to swing to screen right, there is a sudden cut and they are seen going off to screen left. The sequence is continued in this manner for a total of five edits in the space of a little less than a minute of screen time. The pace, of course, is ridiculously slow. Nevertheless, it creates within the viewer the sense of cinematically augmented motion, the production of movement that could not exist without cinema. In later manifestoes, Vertov was to refer to this aspect of his work as the Cinema Eye: "I am eye. I am a mechanical eye. I, a machine, am showing you a world the likes of which only I can see."

While what was to become the Cinema Eye is just barely apparent in *Kinonedelia*, the second of Vertov's major principles, Life Caught Unawares, played a prominent part in the newsreels. As it came to be defined in later writings and films, Life Caught Unawares meant the creation of a sense in the viewer that the activities of the subject on the screen had not been affected by the presence of the camera. The hidden camera, a favourite device of Vertov's cameraman brother Mikhail Kaufman (who did not join Vertov until 1922), played a small role in creating these images. More often, and more significantly, Vertov would depend on his subject being too busy to call attention to the camera's presence. In later films, particularly *Man with the Movie Camera* (1929), this technique was developed into a kind of barometer of social involvement. In *Man with the Movie Camera*, only the social outcast and the NEP-man call attention to the camera, true participants in Socialist activities having no time to "mug."

In *Kinonedelia*, Life Caught Unawares is used as both an organisation and an ideological tool. What now look like rather anodyne shots of people strolling through parks, listening to concerts, and standing in queues in front of city shops, in 1918 and 1919 took on altogether different meanings.

The shots of queues, for instance, worked to counteract a traditional town/country animosity that had intensified in Russia during the period of War Communism. They were evidence to country people that those in the cities were suffering privations similar to their own. Conversely, simple shots of farm activities were aimed at city people alarmed by rumours of rural food hoarding. Taken together, items of this sort were meant to produce the impression of a growing bond between rural and urban areas engaged in a shared struggle against equal hardships. The official admission that these hardships existed undoubtedly helped the credibility of *Kinonedelia* (and of the government that sponsored it). Furthermore, the images of citizens from all over Russia working to achieve Communism created, over the weeks, a continuing travelogue of social progress, a theme more explicitly developed in later Vertov films like *Sixth Part of the Earth* (1926).

Ideologically, this emphasis on the common man as news had ramifications for both Socialist art and cinema history. While cinema itself was nothing new to the Russian people, the idea of a cinema which placed them on a screen so recently reserved for actors and dignitaries was not only a novelty (boosting distribution) but a celebration of their victory in the class struggle. And, just as it was appropriate for the first Socialist cameras to be turned upon the common man, it was equally fitting that Vertov, a neophyte film-maker, should all but quote the earliest works of his medium, the studies of home life and street scenes with which Lumière began world cinema. The images produced by Life Caught Unawares represented the first cinema products since Lumière in which the camera had not been a self-conscious factor in the arrangement of the images it produced. To Vertov, this meant that the film-maker could be accepted into the new society as a fellow-worker rather than as a boss (as he was in fiction film) or a dispassionate observer (as he was supposed to be in contemporary newsreels).

This conception of the film-maker as a fellow-worker may be traced back to the attitude expressed by the Moscow Kino Committee towards their predecessors in *Kinonedelia No. 1*. In the last item of that issue, a shot of the moribund Skobelev Committee was placed after the title: "The Skobelev Committee at the End of the Holiday." Nor did this proclamation of new vigour prove to be an idle boast. By the time the Soviet Government had nationalised cinema production in August 1919, Vertov had not only produced all of *Kinonedelia*[3] but had also edited three short compilation films: *Battle at Tsaritsyn*, *The Trial of Miranov*, and *The Unearthing of the Remains of Sergei Radonezhskogo* (all 1919). At the time of nationalisation, he was working on *Anniversary of the Revolution* (1919), a twelve-reel compilation film chosen by Lenin as one of the first Soviet works of art to be sent abroad. By the time he began work on *Kinopravda* in June 1922, Vertov had, besides supervising film work at the front, edited the thirteen-reel compilation film *History of the Civil War* (1922) as well as the shorter films *All-Russian Elder Kalinin* and *The Agit Train of the Central Party* (both 1921).

These last two films are indicative of Vertov's interest in new methods of distribution. Both grew out of his travels with Soviet President Kalinin on the agit-train *Lenin* in 1920. Using a specially designed film car aboard the agit-train (in much the same manner as Medvedkin some dozen years later), Vertov composed a continually changing travelogue, showing audiences newly edited films while shooting their reactions and their surroundings for insertion into the films they were watching. Vertov repeated this technique during his travel on the agit-steamer *Red Star*, the result being the film *Instructional Steamer "Red Star"* (1924). The technique of including audience response as part of a film's content would be repeated in *Sixth Part of the Earth* and would be a central motif in *Man with the Movie Camera*.

When Vertov returned to Moscow to make *Kinopravda*, he brought with him the ability to liberate film from the conventions of the film theatre and make it part of the architecture of the Soviet City. The Kinoks (practitioners of the Cinema Eye), as Vertov's production group began to call themselves, were as serious about distributing films as they were about making them. *Kinopravda No. 9* shows the Kinoks setting up a mobile projector and having an image on a portable screen in what they claim to be 90 seconds from their time of arrival at any location. Vertov also hoped that accessibility to cinema would not be limited to a passive audience. In 1923, an effort was undertaken to organise clubs of cinema correspondents along the lines followed by the American Newsreel organisation of the 1960s. Unfortunately, the scarcity of materials in the USSR limited this proposed cinema network to films such as *Kinopravda No. 19*, made during the travels of the Moscow-based film-workers.

Exercising his role as a fellow-worker, Vertov's main concern in the first *Kinopravda*s was to help organise public assistance for victims of the 1922 famine. In items concerning the famine, he tempers the shock of images taken in the devastated areas with other images of a Soviet government taking steps to alleviate the situation. As in the *Kinonedelia* item concerning Bochkareva, he experiments with collisions between the message on the title card and the shots that follow. In one instance, we are told that sightseeing flights over Moscow have been organised as a fund-raising device to help the famine areas. But what we actually see on the screen are images of a modern airplane and a vast Soviet city. The sense of urgency produced by the title card collides with the sense of reassurance provided by the images, to leave the viewer with the net impression that the problem will eventually be solved.

The techniques of formal montage which first appeared in *Kinonedelia* were developed to the utmost during the *Kinopravda* period. One typical example of the close cutting was the opening sequence of *Kinoglaz*, a feature made by the Kinoks in 1924. Within the first forty metres of the film, Vertov creates an explosion of no less than 57 shots of dancing, drinking figures. A similar effect is created in the last sequence of *Kinopravda No. 18*. Here, a burst of some 60 eight to four frame shots of faces and mouths and machinery is used to convey a crescendo of enthusiasm.

This particular item illustrates a difference in emphasis between *Kinonedelia* and *Kinopravda*. Within the item, we are shown workers shutting down their machines to attend a ceremony honouring a newly born "October baby." The baby is passed among a small group of Party members, Komsomols, and Pioneers, gifts are presented to the parents, and the singing of the Internationale begins. It is at this point that the machinery seems to set itself in motion and join in the singing, for the montage finale described above.

From the stiff, nervous performances of the participants in the ceremony, it is apparent that Vertov in this sequence has little use for Life Caught Unawares. Nor is this the only *Kinopravda* item which looks posed. In a sequence in *No. 8*, showing eager citizens snapping up news of the trial of the Social Revolutionaries, we see Vertov and his brother in the back seat of a speeding car taking a newspaper from a boy running alongside. Other shots within *Kinopravda* are as, if not more, evidently contrived.

But if Vertov seems in *Kinopravda* at times to abandon Life Caught Unawares, he does so in the fervour of creative freedom which characterises this new stage of his work. The success of *Kinonedelia* and of the compilation films guaranteed him government support (one instance in which the availability rather than the scarcity of stock and equipment encouraged montage experimentation). During the production of *Kinopravda*, Vertov had a large stock of archive material on which to draw. He had a large and competent staff. Producing another newsreel series (*Goskinokalendar*) concurrently with *Kinopravda* gave him a second large stock of facilities, as well as an overview of Soviet current events. At the same time, *Goskinokalendar*, a more conventional newsreel, relieved him of the necessity of presenting "straight" news in *Kinopravda*.

Consequently, *Kinopravda* existed as a purely experimental venture in the cinematic interpretation of current events. The Cinema Eye was given a free hand in constructing and reconstructing those images which the news produced. Cameras were cranked at a multitude of speeds and mounted on every conceivable vehicle. Animation became a regular feature. Vertov remembered having invented entire new genres: "Review films, sketch films, verse films, film poems and preview films made their appearance . . . Considerable work was done in the utilisation of new methods for subtitling, transforming titles into pictorial units equal to the images."

Trying to do everything cinema could do, Vertov inevitably transgressed the boundaries of Life Caught Unawares. He found that one of the most useful capabilities of cinema was that of reproducing a posed or acted event. In *Kinopravda No. 18*, the nature of the story to be covered dictated the filming of people who were all too obviously altering their actions to suit the requirements of the camera.

However much the coverage of ceremonies may have presented a problem in this early work, the idea of the ceremony served in Vertov's later films as an effective compromise between the demands of Life Caught Unawares and the need to present images that furthered the theme of a given film. While, strictly speaking, the orchestra conductor in *Enthusiasm* (1930) is not changing his actions for the benefit of the camera, he is still providing Vertov with the performance called for at that point in the film. This is not to say that the staged scene did not remain a part of Vertov's repertoire of cinematic devices for the rest of his career. It is merely to point out that the staged event, taken in conjunction with the demands of Life Caught Unawares, produced, as a hybrid, an interest in ceremony that provided one of Vertov's most frequently recurring themes.

Another motif running through all Vertov's films is his fascination with machinery, as demonstrated by the use of the machines in *Kinopravda No. 18*. Machines are employed metaphorically in sequences like that in *Kinopravda No. 8*, in which army tanks are almost literally converted into ploughshares as they are used to pull earth moving devices levelling the Moscow airport. Machines may also be used for humour, as in a sequence in *Shagi, Soviet* (1926) in which buses and trucks decide to hold a political rally without their drivers. But as Vertov himself stressed in the manifesto "WE," machines are used most significantly when they are being integrated (via the Cinema Eye) into the life of man:

> WE discover the soul of the machine, we are in love with the worker at his bench, we are in love with the farmer on his tractor, the engineer on his locomotive.
> WE bring creative joy into every mechanical activity.
> WE make peace between man and machine.
> WE educate the new man.[4]

Man and his machinery are thus montage elements in the creation of a cinematic integration which, the Kinoks hoped, would reflect a similarly successful integration in the society of "the new man." In much the same way as man and his machines, man and his history are integrated in what is the longest and perhaps the most powerful of the *Kinopravda* issues. *Kinopravda No. 21* is a 795 metre essay on the effect of Lenin's life and death upon the Russian people. Using the interpretative option of the series, Vertov chose not to treat Lenin's death as a news story but rather to collect all possible relevant images, produce his own animations, and carefully compose a montage around a set of subtitles which read like lines from a Mayakovskian poem.

The size and complexity of *Kinopravda No. 21* indicate Vertov's impatience with the scale and the time limitations of the newsreel genre. Having released his first feature-length non-compilation film a year previously, he felt the time was right to make a full transition to feature productions. By 1925 Soviet feature films were commonplace throughout the USSR; and Vertov, as a pioneer of the Soviet industry and one of its most successful artists to date, might well have felt slighted had he been limited to the production of shorts.

Vertov's later troubles with the Soviet film industry were not to do with the length of his films, but rather were to come about because of contradictory conceptions concerning the importance of non-fiction film. Much to Vertov's chagrin, the Soviet fiction film had emerged in the 1920s as the nation's most highly regarded art form. Against Kuleshov, Pudovkin, Eisenstein, and Dovzhenko in their prime, Vertov's insistence on the Leninist Proportion fell predictably flat. The vigour of his increasingly noisy protests earned him nothing but the continuing enmity of his contemporaries. After 1926, Vertov found himself in virtual exile in the Ukrainian film studios; an exile which was to last until the coming of the Second World War.

While Vertov's own career ended in frustration, the careers of those with whom he worked were in many ways advanced by their contact with him. It was Vertov who made the first demands on the cameramen who were later to make the great Soviet films. Eduard Tisse, Ilya Kopaline, and Boris Frantsisson are examples of cinema workers whose early feedback came from seeing the use that Vertov made of their footage. Similarly, Mikhail Kaufman, an innovator in documentary in his own right, began his film career as a Kinok.

More important than any influence Vertov may have had on those who worked with him, was the impression that his newsreels and early features made on the minds of the Soviet film-makers who later directed works about the Revolutionary and Civil War periods. Few of these men were active film-makers during the period of these events; their impressions both at the time and in later years, when they followed the Soviet tradition of carefully researching historical footage, must have been to some extent shaped by Vertov's selection of images and montage arrangements. One may safely guess that many a re-created demonstration or Party Congress, as well as the costuming and direction of an infinite number of extras, grew out of Vertov's coverage of the original event. In *Kinonedelia No. 10* and again in *Kinonedelia No. 14*, Vertov had preserved, for anyone interested in capturing the spirit of October, the revolutionary activity of pulling down a czarist statue. Other examples are less obvious.

NOTES

1. "The Writings of Dziga Vertov," translated by Val Thalberg. *Film Culture*, No. 25 (Spring, 1962).
2. Alexandre Lemberg, "Dziga Vertov Prikhodit v Kino," *Iz Istorii Kino* (1968).
3. Georges Sadoul questions Vertov's editorship of *Kinonedelias* Nos. 38, 39, 41, 42. See Sadoul's "Bio-Filmographie de Dziga Vertov." *Cahiers du Cinéma*, XXV, 146 (August, 1963).
4. Translated by Lutz Becker in *Art in Revolution* (London, The Hayward Gallery, 1971).

24

DZIGA VERTOV

WE

Variant of a Manifesto (1922)

We call ourselves *kinoks*[1]—as opposed to "cinematographers," a herd of junkmen doing rather well peddling their rags.

We see no connection between true *kinochestvo*[2] and the cunning and calculation of the profiteers.

We consider the psychological Russo-German film-drama—weighed down with apparitions and childhood memories—an absurdity.

To the American adventure film with its showy dynamism and to the dramatizations of the American Pinkertons the kinoks say thanks for the rapid shot changes and the close-ups. Good . . . but disorderly, not based on a precise study of movement. A cut above the psychological drama, but still lacking in foundation. A cliché. A copy of a copy.

WE proclaim the old films, based on the romance,[3] theatrical films and the like, to be leprous.

—Keep away from them!

—Keep your eyes off them!

—They're mortally dangerous!

—Contagious!

WE affirm the future of cinema art by denying its present.

"Cinematography" must die so that the art of cinema may live.

WE *call for its death to be hastened.*

We protest against that mixing of the arts which many call synthesis. The mixture of bad colors, even those ideally selected from the spectrum, produces not white, but mud.

Synthesis should come at the summit of each art's achievement and not before.

WE are cleansing *kinochestvo* of foreign matter—of music, literature, and theater; we seek our own rhythm, one lifted from nowhere else, and we find it in the movements of things.

WE invite you:

—to flee—

the sweet embraces of the romance,
the poison of the psychological novel,
the clutches of the theater of adultery;
to turn your back on music,

—to flee—

out into the open, into four-dimensions (three + time), in search of our own material, our meter and rhythm.

The "psychological" prevents man from being as precise as a stopwatch; it interferes with his desire for kinship with the machine.

In an art of movement we have no reason to devote our particular attention to contemporary man.

The machine makes us ashamed of man's inability to control himself, but what are we to do if electricity's unerring ways are more exciting to us than the disorderly haste of active men and the corrupting inertia of passive ones?

Saws dancing at a sawmill convey to us a joy more intimate and intelligible than that on human dance floors.

For his inability to control his movements, WE temporarily exclude man as a subject for film.

Our path leads through the poetry of machines, from the bungling citizen to the perfect electric man.

In revealing the machine's soul, in causing the worker to love his workbench, the peasant his tractor, the engineer his engine—

we introduce creative joy into all mechanical labor,

we bring people into closer kinship with machines,

we foster new people.

The new man, free of unwieldiness and clumsiness, will have the light, precise movements of machines, and he will be the gratifying subject of our films.

Openly recognizing the rhythm of machines, the delight of mechanical labor, the perception of the beauty of chemical processes, WE sing of earthquakes, we compose film epics of electric power plants and flame, we delight in the movements of comets and meteors and the gestures of searchlights that dazzle the stars.

Everyone who cares for his art seeks the essence of his own technique.

Cinema's unstrung nerves need a rigorous system of precise movement.

The meter, tempo, and type of movement, as well as its precise location with respect to the axes of a shot's coordinates and perhaps to the axes of universal coordinates (the three dimensions + the fourth—time), should be studied and taken into account by each creator in the field of cinema.

Radical necessity, precision, and speed are the three components of movement worth filming and screening.

The geometrical extract of movement through an exciting succession of images is what's required of montage.[4]

Kinochestvo is the art of organizing the necessary movements of objects in space as a rhythmical artistic whole, in harmony with the properties of the material and the internal rhythm of each object.

Intervals (the transitions from one movement to another) are the material,[5] the elements of the art of movement, and by no means the movements themselves. It is they (the intervals) which draw the movement to a kinetic resolution.

The organization of movement is the organization of its elements, or its intervals, into phrases.

In each phrase there is a rise, a high point, and a falling off (expressed in varying degrees) of movement.

A composition is made of phrases, just as a phrase is made of intervals of movement.

A kinok who has conceived a film epic or fragment should be able to jot it down with precision so as to give it life on the screen, should favorable technical conditions be present.

The most complete scenario cannot, of course, replace these notes, just as a libretto does not replace pantomime, just as literary accounts of Scriabin's compositions do not convey any notion of his music.

To represent a dynamic study on a sheet of paper, we need graphic symbols of movement.

WE are in search of the film scale.

WE fall, we rise . . . together with the rhythm of movements—slowed and accelerated,

running from us, past us, toward us,
in a circle, or straight line, or ellipse,
to the right and left, with plus and minus signs;
movements bend, straighten, divide, break apart,
multiply, shooting noiselessly through space.

Cinema is, as well, the *art of inventing movements* of things in space in response to the demands of science; it embodies the inventor's dream—be he scholar, artist, engineer, or carpenter; it is the realization by kinochestvo of that which cannot be realized in life.

Drawings in motion. Blueprints in motion. Plans for the future. The theory of relativity on the screen.

WE greet the ordered fantasy of movement.

Our eyes, spinning like propellers, take off into the future on the wings of hypothesis.

WE believe that the time is at hand when we shall be able to hurl into space the hurricanes of movement, reined in by our tactical lassoes.

Hurrah for *dynamic geometry*, the race of points, lines, planes, volumes.

Hurrah for the poetry of machines, propelled and driving; the poetry of levers, wheels, and wings of steel; the iron cry of movements; the blinding grimaces of red-hot streams.

NOTES

Glosses followed by "ed." or "trans." are additions by the original editor or the translator. Glosses which are not so marked are taken from the Moscow edition without substantial alteration.

1. Kinoks ("cinema-eye men"): A neologism coined by Vertov, involving a play on the words *kino* ("cinema" or "film") and *oko*, the latter an obsolescent and poetic word meaning "eye." The *-ok* ending is the transliteration of a traditional suffix used in Russian to indicate a male, human agent.

   Kinoglaz ("Kino-Eye") is the name Vertov gave to the movement and group of which he is the founder and leader. The term was also used to designate their method of work. It is, as well, the title of the feature-length film that, in 1925, initiates the period of his maturity. We have chosen to use the Russian title in all cases involving specific reference to that film, since it is by its Russian title that the film is generally known to scholars and archivists. This work was the culmination of a development begun in 1922 with the production of a series of shorter newsreel films bearing the same title and devoted to aspects and problems of the new Soviet society. When reference is made to the group or movement as such, we have used the name *Kino-Eye*, both in order to distinguish it from the specific productions and to stress the continuity involved in the production, by Vertov and his group, of the *Kinonedelia* ("Kino-week") and *Kinopravda* ("Kino-truth") chronicles, which preceded the appearance of the film *Kinoglaz*—trans. and ed.
2. Kinochestvo: Another of Vertov's neologisms: the suffix *chestvo* indicates an abstract quality, therefore, the quality of the cinema-eye. While its precise signification is rather vague, it would appear from the context that Vertov is using it, by analogy with *kinok*, in contrast to *cinematography*. In his journal of 1924, he writes, "We almost never used the term *kinochestvo*, as it says nothing and is gratuitous word building." Film theory of the period is characterized, internationally, by a proliferation of terminology, and this particular instance recalls the elaborate speculation surrounding the notion of "photogénie" proposed in France by Vertov's contemporary, Jean Epstein—trans. and ed.
3. Romance: Vertov is referring to a type of sentimental film based on songs ("romances"), popular at that time—trans.
4. Montage: In Russian a single word conveys notions that in English are rendered by the two words *montage* and *editing*. In most instances, one English meaning has been chosen according to the context—trans.
5. Material: This term is frequently used by Vertov and others to mean film footage. Its constructivist connotation is significant with respect to Vertov's theory and practice—trans.

25

JAY LEYDA

BRIDGE (1964)

There is a double content in each piece of newsreel. First of all it contains information of various sorts—the look of world figures at one moment of history, the way people work and play in certain places in certain years, the appearance of a street, of a tragedy, of a new achievement, et cetera almost to infinity. Beyond its information each piece of newsreel has a formal content, unremarked though visible. This includes all the elements that make it possible for the informational content to be communicated to us. At the risk of being obvious, here are some of these: the areas of black, white, and greys that make up the shapes of people and places, the distribution of these areas into compositions (accidental or otherwise), the movement of the people and objects shown, the direction of this movement, and the rhythm of the movement, an element possibly quite distinct from the graphic rhythm of the composition. When there is also, as part of a newsreel piece, simultaneously recorded sound, aural elements have to be counted alongside the visual elements—the pitch of a voice, the response of an audience, etc.—in making the inventory of all that the piece contains. It is this accumulation of two kinds of content that we react to, with only partial consciousness, from our seat in the theatre, as each piece of newsreel comes and goes on the screen.

You cannot rearrange the elements within a piece of newsreel, though you can manipulate them in relation to other pieces—but only if you have studied their whole content. It is from such study and manipulation that the art of the compilation film can grow.

In the preparation of the separate pieces, either new or old, to make a whole newsreel, a consciousness of all their elements rarely plays a part. It is possible for experienced newsreel cutters to develop professional intuitions in regard to the formal content, but this does not often go beyond the aims of smooth continuity and shock effects. In the cutting of past newsreels to present historical concepts or to "agitate" an audience into thinking, it has become obvious today that to neglect the formal content of each piece weakens its informational content, and leaves the audience groping for the purpose of the sequence and the idea of the whole. But in 1927 this necessity for studying the whole content of each newsreel piece and building from its formal elements a carefully engineered bridge to convey information to the audience in the strongest possible way was a totally new idea. Like all new ideas its introduction required effort, even struggle.

By 1926 Kuleshov, Eisenstein, and Pudovkin, with their followers, had applied such engineering principles to the fictional film with a success that challenged any lazier or purely intuitional approach. The Vertov group had pioneered similarly for the documentary film. It was the task of Esther Schub to bring this discipline and strength to the new problems and possibilities latent in the rapidly accumulating store of non-current newsreels.

In 1922, as the Civil War and intervention ended and as NEP began, Esther Schub entered the distribution office of Goskino, her work to be editing and titling foreign and pre-revolutionary Russian films for Soviet audiences.[1] A friend of Mayakovsky and Eisenstein in the Meyerhold group, she brought intelligence, taste, and a sense of social responsibility into this generally despised employment. The first jobs given her were to adapt American serials—with Eddie Polo, Ruth Roland, Pearl White. When she discovered that the faithful Russian audiences did not need the usual swift résumés given at the start of each new chapter of a serial thriller, Schub took these discards to the cutting table she kept in her home, and evenings were spent with film friends there making film jokes with the scraps. (One of her friends was Kuleshov, who had experienced a serious variant of this pastime when he edited newsreels of the Civil War.) Sometimes she would be handed such scraps—without title, subtitles, or any indication of order—to be transformed into a film that could be released; thus Chaplin's *Carmen* landed on her table in the form of a hundred confused little rolls. It was clearly intended as a parody on Bizet's opera, so she supplied it with titles in the same spirit, and she remembered its reception (it may have been Chaplin's introduction to Russian audiences) as gratifyingly hilarious.

More difficult was the transformation of the two-part German thriller, *Doctor Mabuse*, with its lengthy, time-and-metre consuming titles and involved tangle of plots, into a single film that could be followed with less dependence on titles. This required a study of each shot's content and composition, a close examination of each actor's movements and expressions, unattached to the old titles. Rhythm and tempo, of each shot and in relation one to another, became vital factors that could not be ignored, as its director, Fritz Lang, had seemed to ignore them in his original cutting. Schub learned the power of scissors and cement in relation to meaning, and Eisenstein, whose assistance on this job was his first film work, learned too.

When Russian directors saw Schub's value to their own productions, she was transferred to the Third Studio of Goskino to advise and cut new films by Tarich, Ivanov-Barkov, Froelich, Roshal, Mikhin, Molchanov. The most interesting of these was Tarich's *Wings of a Serf* (1926), with Leonidov, as Ivan the Terrible, learning as much from Schub's advice as she learned from his performance. There were also two months of work with Eisenstein, at her home, on the shooting script of *Strike*.

Schub writes that it was the impression made upon her early in 1926 by Potemkin[2] that induced her to seek in newsreel material another film way to show the revolutionary past. She found lists of newsreels filmed in 1917—she learned that the Tsar had maintained his own court cameraman—and she felt sure that she could find enough footage to work with. But the Goskino director, Trainin, answered her every proposal and enthusiasm with "No," and "told me to go on editing fictional films—I might even get an opportunity to make my own film with actors." She turned to the Sovkino Studio, where the livelier minds of Bliakhin and

Shklovsky had some say in policy, and after several conferences they said "Yes."

> At the end of summer, 1926, I went to Leningrad. It was even tougher there. All the valuable negatives and positives of war-time and prerevolutionary newsreels were kept in a damp cellar on Sergievsky Street. The cans were coated with rust. In many places the dampness had caused the emulsion to come away from the celluloid base. Many shots that appeared on the lists had disappeared altogether.
>
> Not one metre of negative or positive on the February Revolution had been preserved, and I was even shown a document that declared that no film of that event could be found in Leningrad.[3]

In spite of such assurances Schub persisted and some of that footage *did* come to light. An old newsreel worker, Khmelnitsky, who had helped her restore some of the damaged footage, brought her small cans of "counter-revolutionary" film that turned out to be the private "home movies" of Nikolai II that she had hoped would turn up some day. In her two months in Leningrad Schub inspected 60,000 metres of film, from which she chose 5,200 metres to take back to work on in Moscow. She spent all her free time in wandering about Leningrad, a new city for her, to feel at home with its geography and appearance in the 1917 shots. Before leaving she supervised the filming of various documents, newspapers and items associated with the events she was reconstructing.

> In the montage I tried to avoid looking at the newsreel material for its own sake, and to maintain the principle of its documentary quality. All was subordinated to the theme. This gave me the possibility, in spite of the known limitations of the photographed events and facts, to link the meanings of the material so that it evoked the pre-revolutionary period and the February days.[4]

After the first private screening (where the section on "World War" was particularly admired) the release title was decided: *The Fall of the Romanov Dynasty*. The only credit on the posters was "Work by E. I. Schub."

In March 1927, as her first "work" was released, Schub began her second. *The Great Road* was to use all Soviet newsreels for the ten years since the October Revolution, beginning (hopefully) with whatever could be found of the Revolution itself. She learned that newsreels of the recent past had been kept just as carelessly, if not more so, than had the oldest Russian newsreels unearthed for her first film. Identification of place and time of shooting was an unforeseen obstacle, but the several living cameramen of the Civil War helped her here. She had more to inspect (250,000 metres) than for the older film, but after 1921–22 the material grew thinner:

> From that date newsreels were shot without much plan and quickly put aside with little comprehension of their historic value, which of course increased with each passing year. Even worse is their change of tone after the Civil War; suddenly the concentration was on parades, meetings, arrivals, departures, delegates, and such—and almost no record was kept of how we transformed the country to a new political economy—or of the resulting construction.[5]

Some precious footage had been sold abroad, without any master copies or negatives having been kept at home—too little raw film in those years to think of such niceties, or of the future. A quantity of early reels had been sent to the United States, as thanks for the work of the American Relief Association during the months of famine. This had fallen into private hands, yet Schub traced this footage and arranged through Amtorg (the Soviet trade office in the United States) for its purchase, for $6,000. (It was cannily copied before the sale, for a future interesting use *against* the Soviet Union!)

> In this lot I found material of the imperalist war, of the funeral of victims of the February Revolution, and—six completely unfamiliar shots of Lenin [filmed in 1920 by an American cameraman]. Soviet audiences saw these intimate scenes of Lenin for the first time in *The Great Road*.[6]

The new film was intended for the celebrations of the tenth anniversary of the October Revolution—in early November. But the new film form discovered and perfected by Schub was not yet on secure ground. Her right as an "author" of these films was challenged, and it was Mayakovsky who publicly ridiculed those who tried in any way to belittle the value of this extremely important work.[7]

The Fall of the Romanov Dynasty had used newsreel material of 1912–17; *The Great Road* continued through the archives of 1917–27. In her searches Schub had found a tempting lot of Russian newsreel from 1896 through 1912, and the Tolstoy centenary to come in 1928 offered her an opportunity to employ it. Her first Tolstoy hope was to depend on the considerable footage that had been filmed of him, but she found only about 200 feet of this—a fifth as much as the footage of his funeral! She decided to place her actual Tolstoy footage in a larger frame of Russia since the turn of the century. The result was *The Russia of Nikolai II and Lev Tolstoy*:

> This montage must serve as an eloquent illustration of the fact that any available acting method for the historical film, no matter how good or talented, has only an ephemeral value in comparison with the chronicle film, which possesses a conviction that can never pale and can never age.[8]

Schub's wisdom and craft were hereafter applied chiefly to new documentary films, but on two occasions before the Second World War (when she had several such occasions) she worked again on materials photographed far from her. The first was *Today* (a "film-feuilleton"), released in 1930. In comparing the capitalist and socialist worlds she made ingenious use of foreign newsreels collected in Berlin. Her second occasion was *Spain* (1939), to be described below.

> . . . what interests us here is not the usual narrative montage, a consequence and corollary of cutting, but expressive montage, above all ideological. It is no accident that compilations so flourish in the USSR. It is natural that the country where the first theories of montage were formulated accords a leading position to the compilation film as an ideological weapon. One should keep in mind that montage is not a simple succession of shots, nor even a sum of their contents, but produces something new, something original. It is a remarkable application of the Marxist law of dialectical change from quantity to quality. Montage rests fundamentally on the interaction of the images . . . *ideological* montage aims at a precise political or moral point in putting together images which have no strictly causal or temporal relationship.[9]

Marcel Martin's search for a definition of the compilation film recalls Eisenstein's effort in 1929 to define "a dramaturgy of the visual film-form as regular and precise as the existing dramaturgy of the film-story," where his enumeration of potentialities ends with "Liberation of the whole action from the definition of time and space"; in illustrating this he gave examples from *October*, from *Arsenal*, and from *The Russia of Nikolai II and Lev Tolstoy*.[10] And it is true that Schub's work provides many examples of a power too rarely used by the compilation film.

In Schub's first three precedent-forming films her cutting ideas usually combined a forcefully simple logic with a minute study of the formal elements in the available footage;[11] the ideas were often built on contrasts that may seem obvious now—but it took imagination to dig them from her raw material. Here is an example,[12] in the *Fall of the Romanov Dynasty*, of one of her direct poster juxtapositions:

> A crowd of elegant idlers are dancing a mazurka on the awninged deck of a yacht.
> The dancing tires some of them. They drink wine.
> Title: "It made me sweat."
> And again they dance.
> Title: ". . . sweat."
> A peasant, exhausted by his work, ploughs a furrow . . .

The admired war sequence in her first film used the newsreels of all combatant countries. For me its climax was another such simple contrast, using two titles: "He who wants war," and "He who is to be sent to war." In *The Great Road* she showed how a newsreel-shot parade could be reconstructed for maximum irony—*without* benefit of sound.

When Schub began this work there were no rules for the physical use of old film materials—it was catch-as-catch-can, and don't worry about either the next need or the future; but Schub's orderly mind evolved its own rules: she never cut a piece of original film, positive or negative, and never employed an original piece—her first move was to make duplicate negatives of every metre she considered using. Later editors were not so scrupulous, not even with Schub's films. Usually pleading some emergency or other, they took whatever they needed[13] so that there are no complete negatives today of Schub's first three films. Among other lessons to be learned from this loss is the necessity for separating documentary archives from documentary film producing studios.

These were the years when Joris Ivens and his friends combated the newsreel's otherwise unchallenged power by borrowing some from Amsterdam or Antwerp theatres on Saturday night, recutting them the whole night to alter their class character, showing them Sunday to a working-class audience, restoring them to their original state that night, and returning them politely on Monday.[14] One immediate result of this stimulating scheme was Henri Storck's satire on the signing of the Kellogg Pact, employing nothing but newsreels related to the event. This compilation, *Histoire du Soldat Inconnu* (1932), was little known until it appeared in the retrospective programmes at the 1961 Tours festival of short films.[15] On that occasion it was seen by Marcel Martin, who describes Storck's film as "*un film de montage très féroce contre la bourgeoisie, l'armée, la religion et le capitalisme; esprit anarchiste et surréaliste plutôt que vision marxiste.*" Perhaps it is necessary to remind oneself that these ideas and attitudes are conveyed entirely through the ingenious juxtapositions of newsreel images.

Béla Balázs tells of a similar activity by a Berlin workers' film society [*Volksverband für Filmkunst*] in 1928:

> It arranged film shows and would have shown newsreels of its own, but the censorship banned them. So they bought old UFA newsreels, which had long finished their run

> and had been approved by the censorship in their time. From these we cut new reels [with a few discreet new titles] . . . Skating rinks and the guests on the terrace of a luxury hotel. "This, too, is St. Moritz": a melancholy procession of ragged, hungry snow-shovellers and rink-sweepers [cut from an earlier place in the reel, before its original audience could note the contrast]. A "Brilliant Military Parade" was followed by disabled ex-servicemen begging in the streets . . . The police were itching to ban these newsreels, but could not do so, as they were all respectable Ufa newsreels, every one of them approved by the censorship. Only the order of showing had been altered a little.[16]

Kracauer[17] underlines the success of the Berlin experiment:

> [The *Volksverband für Filmkunst*] transformed, through mere editing procedures, a set of colorless Ufa newsreels into a red-tinged film that stirred Berlin audiences to clamorous demonstrations. The censor soon prohibited further performances, even though the *Volksverband* based its protest upon the demonstrable assertion that the film contained nothing but newsreel shots already shown in all Ufa theaters without scandalizing anyone.

But this was no more than the excrescence of an interest in the power of the film-editor that was accepted by the film-intelligentsia of Germany since the first shock of *Potemkin*. Walter Ruttmann had moved from a primary interest in the film's abstract movement to an adaptation of this interest to real materials, in *Berlin* (1927). Carl Mayer, whose idea it was to make *Berlin*, objected strenuously to the finished film's anaemic, non-social content, imposed by Ruttmann's "non-objective" tendency. In subsequent works Ruttmann treated archive materials in the same abstract way, sensitive but with neither emotion nor aim. Ruttmann edited two episodes for Piscator's staging of Ernst Toller's *Hoppla! Wir leben* in 1927—a screened war-time prologue to the play, and a review of the world's external progress during the hero's seven-year insanity (1920–27). This dip into the archives may have led him to *Die Melodie der Welt* (*Melody of the World*, 1929), an ambitious *querschnitt* (cross-section) film of all the world's activities (with sound) from love to war—financed as a high-class advertisement for the Hamburg-Amerika Line. All commentators on this film have remarked the peculiar contradiction between the emotional aims of the subject and the neutrality of Ruttmann's result: he had subjected the enormously varied contents of a stock-shot library to an interest in its rhythmic, formal content—and only its formal content. These were the structural materials for a bridge that Ruttmann did not bother to build. He wished to prove that the art of a film has to be separated from its content, yet his work proves a contrary truth.

More concerned with the minds of his audience (though always a small group) was Hans Richter. He came from the same group of "abstractionists" to which Ruttmann had belonged, but Richter was interested in ideas. With his *Inflation*, made in 1928 to introduce a forgotten commercial film, he began a series of "film essays," partly dependent on the same stock-shot libraries that Ruttmann employed. Kracauer describes Richter's film essays as "sagacious pictorial comments on socially interesting topics."[18] He could be as bold and stimulating in his cutting juxtapositions as was John Heartfield in the photomontages published by A.I.Z. in those same years before Hitler.

In a newspaper article[19] written later, as an émigré in Switzerland, Richter distinguished the function of his "film essay" form[20] from the familiar approach of the normal documentary film:

> Films about scenery and quaint customs, winter sports and summer excursions, about the making of a machine-tool or the extraction of dyes from coal-tar, or even about the development of an embryo—all this can be effectively shown by exactly recording in chronological sequence all the visible stages of the process; for a clear understanding of these subjects such a simple chronological approach is even demanded.

But there is another category where this method does not satisfy us.

> I have had to film the subject of the functioning of a stock-exchange. For this an exact record in chronological sequence of all stages of its functioning, no matter how well observed, is not sufficient . . . To make the workings of a stock-exchange understood to your spectator many outside elements have to be indicated—national economy, public needs, the laws of supply and demand, etc. It is not so much a process to be filmed, as it is the ideas behind the complex called "a stock-exchange."
>
> The task given this sort of documentary film is to portray a *concept*. Even what is invisible must be made visible. Acted scenes as well a directly recorded actualities must all be thought of as bits of evidence in an argument, an argument that aims to make problems, thoughts, even ideas, generally understood . . .
>
> In this effort to give body to the invisible world of imagination, thought and ideas, the essay film can employ an incomparably greater reservoir of expressive means than can the pure documentary film. Freed from recording external phenomena in simple sequence the film essay must collect its material from everywhere; its space and time must be conditioned only by the need to explain and show the *idea*.

Ruttmann and Richter were followed into the German film libraries by enthusiastic dozens. In the one year, 1929, at least three large-scale compilations were released in Berlin: *Rund um die Liebe*, compiled by UFA cutters from love episodes from old films; *Die Wunder des Films*, "a neutral cross-section film overflowing with technological optimism"; and *Die Wunder der Welt* (*Miracles of the Universe*), "a patchwork of various explorer films".[21] Many of the unfocused, neutral skills being sharpened in these pre-Hitler years were to be given focus and employment by Dr. Goebbels.

NOTES

1. These details of Schub's career are drawn from her memoirs, *Krupnym planom* (In Close Up) (Moscow, 1959), published shortly before her death.
2. Ibid., pp. 90–1.
3. Ibid., p. 92.
4. In an interview with V. Pfeffer, *Sovietski Ekran*, November 1, 1927.
5. Schub, "Road from the Past," *Sovietskoye Kino*, November–December 1934.
6. An extract from this speech by Mayakovsky is quoted in *Kino*, pp. 229–30.
7. "How the Film Was Made," a drafted article (dated October 1928) by Schub, found in her archives, published in *Iskusstvo Kino*, November 1960.
8. Marcel Martin, "Les films de montage," in *Cinéma 63*, April 1963.
9. Eisenstein, "A Dialectic Approach to Film Form," in *Film Form* (1949), pp. 58–9.
10. Quoted in Ilya Weisfeld's foreword to Schub's *Krupnym planom*, p. 5.
11. Ivens, an unpublished autobiographical manuscript.
12. Reviewed by Derek Hill in *The Observer*, December 17, 1961.
13. Balázs, *Theory of the Film* (London, 1952), pp. 165–6.
14. Kracauer, *Propaganda and the Nazi War Film* (New York, 1942), reprinted in *From Caligari to Hitler* (Princeton, 1947); Kracauer appears to be quoting from *Der Geist des Films*, by Balázs (1930).
15. Kracauer, *From Caligari to Hitler*, p. 194.

16. Richter, "Der Filmessay," *National-Zeitung* (Basel), No. 192, April 25, 1940.
17. Which, we should remember, employed manœuvre newsreel shots of the British Navy in its last reel.
18. Another great woman editor, Helen Van Dongen, gives us a good piece of advice on the close study of footage:

    I cannot emphasize enough how important repeated screenings are in the process of editing. They will not only help you memorize the material but will also make you familiar with the slightest nuances in each shot. ("Three Hundred and Fifty Cans of Film," in *The Cinema 1951*, ed. by Roger Manvell.)

    This increased familiarity she considers more useful *to her* than any written catalogue—though she agrees it may not be feasible in group work.
19. This selfish practice is still with us; in the print that I saw of Leiser's first film several shots had been removed that someone along the way had needed.
20. Today the "film essay" form is almost totally, and incomprehensibly, ignored. The only modern film-maker who employs a witty variation of it is Chris Marker.
21. These three films are mentioned by Kracauer, whose comments are quoted here.

26

MIKHAIL IAMPOLSKY

REALITY AT SECOND HAND (1991)

In 1927 Esfir Shub released *The Fall of the Romanov Dynasty* (*Padenie dinastii Romanovykh*), her first film edited from sequences of pre-Revolutionary newsreels. The film was greeted enthusiastically as a significant landmark and, according to some scholars, heralded the "second period" in the history of Soviet documentary cinema.[1] Almost immediately it became the ideal model for documentary film, a standard of judgement for criticism to be directed against the previous phase, dominated by Dziga Vertov.

The film was made entirely of archive material, a style which from then on was contrasted with the celebrated "life caught unawares" style of Vertov. Direct contact with reality in one form or another was actively being discredited in favour of the editing of archival newsreels. This change in the artistic ideology of the 1920s, which has not usually attracted the attention of scholars, seems to be quite fundamental and requires separate examination.

The chief accusation against Vertov which was widely circulated in the middle of the 1920s was that he had betrayed the document, he had moved away from reality. These reproaches came from the former allies and propagandists of the Left Front and were directed against an individual who had turned the observation of daily reality into his life's cause. But Shub, working on old newsreels, was beyond suspicion. Work on film archival material seemed to contemporaries to be a guarantee of even greater documentary authenticity than work on the real life surrounding film-makers.

Even Vertov's work with old newsreels was criticised. Viktor Shklovsky wrote about Vertov's film *Forward, Soviet!* (*Shagai, Sovet!*, 1926):

> The majority of the shots in this picture were filmed neither by Vertov himself nor on his instructions... But I think that newsreel material is in Vertov's treatment deprived of its soul—its documentary quality.
>
> A newsreel needs a title and date...

> Dziga Vertov cuts up newsreel. In this sense his work is not artistically Progressive. In essence he is behaving like those of our directors (may their tombstones be stolen from their graves) who cut up newsreels in order to use bits in their own films. These directors are turning our film libraries into piles of broken film.[2]

If we think about Shklovsky's accusations, we can see that they are far from trivial. He rebuked Vertov for cutting up old newsreels in order to use them in his own films and thus damaging the film archive collections. The preservation of the archive seemed to Shklovsky to be more important than Vertov's film itself. Izmail Urazov, one of the editors of *Sovetskii ekran* (*Soviet Screen*), defended Vertov in a reply to Shklovsky:

> So they have an archive. But what in fact is an archive? Of course you have to know how to use an archive. But the basic thing is the montage ... a montage of long sequences is bad. It tires you out. You begin to feel that you are in the theatre and not the cinema; it does not exploit all the possibilities of film—its rhythm and tempo.[3]

Urazov of course did not understand that Vertov's celebrated short rhythmic montage was now under suspicion with the onset of the "second period" of newsreels. With the appearance of *The Fall of the Romanov Dynasty*, Shub dotted all the i's; the period of canonisation of "long sequence" montage had begun.

The reaction of left-wing critics to the films of Vertov was determined to a considerable extent by the conception of artistic evolution formulated by OPOYaZ (the Society for the Study of the Theory of Poetic Language) and used by LEF (the Left Front of the Arts). According to this conception, in artistic culture, periods of the dominance of raw material alternate with periods of the dominance of the construction. The LEF group considered that culture was entering a period of the dominance of *material*. Shklovsky wrote at the beginning of 1926: "Soon we will consider a joke to be not a witty communication, but those facts which are published in the trivial information columns of the newspapers."[4] This would mean the final death of construction as the foundation of textual organisation. The newspaper would become a model for the artistic text; and not only the newspaper but also collections of reminiscences, letters, or any documentary material.[5] Osip Brik noted in 1927:

> the integrity [of a work] is achieved by means of the repression of the individual characteristics of the researched material. But with increasing interest in this raw material the extent of this reprocessing should certainly be limited. People will not allow the plot to mutilate the real material, they demand that real material should be given to them in its original State... That is why people prefer to have poorly linked real facts in all their reality to dealing with a well-ordered plot construction into which these facts have been squeezed, like Procrustes' bed.[6]

The poetical montage of Vertov had in essence transcended the autonomy and self-sufficient character of the material, restoring the primary role of the construction.[7] This "recidivist construction" was called by Shklovsky "the infantile disease of plot-less production."[8] The attempt to restore significance to the document as raw material both motivated criticism of the rhythmic and pathetic montage of Vertov and the return to a more simplistic montage of long sequences. Shklovsky wrote: "We are not able to see how the Tungus people eating raw meat wipe their lips and hands with earth, because with Vertov's method in order to show such an incident you would immediately have to show a bourgeois character wiping his lips with some kind of very fine towel."[9]

Raw material remained simply material until it could be carefully examined. This examination allowed the construction to be marginalised in the film. The length of the edited sequence became one of the main formal achievements of Shub. Lev Kuleshov wrote: "Events must be shown so that they can be well examined."[10] He noted this quality in particular in Shub's work, while Mikhail Kaufman "has not grown out of his inclination towards rapid montage." In Kaufman's work "the best sequences are too short—you cannot examine them properly."[11] In 1929 Shub herself formulated the basic aim of her montage: "emphasis on the fact is an emphasis not only to show the fact, but to enable it to be examined and, having examined it, to be kept in mind . . . ."[12]

This emphasis on examination has fundamental significance. She presented the raw material of newsreels as something alienated from the viewer and director, as some kind of unknown, alien and inert object, at which one must look askance. Shklovsky formulated the need for alienation of the material with typical expressiveness: "In art it is most necessary to maintain the pathos of distance and not to tie oneself up too closely. It is necessary to maintain an ironic relationship to one's material and not allow it to get to you. Just as in boxing or fencing."[13] Kuleshov in effect polemicising with Vertov, makes the same point in a different way:

> The non-played film must not demonstrate the subjective impression of the artist on events however correct his artistic convictions may be. The newsreel must accurately demonstrate events and the form of montage of the newsreel is defined not by the author but by the raw material.[14]

This purging of subjectivity from the newsreels, this setting of a distance from the raw material in the cinema of Shub, was achieved by one other essential characteristic: her use of the films of others—that is, ready-made material. A document is identified with reality in such a way that it is understood as material seen by others. The editor's view of the "second-hand" images is substituted for the view of the editor herself on reality. In this context one can see the meaning of Shklovsky's accusations against Vertov that he was ruining the film archives. So in fact the film archive in an unexpected way became an analogue of reality—a place for the preservation of "second-hand" images.

The establishment of film archives became the necessary condition for the further progress of cinema. The archive thus acquired an exclusive significance going far beyond the limitations of a place merely for the preservation of films. As this aspect of film theory in the 1920s has not yet attracted the attention of scholars, it merits closer attention.

Appeals to shoot newsreels were from the very beginning of the 1920s a commonplace of left-wing cinema manifestos. But it was from precisely the second half of the decade that the process of the creation of a film began more and more often to be divided into two stages. The first consisted of a chaotic and total fixation with newsreels which should then be gathered into the film archives and catalogued. The second stage was connected with the editing of these "second-hand" newsreels by a director-editor, the author of the film. The first gathering of material in general was not subordinated to any particular artistic goal. Ideally it would be achieved by thousands of people unconnected one with another. Sergei Tretyakov wrote:

> The masses of photo-enthusiasts, of reporters and thousands of workers' correspondents, for all their greyness and lack of qualifications—these are the potential fact-makers. Their qualifications must be raised and they will then be more valuable for a real socialisation of art than any highly qualified master from the world of art or literature.[15]

The virtue of these little "fact-makers" was that they had no aesthetic context and so could produce an undistorted document.

The experience of Shub showed that from then on the best films had to be made out of the raw material of the film archives. But the scarcity of this material held back the development of the cinema. Mayakovsky called for money to be redirected from art cinema to newsreels: "This will ensure the making of such fine films as *The Fall of the Romanov Dynasty, The Great Way* (*Velikii put'* 1927), etc."[16] V. Fefer agreed with the poet: ". . . newsreels must be filmed not only for the present day but also with a view to future large-scale newsreel compilation films."[17] But Brik was most consistent:

> Of course the most radical step of all would be to close all the cinema studios and send the cameramen out to film real things, then in a short time we would have dozens of such "victories" as that over the Romanov dynasty. But, if that is not possible, then we ought to be able to reduce work in the studios by fully 50% in favour of work on actual reality.[18]

The most striking point in these declarations was the emphasis that work on present-day films should practically stop and that cinema should begin to work for the future so that "in the course of time" they could acquire more masterpieces in the spirit of Shub. The document not only became alienated from the director, it became a *document from the past*. The reflection of contemporary reality became impossible. "The pathos of distance" about which Shklovsky spoke, became the pathos of a *temporal* distance. The "other" is transformed into the "past." When in the discussions in LEF this pathos of temporal distance became generally accepted, one "outsider," L. Esakia, was unable to hold back her surprise:

> Shub declares that, as our epoch is very interesting, we must select from it for the future, i.e. photograph everything and preserve it so that in future people can have some understanding of our epoch. This already becomes simply working for the archives.[19]

Esakia accurately perceived the paradox in the logic: the importance of the present day demanded the storing of raw material for the future. The present epoch could not be reflected on the screen as it had not been turned into raw material for the archives. From this came the imperative demand—speed up the archivisation of present day material. But this conclusion showed that the archival film collection was in essence equated with reality. It had to include as huge a spectrum of phenomena as actuality itself and these phenomena had to be in a "raw" and unworked condition.

The archive had to have an all-embracing character also because at any given time nobody could say what theme would be topical in 10 years' time. All actuality had to be fixed on film without any selection. Tretyakov concluded on this theme in 1927:

> They say now that it was difficult to edit the film *The Great Way* because ten years ago people did not know what was important for them to film. But if, let us say, we win our struggle for newsreels, then are you certain that people will be any happier to receive our archive in ten years'

> time? Perhaps ten years ago people also considered that they were filming in the ideal way... Perhaps in ten years' time the broadening of a vein on the cheek of a People's Commissar during a speech will be very important—but we will not have filmed it.[20]

Posing the question in this way introduced into the cinematic consciousness one essential conflict. This was the conflict between the film as a strictly dated event on the one hand, and of the raw material as a document with a non-temporal, eternal significance on the other. The material must potentially contain all the various possibilities of its interpretation; and on the strength of this it transcended temporal measurement. This transcendental quality was particularly paradoxical because it had to be connected to the time and place of its creation—and catalogued. Tretyakov asserted: "For newsreels it is important to know that a certain person is shown on the screen at a certain time and place doing something. If this 'definition' of the shot disappears, then it becomes generalised and we look at it as de-personalised and typical."[21] But this "definition" of the document irrevocably relating it to the past also provided that alienated distance which made the material eternal and thus distinct from film expressing a transient, topical point of view of the material.

This confict was expressed in the most radical and even fantastic way by Grigori Boltyansky:

> Genuinely eternal "film artefacts," as it is fashionable to say in cinema, cannot be edited out of newsreel material. All such works, edited from raw material according to a particular plan, will be significant only from the point of view of social psychology and the propaganda tasks of a particular year or two. In a year's time somebody else will demand a different form, a different combination of material. But the newsreel film can again and again be revived, broken down into its constituent parts (its raw material) and presented to us in other combinations. The raw material of newsreels has permanent value in contrast to the material of art films. There is no such thing as an "eternal" edited newsreel cine-artefact and here is the tragedy of the greatest master of the editing of newsreel pictures, Comrade Vertov. He cannot understand and will not reconcile himself to the fact that *Cine-Eye* and *Cine-Pravda* will perish after a while and their negatives will be broken up into their original constituent elements. And this is inevitable as only the raw material itself has basic value in the newsreel.... From this arises the effort and struggle to ensure that the raw material, which for decades will provide opportunities for it to be combined in different ways, should be preserved in the same form and under the same title as when it was filmed and in particular that it should be preserved from destruction.[22]

In the choice between film and film archive the preference here was definitely for the film archive as a metaphor of reality—the source of films and the place of their destruction. Films were born from the film archives as from the earth, in order to return again to them. The *eternal* document absorbed the *transient* film. Such a position allowed the question of the limitations of the archival material to be decided in its own way. In so far as the material was understood as raw material for permanent re-combination, the film archive became an endless and inexhaustible source for the future film-maker. The "second-hand" could never be integrated into "one's own"—the real work of the author—sooner or later it would again be alienated from the author's point of view and return to its non-temporal encapsulated autonomy.

As well as the re-combination of material there existed another inexhaustible means for the acquisition of films. Viktor Pertsov proposed that the film collection should be understood as a kind of Borges-like universe: "Of course the theme can cut up the film archive as it were vertically (historically) or in any direction."[23] The dismemberment of the film was turned into an essential phase of the establishment of the film. The specifically archival operation of cataloguing the material began to be understood as a stage in the generation of the text.

Shklovsky described the significance of *The Fall of the Romanov Dynasty* for instance in these terms: "The catalogue of the film [the newsreel material] which was obtained as a result of the viewing was a pure bonus,"[24] and: "In general what lies in the cellars and film collections is passed through a selective, intelligent film-reeler window, collected on montage lists, and is more interesting than what the studio produces."[25] This comment was indicative: the raw material gathered from the montage lists was more interesting than the finished film. The catalogue was more important than the text. Pertsov showed that the catalogue was not the film. But in itself this proof was more than eloquent. He wrote:

> Making the catalogue of cuttings is the job of the archive, which can from time to time make some kind of exhibition of the facts selecting cuttings on a particular theme—for instance an exhibition of filmed landscapes. But such an exhibition has nothing in common with a film picture as an organic whole built up on the basis of montage."[26]

Montage was of course always described as the highest stage of organisation of the text and something organic and ideally complete. But montage as formulated by the LEF-ists in the second half of the 1920s differed little in essence from the principles of archival cataloguing. This was the explanation of Pertsov's attempts to prove that the catalogue was still not a film. The fact is that LEF—and not only they—more and more propagandised the principle of *thematic montage* which was in essence analogous to the thematic selection of material in a catalogue.

The thematic principle was put forward primarily as an antidote to subjectivity in the selection of material, to guard against the danger of abstraction. The selection of material by theme was understood as something arising from the raw material itself and not connected with the will of the artist. The material should catalogue itself so that the will of the archivist doing the cataloguing could in essence be disregarded. Already in 1925 Vertov defended *Cine-Pravda* in the following way:

> Enemies attacking *Cine-Pravda* have mainly pointed out that it is made up of earlier "chance" filmed material. According to us, this means that it is organised from chunks of life into the theme and not the other way round. That is our virtue and not our weakness . . .[27]

In 1929 in the pages of the Leningrad journal *Zhizn' iskusstva* (*Artistic Life*) a polemic developed over the problem of raw material in cinema, which began with an article by Mikhail Bleiman "Down with Raw Material." This polemic is interesting in that it clearly demonstrates the emerging approach to the question of thematic montage. Bleiman seemed to be protesting against the fetishism of raw material: "Being hypnotised by the material prevents the elucidation of what is essentially important in it and an insistent emphasis on that. The raw material of a picture is not regulated, it is not co-ordinated, there is no focus on a conclusion, in fact there is no theme. Most of our pictures are without themes."[28] His criticism of the fetishism of raw material was certainly not made from a standpoint of support for its re-shaping by montage. For Bleiman it was simply a question of the "regulation" of the material according to its themes.

E. Arnoldi entered the discussion and took essentially the same position, but defined it more precisely in his characteristic manner:

> ...facts speak for themselves, but conclusions are drawn by the viewer. The task of the artist is not to pre-digest these conclusions through his attitudes, but to suggest them through the correct selection of facts...Themes grow out of the factual material, they must skilfully select it and not clash with it.[29]

Thus the themes themselves arose out of the raw material. The task of the artist was only to select facts according to the themes that grew out of the material. It was still a question essentially of the same "artistic" cataloguing. Adrian Piotrovsky brought the discussion to an end when he declared that a new period in the development of Soviet cinema had begun, which he called the period of "thematic cinema." He asserted that Soviet cinema was originally formed "in a country overflowing with a gigantic number of new facts, new vital events and phenomena."[30] This flood of facts had led to "the tyranny of documentalism" which now had to be succeeded by the "thematisation" (*tematizatsiya*) of facts.

This growth of emphasis on theme as a montage principle growing out of the material itself, also made it necessary to allow the viewer to examine the material and thus established a montage of long sequences.

In 1930 Shklovsky spoke about his working methods. He hung up sheets of paper giving quotations on the wall of his room and carefully read them for a long time in order to understand them more profoundly: "They hung on the wall for a long time. I grouped them together, hung them side by side and eventually the connections became apparent."[31] Shklovsky organised a distinctive exhibition of "second-hand" film off-cuts like that which the film archivist Pertsov had called for. The "second-hand" material, the film quotations, acquired a self-contained meaning. Fetishism towards the material which, according to this idea, had to be overcome by "thematisation" would become an important stage in the formation of new catalogues. Boris Arvatov criticised LEF for this new fetishism towards the document: "...they teach us to savour the "genuine" peasant and the "genuine" Cézanne; a "chunk" of reality, just like a "chunk" of landscape...[32] Dmitri Levonevsky noted "Objects grow out of their modest essence, swell into fetishes, fetishes secure their immanent development and so the super-Utilitarianism of LEF unexpectedly joins hands with the idealist."[33] Thus the self-definition of the raw material into themes could also be defined as the "immanent development" of a fetish.

Brik, in the end, arrived at a basic formulation of the meaning of raw material: "In newsreels every separate section is comprehensible and complete in itself. Putting the sections in order in the newsreel film only alters the ease and convenience of reading the material as a whole, but the meaning of the material does not depend on it."[34] This 1927 formula declaratively rejected all previous theories of montage from Kuleshov and Vertov to Eisenstein.[35] As "second-hand" material, the film quotations were completely autonomous of the montage, their meaning was encapsulated in them and could not be changed. The model for montage thus finally became cataloguing.

In 1928 LEF issued a manifesto film *The Glass Eye* (*Steklyannyi glaz*) directed by Lily Brik and Vitali Zhemchuzhny. The film was in two parts: first, a parody on a game showing what went on behind the scenes; and then an apologia for newsreels. The newsreel part did not include any newly filmed frames at all and used, as the caption made clear, foreign newsreels and parts of Kaufman's film *Moscow* (*Moskva*, 1927). The most striking thing in the film was the absolute consistency with which the principle of thematic montage was implemented, turning the newsreel part of the film into a perfect imitation of a film archive catalogue. First they showed the coronation of Nicholas II and the Durbar for King George V in India, then fragments of old newsreels and finally they opened the catalogue: "To the Glass-Eye all corners of the world are visible—the Tropics . . . followed by African newsreels. "Countries of the North" with appropriate newsreels, and so on through the catalogue with films under water, scientific films, the towns of Asia and Europe, and so on. It is interesting that one of the characters introduced into the film was that of a cameraman, played by Anatoli Golovnya, who worked with Pudovkin. In this way it was emphasised that the frames of the newsreels were "second-hand."[36] *The Glass Eye* only demonstrated as a principle what LEF had propagandised in other films as well, such as *The Land of the Chuvash* (*Strana Chuvashii*, 1927) directed by Vladimir Korlevich which was also constructed as a catalogue.

This episode from the history and theory of Soviet cinema could be considered insignificant were it not for certain symptomatic indications in it. These were firstly the conscious, declarative retrogression of the cinema form essentially to pre-montage positions and secondly the restoration of the archaic kind of cinema text achieved by the most radical left-wing of the artistic avant-garde from the mid-1920s. It is notable that this restoration was achieved in parallel with a recognition of the impossibility of working with contemporary, actual reality and a principled turn to "second-hand" material. A paradoxical situation arose in which the revolutionary artist was not himself able to look at the world but had to introduce between himself and the world an anonymous and inert mediator. Actuality had to be subjected to a conscious alienation.

It would be easiest of all to explain this situation by reference to the crisis of revolutionary art, its exclusion from the processes of active constructive life. But this crisis apparently had its internal as well as external causes. The LEF artist formulated his task as a task of permanently reconstructing and transforming life. In this perspective, life performed the role of raw material. But the raw material, as something destined for deformation and alteration, could not be their own material, it had to be given as second-hand material. Life demanding re-structuring should be understood only as "second-hand" life. From this arose the paradoxical consequence that the artists who took up the most active positions in life had constantly to subject life to alienation and to convert it into "second-hand" material.

It is significant that in 1926 Sergei Vasiliev, who was later to be the co-director of *Chapayev*, compared his work on the re-editing of foreign films, with the revolutionary transformation of life: "it is now nine years since the proletarian revolution brought out its scissors to 're-edit' in defiance of everything one sixth of the world in its own fashion, and perhaps the time is not far away when the other five sixths will also be taken up with 're-editing.'"[37] To re-edit a *second-hand* film was the same as to re-edit *Soviet* reality.

This situation of *constant* reshaping of "second-hand" material in the tenth year of the Revolution—the apogee of the new tendencies was reached in 1927—developed into a consciousness of the transience of the reshaped text as opposed to the eternalism of the "second-hand" material. The raw material kept its significance, its unchanging character, it was continually returned to the metaphorical film archive at the same time as the films, in which it had been reshaped, aged, disintegrated, and died. The dynamism of the struggle as an unceasing movement paradoxically established the alienated material as eternal and unchanging. The preservation of the character of left-wing art as one of struggle and dynamism up to 1927 was distracted by the involuntary recognition of the stability of actuality. The "second-hand" became eternal.

This crisis of artistic consciousness amongst left-wing artists involuntarily prepared the way for the art of the coming decades, which more and more evidently combined within the limits of Stalinist classicism the alienated stability of the material with the ideology of continuous struggle and progress.

NOTES

1. T. Selezneva, *Kinomysl' 1920-kh godov* (*Film Theory in the* 1920s) (Leningrad, 1972), p. 43. See also: J. Leyda, *Films Beget Films* (London, 1964), p. 41.
2. V. Shklovskii, *Kuda shagaet Dziga Vertov?* (*Where is Dziga Vertov Striding?*), *Sovetskii ekran* (*Soviet Screen*) 14 August 1926, p. 4; translated in: R. Taylor & I. Christie (Eds), *The Film Factory: Russian and Soviet cinema in documents, 1896-1939* (London and Cambridge, MA, 1988), pp. 151–152.
3. I. Urazov, *On shagaet k zhizni, kak ona est'* (*Striding Towards Life as It Really Is*), *Sovetskii ekran*, No. 32, 10 August 1926, p. 6.
4. V. Shklovskii, *Gamburgskii schet* (*The Hamburg Reckoning*) (Moscow, 1990), p. 195.
5. Fetishism towards the "newspaper model" aroused a natural protest from some critics who, with the aim of discrediting the "newspaper" montage of "second-hand" documents, began to place at the centre of the creative process the person of the cameraman, who, as it were, laid down the principle of montage at the time of filming through his composition of the frame. Amongst these critics was D. Borisov who wrote:

   > The author of these lines happened to see how, out of 20 leading articles in a certain newspaper, some fellow made up the twenty-first with the help of scissors. Is this art? No, it's simply a trick. In *A Sixth Part of the World* [*Shestaya chast' mira*, 1926] about 30–40 per cent of the whole film consists of so-called "counter-types" (that is off-cuts from various films), then there are bits shot by dozens of cameramen, filming according to *their own* discretion (usually alongside the cameraman is the director who is also struggling with the composition of the frame), and none of these are linked together by a common artistic approach. The final work of the director here consisted in editorial work with scissors on "second-hand" material, in the shooting of which the director had not participated. And so here again is the same kind of trick.

   D. Borisov, *Shestaya chast' mira (osoboe mnenie)* (*A Sixth Part of the World* [*A Personal Opinion*]), *Kino*, No. 3, 15 January 1927, p. 2.
6. O. Brik, *Fiksatsiya fakta* (*The Fixation of Fact*), *Novyi Lef*, Nos. 11-12, 1927, pp. 48-50, partially translated in: Taylor & Christie, pp. 184-185.
7. Compare this with Ilya Ehrenburg's characterisation of Vertov: "His practice is abstract. . . . The works of Vertov are defined as the fixing of reality. . . . In fact this is a laboratory analysis of the world, complex and poignant. It is what Cubism was to painting'; I. Erunburg, *Materializatsiya fantastiki* (*The Materialisation of the Fantastic*) (Moscow and Leningrad, 1927), p. 17.
8. Shklovskii, *Gamburgskii Schet*, p. 401.
9. Reprinted in: Shklovskii, *Za 60 let. Raboty o kino* (*Through 60 Years. Works on Cinema*) (Moscow, 1985), p. 361.
10. L. V. Kuleshov, *Ekran segodnya* (*The Screen Today*, 1927), reprinted in: *Sobranie sochinenii v 3-kh tomakh* (*Collected Works in 3 Volumes*), Vol. 1 (Moscow, 1987), p. 117.
11. Ibid., p. 118.
12. E. Shub, *Zhizn' moya—kinematograf* (*Cinematography—My Life*), (Moscow, 1972), p. 268.
13. Shklovskii, *Gamburgskii schet*, p. 218. The distancing of the material and the reality identified with it could also take purely physical forms. For instance the Constructivist Alexei Gan thought that the best sequence in Vertov's *Cine-Pravda* was the episode with the display of the German Junkers aeroplane, which "simultaneously . . . served as a subject for observation and also as a means of observing from the air the ground, a town, people, in fact everything in general which could be called our real everyday life"; A. Gan, *Nashe na ekrane* (*Our Life on the Screen*), *Ermitazh*, No. 8, 4–10 July 1922, p. 15. "Real everyday life" was what was seen from the aeroplane and yet was what was at the greatest distance from the observer.
14. Kuleshov, p. 117.
15. S. Tretyakov, *Prodolzhenie sleduet* (*To Be Continued*), *Novyi Lef*, No. 12, 1928, p. 4.
16. V. Mayakovskii, *Polnoe sobranie sochinenii* (*Complete Collected Works*), Vol. 12 (Moscow, 1959), p. 147.
17. V. Fefer, *10 let* (*Ten Years*), *Sovetskii ekran*, No. 44, 1 Nov. 1927, p. 6.
18. O. M. Brik, *Pobeda fakta* (*The Victory of the Fact*), *Kino*, No. 14, 5 April 1927, p. 3.

19. *Lef i Kino* (*LEF and Cinema*), *Novyi Lef,* Nos. 11–12, 1927, p. 66. Brik openly spoke of the need "to film for the archive"; ibid., p. 65.
20. Ibid., p. 52.
21. Ibid., p. 54.
22. G. Boltyanskii, *Mysli o kinokhronike* (*Thoughts on Newsreels*), *Sovetskii ekran,* No. 17, 26 April 1927, p.14.
23. V. Pertsov, "*Igra" i demonstratsiya* ("*Play" and Demonstration*), *Novyi Lef,* Nos. 11–12, 1927, p. 34.
24. V. Shklovskii, *Kartina—dokument* (*The Picture—a Document*), *Kino,* No. 11, 12 March 1927, p. 2.
25. Ibid.
26. Pertsov, p. 35.
27. A. Belenson, *Kino segodnya. Ocherki sovetskogo kino-iskusstva* (*Kuleshov—Vertov—Eisenstein* (*Cinema Today. Essays in Soviet Cinema Art [Kuleshov, Vertov, Eisenstein]*) (Moscow, 1925), p. 35.
28. M. Bleiman, *Doloi material!* (*Down with Raw Material!*), *Zhizn' iskusstva,* No. 32, 11 August 1929, p. 5.
29. E. Arnoldi, *Fakty—veshch' upryamaya* (*Facts are Stubborn Things*), *Zhizn' iskusstva,* No. 34, 25 August 1929, pp. 6-7.
30. A. Piotrovskii, *Kinematografiya temy* (*Thematic Cinema*), *Zhizn' iskusstva,* No. 36, 8 September 1929, p. 6.
31. *Kak my pishem* (*How We Write*), (Moscow, 1989), p. 185.
32. B. Arvatov, *Kinoplatforma* (*Cinema Platform*), *Novyi Lef,* No. 3, 1928, p. 35. Pertsov's "film archive exhibition" was a concrete expression of the tendency towards the alienation of material. Newsreels should be examined in such an exposition in order to elucidate the themes in them, in the sense of some idea and some kind of extra content beyond the obvious. The idea of a cinema museum of the current time had already been expressed in 1925! "Thus a museum. A museum of living people . . ." *Kadr. Kinoletopis* (*The Frame. A Cinema-Chronicle*), *Sovetskii ekran,* No. 7, 12 May 1925, p. 2. Kazimir Malevich in the same year protested violently against a museum approach to actuality in the cinema, considering that Vertov's demonstration of objects "as such" liberated it from an idea (and theme). In this he saw the difference between Vertov and those artists who "think that the human ugly mug is that epitome in which the ideal artistic form exists, and that this ugly mug—and all the everyday rubbish and bazaar hurly-burly which surround it—are the essence of their life": K. Malevich, *Kinozhurnal ARK,* No. 10, 1925, p. 9. He also ridiculed those "factologists" who stood "in the waiting rooms of the deputy directors of life in order to engrave images containing their 'idea.' " In this perspective documents of everyday life had no kind of documentary or archival significance at all. Compare this with the view of Tretyakov who considered that even the veins on the cheek of a People's Commissar should be included in the universal film archive. If one takes the point of view of Malevich then the "abstraction" of the document by Vertov could be understood as a "de-fetishisation" of the document and as the destruction of its exhibition value. Such a document according to Shklovsky "we would not manage to see." It is significant that in 1929 K. Feldman contrasted Vertov as an artist working on reality with those who took second-hand "landscapes" as material: K. Fel'dman, *V sporakh o Vertove* (*The Controversy over Vertov*), *Kino i kul'tura,* Nos. 5–6, 1929, p. 12.
33. D. Levonevskii, *Literatura fakta* (*The Literature of the Fact*), *Zhizn' iskusstva,* No. 33, 18 August 1929, p. 5.
34. O. Brik, *Protiv zhanrovykh kartinok* (*Against Genre Pictures*), *Kino,* No. 27, 5 July 1927, p. 3.
35. Eisenstein was fully conscious of the role thrust on Shub in the discrediting of the montage method espoused by him and ironically referred to it in a letter to her on 15 May 1928: "I had entirely forgotten to whom I am writing. Here we have the non-players, we have the *documenters* . . . Not a word about feelings, my letter is only *documentation* . . . it is not a letter, but an *Abkhazian document* . . . and in so far as construction is still "not in fashion," let it be . . . a *procurement for an Abkhazian document* . . ." Shub, p. 372.
36. The transformation of the cameraman into a character in the film was most consistently pursued in Vertov's *The Man with the Movie Camera* (*Chelovek s kino-apparatom,* 1929) and fulfilled the obvious function of alienating the material. It has something in common with Vertov's ideology of the camera as some kind of super-eye. The material seen by such a mechanical eye is declaratively alienated from the subjective human vision. The person of the cameraman, although he was immersed in the thick of life, paradoxcially gave the material the character of "second-hand" visuals. This cameraman was the hero of the film in contrast to the unseen director-editor. The latter was the bearer of knowledge, the elucidator of the theme which was unknown to the cameraman, who was, as it were, immersed in the material and formed a part of it. In this context the comment of Osip Brik about Vertov's cameraman, Mikhail Kaufman, was appropriate: "Kaufman was not aware of the theme for which he was producing his shots or the meaning these shots were supposed to give to nature." *Ring Lefa* (*The LEF Ring*), *Novyi Lef,* No. 4, 1928, p. 28, translated in Taylor & Christie, p. 226. This fact, that the theme of the shooting was not known to the cameraman, gives his productions the genuine character of "second-hand" material.
37. G. N. & S. D. Vasil'ev, *Sobranie sochinenii v 3-kh tomakh* (*Collected Works in 3 Vols*), Vol. 1, (Moscow, 1981), p. 157.

27

JORIS IVENS

THE MAKING OF *RAIN* (1969)

It took more than one film to teach me to work with actors, but the important accomplishments for me in this film were some successes in photographic ingenuity. In order to film the movement of the sea and the surf in a dramatic, subjective way I constructed a rubber sack with a glass front to contain my head and arms and camera. This enabled me to shoot while breakers rolled over my camera and myself, producing shots of sea movement with a violent quality that nobody had seen before on the screen.

Mannus Franken did much of the direction for me. It was good training to work with faces and human features and with reactions so soon after the mechanized movements on *The Bridge*. Creating certain moods of a fishing community in a minimum of shots was a challenging problem for a young film maker: a lone dog in an empty street; a sleepy pan-shot along the straight lines of the tiny roofs; a single child in a spotless court; a line of dignified fishermen walking stiffly in their black Sunday clothes against the white austere architecture of the village church. For us *Breakers* was a good film—although I remember that we thought the Filmliga audiences didn't like it because they had become a bit snobbish.

My next film started from a far more trivial motive. While on location for *Breakers* we needed the sun, instead we got rain—those long days of rain that you have in Holland. The idea—let's make a film about the damn rain—came quite naturally.

Although this idea arose almost as a joke, when I returned to Amsterdam I talked it over with Mannus Franken who sketched an outline. We discussed and revised the outline many times until it became a film for both of us. Unfortunately, Mannus Franken lived in Paris, so the shooting in Amsterdam was done by me alone. Franken however, came to Amsterdam for a short time to assist in the editing.

In making such a film of atmosphere, I found that you couldn't stick to the script and that the script should not get too detailed. In this case, the rain itself dictated its own literature and guided the camera into secret wet paths we had never dreamed of when we outlined the film. It was an unexpectedly difficult subject to tackle. Many artistic problems were actually technical problems and vice versa. Film experience in photographing rain was extremely limited because a normal cameraman stops filming when it begins to rain. When *Rain* was finished and shown in Paris the French critics called it a *ciné-poem* and its structure is actually more that of a poem than the prose of *The Bridge*. Its object is to show the changing face of a city, Amsterdam, during a shower.

The film opens with clear sunshine on houses, canals, and people in the streets. A slight wind rises and the first drops of rain splash into the canals. The shower comes down harder and the people hasten about their business under the protection of capes and umbrellas. The shower ends. The last drops fall and the city's life returns to normal. The only continuity in *Rain* is the beginning, progress, and end of this shower. There are neither titles nor dialogue. Its effects were intended as purely visual. The actors are the rain, the raindrops, wet people, dark clouds, glistening reflections moving over wet asphalt, and so forth. The diffused light on the dark houses along the black canals produced an effect that I never expected. And the whole film gives the spectator a very personal, and subjective vision. As in the lines of Verlaine:

> *Il pleure dans mon cœur,*
> *Comme il pleut sur la ville.*

At that time I lived with and for the rain. I tried to imagine how everything I saw would look in the rain—and on the screen. It was part game, part obsession, part action. I had decided upon the several places in the city I wanted to film and I organized a system of rain watchers, friends who would telephone me from certain sections of town when the rain effects I wanted appeared. I never moved without my camera—it was with me in the office, laboratory, street, train. I lived with it and when I slept it was on my bedside table so that if it was raining when I woke I could film the studio window over my bed. Some of the best shots of raindrops along the slanted studio windows were actually taken from my bed when I woke up. All the new problems in this film sharpened my observation and also forced me to relax the rigid and over-analytical method of filming that I had used in *The Bridge*.

With the swiftly shifting rhythm and light of the rain, sometimes changing within a few seconds, my filming had to be defter and more spontaneous. For example, on the big central square of Amsterdam I saw three little girls under a cape and the skipping movements of their legs had the rhythm of raindrops. There had been a time when I thought that such good things could be shot tomorrow as well as today; but you soon learn that this is never true. I filmed those girls without a second's hesitation. They would probably never again walk at that hour on the square, or when they did it wouldn't be raining, and if it was raining they wouldn't have a cape, or skip in just that way, or it would be too dark—or something. So you film it immediately. With these dozens of interrelated factors you get the feeling of shooting—now or never.

Even in that ABC exercise of *The Bridge* I had had a taste of the pure joy a film maker knows when playing around with movements and actions. I was filming a train engine waiting to cross the bridge, stopped by the red signal arm. I wanted to photograph the front of the waiting, puffing engine as if it were the impatient snout of a powerful animal. As I released the motor, smoke came out of the chimney and curled up in black and gray puffs into the air. Instinctively I raised my handcamera in a sort of syncopated swing with the lifting movement of the smoke. The result was pretty good, an interesting double movement within the frame that I might never have been able to calculate.

It took me about four months to get the footage I needed for *Rain*. To achieve the effect of the beginning of the shower as you now see it in the film I had to photograph at least ten beginnings and out of these ten make the one *film* beginning. The rain itself was a moody actress who had to be humored and who refused anything but a natural make-up. I found that none of the new color-corrective film emulsions on the market were suitable for my rain problems. The old extra-rapid Agfa film with no color correction at all, and used without a filter, gave the best results. All lenses were used with a fully opened diaphragm because most of the work was done with a minimum of light.

It's remarkable how easy it is to forget the most basic elements of your subject and how important those basic elements are to your work. In *Rain* I had to remind myself constantly that rain is wet—so you must keep the screen dripping with wetness—make the audience feel damp and not just dampness. When they think they can't get any wetter, *double* the wetness, show the raindrops falling in the water of the canal—make it super-wet. I was so happy when I noticed at one of the first screenings of the finished film that the audience looked around for their raincoats and were surprised to find the weather dry and clear when they came out of the theatre.

To give the rain its fullest, richest quality I had to make sure that the sunlight that began and ended the film showed its typical differences. You have to catch the distinction between sunlight before rain and sunlight after rain; the distinction between the rich strong enveloping sunlight before the rain and the strange dreamy yellow light afterwards. I know that this sounds over-subtle but it is important and you have to be aware of it and remember to catch these subtleties with your camera.

In addition to careful photography, these nuances in light quality can be emphasized in movement. For example, I heightened the sharp quality of the sunlight that precedes the rain by keenly defined movements of light and shadow. The sharp dark shadow of a footbridge rips across the wide deck of a boat passing swiftly underneath. This movement is cut off by immediate contact with a close-up of another boat moving in an opposite diagonal across the entire screen. As the rain begins I added to the changes in light, a change in these movements emphasizing the leisurely movement of barges, wet puffs of smoke and waving reflections in the water. When cutting these shots I was careful to avoid abrupt contrasts, letting them build up leisurely on the screen.

Another interesting thing I learned about the values of shots and movements was their relation to humor. In editing I guided the eyes of the audience to the right of the screen by a close shot of water gushing out of a drainpipe, following this immediately by a shot of a dripping wet dog running along. My intention was merely to pick up the movement and rhythm in the pipe shot with the shot of the dog and my simple movement continuity always got a laugh. If I had been a more skillful editor at that time I would have made a more conscious use of such an effect, but I was still learning. I was still too preoccupied with movement and rhythm to be sufficiently aware of the special film capacities for communicating the humorous movements around us.

However, *Rain* did teach me a great deal about film emotion—much more than the emotional story of the *Breakers*. In editing *The Bridge* I had discovered the sad effect achieved by the rhythmic repetition of slow heavy movements. In *Rain* I consciously used heavy dark drops dripping in big pear-shaped forms at long intervals across the glass of the studio window to produce the melancholy feeling of a rainy day. The opposite effect of happiness or gaiety in a spring shower could be produced by many bright small round drops pounding against many surfaces in a variety of shots.

To strengthen the continuity of *Rain* I used the repetition of a second visual motif—birds flying in the sunlight and then as the rain starts, a flock moving against the gray sky (continuing a rhythm indicated in the previous shot by leaves rustling in the wind). During the storm I showed one or two birds flying restlessly about. After the rain has stopped there is a shot of some birds sitting quietly on the wet railing of a bridge.

I shot the whole film with my old Kinamo and an American De Vry handcamera. My assistant was a young Chinese sailor, Chang Fai, whom I had met as a waiter in a Chinese restaurant on the Zeedyk. Chang Fai had jumped a large Indies liner in order to stay in Holland and learn a profession before going back to Asia. His main job as my assistant was to hold an umbrella over my camera.

At that time I was living alone in the large attic of an old Amsterdam house opposite the stock exchange. Anyone who could bring some order to my Bohemian home life was welcome. Chang Fai did not speak a word of Dutch, but with a system of gestures we made the following deal: he would keep house for me and cook and I would teach him photography. He learned a great deal more than holding umbrellas over a moving camera. After a while he was able to buy his own camera and as a parting gift at the end of our deal I gave him all the formulae for fine grain development. I doubt if *Rain* could have been made without Chang's carefully held umbrella and his wonderful black soups that cured the flu—a constant by-product of this film.

Made almost entirely as a cameraman's film, *Rain* proved to be successful with audiences. It followed the same distribution channels *The Bridge* had experienced, and was shown in *avant garde* movie theatres throughout Europe and in many ciné clubs. One thing that spectators always commented on was the film's identity with the simple things of daily life—revealing the beauty in these things. It was, I think, a new field for the close-up which until then had been used only for passionate or dramatic emphasis. These close-ups of every day objects made *Rain* an important step in my development.

The most serious criticism against the film was its lack of "content." In a certain sense this was an exact criticism. I failed to emphasize sufficiently human beings' reactions to rain in a big city. Everything was subordinated to the esthetic approach. In a way I am glad that I laid a foundation of technical and creative perfection before working on other more important elements. I have since seen too many films so exclusively dependent on content that the available means for film making have been neglected with injury to the content itself.

28

JORIS IVENS

REFLECTIONS ON THE AVANT-GARDE DOCUMENTARY (1931)

I.

Documentary expresses reality in terms of causes and effects. I note, first of all, that documentary film is the only means left to the avant-garde *cinéaste* in his battle against the Big Companies [film production companies], not in so far as they represent a large-scale industry, but because documentary expresses reality as it is while the Big Companies generally produce bad films, because they flatter the public's poor taste by adapting to it, indeed by taking inspiration from it, without seeking to provoke the public to reaction or action.

The avant-garde cinema is a cinema that tends to provoke the interest and response of spectators.

And I call avant-garde that cinema which takes the initiative for progress and safeguards it, as the standard-bearer of cinematographic sincerity. The independent cinema, in effect, operates according to an autocritique, which pushes it to advance; the commercial cinema operates only according to a criterion of success, the criterion of a badly educated public.

The commercial cinema brings about only technical progress. The avant-garde cinema augments that with spiritual or intellectual progress.

II.

The talkie forms the nexus for the future possibilities of television and radio. There are new reasons to battle against the motive of bad taste which places the Big Companies in perpetual danger.

III.

Documentary film is the only positive means left the avant-garde *cinéaste* who wishes to commit himself fully to labor, insofar as he represents the expression of the masses or popular expression in his work.

In effect, since documentary exists chiefly on command, and since it is the industrialist's best means of publicity, the filmmaker has to deal only with one man: a businessman, a stranger to the cinema. So it is in the interest of that filmmaker to make a success of his film, whose truth and documentary nature are simultaneously the sole critierion of that success.

By contrast, when he works for the Big Companies, he finds himself struggling against administrative committees, actors, and censorship. He is restricted, he is no longer independent, but works, so to speak, as a kind of slave. In order to escape this enslavement, he must be so clear-sighted, with respect to the production, that he prevails on his spectator, whether his spectator be an industrialist or an illiterate.

IV.

In the current state of the cinema, documentary provides the best means of discovering the cinema's true paths. It's impossible for it to fall into theater, literature, or music hall entertainment, none of which is cinema.

This argument is quite old, but I find it useful to recall and repeat to myself, since now that the cinema includes sound and voice it risks the same danger that it risked at its birth and which it had gradually left behind.

The cinema is a craft. The independent *cinéaste* is a craftsman. He possesses an essential technical skill, which does not at all exclude the spiritual and intellectual. That's why big industry provides so many blessings for us. A good American cameraman brings more to the cinema than a poet does; he senses himself similar to the medieval worker whose task was to realize the grand idea conceived by the intellectual, thanks to his perfect knowledge of the material world in which he worked. A good cameraman makes a better film than a poet does because he knows his material and technique better, and this advantage opens up new possibilities for him. I would even say that the original conception of a poet may be excellent only by chance, for he doesn't possess the necessary cinematic ways of thinking.

V.

It's impossible for the filmmaker of a documentary to lie, not to be true to life. The material world doesn't support deception: a documentary necessitates the development of the human personality of the *cinéaste* since it is the personality of the artist alone which distinguishes him from both reality and simple recording.

The good filmmaker lives surrounded by the material world, by reality. On each occasion he chooses to interpret only a part of that reality, and the success of his film is then dependent on the confidence of the masses in his personality. Stimulated by this confidence, the human personality of an individual who has chosen some part of reality which seems important to him, and nothing but a part, leaves aside all the rest.

In other films, we don't evaluate the personality of the filmmaker or his fidelity to criteria as real or as significant as this.

VI.

Documentary must not be content to be merely a source of emotion, a literary celebration before the beauty of the material world; but it must certainly provoke latent actions and responses.

Through an excess of individualism and aestheticism, Europe is refractory on the matter of social action in documentary.

I believe then that the development of my ideas, of my cinematic ideal, will be achieved only in Russia, where the masses are accustomed to such activities daily and are able to understand the social truth of documentary.

29

TOM CONLEY

DOCUMENTARY SURREALISM

On *Land Without Bread* (1986)

In a certain fashion the cinema of Surrealism conditioned the great narrative styles that dominated film of the 1930s. Today it can offer ways of theorizing narrative in fictional or feature film. Its legacy is important for the study of the history and technique of documentary cinema, where truth generally takes precedence over the rhetoric articulating its realism. The violence of "facts" in documentaries overwhelms spectators by blinding the critical power of the eye to the esthetics that constitute the very basis of its veracity. Analysis of surreal cinema, it seems, re-establishes that power. In this respect, the legacy of Surrealism seems to be perpetually active; it cannot merely be studied as a moment in an evolution of cinema because it persistently questions the order of any history that would pigeonhole it in the European milieu of the 1920s.

The relationship between Surrealism and documentary cinema is exceptionally productive. Surrealism did not actively pursue the documentary or ethnographic cinema to further its manifesto of 1924. Yet with *Land without Bread* (1932, also titled as *Las Hurdes, Terre sans pain, Tierra sin pan, Unpromised Land*), Buñuel, a signatory of the second *Manifeste du surréalisme*, appears to be one of its most important proponents. *Land without Bread* is absolutely crucial to documentary realism and stands, we shall argue, as a model that tests all *cinéma-vérité*. The paragraphs which follow shall examine the junctures, rifts, or punctuations by which its filmic style appears to be fashioned. Attention will be directed away from the subject of the film—a forlorn corner of Spain in the early 1930s—in order to dwell on some modes that convey the disquiet of its documentary. Five aspects will be taken up: (1) the compositional ensemble and its overall

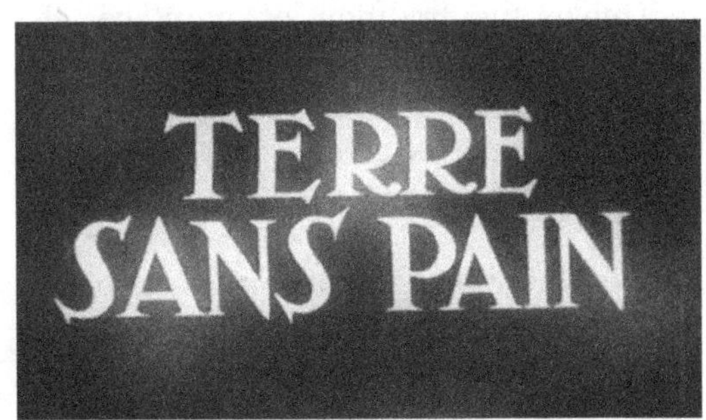

visual effects; (2) the very cursive use of the lap-dissolve; (3) the uncanny framing that both conceals and manifests a cinema of sacrifice (as we shall see, "scapegoating" in a quite literal sense); (4) the breakdown of illusory space through the presence of writing of scripture in the cinematic frame; and (5) the nagging presence of a latently Spanish painterly tradition foregrounding the representation of the Hurdano population.

The Compositional Ensemble

As the appended shot sequence evinces, *Land without Bread* consists of 238 shots over a duration of twenty-seven minutes (or about 865 meters of film). Even if averaged to a mean of seven seconds per shot, the total number would be inordinately high for a documentary. The film abounds with varied shots; its sheer number would lead a viewer to believe that the film is inspired by Eisensteinian montage instead of poetic realism. Cursory viewing proves otherwise, since the impression is one of redundancy, inertia, and unchanging, unmediated portraits of life on the verge of death. It may be that the thematic orientation of *Land without Bread*, dealing unremittingly with a moribund culture that refuses to die in the midst of the "hostile forces" surrounding it, produces an effect of stasis contrary to the liveliness of the *découpage*. Or else, the contradiction between the dizzying ensemble of shots and sequences entirely betrays the deathly interpretation the soundtrack imposes upon the array of images.

Unlike the tradition of montage, the shots rarely depend on each other for their resonance or continuity of meaning. Generally, each is composed as a unified segment carrying rich paradox within itself, as well as in relation to shots both in the immediate context (three to six shots before and after) and in the scope of the entire film (a shot near the end will modulate or rhyme with a scene in the early moments of the exposition). Thus the viewer's eye is asked to extend its field of perception beyond the scope of narrative and montage. Only one sequence shows signs of cross-cutting, and this is in the final seconds (shots 222–236), where the Hurdano household, finishing its evening meal and preparing for slumber, is punctuated by the arrival of an old lady knelling death in an adjacent street. Yet even this hardly appears contrived enough to hasten the viewer to associate the end of the film with a cherished Iberian topos of sleep bringing on dreams of death or monsters. The closeups of the old hag are too deliciously creatural and the bedtime is too staged to allow us to fall into a commonplace. We wonder how the lighting is achieved so well in *contrejour;* how the locals can mime sleep under the glare of light shed upon them; how the extreme closeup of the old soothsayer's wrinkled face has been shot in the illusion of night. Cinematic issues of composition break the sense of movement inherent to cross-cutting, to the point that the spectator can wonder if the bell of death and slumber is apposed to the real death and sleep of the film—that is, its own end. In the mechanism of transfer common to surreal cinema, the contiguity of this sequence in respect to the end of the film suggests that we are being chimed to sleep, that we are seeing ourselves die when the film ends.

Such an obviously loose or open montage could suggest that the director is crafting a double-edged film. On one side, *Land without Bread* is shot in a style that conveys "reality" by virtue of deep-focus photography, where everything in the field of view is focused and subject to documentary report, and where the shot itself has content ample enough to be deciphered patiently. In this latter sense the view of the Hurdano world would depend on the building block of poetic realism, the long take, which is also associated with Renoir, Flaherty, Wyler, or other champions of reality. But the shooting sequence tells us it does not: with the 238 shots in twenty-nine minutes, there is (seemingly) hardly any sign of the long take, or even a shot of teasingly extended duration—from ten to forty seconds—that we would align with the realistic tradition. Hence, the other side: Buñuel forces the viewer to compress the effects of the long take into disgruntling rapidity. Most of the shots suggest careful (as we shall note, painterly) composition, but the editing either does not allow the viewer to comprehend them in rational cinematic terms, or else it radicalizes the realistic style, defining and distorting its principles simultaneously, somewhat before the style gains historical currency.

The latter might be due to the surreal backdrop informing the film. Evidently many visual compositions reiterate scenes from *Un Chien andalou* (shots 11, 102, 136, etc.) and *L'Age d'or* (the bull exiting into the street in shot 11

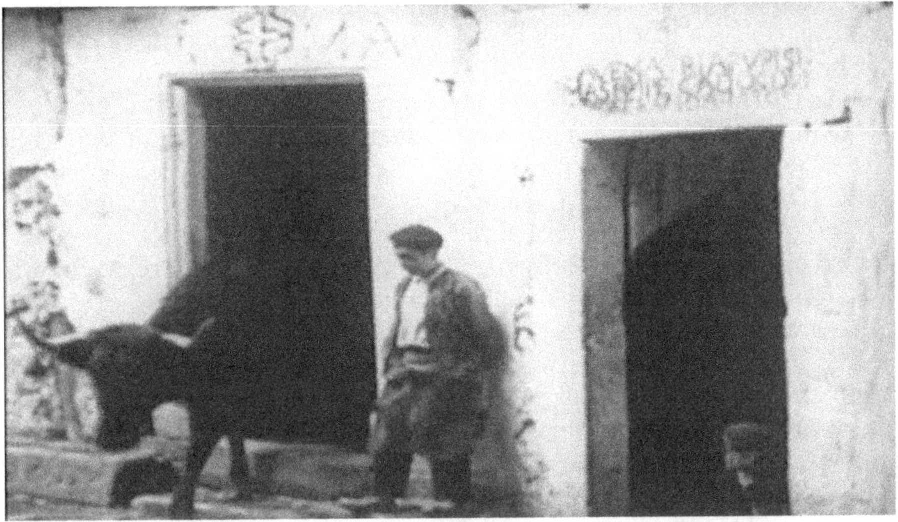

FIGURE 29.1 Shot 11 from *Land without Bread*. Still capture from digital file.

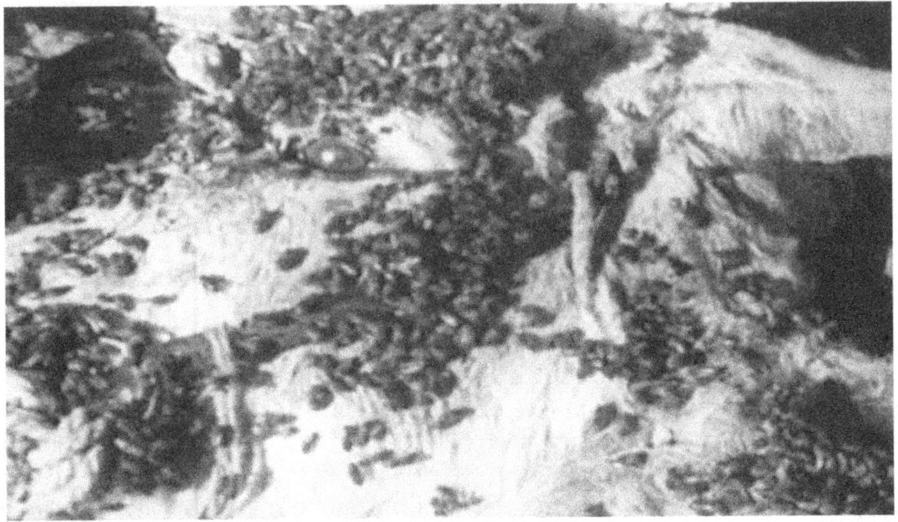

FIGURE 29.2 Shot 136. Still capture from DVD.

recalling the plow Gaston Modot tosses from the apartment window, or the rocky landscape in the mountain goat sequence reiterating the seaside of rocks and bishops' bones), but they are executed in a context of veracity. By reducing the future trademark of realism to a minimum, the film adduces how the oneiric camera, seen in the immense field of unmediated contradictions, yields documentary reality. All the more astonishing—and this point is advanced to insist on the pertinence of *Land without Bread* in the tradition of documentary cinema, which criticism does not emphasize enough—is that truth is always identified with equilibrium.

The shots have pictural austerity in their tensions of form. All the drastic shifts from closeups or medium shots to extreme long shots (in 46–47, 51–52, 88–89, 152–58, 177–78, 236–37, etc.) are contextualized or softened with fade-outs or infrequent dissolves. Countrysides are intermediate scenes separating the sequences depicting the different activities of everyday life. The balance in the compositions is so striking that every shift can only be smooth, no matter how extreme the gaps are from one sequence to another. Most of the cinematography reflects the intensely unremitting glare of the Spanish sun. High contrasts of light and shade would generally produce a jagged tempo of hard edges in succession; yet the equilibrium of the whole is enhanced by the emphasis on absence of penumbra. Humans are portrayed under a bright sky and are deprived of shadows or soft forms that might modify—or humanize—their depiction. The film disallows any visual redemption of mankind in settings that might offer comfort, relief, or any empathy to be shared among viewers and subjects (especially in shots 4, 13, 21, 40, 62, 81, 87, 95, 126, 156, 158, 211–13, 217, and so forth).

The voice-off establishes the documentary continuity. It tends to freeze the images by directing the viewer's eyes to only several of many elements (generally the human as opposed to the natural or organic or seasonal ones) in frame. Betraying, trivializing, or, better, repressing many of the visuals, it marks a difference of consciousness. When the voice reflects the view of a focused, "Western" or industrial view of continuity, history, culture, human kind, or missionary reason, the visuals provide a rich flow of images exceeding—in pleasure, disgust, wonder, Eros, marvel—what the voice or Brahms's accompaniment cannot express about them. A psychoanalytic process emerges from that difference, but in such a manner that, like the synchronous production of *Civilization and Its Discontents* (also issued in 1932), the film implies that the voice cannot be dissociated from repression of optical splendor. The pictogrammatical element avers to be the film's unconscious; it is evident, clear, and immediately accessible. When disaster or plight is reported (in the British accent of the colonizer), oblivious to what is being said of them, children smile at the camera. They contradict the anthropological project of redemption (most evident in shots 21, 61, 71 or in the dwarf sequence). It would be oversimple to observe that the film scaffolds a double bind in the contradiction between voice and image, as *Land without Bread* does not merely question the viewer's right to see the sacred—hence invisible—side of Hurdano culture. It articulates a highly varied tempo of shifts that modulate repulsion and attraction within a unified narrative.

Lap-Dissolves and Extended Perspectives

Not only a basic unit of perspective in Surrealist cinema, the dissolve provides transitions essential for narrative. It also, paradoxically, allows the greatest initial access to the "other" or obverse side of the composition of *Land without Bread*. The dissolve "opens" the obsessions of the film and places all stages of consciousness, history, and documentary on the same surface. In these transitions the stable relation of a figure to a ground is lost; the image becomes of a texture, but also, like a manifest dream, a rebus. In these instants the process of displacement and condensation conditions the rhetoric of the film. The dissolve is clearly a modus vivendi of Surrealism, but less so of documentary. In narrative cinema, it mediates conscious and unconscious realities to the degree it produces the very ideology of the unconscious.[1]

Five dissolves punctuate *Land without Bread*. Each marks the film at a moment seemingly unrelated in time and space to the others. As in the overall impressions lent by the montage, a classical, somewhat restrained use of the transition would also underscore the same documentary motives at the heart of the film. The dissolve never dominates enough to project an oneiric dimension onto the content, as had been the practice in *Un Chien andalou* only four years before. In that film the dissolve is so frequent that distinctions between shots are hard to draw; at least forty mark the duration of twenty-four minutes. In contrast, in the light of realism in this film, the dissolve gives credence to the director's effort to associate each shot with raw, unmediated truth. When the dissolve is used, it would appear "natural" or simply part of a deliberately controlled style.

The first dissolve elides the credits (shots 1–2) into the clouds over which they are written. The second, immediately following (three collages make up shot 3), superimposes a relief map of Europe, Iberia, and Western Spain over one another. In effect, the eye is dissolved into the film before it can witness the ensuing truth which would be located through or beyond the screen. The style in the initial shots virtually slides the viewer from a dreamy, cottony, nebulous condition to the hard edges of the world.

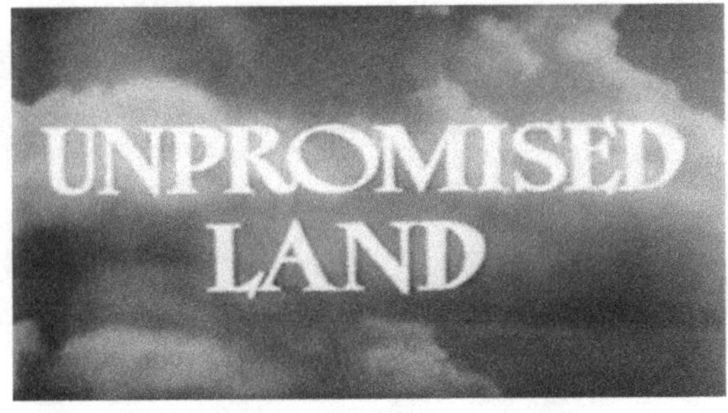

FIGURE 29.3 Shot 1. Still capture from digital file.

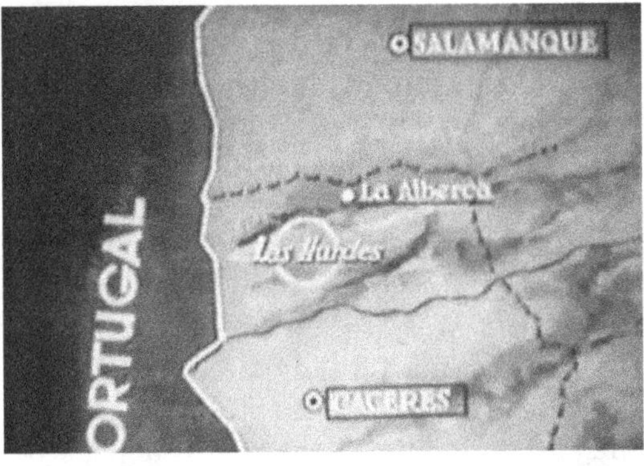

FIGURE 29.4 Shot 3. Still capture from digital file.

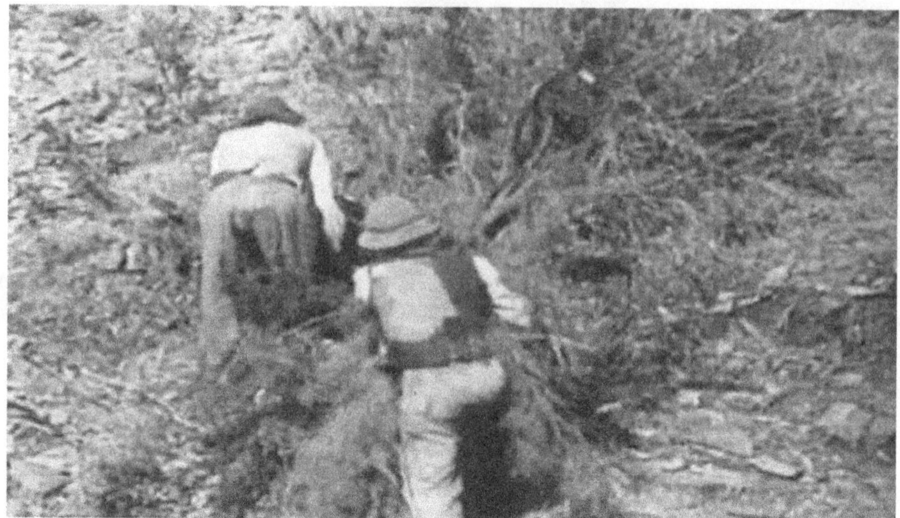

FIGURE 29.5 Shot 147. Still capture from digital file.

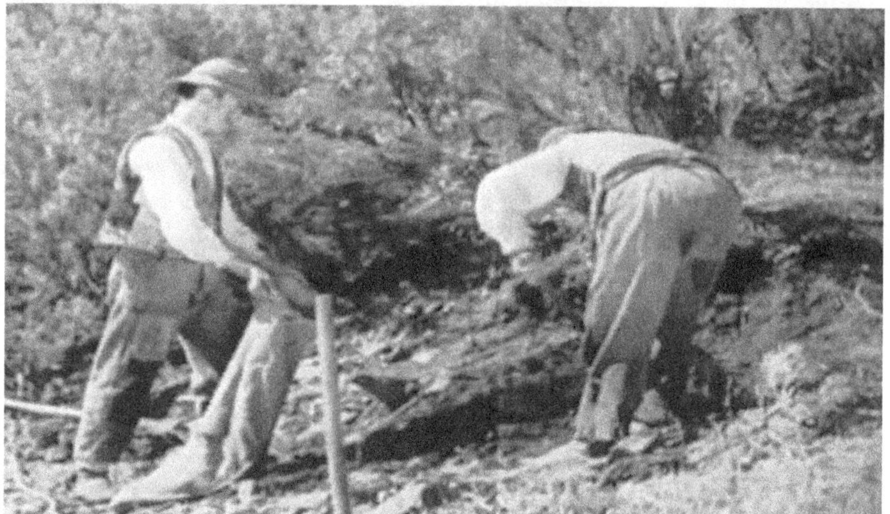

FIGURE 29.6 Shot 149. Still capture from digital file.

Clouds and a protean mass of geographic relief give way to shots of archaic streets in crisp deep focus.

One minute later (in shot 34), in a transition moving from city to country, the fourth dissolve registers a passage from a long shot to a closeup of the Western tower of a Baroque church nestled in a valley. Begun from above, a long track flows from the altitudes into the darker depths of trees growing around the church. Next, in countertilt (from the ground), an attractive, sturdy peasant woman is portrayed. Only near the end of the film do other dissolves recur: one (shot 150), in closeup, moves from a shot of running water at the edge of a river to a man-made embankment of soil held up by rock walls; another, in medium depth (adjacently, in a brief volley in shots 146–49), depicts peasants who are cutting brush. The voice-off explains that these men provide fertilizer for the terraced soil along the edge of the river. The two transitions evoke a culture of gatherers, the passage of agrarian time, and, like the initial dissolves, have nothing particularly striking about them.

Unless the surreal mode of the dissolve is kept in view as a highly charged graphic form, the transition appears only to punctuate the film with balance and restraint. Upon closer view, the dissolves telescope passage of seasons and labors. Shorter, contingent rhythms of change are erased in favor of a temporal oblivion, or a medieval naturalism. Cycles of growth and regeneration mark the image-track exactly when the voice-off reports of endless erosion and futility. Betraying the voice, the transitions effectively disallow the narration from acceding to the status of document. Despite its restrained style, *Land without Bread* is never far in time, space, or history from the experience of *Un Chien andalou* or *L'Age d'or;* their style often depends upon the fugacious emergence of one dissolve from many others. Boundaries between objects and planes of depth are melted in reality as well as in dream; for a moment, forms swim indiscriminately and without apparent contradiction. The dissolve would embody film as automatic writing, where a primary process could be glimpsed, lost, and then retrieved through subsequent viewings.

There is no reason to see why the same device does not advance the principles of cinematic realism. By suggesting that an undeniable flow of force and endless, timeless energy is inaccessible to the eye but ubiquitously visible, surreal cinema could make the unconscious manifest. *Land without Bread* suggests that realism accomplishes the task no less effectively than vanguard experiment.

The fourth dissolve is most obvious; for the great tower of the church is identified with the heroic stature of the peasant woman. Dissolving *into* her, the shot implies that she is a timeless bedrock of the universe. The tower penetrates the female from below at the same time it is identical to her. The vacuity of shadow cast from the rounded arch of the entry to the narthex of the church is situated by her belly, in such a way that the play of the erection, penetration, and containment are absolutely unified within the space of the dissolve. The female is fornicated by the spire, its extension

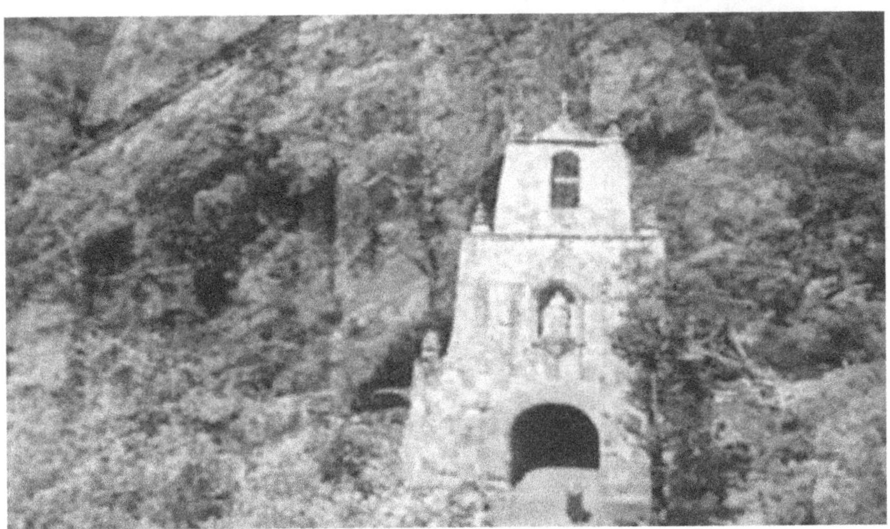

FIGURE 29.7 Shot 33. Still capture from digital file.

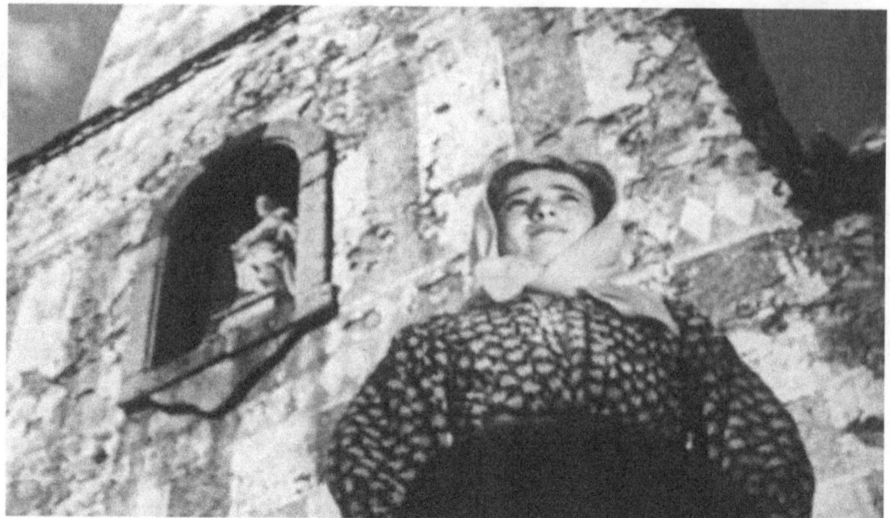

FIGURE 29.8 Shot 34. Still capture from digital file.

traveling up through her body; yet it also is the cavernous area defining her belly. Thus any "subliminal" effect of this penetration is immediately reversed. The dynamic of the transition disallows any symbolic association of one form with a masculine iconography that would be opposed to a female figure, or vice-versa, according to a binary reason. The two are at once mixed, undifferentiated and self-contained within the unit of the dissolve. The ambiguity is all the more trenchant insofar as the high medieval tradition that eroticized luminosity now figures in the cinematic rendering of the edifice and the female. The church has been likened to the Virgin Mary, a wall of stone penetrated by light passing into her body without rupturing her hymen. Here, the same: the photographic equipment in the Spanish hills maculates the female without destroying her, enacting a violence of a sacred order, producing from the dissolve of the steeple and the physical form the very illumination of the film itself. Here tradition, the erotic, and sacred orders establish and sacralize the documentary.

Perspective embodies the same ambivalences. In the establishing shots describing the plights of the Hurdanos in one of their villages (shots of 99–102), the camera looks down a city street that opens onto the mountainous landscape in the background. A staggered row of whitewashed dwellings give way to the vista of hills which descend from the right, behind a wall in shadow, covered by lush tufts of leaves and branches. Almost imperceptible—a second or third viewing reveals the figure—in the street is a tiny, genuflected human form. Within the lapse of the dissolve which moves to a medium closeup of the figure bent over a rock, the eye glimpses the figure simultaneously from far and near. Both are lost in the landscape and merge together from a play of shadows and light. For an instant the camera extends perspective by putting the subject in two places at once. Perceived from near and far, the figure broadens the image. Both lost in the landscape and central to it, the child is the mediating mark of a transition connoting a broad and active process analogy animating the physical and human world. The effect of the dissolve counters the depiction of barrenness when the voice-off on the soundtrack decries the scene: the child, it reports, suffers from malnutrition and dysentery. Where death

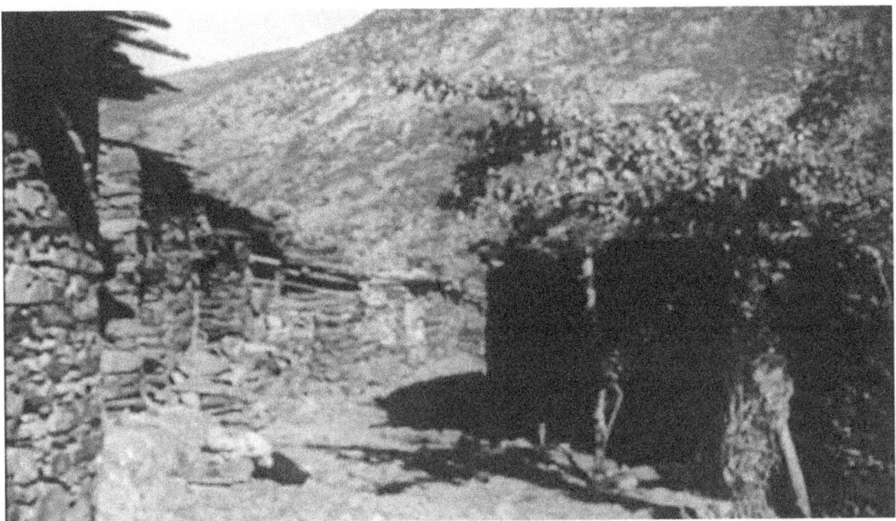

FIGURE 29.9 Shot 99. Still capture from digital file.

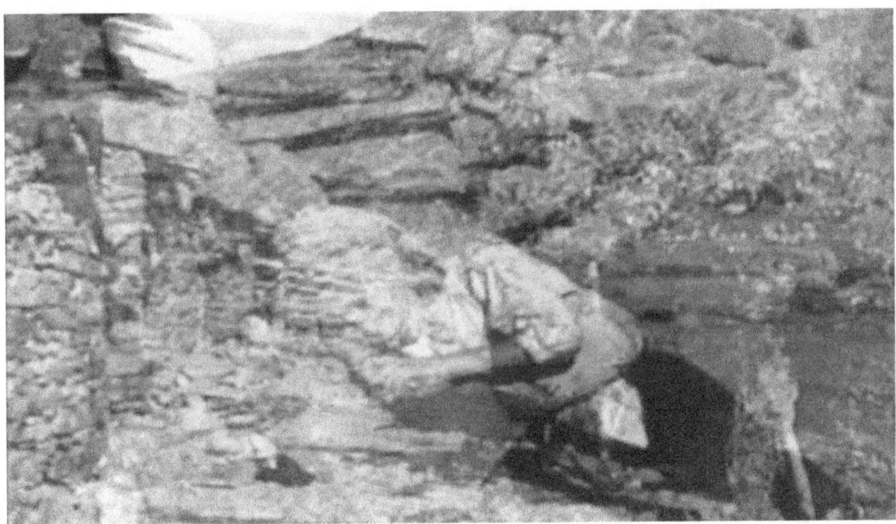

FIGURE 29.10 Shot 100. Still capture from digital file.

is reported, the cinema expands the visual range of the frame.

After the dissolve, for the first and only time in the film, the camera records the presence of the filmmaker. A human, dressed in slacks and a short-sleeved shirt, enters the frame from the left, in the foreground near the camera, and proceeds to inspect the child, who wakes from its slumber, raises her left arm to shield her eyes from the light (or too, possibly from the sight of the cameraman or anthropologist). The voice-off declares that nothing could be done to save the child. After an inspection, seen as a closeup of the child's open mouth, the soundtrack reports that she died three days later. The moral implications of the shooting sequence are obvious: the recording crew did no more than film a calamitous social condition as if it were tourism. It

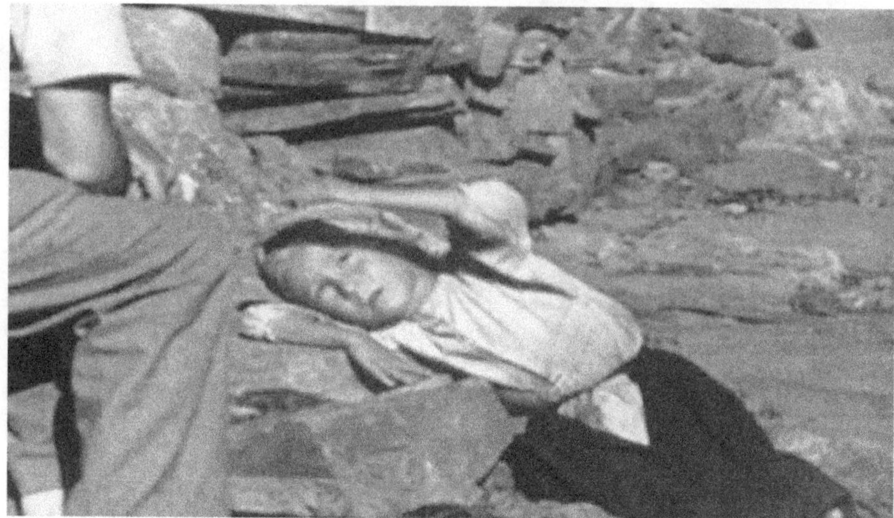

FIGURE 29.11 Shot 101. Still capture from digital file.

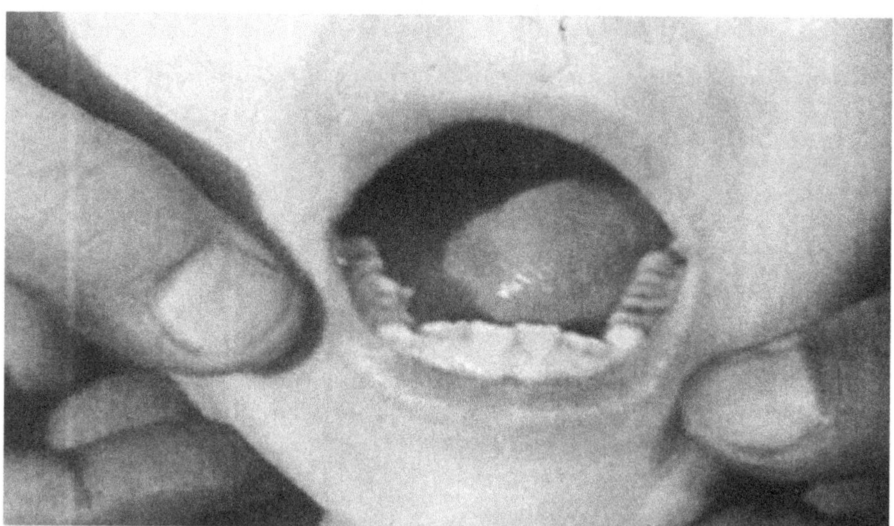

FIGURE 29.12 Shot 102. Still capture from digital file.

invested money in cinema rather than welfare. Even worse, the viewers are rendered culpable for witnessing what they should have remedied, not filmed. The double bind of the human predicament is seen as an esthetic spectacle. Once a relation of voyeurism is established in the relation of the film to the spectator, the unassailable distance held between viewers and subjects disallows any relation of enraged empathy, in this instance, that would have marked the collective perception of the child in its plight.

The sequence overtly specifies the nature of the anthropologist's research and his apparatus. The sight of a sleepy child also identifies a very standard scene, that of the *dormeuse*, that had been a topic of Symbolist painting and lyric from Rimbaud to Valéry. An unabated, favored, intimate view of a dormant beauty allows a voyeur's fantasy to flourish. Here, the sequence begins in the same fashion, with the sight of a subject in profile, who does not look back at the spectator.[2] The sequence ends by carrying the commonplace to what its unconscious dimension never articulated in the eroticized distance kept between the viewer and the figure. The *dormeuse* plays a role in the network of analogies operating elsewhere in the film. The child is likened to a dummy, a doll,[3] or a mannequin that establishes a perspectival field. It also repeats the other scenes of sleeping children who counterpoint the diurnal world to their own of imperceptible dream. The shots in the dissolve-sequence hark back to scenes in Alberca where, in shot 13, local women prepare for Sunday festivities. The foreground captures an old lady knotting the locks of a young girl, while in the background another infant sleeps in exactly the same pose as the child in the Hurdano's street in shot 100. Not unlike the lap-dissolve that perspectivized the relation of the human to the landscape, the film now casts its play of identical forms across the horizontal, narrative geography of the documentary. The infant tends to reflect the view of the spectator. In a state of hazy, dreamy consciousness, it represents the very regress necessary for a view of the film as a field of undifferentiated form, of a manifest surface that a child can apprehend. In one shot (90) of what the voice-off describes as the "turtle-like back" of the rooftops of a Hurdano village, a female holding a child—looking back at the camera—sets a median ground between the animistic texture of the agglomeration and the camera's viewpoint. The infant allows the metaphor to take visual hold and have credibility in the imaginary surface of the film.

The same function marks the procession of the child's funeral just prior to the end of the film (shots 202–21). In that sequence an infant—seen both as a doll and a corpse—is transported across a river to a graveyard overgrown with weeds. Ostensibly portrayed to bring a resonant closure of death to a film about an already dead culture, the penultimate sequence establishes the *other* end of a perspectival topography that uses the sleepy infant as one key to the multiple intersections of dream and document. Once more, what the lap-dissolve embodied in a vertical fashion—in the interpenetration of forms up and through landscapes—the presence of the child analogously reiterates the crisscrossing of narrative lines leading from the city to the province and from the diurnal world of culture (work, play, festival, everyday life) to nocturnal scenes of sleep and death (the beginning of the film bathed in intense Mediterranean light, and the end in deep chiaroscuro).

Framings: A Cinema of Sacrifice

Scenes appear framed according to a great tradition of portraiture reaching back to the seventeenth century, yet the context denies the presence of such heroic sources. No shot fails to articulate a tension between the subjects in view, depth of field, and the borders of the image. The documentary is most effective when it makes these tensions the topic of its montage, when the harsh reality depicted on screen is put into question by the study of the unconscious will or tradition—of modeling a painted world—that lends veracity to an image. Hence the reality is produced by its relation to paintings.

The dynamics of the relation between a classical style of framing and the cinematic recording of brutal reality (we are seeing an archaic world, it is reported, for the very first time) are most visible in the way that one pictural tradition effectively murders and sacralizes the other. The sequence reporting the culinary habits of the Hurdanos is emblematic. We are told that the natives indulge in meat only when, on a rare occasion, "this happens" (shots 108–16). "This" is the sight of a goat suddenly falling from its perch on a ledge on the side of a mountain. To heighten the pathos and improbability of the event, the camera shoots a closeup of the carcass just as it begins to roll and plummet into the valley. The animal recedes from the immediate foreground and is quickly lost from view. The sequence indicates a careful montage. A first shot of the mountainside precedes a medium closeup, shot from a telephoto lens, of two goats on rocky pinnacles. The third depicts them in a medium view on the mountainside, while the fourth reframes the same scene from afar, registering the goat's fall. The fifth shot begins as a closeup of the animal's carcass as it drops away from the camera.

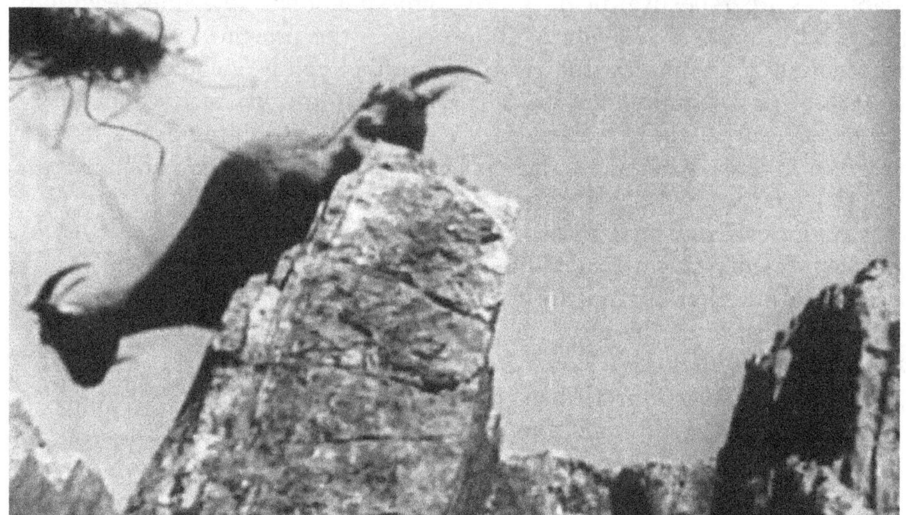

FIGURE 29.13 Shot 108. Still capture from digital file.

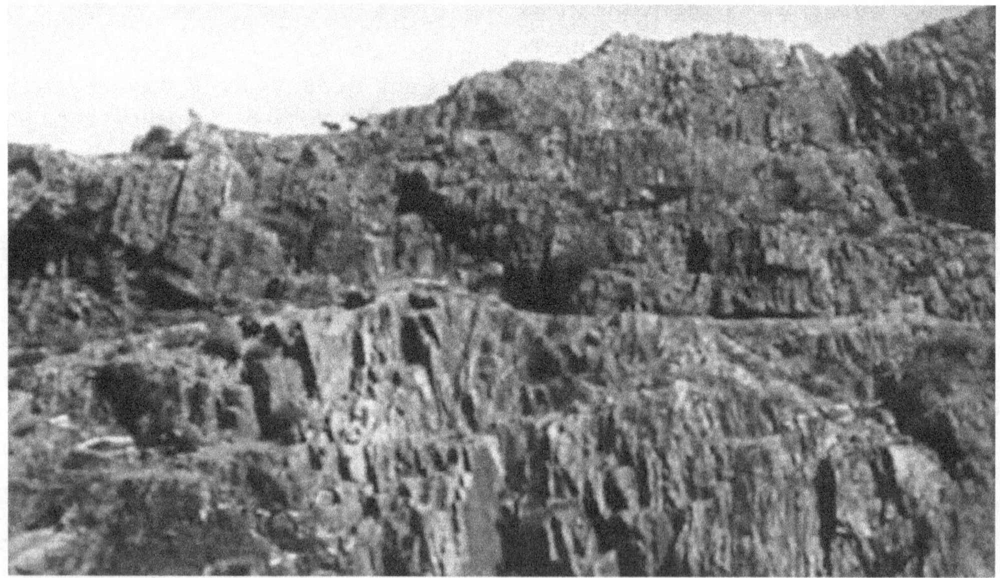

FIGURE 29.14 Shot 109. Still capture from digital file.

Even a passive viewer would not hesitate to note a puff of smoke (in the fourth shot) capturing the goat's fall from its perch. We are baited to ask, upon observing that the animal is sacrificed to precipitate the accident, if the camera is guilty of poor framing: a more carefully positioned lens would have concealed the real cause of the goat's death in order to preserve the illusion necessary for the truth of realism. As such, the sequence seems either patently "sloppy" or uncannily genial. The frame reveals that the crew has murdered the beast in order to produce an outlandishly *documentary effect*. The shot would have been innocuous if it were not underscored by the narrative jump when the camera is placed next to the carcass of the beast in the following shot, recording the fall down the mountainside. The murder becomes a photographic ritual and an exemplary sacrifice.

What seems so far from the world of credibility is cast as a visible form of religious tension. In filmic terms, the two shots of the fall caused by the gunblast and the closeup of the goat's descent underscore the presence of the ritualized murder.[4] The fifth shot virtually explains the other and allows the eye to discern the violence of the edge, where a rift between absence—dream, or primary process—and the world is respected and dissolved. The sequence has analogues everywhere else in the film which also undermine the realism. In the Alberca sequence (shots 13–29), the ritual murder of the cock in the street was depicted identically. A rooster was shot hanging from a cord stretched across the frame, then immediately decapitated by a blow of a razor entering from the right in the closeup. Several shots follow in which men are seen drinking the blood (as wine) of the beast and eating wafers of unleavened bread. A secular Eucharist, clearly mixed within the ritual process of a pagan culture in this initial sequence, counterpoints the spectacle of the goats "scaped" on the Hurdano mountainside. The images betray the narrator's report, or at best they show that the murder is staged by the camera in order to be displaced from the world of archaic life in provincial Spain. The shots of the Albercan youth in regalia on horseback, lighting and smoking cigarettes; their ride through the streets; the long, establishing view of the crowd with the cord stretched across the street with the cock hanging in the center; the closeup of the bird and the sudden entry of the hand; all offer a very logical plan homologous to the mountain goat's astonishing fall from the ledge in the Hurdano mountains. A stage is set, a ritual murder is performed on two levels (both in the field of view and in the cinematic dynamic), and a community is produced in the residue of the collective, somatic absorption of the death.

No images confirm the presence of a community, no doubt because they would work against the process of division at the basis of the framing style. A body is rendered integral when it is cut off; any cohering image of a group would undermine the filmic ritual that produces a community of views in total invisibility and in places far removed from the geography of the film. The framing therefore must not convey delimited or self-contained images of the culture it puts into view; instead, it must render the viewing as something generating confusions of culpability and redemption.

Writings

Few documentaries about illiterate, archaic, or post-neolithic cultures are infused with so much *writing* in the field of view. The map of Europe details all the primitive communities in majuscule in circular form (Tchecoslovaquie, Hongrie, Savoie, Italie, Espagne—all other nations or regions are unnamed). Place-names are carefully written in the last dissolve of the closeup of Southwestern Spain (shot 3). The camera records inscriptions on stone adjacent to skulls in alcoves on the façade of the church in La Alberca (shot 8 or also shot 36). But most important, in the sequence (shots 68–88) in the regional school on one side of the mountains separating the Hurdanos from contemporary civilization, we are led to believe that we have reached the limitrophe regions of Scripture. The shots taken in the classroom mark the last, ultimate line of the Western world. Great care is taken to show a child tracing the Golden Rule in shots 85 and 87. A boy has just walked toward the blackboard washed out by the bright light cast upon it; he raises his right arm to begin drawing the sentences in cursive characters, *Respectad los bienes ajenos*.

The sequence seems bizarre for at least two reasons. As writing always mediates visibility and alterity in the field of an image, wherever script appears in frame, the recognizable world becomes, as it were, a paginal surface. Writing forces the eye to move from illusory apprehension of a simulated three-dimensional volume to one of solely horizontal and vertical extension. In cinema it encourages the spectator to view the images as a pictorial surface that is only real in a compositional sense. Here the long shot of the child writing on the blackboard signals that the reported observations must be viewed as tension rather than the groundings of an apparent reality. The film reveals *its own rules* by breaking down the perspective of illusion. In the dynamic of scripture and anthropology, what the first intertitle scripted as "human geography," the writing paradoxically embodies the double bind of the missionary project it constructs elsewhere. The film ostensively depicts the world of these others, but its presence in their milieu is seen as an element that hardly respects their objects: the daily life in school is disrupted by a camera that catches the children smiling at the lens, or squinting in the mirrored light artificially illuminating the interior. Writing in the image-field bounces onto the spectator a statement that reads, analyzes, or even impugns the camera in the act of filming. The ultimate anthropological lesson being taught in the class is directed at the viewer: stay away, do not shoot a world that ought to be kept foreign; please do not aestheticize the Hurdanos, respect the objects of others.

Respectad los bienes ajenos can also subscribe the film in the manner of an emblem, producing alterity in the image. In this way, an unconscious can be glimpsed in the utter difference between scripture and cinema highlighted throughout the film. One of the many figures of death (and civilization) is the scene of the schoolboy's "writing lesson," which indicates where the relations of power are invested in the ethnographer's optical apparatus. The generics of *Land without Bread* are another case in point: the title is less important than its relation to the image on which it is superimposed. In the English version, UNPROMISED LAND is placed over cumulus clouds. Where the writing indicates land or earth (*Las Hurdes, Tierra sin pan, Land without bread, Pays sans pain* making the same point), the image offers an absence of grounding. The forlorn land is in the sky, in oblivion, absolution or absence; or, too, the unpromised earth is the product of the almost spontaneous generation of scripture over and from an image. Culture is defined by orders of difference and superimposition. These can be coded as repression, stratification, or by other metaphors, but in every event they are conveyed by the absolute alterity offered by scripture in its relation to the palpable world.

Paintings

Despite its portrayal of conditions far from our own, *Land without Bread* flashes many familiar figures before our eyes. The scenes are all recognizable, even agonizingly so. Use of the long shot and extended depth of field throws the film into the great painterly traditions of the Spanish Renaissance and Baroque found in the Prado. The flat, foreshortened view of the country idiots harks back to Velasquez's portraits of four dwarfs in the court of Philip. And, in a shot taken in a village en route from La Alberca (shot 57), a Spanish peasant in the lower right hand corner mimes the frontal stare of one of the Dionysian drunkards in the same painter's rustic scene of "Los Borrachos." Rural streets recall David Teniers. Courbet's "Stonebreakers" marks an obvious visual and conceptual presence (see shot 151). In a different vein, the stark mountainscapes contrasting a dark, jagged outline against bright skies seem reminiscent of the surreal tradition or the broken line of Goya's drawings. The possibility of myriad references points to the fact that most documentary evidence is always filtered through a common cultural conscience formed by esthetic models. These are part of the unconscious "rhetoric" of images that produce the meaning of realism. Akin to an "other" writing with which the filmmaker must work, they mediate the unknown in offering a fragmentary familiarity that aligns the museum with the anthropological tradition. In effect, the more the realistic genre appeals to an esthetic heritage, the more objective—and documentary—the film becomes. In the context of Spain, presence of the treasure from the collection of Philip the Fourth also exacerbates the political dimension of the aesthetic vision. That *Land without Bread* was banned by Republican Spain can be explained by the relation it holds between the presence of a Royalist heritage and the archaic, timeless, equally royal world of the Hurdano culture. Allusive presence of paintings establishes a broad perspectival range, within which the lowest order of the universe is seen in terms of the highest, and vice-versa.

Perspectives serve to reproduce the effect of a loss of grounding where, in many of the shots, the viewer cannot ascertain the vantage point of the camera. Sometimes a closeup of the earth will appear to be an aerial view until a snake or a toad enters the frame in the same or a subsequent shot (see shot 40). Or, in the scenes of street life, the camera often spirals from an extreme closeup of the waterbed to a view from afar (shot 63). The camera marries the low, close perspective to the lofty, omniscient long shot. One modulates the other, just as the presence of art treasures questions the cultural scope of ethnography in the camera's shooting style.

Such appear to be some of the salient traits of the camera in *Land without Bread.* All operate in similarly disjunctive fashions. Further study would probably show how the image and soundtracks persist in betraying one another, how the presence of Brahms deifies the subjects in the film, or how the montage articulates a network of obsessions and allusions to arcana going back to *Un Chien andalou* and *L'Age d'or* and forward to *El Bruto, Los Olvidados,* and *Robinson Crusoe.* At this point it is clear that *Land without Bread* determines much of the ground of the documentary and anthropological enterprise in cinema. Its combinations of theology and montage model a critique of grounding of filmic truth. Its construction offers an acuitous reading of realistic cinema in which objects, figures, voices, or *mises-en-scène* are seen through the art of montage. Most prominently, the film produces an extended perspective within its own styles in the junctures of shots, the composition of individual sequences, the contradictory relation of image and voice, the tensions established through the rapport of the edge to the center of the frame, the redundancy of the scenarios and their abruptness of exposition within a classical frame. For the first time a film sets forth a sacrificial function which both murders and revivifies both viewers and inhabitants of a land without bread.

NOTES

1. On this point, see Francesc Llinas and Javier Maqua's rich discussion of collage in *El Cadaver del tiempo: el collage como transmision narrative/ideologica* (Valencia: Fernando Torres, 1976).

2. The relation of the subject filmed to the spectator is multifarious in the tradition of Surrealism, film and painting. In his *Words and Pictures* (The Hague; Mouton, 1973), Meyer Schapiro notes that humans facing the spectator are generally given a role of power—such as the Pantocrator in the hemicycles of Byzantine churches—while those seen in profile convey a relation of inferiority. They do not look back or offer a view that would disquiet the viewer. The same holds for Degas's early paintings, which never allow the female to gaze upon the spectator; the artist imagines a voyeuristic relation with women who comb their hair without heeding the presence of the painter or viewer. The same relation marks the tradition of invisible editing in the tradition of Hollywood, in which actors are trained never to look directly at the camera or, if they do, to brush their look by the camera en route to fixing upon another subject or object in frame. The tradition of the *dormeuse* in shots 99–102 and elsewhere makes the political, visual, and erotic dimensions of the relation of spectator to subject entirely visible. It is essential for the theory of viewing (and violence) subtending *Land without Bread*.
3. It is both a compositional form that provides visual perspective and a pictographic marker allowing the viewer to engage in a heightened, almost irritable sensibility. The doll-baby will figure similarly in Renoir's work (*Toni*, 1934) and in Italian neorealism (e.g., Puiran).
4. Ritualized murder and cinema are part of a tradition shared with Renoir. We think of the sudden, almost morbid effect that a closeup of a rabbit has when shot during the hunt sequence of *The Rules of the Game*. The camera holds for almost three seconds on the animal as its body clenches into death, when the surrounding shots are more rapid. All of a sudden, the viewer either seizes the baneful gratuity of murder or, closer to Buñuel, the fact that the director has positioned the camera adjacent to a hunter who shoots the freed beast to produce the effect as such. Here the camera murders in order to engage a sense of collective sacrifice with the collectivity of viewers. It is at once deeply religious and cinematographic.

30

JOHN GRIERSON

THE DOCUMENTARY PRODUCER (1933)

The producer's function is to co-ordinate the more or less worldly intentions of backers with the more or less unworldly intentions of artists. He either finds the money for the artists or the artists for the money: differing in honour according to the direction from which he approaches. Sometimes, if he is ingenious, he carries the reputation among the artists of being an artist himself, and among the backers of being tougher than themselves. Sometimes—this is more frequent—he degenerates into a bully or a sycophant, sent by the money-grubbers to mangle and destroy every decent creative effort whatsoever. Sometimes he more blazingly constitutes himself a racketeer and defence organisation for the artists against the money-grubbers. At his best he is just a plain pandar, serving art as best he can within the limits set by the high policy of his organisation. This is almost invariably a low policy.

In documentary there is this difference. The producer does not always serve purely commercial interests; unless, that is to say, you take the Marxian point of view, on which all service of the *status quo* is purely commercial. He can give himself the liberal satisfaction of serving such interests as education and national propaganda: which, on any sensible definition, is itself a species of education. Or the producer may act on behalf of a business concern, large enough in its operations and its outlook, to turn publicity into education, and propaganda into a work of development.

In these special fields the producer's function is that of any other head-master. If he does not himself teach, he sees to it that the parents are satisfied. The only difference in the analogy is that the parents in this case are sometimes too scared of films, or too eminently delighted with any and every film, or too eminently cocksure that they know everything about films. The gentry of the studios, like other criminals, have a simple criterion. They look at the balance sheet and sack accordingly. The gentry of education and propaganda face a balance sheet which can be defined in no such exact terms as are to be found in red columns and black. They have to decide not only about immediate effects in a classroom, but about long-range effects on a generation. They are, as a rule (and except for the eminently expert), satisfied with some such instruction as to "bring this, that, or the other thing alive." This is an ideal formula for a producer, and turns him into the knee-wife he ought to be. His main problem is to see that the director does bring this subject alive and not another. For directors tend to diverge.

But perhaps his functions are, in reality, more complicated. Documentary, or the creative treatment of actuality, is a new art with no such background in the story and the stage as the studio product so glibly possesses. Theory is important, experiment is important; and every development of technique or new mastery of theme has to be brought quickly into criticism. In that respect it is well that the producer should be a theorist: teaching and creating a style; stamping it, in greater or less degree, on all the work for which he is responsible.

Again, because documentary is new, the sponsors of propaganda and education have to be led gently to a knowledge of what is involved. They will instruct you, as like as not, to get a snap of this, add it to a snap of that, and finish triumphantly with a snap of something else; then wonder why the simple sequence which results is not the world-shaking work of art they intended. In that respect it is well that the producer should know how to talk soothingly to children and idiots.

And a third point. The subject matter for education and propaganda is seldom easy. You are not asked to look for the exciting bits and the exciting themes and shoot these. You are generally asked to hunt about in some seemingly dull subject and find a way of putting it on the screen. The producer's job is, by educational or sociological or other reference, to bring his director to the sticking point. This is the most fruitful part of his work, and is the highest justification of those sponsors of education and propaganda who might, on sloppier theories, be considered a plague to honest artists. It is they who force the pace of documentary cinema and extend its range by the very problems they set. Any fool can make exciting films about exciting things. It is they who, in the end, make documentarians. A producer will recognise this.

But only one thing gives the producer importance: the fact that he makes directors and, through directors, makes art. It is the only thing worth an artist's making: money not excepted. Directors can be no larger than the producer allows them to be, and their films no bigger (except by noble accident) than his own imagination permits. Handling, as he may do, men of different outlooks, different temperaments, he must often, like Chesterton's Knight, ride off in all directions. The feat is difficult but, on occasion, spectacular. It involves faith, hope, and charity for each of his directors, in different degrees; and all at the same time. The most important virtue of these is faith: which is to say, footage. The only secret of good results in documentary is that a director be permitted patience with his subject, and persistence. If these do not work once, you may try him again. You may even try him a third time. But you do not carry experiment to Biblical proportions. Round about the third time you decide you have been a bad producer in picking so bad a director. Or you decide he is a genius outside the scope of your imagination. You fire him, or fire yourself, according to your conscience.

31

JOHN GRIERSON

FIRST PRINCIPLES OF DOCUMENTARY (1932–34)

Documentary is a clumsy description, but let it stand. The French who first used the term only meant travelogue. It gave them a solid high-sounding excuse for the shimmying (and otherwise discursive) exoticisms of the Vieux Colombier. Meanwhile documentary has gone on its way. From shimmying exoticisms it has gone on to include dramatic films like *Moana, Earth,* and *Turksib.* And in time it will include other kinds as different in form and intention from *Moana,* as *Moana* was from *Voyage au Congo.*

So far we have regarded all films made from natural material as coming within the category. The use of natural material has been regarded as the vital distinction. Where the camera shot on the spot (whether it shot newsreel items or magazine items or discursive "interests" or dramatised "interests" or educational films or scientific films proper or *Changs* or *Rangos*) in that fact was documentary. This array of species is, of course, quite unmanageable in criticism, and we shall have to do something about it. They all represent different qualities of observation, different intentions in observation, and, of course, very different powers and ambitions at the stage of organizing material. I propose, therefore, after a brief word on the lower categories, to use the documentary description exclusively of the higher.

The peacetime newsreel is just a speedy snip-snap of some utterly unimportant ceremony. Its skill is in the speed with which the babblings of a politican (gazing sternly into the camera) are transferred to fifty million relatively unwilling ears in a couple of days or so. The magazine items (one a week) have adopted the original "Tit-Bits" manner of observation. The skill they represent is a purely journalistic skill. They describe novelties novelly. With their money-making eye (their almost only eye) glued like the newsreels to vast and speedy audiences, they avoid on the one hand the consideration of solid material, and escape, on the other, the solid consideration of any material. Within these limits they are often brilliantly done. But ten in a row would bore the average human to death. Their reaching out for the flippant or popular touch is so completely far-reaching that it dislocates something. Possibly taste; possibly common sense. You may take your choice at those little theatres where you are invited to gad around the world in fifty minutes. It takes only that long—in these days of great invention—to see almost everything.

"Interests" proper improve mightily with every week, though heaven knows why. The market (particularly the British market) is stacked against them. With two-feature programmes the rule, there is neither space for the short *and* the Disney *and* the magazine, nor money left to pay for the short. But by good grace, some of the renters throw in the short with the feature. This considerable branch of cinematic illumination tends, therefore, to be the gift that goes with the pound of tea; and like all gestures of the grocery mind it is not very liable to cost much. Whence my wonder at improving qualities. Consider, however, the very frequent beauty and very great skill of exposition in such Ufa shorts as *Turbulent Timber*, in the sports shorts from Metro-Goldwyn-Mayer, in the *Secrets of Nature* shorts from Bruce Woolfe, and the Fitzpatrick travel talks. Together they have brought the popular lecture to a pitch undreamed of, and even impossible in the days of magic lanterns. In this little we progress.

These films, of course, would not like to be called lecture films, but this, for all their disguises, is what they are. They do not dramatize, they do not even dramatize an episode: they describe, and even expose, but in any aesthetic sense, only rarely reveal. Herein is their formal limit, and it is unlikely that they will make any considerable contribution to the fuller art of documentary. How indeed can they? Their silent form is cut to the commentary, and shots are arranged arbitrarily to point the gags or conclusions. This is not a matter of complaint, for the lecture film must have increasing value in entertainment, education and propaganda. But it is as well to establish the formal limits of the species.

This indeed is a particularly important limit to record, for beyond the newsmen and the magazine men and the lecturers (comic or interesting or exciting or only rhetorical) one begins to wander into the world of documentary proper, into the only world in which documentary can hope to achieve the ordinary virtues of an art. Here we pass from the plain (or fancy) descriptions of natural material, to arrangements, rearrangements, and creative shapings of it.

First principles. (1) We believe that the cinema's capacity for getting around, for observing and selecting from life itself, can be exploited in a new and vital art form. The studio films largely ignore this possibility of opening up the screen on the real world. They photograph acted stories against artificial backgrounds. Documentary would photograph the living scene and the living story. (2) We believe that the original (or native) actor, and the original (or native) scene, are better guides to a screen interpretation of the modern world. They give cinema a greater fund of material. They give it power over a million and one images. They give it power of interpretation over more complex and astonishing happenings in the real world than the studio mind can conjure up or the studio mechanician recreate. (3) We believe that the materials and the stories thus taken from the raw can be finer (more real in the philosophic sense) than the acted article. Spontaneous gesture has a special value on the screen. Cinema has a sensational capacity for enhancing the movement which tradition has formed or time worn smooth. Its arbitrary rectangle specially reveals movement; it gives it maximum pattern in space and time. Add to this that documentary can achieve an intimacy of knowledge and effect impossible to the shim-sham mechanics of the studio, and the lily-fingered interpretations of the metropolitan actor.

I do not mean in this minor manifesto of beliefs to suggest that the studios cannot in their own manner produce works of art to astonish the world. There is nothing (except the Woolworth intentions of the people who run them) to prevent the studios going really high in the manner of theatre or the manner of fairy tale. My separate claim for documentary is simply that in its use of the living article, there is *also* an opportunity to perform creative work. I mean, too, that the choice of the documentary medium is as gravely distinct a choice as the choice of poetry instead of fiction. Dealing with different material, it is, or should be, dealing with it to different aesthetic issues from those of the studio. I make this distinction to the point of asserting that the young director cannot, in nature, go documentary and go studio both.

In an earlier reference to Flaherty, I have indicated how one great exponent walked away from the studio: how he came to grips with the essential story of the Eskimos, then with the Samoans, then latterly with the people of the Aran Islands: and at what point the documentary director in him diverged from the studio intention of Hollywood. The main point of the story was this. Hollywood wanted to impose a ready-made dramatic shape on the raw material. It wanted Flaherty, in complete injustice to the living drama on the spot, to build his Samoans into a rubber-stamp drama of sharks and bathing belles. It failed in the case of *Moana*; it succeeded (through Van Dyke) in the case of *White Shadows of the South Seas*, and (through Murnau) in the case of *Tabu*. In the last examples it was at the expense of Flaherty, who severed his association with both.

With Flaherty it became an absolute principle that the *story must be taken from the location*, and that it should be (what he considers) the essential story of the location. His drama, therefore, is a drama of days and nights, of the round of the year's seasons, of the *fundamental fights which give his people sustenance*, or make their community life possible, or build up the dignity of the tribe.

Such an interpretation of subject-matter reflects, of course, Flaherty's particular philosophy of things. A succeeding documentary exponent is in no way obliged to chase off to the ends of the earth in search of old-time simplicity, and the ancient dignities of man against the sky. Indeed, if I may for the moment represent the opposition, I hope the Neo-Rousseauism implicit in Flaherty's work dies with his own exceptional self. Theory of naturals apart, it represents an escapism, a wan and distant eye, which tends in lesser hands to sentimentalism. However it be shot through with vigour of Lawrentian poetry, it must always fail to develop a form adequate to the more immediate material of the modern world. For it is not only the fool that has his eyes on the ends of the earth. It is sometimes the poet: sometimes even the great poet, as Cabell in his *Beyond Life* will brightly inform you. This, however, is the very poet who on every classic theory of society from Plato to Trotsky should be removed bodily from the Republic. Loving every Time but his own and every Life but his own, he avoids coming to grips with the creative job in so far as it concerns society. In the business of ordering most present chaos, he does not use his powers.

Question of theory and practice apart, Flaherty illustrates better than anyone the first principles of documentary. (1) It must master its material on the spot, and come in intimacy to ordering it. Flaherty digs himself in for a year, or two maybe. He lives with his people till the story is told "out of himself." (2) It must follow him in his distinction between description and drama. I think we shall find that there are other forms of drama or, more accurately, other forms of film, than the one he chooses; but it is important to make the primary distinction between a method which describes only the surface values of a subject, and the method which more explosively reveals the reality of it. You photograph the natural life, but you also, by your juxtaposition of detail, create an interpretation of it.

This final creative intention established, several methods are possible. You may, like Flaherty, go for a story form, passing in the ancient manner from the individual to the environment, to the environment transcended or not transcended, to the consequent honours of heroism. Or you may not be so interested in the individual. You may think that the individual life is no longer capable of cross-sectioning reality. You may believe that its particular belly-aches are of no consequence in a world which complex and impersonal forces command, and conclude that the individual as a self-sufficient dramatic figure is outmoded. When Flaherty tells you that it is a devilish noble thing to fight for food in a wilderness, you may, with some justice, observe that you are more concerned with the problem of people fighting for food in the midst of plenty. When he draws your attention to the fact that Nanook's spear is grave in its upheld angle, and finely rigid in its down-pointing bravery, you may, with some justice, observe that no spear, held however bravely by the individual, will master the crazy walrus of international finance. Indeed you may feel that in individualism is a yahoo tradition largely responsible for our present anarchy, and deny at once both the hero of decent heroics (Flaherty) and the hero of indecent ones (studio). In this case, you will feel that you want your drama in terms of some cross-section of reality which will reveal the essentially co-operative or mass nature of society: leaving the individual to find his honours in the swoop of creative social forces. In other words, you are liable to abandon the story form, and seek, like the modern exponent of poetry and painting and prose, a matter and method more satisfactory to the mind and spirit of the time.

Berlin or the Symphony of a City initiated the more modern fashion of finding documentary material on one's doorstep: in events which have no novelty of the unknown, or romance of noble savage on exotic landscape, to recommend them. It represented, slimly, the return from romance to reality.

Berlin was variously reported as made by Ruttmann, or begun by Ruttmann and finished by Freund: certainly it was begun by Ruttmann. In smooth and finely tempo'd visuals, a train swung through suburban mornings into Berlin. Wheels, rails, details of engines, telegraph wires, landscapes and other simple images flowed along in procession, with similar abstracts passing occasionally in and out of the general movement. There followed a sequence of such movements which, in their total effect, created very imposingly the story of a Berlin day. The day began with a processional of workers, the factories got under way, the streets filled: the city's forenoon became a hurly-burly of tangled pedestrians and street cars. There was respite for food: a various respite with contrast of rich and poor. The city started work again, and a shower of rain in the afternoon became a considerable event. The city stopped work and, in further more hectic processional of pubs and cabarets and dancing legs and illuminated sky-signs, finished its day.

In so far as the film was principally concerned with movements and the building of separate images into movements, Ruttmann was justified in calling it a symphony. It meant a break away from the story borrowed from literature, and from the play borrowed from the stage. In *Berlin* cinema swung along according to its own more natural powers: creating dramatic effect from the tempo'd accumulation of its single observations. Cavalcanti's *Rien que les Heures* and Léger's *Ballet Mécanique* came before *Berlin*, each with a similar attempt to combine images in an emotionally satisfactory sequence of movements. They were too scrappy and had not mastered the art of cutting sufficiently well to create the sense of "march" necessary to the genre. The symphony of Berlin City was both larger in its movements and larger in its vision.

There was one criticism of *Berlin* which, out of appreciation for a fine film and a new and arresting form, the critics failed to make; and time has not justified the omission. For all its ado of workmen and factories and swirl and swing of a great city, Berlin created nothing. Or rather if it created something, it was that shower of rain in the afternoon. The people of the city got up splendidly, they tumbled through their five million hoops impressively, they turned in; and no other issue of God or man emerged than that sudden besmattering spilling of wet on people and pavements.

I urge the criticism because *Berlin* still excites the mind of the young, and the symphony form is still their most popular persuasion. In fifty scenarios presented by the tyros, forty-five are symphonies of Edinburgh or of Ecclefechan or of Paris or of Prague. Day breaks—the people come to work—the factories start—the street cars rattle—lunch hour and the streets again—sport if it is Saturday afternoon—certainly evening and the local dance hall. And so, nothing having happened and nothing positively said about anything, to bed; though Edinburgh is the capital of a country and Ecclefechan, by some power inside itself, was the birthplace of Carlyle, in some ways one of the greatest exponents of this documentary idea.

The little daily doings, however finely symphonized, are not enough. One must pile up beyond doing or process to creation itself, before one hits the higher reaches of art. In this distinction, creation indicates not the making of things but the making of virtues.

And there's the rub for tyros. Critical appreciation of movement they can build easily from their power to observe, and power to observe they can build from their own good taste, but the real job only begins as they apply ends to their observation and their movements. The artist need not posit the ends—for that is the work of the critic—but the ends must be there, informing his description and giving finality (beyond space and time) to the slice of life he has chosen. For that larger effect there must be power of poetry or of prophecy. Failing either or both in the highest degree, there must be at least the sociological sense implicit in poetry and prophecy.

The best of the tyros know this. They believe that beauty will come in good time to inhabit the statement which is honest and lucid and deeply felt and which fulfils the best ends of citizenship. They are sensible enough to conceive of art as the by-product of a job of work done. The opposite effort to capture the by-product first (the self-conscious pursuit of beauty, the pursuit of art for art's sake to the exclusion of jobs of work and other pedestrian beginnings), was always a reflection of selfish wealth, selfish leisure and aesthetic decadence.

This sense of social responsibility, makes our realist documentary a troubled and difficult art, and particularly in a time like ours. The job of romantic documentary is easy in comparison: easy in the sense that the noble savage is already a figure of romance and the seasons of the year have already been articulated in poetry. Their essential virtues have been declared and can more easily be declared again, and no one will deny them. But realist documentary, with its streets and cities and slums and markets and exchanges and factories, has given itself the job of making poetry where no poet has gone before it, and where no ends, sufficient for the purposes of art, are easily observed. It requires not only taste but also inspiration, which is to say a very laborious, deep-seeing, deep-sympathizing creative effort indeed.

The symphonists have found a way of building such matters of common reality into very pleasant sequences. By uses of tempo and rhythm, and by the large-scale integration of single effects, they capture the eye and impress the mind in the same way as a tattoo or a military parade might do. But by their concentration on mass and movement, they tend to avoid the larger creative job. What more attractive (for a man of visual taste) than to swing wheels and pistons about in ding-dong description of a machine, when he has little to say about the man who tends it, and still less to say about the tin-pan product it spills? And what more comfortable if, in one's heart, there is avoidance of the issue of underpaid labour and meaningless production? For this reason I hold the symphony tradition of cinema for a danger and *Berlin* for the most dangerous of all film models to follow.

Unfortunately, the fashion is with such avoidance as *Berlin* represents. The highbrows bless the symphony for its good looks and, being sheltered rich little souls for the most part, absolve it gladly from further intention. Other factors combine to obscure one's judgment regarding it. The post-1918 generation, in which all cinema intelligence resides, is apt to veil a particularly violent sense of disillusionment, and a very natural first reaction of impotence, in any smart manner of avoidance which comes to hand. The pursuit of fine form which this genre certainly represents is the safest of asylums.

The objection remains, however. The rebellion from the who-gets-who tradition of commercial cinema to the tradition of pure form in cinema is no great shakes as a rebellion. Dadaism, expressionism, symphonics, are all in the same category. They present new beauties and new shapes; they fail to present new persuasions.

The imagist or more definitely poetic approach might have taken our consideration of documentary a step further, but no great imagist film has arrived to give character to the advance. By imagism I mean the telling of story or illumination of theme by images, as poetry is story or theme told by images: I mean the addition of poetic reference to the "mass" and "march" of the symphonic form.

Drifters was one simple contribution in that direction, but only a simple one. Its subject belonged in part to Flaherty's world, for it had something of the noble savage and certainly a great deal of the elements of nature to play with. It did, however, use steam and smoke and did, in a sense, marshal the effects of a modern industry. Looking back on the film now, I would not stress the tempo effects which it built (for both *Berlin* and *Potemkin* came before it), nor even the rhythmic effects (though I believe they outdid the technical example of *Potemkin* in that direction). What seemed possible of development in the film was the integration of imagery with the movement. The ship at sea, the men casting, the men hauling, were not only seen as functionaries doing something. They were seen as functionaries in half a hundred different ways, and each tended to add something to the illumination as well as the description of them. In other words the shots were massed together, not only for description and tempo but for commentary on it. One felt impressed by the tough continuing upstanding labour involved, and the feeling shaped the images, determined the background and supplied the extra details which gave colour to the whole. I do not urge the example of *Drifters*, but in theory at least the example is there. If the high bravery of upstanding labour came through the film, as I hope it did, it was made not by the story itself, but by the imagery attendant on it. I put the point, not in praise of the method but in simple analysis of the method.

* * *

The symphonic form is concerned with the orchestration of movement. It sees the screen in terms of flow and does not permit the flow to be broken. Episodes and events, if they are included in the action, are integrated in the flow. The symphonic form also tends to organize the flow in terms of different movements, e.g. movement for dawn, movement for men coming to work, movement for factories in full swing, etc., etc. This is a first distinction.

See the symphonic form as something equivalent to the poetic form of, say, Carl Sandburg in "Skyscraper," "Chicago," "The Windy City" and "Slabs of the Sunburnt West." The object is presented as an integration of many activities. It lives by the many human associations and by the moods of the various action sequences which surround it. Sandburg says so with variations of tempo in his description, variations of the mood in which each descriptive facet is presented. We do not ask personal stories of such poetry, for the picture is complete and satisfactory. We need not ask it of documentary. This is a second distinction regarding symphonic form.

These distinctions granted, it is possible for the symphonic form to vary considerably. Basil Wright, for example, is almost exclusively interested in movement, and will build up movement in a fury of design and nuances of design; and for those whose eye is sufficiently trained and sufficiently fine will convey emotion in a thousand variations on a theme so simple as the portage of bananas (*Cargo from Jamaica*). Some have attempted to relate this movement to the pyrotechnics of pure form, but there never was any such animal. (1) The quality of Wright's sense of movement and of his pattems is distinctively his own and recognizably delicate. As with good painters, there is character in his line and attitude in his composition. (2) There is an over-tone in his work which—sometimes after seeming monotony—makes his description uniquely memorable. (3) His patterns invariably weave—not seeming to do so—a positive attitude to the material, which may conceivably relate to (2). The patterns of *Cargo from Jamaica* were more scathing comment on labour at twopence a hundred bunches (or whatever it is) than mere sociological stricture. His movements—(a) easily down; (b) horizontal; (c) arduously 45° up; (d) down again—conceal, or perhaps construct, a comment. Flaherty once maintained that the east-west contour of Canada was itself a drama. It was precisely a sequence of down, horizontal, 45° up, and down again.

I use Basil Wright as an example of "movement in itself"—though movement is never in itself—principally to distinguish those others who add either tension elements or poetic elements or atmospheric elements. I have held myself in the past an exponent of the tension category with certain pretension to the others. Here is a simple example of tension from *Granton Trawler*. The trawler is working its gear in a storm. The tension elements are built up with emphasis on the drag of the water, the heavy lurching of the ship, the fevered flashing of the birds, the fevered flashing of faces between waves, lurches and spray. The trawl is hauled aboard with strain of men and tackle and water. It is opened in a release which comprises equally the release of men, birds and fish. There is no pause in the flow of movement, but something of an effort as between two opposing forces, has been recorded. In a more ambitious and deeper description the tension might have included elements more intimately and more heavily descriptive of the clanging weight of the tackle, the strain on the ship, the operation of the gear under water and along the ground, the scuttering myriads of birds laying off in the gale. The fine fury of ship and heavy weather could have been brought through to touch the vitals of the men and the ship. In the hauling, the simple fact of a wave breaking over the men, subsiding and leaving them hanging on as though nothing had happened, would have brought the sequence to an appropriate peak. The release could have attached to itself images of, say, birds wheeling high, taking off from the ship, and of contemplative, i.e. more intimate, reaction on the faces of the men. The drama would have gone deeper by the greater insight into the energies and reactions involved.

Carry this analysis into a consideration of the first part of *Deserter*, which piles up from a sequence of deadly quiet to the strain and fury—and aftermath—of the strike, or of the strike sequence itself, which piles up from deadly quiet to the strain and fury—and aftermath—of the police attack, and you have indication of how the symphonic shape, still faithful to its own peculiar methods, comes to grip with dramatic issue.

The poetic approach is best represented by *Romance Sentimentale* and the last sequence of *Ekstase*. Here there is description without tension, but the moving description is lit up by attendant images. In *Ekstase* the notion of life renewed is conveyed by a rhythmic sequence of labour, but there are also essential images of a woman and child, a young man standing high over the scene, skyscapes and water. The description of the various moods of *Romance Sentimentale* is conveyed entirely by images: in one sequence of domestic interior, in another sequence of misty morning, placid water and dim sunlight. The creation of mood, an essential to the symphonic form, may be done in terms of tempo alone, but it is better done if poetic images colour it. In a description of night at sea, there are elements enough aboard a ship to build up a quiet and effective rhythm, but a deeper effect might come by reference to what is happening under water or by reference to the strange spectacle of the birds which, sometimes in ghostly flocks, move silently in and out of the ship's lights.

A sequence in a film by Rotha indicates the distinction between the three different treatments. He describes the loading of a steel furnace and builds a superb rhythm into the shovelling movements of the men. By creating behind them a sense of fire, by playing on the momentary shrinking from fire which comes into these shovelling movements, he would have brought in the elements of tension. He might have proceeded from this to an almost terrifying picture of what steel work involves. On the other hand, by overlaying the rhythm with, say, such posturing or contemplative symbolic figures, as Eisenstein brought into his *Thunder Over Mexico* material, he would have added the elements of poetic image. The distinction is between (a) a musical or non-literary method; (b) a dramatic method with clashing forces; and (c) a poetic, contemplative, and altogether literary method. These three methods may all appear in one film, but their proportion depends naturally on the character of the director—and his private hopes of salvation.

I do not suggest that one form is higher than the other. There are pleasures peculiar to the exercise of movement which in a sense are tougher—more classical—than the pleasures of poetic description, however attractive and however blessed by tradition these may be. The introduction of tension gives accent to a film, but only too easily gives popular appeal because of its primitive engagement with physical issues and struggles and fights. People like a fight, even when it is only a symphonic one, but it is not clear that a war with the elements is a braver subject than the opening of a flower or, for that matter, the opening of a cable. It refers us back to hunting instincts and fighting instincts, but these do not necessarily represent the more civilized fields of appreciation.

It is commonly believed that moral grandeur in art can only be achieved, Greek or Shakespearian fashion, after a general laying out of the protagonists, and that no head is unbowed which is not bloody. This notion is a philosophic vulgarity. Of recent years it has been given the further blessing of Kant in his distinction between the aesthetic of pattern and the aesthetic of achievement, and beauty has been considered somewhat inferior to the sublime. The Kantian confusion comes from the fact that he personally had an active moral sense, but no active aesthetic one. He would not otherwise have drawn the distinction. So far as common taste is concerned, one has to see that we do not mix up the fulfilment of primitive desires and the vain dignities which attach to that fulfillment, with the dignities which attach to man as an imaginative being. The dramatic application of the symphonic form is not, *ipso facto*, the deepest or most important. Consideration of forms neither dramatic nor symphonic, but dialectic, will reveal this more plainly.

32

OTIS FERGUSON

HOME TRUTHS FROM ABROAD (1937)

Paul Rotha, the English film man, has done a lot to solve the problem of independent film making. With John Grierson and others he has got several units under way in England, making documentary, "realistic" two- and three-reelers for whoever will back them. I have just seen several of the more successful ones, of which some are beautiful, some striking, and some just true.

There are difficulties, for these short nonfiction films develop most easily when the subject itself is in motion and presents rudimentary conflict. All there is to do in *Housing Problems* (directed for the gas industry by Arthur Elton and Edgar Anstey) is to show the old rickety houses and the lives within them, crowded and filthy, crawling with vermin, full of the air of decay and back-stairs privies; then set this off against modern developments, built reasonably enough so that the same people can move into them, and get clean for the first time, and sit looking at the four-star luxury of a bath with running water. So this is what they do, a moderate workmanlike job which wouldn't be exciting if it weren't for the people, and the trick of interviewing them with sound-truck and camera.

And these are absolutely the most genuine people I ever saw on the screen, speaking right up in their own words and habits of phrase and no nonsense about it. There is no suggestion of pose; there is above everything a shrewd dignity that keeps them both from whining and from the pathetic little makeshifts with which men and women usually try to hide their poor condition. They are fair sick of the cramping and dirt and stink, they have fought it and never won out and it's not their fault, and they let you have it with both barrels; with cynicism and the eloquence of disgust.

Getting people like this is never accidental and the genius behind this is apparently Ruby Grierson, who got to these people and earned their confidence, smoothed away embarrassment and suspicion, singled out those with a direct voice and a natural twist of word, and worked them over until they would as soon talk to a camera as to Mrs. Flibbity on the next stoop. And that is what makes it really fine.

Children at School was also made for the gas industry, but simply does not come off. The old and the new again, a competent statement of a problem, but no life, no fire—even the kids are stiff. *We Live in Two Worlds* (directed by Alberto Cavalcanti for the Post Office Film Unit) falls in the same category eventually, though it has some very fine pictures of life in Switzerland, and an imaginative treatment of the boundary walls of nationalism.

My favorite among social films is Rotha's production, for the National Council of Social Service, *Today We Live* (direction credited to R. I. Grierson and R. Bond). It opens on the dead mining and industrial region in Wales and (I think) Yorkshire, a perfectly stunning sequence of still wheels and tipples, chimneys with no smoke, no motion except the advance of rust and rot. This is the true wasteland, for nothing will grow in it except people, who grow sparely. So the camera goes to the people living listless and cheap, their rough strong hands bewildered with idleness. In their homes, into their pubs, into their doled pennies.

But the idea of this film was to show how the Council is serving England socially, and of course the Council felt that its work in rehabilitation through community life was enough solution to guarantee a happy ending, the people were being made happy, weren't they? The producers said "Yeah"; but to themselves. It is the implicit irony of their last section that brings it under the wire (and it was a long struggle of conferences to do that), making it serve both the truth and the very distributing facilities that would alone make such truth available. One town gets a social center; the other a center where things can be made and mended. The people work and sing again—and supposedly the chap who keeps hanging back and objecting is just a typical sea-lawyer. But in the end, as the camera shifts from activity to the great mills and mines again, gutted and silent, this chap gets the last word, the word of truth. He agrees it's better than nothing. "But *this* isn't our work," he says; "not the work we want"—and your eyes go involuntarily to the bulge in his coatsleeves and his hands, gnarled from their training, strong and good and useless.

Of all the six I saw (there was a Len Lye color oddity that was quite free and new), the one most naturally effective was *The Night Mail*. You can see the possibilities at once: *The Postal Special* (Basil Wright and Harry Watt did this for the Post Office) leaves London and tears along up through England all night, coming into Glasgow in the morning. All the business of wheels and steam and the counties of England, the whistle for the crossing, the far sound coming nearer, the rush of iron and fire and the mailbag ripped from its patent hanger, and they're out of the sleeping town again, off up the line. The junction, engines shifted and trucks rattling to load and unload letters by the ton, men shouting and heaving and jumping around to beat the schedule. The London crew goes off here and the Glasgow shift takes over, swinging on with familiar banter. Inside the cars there is a steady business of dumping, sorting, resacking, always to beat the schedule—when they pass the first bridge, and then the second bridge, and count the beats of the ninety-five rail-ends, then the sack for that town has to be ready and strapped, tied to its patent davit and swung out; there is a sound like a shot, the davit swings in empty, and *that* town has had its mail delivered in its sleep.

The exposition covers a hundred fascinating details, the knots used, the method of sorting, the stationmaster's telephone, the struggle with faulty addressing—the romance of the ordinary, "the world is so full of a number of things," etc. But there is more than the mechanics of the job; the men work as men actually do work, with deftness here, a bit of puzzlement there, with an economy of phrase and an occasional grunt, always with a little ragging, done with a nudge, a look, a knowing word. And as the crews shift and they get farther into the North, the accents thicken. Well, the mail gets to Glasgow, the post office sells us (painlessly) its bill of goods, and we have got more interest and excitement than if the Postal Special had been wrecked, robbed, and reported by Bette Davis.

Paul Rotha is trying to get something like his and Grierson's multiple-unit system working over here; and this is interesting enough to be gone into later, when I have seen the rest of the films which Rotha is now showing through the Museum of Modern Art, and which you could start setting up a yell for locally.

33

CHARLES WOLFE

STRAIGHT SHOTS AND CROOKED PLOTS

Social Documentary and the Avant-Garde in the 1930s (1995*)

This concern of experimental photography for events close to our own time and society is not a fad, but a flowering.

—Ben Belitt (1937)

The documentary film has a constant hunger for new techniques.

—Ben Maddow (1940)

Documentary cinema from the 1930s has come down to us largely as a genre of social reform: unambiguous in its rhetoric, didactic in its approach, at the service of organizations and agencies with programs to promote or defend. It may thus seem peculiar to link such a cinema to a history of the avant-garde, or at least the avant-garde of high modernism, with its tendencies toward abstraction, fragmentation, distortion, esoteric allusion, perceptual difficulty, and a destabilizing critique of bourgeois norms. Yet documentary and avant-garde filmmaking, if conventionally treated under separate rubrics, have a history of recurring affiliation, dating back to efforts in the 1920s and 1930s to define an "art cinema" distinct from the conventional

*Revised 2015.

practices of the commercial film industry.[1] Moreover, if we are willing to extend our notion of avant-garde cinema beyond the canonic movements of European modernism (Futurism, Expressionism, Cubism, Dada, Surrealism) to encompass more utilitarian and pragmatic strands of modernist thought, the impact of avant-garde experiments of the 1920s on documentary filmmaking in the U.S. in the 1930s comes more clearly into view.

This impact can be traced along several interconnected routes: an evolving critical discourse on film aesthetics in which the concept of documentary cinema took shape; the career trajectories of individual photographers and filmmakers who gravitated toward social documentary projects as the decade of the Great Depression advanced; the organizing of institutional spaces (workshops, exhibition sites) where films produced outside of Hollywood could be showcased and discussed; and the variegated form and style of works to which the label documentary was applied. In the remarks to follow I wish to clarify how these various paths hook up in a network of experimental social documentary practices. Social documentarists in the 1930s were above all future-oriented, committed to the prospect of a better world, whether forged at the anvil of a revolutionary proletariat, enacted through New Deal legislation, or projected upon a technological utopia—the "world of tomorrow," which was the theme of a major showcase for documentary films, the 1939 New York World's Fair. With this mind, we might examine the films they produced as exercises in problem solving, the terms for which were set both by a tradition of formal experimentation in the arts and an ambition to contend with urgent social problems of the day.

In the 1930s, it is important to note, "documentary" was a highly provisional term, employed by critics and filmmakers to explain or advance varied trends in nonfiction filmmaking. Definitions in common circulation by the end of the decade—"the creative treatment of actuality" (John Grierson), "the creative presentation of facts as we find them in everyday life" (Paul Rotha), "the dramatization of facts" (Richard Griffith), "an emotional presentation of facts" (Joris Ivens), "factual photography with the impact of drama" (Arch Mercey)—shared a carefully crafted ambiguity.[2] Reference to the domain of the "factual" or "actual" marked only half of documentary's allure; no less crucial was its invitation to shape such material creatively. Phraseology of this kind loosened, without severing, the indexical bond of documentary images to their nonfictional referents, valorizing a surplus effect: beyond the presentation of mundane "facts" true documentaries were thought to alter or sharpen human perception (the domain of aesthetics), mount persuasive arguments (the domain of rhetoric), and tell compelling stories (the domain of narration). Filmmakers thus could approach work in documentary as an experimental process requiring—and giving expression to—personal or collective knowledge, belief, skill, ingenuity, or artistry. Spectators, in turn, were promised a heightened awareness or emotional experience of the everyday or commonplace. Critical discourse buttressing social documentary filmmaking in the 1930s thus sanctioned a double commitment by filmmaker and viewer alike: to a social sphere worthy of detailed documentation but also to a medium that might bring that world into perspective, structuring knowledge and stirring emotions through creative manipulation of filmic forms.[3]

This entailed less the codification of specific rules or procedures for documentary filmmaking than an eclectic reworking of existing models, including principles of continuity editing found in Hollywood fiction, elements of Stanislavkian performance technique, and the abstract, associative, or conceptual logic of montage experiments by filmmakers associated with the avant-garde. At the same time, social documentary filmmakers sought to distance themselves from antecedent forms of nonfiction found in industrials, educational films, and travelogues. Even Robert Flaherty's carefully staged narratives of life in distant locales, celebrated in art film circles in the 1920s, were critiqued as an adequate model for new social documentary work on both formal and political grounds, their poetic and dramatic effects reinterpreted as signs of an overly studied artfulness that deflected the attention of the spectator from the social turbulence of the day.[4]

At work here, we might surmise, was a process whereby documentary filmmaking was defined in relation not only to its most obvious alternative—the theatrical fiction of Hollywood—but also the very traditions out of which a loose sense of the genre had emerged. The referential appeal of documentary, its very status as a distinct mode of film practice with a privileged relation to the social world, was invigorated by novel claims to be made about the capacity of the medium to lay bare veiled or suppressed social truths. In support of these claims, filmmakers developed compositional styles that tended to be highly contingent, geared to specific projects. Documentary filmmaking hence was concurrently promoted as a discovery procedure, an artistic practice, and a social act.

From Photography to Film: Abstraction, Objectivity, Montage

A conceptual ground for the development of an experimental documentary aesthetic in the 1930s was staked out in the 1920s by artists and critics who found the seeming mechanical objectivity of the camera a source of new ideas about visual perception in an age of mass, technological culture. These ideas were given varied but congruent expression in a cluster of European movements—French Purism, Russian Constructivism, German *Neue Sachlichkeit*—all of which emphasized the material properties of the medium employed, the precision and economy of mechanical processes, and the utility of mass produced forms. In the pages of *Broom*, *The Dial*, and *The Little Review*; at the exhibitions of the New Art Circle, the Société Anonyme, and the Weyhe Gallery in New York; and at film screenings in art film houses in major cities or along the labor-left circuit developed by the Workers International Relief, American photographers and filmmakers had the opportunity to read and view the work of European painters and graphic designers who had responded to new industrial technologies with a call for an objectivist art in which the optical apparatus of the camera played a crucial part.

At the furthest reaches of abstraction were the photographic practices proposed by Lázló Moholy-Nagy, an Hungarian-born constructivist on the faculty of the German Bauhaus, and French cubist painter Fernand Léger. In "Light: A Medium of Plastic Expression," published in *Broom* in 1923, and in more elaborated form in *Painting: Photography: Film*, translated into English in 1931, Moholy-Nagy outlined a scientific approach to photography that embraced the power of the camera to make visible phenomenon that was otherwise imperceptible to the human eye and declared the "primary visual facts" of photography to be gradations of light/dark and color.[5]

In "A New Realism—the Object (Its Plastic and Cinematographic Value)," published in *The Little Review* in 1926, Léger extended this concern for the fundamental materials of photographic art to encompass the contours an object placed before the camera's lens, arguing for the graphic and dramatic beauty of objects *as* objects as well as the unprecedented power of cinema to isolate, fragment, enlarge, mobilize, and juxtapose objects so as to heighten the viewer's contemplation of their shape and form.[6] One in a series of essays by Léger on machine aesthetics that appeared in *The Little Review* in the 1920s, his manifesto on cinema sketched a framework for a fuller political defense of the "realist" dimension to formal experimentation, a defense Léger would himself mount, amid the social upheaval of the Great Depression, in the pages of the American Artists Union publication, *Art Front*, in 1935 and 1937.[7] This new realism, claimed Léger, involved "scientific discoveries" of "pure sensibility" rather than deductive logic, and filled a need for a popular, non-hierarchical, reproducible art.[8]

The cross-breeding of this new formal emphasis on photographic abstraction and rhythmic editing with the subject matter of conventional nonfiction (*actualités*, travelogues, and newsreels) pointed toward a new documentary aesthetic. American filmmakers on the left in particular drew inspiration from the work of Russian documentarists Victor Turin and Dziga Vertov, whose films, and on occasion writings, circulated in left film circles in the early 1930s.[9] Described by French critic Leon Moussinac in the pages *Filmfront* as constituting the "avant- garde of Soviet cinema,"[10] Vertov's "kino-eye" school of cinematography attracted the attention of newly politicized filmmakers in America for its complementary notions of the motion picture camera as a scientific instrument and of filmic montage as an aggressive, complex "language" of visual and acoustic "facts," commensurate with the demands of a revolutionary age. Screened at art film houses as well as smaller film societies clubs, and reported on by the mainstream press, innovative feature-length "city films" like Walter Ruttman's *Berlin: Symphony of a City* (1927) and Vertov's *The Man with a Movie Camera* (1929), provided perhaps the clearest and most conspicuous examples of how a documentary aesthetic might emerge at the point where commitments to social observation, abstraction, and rhythmic and conceptual montage converged.[11]

But there were also precedents closer to home. As early as the late teens, American photographer Paul Strand and painter-photographers Charles Sheeler and Morton Shamberg self-consciously developed a "straight" photography style which emphasized sharply focused, geometrically patterned images over and against diffused lighting or other "pictorialist" effects. Elaborated as an ethos as well as a working method, straight photography stressed equally a faith in the materiality and integrity of a profilmic field and the power of the photographic image to abstract from that field an acutely drawn, clarified image. In its mechanical registration of such an image, straight photography was to serve as a modern antidote to the enervating mannerism and pathos of studio photography. Hence the affinity of straight photography with the modern, "objectivist" poetry of William Carlos Williams and Marianne Moore, composed in reaction to genteel literary traditions, or with the Precisionist paintings of Sheeler, Shamberg, and Charles Demuth, who rejected impressionistic visual effects in favor of a hard-edged graphic style. For these artists, the optics of the camera offered a new metaphor for visual perception that was precise, uncluttered, focused upon the contours and textures of commonplace objects, viewed not as symbols but as *things*.[12]

Among these photographers, all habitués of Alfred Stieglitz's *salon*-style Photo-Secessionist Gallery at 291 Fifth Avenue in New York in the teens, Strand offered the fullest defense of "straight photography" as both compatible with American culture and an antidote to that culture's tendency toward crass materialism. In a series of essays beginning in 1917, Strand argued that the technology of photography, as employed by a cluster of American artists, bridged a now obsolete gap in cultural thinking between the domains of science and art. If the *raison d'être* of photography was "absolute unqualified objectivity," the potential power of which was "dependent upon the purity of its use," the camera, employed by an artist, also constituted a powerful instrument of creative expression; in the very effort to grasp an object pictorially, the photographer's point of view inevitably was registered.[13] By 1922, these ideas had come to undergird a more fully elaborated notion of the contemporary photographer as experimenter, as purposeful and logical as the scientific observer, yet unencumbered by the reductive instrumentalism that increasingly had rendered scientists servants of "a new Trinity of God the Machine, Materialistic Empiricism the Son, and Science the Holy Ghost." At once celebrated and condemned in Europe, this new deity threatened to crush life in modern America where the cult of the machine was driven by powerful economic imperatives. However, by approaching the act of picture-taking with a sensitivity to felt life, the photographer could join "the ranks of all true seekers of knowledge, be it intuitive and aesthetic or conceptual and scientific." Modern technologies of vision thus need not lead to the erasure of human perception and agency or a neurasthenic idolatry of the machine; rather the camera could be placed in service of human need, reason, and design.[14]

Over the next decade, the implications of this approach for motion pictures were explored in commentary by various American critics and social thinkers concerned with the future fate of cinema as a socially useful art. To a certain extent, Strand's argument conformed to romantic conventions of artistic practice: an "objective" sphere was valued precisely to the extent it yielded up an image to the discerning eye of the visionary photographer; in turn, the subjectivity of the artist was invested in the object perceived. In this regard, Strand's position statements on "straight photography" bore the impress of the teachings of Stieglitz, especially Stieglitz's symbolist credo of photographic "equivalents," in which specific emotional or psychological meanings were attributed to visual forms. Yet in his call for photographic practices governed by human needs, Strand also signaled a crucial shift in emphasis from the sensibility of the artist to the well-being of the community, from the cult of the art object to its broader social function.[15]

In the early 1930s, efforts of this kind to articulate a join between mechanical objectivity and social intersubjectivity in cinema took on a new political cast. Given the economic turmoil of the era, David Platt argued in the inaugural issue of *Experimental Cinema* (1930), there was "exigent need of a *force* powerful enough to assist in the presentation of these problems, socially, politically, psychologically, and if possible to transform them to meet the realities of the time." The most appropriate such force was cinema, which penetrated "so deeply into the mystery of reality because of the *instantaneity of vision*."[16] Implicitly placing elements of Strand's earlier argument within a sweeping history of the machine, Lewis Mumford, in his influential 1934 study, *Technics and Civilization*, likewise claimed that cinema was the unrivaled art form of the Neotechnic Age, a third phase of civilization in which machines, no longer "a substitute for God or for an orderly society," would serve "the organic and living."[17] Photography, Mumford proposed, was a form of historical note-taking, allowing the viewer to "grasp spatial relations which may otherwise defy observation." Moreover, the moving picture with its shifting viewpoints registered the flux and variability of human perception and feeling. Hence cinema was "today the only art that can represent with any degree of concreteness the emergent world-view that differentiates our culture from every preceding one."[18]

Mumford's expansive argument for the organic uses of technology at the threshold of the Neotechnic Age—an era in which a Cartesian split between the dead, mechanical body and vital, transcendent soul had been dissolved—would have a major impact on social reform initiatives in the 1930s, including those proposed in one of the most widely viewed documentary films of the period, *The City* (Ralph Steiner/Willard Van Dyke, 1939), for which Mumford served as consultant. Furthermore, Mumford's dauntingly exhaustive history of technology provided the intellectual framework for the widespread acceptance of documentary filmmaking as a progressive social activity. The tenets of straight photography thus were inflected by a new critical discourse on documentary cinema in which the political stakes seemed especially high.

This shift in emphasis from the aesthetics of perception to wider social and historical concerns can similarly be traced along the career trajectories of individual photographers who were central to the 1930s documentary movement. Prescient here again was Strand, who as early as 1921 collaborated with Sheeler on *Manhatta*, a "scenic" view of New York City, pitched, as Jan-Christopher Horak perceptively notes, between Walt Whitman's romantic celebration of Manhattan as a primordial landscape and the abstraction and fragmentation of modernist pictorial arts.[19] Highly praised in art circles throughout the 1920s for the visual density of his deeply textured, sharply focused, platinum prints, Strand also supported himself financially as a freelance newsreel cameraman, honing his skills as a cinematographer in the process. In the 1930s, his circle of collaborators expanded as his film work then took an overtly political turn. Under Strand's supervision, *Redes* (*The Wave*), an acted drama of a fishermen's strike, was filmed on location in rural Mexico in 1933–1934. For this project, he hired two young Austrians émigrés: Henwar Rodakiewicz, a photographer and filmmaker who had attracted attention in amateur circles for an experimental short, *Portrait of a Young Man* (1931); and Fred Zinnemann, a collaborator on the acclaimed German documentary, *Menschen am Sonntag* (*People on Sunday*, 1929), who now worked in Hollywood. In 1936, Strand joined forces with Ralph Steiner and Leo Hurwitz to shoot Pare Lorentz's first New Deal documentary, *The Plow that Broke the Plains*, then assumed a leading role in the formation of Frontier Films, the leading labor-left documentary film unit of the decade, serving as its president until the organization's demise in 1942. Among projects at Frontier, he shot (and Hurwitz edited) the most ambitious left documentary of the period, a feature-length history of the violation of the rights of union workers, *Native Land* (1942).

Steiner, in turn, dated his own maturation as a photographer to his exposure to Strand's work in 1926 ("I was pole-axed; I had never seen prints so rich—with such real texture—and so glorious tonal values").[20] At the end of the decade, under the sponsorship of the Elmhurst Foundation, Steiner embarked on a series of short experimental works (*H2O, Surf and Seaweed, Mechanical Principles*), similar to the abstract films of Eggling, Richter, Ruttman, and Moholy-Nagy. He turned to documentary film work in the 1930s, first briefly at the Workers Film and Photo League in New York, then joining Hurwitz to form an experimental splinter group, Nykino, where ideas about acting and film fiction were explored.[21] After shooting *The Plow that Broke the Plains* in 1936, Steiner followed Hurwitz and Strand to Frontier; a rift eventually led to his departure to make *The City* with Van Dyke and Rodakiewicz in 1938. His influence, like Strand's was widely felt: Irving Lerner and Jay Leyda, both a decade Steiner's junior, worked as his assistants prior to their involvement on major projects at Nykino and Frontier.

Social documentary cinema's debt to straight photography follows yet another route, commencing with the formation of Group f.64 in Oakland, California, in 1932. So named for the camera aperture best able to produce photographic images of sharp focus, f.64 included among its original members Ansel Adams, Imogen

Cunningham, Willard Van Dyke, and Edward Weston. Weston was the group's intellectual leader, Van Dyke its chief organizer, but all members had been recently working in a style that focused on the surface texture and shape of closely viewed objects, cropped or tightly framed against the sky or other neutral background.[22] In commentary that echoed earlier position statements on modern photography, Group f.64's manifesto announced their commitment to "simple and direct presentation through purely photographic methods," a form of "pure photography" not derivative of any other art form.[23]

Although Group f.64 was short-lived, the photographers who came together to form it had an impact on social documentary filmmaking in varied ways. In 1931, for example, the bicoastal film journal, *Experimental Cinema*, published a suite of Weston's photographs accompanied by his brief statement on the power of the photograph to attend to the "direct presentation of THINGS in THEMSELVES." For the journal editors, Weston's "honest eye" explicitly served as a useful counter-example to the "unhealthy artificialism of design" and "conventional technical sentimentalism" of cinematography in Hollywood; in this fashion, straight photography's great nemesis, pictorialism, was now linked to Hollywood's studio style.[24] Weston's son, Brett, formally considered an affiliate of Group f.64, also briefly served as a staff photographer for *Experimental Cinema*, providing illustrations for articles by David Platt on machine aesthetics and Lewis Jacobs on Sergei Eisenstein.[25] On the political front, east and west coasts connected again in 1934 when FPL veteran Lester Balog, having arrived in California to shoot and show documentary footage of migrant labor camps, collaborated with the San Francisco Bay area photographers in a "Photo Commentors" show at the Lilienthal Bookstore under the banner, "Photographs of Social Significance."[26] In 1930, Strand met Adams in New Mexico and over the next several summers researched the terrain of the Southwest, honing an eye for horizontal landscapes that eventually shaped the look of his Mexican documentary, *The Wave*.[27] Meanwhile, Van Dyke, after a brief stint with the social documentary team of Dorothea Lange and Paul Taylor, crossed the continent in the opposite direction, joining Nykino in New York, then working as a cinematographer on Lorentz's second New Deal project, *The River*. He also followed Steiner's path into independent documentary production with *The City* after a stint at Frontier.[28]

As first forays in filmmaking, "scenics" or pattern films allowed experimental photographers schooled in a straight style to explore the arrangement of mass, line, and volume temporally, through the orchestration of patterns of movement within and across individual shots. As Horak has shown, *Manhatta* is comprised in large measure of animated reconstructions of photographs by Strand and Stieglitz; in a sense, the film tests the aesthetic of an evolving New York school of photography against the possibilities of cinema, of regulated movement and kinetic design.[29] Likewise Steiner's shots of water, surf, and mechanical gears in his pattern films add movement to a series of abstract images, the clarity and tectonic precision of which strongly resemble his abstract photographs of the period. Cutting tends to follow and extend patterns of movement within adjacent shots, at times accelerating the pace of the action.

The temporal model for Steiner was music: composer Aaron Copland assisted in the editing of all three films, and they subsequently were screened with musical accompaniment by Marc Blitzstein on a program with French avant-garde shorts at a Modern Music concert in New York. Analogies to music likewise mark Rodakiewicz's *Portrait of a Young Man*, where abstract patterns of waves, rocks, gears, trees, and clouds are explicitly divided into three separate "movements." Influenced perhaps by the title to Ruttman's *Berlin: Symphony of a City*, this musical conceit was echoed in a host of projects suggested for amateurs in the early 1930s. In his 1931 guidebook, *Cinematic Design*, Leonard Hacker proposed that "A film symphony of swaying trees and flowing water with man and animals as part of the surroundings is the finest type of picture that can be made," and presented seven short scenarios for amateurs, including "Symphony Natural," "Symphony Synthetic," and (with no acknowledgment to Léger) "Symphony Mechanique."[30] Leo Hurwitz, who like Steiner claimed to have been "bowled over" by Strand's photographs upon arriving in New York in 1930, referred to his first effort in filmmaking as "a channel of flow of the city" and a "dance film of the subways."[31] For these photographers turned filmmakers, the abstraction of the photographic image now acquired a rhythmic and choreographic dimension.

Social documentary projects, in turn, would offer manifold opportunities to refine and elaborate this style. Crisply focused, carefully composed images is the norm for these filmmakers throughout the 1930s, whether the subject is a western landscape (*The Plow that Broke the Plains*), a New England village (*The City*), or an intricate pattern of slatted, tenement stairs (*The Fight for Life*, Lorentz, 1941). The sustained, rhythmic orchestration of edited shots, cut to music composed for the scene, also is a recurring, even virtuoso, set piece in these films, as when a stream of water gains speed and volume in time to Virgil Thomson's score to *The River*, urban traffic builds to a frenzy to Aaron Copland's score for *The City*, the movement of a tractor is cut to (and the sound of its engine integrated with) Paul Bowles experimental music in *America's Disinherited* (Alan S. Hacker, 1937), or the harvesting of a corn crop is edited to a discordant, heavily cadenced verse chorus by Stephen Vincent Benét in *Power and the Land* (Joris Ivens, 1940). The "conquest of a continent" sequence that opens *Native Land*—with its horizontal tracking shots, vertical counter movements, and diagonally traced lines defining forces in conflict, accompanied by poet Ben Maddow's scripted commentary and Marc Blitzstein's score—amply illustrates how the formal orchestration of complex patterns of movement, given direction and velocity through precise reframing and cutting, flourished under the rubric of social documentary practices.[32]

Hooks and Crannies: Social Reconstruction and Documentary Forms

Experiments in the rhythmic patterning of sharply focused images, however, had limited value in advancing the central goals of social documentary filmmakers. Straight photography required alert, disciplined attention to a field of vision, a profilmic scene, which through selection and abstraction would yield up an image of reality that habitual ways of seeing masked. With social documentary projects, however, stress now fell on the links, pressure points, and relations of power in an invisible social system, residing, as it were, "behind" the world of physical objects, bound together in causal patterns that the social analyst had to work to reconstruct. The scientific analog for documentary inquiry of this kind was less biology or chemistry (recall Steiner's title for his abstract study of water, *H2O*) where microscopic elements could be viewed through optical magnification, or patterns of movement invisible to the eye charted through time- lapse photography, but the *social* sciences, where analyses typically involved a mix of visual documentation, personal testimony, and statistics or charts. Or perhaps the analytical method of social documentary was less a science in any familiar sense than a form of conceptual grasping, closer to the humanistic notion of "understanding," unanchored by an agreed upon set of logical principles or physical laws.

Indeed, social documentary seemed to bring to the fore another model of photographic practice, with roots in Jacob Riis's tenement photographs at the close of the 19th century, published in photo books that attacked the scandalous housing conditions of immigrants; or in the work of Lewis Hine (Strand's first instructor), whose photographs from 1908 through the early 1930s illustrated articles in the social reform journal, *Survey* (later *Survey Graphic*), the massive, six-volume *Pittsburgh Survey*, and the brochures and pamphlets of the National Child Labor Committee.[33] Pattern films, in effect, dehistoricized documentary photography, closing down the multiple temporal registers that a work of cinema might mobilize for an image, focusing attention on, and intensifying the spectator's sensation of, an immediate act of perception. City films, in contrast, often cued other temporal patterns by establishing, say, a time of day for the action (dawn to dusk was a typical formal structure), or alluding to economic tensions in a modern urban landscape. Leyda's *A Bronx Morning* (1931), for example, edges away from a strictly "symphonic" format for the city film by focusing on hand made signs ("fire sale," "prices down . . . the bottom") and incorporating a running series of intertitles ("The Bronx does business . . . and the Bronx lives . . . on the street") that cast the neighborhood as a public space marked by economic fluctuation and change. In a similar vein, Conrad Friberg in *Halsted Street* (1934) foregrounds economic and ethnic divisions along a city-long Chicago street in the era of the Great Depression. Opening with the laborious movement of a plow horse through farmland to the south, and closing with the leisurely gait of equestrian riders in park land to the north, *Halstead Street* reconstructs a dense social milieu through the juxtaposition of commercial billboards, movie marquees, ethnic storefronts, church missions, and political posters and placards, and caps the recurring image of a burly man walking briskly northward with his arrival at a solidarity march. In full-scale social documentaries, historical trajectories of this kind gain dominance. Thus, while straight photographers and social documentarists both rejected traditions of genteel refinement and decoration in the arts, new documentary film work relied on conceptual schema—social typing, social conflict, allegories of social transformation—that straight photographers had jettisoned in favor of strict attention to "the thing itself."

In 1940, veteran documentarist Joris Ivens put the problem this way: "Films on wood-structure, or in the operation of a bridge should have no trouble in touching the reality of their subject. But films on larger, more important themes, require a deeper approach. In my opinion, it's necessary to find the social reality, then to find the essential drama of that reality."[34] Where precisely was *this* reality to be found? To a certain extent, the historical significance of social events was presupposed by the political or philanthropic organizations with which filmmakers often where aligned. The task of the documentarist was to invest these propositions with a sense of immediacy, density, lyricism, wit, or persuasive appeal. Yet the process of filmmaking itself could alter one's grasp of an inherited proposition about the world, complicating or even skewing any simple message a sponsor might wish to promote. For the ambitious practitioner, documentary filmmaking thus involved the dynamic interaction of inherited propositions, the specific social topic under scrutiny, and the properties of the medium through which social material was to be given dramatic force.

That this required the discovery or cobbling together of *new* forms of cinema was a widely shared viewed. On the left, the rhetoric of the Workers Film and Photo League easily absorbed the avant-garde's cultural critique of Hollywood cinema as philistine and dull, to which was added a sharpened economic critique of Hollywood's factory system of production and the money interests the film industry served. Organized two doors away from the old Biograph studios on East 14th Street, where D. W. Griffith had first risen to fame, and modestly funded by Workers International Relief, the New York FPL boldly sought to reclaim American cinema for the working class, announcing a program to expose "reactionary" films, champion "artistic and revolutionary Soviet productions," and "produce documentary films reflecting the lives and struggles of the American workers."[35] Harry Alan Potamkin, a vigorous advocate of avant-garde experiments of the 1920s, argued for the potential of films of "*montage* and document" to sharpen the technical skill, formal sensibility, and powers of political analysis of the amateur of modest means. "Bread lines and picket lines, demonstrations and police attacks," Potamkin proposed, were appropriate subject matter for aspiring working class filmmakers. Workers' groups, moreover, were strategically placed to provide support for pioneering efforts of this kind.[36] At the FPL, Hurwitz later recalled, "the great mystique of craft was being dissipated" as filmmakers taught themselves in an ongoing workshop and loose apprentice system.[37] Experimental films from Europe and America, along with the work of Soviet filmmakers, were screened, discussed, and mined for ideas and techniques. To an excitement with new forms of spatio-temporal perception made possible by the modern medium of cinema, Marxist political theory added the promise of a revolution in historical consciousness, a theme sounded in the pages of *Experimental Cinema*, published by Lewis Jacobs and David Platt in association with their amateur film club, the Cinema Crafters of Philadelphia, and echoed later in *Filmfront* and *New Theatre*, both of which were affiliated with the Film and Photo League. The infusion of amateur experimentation with new political commitments was for many young filmmakers a heady mix, as they envisioned the concurrent dawning of a new cinema and a new world. The 1920s amateur thus was recast as the 1930s cineaste-activist, with energies redirected to contemporary political concerns.[38]

As documentary production spread to other sites during the second half of the decade, rhetoric became more temperate. On the left, Popular Front politics muted calls for revolution, in cinema houses as well as in the streets. Meanwhile, social documentary was embraced as a defensible (if at times controversial) medium of persuasion by government agencies, labor unions, reform groups, and private foundations. The New Deal documentaries of Pare Lorentz, in particular, attracted wide acclaim for their forceful treatment of regional American themes. Yet even as debates concerning social documentary entered mainstream channels, the notion that documentary practices were necessarily experimental remained a recurring refrain. Over the horizon might reside an era of documentary guidebooks and manuals, but working filmmakers emphasized the contingent nature of their enterprise and, when opportunities arose, sought ways to expand the range of effects a documentary film might be thought able to achieve. "It was part essay, part poem, part political speech," Hurwitz later said of this new effort, "it was an attempt to create an emotional impact out of ideas, contradictions and conflicts."[39]

Viewed retrospectively, the principles governing experimentation by these filmmakers roughly match those David Bordwell has identified in the work of Soviet filmmakers of the 1920s.[40] American social documentary filmmakers, for example, considered the "art" of cinema a vital component of their work; debate centered on how aesthetic effects could best serve pragmatic ends. In these films, narration tends to be overt, foregrounding the relation of the film to an anticipated spectator, and often inviting that spectator to become one with a broader community the film posits and privileges. Causality is supra-individual, with the behavior of characters strongly marked according to social type. Abstract or associative patterns serve wider persuasive goals, as poetics and rhetoric converge. Social documentary projects, moreover, often draw on a prescribed set of argumentative commonplaces—the need for working class solidarity, for restoring depleted soil, for fighting fascism at home and abroad—which filmmakers sought to render vivid through experimental techniques. Thus while an argument, in broad outline, might be highly familiar, its unfolding on film could be fresh, unpredictable; should a technique seem inappropriate, the effect also could be deemed peculiar or strange.

Indeed, we might say that the effort to restore a social and historical dimension to the representation of "things" encouraged documentarists in the 1930s to crook, torque, or detour an argument or narrative in an effort to invest it with greater social texture, open up an unpredictable line of inquiry, or achieve a particular dramatic effect. To make a direct assertion, a simple slogan might suffice. But to represent a plausible social world on film entailed dividing, stratifying, and recombining elements in complex forms. In social documentary, as in historiography more broadly conceived, the tensions generated by competing patterns of imagery, emplotment, and rhetoric could powerfully evoke a sense of the density and mutability of social experience and the associative pathways of memory. In raiding the storehouses of both avant-garde and classical narrative techniques, early social documentarists thus explored forms of comprehension not restricted to straightforward, transparent description, even as they sought to authenticate these accounts by treating the photographic image as empirical evidence.

Consider, for example, one recurring pattern in these films, the forceful juxtaposition of contrasting social elements: worker/capitalist, farmland/dustbowl, illiteracy/schooling, peace/war, etc. At the local level, through rapid cutting, conceptual contrasts of this kind are sometimes invested with a brute perceptual force, as in the prologue to *Bonus March* (FPL, 1932) when a series of peacetime, military "travel" posters, swinging in the breeze, are abruptly intercut with

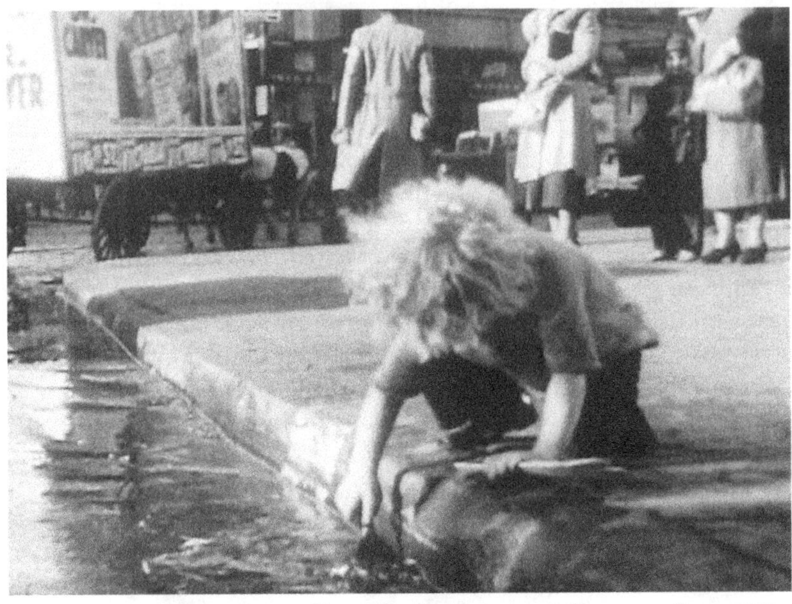

FIGURE 33.1 Scene from *The City*, directed by Willard Van Dyke. Still capture from DVD.

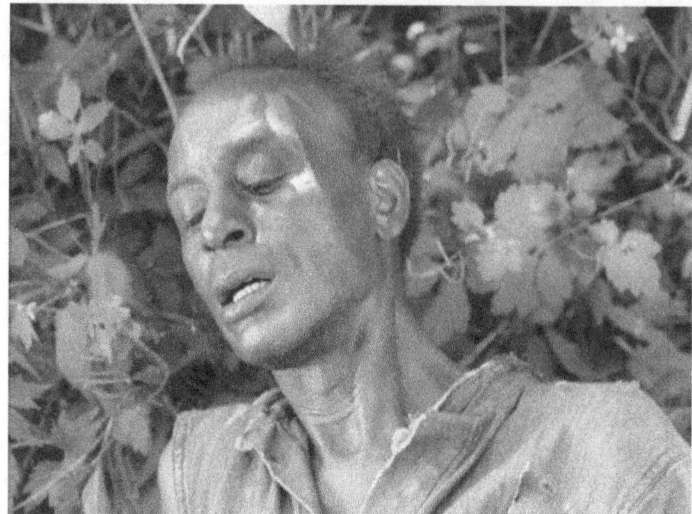

FIGURE 33.2 Scene from *Native Land*, directed by Leo Hurwitz and Paul Strand, with Louis Grant. Photo by Elinor Mayer. Still capture from DVD.

newsreel footage of destruction and carnage from World War I. These contrasts may also underpin broader principles of construction, as in the five-part division of *The City*, based upon alternative patterns of social organization, each composed in a different style, with the final segment, a modern Greenbelt village, graphically linked to the first, an old New England town, and culminating in a series of summary cuts that distill the large scale argument posed by the commentator: Urban slum or suburban utopia? "You take your choice." More complex, and unique among films of the period, is the structure of *Native Land*, in which an elaborate detective plot is built up from discrete sequences arranged to foreground bold stylistic shifts: in musical tone (upbeat, downbeat), *mise-en-scene* (light, dark), and narrative style (verbal recounting, dramatic reenactment). The most wrenching transition, moreover, is reserved for the penultimate scene, when a holiday ride on a merry-go-round is ruptured without warning by a montage of still photographs, reconstructing from fragmentary evidence the slaying of workers at the Republic Steel factory in Chicago on Memorial Day, 1937. In this instance, stylistic contrasts at the local level hook up with a broader, cyclical pattern of victory and defeat, motion and stasis, celebration and mourning that defines *Native Land*'s metahistorical ground.

Juxtapositions may also cut a different way, suggesting analogies or metaphors. In *The Plow That Broke the Plains*, tractors are likened to tanks, and grain spouts to cannons, as American agriculture goes to war. Later, flowing grain matches streaming ticker tape, and the quick hands of a jazz drummer are intercut with a vibrating ticker globe. A connection between economy and ecology is then sealed: the glass globe topples and shatters; fade out / fade in on parched, cracked, bone-strewn earth. *Men and Dust* (Dick, 1940) compares the diseased lungs of Ozark miners to eroded land by exploiting the overlapping term in "coal dust"/"dust bowl." As farmers dig irrigation ditches in *The Spanish Earth* (Ivens, 1936), soldiers dig trenches, linking civil war in Spain to land reform. Civilian and military life are bridged at the close of *Heart of Spain* (Kline, 1937) through a metaphor for the body politic drawn from the film's title: as blood is extracted from the arms of donors, new recruits march boldly to the front, acts of common sacrifice by a people unified by war. Hands, at first seen idle, turn to labor, then to commerce, in *Hands* (Steiner/Van Dyke, 1935), a promotional short for the Works Progress Administration (WPA); isolated and multiplied in quadrants and prismatic frames, these gestures stand in synecdochically for a recovering U.S. economy. At the close of *People of the Cumberland*, the outstretched arm of a young athlete, crosscut with the flow of water through a TVA dam, is replayed as a gesture of solidarity and political optimism by backwoods youth about to come of age.

Efforts to invest social arguments with emotion also motivate striking stylistic strategies. Here, again, montage principles dating back to the silent era are in evidence. Lewis Jacobs's published notes for *Highway 66*, an unproduced documentary, consist of fragmentary descriptions of urban prowling, billboard slogans, and rural despair; readable as disjunctive poetry, this loose scenario suggests the degree to which the shock effects of a modernist aesthetic seemed an appropriate vehicle in the early 1930s to express the disorientation of the Great Depression across regional lines.[41] *Ford Massacre* (Detroit FPL, 1932) argues for worker solidarity by including footage of a police attack on Dearborn auto workers, viewed at ground level by participating filmmakers. Close-range, hand-held camerawork and abrupt, discontinuous cutting, provide a visceral sense of violent disruption, of a struggle marked by high drama. Edited battle footage in *The Spanish Earth*, *China Strikes Back* (Frontier, 1937), and *Crisis* (Frontier, 1938) likewise emphasizes the percussive, disorienting force of attack and counterattack, adding a sense of urgency to partisan reportage and, in the process, establishing the model for many U.S. combat films of World War II.

Social documentary sound tracks often extend the range of these effects, in part through the sensory impact of sound effects and music, but also by way of the expressive function of the human voice. In the early 1930s, technological constraints limited sound recording, but lip-synchronized speech was on occasion employed to remarkably idiosyncratic effect. In The *Strange Case of Tom Mooney* (Los Angeles FPL, 1933) veteran Vitaphone director Bryan Foy withholds a lip-synchronized statement by Mooney until the closing moments of the film. With no more plot to be recounted, the incarcerated labor leader simply reminds his supporters that he is not getting any younger; his tremulous voice then yields to hauntingly silent footage shot at the time of his arrival in prison seventeen years before. ("It is a moment," one reviewer noted, "which some centuries of Hollywood could not erase from my mind.")[42] In the opening, nonvocal section of *Millions of Us* (American Labor Film, 1935), Slavko Vorkapich's impressionistic montage establishes a transient's hallucinatory state of mind, as images of food are superimposed upon his sleeping body. Then, in the final segment, the unemployed worker joins a union and his envisioned fantasies are replaced by lip-synchronized dialogue and his possession of a new collective, public voice.

By the late 1930s, thanks both to the critical success of Lorentz's poetic commentary for his New Deal documentaries and the greater resources documentarists had at their disposal, vocal patterns emerged as a carefully planned component of the formal design of these films. Beyond exposition and argument, voice-over narration often serves various expressive functions. Vocal commentators assume the voices of characters in *The Spanish Earth*, *Men and Dust*, *Power and the Land*, and *The Land* (Flaherty, 1942). Writer Ben Maddow and composer Marc Blitzstein designed the sound track to *Native Land* as an oratorio for the rich bass voice of Paul Robeson, who alternates between poetic commentary and songs. In his score for *Valley Town*, Blitzstein included recitatives for an unemployed mill worker and his wife; sung as interior monologues, the music recalls Kurt Weill's for Bertolt Brecht—and was altered by *Valley Town*'s disconcerted sponsor when the film first was released. Midway through *People of the Cumberland*, exposition unexpectedly gives way to breathless, first-person narration, as we witness a reenactment of the entrapment and slaying of a union organizer by anti-labor thugs. A scored double heartbeat, maternal and fetal, establishes the pace of an ominous childbirth scene at the outset of *The Fight for Life*.[43] Later, as a doctor wanders the night streets of Chicago, his soliloquy is counterpointed by Joe Sullivan's jazz score. In this instance, social documentary cinema anticipates the stylistic effects of *film noir*.

It may be appropriate, then, to speak of a tension in social documentaries of the 1930s between the assertion of direct propositions concerning social reality and something more open-ended, eclectic, and loose-fitting in the way in which the social problems are recounted and future solutions set forth on the screen. Strand's early effort to locate in straight photographic a human dimension—a way of thinking, an emotion felt—resurfaces in social documentary practices in patterns that are compound, oblique, and interlaced—in short, in a form that finally is anything but "straight." Even a film like *The River*, today often put forth as exemplary of a "classic" documentary style, achieves a sense of unity only through the strenuous orchestration of a wide range of diverse elements, across a series of discrete segments, incorporating natural, economic, and social histories of the Mississippi River bed through intricate variations on visual, vocal, and musical themes. Moreover, even when efforts to generate a sense of human drama and emotion brought documentary filmmakers into close contact with the conservative dramaturgical conventions of Hollywood fiction and Socialist Realism, these films tend to foreground an exploratory or experimental dimension to performance. In neither of Nykino's extant works, for example, does the psychology of individuated characters principally structure the film: *Pie in Sky* (1935) uses acting for improvisational satire; *The World Today* uses it to dramatize newsreel material, in the mixed format of *The March of Time*. Likewise, dramatic reenactments in *People of the Cumberland* and *Native Land* stress the localized, discrete effects the work of actors can achieve; within this context performance functions as simply one among several ways in which history may be reconstructed, dramatized, and assessed.

These examples, moreover, argue against the commonly held view that documentary filmmakers, historically, have sought to perfect an invisible style. Rather, it seems plain, varied conceptions of realism underpin the use of different techniques, some of which are foregrounded, others masked. *Nanook of the North* surely gained a wide audience in part because of Flaherty's mastery of conventions of seamless, continuity editing, but *Nanook*, *Moana* (1926), and *Man of Aran* (1934) also earned high marks from critics for their exceptional *compositional* beauty, which set the films apart from routine travelogue films. Moreover, in rejecting Flaherty's exotic imagery and domestic plots, a new generation of documentarists on the left in the 1930s privileged dynamic editing patterns that were highly pronounced, in search of perceptual effects and a conceptual logic that seemed commensurate with the acts of aggression, victimization, and resistance that these filmmakers took as their principle themes. Likewise, documentaries of liberal reform staked their claim to represent social reality in part on an exorbitant style; unexpected juxtapositions, dramatic set pieces, and odd transpositions in verbal diction or forms of address offer a more textured and conflicted view of social relations than do events more peaceably depicted or described.

To label social documentary in the 1930s as a utopian project is to call attention to both the formal ambitions of the filmmakers and their faith, unparalleled perhaps in the history of documentary cinema in the U.S., in new social compacts and the inextricable bond between political destiny and human design. Filmmakers, like the social theorists they sometimes quoted, were motivated by a passion to construct, with construction understood not as a mechanical or even necessarily efficient process but as a human activity involving dynamic experimentation with old and new forms. In these films, the power of social and technological innovation is repeatedly linked to the raw force and fecundity of nature, an image true to the organicist view of engineering articulated most fully by Mumford, whose Neotechnic Age was to be rational, not rationalized, inventive, not mechanized, cut to the measure of human hopes and desires, most especially the aspiration to make the world new.[44] Informed by a romantic streak that American modernism never fully shook off, these films are sometimes bleak but never nihilistic; even as scenes of poverty, disease, and despair are graphically rendered, future possibilities seem imminent. In part this is attributable to a recurring rhetorical trope: a closing call for commitment to a political program. But more persuasive than upbeat codas, appended to frankly dark reports, is a general commitment to problem solving to which stylistic shifts themselves give evidence.[45] Uneven in execution, experiments in documentary composition, convey, if nothing else, a sense of purposeful probing, a searching (and occasionally searing) quality that exceeds any simple effort to demonstrate a point. Like the picture of the Mississippi presented in *The River*—bent out of shape by failed social policies, but capable of alleviating social ills through better planning and design—the forked and twisted structures of these films exemplify both a sense of social disturbance and a human power to put things (back) together, drawing on past experience to order material in new and productive ways. Here formal experimentation seems part and parcel of social documentary's defense of the realm of social imagination, of the power to make palpable the corrosive effects of social ills and to plan and project a better world.

NOTES

1. For contemporary comment see Ben Belitt, "The Camera Reconnoiters," *The Nation*, 20 November 1937), pp. 557–558; reprinted in *The Documentary Tradition: From Nanook to Woodstock*, ed. Lewis Jacobs (New York: W. W. Norton, 1971), pp. 141–145; and "David Wolff" [Ben Maddow], "Film Intensity: *Shors*," *Films*, Spring 1940, p. 57. Consider, for example, the central role of Emile de Antonio, Lionel Rogosin, Shirley Clarke and Robert Frank in the formation of the New American Cinema Group in the early 1960s; or in recent years the conscious blurring or effacing of any workable distinction between documentary and avant-garde practices in films by Agnes Varda, Chris Marker, Raoul Ruiz, Trinh T. Minh-ha, Yvonne Rainer, Su Friedrich, Marlon Riggs, James Benning, and Morgan Fisher, among others. On the ties between the avant-garde and political documentary filmmaking in the 1960s and 1970s, see Michael Renov, "Newsreel: Old and New—Towards an Historical Profile," *Film Quarterly* 41, no. 1 (Fall 1987): 20–33 and David E. James, *Allegories of Cinema: American Film in the Sixties* (Princeton, N.J.: Princeton University Press, 1989), pp. 166–236.
2. John Grierson quoted by Paul Rotha in *Documentary Film* (London: Faber & Faber, 1939), p. 68; Paul Rotha, "The Documentary Method in British Films," *National Board of Review Magazine* (November 1937), p. 3; Richard Griffith, "A Note on Documentary Film," program note accompanying Museum of Modern Art retrospective, "The Non-fiction Film: From Uninterpreted Fact to Documentary," November 1939–January 1940, in File M257, Thomas J. Brandon Collection, Film Study Center, Museum of Modern Art (MoMA), New York City; Joris Ivens, "Notes on the Documentary Film," *Direction* 3, no. 4 (April 1940), p. 15; Arch Mercey, "New Frontiers for the Documentary Film," *Journal of the Society of Motion Picture Engineers* November 1939, p. 525.

   Film historians frequently have traced the foundation of a social documentary aesthetic to Grierson, but the impact of the work of Grierson and the British documentary school was not felt in the U.S. until later in the decade, thanks in large measure to Rotha, author of the first book-length study of documentary, who as a Rockefeller Fellow lectured on the topic and organized screenings at the Museum of Modern Art in 1937–38. It might be more appropriate, then, to view Grierson's initiatives in Great Britain (and later Australia and Canada) as symptomatic of a more global effort to define, refine, and promote a documentary film aesthetic in an era of mounting interest in the power of nonfictional cinema to shape a sense of social reality for a community of spectators. For a discussion of some common patterns among radical documentary film groups in Germany, France, England, and the U.S., see Jonathan Buchsbaum, "Left Political Film in the West: The Interwar Years," in Robert Sklar and Charles Musser, eds., *Resisting Images: Essays on Cinema and History* (Philadelphia: Temple University Press, 1990), pp. 126–148.

3. Efforts to recast documentary as a medium of filmic experiment also inspired a backlash. Oswell Blackstone in *Close-Up*, for example, argued that the power and lucidity of photographic observation had been spoiled by extravagant cinematic techniques: "We want documents which will show, with the clarity and logic of a scholar's thesis, the subjects they are supposed to tackle: we want no more filtered skies, 'Russian' montage and other vulgarities in our educational productions." See "Manifesto on the Documentary Film," *Close-Up* 10, no. 4 (December 1933): 325–326.
4. See Irving Lerner, "Robert Flaherty's Escape," *New Theatre*, December 1934, reprinted in *New Theatre and Film, 1934 to 1937*, ed. Herbert Kline (New York: Harcourt, Brace, Jovanovich, 1985) pp. 307–310; E. K. [Ed Kennedy], "The Films Look at the Worker," *Filmfront*, 24 December 1934, p. 6; and Sidney Meyers, "An Event: *The Wave*," *New Theatre and Film* November 1936, reprinted in Jacobs, ed., *The Documentary Tradition*, pp. 118–122. A similar critique of Flaherty was pursued in Great Britain; see David Schrire and John Grierson, "Evasive Documentary," *Cinema Quarterly* 3, no. 1 (Fall 1934): 7–9, followed by Grierson's qualified defense of Flaherty, pp. 10–11. Schrire's critique also included a polemic on how documentary was best to be defined, and excluded Flaherty's films from that definition.
5. Lázló Moholy-Nagy, "Light: A Medium of Plastic Expression," *Broom* 4, no. 4 (March 1923): 283–284; *Painting: Photography: Film* (Boston: American Photographic Publishing Co., 1931), first published as *Malerei, Fotografie, Film*, volume 8 in the Bauhaus book series (Munich: Albert Langen Verlag, 1925; rev. ed 1927).
6. Fernand Léger, "A New Realism—The Object (Its Plastic and Cinematographic Value)," *Little Review* 11, no. 2 (Winter 1926); 7–8; reprinted in *An Introduction to the Art of the Movies*, ed. Lewis Jacobs (New York: Noonday, 1960), pp. 96–98.
7. See Fernand Léger, "The Esthetic of the Machine: Manufactured Objects, Artisan, and Artist," *Little Review* 9, no. 3 (Spring 1923: 45–49), and continued in *Little Review* 9, no. 4 (Autumn–Winter 1923–1924): 55–58; "Film by Fernand Léger and Dudley Murphy," *Little Review* 10, no. 2 (Autumn–Winter 1924–1925): 42–44; see also "The New Realism," *Art Front* 2, no. 8 (December 1935): 10:11, reprinted in *Functions of Painting*, ed Edwary F. Frye (New York: Viking, 1973), pp. 109–113; and "The New Realism Goes On," *Art Front* 3, no. 1 (February 1937): 7–8.
8. Suggestively, Léger repeatedly insisted on the label "realism" over and against a term like "abstraction," perhaps because the latter undercut the concrete, worldly dimension to formal elements that he sought to promote. The theme endured in his writings over several decades. Modern notions that art should strip itself of representational trimmings and limit itself to its plastic, compositional elements, he observed in 1913, "is not simply a passing abstraction, valid only for a few initiates; it is the total expression of a new generation whose needs it shares and whose aspirations it answers." "The Origin of Painting and Its Representational Values," *Montjoie* (1913), reprinted in *Functions of Painting*, p. 10.
9. See Victor Turin, "The Problem of a New Film Language," translated by Christel Gang, *Experimental Cinema* 1, no. 3 (1931): 11–12; Mikhail A. Kaufman, "Cine Analysis," *Experimental Cinema* 1, no. 4 (1932): 21–23; "Dziga Vertov on Kino-Eye: Excerpts from a Lecture Given in Paris in 1929," *Filmfront* 1, no. 2 (7 January 1935): 6–8; Leon Moussinac, "Dziga Vertov on Film Technique," *Filmfront*, 1, no. 3 (28 January 1935), pp. 7–9. For responses to Vertov's films in the U.S, also see Simon Koster, "Dziga Vertoff," *Experimental Cinema* 1, no. 5 (1933): 27–28.

   In his commentary on contemporary cinema for a wide range of publications in the early 1930s, Harry Alan Potamkin also alerted the attention of readers in the U.S. to Soviet experiments in documentary, including Esther Shub's *The Last of the Romanoff Dynasty* (1927), Yakov Blok's *The Shanghai Document* (1928), and Mikhail Kalatozov's *Salt for Svanetia* (1930), as well as *Turksib* and *Man with a Movie Camera*. See especially "The Montage Film," *Movie Makers* (February 1930), reprinted in *The Compound Cinema: The Film Writings of Harry Alan Potamkin*, ed. Lewis Jacobs (New York: Teachers College Press, 1977), pp. 70–73; as well as 472–473, 59–65, 313–317. More generally on the distribution of, and critical response to, Soviet films in the U.S. during this period, see the "Hollywood Bulletin" column in *Experimental Cinema* 1, no. 2 (June 1930): 12–14; 1, no. 3 (1931): 22–23; and 1, no. 4 (1932): 54–60; Herman J. Weinberg, "The Foreign Language Film in the U.S." *Close-Up* 10, no. 2 (June 1933): 187–191; and Vlada Petric, *Soviet Revolutionary Film in America* (Ph.D. diss., New York University, 1973).
10. Moussinac, "Dziga Vertov on Film Technique," p. 7.
11. Both *Berlin: Symphony of a City* and *Man With a Movie Camera* were reviewed by Mordaunt Hall in *The New York Times*, the latter film twice. See "The Soul of a City," 14 May 1928, p. 25; " 'Moscow Today' Hailed," 13 May 1929, p. 27; and "Floating Glimpses of Russia," 17 September 1929, p. 36. On *The Man With a Movie Camera*, also see Jere Abbott, "Notes on Movies," *Hound and Horn* (December 1929): 159–162; and Evelyn Gerstein, "Three Russian Movies," *Theatre Guild Magazine* (October 1929): 14–16. The crucial role of *Berlin* in establishing documentary as a different kind of experimental cinema is evident in Potamkin's

suggestion in 1930 that among films where the "logic of images [are freed] from the logic of words . . . the practices are, for the most, either documentary (as in the composite newsreel *Berlin*), or effetely fanciful, an *atelier* experiment, as in France." See Potamkin, *The Compound Cinema*, pp. 45–46. In his discussions of Soviet documentary, Potamkin also frequently cites *Berlin* as precursor to Russian experiments.

12. On the relationship of straight photography to "objectivist" poetry, see Peter Schmidt, *William Carlos Williams, the Arts, and Literary Tradition* (Baton Rouge: Louisiana State University Press, 1989), pp. 10–47. On Precisionism, see Karen Tsujimoto, *Images of America" Precisionist Painting and Modern Photography* (San Franscico Museum of Modern Art, 1982). On the effort of 20th century photographers to reconcile science and art, see Peter Wollen, "Photography and Aesthetics," *Screen* 19, no. 5 (Winter 1978–79): 9–28.
13. Paul Strand, "Photography," *Seven Arts* (August 1917): 524–526; reprinted in Nathan Lyons, ed., *Photographers on Photography* (Englewood Cliffs, N.J.: Prentice-Hall, 1966), pp. 136–137.
14. Paul Strand, "Photography the New God," *Broom* 3, no. 4 (1922): 252–258; reprinted in Lyons, *Photographers on Photography*, pp. 138–144.
15. On the social dimension of Strand's style of documentary portraiture, see John Berger, "Paul Strand," *New Society* (1972); reprinted in *About Looking* (New York: Pantheon, 1980), pp. 41–47. The placement of Strand's camera, Berger writes, "is not where something is about to happen, but where a number of happenings will be related. Thus, without any use of anecdote, he turns his subjects into narrators" (p. 43). On the relationship of Strand's work to traditional views of technology and nature in America, see Ulrich Keller, "An Art Historical View of Paul Strand," *Image* 17, no. 6 (December 1974): 1–11.
16. David Platt, "The New Cinema," *Experimental Cinema* 1, no. 1 (1930): 1–2.
17. Lewis Mumford, *Technics and Civilization* (New York: Harcourt Brace Janovich, 1934), p. 5.
18. Ibid., p. 342.
19. Jan-Christopher Horak, "Modernist Perspectives and Romantic Desire: *Manhatta*," *Afterimage* 15, no. 4 (November 1987): 8–15.
20. Ralph Steiner, *A Point of View* (Middletown, CT: Wesleyan University Press, 1978), p. 10. John Grierson, in turn, would praise Steiner at the time of the release of *The City* "for a visual sense of things that must be one of the greatest influences in our observations today." See "Dramatizing Housing Needs and City Planning," *Films* 1, no. 1 (November 1939): 88.
21. An effort to reposition Steiner's photography within the framework of social documentary is evident in a four-page section devoted to his work in *Theatre Arts Monthly* 14 (January 1930): 77–81. Opening with strips of images from his recent films, the series proceeds to link Steiner's photographs in a logical sequence leading from "Nature's Own Design" (trees and clouds) through "Power from Nature" (electrical power lines) to "Nature Left Out" (a tattered poster for a Hollywood "talkie"). In short, the series is constructed as a proto-documentary montage on a theme central to social thought of the period.
22. Original members also included John Paul Edwards, Sonya Noskowiak, and Henry Swift. Invited to join the group for its first show at the De Young Museum in San Francisco in November 1932 were Conseulo Kanga, Alma Lavenson, Preston Holder, and Brett Weston. On the organization of the group, see Therese Tauh Heyman, ed., *Seeing Straight: The Group f.64 Revolution in Photography* (Oakland, CA: Oakland Art Gallery, 1992); and Michel Oren "On the 'Impurity' of Group f/64 Photography," *History of Photography* 15, no. 2 (Summer 1991): 119–127.
23. "Group f.64 Manifesto, 1932," in Heyman, ed., *Seeing Straight*, p. 53.
24. "Edward Weston," *Experimental Cinema* 1, no. 3 (1931): 13–15. Initially edited Platt and Jacobs in Philadelphia, *Experimental Cinema* had extensive coverage of Hollywood by Seymour Stern in Los Angeles. Potamkin originally served as New York editor, but split with the journal over a complicated dispute between *Experimental Cinema* and *Close-Up* after the first two issues. See "Editor's Note," *Experimental Cinema* 1, no. 3 (1931): 34.
25. David Platt, "Focus and Mechanism," *Experimental Cinema* 1, no. 2 (1931): 2–3; Lewis Jacobs, "Eisenstein," *Experimental Cinema* 1, no. 4 (1931): 4. In its second issue, *Experimental Cinema* also listed among its staff photographers Lázló Moholy-Nagy, Man Ray, El Lissitzsky, George Grosz, Ralph Steiner, and Charles Sheeler. However, the work of none of these photographers was published in the journal.
26. According to Balog, other members included Imogen Cunningham, Ansel Adams, Otto Hegel, Consuela Kanaga, Peter Stackpole, and briefly Dorothea Lange. Although asked to join, Weston reportedly declined: Balog interview with Tom Brandon, 18 March 1974, File I158, Brandon Collection, MoMA.
27. Calvin Tomkins, "Profile" and "Excerpts from Correspondence, Interviews, and Other Documents," in *Paul Strand: Sixty Years of Photographs* (Millerton, N.Y.: Aperture, 1976), pp. 24–25, 152–153.
28. See Amalie R. Rothschild's 1981 documentary, *Conversations with Willard Van Dyke*; "Thirty Years of Social Inquiry: An Interview with Willard Van Dyke by Harrison Engle," *Film Comment* 2, no. 2 (Spring 1965): 23–37; interview by G. Roy Levin, *Documentary Explorations: Fifteen Interviews with Filmmakers* (Garden City, N.Y.: Doubleday, 1971), pp. 175–193; and interview by Tom Brandon, Brandon Collection, File K223, MoMA.
29. Horak, "Modernist Perspective and Romantic Desire: *Manhatta*," pp. 8–15.
30. Leonard Hacker, *Cinematic Design* (Boston: American Photographic Publishing Company, 1931), pp. 73–112, 149–158.

31. On Strand's influence, see Leo Hurwitz, "One Man's Journey: Ideas and Films in the 1930s," *Cinema Journal* 15, no. 1 (Fall 1975): 6. Hurwitz's first film is described in his interview with Tom Brandon, 8 November 1975, File I183, Brandon Collection, MoMA.
32. At a 1940 symposium on film music, with Copland, Thomson, Blitzstein, Bowles, Hanns Eisler, and Benjamin Britten participating, the consensus of the panelists was that documentarles fostered more innovative collaboration between filmmaker and composer than did commercial film work. See "Music in Films: A Symposium of Composers," *Films* 1, no. 4 (Winter 1940): 5–19. In response to a major documentary retrospective at the Museum of Modern Art in the winter of 1939–1940, and two programs at the American Music Festival organized by radio station WNYC, music critic Kurt London came to a similar judgment, noting: "In this era of commercialized entertainment, it is the documentary more than any other form that allows musical and sound experimentation . . . The progressive documentary without a progressive use of sound or music is the exception and not the rule." See "Film Music of the Quarter," *Films* 1, no.2 (Spring 1940): 45. Participants at an evening of film music in New York sponsored by the League of Composers, London later reported, "were pretty well agreed that experimentation was possible only in the documentary field." See "Film Music of the Quarter," *Films* 1, no. 4 (Winter 1940): 26.
33. Jacob Riis, *How the Other Half Lives: Studies Among the Tenements of New York* (New York: Charles Scribner's Sons, 1890; reprint ed., New York: Dover, 1971).
34. Joris Ivens, "Collaboration in Documentary," *Films* 1, no. 2 (Spring 1940), p. 32. Ivens speaks here from personal experience, having made an abstract study of a bridge (*De Brug*) while still in the Netherlands in 1928. For earlier commentary on the logical connection between avant-garde and documentary filmmaking, see Ivens, "Some Reflections on Avant-Garde Documentaries," originally published in *La Revue des Vivants* 10 (October 1931), and reprinted in *Joris Ivens: 50 Years of Film-making*, ed. Rosaline Delmar (London: British Film Institute, 1979), pp. 98–100.
35. "Workers Films in New York," *Experimental Cinema* 1, no. 3 (1931): 37.
36. Harry Alan Potamkin, "Workers Films," *Daily Worker*, 31 May 1930, p. 3. Also see *The Compound Cinema*, pp. 397–398. As Patricia Zimmermann has argued, Potamkin helped to shift critical discourse on amateur filmmaking away from a preoccupation with domestic and leisure-time pursuits toward more public, political activity. See Zimmermann, "The Amateur, the Avant-Garde, and Ideologies of Art," *Journal of Film and Video* 38, nos. 3–4 (Summer/Fall 1986): 75–77. Similar advice was offered to amateur filmmakers in Great Britain: see EMBFU [Empire Marketing Film Board], "A Working Plan for Sub-standard," *Cinema Quarterly* 2, no. 1 (Fall 1933): 19–25.
37. Hurwitz, "One Man's Voyage," p. 10.
38. This sense of political urgency can be found in the evolution of an organization as innocently named as the Nature Friends Photo-Group in New York. In 1935, members reported that they had collaborated on their first 16mm film, a four-reel production contrasting scenes of crowding and breadlines in New York City with recreational activities in their rural campgrounds. "League News: Nature Friends Photo Group Challenges," *Filmfront* 1, no. 3 (28 January 1935): 14–15.
39. Hurwitz interview with Brandon, Brandon Collection, MoMA.
40. David Bordwell, *Narration in the Fiction Film* (Madison: University of Wisconsin Press, 1985), pp. 234–273.
41. Lewis Jacobs, "*Highway 66*: Montage Notes for a Documentary Film," *Experimental Cinema* 1, no. 4 (1932), pp. 40–41.
42. Robert Littella, "Sound Without Fury," *New Republic* 71 (6 September 1933): 102.
43. For Pare Lorentz's conception of the soundtrack for this passage, as well as other instructions concerning the score, see Lorentz's notes to composer Louis Gruenberg, published in *The Best Film Plays, Vol. II*, ed. John Gassner and Dudley Nichols (New York: Garland, 1977), pp. 1082–1087.
44. Critics pursued organic metaphors as well. Consider the comment by Ben Belitt, quoted at the outset of this essay. Belitt's image of experimental photography on social themes as "not a fad, but a flowering" suggests that innovative work by documentarists, instead of being chic or fashionable, was earthbound. However colorful, vivid, and varied, it was rooted in the land, where social experience (as so many documentaries of the period sought to make plain) properly began. So grounded, Belitt proposed, documentary films reconnected social actors with the drama of their historical moment, offering (in a phrase Belitt takes from Peter Quince in *A Midsummer's Night Dream*) "a marvelous convenient place for our rehearsal." See "The Camera Reconnoiters," p. 558.
45. On the process by which technology is linked to nature in New Deal documentaries, see *Paul Arthur*, "Jargons of Authenticity (Three American Moments)," in Michael Renov, ed., *Theorizing Documentary* (New York: Routledge, 1993), pp. 108–134.

34

SAMUEL BRODY

THE REVOLUTIONARY FILM

Problem of Form (1934)

The question: What is the medium of revolutionary film production in capitalist countries such as America? The answer: First and foremost the filmed document. Movie reportage. Reality recorded on film strips and subjected to the painstaking technical operations, montage, whereby these strips are built up into wholes embodying our revolutionary interpretation of events. This is neither a makeshift nor a degradation of the creative potentialities of the cinema. The bourgeois film has vulgarized and perverted the greatest faculty of the movie, never having raised it above the level of the newsreel.

Are we for the documentary simply because the studio-acted film is beyond our material reach? No. Strange as it may seem our orientation in this question is one of principle based on what we think is the most convincing and effective medium for "the camera in the class struggle." It is true that the method of the revolutionary filmed document will lead us miles away from the forms and requirements of the enacted studio film. This may cause many to shed a tear. It is, in fact, already causing tears. Our answer? We are forging the film into a working class weapon. And workers' films will be most art when they are most weapon.

In the film there exists no "happy medium" between the histrionic recreation of reality and directly recorded reality itself. "The illusion of reality in the cinema," writes Leon Moussinac, "must remain constant, even in the domain of the fantastic. In other words, in the cinema the sensation of reality is indispensable to emotion." Associate filmed reality and its reconstructed counterpart into a unified structure and you find "the sensation of reality" irremediably disrupted.

We are practical people. Our theories are acquired at the cost of badly burned fingers. Exhibit A: The Struggle For Bread.

We have, on the other hand, long ago discovered and tested the power and effect of simple and direct visual reporting.

Our records of the Detroit Ford Massacre, the Scottsboro Case, the Bonus March, etc., are ample proof that even when we abstain from "constructively editing" our photographed documents, they nevertheless retain an inestimable importance if for no other reason than that they are irrefutably convincing exposes. The Pathe Newsreel of the Ambridge massacre is a supreme example of the political value to us of motion picture reportage. We must train working class camera-men whose function in the workers' film movement will correspond to that of worker-correspondents in the field of revolutionary journalism.

We have as yet accomplished little in the sphere of the documentary film in which it is essential for us to intervene; to organize the raw material into a unified revolutionary interpretation. This represents an almost totally unexplored form calling for the highest degree of skill and talent in the realm of cinematic creation. Our best teachers in this respect are the Soviet directors of the documentary school who have tremendously enriched the arsenal of revolutionary film culture with such masterpieces as *Shanghai Document*, *Spring*, etc. Our own *Washington Hunger March* and the sparklingly brilliant strip on the Washington Farmers Convention represent significant attempts in what must become the broad pattern for the production of films in the American working class film movement.

The resolution of the first conference of the Cinema Bureau of the International Union of Revolutionary Theatre suggests the didactic short film as an important form of our production. Match the moving diagram, chart or graph for workers study groups, if you can. We have completely neglected the educational short. We must build up a 16mm film library which will comprise a complete course in political education for workers. A joint task for the Film and Photo League and the faculty of the Workers School. In this connection we can avail ourselves of the mass of data and, research compiled by departments of visual instruction in various institutions of bourgeois learning. Important scientific discoveries on methods of education through the moving image have been made during the last few years. These we must dig out of the specialized spheres of college laboratories where they are doomed to remain by virtue of their narrow and exclusive application (does Hollywood need them?) and use them for our purpose. Three distinct branches of the documentary method, therefore, comprise the scope of our production. Film reporting, or the recording of highlights in the class struggle which are of political value as events over-flowing the frame which merely acts as the carrier, Ambridge, Scottsboro, Detroit Massacre, Tom Mooney Run, etc. The synthetic documentary, the effect and intent of which is one hundred percent dependent on the intervention of the "editor," *The Land of The Free, Imperial Valley*, etc. The frankly educational film for purposes of direct political economic instruction.

The Film and Photo League is beginning to assume a status more commensurate with its great cultural-political importance in the struggles of the working class.

The Hollywood machine is being geared to the political and economic policies of its Wall Street owners. The production of reactionary, openly pro-war films is no longer the exception but the rule. The League's program of struggle against Hollywood is clear. We have already tested this program in action. There exist among us no political differences concerning methods of agitation and propaganda to be employed in struggling against the films of the enemies of the working class.

35

LEO T. HURWITZ

THE REVOLUTIONARY FILM

Next Step (1934)

The film movement in America has for some time been faced with the problem of what film forms are its true concern. The Film and Photo Leagues have up to now produced mainly newsreels. They are necessary because of the rigid censorship and the malicious distortion that the capitalist film companies use in their treatment of events relative to labor and labor's struggles. These newsreels serve an agitational and revelational function to arouse the working class, and as a corrective for the lies of the capitalist agencies. A strike, demonstration or hunger march is shown with the full brutalities of the police, with the full heroism and militancy of the workers, without the distractive mocking comment of the bourgeois announcer.

Because newsreels are fractional, atomic and incomplete, the revolutionary movement has required a more synoptic form to present a fuller picture of the conditions and struggles of the working class. And so the synthetic documentary film has become an important form for film workers in the revolutionary movement—a form which allows for more inclusive and implicative comment on our class world than the discursive newsreel. For this great and rich medium the bourgeois filmers have had little use, since they cannot face the truths that the documentary camera can report. Their lies are better served by a more closely supervised camera in a shadowed studio under the kind sun of California. Aside from a few reels on sports, some shorts of believeitor-nots, and the half-truth-half-lies of industrial and "educational" films, Hollywood has ignored the vast possibilities of the synthetic film document.

Another factor, besides its great effectiveness, has determined the preoccupation of the radical movie-makers with the documentary film. At this time, with the radicalized working class as small as it is, it is almost impossible for economic and technical reasons to undertake the vast task of producing and distributing revolutionary dramatic films, which, in some ways, are capable of going beyond the document (as the synthetic document transcends the newsreel) in its width of scope, its synoptic approach, in its ability to recreate events and emotions not revealable to the camera in the document.

The problems of documentary montage are very different from that of the dramatic film. The former may be called *external* montage, the creative comparison, contrast and opposition of shots, externally related to each other, to produce an effect not contained in any of the shots—or, as Samuel Brody has well described it, "reality recorded on film strips and built up into wholes embodying our revolutionary interpretation of events." For this type of cutting, *The Man With the Movie Camera* is the textbook of technical possibilities. The dramatic film presents the problem of what may be called *internal* montage, which is essentially a recreative analysis and reconstruction of an internally related visual event in terms of shots of film, to reveal best the meaning of the event. The documentary film embodies the reporting on film of actual events and the creative addition of these bits of cinematographed reality to render an interpretation of that reality. The dramatic film involves in its cinematography the interpretive breaking-up of the recreated reality, and, in its montage, the synthesis of these analysed elements to recreate the event on film from a given point of view.

Any acted sequence in an ordinary film will serve as an illustration of internal montage—any direct succession of acts to render a dramatic event. An example of external montage may be taken from a recent newsreel compilation by the New York Film and Photo League. The newsreel shots are sure: President Roosevelt signing a state paper and looking up at the camera with his inimitable self-satisfied smile, and a shot of fleet manoeuvers—two shots taken in widely separated times and places and not essentially (but *externally*) related to each other. By virtue of splicing the shot of the warships just after Roosevelt signs the paper, and following the threatening ships of war, with the rest of the first shot (Roosevelt looks up and smiles), a new meaning not contained in either shot, but a product of their new relation on film, is achieved—the meaning of the huge war preparation program of the demagogic Roosevelt government.

External and internal montage, as described here, are by no means mutually exclusive. Both may be used, and in fact have been used frequently to complement each other—sometimes with emphasis on the document as in *Ten Days That Shook The World*, sometimes with the emphasis on the recreated drama, as in *The End Of Saint Petersburg*.

A mixed form of the synthetic document and the dramatic is the next proper concern of the revolutionary film movement: to widen the scope of the document, to add to the document the recreated events necessary to it but resistant to the documentary camera eye—a synthetic documentary film which allows for material which recreates and fortifies the actuality recorded in the document and makes it clearer and more powerful.

The training of revolutionary film makers in America has come wholly from their experience in the newsreel and documentary film. What has been learned of the problems of shooting and cutting has been learned in the crucible of events, in preparing films of workers' struggles to be used in turn as a weapon in these struggles. In order to study the problems of internal montage and to prepare for the making of the type of film indicated above, ten or twelve members of the Potamkin Film School, under the technical direction of Ralph Steiner, are working in an experimental group at the Film and Photo League. They have set themselves a series of problems, each involving the writing of a shot-by-shot continuity for the sequence to be filmed, photographing of the sequence and the final editing. Two problems have so far been completed. The first, to render the simple act of an unemployed man entering his room after an exhausting day of job-hunting, sitting down, tired, worn and without hope. The second, a continuation of the first, the landlord entering the room to serve the tenant with a dispossess for non-payment of rent. This group works wholly with non-actors in order to duplicate conditions which will occur in making films later. The great task is to learn how to make the camera eloquent, how to make use of the natural acts of an untrained actor to serve the needs of the scenario.

It is too early to indicate the nature of the films which will be made along the lines indicated here. However, the plan is to develop this experimental group into a production group within the Film and Photo League for the purpose of making documentary-dramatic revolutionary films—short propaganda films that will serve as flaming film-slogans, satiric films and films exposing the brutalities of capitalist society.

36

RALPH STEINER AND LEO T. HURWITZ

A NEW APPROACH TO FILM MAKING (1935)

Last winter Lee Strasberg, one of the directors of the Group Theatre, gave a course in theatre direction at the Theatre Collective school.* We, as film makers, with no opportunity to learn the principles of our craft except by (expensive) trial and (mostly) error derived so much benefit from his patient, brilliant, analytical lectures that we are moved to present something of what we have learned to other film makers. With no film school in America led by an Eisenstein we feel that revolutionary movie makers must go for help to theatre workers like Strasberg and others who have thought deeply on the problems of films.

Although we film makers have problems some of which relate to those of the theatre and others which are of necessity different, since we work in a different medium, this course has given us what amounts to a completely new approach to both. In addition it has given us concrete methods of attacking a number of these basic problems. Not only did we get a clearer view of the main objectives toward which we have been groping but also an equally clear indication of the means by which they can be achieved in terms of the screen.

In the first place Strasberg emphasized the necessity of getting at the basic meaning of the scenario—of defining with the utmost clarity what must be said with the film as a whole. For instance: two theatres in Moscow produced Gorki's *Yegor Buletchev* and though in both the actors spoke the same lines each theatre gave the play an entirely different meaning; the Moscow Art Theatre produced a play about the death of a man by cancer; to the Vaghtangov Theatre the same play was not only about the death of a man but also the disintegration of a whole class of society. Strasberg gave us a

*This article is based on report given at the conclusion of Lee Strasberg's course.

method of research to determine the basic idea of the script when it is not discoverable from the scenario itself. This research tries to determine what in the life and time of the author led to the writing of the scenario and effected and conditioned its contents.

Secondly, with the basic idea determined Strasberg suggested a method of applying it to the production in order to obtain interest and reality: how the basic idea determines the style; how to work on the problem of the sets and background in relation to the idea; how to work with the actor and how to invent his activities.

Third, he made us conscious that every step in film making, must be related to an audience. He made us realize that the film is *theatrical*—that is, it communicates its meaning by the recreation of dramatic situations in filmic time and space, and depends for its effectiveness on the emotional involvement of the audience in these situations. That unless this audience response is obtained, films, however profound and socially important in subject, will be lifeless and socially ineffectual.

The significance of this whole approach to us and to other film makers can be better understood by indicating our previous histories as film makers and the major influences which effected our point of view. There were three main factors in our development each of which contributed influences of definite positive value but each of which also warped our basic attitude toward the film medium.

The Formal Revolt from Hollywood—During the twenties we grew disgusted with the philistinism of the commercial film product, its superficial approach, trivial themes, and its standardization of film treatment: the straight-line story progressing from event to event on a pure suspense basis, unmarred by imaginative use of the camera, unmarred by any freshness in editing or any human or formal sensitivity. Our reaction, which we shared with the young generation of experimental film makers, was a more or less aesthetic revolt from the current manner of film production. The important thing, we felt was to do those things which the film was capable of, but which the commercial film didn't and couldn't possibly do. There seemed unbounded possibilities for the use of the films as a visual poetry of formal beauty.

The potentialities of the camera were explored: angles, lens distortions, camera tricks; the play of light, the magnificence of objects and objects in motion; the eloquence of things, rhythmic possibilities, and symphonic treatment.... It was a period in which much was learned and explored about the technical resources of cinematography and montage, but the whole emphasis was on the beauty, the shock, the effectiveness of OBJECTS, THINGS—with no analysis of the effect on an audience. In fact, the quick demise of this movement is proof that the audience got next to nothing out of it, though, certainly, technical advances were made. It could lead to nothing else but ivory tower aesthetic films, unrelated to contemporary life. The film had been depersonalised, inhuman; the THING, technique and formal problems were supreme. Even people were considered externally, as objects rather than as human beings. Those who went through this period had for a time a definite mark left on them even though they came out of it disillusioned into a more salutary field.

Pudovkin's Film Technique—The second main influence was Pudovkin's book, *On Film Technique*.The book itself, one of the first and best theoretical analyses of the film medium, satisfied an important need in the young and immature art of the movies. But its whole concern quite naturally was with the special problems of film technique, those problems that *differentiate* the film from any other medium. It did not concern itself with the basic dramatic principles that are *common* to all the theatrical arts. We made the error of overlooking the fact that

Pudovkin was presupposing this base, and we considered the book a Bible of *film principles* rather than a series of collected essays on *film technique*. It is easy to see what errors might flow from laying the entire emphasis, as we did, on the secondary principles of film technique without grasping or even realising there exist the primary dramatic principles without which a theatrical art cannot affect and involve an audience.

Pudovkin's concern with the end problems—the detailed shooting script, the taking of the shot and the final editing—did not give us the basis for the primary step—the conception and rendering of the story, mood or idea in dramatic terms (theatricalization).

What we came away with from Pudovkin was briefly this: The basic thing in movie making is *editing* (montage). Editing gives life and meaning to dead strips of film by virtue of the context—just as a sentence in a poem vitalises and gives new meaning to the individual words that, taken by themselves, are lifeless and without overtones. The content of a shot is relatively unimportant; its effect is the result of what comes before and after, the elements that react with it. You can take a shot of a man with a blank expression, as Kuleshov did, and edit the same piece of film with a shot of a plate of soup, or a woman lying partially nude on a bed—and the same piece of film takes on two different meanings in the different contexts. In the one he appears hungry; in the other he appears lustful. The whole series of Kuleshov-Pudovkin experiments in cutting and the principles that were deduced have a tremendous value, but in so far as they taught us that the content of the shot was unimportant that the meaning of a sequence depended on editing, they gave us an approach which led us off on the wrong track.

This point of view "made it unnecessary" for us to think about the main problem of film making: the theatricalization of human ideas and situations (*mise en scene*)—in the words of Leo Strasberg, "...the creation of circumstances which make a scene possible, alive and full of suspense...the building up of the circumstance, character, etc. so that the action becomes not only plausible but necessary..." Pudovkin, as a movie director, is brilliant in his invention of such circumstances and activity, but in his book he is concerned not with the problem of their invention but largely with the technical problem of how they are executed in production and editing. For example, in his book Pudovkin describes how he made an extraordinary scene in *Storm Over Asia*, the scene at the trading post where the hero brings in the valuable silver fox, which is envied by all the other trappers. Pudovkin does not tell us the process of the theatricalization of the scene with all its circumstances from the scenario; he rather describes *how* he got the special effect that he wanted by using jugglers and magicians to fascinate the crowd of trappers with their tricks, and photographing their hypnotically fascinated faces without their knowledge. He edited this piece of film with some shots of the valuable silver fox, and the effect in the film was to make the fox appear tremendously valuable in their eyes. It can easily be seen what the effect of this type of emphasis on the *technique of execution* (the results obtained by placing together unrelated pieces of film to create a new unity), would have on film makers who did not first understand the primary dramatic problem of constructing the scene in space and time from the words of a scenario. Our whole orientation was toward editing or montage and toward special filmic techniques, without understanding that these were only the *means* for the shaping and communication of a *basic dramatic stuff*. It reemphasized our already formal approach.

As a result of this attitude we were unable to understand or utilize the problems that were sent to us from Eisenstein's classes in the Moscow Film School. Once of the problems was to stage, to create, the *mise en scene* of a situation in which a soldier comes back from two years at the front to find his wife with a new-born baby. We could see no profit in attempting to conceive this situation for the stage, nor how it would aid us in the making of films. Had we been asked to do a shot by shot camera script of the incident we would have seen some point in it. We did not realise that the staging—the invention of activity and circumstances to recreate the scene in space and time—was a necessary step before a shooting script could be made. Without this step a shooting script might result in an interesting camera and montage treatment, but would never bring the situation to life for an audience.

The Documentary Film—It is natural, out of this background, after the first flush of excitement in the purely formal experimental film, and after we arrived at our conception of the movie as a class weapon, that our interest would be concentrated in the documentary film—the film that catches reality on the wing as it passes by. In making a documentary film, as we then conceived it, you photographed the event and the things that were relevant to it, and then by means of clever editing you could do most anything in making the film effective. In brief this was our approach: You were going to do a film about the Scottsboro case, or New York Harbor. You knew what the film was going to say. Then you took your camera and attempted to capture completely as you could the most meaningful visual aspects of reality. Then, to the cutting room, where you pieced the film together in a brilliant and cogent montage to make it a moving document of life. Only somehow it was never really moving. At best it turned out to be a conceptualized statement, a film concerned with objects and the purely external manifestations of people without their emotions or motivations, a pamphlet on the screen, to which you could say "yes" with your mind, but your emotions weren't involved.

In our documentary films, we relied on the idea that photographed reality contained its own dramatic punch, and while it is certainly true that documentary material has a finality and incontrovertability and carries with it a special persuasiveness, we did not realise that this was not enough to involve an audience's emotions, to create drama. We did not realize that even in a documentary film it is still necessary to use theatrical means of affecting an audience—suspense, build, dramatic line, etc.

With this background and the feeling that something was missing, we entered Strasberg's course in direction. The specific techniques applicable to all phases of film making, from scenario writing to directing the actor, which we found there, we have tried to indicate briefly. But most important of all we found a basic approach toward film making, which if put into practice can raise the revolutionary film far above its present low level. We learned that the film as a dramatic medium cannot merely concern itself with external happenings even though they be revolutionary happenings, but must embody the conflict of underlying forces, causes. That to achieve this the making of a film involves not merely: (1) knowing what you want to say, (2) a scenario, and (3) shooting and cutting it, but the intermediate steps of theatricalizing the events through the invention of circumstances and activities which transform concepts, relationships and feelings into three dimensional happenings that are plausible, effective and rich in significance. Only in solving problems does it seem likely that a film conduit can be constructed which can carry our revolutionary viewpoint to an increasingly receptive audience, one that is really moved because in the life on the screen it finds its own aspirations and struggles, its own failures and successes, its own truths.

37

WILLARD VAN DYKE

LETTER FROM KNOXVILLE (1936)

Knoxville, Tennessee

So far, Pare and I have gotten along famously. He trusts me to do this job in the South without him and has indicated he has a lot of faith in my work. It is too early to say anything yet, but I have a vague suspicion that this will not be a completely bad picture from any point of view. Which is another way of saying that I think he knows more of what he wants than he has been given credit for. If, as I said before, you can try to translate what he is saying into visual terms, you're okay. Of course it isn't always easy.

The valleys are flaming with color, and the somber mood of the earth stirs old memories and old nostalgias. Life has meaning; arising out of ancient death and decay giving way to new life.

It is very hard to say what the chances for the future are in this thing. One can't know what the people in Washington are thinking. It seems that Pare gets along well with Tugwell, and that Tugwell is interested at least in this picture if not in a permanent program. I feel that if this one thing is good, it will mean a big step toward the ultimate establishment of a film producing section in the government. I don't think it will happen tomorrow, though. And I don't think it will be like any other department the government now has. But that is all a long story, and one that will take much time in the telling. One thing you can be sure of—if there is a permanent program, and if there is a guy named Lorentz connected with it, there will be a cameraman who will soon be a director and whose name is Van Dyke also connected with it. Pare is sold on my ability to direct people and that is why I am down here alone to do this job. Not that I feel I know anything about directing yet—you know I don't feel that, but I do know more that he does. I have had long talks with him about Faulkner, Dos Passos, Caldwell, Farrell and the rest of the boys, and I find that he has a very clear critical analysis ready for all of them. He isn't dumb about literature a bit, and he thinks I am pretty unusual to have read what I have and to agree with him so thoroughly. In other words, I really like the guy quite a lot.

But if nothing ever happens in the future, the gold and red of the trees, the somber quiet skies and the feel of myself traveling over the earth will be a memory I shall always cherish. It is a good earth and a good life and there is much to be done. Could I ask for more?

38

RALPH STEINER

LETTER TO JAY LEYDA (1935)

October nine

Dear Jay:

We (Paul Strand, Leo & I) are out here making (God help us) a film for the Resettlement Administration of the government. It isn't going to be much of a film as the man who is running it, Pare Lorentz—film reviewer for *Judge*, is a completely mush minded individual. The film has possibilities: it's about the cause of the dust storms which is the exploitation of the soil—unthinking of the future and ruthless, but not much will come out of it. We did a scenario but it didn't look important enough to Lorentz who doesn't realize that with two reels on such a big subject the film has to be simple. He has given us a scenerio with suggested shots that none of us can puzzle out. He has a curious mind that is always in such a hurry to get to step B that he never does step A—always telephoning twenty people about arrangements for shooting or travelling right through a scenerio [*sic*] conference. He wires us that he has shipped us film and hasn't, sends telegrams by the score most of which communicate nothing to us and makes twenty dollar calls to tell us to take shots we've told him we're already made. He wants mostly shots and hopes they'll fit together in the cutting room. We are all three government employees, sworn to uphold so help us God without mental reservations the constitution of the U.S. and get $25 per ("dime" as they say it in Washington) day plus our rail road passes and 5 a day for subsistance. The job is so Alice in Wonderland that we are sort of girl schoolish and make endless bad puns practically all the time. The country is very swell around here—the people aren't really tougher than those in the East nor do, as we heard, the birds make nests out of barbed wire but the country is rougher and enormous: a man tells us to look at his hay meadow and we find it fifteen miles long and five wide, his pasture is fifty five miles long. They don't like dollar bills "folding money" but clank with silver dollars. There's a chief Four Balls (testes) in town and actually a "shits-behind-the-Teepee" on the reservation. We go today to Texas for a few weeks and then back to N.Y. perhaps to make a film for the new masses. Paul has become a member of the full time section of NYKino and should be a great help to us. By the way, what happened in the Eisenstein-Strand business, and why

14 MILES FROM CUSTER BATTLEFIELD IN THE HEART OF THE CROW INDIAN COUNTRY

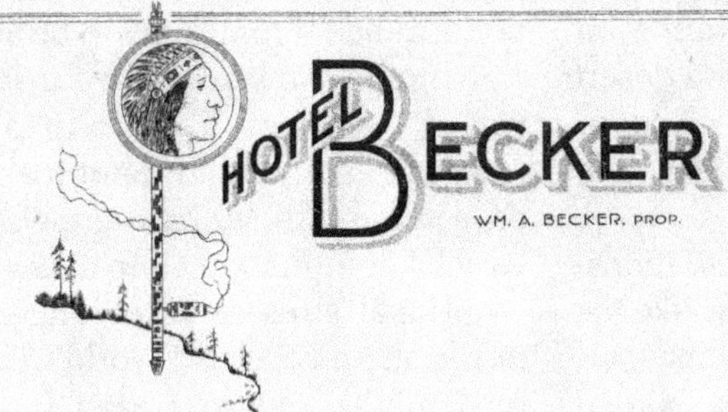

MODERN THROUGHOUT

[1930s]

Hardin, Montana

October nine

Dear Jay:

We (Paul Strand, Leo & I) are out here making (God help us) a film for the Resettlement Administration of the government. It isn't going to be much of a film as the man who is running it, Pare Lorentz - film reviewer for Judge, is a completely mush minded individual. The film has possibilities: it's about the cause of the dust storms which is the exploitation of the soil - unthinking of the future & ruthless, but not much will come out of it. We did a scenerio but it didn't look important enough to Lorentz who doesn't realize that with two reels on such a big subject the film has to be simple. He has given us a scenerio with suggested shots that none of us cam puzzle out. He has a curious mind that is always in such a hurry to get to step B that he never does step A - always telephoning twenty people about arrangements for shooting or travelling right through a scenerio conference. He wires us that he has shipped us film and hasn't, sends telegrams by the score most of which communicate nothing to

FIGURE 38.1 Detail of letter from Ralph Steiner to Jay Leyda, October 9, 1935. Courtesy of Tamiment Library, New York University, and the estate of Jay Leyda.

couldn't he get a worker's visa or why couldn't or why didn't Eisenstein want to (if it was a case of that) and why did you desert Paul at the end and not answer his please to know what was wrong and why Eisenstein wouldn't answer his telegrams?

I don't know if you've heard of the National Film alliance which is supposed to be like the New Theatre League, to stimulate and promote anti war and Fascist films. It was started by a big blow up at the F & Ph. League at which all the big theatre and cultural directors of the party were. All the films for years back were shown in an all day and a night session. Some F & P people and Leo, Irving & I were in on it, but I've resigned (I could since I'm not a party member) as the F & P members are again (like Brandon) more interested in power and playing politics than in stimulating film production. After a couple of dirty dishonest deals I quit and asked to have my name withdrawn from the list of directors and sponsors. That helped some and the party organizer Merritt Crawford, an old film man—founder of some of the film papers is now bearing down on the lice. What is especially bad is that the two bad influences are party members and the whole thing is a united front movement. It got to be just like the old hysterical Brandon-Brody days with rail roadings of people (dopes) like Irving Browning onto the executive committee when we need people like George Sklar, Paul Peters, Herb Kline etc. If they can throw out the two worst elements I'll come back and work. Your old friend Frank Ward is in on it and kissed the asses of the boys who talk loudest and fastest. They tried at one meeting where Leo was missing, to pull the old Brandon line about class struggle etc, etc. and what Karl said on page 376 but I've gotten to the point where I know enough about the class struggle and the party line to separate dopey or dishonest ideas from the left wing lingo.

One of the best stunts is to (a German by the name of Tisch pulled it on me) preface a phoney idea with the statement with: "my political belief forces me to be a realist. . . ."

I in enclosing part of your last letter for you to read. I could go to great lengths to say what I think but I'll put it simply: in the days when I knew you there were incidents which demonstrated that under certain emotional stresses your judgements were not based on the real world of things, people, and the laws governing them that I was familiar with. This was not only my opinion but was shared by more than one of your associates (and friends). This seems to me to be a clear case of your going off into some strange Dayton–childhood–Leyda world in which things aren't as they are to most of us. I can say this: that you haven't any stauncher friend than Leo, that the last thing in the (this) world that he is a devil or a person that would stab anyone in the back much less you of whom he is very fond. I say trust me in this and write him an apology.

Did you or are you going to make a film in China or has the Eisenstein still work prevented? We had Pabst and Ermler see *Pie in the Sky* and they both liked it but Ermler peed all over us for not thinking out more clearly our line before making the film. The film is very good in some of its acting and very imaginative but is too "sacriligious" for any but very left conscious audiences.

What did you think of the thing Leo and I did in new Theatre? We learned a lot from Leo and from Gadget Kazan's class at new Theatre League, even if you might not guess as much from the article.

Don't you have to come back some day to retain your citizenship? Come back just in time to "turn the guns the other way" in the next world war. Lots of affectionate greetings. How, if and when, are you going to pay your way back?

Ralph

39

JOHN T. MCMANUS

DOWN TO EARTH IN SPAIN (1937)

Joris Ivens, the aware little Dutchman who is continuing, through the medium of the documentary motion picture, the art tradition of the Dutch and the Flemings in realism, is currently in Manhattan, back from having shown his latest film, *The Spanish Earth*, to President Roosevelt and to Hollywood.

Mr. Ivens made *The Spanish Earth* under the sponsorship of Contemporary Historians, Inc., a group headed by Lillian Hellman, Archibald MacLeish, John Dos Passos, Ernest Hemingway and others passionately concerned with the struggle of the people of the Spains to quell their country's insurgents and all they represent.

The conception of *The Spanish Earth* is Mr. Ivens's own, however, and it is concerned primarily with the efforts of a peasant people to reclaim for themselves, by irrigation and toil, a land that had been neglected through generations of absentee ownership, while the struggle to preserve their new liberties, their new right to make the soil yield for themselves, goes on virtually at their doors. This, says Mr. Ivens, is the meaning of the war in Spain. It is, he says, a war for melons, tomatoes, onions—not one for broad principles of ideology.

The first one to see *The Spanish Earth* outside of the laboratory projection room was President Roosevelt, who viewed it on July 7. Mr. Ivens was particularly gratified at the President's expert appreciation of film values. Without reporting his entire chat, he said the President remarked on the "fine continuity" of the picture, and had been impatient with a White House aide who disturbed him several times during the screening.

* * *

The Hollywood showings—there were several—netted the sponsors $20,000, which will be spent for ambulances for the Spanish war area. The first was held at the Ambassador in Los Angeles on Sunday afternoon, July 11. Mr. Ivens and Mr. and Mrs. Hemingway had flown out with a print. Hollywood's great names paid $5 each, 200 of them to attend this showing, and the next night, at Frederic March's home, a gathering of Hollywood's best-known figures, people like Robert Montgomery, Luise Rainer, Silvia Sidney, Miriam Hopkins, Lewis Milestone, Alan Campbell Dorothy Parker, Fritz Lang, Anatol Litvak, Ernst Lubitsch, Miss Hellman, King Vidor, Dashiell Hammett, Arthur Kober, Errol Flynn, Joan Bennett, Donald Ogden Stewart, Lionel Stander and others were so impressed that word zipped through the studios that this picture was a "must."

The next evening, Tuesday, found the Philharmonic Auditorium packed to its 3,500 capacity at a $1.10 top. Twenty-five hundred were turned away. Mr. Ivens, bringing the reels, was a little later than he had expected to be, and was pretty nearly turned away himself. Los Angeles policemen are apparently easier to convince than New York's finest, however, and he was finally permitted to enter. Later it was shown privately for Joan Crawford and Franchot Tone, and subsequently for John Ford and for Darryl Zanuck. Hollywood was a little amazed to learn that the total cost of the film had been a mere $12,000, impressed as they were with the interesting treatment of the sound and the high professional quality of the production.

The only untoward incident Mr. Ivens reported during the Hollywood visit was the precipitate disappearance from the March home, via the men's room, of a noted actor-adventurer just before Donald Ogden Stewart requested contributions after the showing there. New York will see the film, with narration written and delivered by Ernest Hemingway and a score of Spanish native music arranged by Marc Blitzstein, as soon as its sponsors find a suitable theatre.

* * *

The Spanish Earth was made largely in the village of Fuentadueña, forty kilometers from Madrid on the Valencia road. Mr. Ivens got to Madrid in December with his camera man, John Ferno, selected the village as a likely point for the fight for control of the road to concentrate, and set about acquainting himself with his cast. His cast were the villagers. The procedure there, Mr. Ivens says, was to sit in the inns, to learn "the names of the kids," and to convince the people that one was not seeking to exploit them or to capitalize on their misfortunes.

The confidence of the subjects in such work is extremely important, Mr. Ivens has found, and winning that confidence and thenceforth accustoming people to go their natural ways with the eye of the camera always on them is the art of the successful photographer of realism. "Just as a Hollywood director has to direct actors, so, in my profession, I must direct people," he says. "There can be no retakes, one after the other. With actors, it is different. As they do a scene over and over, it gets better and better. People become self-conscious, and get worse and worse. Sometimes, two or three days later, when the light is right again and the situation is similar, maybe I will say 'Do again what you did the other day,' and I may get a better scene. But it must be spontanic [*sic*]; it cannot be rehearsed. It is an interesting sport. It is like stalking. The camera wanders here and there, and suddenly, pounce! and we have the real thing."

After the preliminary work had been done, he and Ferno went to Paris to supervise the processing of the negative they had already taken. There they met Hemingway, heading for Madrid as a correspondent. He returned with them, and they found the sturdy novelist an excellent "grips," as well as an interpreter. Mr. Ivens gives much of the credit for *The Spanish Earth* to a most unexpected ally, however Sidney Franklin, the bullfighter from Brooklyn. Franklin, Ivens reports, is lionized in Madrid, and is, in consequence, the finest liaison man conceivable. Franklin cut through red tape with sure matador strokes when the occasion demanded, and got gasoline, passes to the front, and transportation for the crew when all other methods had failed. Bullfighting is out for the time being, Mr. Ivens reports, the idea being that lives oughtn't to be risked in the bull ring when there are more suitable places to risk them.

Mr. Ivens's picture is, to use his words, a document of a people, a drama of the soil, with a back-ground of war. Fuentaduena, on the Tajos, was not itself in the front line. Mr. Ivens missed on his calculations there by 25 kilometers. But the air raids came periodically and the war hung over Fuentaduena just as truly as over the towns nearer the line. Mr. Ivens checked on that, as a matter of integrity. The war scenes were filmed at the front line along the Madrid-Valencia road, and in Madrid itself.

* * *

Mr. Ivens made this last point very graphic. This reporter talked with him in the roof garden at the Luncheon Club, a story or so above the Rainbow Room, sixty-odd floors over midtown New York. Below us lay Central Park, stretching two or three miles to the north. Mr. Ivens walked to the parapet and indicated 110th Street.

"From the Telefonica (Madrid's eighteen-story skyscraper) the Fascist line in University City appears right up there," he pointed. His arm swung in an arc, as if preparing to point out something else. It found a distant Broadway street car. "There, over there," he said, "the street car. Five minutes to the front line."

War has become a normal state in Madrid, he says, although not for him. "When we wanted quiet, we went to the front. At the front bursting shells are the normal thing. You expect them; you anticipate them. You know where to hide. The soldiers dread leave in the city. In town it is all quiet, and then, bumph! there is a shell in the street. It has nothing to do with the town. It is stupid."

Mr. Ivens's own views on the Spanish situation are that the conflict will last as long as the rest of Europe permits it to. Should the non-interventionists succeed in halting German and Italian activity on behalf of the rebels, the government would suppress the revolt quickly, he thinks. If the Fascist countries are permitted to continue their support, however, he believes the Loyalists will be defeated. Russian support of the Loyalist cause has been a support of paid-for materials and instruction in their use, not one of man power, he says.

* * *

The fall of Madrid or Rebel control of the Valencia road would end the conflict, he thinks, but he nevertheless doubts that a Franco government could control the country without "murdering 50,000 people to quell opinion so they can have a quiet night." Even then, in his opinion, the Spanish peoples, having for a time tasted freedom from the oppression of a feudal system, would eventually force the formation of the government along the lines now indicated by the Popular Front government.

"But this would be the long, the roundabout way," he says, "and it must not be so. When you are close to the fighting it becomes the most important thing in the world to win the war for the Spanish people. It is most important, for democracy to survive, to keep Spain democratic. Fascism is murdering every cultural development in Europe."

In the event of a Loyalist victory, Mr. Ivens sees the Spain of the future, after mutations which may include first a period of democracy and perhaps a period of socialism, as a democratic State with a popular front.

The attitude of the Spanish people toward the church is bitter, he found, with resentment toward the physical evidences of an organization that people had identified with a distasteful government, with taxes and with oppression. But adherence to the basic concepts of Christianity is too deeply rooted to be disturbed, and the church will come back quickly for this reason, he is confident.

40

CHARLES WOLFE

HISTORICIZING THE "VOICE OF GOD"

The Place of Voice-Over Commentary in Classical Documentary (1997)

In critical and historical accounts of documentary film practice, voice-over commentary in the "classical" documentary of the 1930s and 1940s is commonly equated with a "Voice of God." Disembodied, this voice is construed as fundamentally unrepresentable in human form, connoting a position of absolute mastery and knowledge outside the spatial and temporal boundaries of the social world the film depicts. Vocal commentary for *The March of Time* often serves as the prototype: stentorian, aggressive, assuming a power to speak the truth of the filmic text, to hold captive through verbal caption what the spectator sees. In the 1950s and 1960s, most histories tell us, the technique was rejected as authoritarian, didactic, or reductive by filmmakers who, committed to new strategies of observation (direct cinema, *cinéma vérité, cinéma direct*), opted for location sound, the authenticity of which was presumably commensurate with that of the photographic image. To the extent that vocal narration remains in use—by filmmakers schooled in the *vérité* critique but seeking to recover some of the power of the voice to narrate or explain—voice-over typically is considered less assertive or homogenous than in documentaries of an earlier era; voices are personal or casual, multiple or split, fragmentary or self-interrogating, lacking a full knowledge of events or the motives and causal logic that a classical documentary would claim to disclose.[1]

The remarks to follow query standard accounts of the history of documentary voice-over from two perspectives: first, by exploring some general issues suggested by the language we currently use to describe a commentating voice in documentary; second, by considering the range of vocal strategies found in American documentaries in the early years of sound, with particular attention to *The Spanish Earth* (Ivens, 1937) and *The Battle of Midway* (Ford, 1942). If the notion of a "Voice of God"—accepted, rejected, or deflected and dispersed—plays a central role in the way the history of documentary has come to be written, this concept also may mask those elements of sound film practice in the 1930s and 1940s that are most intriguing and instructive—instructive for what they tell us about both changing conceptions of documentary style and a field of historical cross-references that to the modern viewer may be lost.

Voice-Over as Metaphor

A key term in our contemporary critical vocabulary, "voice-over" designates a *place* for vocal commentary by way of a metaphor that is at once spatial and hierarchical: voices are heard *over*...what? Over images, we may be tempted to say, but I think this is only partially right. As the felt need for a distinction between voice-*over* and voice-*off* makes plain, at issue here is not simply synchronisation (whether vocal utterances are matched to moving lips on the screen), nor a particular sensory dimension (audition versus vision), but rather our interpretation of the relationship of voices that we hear to a world that a documentary takes as its object of regard.[2] The source of a voice heard "off," while not visible within a given shot, is assumed to originate within a proximate visible field—off frame but from a space contiguous to and a time continuous with the depicted action. In contrast, voice-over comes from *else*where (the question of *where* else, I will take up shortly) and may entail the hierarchical relation of a voice to other sounds as well. Those who speak in voice-over may know, comment on, or drown out sounds from the world a film depicts, but the relationship is asymmetrical: voices from that register have no reciprocal power to introduce or comment on the voices that overlay this world. We might want to say, then, that voice-over covers the world of the "diegesis"—a term as appropriate to an analysis of narrative documentaries as to narrative fictions. While the power of documentary cinema may depend in large measure on our faith in the particular recording capacities of camera and microphone, our comprehension of a "talking" documentary film, and of those claims it makes on our attention, requires that we locate what we hear in relation to a postulated world. In short, the idea of "voice-over" depends upon our sense of the film as a text, capable of being partitioned in ways that are conceptual or structural, not simply technological or material.

In the compound term "voice-over," the spatial and hierarchical implications of the preposition "over" also are joined to a word which itself connotes a certain measure of power. In common usage, "voice" refers not simply to the physical phenomenon of a vocal utterance—the sound produced by lungs and larynx—but to the very capacity to speak, to give formal and open expression to an idea, emotion, wish, choice, or opinion. Furthermore, "voice" may refer to the governing perspective of a text, a source or founding impulse responsible for the organisation of its surface features. This is the sense of the term, for example, employed by Bill Nichols and Jeffrey Youdelman in separate essays on voice in documentary, published in the early 1980s, in which each argues that the abandonment of the tradition of voice-over commentary by *vérité* filmmakers in the 1960s resulted in a loss of "voice" in a larger, figurative sense.[3] Here voice is conceived, in Nichols' apt formulation, as "that which conveys a text's social point of view," unrestricted to "any one single code or feature, such as dialogue or spoken commentary. Voice is perhaps akin to that intangible, moiré-like pattern formed by the interaction of all a film's codes."[4] In this fashion, the optical metaphor of "point of view"—central to contemporary theoretical and critical writing on cinema fiction—is subsumed by one that is vocal, an appropriate choice perhaps for a genre in which a rhetorical function has often been stressed. This chain of connotations makes imaginable an acoustic equivalent to what Edward Branigan (elaborating on the optical metaphor) has labelled a text's "point of *over*view"—perhaps an "over-voice"—discernible as we ascend various "levels" of narration to the uppermost limit of authority in a given work.[5] Or, to put this another way, we might say that voice provides a master trope for theorising the founding principles of documentary narration and rhetoric, governing the formal construction of a work of non-fiction across different stylistic registers.[6]

But I find my metaphors mixing. Can "voice-over" seem to function as the keystone or foundation of a documentary text, *anchoring* its construction, and at the same time hover over the world upon which it comments, *covering* it like canopy? Here our attention is drawn to the fact that, as a spatial metaphor, "voice-over" tells us nothing about the source of the voice we hear, orienting us only in terms of a negation: voice not from the image, nor from that surrounding diegetic space that images and sounds imply.[7] Where then from? Many possibilities can be cued by a film, ranging from "places in time" subsequent to the events depicted (as with voice-over by a character, recalling an earlier event) to an extradiegetic register devoid of precise spatial or temporal definition. Pascal Bonitzer has proposed that it is precisely the lack of specificity to the origin of a vocal commentary in documentary—its nonreferential aspect—that is central to its power. From an undetermined place, evading scrutiny or critique, the disembodied voice disposes of the image.[8] From this assessment it is perhaps only a small step to the notion of a disembodied "voice of God." A more richly figurative label than "voice-over," "voice of God" also may seem to resolve the ambiguous implications of a voice at once over and under, hovering and anchoring. Omniscient, omnipresent (that is to say everywhere and nowhere in particular), God may be thought of as both celestial (watching down on us) and terrestrial (inhabiting the world in all its details). The authority to describe, narrate, or interpret a world already known is thus attributed to a transcendent force.

No one, I assume, takes the "voice of God" metaphor literally. My question is: do we even take it seriously? Whose voice would be like the voice of God? That of Cecil B. DeMille? Orson Welles? Charlton Heston?[9] Suggestions of this kind, provoked by our familiarity with roles played by these highly public personalities on and off the screen, typically are treated as jokes. Signalling the bald aspiration of the male *basso profundo*—pompous, overbearing—the term "voice of God" carries with it an element of ridicule. Perhaps this is why it is commonly capitalised, in mock aggrandisement, pricking its pretense to authority, or is placed in quotation marks, as if culturally suspect, not to be taken at face value. At the very least, this element of pretense cues us to treat such aspirations as a fiction, a playing with God-like powers.[10]

The impulse of *vérité* critics to reject vocal commentary in documentary as not simply authoritative but authoritarian, and hence to resist it, carries with it the assumption that voices layered over recorded images and sounds are in some sense detachable from the authentic filmic document. Prejudice against the immoderate ambitions of an "over-voice" thus may betray a more fundamental, unspoken faith in the authenticity of "unnarrated" image and sounds, repositories of a truth that can be discerned without the interruptions or interference of an invisible interpreter.[11] Amplified in motion picture theatre, imposing comment not simply over the images but upon the unreceptive and immobile viewer, such a voice may convince us all the more strongly of the artifice behind its claim to mastery. The truly insidious voice,

Bonitzer provocatively suggests, is the one that does not say much; without affectation or inflection, it whispers in our ear: "It is a layer protecting the film's image, lubricating it, not forcing it."[12] In contrast, the passionate voice, or differentiated voice, at least partially restores a body to the voice; its contours and place of origin are imaginable. Identifiable, it encourages response and may be easier to resist.

Non-Fiction Talkies

Rarely do early sound documentaries from the 1930s and 1940s feature voices that whisper in our ears, and we may be inclined to resist more than a few. Yet to characterise these voices collectively as God-like is to efface the spectrum of vocal strategies employed during this period and the range of social implications these voices generated. Many of the most celebrated documentary filmmakers of the period—Pare Lorentz, Willard Van Dyke, and Ben Maddow in the United States; John Grierson, Alberto Cavalcanti, Paul Rotha, and Humphrey Jennings in Great Britain—viewed the vocalisation of the non-fiction film as an opportunity for experimentation.[13] The very technological difficulties of recording lip-synchronised location sound prompted exploration of varied ways to match voices to documentary pictures. In an era of highly focused concern for the social dimension of the arts, close collaboration among filmmakers, writers, composers, and actors often centred on spoken narration as a key ingredient of a new kind of audio-visual work—not simply a routine travelogue or instructional film, but a vocalised "documentary."

In recent years, these collaborative undertakings have attracted renewed attention, as film historians have sought to reconstruct the circumstances of production in which self-consciously artful social documentary filmmaking occurred in the 1930s and 1940s.[14] Less well known, but of considerable importance to the topic at hand, are the earliest efforts of non-fiction filmmakers to adapt the technology of "talkies" to the established format of silent travelogues and compilation films. Although many of these films do not survive, or have yet to be unearthed, press coverage of travelogues, newsreels, and films of diverse political persuasion in the 1930s hint at a wider field of activity in need of charting.[15] At the very least, reviews in Variety and the *New York Times*, if often sketchy, provide a sense of how the spoken word was assimilated into conventional ways of describing and evaluating non-fiction films.

Searching for a new vocabulary, reviewers tried out a wide range of labels for what we now routinely call "voice-over": "canned monolog," "running monolog," "running comment," "synchronised dialogue," "descriptive talks."[16] By the mid-1930s, however, the preferred terms were "commentary" or "narration." Moreover, reviewers tend to describe the voice as occurring not "over" the depicted action but "off-screen" or even "off-stage"-adjectives used not in the contemporary sense of "voice-off," but rather to designate a place for the voice external to events on the screen. Thus the Variety reviewer of a 1935 documentary on the search for a Jewish homeland, Land of Promise, praises commentator David Ross for giving the film "a corking finishing touch with his splendid, sympathetic off-screen narration."[17] Less happy with the results, the reviewer of *Taming the Jungle* (Paul D. Wyman, 1933) observes: "Now and then an off-stage voice makes some comment, which is no help whatever."[18] During the first years of talkies, in particular, terms such as "off-screen monologue," "off-stage lecture," and "off-screen interlocutor" also frequently were employed.[19]

Subdued or restrained voices also tend to earn higher marks than those that are pompous, imperious or overwrought. Frank S. Nugent faulted the World War I compilation documentary, *Hell's Holiday* (1933), for having "stridently nationalistic" commentary; a Variety reviewer accused the same film of mistaking "hysterics for histrionics in the lecture."[20] In contrast, the "off-screen narrative" of Lest We Forget, produced by the Canadian Legion and released by Columbia Pictures in 1935, was praised in the pages of Variety for "simple language" of a kind that neither tried to "show for effect" nor "gloss over the gruesomeness of war."[21] If vocal commentary sounded implausible or otherwise ill suited for the images, critics also took note. "They tell you that this group of furred people half buried in the snow of a blizzard are facing death," noted a reviewer of *Igloo*, an Arctic Circle travelogue by Ewing Scott, released by Universal in 1932. "But the plump and cheerful looking natives don't look it. It's a case where the bare actuality, unsupported by artistic and literary trickery, doesn't register."[22] Likewise *Gow*, E. A. Salisbury's South Seas chronicle produced the following year, was criticised for "dialog buildup that attempts to give [the film] punch the photographed matter lacks."[23]

Evident here is an effort to talk about the new acoustic experience of synchronised sound by way of an older tradition of the illustrated lecture, a tradition out of which the popular genre of the travelogue talkie directly emerged. Labels such as "off-stage lecturer" or "off-screen interlocutor" evoke the pre-talkie slide and motion picture lecture circuit, with silent pictures accompanied by a commentator purported to be familiar with the topic at hand. The voice of this lecturer had a visible place of origin: at the lectern or podium, likely to the side of the pictures. With early talkies, the absence of this lecturer may have further diminished, rather than enhanced, the authority of the voice, especially if the commentary seemed gratuitously, or otherwise inadequately, tacked on.[24] In contrast to the contemporary term "voice-over," references to an "off-screen" voice emphasised origin over destination, signalling more strongly the sense of a voice from a place apart.

The vocal style of *The March of Time*, in contrast, was modelled after radio drama, including the radio series of the same title launched by *Time* magazine in March 1931. As Catherine L. Covert has demonstrated, cultural discourse on radio reception in the 1920s often featured analogies between the wireless transmission of voices and supernatural forces.[25] Part of the cultural work of radio during its early commercial development was the rerouting of the fascination of listeners with the seemingly magical quality of radio transmission toward an attraction to radio personalities, familiar voices heard regularly "on the air."[26] Amid these developments, *The March of Time* carved out programming space for a unique kind of dramatic newscasting featuring professional actors (many of whom would go on to careers in motion pictures) re-enacting events of topical interest. Narrating the series was "The Voice of Time," a role initially performed on radio by Ted Husing and Harry Von Zell. With the commencement of a screen version under the direction of Louis de Rochemont in 1935, Westbrook Van Voorhis assumed the narrator's role, quickly mastering the eccentric ("Timespeak") syntax, odd inflections, teletype cadence and often ironic tone that the part required. Soon a celebrity in his own right, Van Voorhis travelled and lectured extensively as a company spokesperson. As the Voice of Time, he also frequently was parodied, most famously perhaps by William Alland in the "News on the March" segment of *Citizen Kane* (Welles, 1941).[27] Offering an arch variant on the portentous reporting of Lowell Thomas, Graham MacNee, and other radio personalities turned newsreel commentators, Van Voorhis's voice came to represent a limit case for the theatrical embellishment of news narration on the motion picture screen.[28]

No less important a legacy than the Voice of Time, however, was the original radio program's emphasis on the distribution of speaking parts among a group of professional performers, some of whom were capable of impersonating the voices of leading figures in the news. Non-fictional radio drama, like fictional programs, entailed the orchestration of an ensemble of disembodied but easily characterised voices, the success of which was as much a matter of casting as writing. To the extent that documentary filmmakers in the 1930s and 1940s felt compelled to experiment with various mixes of vocal narration, music, and sound effects, studio broadcasting provided a workshop for exploring new ideas. The "airwaves," in effect, came to function as an imaginary social space for vocal commentaries and the cultivating of personalities across radio and talking films.

Two distinct vocal traditions, then, can be observed here. Early travelogue talkies, ranging from the low-budget jungle films of Martin and Osa Johnson (*Congorilla* [1932], *Baboona* [1935], *Borneo* [1937]) and Frank Buck (*Bring 'Em Back Alive* [1932], *Adventure Girl* [1934]) to photo-journalist Margaret Bourke-White's politically slanted *Eyes on Russia* (1934), drew heavily on the lecturer format. By including Bourke-White, Buck, or the Johnsons within a documentary diegesis, these films linked off-screen, first-person commentaries to figures traversing exotic locales. More dramatic effects were achieved, however, through strategies of vocal re-enactment, with roots in radio drama. In social documentary films, a single narrator might speak for voiceless figures (*The Land* [Flaherty, 1941]); or interpolated voices express the thoughts or feelings of characters (*People of the Cumberland* [Meyers and Leyda, 1938], *Valley Town* [Van Dyke, 1940]); or dialogue be exchanged across different levels of narration (*A Place to Live* [Lerner 1940], *Fight for Life* [Lorentz, 1940]). Radio drama also seems central to the effort to soften, poeticise or diffuse narration, as with Lorentz's integration of cadenced commentary with Virgil Thomson's folk-styled score in *The Plow That Broke the Plains* (1936) and *The River* (1937); or Stephen Vincent Benét's folk-verse commentary, read by radio actor (and *March of Time* veteran) William P. Adams, in *Power of the Land* (Ivens, 1940); or the dividing of commentary between actor Walter Huston and a less polished Anthony Veiller throughout Capra's *Why We Fight* series; or among a quartet of voices—two narrators and two soldiers, two British and two American—in the Anglo-American co-production—*Tunisian Victory* (Capra and Hugh Stewart, 1944).

Sometimes awkward or stagy, devices of this kind nevertheless point to a recurring interest in finding ways to speak across and bind the separate spaces of (1) a documentary diegesis, (2) the motion picture theatre, and (3) an indefinite, mutable, and potentially fictional realm of vocal commentary that a post-synchronised soundtrack established in between. Into this last space, a variety of voices are cast. In part, vocal commentaries develop a zone of inferiority, of character subjectivity, after the fashion of narrative fictions but in support of a documentary plot. But the echo of external voices in this "off-screen" zone also may open up the film to other narratives and other social worlds.

Casting Voices: *The Spanish Earth* and *The Battle of Midway*

Consider, for example, the strategic use of vocal commentary in two of the most celebrated documentaries of the period, *The Spanish Earth* and *The Battle of Midway*. The production histories of the films bear some resemblance. Shot under battlefront conditions by a crew of partisan filmmakers, both works assumed their final shape in the editing room as rare combat footage was integrated with more carefully composed images and post-synchronised sound effects, music and vocal commentary. Both films target an audience at a distance from the scene of conflict and seek to stir sentiments on behalf of a combined civilian-military campaign. Of considerable topical interest, both films were screened for Franklin and Eleanor Roosevelt in the White House, then found wider American distribution and attracted notice, in the press. Although restricted in the main to art film houses and an expanding left-labour exhibition circuit, *The Spanish Earth* raised medical relief funds to aid the Spanish Republican cause, and helped to forge an alliance of anti-fascist, popular front groups in the United States prior to the onset of World War II. Distributed nationally by Twentieth Century-Fox, *The Battle of Midway* was a stimulus to a billion-dollar bond drive by Hollywood's War Activities Committee in September 1942.[29] In short, both were successful films of persuasion, made under difficult conditions to achieve concrete political goals. The patterning of vocal commentary in the two films, however, differs in ways that help to illustrate the kinds of connections and the spectrum of associations an alert spectator of documentaries could be expected to make.

Written and spoken by Ernest Hemingway, vocal narration in *The Spanish Earth* serves several conventional functions. Hemingway identifies key locations (the village of Fuentedueña, Valencia, the Tago River, the city of Madrid) and historical personages (Enrique Lister, José Diaz, Gustav Regler, La Passionária). Shifting tenses freely, he shuttles back and forth in time, most poignantly perhaps when, after identifying a former civilian lawyer and now "brave and skillful" rebel commander, Martinez de Aragón, Hemingway reports that the officer later died during the attack on Casa del Campo. He provides sensory information the camera cannot register, as when he observes, over a long shot of a Madrid street under aerial attack, that the "smell of death is acrid high explosive smoke and blasted granite." He explains military tactics ("Madrid by its position is a natural fortress and each day the people make its defence more and more impregnable"), translates politically coded gestures ("the clenched fist of Republican Spain"), and underscores the structural link the film works steadfastly to draw between an irrigation project in the country and the battle for Madrid. Knowledgeable through out, he helps to orient the viewer, to clarify narrative conflicts, and to interpret the significance of events that are depicted and juxtaposed visually.

Hemingway also employs several novelistic devices that serve to psychologise the action. We are given access to the motives of a young rebel soldier, "Julian," whose journey home to see his family in Fuentedueña strengthens the link between city and country, military service and farming. Footage of an evacuation, deftly edited by Helen Van Dongen, gains emotional power as Hemingway assumes the voice of an aging woman who is imagined to ask, "But where will we go? . . . Where can we live? . . . What can we do for a living?," then another who is imagined to reply, "I won't go. I'm too old." More elaborate still is a leave-taking sequence, in which a contingent of soldiers depart for war. A soldier and a woman sit on a running board, with a small child standing on one side and an uninvolved soldier on the other. The narrator observes:

> They say the old-goodbyes that sound the same in any language. She says she'll wait. [Cut to another soldier and two women, one looking toward him and the other away.] He says that he'll come back. He knows she'll wait. [Cut to a soldier standing beside a woman and four small boys.] Who knows for what, the way the shelling is. [Cut to a woman holding an infant, framed by two soldiers, one who looks toward the camera.] Nobody knows if he'll come back. [The soldier turns toward the woman, blocking her from camera view.] Take care of the kid, he says. I will . . . [cut to a military truck, as a group of women pass by in the

fore-ground] . . . she says but knows she can't. They both know that when they move you out in trucks, it's to a battle.

With great economy, the commentary captures an interior tension between thought and speech, between what is promised or asserted and what is known to be true. Differently configured, each grouping is attended to separately by the camera, whose presence at this inescapably public moment is acknowledged by a glance. Based on the small, distinctive gestures of these men and women, it is possible to conjecture that each family has a different story to tell. At the same time the pressures and protocols of wartime parting—which inevitably leave complex feelings unexpressed—is evoked as a common, shared experience. Like the Spanish choral music we hear over the prologue, during Julian's travels home, and at the very end, Hemingway's commentary foregrounds collective emotions and patterns of thought.

Do we construe this voice as the "voice of God"? Hemingway's authority is never called into question. He is not restricted to a single location and he moves back and forth in time. He has the power to narrate and explain events and speak for silent figures on the screen. Yet as Tom Waugh has noted in a richly suggestive discussion of *The Spanish Earth*, Hemingway's commentary is much closer to the tradition of documentary experiments in the 1930s and 1940s than a conventional newsreel style.[30] To begin with, Hemingway's voice does not seem to descend from on high. In part this is because of the forms of address he adopts, as when, for example, he responds acidly to a close-up of the identification plate of a downed plane, "I can't read German either," implicitly aligning himself with the American spectator while linking the Spanish Fascists to an emergent Axis threat. At times he places himself among the villagers and foot soldiers, and invites the viewer to do so also, executing subtle shifts between the third and first persons. "This is the moment that all the rest of war prepares for," he notes in the closing section, "when six men go forward into death to walk across a stretch of land and by *their* presence on it prove—this earth is *ours*" (my emphases). Reduced in number, the soldiers dig in to protect the irrigation project along the road from Valencia to Madrid. "The bridge is ours. The road is saved," the narrator tells us, an assertion of collective triumph that can be shared by supporters of the Republican cause around the globe.

Hemingway's voice also is never thunderous or overbearing. His spoken commentary, akin to his distinctive prose style, is concise and restrained. For long stretches, the narrator falls silent, yielding to Spanish folk songs (reworked in the style of Virgil Thomson's regional Americana and Marc Blitzstein's brasher, sometimes dissonant scoring); the fabricated sounds of gunfire, aeroplanes, sirens and shattering glass (under the direction of effect: editor Irving Reis of the CBS radio workshop); the speeches of leaders (some translated, some not) and anxious cries of warning or anguish ("¡Avación!," called out five times, by voices of different volume, timber and pitch).[31] Sometimes the very silence of the soundtrack is unnerving, as when victims of a bombing raid scurry down city streets, in anticipation of another explosion, the sound of which we too await. This sequence seems the inspiration for the playbill cover for the American premiere of *The Spanish Earth* at the 55th Street Playhouse in August 1937, which featured an abstract rendering of a woman and child, the mouths of both open in wide black circles, beneath the outline of three soaring airplanes. At the bottom of the page, under the title of the film, Hemingway is credited with the "commentary and narration." This cover artwork neatly captures the reciprocal relation between Hemingway's literate commentary, supportive but understated, and the pictorial representation of war-time anguish, for which there are no words.[32]

For many commentators in the 1930s, moreover, the casting of Hemingway as reader of his own scripted commentary reinforced the authenticity of his remarks. A rather different effect reportedly was achieved with an earlier recording of the commentary by Orson Welles, recruited by the film's sponsors in an effort to capitalise on the celebrity status of this *wunderkind* of the Federal Theatre Project and rising radio star of Archibald MacLeish's radio verse plays *Panic* (1934) and *The Fall of the City* (directed by Reis in 1937) and *The March of Time* and *The Shadow* radio series. Although this version of *The Spanish Earth* was shown at the White House and at various benefit screenings in Los Angeles, Ivens discarded it prior to *The Spanish Earth*'s general release. Its weakness, the filmmakers agreed, was largely one of tone. Van Dongen later recalled that Welles' narration was like the "voice of God," demanding all the attention, clashing with the picture. As far as I was concerned it wrecked the film.[33] Persuaded by Van Dongen and others, Ivens opted to let the author read his own script. Hemingway's "lack of a professional commentator's smoothness," Ivens later remembered, "helped you believe intensely in the experience on the screen."[34]

Above and beyond the differing qualities to their voices, Welles and Hemingway also brought different personae to their casting in the film. Welles was a brilliant young showman, Hemingway an established man of letters. Well known in literary circles for his fascination with Spain, as evident in works of fiction (*The Sun Also Rises*, 1926; "A Clean, Well-Lighted Place," 1933) and non-fiction (*Death in the Afternoon*, 1932), Hemingway had spent much time in that country.[35] Prior to working on *The Spanish Earth*, he assisted writers Prudencio de Pereda, John Dos Passos and Archibald MacLeish in composing the commentary for *Spain in Flames*, a tendentious (and heavily censored) documentary edited by Van Dongen from newsreel footage of the Spanish Civil War. His eyewitness reporting of the Spanish conflict, while travelling with Ivens, also appeared in the *New Republic* and via dispatches for the North American Newspaper Alliance in the months prior to and during the release of *The Spanish Earth*. In this sense, Hemingway's vocal performance was in the tradition of the informed, well-travelled, credentialled lecturer. His commentary, in Ivens' judgement, was akin to that of "a sensitive reporter who had been on the spot and wants to tell you about it—a feeling that no other voice could communicate."[36] While reviewers in 1937 were not of one mind in assessing the commentary's effectiveness—some found it insufficiently flamboyant or bipartisan—most reviewers paid close attention to Hemingway's vocal style, many detecting in it an echo of his terse, poetically understated and, at times, caustic prose.[37]

Vocal commentary in *The Battle Midway* functions rather differently. Ford, who had been wounded while filming the battle with his Office of Strategic Services Field Photo Unit, provided preliminary ideas for a script, but solicited successive drafts from two former collaborators, screenwriter Dudley Nichols and MGM executive James Kevin McGuinness. Working like a radio director, Ford then assigned parts from the script to four actors—Donald Crisp, Irving Pichel, Jane Darwell, and Henry Fonda—and coached them in their reading of individual lines.[38] Each of the quartet has a distinct vocal personality. Crisp's voice tends to be lilting and a bit urgent, and is most closely aligned with aerial missions. Pichel's is more formal and solemn, and he often comments on the aftermath of combat from a perspective on the ground. At the same time, both function as conventional narrators, defining settings, placing events in a temporal sequence, and attributing thoughts or emotions to individual figures (including, with laboured irony, the "anxious" birds of Midway Island) as they are depicted on the screen.[39] The temporal mobility of Crisp and Pichel is suggested by their use of the historical present (as when Pichel intones: "An historic council of war is held"), or by adroit shifts in tense, as when Crisp's assertion, "Meanwhile our ships stopped the Jap fleet," is followed by the excited announcement, "Suddenly the trap is sprung!". Much more explicitly than does Hemingway, Crisp and Pichel also acknowledge the geographical distance between the action described and the location of the spectator, while at the same time articulating a social relationship between these separate sectors.

Defined explicitly as battlefront and homefront, these worlds are connected by the common experience of war. "It's our outpost, your front yard," Crisp announces as we are given our first aerial view of the islands, the scene of a once and future battle, aligning himself with the naval pilots stationed far from home. But then, after victory, he crosses the boundary he had earlier drawn, reminding us collectively that "our front yard is safe." Never forced to settle on one side of the battlefront/homefront divide, Crisp and Pichel provide an overview (if not at times an over-voice) for the domestic spectator, transforming what might at first appear to be an exotic travelogue into a narrative account of heroic labours along a new global "porch front"—the Pacific theatre of war. "Men and women of America," Pichel announces somberly as surviving pilots return, "here come your neighbours' sons, home from a day's work. You'll, want to meet them." Vocal commentary thus provides the opportunity for a new form of greeting across a spatial gap and temporal lag that motion pictures, viewed retrospectively, inevitably disclose.

The multiplying of speaking parts, moreover, allows Ford at once to dramatise and bridge this divide. Here the voices of Darwell (overtly maternal) and Fonda (chipper, well-mannered) play crucial roles. During their initial exchange, just prior to the first round of battle, Darwell excitedly observes that a pilot resembles her "neighbour's boy" precisely at the moment he comes into view for the spectator, foreground left. As the camera pans over to a plane, Darwell then inquires if it is "one of those flying fortresses." Fonda politely replies, "Yes, ma'am it is." Darwell names the pilot ("Why that's Will Kinney"), identifies his hometown (Springfield, Ohio), and wonders aloud if Kinney will "fly that great big bomber." Again, Fonda responds with plain-spoken courtesy: "Yes ma'am, that's his job. He's the skipper."

From what place do these characters speak? Where does their colloquy occur? The question seems relevant in a way that it doesn't for Crisp and Pichel. First of all, Darwell and Fonda's relationship to what we are watching in the film seems more circumscribed. Neither are empowered to narrate events concerning the battle: to establish temporal, spatial or causal links, or to instruct us (even indirectly) in the historical significance of what has transpired/is transpiring. Moreover, while the commentaries of Crisp and Pichel room freely over events, those of Darwell and Fonda are limited to two occasions: the departure of pilots from Midway Island into battle, and the return of survivors in its aftermath. Furthermore, Darwell and Fonda seem engaged in an off-screen drama; they exchange dialogue, act out roles. Indeed, a logical hypothesis might be that they are watching footage from *The Battle of Midway*, perhaps sitting before us. From this place, Darwell speaks for the watchful American mother, capable of discerning in the slightest gesture—a certain gait—a telling sign of familiarity, and hence the possibility of restoring familial bonds. In counterpoint, Fonda (a serviceman on furlough? a self-educated new recruit? a military escort for Darwell?) supplies professional information—that, say, such and such a plane is indeed a flying fortress, or that piloting the bomber is young Will Kinney's job.

Darwell's comments, however, do not simply respond to the images. Her remarks seem briefly to influence the direction the film takes. She reveals more about the Kinneys of Springfield: "Will's Dad is an engineer, 38 years on the old Ironton railroad"; his mother, sitting and knitting, with a service star on the wall behind, is "just like the rest of us mothers in Springfield or any other American town"; his sister Patricia, chatting on the telephone, is "about as pretty as they come." In this fashion we are taken on a short excursion from Midway Island to Springfield where, long in advance of Pichel's invitation to meet "our neighbours" sons', Darwell introduces homefront spectators to people "just like themselves." Does Darwell now function as an embedded narrator, in some sense authorising the images of the people from Springfield she describes? Do these images represent her memory of these people, triggered by her recognition of Will? Are they Fonda's images too? Or does the screen now anticipate and respond to Darwell's comments, the images slotted into place by some higher-level narrator to keep pace with the verbal information she supplies? The detachment of voices from specific bodies (but surely not from the specific connotations of gender and age) thus may occasion a curious effect, whereby recorded voices, projected from theatre speakers, circulate through surrogate spectators on their way to "covering" a diegetic plane.

However we choose to chart the flow of voices, what transpires is a fiction—on at least two counts. First, unlike the battle fought at Midway, no referent is specified for this exchange. The placeless space of voice-over is filled temporarily by an imaginable homefront vignette from which we may take pleasure or instruction, or even umbrage, but which has no concrete relation to the events that occurred at Midway, on 4–6 June 1942. Moreover, to the extent that the voices of Darwell and Fonda are highly recognisable, their exchange calls to mind a vocal intertext of film fictions. Indeed, the most proximate referent for their conversation is surely Ford's *The Grapes of Wrath*, in which Darwell and Fonda had appeared two years before: Darwell in the Academy Award-winning role of Ma Joad, espousing a family-based notion of community in a Depression-era story of social dislocation; Fonda as her son Tom, who possesses a wider range of social knowledge and by necessity breaks with the family in pursuit of social justice, taking on the burden of a larger cause at the close. Without grounding itself in the plot of this particular fiction, the exchange between Darwell and Fonda nevertheless trades in the repository of associations that this vocal intertext supplies.[40]

A trail of associations—if more faintly felt—is evoked by the performances of Crisp and Pichel as well: Crisp in his Academy Award-winning role as the patriarch of a Welsh mining family in Ford's *How Green Was My Valley* (1941); Pichel heard (but never fully seen) as the adult narrator of the same film, whose leave-taking from the valley inaugurates the retrospective telling of the story.[41] Perhaps because Crisp and Pichel themselves never engage in a fictional exchange with one another, their voices retain an autonomy that underscores their function as documentary narrators. When the pilots return to Midway Island, Fonda follows up on remarks by Crisp and Pichel, and a fervent plea by Darwell to get the injured pilots to a hospital (uttered as if it might affect the outcome of these documented events) inspires biting commentary by Crisp on the destruction of the hospital by the Japanese. But Crisp and Pichel never themselves assume the role of characters, never descend—so to speak—into Springfield. Amid the densely orchestrated sounds of combat once the battle has commenced, Pichel intervenes to announce, "this really happened," as if to cordon off this segment from the previous colloquy.[42] In doing so, he aligns his own commentary with a passage that is visually coded as authentic, as shock waves are registered both by an unsteady camera and by the presentation of frame lines, as if the gate of the printer, or perhaps the projector at the site of reception, has been knocked ajar by the force of an explosion.

At work here is an inversion of the interpolation of documentary passages in Hollywood fiction of the period, of say the broadcast reporting of celebrated radio news commentator Hans Kaltenborn in *Mr Smith Goes to Washington* (Capra, 1939), who is recruited to add a trace of authenticity to the story of a senate filibuster, yet whose presence never throws the fiction off course.[43] Although *The Battle of Midway* bills itself at the outset as simply a record or report by Navy photographers, the labours of Ford, his writers, and his stock company of actors point to a rather different notion of what can count as an appropriate documentary experience. For spectators in a commercial motion picture theatre, *The Battle of Midway* traded overtly with the conventions of Hollywood fiction. Vocal commentary by Darwell and Fonda, in particular, is less a ground of authority than a tool to expand the ways in which authenticated images can be interpreted, with narrators and proto-characters interposed between the spectator and a presupposed, projected world. In this fashion, *The Battle of Midway* imports from fiction elements of melodrama even as it anticipates, in its memorable combat footage, the expressive immediacy of *vérité*, whose practitioners rejected theatrical vocal effects.

Recasting the "Voice of God"

Unlike reflexive, modernist, or postmodern documentaries of more recent vintage, both *The Spanish Earth* and *The Battle of Midway* secure a causal logic for the action they depict, and never call the authority of their vocal commentaries into question. But in a way that the notion of "Voice of God" narration does not suggest, these documentaries also employ forms of verbal address and verbal tenses that define a complex spatial and temporal relation among commentator, spectator, and documented events. Moreover, the films seem keenly aware of the social qualities and distinctions that a disembodied voice can evoke and draw on familiar personalities precisely for the associations their voices provide. Conventional notions of voice-over narration notwithstanding, this should not surprise us. As Sarah Kozloff has observed with respect to the use of voice-over in classical Hollywood fiction, nothing prevents a third-person narrator, however disembodied, from revealing something about his or her world, nor the spectator from scrutinising and evaluating what this narrator has to say. Concomitantly, the grounding of a visible narrator in a particular location does not necessarily delimit the range of knowledge nor diminish the potential authority of that figure. In either case, spectators make judgements about the reliability and import of what they hear. As Kozloff notes, "the moral and political questions concerning voice-over, do not revolve around its unique essence, but around how filmmakers use it—what they have the narrator say, and in what manner."[44] It is the very specificity of the use of vocal narration in persuasive documentaries such as *The Spanish Earth* and *The Battle of Midway* to which we must attend.

Judgements concerning the pertinence and explanatory power of vocal narration in a documentary involve many factors, only one of which—and perhaps not always the most compelling given the sensory pleasures and motor force of motion pictures—is the logic of an argument. Above and beyond and even against matters of coherence and plausibility, we may also find vocal commentary attractive for its felicitous language, appealing verbal rhythms, or fresh expression of familiar sentiments. Interplay among a variety of voices likewise may arrest attention. Many social documentary filmmakers in the 1930s and 1940s were willing to explore and exploit these attractions, to experiment with poetic or colloquial language, diffused authority, and polyvocalism. In part, this seems inspired by a desire to produce the kind of variegated subjectivity common to classical fiction. But it may also reflect an impulse to expand the range of narrational options through the interpolation of extrinsic, ambiguously situated voices. In contrast to classical fiction, the effect often is to render fuzzy the boundaries of the non-fictional world upon which a documentary film is premised. Imported voices thus may invoke complementary worlds (including the imagined worlds of fiction) which the viewer is invited to consider in relation to the main, documented event.[45]

Faced with a potential disjunction between a documentary's referential field and the uncertain ground for disembodied voices, a spectator is encouraged to locate, and infer connections across, a variety of social markers. The invisible realm of "voice-over" thus should itself be construed as preeminently social, an historical understanding of which demands the reconstruction of a broader vocal intertext encompassing fiction films and radio dramas. To chart such a space is not to presume that we can know the horizon of expectations of all historically situated spectators—a task itself without boundaries. Nor is it to specify the necessary effect of any particular vocal strategy—a generalisation built on quicksand. Nevertheless, accounts of reception may bring into relief associations and assumptions that have lost salience over time. Having no difficulty identifying Ford's allusion to the Joad family in *The Battle of Midway*, for example, several (male) reviewers found Darwell's dialogue in particular to be excessive and overwrought. Critic Manny Farber, seizing an opportunity to scold wartime documentary filmmakers for emphasising words at the expense of images, in a review that anticipates a *verité* critique, ridiculed the vocal commentary in *The Battle of Midway* as "high school dramatics," incommensurate with the compelling images of men in battle.[46] Yet the film's editor, Robert Parrish, recalls hearing women sob at the film's Radio City Music Hall premiere, an event that fulfilled Ford's ambition to open up an entry point in the story of the battle for "the mothers of America."[47] The fictive space Darwell and Fonda occupy, if variously judged, thus takes on definition by way of references extrinsic to the film's ostensible subject and largely unavailable to the modern viewer.

Construing the placeless space of vocal narration in documentary as fundamentally social and historical brings to light the limits of "voice-over" as a metaphor to describe the varied kinds of work that vocal commentary performs. It draws our attention to a field of vocal references in which the non-fiction "talkies" of the period circulated, a lateral file of vocal possibilities from which these films drew, and brings info sharper focus the stress points in those works for which a necessary and sometimes awkward split between sound and image occasioned an experimental approach. It encourages us to explore precisely those features that are occluded by the conventional notion of "voice of God" narration, retrospectively and uniformly applied: the historical resonances of vocal acts—how accents, inflections, and forms of speech reverberate across and double back over fiction and non-fiction, film and radio, in the media dialect and dialogue of another era.

Acknowledgement

I wish to thank Edward Branigan, Nataša Durovicová, and Michael Renov for their comments on a previous version of this essay.

NOTES

1. For an influential topology of modes of documentary representation based on an historical sketch of this kind, see Bill Nichols, "The Voice of Documentary,"

Film Quarterly (Spring, 1983), 17–29, reprinted in *Movies and Methods*, vol. 2, ed. Nichols (Berkeley: University of California Press, 1985), 258–273, and revised in Nichols, *Representing Reality* (Bloomington: Indiana University Press, 1991), 32–75. Nichols takes pains, however, to stress that the four modes are not exclusive to any single historical period.

2. On the utility of the distinction between voice-off and voice-over, see Mary Ann Doane, "The Voice in the Cinema: The Articulation of Body and Space," *Yale French Studies*, 60 (1980): 33–50, especially 37–43.
3. Nichols, "The Voice of Documentary"; Jeffrey Youdelman, "Narration, Invention, & History: A Documentary Dilemma," *Cineaste*, 12, no. 2 (1982): 8–12. Youdelman prefaces his remarks with a useful discussion of some prototypes from the 1930s and 1940s, including *The New Earth* (Ivens, 1934), *Night Mail* (Wright and Watt, 1936], *The River* (Lorentz, 1937), *The City* (Van Dyke and Steiner, 1939), *Native Land* (Strand and Hurwitz, 1942), and *Strange Victory* (Hurwitz, 1948).
4. Nichols, "The Voice of Documentary," 18. In his revised discussion of the topic, Nichols chooses to replace the term "voice" with "argument," as carried by both "commentary" and "perspective." A "loss of voice," then is reformulated as "a deferential perspective, one that chooses to present evidence of the world as witnesses describe it rather than add a contrapuntal argument or voice of its own" (*Representing Reality*, 281, endnote no. 17). In opting for a term unencumbered by the acoustic connotations of "voice," Nichols thus chooses to emphasise the polemical, rather than more broadly expressive, dimension of a documentary's underlying "social point of view."
5. Edward Branigan, *Narrative Comprehension and Film* (London: Routledge, 1992), 115.
6. Carl Plantinga adopts just such a trope in *Rhetoric and Representation in Non-Fiction Film* (Cambridge University Press, 1997), in which he usefully outlines three broad epistemological functions for documentary, based on the degree of narrational authority, and labels these the "classical," "open," and "poetic" voices of non-fiction.
7. That we can respond to sound waves, but not light waves, without knowing their source suggests the rather different ways we think about audition and vision. As Edward Branigan notes, while we tend to believe that sound waves travel to our ears, we conceive light waves as a property of an object viewed; hence, for example we imagine that the "red" cover of a book retains its colour even in a lightless room. "When we see a 'lamp' and can name it, the identification is complete but a 'whistling' sound still needs to be specified: the whistling *of* what? *from* where?" See Branigan, "Sound and Epistemology in Film," *The Journal of Aesthetics and Art Criticism*, vol. 47, no. 4 (Fall, 1989): 311.
8. Pascal Bonitzer, "Les Silences de la voix," *Cahiers du cinéma*, 246 (February–March 1975), translated as *The Silences of the Voice* (*A Propos of Mai 68* by Gudie Lawaetz)' in *Narrative, Apparatus. Ideology: A Film Theory Reader*, ed. Philip Rosen (New York: Columbia University Press, 1986), 324. Bonitzer's ideas are elaborated upon by Doane in "The Voice in Cinema," 42; and Kaja Silverman in *The Acoustic Mirror; The Female Voice in Psychoanalysis and Cinema* (Bloomington: Indiana University Press, 1988), 48–49, 51–54, and 163–164.
9. It is interesting to note that in *The Next Voice You Hear* (Wellman, 1950), a fiction film that seeks to take seriously the question of God's vocal intervention in the lives of ordinary American citizens by way of the radio, God's voice is precisely the one that we do not hear. Instead, we learn of God's advice from characters, tuned to their radios, while the spectator through various plot devices is kept out of earshot.
10. In a work of non-fiction, what do we make of this pretence to God-like powers? Can a non-fictional world be construed as "authored" by the same force a vocal narrator represents? Or does the non-fictional status of the image strain any claim such a narrator might make about its creative powers? Note, for example, this scripted disclaimer of authorship in the credits to *With Car and Camera Around the World*, a silent travelogue by "Aloha and Walter Wanderwell," released in 1929: "Author, God, for he created the earth and its people. Scenario by All Peoples" (quoted in *Motion Picture News* [21 December 1929]: 40).
11. Explaining his aversion to "Voice of God" narration, Ricky Leacock notes: "When I become intrigued by theatre or film or even education, it is when I am not being told the answer. I start to find out for myself... The moment I sense that I'm being told the answer I start rejecting" (James Blue, "One Man's Truth—An Interview with Richard Leacock," *Film Comment* [Spring, 1965]: 16). Bonitzer and Doane critique the naivety of such a view. A lively defence of authoritative vocal commentary, moreover, can be found in J. Ronald Green, "The Illustrated Lecture," *Quarterly Review of Film and Video*, vol. 15, no. 2 (1994), 1–23.
12. Bonitzer, 327.
13. See especially Willard Van Dyke, "The Interpretive Camera in Documentary Film," *Hollywood Quarterly*, vol. 1, no. 4 (1946): 405–409, reprinted in *Nonfiction Film Theory and Criticism*, ed. Richard Meram Barsam (New York: Dutton, 1976), 342–349; Ben Moddow, "The Writer's Function in Documentary Film," *Writers' Congress: The Proceedings of the Conference Held in October 1943 Under the Sponsorship of the Hollywood Writers' Mobilisation and the University of California* (Berkeley: University of California Press, 1944), 98–103; Pare Lorentz, *FDR's Moviemaker: Memoirs and Scripts* (Reno: University of Nevada Press, 1992); John Grierson, "The G.P.O. Gets Sound," *Cinema Quarterly* (Edinburgh), vol. 2, no. 4 (Summer 1934): 215–221, and "Two Paths to Poetry," *Cinema Quarterly*, vol. 3, no. 4 (Summer, 1935): 194–196; Alberto Cavalcanti, "Sound in Films,"

Films (November, 1939): 25–39; and Paul Rotha, *Documentary Film* (London: Faber & Faber, 1939, 2nd edn.), 201–223. Although my comments in this essay are restricted to documentary filmmaking in the United States, they are applicable to much British (or "Griersonian") documentary from the same period.

14. William Alexander, *American Documentary Film from 1931 to 1942* (Princeton, N.J.: Princeton University Press, 1981); Russell Campbell, *Cinema Strikes Back: Radical Filmmaking in the United States, 1930–42* (Ann Arbor, Michigan: UMI Research Press, 1982); Jonathan Buchsbaum, "Left Political Filmmaking in the West: The Interwar Years," in *Resisting Images: Essays on Cinema and History*, ed., Robert Sklar and Charles Musser (Philadelphia: Temple University Press, 1990); Paul Arthur, "Jargons of Authenticity (Three American Moments)," in *Theorizing Documentary*, ed. Michael Renov (New York: Routledge/AFI Film Readers, 1993), 108–134; Charles Wolfe, "The Poetics and Politics of Nonfiction: Documentary Film," in *Grand Design: Hollywood as a Modern Business Enterprise, 1930–39*, ed. Tino Balio (New York: Charles Scribner's Sons, 1993), 351–386, and "Straight Shots and Twisted Plots: Social Documentary and the Avant-Garde in the 1930s," in *Lovers of Cinema: The First American Film Avant-Garde, 1919–45*, ed. Jan-Christopher Horak (Madison: University of Wisconsin Press, 1996), 234–266.
15. For important new work in this area, see Dana Benelli's superb PhD dissertation, "Jungles and the National Landscape: Documentary and Hollywood Cinema in the 1930s" (University of Iowa, 1992).
16. Anon., review of *The Break Up*, *Variety* (6 August 1930): 35; Frank S. Nugent, review of *Hell's Holiday*, *New York Times* (15 July 1933): 14; "Land.," review of *Bring 'Em Back Alive*, *Variety* (21 June 1932): 14; "Char.," review of *Explorers of the World*, *Variety* (22 December 1931): 19.
17. "Bige.," review of *Land of Promise*, *Variety* (27 November 1935): 30.
18. "Chic.," review of *Taming the Jungle*, *Variety* (6 June 1933): 14.
19. "Shan.," review of *Hei Tiki*, *Variety* (5 February 1935): 31; "Rush.," review of *Igloo*, *Variety* (26 July: 1932): 17.
20. Nugent, 14; "Kauf.," review of *Hell's Holiday*, *Variety* (18 July 1933): 37.
21. "McStay.," review of *Lest We Forget*, *Variety* (17 April 1935): 15.
22. "Rush.," review of *Igloo*, 17.
23. "Char.," review of *Gow*, *Variety* (5 December 1933): 17.
24. One reviewer, for example, complained that the Cameo Theatre in New York misleadingly promoted travelogues as entertaining, rather than strictly educational, films by advertising those with vocal accompaniment as "all-talking" (Anon., review of *The Bottom of the World*, *Variety* [16 July 1930]: 29).
25. Catherine L. Covert, "American Sensibility and the Response to Radio, 1919–24," in *Mass Media Between the Wars: Perceptions of Cultural Tensions, 1918–24*, ed. Covert (Syracuse, N.Y.: Syracuse University Press, 1984), 199–220.
26. Erik Barnouw, *The Golden Web: A History of Broadcasting in the United States, 1933–53* (New York: Oxford, 1968), passim; Hector Chevigny, "Commercial Radio Writing in Wartime," *Writers' Congress*, 141–152.
27. Raymond Fielding, *The March of Time, 1935–51* (New York: Oxford University Press, 1978), 102–110, 220–221, 260–262; Bruce Cook, "Whatever Happened to Westbrook Van Voorhis?," *American Film* (March 1977), 25–29.
28. Less celebrated, but notable for the pattern of migration from radio journalism to film their careers illustrate, were Malcolm La Prada, a radio travel talk narrator who provided vocal commentary for Bray Pictures' *Rambling Reporter* travel talk film series in 1930; NBC's Alois Havorille, narrator for *This is America* beginning in 1933; and NBC's Floyd Gibbons, commentator for *With Byrd at the South Pole* (1934).
29. On the production and distribution history of *The Spanish Earth*, see Joris Ivens, *The Camera and I* (New York: International Publishers, 1969), 103–138, reprinted as "Spain and *The Spanish Earth*," in Barsam, 349–375; Thomas Waugh, "Men Cannot Act in Front of the Camera in the Presence of Death: Joris Ivens' *The Spanish Earth*," *Cineaste*, vol. 7, no. 2 (1982): 30–33 and vol. 7, no. 3 (1983): 21–29; Thomas P. McManus, "Down to Earth in Spain," *New York Times* (25 July 1937): x:4; and Ben Bellitt, The Camera Reconnoiters, *The Nation* (20 November 1937); reprinted in Lewis Jacobs, ed., *The Documentary Tradition* (New York: W. W. Norton, 2nd edn., 1979), 142. On *The Battle of Midway*, see Tag Gallagher, *John Ford: The Man and His Films* (Berkeley: University of California Press, 1986), 200–213; Robert Parrish, *Growing Up in Hollywood* (New York: Harcourt, Brace, Janovich, 1976), 144–151; "TMP," "Film of 'Midway' Released by Navy," *New York Times* (20 September 1942): 19; Anon., "18 Minutes of Midway," *Newsweek* (21 September 1942): 80. Prior to the film's general release, *The Spanish Earth* was widely seen in Hollywood, where its audience included director John Ford (McManus, "Down to Earth in Spain": x: 4).
30. Waugh, *Cineaste*, vol. 7, no. 3 (1983), 25–26.
31. Irving Reis devised the sound of a bombardment in *The Spanish Earth* by recording in reverse an earth-quake effect from *San Francisco*, the popular fiction film released by MGM the previous year (Ivens, 129). Reis' background in radio drama paved the way for his work as a screenwriter at Paramount in 1938 and his career as a Hollywood director to follow.
32. A copy of the playbill can be found in file H 139, Thomas Brandon Collection, Film Study Center, Museum of Modern Art, New York.
33. Ben Achtenberg, "Helen Van Dongen: An Interview," *Film Quarterly* (Winter, 1976–77): 52.
34. Ivens, 128.

35. Carlos Baker, *Ernest Hemingway: A Life Story* (New York: Charles Scribner's, 1969), 299; Edward F. Stanton, *Hemingway and Spain: A Pursuit* (Seattle: University of Washington Press, 1989), 150-154; Robert O. Stephens, *Hemingway's Nonfiction: the Public Voice* (Chapel Hill: University of North Carolina Press, 1968), 88–108; Alexander, 151–152.
36. Ivens, 129. Many critics agreed: "So simple, so real, so patently the voice of truth" (Cedric Belfrage, excerpted review, File H139, Thomas Brandon Collection); "The beauty of simple things and felt simply said" (*London Observer*, File H139, Thomas Brandon Collection); "Hemingway's voice—for he speaks the commentary himself—cuts through the sound of crackling battle" (Basil Wright, "*The Land Without Bread and The Spanish Earth*," *Film News* (December 1937), reprinted in Jacobs, 147). Alberto Cavalcanti found Hemingway's commentary the fulfillment of Wordsworth's definition of poetry: "emotions recollected in tranquillity" (29).
37. "JTM" [John T. McManus], "The Screen," *New York Times* (21 August 1937): 7; John T. McManus. "Realism Invades Gotham," *New York Times* (22 August 1937): x, 3; James Shelley Hamilton, *National Board of Review* (October 1937, reprinted in Stanley Hochman, ed., *From Quasimodo to Scarlet O'Hara: A National Board of Review Anthology* (New York: Frederick Ungar, 1982), 262–263; and reviews by "JDH" in *New York Sun* (23 August 1937), by Gould Cassel in *The Brooklyn Daily Eagle* (24 August 1937), and anonymously in the *London Times* (9 November 1937), excerpted and collated in File H139, Thomas Brandon Collection. Hemingway's text subsequently was published in book form as *The Spanish Earth* (Cleveland: J. B. Savage Co. 1938).
38. Parrish, 146–150. Nichols previously had worked with Ford on nine features and had written the commentary for Joris Ivens's *The 400 Million* (1939), a compilation documentary made in support of China's struggle against Japan in the 1930s.
39. In a perceptive discussion of *The Battle of Midway* in *Rhetoric and Representation in Nonfiction Film*, Carl Plantinga draws a distinction between the voice of Crisp, a zealous patriot describing combat in a tendentious fashion, and that of Pichel, a gentle father or spiritual leader possessing moral authority (160). An extrapolation of character traits of this kind is interesting to consider in light of the separate contributions of writers Nichols, a political liberal and McGuire, a conservative, and the tension between military ardour and moral authority in several of Ford's fiction films, including *Drums Along the Mohawk* (1939), *They Were Expendable* (1945), *Fort Apache* (1948), *She Wore a Yellow Ribbon* (1949), and *The Horse Soldiers* (1960). While Ford's fiction films tend to plot this tension as narrative conflict, the voices of Crisp and Pichel serve complementary functions here.
40. Ford was identified as the director of both *The Grapes of Wrath and How Green Was My Valley* in the first news item on *The Battle of Midway in New York Times*, "Footnotes on Headlines" (20 September 1942): 4, 2. At the time that Darwell and Fonda were recruited for vocal roles on *The Battle of Midway*, they were working together on *The Ox-Bow Incident* (Wellman, 1943) at Twentieth Century-Fox. Shortly thereafter, Fonda enlisted in the Navy and served in the Pacific. Darwell later reprised her role as Ma Joad in a radio version of *The Grapes of Wrath* on NBC's *University Theater* on New Year's Day, 1 949.
41. Pichel's vocal authority similarly was exploited in *Happy Land* (1943), a wartime drama directed by Pichel, in which his voice is heard over a radio, announcing news of the outbreak of war in Europe.
42. According to Parrish, this line was initially uttered by Ford during a screening session with Nichols (147).
43. From this perspective, Kaltenborn's vocal and physical performances as noted commentator across radio and film, and fiction and non-fiction, warrant further study. Consider, for example, his casting by Orson Welles in *Julius Caesar* for a *Mercury Theater of the Air* radio broadcast in the fall of 1938, or Kaltenborn's appearance as a radio commentator, interviewing a Nazi official played by an actor, in *The March of Time* episode, "On Foreign Newsfronts," in September 1940. Gaining great public prominence for his dramatic reports on the Munich Conference in the summer of 1938, Kaltenborn also was a CBS analyst in Spain during the Civil War (see Barnouw, 74–75). I explore the implications of Kaltenborn's appearance as a nonfictional character within the fictional context of "*Mr Smith Goes to Washington*: Democratic Forums and Representational Forms," *Close Viewings: An Anthology of New Film Criticism*, ed. Peter Lehman (Tallahassee: Florida State University Press, 1990), 321–326.
44. Sarah Kozloff, *Invisible Storytellers: Voice-Over Narration in American Fiction Film* (Berkeley: University of California Press, 1988), 97.
45. Drawing a distinction between the tests we apply to fictional and non-fictional narration, Edward Branigan proposes that with fiction we start with lower level pictures or words from which we seek to infer "a plausible set of higher mediations with which to justify depicted events," while with non-fiction we start with beliefs in a historically real, unmediated event and the recording capacities of camera and microphone, and infer from this what "lower" level pictures or words plausibly could be known about that event. "Both classical fiction and classical non-fiction," he writes, "attempt to discover meanings that lie 'behind' (beyond, below) events; they merely start in different places and one expands, while the other contracts, the levels of narration" (*Narrative Comprehension and Film* [London: Routledge, 1992], 204–205.) Note the two qualifying prepositions for "behind" suggested here. "Beyond" (but not "below") opens up the possibility that meanings may relate to one another not only hierachically (more or less deeply embedded in the text) but perhaps also

to the side (or outside?) of the documentary diegesis.

46. "TMP," "Film of 'Midway,'" 19; Bosley Crowther, "Citation for Excellence," *New York Times* (20 September 1942), sec. 8: 3; Sam Harold, "Disappointed in 'Midway' Film," *New York Times* (18 October 1942), sec. 8: 5; Manny Farber, "Memorandum to Hollywood," *New Republic* (5 October 1942), 414–415. Assuming the voice of an unhappy respondent to *The Battle of Midway*, Farber speaks directly to the filmmakers: "So plus everything else, it's a quiz show you give us: who belongs to the voice? Up till now one voice would do you. In 'Midway' you have most of the Joad family, in addition to a character actor I haven't guessed yet. Donald Crisp, Henry Fonda, Jane Darwell and Mr X. A symphony of discord" (414).

47. Parrish, 151.

41

STEVE NEALE

TRIUMPH OF THE WILL

Notes on Documentary and Spectacle (1979)

Introduction

Triumph of the Will was commissioned by Adolph Hitler on behalf of the Nazi party in Germany as a record and celebration of the 1934 Party Rally in Nuremberg. It was shot by a team of cameramen, soundmen and other technicians under the direction of Leni Riefenstahl and subsequently edited by her. It was premiered in Berlin on 28 March 1935 and was awarded the National Film Prize by Goebbels during the Festival of the Nation in May 1935 and the Diplome de Grand Prix at the Exposition Internationale des Arts et des Techniques in Paris in July. This latter event, in particular, is of significance for the film's later inscription into cinema history. *Triumph of the Will* has often been damned for its political content and for being a Nazi propaganda film. Just as often though, it has been hailed, albeit ambivalently, as a cinematic masterpiece. Neither of these assessments, however, has produced a substantial analysis either of the film and its own internal codes and systems or of its conjunctural functioning and effectivity: in all the discussions of the film that I have come across consideration of one of these aspects has come to dominate (or eliminate) consideration of the other. This has evidently a lot to do with a compartmentalisation of art on the one hand and history on the other, but even more crucially it has a lot to do with the lack of any concept of discourse, of any concept of discursive relations or discursive effectivity. In my view, the balance certainly needs to be recast—film and conjuncture need to be integrated more effectively. But a necessary preliminary to this is an examination of the film's textual organisation and discursive systems; it is only from there that conjunctural analyses can proceed. What I aim to do in this article is to initiate such an examination, concentrating in particular on two areas of systematicity—spectacle and looking—which have often rather vaguely been discussed by the film's critics but which have never been analysed thoroughly at all. In so doing, I shall proceed initially by interrogating some of the terms and concepts deployed by these critics. This article, then, is neither an ideological reading of the film, nor an analysis of its conjunctural positioning. It is rather an analysis of some of the major conditions necesary for both.

I

> In short, *Triumph of the Will*, like *Birth of a Nation*, embodies an overwhelming contradiction: it is cinematically dazzling and ideologically vicious. (Richard Meran Barsam, *Filmguide to Triumph of the Will*, Indiana University Press, 1975, pp 17–18.)

This quotation is typical of most critical comment on *Triumph of the Will*. It is damned for its "ideology" on the one hand and praised for its cinematic artistry on the other. Hence:

> Two conclusions cannot escape anyone seeing *Triumph of the Will*; it could never have been made by anyone not fanatically at one with the events depicted, nor equally could it have been made by anyone not profoundly encompassed by the medium. (David Gurston, "Leni Riefenstahl," *Film Quarterly*, v XIV n 1, Fall 1960, p 15.)

> Some viewers may question the sincerity of the mass emotion expressed at the rallies, or find themselves alienated by the party rhetoric, but most agree on the cinematic power of the film. Ultimately, the modern audience is stunned both by the film's artistic power and by its political content. (Barsam, op cit, p 27.)

> As there is terror in *Triumph of the Will* when one thinks of what the production helped stabilize and bring about, there is also the stamp and invisible signature of authentic genius. (Marshall Lewis, "*Triumph of the Will*," *Film Comment*, v 3 n 1, Winter 1965, p 23.)

In structuring these two aspects of the film as a "contradiction," this kind of criticism is able both to separate one aspect from another (cinematic power is different from ideology; they are separate in themselves and can thus be separately discussed), and yet simultaneously to hold them together in a notion of contradiction that in effect differs little from notions like "paradox" or "ambiguity"—terms which, in traditional criticism of the arts, serve less as analytical concepts than as marks of confusion or, even, of quality.

Despite the separation, however, the nature of "the cinematic power" of *Triumph of the Will* is never subject to detailed discussion. It is recognised. It is also celebrated. But its specificity, its systematicity and its effects are never fully analysed. One of the reasons for devoting attention to the film lies, therefore, not only in the need to pull the terms "cinema" and "ideology" back together but also in the need for some kind of initial analysis of its cinematicity: what is it that these critics find so overwhelming and so deserving of praise—despite their liberal consciences? Why—and how—is the film so "cinematically dazzling"?

There is another reason too, one which is ultimately and intimately related, in my opinion, to these kinds of questions, though it is one which is admittedly rather more speculatively based. It derives from a juxtaposition of a series of related conceptions of film, documentary and propaganda, a juxtaposition which is not in fact explicitly made or explicitly recognized by the critics of *Triumph of the Will* (perhaps for symptomatic reasons) but one which, once it *is* made, generates a number of interesting and important contradictions, centring in particular on notions about (and definitions of) the relationship between documentary, cinema and vision. Before discussing this more fully, I want to spend some time in looking at the opening section of the film and in examining in particular the inscription of a twin system of spectacle and looking. Since in my view it is these elements which give the film both its cinematic *and* its ideological power. They also simultaneously, provide the terms and the basis needed to discuss the kinds of contradiction I have in mind.

The opening section of *Triumph of the Will*, lasting some 10½ minutes and comprising 113 shots overall (discounting titles and credits) can be subdivided into three main segments, as follows: (1) The flight into Nuremberg and the landing of Hitler's aircraft. (2) The motorcade. (3) The arrival at the hotel. As will become evident, this segmentation derives not only from diegetic criteria (criteria involving the specification of the spatio-temporal unity of events), but also from distinct stages in the inscription and/or the re-marking of the systems of spectacle and looking that traverses the film overall.

The first of the shots in this section consists of a view through the cockpit window of the aircraft, panning slowly left as the aircraft moves forward (Figure 41.1). This is followed by eight more shots from the plane, each of them focused on different aspects/moments of the cloud formation visible from the aircraft window, and each of them, at one point or another, including within the frame visible evidence of the presence of the aircraft itself.

The imbrications of framing, composition, movement and clouds in these opening shots function to install *spectacle* as the principle of the film's operations. That is to say a signifying system is installed whose basis lies in a specific form of the evocation and satiation of the scopic drive, a system which is especially concerned both to stress, to *display*, the visibility of the visible, and to produce, as far as is possible, an elision between the look of the spectating subject and the look of the other across the instance of the visual field of the image[1] through the mobilisation of precisely those of particular codes of spatial scale (monumentality and extreme contrast); of light (chiaroscuro or extremes of luminosity); of elaborate and/or (heavily marked-displayed) composition;[2] and so on.

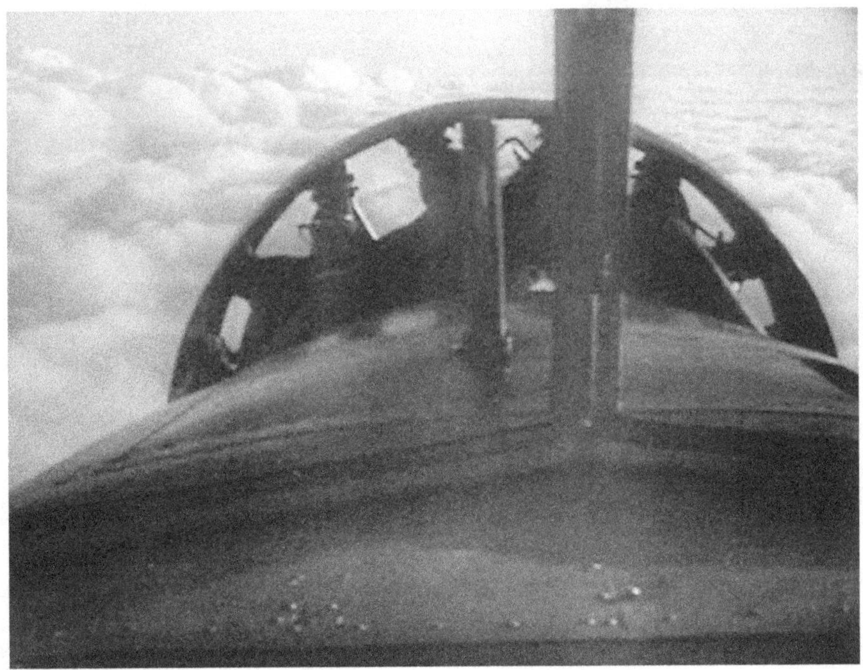

FIGURE 41.1 Still capture from DVD.

All these forms of codification are designed to *exhibit* the image for the gaze of the spectator and for the scopic drive that sustains it, designed, precisely, to "catch" (to lure) the eye. The cloud formations in particular here are both important and indicative. As Hubert Damisch has argued in his book *Théorie du nuage* (Paris 1972) clouds have been an essential ingredient in the whole apparatus of spectacle in European art. In offering to the spectator's gaze a set of forms which mask and fill an otherwise empty and potentially infinite space (the sky) while simultaneously signifying the very emptiness and infinity that they mask, clouds have come to function, in a sense, to signify spectacle itself. This double functioning illustrates particularly well the contradiction that spectacle involves. The traces of the cockpit in the image have an interesting significance and role in relation to this. If the spectating subject is inscribed, via the spectacle of the cloud formations, in interrelationship with an easily flowing and effortless series of movements (both of the aircraft and of the panning camera within it)—the gaze able almost to encompass the infinite, such is its position of visual privilege—the traces I am referring to function so as to *circumscribe* its apparently limitless power, to indicate and demarcate its limits. They are, in this sense, almost overtly indicative of the flaw at the heart of the scopic drive, of the insistence of the other in the visual field, of the impossibility of the very position of visual mastery inscribed in the other codes that organize the sequence. In *representing* these limits, these traces themselves function to fill the lack. In their very repetition they stabilize as unproblematically signified elements of the diegesis, coming simply to represent the presence of the aircraft itself. Moreover, in coming so close to (yet so far from) the flaw in the scopic drive, the film can all the more effectively engage the

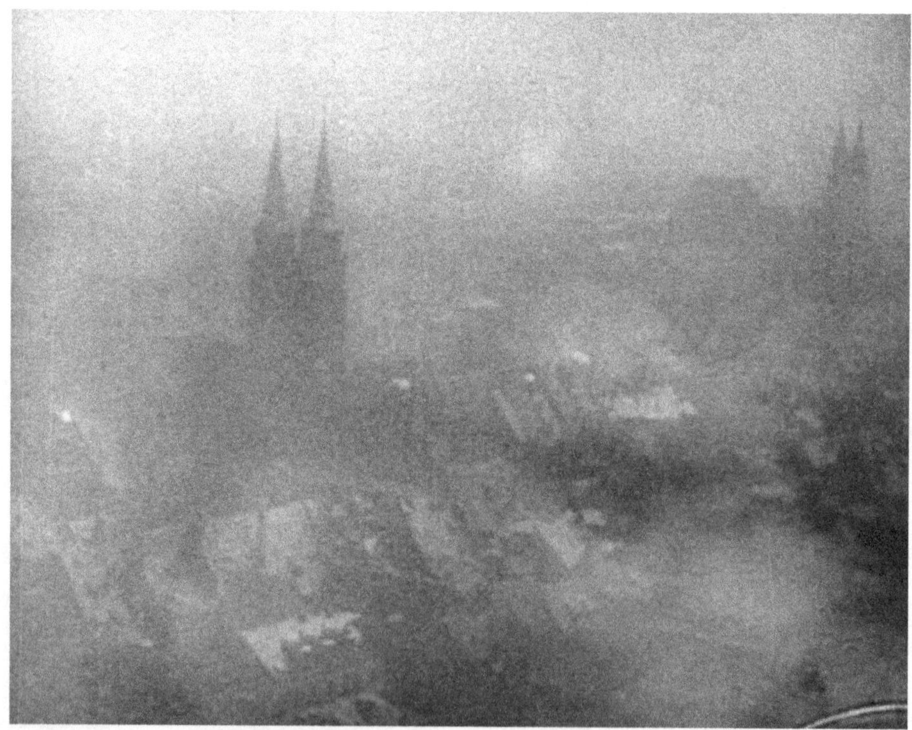

FIGURE 41.2 Still capture from DVD.

drive's dynamic—pulling the subject into the metonymic flow of the spectacle across fluctuating instances of "imperfect" vision which—precisely because of the "imperfection"—can promise the impossible plentitude elsewhere provided by the plentiful instances of unblemished spectacle that soon come to fill the film.

In shot 9, the aircraft's forward movement through the clouds and down towards Nuremberg marks the first point of re-orientation of the film's visual system. As the plane descends, the clouds appear to dissolve, to draw apart like a stage-curtain,[3] to reveal the aerial spectacle of the city itself, spread out below for our gaze (Figure 41.2). Four more shots, each repeating an arc-like movement around a particular building or monument, re-mark the instance of spectacle across its new diegetic space before, in shot 14, there occurs a view of the plane itself, a view which pulls the fragments and traces previously visible (and vaguely troubling) into the plentitude of the image and its composed visual field. In so doing it not only fully stabilizes, in retrospect, those previous fragments and traces, it also fully establishes that the register and position of the gaze of the spectator is one of privileged mastery, now detached from and transcending any specific, identifiable and circumscribed place. The gaze is now inscribed as limit*less*, and is specifically re-inscribed as such in the following (famous) shot in which the plane's shadow passes over the street and its parading troops. The plane's diegetic presence is re-marked while the spectator's gaze (above the crowd, above the city, comprehending both the plane and its shadow) is re-inscribed in its position of all-encompassing mastery—all the more so in a shot whose strikingly contrived, composed, almost especially arranged, effect functions precisely to catch the eye.

The following sequence of shots (15–23), alternating views of the plane in flight as it comes in to land with successively closer shots of the city and its parading troops and massed crowds (and thereby folding the one into the other, integrating the two into a common diegetic space itself heavily marked by the instance of spectacle (the troops on parade)), leads on to a shot (shot 23, Figure 41.3) which initiates a system of looking that runs throughout the remainder of the film and that dominates its visual articulation. This shot consists, simply, of a crowd gathered behind two Nazi guards gazing up and out of frame right (ie watching the arrival and landing of the plane). It is at this point that the activity of looking is inscribed into the diegesis itself, and that its privileged object begins to be established. Thirteen shots later—a delay that functions emphatically to mark its importance—the anticipated object of the look, the figure of Adolph Hitler, comes initially into view (shot 36, Figure 41.4). In other words, the first clearly identifiable (seeable) instance of intra-diegetic looking is co-incident with the initial appearance of Hitler, with the latter as that which gratifies the former, filling the space implied by the eye-line in shot 23, completing the visual and dramatic impetus of the sequence as a whole.

This initial segment closes, importantly and significantly, with a sequence of shots which firmly establish that the *political* relationship between the crowd and Hitler, as signified in the film, is one, precisely, that hinges on looking: Hitler's status *in the film* derives from, and is motivated and signalled by, the fact that he is structured and marked as the privileged object of the gaze, that he himself is the ultimately significant spectacle—for the crowds *in* the film and for the spectators *of* the film. Hence the significance of shot 41. Here, Hitler is framed in close-up, returning the gaze of the saluting crowd and, thus, acknowledging his visual as well as his political function. It is the spectator's look which joins the two spaces (that of the crowd and that of Hitler) and the two instances of looking together.

From here the film moves into its next segment, the street cavalcade, a segment

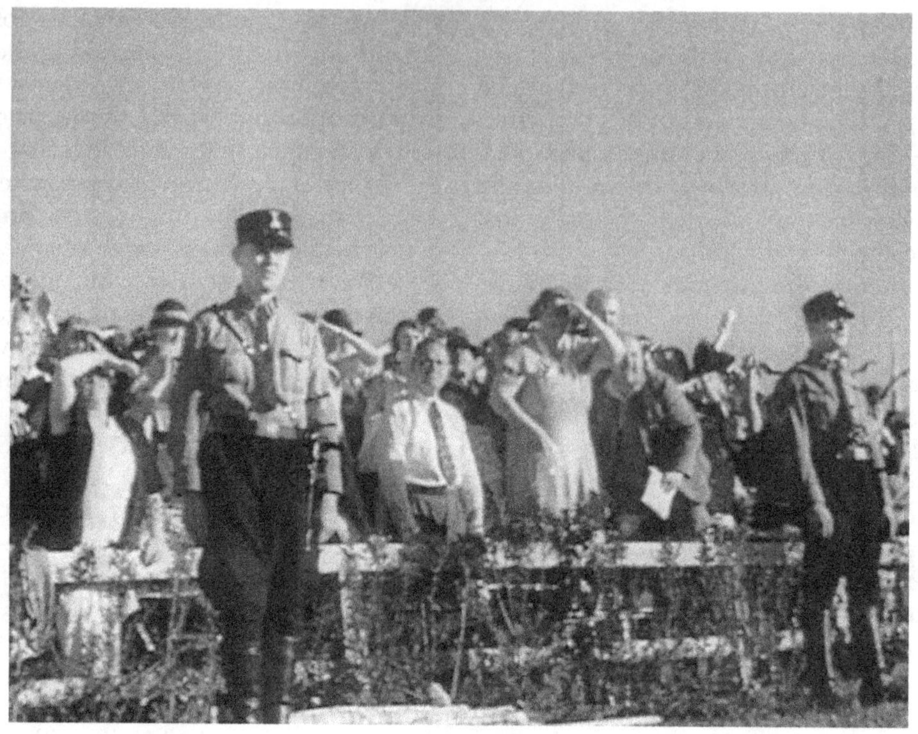

FIGURE 41.3 Still capture from DVD.

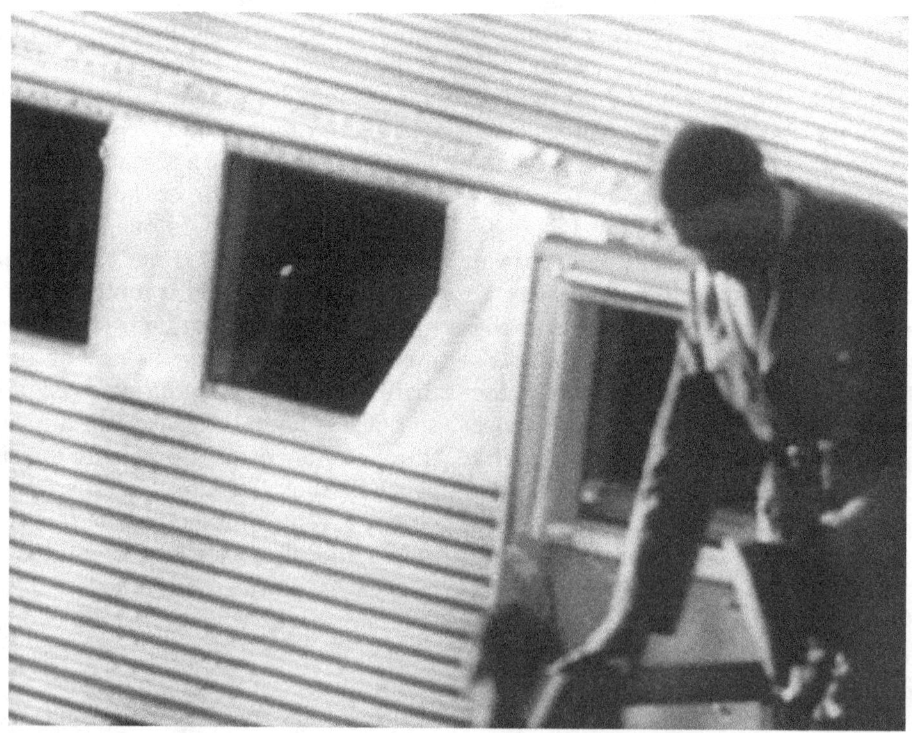

FIGURE 41.4 Still capture from DVD.

which serves above all to re-mark and to emphasize Hitler's function *vis-à-vis* the intra-diegetic crowd, the filmic spectator and the system of spectacle which it anchors. Consisting largely of a series of alternating shots of the crowds watching and saluting and of Hitler standing in his car (occasionally but significantly punctuated by more distant views encompassing both instances—continuing the inscription of spectacle in its mode as spatial scale in conjunction with a mastering distance of gaze), it insists over and over again not only upon the activity of looking as the basis of the relations between the actants the sequence signifies, but also upon looking as the key term in the articulation of its own internal consistency: in a manner very similar to that of classical "fictional" cinema. The sequence under discussion here depends absolutely for its clarity and intelligibility upon a non-contradictory articulation of intra-diegetic looks across the look of the camera and the spectator; given the absence of a plot, and given the absence of dialogue and commentary, the role of this relay of looks in the provision of a position of intelligibility for the spectator and in the location of events in a clear spatio-temporal milieu is all the more heavily weighted. (The striking instances of a "play" with looking and its cinematic articulation in this segment—as for instance in the "exchange of looks" between Hitler and a cat (shots 78–80) and in the apparently animated looking of a statue (shot 67)—indicative of this weight and of the ease with which it is borne; an index of its "artistry" and "style.")

As regards the functioning and importance of the figure of Hitler with respect to the relay of looks and the film's system of spectacle, two aspects of the segment under discussion are especially interesting and significant. The first might appear "accidental" from a purely technical point of view, but its recurrent insistence throughout the segment suggests that it is symptomatically crucial. The first shot in the segment as a whole is a moving high angle shot of Hitler's car driving toward the camera along a crowd-lined road: all the functionally important components in the segment thus assembled for the encompassing gaze of the spectator. The second shot, taken, it would seem, from the car itself, shows only the saluting crowd. The third shot (shot 45) is taken from a camera placed head-on in front of the car, its driver on the right, the standing and saluting figure of Hitler on the left. During the course of the shot, as the car moves forward and the camera back, the camera pans right towards the crowd lining the street, so that Hitler actually moves out of frame. This is the first of a number of shots in which Hitler dominates the frame only subsequently to be lost from it, usually as a result of camera movement. Shot 55, for instance, is a close-up of Hitler taken from behind, the crowd visible in banks to the right. The camera here, again, pans right toward the crowd and Hitler moves out of view. In shot 58, again framed from behind Hitler's head, but this time with the camera tilted upward slightly to include within the image figures on a flag-lined bridge, the effect is achieved by a further tilting of the camera to hold the bridge in frame as the car moves forward. In shot 61 Hitler does not, in fact, move out of frame at all. Instead, he is lost in darkness as the car passes under the bridge. It moves back into light (and vision) as the car emerges at the other side. Finally, in shot 89, taken from the side of the car as it moves left, the camera tracks past Hitler, slows down to re-frame him from a closer position and then, finally, moves past him again to focus on the crowds behind him.

Each of these instances articulates the primary elements structured by the segment as a whole—Hitler and the crowd. Given the relay of looks that holds these elements together coherently, and given Hitler's role in anchoring that relay, their significance lies in the way in which they vary that articulation, and, especially, in the way in which they institute an oscillating play with Hitler's presence in/absence from the frame. Thus the first of these instances is preceded and followed by shots of the crowd alone, its gaze in a sense functioning to re-mark Hitler's absence from the spectator's visual field. He returns, however, centrally and dominantly framed, two shots later. And this tends to be the pattern throughout. In other words, given the variations (and these are important in contributing to that sense of style and visual dynamism noted by the film's critics), the oscillation between Hitler on the one hand and the crowd on the other is articulated across an oscillation between Hitler's presence in/absence from the frame in such a way as insistently to highlight his function as privileged object of the look and as a principle of visual orientation and coherence.

The second feature of this segment to which I want to draw attention concerns four particular shots (47, 59, 61 and 85). In each of these shots Hitler's body is, in one way or another, specifically marked by a lighting effect, and in each case the effect serves, to highlight Hitler as object of the look. As with the presence/absence oscillation discussed above, each instance is subject to some variation: in the first the light is marked, almost like a halo, on Hitler's head; in the second it is marked on his head and shoulders (shot 59, Figure 41.5); in the third it is that into which he enters after passing into the darkness under the bridge, while in the fourth, again, the focus is Hitler's head. In each case, the shots in question occur after a sequence from which Hitler's figure has been absent (shot 59 being slightly different in that it is one of the instances of oscillation noted above). In fact there is only one example throughout the whole segment in which Hitler's body remains unmarked after an absence of three or more shots, and this, occurring as it does during the sequence in which he is presented with flowers by a little girl, is a very particular case. Indeed, it might be maintained that sequence as a whole performs an analogous marking function, especially as the three shots that do occur during Hitler's absence from the screen are each individualised images of girls watching and smiling at the apparently impromptu ceremony. It should be noted, incidentally that there are other instances of "play" with the cinematic articulation of looks in the film apart from those involving the cat and the statue. I have in mind, in particular, a sequence during the final street parade in which three differently angled shots of marching troops are linked together through a matching of eye-lines produced by interleaving them in sequence in the editing with a medium shot of a group of people watching from a window—two gazing off to the left and two, through binoculars, to the right—and with a medium close-up of Hitler who initially is gazing out of screen left and who then turns to gaze out of frame right, thus producing, on top of the matching of eye-lines, a visual rhyme which serves to bind the sequence together all the more tightly (figures 6–11)—and all the more stylishly, so also are there other instances in which Hitler's body is marked as object of the look by a particular effect of light. Indeed, this is one of the film's most insistent, most evident and most important figures. Examples occur, in particular, and for obvious reasons, during the night sequences in the Nuremberg stadium and the congress hall (see Figures 41.12, 41.13 and 41.15): one of the primary functions of the motorcade segment, therefore, can be seen to be that of initiating the inscription of this figure in the context, overall, of the marking of Hitler as the basis and centre of its system of spectacle.

The last segment I wish to discuss centres on the arrival of Hitler at his hotel. It represents the culmination not only of an ongoing diegetic action—that which might loosely and simply be termed "the arrival of Hitler in Nuremberg"—but also of the initial inscription of those systems of spectacle and looking that traverse the film as a whole—giving it the visual unity that its

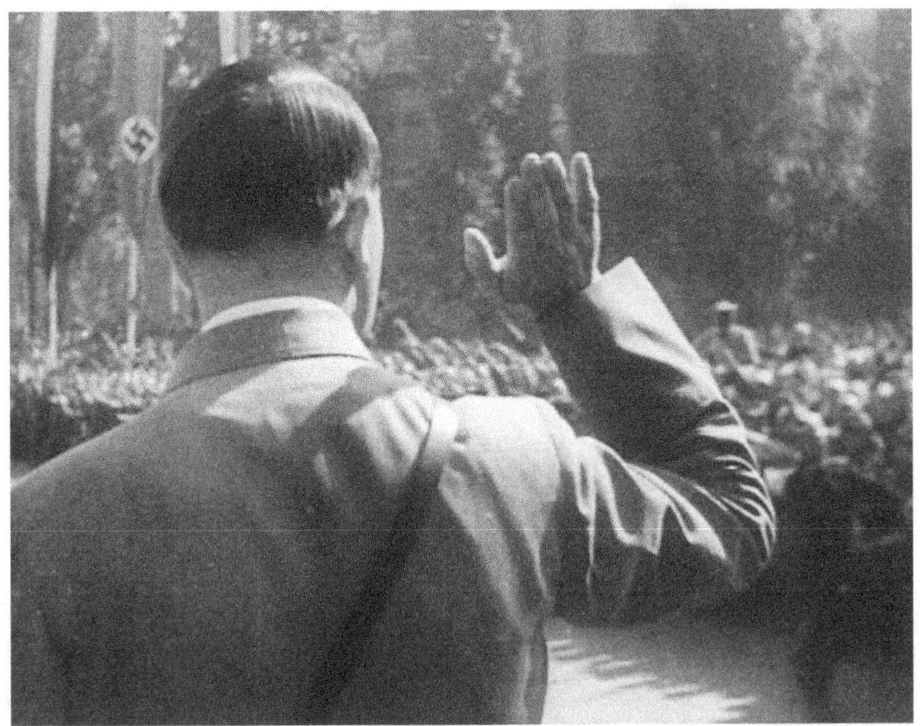

FIGURE 41.5 Still capture from DVD.

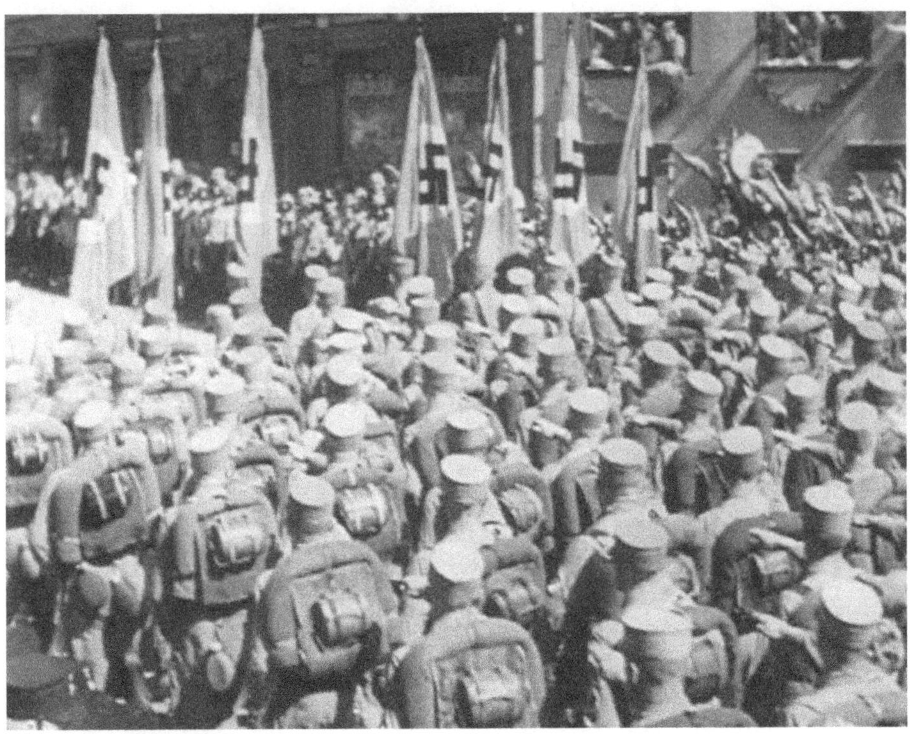

FIGURE 41.6 Still capture from DVD.

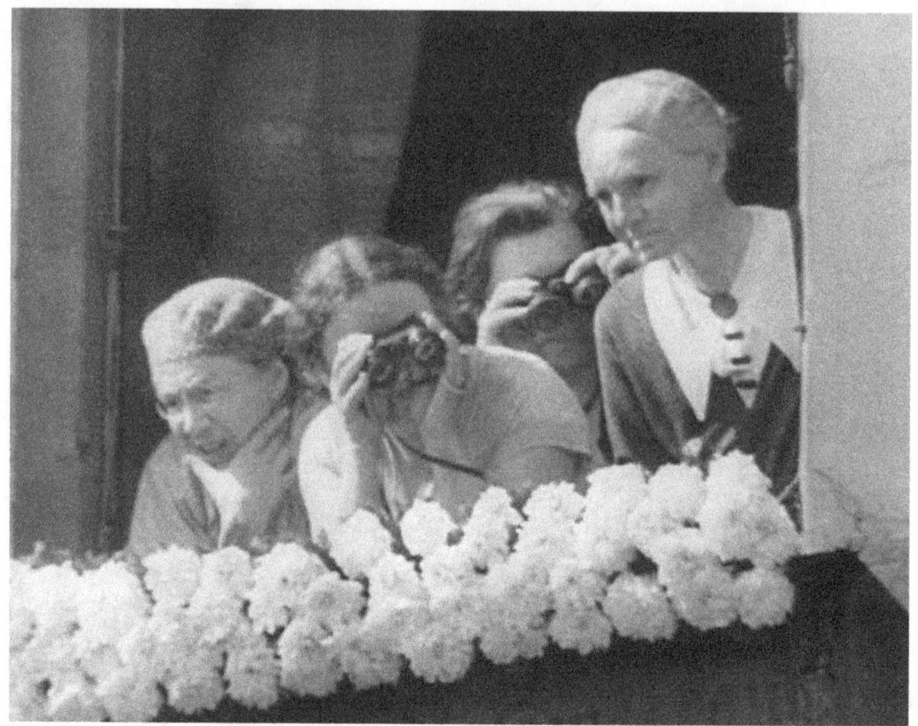

FIGURE 41.7 Still capture from DVD.

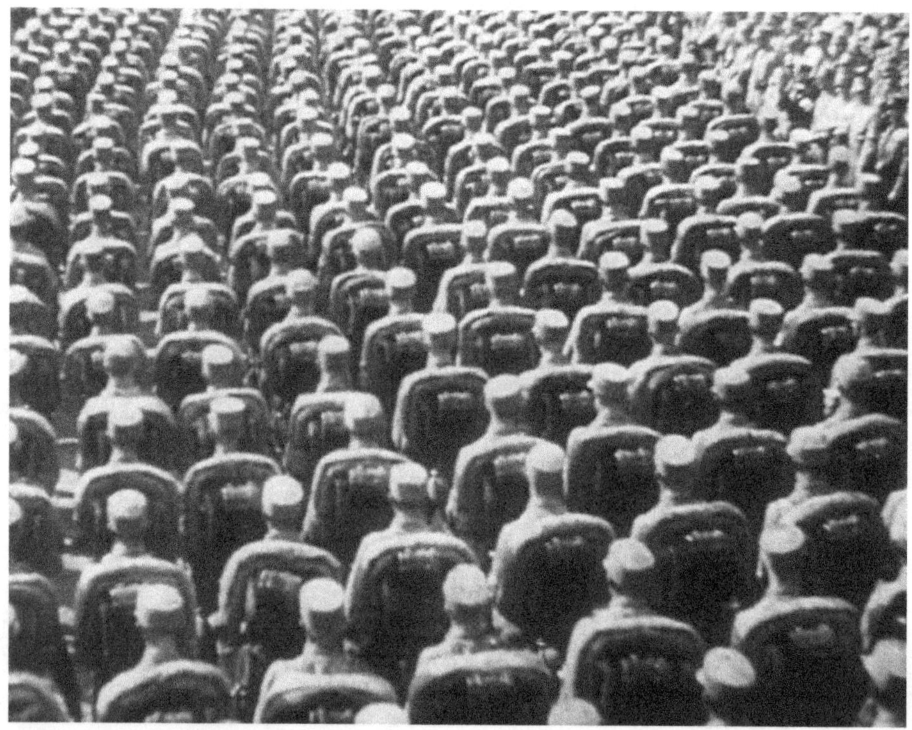

FIGURE 41.8 Still capture from DVD.

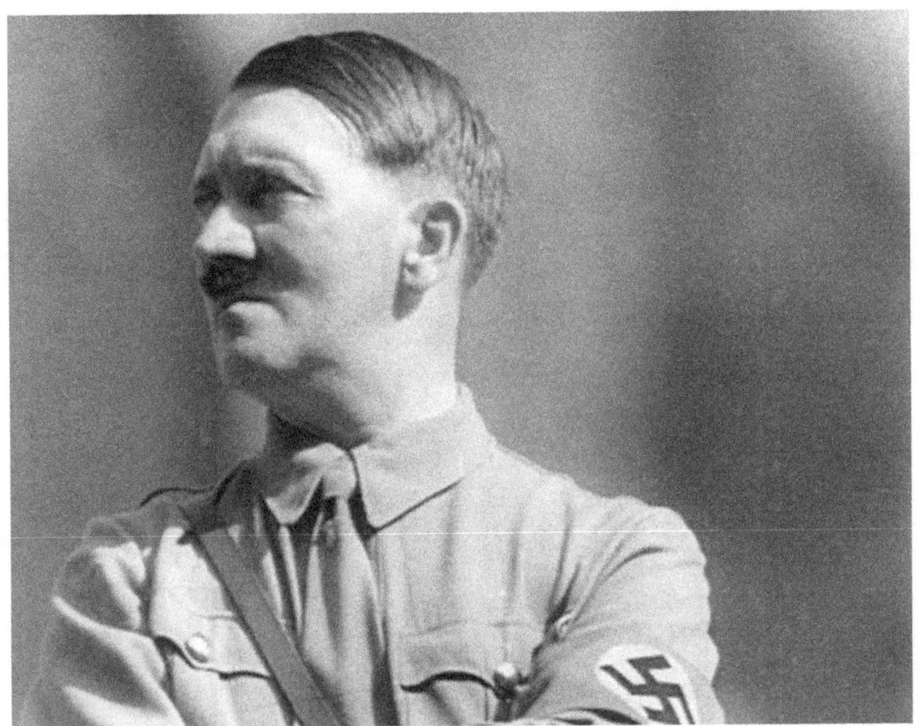

FIGURE 41.9 Still capture from DVD.

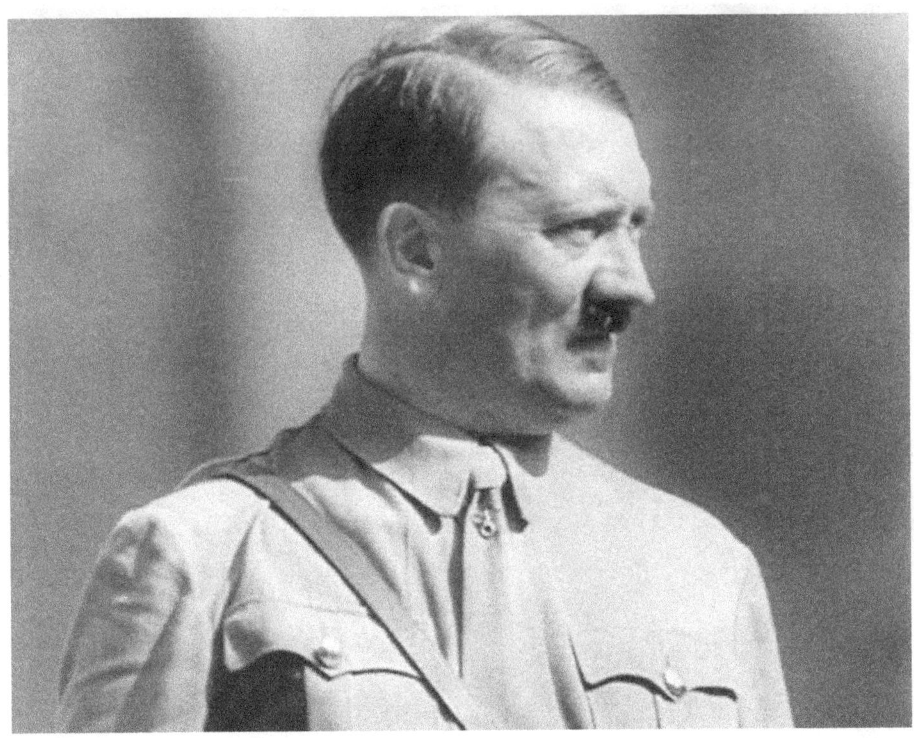

FIGURE 41.10 Still capture from DVD.

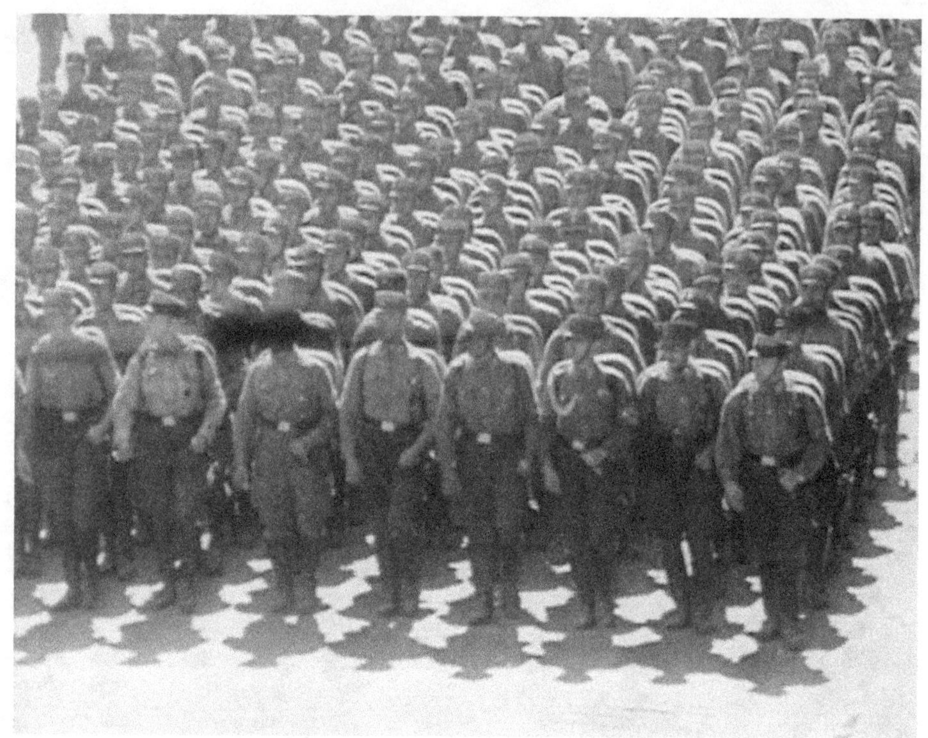

FIGURE 41.11 Still capture from DVD.

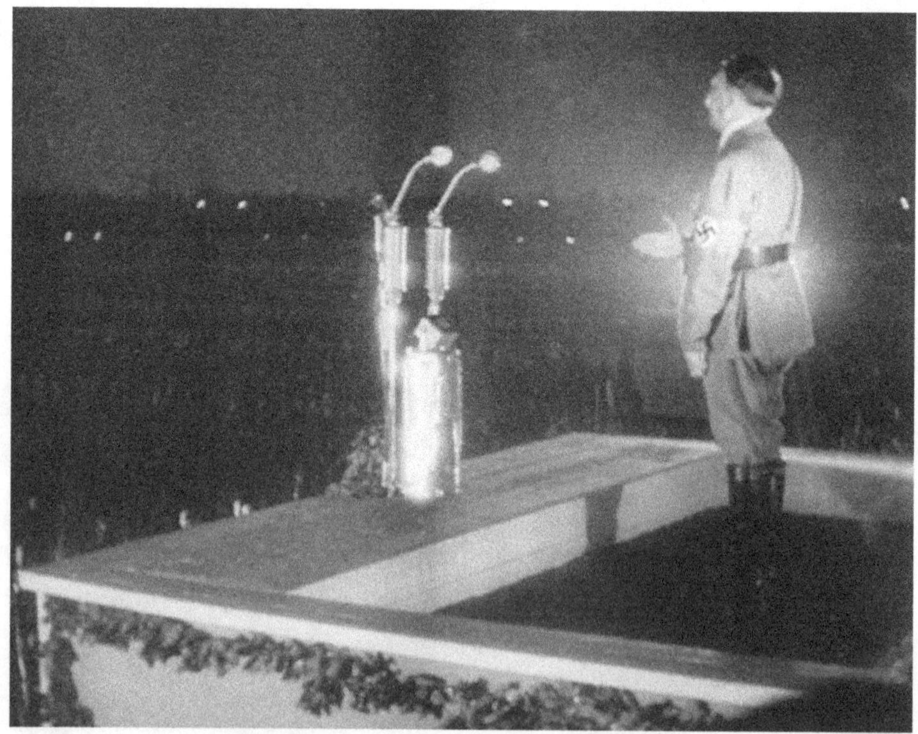

FIGURE 41.12 Still capture from DVD.

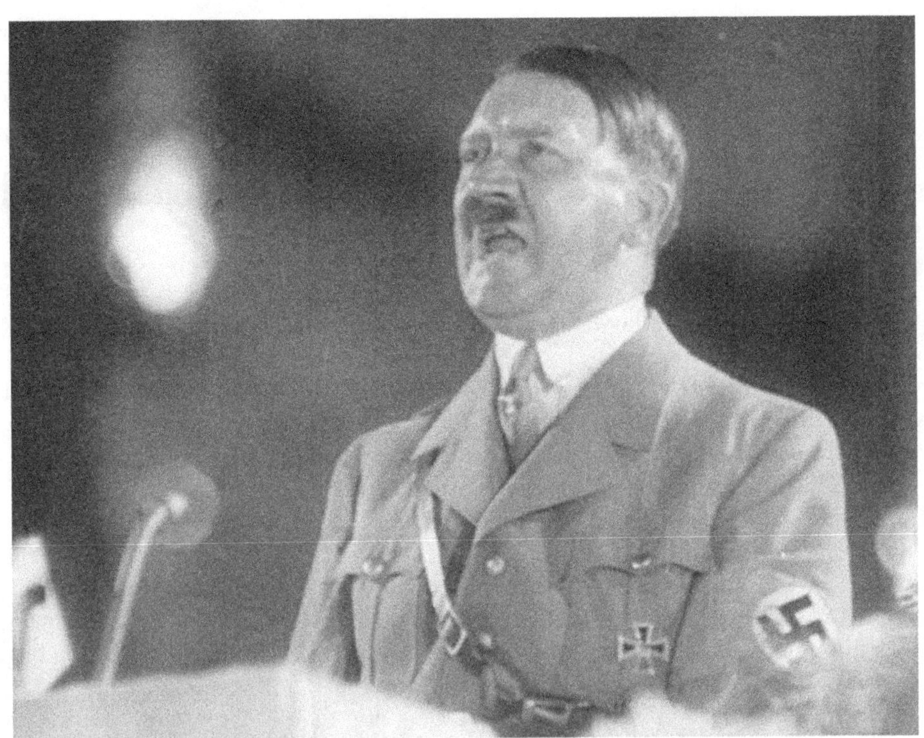

FIGURE 41.13 Still capture from DVD.

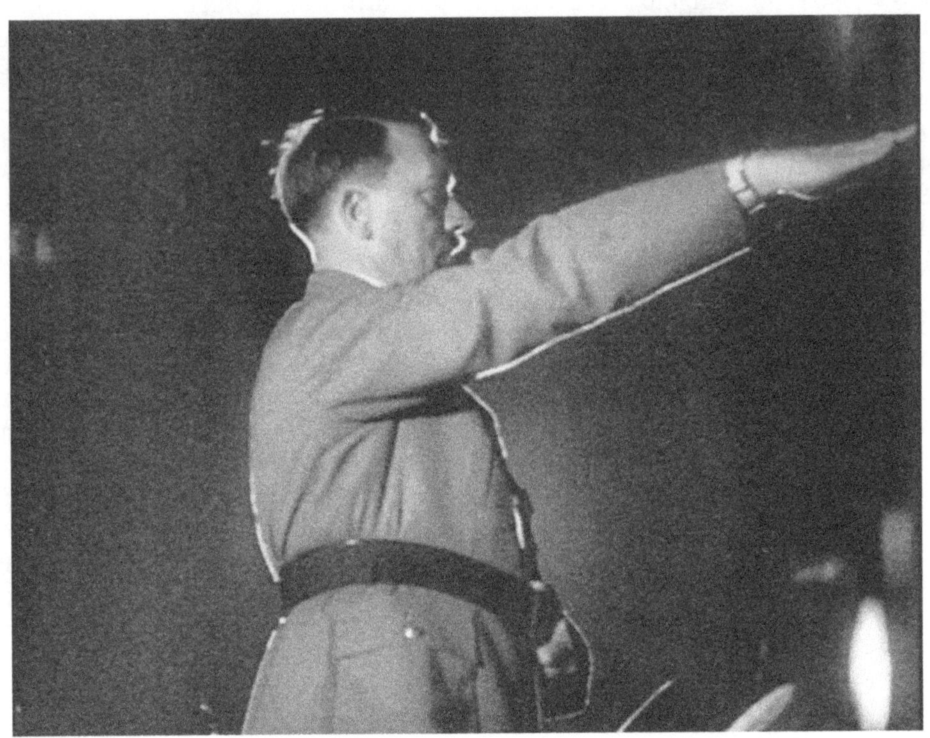

FIGURE 41.14 Still capture from DVD.

critics find so overwhelmingly powerful and so worthy of praise.

Two moments in particular are of significance here. Firstly, following a sequence in which Hitler's car drives to halt outside the hotel, initially taken in a series of high-angle long-shots (which, throughout, have functioned simultaneously to turn the events they focus into a "composed" and complete visual scene, laying out its components for an all-encompassing and all-comprehending spectatorial gaze) and following his descent from the car, there occurs both one of those instances of a play with cinematic looking referred to above and, in the midst of this, an instance of the marking of Hitler's body by light.

The play with looking is particularly interesting in that it serves, like the other instances in the film, to highlight both the activity of looking in itself, and the skill with which it is here articulated cinematically, while, in the particular context of the segment, opening a kind of sub-system of visual suspense, refusing to close-off the spatial organization of the scene by refusing any final spatial coherence in its matching of diegetic looks. The sequence runs as follows: shot 94 shows a close-view of a section of the crowd looking at Hitler and waving. Shot 95 (Figure 41.12 the shot in which Hitler is "halo'd" by light) shows a close view of Hitler gazing to the right (away from the crowd as shown in the previous shot). Shot 96 returns to the crowd. Shot 97 returns to Hitler, shot 98 to the crowd. Shot 99 shows Hitler turning his head and gazing off to the right of the camera, while, finally, shot 100 shows a close-up of a helmeted soldier. Like Hitler he is turning his head left, but here the head (and the gaze) are directed right round, and out of frame left. The various gazes, then, do not fully match one another, do not overlap and intersect with one another sufficiently either to define an enclosed and self-sufficient space or, therefore, to complete the scene they articulate. Because of this the sequence is dynamised, kept open, but the terms and conditions for its eventual closure have been set: a series of looks have eventually to be bound together into the spatial coherence of a scene; moreover, they have to articulate together in such a way that Hitler has to be placed at the point of their intersection—almost literally at the centre of the scene.

It is this that is achieved in the final sequence of shots, Having entered the hotel, 5 shots (shots 106–110) follow of the watching, waiting and saluting crowd. In each case, the gazes of the members of the crowd are directed out of frame right, a repetitious insistence which articulates an overwhelming "demand," so to speak, for the implied but absent space those gazes define to be filled in, for the object of the gazes to be shown, for the gazes to be returned and for the scene thus to be completed and closed off. Shot 111 begins to fill the gap. Beginning with a close-up of a flag near one of the hotel windows, the camera moves left to frame the window itself, with the sign "Heil Hitler" plainly visible, indeed displayed, beneath it. But the gap is still not quite filled. In fact, it is itself signified precisely by the empty window frame. It is then at the end of the shot, that Hitler begins to appear. As he comes into view, however, we cut back to a shot of the crowd—again gazing off-screen right, the delay simply emphasizing the lack in a suspense of looking. Then, at last, we return to Hitler, finally centrally and dominantly framed in the window, marked as such for the gaze of the crowd and the spectator (shot 113, Figure 41.15). He looks firstly to the right and then to the left, acknowledging the look of the crowd and completing the spatial articulation of the scene. Spectacle is marked here in the artifice of the double frame (ie the frame of the window as well as the frame of the image) and in the strong suggestions of theatricality evident in the disposition of the scene (Hitler at the window, elevated above the crowd as if on a mini-stage). Two more shots of the crowd and then we return, for the last shot of this opening section of the film, to Hitler at the window. His arms are

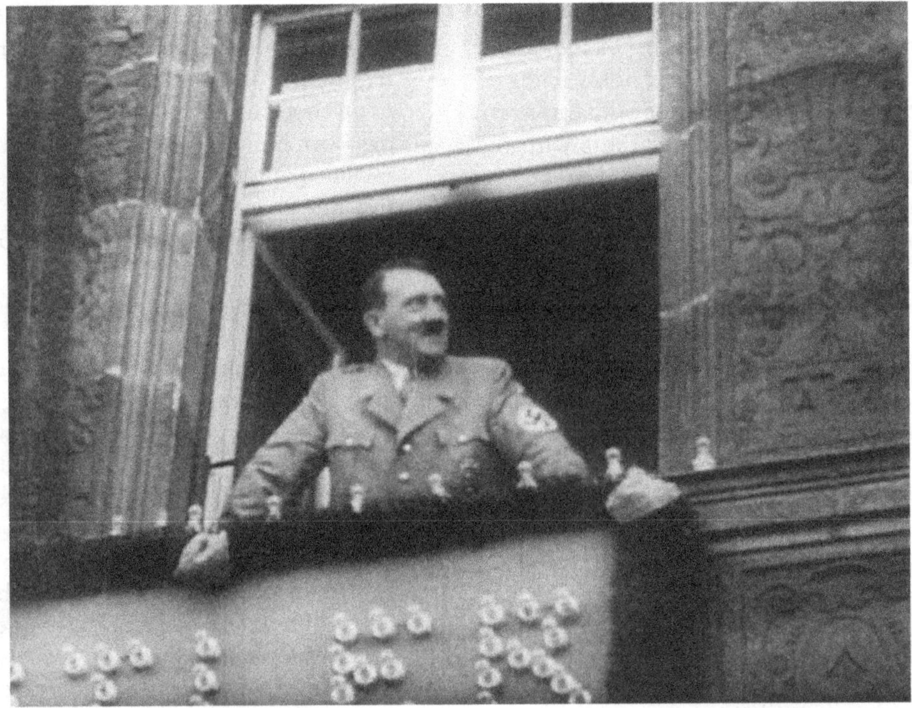

FIGURE 41.15 Still capture from DVD.

outstretched on the window-sill and his gaze is directed out of frame right, a gaze which, unspecified as to its object, serves less to suggest a concrete off-screen space than to indicate a state, almost of reverie. Thus it re-marks Hitler's function as spectacle, as object of the look: he seems to turn his head not in order to look at something specific, but in order that the gaze itself can be properly and fully looked at, undisturbed by any possibility of its being caught within a specific action or event, which would direct our attention and our gaze away, or absorb it into a function conflicting with the one that it in fact performs, soliciting the look of the spectating subject.

II

From the preceding analysis a number of points about the terms set by the opening section of *Triumph of the Will* have emerged, terms which are taken up, re-stated and elaborated during the remainder of the film, and which go some way toward specifying what its critics mean when they speak of "artistic power" and "authentic genius" and use terms like "cinematically dazzling." The terms—clearly—are "spectacle" and "looking." The former emerges as a precise system for emphatically engaging the scopic drive and filling it with satisfying images (with "emphatically" here as indicative not only of an unequivocality, but also of the very figure—hyperbole—which predominantly systematizes the various visual codes involved). Hence the fact that nearly all of the film's scenes and sequences are constituted—diegetically—as displays: the folk parade, the cavalry parade, the Youth and Labour Rallies, the Storm Troopers Rally, the ceremony for the war dead and so on. These displays are then re-marked as *cinematic* displays, as cinematic spectacle, by the visual codes deployed and of course, in particular, by the structure of looks and the emphasis this is given. Looking, therefore, the second term, is not only the foundation of spectacle in its relations with the spectating subject, it is also the means by which the film coheres as a film—linking the images together and to a large extent specifying their meaning. The film articulates these two terms in a particular way, such that each becomes the support and function of the other, the two held together in a dynamic balance which both lures and entertains the scopic drive, and such that a very classical rhythm and economy sustains its visual effects, regulating according to a mode of dynamised homogeneity that thus becomes the sign of that very mode of cinematic artistry celebrated by the critics, particularly insofar as they function to display, as it were, the film itself, insofar as they function as *style*.

Hence the importance and significance of those instances of play with the cinematic articulation of looks pointed to above the film, at points like these, displays its own processes of articulation enough to firmly inscribe a sense of style in its basic systems and structures, while nevertheless containing them precisely as style, as a mode of unity of those system and structures rather than as a mode of heterogeneity that cuts *against* them, pulling them out of their function as structures of identification.

The classicism, as well as the particularity, of the film's rhythm and economy can be indicated by discussing in the light of Bellour's analysis of a sequence from *The Big Sleep* ("The Obvious and the Code," *Screen* v 15 n 4, Winter 1974/5) a sequence that occurs after the opening section, during the ceremony for the war dead in the Nuremberg stadium. The sequence centres diegetically on Hitler's speech after the laying of wreaths at the monument, and comprises overall some 21 shots in sequence as follows:

1. Very high angled long shot of the podium from which Hitler speaks in its setting of regimented soldiers and crowd.
2. Long shot, taken from a low angle, of Hitler at the podium, with a figure included on the right hand side of the frame.
3. Massed flags being carried forward by troops.
4. Very high angled long shot of troops marching.
5. Medium close-up of Hitler at the podium, arms held together in front, and facing right.
6. View of the serried ranks of troops, with high ranking officers prominent in the centre and right of the frame. (Figure 41.16).
7. Long shot of Hitler at the podium, angled from below. This shot is similar to shot 2, but different in that it is both more distant from the podium and, evidently, taken from the other side. The figure included in shot 2 is not visible here. The right hand side of the frame is instead dominated by a sculpture of an eagle.
8. High angled long shot of troops arranged in serried and regimented ranks.
9. Shot of Hitler at the podium. The shot is again, as in shot 7, taken from the left-hand side, but here the camera is closer. Neither the figure included in shot 2, nor the eagle in shot 7 is visible.
10. Troops standing with flags, the eagle dominantly present in the centre background of the frame.
11. Shot of Hitler that is similar in most respects to shot 5 except that the camera appears to be slightly further away.
12. Shot of flag-bearing troops with three huge flags displayed in the centre right background of the image.
13. Long shot of Hitler at the podium taken from the left-hand side again but from a noticeably less oblique angle and from a further distance than before, thus including not only the eagle, but more of the troops bearing flags assembled to the right of the frame.
14. Long shot similar to 12, but taken at a greater distance and including more of the troops,

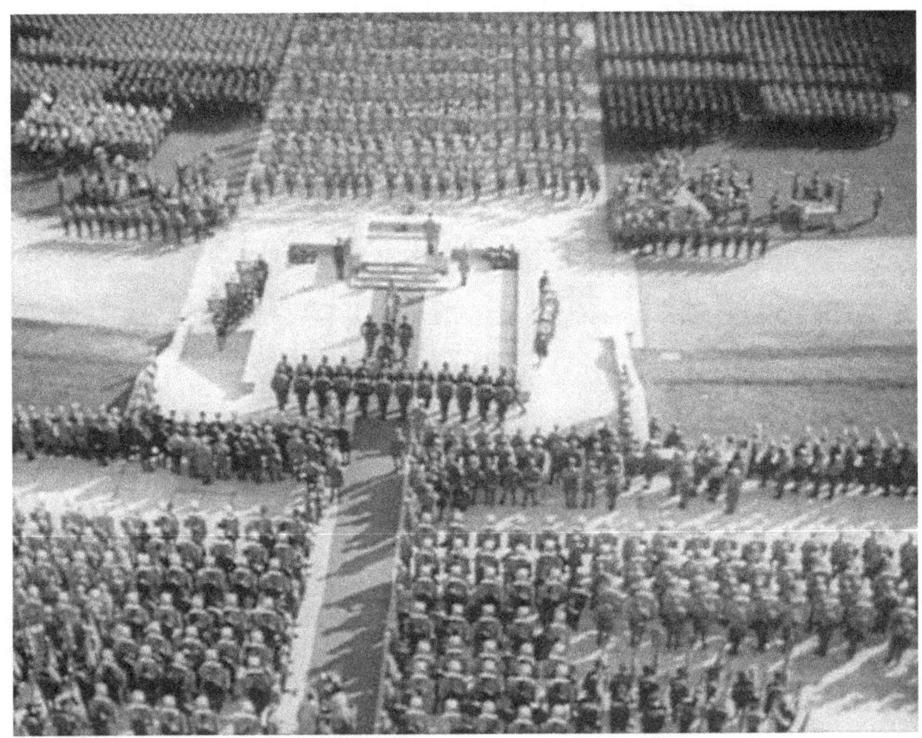

FIGURE 41.16 Shot 1. Still capture from DVD.

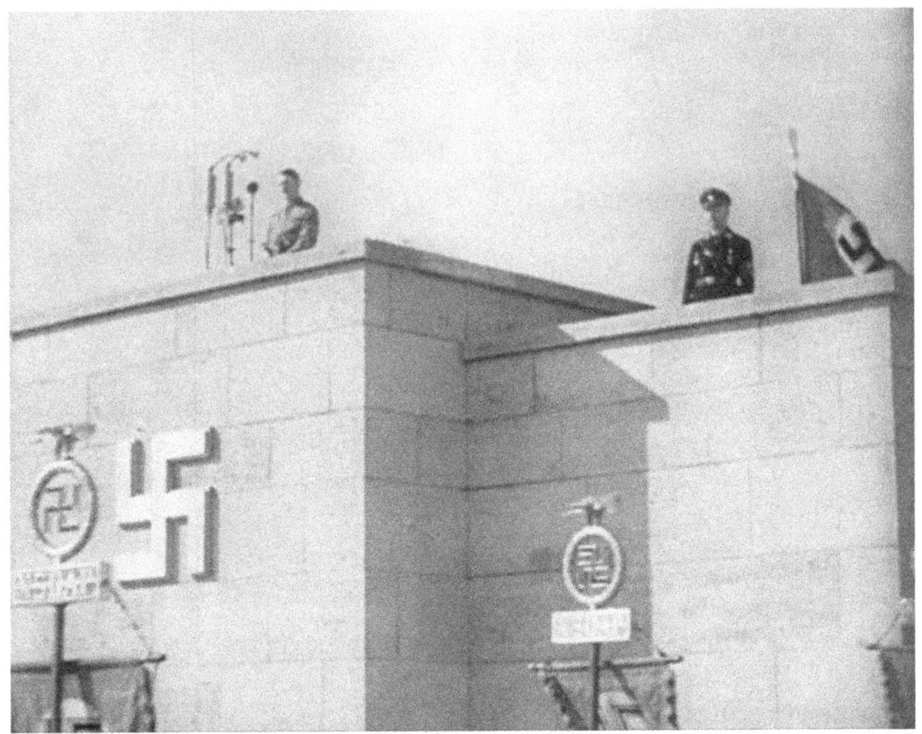

FIGURE 41.17 Shot 2. Still capture from DVD.

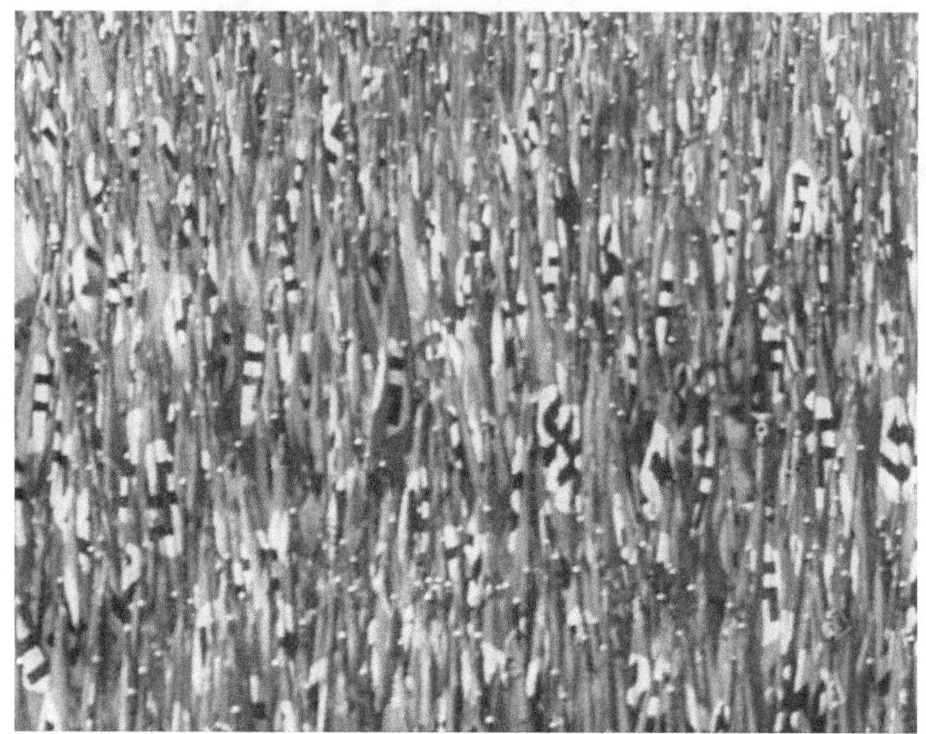

FIGURE 41.18 Shot 3. Still capture from DVD.

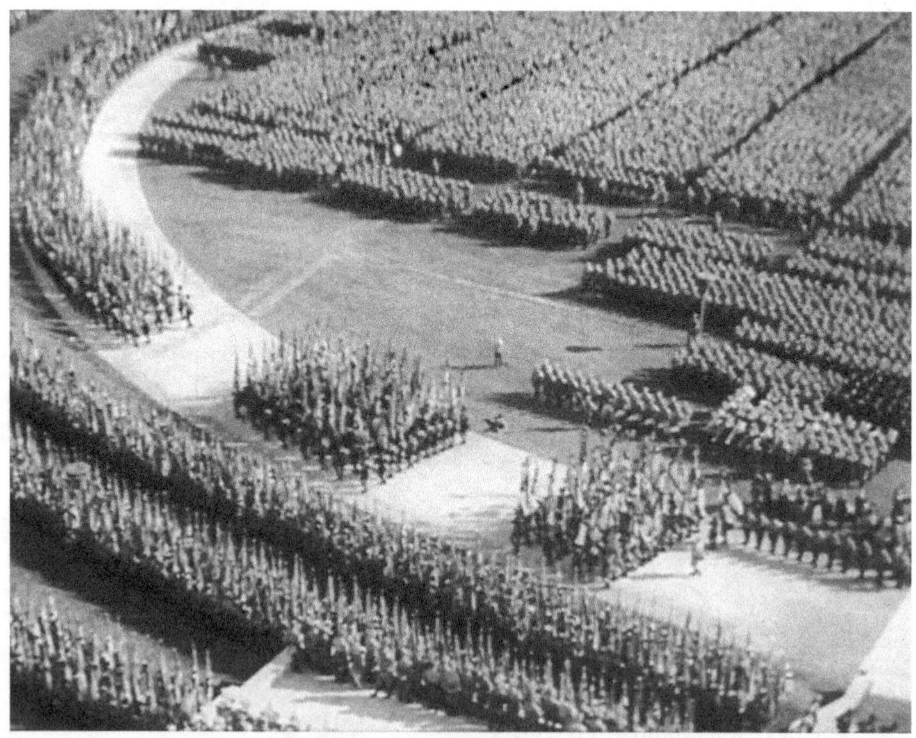

FIGURE 41.19 Shot 4. Still capture from DVD.

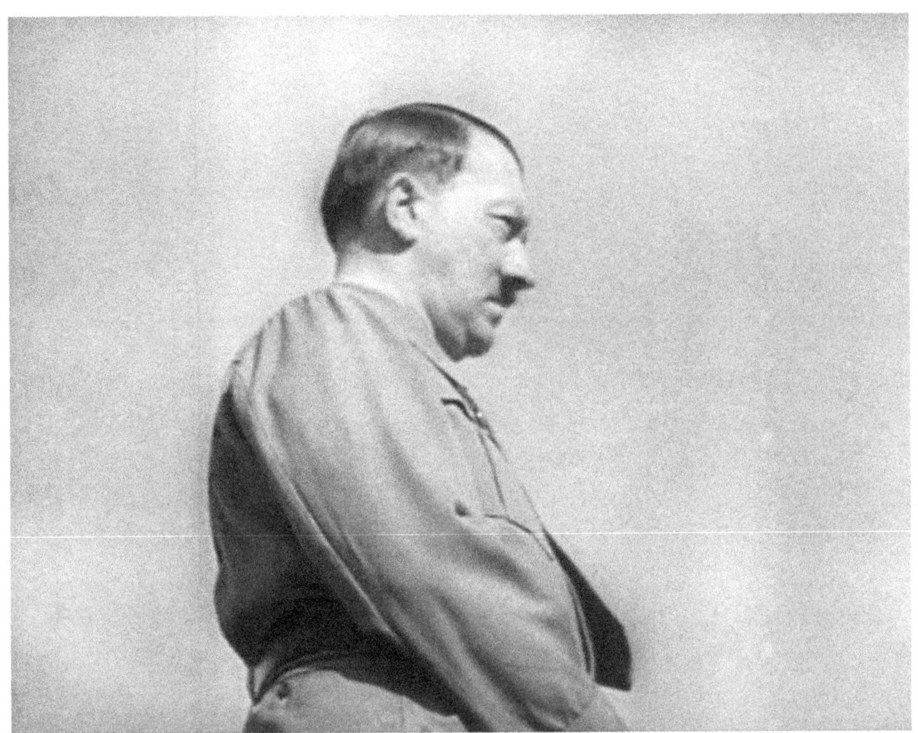

FIGURE 41.20 Shot 5. Still capture from DVD.

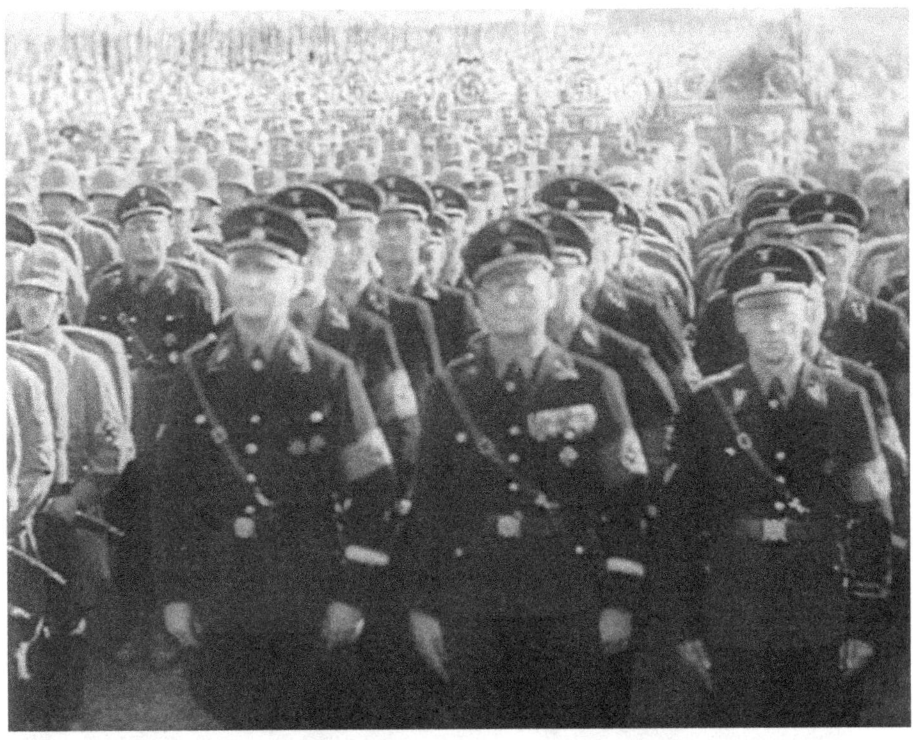

FIGURE 41.21 Shot 6. Still capture from DVD.

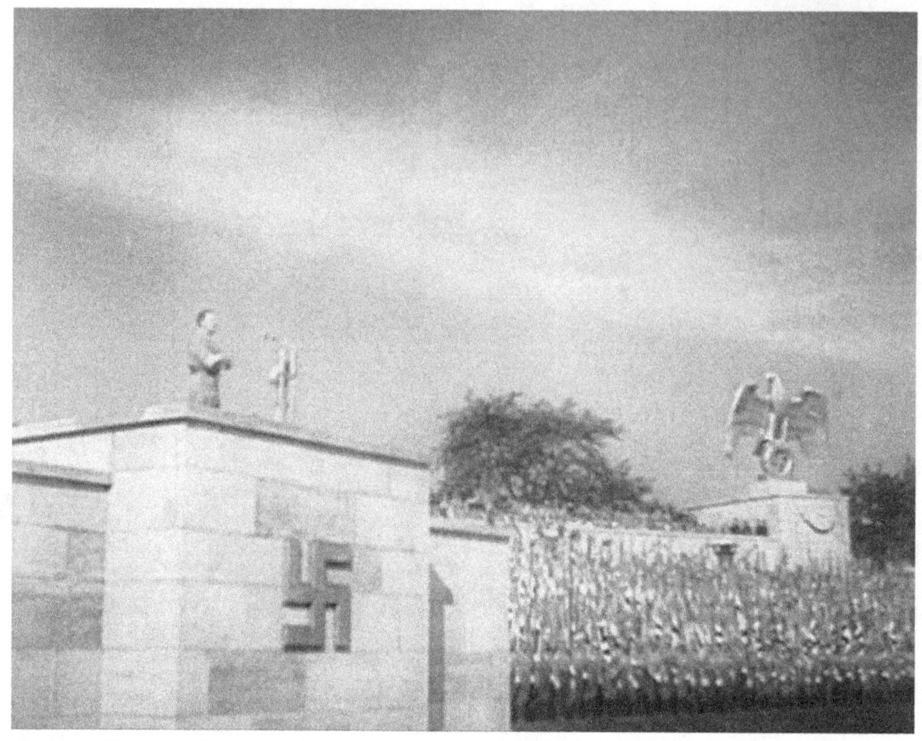

FIGURE 41.22 Shot 7. Still capture from DVD.

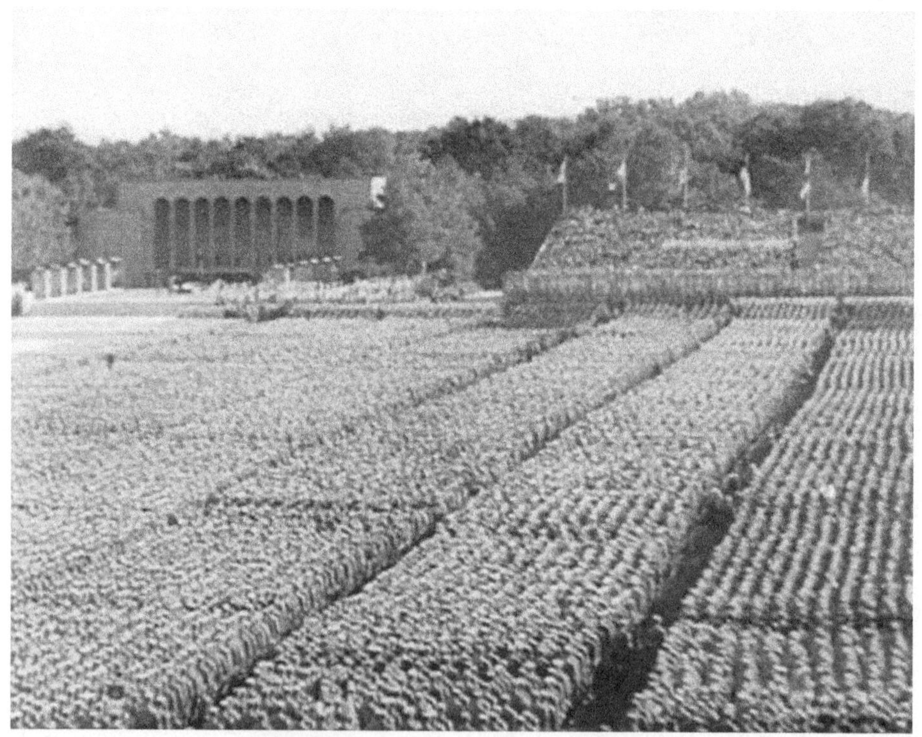

FIGURE 41.23 Shot 8. Still capture from DVD.

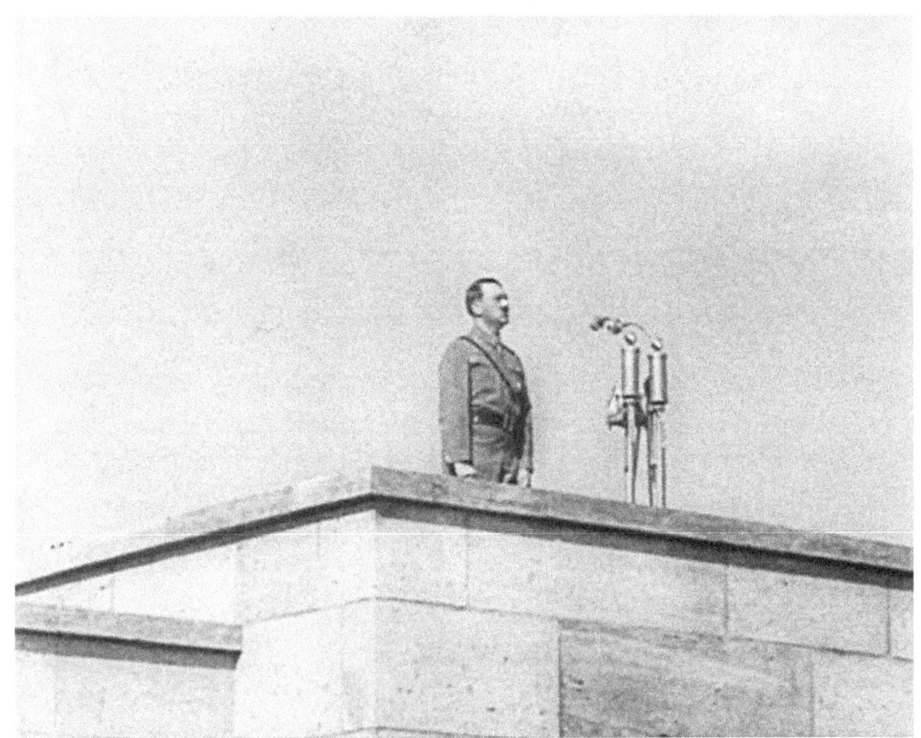

FIGURE 41.24 Shot 9. Still capture from DVD.

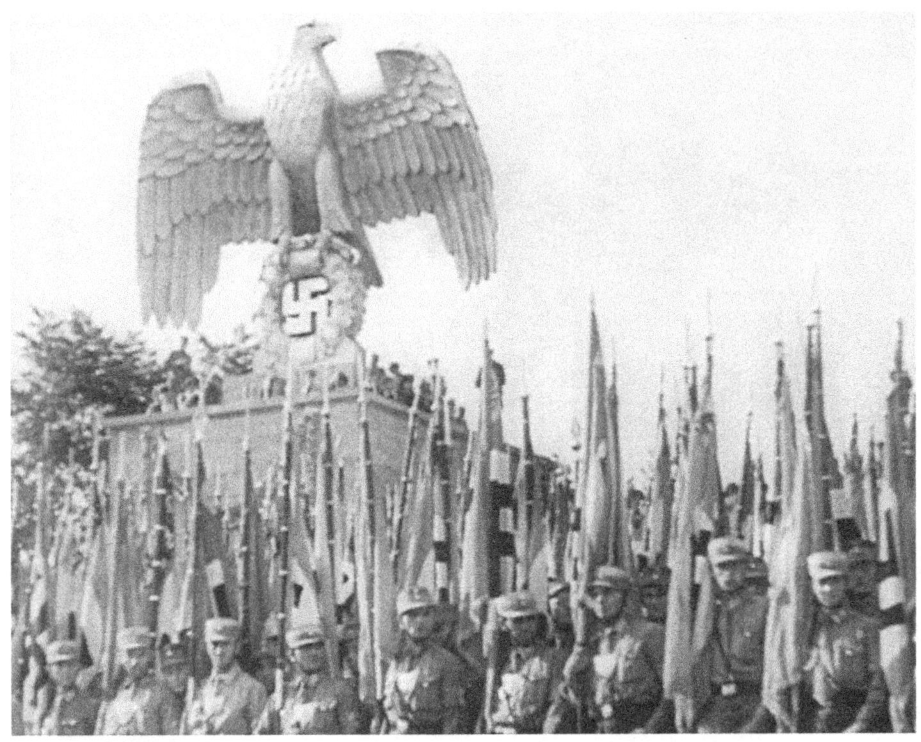

FIGURE 41.25 Shot 10. Still capture from DVD.

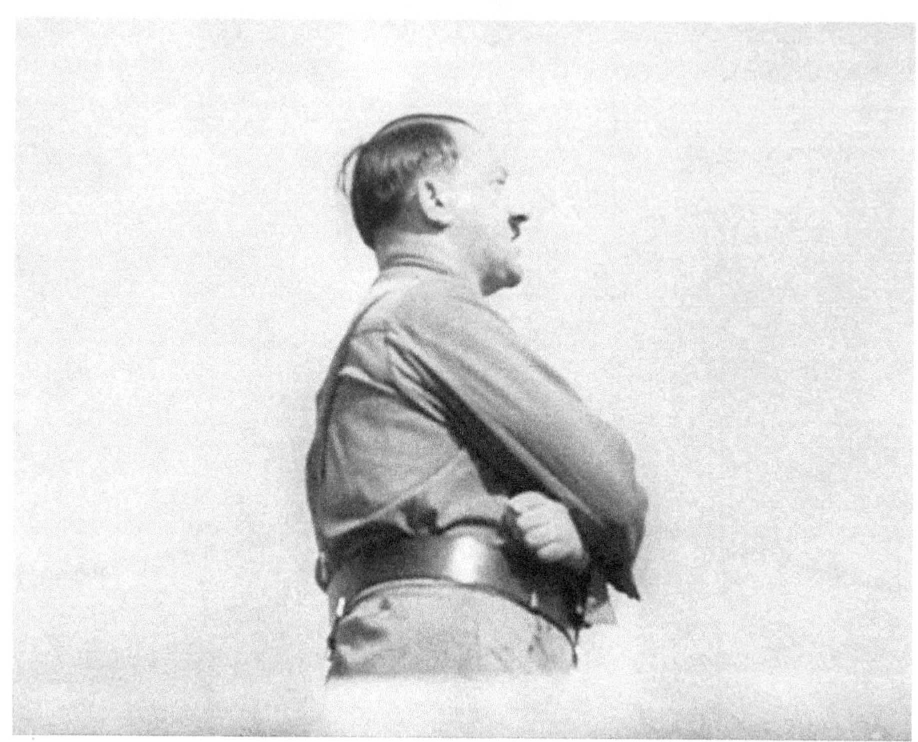

FIGURE 41.26 Shot 11. Still capture from DVD.

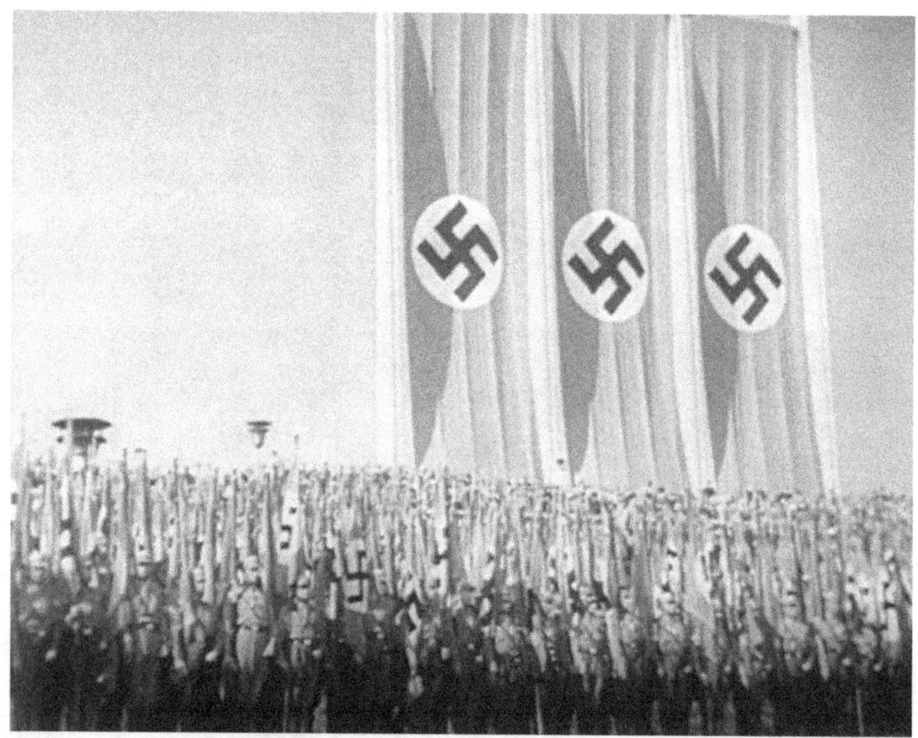

FIGURE 41.27 Shot 12. Still capture from DVD.

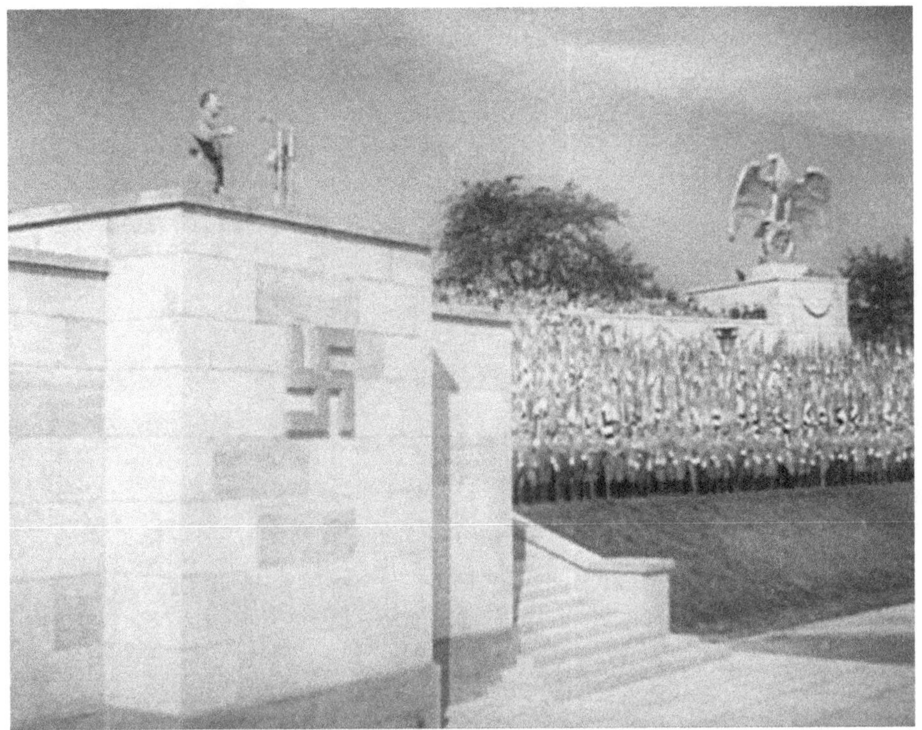

FIGURE 41.28 Shot 13. Still capture from DVD.

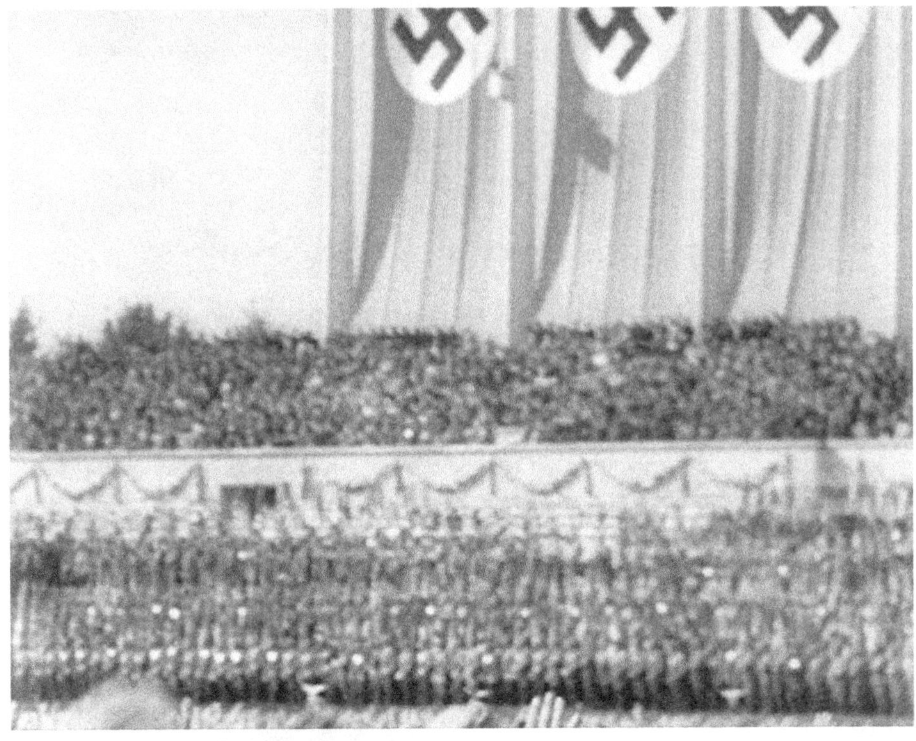

FIGURE 41.29 Shot 14. Still capture from DVD.

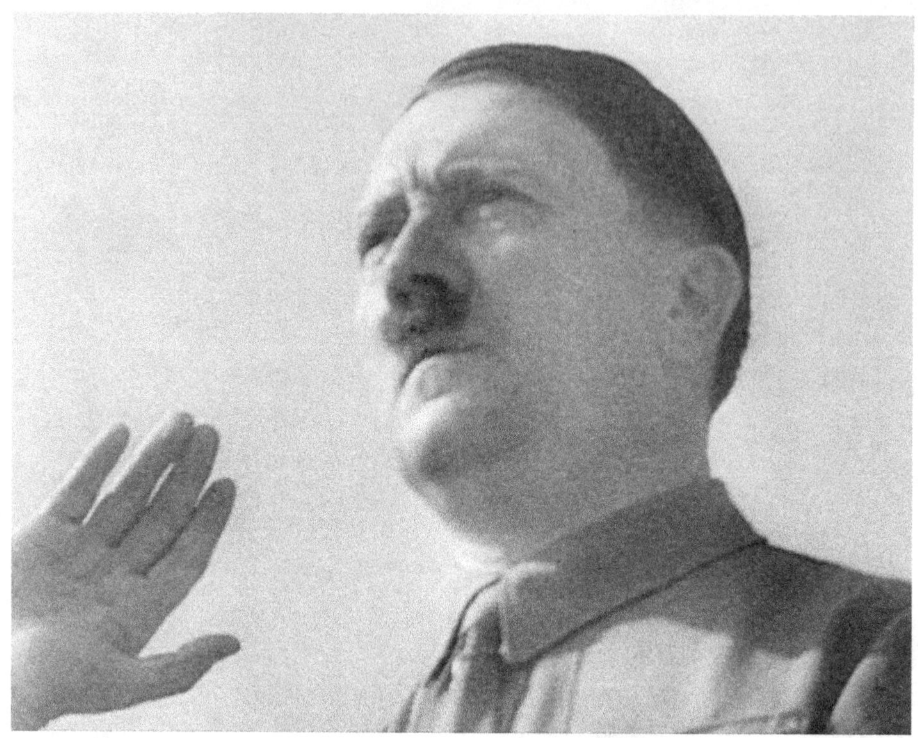

FIGURE 41.30 Shot 15. Still capture from DVD.

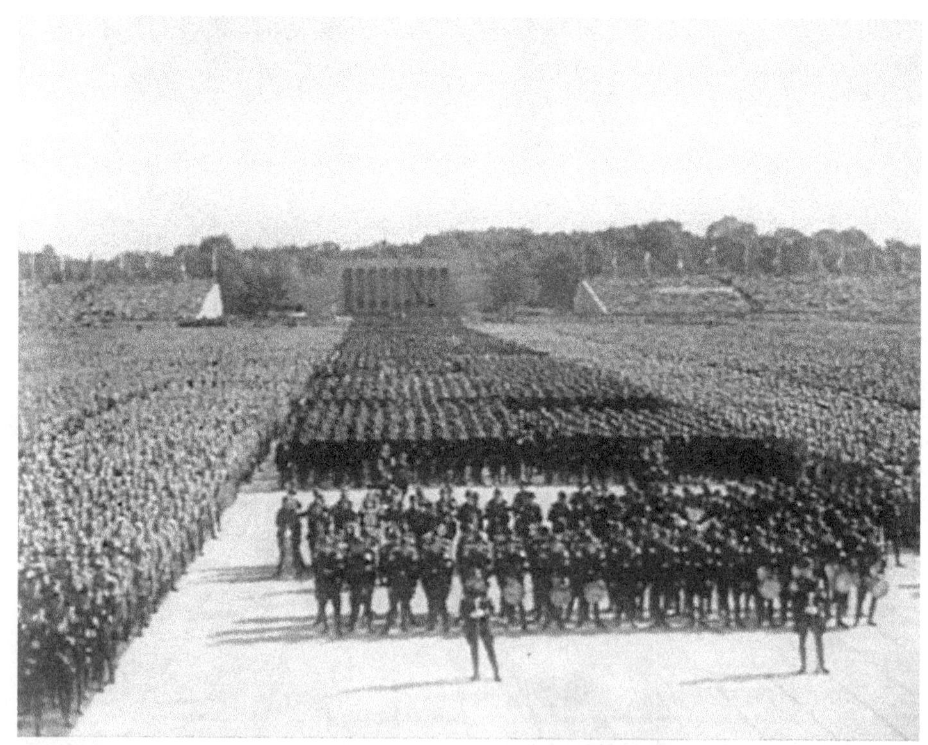

FIGURE 41.31 Shot 16. Still capture from DVD.

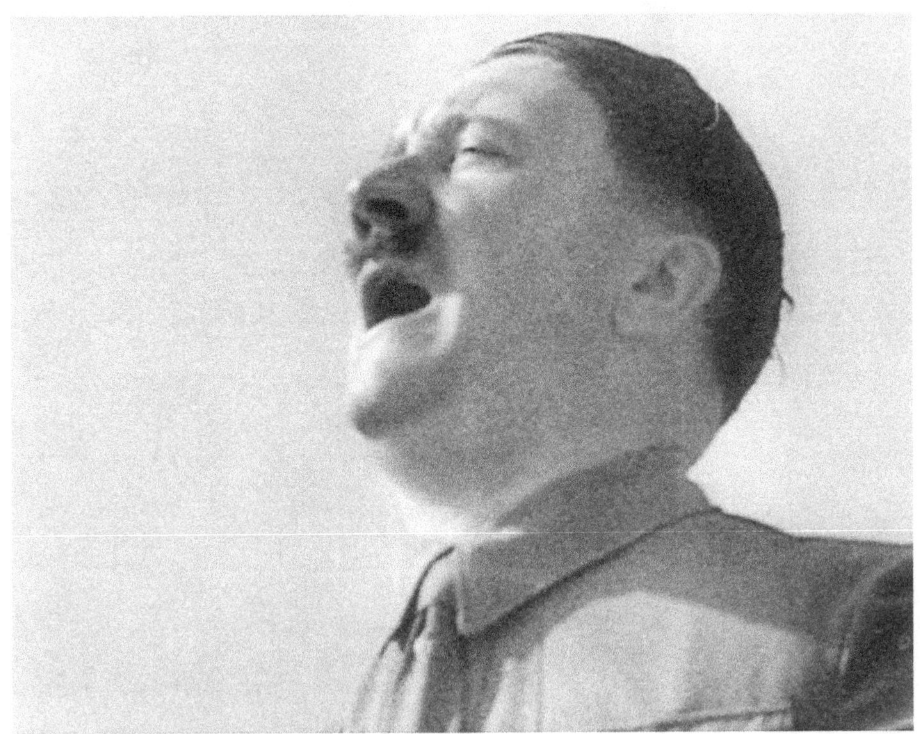

FIGURE 41.32 Shot 17. Still capture from DVD.

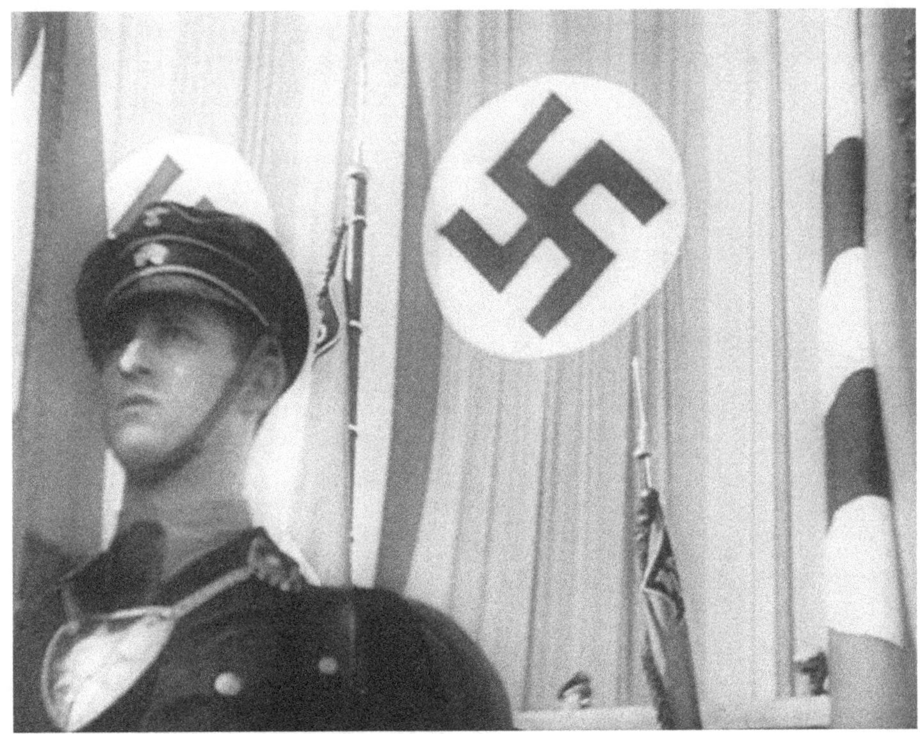

FIGURE 41.33 Shot 18. Still capture from DVD.

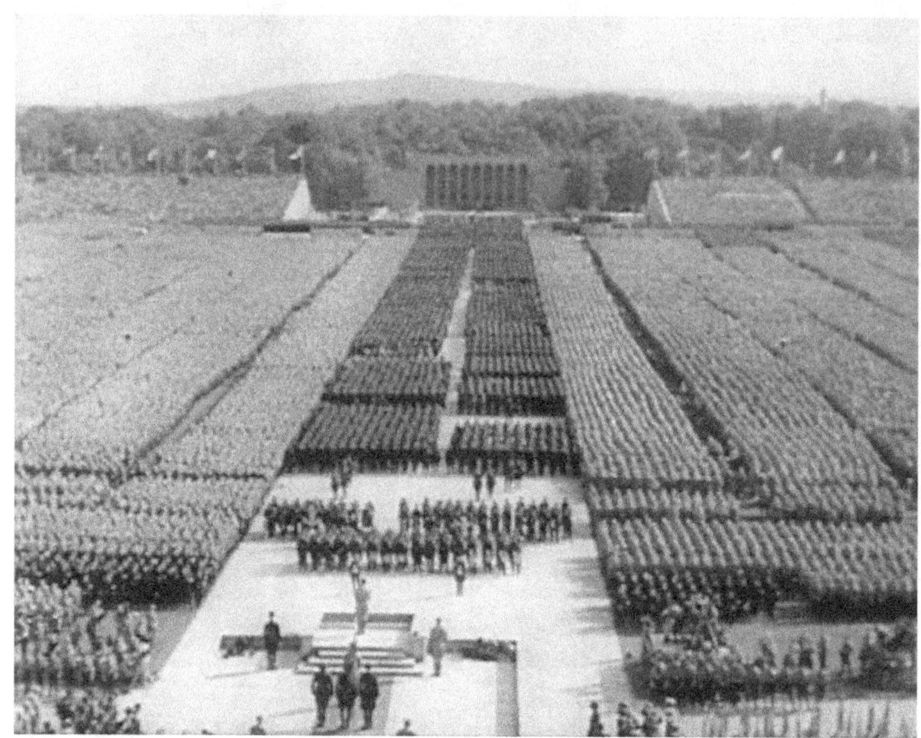

FIGURE 41.34 Shot 19. Still capture from DVD.

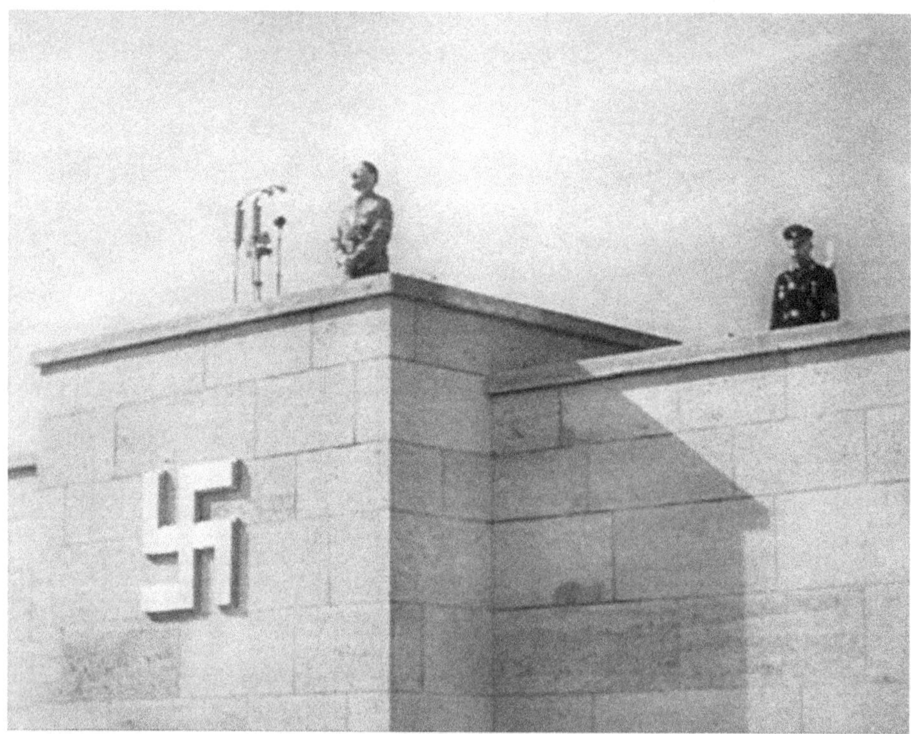

FIGURE 41.35 Shot 20. Still capture from DVD.

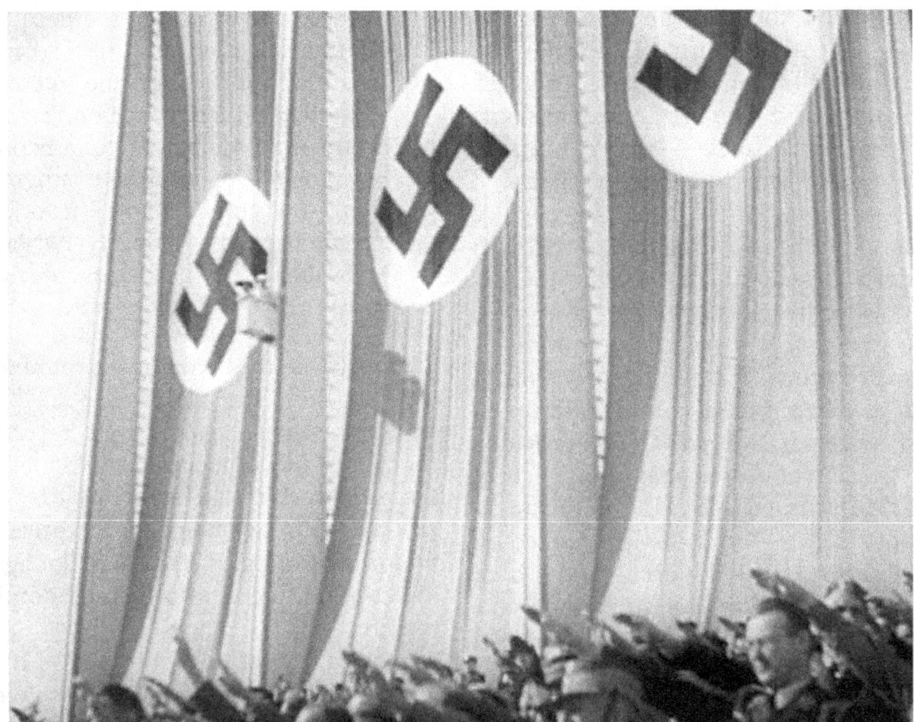

FIGURE 41.36 Shot 21. Still capture from DVD.

whose spatial disposition in the stadium is thus clearer and more intelligible.

15. Close-up angled view of Hitler, taken from below and from the right and including his raised right hand.
16. Long shot of troops.
17. Close-up of Hitler, whose face is here more sideways on than in 15. His hand is not visible.
18. Medium close view of an individual soldier holding a flag. Two of the large flags visible in previous shots are dominant behind him.
19. Very high angled long shot of podium and troops and crowds, very similar to shot 1, but taken from a slightly lower angle.
20. Low angled long shot view of the podium, almost identical to shot 2 but different in that the flag visible next to the figure on the right in shot 2 is here excluded from the frame.
21. Final shot of the three flags. Medium shot, angled from the right.

As is evident from the stills included here and from the descriptions provided above, the sequence comprises a set of minimal (but significant) differences articulated across a set of basic and insistent repetitions (the differences measured against the repetitions rather than vice-versa, as if there were a hierarchy between the two). Or rather, to be more accurate, there are two structures of repetition/difference, the one crossing the other. The first is established in the sequencing of the images as such, those including Hitler alternating with those of the scene around him, Hitler's presence alternating with his absence. Here the repetition lies in the alternating pattern itself, varied only at the point at which two shots of the scene rather than the usual one intervene between shots of Hitler (i.e. shots 3 and 4). The second concerns the images themselves, the paradigm constituted by shots of Hitler on the one hand and that constituted by shots of the scene around him on the other. With the former the repetition is all the more strongly marked in that there is a specific and identifiable focus for each image—Hitler himself. Variations are established in a variety of ways—scale and distance, angle, gesture and so on, each measured against the fact of Hitler's presence. With the latter there is no such specific focus running across each of the images. In a sense, their unity is constituted precisely out of the absence of Hitler, that being their common factor. It is also, more positively as it were, provided by a repetition of those codes and effects of spectacle discussed in relation to the opening shots of the film: codes and effects of scale and composition—each shot is both breath-taking and eye-catching in a way which a number of the images of Hitler himself are not.

The economy of the structures of repetition and difference evident here deviates very little from that of the classic Hollywood fiction film, [. . .] precisely that economy of process which is the mark, *par excellence,* of classical cinema, an economy whose general characteristics and significance have been described by Stephen Heath as follows:

> The coherence of any text depends on a sustained equilibrium of new informations, points of advance, and anaphoric recalls, ties that make fast, hold together. One part of the particular economy is the exploitation of narrative in film in the interests of an extreme tendency towards coalescence, a tightness of totalization; the film is gathered up in a whole series of rhymes in which elements—of both 'form' and 'content'—are reproduced, shifted, and turned back symmetrically, as in a mirror . . . Yet this symmetry . . . is an effect of the elaboration of the narrative which gives at the same time the necessary advance, an order. [. . .] The narrative join of a film recasts repetition—difference, the interminable flux of desire, the horizon of death—into the balance of a fiction (an integrity of recall and progression), thus maintains the historical function of the subject . . . ("Film Performance" in *Cine-Tracts,* n 2, pp 13–14).

If this is the economy profoundly at work in the sequence, indeed in the film as a whole, it is marked by a particularity in its *emphasis* on spectacle and looking as a means, in the absence of a plot, of holding the film together, and, especially, by their functioning in relation to the figure of Hitler—the figure who literally dominates the film.

Now it is precisely at this level that the ideological operation of *Triumph of the Will as a film* is to be sought. It is only from here that the specificity of the inscription of the political ideology of Nazism can begin to be approached, since those political/ideological discourses already constituted outside the text are transformed in their very inscription, both by their figuration together and by their cinematic articulation. Moreover, of course, it is in that articulation that the effect of the text *vis-à-vis* the spectating subject can be traced. The functioning of the separation made between ideology and politics and the cinematic by those critics cited at the beginning of this article can be seen to be one which actually disavows the functioning of the film's "cinematic power," despite all the phrases about its artistry and genius.

It is at this point, finally, that I would like to return to and elaborate more fully my earlier point about the contradictions that exist within and between certain predominant conceptions of documentary, propaganda and film insofar as they centre on cinema and vision.

III

Triumph of the Will, of course, is a classic of progaganda. Propaganda is avowedly intentional. It concerns itself with the productions of *effects* (in the interests of persuasion and manipulation). Evidence of technique, form and style, evidence of a mode of semiotic work, is both easily detectable and comfortably admissable, contained within the problematic. (Indeed, in a sense it is demanded by it. Problems only come when technique, form and style transcend the crudities of propagandistic rhetoric. Then they become art. Hence the ambivalent attitude towards Riefenstahl.)

There is a contradiction, however, between propaganda and *documentary.* Film critics constantly find themselves attempting to sever those connections between the two that propaganda films themselves persistently make. The only way they can find of doing so, usually, is to ascribe a set of cynical intentions to the films and their makers: they use the connotations of veracity that documentary overwhelmingly produces in order to give spurious substance to a set of dubiously biased arguments and in order to dupe their audience, thereby betraying the "documentary ideal," which thus is restored to a place where its truth is uncontaminated.

One of the main reasons for the critics' concern, of course, is that these films demonstrate uncomfortably that documentary is a process of construction, rather than a process of reflection. (This is not, of course, to maintain that propaganda films are therefore necessarily progressive, even in this context: precisely because they trade upon, rather than challenge and open to question, the contradictions involved in documentary and its ideologies, they tend always to remain fundamentally complicit in its perpetuation.)

The role of technique, form and style can, therefore, insofar as they contribute toward the definition of propaganda, and insofar as they highlight an instance of construction within it, be seen to be odds with documentary and the liberal critics' "documentary ideal." As Annette Kuhn has argued, this ideal involves, as far as possible, an *effacement* of these traces of semiotic work:

> The absence of marks of meaning production in such films, their presentation of themselves as transparent, entails also an apparent lack of any language other than that of everyday speech (of natural/naturalized language). The signs of the production of meaning in fiction films [or in propaganda films] may be contained but nonetheless displayed to some extent—as 'style' for instance. In the documentary, however, they are simultaneously disavowed and subject to a work of effacement: 'style' is inappropriate, the image 'speaks for itself.' ("The Camera I—Observations on Documentary," *Screen* v 19 n 2, Summer 1978, p 72.)

Now if we here take spectacle, with its marks in an evidence of visibility and looking, as one particular mode of cinematic style, as compatible with propaganda documentaries, but as incompatible with documentary itself, a curious contradiction begins to emerge. Spectacle focuses exactly those two aspects of cinema—visibility and looking—which otherwise function as the very foundation of the ideology of cinematic documentary, and which articulate in that ideology as follows:

> All forms of documentary, whether or not they also embody any direct verbal address inscribe spectator positions which hinge on various articulations of the instance precisely of observation. They work in such a way by posing a variety of relationships between the eye or the look of the spectator, that of the camera, and that of the camera

> operator. Because in documentary film the apparently self-evident and unmediated "truth" of the visible is fetishized, the spectator is placed in a relation hinging upon his or her command of that which is observed. The spectator becomes the observer *par excellence*. (Ibid., p 82.)

If this is the case, why should *evidence* of the visible and of observation, the *display* of their articulation together, come into contradiction with documentary?

The answer lies, I think, in the fact that such evidence and such display not only highlight the instance of the construction of a position of looking and visual command, not only highlight the instance of the construction of the visible itself, but also displace knowledge, the essential ingredient in documentary, in favour of the construction of a mode of visual pleasure. Spectacle is content neither with simply rendering visible the observable nor with inscribing the spectating subject simply in position as observer. It is much more concerned with the processes of rendering visible and of looking themselves. What counts in spectacle is not the visible as guarantee of *veracity* (of truth, of reality), but rather the visible as mask, as lure. What counts is not the instance of looking as *observation*, but rather as fascinated gaze. It addresses the imbrication of looking and the visible not as the prior condition to the construction of a form of knowledge about a particular subject or issue, but rather as that which hovers constantly across the gap between the eye and the object presented to it in the process of the scopic drive. Documentary disavows the gap altogether, subordinating both instances to that set of essentially empiricist codes of exposition required to produce its knowledge effect. Spectacle, on the other hand is essentially concerned with the gap itself, the concern being not to challenge its unproblematic elision, not to construct a mode of distanciation, holding the gap as a contradiction addressed to the spectating subject, but to institute an oscillating play between vision and the visible in order to address scopic drive exclusively, to lure the gaze of the spectator and fill that gaze with plenitude of the image itself. Hence, to refer back to *Triumph of the Will*, the oscillating play with the traces of the presence of the plane in the opening shots, the play with Hitler's presence in the motorcade sequence; hence, also the heavily composed images (the sign of the plenitude itself), and to take a final example, the shot of the moving flags intercut with Hitler at the podium in the sequence from the ceremony for the war dead discussed above (shot 3'): the shot is temporally constructed so that it is initially unclear as to what is being shown; it only gradually emerges that the patterns of light and shade are in fact flags being carried by the troops. The pattern, and the uncertainty as to their identity lures the spectator's gaze, the gaze is only satisfied once it is clear that they are flags. It is relation between the two, their articulation together, that characterizes spectacle, an instance of that hovering over the gap between vision and the visible indicated above.

In the particular case of *Triumph of the Will*, the contradiction between documentary and spectacle is dealt with by recourse to notions of artistry and style. Displacing issues of truth, reality, manipulation and so on, the film emerges simply as "cinematic poetry" (Barsam, op cit, p 29). But this, in turn, emerges as in contradiction with the "ideology" of the film, a contradiction which insists in the discourse of the critics, but which is manageable insofar as it is handled in terms of form on the one hand and content on the other. It is only when that particular division is challenged, and only when the nature of the film's "cinematic power" is closely examined as an integral part of its ideological operation, that the contradictions begin to emerge. As they have done so, we have seen that the key term—spectacle—itself involves contradictions, ones which provide another theoretical means with which to challenge documentary and its ideology at their very basis, that is at the level of vision and the visible.

NOTES

1. For an elaboration of the concept of the look see Jacques Lacan, *The Four Fundamental Concepts of Psychoanalysis*, Hogarth Press, London 1977, pp 67–119; Stephen Heath, "*Anata Mo*," *Screen* v 17 n4, Winter 1976/7, pp 55–56 and 62–63; and Constance Penley, "The Avant-Garde and its Imaginary," *Camera Obscura* n 2, pp 21–23. [. . .]
2. This is the significance and context of Victor Burgin's remarks on composition and monocular perspective in photography [. . .] ("Looking at Photographs," *Screen Education* n 24, Autumn 1977, pp 23–24). The "authority of the other" here is linked precisely to the issue of the mastery, by the spectating subject, of the visual field of the image. The *intrusion* of the frame is the mark of the lack of that mastery.
3. Theatricality—in all its artifice—is crucial to the particular mode of spectacle I am referring to here, a mode whose traditions stem from, and are exemplified by, Baroque painting, theatre and opera. Centring in particular on the stage itself (the designated site of exhibition and display) and on the stage-curtain (i.e. that which is lifted to show the display—and that which therefore functions, importantly, as the mark *par excellence* of the lure of spectacle itself), it is a mode which seems to involve an oscillating play between not only the exhibition of a visual illusion or effect as such, but also the exhibition of the means—the tricks—used to produce it. An awareness of artifice therefore, at some point, seems to be essential to the overall effect. [. . .]

42

RICHARD GRIFFITH

FILMS AT THE FAIR (1939)

In announced intention, the New York World's Fair of 1939 is devoted to social prophecy. Its two slogans, "The World of Tomorrow" and "The Golden Age of Science," prevision a society whose direction is determined by the effort to organize nature, human machinery, and human beings themselves into a relationship which will fulfil human needs on a wider scale than is at present possible. The form of that relationship and the means used to bring it into existence are the subject of the Fair itself, and are presented through every known medium of dramatic projection. Architecture, lithography, photography, painting, sculpture, music, the stage, all play their parts and are used with considerable freedom.

It is natural to assume that the motion picture would lead the van in this large-scale experiment with the propagation of ideas. A new invention still in process of development, it has more associations with the future than with the past. Its unique technical resources permit it to present the impossible as well as the actual, making it an ideal channel for prophecy and speculation. Its capacity for mass-persuasion was long ago demonstrated. Moreover, it possesses in the form of the documentary film a technique capable of representing the world of tomorrow in terms of present tendencies.

Of all the forms of film, this documentary function is the one most appropriate to Fair aims. By very hypothesis, it stands for what Thomas Mann has called "the will toward the future." It sees life in terms of change. As John Grierson has premised, "the only reality is in the fellow who needs, in security for all and living decently in pride with one's neighbors." With its roots in this primary reality, documentary film dramatizes the *means* of meeting need, by the reform of institutions, by cultural contact, by economic organization. And in thus showing exactly how the future can be built, documentary provides an assurance that it *will* be built. Here, perhaps, is where the film of dramatized fact could have been of greatest service to the Fair. Its interest in practical possibilities, the actuality of its material, the immediate urgency of its subjects, might have lent a sense of reality to the wonderland of Flushing.

The Fair Corporation itself and its subscribing exhibitors have partially realized the possibilities of the film in this reference, and have used it extensively; more than five hundred motion pictures are shown throughout the various exhibits. Moreover, there has been unanimous recognition that the fact film is best adapted to serve Fair purposes, and films of pure entertainment are confined to the Amusement Area. The remaining exhibitors, comprising the three divisions of World's Fair Buildings, Government Pavilions, and Commercial Exhibits, have used all the varieties of the factual film to propagandize their individual interests in relation to the World of Tomorrow. With commendable restraint, they have avoided using cinematic tricks to create a Jules Verne conception of the future. On the contrary, films at the Fair are largely devoted to immediate issues. They try as best they can to reveal the relation between present and future as a ceaseless process of transition. And most of them attempt to achieve some feeling of reality in their methods of presentation.

But though the World's Fair is the best opportunity documentary has ever had, and though it offers the largest number of fact films ever seen in one place at one time, it does not fulfil the major possibility open to it: that of experiment. A relatively small number of films were produced especially for the Fair, and the motion pictures displayed there actually represent the film of yesterday rather than tomorrow. Because this is true, the primary function of the present report must be that of evaluating present tendencies in the use of the fact film. Despite the large number of films which had to be seen and judged, those tendencies are relatively simple and clear.

Perhaps the most important of all the factors which govern these tendencies is the conception of propaganda held by sponsors. The World's Fair experience has thrown this factor into high relief and revealed its true weight in determining the quality of a film. It is axiomatic among followers of the documentary film that the social and educational value of any production is determined by the motives of its sponsor. But in the actual making of films, motives may count for considerably less than an intelligent grasp of propagandist methods. Certainly it is true that the most successful motion pictures at the World's Fair are those which see the Fair itself as an opportunity to use new ways of challenging popular attention.

Science and Society

The buildings and exhibits sponsored by the World's Fair Corporation naturally have offered the best use of films embodying the documentary ideal. The function of these exhibits is that of projecting society's methods of meeting basic needs—Food, Medicine, Education, Communication. In each building sponsored by the Fair itself there is a "focal exhibit" which is designed to crystallize the ideas utilized in the exhibit as a whole. An intelligent plan for the use of film in these focal exhibits was developed, and several freely experimental pictures were produced. Ralph Steiner and Theodore Lawrence edited library material intended to be used as an integral part of a "Story of Communications" exhibit, with commentary by Gilbert Seldes. The Department of Agriculture produced several "zoom" films to be used in the Food Building to exemplify the problems involved in the production and distribution of foodstuffs. For the "Three-Thirds of a Nation" focal exhibit in the Consumers Building, Wilding Pictures produced a "cinematic mural" consisting of seven films projected simultaneously side by side, the action shifting rapidly from one frame to another. With the exception of the Communications material, the experimental tendency of these films seems directed toward playing with the tricks of the medium for sensational effect, rather than developing a valid technique for the dramatization of fact. They were, however, admirable in general aim, and it is unfortunate that their projection proved too costly for the Fair budget. None of these were shown for more than a few days after the opening of the Fair.

The only focal exhibit of films in operation throughout the Fair was that contained in the Little Theatre of the Science and Education Building. This program, supervised by Philip McConnell, is worth extended analysis. It made a valiant effort to gather and show all the most important films on its thematic subjects, science, education, medicine, and social problems, and therefore provides a key to the extent to which the motion picture is serving these activities today.

The exhibit's most famous film is, of course, *The City*. Much has already been written concerning the value of this picture, but I think too little account has been taken of the fact that it was produced especially for showing at the Fair, a fact which has had much to do with determining its nature and quality. Pare Lorentz's scenario characteristically demonstrates that the problem of civic planning is one of conceiving a city organization which will serve everyday needs as functionally as did the old American town—a valid film idea, since the community advocated resembles closely the village of the past and can be compared to it cinematically. In addition, the decentralized town which the film propagandizes is generally accepted by experts as the proper solution for the problem of city planning. As a paper project, then, *The City* is unassailable. It begins to reveal its weakness when it goes beyond abstract discussion of design and tries to motivate decentralization in terms of human values. Here it is much more concerned over the inconvenience which traffic congestion causes the motorist than with the dirt and disease of the slums. The contemporary city is bad because it is hurried, crowded, anonymous; the decentralized town is good because it provides space, leisure, and an organic community life. Chaotic metropolis or summery suburb—"each of them is real, each of them is possible. You can take your choice." *Who* can take it? *The City* proceeds as though everyone could, as though it had only to convince us of the *value* of the future town. But people do not live in slums by choice. They need to be shown not only what they ought to have but how they can get it. And this the film does not mention.

But on the credit side, *The City's* record bulks large. The American way in documentary has been all too frequently the way of symbolism and *The City*, following precedent, might have been a symphony of construction, a hymn to the building of the future beehive. Its directors have instead preferred to reveal the meaning of the city in terms of human feeling. Their rendering of life in the unplanned metropolis is humorous when it should have been tragic, but at least it moves the spectator. And we learn what it will be like to live in the decentralized town, not through the commentary's decorative rodomontades, but from what we see on the screen. There we meet people at work and play, doing things we have done ourselves, and, coming close to them, we perceive what it is like to perform the familiar tasks and seek the familiar satisfactions under the conditions of a planned environment. For the first time in America, perhaps for the first time in the world, the camera technique of Robert Flaherty has been applied to the material of contemporary life. The result is a film whose human intimacy has made it liked by all kinds of audiences. Van Dyke and Steiner have here instigated a revolution in method which, more than anything else, will bring the strength of popularity to the documentary film.

Other films in the Little Theatre's social problems series are concerned with immediate subjects and the technical problems they raise. Pare Lorentz's famous and popular government films, *The Plow That Broke the Plains* and *The River*, represent well what documentary has done to dramatize the conservation of national resources. Though they are romantic rather than scientific in approach, though the solutions they offer are not adequate,[1] they do give full statement to their problems—a statement expressed, moreover, in terms of urgent need. The British documentary movement has sent a selection of films representing its approach to social problems as expressed in such subjects as nutrition (*Enough to Eat?*), housing (*Housing Problems, Kensal House*), local government (*The Londoners*), and education (*Children At School*). Of unequal merit technically, these films indicate the magnitude of the task the British movement has tackled. The wide range of subjects reveals a disposition to present a complete picture of the modern effort to reorganize society on a scientific basis. Some of them, like *Housing Problems* and *Enough to Eat?* have already influenced national policy, and all of them have contributed to the reputation of the documentary film as an agency for bringing the ordinary citizen in touch with the forces which govern his life.

In the field of screen journalism, The March of Time contributed *Men of Medicine*, an excellent piece of *reportage* with clear-cut educational value. Several important political films (*The Spanish Earth, Return to Life, The 400,000,000*) were shown at the Little Theatre for awhile and represented the use of the documentary approach to dramatize issues drawn from the news. All of these films on social problems are well-considered efforts to instruct audiences. The other programs at the Little Theatre, however, are significant of the inadequacy of the contemporary educational film.

The series on medicine is deplorable. Aside from a good March of Time item, *Heart Disease*, not one film shows any comprehension of how to do its job. Two pictures on pneumonia, *A New Day* and *Serum to Wyndham*, may be taken to represent the ideas and methods involved. Both are devoted to convincing audiences that pneumonia is a disease so dangerous that it must be treated immediately on its inception. *A New Day* imports Hollywood actors to give a gloss to this theme, and thereby nullifies the audience's disposition to regard what it sees as a real occurrence. *Serum to Wyndham*, unconscious of the inherent drama of its theme, tacks its narrative to a "race for life" conceived in terms of wildest melodrama. Films on the advancement of science and technology, as exemplified by Dr. Irving Langmuir's *Surface Chemistry*, eschew this Hollywood approach but achieve equal remoteness from life by presenting their ideas in a tired classroom manner. The program on progressive education is worst of all. With the exception of *School*, a well-made but random film, none of its pictures achieved even mechanical competence. They were greeted derisively by audiences which, if they demand nothing else, expect to see and hear what is presented on the screen.

The Little Theatre's program on social problems might well pretend to represent the best achievement of the documentary film. The high standard here may be attributed largely to the fact that documentary technicians themselves are deeply interested in such subjects. They have fought to make these films, and the results come from their efforts rather than the exactions of sponsors. The inspiration of the films on medicine, science, and education, on the other hand, comes from the sponsors themselves. Besides being technically incompetent,[2] these films produced and closely supervised by health services and scientific societies are for the most part remote from the realities they try to serve.

The focal film exhibit at the Science and Education Building, then, embraces the best films on its thematic subjects and reveals that best to be none too good. Other films in the Fair Corporation Buildings (sponsored by philanthropic societies or industrial firms whose work is related to the theme of the building) are even less worthy of consideration. *Good Neighbors*, produced for the U. S. Maritime Commission and shown at the Maritime Building, is a dull exposition of national policy toward South America, dramatized in a feeble dilution of the March of Time style by technicians from that film unit. The Aviation Building displays an Air Force recruiting film and one on aeronautical science, neither interesting enough to hold the passerby before the booths in which they are projected. *Shadow On the Land* in the syphilis exhibit at Medicine and Public Health, the Cancer films in the New York City Building, and the Aetna and Metropolitan Life Insurance health and safety pictures, are similar to the medical films at the Little Theatre and subject to the same criticisms. In the Consumers Building, the Household Finance Corporation displays two ambitious films on home economy, *Heap O' Livin'* and *Happily Ever After*. The former is produced in Hollywood style, "starring" Edgar A. Guest, but *Happily Ever After* is a sensible, if not extraordinary, dramatization of analytical purchasing. As though to offset this intelligent example of the public relations film, Macfadden Publications has conferred upon the Communications Building one of the most preposterous movies at the Fair. *I'll Tell the World* employs professional actors to tell a "human interest" story pointing the great truth that advertising is a boon to the consumer, the producer, the middleman, the government, and everybody else. The remainder of the Fair Corporation Building films frankly plug a product, using the tricks of the medium, and especially the cartoon, in the service of conventional advertising approaches. A summatory title is *The Amazing Recovery of Inbad the Ailer*, produced by the manufacturer of a laxative.

"National Projection"

Two major propagandist conceptions seem to determine the use of film by government exhibits at the World's Fair. The first may be described as an apologetic or public relations approach: that of presenting the history, social structure, cultural achievement, and foreign policies of each nation in a presumptively analytical but predominantly favorable light. The second, more frequently used, approach is closer to pure advertising; it consists of films designed to stimulate buying of commercial products or to attract tourists. The extent and nature of foreign programs are largely determined by the quality of general film production in each country. From the point of view of both propaganda ideas and technical style, the programs display marked national characteristics.

[. . .]

Of all the government exhibits at the Fair, the British Pavilion probably had the best opportunity to gain prestige by appealing to special groups of the film public. The British documentary film is world-famous, and educators, publicists, and technicians have long been curious to see examples of its work. Instead, only a small group of documentaries is to be seen, and the selection is random. *Song of Ceylon* is there, and *Shipyard* and *The Londoners* are occasionally shown, but such historically important pictures as *Industrial Britain, Coal Face* and *The Saving of Bill Blewitt* are absent. *Housing Problems* and *Enough to Eat?*, which are the most socially important, the most influential, and the most British of these films are shown at the Science and Education Building but not at the national exhibit. In place of these, the Pavilion offers a heterogeneous collection of travelogues and "interest" films, incompetent enough and dull enough to alienate the most passionately Anglophile group, much less a lay audience accustomed to the tempo of American films.

So many of these pictures are below the lowest possible level of audience acceptance that one at first imagines them to have been selected at random by men who had never seen any of them. But repeated visits to the exhibit gradually reveal a motive for the choice, focussed in the British Newsreel which opens each program. Before the outbreak of the war, the items in this reel were devoted almost wholly to such "events" as the changing of the guard at Buckingham Palace, the visit of Their Majesties to a children's camp, the opening of a garden party by the Duchess of York. Since war was declared, the reel has displayed the might of the military. As with the newsreel, so with the rest of the program: these unimaginative and rather pompous films on British landscapes, monuments, and sports, project the England of tradition and stability. They summon the past to reinforce the present, saying with J. B. Priestley in *English Journey*, "Damn you, I'm all right."

The documentary movement in England has devoted itself over a period of ten years to dramatizing the Britain of today. Whatever the success or failure of its more ambitious aims, it has never failed to do the primary job of urging the citizen to accept social responsibility. An excellent example of the way this job has been done under present conditions of sponsorship is contained in the new film, *Men of Africa*. Presented by the Colonial Empire Marketing Board, the film is intended by its sponsors as a defense of British colonial government. Using the same propagandist methods as those employed in the Hall of Colonial Administration at the British Pavilion, it tells how England is trying to raise the living standard of her primitive subjects. By medical care, by education, by scientific agriculture, tropical colonies and their inhabitants are put on an equal footing with the rest of the Empire. The film thus states that Britain's right to govern colonies is determined by the extent to which she fits them to govern themselves. In articulating this idea (which was hardly the intention of the sponsors) Alexander Shaw's direction has transformed the film from an apology for the British Empire into an inculcation of England's responsibility toward subject populations.

Few of the important documentaries embodying this approach are at the British Pavilion, and the films actually shown there have little relation to England today. They are, in fact, wholly opposed to the function for which the documentary film has become famous. Nevertheless, the British Cinema is one of the best-attended theatres at the Fair. This may be partly accounted for by the fact that, even at its worst, the technical ingenuity of the British fact film is higher than the average of the Fair. Most popular of all films at the British Theatre are the instructionals—Mary Field's and Percy Smith's *Secrets of Life* series, the Strand films of the London Zoo, and two remarkable engineering pictures by Arthur Elton, *The Transfer of Power* and *Springs*. Only in this category is the best of Britain's film work to be seen at its national exhibit.

The United States is represented at the World's Fair by Hollywood's conception of the documentary film. *Land of Liberty*, edited by Cecil B. DeMille from 125 historical films, was presented to the U. S. World's Fair Commission by the motion picture industry of the United States, and is, being 14 reels long, the "big" American film at the Fair. Undeniably it is a big film, covering the whole field of American history in considerable detail. It embodies, too, a viewpoint often called "typically American" in its veneration of the past, its dogged belief in democracy, and its sense of confusion and defeat at the present state of world affairs. But sincere as *Land of Liberty* is in its effort to capture the spirit of America, it can scarcely be accepted as an adequate historical film. All of its material comes from fictional pictures, where events are recited at second hand. Few of its excerpts have any sense of history, and none of them any feeling of reality. The result, if not uncharacteristic of the American film, is hardly informative, much less scholarly. Yet *Land of Liberty* is the only important film shown exclusively at the Federal Building. With it go a few government shorts on forestry and fishery and such. They do nothing to revoke the judgment that the "educational" films produced by government bureaus are about as powerful as virgin celluloid. On the contrary, their dull incompetence shows how desperate is the need for the reorganized government program proposed by U.S. Film Service for which Congress has yet to make an appropriation.

[. . .]

Commerce and Industry

Contrary to general expectation, few new films were produced especially for the World's Fair by commercial and industrial exhibitors. Consequently the programs on view largely typify past conceptions of the public relations and advertising film rather than contemporary experiment. This presents a gloomy prospect to the initiate whose experience of commercial films has taught him that their informational and entertainment value is generally nil. Yet in many of the pictures made within the past five years new influences can be observed at work—influences far more valuable than those which inform the majority of scientific films. To a surprising extent, these new ideas are pushing the public relations film toward the documentary ideal.

Indeed, the model public relations film is being displayed at the World's Fair. It is a *History and Romance of Transportation*, produced by Frontier Films for the Rocket Port Exhibit at the Chrysler Building. Edited chiefly from library material, the film tells the story of transport from earliest times to the present. Cunningly cut on lines of accelerating movement, it builds a tension which is released by the actual launching of a miniature rocket ship, the climax of the exhibit proper. In representing the development of transport as a fulfilment of a human need, this short document gives the citizen an understanding of his vital stake in this commonly accepted convenience of daily life. Unfortunately the sponsors cannot claim credit for the excellence of the film. The entire Rocket Port exhibit was originally produced for the Fair Corporation and was transferred to the Chrysler Building at the last moment. Perhaps its popularity will show its new sponsor where the logical next step of his public relations film lies.

If *Transportation* represents the ideal goal of the publicity film, the series of pictures shown at the General Motors Theatre stands for its transitional phase. One group of these films dramatizes safety in driving; another is dedicated to the idea that scientific research is the source of all automotive progress, and that it is the responsibility of manufacturers to support research. Both conceptions approach documentary; they state that road transport is within the domain of public interest, and at the same time that the maker of motor cars must look upon his position as an obligation to serve social aims. These films still have something of the sense of furtive apology for industry rather than a positive statement of public service, but they are a great advance on previous public relations concepts. Their technique is another matter. Here safe driving methods are dramatized in terms of cartoon characters, with symbolic Caution as hero and Man-Mountain-Momentum as villain. Films on the progress of automotive engineering are rendered in the hoary style of the "oddity" film. Admirable as the General Motors films are in idea, their treatment removes from them the sense of fact which would persuade audiences to take them seriously.

Such comparatively enlightened films are rare at Flushing, nevertheless. The vast majority of publicity films—and there are scores of them on view—follow an older public relations concept, typified in *The Story of Lucky Strike* and *Men Make Steel*. The former is a straightforward *reportage* of the making of cigarettes, appealing to curiosity only. The latter demonstrates that a blast furnace in Technicolor is still a blast furnace, used for pictorial values only.

Advertising films at the Fair provided an opportunity for experiment which, curiously, few exhibitors were moved to grasp. The success of European producers in using film tricks to ensure acceptance of an advertising plug was an obvious vein to work, but the majority have preferred to follow the line of previous (unsuccessful) experience with film advertising. The most ambitious experiment at the Fair in this line is the oil industry's *Pete Roleum and His Cousins*. Almost this picture asks acceptance as a public relations-documentary concept. Its bland message assures us that petroleum in its various forms is the basis upon which rests all modern industry and science and, to prove the point, we are shown the necessary result of the sudden disappearance of oil—namely, the collapse of Western Civilization. Furthermore, the oil industry's contribution to our life is almost wholly philanthropic; most of its income goes for wages and taxes, only a tiny fraction being retained as profit. Since this evaluation of the importance of petroleum could not possibly be accepted as cold fact, it is offered as fancy, with a puppet Pete Roleum and his derivative cousins representing the various functions of oil. The film is thus divided against itself; its message is all but statistical, its treatment intentionally unreal.

In itself the treatment is noteworthy. Joseph Losey's production has created a fantastic puppet world much more carefully than it has ever been done before on the screen. The characters have something of the imaginative anthropomorphism which distinguishes Disney's work, and they move in a musical and scenic setting that invokes the wavering perspective of fancy. Continental producers, following the same methods, have achieved excellent results. Employing all the tricks of the medium, they create a topsy-turvy world in which the sales message is kidded along with everything else. This Losey's film does not achieve. The sponsor's heavy-handed message prevents enjoyment of its fantasy. Its technique, however, is perfectly valid in a proper sphere, and *Pete Roleum* thus testifies that film fancy should not be used in the interests of a phoney apology for industry.

Valid use of film trickery is exemplified in the Chrysler Building's *In Tune With Tomorrow*. Here a Plymouth car is seen to assemble itself as if by magic, and in three-dimensional cinematography. This picture, with Disney's *Mickey's Surprise Party*, a cartoon plugging Nabisco Products, appreciate the value of humor. Most of the others, however, are in deadly earnest. They tell "human interest" stories which, in the manner of magazine advertising, try to sell a product by appealing to basic sentiments—fear, vanity, sex. This is the time-honored tack of the advertising film and nothing remains to be said of it except that Fair experience once more demonstrates its mistaken logic. Audiences expect either fact or fantasy from the non-fiction film; offering them fact disguised in fiction invites the cynical reaction most of these pictures receive.

Conclusions

A few, a very few, of the films at the World's Fair offer a Utopian vision of a world far off in time, basing their suppositions on unused scientific knowledge and on the premise that mechanical progress will continue at an accelerated rate. A second, not much larger, group dramatizes a world in transition, dealing with present processes in terms of their meaning for the future. Thirdly, the vast majority of Flushing's films consider present and potential developments in relation to the individual interests of their sponsors. The second group of films at once approaches the documentary ideal and fulfills that "will toward the future" which is the World's Fair's soundest inspiration. The Fair Corporation, in its own films, adhered to this ideal, employing accredited documentary makers and allowing them latitude for experiment. Other exhibitors, of whatever type, have largely failed to make use of the talent and experience at hand. In the main, their films are either visionary or obsolescent. Consequently it cannot be the verdict of this report that the World's Fair films realize the very great opportunity offered them by the essential purpose of the Fair itself. Out of the reasons for this failure, however, comes an illuminating insight into the prospects of the documentary film.

Factual films sponsored by scientific, educational, and medical authorities are documentary almost by definition. What stands between them and rightful claim to that label is, in every case, the appallingly bad technique in which they are couched. Had the large number of these films been produced by experienced men, the fact film would have served Fair ends with distinction. The case of the public relations film is essentially similar. These pictures are primarily produced to serve special interests, but the example of the General Motors and Chrysler displays indicates that industry is rapidly becoming convinced that, in publicity at least, it must assume social obligations to win public good will. The best public relations films at the Fair show development toward the documentary conception. The reason that they are not documentary in fact is that their ideas are rendered in a half-hearted fictional technique which insists on sugar coating the pill to the point of nausea.

The essential failure of the sponsors, then, would seem to be that of ignoring available methods and experienced talent. But I do not think they are to be blamed for that. They are, after all, not film experts and their conception of the right use of film is governed by the status of the motion picture in present-day society. The film as education and journalism has a modicum of prestige, but the fiction movie is the mightiest entertainment on the face of the earth. It is not unnatural, therefore, that Fair exhibitors, wishing to utilize this great power to please and persuade, have gone to its apparent source. To them as to most people the fact film, if it is known at all, is associated with dull didacticism. The excitement and glamour, therefore the persuasive power, of the movie seemingly lie in entertainment. Wishing to borrow that persuasion, the Fair's exhibitors naturally turned to Hollywood technicians on the one hand and to commercial film makers on the other. These latter (who in fact produced the great majority of all types of films at the Fair) guarantee only a sort of minimum audience acceptance for the ideas they undertake to project. Their production method represents a compromise between information and propaganda, which the public is supposed to resent, and amusement, which it is supposed to embrace whole-heartedly.

This compromise misses the fundamental purpose of the Fair, and audience reaction to films so produced must have surprised their sponsors greatly. For years the commercial film companies have turned out an endless stream of scientific, educational, and publicity films. Though none of these pictures became famous, they apparently were acceptable enough to sales conventions, conferences of scientific societies, and to an occasional lay audience which tolerated them because they were brief and the admission was free. But, dragged from this innocuous desuetude into the limelight of an international exposition, they are tried and found wanting by a more discriminating public. Visitors to the Fair are in search of entertainment of a kind, it is true. But the very fact of their assistance at the birth of the World of Tomorrow demonstrates their interest in reality rather than fiction. Many of the hundred thousand who daily pass through the turnstiles make a beeline for bar or midway, and maybe they stay there till closing time. But if by chance they happen into an industrial or governmental or scientific exhibit, they are seeking information rather than still more amusement. They want to know what tomorrow holds for them as individuals and members of society, and they ask to be told in terms of work in progress. That is why *The City* is the most famous film at the Fair, and *The Plow* and *The River* among the most popular. That is why those government exhibits which dramatize national endeavor rouse interest, while those which entice tourists are received passively. That is why the crowds jam the General Motors Theatre and pass Macfadden Publications by. If the Fair is a field day for the commercial movie rather than the documentary film, it at least demonstrates the slight impact of the one, the intrinsic interest of the other.

There *is* a public interest in facts as well as a public appetite for entertainment, and it is the opinion of this survey that films which serve the former are demonstrably more successful with Fair audiences than those which pretend to satisfy the latter. The record on this point is sufficiently clear to impress the most timid of sponsors. The Fair provided the documentary movement with an unparalleled opportunity to show before all the world that it possesses a propagandist technique which has no equal among the expressive media. That this opportunity has gone begging is not alone the fault of the timidity and conservatism of sponsors. The ideas in many of their films reveal an identity of viewpoint with documentary aims. Had they been made sufficiently aware that there exists a method of film making eminently adapted to serve these aims, they could not have failed to avail themselves of that method and of the talent dedicated to its service. It is to be hoped that the first success of the newly formed Association of Documentary Film Producers will be to inform all potential sponsors that there is a group of responsible, energetic film-makers ready to project their ideas filmically.

The film situation at the Fair points again the fact that the major problem of documentary today is one of sales promotion. If the Fair of 1940 is to muster a better showing of fact films, if the documentary movement is ever to secure a firm sponsored basis, the problem must be met now. Its traditional difficulties are no less today. Possibly they are even increased by a world crisis which threatens to sabotage the Fair itself. But that is the job to be done.

The preceding article is based upon a survey prepared by the author for the American Film Center.

NOTES

1. The original ending of *The Plow That Broke the Plains*, showing soil conservation efforts in the Dust Bowl, had been removed from the film as shown at the Science and Education Building, thus leaving the problem wholly unresolved.
2. At the risk of redundancy, it seems necessary to emphasize that the majority of films on medicine, science, and education at the Little Theatre and throughout the Fair are among the worst examples of photography, sound, direction, and editing ever seen. If this incompetence is caused by inadequate financial resources, it is perhaps not blameworthy. On the other hand, one wonders why such necessarily ineffectual films were produced at all.

SECTION III

DOCUMENTARY PROPAGANDA

World War II and the Post-War Citizen

43

JONATHAN KAHANA

INTRODUCTION TO SECTION III

Although section III is the shortest in this volume, the issues it deals with are substantial, and important for later developments in documentary theory and practice. In historical terms, this section concentrates on the relatively brief period framed by the years of the Second World War. It highlights some unique aspects of state-sponsored modes of documentary production—which, for our purposes, includes the production of policy and of aesthetic and critical discourse—during a national mobilization of labor, industry, culture, and thought. And it follows these developments into a world reshaped by international conflict.

As André Bazin writes at the start of an essay on the U.S. Army's *Why We Fight* series, this war was "at the heart of a decisive new revaluation of documentary reporting" (60). But how this "revaluation" of documentaries so well-known and widely-seen, and yet so roundly dismissed by critics, historians, and theorists, would proceed was, and still is, an open question. So when we ask what happened to documentary films and audiences during and the Second World War (as did public relations expert Wesley Pratzner in a 1947 article for *The Public Opinion Quarterly*, reflecting on the massive wartime enterprise of documentary production and exhibition[1]), we do well to approach the materials of this section with the open mind of movie reviewer and documentarian James Agee, who spoke in 1945 of his "perplexity" when faced with images and sounds that were the "best and most terrible" he had seen.

The nationalization of documentary cinema that occurred in many Allied and Axis countries, under which the means of making non-fiction media for public consumption were commandeered by government agencies and operatives, a state of affairs complemented by the special wartime conditions on truthful speech in general, can be seen, from the perspective of Western liberal democracies, as a brief emergency, a suspension of the usual bourgeois-individual liberty to create and circulate ideas that was necessary for national security. The effects of the emergency on the critical reception of documentary are the subject of materials in the first half of this section. This crisis seemed to be rectified by the gradual return to the international marketplace of ideas and of goods after 1945. But as the essays and statements in the second half of the section suggest, documentary structures and problems broached in an original way during the propaganda and counter-propaganda campaigns of the war continued, well into the 1950s and beyond, to haunt documentary producers and the institutions that housed them, as these intelligence workers found their way back into the peacetime social fabric and into postwar cultures and industries of non-fiction film and television.

Critics, scholars, and producers have sometimes treated wartime as a state of exception in the documentary tradition. At least since photographers of the Crimean and American Civil wars, documentary has been seen as a way to record, with some degree of independence from the states waging battle, the terrible experience of military combat. Yet with some justification, the use of documentary methods *by* belligerents shooting their own history has been seen as something of a betrayal of a traditional documentary ideal of freedom from state and corporate power and ideology. In part, this is because wars seem to suspend the cultural contract of liberal societies. Wars demand unanimity, if not blind trust, in the people in whose name they are fought. They seem also to justify the interruption of processes we think of as central to the social and political function of documentary: like publicness, which in peacetime will often take the form of expressions, in the press and elsewhere, of citizens' doubts about authority and institutions, or the valorization of individual and local differences, of "community," over the homogeneity of the national whole. And to viewers and critics alike, especially when they look back on these accounts from peacetime, the access documentary producers are given to military installations and the rarified, dangerous conditions of the battlefront can look like a compromise, or a mass deception. As we saw in the cases of *Battle of the Somme* (1916) in section I and *Triumph of the Will* (1935) in section II, films justified in their moment as works of non-fiction made by artists with privileged perspectives on national and popular causes can strike us later as something less noble.

Of course, "propaganda" did not always have the obscene connotation it does now. The writing collected in this section, both from the period and looking back, makes frequent use of the term "propaganda," and just as often in a purely descriptive, or even affirmative way as in judgment or condemnation. Even outside of wartime, documentary producers before and for some time after 1945 were comfortable describing their work as propaganda; and one lesson to take from this section is the value of this concept and all it entails for the production and the study of documentary, starting with the recognition that documentary is a language of persuasion—a language that is also artful. In James Agee's review for *The Nation* of the work of anonymous newsreel producers, and in Jim Leach's and Jennifer Horne's discussions of "hot" and "cold" war *auteurs* Humphrey Jennings and James Blue, we encounter a very different picture of the documentary propagandist than the stereotype of the artless state functionary, grinding out shrill, cold-blooded lies to break the will of a people.

Another valuable point to be taken from the study of wartime documentary and postwar documentary, and from the careers of filmmakers like Jennings and Blue, is the one made succinctly by another filmmaker who worked both with and against state and corporate powers, George Stoney. In his one-page rejoinder to Jack C. Ellis's history of documentary film, *The Documentary Idea*, Stoney underscores the economic and material continuities between wartime and peacetime (or institutional and independent) production in the mid-century documentary world. As Stoney points out, many filmmakers we think of as independent voices contributing to a public sphere of political or civil discourse in the U.S., the U.K., and other liberal or welfare-state democracies made the transition from radical left, anti-state and anti-capitalist documentary of the 1930s quite easily and seamlessly into positions in the state agencies of information during the Second World War. And for these producers and others, like the Canadian and Indian documentary units discussed by Zoë Druick and Srirupa Roy, or the African-American and white liberal intellectuals responsible for the making of the U.S. Army training and morale film *The Negro Soldier* (1944), state and corporate communications apparatuses could serve as proving grounds for the many kinds of independence movements that blossomed around the world in the decades after the war.

A third new idea to be found in this section, particularly among historians writing under the influence of political theory, is that of an ideological continuity that spans wartime and peacetime societies through documentary film, as much through the form of its address as through its content. Druick, Roy, and Horne all suggest the presence, in the Cold War–era national and transnational documentary projects they describe, of a subdued but no less effective appeal to citizenship that carries over from the command-and-control structure of wartime national defense to a bio-political measure of concern for healthy national bodies. And in Druick and Roy, a dulling of the documentary senses that threatened to return to non-fiction cinema, after the excitement of war is finally given its due as an aesthetic property. Against the emergency of wartime, the routine, workaday spirit that struck commentators closer to the period, like Pratzner and Stoney (and, in the next section, Jean Painlevé, who calls it "castration") as a liability of its pre- and post-war modes of production is here theorized as a rhetorical weapon of institutional and civic documentary at mid-century.

NOTE

1 Wesley F. Pratzner, "What Has Happened to the Documentary Film?," *The Public Opinion Quarterly* 11, no. 3 (Autumn 1947): 394–401.

44

JAMES AGEE

REVIEW OF IWO JIMA NEWSREELS (1945)

The Paramount newsreel issue about Iwo Jima subjects the tremendous material recorded by Navy and Marine Corps and Coast Guard cameramen to an unusually intelligent job of editing, writing, and soundtracking. I noticed with particular respect a couple of good uses of flat silence; the use of a bit of dialogue on "intercoms," recorded on the spot, in a tank; and the use, at the end, of a still photograph down whose wall the camera moved slowly. Still photographs of motionless objects have a very different quality from motion-picture photographs of motionless objects; as Jean Cocteau observed, time still moves in the latter. The still used here was of dead men, for whom time no longer moved. The device is not a new one; Griffith (or William Bitzer) used it for the same purpose at the end of a battle in *The Birth of a Nation*, and René Clair used stop-shots for a somewhat related purpose in *The Crazy Ray*. But it is a device too basic to poetic resource on the screen to discard as plagiarized, and I am glad to see it put back into use so unpretentiously and well.

The Fox version of the same battle—the only other version I could find—drew on the same stock, and is interesting to compare with the Paramount. In one way it is to its credit that it is much less noisy and much less calculated to excite; it is in other words less rhetorical, and the temptations to rhetoric must be strong in handling such material, and usually result in falseness. But in this Paramount issue it seems to me that rhetoric was used well, to construct as well as might be in ten hours' work and in ten minutes on the screen an image of one of the most terrible battles in history. And that is not to mention plain sense: the coherent shape of violence in the Paramount version, which moves from air to sea to land; its intact, climactic use of the footage exposed through a tank-slit, which in the Fox version is chopped along through the picture; and its use of the recorded dialogue, which Fox didn't even touch.

The Fox version does on the other hand have two shots—a magically sinister slashing of quicksilvery water along the sand, and a heartrending picture of a wounded Marine, crawling toward help with the scuttling motions of a damaged insect—which I am amazed to see omitted from a piece of work so astute as Paramount's.

Very uneasily, I am beginning to believe that, for all that may be said in favor of our seeing these terrible records of war, we have no business seeing this sort of experience except through our presence and participation. I have neither space nor mind, yet, to try to explain why I believe this is so; but since I am reviewing and in ways recommending that others see one of the best and most terrible of war films, I cannot avoid mentioning my perplexity. Perhaps I can briefly suggest what I mean by this rough parallel: whatever other effects it may or may not have, pornography is invariably degrading to anyone who looks at or reads it. If at an incurable distance from participation, hopelessly incapable of reactions adequate to the event, we watch men killing each other, we may be quite as profoundly degrading ourselves and, in the process, betraying and separating ourselves the farther from those we are trying to identify ourselves with; none the less because we tell ourselves sincerely that we sit in comfort and watch carnage in order to nurture our patriotism, our conscience, our understanding, and our sympathies.

45

JAMES AGEE

REVIEW OF *SAN PIETRO* (1945)

San Pietro is the record of the part which one regiment of infantrymen took in one of several fights which resulted in the capture of one village, the key to an Italian valley. At the end of the fight the seven-hundred-year-old village was chaos, and the regiment required 1,100 replacements. *San Pietro* runs only half an hour, and still leaves much of a world open to the most highly imaginative use of its kind of material. But it is in every way as good a war film as I have seen; in some ways it is the best.

It was made by six Signal Corps camera men under the command of Major John Huston, who also designed the scenario and wrote and spoke the narration. Most of these men were veterans. That fact presumably helps to explain a number of things: how they all lived through the shooting of the film; how deep inside the fighting some of it was made; how well they evidently understood what to expect, how to shoot it, what it was good for, and its weight and meaning in the whole picture. But remarkable as the camera men evidently were, it is fairly clear that the main credit for the picture goes to Major Huston. He moved continually from one of his men to the next, showing them what he wanted and where to go for it; he kept planning and revising his scenario and his narration in spare time during the days and nights of fighting; he had to work blind, for the film was developed and printed in Washington and he saw nothing he had—or had lost—until he got back to this country. Yet Huston and his camera men understood so well what they were after that when he did return, to assemble the film, he had to make very few changes in his narration.

The attitudes which have pervaded most of our combat films are seldom questionable and usually something to be proud of; but there is a major advance here. It is clear that Huston understood what he was recording, and how to record it, with a wonderfully vigorous and whole maturity, at once as a soldier and an artist and a man. No war film I have seen has been quite so attentive to the heaviness of casualties, and to the number of yards gained or lost, in such an action; none has so levelly watched and implied what it meant, in such full and complex terms—in military terms; in terms of the men who were doing the fighting; in terms of the villagers; and of their village; and of the surrounding country; and of the natural world; and of human existence and hope.

Huston's narration is a slightly simplified technical prose, at once exact and beautifully toned and subtly parodistic; it is spoken with finely shaded irony, equally free of pompousness and optimism and mawkish generalizations and cheap bitterness. Against the images he has chosen, their always satisfying arrangement, and their beautiful over-all plan and implication, this text points itself so richly and flexibly that for once wordiness in a film more than earns its way. As for the over-all plan and implication, I don't see how that of any post-war film is going to improve on it, and I rather doubt that any will come quite up to it. For at one and the same time, without one slip along the line, from the most ticklish fringes of taste to the depths of a sane mind and heart, it accepts the facts and treats them as materials relevant to anger, tenderness, pride, veneration, and beauty. Somewhere close to the essence of the power of moving pictures is the fact that they can give you things to look at, clear of urging or comment, and so ordered that they are radiant with illimitable suggestions of meaning and mystery. Huston's simple, wordless use of children, toward the end of this film, does that, and seems to me the first great passage of war poetry that has got on the screen. In emphatic agreement with some recent comments by Bernard Haggin, however, I do want to object to one thing; music can only vitiate this kind of film. Here, with all words and irony at last withdrawn, as you watch the faces of the children, each one unimaginably beautiful and portentous, and ordered and timed into their culmination as nobly as the words in a great tragic line, it is as infuriating to have to fight off the emotional sales pressure of the Mormon Choir as it would be if all the honored watches and nasal aphrodisiacs insisted on marketing themselves against a Toscanini broadcast.

46

THOMAS CRIPPS AND DAVID CULBERT

THE NEGRO SOLDIER (1944)

Film Propaganda in Black and White (1979)

After years during which blacks and police engaged in pitched battles in small Southern towns and large Northern cities, Nicholas Katzenbach, Attorney General under Lyndon B. Johnson, termed television "the central means of making a private moral conviction public, of impelling people all over to see and confront ideas they otherwise would turn away from." Black activists considered television, in the words of a network producer, "the chosen instrument of the black revolution."[1] But television was not the first electronic medium used to further social change. The United States Army's orientation film, *The Negro Soldier*, released in January 1944, is one of those rare instances which allows the historian of mass media to speak confidently about conception, execution, and—to a degree—results both intended and unintended, of a specific controversial film. The uses eventually made of the Army's motion picture illustrate the difficulty of gauging in advance the impact of mass communication on social change.

During World War II the Army was officially committed to maintaining existing patterns of segregation. But the liberal rhetoric of official war aims proved fatal to thoughts of maintaining the *status quo* at home. By inducting 875,000 Negroes into a fighting force of some twelve million, the Army discovered that it was operating a social relations laboratory.[2] In spite of the wishes of many whites, the Army became a half-way house for those who believed that wartime should bring substantial racial progress.

The relationship between racial tensions and film can best be explained by a metaphor. The biologist defines symbiosis as an association of two different organisms which live attached to each other and contribute to each other's support. This article will describe the making and distribution of *The Negro Soldier* as an example of social symbiosis, for the idea did not come from one person, but emerged from a coalition of four wary interest groups which came together in antagonistic cooperation. The film offered important lessons to those who made post-war Hollywood "message" films, while black pressure groups discovered a new way to further social change through the distribution of motion pictures.

In retrospect, the four groups and their aims are easy to identify. First is the Army itself. By the time of Pearl Harbor both civilian and military leaders in America recognized motion pictures as a significant propaganda medium; they believed film could instill in citizens a spirit of patriotism and a will to fight.[3] Chief of Staff George C. Marshall believed that film should play a major military role in wartime.[4] Convinced that lectures about patriotism and recent history generally made no impact on draftees, he concluded that film could present serious material in a lively and interesting fashion. Thanks to Marshall, the Army chose Hollywood's Frank Capra to head an elite film unit assigned to make feature-length morale films intended to build enthusiasm for official war aims. To Marshall the key to morale for the educated soldier was to give a reason for fighting.[5] Capra's *Why We Fight* series, mandatory viewing for every soldier, defined official war aims in a way no other medium could match. Marshall hoped that a Capra-unit film about the Negro would provide a reason why racial tolerance was necessary to a unified military effort.

Capra's credentials for his assignment were considerable. A Sicilian immigrant, he began his Hollywood career by working on comic short subjects. Every film he made in the 1930s showed the "little guy" as eventually triumphant, a message bound to find a sympathetic reception in hard times. Above all, Capra's name became synonymous with the box office: no other Hollywood director could match his unbroken string of hits: *It Happened One Night* (1934), *Mr. Deeds Goes to Town* (1936), *Lost Horizon* (1937), *You Can't Take It With You* (1938), *Mr. Smith Goes to Washington* (1939), and *Meet John Doe* (1941). Capra was living proof that the American Dream did come true; to him patriotism was a high calling, though he masked his ardor with a deft comic touch. Capra's War Department film unit quickly attracted many of Hollywood's most talented cutters, scriptwriters, and directors. When the unit's first *Why We Fight* film, *Prelude to War*, appeared in November 1942, Capra's preeminent position in military filmmaking was assured.[6]

The second group is the blacks themselves, who saw World War II as a time to bring an end to longstanding discrimination. To black America, Franklin D. Roosevelt's Four Freedoms—freedom of speech, freedom of religion, freedom from fear, and freedom from want—were totally incompatible with segregation. The desires of black America must not be measured by the standard of today's activist rhetoric. In World War II most Negroes sought "racial tolerance" as a first step. Though there was violence, particularly race riots in Detroit and Harlem, the National Association for the Advancement of Colored People (NAACP), headed by Walter White, looked to the courts, and to white liberals, to bring about gradual change.

Earlier government films relating to blacks suggested progress more glacial than gradual. In World War I official Signal Corps footage used Negroes for comic relief. During the 1930s, Pare Lorentz's conservationist films, *The Plow That Broke the Plains* and *The River*, contained only a few black faces. The first two years of the war saw little change. Blacks were patronized in the few films with specific Negro themes released by federal agencies, either by overpraising Jim Crow schools (*Negro Colleges in Wartime*), or by celebrating "safe" heroes such as George Washington Carver.

Henry Browne, Farmer, a Department of Agriculture film, failed to convince anyone that racial tolerance was desirable. Browne was the perfect obedient Negro: possessor of forty acres, some chickens, a son in the black 99th Pursuit Squadron, and a willingness to grow peanuts because his country needed their oil. To make matters worse, a low budget made the entire enterprise look second-rate. The Negro journalist who originally suggested the idea termed the finished product "an insipid little story far from our original purpose."[7]

Something more substantial was needed because the 1940 Selective Service Act prohibited racial discrimination. The Army looked to Negro manpower. At the same time, military compliance with segregation somehow did not, as the approved Army manual phrased it, "endorse any theory of racial superiority or inferiority."[8] The resulting situation was made worse by a pervasive hostility toward Negro soldiers, who tended to score lowest on the Army General Classification Tests. Deputy Chief of Staff Joseph T. McNarney voiced a prevalent Army attitude: "there is no use having colored troops standing by and eating their heads off if their lack of aptitude is such that they can never be used overseas."[9]

Bitter racial prejudice did not distinguish among aptitude scores. Lacking an effective means of mass persuasion, the Army could only place "excessive faith in the effectiveness of hortatives" as a means of encouraging black and white soldiers to fight together for democracy. This approach was not enough. Secretary of War Henry L. Stimson's Civilian Aide for Negro Affairs, William Hastie, collected a file of outrageous racial incidents in which black soldiers, trained for the most part in the South, had been beaten by local rednecks. Such incidents, reported in the black press, offered a compelling reason for Negroes to reject official pleas for wartime unity.[10]

A group of leading social scientists employed by the Army's Information and Education Division (I&E) felt that scientific research could identify precisely what kind of film might bring white and black America closer together; these civilians made up the third group, and they wanted a documentary film about the Negro.[11] The idea for using motion pictures for persuasion was greatly aided by the fact that Capra's unit and the Research Branch worked side-by-side in I&E.

Brigadier General Frederick H. Osborn headed the Division. A wealthy New Yorker without prior military service, Osborn had family connections and a flair for administration. His father was one of Stimson's close friends, and an uncle, Henry Fairfield Osborn, had been largely responsible for bringing New York's Museum of Natural History to international prominence. Osborn, a board member of the Social Science Research Council (SSRC), had a scholarly study of eugenics to his credit. He came to the Army persuaded that morale could be determined by scientific means, and that traditional morale boosters—sports, camp songfests, "decks of cards and dice and tonettes"—belonged to a bygone era.[12] Osborn's advocacy, together with the support of both Marshall and Stimson, proved crucial to the military's adoption of both film and social science research.

Osborn was in an ambivalent position. Personally interested in statistical research, he headed a division concerned more with practical education and morale services within the Army than matters of sampling technique. I&E represented an unstable alliance between Capra's faith in film as entertainment, and faith in film as pedagogical tool, the latter the attitude of Samuel Stouffer, the University of Chicago sociologist who headed the professional staff of the Research Branch.[13]

At the same time, everyone in I&E shared an ardent belief in salesmanship. Wartime was no time for recondite speculation. Ideas were measured by their practical value. Capra needed no instruction in sales techniques: since the days of *Mr. Smith Goes to Washington* (1939) he had been selling democracy in his feature films. Less familiar, however, is the hucksterism of the social scientists. The Research Branch published its findings in *What the Soldier Thinks*, where numerous graphs and charts promoted the technique of "scientific" sampling along with practical results assured by asking questions incapable of complex answers.[14]

The social scientists realized that a morale film about race relations was a perfect place to test ideas about social engineering.[15] This outgrowth of behaviorial psychology argued that human behavior could be manipulated towards socially desirable goals. Critics of industrial societies had long complained that as technology spread its benefits, it also eroded traditional values. Stouffer and Donald Young, the War Department's official expert on race relations, believed that a "humane" or "liberal" use of film could reaffirm the values of a democratic society.[16] They also accepted a doctrine employed by most American propagandists in World War II—the "strategy of truth" or "propaganda of fact."[17] One was scrupulous about that which supported one's side while passing over the rest in silence. The result often sounded like a lawyer's brief pretending to objectivity.

The fourth group was the Hollywood film community. The fact that Capra's unit was staffed with regulars from the major studios, and that the films were actually made in Hollywood, meant that military filmmaking was followed on a daily basis. *The Negro Soldier* played a significant part in furthering a dramatic shift in the kinds of roles blacks received in feature films; after 1945 the era of the "message" film was at hand. Only *The Negro Soldier*, of all wartime films depicting blacks, actually tried to weave the Negro into the fabric of American life; this characteristic made the Army's film a model for filmmakers wishing to break through ingrained industry stereotypes.

Before 1939, virtually every black role was intended as comic relief.[18] The War Department's officer's training manual, *Leadership and the Negro Soldier*, described this stock figure vividly: "When the Negro is portrayed in the movies, or elsewhere, as a lazy, shiftless, no-good, slew-footed, happy-go-lucky, razor-toting, tap-dancing vagrant, a step has been taken in the direction of fixing this mental picture of the Negro in the minds of whites."[19] The NAACP's Walter White went to Hollywood twice in 1942 to urge a better future for blacks in feature films.[20] White, according to producer Darryl F. Zanuck of Twentieth Century-Fox, wanted Negroes "used as often as possible in the more heroic roles—in the positions which they occupy in real life."[21] In *Sahara* (1943), a black even acted as spokesman for democratic values. But such roles, however well-intentioned, were but more sophisticated versions of earlier attempts which overpraised Negro colleges.

To understand *The Negro Soldier* as a product of Hollywood technique and social science prescriptions, it is necessary to follow the evolution of the script. In March 1942 Frank Capra asked the Research Branch to draw up a list of "do's and don'ts" regarding the cinematic depiction of blacks. Sociologist Donald Young, who had devoted his pre-war career to the study of racial minorities and the impact of motion pictures, prepared a memorandum filled with well-meaning cautions, the ideas of a liberal who above all sought racial tolerance: avoid stereotypes such as the Negroes' alleged affinity for watermelon or pork; also avoid strong images of racial identity ("play down colored soldiers most Negroid in appearance" and omit "Lincoln, emancipation, or any race leaders or friends of the Negro"). Young also favored intraracial politesse: "Show colored officers in command of troops, but don't play them up too much. The Negro masses have learned that colored men who get commissions tend to look down on the masses."[22]

The first script for *The Negro Soldier* was prepared by Marc Connelly. As writer for *Green Pastures* (1930) he had a reputation for sympathetic treatment of Negro themes.[23] Connelly began working in Washington in May 1942 and followed Capra to Hollywood when the unit moved there in June. The script, which has disappeared, was deemed "too dramatic" for the Army's tastes. A second draft, prepared by Ben Hecht and Jo Swerling, was also rejected because I&E continued to insist that the Negro film be "documentary"—i.e., an example of the "propaganda of fact."[24]

During script revisions, Capra gave little attention to the project; in fact, he planned to assign the film to his friend William Wyler, but the latter "got a better offer from the Air Force." In the fall of 1942 Capra chose Stuart Heisler, a comparatively young director.[25] Heisler already had extensive experience as a studio technician and seemed knowledgeable about racial matters after having made *The Biscuit Eater*, a 1940 film shot on location in Georgia with an interracial cast. Heisler immediately accepted the offer, asking only that Capra provide him with "somebody that *really* knows the background of the Negro."[26]

As a result, Carlton Moss, a black writer, was pressed into service. Moss had attended Columbia University and had worked for the Federal Theater Project under John Houseman, who in turn recommended him to Capra. According to both Heisler and Moss the two "hit it off like magic." Moss remembers working on his version of the script in Washington at the Library of Congress, but not because it put him near the books he needed. It was hard to write about racial harmony while eating in Jim Crow restaurants; the Library's cafeteria was an unsegregated "oasis."[27]

Shooting began in January 1943. Heisler, Moss, Research Branch representative Charles Dollard, and a camera crew travelled the United States, visiting nineteen Army posts, virtually every location where black troops trained in large numbers. In Philadelphia, Donald Young arranged for added scenes to be shot at the homes of prominent Negroes. Heisler prepared a number of sequences in which black officers directed the training of soldiers. Most of this footage never appeared because the final version relied more on a docudrama than a documentary style.

The finished film, 43 minutes long, received official approval in January 1944.[28] *The Negro Soldier* (OF 51) unfolded in classic studio style, with a narrative spinning out

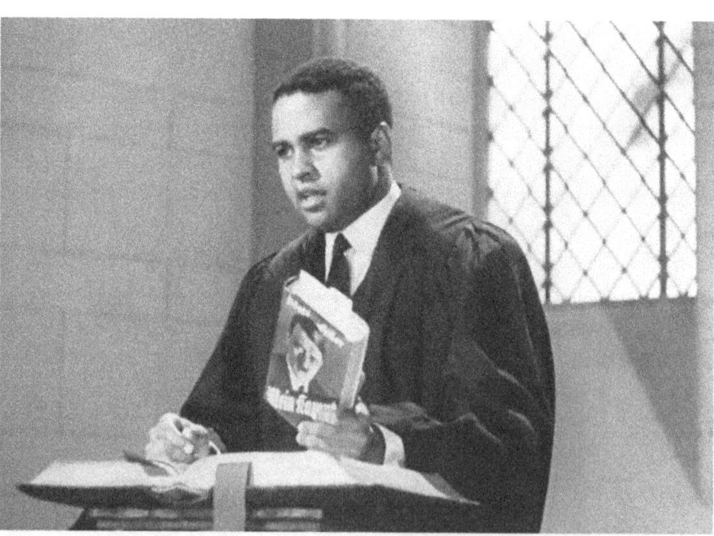

FIGURE 46.1 Carlton Moss in *The Negro Soldier*. Screen capture from digital file.

a flashback device, flawless lighting, and technically perfect optical effects punctuating the sequences. To black audiences, in particular, this technical quality was especially significant. Never before had a film purporting to document black American achievement been made with such professional competence. At the same time, the movie served the Army as propaganda for both black and white troops and as a teacher of comradely regard across racial lines without explicitly violating Army policy toward racial segregation.

A summary of the film's visual content shows how this was accomplished. Neat, clean, orderly, responsible, patriotic: these are the middle-class values which the film presents in image after image. Following the opening credits, a wide establishing shot places us in a splendid stone Gothic church. From the point of view of the congregation we see a black soldier, in uniform, singing a solo; we hear a chorus of extraordinary ability. As the last notes fade away a handsome young preacher (played by Carlton Moss) turns from his prepared text to introduce representative soldiers in the pews.[29] The camera cuts to a sailor, a soldier, even a beautiful light-skinned WAC, "Private Parks, First Class." "First class, indeed," says the preacher with undisguised pride.

The well-dressed, attentive congregation, full of servicemen in uniform, inspires Moss to reflect on the achievements of black Americans: newsreel clips show Joe Louis with his "American fist" recovering the heavyweight championship from Max Schmeling; black athletes defeat Nazi Germany's best at the 1936 Berlin Olympic games. It seems that black America is showing the world what democratic competition can do, and what happens when a Negro gets a fair chance to compete on equal terms. Moss reminds his congregation that the war is being fought to defend the American way of life. A Nazi training film shows Schmeling learning to be a parachutist; more newsreel footage shows Joe Louis, in uniform, going through Army basic training. Moss produces a copy of *Mein Kampf* and reads a passage in which Hitler describes the futility of teaching a "half-ape" to be a doctor or lawyer (see Figure 46.1). The congregation looks appropriately shocked to learn what the Nazis really think about Negroes.

Moss then reflects upon the heroism of blacks in earlier American wars. To recreate historic battles, Heisler used neither complete reenactment nor mere reproduction of old paintings and engravings. The shooting script called for transparencies or "glass shots" made from contemporary illustrative materials, while black and white actors dressed as soldiers passed in the foreground carrying powder and shot to their cannons.[30] The "glass shots," intercut with interracial closeups for emphasis, illuminated the black role in earlier wars, along with the settlement of the West. To Negroes the very idea of any black past other than slavery was for the most part a complete surprise. Here was visual proof that America owed its freedom to its entire population. This lesson in race pride made an indelible impression on those whose education included virtually no mention of black history.

For events after 1898, it was possible to use newsreel footage. Flickering images drawn from archival film allowed audiences to see documentary evidence of Negroes in Cuba and laborers digging the Panama Canal. A wonderful character ("Hi, I'm Jim"—who looks old enough to have fought in 1898) is superimposed over the documentary footage. He tells us about "cleaning up" in Cuba and digging the canal. He sounds so matter-of-fact that we are swept along into accepting the unspoken message: patriotic, dependable blacks have been working to keep America safe all along. For World War I there is footage of the 369th National Guard in the uniform of the French Army. The historical account ends with a staged sequence featuring a black sailor, sure to be taken for Dorie

Miller, a steward in the segregated Navy who had taken up a fallen gunner's weapon at Pearl Harbor and became the first black in World War II to fire at the enemy. The Japanese attack provides Moss with an opportunity to make another point: "And there are those who will still tell you that Japan is the saviour of the colored races," thereby suggesting the opposite—neither Hitler nor Hirohito have anything but contempt for Negroes.

The film now makes an abrupt transition from past performance to present opportunities. Mrs. Bronson, a handsome middle-aged woman wearing a suit and small fur stole (a scrupulous middle-class image in keeping with Donald Young's prescription), stands up in church to read a letter from her son who has just become an Army officer. As she reads the letter, the film cuts to scenes of basic training. Young Bronson is the very picture of light skinned, muscular leadership. He drills in the snow, goes to a segregated dance, meets a nice young girl, and back at camp, is introduced to the poetry of Langston Hughes. After soldiering all week Bronson heads for church on Sunday. The camp chaplain offers a pep talk describing improbably broad opportunities for blacks to get into Officer Candidates School and even West Point; Army units are shown as eager to accept black recruits (see Figure 46.2). The film ends back in Mrs. Bronson's church as the congregation rises to sing "Onward Christian Soldiers" which segues into "Joshua Fit' de Battle ob Jericho," over which we see a montage of marching men and women. The songs and images combine in a final emotional appeal for wartime unity.

At first, *The Negro Soldier* was intended solely for black troops. Donald Young wrote an official manual, *Leadership of Negro Troops*, to be used by the white officers who commanded black units in World War II.[31] But even before the film was released, two of the four groups, the social scientists and the blacks, began to agitate for wider military and civilian distribution.

Such talk resulted in an extraordinary amount of official debate. The film's director, Stuart Heisler, remembers representatives of more than fifty federal offices screening the rough cut and reading revisions of the script.[32] Nobody seemed sure what the impact of the film might be on

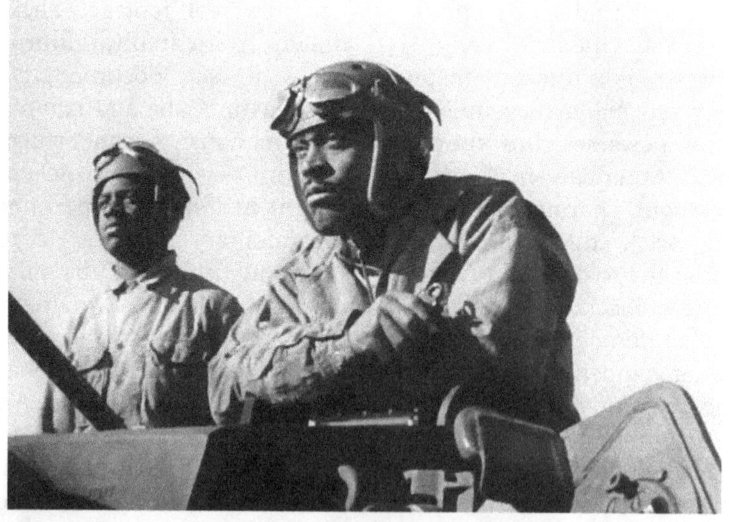

FIGURE 46.2 Location footage of black troops revealed a wide range of military specialties and roles for blacks, along with continuing segregation. Screen capture from digital file.

black soldiers. To learn if the film would encourage rioting by Negro troops, Heisler, Moss, and Charles Dollard, the Research Branch representative, took their product to a "Negro camp outside of San Diego." The commander, who "knew" his men, insisted that the film would provoke violence. He brought in a special unit of nearly one hundred military police to prevent trouble. The result was hardly what the commander expected. Enthusiastic black recruits threatened to riot unless *all* Negro troops on the post saw the film.[33]

White soldiers offered a different problem. Here another group, the Army leadership, took a direct hand to ensure that the final product would be safe enough to appeal to the widest possible audience. Anatole Litvak, Heisler's superior in the Capra unit, hand-carried the completed "answer print" of *The Negro Soldier* to the Pentagon in October 1943. Marshall, Stimson, Osborn, the head of the Army's Bureau of Public Relations, General A. D. Surles, and Assistant Secretary of War John J. McCloy personally viewed the film. On November 1, after much discussion, Litvak received a detailed memorandum outlining specific changes intended to make the film more factually accurate and to mollify racial sensibilities of audiences.[34] Heisler had already been ordered to cut the footage showing men "under the command of Negro officers."[35] War Department officials insisted that a section of the film dealing with World War I include "a small amount of footage which would show that Negroes did something other than engage in combat in the front line." Emphasis on black combat experience in the current war also had to be "toned down" since it "would give an erroneous conception of the overall job of the Army." Finally, every nicety of customary racial etiquette was to be preserved. For example: "The sequence showing a [white] nurse or physiotherapy attendant massaging the [black] soldier's back will be eliminated."[36] This momentary visual breach of racial and sexual taboos could not be shown though the Army did use white staff to treat injured black soldiers.

In January 1944 the Army agreed to use the film in basic orientation for Negro troops, while continuing to debate further distribution.[37] The Research Branch conducted a "scientific" survey to see what statistics might say about wider reception. This was the wartime pattern: what individual commander's prejudice could compete with the scientifically measured opinion of the entire Army? The survey reported that almost ninety percent of black soldiers questioned wanted the film shown to white soldiers as well as black. Almost eighty percent thought civilians should see it. The surprise came in the white response, for almost eighty percent of those questioned favored showing the film to both black and white troops; nearly eighty percent wanted the film shown to white civilians.[38] Still, some military leaders insisted that the film be accompanied by printed material designed to blunt the message of racial tolerance. The Research Branch, particularly through the efforts of Donald Young, successfully insisted that the film stand alone.[39] In spite of itself, and in opposition to the wishes of some military leaders, the United States Army had a film based on social engineering precepts to teach racial brotherhood.

In the end, OF 51 became "mandatory" viewing for all troops at replacement centers within the United States.[40] Between February 1944 and August 1945, when the order was rescinded, almost every black in the Army and Air Corps saw this film; millions of white soldiers also viewed it as part of I&E's standard orientation program.[41] Though overseas combat zones could not enforce mandatory viewing for all soldiers, the Army still used the film late in 1946. Harry Truman's 1948 desegregation order marked the end of OF 51's official usefulness.[42]

The film had been made for military audiences. What would happen if it joined the ranks of a few other Army orientation films (including *Prelude to War* and *The Battle of Russia* from the *Why We Fight* series) and found commercial distribution to movie theaters all over the United States? Would white patrons pay regular admission to see a film about racial tolerance? Distributors felt sure the answer was no. Blacks thought otherwise; they recognized that the official nature of the film would make it an effective weapon in the struggle for civil rights if it were widely seen by civilians.

The first step was official approval from Elmer Davis, head of the Office of War Information (OWI).[43] He and several members of his staff screened *The Negro Soldier* and demanded yet a few further changes. Davis concluded that the film "probably would be perfectly passable in any theatres whatever in the North; and that the only risks . . . would be attendant upon showing it in, say, Atlanta, or some such Southern center." One member of his staff introduced a new area of possible opposition—whether or not "the Negro press" might consider the film "just icing."[44]

OWI fears led in January 1944 to a private showing at the Pentagon for nearly two hundred black journalists. Frank Capra, though he had little to do with the film, arrived in Washington to show "his" production. Most of the audience wrote favorable—even glowing—reviews, passing over the omission of slavery and the realities of discrimination. Activist groups such as the NAACP and the National Negro Congress praised the film as "the best ever done" and called for its widespread distribution.[45] In April 1944 the Army officially released the film to civilian audiences.

It was one thing to make the film available to civilians, another to have it seen. From April 1944, the fate of *The Negro Soldier* increasingly turned on the activities of blacks, in particular Carlton Moss and Truman K. Gibson, now Stimson's Civilian Aide for Negro Affairs. Both proved adept at rallying Hollywood opinion in the film's favor, and overcoming a mixed critical response. Bosley Crowther of the *New York Times* thought the film "questionable" because it "sugar coats" and "discreetly avoids the more realistic race problems." James Agee, the Southerner who covered cinema for the liberal *Nation*, termed the film "pitifully, painfully mild" although he recognized that blandness made it more saleable. Few white critics shared Agee's insight into black attitudes toward the film. "Straight and decent as far as it goes," he wrote, it "means a good deal, I gather to most of the Negro soldiers who have seen it." Moss agreed, telling a *Time* reporter that the movie would "mean more to Negroes than most white men could imagine."[46]

Civilian distribution depended on resolving a longstanding debate between the Army and the War Activities Committee (WAC), the group representing commercial distributors in negotiations for circulation of government films.[47] *The Negro Soldier*, at 43 minutes, or roughly half of normal feature length, would remain unpopular with bookers because no matter what its merits, the film required a change in the standard length of programs.[48] To combine an educational film of "excessive" length with OF 51's subject seemingly restricted viewing to black theaters.[49] But Army enthusiasm prevailed over WAC opposition. *The Negro Soldier* was released to those theaters which requested it from a national total of 16,203 "pledged" commercial houses. Accurate attendance records, kept in part to stave off possible government regulation, revealed that in calendar year 1944 the film was a commercial bust. It played in only 1,819 theaters in contrast to most OWI shorts which played in more than 13,000 theaters, or the Air Corps combat film *Memphis Belle* (in Technicolor), seen in over 12,000 theaters the same year.[50] Because of its awkward length, fears of resentment of its special pleading, and the normally low grosses generated by slack summer attendance, OF 51 in its first run seems to have done more poorly than any other film released by the government for commercial distribution.

Leading Hollywood producers, urged on by Moss and Gibson, tried another way of beefing up attendance. Litvak and Heisler re-cut the film to a 20-minute two-reeler, enabling the Army to offer two lengths of the same film to civilians, beginning in July 1944.[51] As OF 24, but with the same title, the film is virtually identical to OF 51, though omitting entirely Mrs. Bronson and her son's experience at Officer Candidates School. At the end a few added shots of black pilots and black construction workers in India helped give a wider visual sense of Negro involvement in the war. Only *The Negro Soldier*, of all films produced by the military during the war, was available in two versions at the same time. Moss estimated that possibly 5,000 theaters eventually showed the shorter version.

Civilian distribution still faced one last hurdle, a lawsuit from a white Jewish filmmaker who had also made a movie about race pride. Jack Goldberg, president of The Negro Marches On, Inc., for years had produced "race movies," a genre of cheaply mounted productions for distribution in Negro neighborhood houses. He sued in federal court to restrain the WAC from booking *The Negro Soldier*, claiming that it competed unfairly with his own film, *We've Come a Long, Long Way*, which dealt with roughly the same subject. Goldberg's film possessed a certain credibility in black circles owing to its sponsorship by Elder Solomon Lightfoot Michaux, a radio evangelist well-known to Negro listeners.[52]

At this point the NAACP entered the controversy. Roy Wilkins helped Truman Gibson assemble a "confidential" list of white liberals to "assist distribution," including Nelson Rockfeller, Fiorello La Guardia, Cardinal Spellman, and the *New Yorker's* Harold Ross. NAACP special counsel Thurgood Marshall joined Gibson in filing an *amicus curiae* brief, insisting that the WAC provided "the only available medium" for circulating a film that "proceeded on the premise that racial prejudices which divide our population will have their effect minimized by the dissemination of facts." Marshall and Walter White then prodded the liberal Hollywood Writers' Mobilization into endorsing the film as a "real contribution to national unity" and a repudiation of "racist lies."[53] Gibson and Moss arranged for gala Hollywood receptions in May and June 1944 to drum up support for both versions of "their" film. Black actress Lena Horne praised the film and major Hollywood producers provided blurbs, most more convincing than that offered by Columbia's Harry Cohn: "the greatest War Department Picture ever made."[54]

The NAACP, which had nothing to do with the making of OF 51, now promoted the film as if it were its own. "NAACP Deplores Legal Action Against Film *The Negro Soldier*," declared a press release which claimed that Goldberg's film was "insulting to Negroes," in contrast to *The Negro Soldier's* "enormous potentialities for good in stimulating the morale of American Negroes and in educating white Americans." White also persuaded liberal Jewish groups to repudiate Goldberg, thereby avoiding the appearance of a "Jewish vs. Negro situation." Goldberg was termed a longtime exploiter of black audiences. In the end Goldberg lost in court and settled for a few days' "clearance" to allow his film a brief run and give him a chance to get back part of his investment.[55]

The Negro press continued its campaign to gain wider distribution. It urged the National Council of Negro Women "to rally the public and force the special film, *The Negro Soldier*, to be released in full to audiences of both races." In Los Angeles press support led to a preview under the auspices of the mayor's Civic Unity Committee at a leading hotel.[56] Educators invoked the arguments of the scientific sample to promote the film. They tested OF 51 as a tool for teaching "inter-cultural education" and "living together," and ranked it third in effectiveness out of seventeen films studied.[57]

The campaign soon included plans for distributing the film to civilian audiences outside the commercial circuit. The coming of age of 16 millimeter film (at the time still called "substandard" film) proved a major means for spreading government information throughout the country. Indeed World War II marked the apogee of non-commercial distribution of films in the United States.[58] The OWI and the Army's Public Relations Bureau waged a tedious administrative battle over distribution. In April 1944 the OWI won the right to distribute the long version (OF 51) nontheatrically to a network of film departments in public libraries, schools, and colleges in every state.[59] The Film Library of the Museum of Modern Art in New York, which developed educational distribution of "classic" films in the late 1930s, helped promote *The Negro Soldier* by including it in a special series of Capra-unit films shown in New York to capacity audiences in July 1944.[60]

Black groups throughout the country were soon enthusiastic over "their" film and eagerly booked it for church and civic functions.[61] *The Educational Film Guide for 1945*, a standard guidebook for users of documentary film, praised OF 51's technical quality: "good photographs, a nice variety of scene, some flashes of humor and excellent musical background."[62] The film's superb technical quality made it the hit of the season in nontheatrical distribution. The film bureau of the Cleveland Public Library, for example, indicated frequent requests for the film in its monthly reports to the OWI, listing such groups as the "Woodbridge School & PTA" and the "Zion Methodist Church."[63] Not every report indicates attendance figures—nor are such figures capable of verification—but yearly estimated attendance at OWI films distributed nontheatrically numbered over 7.5 million, and that represents only domestic distribution.[64] The film was also used extensively in Latin America, particularly in Haiti, with its predominantly black population.[65]

With the release of OF 51, Moss lobbied for a second film, eventually called *Teamwork* (OF 14), a more self-conscious advocate for racial integration. The motion picture shows blacks in combat against the Nazis. A sequence shot on a Hollywood back lot has Nazi cannoneers shell black troops with a flurry of leaflets reminding them of the "lousiest" jobs and housing awaiting them at the war's end. The blacks toss aside the flyers, as they advance under fire. The narrator grants that "nobody thinks the United States is perfect."[66] Joe Louis is quoted as saying "there's nothing wrong with America that Hitler could fix!" A timid, much less elaborate production than OF 51, *Teamwork's* modest "message" about integration nevertheless alarmed some in the Army. The film received belated military release only in January 1946, thanks in part to the efforts of the NAACP. Roy Wilkins attended a sneak preview of the film at the Signal Corps Photographic Center on Long Island. Wilkins lobbied for release and the NAACP felt the film could "do much to promote racial unity *now and for the future*." By the summer of 1946, *Teamwork* also went into civilian distribution.[67]

What in retrospect can be concluded about the direct and indirect impact of *The Negro Soldier* on postwar American race relations? We believe this film represented a watershed in the use of film to promote racial tolerance. *The Negro Soldier's* influence can be seen in three areas: promotion, production, and the demise of "race films."

1) Promotion. Black pressure groups learned that film was a tool for social change. The Army did not recognize how much the technical quality of the film suggested to viewers a military commitment to equality of opportunity. The existence of such a film indicated change within the Army—why

not also in the civilian world? Carlton Moss, handsome and eloquent, was the educated preacher who moved his listeners with facts and force of logic. Mrs. Bronson, in her suit and fur, seemed to prove that a black mother was the same as other middle-class women, save for a slightly darker skin color. Moreover, the Army considered Mrs. Bronson's son a valuable asset and trained him thoroughly. His hard work paid off in an officer's commission. Was not this visual evidence of equality of opportunity? How about Private Parks, First Class—wasn't she attractive and competent no matter what her racial background? And that fine church and all those well-dressed people who took their civic responsibilities seriously—all America could see these were valuable citizens. Such images provided visual proof of why racial equality was not just morally but logically justified. Why not everywhere? As Moss put it, he set out to "ignore what's wrong with the army and tell what's right with my people," which, he hoped, would cause whites to ask "what right have we to hold back a people of that calibre?"[68]

The NAACP now understood how potent indirect messages in films could be. It produced a brochure promoting "audio-visual aids" for "teaching democracy." It formed a new national committee to deal with matters of film propaganda and encouraged film distributors to circulate inventories of films urging "tolerance" and "brotherhood" such as *Teamwork* and *Americans All*, produced by *The March of Time*. The National Conference of Christians and Jews joined what promised to be a new movement, discussed in journals with titles like the *16mm Reporter*.[69] Getting films off of shelves and before commercial and non-commercial audiences was a specific goal capable of fulfillment by any number of black pressure groups. The NAACP could echo the sentiment of an earlier enthusiast for social experimentation: "I have seen the future and it works."

2) Production of "message films." A black journal's headline at the time of OF 51's release makes the point: "Army Shows Hollywood the Way."[70] The postwar era of feature films with "messages" about racial liberalism can be traced directly to the humane, natural realism of *The Negro Soldier*, though it would be simplistic to insist that a single film was the sole cause of every "message" motion picture produced after 1945. A number of examples demonstrate the connection.[71] Jester Hairston arranged the choral parts for *The Negro Soldier*. After 1945, Dimitri Tiomkin, who wrote OF 51's score, used Hairston for entire films, a startling change from "before the war [when] the studios only called us when they had 'Negro music' to be sung."[72] Stuart Heisler, director of *The Negro Soldier*, went on to make *Storm Warning* (1950), a harsh indictment of the Ku Klux Klan. Ben Maddow came from a background in wartime documentary film to write the screenplay for Faulkner's *Intruder in the Dust* (1949), an urgent plea for mutual respect across racial lines in the South. Carl Foreman, who began the war by writing the Dead End Kids' *Spooks Run Wild*, worked for Frank Capra's film unit. Afterwards he wrote *Home of the Brave* (1949), in which the black hero was named "Mossy" as a tribute to a wartime friendship with Carleton Moss. Stanley Kramer, the producer of *Home of the Brave*, had worked at the Signal Corps Photographic Unit on Long Island during the war. His entire postwar career was devoted to "message" films, including *The Defiant Ones* (1958) and *Guess Who's Coming to Dinner?* (1967), both vehicles for Sidney Poitier and racial liberalism.[73]

3) The demise of "race movies." The failure of Jack Goldberg's suit signalled an end for the "race movie." When feature films began to depict blacks as human beings, there was no longer a need for third-rate films designed especially for Negro audiences. After 1945 it was soon hard for anyone, black or white, to remember when as a matter of course separate-but-unequal "race movies" were a staple of the American scene. The humanity of *The Negro Soldier* had done its work well.

The historian is always interested in cause and effect, but perhaps a sense of irony is essential in understanding the impact of *The Negro Soldier.* Who would have thought that the Army, officially committed to segregation, would end up with a film which symbolically promoted the logic of integration? Who would have predicted that a documentary-style film about black history and opportunities for military advancement would spawn a generation of feature films calling for racial tolerance? Who would have thought that a military orientation film would make black civilians glow with pride? Minority pressure groups cannot help appreciating such ironies. Merely to show a film is no guarantee of anything, but screening a "message" film for a variety of audiences clearly can achieve results not originally conceived of. This is arguably the symbiotic potential of all mass media, a potential realized in the midst of total war, when the Army used film to show not just Hollywood but all America that civil rights was not only a moral but also a logical necessity. Such conclusions led Walter Fisher, one of a handful of black officers assigned to I&E, to remember this pioneering film a third of a century later. Although "we knew ... the day of jubilee had not arrived," he considers *The Negro Soldier* "one of the finest things that ever happened to America."[74]

Acknowledgments

We would like to thank the Woodrow Wilson International Center for Scholars, Smithsonian Institution, Washington, D. C., for support in preparing this essay.

NOTES

1. Quoted in Thomas Cripps, "The Noble Black Savage: A Problem in the Politics of Television Art," *Journal of Popular Culture,* 8 (Spring 1975), 687–95.
2. See Ulysses Lee, *The Employment of Negro Troops: Special Studies* (Washington, D. C.: Office of Chief of Military History, U.S. Army, G.P.O., 1966), a volume in the official series, *The United States Army in World War II;* see also Richard M. Dalfiume, *Desegregation of the United States Armed Forces: Fighting on Two Fronts, 1939–1953* (Columbia, Mo.: Univ. of Missouri Press, 1969); and Alan M. Osur, *Blacks in the Army Air Forces During World War II: The Problem of Race Relations* (Washington, D. C.: Office of Air Force History, G.P.O., 1977).
3. Roger Manvell, *Films and the Second World War* (South Brunswick, N. J.: A. S. Barnes, 1974); David Culbert, "Walt Disney's Private Snafu: The Use of Humor in World War II Army Film," in Jack Salzman, ed., *Prospects: An Annual Journal of American Cultural Studies,* 1 (Dec. 1975), 80–96, and Richard Dyer MacCann, *The People's Films: A Political History of U.S. Government Motion Pictures* (New York: Hastings House, 1973).
4. For an introduction see Richard Griffith, "The Use of Films by the U.S. Armed Forces," in Paul Rotha, *Documentary Film* (3d ed.; London: Faber and Faber, 1952), 344–58; on Marshall see Forrest C. Pogue, *George C. Marshall:* Organizer of Victory 1943–1945 (New York: Viking, 1975), 91–92; Frank Capra, *The Name Above the Title: An Autobiography* (New York: Macmillan, 1971), 325–70; and three official histories from *The United States in World War II*: Dulany Terrett, *The Signal Corps: The Emergency (To December 1941)* (Washington, D. C.: Office of the Chief of Military History, U.S. Army, G.P.O., 1956), 78–82, 223–30; George Raynor Thompson et al., *The Signal Corps: The Test (December 1941 to July 1943)* (Washington, D. C., 387–426; and George Raynor Thompson and Dixie R. Harris, *The Signal Corps: The Outcome (Mid-1943 Through 1945)* (Washington, D. C., 1966), 540–79.
5. There is a vast literature about morale and its importance. See Wesley Frank Craven and James Lea Cate, eds., *Services Around the World,* vol. VII of *The Army Air Forces in World War II* (Chicago: Univ. of Chicago Press, 1958), 431–76, for a good introduction to the problem. The scientific study of morale was an outgrowth of World War I. See Edward L. Munson, *The Management of Men: A Handbook on the Systematic Development of Morale and the Control of Human Behavior* (New York: H. Holtand Co. 1921); Munson's son became Capra's superior in I&E; he too wrote a widely used guide to morale: Colonel Edward Lyman Munson, Jr., *Leadership for American Army Leaders, in The Fighting Forces Series* (rev. ed.; Washington, D. C.: The Infantry Journal, 1944).
6. Production files for "Prelude to War" are located in 062.2 ocsigo, Box 1, Records of the Chief Signal Officer, RG 111, Film Section, National Archives, where a viewing print may also be found [hereafter FS-NA]. See also 062.2 ocsigo, Box 12, A52-248, Washington National Records Center, Suitland, Maryland, for additional production material [hereafter WNRC-Suitland]. Concerning the optimism of Capra's films see Robert Sklar, *Movie-Made America: A Cultural History of American Movies* (New York: Vintage Books, 1976), 205–14.

7. Claude A. Barnett, head of the Associated Negro Press, to Victor Roudin, copy, March 26, 1953, in Barnett MSS, Chicago Historical Society, Chicago, Ill. As one black critic suggested, "Is there only one Negro family in the war and is the only thing they are doing farming?" William Ashby, Springfield [Ill.] Urban League, to Elmer Davis, Box 1431, entry 264, RG 208. Prints of both films are located in FS-NA. An official OWI analysis of *Negro Colleges in Wartime* is located in Box 1490, entry 271, RG 208; the script is in Box 1569, entry 302, RG 208; Box 1571, entry 302, RG 208, has nearly fifty photographs "taken for Negro Colleges but scenes not included in film"; stills from *Henry Browne, Farmer* are in Box 1569, entry 302, RG 208; the lack of appeal of *Negro Colleges in Wartime* is discussed in "Distribution of and Use of OWI Non-theatrical Films in April 1943," Box 1483, entry 268, RG 208, where only one film of all in OWI distribution had fewer bookings per print. All in WNRC-Suitland.
8. [Donald Young], *Leadership and the Negro Soldier*, Manual M5 (Oct. 1944), 4. In keeping with wartime practice the author's name is not given. Culbert interview with Donald Young, Macungie, Pa., February 13, 1977. A copy of Manual M5 is located in Box 1011, Records of the Assistant Secretary of Defense, Manpower Personnel & Reserve, Record Group 330, Modern Military Records, National Archives, Washington, D. C. [hereafter MMR-NA].
9. Secret Minutes, Meeting of General Council, May 31, 1943, 3–4, 334 cos, Box 30, Records of the Office of Chief of Staff, RG 165, MMR-NA.
10. Lee, *Employment of Negro Troops*, 330.
11. For a fine discussion of I&E see Neil Minihan, "A History of the Information and Education Division," manuscript loaned to Culbert. Also helpful is "Study of I&E Activities in World War II," typewritten, copy in Box 1, Francis Spaulding MSS, Archives of Harvard University, Cambridge, Mass.
12. Interview with Donald Young, February 13, 1977; telephone interview with Frederick Osborn, November 5, 1976; telephone interview with Paul Horgan, November 10, 1976; Osborn, *Preface to Eugenics* (New York: Harper, 1940).
13. Culbert interview with Donald Young, February 13, 1977; letter of Young to Culbert, December 27, 1976.
14. Stouffer publicized his attitude surveys in *What the Soldier Thinks*, complete copies of which are found in RG 330, MMR-NA, along with supporting unpublished data. In summary form they appear in Samuel A. Stouffer, et al., *Studies in Social Psychology in World War II: Vol. I, The American Soldier: Adjustment During Army Life; Vol. II, Combat and Its Aftermath; Vol. III, Experiments on Mass Communication; Vol. IV, Measurement and Prediction* (Princeton, N. J.: Princeton Univ. Press, 1949–50). The methodology of these surveys is brilliantly attacked in Jacques Ellul, *Propaganda: The Formation of Men's Attitudes* (New York: Vintage, 1973), in particular 259–302.
15. A good discussion of social engineering is found in Robert K. Merton, *Social Theory and Social Structure* (rev. ed; Glencoe, Ill.: Free Press, 1957), in particular chapter 16, "Science and Democratic Social Structure." See also Alvin M. Weinberg, "Can Technology Replace Social Engineering," in Albert H. Teich, ed., *Technology and Man's Future* (New York: St. Martins, 1972), 27–35. For the origin of the term see H. S. Person, "Engineering," in Edwin R. A. Seligman, et al., eds., *Encyclopedia of the Social Sciences*, volume V-VI (New York, 1931), 542.
16. For Young's pre-war work see his *Motion Pictures: A Study in Social Legislation* (Philadelphia: Westbrook, 1922); he also edited two special issues of the *Annals of the American Academy of Political and Social Science: The American Negro*, 90 (1928) and *Minority Peoples in a Nation at War*, 223 (1942).
17. For a good discussion of the problem see Paul F. Lazarsfeld and Robert K. Merton, "The Psychological Analysis of Propaganda," in *Writers' Congress. The Proceedings of the Conference Held in October 1943 under the Sponsorship of the Hollywood Writers' Mobilization and the University of California* (Berkeley, Cal., 1944), 362–80.
18. Thomas Cripps, *Slow Fade to Black: The Negro in American Film, 1900–1942* (New York: Oxford Univ. Press, 1977).
19. *Leadership and the Negro Soldier, 4*.
20. Cripps, *Slow Fade to Black*, 375–76.
21. Zanuck to screenwriter Eric Knight, July 22, 1942, Eric Knight MSS, Quakertown, Penna.
22. "Suggested Motion Picture of the Negro in the U.S. Army," n.d. [Mar. 1942], copy in Young to Culbert, December 27, 1976; the final memorandum is discussed in Lee, *Employment of Negro Troops*, 387; Culbert interview with Donald Young, February 13, 1977.
23. Capra, *Name Above the Title*, 337.
24. Carlton Moss to Donald Young, August 26, 1942; Box 224, Records of the Civilian Aide to the Secretary of War (Hastie File), RG 107, MMR-NA.
25. Cripps interview with Frank Capra, La Quinta, Cal., December 31, 1976; Axel Madsen, *William Wyler: The Authorized Biography* (New York: Crowell. 1973), 224–25.
26. Cripps telephone interview with Stuart Heisler, February 17, 1977.
27. Cripps interviews with Carlton Moss, Hollywood, Cal., June 1970; Boston, Mass., April 1973; Iowa City, Iowa, July, 1974. Moss attended Morgan State College and wrote radio scripts for Dr. Channing Tobias, head of the black YMCA.
28. A copy of the original version of OF 51 is found in FS-NA.
29. A complete copy of the final photographic scenario, May 31, 1943, plus an earlier version dated September 17, 1942, may be found in proj. 6022, 062.2 ocsigo, Box 12, A52-248, WNRC-Suitland. Moss ended up playing the preacher himself only after rejecting a succession

of Hollywood Negroes who seemed tied to traditional black acting styles.

30. The script's shooting instructions for achieving this result are instructive: "(NOTE: This scene will be used as a transparency to work in two or three Negro soldiers with white soldiers passing in the foreground carrying shot and powder for cannons.)"; "(NOTE: Beginning with the Revolutionary period, down through all the wars, including World War I IMPRESSIONISTIC CLOSEUPS—white and Negro—mostly recognizable Negro faces—will be shot for dressing up and emphasizing that there were Negro soldiers in all of these wars.)" Script, May 31, 1943, p. 12, A52-248, WNRC-Suitland. The official production budget under the heading "Bits and Extras" called for "Battle of New Orleans. 5 Negroes 1 day at $10.50 a day." Copy in 333.9, ig, Box 1160, Records of the Inspector General, RG 159, WNRC-Suitland.
31. Osur, *Blacks in the Army Air Forces*, 80-81, notes opposition within the Army to issuing Manual M5. The foreword to *Leadership and the Negro Soldier*, p. iv, specifically suggests that *The Negro Soldier* be shown as part of the course of instruction, "preferably the second meeting," and also suggests, p. 64, that one of the Capra *Why We Fight* films, *Divide and Conquer*, be shown to combat racial "hate" rumors within the United States. Gunnar Myrdal's *An American Dilemma: The Negro Problem and Modern Democracy* (New York: Harper, 1944), is given particular emphasis in the manual's list of suggested readings, p. 101.
32. Cripps telephone interview with Heisler, February 17, 1977; *The National Film Board News Letter*, February 4, 1944, 2, reported that "in Washington there are about sixty different bureaus or sub-bureaus of the U.S. Government concerned with either the production, distribution, or utilization of films." Copy in Box 1486, entry 269, RG 208, WNRC-Suitland.
33. Cripps interview with Heisler, February 17, 1977.
34. Munson to Litvak, November 1, 1943, 062.2 cos, Box 304, Records of the Chief of Staff, Troop Information & Education, RG 319, MMR-NA.
35. Cripps telephone interview with Heisler, Feb. 17, 1977.
36. Munson to Litvak, Nov. 1, 1943, Box 304, RG 319, MMR-NA.
37. Karl Marks to John Hubbell, Jan. 12, 1944, copy in OF 51 production files, 062.2 ocsigo, Box 14, RG 111, FS-NA.
38. Report B-102, "Reactions of Negro and White Soldiers to the film *The Negro Soldier*, April 17, 1944. 439 blacks and 510 whites at Camp Pickett, Virginia, previewed the film. In addition almost 91 percent of the whites described it as "very good." Copy in Box 992, RG 330, MMR-NA.
39. Memorandum, Maj. Gen. Ray Porter, Assistant Chief of Staff G-3, to Osborn, May 4, 1944, 413.53 ag, Box 3241, Records of the Adjutant General, RG 407, MMR-NA; Karl Marks to ocsigo, Apr. 15, 1944, 062.2 ocsigo, Box 44, A45-196, WNRC-Suitland.
40. War Department Circular 208, May 25, 1944, 413.56 ag, Box 3241, RG 407, MMR-NA.
41. War Department Circular 283, September 19, 1945, 413.53 ag, Box 3237, RG 407, MMR-NA.
42. Brig. Gen. C. T. Lanham, Director, I&E Div., to Karl Korter, June 6, 1946, 062.2 cos, Box 374, RG 319, MMR-NA.
43. A good introduction to the OWI is Allan M. Winkler, *The Politics of Propaganda: The Office of War Information, 1942–1945* (New Haven: Yale Univ. Press, 1978); for Davis' pre-war radio experience see David Holbrook Culbert, *News for Everyman: Radio and Foreign Affairs in Thirties America* (Westport, Ct.: Greenwood, 1976), 125–52.
44. Paul Horgan to Lyman Munson, Nov. 6, 1943, 062.2 cos, Box 304, RG 319, MMR-NA.
45. Capra, *Name Above the Title*, 358–62. Mabel R. Staupers, NAACP, to Maj. Gen. A. D. Surles, February 25, 1944; and telegram, National Negro Congress to Surles, February 19, 1944, RG 107, MMR-NA.
46. *The New York Times*, Apr. 22, 1944; *Nation*, March 11, 1944, 316; *Time*, March 27, 1944, 94, 96.
47. For an excellent discussion of how the WAC functioned see mimeographed analysis of theater booking practices prepared for War Manpower Commission, n.d. [July 1944] in Taylor Mills to Francis Harmon, July 22, 1944, Box 1488, entry 269, RG 208; see also Mills to Truman Gibson, May 1, 1944, Box 1484, entry 268, RG 208, both in WNRC-Suitland.
48. War Activities Committee, *Movies at War 1945* (New York: War Activity Committee, 1945), 42, copy enclosed in Francis Harmon to Culbert, January 26, 1977; information about exact bookings of OF 51 in each of thirty-one exchanges is found in Box 1485, entry 269, RG 208, WNRC-Suitland.
49. Peter Noble. *The Negro in Films* (New York: Amo Press, 1970), 99–100 lists numbers of black theaters by state.
50. Telegram, Lehman Katz to Lyman Munson, n.d. [June 19, 1944]; unsigned memorandum, n.d. [June 28, 1944], both in proj. 6024, 062.2 ocsigo, Box 12, A52-248, WNRC-Suitland. The short and long versions were both made available to commercial distributors in July 1944. Publicity release WAC, July 21, 1944, copy in Box 1, Albert Deane MSS, Museum of Modern Art Film Library, New York, N. Y. A print of 24 is available from the Army Training Support Center, Tobyhanna, Pa.
51. "Weekly Report on Film Production Activities," Lehman Katz to Paul Horgan, May 3, 1944, 319.1 cos, Box 370, RG 319, MMR-NA. Specific suggestions from the producers are quoted in Gibson to Anatole Litvak, Apr. 14, 1944, proj. 6024, 062.2 ocsigo, Box 12, A52-248, WNRC-Suitland.
52. The Goldberg film was based on the OWI pamphlet *Negroes and the War*. Jack Goldberg to Francis Harmon, February 28, 1944, Box 1488, entry 269, RG 208.
53. Wilkins to Gibson, January 3, 14, 15; February 1, 3, 1944; Wilkins to Maj. Homer B. Roberts, February 9, 1944; United States District Court,

Southern District of New York, *Negro Marches On*, Plaintiff, v. War Activities Committee, Defendants, copy, n.d.; Gibson, *amicus curiae* brief, 2 pages, n.d.; Thurgood Marshall to Pauline Lauber, executive secretary, Hollywood Writers' Mobilization, May 2, 1944; Robert Rossen to Frank Capra, March 30, 1944, all in Box 277, Records of the National Association for the Advancement of Colored People, Manuscript Division, Library of Congress, Washington, D. C. [hereafter NAACP Records].

54. Quoted in Gibson to Anatole Litvak, April 14, 1944, proj. 6024, 062.2 ocsigo, Box 12, A52-248, WNRC-Suitland.
55. Goldberg to Congressman Andrew J., May, April 1, 1944; Goldberg to White, May 25, 1944; Ralph Cooper to White, June 8, 1944; Julia E. Baxter to Wilkins, November 4, 1943; press release dated April 27, 1944; White to Marshall, May 4, 1944; all in Box 277, NAACP Records.
56. Clippings from black press; and invitations to Moss from the Civic Unity Committee and Charles U. Shellenberg, Los Angeles YMCA, April 24, 1944, in personal files of Moss, copies sent to Cripps; trade paper clippings in Stuart Heisler MSS, Theater Arts Library, UCLA.
57. Discussed in Leonard Bloom, *California Eagle*, March 16, 1944; and Esther L. Berg, "Films to Better Human Relations," reprinted from *High Points* (New York: Brooklyn Jewish Community Council, n.d. [1945]), copies from personal files of Moss sent to Cripps.
58. RG 208 has the extensive records of OWI's Non-theatrical Division of the Motion Picture Branch. See also Film Council of America, *Sixty Years of 16mm Film 1923–1983: A Symposium* (Evanston, Ill., 1954), 148–59.
59. Curtiss Mitchell to Stanton Griffis, April 12, 1944, Box 1484, entry 268; Taylor Mills to Edgar Baker, June 8, 1944, Box 1486, entry 269; methods of distribution are discussed in C. R. Reagan to Congressman Louis Ludlow, June 10, 1944, Box 1581, entry 305; all in RG 208, WNRC-Suitland.
60. Iris Barry, Curator, Museum of Modern Art Film Library, to Rudolph Montgelas, Bureau of Public Relations, n.d. [Aug. 1944], War Dept, folder, Central Files, Museum of Modern Art Film Library, New York, N. Y. 3,250 persons saw OF 51 (from July 24–30, 1944).
61. Not every group had a choice: "Mr. E. J. Welch, D. C. Reformatory, Lorton, Va., is anxious to obtain the film, THE NEGRO SOLDIER, for a showing at the reformatory." Catherine Preston, to Joseph Brechsteen, September 13, 1944, Box 1483, entry 268, RG 208, WNRC-Suitland.
62. Dorothy E. Cook and Eva Rahbek-Smith, compilers, *Educational Film Guide* (New York, W. W. Wilson, Co., 1945), 152. This annual compilation first appeared in 1936.
63. "OWI Monthly Report of Government Film Showings for October 1944," Cleveland Public Library, Box 1640, entry 362, RG 208, WNRC-Suitland. Boxes 1624-1647 cover every state with varying degrees of completeness on a monthly basis.
64. C. R. Reagan stated that he distributed 138 of his 150 16mm prints for 15,600 showings with an estimated total audience of 3,220,000 between June 15, 1944 and January 1, 1945. Reagan to Gibson, January 4, 1945, Box 224, RG 107 (Hastie File), MMR-NA.
65. In June 1945 OF51 had been shown 69 times to 43,025 persons in Haiti. See monthly "16mm Films-Latin American Program-Summary by Title," Copy in Box 218, central files 3, Records of the Coordinator for Inter-American Affairs, RG 229, WNRC-Suitland.
66. There is a print in FS-NA. The Script and production records are found in proj. 11, 015, 062.2 ocsigo, Box 19, A52-248, WNRC-Suitland.
67. Wilkins to Surles, August 22, 1945; White to Marshall, Harrington and Wilkins, April 17, 1946; White to Arthur Mayer, May 21, 1946; White to Robert Patterson, May 9, 1946; Jeannette E. Samuelson, public relations director, Arthur Mayer and Juseph Burstyn Theatres, to "Friend," mimeographed, July 11, 1946; Ida Long, 20th-Century Fox to Fred S. Hall, December 27, 1944; Hall to White, December 29, 1944; Wilkins to Maj. Homer B. Roberts, January 2, 1945, all in Box 277; White to Wilkins, Marshall and Harrington, April 24, 1946; Wilkins to Julia E. Baxter and Harrington, October 21, 1946; White to Patterson, April 24, May 9, 1946, all in Box 274; all in NAACP Records. Samuelson to W. W. Lindsay, Army Pictorial Service, June 12, 1946, proj. 11, 015, ocsigo, Box 19, A52-248, WNRC-Suitland.
68. Moss clipping file, March 1944, in personal files of Moss, copies sent to Cripps.
69. Press clippings in Box 274, NAACP Records.
70. *Negro*, II (Sept., 1944), 94, Johnson MSS.
71. The tendency is described in Samuel Goldwyn, "How I Became Interested in Social Justice," *Opportunity*, 26 (Summer 1948), 100–01.
72. "Movie Choir," *Ebony*, 4 (Oct. 1949), 25–27.
73. Cripps telephone interview with Carlton Moss, July 8, 1977; Cripps telephone interview with Stanley Kramer, July 11, 1977; Cripps telephone interview with Carl Foreman, July 12, 1977.
74. Culbert and Cripps interview with Walter Fisher, Washington, D. C., July 12, 1977.

47

ANDRÉ BAZIN

ON *WHY WE FIGHT*

History, Documentation, and the Newsreel (1946)

War and the apocalypse it brings are at the heart of a decisive new reevaluation of documentary reporting.[1] The reason is that, during a war, facts have an exceptional amplitude and importance. They constitute a colossal *mise-en-scène* compared with which that of *Caesar and Cleopatra* (Gabriel Pascal, J. Arthur Rank; GB, 1945) or *Intolerance* (D.W. Griffith, Wark; US, 1916) looks as though it were the set for a small show touring the provinces. But these facts also constitute a real *mise-en-scène,* which is used only once. The drama also takes place "for real," for the protagonists have agreed to die at the same time as they are shot by the camera, like enslaved gladiators in the circus arena. Thanks to film, the world is cleverly saving money on the cost of its wars, since the latter are used for two purposes, history *and* cinema, thus reminding us of those less-than-conscientious producers who shoot a second film on the overpriced set of the first one. In this case, however, the world is right. War, with its harvest of dead bodies, its immense destruction, its countless migrations, its concentration camps, and its atomic bombs, leaves far behind the creative art that aims at reconstituting it.

The craze for war reports seems to me to derive from a series of psychological and perhaps also moral exigencies. Nothing suits us better than the unique event, shot on the spot, at the very moment of its creation. Such a theater of operations, when compared with the other one, has the invaluable dramatic superiority of inventing the play as it spontaneously unfolds. It is a kind of *commedia dell'arte* in which the scenario itself is always being reworked. As far as the technical means are concerned, there is no need to insist on their unerring efficiency. I would simply like to underline the fact that these means reach a cosmic scale and that they need fear only earthquakes,[2] volcanic eruptions, tidal waves, and the Apocalypse itself. I say this without irony, because I think that the number one broadcast in the series *News from Heaven* will certainly be devoted to a lengthy report on the Last Judgment, compared to which the report on the Nuremberg trials will somehow look like the Lumières' *Workers Leaving the Factory* (France, 1895).

If I were pessimistic, I would add a slightly Freudian psychological factor that I would call the "Nero complex" and define as the pleasure experienced at the sight of urban destruction. If I were optimistic, I would allude to the aforementioned moral factor and say that the cruelty and violence of war have taught us to respect—almost to make a cult of—actual facts, in comparison with which any reconstitution, even made in good faith, seems dubious, indecent, and sacrilegious.

But the war report above all fulfills another need, which explains its extreme popularity. The taste for such documentary news, combined with that for the cinema, reflects nothing if not modern man's will to be there, his need to observe history-in-the-making, not only because of political evolution, but also because of the evolution as well as irremediable intermingling of the technological means of communication and destruction. The days of total war are fatally matched by those of total history. The governments of the world have understood this very well; this is why they try to show us film reports of all their historical acts, such as the signing of treaties or the meetings of the various superpowers. As history is not at all a ballet that is fixed in advance, it is necessary to plant along the way as many cameras as possible so as to be able to film it in the act (in the historical act, of course). Thus nations at war have made provisions for the cinematic equipment of their armies, just as they have made provisions for the truly military equipment of those armies. The camera operator accompanies the bomber on its mission or the infantrymen during their landing. The armament of the fighter-bomber contains an automatic camera placed between its two machine guns. The cameraman runs as many risks as the soldier, whose death he is supposed to film even at the cost of his own life (but who cares, as long as the footage is saved!).

Most military operations now include a detailed filmic preparation. Who, then, is able to say to what extent strictly military efficiency differs from the cinematically effective spectacle that we expect from it? In a lecture on the art of the documentary, the French film critic and director Roger Leenhardt imagined that, next time, Commander Humphrey Bogart or Sergeant Spencer Tracy, playing the parts we have come to expect of them, would be the protagonists of some grand semi-fictionalized report. A crew of cameramen would be responsible for filming the course of the actual military operations that Bogart or Tracy would really command at the patriotic peril of his life. Shall we say that we haven't reached this point yet? I ask you to think about the bombing of the Bikini atoll and about the naval theater boxes nearby, to which only special guests had access (somewhat as they do for live programs on television) while numerous cameras were filming for you and me the sensational moments. I ask you also to think about the Nuremberg trials, which took place under the spotlights, as though they were the enactment of some murder trial in a detective film.

We live more and more in a world stripped bare by film, a world that tends to peel off its own image. Hundreds of thousands of screens make us watch, during the news broadcasts, the extraordinary shedding performed each day by tens of thousands of cameras. As soon as it forms, history's skin peels off again. Before the war a filmed news report used to be called "the eye of the world." Today this title is hardly pretentious as countless Bell-and-Howell lenses, placed all over the world where important events take place, prey on the picturesque, bizarre, or terrible signs of our destiny.

Among the American films released in France right after the Liberation, the only ones that have elicited unanimous approval and inspired a boundless admiration are those in the series *Why We Fight*. They had the merit not only of introducing a new tone into the art of propaganda, a measured tone that convinced without violence, at once didactic and pleasant; but also, although they consisted only of newsreels, they knew how to capture attention like a detective novel. I think that, for the film historian, *Why We Fight* has created a new genre: the edited ideological documentary. I don't mean that such a use of editing is new. The great German or Soviet editors have long since demonstrated the use one could make of it in documentaries, but the Capra films display a new originality: none of the images of which they are composed (except for a few connecting shots) were photographed for these films. The editing thus aims not so much at showing as at making a point. These are abstract, purely logical films that paradoxically use the most historical and the most concrete kind of document: the newsreel. They have established for good, with a perfection that will probably never be surpassed, that the *a posteriori* editing of film shot for other purposes can achieve the flexibility and precision of language. The best-edited documentaries up to now have been only narratives; those under consideration are speeches.

The films in the series *Why We Fight* (along with a few other American and Russian documentaries) have been made possible only by the enormous accumulation of documentary footage from the war; they are the result of the search for people and events, which more and more has become an official institution. To make these films, an enormous selection of newsreels from international archives was necessary, and these archives had to be complete enough to contain an event as intimate in its historical nature as Hitler's war dance at the Rethondes Crossroads (in northern France). One can conclude from this that Dziga Vertov's theory of the Cine-Eye is beginning to be confirmed in a sense that even the Soviet theoretician had not foreseen. But the camera, unique as it is among the picture hunters of the world, could not have reached this omnipresence in space and time by itself—an omnipresence that today permits us to catch in our nets an enormous number of documentary images. Naturally, human intervention was necessary.

It has been said how good these films are as much from a strictly cinematic point of view as from a political one. However, it turns out that probably not enough time has been spent on an analysis of the intellectual and psychological mechanism to which they owe their pedagogical efficiency. This mechanism is well worth examining, though, because its main force seems to me to be particularly dangerous for the future of the human spirit and should therefore not be excluded from any careful study of the rape of the masses.

The principle behind this type of documentary essentially consists in giving to the images the logical structure of language, and in giving to language itself the credibility and proof of photographic images. The viewer has the illusion of watching a visual demonstration, whereas this demonstration is in reality only a succession of equivocal facts held together merely by the cement of the words that accompany them. The essential part of the film is not in its projection but in the soundtrack. Shall we say that this is nothing new and that every single elucidation of a visual text, every single pedagogical documentary, does the same? I don't think so, because, in the case of the pedagogical documentary, preeminence is given either to the pictures or to the language. By contrast, a documentary on trawl fishing or on the building of a bridge shows *and* explains. There isn't any intellectual deception in the process; the intrinsic and distinct values of the words and of the pictures are preserved. Here, however, the film rests on the absolute opposite: the subordination of the events pictured on screen. Please, understand me well: I am not posing the problem of content but of form. I am denying neither the rightness of the arguments not that the right people have to try to convince us, but solely the honesty of the method used. These films, which start with a favorable *a priori*, that of using logic, reason, and the evidence of the facts, in actuality rest on a grave confusion of values, on the manipulation of psychology, credulity, and perception.

One could closely analyze a scene like the battle before Moscow (the fifth film in the series) for evidence of what I am saying. The comments on the soundtrack clearly explain the facts: the retreat of the Russians, German offensive, Russian resistance, stabilization of the front line around the latest lines of retreat, Russian counteroffensive. It is evident that a battle of this size could not be filmed *in toto*. One could pull from it only extremely fragmentary shots. The work of the editor has been essentially to choose shots from German newsreels, which supposedly had been taken right outside Moscow and which gave the impression of a victorious German offensive: rapid movement of soldiers, tank attacks, and Russian corpses in the snow. Then, in the Russian counteroffensive, the editor found impressive scenes of soldiers rushing forward, being careful, of course, to position them on screen in the opposite direction from the Nazi infantrymen in the preceding shots. The mind makes of these apparently concrete elements an abstract outline and reconstitutes an ideal battle, since it has the indubitable illusion of seeing this battle as a kind of duel. I have chosen on purpose a sequence in which such a concrete schematization was inevitable and in this case completely justified, since the Germans did indeed lose the battle. But if we extrapolate this device, we understand that we can thus be convinced we are watching events whose outcome and meaning have been completely invented. Shall we say, then, that we should have at the very least a guarantee of the filmmaker's moral honesty? In any event, this honesty can bear only on the ends, since the very structure of the means renders them illusory.

The shots used in these films are in a way straight historical facts. We spontaneously believe in facts,[3] but modern criticism has sufficiently established that in the end they have only the meaning that the human mind gives to them. Up to the discovery of photography, the "historical fact" was reconstituted from written documents: the mind and human language came into play twice in such reconstitutions: in the reconstruction of the event and in the historical thesis it was adduced to support. With film, we can refer to the facts in flesh and blood, so to speak. Could they bear witness to something else other than themselves? To something else other than the narrative of which they form a part? I think that, far from moving the historical sciences toward more objectivity, the cinema paradoxically gives them the additional power of illusion by its very realism. The invisible commentator, whom the viewer forgets while watching Capra's marvelously edited films, is tomorrow's historian of the masses, the ventriloquist of this extraordinary prosopopeia that is being prepared in all the film archives of the world and that wills the men and the events of another time back to life.

NOTES

1. [Editor's note]: This article was first published in French in *Esprit* (1946), then reprinted in Vol. 1 ("Ontologie et language") of Bazin's four-volume *Qu'est-ce que le cinema?* (Paris: Editions du Cerf. 1958–1962), pp. 31–36. It is translated into English here for the first time with the permission of Madame Janine Bazin.
2. Even more than that! An H-bomb today is equivalent to a hundred big earthquakes.
3. But then again, with a very British sort of humor John Grierson has just revealed (in the newspapers of October 13, 1958) that he was the creator of Hitler's war dance at the Rethondes Crossroads. Hitler was simply lifting his leg. By redoubling the shot, as in the anti-Nazi burlesque titled *The Lambeth Walk* (Albert de Courville. CAPAD/Pinebrook; GB, 1939), the famous English documentarian made Hitler dance his now famous Satanic jig, which has thus become "historical." [Editor's note: Bazin added this note to his 1946 article when he collected it in the first volume of his *Qu'est-ce que le cinéma* (1958).]

48

JIM LEACH

THE POETICS OF PROPAGANDA

Humphrey Jennings and *Listen to Britain* (1998)

The films made by Humphrey Jennings during World War II are widely regarded as the peak of his achievement as a filmmaker. In particular, *Listen to Britain* (1942), *Fires Were Started* (1943), and *A Diary for Timothy* (1945) have been recognized as key examples of a "poetic" style whose beautiful images and striking montage effects seem to challenge John Grierson's emphasis on the social purpose of documentary. When *Listen to Britain* was released, it was dismissed by Edgar Anstey, one of Jennings's colleagues at the Crown Film Unit, as a work of great beauty which "will not encourage anyone to do anything at all" (quoted in Sussex 144). After the war, however, it was this "poetic" approach that appealed to a group of young critics opposed to the Grierson tradition. In an influential article published in *Sight and Sound* in 1954, Lindsay Anderson not only celebrated Jennings's "poetic style" but also argued that he was "the only real poet the British cinema has yet produced" (53).[1]

Even though Anstey and Anderson arrived at opposing conclusions with regard to the value of the films, they shared the assumption that poetry and propaganda are incompatible. Yet the depiction of the war effort in these films is closely associated with the enduring myth of the "people's war," and Andrew Britton has recently argued that Jennings was creating propaganda for "the British Imperial Myth" which is "still incorrigibly there to this day" and which "emphasizes . . . the homogeneity, the unambiguous political unity, of British wartime society" (38). Jennings is thus seen to be complicit with a myth that created the illusion that the British class system had been swept away and sought to dupe the people into believing that no further social change would be required once the war had been won.[2]

While Britton does show how both the films and the myth were appropriated by the conservative ideology of the Thatcher years, I believe that he misrepresents how the films work as poetic documentaries and, in so doing, tends to downplay the complexity and contradictions in their relationship to the myth which they reflect and help to construct. In this essay, I will offer a close reading of *Listen to Britain* to suggest how its poetic style and propaganda purposes unsettle and enrich each other, and I will outline some general principles regarding the relationship of poetry and propaganda within the documentary mode.

Although the opening credits assign joint responsibility for the direction and editing of *Listen to Britain* to Jennings and Stewart McAllister, I will continue to refer to Jennings as the film's author, partly for the sake of convenience but also because the film clearly anticipates the two later films with which it forms an informal trilogy documenting the progress of the war effort in Britain. Jennings received sole credit for directing both films; McAllister edited *Fires Were Started* but not *A Diary for Timothy*. The joint credit on *Listen to Britain* acknowledges the difficulty of separating direction from editing in a film which, as we will see, depends so heavily on montage effects. Clearly, others also contributed significantly to these Crown Film Unit productions, but they are all centrally informed by a sensibility which derives from Jennings. In any case, my concern here is not with questions of authorship but with how this sensibility has been defined through the categories of "poetry" and "propaganda."

Poetry in Motion

Recent historians and theorists of documentary continue to place Jennings in what Stuart Legg once called "the poetic line" (quoted in Sussex 159). Thus Paul Swann refers to "a uniquely poetic element" in Jennings's films and Bill Nichols identifies "a poetic form of exposition" in *Listen to Britain* (Swann 163; Nichols 179). Although Swann's wording suggests that Jennings's work stands apart, it is clear that, by the 1940s, the "poetic line" already encompassed a wide range of films, including the city symphonies, the films of Leni Riefenstahl and Robert Flaherty, and even a few British documentaries such as Harry Watt and Basil Wright's *Night Mail* (1936), which incorporated verse by W. H. Auden and music by Benjamin Britten. My analysis of *Listen to Britain* will, therefore, not offer a comprehensive account of the possibilities of the poetic documentary but rather will try to pin down exactly what it means to call this particular film "poetic."[3]

While the usual implied opposite of poetry is prose, the literary analogy is rarely rigorously employed and is often blurred by equally vague allusions to painting and music. Jennings was called an "unrepentant impressionist," and *Listen to Britain* has been described as "a 'symphony' of the sounds of Britain at war" (Hardy 171; Barsam 172). In Jennings's case, such analogies were especially plausible because of his work in other media, as a poet and a painter and as an organizer of the London surrealist exhibition of 1936. He had already spoken out in "defence of the poet" and against a general tendency in the arts of the 1930s toward an emphasis on the "social and useful" (Hillier 70-71).

There are clearly problems involved in transferring the literary category of "poetry" to an audio-visual medium, and it is certainly not clear that propaganda needs to be associated with prose. A more pertinent opposition might be that suggested by Claude Lévi-Strauss between poetry and myth: the density and complexity of poetic speech means that it can be translated only "at the cost of serious distortions," while the substance of myth lies not "in its style, its original music, or its syntax, but in the *story* which it tells" (Lévi-Strauss 210). It may seem to make little sense to ask whether *Listen to Britain* could be translated, but this formulation does suggest the way in which its "poetic style" works with and against what Roland Barthes, building on the ideas of Lévi-Strauss, has called the "frozen" speech of myth which sets out to "immobilize the world" (129, 155).[4]

Before looking at specific examples of how this "poetic style" functions in *Listen to Britain,* I will briefly review three criteria for identifying the "poetry effect" which emerge from the discourse surrounding Jennings's films. According to Anderson, there is no doubt that the primary criterion should be the filmmaker's ability to develop a personal vision. While admitting that Jennings's films were "official, sponsored propaganda," Anderson valued them because the "manner of expression was always individual" (53). This idea was taken up by Jim Hillier, who compared Jennings to John Ford, another director whom Anderson greatly admired, arguing that each director develops a "personal vision" within the constraints of "the propaganda documentary" and the Hollywood genre system, respectively (Hillier 70). More recently, Kevin Jackson has reiterated this argument, claiming that Jennings "used the most seemingly anonymous of all film forms to work out an unmistakable personal language" (x).

Anderson's allusion to Ford underlines the links between this line of argument and Andrew Sarris's use of personal vision as one of the criteria in his version of the auteur theory. Indeed, in Hillier's account, Jennings emerges as "the British cinema's one undoubted *auteur*" (Hillier 62). Since the auteur theory has subsequently been widely attacked as a vestige of a Romantic investment in the notion of individual creativity which ignores not only the industrial basis of film as a medium but also the extent to which the meanings generated by any work of art are produced by its cultural context, its application to Jennings might seem to confirm the doubts of those who rejected his work as anachronistic and socially irrelevant. The criterion of personal vision would thus seem to be quite consonant with Edgar Anstey's judgment that a poetic documentary like *Listen to Britain* is "a figment of the romantic imagination" (quoted in Sussex 144).

Without denying that Jennings's films do exhibit recurring motifs and preoccupations which reflect the sensibility of their prime author, I want to suggest that this criterion is of limited value in distinguishing a poetic documentary. What is the point of stressing the "personal vision" in *Listen to Britain* when the film itself goes to great lengths to conceal the presence of the filmmakers, developing what might even be called an "impersonal" style in order to suggest that the "personality" which it documents is that of the British people? This impersonality certainly has ideological implications, which will be examined later, but there seems to be nothing intrinsically "poetic" about it.

I do not want to reject the category of the "personal" out of hand, however, since it emerges in a new form from a consideration of the other two criteria which have been most often used for identifying the poetic style in these documentaries. For many critics the most telling sign was a negative one: the lack of an omniscient voice-over commentary. In the Griersonian tradition, the "voice" of the documentary is identified with that of the male voice-of-God commentator, whose claim to authority and omniscience depends on the denial of a personal viewpoint.[5] The film's argument is conveyed through the commentary, and the images are subordinate to its demands. Although the commentary claims to explain the images, it actually determines their structure, just as the narrative does in popular fiction films.

Jennings consistently resisted the dominance of the voice-of-God commentator in his major work. After eliminating commentary completely from *Listen to Britain,* he moved toward the indirect address of classical narrative cinema in *Fires Were Started* (following the lead of Robert Flaherty), and used second-person address (ostensibly to a baby born at the end of the war) to complicate the spectator/commentator relationship in *A Diary for Timothy.* The absence of a commentator in *Listen to Britain* leads to a sense of "ambiguity," often seen as one of the hallmarks of poetic language.[6] Since the relationships between the images are no longer determined by a verbal discourse, the editing must create its own continuity which, however, is at least partially open to interpretation. Thus Hillier refers to the "rich ambiguity" of Jennings's style in which "the meanings of an image, or more frequently the connections between images, are left to the audience's emotions for interpretation" (Hillier 87). This refusal to impose meanings implies both a respect for the personal freedom of the spectator and an awareness that meanings are always complex and plural.

From this perspective, the poetic activity involves encouraging new ways of seeing, as suggested by Mick Eaton's claim that the use of "montage both within and between shots" in Jennings's films works to "transform the familiar iconography of British life through the revelation of the bizarre in the everyday" (81). I would suggest that what is revealed is more often incongruous than bizarre, but Eaton's formulation does suggestively link the surrealist influence on Jennings to his involvement with Mass Observation, an organization dedicated to the anthropological investigation of everyday life and culture in Britain. In a radio talk broadcast in 1938, Jennings expressed his concern that modern poetry and everyday life "have got out of touch with each other," and his wartime practice as a filmmaker can be seen as an attempt to reunite them (quoted in Jackson 255).

In the absence of a commentary, the spectator must seek meanings in the images and sounds and in the linkages established between them. To some extent, this effect recalls Sergei Eisenstein's famous definition of montage: "from the collision of two given factors *arises* a concept" (37). In discussing the implications of this idea for Jennings's films, Eaton argues that this "concept" can never be "completely circumscribed in advance" and that "it must always oscillate between the personal and the social" (82). If the poetic discourse of *Listen to Britain* is, as I have suggested, impersonal, it is because the style is supposed to emanate not from the director's personal vision but from the "power of poetry" which Jennings attributed to the English people and which thus encompasses both the director and the spectator.[7]

The implication of the spectator in this "contamination" of the social with the personal is closely related to the third criterion which has been used to define the poetic documentary. According to Andrew Higson, documentary is normally confined to the "public gaze," unlike fiction films which can use point-of-view shots to encourage identification with characters (77). The poetic effect of Jennings's wartime films is associated with what might be called the introduction of a "private eye."

Anderson argued that Jennings developed a "style based on a peculiar intimacy of observation" in which the "commonplace" is made significant (54). In *Listen to Britain,* the war has created a context within which everyday life gains a new significance because its patterns can no longer be taken for granted. What is at stake is what Bill Nichols has called "the social subjectivity of viewing, or listening" to which the film draws attention through a style that "fractures the time and space of its scenes from the visible world of wartime Britain into a large number of dissociated impressions" (179–80). If we couple Nichols's description with Gavin Lambert's much earlier claim that "the technique of *Listen to Britain* is based completely on the power of association" (25), the film's "intimate" address can be seen to disturb the ideological continuity of the public sphere and to generate a psychological tension around the competing forces of association and dissociation, continuity editing and montage.

"Only Connect"

Although it is only about eighteen minutes long, *Listen to Britain* is made up of over two hundred shots, organized into seventeen sequences of varying lengths whose boundaries are, however, often obscured by ambiguous transition shots and overlapping sound. The frequent shifts—from country to city, from work to leisure activities, from noise to music—promote an alertness to the possibility for unusual and ambiguous linkages between shots, even when the editing within sequences seems to conform to more conventional continuity rules, an alertness that also extends to juxtapositions within single shots. While the spectator is caught up in the flow of images and sounds, however, the film does intermittently draw attention to the act of looking through the use of point-of-view editing which works both to focus the spectator's viewing and to draw this viewing into the "social subjectivity" that supposedly grows out of the experience of living in wartime Britain.

The film opens with two images of the countryside, the first of trees with leaves blowing in the wind, the second of wheat rippling in a field. While this second image introduces the idea of cultivated nature, both carry connotations of a traditional image of rural Britain as a "garden." However, these connotations are disturbed by the noise of planes on the sound track, and the third shot duly shows planes flying across the sky. The human presence and the look are then introduced into the film as we see three land workers looking at something outside the frame and then two shots of men at an anti-aircraft installation peering up into the sky. Another shot of planes is followed by a shot of a tractor working close to the anti-aircraft gun, and the noise of the tractor drowns out that of the planes. The sequence ends with a closer shot of the tractor and a shot of the sky with planes at high altitude.

This opening sequence, which consists of eleven shots and lasts a little more than one minute, quickly establishes the kind of spectatorship that the film will invite. The contrast between rural peace and intimations of war is fairly obvious, but the meaning of the contrast depends on whether we emphasize the visual and aural dissonance or the harmony implied by the war effort. If the land workers and gunners contribute to this effort in their different ways, their unified purpose is expressed through their looks at the sky, implying the need for alertness against an enemy who will remain unseen and unmentioned throughout the film. Rather than instigating a paranoid search for an enemy, however, this sequence prepares for a film that will encourage a similar alertness in the spectator, who is asked to reflect on the experience of unity within difference.

The next sequence is anticipated by a beep heard over the end of the last shot of planes and then, as we see a house framed by trees and a fence, a radio announcer introduces the news. However, instead of news, his voice is followed by lively dance music, which is soon located in a dance hall where the floor is filled with couples dancing to "Roll out the Barrel." Shots of the dancers are intercut with shots of civil defense crews looking out to sea, silhouetted in the moonlight, and of a young woman showing a photograph (which we do not see) to a soldier as they sit beside the dance floor. The communal activity of dancing in couples mediates between intimate (and private) looks and the social need for continued watchfulness.

The following sequences alternate between work necessary for the war effort and leisure activities which provide temporary relief from this effort. After shots of coal miners at work, a train stops at a signal, and Canadian soldiers pass the time by playing cards and singing "Home on the Range." As the train pulls away, a sound overlap bridges the transition to an aircraft factory where three shots of a plane being assembled are followed by one of a plane taking off. The camera then pans to a sign identifying "Ambulance Station 76" while a woman's voice is heard singing to a piano accompaniment. A middle-aged woman in uniform is then shown performing for a group of younger women who tentatively join in as she sings the traditional song, "The Ash Grove." The ambulance station is located in what seems to be a museum, with a large statue looming over the women, but a cut-away to a close-up of hard hats hanging on the wall places both folk music and classical art in the urgent context of the war effort to preserve these traditions.[8]

Tradition is also invoked by the next shot of Big Ben and by the synchronous sound of its chimes. But this sound is then relocated to a radio broadcast as an announcer declares, "This is London calling," and the theme music of "The British Grenadiers" is heard. A rapid montage sequence then illustrates the work of the BBC World Service by presenting snatches of foreign-language programs over shots of radio equipment, an effect that evokes both Britain's traditional role as a world power and the role of modern technology in maintaining it.

Having broadened its perspective to include the international scope of the war effort, the film then includes a sequence in which the "private eye" comes into its own. The montage of radio equipment is followed by a shot of the countryside at sunset while a woman's voice reads a message for the armed forces overseas. A fade leads into shots of the country at dawn, with the sound of birds singing on the soundtrack. These sounds then merge into the noise of horses' hooves, and a man is shown leading a horse past a factory which workers are entering. The motif of "morning" continues as the camera pans over a city, recalling similar imagery in "city symphony" films such as Ruttman's *Berlin: Symphony of a Great City* (1927) and Vertov's *Man with a Movie Camera* (1929). A male voice calls out instructions for physical exercise to the rhythmic accompaniment of a piano, while the camera follows another man walking briskly along a city street wearing a bowler hat and carrying a hard hat as well as a briefcase.

Three shots of industrial buildings accompanied by factory noises are followed by a shot of a tree in sunlight as a piano begins to play. The next shot shows a woman preparing tea in a domestic interior. Her look out of the window cues a reverse-shot of children dancing in a school playground from which (presumably) the sound of the piano is coming [Figure 48.1]. Just before a cut back to a close-up of the woman looking out of the window [Figure 48.2], a girl's voice calls out "Mummy!" Another shot of the children dancing is followed by a cut back to the woman, who now looks away from the window, cueing a second reverse-shot of a framed photograph of a man in uniform [Figure 48.3]. By inviting identification with the woman's private experience through the use of point-of-view shots, the film temporarily adopts the strategies of fiction cinema and implies that both empathy and detachment, private eye and public gaze, are required to adequately comprehend the impact of war as a public event on people's lives.

While the child's cry anchors the sequence firmly within the emotional and ideological framework of the "family," its meanings are immediately opened out again. The framed image of the "father" is not followed by a cut back to the "mother" but by a closer shot of the children in the playground. This shot is bound to the next shot of armored vehicles moving through the streets by the continuation of the piano music which only gradually gives way to the noise of the vehicles. Once again, the present reality of war impinges on a space associated with peace and tradition, the latter here represented by several shots of a building of Tudor design which a sign reveals to be a "Guest House and Tea Room." Just before this sequence ends, a close-up of a young girl watching the troops

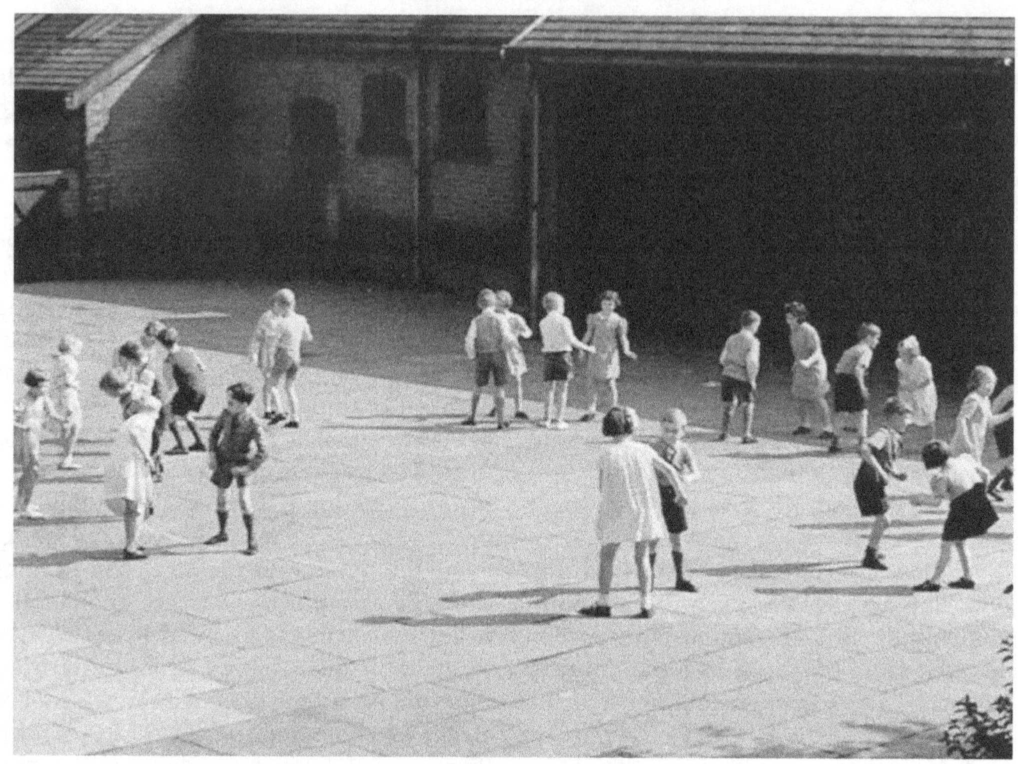

FIGURE 48.1 *Listen to Britain* (1942). Screen capture from DVD.

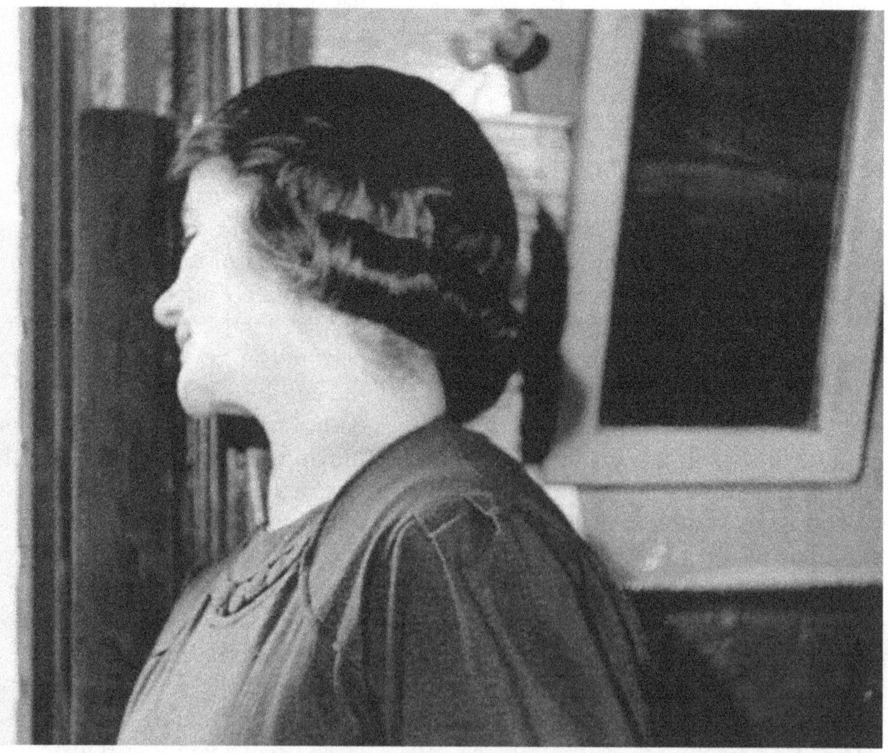

FIGURE 48.2 *Listen to Britain* (1942). Screen capture from DVD.

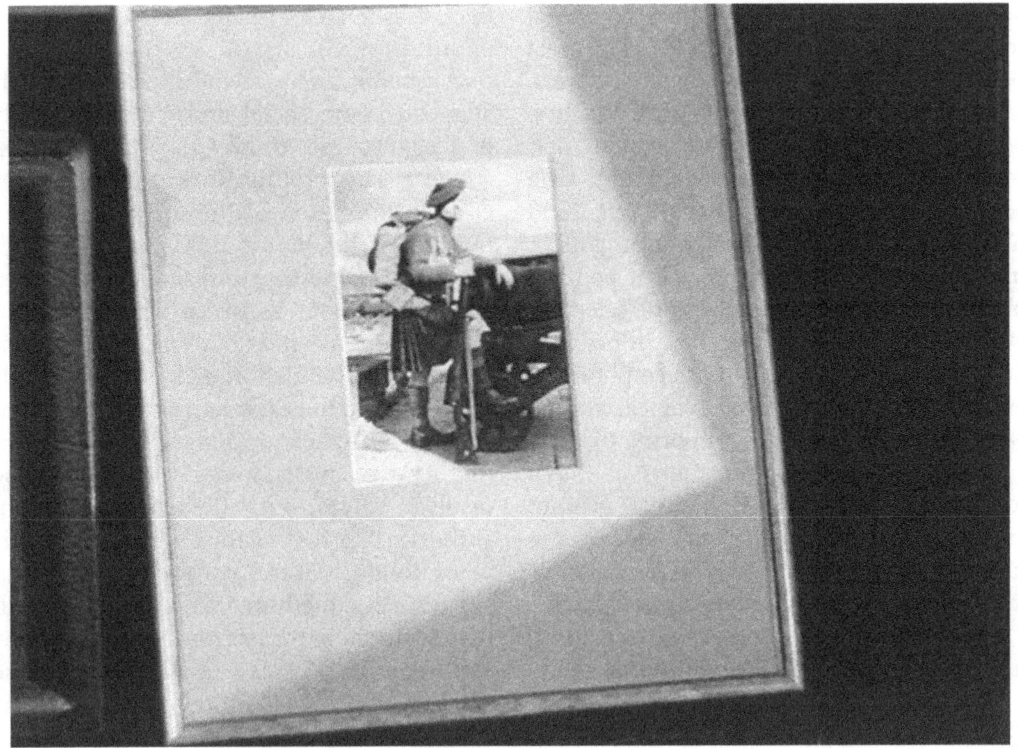

FIGURE 48.3 *Listen to Britain* (1942). Screen capture from DVD.

pass by links its meanings to the "family" motif of the previous sequence.

Ideology and Utopia

At this point, just before the film's concluding and most famous sequences, I want to break off my analysis to address the issues of propaganda and ideology which have so far remained largely implicit. To some extent, the film's "poetic" address masks its propaganda function; but *Listen to Britain* was clearly made as a contribution to the war effort, and we now need to examine the implications of the interaction of poetry and propaganda.

As we have seen, Edgar Anstey felt that the film's poetic style was incompatible with its intended use as propaganda. He argued that "it will be a disaster if this film is sent overseas" because "our Allies" would be appalled to "learn that an official British film-making unit can find time these days to contemplate the current sights and sounds of Britain as if the country were some curious kind of museum exhibit" (quoted in Sussex 144). When the film was released in the United States, its ambiguity was reduced by a strident verbal introduction, apparently added by "a nervous civil servant" (Hodgkinson and Sheratsky 59), and Anstey later admitted that it "had enormous influence overseas" (quoted in Sussex 145).

The apparent success of *Listen to Britain* in influencing public opinion suggests both that propaganda should not be too narrowly defined and that the boundary lines in the debate over social utility and aesthetic pleasure are not as distinct as they might seem. Grierson seems to have assumed that documentary could combine propaganda with social responsibility because of its close ties to actuality, but there is no doubt that documentaries can reflect and construct myths as much as fiction films do. In most fiction films, and in many documentaries, these myths function ideologically as hidden assumptions, but propaganda normally makes its intentions apparent. In a sense, then, propaganda is more open and honest about its ideological workings than films which disclaim any social or political purpose, although the process of selecting evidence for use in propaganda films may be governed by ideological assumptions or assumptions about the ideological framework which the spectator will bring to bear.

In assessing the implications of *Listen to Britain* as propaganda, then, we need to attend both to the myths circulated in the film and to the ways in which it envisages the spectator's relations to these myths. There can be little doubt that the most pertinent myth to which *Listen to Britain* contributes is that of the "people's war." Leonard Quart situates the film in relation to this myth when he describes it as "a portrait of a nation where all classes (despite the existence of clear class divisions), sounds, and images act as one against a common enemy" (63).[9]

Andrew Britton adopts a similar view but argues that this vision of national unity serves the interests of "the dominant class culture" (44). He refers to "the imperialist content of the war myth" as "Churchillian" and links it to Thatcherist rhetoric during the Falklands crisis (38–39). By simply eliding the "people's war" with the conservative ideology that dominated Britain in the 1980s, however, Britton ignores the contradictions which the myth was struggling to contain. While he does admit that the Labour Party's victory in the 1945 General Election and the establishment of the Welfare State testify to "the material content of the popular aspirations which secured the united British nation," Britton does not allow that these aspirations may have been incorporated into what he calls "the *ideology* of war unity" and, in fact, may be a major factor in its effectiveness and endurance (38).

As my analysis of the film has already suggested, the social and cinematic unity is less assured than Quart and Britton suggest. The attempt to read the film as a simple expression of the myth misses the fragility of the connections made through montage in *Listen to Britain.* Questions about the extent to which similarity overrides difference and about the permanence of the social bonds forged by the war effort are central to the experience of the film and even to its ideological meanings, since it implies that such an uncertainty could be resolved only through the imposition of an authority like that against which the war is being fought. Thus Geoffrey Nowell-Smith suggests that the film's vision is "consonant with Churchillian rhetoric, but by no means equivalent to it" since "it both holds more together and shows more awareness of its own instability" (330).

Clearly, this "instability" is related to the "ambiguity" of the film's poetic effect. What this suggests is that the ideological implications of a film cannot be separated from its formal strategies. Thus, in Leni Riefenstahl's *Triumph of the Will* (1935), for example, the film's rhetoric becomes an extension of the documented event (most visibly apparent in those shots which show cameras moving up and down on elevators in the walls of the stadium). While this film has also been regarded as a poetic documentary and also has no commentary, there is little room for ambiguity in its style, which draws on and extends the monumentality of an event staged by Hitler as a propaganda statement glorifying his authority.

While Riefenstahl's aerial shots and panoramic views of the Nuremberg spectacle evoke what Michel de Certeau has called the "totalizing eye," *Listen to Britain* offers instead the view from " 'down below,' below the thresholds at which visibility begins" (92–93). The camera observes, poised between involvement and detachment, activities which the shifting flow of the editing designates as parts of a larger reality, setting up a tension between the fragmentation of the representation and the implied unity of the whole, between what can be seen and what can be imagined. Of course, the title of the film directs us to "listen," and the pull between sight and sound adds to the fragility of the film's discourse. The result is something very like what Raymond Williams has called the "subjunctive mode," a mode which tries to identify the utopian possibilities that cannot be detected by works in the "indicative" mode which simply "state that this is what reality is like" (218).

Poetry, Propaganda, and Myth

Listen to Britain does have its blind spots, some of which it shares with the myth of the "people's war." Yet this myth was so successful because it did address an important aspect of many people's experience of the war: it tried to reconcile the contradiction between the need for social change, if only to gain support for the war effort, and the forces resistant to such change. What I am suggesting is that *Listen to Britain* activates the tensions involved in the very construction of the myth and builds them into the spectator's experience of the film. Its ideological limitations thus need to be assessed in the context of its refusal to settle for either reality or myth or to elide the differences between them.

One of the blind spots seems to emerge in the sequence involving the woman's look at child and husband which I had just reached in my analysis of the film. While many women are depicted in uniform or at work, the representation of this woman as housewife and mother seems to anticipate the ideological pressures for a return to more traditional gender roles once the war was over. That there is an element of strain in the film's discourse is indicated by the rather artificial device of adding the cry of "Mummy" to the soundtrack to reinforce the effect of the point-of-view editing which situates the woman clearly within the framework of the family unit. The elimination of the possibility of ambiguity here is out of keeping with the general tendencies of the film's style. But, as we have seen, this is also the sequence in which the tension between public and private is most fully resolved in favor of the latter. By adopting the strategies of classical narrative at the moment of its most conservative representation of gender relations, the film implicitly points to the ideological limitations of the private eye. Yet this sequence does invite identification with the way the war was actually experienced by many women without denying other possibilities, some of which the film also represents.

The complexities of the subjunctive mode become most apparent in the film's next movement, which includes its most celebrated effect, the sound bridge that merges the conclusion of a song by the music hall team of Flanagan and Allen into the introduction of a Mozart piano concerto played by Myra Hess. These concerts make up the two longest sequences in the film, but music is also prominent in the sequence that introduces them. Over a shot of an armored vehicle passing a group of people watching from a doorstep, a fanfare is heard and lively music begins. A dissolve leads into an aerial shot of the countryside (one of the film's few views from above), and a radio announcer is heard, "Calling all workers." As if in response to this call, the film bursts into a flurry of movement: a truck passes under a freight train crossing a bridge, the camera moves rapidly past terraced houses, and a close-up of a wheel spinning on a machine takes us into a factory. Women working and singing are then intercut with the loudspeakers from which the music is supposedly coming. Appropriately, in view of the "family" sequence which has just ended, the song is "Yes, My Darling Daughter."

This sequence is built out of a cluster of meanings related to music, gender, and technology, all of which refer back to earlier moments in the film and gain new resonance through their present juxtaposition. Then, as the camera once again moves rapidly past rows of houses, the music fades out and is replaced by station noises which cue four brief shots of men and women in uniform waiting at a train station, another aspect of wartime experience. This brief lull leads into a performance by Flanagan and Allen of one of their most popular songs, "Underneath the Arches," for an enthusiastic audience of workers on their lunch break. This concert is linked, via the famous shared chord, to one of Myra Hess's lunchtime performances at the National Gallery in which she is accompanied by an orchestra of musicians from the Royal Air Force.

The juxtaposition of these two concerts, one decidedly "popular" and the other the product of "high" culture, has been seen as the climactic point in the film's drive to forge links between all elements of British society. As David Thomson puts it, the effect is "a way of saying all people, all classes, have their music" (58). Yet, while the sound overlap does reveal a basic affinity at the level of musical language, the unity created in the editing does not eliminate the need to notice the differences as well as the similarities which the film finds in its representation of the two concerts as musical and social events. Geoffrey Nowell-Smith captures the complexity of the sequence when he argues that its meaning is "left open" so that "the union of popular and high culture and their possible divergence" can be "held in the balance" (331).

The lunchtime concerts by Myra Hess did become part of the myth of the "people's war" because they attracted many people who had not attended concerts of classical music before. Another concert is featured in *Diary for Timothy* where Hess's performance of music by Beethoven prompts the commentator to remind "Tim" that this is "German music" and that he will have to think about this apparent contradiction when he grows up. The Mozart piano concerto heard in *Listen to Britain* is not quite "German music" (given Mozart's Austrian origins), but it is close enough to raise similar issues, especially since it follows the evocation of familiar London sites in "Underneath the Arches" (although the only arches that the film actually shows are those in front of the National Gallery). The power of music to transcend class and national boundaries is affirmed, but significant differences remain.

These differences emerge precisely because of the similarities in the way that the two concerts are represented. Both are introduced by signs which appear shortly after the music has begun, and both intercut shots of the performers on stage with shots of the audience. Yet parallels also reveal differences: thus a menu chalked on a blackboard at the first concert finds its equivalent at the second in a program listing the order in which the music will be played. Both audiences obviously enjoy the music, but the workers sit at tables and sing along as they eat while, at the National Gallery, some people eat discreetly on the margins of the audience but most concentrate on the performance. Two shots reveal the queen as a member of this audience, suggesting either or both the closeness to the people of the British royal family or the cultural distinctions that make the National Gallery rather than a workers' canteen an appropriate site for the queen to visit.

This last distinction may well have been qualified for the original audience who would know that, under the right circumstances, members of the royal family would attend performances by popular entertainers. Of course, these would then tend to become more formal occasions, but formality is not completely absent even in the workers' canteen. After Flanagan and Allen have appeared in medium shot, singing in a gently relaxed manner, a long shot from the audience reveals them on stage in front of a grand piano and orchestra. Such details suggest influences flowing both ways across the divide between popular and high culture, and their effect could be complemented by the specific extra-textual knowledge that a spectator might bring to the film, as suggested by Nowell-Smith's comment on the Jewish backgrounds that link Bud Flanagan and Myra Hess (331).

The symmetry between the representations of the two concerts is disrupted when the camera's attention wanders away from the Mozart performance (which continues on the soundtrack) and follows a sign to a War Artists' Exhibition where a sailor is seen examining a painting of a ship in harbor. After a brief return to the concert, we are shown sandbags and the empty frames of paintings which have been removed to protect them from bomb damage, both digressions extending the concern with the impact of the war on art. The exhibition suggests the need for painters (and filmmakers like Jennings) to record the experience of war, while the empty frames attest to the threat to the cultural heritage. In a sense, the persistence of music-making compensates for the removal of the paintings but, if the cultural and economic value of the originals has led to their absence, they return in the form of reproductions (presumably) which decorate the concert area and which (at least to the camera eye) are indistinguishable from the originals.

As the concert sequence comes to an end, the camera moves outside the National Gallery, and we see two shots of the statue of Nelson atop the column in Trafalgar Square, reminding us of an earlier war. The music continues even into the next sequence, which shows men and women building tanks, and is only gradually drowned out by the factory noises. A single shot of a military band leading a parade through city streets cues the return of music to the sound track but, even before the shot ends, industrial noises once again fade in, cueing a sequence in a blast furnace which includes shots of a molten ingot from the point-of-view of the workers. The interaction of music and noise, the slight disjunctions between sight and sound, the move from public gaze to private eye, all work to stress the range of experiences tenuously held together by the war effort.

Over the final shots of the blast furnace, music again returns as the voices of a choir emerge from the industrial noise. The music swells up over shots of factory chimneys, wheat rippling in the wind (a reprise of the second shot), and cooling towers at a power station, and the film ends with an aerial view of the countryside. Some clouds pass in front of the camera, rhyming with the smoke and steam of the chimneys and cooling towers, but move away to leave an unimpeded view of land and sky, with no sign of the planes of the opening sequence (their noise replaced by the triumphal music). The effect is a rather rapid but powerful movement toward closure: Hillier points out that the music here is "the only sound whose source is not identified in the film" so that "it seems to well out from *all* the elements of the film" (89).

However, this ending does seem to violate the rule of ambiguity which operates throughout the rest of the film, especially since the powerful concluding music is a performance of "Rule Britannia!" David Thomson thus questions the effect of the ending because "there's no sight of the choir, and too little thought of what 'Rule' means" (58). It is not quite true that this is the only sound whose source is not identified, since the voice of the fitness instructor also comes from nowhere, although we are clearly meant to assume that the source is a radio broadcast. However, the use of one of Britain's unofficial national anthems in the ending, even if it may also emanate from a radio broadcast featuring one of the country's many amateur choirs, does carry imperialist connotations which have not been emphasized in the rest of the film.

The final shot, too, seems to verge on a "totalizing" view, although the cuts back and forth from city to country imply that the whole still cannot be encompassed by a single shot. Perhaps it also makes a difference that the only "waves" we see are in a wheat field and that the music may be broadcast over the airwaves which have earlier been shown to be an important part of the war effort. Even if propaganda wins out at the end of *Listen to Britain,* the rather abrupt closure and the "poetic" openness of all that has gone before make this victory itself somewhat ambiguous. The film documents a historical moment in which the claims of poetry and propaganda come together in the evolving myth of the "people's war," and this unstable partnership signals a challenge both to the nation and to the documentary form.

NOTES

1. The critics, including Gavin Lambert and Lindsay Anderson, who defended Jennings were paving the way for a new approach to documentary which would eventually become known as Free Cinema. Since Jennings died in an accident in 1950 and his postwar films disappointed even his admirers, his influence on the Free Cinema filmmakers was almost entirely confined to his wartime films.
2. For a thorough treatment of the historical and cultural contexts of the myth of the "people's war," see Angus Calder, *The People's War: Britain 1939–1945* (London: Jonathan Cape, 1969).
3. One of the most suggestive treatments of the "poetic" in cinema is still Pier Paolo Pasolini's "The 'Cinema of Poetry,'" in Pasolini, *Heretical Empiricism*, trans. Louise K. Barnett (Bloomington: Indiana University Press, 1988), 167-86. Jennings's films might be usefully discussed in relation to Pasolini's argument that people "'read' reality visually" through their encounters with "objects and things that appear charged with multiple meanings and thus 'speak' brutally with their very presence" (168); but, as Pasolini made clear in a later essay, he was interested only in "narrative poetry" and opposed to "a cinema of lyric poetry obtained through editing and the intensification of technique" (251–52). The "poetic" style of Jennings's wartime documentaries is approached through the linguistic theory of Juri Lotman in Bjorn Sorenssen, "The Documentary Aesthetics of Humphrey Jennings," in *Documentary and the Mass Media*, ed. John Corner (London: Edward Arnold, 1986), 47–63.
4. The issue is far from simple, however, because there is a clear parallel between Jennings's "poetic style" and Lévi-Strauss's argument that meaning "cannot reside in the isolated elements which enter into the composition of a myth, but only in the way those elements are combined" (Lévi-Strauss 210). The relationship of poetry and myth is approached in a rather different way in Barry K. Grant, "Tradition and the Individual Talent: Poetry in the Genre Film," in *Narrative Strategies: Original Essays in Film and Prose Fiction*, ed. Syndy M. Conger and Janice R. Welsch (Macomb: Western Illinois University Press, 1981), 93-103.
5. Bill Nichols defines the "voice" of a documentary as "that which conveys to us a sense of a text's social point of view, of how it is speaking to us and how it is organizing the materials it is presenting to us." "The Voice of Documentary," *Film Quarterly* 36, no. 3 (spring 1983): 18.
6. Hillier notes that "Jennings was a product of the I. A. Richards school of criticism that produced Empson's conception of the ambiguity or multiplicity of poetic statements" (87). William Empson's influential *Seven Types of Ambiguity* was first published in 1930.
7. The reference is to a 1947 review by Jennings of a book on the "English character" in Jackson, *Reader*, 238; Jennings takes his lead from the book in referring to the "English" but, as the title of *Listen to Britain* suggests, he normally sought to invoke the national unity of the "British" people.
8. This sequence was apparently shot in the basement of the Old Bailey (Hodgkinson and Sheratsky 58).
9. Quart's formulation here suggests the need to compare the apparent unifying effect of the war in Jennings's films with the depiction of male groups, in British and Hollywood war films of the postwar period, who overcome social and/or racial differences for the sake of their struggle against a common enemy.

WORKS CITED

Anderson, Lindsay. "Only Connect: Some Aspects of the Work of Humphrey Jennings." In *Humphrey Jennings: Film-maker, Painter, Poet*, ed. Mary-Lou Jennings, 53–59. London: British Film Institute, 1982.

Barr, Charles, ed. *All Our Yesterdays: 90 Years of British Cinema.* London: British Film Institute, 1986.

Barsam, Richard Meram. *Nonfiction Film: A Critical History*, rev. ed. Bloomington: Indiana University Press, 1992.

Barthes, Roland. *Mythologies*, trans. Annette Lavers. London: Jonathan Cape, 1972.
Britton, Andrew. "Their Finest Hour: Humphrey Jennings and the British Imperial Myth of World War II." *CineAction* 18 (fall 1989): 37–44.
de Certeau, Michel. *The Practice of Everyday Life*, trans. Steven Rendall. Berkeley: University of California Press, 1984.
Eaton, Mick. "In the Land of the Good Image." *Screen* 23, no. 1 (May–June 1982): 79–84.
Eisenstein, Sergei. *Film Form: Essays in Film Theory*, trans. Jay Leyda. New York: Harcourt. Brace and World. 1949.
Hardy, H. Forsyth. "British Documentaries in the War." In *Nonfiction Film Theory and Criticism*, ed. Richard Meram Barsam, 167–72. New York: E. P. Dutton, 1976.
Higson, Andrew. 1986. "'Britain's Outstanding Contribution to the Film': The Documentary-Realist Tradition." In *All Our Yesterdays: 90 Years of British Cinema*, ed. Charles Barr, 72–97. London: British Film Institute, 1986.
Hillier, Jim. "Humphrey Jennings." In Alan Lovell and Jim Hillier, *Studies in Documentary*, 62–132. London: Seeker and Warburg, 1972.
Hodgkinson, Anthony W., and Rodney E. Sheratsky. *Humphrey Jennings: More Than a Maker of Films*. Hanover: University Press of New England, 1982.
Jackson, Kevin, ed. *The Humphrey Jennings Film Reader*. Manchester: Carcanet Press, 1993.
Jennings, Mary-Lou, ed. *Humphrey Jennings: Film-maker, Painter, Poet*. London: British Film Institute. 1982.
Lambert, Gavin. "Jennings' Britain." *Sight and Sound* 20, no. 3 (May 1951): 24–26.
Levi-Strauss, Claude. *Structural Anthropology*, vol. 1, trans. Claire Jacobson and Grundfest Schoepf. New York: Basic Books, 1963.
Nichols, Bill. *Representing Reality: Issues and Concepts in Documentary*. Bloomington: Indiana University Press, 1991.
Nowell-Smith, Geoffrey. "Humphrey Jennings: Surrealist Observer." In *All Our Yesterdays: 90 Years of British Cinema*, ed. Charles Barr, 321–33. London: British Film Institute, 1986.
Quart, Leonard. "Wartime Memories." *Cineaste* 20, no. 3 (1994): 63–64.
Sussex, Elizabeth. *The Rise and Fall of British Documentary*. Berkeley: University of California Press, 1975.
Swann, Paul. *The British Documentary Film Movement. 1926–1946*. Cambridge: Cambridge University Press. 1989.
Thomson, David. "A Sight for Sore Eyes." *Film Comment* 29, no. 2 (March–April 1993): 54–59.
Williams, Raymond. *Politics and Letters*. London: New Left Books, 1979.

49

GEORGE C. STONEY

DOCUMENTARY IN THE UNITED STATES IN THE IMMEDIATE POST-WORLD WAR II YEARS (1989)

Throughout this book* Dr. Ellis contends that the American documentary movement was carried forward very largely by people "on the left" and I will not dispute this. But he leaves the unwary reader with the impression that, therefore, most of the documentaries seen in this country conveyed those sentiments, which is untrue. In the years after the Second World War sponsorship by industry and institutions determined the nature of the bulk of the films that circulated out of the 16mm libraries. Many of these were politically "neutral" but many, including some of them made by those of us whom Ellis rightly describes as tending toward the left politically, were far from neutral. Examples:

Almost every child in the country saw *The American Road*, produced in 1953 by M.P.O. (a large industrial film production company) to celebrate the Ford Motor Company's fiftieth anniversary. It is as fullhearted a celebration of the free enterprise system as one could make and enshrines Henry Ford as a folk hero. This film has been projected daily in the "Futurama" in Dearborn. I directed the historical re-creations. Joe Marsh, a blacklisted Hollywood writer, did the script. Alex North, the famous Hollywood composer (then blacklisted also), did the music. We all needed the money.

Almost every other documentary director active at the time has similar films to his credit. Sidney Meyers did Monsanto's *Decision for Chemistry* and lots more. Willard Van Dyke did a series for the National Rifle Association. Lee Bobker did an apology for

* Originally published as "Appendix" to Jack C. Ellis, *The Documentary Idea: A Critical History of English-Language Documentary Film and Video* (Englewood Cliffs: Prentice Hall, 1989), 302.

strip mining for the Peabody Coal Company. Even Robert Flaherty's *Louisiana Story* is essentially a folksy apologia for Standard Oil's exploitation of wetlands that today we know should be protected as sources of fresh water.

My hunch is that, however justified we thought we were in making these films, by doing so we lost the respect we once had as documentary filmmakers on the part of the intellectual and artistic community. This began to be redressed when there was a new approach ("direct cinema") and a new concept ("the independent Filmmaker") to inspire us and refresh our resolves. For, in truth, the disillusionments of the late 1940s and the intimidations of the McCarthy period that followed destroyed our political underpinnings.

ZOË DRUICK

DOCUMENTING CITIZENSHIP

Reexamining the 1950s National Film Board Films about Citizenship (2000)

Despite recent assessments debunking the radical politics of John Grierson and the early years of the NFB (National Film Board),[1] in terms of documentary form, the 1950s are still commonly seen as the decade in which the NFB finally shuffled off the aesthetic shackles of its founder, John Grierson, and started pushing the envelope of style. In the standard account of the decade, D. B. Jones writes, "In the relative quiet of the nineteen-fifties, the Film Board—or, more precisely, a small group of filmmakers within it—began to reach toward 'the creative treatment of actuality,' although they wouldn't have put it that way."[2] Jones is referring primarily to the work of Studio B; of the five films of the 1950s that he discusses, three were made in that unit: *Corral, Paul Tomkowicz: Street-railway Switchman* and *City of Gold.* (Production information on these and other films mentioned below can be found in the Filmography at the end of this article.) Two films from the animation department also merit mention: *Neighbours* and *The Romance of Transportation in Canada.* In his book covering the same period, *In the National Interest,* Gary Evans limits his discussion to an almost identical set of films.[3] There can be no argument that during this decade, NFB output, including the films of Studio B, the animation of Norman McLaren, and the innovations of the O[ffice] N[ational du] F[ilm], included some of the finest short film work that has ever been produced in Canada.

Yet historians tend to focus on these aspects of the NFB's history at the expense of a real analysis of the governmental rationale and intention of the Film Board after the war. The NFB produced hundreds of little-known films in the 1950s, most of them both unexceptional and unmemorable. In an unpublished study, film historian Peter Morris found that films dealing broadly with "people and places," "leisure" and "people and problems" represented 71% of NFB films in circulation in 1948 and was a still-healthy 63% in 1961.[4] The majority of these unremembered films from the 1950s are concerned with the everyday life of citizens. Yet this production focus—ultimately, I will argue, a welfare state policy objective—is rarely examined and never explained. In their focus on aesthetic excellence or political chicanery, histories of the NFB have tended to overlook the rationale behind government funding of this institution and the characteristics of its most common type of film: the tale of citizenship. It is not that government funding was used to produce many films in hopes that a few would achieve aesthetic success. It was, rather, that a few filmmakers were able to bend government film objectives enough to create works of art.

In this paper I will argue that rationales for government funding of film production sprang not from a desire to produce innovative films but, rather, from reasoning derived from the new social scientific thinking about education and citizenship in the welfare state. The influence of the social sciences may be seen in both the form of the majority of the documentaries made in the 1950s and in their subject matter. The reason for the use of film by government may be illuminated by Michel Foucault's notion of "governmentality" which he defined in a 1979 lecture as "The ensemble formed by the institutions, procedures, analyses and reflections, the calculations and tactics that allow the exercise of this very specific, albeit complex form of power, which has as its target population, as its principle form of knowledge political economy, and as its essential technical means apparatuses of security."[5] According to Foucault, individuals and their coming-into-subjectivity, or "subjectivization," are the ground on which the nation exists and, therefore, the site for practices of government. Individuals are produced as subjects at the level of the everyday by their experiences within discursive regimes and practices which strive to regulate their conduct. This regulation can reduce politics, according to Barry Smart, "to a technical question of social management."[6]

The 1950s marked the high point in the ideological Cold War and gave new reasons for production of national security through loyal citizens. As Kevin Dowler has observed in a study of Canadian cultural policy during this period, "From the perspective of security, identity is simply one of the desired outcomes of state security aims."[7] In Foucault's view, the liberal state is necessarily a security state, where liberty is both an extension of security and one of its preconditions.[8] Foucault commentator Colin Gordon has observed that, "Liberalism discards the police conception of order as a visible grid of communication; it affirms instead the necessarily opaque, dense autonomous character of the process of population. It remains, at the same time, preoccupied with the vulnerability of these same processes, with the need to enframe them in 'mechanisms of security.' "[9] The discourse of security and its implementation occurs at the level of the subject, rather than territory, and thus, historically speaking, implies a whole new series of practices for government.

There is no doubt that film was used as a form of government communication in Canada before the advent of the National Film Board in 1939,[10] yet the NFB brought about important differences. Films produced by the Canadian Government Motion Picture Bureau (1917–1941) were concerned primarily with land settlement and tourism: territorial concerns in the most literal sense. With the establishment of the NFB, by contrast, government film production was reoriented toward material problems of citizenship: war, nutrition, labour, family life, insanity, ethnicity and so on. This shift in national representation marks a change in the conception of the nation—from territory to population—with real effects on how it was to be governed.[11]

In the development of the welfare state after the war, the Liberal government tabled an array of new social policy legislation, including initiatives around housing, health, family benefits and Indian affairs.[12]

Although there is no indication that the NFB was *officially* compelled to document these initiatives, after suffering years of attacks in the House of Commons,[13] as well as an RCMP investigation of employees, followed by a purge of "radicals" from its ranks,[14] not to mention an external management audit in 1949 (*National Film Board: Survey of Organization and Business Administration* [1950]) and a special parliamentary investigation in 1952 (Special Committee on the National Film Board [1952]), it would be reasonable to speculate that the Board was interested in pleasing its sole funding source.[15]

Even more perplexing than the question why was the NFB founded? is the question: was it maintained in the late 1940s after its wartime usefulness had been exhausted and at a moment when it was embroiled in politically uncomfortable scandals? Although it is a question historians of the NFB have judiciously avoided, it deserves to be addressed. I propose that we must look again at both the development of the new social science in the United States and the use of documentary film in England. Comparing the two discourses—of social scientific government and of Empire publicity—it seems at least probable that the plethora of NFB peace-time films about citizenship made in the 1950s was justified by the adoption of techniques of social science and public relations as strategies of government in the welfare state. Grierson, who had studied social science during his sojourn at the University of Chicago, can be seen as a crucial cross-Atlantic link between American social science, British "marketing" of Empire and the growth of the Canadian welfare state.

Social Science, Film and Government

Established at the turn of the century in American universities, social science departments with new academic objectives soon developed new methods of knowledge-production as well. Primary among them was the measurement of observable phenomena. Statistical and observational social scientific research of the 1920s attempted to predict, and thereby control, behaviour. Based in large part on the kinds of studies of the population carried out by governments in the census, social scientists, journalists, and statisticians banded together, often with largesse provided by private donors like the Rockefeller and Carnegie Foundations,[16] to discover the effects competing messages could have on behaviour. Coinciding with the rise of both mass society and the mass media, these studies were linked to the concept of government through their concern with (1) the organization of mass populations and economies, and (2) the conduct of individuals. Correlatively, then, it comes as little surprise that social writing of the 1930s was characterized by two types of facticity: facts presented in general terms, abstractly quantified (statistical); and specific facts which made claims to be representative (descriptive).[17] Descriptive methods included the case-study, the participant-observer report and the informant narrative.[18] These epistemological experiments of the social sciences laid the foundation for narrative strategies being deployed by the newly invented documentary films.

A man of his generation, Grierson was brought into contact with the architects of the New Deal at the University of Chicago in the mid-1920s. Pursuing his master's degree in Sociology and Political Science, he was the recipient of a Rockefeller Foundation fellowship in 1924 which encouraged students to travel around the United States conducting research. His original subject of study was "immigration and its effects on the social problems of the United States," a popular subject at the Rockefeller Foundation. After working with his supervisors Charles Merriam and Robert Park, two of the most influential social scientists in America,[19] Grierson modified his subject first to "Public Opinion—Social Psychology" and then to "Newspaper Psychology."[20] Even after his interest in film and democracy was piqued by Walter Lippmann,[21] Grierson's writings show clear affinities with social scientific and managerial government ideas of his day.[22] In 1930 Grierson wrote,

> We have all been abstracting our arts away from the personal, trying to articulate this wider world of duties and loyalties in which education and invention and democracy have made us citizens. . . . [T]here is an urgency in the problem of articulating it to ourselves which is without parallel in the history of citizenship. What sentiments will we have in this new world to warm and direct our will in it? How shall we crystallize them and teach them if we are to stave off chaos?[23]

The new social scientific ideas to which Grierson was exposed at the University of Chicago help to explain more than just his commitment to film and public education. Closer examination helps us to understand the narrative strategies of the documentary films themselves. Films influenced by Grierson, which includes the majority of NFB documentaries produced in the 1950s, are concerned with anonymous individuals typical of particular population or occupation groups. In many ways, they resemble the statistical method favoured by sociology and political science at Chicago. Ideas prevalent in this new scientific study of society included: a modified Darwinism that focussed on the effect of the environment on the labour and life of the community; an emphasis on measurable results produced in empirical studies which could be used to devise plans of social intervention; a growing mobilization of the anthropological conception of "culture" as the fount of individual beliefs and opinions; and an emphasis on education as the democratic method of immigrant integration. These approaches are all there to be found in NFB films. Thus, despite his departure from the academy (incidentally, without ever completing his degree), Grierson did not discard his academic training. His biographer Forsyth Hardy accurately notes that, "For [Grierson] documentary was never an adventure in film-making at all but an adventure in public observation."[24]

Throughout the 1920s, Grierson's supervisor, Charles Merriam, oversaw an international comparative study on citizen training. In his overarching synthesis, *The Making of Citizens* (1931), Merriam postulates that the most pressing question for modern society is deciphering the development and disintegration of groups in order to determine what are "the essential elements in the texture of group cohesion?"[25] A brief examination of this seminal international study of education and citizenship sheds light on ideas later propounded by Grierson and fundamental to the theoretical underpinning of the Film Board after the war.

[. . .]

In Merriam's view, the cornerstone of the modern state is the reliable and efficient citizen. "Vigorous citizenship rests upon soundly constituted types of personality, and the nature of this fundamental soundness is an important part of the making of the future citizen" (378). In this regard, civic education figures prominently:

> [. . .] It is possible to build the citizen from the ground up, using as a point of departure the controls of body and mental balance now emerging from scientific studies to revolutionize our knowledge of political nature and our ability to deal with it successfully. An admirable beginning has already been made in the development of medical care for school children, but it will be necessary to extend this to cover new types of

> attention based upon new studies of the human constitution, physical and mental; and to adjust the organization of civic training to this new basis in the new realism. (382)

For Merriam, the mental and physical "hygiene" of the individual was tied to the health of the nation: education and citizenship training relied upon the sound basis of managed health.

[. . .]

Grierson used these ideas to sell the idea of documentary film as an Empire-unifier to the Empire Marketing Board and, subsequently to convince the Canadian government that public education through film could produce both Canadian unity and distinction from the United States.

Grierson's ideas about representativeness, which can be clearly seen in the anonymous types that populate his films, correspond to the ideas of his other committee member, the widely influential Robert Park, often considered the "architect of the Chicago School."[26] [. . .] Park and his followers attributed to people's circumstances the determining causes of their occupations and outlook. Although mechanistic and potentially naïve, this was a radical re-thinking of the analysis of poverty by nineteenth-century geneticists, which had attributed slum living to inherent degeneracy and defectiveness. The upshot of such a rearranging of causes and effects was the possibility for reform, not on a case by case basis, but through the grand gestures of urban and social planning. According to this theory, by improving impoverished parts of the city (or the nation), life would be ameliorated, regardless of relations of economic inequality which had produced poverty to begin with.

Park was a strong supporter of publicizing government services in the attempt to affect public opinion. In order to "get and keep" the interest and cooperation of the public, he believed public institutions "must advertise" and "sell" their services.[27] This view was linked to new imperatives of democracy to keep people informed about the use of their taxes. In a complicated rhetorical manoeuvre entailing both service to and manipulation of the public, Park noted in 1918, "Any institution supported by the public, will no longer expect to take money from the community, either in the form of gifts or taxes, except upon condition that it can make the people of the community intelligent and responsible participators in its enterprises and its tasks."[28] Members of the public are thus treated as shareholders or consumers of the welfare state. Park suggested that "one way to interest the public in the work of the social agencies is to state social problems in definite terms of profit and loss to the community."[29]

Grierson undoubtedly felt the influence of Park's commitment to empirical research as a basis for centrally organized reform, his use of government publicity to exact public support, and his view of human ecology, in which the environment rather than politics or economics is seen to be paramount in the influence on individuals. Chicago School thinkers adopted an instrumental pragmatism: because the world was ever-changing and people were continuously adapting themselves, understanding society's "natural evolution" would provide insight to "guide social development towards the best ends."[30]

While the Chicago School's influence on Grierson is absent from what Joyce Nelson has termed the "Grierson legend," his affinity with the American publisher and democratic theorist Walter Lippmann is often noted.[31] In a statement that is antithetical to the democratic pragmatism of the Chicago school, Lippmann declared in 1922 that the pursuit of the "ideal, omnicompetent, sovereign citizen" was "useless."[32] "The individual man," he wrote, "does not have opinions on all public affairs. He does not know how to direct public affairs. He does not know what is happening, why it is happening, what ought to happen."[33] In 1925, the year after Grierson arrived in the United States, Lippmann published *The Phantom Public* in which he went so far as to posit that education was not the answer to the problems of democratic citizenship, asserting that "the problems that vex democracy seem to be unmanageable by democratic methods."[34] These views are the polar opposite of those of Merriam and Park which encourage the selling of democratic ideas to the public and the use of education and social science to indoctrinate citizens into some semblance of a fully functioning democracy.

Many of Grierson's own writings grapple with Lippmann's pessimism as he tries to take into account the limitations of a democratic populace and the need to educate it: "The key to education in the modern complex world no longer lies in what we have known as education but in what we have known as propaganda," he was to conclude in 1941.[35] Grierson's views were thus actually formed in *contradistinction* to Lippmann's republican nostalgia; they were the views of a young man in a new century where the study and guidance of human behaviour promised understanding, efficiency and progress. Grierson shared with Merriam a belief in the indoctrinating role of education in a multi-ethnic society. He also shared his supervisor's ability to acquire funding from the private sector and the government alike by arguing for the applicability of social science research to problems of both modern government and society.

The Empire Marketing Board

[. . .]

By the 1920s, British politicians had modified the nineteenth century slogan "trade follows the flag" to the more sardonic "trade follows film," which they used as a justification for placing quotas on American film imports and injecting funds into national production.[36] Grounded in these concerns, the Empire Marketing Board (EMB) was established in 1926 to publicize Empire products and promote intra-Empire trade through the cultivation of voluntary consumer preferences based on Empire loyalty.[37] The next year, upon his arrival home from the University of Chicago, John Grierson was hired to develop the film wing of the EMB and with his hiring, the so-called documentary film movement was born.[38] From its inception, then, government documentary was used to promote the distinctness of Empire values over American ones for the purposes of influencing consumer choice.

It was not long before John Grierson visited Canada as part of his EMB work. The EMB was concerned to ensure that the Dominions were promoting loyal Empire messages, and in 1930 Grierson was sent to investigate the state of Canadian government filmmaking and distribution, at that time under the control of the Ministry of Trade and Commerce in the form of the Canadian Government Motion Picture Bureau.[39] With the demise of the EMB due to Depression-era funding cuts, his connection to Canada lapsed in 1933, but in 1938 Grierson was given a new home at the Imperial Relations Trust,[40] which had been established with an anonymous donation of £250,000 to carry on the work of the EMB and "strengthen the ties which bind together the Dominions and the United Kingdom."[41] In 1938, when he was invited by the Canadian government, at Vincent Massey's urging,[42] to assess the state of the Canadian film industry, Grierson took the opportunity to simultaneously evaluate the Canadian film situation for the benefit of the Imperial Relations Trust.[43] The most famous result of this visit was Grierson's recommendation for the establishment of a National Film Board to centralize the organization of Canadian film production and distribution, along the lines promoted by the Imperial Relations Trust.[44]

There were clearly Empire-building objectives in the Trust's support for domestic and even nationalistic film-production in the Dominions. For example, in a 1941 letter to Imperial Relations Trust chairman Sir Stephen Tallents, Grierson describes the benefit of the newly established Canadian Film Committee to the Imperial mandate:

> This new organization, representing as it does, all the national organizations, apart from Government departments, interested in the education and cultural uses of the film is a valuable development. It provides organizations in Great Britain with an ordered access to Canadian audiences and an instrument through which they can, with economy and efficiency, operate in Canada. It gives the Canadian Government valuable aid in developing Canadian audiences for films of national educational value. It may, therefore, be expected to play a considerable part in breaking down the sectional outlook now prevalent in Canada.[45]

Two years after the creation of the Film Board, Grierson reiterates that Canada's interest in him happily coincides with the Trust's mandate, stating: "Circumstances are, of course, very favourable but we have at least had the wit to use them."[46] Clearly, the Imperial Relations Trust and the Canadian Government were agreed that film could be used to promote patriotism which might affect, among other things, consumer choices. However, the two governments also wanted to promote unity in the face of, on one hand, a fractious Empire and rising American power, and on the other hand, an embryonic nation composed of distinctive regions and a large and diverse immigrant population.

Canadian Citizenship

While waves of immigration created problems for the Canadian government that were somewhat analogous to those of the British Empire, in attempting to deal with cultural diversity, Canadian academics and government policy makers alike increasingly turned for solutions to the work being done in American social science. Bridging the two discourses, John Grierson was well-armed to bolster his ideas for a centralized national film institution. Integrating immigrant communities through public information—a combination of Merriam's ideas of governance through the management of public opinion and the Empire Marketing Board's attempt to use publicity to consolidate the British Empire—became entrenched in Canada during the Second World War, with no small help from John Grierson. In 1941, J. T. Thorson, head of the Bureau of Public Information, established the Committee on Cooperation in Canadian Citizenship (CCCC)[47] in an effort to spread information about the Canadian war effort to various ethnic communities.[48] These efforts eventually led to the establishment of the Nationalities Branch of the Department of National War Services,[49] the progenitor of the multiculturalism apparatus of the Department of the Secretary of State.[50] "More was done to involve ethnics in Canadian life in 1940 and 1941," notes one observer, "than had been done in the nearly three-quarters of a century since Confederation."[51] It is against this background that we must assess the governmental aims behind the establishment and the continued development of the NFB.

The idea for the Film Board was warmly received in Canadian political circles, no doubt because of the social scientific, nation-building role it was seen to be able to play. Indeed, parliamentary debates about the establishment of the NFB display a wide base of support for an initiative to "advertise Canada" with "national," "prestige-building" films. As W. D. Euler, Minister of Trade and Commerce, stated during the first reading of the Film Act in March 1939, "While the bill is largely according to [Grierson's] recommendations, it was framed only after the deputy ministers of the various departments concerned had carefully canvassed the whole situation, discussed the merits of the scheme advanced and adopted it unanimously."[52]

The somewhat counter-intuitive drive to make democracy more predictable and less unruly was the project assigned to the Film Board's general and documentary production, most especially in the 1940s and 1950s. Paradoxically, the public information disseminated by the Board was seen to be useful in publicizing representative democracy itself. Grierson embraced this paradox, and was quite explicit about his somewhat authoritarian views. A strong supporter of public opinion polling,[53] Grierson was quite famously an advocate of "democratic propaganda." "We can, by propaganda," he wrote in 1942, just prior to his appointment as head of the War Information Board,

> widen the horizons of the schoolroom and give to every individual, each in his place and work, a living conception of the community which he has the privilege to serve. We can take his imagination beyond the boundaries of his community to discover the destiny of his country. We can light up his life with a sense of active citizenship. We can give him a sense of greater reality in the present and a vision of the future. And, so doing, we can make the life of the citizen more ardent and satisfactory to himself.[54]

By 1952, the potential of the Film Board for educating immigrants about the Canadian way of life was paramount. Tory leader, George Drew, suggested in the House of Commons that, "Films which illustrate in pictorial form certain types of our system of national, provincial and educational government, certain types of our own characteristic Canadian way of doing things in different parts of the country, would all be very helpful in connection with these programs."[55]

Following from its fundamental indebtedness to the social sciences, the NFB of the 1950s determined that the most important topics of its films would be (1) labour-management relations, (2) the birth and growth of the nation (frontiers), a subset of which is the integration of immigrants, and (3) the eugenic emphasis on the link between physical, mental and environmental health. Yet for all the apparent diversity of these topics, they can be linked through the concept of modern Canadian citizenship that was developing concurrently with the Film Board itself. Indeed, the Film Board can be best understood not only as a response to the American film industry (a point widely agreed upon by NFB historians of all stripes), but also as an attempt to understand what being a Canadian has meant. The questions which guide the films are not only the classic Canadian queries "Who am I?" and "Where is here?" but also "Who are those *other* citizens?" Examining the NFB's role in producing tales of citizenship for both self and others is crucial to understanding its service to the Canadian government and, reciprocally, the government's continued support of the Board's filmmaking activities.

An Archive of Typicality

Contrary to the sense you would get reading most NFB histories, the bulk of NFB films from the 1950s are actually concerned with citizenship and governmentality. People are profiled in ways which accentuate their regional or ethnic typicality and their exemplary willingness to fit into the Canadian amalgam. A few examples should demonstrate the governmental social scientific narrative strategies of 1950s NFB films about the population.

Addressed to the imagined central Canadian, *Prairie Profile* examines the life of

Abernethy, Saskatchewan, a "typical" prairie town. Indeed typicality is what the film strives to depict, as is indicated by the first question posed by Fred Davis to a member of the town: "Would you call this an average community?" To which the man replies, "Perhaps there is no such thing as a typical prairie district, but we *are* representative." This desire for representativeness, this need to make a grand claim of typicality must be seen as part of the postwar NFB strategy of *significance* for its stories about ordinary citizens from different regions and backgrounds. Otherwise, the film's exploration of the development of farming techniques and local decision-making in the town would appear to have no relevance to a wider audience.

In *Men of Lunenberg*, one of the *Peoples of the Maritimes* series, the significance of the present-day community is established for the rest of Canada through a telling of their "heritage story": they are descendants of the Protestant Germans who settled the south shore of Nova Scotia in the 1750s. Typically, before the film profiles the present community with a participant-observer report, a male narrator initiates the story with a short version of how this group first made its way to Britain's colony, and like so many films made by the NFB in those years, the emphasis is on exploring regionality. This reflects, of course, one of the principle mandates of the NFB, as stated in the 1939 Film Act: "to help Canadians in all parts of Canada to understand the ways of living and the problems of Canadians in other parts."

Moreover, the focus on labour and culture related to location, corresponds to Robert Park's ideas about the effect of environment on its inhabitants and the hardships of frontier living. Not only were these ideas about Canada's frontier of interest to Americans and Europeans, they also came to be one of Canada's most imposing myths of self-understanding. The actual experience of the Germans in Nova Scotia or the fishermen in Gaspé (*Gaspé Cod Fishermen*) or the prairie farmers is of less importance than how these stories may be used in the present moment for purposes of multicultural government. Indeed, a great deal of forgetting must occur in order to make formerly repudiated or marginalized communities into mosaic tiles in the big picture of the centrally administered federal welfare state.

The "terra incognita" of political life, citizen education for immigrants figures in many NFB films. Good immigrants are the subject of films highlighting Canada's tolerance for difference in the postwar world. In 1949, for example, the series *Canada Carries On* presented *Passport to Canada*, a film with a vision of Canada as a multicultural utopia. Beginning with the usual platitudes about Canada as a land of immigrants, a political line which tends to downplay the varied conditions subtending different waves of immigration, the film proceeds to discuss the current influx of so-called displaced persons "flocking" to Canada from Europe: "They come to live a new life. They come here for peace, freedom and a bit of permanence." Immigrants are shown in the customs office, and speeding to their destinations on trains. Voice-overs by people with different accents express hope and excitement. An anglophone male voice-over explains the use of adult education for acquiring language skills and knowledge about the Canadian way of life. The film ends with a recurring trope: a scene of a teacher addressing her class about the similarity of all peoples around the world regardless of superficial differences; close-ups of visibly different students united through their hopeful looks at the teacher, visually demonstrate the substance of the narration. Not only immigrant adults and children are anchored by the Canadian authority of narrator and school-teacher alike, but the film enters into a regress of exemplarity as it was no doubt made to be shown to immigrants in the context of a language-acquisition class. The film thus expressly uses images of typical students in order to offer exemplary subject positions to new immigrants.

A tool for citizenship education sponsored by the Department of Citizenship and Immigration, *The Newcomers* reiterates the message of most films about immigrants from the 1950s: white European immigrants bring both willingness to start again (a desirable feature in an immigrant) and a knowledge of European culture (a desirable feature in a Canadian). Such films offer not reality so much as a possible narrative of integration. *The Newcomers* is also aimed at a general population, although it is less likely that people outside of the institutional settings where government film distribution was focussed would have been in the audience. With a strategy reminiscent of Park's governmental pragmatism, the economic benefits of immigrants are emphasized: "Canada is less dependent upon external sources for trade; immigrants are a vast new market." As was emphasized by citizenship education lobby groups such as the Committee on Cooperation in Canadian Citizenship, rural schools are depicted as important links in enculturation, teaching immigrant children Canadian ways. Yet the film makes an interesting slippage between providing citizenship education and demonstrating the apparatus of such pedagogy. Why would new immigrants in rural schools be shown films about people in the same situation as themselves? What the film actually serves to do is publicize the work of government institutions in the daily life of the population. The film ends with the refrain that Canada is a nation of immigrants: "All Canadian families come from across the sea," says the narrator. This statement, commonly echoed in multiculturalist education, tends to mystify, even while pretending to clarify, the politics and the history of the Canadian "mosaic."

Frontier College demonstrates the role that conscientious Canadians can play in educating adult immigrants. The story concerns a typical college student who is awakened to his larger civic duties by spending a summer as a Continuing Education instructor on a railway construction site. The railway camp is divided between men of Canadian origin and immigrants from Italy and Germany who are in conflict at the camp. As the teacher gains the trust of the opposing groups, he is able to help them overcome their conflicts through learning about Canadian ways. This development is expressed metaphorically by the immigrants replacing their home-country songs—discordant when sung simultaneously—with an indigenous railway song learned in class: "I've Been Working on the Railroad." *Frontier College* emphasizes the link between citizenship and education and stresses the importance of overcoming ethnic and sectional differences. It depicts culture in both an anthropological sense, as that which differentiates the immigrants from the Canadian narrator, and as something ennobling and universal, which may be achieved through art appreciation and the learning of Canadian ways. The two senses of the word meet in the schoolroom where Italian immigrants are invited to share the appreciation of Italian high art forms, like opera, with the class. In effect, the protagonist-narrator sorts out the elements of the workers' home "cultures" that may be successfully maintained in Canada. Perhaps most importantly, loyal citizenship, or the forging of national allegiance, in Charles Merriam's terms, is shown to be a source of national stability and even defence.

One of the most celebrated NFB films, *Paul Tomkowicz: Street-railway Switchman,* also offers an example of pairing an immigrant with a typical occupation. Often cited for its award-winning lyrical visual qualities, the film contains an interesting contradiction which usually goes uncommented upon. The subject of the film is shown working a night shift on the streets of Winnipeg while his reflections are heard in voice-over. Paul Tomkowicz was indeed interviewed by Roman Kroiter, but because of sound problems with the original tape, the voice-over one hears was actually read by an uncredited actor.[56] This substitution is significant in that the actor's voice, directed by Kroiter, produces another delivery, another text, out of Tomkowicz's words. This is symbolic of the representation of immigrants in so many NFB films: the films tend to craft a particular type of story that is largely independent of the actual people being shown. The narrator is most often a non-immigrant, but when he does take the immigrant's voice it may be read by an actor. In that the immigrant represented is made into the imaginary immigrant by the government film institution, these films become documents of "typifying" narratives.

One such narrative offered by film after film derives from the "making of citizens" rhetoric of the social sciences, in which children are the key to national re-integration. For example, *Threshold: The Immigrant Meets the School,* a film sponsored by The Ministry of Citizenship and Immigration, tells an exemplary story of postwar immigrants adapting to life in Canada. The sympathetic anglophone narrator observes that "the children are adapting faster than the parents can or will." After the immigrant family goes through a "normal" stage—"the period of tension"—which afflicts so many newcomers, the narrator sums up this shift: "Growth and change are constant in this young country." Although change is constant, it is the management of that change which interests social scientists and eugenic planners, and guides the narrative of a number of NFB documentaries of the period.

By and large, films on immigration impose one of two stories onto their subjects. (1) While immigrants must be prepared for a rough transition, their children will adapt without any problem. (2) Canadians are all immigrants, so tolerance for these necessary economic units is advisable. In the context of the films, the immigrant's economic necessity is seen to outweigh the distress their cultural difference might provoke. Not simply telling stories of typical recent arrivals, these films also often project into the probable future when more immigrants will be required to build civic works, consume products and/or contribute to Canadian culture. In order to secure consensus about the meaning of immigrants, therefore, the films reproduce the same narratives again and again.

By the mid-1950s, the reserve system for Native Canadians was an embarrassment which could only be rectified by complete integration of aboriginal people into mainstream Canadian society. In *No Longer Vanishing/Indiens du Canada,* sponsored by the Indian Affairs Branch of Immigration and Citizenship, an anglophone male voice-over says: "This is a story of the original Canadians who preceded the white man." Originally, we are told, reserves were designed to shelter Indians while they learned the white man's ways; instead they stayed there. However, well-intentioned mistakes of the past can be rectified by good will today; for example, the full value of Indian arts and culture is coming to be respected. Scenes of the reserve are acted out, highlighting poverty and filth. "Isolation, paternalism have hurt them, made them dependent," concludes the narrator. A First Nations male narrates in voice-over his return visit to the reserve. The people depicted as refusing to believe that he doesn't experience discrimination in the city are labelled "bitter Indians." In another case study, a First Nations woman who has become an urban nurse is interviewed. While she watches buffalo being fed at the zoo, she says in voice-over, "They've stopped dying out and are coming back, like our own people." According to the narrator, education in mixed schools is one of the best ways to help aboriginal people make "the transition." "Old prejudices are falling away in mixed classes," we are told.

Like so many films about "Native problems," *No Longer Vanishing* has several intentions: to exonerate the reserve system by situating it as a transitional model; to claim that there are no biological bases for prejudice even while repeatedly evoking the spectre of innate aptitudes; and to present state education as the site *par excellence* of "transition" into mainstream life. For this type of film, an early mainstay at the Film Board, the central question is one of government. How, the films ask, are "we" to help aboriginal people help themselves? What is the best way to craft citizens out of wards? These films are primarily produced for the non-Native population. Their message is thus a combination of multiculturalism and the immigrant discourse extended to First Nations "others."

Influenced by ideas from environmental urban sociology, governments—at various levels—often linked housing to social problems and, therefore, to the need for civic engineering. NFB films dealing with these issues highlight the public interest in the private domicile. For example, *On a Day Off*, sponsored by Central Mortgage and Housing, uses a fictionalized story about typical working class families to prove not only that with the help of the federal agency working class people might one day own their own homes, but also that with better homes come "better families."

Dealing with a variety of social "problems" and basing their approach on social scientific research methods, documentary films about citizenship produced by the Film Board in the 1950s commonly adopted the narrative strategy of recounting a typical, and therefore representative, case study using either actors or "real" people, and often both. Commonly, anonymous individuals are made to stand in for their social categories, the same categories required by the administrative apparatus of the liberal welfare state. Unsurprisingly, then, one finds that stories about the behaviour of citizens fall more or less neatly into a series of public policy categories: housing, labour, health and welfare, citizenship and immigration, Indian affairs and so on. The NFB films about the everyday life of citizens—by no means a description of all the films produced by the Board, but certainly one of its principle concerns in the 1940s and 1950s—produce narratives of citizenship in which individuals are subordinated to group identities smaller than that of the nation-state: "native," housewife, Québécois, farmer, immigrant. Based on the kind of statistical information produced by the census and marketing studies, these NFB films amount to hegemonic inscriptions of difference within the federation of the state.

Conclusions

The desire to categorize and govern is not solely a product of social scientific welfare state planning in Canada; it is also a legacy of colonial administration in general and the British North America Act in particular.

Historian Allan Smith has observed that the British North America Act attempted to achieve a new sort of nation-state, one built on a confederation of different and often polarized groups:

> Confederation created a political entity which owed its birth to the concern of its people, both French-speaking and English-speaking, to preserve a British civilization in North America, one which would, in time, assume the status and dignity of a great state. There would be a consensus in this new society, as there must be in any society, but it would not derive from a particular culture or set of values narrowly conceived. It would be a consensus which did not limit but rather encouraged diversity and freedom, and this not merely of individuals but of groups.[57]

Smith explains that "pluralism made necessary the construction of a political system that would accommodate it."[58] Within this liberal model, the public sphere is one site where discourse is incited through governmental technologies.

Nevertheless, social science-inspired 1950s documentary film production by the NFB played a crucial role in the mobilization of liberal social discourse and its attendant policies, particularly through the evocation of everyday life as the canvas on which scenes of good citizenship might be depicted. To paraphrase Adorno and Horkheimer on the culture industry, in these documentaries, not reality is offered, but evidence of its existence.[59] In the case of the NFB, filmic "evidence" of a well-managed Canadian society was seen to help create a sense of Canadian reality both at home and abroad. This vision is especially apparent in films which depict Canadian citizens in relation to government agencies, and the assumption of documentary transparency lent credibility to notions of political transparency in Canada.

NFB historians of the postwar period have, by and large, ignored the governmental function of the NFB, choosing instead to focus either on rare "great" films or on the thwarting of a feature film industry. Indeed, Grierson himself would no doubt have been much more forthright about the political objectives of NFB documentary films than are any of his chroniclers. For Grierson, documentary film produced by government was a way of achieving social compromise between polarized groups such as labour and management. For many who have written about Grierson and the Film Board, it would seem that the utopian goal of making films outside of market relations has nothing to do with political and social conflicts. Grierson, on the other hand, was proud of the role government documentary film production could play in the ambivalent project of selling Canada to itself. It is time that the NFB's connection to these governmental objectives be recognized.

Filmography

Corral (Canada, 1954, Colin Low)
City of Gold (Canada, 1957, Wolf Koenig, Colin Low)
The Days Before Christmas (Canada, 1958, Stanley Jackson, Wolf Koenig, Terence Macartney-Filgate)
Frontier College (Canada, 1954, Julian Biggs)
Gaspé Cod Fishermen (Canada, 1944, Jean Palardy)
Men of Lunenberg (Canada, 1956, director uncredited)
Neighbours (Canada, 1952, Norman McLaren)
The Newcomers (Canada, 1953, David Bennett)
No Longer Vanishing (Canada, 1955, Grant McLean)
On a Day Off (Canada, 1959, Erik Nielsen)
Passport to Canada (Canada, 1949, Roger Blais)
Paul Tomkowicz: Street-railway Switchman (Canada, 1954, Roman Kroiter)
Prairie Profile (Canada, 1955, Gordon Burwash)
The Romance of Transportation in Canada (Canada, 1953, Colin Low)
Threshold: The Immigrant Meets the School (Canada, 1959, George Bloomfield)
The Transition (Canada, 1964, Mort Ransen)

Acknowledgments

I would like to acknowledge the Grierson Archive, Stirling, Scotland, for permission to cite from documents in their collection. My thanks to the anonymous readers of the journal for their insightful comments on earlier drafts of this essay. All photos are courtesy of the National Film Board of Canada.

NOTES

1. See for example, Pierre Véronneau, *Résistance et affirmation: la production francophone a l'ONF—1939–1964* (Montréal: Cinémathèque Québècoise, 1987); Joyce Nelson, *The Colonized Eye: Re-thinking the Grierson Legend* (Toronto: Between the Lines, 1988); Peter Morris, "Re-thinking Grierson: The Ideology of John Grierson," in *Dialogue: Canadian and Quebec Cinema*, ed. Pierre Véronneau, Michael Dorland and Seth Feldman (Montréal: Mediatexte, 1989), 24–56; Peter Morris, " 'Praxis into Process': John Grierson and the National Film Board of Canada," *Historical Journal of film, Radio and Television* 9.3 (1989): 269–282; Scott Forsyth, "The Failures of Nationalism and Documentary: Grierson and Gouzenko," *Canadian Journal of Film Studies* 1.1 (1991): 74–82.
2. D. B. Jones, *Movies and Memoranda: An Interpretive History of the National Film Board of Canada* (Ottawa: Canadian Film Institute, 1981), 60.
3. *Paul Tomkowicz: Street-railway Switchman, Neighbours, Corral, The Romance of Transportation in Canada, The Days Before Christmas.*
4. My thanks to Peter Morris for sharing these raw data with me.
5. Michel Foucault, "Governmentality," in *The Foucault Effect*, ed. G. Burchell et al. (Chicago: University of Chicago Press, 1991), 102.
6. Barry Smart *Foucault, Marxism and Critique* (London: Routledge and Kegan Paul, 1985), 121.
7. Kevin Dowler, "The Cultural Industries Policy Apparatus," in *The Cultural Industries in Canada: Problems, Policies and Prospects*, ed. M. Dorland (Toronto: James Lorimer & Co., 1996), 330.
8. Colin Gordon, "Governmental Rationality: An Introduction," in *The Foucault Effect*, 19–20.
9. Ibid., 20.
10. By the turn of the century, The Canadian Pacific Railway, Massey-Harris, and the Canadian Government were already involved in film: "This early involvement by both commercial companies and government is of interest because it, too, set a pattern that continued to mark Canadian production over many decades. Indeed, it seems to have been realized almost from the beginning in Canada that film could be used for more than just entertainment" (Peter Morris, *Embattled Shadows* [Montréal: McGill-Queen's Press, 1978], 33).
11. Foucault, "Governmentality," 100.
12. See, for example, R. Blake and J. Keshen, eds., *Social Welfare Policy in Canada: Historical Readings* (Toronto: Copp Clark, 1995).
13. Reg Whitaker and Gary Marcuse, *Canada's Cold War* (Toronto: University of Toronto Press, 1994), 134.
14. Gary Evans, *In the National Interest* (Toronto: University of Toronto Press, 1991), 9.
15. This speculation is supported by the series of films planned for the Psychological Propaganda series which, although never filmed, bears a close resemblance to many of the films made as the decade progressed as part of series such as *Faces of Canada*. See Evans, 349.
16. "In 1921 one hundred foundations granted slightly over $180,000 for research and advanced education in the social sciences and history. By 1927 that benevolence had burgeoned to almost $8 million" (Edward Purcell Jr, *Crisis of Democratic Theory* [Lexington: University Press of Kentucky, 1973], 28).
17. William Stott, *Documentary Expression and Thirties America* (New York: Oxford University Press, 1973), 153.
18. Ibid., 160.
19. Purcell Jr., 17, 19.
20. Forsyth Hardy, *John Grierson: A Documentary Biography* (London: Faber and Faber, 1978), 31.
21. John Grierson, "Propaganda and Education," in *Grierson on Documentary*, ed. Forsyth Hardy (London: Faber and Faber, 1979), 149–151.
22. Grierson reportedly kept a copy of Charles Merriam's *American Political Ideas* handy until the end of his life (Hardy, 34).
23. John Grierson, "The Russian Example," in *Grierson on Documentary*, 23–4.
24. Hardy, *John Grierson*, 59.
25. Charles E. Merriam, *The Making of Citizens* (Columbia: Teachers College Press, 1966), 34 (originally published 1931). All subsequent references will appear in the text as page numbers.
26. Marlene Shore, *The Science of Social Redemption* (Toronto: University of Toronto Press, 1987), 85–6.
27. Robert Park, *Race and Culture* (Glencoe: Free Press, 1950), 144.
28. Ibid., 144.
29. Ibid., 146.
30. Shore, 98.
31. Evans, 31; William Young, "Making the Truth Graphic: The Canadian Government's Home Front Information Structure and Programmes During World War II" (Ph.D. diss. University of British Columbia, 1978), 52.
32. Walter Lippmann, *Public Opinion* (New York: Free Press, 1922), 39.
33. Ibid., 39.
34. Walter Lippmann, *The Phantom Public* (New York: Harcourt, Brace & Co. 1925), 189.
35. John Grierson, "Education and Total Effort," in *Grierson on Documentary*, 139.
36. Paul Swann, *The British Documentary Film Movement 1926–1946* (Cambridge: Cambridge University Press, 1989), 10.
37. Ibid., 21; see also Stephen Constantine, " 'Bringing the Empire Alive': The Empire Marketing Board and Imperial Propaganda, 1926–1933," in *Imperialism and Popular Culture*, ed. John Mackenzie (Manchester: Manchester University Press, 1986), 192–231.
38. Ian Aitken, *Film and Reform: John Grierson and the Documentary Film Movement* (London: Routledge, 1989), 96.
39. James Beveridge, *John Grierson: Film Master* (London: Faber & Faber, 1978), 135.
40. Swann, 144.

41. Imperial Relations Trust, *Annual Report, 1938-1939*, 9.
42. Gary Evans, *John Grierson and the National Film Board of Canada* (Toronto: University of Toronto Press, 1984); Marjorie McKay, *History of the National Film Board of Canada* (National Film Board Archives, n.d.).
43. "The Trustees were fortunate in securing the services of Mr. John Grierson as their Film Officer. In May 1938 Mr. Grierson went to Canada. He had been invited by the Canadian Government to advise on certain aspects of the Government's film activities and he was able, at the same time, to investigate for the Trustees the position in regard to the distribution of British and other Dominion films in Canada, and to study the question of the production of Canadian films suitable for distribution to the United Kingdom and other Dominions" (Imperial Relations Trust, *Annual Report* [1938-39], 10).
44. John Grierson, *Report on Canadian Government Film Activities*, 1938 (National Archives of Canada, RG 20, Vol. 578, file T-A-383 Vol. 1). Another equally important upshot of Grierson's visit was the granting of Imperial Relations funding to the National Film Society of Canada and the Canadian Association for Adult Education in order to sponsor a conference on educational uses of the non-theatrical film, which took place in Winnipeg in September 1938 and resulted in the establishment of the civilian Canadian General Film Committee, described by the Trust as "a co-ordinating body representative of institutions and organizations interested in the production and use of films for educational and cultural purposes" (Imperial Relations Trust, *Annual Report* [1938-39], 10).
45. John Grierson, "Letter From Grierson to Stephen Tallents," in the Grierson Archive G4: 25: 2 (January 9, 1941), 3; italics mine.
46. Ibid., 3.
47. Young, 33; N. F. Dreisziger, "The Rise of a Bureaucracy for Multiculturalism: The Origins of the Nationalities Branch, 1939–1941," in *On Guard for Thee: War, Ethnicity, and the Canadian State*, 1939–1945, ed. N. Hillmer et al. (Ottawa: Canadian Committee for the History of the Second World War, 1988), 20.
48. William Young, "Chauvinism and Canadianism: Canadian Ethnic Groups and the Failure of Wartime Information," in *On Guard for Thee*, 37.
49. Ibid., 38.
50. Dreisziger, 21.
51. Ibid., 23.
52. Canada, *Hansard Parliamentary Debates*, 4th Session, 18th Parliament, Volume II (March 8, 1939), 1737.
53. Daniel Robinson, "Polling Consumers and Citizens" (Ph.D. diss., York University, 1996), 202.
54. Grierson, "The Nature of Propaganda," 108. Significantly, the Massey-Lévèsque Report reiterates these sentiments about adult education in 1951: "In a democratic state, national effort in war and national unity in peace are maintained only by the informed conviction of its citizens. No democratic government can afford to neglect at any time a means of public information so far-reaching and so persuasive as the film. The provision and distribution of films by the national government is as little open to question as the issue of the white paper or the blue book (*The Royal Commission on National Development in the Arts, Letters and Sciences* [1951], 310).
55. Canada. *Hansard Parliamentary Debates*, 6th Session, 21st Parliament, Volume IV (July 4, 1952), 4278.
56. Evans, *In the National Interest*, 75.
57. Allan Smith, "Metaphor and Nationality in North America," *The Canadian Historical Review* 51.3 (1970), 254–5.
58. Ibid., 255.
59. The exact quotation is, "Not Italy is offered, but evidence that it exists" (Theodor Adorno & Max Horkheimer, *Dialectic of Enlightenment*, trans. John Cumming [New York: Continuum, 1990], 148).

51

SRIRUPA ROY

MOVING PICTURES

The Films Division of India and the Visual Practices of the Nation-State (2007)

[. . .]

My specific focus here is on the history, practices, and productions of the Films Division of India, which was established as a branch of the state Ministry of Information and Broadcasting in 1948—shortly after independence. In the fifty-odd years of its existence, it has produced over eight thousand documentaries, short films, and newsreels, or an average of one new film every three days, making it the single largest producer of documentary films in the world. Until 1994, under the terms of a compulsory exhibition and licensing policy, owners of commercial movie theaters throughout India were required to screen a state-approved documentary film or newsreel before the start of any commercial feature film. In addition, the Films Division supplied prints to several central ministries such as the Ministry of Welfare and the Department of Field Publicity (a branch of the Ministry of Information and Broadcasting that was constituted to generate rural support for the project of economic planning) for free screenings in rural areas. With this framework of distribution in place, the Films Division could claim an average audience strength of eighty million viewers every week.

However, as a review commission noted as early as 1967, the prodigious output of the Films Division and the ambitious scope of its distribution scheme did not necessarily translate into, and may even have militated against, the meaningful reception of its visual texts.[1] The national distribution scheme paid little attention to the specific conditions under which different groups of subnational audiences actually receive or engage with the films. Reflecting this disinterest in questions of effect, most Films Division documentaries are characterized by their ponderous and heavy-handed style; for the most part, they lend themselves all too readily to charges of clumsy propaganda and bureaucratic ineptitude. When we examine the spectacular and enchanted dreamworlds of "Bollywood" or Hindi commercial cinema with which they compete for attention, the credibility of such dismissals is further heightened. What explains this phenomenon of "production for its own sake?" Why are Films Division documentaries so boring?

By way of answering these questions, in this chapter I undertake a close investigation of an apparently paradoxical phenomenon: the "disenchanted imaginary" produced by the Films Division of India in the first two decades after Indian independence. Through a discussion of the origins, governing imperatives, formal treatment, and thematic choices made by the state producers of documentary film during the first few decades after independence, I show how the Films Division enabled the constitution of a distinct identity for the state as an authoritative representative of the Indian nation—an identity that could be recognized both by nonstate audiences and by state elites themselves. In this project of state identification, the content of the visual representations produced by the Films Division were of considerable importance—the ways in which the Films Division quite literally allowed national audiences to "see the state" and the concrete activities that it was undertaking on behalf of the nation. Of equal importance, however, was the distinctive filmic idiom that it deployed. As I demonstrate below, it was through the elaboration of a distinctive filmic genre of the state documentary—through the formal differentiation produced by effects of "boredom," "disenchantment," and "nonresonance"—that the distinctive authorial flourish of the state's signature was secured.

Lineages of Documentary Film

I begin here with a discussion of the origins of the Films Division and of the multiple imperatives and actors that shaped the relationship between state and film in the early years of postcolonial India. Although the Films Division was formally established by the postcolonial state shortly after the transfer of power from imperial to sovereign national hands in 1947, the practice of state involvement in the production of film has an older colonial history. To quote a publicity brochure issued by the Films Division in 1969: "Like the roads and the railways, the posts and telegraphs, the administrative system and the armed services, which the British built up primarily in the interests of Empire and secondarily in the interests of the ruled, the Documentary film and the Newsreel too were brought in. And in the transplanted soil, both seemed to have thrived well."[2]

Both state and nonstate actors were involved in this exercise of transplantation. If documentary film played a key role in disseminating visual representations of nation and state in India, this was not so much an outcome engineered by state propaganda agencies as it was a "coproduction" authored by a motley crew of bureaucrats, independent filmmakers, civil society associations such as the Documentary Unit of India and the Independent Documentary Producers Association that were established as production consortiums and lobby groups for documentary filmmakers, and international organizations such as UNESCO and the Ford Foundation that played a critical role in encouraging the use of audiovisual technologies in the "new nations" of the third world.[3]

The term "documentary" was first used by the filmmaker John Grierson to describe Robert Flaherty's film *Moana* (1926). For Grierson, a documentary film was one that entailed "a creative treatment of actuality,"[4] and it is this notion of portraying "actuality" or accurately depicting reality that informed the earliest efforts at documentary filmmaking in India. The existing tradition of filmmaking in India already included "topicals," or short films on real events,[5] but these were nonreflexive, "random filmings of scenes" devoid of any overarching structure or message.[6] The return to India of three Indian filmmakers—P. V. Pathy, K. S. Hirlekar, and D. G. Tendulkar, from Paris, Berlin, and Moscow, respectively—led to the initiation of the Indian documentary movement in the

1930s.[7] Inspired by the example of German *kultur* films; by Soviet cinema (primarily the work of Sergei Eisenstein); and by the work of John Grierson and Paul Rotha in England and Robert Flaherty and Pare Lorentz in the United States, these Indian filmmakers felt that film should have a definite social purpose of instruction, information, and motivation. The choice of appropriate "topics" and their "creative treatment" therefore required careful attention. Accordingly, the earliest Indian documentaries were films made for "the education and enlightenment of the people."[8] These included films on the Indian nationalist movement (*The Haripura Congress Session*, 1938), films appealing for funds for earthquake victims (the Imperial Film Company's film on the Quetta earthquake), films publicizing the railway system in India (the travelogues of K. Subramaniam), and films that focused on a specific cultural or historical aspect of Indian reality (including works such as Mohan Bhavnani's *Mysore—Gem of India*; as well as the film *Keddah*, on elephant trapping, and *Wrestling*, on "the various peculiarly Indian techniques of this popular sport").[9]

For the practitioners of documentary making in India in the 1930s, the medium could be an agent and instrument of social change, with filmmakers emulating the documentarian Paul Rotha's self-description as a "legislator of mankind" or a builder of a new social order.[10] However, this impulse of social reform did not interrogate the authority of the colonial state, and the aim of "educating and enlightening" the people did not disrupt the civilizing presumptions of colonial rule. Thus the universal themes of modernization (the railways; the notion of voluntary civilian donations to help the underprivileged; and even the existence of impulses of political modernity such as the Indian National Congress) were showcased in an effort to trace the movement of the Indian people in the direction of development and progress under the guidance of the colonial state. India itself found particularist meaning as a conglomeration of culturally diverse and custom-bound groups.

The colonial state had similar views on the instructive nature and social function of the documentary film, and it was the state's utilization of the documentary genre as part of its "war effort" during World War II that gave the Indian documentary movement its first institutional support structure. With the onset of the war in Europe, the state turned to its subjects for crucial assistance in the form of manpower and strategic supplies. In 1940 the Imperial Department of Information, through its chief bureaucrat, Desmond Young, authorized the creation of a Film Advisory Board (FAB). The FAB's mission was to produce films that would publicize the urgency and the requirements of the war situation, as well as appeal for popular support.[11] Despite its explicitly imperial concerns, the FAB was supported by a number of individuals sympathetic to the nationalist cause, for whom the importance of engaging in an immediate battle against fascist forces in the international arena overshadowed more localized concerns. The films produced by the FAB include war-related documentaries on topics such as military recruitment (*He's in the Navy*) and military technology (*The Planes of Hindustan*), as well as nonstrategic documentaries on general themes that would both be of interest to and inform the Indian public (*Women of India; Industrial India*). However, even the latter category of "nonpropagandist" films linked the representations of India to the presence and activities of the British state, which was presented in both *Women of India* and *Industrial India* as the central protagonist—that is, as the progressive and developmentalist institutional authority that enabled India and Indians to move forward.

Further, the particular filmic form favored by FAB officials was one that underscored a vertical or hierarchical relation of authority between filmmaker and film viewer and, by implication, between state and society. The company Time-Life Inc. sponsored the documentary series *The March of Time* (produced by Louis de Rochemont in 1938), and its authoritative conventions such as the use of "voice-of-God" interpretive narrations, the tendency to summarize personal interviews with explanatory comments, diagrams, and charts, and the focus on "important people" had a strong impact on the FAB chairman, Ezra Mir, who actively encouraged the production of similar films for an Indian audience. The FAB was eventually replaced by a set of three specialized organizations: the Information Films of India (IFI), Indian News Parade (INP), and the Army Film Centre (AFC). While newsreels and films related to war propaganda were those most frequently produced, the occasional creative and nonpropaganda ventures were also supported by the British state (e.g., Mohan Bhavnani's *The Private Life of a Silkworm*, and Paul Zil's *Bombay: The Story of Seven Isles*). These films attempted to portray some aspect of Indian life to domestic audiences, and education and information were once again the primary motivations. The state also turned its attention to the distribution of films and enforced rule 44A of the Defence of India Rules to mandate compulsory exhibition of state-produced films by private exhibitors all over India.

The colonial state's documentary production and distribution efforts ceased in 1946 because there was no longer a need for war propaganda. Moreover, in the particular conjuncture of the "endgame of empire," the state increasingly resorted to coercive measures, thereby abandoning its project of persuasion and the quest to secure the normative compliance of the subject population. Nevertheless, as the film historian Sanjit Narwekar notes, many Indian nationalists continued to view with suspicion the FAB and the IFI, and by association, the broader enterprise of the official documentary film, accusing these organizations of "try[ing] to dragoon an unwilling nation into the war."[12]

The task of reinventing the documentary film as the handmaid of a national rather than a colonial state was part and parcel of a larger enterprise of reimagining the new, postcolonial India. The redefinition of the state as national rather than colonial, of the relation between the state and its people in terms of citizenship rather than subjecthood, and even of the national community itself (given the geographical and demographic reconfiguration of India after the partition in 1947) were pressing tasks confronted by the postcolonial polity. Moreover, the state was presented as the key agent in this process of national becoming; a new, sovereign state, that, unlike its colonial predecessor, could be visibly shown to undertake activities that were "truly representative" of the Indian people.

In postcolonial India, this imperative of visibility was served through the adoption of a "monumental"[13] style of state making, or the undertaking of large-scale technological and industrial projects. India after 1950 was a nation that was defined through the big dreams of its state. On the domestic front, this view translated into a commitment to planned development through the construction of institutions, expertise, and material artifacts that could quite literally be seen to command the economy from a transcendent, directorial vantage point. Science and technology also enabled the dreams of greatness to be literalized: the new India could, and did, build big dams, big bridges, big railway coach factories, big power plants, and big atomic reactors. And these projects were all proclaimed to exist because of the representative labors of the sovereign state. In official public discourse as well as in the contemporary media landscape, the state facilitation of big development, big science, and big technology received maximum emphasis and was upheld as visible evidence of the representative commitments of Indian independence. But this logic of visible representation could make sense only in the eyes of a viewer; only if a particular way of seeing could be presumed. From April 1948 onward, the Films Division and its documentary films and newsreels were harnessed in the task of consolidating this gaze. With this, the national value of the documentary film no longer needed to be the subject of impassioned pleas put forth by documentary filmmakers. They could now be nation builders, and the state could now be a documentary filmmaker.

In sum, the decision to establish the Films Division in 1948 was shaped by the interplay of varied imperatives and stakes that structured the political field of decolonization. The emulation of colonial governance practices; the particular exigencies of "postcolonial anxiety" in India; contemporaneous inspiration from the use of documentary film by other nation-states such as Britain, the United States, Canada, and the Soviet Union;[14] and pragmatic calculations about the value of audiovisual pedagogy in a country characterized by a high level of illiteracy all played a role in authorizing the state's use of documentary film.

[. . .]

Seeing India

In terms of its organizational structure, the Films Division resembled all other bureaucratic organizations, with little to distinguish its particular mandate of aesthetic labor. Its headquarters were in Bombay, with three nodal field offices in Delhi, Calcutta, and Bangalore and several branch offices in other metropolitan centers in India.[15] The organization was headed by the chief producer, and while the first few heads were professional filmmakers, in later years the post was filled by generalists drawn from the Indian Administrative Services who did not necessarily have any prior filmmaking experience.

In its initial years, the Films Division consisted of a production wing and a distribution wing. Film topics were suggested by different ministries, government agencies, and state governments. There was also an annual interministries meeting where coordinated topics were suggested, and on the basis of this meeting an annual production plan was finalized by the Ministry of Information and Broadcasting. The responsibilities for documentary production were shared by three producers: one in charge of documentaries; one in charge of newsreels; and one in charge of commissioning productions by independent filmmakers.[16] With the state as the biggest patron of the short film in the 1950s and 1960s, filmmakers were eager to sign contracts with the Films Division and they viewed its work in very favorable terms. The relation between the Indian state and the independent artist was thus a collaborative and accommodative one in the immediate post-independence period—for the most part, both parties shared common understandings about the nature and purpose of documentary film as a tool that could bring awareness to "ethically incomplete"[17] national audiences. Filmmakers interested in establishing themselves as the creators of serious or intellectual cinema frequently turned to the Films Division for sponsorship and financial support.[18] A list of directors and producers of Films Division documentaries over the past fifty years includes names like Satyajit Ray, Mrinal Sen, Shyam Benegal, K. A. Abbas, Sukhdev, and other pioneers of independent Indian cinema.

The distribution wing coordinated the complicated process by which forty thousand prints were screened in cinema theaters throughout the country every year. A hundred new newsreels and another hundred new documentary prints in the thirteen official languages were released weekly to two hundred different "first-run" cinema houses throughout the country. After one week, the first-run houses that had initially received the documentaries would receive the newsreels, and those initially receiving the newsreels would receive the documentaries. Once this circuit had been completed, the prints would be sent on to the second-run houses and so on until over the course of a year all of the national cinema houses in the country had received the prints. From each cinema house, the Films Division would collect 1 percent of the total box-office earnings as a rental fee for the screening of its documentaries and newsreel films. In addition to this revenue-generating process of film circulation, prints were supplied to the Field Publicity Directorate for free showings to urban and rural audiences.[19] The scope andambition of this distribution scheme led at least one critic to estimate that the Films Division films had an "audience potential" of over ten million individuals every week.[20]

To what extent did this audience potential translate into lived experience? Further, what did the viewing of a Films Division documentary entail—that is, what was illuminated and what in turn was obscured? Finally, who was addressed, by whom, and how? To answer these questions, I turn to the actual films themselves along with the specific choices of form and content, the production practices, and the visual treatment that together enabled the Films Division to chart a distinctive line of sight in postcolonial India.

According to the Films Division's own classificatory scheme, it produced several different kinds of films for the "people of India."[21] These categories include: art and experimental films; biography and personality films; classroom films and children's films; educational and motivational films; Defence Ministry films; export and tourist promotion films; and "the visit" films, or documentaries on official trips taken by Indian state officials to other countries. A somewhat different categorization scheme informs Table 51.1, which is based on thematic distinctions that were endorsed by the Films Division at the time of a comprehensive review of the approximately seventeen hundred documentaries that had been produced by 1972, commemorating twenty years of its establishment. As the table indicates, approximately 8 percent of the documentaries were on topics of art and culture; 18 percent on citizenship and reform; 17 percent on defense and the "international scene"; and 38 percent on development and planning. The remaining films were an assortment of biographical documentaries, children's films, documentaries on "geography and travel," and experimental films. It is useful here to take a closer look at some of these efforts to document different aspects of Indian reality and the visions of India and Indians that were elaborated for audiences across the nation, whether in the plush air-conditioned environments of colonial cinema houses in the major metropolitan centers, or in the open-air *maidans* (fields) in small towns and villages.

The art and culture documentaries portrayed India's natural regional cultural diversity. These films represented culture as a tangible artifact, object, or visible practice that could be located in a specific time and place: for example, Madhubani paintings from Bihar in eastern India, temple carvings from the Ajanta caves in western India, or Kathakali dancers from the southern state of Kerala. On display were the discrete, almost hermetically sealed worlds indexed by each of these distinctive cultural forms and practices. Further, in reflecting the nationalist predilection for the folk, the location of culture was invariably nonurban. The gaze of the Films Division was almost exclusively directed toward prelapsarian vistas of colorful exuberance that constituted Indianness as a collection of exotic others. No matter who the audience was, there was always some "forgotten," "unknown," or "hidden" cultural community that could be presented before it as a result of what Films Division officials described as their painstaking labors of cultural recuperation and excavation.

The depictions of folk cultural diversity created a spatial distance between

TABLE 51.1 Categories of Films Division Documentaries, 1949–1972

CATEGORY	NUMBER OF FILMS
Art and Culture	139
Archaeology and monuments	30
Arts	55
Crafts	9
Festivals	13
People of India	32
Citizenship and Reform	314
Civic education	35
Government and citizenship	59
Health and hygiene	137
Education and youth activities	78
Coins, weights, and measures	5
Development and Planning	696
Agriculture	137
Community development and cooperation	59
Cottage industries	20
Fisheries	12
Five-year plans and their projects	65
Housing	10
Industry	89
Labor and employment	25
Relief and rehabilitation	27
Savings	43
Science and technology	40
Social welfare	35
Trade and commerce	29
Transport and communications	105
Miscellaneous	304
Biography	50
Children's films	11
Classroom films	15
Current history	28
Experimental films	18
Food	28
Geography and travel	115
Natural resources	13
Sports, pastime, and recreation	26
Defense and International	289
Defense	121
International scene	168
TOTAL	1,742

Source: Pati, *Films Division Catalogue of Films*, 1949–1972.

the audience and the subject of films on painting, music, and dance, contributing to the sense that "real culture" was inevitably located elsewhere. A series of films on architecture created a similar effect of temporal distance, as they located culture in a remote past at considerable remove from the time-space of the contemporaneous viewer. Here, too, the diversity of architectural form was the dominant theme, with

Indians urged to contemplate their heritage as a constellation of singular monumental forms scattered throughout national territory, united only by the eye of the statist camera. The state's role as the unifier of the nation, or the fact that only state-sponsored cultural activities could bring forth an undifferentiated sense of being Indian, was underscored through another set of art and culture films—namely, those that turned their lens on the "festivals of India." Here, the only festival that enjoyed the unqualified or uninflected label of Indianness was that of Republic Day. All others were marked by their distinctive religious and regional particularities: a Buddhist commemoration, a Punjabi marriage, or a carnival in Goa, all of which were described as "festivals of India" even as—and in fact because—they belonged to discrete, subnational cultural universes. In a similar vein, alongside the documentaries that highlighted the diversity of regional musical instruments and forms were the films that showcased the efforts of the state-owned All India Radio to promote a genre of "national music," drawing attention to the unique ability of the state to integrate the culturally diverse nation.[22]

A second set of documentaries addressed various aspects of "citizenship and reform." The understanding of citizenship that informed the cinematic imaginary of the Films Division was one that emphasized the proximity, rather than the distance or the autonomy, of the citizen from state institutions. The ideal citizen was characterized by her or his ability to obey, comply with, and otherwise follow the instructions of the state, and the practice of citizenship was depicted in tutelary and pedagogical terms as a learning activity or an ongoing process of acquiring skills and attributes rather than an already-possessed right or claim that could be exercised in the present.[23] The Films Division imparted a wide range of citizenship lessons. Some documentary films undertook the task of familiarizing audiences with the technologies of citizenship in the most literal sense of the word by providing instructions on how to mark ballot papers and how to use ballot boxes.[24] Others called for various forms of behavioral reform that would invest selfish individuals with a sense of social responsibility and enable them to appreciate and fulfill the manifold duties of citizenship. Individuals were "motivated" to realign their private values with public ones, and to redefine self-interest in terms of the national rather than the individual self. For instance, in *The Case of Mr. Critic* (1954), the ideal citizen was depicted as one who refrained from engaging in "socially unproductive acts" of criticism and was mindful of the "damage caused by loose and irresponsible talk."[25] A similar exhortation informed *Dilly Dallying*, a film produced in 1957 that purported to convey "how the habit of delay can ruin a man" and can cause considerable damage to the larger national project of social and economic advancement.[26]

The theme of "exemplary Indians" was the explicit focus of another category of films, the "biography and personality" documentaries. Unlike the anonymous address of the citizenship films, this set of documentaries focused on named, individual exemplars. According to the Films Division's own summary, the selection of individuals included "those who fought the British, emancipated the women, unravelled the mysteries of science, expounded the philosophy of Hinduism, and enriched Indian art and culture."[27] Crucial significations of ideal Indians were embedded in these choices, with the individuals deemed worthy of emulation as those who uphold the values of national sovereignty (fighting the British), rationality and science ("unravelling the mysteries of science"), and above all leadership/guidance and instruction (philosophers, artists, emancipators of women). The choice of exemplary individuals also took into account the representation of regional diversity. In portraying the lives of "great men and women," both their contributions to the greater national good as well as their distinct regional origins received equal emphasis—thus the Nobel Laureate Rabindranath Tagore is depicted as both a national poet and a "son of Bengal."[28] In this way different regions were presented with their "own" national hero: the act of exemplification at once totalizing and fragmenting in its effect and import.

While films on art and culture, citizenship and reform, and biography documented "the people of India" and their varied cultural and civic practices, a significant number of films showcased the forms and feats of state institutions and officials. In the "defence films" and the films on "the international scene" (these covered the visits of Indian presidents and prime ministers to other countries and the reciprocal visits of "foreign dignitaries" to India), the protagonists were the office bearers of the state rather than ordinary—or in the case of the biography films, extraordinary—civilians. If the Films Division may be seen to have consolidated a statist vision of nationhood, tying national identity to the presence and actions of the state, then these films advanced this vision in the most explicit way. Armies and prime ministers stood in for the state, which then stood in for, and as, the nation and its citizens.[29]

Finally, the single largest category of Films Division documentaries, representing more than a third of the total output of documentary films in the first two decades after independence, were those that addressed the themes of planned development and various aspects of social and economic modernization. The specific treatment of these themes was realized in a variety of different ways. In some films the abstract ideals of the Nehruvian imaginary of modernization and planned development took concrete visual form and were materialized either as distinct artifacts such as dams, steel plants, locomotive factories, or agricultural equipment, or as specific sets of embodied practices: thus we see farmers using new water pumps in *Partners for Plenty* (1955); women in *salwar kameezes* adeptly handling test tubes in *The Black Gold*, a film made in 1965 about "oil exploration in India"; and engineers engaged in dexterous labors of "flood control" along the embankment of a rapidly rising river in *Fight the Floods* (1955), a film that "dramatically presents the havoc wrought by floods in various parts of the country and highlights the work of the Central Flood Control Board."[30] The accompanying narrative commentary located these images in the contemporaneous time-space of the viewer, with progress, modernity, and development described not as idealized future horizons but as immediate, tangible substances. The monumental edifices of the Bhakra Nangal dam towering over an empty landscape (*A Symbol of Progress*, 1965); the glowing furnaces in steel plants that "took one's breath away";[31] and the smiling farmers steering gigantic tractors with studied ease and nonchalance in *Where the Desert Blooms* (1962), a film on the Central Mechanised Farm in Suratgarh, Rajasthan, were all a part of the Films Division's distinctive elaboration of a modernity that was "spectacular" in both senses of the term—visible as well as grand.

In contrast to this spectacular and "fetishized figuration of modernity,"[32] other Films Division documentaries presented modernity and development as imperceptible phenomena that left no material traces in the present. In films such as *Our Regulated Markets* (1960), a film on the "hardships and losses inflicted on the producer-sellers by the middlemen and efforts made to eradicate them in the form of regulated markets,"[33] or in *Dry Leaves* (1961), on the "dowry system" and how "this age-old custom has ruined many a home,"[34] the present was characterized not by the concrete achievements of modernity but by backwardness, negation, and loss. Where other films emphasized the successful grasping of modernity in the present—thus India today has a steel plant, a dam, a self-sufficient economy—these films elaborated a different vision of a deferred modernity, reproducing images and narratives of problems and obstacles rather than solutions and triumphs. Suggesting that the temporal logic of official developmentalist discourse is more doubled or ambivalent than teleological, this set of films depicted the present as an uncertain "waiting room,"[35] rather than a definitive and triumphant "moment of arrival."[36]

The question of agency in processes of development and modernization also met with multiple responses in Films Division documentaries. Who or what was the agent of development and modernity—the state or the people? Or did agency and intention not matter at all, and were development and modernity occurrences that were structurally determined and inevitable? The documentary films of the state endorsed all of these positions, and elaborated visions of "assisted progress" as well as "natural progress." Some films focused on the state's essential role in initiating and promoting modernization and development (*Phosphate for Plenty*, 1970). Others emphasized instead the autonomous initiatives of ordinary people (*Your Contribution*, 1954). Still others departed from these agent-centric understandings altogether in their elaboration of the unstoppable and self-propelling dynamics of modernity (*Kisan* ["The Farmer"], 1967).

Of significance is the simultaneity or the coexistence of these differential visions, and the fact that the ambivalent and fissured constitution of modernity ostensibly stemmed from the singular institutional source of the state. Calling into question the monolithic presumptions of James Scott's influential metaphor of "seeing like a state," the contending imaginaries produced by the Films Division drew attention instead to the fragmented nature of the statist vision—to the blurring rather than the "legibility" of "social mapping" practices.[37] In their representation of development, progress, and modernity as simultaneously achieved and unachievable, material and ephemeral, specified and anonymous, triumphant and anxiety-laden, and assisted and self-generating, these films reflected the complex constellation of competing imperatives, governance levels, policy frameworks, and political actors that constituted the postcolonial Indian state.

[...]

The decade of the 1960s saw the emergence of a new set of visual vocabularies. Even as Films Division documentaries continued to imagine India in terms of the constitutive and indissoluble link between nation and state, the representations of nation and state registered several significant shifts. For instance, the specific conjuncture of India's war with China in 1962 led to the production of films in which martial strength was the defining attribute of the state; vulnerability the distinguishing characteristic of the nation; and sacrifice and bravery the constitutive features of the ideal citizen.[38] A trailer with the no-nonsense title of *National Anthem-cum-Flag* was produced by the Films Division in 1963 at the behest of the Committee for Emergency Publicity (in existence from 1962 until 1968) and the National Defence Council, a multipartisan group constituted to coordinate civilian defense efforts. All commercial film screenings were required to conclude with an exhibition of this one-minute film. The national sound waves were also harnessed by the new requirement of increasing the visibility of official emblems, and a new practice of playing a recording of the national anthem at the conclusion of the daily broadcast of All India Radio was introduced in March 1963 at the same time as the mandatory screening of the anthem/flag film.[39]

Other films undertook the task of meaning making. It was not enough simply to disseminate the sights and sounds of the state, but their correct national significance also had to be specified. As the annual report of the Ministry of Information and Broadcasting (the parent organization of the Films Division) noted in 1965, it was imperative to produce films that could effectively communicate and explain "the necessity of maintaining decorum whenever the national anthem is sung."[40] If in the documentary films from the 1950s a dam, a laboratory, or a census survey stood in for the relationship between nation and state, the entry of a new discourse of "national security" in the 1960s occasioned an additional set of signifying practices. The feats of the armed forces, the chords of the national anthem, and the fluttering tricolor flag now became familiar presences in Films Division documentaries, with Indians urged to contemplate not what the state could do for them but what they could do for the state.

Amid these many transformations in the cinematic vision of the state that reflected the dynamic, processual character of the nation-statist project in postcolonial India, certain representational themes and devices remained unchanged over time. In particular, and despite the significant changes in political, economic, and social structure and practice that took place between the Films Division's founding in 1948 and the major retrospective organized in 1972 to celebrate two decades of its existence, the cinematic representations of "the Indian Muslim"—or rather, the aporias and elisions of these representations—remained remarkably constant. The catalogue of films produced by the Films Division in 1972, covering twenty-two years of documentary film production, describes in detail an impressive total of 1,742 documentaries. [...] Only seventeen of these films, or less than 1 percent, had anything to do with the presence of Muslims in India.

Moreover, although these films differed in terms of their subject matter, they all contributed to a common understanding of the status of Muslims as special minorities set apart from the national mainstream in one way or another. The Films Division documentaries from the 1950s and 1960s invariably constituted "Muslimness" as a special or qualified national presence. Some films celebrated the lives of exemplary, famous, and "good Muslims"—for example, the Mughal emperor Akbar, the poet Ghalib, and the musicians Zakir Hussain, Allah Rakha, and Allaudin Khan. In another instance, *Bound for Haj* (1959), the visibility of Muslims served to illustrate the protective beneficence of the state in facilitating the sacred pilgrimage to Mecca. The theme of select Muslims as ideal citizens was furthered as well in *A Muslim Festival in Secular India* (1965), a film depicting the Id festivities at the official residence of then-president Zakir Hussain. *A Muslim Festival* stood in marked contrast to the unqualified and generalized address of *The Faith* (1967), a film about the Hindu pilgrims at the Kumbh Mela festival along the banks of the river Ganges in Allahabad. A final set of films evacuated contemporaneous subjectivity and agency from Muslims altogether, with architectural monuments (the Taj Mahal, the Qutb Minar) and "cultural heritage" (Hindustani music, Kathak dance) standing in for Muslims in India. In this manner, and to use the agency's own words as quoted at the opening of this chapter, the "memory of the nation" encapsulated within the "storage vaults" of the Films Division attests to the graded hierarchies of diversity displays in postcolonial India. Even in the "golden age" of Nehruvian secularism, then, the light of Indianness shone in a selective and partial manner, as encounters with the nation-state consistently illuminated some experiences of national belonging and obscured others.[41]

Shifting Visions II: Contending Imperatives

Not all variations in the documentaries produced by the Films Division could be explained by temporal shifts in the political field. As noted in the previous section, the Films Division also produced significantly different representations of state and nation within the same time period. With the postcolonial state itself constituted as a multi-layered arena informed by different, even contending, imperatives, the Films Division played several different roles at any given point in time. For instance, while the Films Division embodied a productive or positive relationship between the state and film—that is, the state as filmmaker—a significant set of negative restrictions and prohibitions were also put in place at the same time, from the rationing of film stock and the activation of colonial censorship laws to the state control of venues and channels of film distribution. Engaged in the work of film production at a time when the access of filmmakers to raw film stock was severely restricted,[42] the Films Division was charged with the responsibility of presenting the "right" cinematic vision, and of working in tandem with the censorship agencies of the state and their mandate of preventing the "wrong" visions from gaining public exposure.[43] In supplementing the negative or prohibitory impulses of state power, the Films Division was assigned a role in the postcolonial project of producing an interventionist state that was at the same time accountable and limited: one that would not be characterized by the heavy hand of coercion alone.

Thus on the one hand the documentary films produced by the Films Division addressed themselves to the pedagogical mandate of the state by upholding exemplary visions of India and Indianness before an infantile nation in need of reform and development. On the other hand, the structuring influence of a "democracy mandate" undercut such assumptions about national backwardness, emphasizing instead autonomous choices made by ordinary citizens to watch and appreciate these documentaries. In the initial years after independence, the official descriptions of documentary film deployed economic metaphors of monopolistic domination as well as those of free-market competition in discussing the role and significance of state-produced film;[44] descriptions that in turn drew upon and reproduced substantially different understandings of the "maximalist" and "minimalist" state respectively.[45]

[. . .]

In highlighting its work as a nonpartisan publicist and information provider, the Films Division endorsed a limited vision of its own agency as a mere vehicle for communicating preexisting truths, with its role restricted to the passive reflection of exogenously determined realities alone. Discussions about the state's work of publicity and information provision in fact invested agency in the people rather than in the state through the repeated assertions of how, once they were in possession of the truth about the national projects being undertaken by the state, ordinary Indians would be galvanized into action and become nation builders on their own accord. At the same time, however, and in what amounted to a direct refutation of the "limited messenger" role described above, the Films Division was also authorized as an agent of social education, transformation, and motivation. In fulfilling these tasks, documentary films were required to play an active role in the project of nation building, instead of merely reflecting or communicating the details of the project. As a review commission would note in a 1967 report on the workings of the Films Division, "mere publicity" alone was not enough: persuasion was another, and key, task at hand.[46]

Recognizing the State

If the content and themes of Films Division films consolidated a particular, if ambivalent, vision of India around the sights and sounds of the state, it was the form of these films that definitively established the state as the author of the national vision. Despite their varied choices of content, topic, and exposition, Films Division documentaries and newsreels were instantly recognizable as Films Division documentaries and newsreels. It was precisely their unmistakably state-produced style that played a key and constitutive role in the project of state identification, enabling as they did the public recognition of the state's distinctive vision and register of address. The practices of "state reification" that produce the state as a distinctive social actor as well as the authorized representative of the nation are not exhausted by microlevel, disaggregated, and invisible or "interiorized" interventions.[47] In Ann Anagnost's words, the "hypervisibility of the apparatus of power and its operations on the social body,"[48] that is, the continual and visible demonstrations of the state's ability to make claims on behalf of the nation, are equally important.

Beginning with their introductory sequences, the Films Division documentaries addressed this imperative of state recognition in a variety of ways. Just as the familiar sight of the torch-bearing figure of Columbia or the roaring lion of MGM serves as a particular visual cue for audiences of Hollywood films about the nature of the film-viewing experience that awaits them, so too did the logo of the Ashokan pillar with its four-headed lion motif (designated as the official emblem of the Indian state in 1950) and the accompanying legend "Films Division of India presents" frame the expectations of spectatorship through repeated exposure. In a similar vein, the distinctive aural address of Films Division documentaries established the films as "official texts," where a disembodied exegetical voice-over explained, contextualized, summarized, and otherwise narrativized the visual events unfolding on the screen—an effect that was once again secured through iteration.

Although the content differed from film to film, most Films Division documentaries were characterized by a common narrative style. An introductory statement usually predicated at the highest level of generality would open the film once the title credits had faded to black, with the voice-over either unfolding in tandem with the visual sequences or coming in as an explanatory interjection after a silent montage had quickly flashed across the screen. "The glory that was India attracted people from different lands," declared *The Road to Freedom*, as the solid colors of a two-dimensional standard-issue map of India gradually faded away until the outline of the map was all that was discernible—a boundary around the grainy images of kings, pilgrims, horses, ships, and marching soldiers that now filled the interiors of the map. In the opening sequences of *Destination India* the pithy announcement "Welcome to India" followed a rapid montage of Hindu pilgrims bathing in the Ganges at Benaras, a panoramic shot of the *Taj Mahal*, a near shot of the Buddha's face, and a tight close-up on an elaborate stone trellis that panned out to a wider view of the inner walls of St. Paul's Cathedral in Calcutta. The commentary continued throughout these films, interrupting the flow of images at times with a laconic description ("India became free at the stroke of midnight"), at others with a detailed exegesis that cast the images in an explicitly pedagogical light ("There is a diversity and freedom of expression in our democracy, freedom we must cherish if democracy is to have any meaning"). While the visual representations embodied and materialized the meaning of nationhood in specific and localized terms, the accompanying commentary invariably addressed its audience as an undifferentiated and abstract collectivity, alternating between a collective first-person and a third-person mode of address: thus "we are" and "India is."

In its early years, the Films Division would rely on the same individuals to record voice-overs for as many of its films as possible. As a result, the "sound" of the state came to acquire a distinctive and recognizable quality: the distinctive tone and enunciations of the Anglicized baritones of Romesh Thapar and Sam Berkeley-Hill or the modulations of a Sanskritized Hindi.[49] The effort to establish a regionally unmarked "voice from nowhere" had the effect of constituting a "voice from somewhere," enabling as it did the identification of how "the state states."[50]

In this regard, the specific idiom of state speech is of note—the fact that Films Division commentaries consistently drew upon the registers of "policyspeak" that informed official discourse and practice in a wide range of arenas—from the commentary broadcast on Rajpath during the annual Republic Day parades and the programs on All India Radio to the voluminous texts produced by the Planning Commission. Like these other statist articulations, the commentaries of the Films Division were characterized by their use of specialized terminology, neologisms, and acronyms; hyperbolic pronouncements; and ponderousness.

If the Films Division played a significant role in establishing a distinctive sound for the state through its use of a specific style of commentary, its development of a familiar visual repertoire facilitated the social recognition of the gaze of the state, so that over time a particular set of images came to be identified with an official envisioning of nationhood. The same images appeared over and over again in state-produced documentary films and newsreels, and filmmakers drew upon a common archive of stock shots despite the fact that there were significant variations in the actual topic of the films being made. The familiar montages of India's natural and cultural diversity—from turbaned men on camels against a desert backdrop to fisherwomen on the coconut palm-fringed shores of Kerala's backwaters; the recurrent image of a "simple peasant"; the teeming "crowd shot" that stood in for the Indian masses—all established a specific way of seeing India, one that could be unambiguously identified as the vision of the state.

The State as Critic

Just two decades into the Films Division's existence, the state itself noted that its envisioning of nationhood was more ponderous and disenchanted than resonant and believable. In 1967, the Ministry of Information and Broadcasting, the parent organization of the Films Division, convened an investigative commission, referred to as the Chanda committee, to evaluate the various "publicity wings" of the Indian state: the Films Division, the Directorate of Advertising and Visual Publicity, and the Press Information Bureau. In its mission statement, the committee described its task as one of explaining the paradox of state attempts to monopolize and regulate public information in a democratic polity. In reflecting its central concern with the contradictions of an "official information agency in a democratic society," the indictment of "propaganda" dominated the committee's review of the Films Division, and the call to produce nonpropagandist films was among its chief recommendations. The understanding of what constituted propaganda drew upon the familiar dichotomy between political and nonpolitical activities and expressions. According to the Chanda committee report, the portrayal of "*questions above public dispute* such as literacy, agricultural production, sanitation etc." did not constitute propaganda—a statement that recast contested policy formations that were mired in partisan contests as transcendent and consensual expressions of the national interest.[51] On the basis of this distinction, films that advanced partisan perspectives, showcasing the achievements of particular political leaders and political parties, were denounced as examples of political propaganda, while films that depicted the "neutral" activities of the state were upheld as examples to emulate: "In a developing country the raison d'etre of the Films Division is to propagate the aims and portray the activities and achievements of a welfare state. But this does not imply that the films should depict largely the activities of the political leaders and the meetings and projects in which they participate."[52]

Along with the recommendation to produce documentary films on impartial themes, the Chanda committee called for a transformation in cinematic style, and also deliberated on the question of effect and reception. It was not enough to passively depict "the activities and achievements of a welfare state," but also the goal of "provok[ing] constructive thinking" had to be addressed. In the words of the committee: "It is necessary that the objectives of the planning effort should be presented with subtlety, [and be] able to hold the attention and make an impact on the viewing public. They should be provocative and pose a challenge to the community . . . they should portray the realities of life, pose the problems boldly."[53]

Several factors were held to be responsible for the palpable lack of resonance of Films Division documentaries, or their failure to "hold the attention and make an impact on the viewing public." First, there were significant flaws in the organizational structure of the Films Division and in its mode of operation. It lacked organizational autonomy and thus produced the bulk of its documentaries in response to the requests it received from different ministries instead of being able to chart out an independent cinematic vision. Related to this issue was the problem of personnel. Decision making within the Films Division was undertaken primarily by bureaucrats instead of by trained filmmakers. At the time of the review, the practice of hiring graduates from the Film and Television Institute of India had been discontinued for over five years, and the directorial positions within the organization were occupied by nonspecialist civil servants who were impervious to aesthetic concerns.

Another factor was related to problems in the production practices of the organization. Not only was the availability of technological infrastructure inadequate, leading to the production of films that the committee described as "stuck in the 1930s," but the existing system of commissioning films actually provided incentives to make films that failed to hold the attention of audiences. Filmmakers were paid according to the footage of film they produced, which meant that it was in their interests to produce films that were as long as possible. Moreover, the practice of commissioning films according to a "lowest-tender" system meant that thriftiness or the ability to generate the lowest-budget figures rather than considerations of aesthetic skill informed the selection of filmmakers, and thus further contributed to the low quality of Films Division films.[54] The Chanda committee cited specific examples of this aesthetic lack: the penchant for spoken commentary at the expense of visual content; the absence of "human interest" stories in newsreels; and the absence of humor, satire, suspense, and drama in documentaries.

Finally, the distribution scheme of the Films Division also occasioned extended criticism. According to the Chanda committee, the compulsory distribution policy did not advance, and in fact obstructed, the meaningful reception of films. Instead of allowing exhibitors (the owners of film theaters) to choose documentaries and newsreels that were appropriate for their audiences, the centralized process of distribution allocated films on an arbitrary basis that did not take the specific local context into account. This led to situations that, far from eliciting support and loyalty for the "disinterested" state, might in fact have fostered disaffection and anger for the indifferent state. The incident of a film on floods being screened before audiences in Orissa at a time of extended drought was one such example cited by the committee. A parallel example, though less extreme, was the screening for elite audiences in urban theaters of instructional films on the application of fertilizers, or films demonstrating the superior performance of the latest tractors made in India.[55]

In this regard even the scheme of distributing free film prints to rural areas had significant flaws. For example, the small number of free prints produced was not commensurate with the size of the rural population.[56] Moreover, with the absence in many Indian villages of film-screening equipment, and the even more basic lack of electricity, films could only be screened in rural areas through the use of mobile cinema vans. This in turn was possible only if "motorable roads" were in existence, a requirement that, according to the Chanda committee's calculations, effectively reduced the rural outreach of the Films Division to a mere 500,000 people.

Language was another limitation for rural distribution. The films were dubbed in the thirteen official languages of India, which meant that they were not easily understood among India's many "dialect communities."[57] In sum, twenty years after its existence, at approximately the same time that the Films Division published a catalog listing its "impressive achievements" of producing almost two thousand documentary films, another state agency issued an emphatic and scathing indictment of the limited reach, the dullness and unimaginativeness, the heavy-handed bureaucracy, and the singular lack of resonance of the "moving pictures" of nationhood in Nehruvian India. If the state was an autoenthusiast, it was also its own biggest critic.

In itself, the existence of an official committee report that is critical of the state is hardly remarkable. In fact, the ability to produce and circulate such critical commentaries is widely regarded to be the distinctive feature of an accountable, democratic regime and an "open society." What is of interest here is the ways in which the Chanda committee, like the countless other review commissions that have been convened in India, drew upon and reproduced a distinctive set of repertoires or rituals that furthered the "myth of the [nation]-state."[58] The committee was a theater of state power where, through the proliferation of discourses about the manifest failures of the state to further the interests of the nation, the abstractions of state and nation assumed concrete form and the link between state and nation—the idea that the nation "needs" a state—was consolidated and secured. Here, the nonresonance of the Films Division documentary—the fact that it was boring, heavy-handed, and disenchanted—played a constitutive role, enabling as it did the looping or recursive exercises of review, recommendation, failure, and review again.

[. . .]

Conclusion

[. . .]

In this chapter, I have confirmed but also departed from [James] Scott's discussion of "map making" or "seeing like a state" as a productive exercise of state power. In agreeing with Scott I have drawn attention to the state simplifications that were produced in and through the medium of documentary film, or the ways in which the Indian state produced reductive visual representations of national realities, and presented its fictions and fantasies as fact. At the same time, I have moved away from the discussion of how these statist practices impact society, and the related understanding of "state" and "society" as preformed or given entities. Instead, I have considered the state-constituting effect of such practices, or the ways in which these acts of mapping have actually produced the state as a particular kind of authoritative entity.

For more than fifty years, the Films Division has played a key role in the project of seeing like a state. In the first instance, this entailed the production and circulation of visual representations of the state itself whether as object, idea, or activity, and of the intimate and indissoluble bond between state and nation. A monumental dam; a prosperous farmer; a tricolored flag planted on Mount Everest; the signing of a constitution; the bullet-ridden corpse of a prime minister; the protection of folk art forms; a dream for which thousands of "our ancestors" have laid down their lives—these were just some of the myriad images of state and nation that confronted the audiences of Films Division documentaries and newsreels.

Second, to see like a state was also to see the state as a distinctive viewer. It was to come upon a particular line of sight and to recognize its authoritative provenance. Here, the "boredom effect" of the Films Division documentaries played a constitutive role, securing widespread social recognition of the unmistakable style of the official documentary. With the repetition of stock shots in different films; the use of a common "voice from nowhere" style of exegetical commentary; the unchanging quality of the voice itself; and the familiar doubled narrative of state-led nation-building as a task both achieved and deferred, possible and impossibly arduous, the Films Division established a distinctive genre or style of filmmaking that was immediately recognizable: there was no ambiguity about who or what was doing the seeing and the talking.

Third, seeing like a state was about the obstruction of vision. As the custodian of the largest archive of audiovisual material in India, the Films Division has the discretionary authority to grant or refuse permission for the use of its material.[59] In many instances these comprise the only visual records of significant events that have taken place over the past fifty years. With the official camera as the sole witness to numerous episodes in postcolonial history, it is through the lens of the Films Division that we view Gandhi's assassination, the pageantry of Republic Day, nuclear tests, wars, floods, famines, and dams, even if the film we are watching has been produced by the BBC. If the written record of official history erases all fissures, slippages, and ambiguities from its seamless narration of the past, the visual texts of the state constrict our vision in even tighter ways. The outtakes of the Films Division have long been destroyed, and there was no second-camera unit present at the recording of history.

The constricting effects of the state's tunnel vision are not restricted to the domain of history. As this chapter has shown, the Films Division has also taken culture as its canvas, elaborating vivid visual representations of India's cultural diversity. The stereotypical projections of identity and difference that this vision of Indian diversity reflected and fostered have traveled far beyond the confines of official celluloid to structure the representational worlds of Hindi commercial cinema and of multinational advertising. Although the compulsory screening policy of the Films Division was discontinued in 1994, its distinctive visions continue to proliferate. The colorful montage of India's geographic, historic, cultural, religious, and ethnic diversity—the intercuts and dissolves that link coconut trees to the Himalayas, dancing peasants to praying Brahmins, the Taj Mahal of Mughal Agra to the Victoria Terminus railway station in Bombay—is today reproduced in marketing campaigns for Coca-Cola and a promotional video for the MTV India television channel.[60]

Like their statist counterparts, these images invite us to gaze upon a reality that we do not encounter in our daily lives.[61] All traces of polyester and plastic, violence and inequality, and power and resistance have been air-brushed from their colorful vistas. As the historian Shahid Amin has trenchantly observed in a recent discussion of the representational devices of nationhood in India: "The face on the poster does not match the man on the street."[62] The mismatch that Amin highlights is about the arbitrary logics of visual representation. For instance, in the imagery of the "national integration" poster, a staple of Nehruvian secular nationalism,[63] Muslim identity is invariably symbolized by a fez, even though Indians would be hard pressed to cite a single instance when they have actually seen a person wearing one.[64] As we have already seen, this observation about the "[mis]representation of the Mussalman"[65] can be extended to Films Division documentaries as well, which furthered the understanding of the exceptional presence of Muslims in postcolonial India. In this regard, we can say that to see like a state in Nehruvian India was to see Muslims as permanent minorities marked by an essential difference. Although this difference involved the valorization of Muslim identity rather than its stigmatization—thus the Films Division turned its lens on "good Muslims" rather than "bad Muslims"—the qualified or special nature of Muslims remained a persistent theme.

Finally, to see like a state was to partake of a constitutive fear of politics. Although the vibrancy and density of civic associational life in India and the active engagement of ordinary Indians in innovative forms of political participation have been a staple theme of academic discussions about the health and durability of Indian democracy,[66] the Films Division's imagination of the Indian citizen was eviscerated of any such signs of political vitality. It was instead her or his ability to patiently "stand in queue" instead of milling around in a disorderly fashion; to willingly discard "traditional" techniques of measurement for the universal coordinates of the Metric system; to participate selflessly in the "social uplift" of the "disadvantaged sections"; and to realize the "dignity of manual labour."[67] Like the "naturally diverse nation" and the "transcendent state," the ideal citizen of Nehruvian India would also be imagined along extrapolitical, antipolitical lines.

[. . .]

NOTES

1. *Report of the Committee on Broadcasting and Information Media on Documentary Films and Newsreels*, 1967, Ministry of Information and Broadcasting, New Delhi; hereafter referred to as the Chanda Committee Report 1967.
2. Quoted in Mohan, *Two Decades of the Films Division*, 10.
3. For a discussion of the specific cultural mandate of UNESCO during this period, see Girard, *Cultural Development*; and Sewell, "UNESCO." For a general discussion of the Ford Foundation's ideological practices of development and philanthropy, see Berghahn, "Philanthropy and Diplomacy in the 'American Century.'" The documentary filmmaking effort in India also benefited from the corporate sponsorship of organizations such as Burmah Shell, the petroleum conglomerate in South Asia. Burmah Shell's publicity/filmmaking unit in India was headed by James Beveridge of the National Film Board of Canada and employed several independent documentary filmmakers to make publicity and training films for the organization, but also films of "aesthetic merit" that traveled to international festivals. See Mohan, *Two Decades of the Films Division*, and Woods, "From Shaw to Shantaram."
4. Cited in Barsam, *Nonfiction Film*, 2.
5. For example, *Reception Given to Senior Wrangler, Mr. R. P. Paranjpe* (1902); *Great Bengal Partition Movement and Procession* (1905); *Bal Gangadhar Tilak's Visit to Calcutta and Procession* (1906); *The Terrible Hyderabad Flood* (1908); *Delhi Durbar and Coronation* (1911); and *Cotton Fire at Bombay* (1912).
6. Narwekar, *Films Division and the Indian Documentary*, 12.
7. Ibid., 16.
8. Pathy, "A Document on Indian Documentary."
9. Narwekar, *Films Division and the Indian Documentary*, 15–16.
10. According to Richard Barsam, Rotha's "humanistic" vision of the documentary film and its creator derived inspiration from Percy Bysshe Shelley's vision of the true artist as a "legislator of mankind." See Barsam, *Nonfiction Film*, 10.
11. For a discussion of the war propaganda filmmaking effort, see Woods, "Chappatis by Parachute."
12. Narwekar, *Films Division and the Indian Documentary*, 23. In fact, there was no official film production unit present to record the transfer of power at midnight on August 14–15, 1947. The event was documented by international camera units and, in India, by a two-person team of independent Indian filmmakers. Mohan, *Two Decades of the Films Division*.

13. Abraham, "Landscape and Postcolonial Science," 164.
14. For a discussion of the state-documentary partnership in other contexts, see Barnouw, *Documentary*; MacCann, *The People's Films*; Swann, *The British Documentary Film Movement, 1926–1946*; Roberts, *Forward Soviet*; and Taylor, "Now That the Party's Over" and *Film Propaganda*.
15. In addition, a cameraperson affiliated with the Films Division was stationed in each state capital to provide on-the-spot coverage of news events for the production of newsreels. See Mohan, *Two Decades of the Films Division*.
16. In the first twenty years of its existence, approximately 75 percent of Films Division productions were done "in house," and the rest were produced by individuals who were not formally affiliated with the organization. See Mohan, *Two Decades of the Films Division*; see also Garga, "Turbulent Years" and "Is Anyone Watching?"
17. For a different but related discussion of how citizenship discourse in capitalist states invariably addresses an "ethically incomplete" subject that "needs" improvement and managerial intervention, see Miller, *The Well-Tempered Self*.
18. Apart from commissioning work from individual filmmakers, the Films Division also distributed films received from a range of different national and international agencies, including state governments, central government organizations such as the Khadi and Village Industries Association, civil society organizations such as the Independent Documentary Producers' Association, and international sources such as the United Nations Film Board, the United States Information Services, and the World Health Organization. See Mohan, *Two Decades of the Films Division*, 62–63.
19. A total of 12,000 such films were distributed for free (one print for every 250,000 people), and therefore each print required 12,000 projections in order to cover the entire population. But the life of each print was only 200 projections, as the Chanda committee noted in its 1967 report, thus effectively limiting coverage to only 10 percent of the population. According to the committee, the lack of "motorable roads" in rural areas also limited the viewership of Films Division documentaries.
20. Narwekar, *Films Division and the Indian Documentary*, 25.
21. "The word 'People' is an expansive word representing the people inhabiting the length and breadth of the country with their languages and economic systems, determined by geography and agro-climatic divisions" (Mohan, *Documentary Films and National Awakening*, 93). This book was commissioned by the Films Division and provides a discussion of the Films Division and its activities from the perspective of the organization itself. Further, the author of the book, Jag Mohan, was actively associated with the Films Division for many years and produced several films for them.
22. *Vadya Vrinda* (1956) is a documentary about the All India Radio's "unique experiment" in creating a national orchestra of musical instruments from different regions of the country.
23. The Nehruvian state's tutelary discourse on citizenship both resembled and departed from the "infantile citizenship" ideal in the United States and the "socialist paternalism" of Romania. For the former, see Berlant, "The Theory of Infantile Citizenship"; for the latter, see Verdery, "Whither 'Nation' and 'Nationalism.'"
24. For instance, *Democracy in Action* (1951) introduced citizens to the procedures of voting and elections in anticipation of the first general election of 1952. In 1956, six five-minute films detailed the mechanisms of different types of ballot boxes, and in 1959, *New Way to Vote* depicted the use of a new type of ballot sheet.
25. "The Case of Mr. Critic," quoted in Pati, *Films Division Catalogue of Films*.
26. For instance, in *Ideal Citizen* (1959) the title was given meaning through depictions of exemplary individuals who "[kept] their surroundings clean," organized schools and dispensaries, paid their taxes, exercised their right and duty to vote, and cooperated with the police.
27. Mohan, *Documentary Films and National Awakening*, 96.
28. *Rabindranath Tagore* (1961) was directed by the eminent Indian filmmaker Satyajit Ray.
29. For instance, *Magic Moments* (1962) on the visit of Jacqueline Kennedy to India; *Mitrata Ki Yatra* (*Journey of Friendship*, 1955) on Nehru's visit to the USSR; and *Out of the Blue* (1963, a defense film about helicopters.
30. Pati, *Films Division Catalogue of Films*, 96.
31. Narwekar, *Films Division and the Indian Documentary*.
32. Sundaram, "The Bazaar and the City."
33. Pati, *Films Division Catalogue of Films*, 31.
34. Ibid., 412.
35. We can in fact describe this as the emergence of a new postcolonial narrative of temporality and progress (the saying of "not yet" to ourselves, to rephrase Dipesh Chakrabarty), which had ambivalent political effects, empowering as well as marginalizing the agency of ordinary citizens. See Chakrabarty, *Provincializing Europe*. In chapter 3 I develop this point in further detail through a consideration of the "diffident developmentalism" of Nehruvian India.
36. However, despite the divergent constructions of the here and now as certainty and uncertainty respectively, both the representation of spectacular modernity and that of deferred modernity evacuated the present of substantial, lived meaning. Thus, while in *My Land My Dreams* (1968) it was the "struggles" of the past or what was described as the "historical exploitation of farmers" that invested their present freedom with meaning, in *Grow Hybrid Maize* (1967) the significance of the present was as a harbinger of future prosperity.
37. See Scott, *Seeing like a State*. In a similar vein, and despite the difference in their understandings of state autonomy, Marxist theories of the state as well as the scholarship

on "bringing the state back in" have failed to disaggregate the state along levels of governance and have overlooked the multiple and contradictory effects of "stateness." "The capitalist state" was theorized as a (mostly) singular formation in the Poulantzas-Milliband debates of the 1970s, and the "statist" scholarship of Skocpol and others took the state to be a unitary actor. See Poulantzas, "The Problem of the Capitalist State"; Miliband, "The Capitalist State"; and Skocpol, "Bringing the State Back In."

38. As the introductory chapter has noted, the China war saw the emergence of militarist rhetorics of citizenship and nationhood and a more unitaiy conception of the nation-state. The production list of the Films Division reflected this shift, with a flurry of films produced between 1963 and 1965 that emphasized "national security" as the primary issue at hand.

39. The films that were produced between January and March 1963 under the "national emergency" scheme all related to various aspects of the war effort: official explanations of the causes or reasons for the war; appeals for public support; and foregrounding the prowess, sacrifice, and bravery of the military. See, for instance, *Shifting Line* (explaining India's position on the international border dispute), *Road to Victory* ("people's reaction to China aggression"); *Service before Self* ("supporting the armed forces"); *Letter from the Front* ("what to donate and what type of work to do"); *A Proud Tradition* ("Hero of Chusul: Late Major Shaitan Singh"); *Meet the Challenge* ("role of women in national emergency"); *They Are Not Alone* (role of panchayats [village assemblies] in national emergency); *A Privilege* ("officer recruitment"); *Careless Talk* ("security consciousness"); and *An Unavoidable Internment* (Chinese internees in India). See Government of India, *Annual Report*, 1962–63.

40. Government of India, *Annual Report*, 1964–65, 4.

41. The Indian constitution promulgated in 1950 did not provide a definition of secularism, and the term is itself missing from the constitutional text (the existing preambular definition of India as a "sovereign socialist secular democratic republic" was introduced by the 42nd amendment in 1976). Despite this formal constitutional absence, however, secularism understood as "equal respect for all religions" (and thus distinct from both the Anglo-Saxon variant of the "wall of separation" between churc h and state and the French *laic* variant of "civil religion"), served as the normative as well as pragmatic touchstone of legislative reform and social and cultural policy making in Nehruvian India. While the secular embrace of India's multireligious composition is at considerable remove from the Hindu nationalist vision of India as a Hindu nation in which non-Hindus are "second-class citizens," the internal distinctions of secularism are not without their own problems. As this brief discussion of visual representations of religious diversity has suggested, Nehruvian secularism had a particular "minoritizing" effect, whereby certain communities were constituted as the object of secular laws and policies (those requiring tolerance) while others were authorized as secular subjects (those invested with the power to tolerate). For an extended discussion of the powered dimensions of discourses and practices of tolerance and diversity, see Hage, *White Nation*.

42. The allotments were 12,000 feet of raw film stock for the eastern region, 13,000 feet in the south, and 400 feet for trailers. See Government of India, *Annual Report*, 1950–51.

43. Placing the positive injunction of the Films Division alongside the censorship prohibitions of the Indian Cinematographic Act of 1952 is instructive in this regard, as all the "shall nots" of the act are transformed into "shall dos" when it comes to Films Division films. For example, the statement that "the sympathy of the audience shall not be thrown on the side of crime, wrong-doing, evil or sin" authorized the production of films that elicited audience sympathies with "the side" of goodness and truth. For a discussion of the policies and effects of cinema censorship in India, see Vasudev, *Liberty and License in the Indian Cinema*; and for a different discussion of the "productive" power of film censorship, see Gopalan, *Cinema of Interruptions*.

44. As Nehru observed during his remarks to the 1955 Film Seminar (the national meeting of representatives from the film industry and state officials in New Delhi that was convened to discuss "the role of film in nation-building"), the government will compete through the production of documentaries "not . . . with the desire to compete, but to some extent the results might be a setting up of standards by a certain measure of competition" Sangeet Natak Akademi, *Seminar on Film in India*, 15.

45. For a discussion of the unique complex of "high and low stateness" that characterized the Indian state, see Rudolph and Rudolph, *In Pursuit of Lakshmi*.

46. Chanda Committee Report 1967.

47. According to Foucault, these are the distinctive features of disciplinary power, in contrast to the centralized, exterior, and visible or "spectacular" operations of juridical-sovereign power. See Foucault, *Displine and Punish*; and Faubion, *Power*, vol. 3.

48. Ann Anagnost discusses the imperative of visibility in her examination of the formation and legitimization of the party-state in China. See Anagnost, *National Past-Times*, chapter 4. Her account modifies the Foucauldian premise about the invisibility of modern disciplinary power, which was based on an understanding of how the Benthamite panopticon allows an authority figure to observe a prison inmate without being observed himself. As Anagnost continues, "The tower at the center is not entirely a darkened space inhabited by an invisible gaze but an illuminated stage from

which the party calls, 'Look at me! I make myself visible to you. Your return gaze completes me and realizes my power'" (116).

49. "The cold words written by the commentary writers turn flesh when the commentators take over. It is they, who with their accents, pauses and exclamation convey to the 'captive audience' the importance and significance of the visuals. Sam Berkeley-Hill, the late Nobby Clarke, Romesh Thapar, Zul Vellani and Partap Sharma have done the salesmanship for the Films Division in the English language." Mohan, *Two Decades of the Films Division*, 50. See also Thapar, *All These Years*, for a vivid autobiographical reminiscence of her husband Romesh Thapar's audio commentaries for the Films Division.
50. As Philip Corrigan and Derek Sayer have observed in their examination of the distinctive cultural repertoires and practices of state formation in England, "States, if the pun be forgiven, state; the arcane rituals of a court of law, the formulae of royal assent to an Act of Parliament, visits of school inspector, all are statements. They define, in great detail, acceptable forms and images of social activity and individual and collective identity; they regulate, in empirically specifiable ways, much . . . of social life. Indeed, in this sense, 'the State' never stops talking" (Corrigan and Sayer, *The Great Arch*, 3).
51. Chanda Committee Report 1967.
52. Ibid.
53. Ibid.
54. The commissioning policy of the Films Division replicated the general bureaucratic practice of awarding government contracts to the most "economical" bidder. In the case of the Films Division, this meant the commissioning of filmmakers with the lower budget, rather than on creative-aesthetic grounds. See Chanda Committee Report 1967.
55. The following example from my own life is illustrative of this "crossed signals" effect. My memory of a family outing to see the Hindi film *Sholay* in Calcutta in the mid-1970s is vividly associated not with images from the film but with black-and-white visions from a pre-film documentary about a *gobar* (cow dung) gas-producing contraption surrounded by smiling farmers. I cannot recall the title, the location, or any other details of the Films Division documentary, the source of these images. However, the imagery of the farmer and the fantastic piece of technology, and the combination of fascination and queasiness that the notion of a cow-dung-powered machine elicited, are strangely easy to relive thirty years later.
56. The Films Division provided only 12,000 free prints, or one print for every group of 250,000 people. However, since the life of a film print was approximately two hundred screenings (it would wear out after this point), significant numbers of people were left "uncovered" by the distribution scheme.
57. In discussing the limits of the Films Division's linguistic reach, the Chanda committee drew particular attention to its neglect of the (unspecified) "tribals of India": a lapse that it deemed especially problematic given their palpable "need" for modernization.
58. Hansen, "Governance and Myths of the State in Mumbai."
59. The considerable revenue-earning potential of such international sales influenced the decision to create a "customer friendly" Web site containing sample clips of documentaries in 2002; see http://www.filmsdivision.org.
60. Elsewhere I have examined these contemporary (nonstate and transnational) reproductions of the diversity imagination, and I argue that there are significant points of convergence with established idioms of official nationalism. See Roy, "Nation and Commemoration."
61. For related discussions about the "misrepresentations" of multiculturalism, see Mackey, *The House of Difference*; Povinelli, *The Cunning of Recognition*; and Hutnyk, *The Critique of Exotica*.
62. Amin, "On Representing the Musalman," 95.
63. For a rich discussion of the calendar art and posters of Nehruvian India, and the popular cultural visualization of "unity in diversity," see Uberoi, "Unity in Diversity?"
64. As Hasan and Menon have documented, the categorical logic that informs discussions about "Muslim women" obscures the host of regional, class, and other differences *within* this apparently monolithic group. See Hasan and Menon, *Unequal Citizens*.
65. Amin, "On Representing the Musalman."
66. India's "healthy" and "vibrant" democratic tradition has been a staple theme of media discourse, and it has also informed scholarly analyses for the past half century. For a recent reiteration of this argument, see among others, Khilnani, *The Idea of India*; Kohli, *The Success of India's Democracy*; and Linz, Stepan, and Yadav, "Nation-State or State-Nation?"
67. See, for example, *Say It With a Smile* (1960), a film that depicts the ideal civic behavior of "courtesy for others' feelings"; *Vital Records* (1964), on birth and death registration procedures; *With Your Own Hands* (1956), on the dignity of manual labor; and *Withering Flowers* (1963), on the institutional reform and "uplift" of "delinquent children."

BIBLIOGRAPHY

Abraham, Itty. "Landscape and Postcolonial Science." *Contributions to Indian Sociology* 34 (2000): 163–87.

______. *The Making of the Indian Atomic Bomb: Science, Secrecy, and the Postcolonial State*. New Delhi: Orient Longman, 1998.

Amin, Shahid. "On Representing the Musalman." *Sarai Reader* 04: *Crisis/Media*. New Delhi: Sarai, 2004.

Anagnost, Ann. *National Past-Times: Narrative, Representation, and Power in Modern China.* Durham, N.C.: Duke University Press, 1997.

Austin, Granville. *The Indian Constitution: Cornerstone of a Nation.* New York: Oxford University Press, 2000.

Barnouw, Erik. *Documentary: A History of the Non-Fiction Film.* Rev. ed. New York: Oxford University Press, 1993.

Barsam, Richard Meran. *Nonfiction Film: A Critical History.* New York: E. P. Dutton, 1973.

Berghahn, Volker. "Philanthropy and Diplomacy in the 'American Century.'" *Diplomatic History* 23.3 (1999): 393–419.

Berlant, Lauren. "The Theory of Infantile Citizenship." *Public Culture* 5.3 (1993): 395–410.

Chakrabarty, Dipesh. *Provincializing Europe: Postcolonial Thought and Historical Difference.* Princeton, N.J., Princeton University Press, 1998.

Chakravarty, Sumita S. "National Identity and the Realist Aesthetic: Indian Cinema of the Fifties." *Quarterly Review of Film and Television II* (1989): 31–48.

______. *National Identity in Indian Popular Cinema.* Austin: University of Texas Press, 1993.

Chatteijee, Partha. *Nationalist Thought and the Colonial World: A Derivative Discourse?* Minneapolis: University of Minnesota Press, 1991.

Corrigan, Philip, and Derek Sayer. *The Great Arch: English State Formation as Cultural Revolution.* Oxford: Blackwell, 1985.

Foucault, Michel. *Discipline and Punish.* Trans. Alan Sheridan. New York: Vintage, 1995.

Ganti, Tejaswini. "Casting Culture: The Social Life of Hindi Film Production in Contemporary India." Ph.D. dissertation, New York University, 2000.

Garga, "B.D. Is Anyone Watching?" *Cinema in India* 2.3 (1988): 26–30.

______. "Turbulent Years: The Indian Documentry." *Cinema in India* 2.2 (1988): 32–36.

Girard, Augustin. *Cultural Development: Experiences and Policies.* Paris: UNESCO, 1983.

Gopalan, Lalitha. *Cinema of Interruptions: Action Genres in Contemporary Indian Cinema.* London: British Film Institute, 2002.

Government of India, Ministry of Information and Broadcasting. *Symposium on Historical and Biographical Film.* 1956.

______. *Annual Report of the Ministry of Information and Broadcasting.* 1950–51, 1962–63, 1964–65.

Hage, Ghassan. *White Nation: Fantasies of White Supremacy in a Multicultural Society.* London: Routledge, 2000.

Hansen, Thomas. "Governance and State Mythologies in Mumbai." In *States of Imagination: Ethnographic Explorations of the Postcolonial State,* ed. Thomas Hansen and Finn Stepputat. Durham, N.C.: Duke University Press, 2002.

______. *The Saffron Wave: Democracy and Hindu Nationalism in Modern India.* Princeton, N.J.: Princeton University Press, 1999.

Hasan, Zoya, and Ritu Menon. *Unequal Citizens: A Study of Muslim Women in India.* New Delhi: Oxford University Press, 2004.

Hutnyk, John. *The Critique of Exotica: Music, Politics, and the Culture Industry.* London: Pluto Press, 2000.

Indian Institution of Mass Communications. *Proceedings of the Seminar on the Role of Film in National Development.* New Delhi: Indian Institute of Mass Communications, 1976.

Kapur, Geeta. "Cultural Creativity in the First Decade." *Journal of Arts and Ideas* 23–24 (1993): 17–49.

Khilnani, Sunil. *The Idea of India.* London: Hamish Hamilton, 1997.

Kohli, Atul. ed. *The Success of India's Democracy.* Cambridge: Cambridge University Press, 2001.

Krishna, Sankaran. *Postcolonial Insecurities: India, Sri Lanka and the Question of Nationhood.* Minneapolis: University of Minnesota Press, 1999.

Linz, Juan, Alfred Stepan, and Yogendra Yadav. "Nation-State or State-Nation? Conceptual Reflections and Some Spanish, Belgian and Indian Data." *Human Development Report Background Paper.* New York: United Nations Development Program, 2004. 20–21.

MacCann, Richard Dyer. *The People's Films: A Political History of U.S. Government Motion Pictures.* New York: Hastings House, 1973.

Mackey, Eva. *The House of* Difference: *Cultural Politics and National Identity in Canada.* London: Routledge, 2000.

Miller, Toby. *The Well-Tempered Self: Citizenship, Culture, and the Postmodern Subject.* Baltimore: Johns Hopkins University Press, 1994.

Mohan, Jag. *Documentary Films and National Awakening.* New Delhi: Publications Division, 1900.

______. *Two Decades of the Films Division.* New Delhi: Ministry of Information and Broadcasting, 1969.

Mukherjee, Rudrangshu, ed. *The Penguin Gandhi Reader.* New Delhi: Penguin Books 1995.

Narwekar, Sanjit. *Films Division and the Indian Documentry.* New Delhi: Publications Division, 1992.

Parekh, Bhikhu. *Colonialism, Tradition and Reform: An Analysis of Gandhi's Political Discourse.* New Delhi: Sage Publications, 1989.

Pathy, P. V. "A Document on Indian Documentary." *The People* (July 2, 1950): n.p.

Pati, Pramod. *Films Division Catalogue* of *Films,* 1948–1972. Bombay: Films Division, 1974.

Povinelli, Elizabeth. *The Cunning of Recognition: Indigenous Alterities and the Making of Australian Multiculturalism.* Durham, N.C.: Duke University Press, 2002.

Prasad, M. Madhava. *Ideology of the Hindi Film: An Historical* Construction. New Delhi: Oxford University Press, 1998.

Roberts, Graham. *Forward Soviet: History and Non-Fiction Film in the USSR.* New York: St. Martin's Press, 1999.

Roy, Srirupa. "Nation and Commemoration: Celebrating the Fiftieth Anniversary of Indian Independence." *Interventions: The International*

Journal of Post-Colonial Studies 3.2 (2002): 251–65.
Rudolph, Lloyd, and Susanne Hoeber Rudolph. *In Pursuit of Lakshmi: The Political Economy of the Indian State*. Chicago: University of Chicago Press. 1987.
Sangeet, Natak Akademi. *Seminar on Film in India*. New Delhi: Sangeet Natak Akademi.
Scott, James. *Seeing like a State: How Certain Schemes to Improve the Human Condition Have Failed*. New Haven, Conn.: Yale University Press, 1988.
Seth, Sanjay. "Nationalism, National Identity, and 'History': Nehru's Search for India" *Thesis Eleven* 32 (1992) 37–54.
Sewell, James. "UNESCO: Pluralism Rampant." In *The Anatomy of Influence: Decision-Making in International Organization*, ed. Robert Cox and Harold Jacobson. New Haven, Conn: Yale University Press, 1974. 139–74.
Sinha, Subir. "Development Counter-Narratives: Taking Social Movements Seriously." In *Regional Modernities: The Cultural Politics of Development in India*, ed. K. Sivarama-krishnan and Arun Agrawal. New Delhi: Oxford University Press, 2003.
Srivastava, Sanjay. "Voice, Gender and Space in Time of Five-Year Plans." *Economic and Political Weekly* (May 15, 2004).
Sundaram, Ravi. "The Bazaar and the City: History and the Contemporary in Urban Electronic Culture." 1999. Available online at http://www.monoculartimes.co.uk/architexts/bazaarandcity–1.shtml.
Swann, Paul. *The British Documentary Film Movement, 1926–1946*. Cambridge: Cambridge University Press, 1989.
Taylor, Richard. *Film Propaganda: Soviet Russia and Nazi Germany*. 2nd ed. London: I. B. Tauris, 1998.
______. "Now That the Party's Over: Soviet Cinema and Its Legacy." In *Russia on Reels: The Russian Idea in Post-Soviet Cinema*, ed. Birgit Beumers. London: I. B. Tauris, 1999, 34–42.
Thapar, Raj. *All These Years: A Memoir*. New Delhi: Seminar Publications, 1991.
Uberoi, Patricia. "Unity in Diversity? Dilemmas of Nationhood in Indian Calendar Art." In *Beyond Appearances: Visual Practices and Ideologies in Modern India*, ed. Sumathi Ramaswamy. Delhi: Sage Publications, 2003.
Vasudev, Aruna. *Liberty and License in the Indian Cinema*. New Delhi: Manohar, 1978.
Vasudevan, Ravi. "Addressing the Spectator of a 'Third World' National Cinema: The Bombay 'Social' Film of the 1940s and 1950s." *Screen* 36.4 (1995): 305–24.
Verdery, Katherine. "Whither 'Nation' and 'Nationalism.'" *Daedalus* 122.3 (1993): 45.
Woods, Philip. "Chappatis by Parachute: The Use of Newsreels in British Propaganda in India." *South Asia* 23.2 (2000): 89–109.
______. "From Shaw to Shantaram: The Film Advisory Board and the Making of British Propaganda Films in India, 1940–1943." *Historical Journal of Radio, Film and Television* 21.3 (2001): 293–308.

52

JENNIFER HORNE

EXPERIMENTS IN PROPAGANDA

Reintroducing James Blue's Colombian Trilogy (2009)

In a newspaper column published in April 1953, the American social critic Walter Lippmann sharply criticized the creation of a newly bureaucratized government propaganda agency by noting the ineffectiveness of counterpropaganda tactics. "As a way of stimulating the appetite for the American way of life," Lippmann wrote, "it is like serving castor oil as a cocktail before dinner."[1] Fundamentally opposed to the creation of a mass media monopoly, but more concerned that exporting state propaganda was simply counterproductive, Lippmann seized on the obvious falseness of the gesture: "Foreigners are in more ways than one a good deal more like Americans, and certainly like us in that they do not wish to feel they are being manipulated and made fools of by someone with something to sell." Nevertheless, or perhaps precisely because of the common desire people have to not be manipulated, in the years to follow, a semantic forest would spring up to complicate and obscure the operations of the United States Information Agency (USIA; or USIS, for United States Information Service, overseas), the government office that was established as its own entity outside of the Department of State in August 1953 and shuttered in 1999.

Those who worked for this agency no longer referred to themselves, in the direct language Lippmann might have preferred, as propagandists. The nomenclature invented to describe the work of influencing foreign opinion and other state-to-state activities was nuanced and muted: USIA agents now worked in *public diplomacy*, *cultural diplomacy*, *public affairs*, and *cultural affairs*. At the same time, combining in one agency the opposing pursuits of multilateral cultural education and propaganda meant that while the job of the cultural attaché was recast in the language of informatics, the overseas communications fieldworkers, too, had to adjust to older notions of cultural diplomatic practice. Over the years, the USIA hired an array of specialists for work in both fast and slow media who had backgrounds in entertainment industries, information and library science, journalism, and media technology. Information transmission was the supposedly unproblematic nature of the agency's mission. But it was the other side of the communications dynamic, its encounter with culture, the public, and the affairs it conducted on foreign soil—its ideological and psychological operations—that came to epitomize and symbolize the Cold War bureaucracy.

Indeed, between 1946 and 1974, even as the CIA conducted its own covert propaganda efforts, the USIA experimented with an array of cultural and educational programs designed to export and celebrate American culture.[2] While Voice of America was the agency's audio emblem, the lesser-known Motion Picture Service incorporated experiments with documentary into its operations, with some notable success. Among the filmmakers recruited for this program in creative propaganda were a number of well-known, or soon to be well-known, American auteurs of independent documentary and avant-garde cinema. Comparable to the work of studio directors such as Frank Capra, John Ford, and John Huston on behalf of the U.S. military during World War II (WWII), the participation of filmmakers such as Ed Emshwiller, Charles Guggenheim, Bruce Hirschensohn, and Leo Seltzer in the Cold War work of the USIA has been—like the films themselves—a well-kept secret. The purpose of this short essay is to shed light on this remarkable alliance, and to provide historical and political context for the propaganda work of one such Cold War artist, the documentary filmmaker and writer James Blue. The 2008 Orphan Film Symposium provided the occasion to reintroduce three of Blue's USIA films to the viewers, who watched the projection of pristine 35mm prints, loaned from the collections of the National Archives and Records Administration (NARA) in Washington, DC.

USIA was a complex and ideological entity, divided in both its mission and its internal operations. On the one hand, the agency was rooted in the foreign affairs traditions of state envoys and the arts of ambassadorship and reflected the hierarchical structure and mission of the Department of State. On the other, it was a media organization attempting to modernize international communications and shape world opinion. President Dwight D. Eisenhower had referred to the USIA as having "P-programs" (i.e., propaganda) but simultaneously celebrated it as a "people-to-people" organization. Anecdotes told in career memoirs and professional reflections similarly reflect this confused identity, one that stemmed from a crucial and persistent lack of clarity within the organization of the distinction between culture and information.

This conflated philosophy was a defining feature of the USIA, one that might allow us to better understand how experimental filmmakers and documentarians might have been able to thrive in an otherwise restrictive and message-oriented workplace. The lack of subtlety in the agency's operating around the notion of culture is particularly worth examining, for so much of what is contained in the moving image archive of the USIA can be understood as historically peculiar recordings of culture. Rather than seeking to clarify what was possibly the most palpable symptom of the agency's conflicted self-understanding, we might instead allow this murky definition to be the prism through which we examine the moving image artifacts of the agency.

Former USIA envoy Richard Arndt has instructively pointed out that in the lexicon of the USIA, the words *culture* and *cultural*—especially where connected to the words *affairs, diplomacy, attaché,* or *policy*—belonged to the arts and education "side" of the agency. Arndt explains the functional ambiguity of the ideas of culture and information, observing how the official location of the agency could matter more than clarity of purpose.[3] Inside the Department of State, cultural programming sounded menacing. Moved outside of the Department of State, information could become the not-so-secret cover for cultural programming. But genuine cultural diplomacy, respectful conversation among representatives of different ways of life, diminished as the number of sponsored programs increased in the late 1950s. This increase was seen especially in displays and exhibits at international expositions and smaller trade fairs promoting American agricultural and industrial exports, an innovation in which the USIA excelled. Internationalism itself, it seemed, had lost traction as an idea, and certainly the agency's ability to fulfill its mission suffered. At the core of the agency was a field structure idealistically geared toward international cooperation and a belief in the possibility of cultural relations, objectives that were at continuous odds with the mission of promoting American foreign policies abroad. Throughout its existence, however, the USIA contained within it these two distinct cultures.

The gradual transformation of what was to become the USIA can be traced back to key periods of information campaigning during international conflict: President Wilson's appointment of journalist George Creel to head the short-lived Committee on Public Information in 1917, for instance, or President Roosevelt's creation of the lesser-known Agency for Foreign Intelligence and Propaganda in 1941. Fundamental to the politicization of the agency was the U.S. Information and Educational Exchange Act, referred to as the Smith-Mundt Act, which President Truman signed into law in 1948. In keeping with the peculiar partnering of information with cultural affairs, this legislation sought to extend the Fulbright educational exchanges begun in 1946, but the law also prohibited the presentation within the United States of any state-funded American propaganda intended for foreign audiences.[4] In 1953, under the authority of the Reorganization Act of 1949, the Eisenhower administration made the USIA an entity independent of the State Department.[5] The agency was authorized to exert American influence abroad in print media, radio broadcasts, libraries, book publishing, television, exhibits, the teaching of English, and personal contacts. Through each medium, it was to communicate to targeted audiences a favorable impression of U.S. foreign policies and the American way of life. Crucially, the USIA was more than just a communications conglomerate. An information-age entity with a social science agenda, it was imagined as both sender and receiver. Its offices and overseas outposts would collect masses of information on the entertainment and information consumption patterns of foreign audiences. Most importantly, if the information gathered was deemed important to foreign policy, it would be brought to the attention of the president.[6]

Unlike other cultural affairs operations, the USIA had been placed in a contentious location close to the office of the president and his security council. In a White House memo dated January 25, 1963, President Kennedy affirmed this advisory role, stating that while "the Director of the U.S. Information Agency shall take the initiative in offering counsel where he deems it advisable, the various departments and agencies should seek such counsel when considering policies and programs which may substantially affect or be affected by foreign opinion."[7] A few months later, before a House of Representatives Committee on Foreign Affairs subcommittee hearing titled "Winning the Cold War: The U.S. Ideological Offensive," Edward R. Murrow was asked to state the mission of the agency. As the USIA director at the time, he recited the agency's singular purpose: to communicate American foreign policy "as enunciated by the President and the State Department."[8] "We do this in two ways," Murrow explained to the committee, "first, by influencing public attitudes abroad in support of these objectives, and second, by advising the President and the executive branch on the implications of foreign opinion for current and contemplated U.S. policies and programs." A year after the hearings, Representative Dante Fascell (D-FL) submitted his subcommittee's findings to the House Committee on Foreign Affairs. Assailing a "fuzziness of concept" at work in what it referred to as the "third dimension of foreign policy," the report nonetheless reasserted the strategic value of the USIA's presence at national security meetings with the president. At the same time, the report, citing the Kennedy memorandum, raised the concern that "[the agency's consultative power] can create confusion and uncertainty about the reallocation of authority and responsibility."[9]

Framed in this controversial manner, the agency's dual propagandistic and advisory role opened a new chapter in American foreign diplomacy. This feedback loop raised the ire of many outside the agency, but the power to advise the president on the temperature of foreign opinion and thereby influence foreign policy was one most treasured by staff members. In defense of the agency's unique position within the executive branch, former USIA officer Fitzhugh Green recalled in 1988 that the

> USIA featured prominently in defusing reactions to the Bay of Pigs fiasco and announcing the triumphant resolution of the Cuban missile crisis. Bruce Herschenson [*sic*], USIA's talented moving picture chief, produced hard-line propaganda films. One, *Five Cities in June* [i.e., *The Five Cities of June*, 1963], sneered at the obviously inaccurate Russian portrayal of their space exploits and touted the brilliant U.S. space achievements. When I screened this film at the U.S. Mission to the U.N., the Soviet guests left the theater in a huff, understandably irritated over the space commentary.[10]

In January 1970, the *Washington Post* reported that the agency's influence "in the making of policies it must justify abroad" had been discernibly reduced, in part an outcome of the Nixon administration's exclusion of the USIA from National Security Council meetings.[11] In 1977, the agency was briefly renamed the International Communications Agency and reoriented towards a new goal of so-called public diplomacy. Continuing many of the policies of the Nixon and Ford administrations, but heralding a rhetorical sea-change in response to the public distaste for the idea of state propaganda, President Jimmy Carter declared, "the Agency will undertake no activities which are covert, manipulative or propagandistic."[12] In 1982, President Ronald Reagan returned the agency name to the USIA. In 1999, the State Department took over the agency's duties and the USIA was officially closed.

Outside of a handful of career memoirs, the agency's history has remained largely obscure and piecemeal.[13] The surviving material history of the agency could support a wealth of studies in a variety of academic disciplines. As Nicholas J. Cull points out, the substantial documentary film output of the USIA Motion Picture Service has received scant scholarly attention.[14] This curious absence from American film and television histories is due in large part to the 1948 Smith-Mundt Act, which included a ban on exhibiting USIA productions inside the United States (except to members of the press and under congressionally approved circumstances). There was a failed attempt to lift the ban in 1972. The law was successfully amended in 1990, when Congress gave the Archivist of the United States the ability to distribute USIA "motion pictures, films, and videotapes" twelve years after the date of dissemination abroad or, if never disseminated, twelve years after production. But academic and historical neglect of these "impounded" federal films also persists because of the difficulties of archival access.[15]

After the USIA had been decommissioned, its productions, libraries, administrative files, and records were classified, discarded, sent to cultural affairs offices within the State Department, or moved to the NARA. Those accessioned by NARA have been broken up into separate collections areas. An estimated thirty-five thousand reels of USIA motion picture material alone (finished films, unedited footage, and outtakes) are held at the National Archives. Its catalog describes Record Group 306, the Records of the U.S. Information Agency, as containing "96 motion image series, of which 84 contain film titles." Detailed descriptions of series are yet to be produced. Musical rights clearance continues to inhibit industrial and other repurposing of the material. Nevertheless, among the myriad forms of evidence it might supply, the USIA's multitopic moving image record could significantly enrich our understanding of the nation's unique cinematic and televisual address to the rest of the world during the Cold War.[16]

That the collection is highly underutilized today by researchers is not surprising. Even at its zenith, when it benefited from Murrow's high-profile persona, the USIA remained sheltered from view. At the time, even many congressional representatives had difficulty distinguishing the operations of the USIA from the daily functions of USIS reading rooms and bookmobiles, construing the motion picture division as a 16mm rental library and thinking of its head as a librarian.[17] In a 1963 hearing of the House Subcommittee on International Organizations and Movements, Representative Frances P. Bolton (R-OH) asked Murrow two questions: Did the Films Division dispose of badly worn prints? And, were audiences tired of watching westerns?[18] We could attribute the congresswoman's vague understanding of this agency to the ban on the U.S. exhibition of the films, which had very effectively removed almost any discussion of them from the American mediascape.

The moving image holdings at NARA are only a partial representation of the agency's total film output. Arguably, under Murrow's directorship (1961–63) and for a few years after his death, morale within the agency was at its peak, and film production at its highest quality. In 1962, the USIA annual operating budget was $121 million. Of that, $1 million was earmarked for the creation of release prints, a mere $500,000 for the operation of mobile and four-walled exhibition venues, and a budget line of $92,000 was specified for the Disney-designed Circarama system, a 16mm panoramic projection onto a continuous, circular screen.[19] For the dozen or so USIA films made every year, production was mostly done by private motion pictures companies, on a contract basis. In-house staff worked on editing and sound recording, publicity, translation, and distribution. In addition to documentaries, newsreels, and short subjects, the agency produced a monthly screen magazine called *Today,* for dissemination in African regions. The organization boasted that 60 million viewers watched its export-only films in 746 theaters and that a Soviet publication called the program "anti-communist propaganda."[20] At this time, the agency claimed eleven thousand workers on its payroll, operated 239 offices in 105 countries (claiming that its presence was increasing in the decolonizing areas of the world), and broadcast Voice of America in thirty-six languages 761 hours a week. Under Murrow, television transmission had expanded to Liberia and the Philippines.[21] In 1964, the agency reported that it serviced some 226 "film centers" in 106 countries, requiring the use of more than seven thousand five hundred projectors and nearly three hundred mobile-unit trucks to facilitate film distribution and rural exhibition. Films in the field were exhibited in more than fifty languages and dialects. In some cases, USIA pictures were put into theatrical distribution and even submitted to film festivals. At that time, the Motion Picture Service was staffed by 158 positions. Although not included in the distribution staff of the Motion Picture Service, the USIS film libraries abroad were critical to the hub-and-spoke system of film circulation, making the actual total number of staff committed to the film operation larger.[22]

The most consistent definition of the agency's mission across its years of operation and under different directors was that it would "submit evidence to peoples of other nations by means of communications techniques that the objectives and policies of the U.S. are in harmony with and will advance their legitimate aspirations for freedom, progress and peace." This evidentiary purpose might suggest that the proscribed film style would be the expository mode. Indeed, four imperatives also emphasized a show-and-tell approach to foreign audiences: explain U.S. policies; demonstrate how those policies "harmonized" with other nations' goals; counter propaganda against the United States; and "delineate" aspects of American life that would help to clarify U.S. policies.[23] Those obtusely worded guidelines (with the exception of the order to "counter hostile propaganda") resulted in documentary portraits such as *In Search of Lincoln* (1956), *Robert Frost* (1960), and a panorama of American historical sites called *Pilgrimage of Liberty* (1958). Budgetary restrictions also shaped house style. Under Theodore Streibert, one of Murrow's predecessors, Turner Shelton headed a motion picture unit (then called International Motion Picture Service) hamstrung by accounting procedures ill suited to creative production. Newsreel reports, recordings of speeches, and documentary projects were all assigned on a "low bid" contract. George Stevens Jr., the idealistic head of Motion Pictures hired by Murrow, would turn this restriction into an advantage, bringing in young filmmakers, pressuring the contracted producers to hire the pricier creative talent, and using "creative accounting."[24]

Many credit the unusual aesthetic experimentation of that period to the leadership of Murrow and/or Stevens, or to the chemistry between them—and between Murrow and Kennedy as well. Stevens, who later became the founding director of the American Film Institute, recalled that at the time, "relatively few had their eyes on filmmaking." "In the film-crazed world of today, where even minor directors are celebrities, it's hard to comprehend how different the landscape was in the early 1960s. Films were considered by the elite to be an avenue of middle-class escape, a lower form of entertainment than theater, ballet, and opera."[25] As Richard Dyer MacCann has noted in his analysis of the unit as it operated from 1962 to 1967, "the art of the film was notably, if somewhat secretly, enriched."

> Whatever one might say about the individual films, the essential thing was that an atmosphere of experimentation was maintained in the very midst of a mundane propagandist mission. In the tradition of John Grierson, Stevens managed to draw into a program of national publicity a variety of individualists. The U.S. Information Agency became the only place in the United States where young film-makers might advance from college projects or first efforts for industrial sponsors to a filmic statement on a broader theme.[26]

MacCann's book *The People's Films: A Political History of U.S. Government Motion Pictures* (1973) offers the most complete film-historical account of George Stevens's

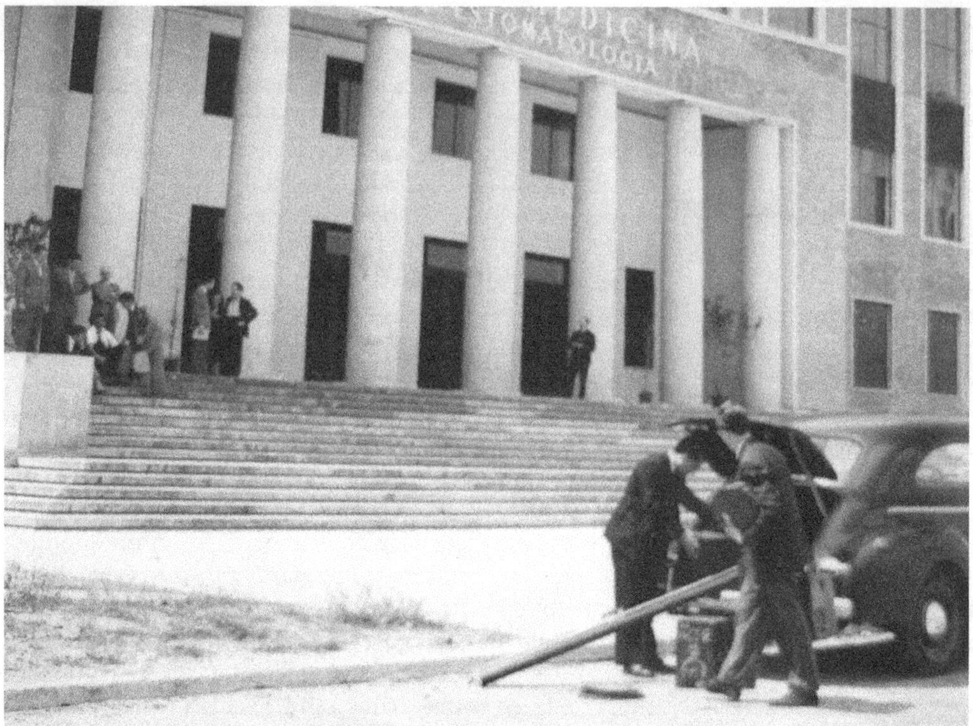

FIGURE 52.1 Film delivery for a United States Information and Educational Exchange program screening in Spain, 1949. Photograph. Courtesy of the National Archives and Records Administration.

creative leadership as head of the USIA filmmaking division. Stevens was twenty-nine years old and working as an associate producer on his father's Hollywood films, *The Diary of Anne Frank* (1959) and *The Greatest Story Ever Told* (1965), when he accepted an invitation from Murrow to put into practice his notion of "how motion pictures and filmmakers might contribute to the New Frontier."[27] In his own writing and in interviews, Stevens credits his inspiration and success to Murrow and to JFK and, to this day, still recites the five policy ideals which guided public service under that administration: (1) the pursuit of peace, (2) strength and reliability, (3) free choice, (4) the rule of law, and (5) the support of the United Nations.

If we think of his efforts to revitalize government documentary filmmaking as a product of Cold War hostilities, we neglect the degree to which Stevens's choice of topics was driven by his producer's sensibility. Among the many talented filmmakers Stevens hired during his five years at the USIA were Bruce Herschensohn, Ed Emshwiller, William Greaves, Charles Guggenheim, Leo Seltzer, Terry and Denis Sanders, Carroll Ballard, Kent Mackenzie, Haskell Wexler, and James Blue. Stevens created a competition for filmmaking students to create a short documentary about their school directed at foreign audiences. Internal diplomacy was often how he succeeded in seeing films to completion. According to MacCann, Bruce Herschensohn's short documentary *The Five Cities of June* (1963, produced by Hearst Metrotone's *News of the Day* crew) was popular overseas, admired by Kennedy, and nominated for an Academy Award. *The Five Cities of June,* Nicholas Cull writes, "offered a society that was capable of reform, unafraid to discuss its problems in public, and whose values came together in the person of a dynamic president, who was prepared to confront the Soviet threat resolutely and in the name of freedom."[28] Herschensohn made the first feature-length USIA documentary, *John F. Kennedy—Years of Lightning, Day of Drums* (1964), after making a small, poignant film about Lyndon Johnson called *The President* (1964).[29] In 1967, Stevens became the founding director of the American Film Institute.

In 1964, the USIA released a controversial documentary treatment of the August 1963 civil rights march on Washington called *The March*. In anticipation of the event, Stevens had arranged for Hearst Metrotone cameramen and brought in the young filmmaker James Blue to direct. According to Nicholas Cull, Blue instructed the camera operators to avoid the newsreel habit of moving from one scene to the next to capture facial expressions and reactions in the crowd. He shot handheld footage of the arrival of marchers on buses the day before and of the speakers on the steps of the Lincoln Memorial. Controversy surrounded the film upon its release, displeasing President Lyndon Johnson. In a compromise between the White House and the USIA, a stiff USIA Director Carl T. Rowan delivered a filmed prologue.[30] MacCann notes that the thirty-three minute film "has something of the epic quality of *The River*, and in the manner of that poetic government documentary, it reflects the sharp excitement of a great contemporary issue."[31]

While *The March* has the distinction of having been named to the National Film Registry in 2008, there is perhaps no better illustration of the Motion Picture Service's creative approach to the information film than the three short films about Colombia that it produced in 1963. Filmmakers James Blue and Stevan Larner had met in Paris in 1956 while studying film on the G.I. Bill. Stevens had seen Blue's feature film about an Algerian family, *The Olive Trees of Justice* (1962), at Cannes and hired both men to come to the USIA. To serve the Kennedy Administration's "Alliance for Progress," Stevens sent Blue and Larner to Bogatá, Colombia.[32]

Part of Kennedy's foreign policy mission in the region was to stimulate economic self-sufficiency with a partnership between the Colombian government and American entrepreneurs and businesses.

Using a Nagra audio tape recorder and a 35mm camera, the two returned with material for three films, which Blue then edited into lyrical and unexpectedly self-reflexive essay films on health reform, education, land reclamation, and housing. The resulting works—*A Letter from Colombia, Evil Wind Out,* and *The School at Rincon Santo*—are similar enough in theme and style to be considered a trilogy, even if they were never intended to be seen as such. *The School at Rincon Santo* won documentary prizes at film festivals in Bilbao and Amsterdam. *A Letter from Colombia* received a special award in 1963 from the Centre for Human Relations in Venice. Larner recalled his time making films for USIA:

> I was hired to create segments for a theatrical news magazine, called *Horizons* (*Horizontes*) in a newsreel format (the other contractor was Hearst-Metrotone news) to be distributed in Latin America by the United States Investigations Service [*sic*] (USIS). I was to travel to Colombia and Central America, spend two to three weeks in each country, developing three to seven minute stories, shoot them, and send the exposed 35mm black and white negative back to Hearst-Metrotone, along with script notes, shot lists, etc. for editing and voice-over narration. Also I was to use a local as my assistant and train him or her to be able to generate other stories after I left.[33]

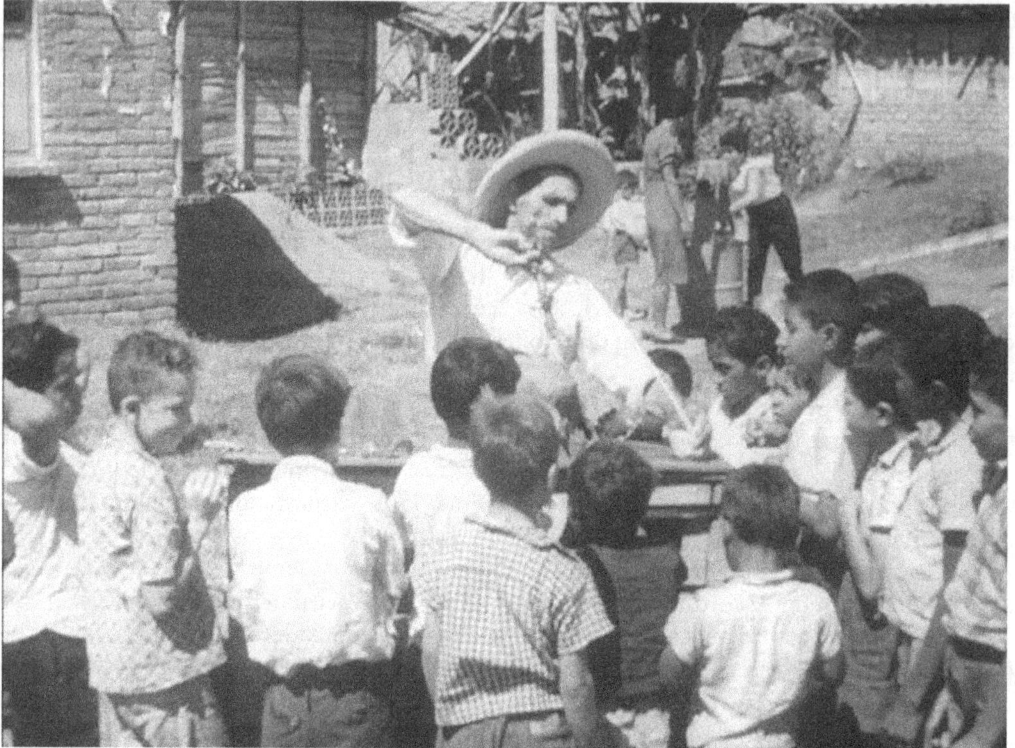

FIGURE 52.2 Reimagining progress, property, and community in *A Letter From Colombia* (James Blue, 1963). Screen capture from DVD. Courtesy of the National Archives and Records Administration.

In tone and in sentiment, the films offer photographic evidence that Larner and Blue went beyond their assignment and practiced a kind of cultural diplomacy through their filmmaking. *A Letter from Colombia* promotes the Alliance for Progress only through the general respect that it shows for large-scale state modernization programs.

The film's skeptical, essayistic structure does not suppress the human costs of industrialization. For example, at the start of the film, we are shown a woman moving small boxes that are then revealed to be child-sized coffins. Over these images, James Blue's reticent narration comes across as that of an outsider with a guilty conscience: "I have come here to make one of those films about progress that you see from time to time. New housing, industry, machinery: progress with a big *P* that you can measure in tons of bricks and miles of road. This is about my search for that progress, what I found, and where I looked to find it." After declaring that symbols of progress "all look alike," Blue pauses to make fun of newsreels and government-sponsored films that sell the notion of industrial progress and "better living" as if anyone could be against the idea, a gesture that makes cinematic sense but likely did not win unanimous support in Washington.

In *Evil Wind Out*, a cigarette-smoking doctor comes from a national public health service to a town suspicious of modern medical practices; the film concludes with the dedication of a new health center. *The School at Rincon Santo*—which displays perhaps the most virtuosic use of non-actors in Blue's USIA films—relates the story of the

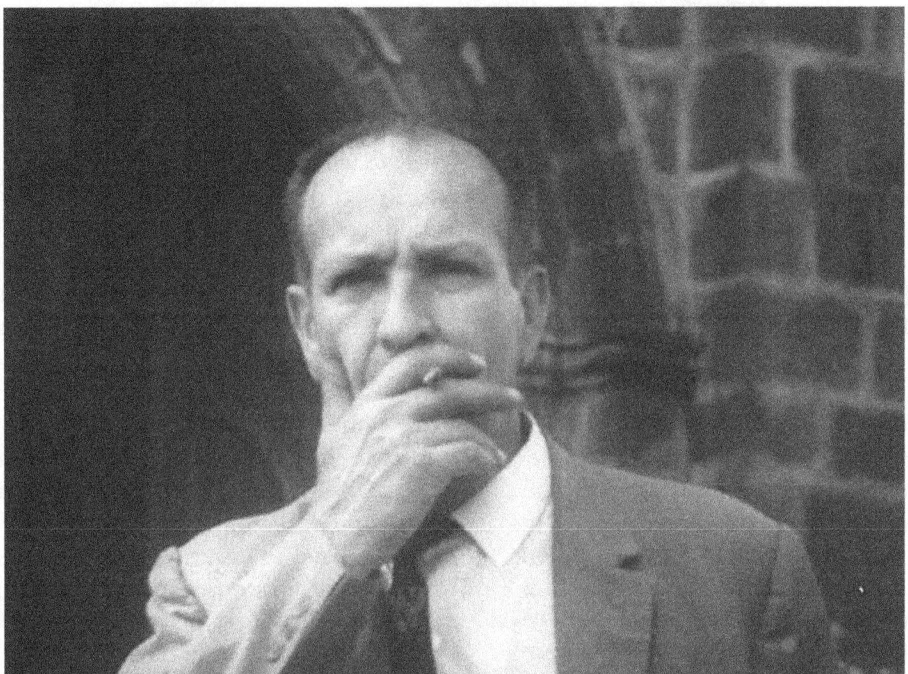

FIGURE 52.3 The cigarette-smoking doctor "from the nation's public health service" arrives in the rural village and waits on the steps of a church in *Evil Wind Out* (James Blue, 1963). Screen capture from DVD. Courtesy of the National Archives and Records Administration.

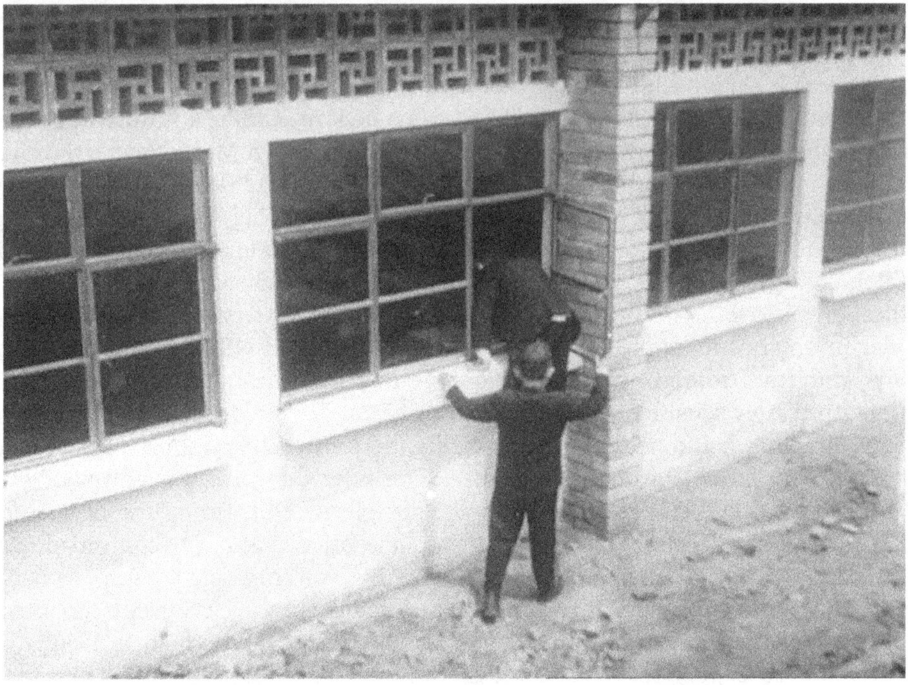

FIGURE 52.4 "Never has a one-room schoolhouse meant more than the new school at Rincon Santo," the voice-over narration tells us in *The School at Rincon Santo* (James Blue, 1963). Screen capture from DVD. Courtesy of the National Archives and Records Administration.

construction of a rural community's first schoolhouse.

In an interview Blue gave while he was still working under Stevens at the USIA, he said he was especially fond of *The School at Rincon Santo*:

> It was a wonderful experience; they [the USIA] gave me carte blanche. The theme is people helping themselves to progress. I worked as I always work: finding the essential elements of a situation which, when brought together, express something about the situation without my having to intervene in it. . . . I'm always very proud of myself when I do that entirely. There's one film in this group where I brought everything out of the existing materials. It's called *The School at Rincon Santo*, and it is the most successful of the three films.[34]

We might think of the shot just after the title sequence in *The School at Rincon Santo*, two boys surreptitiously slipping into the side of a state building, as a metaphor for Blue and Larner at the USIA, drawn into the institution by a mischievous curiosity. Years later James Blue said that he had always aspired to do "regional filmmaking—to reflect a region to itself," a goal which cut against the very aims of its ideological purpose.[35]

For documentaries meant to explain and promote American foreign policy, these films are surprisingly sensitive and compassionate. In fact, they could be thought of as ambassadors who do not hesitate to speak out of turn, subverting their diplomatic mission. *The School at Rincon Santo* inhabits the social imaginary of a small Colombian village. In *Evil Wind Out*, there is oversimplification, but in the service of community theater. And in *A Letter from Colombia*, parody of the expository voice itself. The personal view and intimate voice-over, the association of dreaming and development, the clear references to Chris Marker, Luis Buñuel, and other filmmakers—somehow, these expressive qualities survived the bureaucratic scrutiny to which they were submitted.

In comparison with other agency-produced media depicting American foreign policy in a more didactic manner, Blue's films were radical statements.

But they can also be understood using the deprecatory terms that USIA staff borrowed from anthropology to refer to officers who made themselves too much at home while abroad. They were said to be "going native" or had contracted "localitis."[36] With a little less condemnation, this agency-speak could also be used to describe Blue's rogue identificatory narration, especially his explicit interest in creating films that would speak directly to local audiences by attempting to present their realities and their fears about modernization. After all, just a few years later, ethnographic filmmaker David MacDougall would celebrate James Blue and Stevan Larner's final collaboration for the USIA, *A Few Notes on Our Food Problem* (1968), for exemplifying the desire for a more intersubjective documentary ethics, what he termed Blue's "unprivileged camera style."[37] Margaret Mead had served as a consultant on that project, a prescient meditation on the global food crisis that required months of shooting in Brazil, Uganda, India, and Taiwan, and six months of editing upon return. *A Few Notes on Our Food Problem* was one of the many USIA productions to garner significant critical attention in festivals and received an Academy Award nomination in the documentary short subject category. Soon after that film was completed, James Blue left the USIA in protest of U.S. foreign policies in Vietnam. He continued to maintain his working relationship with George Stevens Jr., however. Stevens recruited Blue to join the film production faculty of the American Film Institute in its first year.

The vast and underutilized collection of USIA moving image material at

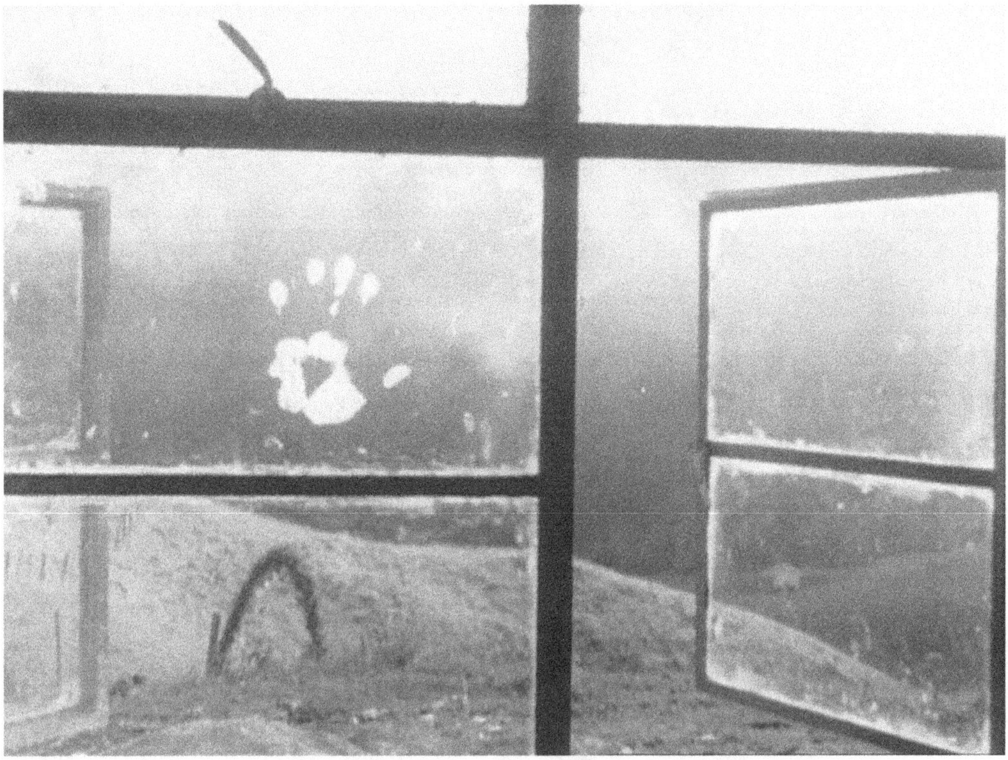

FIGURE 52.5 Layered voice-over in *The School at Rincon Santo* translates the voice of a community member into English: "We worked with our own hands, nothing more." The handprint on the window was left by James Blue. Screen capture from DVD. Courtesy of the National Archives and Records Administration.

the National Archives holds many more examples of what we might productively consider American "foreign" films. And no doubt additional USIA films are to be found in private collections and outside the United States as well. As I have tried to suggest here, these films range widely in tone and in message. Each film is representative of a fraught government agency, its relationship to changing American foreign policy, and its ever-present struggle over the definition of cultural diplomacy. In particular, the USIA films made during the five years of George Stevens Jr.'s directorship can be seen as both the reflections of failed foreign policies and their subtle contradiction. In this way, all of these films will remain important meditations on foreign relations: the relations between cultures, between citizens, and between the viewer and the viewed.

Acknowledgment

I wish to thank Dan Streible for his generous editorial feedback, and Leslie Waffen, William T. Murphy, Gerald O'Grady, and George Stevens Jr., for sharing their time, expertise, and reminiscences about the NARA collections, the USIA, and James Blue's life and work with me during the preparation of this article.

NOTES

1. Walter Lippmann, "Abolish the Voice of America," *Washington Post*, Apr. 27, 1953.

2. Michael Kammen, "Culture and the State in America," in *The Arts of Democracy*, ed. Casey Nelson Blake (Washington, D.C.: Woodrow Wilson Center Press, 2007), 69–96.
3. Richard Arndt, The First Resort of Kings: American Cultural Diplomacy in the Twentieth Century (Washington, D.C.: Potomac Books, 2005), xvii–xx.
4. Foreign Relations and Intercourse Act, U.S. Code 22 (1948) §1461-1a.
5. Edward T. Folliard, "Ike Revamps Information, MSA Setups," *Washington Post*, June 2, 1953.
6. Wilson P. Dizard Jr., *Inventing Public Diplomacy: The Story of the U.S. Information Agency* (Boulder, Colo.: Lynne Rienner Publishers, 2004), 67.
7. House of Representatives Committee on Foreign Affairs, Subcommittee on International Organizations and Movements, *The U.S. Ideological Effort: Government Agencies and Programs*, study prepared by the Legislative Reference Service, Library of Congress, 88th Cong., 1st sess., 1964, Committee Print, 9.
8. House Committee on Foreign Affairs, Subcommittee on International Organizations and Movements, Winning the Cold War: The U.S. Ideological Offensive: Hearing before the Subcommittee on International Organizations and Movements of the Committee on Foreign Affairs, 88th Cong., 1st sess., Mar. 28–29 and Apr. 2–3, 1963.
9. House Committee on Foreign Affairs, *Report on Ideological Operations and Foreign Policy*, 88th Cong., 2nd sess., 1964, Rept. 1352, 9–13.
10. Fitzhugh Green, *American Propaganda Abroad* (New York: Hippocrene Books, 1988), 36–37. The erroneous reference to Bruce Herschensohn as "motion picture chief" underscores the problems of the career memoir for history writing. For a more authoritative account of *The Five Cities of June*, see Nicholas J. Cull, "Auteurs of Ideology: USIA Documentary Film Propaganda in the Kennedy Era as seen in Bruce Herschensohn's *The Five Cities of June* (1963) and James Blue's *The March* (1964)," *Film History* 10, no.3 (1998): 295–310.
11. A. D. Horne, "Little Change Is Discernible under New Regime at USIA," *Washington Post*, Jan. 2, 1970.
12. Arndt, *First Resort of Kings*, 499.
13. I have relied heavily on these sources for both historical context and internal commentary: Arndt's First *Resort of Kings*, Green's *American Propaganda Abroad*, and Dizard's *Inventing Public Diplomacy*, as well as Lois W. Roth and Richard T. Arndt's, "Information, Culture, and Public Diplomacy: Searching for an American Style of Propaganda," in *The Press and the State: Sociohistorical and Contemporary Interpretations*, ed. Walter M. Brasch and Dana R. Ulloth (New York: University Press of America, 1986).
14. Cull, "Auteurs of Ideology," 295. The journal *Film Comment* published animated discussions of USIA filmmaking, especially regarding the controversial practice of footage reuse. See issues Summer 1965, Spring 1966, Fall-Winter 1967, Spring 1969, and Spring 1970. *Film Comment*'s 100th issue recounted the journal's editorial history, including its tackling of USIA film debates. Gordon Hitchens, editor of *Film Comment* from its inception in 1962 until 1970, also worked on six USIA films himself. Hitchens recruited James Blue to contribute regularly to the magazine, beginning in 1963. See Cliff Froehlich, "Inside *Film Comment*," Jan.–Feb. 1984, 33–40.
15. See Foreign Relations and Intercourse Act, U.S. Code 22 (1948), and Code of Federal Regulations, 36, Part 1256.98, "Domestic Distribution of United States Information Agency Audiovisual Materials in the National Archives of the United States." There still exists a duplication restriction covering much of the copyrighted material. Richard Dyer MacCann refers to the USIA films as "impounded" in *The People's Films: A Political History of U.S. Government Motion Pictures* (New York: Hastings House, 1973), 174.
16. For an example of other subject area contributions of the collection, see Donald Roe, "The USIA Motion Picture Collection and African American History: A Reference Review," *Quarterly of the National Archives and Records Administration* 29 (1997): 154–61.
17. House Subcommittee, *Winning the Cold War*, 14–16.
18. House Subcommittee, *Winning the Cold War*, 14–15. George Stevens Jr., was head of the Films Division at the time.
19. For a description of the Disney system, see John Belton, "The Curved Screen," *Film History* 16, no. 3 (2004): 284.
20. House Subcommittee, *Winning the Cold War*, 17.
21. House Subcommittee, *Winning the Cold War*, 5.
22. House Subcommittee Committee Print, *U.S. Ideological Effort*, 19–20.
23. Arndt, *First Resort of Kings*, 275.
24. MacCann, *The People's Films*, 178–85. It was Theodore Streibert who had brought in Cecil B. DeMille to advise on the agency's film operations. According to Dizard (*Inventing Public Diplomacy*, 66), DeMille made one trip to Washington in which he delivered a speech about the power of film.
25. George Stevens Jr., *Conversations with the Great Moviemakers of Hollywood's Golden Age at the American Film Institute* (New York: Vantage, 2006), xii.
26. MacCann, *The People's Films*, 195.
27. Stevens, Jr., *Conversations*, xi.
28. Cull, "Auteurs of Ideology," 301.
29. Some documents related to the release of *John F. Kennedy—Years of Lightning, Day of Drums* to American viewers have been included in *Film and Propaganda in America: A Documentary History*, vol. 4, ed. Lawrence H. Suid (New York: Greenwood Press, 1991). In *American Propaganda Abroad*, Fitzhugh Green offers the following anecdote George Stevens told him about the filming of *The President* which demonstrates the

similarities between Washington and a fiction film set: "USIA cameramen shot Johnson from various angles as he sat at his desk one evening in the Oval Office. While the cameras shirred, the president scratched his fountain pen across white sheets of paper. Stevens wondered if he might be writing a speech and surreptitiously peeked over his shoulder. He saw that every page was covered only with . . . Lyndon B. Johnson, Lyndon B. Johnson, Lyndon B. Johnson, Lyndon B. Johnson" (38).

30. Cull, "Auteurs of Ideology," 302–9. I have kept my discussion of *The March* brief, in part because Cull has offered such a lengthy and careful discussion of it already.
31. MacCann, *The People's Films*, 192.
32. Blue made five films for the agency, including *A Few Notes on Our Food Problem* (1968), which was nominated for an Academy Award.
33. Stevan Larner, "Remembering James Blue," in *James Blue: Scripts and Interviews*, ed. Gerald O'Grady (Houston: Southwest Alternate Media Project, 2002), 6–7.
34. Mary Batten, "An Interview with James Blue," in *James Blue: Scripts and Interviews*, 17.
35. Mark Mikolas, "Crisis in the Fourth Ward: An Interview with James Blue," in *James Blue: Scripts and Interviews*, 28.
36. Arndt, *First Resort of Kings*, 427.
37. David MacDougall, "Unprivileged Camera Style," *RAIN* (Royal Anthropological Institute newsletter, London) 50 (1982): 8–10.

53

PETER WATKINS WITH JAMES BLUE AND MICHAEL GILL

PETER WATKINS DISCUSSES HIS SUPPRESSED NUCLEAR FILM *THE WAR GAME* (1965)

WATKINS: Here you have a country of 52 million people, Great Britain, where probably not more than ten thousand know anything at all about the present world nuclear situation, the world nuclear stockpile, what their own national deterrent is, what radio-activity is—and it will all catch up with them before they even know. This is grossly undemocratic—a rather weak word to use—and so my film is *telling* people, if they want to listen. Not only on the national basis, but about the whole present situation as it is *now* being *legalized and formalized and analysed* by such people as Herman Kahn [author, *On Thermonuclear War*, formerly with Rand Corporation].

I reckon as somebody said—"Everyman before he dies has a right to know what he's running from"—and I believe that very much. Not more than a microscopic percentage of the people in this country know anything about their present situation at all.

It's not so much that facts are deliberately withheld from people as there being a gentleman's agreement not to tell people—and this is why my film, *The War Game*, will really curl the eyeballs of a lot of higher ups. They will have to decide that it is not right for people to know these things, because "this will effect the war morale of Britain," and that's going to be a hell of a thing to decide.

This is the avenue I'm crowding them into. That's going to be a very nice, juicy situation. They will have to *admit* that what the film says is true. I can say to any of these gentlemen—"How many books on radio-activity or thermonuclear weapons have you read?" And not more than point five percent will have read more than half the books. A lot of the facts in the film will be fairly new to them, and this in itself will be a very interesting revelation to them. And they can only admit—unless they actually lie—that it is quite likely that there are a lot of British citizens in their position. In other words, *is the withholding of knowledge a good thing?* And the only kind of argument they can put forward, if they reject the film, is—"You musn't frighten people." And this, I will say, "doesn't wash." And they will have to repeat—"You mustn't frighten," and then we shall really be going to town.

An interesting situation indeed. We are living in this gross lie and delusion because, of course, the full political structure rests on this thing. I, at least, feel that citizens have *a right to know what that structure is,* before they then decide whether it's a good thing or a bad thing. Lots of people will probably see my film and say—"Well, I still believe that the thermonuclear posture is a very good thing to prevent happening the holocaust that your film shows happening." At least that person can say that with some knowledge *now,* because formerly when anyone put a cross on a ballot-sheet it was without any knowledge at all. In the past, our ignorance might not matter so much, when nations could recover from wars. But thermonuclear war is "recoverable-from" only in a limited degree. So we're going to catch up with it.

The film is four-fifths ready now. The problems will start when the hierarchy sees it, which should be in about two weeks time. I can't "prepare" myself. It's just sort of . . . well, I *have* prepared myself. I've got all sorts of counter-arguments, and I think I'm going to get them into a very difficult position.

BLUE: What exactly will we see in this film?

WATKINS: It's about a nuclear attack on Britain—probable causes of, and effects of. It's great fun. Action is in Kent, as part of a country-wide tactical nuclear strike. As you know, no film can look at the entire country. I'll just take Kent as a working example.

BLUE: How are you able to predict what might happen in such an attack?

WATKINS: This is why the film is going to be attacked like hell when it goes out. It's based on conjecture, but conjecture based on the arithmetic of Britain, based on the arithmetic of how many targets we've got, versus our resources, versus this, versus this, versus this. You can't really cheat these figures. This is information spread over many, many, many books. There are probably well over a hundred different books—books on the effects of thermonuclear weapons, books on the crippling doses of Strontium-90, books on what thermoradiation does to your eyeball at certain distances, books on any number of very unpleasant subjects.

BLUE: Does *The War Game* deal with the responsibility of the government to inform the public?

WATKINS: Yes, this the film does in at least two of three chunks, quite specifically. There is one sequence where I put forth something with which the audience will immediately identify themselves—because they will realize their own lack of information. The camera spends five minutes with a crowd of survivors who are undergoing various minor psychological "kickbacks" from what they've been through—they're in fairly harmless states of daze and apathy. They have come from a radioactive Z zone. The commentary says—"It is likely that a few of these people will even know what a radioactive Z zone is," but the commentary doesn't explain what it is. Then it goes on—"It is likely that a few of them will know what 'Beta Burns' and 'Cell Division' and 'Polution' are." But the commentary doesn't define these terms. And if it works, I can see the minds of viewers who are honest with themselves—"I don't know what these terms are either! What is ID-131 and Cobalt-60—what is Carbon-14?"

I don't need to explain these terms. The film does show what radio-activity does to the human body, and in quite horrifying detail, but with Carbon-14 and all this I'm sort of titillating the audience. The authority of the film is that the chap on the Board of Governors won't know these terms either and hasn't had them explained to him.

In the film, I quote from the British manual of the Home Office—these are really the villains of the piece—it's written in 1959—"British public knowledge in the affairs of radio-activity will be made progressive in the next few years." I then go to a totally genuine street-interview, and I ask a woman—"Do you know what Strontium-90 is?" and she says—"I think it's a sort of gun powder, isn't it?" Most people said they didn't know. It's appalling, absolutely appalling.

Now I've got the film roughly cut, and I've got my escalatory system—Vietnam, Berlin and all that jazz—and then Herman Kahn, God bless him, publishes this thing in the *Times* two weeks ago which I'm now going to put in the front of the film. Kahn's piece is called *Thirty-Eight Rungs to Spasm—Or Insensitive Wars.* Five of my scenarios are exactly there within it. The point is that the government is going to feel that this undermines civil authority, because civil authority in this particular subject seems to rest partly on the public's lack of knowledge. The key burning issue is this—if people really understood thermonuclear posture and the results of it and the way the results can affect a small country like this, as opposed to thinking in insular terms, then would the people stand for it? Or would they accept nuclear war? It's possible they might, but it's also possible they might not. So basically *nobody* has the knowledge even to decide that. That's where it's an undemocratic situation. And that's what is going to bother the government.

BLUE: *The War Game* then is directed more at the governmental question than at the Bomb itself?

WATKINS: I attack the Bomb with all my might. If anyone sits through this film and comes out liking the Bomb, then they must have sat through it with both eyes shut. But I do not come out and say—"Britain must unilaterally disarm." I leave *that* to the viewer himself.

I think the whole thing is a mad situation. It's not just Britain, it's the whole world. Expense. Do you know that I found out that one-tenth of the American labor force is on the payroll of the military?—in one sense or another, with defense, installations, manufacturing projects, one way or another.

BLUE: Let's discuss the problems of shooting *The War Game.* Try to tell us how you went about things—people, camera, etc. I'm interested not only in what you finally said to the actors, but also in the general movement toward getting the results.

WATKINS: Well, really getting down to basic roots, my sort of film is a gross cheat. You *could* say that it is life as Peter Watkins sees it, and yet in a way it isn't, because I've never seen an atomic attack. A lot of people will object to this film on these grounds. For example, there is a sequence on the problems that will inevitably arise should civilian evacuation be put into motion. Now, how do I *know* how survivors will react? How much of this is just *myself,* saying what I want to say? But I try not to. I've intensely researched the subject. I show civil authorities putting into practice certain restrictions—rationing and all sorts of things—because they are going to receive a very large number of evacuees. This I *know* will happen, because if the government puts evacuation into process, then they have to put people somewhere. Of fifty-two million people in the country, there is little point in beginning evacuation unless you evacuate fifty or sixty percent of the twenty-five cities in this country that are key "counter-city" targets. So all this is mathematical logic—not completely, but almost. These evacuees have to go somewhere that is considered a non-target area. They can't go into the sea—they have to go somewhere on the land mass. The number of places in this country that can put up and feed and shelter ten million people are very limited—those places that aren't themselves under the radio-active lea of, or the blast range of, either airfields, ports, air bases or cities. The number is very limited.

So this is my way of getting ready to film. The civil authorities have to put certain restrictions into play, such as rationing, otherwise you'll never feed these people. Now, if they do this, then they have to set up restrictive road movement and all this sort of business. So for my film purposes, which do you imagine a policeman saying?—"Yes, we've got to have roadblocks, and I don't care if Father who is outside the roadblocks wants to come in to be with his wife—I stop him!" Or do you imagine the policeman saying—"This is absolutely bloody nonsense—you can't stop husbands getting to wives at a time like this!" My policeman says the second thing, because I think it's a more humane thing for a policeman to say and I think any man would say that. But I don't *know* that a policeman would say that, so I also have a policeman saying something like the opposite. In the film, they do actually set up roadblocks but the thing doesn't work very well.

BLUE: What about the behavior of the people in the encampment?

WATKINS: All I can do is imply that about fifty or sixty percent of the people stay and another half immediately lights out. So that you can look at both sides of it. But in actual fact I could be grossly wrong—100% might stay, or flee. You just don't know. This is unlike *Culloden*, my earlier historial war film, where at least I have a record of what people did. As the director of a film like *The War Game*, you have to be convinced that what you do, even without an historical record, rings true—*true* because it stems from this "mathematical pyramid." This pyramid is the foundation of *The War Game*—just as, for *Culloden*, British history was the foundation.

BLUE: Was it easier to direct your people in *Culloden*, because it was based on a history familiar to the non-actors you used?

WAKTINS: I don't think that makes a lot of difference, because when you get down to actually putting human beings in front of this awful camera lens, any legend or anything else all goes straight away out of his mind. He's so worried about the whole thing, you really have to start from scratch. Basically you can only work on the assumption—he must come across as a real person and not as someone acting. And the key thing in this is trying to get *nothing* out of that person that is not right for him as a character. If a person has only got to open his mouth and say two lines, it really is *chi-chi* nonsense to go into all the background of his personality. I haven't got the time, and this is nonsense. He is, in a way, not only a *person*, but he is *representative of people in his circumstance*. And having him recognize that, you have to show him that what he says is as underplayed and as believable as possible. This is not easy when people are being angry into the camera—"How the hell do you expect me to do this or that?"

I did not scene last Monday—a very difficult scene—I had a crowd of about twenty children, in age from six to about fifteen, boys and girls with mothers and a couple of fathers. I haven't seen the rushes so I'm not sure—but it looked very horrifying. This is the one scene in the entire two-hour film where the camera says—"You are now looking at the debris of thermonuclear war. These are the injuries. These people have been gassed. These people have suffered from heat stroke. These have been impaled by flying debris. These have been burnt. These have had their clothes set on fire by radiation." We just went along, sort of laying it on the line like that. I mean it's rather like tossing a clump of humanity into a corner and letting them writhe. They had to scream and cry and do things that normally are the most difficult things to get an untrained person to do. I spent about a quarter of an hour getting it out of them. They were made up, but no one told them what they were supposed to do. They trundled down to this little sort of wrecked corner of a barracks where we were filming, and we laid them all around in positions without explaining the scene yet. I plumped them down and then said: "You have been soandso and soandso." I explained the condition they were in. I then went to each person individually. It's a wide-angle shot, hand-held, and goes past people and sometimes someone goes past and bangs into the camera and says "excuse me." Although we laid the people out and planned the camera movement, if the thing works it will look totally unorganized.

I tried to get from each of them a different sort of shock or paralysis or crying or fear or pain-reaction—extremely difficult to do and I don't know if it worked or not. To look at someone in film and really *believe* that he is in pain is most difficult to do.

We were running on sound and I said that the sound is very important—"I'm only going to be passing your face for about five seconds and I want you to be giving forth." Except for one woman who couldn't do it for more than ten seconds without actually giving herself a rupture, to most of them I said—"I want you to give forth for all of the one minute that this shot is going to last, whether you are in the camera's range or not." So they all got this noise coming out of them. It was awful—a sort of animal-like noise—and I was watching them and it was absolutely incredible. Something clicked. The scene clicked, they knew what they were supposed to be doing and they really went to town, all sort of people.

A little kid was looking bolt-eyed into the camera. I had worked this all out—you cheat to start with. I have a sort of basic formula that sounds like a factory method—if you get someone breathing very quickly, this starts something going inside them, it opens the mouth and something happens to the eyes and then if you build something on top of this, the results can sometimes be not bad at all for pain or exhaustion. This sounds like Physical Exercise Number Five, and some people will say this doesn't go at all. But I'd do it even with a professional actor, because that is a psychosomatic thing anyway—breathing fast—it does produce certain things. But I got some kids doing just that—bolt-eyed into the camera. Other kids I got to pretend they were crying. And when the noise of everyone was awful, they lost inhibition and went to town on it a bit and made noises that people don't normally make, a vicious mélange of this sort of thing.

Although I go on about the difficulties, it is probably easier than a subtle scene when you have one person isolated in front of the camera and the whole thing depends on the right sort of flick of the eyes. Things either work or they don't work, and the depressing thing about this sort of film is that you can never tell whether it has worked until you see it on the screen.

BLUE: You say you're after an unorganized result.

WATKINS: Organized unorganization.

BLUE: What does that look like, in terms of the image?

WATKINS: You completely avoid the "well-framed" look. Things in my film must be "flat-on"—this doesn't denigrate dramatic effect at all. But if I film someone talking to camera, I prefer to film them "nicely framed" in a fairly tight closeup. And never an *extreme* closeup—there you begin to get into the field of drama. I like to keep people back a bit so that you can look at them. My people always look straight into your eyes because they are looking into the lens. They are not looking off. In a raw situation to go flat onto someone saying into the camera "I think so and so"—this is where you are using a real person, this is direct, no phony dialogue scenes.

This sort of film has to be incisive, has to make points and move ruthlessly. The traditional low-angles or the traditional angles of westerns looking up past the gun holster just don't fit this sort of film. Seldom if ever an "over the shoulder." You constantly say to yourself—"You are in a newsreel situation. What is the sort of thing that you would have taken if you were there." This is a fairly good criterion—then you cheat sometimes on that. Because you can say, as I did when directing *Culloden*—"There were no newsreel cameras in 1746 and a cameraman would never have been in front of charging men." But if you film it in such a way that it looks real, then that question usually doesn't arise.

BLUE: When you say "looks real," what do you mean?

WATKINS: That life is existing on *both* sides of the camera. I had a shot going through a whole stack of people and you hear someone saying near the camera "excuse me, please"—this does things, I assure you. Or if someone comes up and looks in the camera and the camera sort of "bumps" and moves away from him just as you see him—this is the technical nuts and bolts of it. You've got to make sure it's not overdone, that it's right for the scene and you've got to use different ways of doing it, because you see it twice and it looks wrong. Once in a film is just about right. Hand-held is half the answer to the whole thing.

Never, never, never in this sort of film do a track, a smooth track. I have one track in *The War Game*. It takes six minutes; however, it looks real. A shot in sync; the camera is on the back of a motor-bike looking over a police-dispatch rider's shoulder. He drives about two-hundred yards very fast down the road, stops, gets off the motor-bike, goes up to two policeman with a message, they say "take it straight up there," the camera follows him up the flight of steps, through swing doors, into the vestibule of a big county-hall, across the floor, up a flight of steps, around a corner, up another flight of steps, down a corridor, into a room—all in sync—listens to two people talk to each other for a moment, follows a man across a floor, circles around a table where four men are sitting, then down behind the table where someone starts to talk in dialogue. All that happens in one shot. It works because it's handheld, because people look into the camera as they pass, people react normally, because the dialogue isn't always crystal-clear, because all sorts of things happen that are justified. You might get a light flair into the camera. This is real.

BLUE: Tell us about your selection of non-actors for your film. You are looking for people who will make us say upon seeing them—"Those are real people" and not "Wow, what a great performance!"

WATKINS: Yes. In *The War Game* I have a series of people, each having only one and two sentences to say. Each talks about domestic trivia—what it's like not to have heat, or not very much food, or to have unclean washing water. None of the people who played these roles had ever been in these circumstances before, but somehow they understood what I wanted. This is a thing one shouldn't really say, I suppose—but it's partly an audience delusion as well. Because if you have a woman very quietly and simply say—"We've been eating out of tins for the last three days and it's been cold," then you think to yourself—"My God, that could happen to me," because it's a normal thing. She says it quietly and she looks dead tired and it's totally unacted in the accepted sense, then the audience will help that by reading a tremendous lot into it. Getting right down to the mechanics of it, you've taken an ordinary person, you've gotten her to repeat it two or three times until she says it quietly and simply enough, and with fatigue enough, and then you've got it. It is a cheat in a way.

I usually do this: I say—"I want you to say it like this" and then I say it. And "I want you to be tired and play it down"—you have to keep holding people down. Some people—some ordinary housewives—surprised me like hell. They came out with a marvelous thing the first time. Some people were good at about take seven. It's the basic simplicity of it, it's dialogue that I've thrust into their palm about ten minutes before the take, telling them—"Now go and learn that." They know they are to act housewives—they are in a way standing for a lot of housewives who will be in this position. The point has to be made in about four seconds flat. I explain exactly what she has got to do. What she says must be relevant. If it's a housewife explaining about the lack of washing-up water, then that is all that needs to come out.

But there are also more difficult things. I have a man who plays a police inspector who must explain in a one-minute take straight into the lens in a rather quiet and shacked-out way, as though it is literally two months after a thermonuclear strike, the process of moral breakdown. An interviewer asks him about the way people are behaving; and he looks straight into the camera and says—"Well, before the strike, people behaved in such and such a way, but now people are getting worse because . . ." and then he tries to explain. It helps to have a fairly intelligent amateur actor.

Of the amateur actor there are two categories—those who over-project like mad and are literally useless and those with tremendous intelligence who immediately grasp this totally different technique they've never used before. The camera and microphone are close, so you have to put yourself forward in another way. Their acting experience really helps in all sorts of technical things, such as emphasis, the intelligent grasp of where and why pauses come in.

Usually I write my text all the way down to putting the pauses in. And I write the "uhs" in. People generally forget these but get the idea. If you write it "I . . . I . . . well, uh . . ." and explain that this is how you want it said, then they usually don't have to copy you exactly and they might even change the words slightly. I usually say the thing over and over as I write it until I feel if the reality is coming out of it.

BLUE: How do you introduce your non-actors to their text?

WATKINS: With sympathy and intelligence, that's all it is. I may let him see the script first. I tell him the sort of man he is supposed to be. I don't go into character a lot. I don't believe in that for this sort of film. I believe a man is a man and he'll come out as he is. And if I say—"You have fifteen children"—this is irrelevant because he has forgotten that. The audience is not going to look and say—"He's got fifteen children, hasn't he? I can see it in his eyes!" As long as he knows the circumstances, then basically the sort of man he is as the performer *is* the sort of character he is. I seldom attempt "character playing." People are themselves. As long as he knows the circumstances he is in and the way he would react, then you are realy most of the way there.

BLUE: What about directing emotional responses other than screaming and yelling?

WATKINS: Emotions in this sort of film tend to be fairly basic and uncomplicated. Here's an example, concerning one woman. It was supposed to be a crowd scene, a riot, and a rather fascist citizens auxiliary corps drives up a truck and runs a child down. This precipitates a mass reaction from the crowd. I actually used a woman with her real son. I said to her—"You are in this situation, the truck drives up, and we'll put your boy under the truck. The camera will approach from the back, by the time the camera charges through the crowd to the front you'll just be picking your boy up from under the wheels of the thing. And because the truck has gone over the curb, it will look as though it has hit someone in the crowd. By the time the camera charges through we'll see you picking him up and we'll know it's your boy." And she was dead worried about this because the truck has to come screeching up and then she has to put her boy underneath. We tried it once and the brakes weren't right and you swore that another six inches and it would have really hit him. And I said—"I then want you to pick this boy up and I want you to go bloody, animal mad! You're two months hungry, two months of deteriorating conditions, low on rations, and then *this* happens! And you've got a boy lying there who feels odd in your arms and there is some blood coming out of his mouth because of the internal puncture. Now I want you to go *mad* at these people in this truck!" But could she do this? I shouted and screamed, I ruptured myself, the crowd was going berserk. The conditions couldn't have been better, and she just looked like somebody out of a girls' school hockey-team. So I finally had a man do it, someone who wasn't the boy's father at all! He looks marvelous! He looks as if he's going to go castrate everyone of them. He had this sort of intelligence and he grasped it. To make the woman react, I had almost kicked the boy in the teeth, but she couldn't do it. Being a mother doesn't always have any advantage whatsoever. You need this basic sort of *click*—"I understand," *click*—"I'll forget inhibitions," *click*—"I can do it." In some people no click takes place at all.

I have another scene that worked but not as well as it should because the woman just wouldn't give. A house thirty miles from a series of megatonic explosions in an airfield. Nothing is happening in that house really, other than the place is under the prolonged blast wave, so that means that everything is going like this [Watkins rattles an ash-tray on the desk to simulate an earth tremor] and this goes on for 45 seconds. And all this family is doing—the boy's been out in the field—and of course they don't hear the sirens and he suffers from the flash and they pick him up and the camera rushes inside the house with them. And then the rattling starts and they just grab onto the table. And when they charged into the house they had one boy in their arms and there was a little baby on the floor screaming his bloody head off when we were filming this. The scene looks horrifying! Because you've got *this* [Watkins imitates baby scream] and the camera is bouncing and we've got all the crockery on the mantle rattling. But the woman's face wasn't right and I couldn't do this again because I'd got her out there with a lot of great palaver and whatnot. And she just didn't *give* something, she couldn't. But the scene is luckily over-all not bad. I wanted an awful non-comprehensive gape from her, which is very difficult to get from some people. But since you don't really see her, and the baby is screaming and the other little kid is going [Watkins imitates the short bursts of cries], it works all right.

GILL: Did you aim for a complete shooting script with dialogue before actual production started?

WATKINS: Yes, I get it all on paper, and then I shoot and it all changes because of special circumstances of weather and people and all sorts of things. But I certainly try to start with a very detailed script, because you can't improvize this sort of thing. It's difficult enough to organize with a working script, but without it would be chaos. You're not working with professional actors, so you've got to organize private people who are coming on their own time and the thing is an immense jigsaw puzzle to work out, to shoot.

BLUE: How do you find your non-actors?

WATKINS: You just find people. I'd decided the areas to do it—three fairly big towns in Kent. I went to these towns and got the ball rolling by finding the local dramatic societies, or the local cine-societies. And these people bring in all their uncles and dads and the whole thing just snowballs, snowballs into a series of large meetings held in each town with usually a hundred or a hundred and fifty people attending, mostly from local drama groups—and I try and get them organized into the film. This usually works very well. I suppose if you count heads, I had about three hundred and fifty people in my last film.

GILL: What do you think of *Doctor Strangelove*?

WATKINS: I don't know ... whenever I open my mouth about that, there are all sorts of people who . . . I liked *Failsafe* far better.

GILL: Isn't *Failsafe* much more conventional?

WATKINS: Don't under-rate it. Sidney Lumet has got his head screwed on. It's a very well made film. I haven't seen *Twelve Angry Men* and I haven't seen *The Hill*. But *Dr. Strangelove* . . . I don't know. I thought at the time it was a well made film, but I keep hearing people say how bloody awful they thought it was, so I keep having doubt. I heard a woman coming out in the foyer at the end of that film and she said—"Oh, ho, my dear, I did enjoy that!" And so that's why the film fails! I just have certain feelings about the *present* nuclear situation to not think it's awfully funny. *Basically Dr. Strangelove* is an *acceptance* film. I mean the full title means more in actual fact than people give it credit for—*How I Learned to Quit Worrying and Love the Bomb*.

BLUE: You feel that this represents a particular danger?

WATKINS: Getting down to nuts and bolts as far as the next bloody well war goes, Mate!, it will be your people and the Russian people who will really be more particularly involved. And we British shall be there purely as a crisped-up side-kick.

But in America you have a far greater dissemination of public knowledge on the effects of nuclear weapons. We've got nothing at all in this country. Mr. and Mrs. Bloggs know nothing about it whatsoever. This is why I'm making *The War Game*.

Regarding the effects of *Dr. Strangelove*, I don't think many people have seen it here. Basically, it sends you out—if you don't know the ends and outs of nuclear weapons, if you don't know what they can do, if you don't know what the present stockpile is, if you don't know all these things, and most people don't! . . . then *Dr. Strangelove* sends you out laughing. *And that ain't on*. How many ordinary people say—"That film frightened me," as opposed to saying—"Do you remember the scene with the Coca Cola machine?" But how many people have said to you—"That could actually happen." Now, come on, how many?

There is an acceptance of thermonuclear war, especially in the United States, and this seems to measure a certain degree of thinking, particularly top-level thinking. I know a little bit about this now, after *The War Game*, I mean this whole "limited-phase" thing, all this whole business. It's just nonsense. But there is an acceptance of thermonuclear war as something that can "possibly be absorbed."

SECTION IV

AESTHETICS OF LIBERATION

Free, Direct, and *Vérité* Cinemas

54

JONATHAN KAHANA

INTRODUCTION TO SECTION IV

In the delightful screed that opens this section, "The Castration of Documentary," French non-fiction film pioneer Jean Painlevé laments the sorry state of documentary, circa 1953:

> Nowadays just about anything is deemed a worthy subject for a film: the search for a missing person, a shipwreck, etc. Confusion reigns everywhere. Athletic feats pose as cinema. Filmed testimonials pose as sociology. Lines between different forms of media have been obscured as well: radio personalities now appear as television hosts; filmmakers now appear on radio.

Although Painlevé was most concerned with the "lack of sincerity, inventiveness, and . . . energy" he found in the contemporary cinema of science and nature, his plaint expresses the impatient spirit of documentary filmmakers everywhere in the 1950s—or at least those who would participate in the liberations referred to in the title of this section, a freeing of documentary from different industrial and aesthetic constraints. Towards the end of the decade in which Painlevé was writing, and for at least the next ten or fifteen years, filmmakers who had been chafing at conventions formed in what we might now call the "classic" period of documentary film—roughly 1930–1960, the years when formal, professional, and political institutions of documentary cinema were being established—sought new ways of making a documentary, new subjects to make documentaries about, and new audiences to show them to. This section introduces the reader to some of the international varieties of this effort, and to some attempts to think critically about the impact of these attempts to free documentary and discover new social truths.

It would be hard to find a consistent political or ideological impulse or meaning in these scattered renovations. And in that sense, what's outlined in this section is less a movement than a number of simultaneous experiments with topic, style, and technology, some of which happened to share personnel, ideas, or equipment. Nevertheless, we can still see British "Free Cinema," Canadian "Candid-Eye," French "*Cinéma-vérité*," American "Uncontrolled" or "Direct Cinema," and all their cognates elsewhere in the world as a widely-distributed cinema of protest.

To be sure, many of the same causes and events inspiring the overtly political filmmaking addressed in the section following this one were on the minds of those calling for the liberation of documentary from the old rules. In a 1966 *Village Voice* column on the topic of the new amateur newsreel, Jonas Mekas pointed to the "things happening round us, from the ghettos of L.A. to the smoky outskirts of Chicago and all across the country and in Vietnam, and in our own small city—big things, and small things, ugly things" as the reason to take small non-professional cameras into places cameras hadn't been before and "show everything, everything." And a number of these filmmakers, especially in France, drew on the idea of the "kino-eye," which they took from the newly rediscovered work of Dziga Vertov, an explicitly political filmmaker whose work was made possible by its association with a state revolutionary movement. (The term *cinéma-vérité*, which Edgar Morin claims to have invented in 1959 or 1960, translates into literal French the title of the Soviet newsreel on which Vertov first worked, *Kino-Pravda*.) But the revolution addressed in this section was aesthetic, subjective, and rather modest by comparison with the world-changing aspirations of the radicals and the collectives of the 1970s. The goal Lindsay Anderson has in mind, for instance, in his 1957 appeal to "Free Cinema" is, above all, official and mass-cultural respect for documentary: he and his compatriots protest the domination of film culture in England by the commercial fiction film and the lack of state support for an alternative to this entertainment-based cinema. One might even say that, despite the anarchic sound of manifestos like cinematographer Ricky Leacock's 1961 "For an Uncontrolled Cinema," this was a somewhat conservative revolution, in that it returned documentary to the aims stated by Grierson in the 1930s: take the apparatus out of the studio, and use it to tell the unique story of a location.

In fact, even though its partisans liked to declare their commitment to recording only the present moment, some of the formative statements and gestures of this new documentary style *did* look back to earlier, perhaps unrealized conceptions of documentary in its classical era, pulling at some of its loose threads and unconscious thoughts. The English author, artist, and filmmaker Humphrey Jennings, who worked unhappily under John Grierson for a while, was the patron saint of Anderson and the other "Free Cinema" filmmakers. (Jennings's surrealist-inspired study of working-class amusements, *Spare Time* [1939], could be seen as a precursor to the *vérité* cinemas examined in this section.) Likewise, the unclassifiable documentary work of George Franju, like his 1949 portrait of a French stockyard, *Blood of the Beasts*, anticipates the spontaneity and playfulness of "direct" cinemas with its eye for what Jean Cocteau, in a 1963 essay, calls the "everyday miracle." And although they are not usually discussed in the company of films about the everyday habitats of ordinary people, Alain Resnais's harrowing 1953 film about the Nazi concentration camps, *Night and Fog* (*Nuit et Brouillard*), and Forough Farrokhzad's equally disquieting 1963 film *The House Is Black*, a portrait of an Iranian leper colony, both make such unconventional, ironic use of classical Western documentary form and discourse—including ceremonial cinematography and narration, music, a "Voice of God," and the idea that medicine and science serve universal, humanistic ends—that we can think of them as participating in the general overturning of documentary institutions and customs that begins in the 1950s.

Of course, it wasn't long before this candid camera revolution had generated its own doctrines and detractors, and much ink has been spilled in the years since Anderson et al. published their declarations of independence on the question of just how *vérité* these new forms of documentary actually were. Some critics writing at the time doubted that there was anything particularly inventive about these films, and remained unimpressed by their makers' claims for them; and some historians since have wondered whether the significance of these experiments was and has been overstated in the critical literature.[1] Mekas's essay and Margaret Mead's *TV Guide* article trumpeting the importance of the *cinéma vérité* television series *An American Family* (1973), reproduced here, are exemplary of this outlook. Pauline Kael takes a very different, and much dimmer, view of *cinéma-vérité* and its legends in her *New Yorker* review of the Maysles brothers' Rolling Stones film *Gimme Shelter* (1970). In her thorough analysis of one of the period's touchstones, the Robert Drew Associates film *Primary* (1960), Jeanne Hall addresses such arguments, and points out that many of them—including ones made by the filmmakers themselves—don't quite synch with the film they describe, and express aims and ideals more than documentary realities. Hall's excellent essay can be read together with together with the essay by Canadian filmmaker and aesthetic philosopher Bruce Elder, "On the Candid-Eye Movement," where Elder engages in an astute comparison of national variants of this style, attributing their differences to sociological and ideological factors. Similarly, Tom Whiteside's report on the television interview, *vérité*'s foremost rival in the quest to reach new depths of documentary intimacy in the 1960s, makes plain how much work went into these spontaneous revelations of character (as does Paul Arthur's review of American "jargons" of authenticity in section VI). Their critiques challenge us to rewatch, reread and reconsider, neither to praise nor to bury but to better understand the mythology, and the persistent appeal, of *vérité* style.

NOTE

1. See, for instance, the dossier of conflicting views published in the Summer 1964 issue of the journal *Film Quarterly*, or, more recently, Michael Curtin's dissenting opinion of *cinéma vérité*'s historical significance, in *Redeeming the Wasteland: Television Documentary and Cold War Politics* (New Brunswick, NJ: Rutgers UP, 1995).

55

JEAN PAINLEVÉ

THE CASTRATION OF DOCUMENTARY (1953)

What is a documentary? "Any cultural film." "A nontheatrical film." "A short subject." "A reduced format film." That is just a partial list of answers international experts have offered. Faced with this confusion, the World Union of Documentary Filmmakers thought it worthwhile to formulate the following definition in 1947:

> Documentary: any film that documents real phenomena or their honest and justified reconstruction in order to consciously increase human knowledge through rational or emotional means and to expose problems and offer solutions from an economic, social, or cultural point of view.

Unfortunately, much time will pass before we can truly appreciate this definition and put it to use. In the meantime, audiences will mature while the documentary will degenerate. In the old days, the documentary was hissed at, scorned because of its noble pedigree (some unlikely third-rate films profited from this perception, though far less often than in today's glut and, moreover, those who used to make documentaries still had sincere intentions). Back then everybody, even the intelligentsia who frequented the so-called avant-garde movie theaters, complained about documentaries. "Oh no!" I once heard the former nursemaid of novelist Raymond Radiguet groan while sitting behind me at the Ursulines in 1927, "Another film by Michel Zimbacca!" Eventually it became fashionable to arrive late and skip the documentary altogether. Today, however, the man of taste who finds himself at a cinematic event feels compelled to applaud the documentary, no matter what it is, for he has finally learned—indeed, we have drummed it into him—that the documentary is cinema at its purest. There is even an elite that claims to like nothing but documentaries. Except for a few true cinephiles, it is precisely these documentary lovers who are the enemies of cinema. Still, all of them put together represent but a tiny segment of the moviegoing "clientele," or cinema's real market. We have even tried to widen our audience, but in doing so we have come to endorse the most disgusting type of conformity, and not just to sell inferior merchandise. It is enough to make me start hissing myself, but that would give too much pleasure to those still contemptuous of the genre and who ignore the obvious fact that there are just as many lamentable feature films as mediocre documentaries. (And with the added decline of animation, despite technical innovations being employed in other genres, I often find myself waiting in anticipation for the intermission so I can view the next installment of the commercial "White Teeth.")

Currently, there are close to a thousand documentaries waiting to be released, clogging up the French market. (Those anxious to implicate me can relax: I have not made a documentary for a general audience in six years and therefore do not contribute to this bottleneck.) This glut of documentaries pending distribution can be explained not only by competition from other genres and foreign releases but also, and this may be the most important, by a cancerous proliferation of "short subjects" by beginners who view them as an easy way to get started. Some blame must also be placed on the relative ease in securing funding through private or governmental sources (although this is beginning to dry up). Even then, a documentary is an investment of the most risky sort, given the state of the market and the public's moviegoing habits. Documentaries not sponsored by the govemment or large companies risk early death. Indeed, to survive, a documentary is forced to become a public servant or a private one; that is, the filmmaker must walk a straight line. Given that the most banal and uninspired documentary, one that neither challenges the viewer nor drains the producer's money, already has difficulty making a profit, one can imagine what happens to innovative films: they are hidden away, treated worse than poor relatives who are at least tolerated. It is hardly an encouraging state of affairs for the rare producers, generally ex-filmmakers themselves, who want to support a quality effort. We need the genius of a Robert Flaherty or a Joris Ivens or the surprising novelty of a *Kon-Tiki* to break through the current barrier of indifference.

Money alone does not guarantee a successful film. It is the general public, the audience that keeps cinema alive, and they will only come for a fiction film. A theater owner knows this and exploits it. Naturally he does not actually watch all the films that a distributor foists upon him: he has better things to do than waste time in a movie theater. Instead, he listens to what his customers tell him and studies the effects the films have on his neighborhood. This civic-minded gent might be fascinated, for example, with the effect a particular film might have on children. He determines, just by looking around, whether or not the week's movie appealed to children. When, after a certain movie called *Bloody City*, little boys began tormenting and knocking down little girls, he realized it was because they liked the movie. This well-informed man will never push for a documentary: it exhausts the mind when what people really want is to be entertained. Let us also not forget the distributor who is only interested in making money from a big film. There are so many obstacles. Yet these only partly explain the current deterioration of the documentary. The number of producers and filmmakers continues to increase (Do they believe in their own genius or in Father Christmas?), some lasting only long enough to cash their checks and deliver shoddy merchandise. One might, at first glance, view this profusion of films as a positive development: offering a variety of choices and a chance for a few flowers to bloom. Unfortunately, this is rarely the case since the conditions are fundamentally rotten (true not only in cinema, rest assured). Moreover, we have not been able to rid ourselves of such childish antics as distributing prizes at festivals that are not even organized by the profession, although some professionals do serve on the juries. (Nothing disgusts me more than a man of the trade getting mixed up with award ceremonies. As evidence, I point to a dilettante in the medicoscientific field: his first act was to create a "Grand Prize"—then promptly award it to one of his own films! This also brings to mind Anquetil, a great singer from the twenties, who founded the "Grand Prize of the Society of Nations for Virtue," and awarded it to one of his own books, a book, incidentally, whose tone of righteous indignation could not disguise its true subject: pornography.).

So a question arises: are filmmakers completely devoid of new ideas or are they just spineless individuals in the pockets of producers whose sole concern is commerce? Although it is not fair to demand that every film have the incisiveness of Georges Franju's *Hôtel des invalides*, the intensity of Michel Zimbacca's *L'Invention du monde*, or the sweeping breadth of Albert Lamorisse's *Bim*, it is unthinkable that a filmmaker would have nothing to say about his subject. I hear some whisper that their subject was forced upon them—that is too easy. Others, lacking a better justification for their work, point to an alibi called "beautiful photography," which modern technology has made available to even the most ignorant amateurs. The unexpected, the unusual, the lyrical—all have vanished, replaced, I would argue, by "beautiful photography." So, for example, you can sit through an entire film about an abbey and still not know where it is located! Another formula that has become popular: rather than showing something, simply suggest it. "Close your eyes and imagine . . ." (A familiar refrain!) But we know better. We can get words without images from literature. At other times, we are invited to invisible battles, far away, to contemplate a hundred thousand men we cannot see. "What about poetic license, artistic liberties?" one might ask. That is not what is happening here. Rather, it is proof of cinematic impotence and fraud. It is also fraud, though it is often camouflaged as "reportage," to make a "documentary" about a country that ignores everything except secondhand reports from books or travelers. The element of adventure is stripped away in favor of a few exotic effects, and the subtle expressions of a country or population are reduced to poorly digested footage. Rivers, the sea, mountains, forests, animals, furry or fierce, are all slapped together to form a miniature eclectic bazaar, perfect for moviegoers hungry for shivers of fear or heroism while safe in their movie theater seats. Indeed, so artificial are these wild exploits, one expects them to culminate in an advertisement for a shirt that prevents rheumatism, or that the dead hero of Alphonse Daudet's *Port-Tarascon* will suddenly rise up and sing the praises of Mathurin spinach.

Nowadays just about anything is deemed a worthy subject for a film: the search for a missing person, a shipwreck, etc. Confusion reigns everywhere. Athletic feats pose as cinema. Filmed testimonials pose as sociology. Lines between different forms of media have been obscured as well: radio personalities now appear as television hosts; filmmakers now appear on radio.

At least the pioneers of cinema were more discreet. Think of Marquis de Wawrin's *In the Land of Headhunters* (*Au pays du scalp*), or Titayna's *Indians, Our Brothers*, or even the older *Symphony of the Virgin Forest* whose director, August Bruckner, died while making it. This is to be distinguished from the deplorable Nazi film *The Hell of the Virgin Forest*, which appeared seventeen years later in 1942 and whose wonderful sequence of a giant otter almost compensated for the paucity of the whole. Films with grand *mise en scènes* that were panned immediately such as Hoefler and Futter's *Africa Speaks to You* or Willard Van Dyke's *Trader Horn*—where, for the benefit of the camera, a guide was sacrificed to a rhinoceros—were no more artificial than certain recent much-ballyhooed "documents." (Despite the drama, conditions on reserves are actually less dangerous than a circus trainer in a cage of performing cats.) And if one looks to other documentary genres, one will discover young filmmakers worthy of a Marcel Ichac or a Jacques Cousteau have not yet given signs of life.

In all the imitators, one finds a complete lack of sincerity, inventiveness, and the energy necessary to capture difficult-to-achieve effects. At one time, some of them may have been innovators, but once a filmmaker repeats himself, his work loses its original purity and quickly becomes formulaic. Would it be so awful to try something new and original? After all, cinema is not cooking where warmed-up leftovers often taste better than the first time. I apply my argument to big movies as well. And why shouldn't I? Other critics have always applied their ignorance to all of cinema. One of them, in fact, discovered science films in 1951 through a Walt Disney film *The Little Corner of the Earth*, a charming though highly unscientific montage of images, some of which were sensational, but as for the whole, I can not remember a thing. Perhaps this young critic never considered the German Ufa documentaries or others that graced screens for twenty years and are still shown today from time to time, or, more recently, Soviet films, such as *Reanimation of the Organism, Sands of Death*, etc., which since 1945 have been well-received by all sorts of audiences. And when a critic praises Fred Astaire, is it for the charming *Gay Divorcée*? No, it is for the subpar *Top Hat*. And if another wants to recommend a tawdry musical—Oh great Armontel, what were you doing in one of these concoctions?—he can not use the excuse that *Tourbillon de Paris* is too old. Original and still fresh, it continues to be shown periodically, despite being fifteen years old. And when speaking of *The Spy*, no critic mentions the much superior *Lights*.

Ever since Luciano Emmer and Enrico Gras created in 1941 the masterpiece *Earthly Paradise* based on a Bosch painting, others have tried to do the same. But for the most part, this practice is a form of misrepresentation, justifiable only in cases where the frozen action of a work—a painting, for example—is used to inspire a screenplay, as was the case when Alain Resnais, with much skill, used Picasso's *Guernica*. Otherwise, simply representing an artist's work is not a legitimate way to bring a painter back to life. What is unique to Van Gogh? That upon leaving a brothel, he cut off his ear? That his brother Theo may have been an awful man? I do not know, I have not ironed out my question, and I certainly do not want to make family dramas, I am simply trying to point out that even the most skillful montage of Van Gogh's paintings will not make the man come alive. Indeed, except for Resnais's excellent production, there have only been failures, useless and base efforts, films of disjointed cuts where among other things we see a raging sea, a ship, someone aboard singing the nursery rhyme "There was a small boat . . . ," then a palm tree (Martinique!), then someone singing "My sweetheart has left . . ." Lack of money cannot excuse this lack of imagination. And it is bad enough when paintings are filmed in black and white (The excuses? Cost, technical difficulties, incorrect rendering. Even so . . .), but it is made worse by a passionless narrator, some poor hack who has not studied, understood, or felt what he purports to be showing! We too often forget that while any subject can be filmed, few are truly cinematic. You can tie your brain into a Louis XV knot trying, but you will still end up with a forgery.

Works such as Charles Dekeukeleire and Henri Storck's *Ancient Faces, Modern Faces* or Paul Haesaerts's *From Renoir to Picasso* proved that cinema could be used to present a thesis, though a viewer might not always agree with it. But this new use was quickly ambushed by the simplistic and pointless works that followed. And then there are those who have sought refuge in the once-marvelous genre of educational films, or those who have flocked to the medico-surgical field only to systematically bleed it dry. And do not think that a subject matter's technical nature precludes lyricism: see the impeccable *Circular Loom* or the remarkable *The Jetty of Zonguldac* for just two examples of superior technical films. But like the shoddy documentaries made for mass audiences, most so-called specialized films also lack cinematic taste and the basic understanding of how to explain something to a general audience (whenever a documentary is made, one must determine for whom and why) and are devoid of any connection between filmmaker and subject.

Though expositional films can often fail, there is a subset that can succeed: those that are made for a cozy group of insiders, a coterie of initiates. These films, of course, require that viewers know all of an author's work (if the film is about a writer), the intimate details of his love life, and the underside of Parisian life in a bygone era. The uninitiated catch only fleeting flashes, illuminating . . . nothing! Sure, the film might touch a few hundred people living in the same mental landscape and displace a few thousand snobs, but what about the rest of the public? (This reminds me of traveling salesmen who trot out the same stories year after year, bursting into fits of laughter at the mention of a single word.)

Sure, it is easy to blame the producers, distributors, exploitative theater owners, the audience, etc., for all the evils, but ultimately it is the filmmaker who must take responsibility. Some plead the "I'm just trying to put food on the table" argument. Well, that argument has run its course: it is a cynical rationalization, at least for those who only pretend to try to overcome difficult conditions in order to create influential work. There are those throughout our profession who make a living by this rationalization, even scorning it if necessary, as is the case with important playwrights and theater actors when they work in cinema. But there are others, those who press on despite the obstacles. I am addressing this minority in particular. You who do not practice the defeatist motto: "It's better than nothing"; you who have a strong enough cinematic eye to impose it on subjects you feel something for; you who will not agree to make a film about sugar production for the simple reason your grandfather was diabetic; you who scorn saccharine sentimentality and refuse to disfigure a work with it. It is you who hold the fate of the documentary—battered and bruised by a thousand blows from all sides—in your hands. But do not forget that a good theme is not enough to ensure a good film: the worst clichés will still kill it. Granted, except for a few rare and modest opportunities for technical or aesthetic research, the economic realities that currently affect French cinema will make it difficult for you to express yourself fully. But if, in the hope of finding provocative debate, you have read this far, all the way to the end of these intentionally polemic lines, then reread the definition at the beginning. You will find in it a solid framework for your film projects, one that will allow you to bring forth, with a clear mind, your ideas and desires.

56

JEAN COCTEAU

ON *BLOOD OF THE BEASTS* (1963)

[Translator's note: Jean Cocteau's writing is polysemic, musical and imposing. It moves and pulsates, much like the work of Zola and Franju to which it refers. As his contemporary Walter Benjamin asserts, the "task of the translator" is to preserve ambiguity when several interpretations are possible. In this regard, I have tried to respect multiple meanings in the text, and to preserve the elements of Cocteau's rhythmic style in the original French, including redundancies and fragments, except where they impede comprehension.]

Zola is a great poet and a great filmmaker. Few people realize this. Illustrious, he is damned in his chosen medium: the locomotive that dies in the snow, the white horses of the mine, the girl emptying her pockets in the tunnel, the little boy bleeding beneath the Épinal images,[1] the drunkard in flames, so many strange gags, whose misunderstood intensity can be captured by the cinema alone.

I was thinking about this while watching George Franju's admirable documentary on slaughterhouses. There is not one shot that does not move us, almost without reason [*sans motif*],[2] solely through its stylistic beauty and great visual writing. Of course, the film is hard to bear. He will undoubtedly be accused of sadism because of the way he grabs hold of the drama with both hands without ever avoiding it. He shows us the killers without hate of which Baudelaire spoke.[3] He shows us the sacrifice of innocent beasts. Sometimes he manages to generate tragedy with the terrible surprise of unknown gestures and attitudes that he brutally pushes us to face. The horse struck right on the head [*de front*][4] that falls onto its knees, already dead. The reflexes of decapitated calves that convulse and seem to struggle. In short, a noble and ignoble world that spills its last wave of blood onto a white tablecloth where the epicure is to think no longer of the suffering of the victims in whose flesh he plants his fork.

Around the sacrificial table lies the city made up of several cities and villages, the city we think we know, and yet don't know, its maritime and lugubrious sky over the disquieting setting of the Ourcq Canal.[5]

Never will you forget the interminable barge bedecked with linens nor the shrouds from the animals' morgue, shrouds made of their own hide.

Once again, courageous filmmakers not driven by success prove to us that the cinematograph is the tool of realism and lyricism and that everything depends on the angle from which life's spectacles are observed. Through this angle they require us to share a particular vision of things while underscoring for us the everyday miracle.

NOTES

1. Épinal images [*les images d'Épinal*] refers to the clichéd and emphatically naïve depiction of popular subjects (historical, religious, and literary) that characterized the brightly colored prints of the Épinal region made famous by illustrator and printer Jean-Charles Pellerin at the end of the 18th century.—Trans.
2. "Without reason" [*sans motif*] could be interpreted simply as "without cause." However, it also seems to imply that each shot affects us almost "inexplicably," "illogically" or even "untendentiously."—Trans., with thanks to Dana Polan.
3. A reference to Charles Baudelaire's poem "*L'Héautontimorouménos*" [The Self-Tormenter] from *Les Fleurs du mal* (1857).—Trans.
4. "*De front*" has a double meaning here, both literal and figurative. As we see in the film, Cocteau is referring to where the horse is struck: on the head. But *de front* could be translated as "head on," in the sense of directly, or unceremoniously. However, the English phrase "head on" also suggests the collision of two equal bodies, and Cocteau is clearly aware of Franju's sensitivity to the inequalities inherent in the situation. My compromise loses some of Cocteau's poetry, but incorporates both meanings.— Trans.
5. This 110 km historically industrial waterway that begins in northeastern Paris was constructed in the early 19th century under Napoleon's reign. Until 1962, when the last freight boats ceased operation, it functioned primarily to supply Paris with water, and to transport cargo to local industries. In recent decades, its industrial character has gradually begun to subside, as shops, leisure parks, and pleasure crafts have become increasingly more common on and around the Canal.—Trans.

57

LINDSAY ANDERSON

FREE CINEMA (1957)

When people ask you what you do, and you tell them you work in films, their reaction is predictible. "Oh! That must be very interesting . . ." They mean it, too. But then go on, and tell them you make documentaries, and you get a different response. The light of interest fades from their eyes and conversation flags. Sometimes they say: "Wouldn't you like to make real films?"

This sort of standard response is the measure of the failure of British Documentary—a failure for which the responsibility must be shared by many of us. Not by the film makers alone, but by distributors and exhibitors too. By the politicians who connived at the destruction of the Crown Film Unit; and by the public and the critics who continue to accept a situation in which the production of quality documentaries about Britain is a financial impossibility—and remain content to sit through appalling travelogues and third-rate imported shorts without raising a murmur.

Documentary should not be—it certainly need not be—synonymous with dulness. It should be one of the most exciting and stimulating of contemporary forms. After all, the cinema started with it. Lumière's first films are all admirable documentaries: trains pulling up at stations, workers leaving their factories: still interesting to look at today. But the cinema was soon captured by drama, and with relatively few notable exceptions artists have preferred fiction to the exploration and interpretation of the "actual", living material. Yet think how rich, fantastic, unexpected and significant "actual" life can be. Our own documentary movement began to say something in the thirties: and films like *Song of Ceylon, Housing Problems, Night Mail* still carry their message today. During the war Humphrey Jennings emerged as the British cinema's most eloquent and individual poet: *Listen to Britain, Diary For Timothy* and *Fires Were Started* should be compulsory viewing for every British schoolchild. (How many readers of this review have seen them, I wonder?) But in recent years—conformism, publicity more-or-less disguised, the deadness and the dishonesty of the "official" vision.

The problem is twofold: creative and economic. British film makers are not blameless. Energetic and radical in their youth, the surviving members of Grierson's band of pioneers (many of them now established in positions of influence) have abandoned the treatment of contemporary life in their films. This retreat they are apt to rationalize: there are no problems today—or the problems are different—things are more complex—we must think dialectically, internationally, intellectually.... Yet people still exist, and housing problems, and night mails—as well as Teddy Boys, new schools, automation, strikes and sex crimes. All these are subjects for documentary, and of the right kind: the human kind.

Admittedly the economic problems are formidable. The Conservative Government dissolved the Crown Film Unit in 1952, and since then the official policy is that the country does not sponsor documentaries for home consumption, except in special cases, for specific propagandist or informational purposes. But the present system of distribution and exhibition in the commercial cinemas makes the speculative production of documentaries quite impossible: either they are not booked at all, or you get twopence for them. Some kind of sponsorship *has* to be found.

It is in this connexion that the movement which we have called *Free Cinema* is significant. Three programmes of these films have so far been shown, all at the National Film Theatre: two of them have been made up of films made in and about Britain, one of films from abroad. They are all relatively modest pictures, in means if not in ambition: most of them have been shot on 16 millimetre. (This is the "substandard" gauge of film, as used on portable projectors as opposed to the standard 35mm film used in normal commercial production.) They have not been made according to any plan or programme: instinct came first, and we discovered our common sympathies after. But all of us want to make films of today, whether the method be realist or poetic, narrative or montage. And we all believe that "objectivity" is no part of the documentary method, that on the contrary the documentarist must formulate his attitude, express his values as firmly and forcefully as any artist. The result has been a group of films on diverse themes: a poetic fable about two deaf mutes in the East End of London: studies of Amusement Park and Jazz Club: Piccadilly on a Saturday Night and Covent Garden all round the clock. These are not intended as picturesque films (although of course they are written about as though they are, very often); nor as simple slices of life. Slices, if you like, but cut with a bias. All of them say something about our society, today.

This programme is presented not as an achievement, but as an aim. We ask you to view it not as critics, nor as a diversion, but in direct relation to a British cinema still obstinately class-bound; still rejecting the stimulus of contemporary life, as well as the responsibility to criticise; still reflecting a metropolitan, Southern English culture which excludes the rich diversity of tradition and personality which is the whole of Britain.

With a 16 millimetre camera, and minimal resources, and no payment for your technicians, you cannot achieve very much—in commercial terms. You cannot make a feature film, and your possibilities of experiment are severely restricted. But you can use your eyes and ears. You can give indications. You can make poetry.

The poetry of this programme is made out of our feelings about Britain, the nation of which we are all a part. Of course these feelings are mixed. There are things to make us sad, and angry; things we must change. But feelings of pride and love are fundamental, and only change inspired by such feelings will be effective.

"We have the Welfare State and the domestic upheavals of the Huggetts . . . Bleak, isn't it? . . ." So someone wrote in a letter to the *Observer*, "explaining" why vital art is no longer possible in this country. This kind of snobbish, self-derisive, pseudo-liberalism is the most pernicious and sapping enemy of faith. We stand against it.

Our aim is first to look at Britain, with honesty and with affection. To relish its eccentricities; attack its abuses; love its people. To use the cinema to express our allegiances, our rejections and our aspirations. This is our commitment.

When you are making a film like *Every Day Except Christmas*—or rather while you are editing it, waiting for a reel to be joined, or reprints to come in from the lab—it is easy to talk about what you are trying to do. But when you have finished, it is difficult. The film speaks for itself, you feel; and if it does not, you have failed, and statements of intention are merely pretentious.

But perhaps I should say what I was *not* trying to do. I was not trying to make an information film, or an instructional film. And I was *not* trying to make a picturesque film. When John Grierson first defined the word "documentary," he called it "the creative interpretation of actuality." In other words the only vital difference between making a documentary and making a fiction film is that in documentary you are using "actual" material, not invented situations and actors playing parts. But this actual material still has to be interpreted, worked on creatively, or we are left with nothing but publicity. And if we are to interpret, we must have an attitude, we must have beliefs and values. It is in the light of my belief in human values that I have endeavoured to make this film about Covent Garden market. I hope it makes my commitment plain.

I have been reproached on the one hand for not giving more "information" about the people in the film; and on the other for not making a more explicit social comment. I have nothing against information films, and no doubt there are some very interesting ones to be made about Covent Garden (statistics, dates, weights, wages, etc.). But this is not the kind of information I wanted to give about these people—and about people in general.

Similarly with social comment. I feel that at the moment in this country it is more important for a progressive artist to make a positive affirmation than an aggressive criticism. (The criticism will be implicit in the affirmation anyway, if it is a genuine one.) In aggressive criticism there is too often a sense of inferiority. The Left in Britain suffers too much from such complexes of opposition. I want to make people—ordinary people, not just Top People—feel their dignity and their importance, so that they can act from these principles. Only on such principles can confident and healthy action be based.

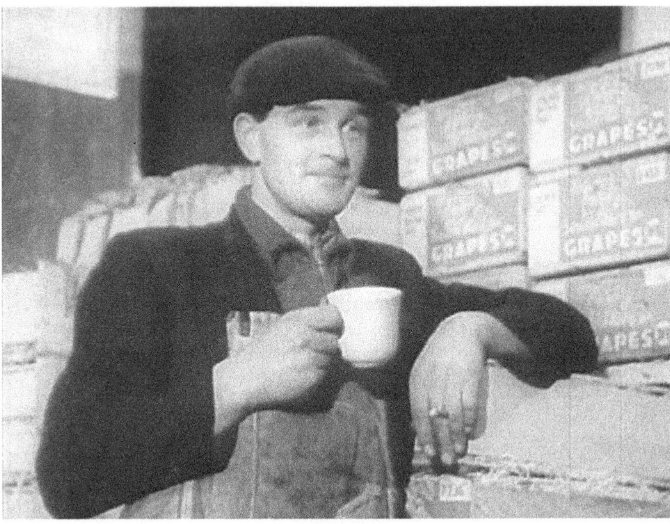

FIGURE 57.1 *Every Day Except Christmas* (Lindsay Anderson, 1957). Screen capture from DVD.

Luck and Sponsorship

Who pays for these films? One of them was privately financed (*O Dreamland*); *Together, Momma Don't Allow* and *Nice Time* were paid for by the British Film Institute's Experimental Fund; and *Every Day Except Christmas* was commissioned by the Ford Motor Company. There is food for thought here. The Institute's Fund is a remarkable thing, but of course its scope is limited. None of the film makers who avail themselves of it can be paid anything for his work, and budgets are only adequate for relatively modest productions, generally on 16mm. This is why Ford's sponsorship of *Every Day Except Christmas* is so important. Directors have grown accustomed to think of their sponsors as automatically unreasonable, narrowly utilitarian, and essentially unimaginative: undertaking a subject commissioned by an industrial concern, they are defeated before they start. Yet here is a film made for an industrial sponsor which—whatever its artistic value—has been made completely without interference or pressure, with its director allowed, even encouraged, to express himself as he feels. (It is unthinkable that a film should today be made for a Government department, or for the Central Office of Information, under conditions so liberal and so enlightened.) I am quite conscious of my extraordinary luck in having been able to work like this, and of my debt to Leon Clore of Graphic Films, who undertook the further responsibility of extending the picture from its original twenty-minute conception to its final forty-minute length. But—I cannot help wondering—should the existence of films of this kind in Britain have to depend on luck, or on the courage, principle and imagination of an individual producer or industrial sponsor? If so, there will not be many of them.

A number of questions, in fact, present themselves, not merely to film makers and enthusiasts, but to anyone seriously concerned with present-day realities in our country. And I presume this means all readers of the *Universities and Left Review*. For instance: Why do we not use the cinema; and what are the implications of this neglect? Is it not strange that at a time when so much emphasis is being put on ideals of community, this medium (above all potent in the service of such ideals) should be abandoned to irresponsible commerce? Why does the Left not take a more active and creative interest in an art so popular? And is it not time that artists whose convictions are progressively started to consider a little more seriously their relationship with their audience, the kind of use that can best be made of these mass-media, so that their art be neither exclusive and snobbish, nor stereotyped and propagandist—but vital, illuminating, personal and refreshing?

58

TOM WHITESIDE

THE ONE-TON PENCIL (1962)

Notwithstanding the many false faces of life that television casts upon the home screen, it is a medium that has a peculiar capacity for conveying glimpses of the real world, and sometimes, when its cameras and microphones are used for the purpose of dealing with actualities rather than of passing along the canned daydreams that make up most programs, the results can prove absorbing even to people who normally don't bother with the medium. The bulk of the networks' journalistic activities consists in covering the day-to-day news and such big special events as the political conventions and the national elections. Beyond this area, however, the broadcasters have lately been increasingly active in the production of live or filmed documentary programs that survey aspects of contemporary affairs not necessarily in the immediate news. Ordinarily, a documentary is presented not as an isolated production but as a part of a series of factual programs bearing some proprietary title—for example, "N.B.C. White Paper," *C.B.S. Reports*, or the American Broadcasting Company's *Close-Up!* The contents of documentary programs are extremely diverse. Within the past year or so, a viewer could have encountered on the network of the National Broadcasting Company a program on the problems of the declining American railroad industry, or one on the Peace Corps. If he had chanced to turn to the Columbia Broadcasting System, he could have spent an hour learning about the imminent world water shortage, or about the state of our civil defense. And on A.B.C. he could have come across an exposition of the intricacies of automation, or of the problem of student dropout in the public schools. Documentaries are nothing new to network television, but the current profusion of them is. Three years ago, the documentaries on the air were so few as to be hardly noticeable, but since then—and since the quiz scandals that caused such a public outcry against the industry—the networks have been expanding their journalistic operations, and right now the production of television documentaries is flourishing as it has never flourished before. In fact, putting together such programs seems to have grown into a journalistic profession in itself—a clamorously active occupation, distinct from ordinary newscasting, from the show-business end of television, and from printed-word reporting—which has been developing its own forms of expression, its own stylistic techniques, and its own breed of journalist.

Of all the people who have been responsible over the past few years for developing the television documentary, none is more active, or better known in the industry, than Fred W. Friendly, of C.B.S. Friendly has been working with the television-documentary form for as long as the networks have been sending their programs across the continent. For seven years, beginning in 1951, he was co-producer, with Edward R. Murrow, of *See It Now*, a C.B.S. series that was probably most memorable for a study of Senator Joseph McCarthy (1954) and for an interview with Dr. J. Robert Oppenheimer (1955). Since 1959, Friendly has been the executive producer of *C.B.S. Reports*, a series of documentaries, most of them an hour long, presented, on a variable schedule, approximately three times a month, under titles that have included "The Population Explosion," "Biography of a Missile," "Biography of a Bookie Joint," "Censorship and the Movies," "Eisenhower on the Presidency," "Can We Disarm?," and "East Germany: The Land Beyond the Wall." As the man responsible for *C.B.S. Reports*, Friendly controls the biggest single documentary operation in television and he supervises the activities of ten subordinate producers and a score of assistants, who make up a semi-autonomous unit within the C.B.S. news department. During the present season, these production people will put together, under Friendly's direction, twenty hour-long and four half-hour-long programs—a formidable task in the face of difficulties that include months of filming on location for many of the documentaries, and extraordinary exertions to produce others under emergency-deadline conditions.

In the process of getting this task accomplished, Friendly, a big, loose-limbed man of forty-six, tackles his highly variegated duties with a hustling energy and enthusiasm unusual even in the television business. He has a sense of mission that he tends to apply full blast to any project that he undertakes, and since he is always involved in as many as a dozen widely scattered projects—recently these included keeping in touch with a crew he had dispatched to the Tigris and Euphrates to investigate the problem of water conservation ("The Water Famine"), with a crew he had sent to London to interview Angry Young Men ("Britain: Blood, Sweat, and Tears Plus Twenty"), and with a crew who had gone to the Amazon Basin to investigate the political, economic, and social situation in that region ("Brazil: The Rude Awakening")—he exists in a state of compound excitement that seems incapable of diminution. Michael Dann, the C.B.S. vice-president in charge of East Coast network programming, says of Friendly, "I never knew a man who could get so worked up about a subject. Gee, when he was working on Polaris ["The Year of the Polaris," a documentary about our submarine-launched missiles], he sounded as though he was going to get one for his back yard." Most of the time, Friendly's energies emanate either from his office, on the seventeenth floor of the C.B.S. building, on Madison Avenue, or from a C.B.S. screening room, on Ninth Avenue, where he views nearly all the film that his camera crews turn out; however, he also spends a considerable amount of time out of town, overseeing filming on location, and on these missions, too, his hustling qualities quickly make themselves apparent. "Fred Friendly always looks as though he had just got off a foam-flecked horse," Carl Sandburg once wrote in *Variety* after a few meetings with Friendly on location in North Carolina. Friendly's get-it-done quality was much in evidence when, last spring, he flew down to Huntsville, Alabama, in the process of making a *C.B.S. Reports* documentary entitled "Why Man in Space?" There, at the National Aeronautics and Space Administration's George C. Marshall Space Flight Center, he ordered his camera crew into a building where technicians were assembling a Saturn rocket booster. Inside, to the sound of riveting guns and so forth, the rocket people were swarming all over the recumbent rocket, the high priority rating of the project impelling them to maximum effort, but within a few minutes after Friendly got into action, striding here and there and ordering his cameramen about ("Get those engines! I want all eight of them in the shot! And I want a pan shot right along here. I want the works!"), the C.B.S. producer and his crew looked to be by far the busiest men in the place.

Friendly's talent for pouring out energy is an invaluable one in a profession where the problem of just getting from one place to another is so much more complicated than it is for people who work in printed journalism. As a rule, when a reporter for a newspaper or magazine goes out on the job, the basic tools he needs for describing what he sees and hears—assuming that he wants to make notes on the spot—can easily be carried in his pocket; if the assignment takes him to another city, he may take a portable typewriter along. But when a man who is making a television documentary goes out to record a scene or an interview, a typewriter, if he brings one at all, is the least of his burdens. His business requires him to be accompanied by a tremendous clutter of equipment—one or two thousand pounds of motion-picture cameras, extra lenses, big lights and reflectors, power converters, great coils of cable, bulky boxes of film, microphone hookups, and sound-recording equipment. And he must also be accompanied by the people who operate all these devices, at the very least a cameraman, an assistant cameraman, a sound man, and an electrician. Since the making of each documentary program involves the filming of dozens or scores of scenes, at spots that may be far apart—and are sometimes continents apart—the sheer logistic work necessary to keep half a dozen documentaries in active production at one time is something like the job of keeping a small but perpetual Berlin airlift going. Friendly regards such arduous exercises as a natural and unavoidable part of his everyday existence. "We work with a one-ton pencil," he says of his brand of journalism.

The amount and unwieldiness of the equipment that Friendly finds necessary in the production of documentaries inevitably affect their form and, to a certain extent, the programs' content. The television documentary, to begin with, is not a particularly flexible form of expression, since its scope tends to be limited by the very thing that gives television its unique power; namely, visual directness. Then, because of the nature of the medium, every word spoken on it ordinarily has to be accompanied by some sort of image, whether it is the image of the man who is doing the speaking or an image connected with what he is speaking about, and this situation makes for difficulties in the verbal presentation of ideas that can't readily be matched to pictures on the screen. It is difficult to attempt to make, and almost impossible to succeed in making, any detailed reconstruction of events that have not already been extensively recorded on film. The producers of documentaries like those in the C.B.S. historical series *The Twentieth Century* can make interesting use of old film clips from, say, the First World War, but the producer who is concerned with performing a contemporary journalistic function, as distinct from a historical one, cannot command anything like the flexibility of form that is possible with the printed word. He doesn't have the same liberty to fuse subjective observations and objectively described action. He doesn't have the same freedom to summarize what he sees, for he can't compress the film he shoots, as a writer can compress his observations; he can only slice the film up into smaller pieces and reconnect some of them, possibly using some narrative material as a kind of verbal cement. He has the means of quoting a subject with undeniable accuracy—all too undeniable, sometimes, for the tastes of some politicians—but he can't paraphrase what his subject is saying except through some such rather awkward device as background narration. And since for most practical purposes he can't readily move back and forth through time as an observer, the tense in which he expresses himself—if the television image can be said to have tenses—is pretty much limited to the present. Nor is this all, for while the maker of television documentaries has the means of recording with great precision what appears in front of his cameras, the very equipment that enables him to do this also encumbers him in his attempt to depict every situation truly. A conventional journalist can go into a room, get interviews with some of the people present, and then depart without having noticeably intruded upon the proceedings. The arrival of a network television camera crew, however, is an event in itself, and for many people in a room may overshadow in importance anything else that is taking place there. People stop what they're doing; they're going to be on TV. The place, packed with lights, cables, cameras, recording equipment, and camera crew, is transformed from a room into a motion-picture set, and into the middle of this set, when all is ready, the interviewees, one by one, are finally led, a lapel microphone hung around each man's neck like a noose, to be questioned under the stare of the lenses and hot lights.

Holding the mirror up to nature under such circumstances is not easy, and this is particularly so in Friendly's case, because most of his documentaries consist in large measure of interviews. Friendly is well aware of this inherent difficulty, and he uses a number of countermeasures for minimizing it—and, he believes, in many cases overcoming it. The principal countermeasure is his method of selecting people who are going to appear and talk on the screen. Because he realizes only too well that the paraphernalia of television film-making have an intimidating effect on many subjects—some people are simply floored by the experience of being faced by all the lights, the lenses, and the microphones—he does his best to choose people who feel so strongly about what they have to say that their sense of conviction will override their natural uneasiness in the face of the mass of equipment pointed at them. Friendly is assisted, of course, by the subject matter of his documentaries, which frequently involve issues that invite firm expressions of opinion. However, he must be constantly on the lookout for the sort of personal forcefulness that will not dissolve—or, better yet, is even capable of blooming—under lights that total three thousand watts, no matter what the subject matter may be. "We want to deal with people who are *involved*" is one of Friendly's several ways of describing the kind of person he tries to get on camera. Among his other ways of putting it are that the subject must be "able to communicate," or must "come through," or that he should be "a man with fire in his belly." Not everybody who is "involved" necessarily has the ability to "come through," however. The fire that is in a man's belly may not necessarily flare up on the screen. Some people who meet Friendly's specifications for strong involvement falter under the lights—one of them has described the business of being interviewed amid all the gear of a Friendly production as "a shattering experience"—and they fail to project themselves any farther than a scrapfilm bin in the cutting room. A series of such near-misses on the part of people interviewed for a particular program can cause Friendly to drop the project in question altogether. There is little room in his scheme of things for people who have a passive attitude toward the world—a category that today seems to be a fairly large one—or for people whom he regards as being stoically inclined. For years, Friendly has been thinking of doing a *C.B.S. Reports* documentary on the Navajo Indians, in Arizona, but so far he hasn't been able to find any Navajos who seem talkative enough for his purposes. For this reason, among others, the Navajo project has yet to be carried out. "I wish we could get hold of more Indians with fire in their bellies," Friendly said thoughtfully a while ago to one of his producers.

The presence of inner fire and the faculty for communicating or coming through are among the first things Friendly inquires about when he is thinking of asking someone to appear on *C.B.S. Reports*. Early last summer, for example, he got the idea of making a documentary on ancient Greece in which viewers would have as their guide and commentator an authority on that civilization. He thought of asking Robert Graves to serve as the commentator, and since Graves happened to be in New York, where he was to give a lecture at Columbia in a day or so, Friendly had a talk with him and then dispatched his right-hand man, Palmer Williams, director of operations for *C.B.S. Reports*, to hear the lecture. "Palmer, does he *communicate*?" Friendly asked when Williams returned from the lecture. Williams indicated that he wasn't altogether sure. That seemed to settle the poet. A few days later, Friendly spent an evening with Edith Hamilton, and was highly enthusiastic. "She's *got* it!" he said. "To hear her recite a few words of Aeschylus! And just the thought of transporting this frail ninety-four-year-old woman by jet to Athens! Just think of it!" Friendly is still just thinking of it.

When Friendly believes he has found a person in whom the qualities of involvement and communicativeness are present to a sufficient degree, he demonstrates a remarkable ability to get that person stirred up about television. Friendly moves in with such energy and enthusiasm that resisting his overtures can become a very difficult matter. Among those who have initially held out against Friendly's suggestions that they appear on his programs and have later surrendered are such diverse personalities as General Dwight D. Eisenhower, Walter Lippmann, and Admiral Hyman Rickover. General Eisenhower, a rather diffident and frequently stumbling speaker on television when he was President, was at first very dubious when Friendly, with the backing of William S. Paley, chairman of the board of C.B.S., suggested that he allow himself to be the subject of a series of interviews on *C.B.S. Reports*, but when Friendly had completed the project, after a total of some ten days of filming in Gettysburg, Eisenhower conveyed on the screen a personal warmth such as was perhaps unmatched in any of his television appearances during his Presidency.

Admiral Rickover, who does not have the reputation of being an easy man to handle, had his first encounter with Friendly in 1956, when Friendly called on him to ask his cooperation in the production of a program, for the C.B.S. series *See It Now*, dealing with the Navy's atomic-submarine building program. The Admiral greeted Friendly by looking the producer hard in the eye and saying, "Friendly, I don't need you," but within a few weeks he was so deeply involved in the project that he was telephoning Friendly at all hours. ("Fred? Got a pencil? Take this down!") Four years later, Rickover was similarly cooperative when *C.B.S. Reports* made "The Year of the Polaris."

Walter Lippmann, who through most of his career made a point of avoiding personal public appearances, for years spurned all sorts of attempts by television networks to get him to make an appearance on the screen. In the fall of 1960, Friendly went after him, and after a struggle Lippmann, as Friendly puts it, "was dragged in kicking and screaming" to be interviewed for an hour-long program. Lippmann himself puts it this way: "Friendly came to lunch with me in Washington and began to draw me out about appearing on a filmed program. He pushed—he's a tremendous salesman, this fellow. Finally I said, 'I'll think about it, but if I do it I want to have control over what comes out.' He said, 'I'll give you an agreement and if you don't like the result we'll burn the film.' That was a challenge." The result was a program entitled "Walter Lippmann on Leadership," in which Lippmann, interviewed by Howard K. Smith, talked for an hour on the eight years of the Eisenhower administration and on other matters. The program was so successful that Lippmann made another hour-long appearance on *C.B.S. Reports* last summer, and a half-hour appearance in December, and there is a good chance that such talks will become an institution.

Such successes on Friendly's part are due not only to his energy and persuasiveness but also to his production techniques. What Friendly sets out to do with people who become subjects of his documentaries—whether, like Eisenhower, Lippmann, or Carl Sandburg, they are on the screen for a whole hour at a time, or whether, like a number of Negro and white Southerners on a program called "Who Speaks for the South?," they appear only briefly—is to make the best use of television's unusual ability to emphasize essential personal qualities. Anybody who has watched a man being interviewed for a Friendly production and has then seen the same interview on television cannot help being struck by the contrast between the relatively ordinary, everyday quality of the man's voice and demeanor when he is observed from just behind the semicircle of paraphernalia during the interview and the active, engaged, responsive air the same subject seems to acquire when he is seen in a closeup on the television screen. In the flesh, a man's face is, after all, only part of him, but in a closeup it becomes, suddenly, all of him. Every facial movement or gesture is heightened in effect, and every accompanying vocal inflection is correspondingly stressed, with the result that the whole personality of the man is peculiarly concentrated and revealed. This ability of television to accentuate character gives Friendly an opportunity to make his subjects, as he puts it, "larger than life," and it is into the job of encouraging this mysterious magnifying process that Friendly flings the full force of his professional energy.

Essentially, Friendly's art consists in selecting and juxtaposing various filmed sequences taken from the enormous mass of such material that is gathered on whatever subject he tackles. His method is such that he does not attempt to put words in the mouth of anyone who is interviewed, nor does he really attempt to control a man's demeanor before the camera. But before a single shot is made he does devote a great deal of care to the manner in which the subject of an interview will be questioned by the interviewer, to the manner in which the subject will be photographed while he talks, and to the physical arrangement of the apparatus. As things are arranged in a Friendly production, the equipment can be operated with so little waste motion that its obtrusiveness is reduced to a minimum; on the other hand, its presence can, if necessary, be used as a psychological means of prodding the man being interviewed into greater communicativeness. Last spring, when Friendly and a production crew went down to the Eisenhower estate at Gettysburg, Friendly knew in advance, thanks to his production men's efforts, just how the interviews were to be conducted, and where. The room in which most of the shooting was to take place—Eisenhower's office—had already been chosen, and the entire layout of cameras, lights, recording equipment, and so on, had been blocked out on an architect's plan of the house. And thanks to work done with Walter Cronkite, who was to conduct the interviews, and with Ed Jones, the producer assigned to the project, he also knew substantially what questions were to be put to Eisenhower. Every man in the production crew knew not only just what to do but how to do it with a minimum of physical movement, and how to keep the mechanical distractions of the filming process at the lowest possible level. Friendly even instructed his men to dispense with the noise of the clapstick—the diagonally striped wooden bar, hinged to the top of a slate, that a camera assistant ordinarily claps down smartly at the beginning of each scene—an unusual concession, since the clapstick is considered necessary to enable people in the cutting room to synchronize the film image with the accompanying sound track, each of these customarily being recorded on separate reels of film. Friendly used two thirty-five-millimetre cameras for the interviews, and he was able to avoid the normal interruptions required for changing film (a thousand-foot reel of thirty-five-millimetre film lasts for eleven minutes of continuous shooting) by operating the two cameras so that one was always going while the film in the other was being replaced. The first day, Friendly kept the cameras running for a total of four hours, with only one five-minute break at the end of two hours. By the time that break came, the camera motors were so hot from continuous use that they had to be changed. As for Eisenhower, he seemed very much at ease during the entire four hours. He was amazed that a television appearance could go so smoothly and with so little fuss, he told Friendly later.

The lengths to which Friendly was prepared to go for the purpose of getting the most out of the Eisenhower interviews were admittedly unusual by his own standards, yet they did not result in arrangements very different from the ones he normally makes in filming a long interview with somebody like Lippmann or Sandburg—and for that matter, even during relatively minor interviews his production men are careful to make the subjects feel at home. While Friendly has no control over what a subject may say on camera, he does have complete control over the selection of the interviewer, and interviewers who know his working methods—the most skillful of these, outside of Edward R. Murrow, has probably been Howard K. Smith, who recently resigned from C.B.S. as the network's chief Washington correspondent—are able to give him a great deal of help in getting his subject to talk freely. Such an interviewer knows, for example, that he must avoid anything like a rehearsal with the subject, because an interviewee will never answer a question the second time with the conviction he displays in answering it the first time. The interviewer also understands why Friendly, for all his attempts to make his subjects feel at home under the lights, believes there are occasions when the very presence of all the apparatus is useful in making a subject more vocal. This principle is demonstrated when a subject, in replying to a question, says something that the interviewer suspects can be said more succinctly or interestingly; in this case, the interviewer, instead of going on to the next question, pauses, deliberately saying nothing, and sits and waits long enough for the subject to become aware of the television equipment around him and of his own silence. As likely as not, the interviewee will be sufficiently goaded by his own momentary self-consciousness and by the whirring of the cameras to come out with something like "What I mean is—" and then go on to make his point more cogently. Friendly says, "You wait three seconds and then the pure gold starts to come."

The people Friendly uses as interviewers on *C.B.S. Reports* may be chosen from among the regular members of the C.B.S. news department, or from among the producers who assist him on specific projects, but whoever they are, their roles on the screen during the interviewing process are always carefully subordinated to those of the people being interviewed. This concept of the interviewer's job differs from that in evidence on some other documentary series, where the interviewer is often shown standing side by side with his subject, carrying on a conversation in a domineering manner. In Friendly's programs, the interviewer is ordinarily a relatively shadowy figure; his back is partly turned to the camera, and he is well to one side of the person he is interviewing. (At other times, he may be shown from the front, alone, in the act of asking questions, but since under most shooting conditions there is no way of obtaining such full-face shots without stationing an extra camera somewhere behind the subject, these frontal shots are almost always made after the actual interview.) However shadowy the interviewer may seem, his presence is nevertheless a vital factor when someone is talking before the *C.B.S. Reports* cameras, because Friendly believes the subject should be shown responding to a particular human being rather than to a load of equipment. "We are not in the watch-the-birdie business," he says. "We don't want to have people making speeches to the camera. You can't turn them into actors. Anyway, making a speech is never a natural thing to do. It was designed as a way of reaching several hundred or several thousand people at a time. Nowadays, with television, what a man says can reach four or fourteen or forty million people at a time, and the way he can do that best is not by making a speech to everybody but by talking to one man."

When someone is in the process of talking to one of Friendly's interviewers, surrounded by the full complement of two cameras and the customary lights and recording equipment, part of the technique that Friendly uses to bring the subject's essential qualities to the screen is evident from the movement of the cameramen. As the subject talks, these men silently go about their business; while one camera focusses on the subject's face and shoulders, the other, taking what Friendly's people call "grab shots," from time to time goes after supporting detail—a closeup of a gesture of the subject's hand, for example, or even of his shoes, if there is something interesting about them. The grab camera will also pick up, with one or another of the several lenses mounted on its lens turret, a series of extreme closeup shots or a series of medium shots of the subject, of the subject and the interviewer together, and, occasionally, of the interviewer alone. The cameramen thus provide Friendly with the material he needs not only for compiling the basic record of the interview but for imparting visual emphasis to things that strike him as significant and for making a transition from one section of the interview to another.

Perhaps eight or ten times as much film may be shot in the course of an interview as Friendly can conceivably use in the finished program, but his policy is to shoot, shoot, and continue shooting until he feels that his subjects have expressed themselves to his satisfaction, at which point he is ready to begin editing his material into its much shorter, finished form—a process that involves long and tedious sessions in the cutting room. Here his job is, in essence, to telescope a long talk by selecting a series of verbatim passages and joining them together. But joining together a series of shots from an interview is a considerable technical problem, because when a man is talking his head doesn't stay still, and when a television producer wants to eliminate a stretch of extraneous matter, he will find that the cutting and splicing causes the subject's face to make sudden, disconcerting jumps from one position to another. What the producer has to do to get rid of this effect is to insert some brief transitional shot, and this is a technique that Friendly often uses in a manner sufficiently forceful to turn a technical handicap into a professional virtue. By Friendly's process of editing, a comparatively static scene of a man talking at length to an interviewer will become a series of vignettes in which the audience sees the subject from a variety of aspects. At one moment he will be seen from a few yards away, and at another in closeup, first from the right and then from the left; at other moments, the subject's voice will be carried in simultaneous juxtaposition with shots of his hands gesticulating or of the interviewer listening. Moreover, the whole succession of shots is manipulated so as to give emphasis to particularly meaningful words and gestures, and at the same time a certain rhythmic pattern is created by a system of visual and aural punctuation, in which a smile, a frown, a gesture of the hand, or an ironic laugh may be used in the manner of a comma, a semicolon, or a period, a marker at which a shot can be ended and set off from the one that follows.

Friendly relies on the technique of juxtaposition not only in depicting the subjects of interviews but also in relating what they say or do to the action shots with which, on most of his programs, the interviews are interspersed. His use of this technique is seen at its most effective when he is dealing with a dramatic subject, like the countdown at the launching of a rocket. In "Biography of a Missile," for example, a 1959 program in which Friendly and Murrow followed step by step the making and launching of a Juno II, an exciting sequence juxtaposed shots of the tense faces of the engineers in the firing blockhouse with shots of the actual launching. Similarly, in "The Year of the Polaris," the audience was able to see not only the first launching of a Polaris missile from an atomic-powered submarine as it appeared from the surface of the ocean but also, intermittently, the scene in the launch-control area within the submarine—a scene memorable for a splendidly juxtaposed closeup shot of Admiral W. F. Raborn, the man in charge of the launching, carefully crossing two fingers of his right hand as the countdown approached zero.

Still another way in which Friendly makes strong use of juxtaposition is in his treatment of controversial topics. Out of a series of interviews in which various people express differing views on a given issue, he may extract shots in which sharply conflicting attitudes are expressed and present them one against the other, as a means of indicating the range of opinion on the issue involved—for example, in "Who Speaks for the South?," shots of Negroes and whites commenting on segregation in the public schools of Georgia; in "The Keeper of the Rules: Congressman Smith and the New Frontier," shots of Republican and Democratic congressmen delivering their conflicting opinions on the political tactics of Howard W. Smith, the chairman of the House Rules Committee; and in "The Population Explosion," a documentary filmed largely in India, shots of laymen, physicians, and Roman Catholic clergymen presenting their views on birth control.

With its ability to juxtapose individual shots in dramatic contrast, and also to convey the intensity of people's convictions, television is extraordinarily well suited to dealing with controversial matters, and Friendly has never hesitated to use the medium for this purpose. In addition to the documentaries just mentioned, some of the most notable fruits of this policy have been the Murrow-Friendly program of 1954 that tartly depicted the career of Senator Joseph McCarthy; "Harvest of Shame" (1960), which was produced by David Lowe, and which cast a harsh light on the lot of migratory workers in this country; "The Business of Health: Medicine, Money and Politics" (1961), which was produced by Stephen Fleischman, and which dealt with the high cost of medical care and the various means of coping with it, ranging from prepaid medical insurance to the Kennedy administration's plan for medical care for the aged through Social Security deductions; and "Who Speaks for Birmingham?" (1961), which was concerned with the process of racial desegregation in that city. Indeed, Friendly's fondness for using controversial subject matter in *C.B.S. Reports* has caused some of the programs themselves to become subjects of public controversy, bringing him and his producers under attack by various powerful interests. Thus, the American Farm Bureau Federation denounced "Harvest of Shame" as a "rigged documentary" and a "highly colored propaganda job" through which, the Federation claimed, "the public relations of farmers were irreparably damaged." "The Business of Health" prompted the Board of Trustees of the American Medical Association to issue a statement asserting that the program was filled with "misrepresentations, bias and distortions," constituting a "caricature of medicine and its aims." "Who Speaks for Birmingham?" so nettled several powerful white citizens of that city, including the chief of police, that they brought suit against C.B.S. for damages of $1,500,000, on the ground that the program had defamed them. (The case is still pending.) And "Biography of a Bookie Joint," which, by means of concealed cameras, showed such a truly astonishing number of customers (including men in police uniform) parading daily in and out of a Boston key-making store that the program identified as a front for bookmaking, that it caused no less a figure than Richard Cardinal Cushing to declare at a Boston police ball that "whoever was behind [the program] owes an apology to the City of Boston." His Eminence also complained, "We all have our failings and faults, but why hang them, as it were, like dirty linen on a clothesline from one end of the country to the other?"

Friendly regards such criticisms as an inevitable by-product of any television journalism that attempts to come to grips with current issues. If in *C.B.S. Reports* programs dealing with political matters the right wing doesn't usually show up too well, this is not, Friendly maintains, because of any built-in political bias on his part. "We have to be sixty-five per cent against both the Democrats and Republicans," he likes to say, and he is also fond of saying that while there has never been any intention on the part of his organization to injure anybody's reputation, some people have contrived to injure their own reputations by expressing their views on his programs. Friendly does admit, however, that some of his programs have what he calls "a point of view," and since his own social outlook is marked by a general attachment to the cause of the underdog and by strong feelings about poverty and oppression in the world, it is not surprising that a *C.B.S. Reports* program dealing with racial segregation should possess a sharpness that rattles some Southern whites, or that one on migratory labor should cause the farm lobby to react violently. But if Friendly's work reveals him to be something of a moralist, he seems to stop short of salvationism, and it appears to be a matter of professional pride with him that he feels he can resist, in the editing process, the temptation to emphasize on screen those portions of interviews that tend to harmonize with his own personal attitudes.

In making preparations for interviews and for *C.B.S. Reports* programs in general, Friendly does not draw up any detailed plan. There is no basic script to be followed but only a general idea of what the program is to be about; the actual course of its development is determined by the nature of whatever raw material Friendly's producers, interviewers, and cameramen turn up. The documentary that reaches the screen is primarily a product not of a scriptwriter but of a producer, who has compiled it by picking and choosing slices of film and piecing them together. In contrast to most other documentary series, in each program of which a writer is given credit on the screen for having prepared a script, *C.B.S. Reports* rarely has listed the name of a writer, because Friendly doesn't have any writers, as such, on his staff. What little writing is done for a typical Friendly production consists of expository passages composed by the news correspondent who will deliver them in introducing the interviews he conducts, and of passages that are usually banged out on a typewriter during the last stages of the editing process by Friendly or by the producer and staff of the program for use either as narrative bridges between one section of the documentary and another or in the "shirttail," as Friendly's people call the opening section, which is made up of brief excerpts from the material that is to follow.

In the opinion of quite a few of the documentary producers for other networks, who are used to working from comparatively tight outlines drawn up before they start filming their programs, Friendly's habit of shooting on and on at everything in sight until he gets what satisfies him is a grossly inefficient one, even if it does enable him sometimes to achieve striking results. They also consider him rather rigid in his methods, and particularly in his insistence on using heavy thirty-five-millimetre cameras, for while these obtain shots of high technical quality, they deprive him of the freedom of movement that light, highly portable sixteen-millimetre cameras afford their crews. With such equipment, these producers maintain, their men can obtain shots of reasonably high quality while dispensing on occasion with the elaborate lighting that must be used in thirty-five-millimetre filming. For example, the use of lightweight equipment enabled N.B.C. to send a couple of reporters on foot deep into the jungles of Angola, where during a march of some three hundred miles they shot a number of dramatic sequences for an "N.B.C. White Paper." Similar methods enabled A.B.C. to put a cameraman in the White House to make a continuous visual record of President Kennedy at work—sitting at his desk using the telephone, moving about his study, and even going from one room to another. One of Friendly's critics in the business has called his television "big-head TV"—a world bounded, in Friendly's endless closeups of people, by the chin and the eyebrow—a form of representation in which the camera is accepted as a great, clumsy machine, into whose glassy visual range the subject has to be taken, rather than being made a truly flexible and mobile instrument that can reach out to the subject and readily travel with him. They seem to feel that while Friendly may be a highly talented documentary producer, he is slightly old-fashioned.

For his part, Friendly firmly maintains that he is willing to sacrifice whatever extra mobility he might obtain by using sixteen-millimetre equipment for the sake of the high technical quality of the film he gets by working with thirty-five-millimetre cameras and what he considers proper lighting. Clear photography, clear sound, and effective lighting are universally conceded to be among the hallmarks of the Friendly documentary. Beyond these purely technical considerations, Friendly's work is also recognized as noteworthy for the quality of its reporting, for editing that gives it a characteristic crispness and pace, and for the authenticity of its content. Some network documentary producers are not above the use of occasional hanky-panky to achieve continuity or dramatic effect. Sometimes when the viewer thinks he is seeing a continuous sequence of real events, he may actually be seeing some genuine material onto which has been grafted a set of old stock shots lifted from some film library. Or the sound that the audience hears while viewing, say, the scene of a street riot may have nothing to do with that particular riot but may have been merely thrown in from a sound-effects library, the film itself having been shot without sound. Whatever the intent of the producer may be in such cases, the effect is to mislead the viewer.

Friendly does his best to avoid this sort of thing, and the one or two instances in which, over the years, he feels that he hasn't played altogether fair with the viewer in the matter of a stock shot have caused him to indulge in considerable self-reproach. Aside from such past exceptions, and from the practice—in itself perhaps harmless, though it is not difficult to see how it could become harmful—of presenting as part of a continuously filmed interview shots actually made after it of reporters repeating certain questions, Friendly insists quite strictly on authenticity. "If we show, as we did during the Korean War, a view of a hundred-and-five-millimetre howitzer in action, we make sure that the sound accompanying the shot is the sound of *that* howitzer," Friendly says. "You could do it the easy way, and shoot silent film and then get the sound made in a studio, but it wouldn't be right. When we do a space-research show and set out to get a shot of the test-firing of a balsa-wood ball that the scientists hope they can land on the moon at a hundred and fifty miles an hour, we make sure that we record the right sound at the right time, because there's only one kind of noise that a balsa-wood ball makes when it hits a target at a hundred and fifty miles an hour. We try to give the viewer grounds for telling himself as he sees the show, 'This is as it really happened.' If you don't work that way, you don't know where you will wind up." [. . .]

In conformity with his striving for authenticity, Friendly, unlike a number of his confreres, does not allow the use of background music as a means of heightening an effect on the screen; he considers such music a theatrical device that has no proper place in journalism, and except for a regular introductory musical theme—a few bars from Aaron Copland's "Appalachian Spring"—that accompanies the display of the *C.B.S. Reports* title, he permits music only when it happens to be part of the sound of whatever scene his people are shooting.

C.B.S. Reports is a more or less direct outgrowth of *See It Now*, which Friendly began producing jointly with Edward R. Murrow on a half-hour, once-a-week basis in 1951. *See It Now* began as a sort of weekly television news review. Although in the early days its production methods were crude by Friendly's present standards, it was the first television documentary series of any consequence that attempted to deal with current affairs. Previously, Friendly's experience with the airwaves had been confined mostly to radio, which, with the exception of four and a half years of wartime Army Service, he had been in since 1936. In prewar years he had been the producer of a series of dramatized biographical sketches for a program called "Footprints on the Sands of Time," which was broadcast over a station in Providence, Rhode Island, his home town, and later, after the war, he was the originator and producer of a weekly news-quiz program called *Who Said That?*, which ran on N.B.C. in 1948 and 1949. Friendly's association with Murrow began in 1948, when, after they had been brought together by an agent named J. G. Gude, they collaborated on the production of a record album, called *I Can Hear It Now*, which was a collection of excerpts from recordings of the voices of famous people, done in the general spirit of Frederick Lewis Allen's *Only Yesterday*. *I Can Hear It Now* quickly became a best-seller, and Friendly and Murrow followed it up with three more similar albums and then with a comparatively short-lived radio news program called "Hear It Now." With the rise of television, the idea of a weekly *See It Now* program developed naturally. *See It Now* went on the air on November 18, 1951, with Murrow as its narrator, and on that first program the producers, to celebrate the recent linking by microwave of the East and West Coasts, displayed simultaneously, by a split-screen technique, live shots of the Atlantic and Pacific Oceans. In the seven years of the program's existence, Friendly, who had already formed the habit of, as Murrow puts it, "taking off without warming his motors," charged all over the world with his one-ton pencil in pursuit of reality: to Ann Arbor, Michigan, on the day the discovery of polio vaccine was announced, for an interview with Dr. Jonas Salk; to the waters of Israel, where he ordered his men to light up the Sea of Galilee by night in order to photograph nocturnal fishermen at work; to Berlin; to Suez; to a meeting hall in Pine,

Colorado, where voters were assembled for a school-bond election; to Stagg Field, in Chicago, for a gathering of nuclear scientists; and to any other spot he could think of where some sort of social or technological upheaval was going on. His cameras took notes on interviews with all sorts of leading figures in the world: with Nehru, in New Delhi; with Nasser, in Cairo ("There's a good picture somewhere of me lecturing Nasser," Friendly says); with Ben-Gurion, in Israel; with Chou En-lai, in Rangoon; with Macmillan, in London; and with Truman, in Islamorada, Florida. His cameraman went up in an Air Force plane and flew into an atomic cloud over Yucca Flat, Nevada, to give viewers an idea of what radioactive fallout looked like from the inside. They went overseas on good-will tours that included a tour of India by Marian Anderson, a tour of North Africa, Turkey, and Israel by Danny Kaye, and a tour of West Africa by Louis Armstrong.

In domestic waters, Murrow and Friendly ("Murrow on the bridge; Friendly running the engine room—that's the working relationship they had," a C.B.S. man recalls) sailed into the area of political controversy—an area that television up to then had timorously avoided—by taking up matters having to do with civil liberties. In 1953, for example, they espoused the cause of Milo Radulovich, a U.S. Air Force Reserve lieutenant who, although nobody questioned his personal loyalty, had been officially designated as a security risk, suspended from the Air Force Reserve, and recommended for dismissal, because of political activities that his sister had engaged in and because his father had subscribed to a pro-Tito Serbian-language newspaper. In a half-hour program, Murrow, as narrator, presented the entire history of the affair and sketched the dilemma of a man faced with a particularly egregious charge of guilt by association. As a result of the program, which caused a considerable stir in the press, the Air Force reversed its findings on Lieutenant Radulovich a few weeks later, and restored him to active duty. In 1954, during the heyday of McCarthyism, Murrow and Friendly struck a further blow for civil liberties with their acidulous study of the methods used by McCarthy in his rise to power—a study highlighted by a shot of the Senator from Wisconsin making a 1952 campaign speech against Adlai Stevenson. "I perform this unpleasant task," the shot caught McCarthy saying, "because the American people are entitled to have the coldly documented history of this man who says he wants to be your president. But strangely, Alger—" Here the Senator paused, and the crowd roared. "I mean, Adlai—" The crowd laughed again, briefly; then, in the ensuing quiet, McCarthy became seized by wave after wave of hysterical giggles, which Murrow and Friendly coolly held on screen until the last, painful spasm died away. McCarthy struck back a couple of weeks later, in air time that the network made available to him, but there is little doubt that the first program rubbed some of the varnish from the shield of McCarthyism. Within a few days of the Murrow-Friendly broadcast, C.B.S. had received a hundred thousand responses, by wire, mail, and telephone, most of them favorable, although a few were highly abusive. As for the C.B.S. management's attitude toward the program, Friendly indicates that the brass looked the other way in embarrassment—in fact, it refused to place newspaper ads announcing the documentary, whereupon Murrow and Friendly, to insure that it would be widely viewed, prepared ads of their own and paid for them out of their own pockets. "The morning after the McCarthy show," Friendly says, "when the newspapers were running banner headlines about it and the C.B.S. switchboards and mail rooms were jammed with messages from the public about it, I rode up in the elevator with the man who was then in charge of C.B.S. Television. He didn't say a word to me on the subject—just asked me how I'd been. In fact, I suppose I could count on the fingers of one hand all the calls we had from upstairs during the seven years that *See It Now* was on the air."

From 1951 to 1955, *See It Now* was sponsored by the Aluminum Corporation of America, which Friendly has described as "a dream sponsor," meaning that it made no attempt to interfere with the editorial content of the program, however controversial it might be. But at the end of the 1954–55 season, Alcoa felt it necessary to seek a wider audience than it was reaching with the Murrow-Friendly show, and withdrew its sponsorship. *See It Now* never had another full-time sponsor. Scores of potential ones were approached, only to shy away at the thought of advertising on a program that not only had a relatively small network audience but regularly dealt with controversial subject matter, and particularly with such controversial subject matter as McCarthyism. The C.B.S. management, too, although it frequently trumpeted the virtues of *See It Now* in institutional advertising and in reports to Congress and the Federal Communications Commission on its record of public-service programming, apparently took a lukewarm attitude toward the program. "After a good show, we would sit and wait for a phone call from upstairs, and for years it never seemed to come," Friendly recalls. The end came in 1958, when the networks were making a killing in the audience-rating books with big-money quiz shows and with dramatic programs purveying sadism and violence as stock commodities. The last *See It Now* program to go on the air, in July, 1958, was called "Watch on the Ruhr;" it was a documentary on Germany's economic and political resurgence, and it included a memorable sequence of closeups of members of a German theatre audience watching the climactic scene in a performance of "The Diary of Anne Frank."

After the demise of *See It Now*, Murrow and Friendly attempted to take up some of the slack with "Small World," a program featuring a series of discussions, moderated by Murrow, between people in different parts of the world, who conversed by means of a radio or telephone hookup while cameras recorded each end of the conversation. It was a complicated idea for a program and a far cry from the documentaries that Murrow and Friendly had been doing; "Small World" ended, with hardly a murmur of protest from anybody, at the close of the 1959–60 season.

In the meantime, however, the big quiz shows, on which the networks had come to rely so heavily, were blowing up in their faces, and, in the accompanying atmosphere of shock, scandal, and investigation, the C.B.S. management again became aware of the virtues of the television documentary. In 1959, Frank Stanton, the president of C.B.S., revived *See It Now* under the name of *C.B.S. Reports*, and installed Friendly, who had managed to keep most of his old staff together, as executive producer of the series. (Murrow, who had been at odds with Stanton over various matters and who had already announced his plans to take a sabbatical leave for a year, was not appointed co-producer, although he later appeared as reporter-narrator on a number of *C.B.S. Reports* programs. Early last year he resigned from C.B.S. to become director of the United States Information Agency.)

C.B.S. Reports is a great show-piece for the C.B.S. management. Because the series has no regular sponsor, and attracts comparatively few sponsors for its individual programs in the course of a season, it brings in only about half a million advertising dollars, while its production costs come to about two million dollars, and it occupies air time worth about twice that sum. Such losses are not matters of excessive concern to the network, whose income from the presentation of such shows as "Gunsmoke," "Have Gun, Will Travel," "The Twilight Zone," "The Garry Moore

Show," "Perry Mason," "Rawhide," and "The Defenders" has helped to raise the net profits before taxes of C.B.S., Inc., from $9,555,000 in 1950 to $51,335,000 in 1960. Unlike *See It Now,* which for much of its existence was relegated to what was then the chronological Siberia of the airwaves, late Sunday afternoon or early Sunday evening, *C.B.S. Reports* is assigned to prime evening time—10 to 11 P.M. on Thursdays, when it is theoretically available to a very large audience. As it happens, though, the program coincides with N.B.C.'s "Sing Along with Mitch," which regularly attracts about twenty-five million viewers, and with A.B.C.'s "The Untouchables," a panorama of gangland slaughter that has a regular audience of about twenty million. According to the C.B.S. statistical people, *C.B.S. Reports* has an average audience of six million.

What with its audience rating, contemptible by the standards of the big commercial programs, and its habit of dealing with controversial subject matter—or, as Friendly has put it, of "saying upstream things"—*C.B.S. Reports* has had chronic sponsor trouble. Friendly doesn't quite understand the attitude of the big corporations toward sponsoring documentaries. "One of these advertisers will come in and say he can't sponsor a show that deals with the problems of segregation, or a show on the crisis in Algeria, or a show on radioactive fallout, because he can't risk having his corporate image hurt by controversial subject matter. Then he'll turn around and sponsor a dramatic series that has nothing but bloodletting and eye-gouging in it," he says with some puzzlement. Because of the paucity of sponsors, Friendly is under considerable pressure to make compromises in dealing with potential ones, the most frequent demand being that he agree to let them see programs before they go on the air. With other, and more marketable, kinds of program, this is, of course, not only a normal procedure but a mandatory one, yet it is one that Friendly stubbornly holds out against, on the ground that it might tempt advertisers to suggest editorial revisions as a condition of their sponsorship. "We've lost some pretty good sponsors because we wouldn't say we'd let them see shows ahead of time," he says. "A magazine editor would probably kick any advertiser right out of his office who wanted an advance look at the articles he was running before he decided to place an ad. The trouble with TV is that there's no tradition of independence. It isn't easy to say no and hear the guy from the sales department say, 'O.K., Fred, but your integrity is going to cost us two hundred thousand.' Just the same, I think we have to say no, until it gets to be a habit that everybody accepts." Such pressures for compromise do not all come from advertisers; they also come from within the network, which has its own commercial position to maintain, and its relations with its affiliated stations to think of, and which, finally, must meet the tricky F.C.C. requirements concerning the provision of equal time for presentation of opposing points of view on the airwaves. It was not a particularly new experience for Friendly when, last spring, before putting "Who Speaks for Birmingham?" on the air, he had to attend a series of angry meetings of network brass and defend the program against the charges of one vice-president that it presented the Birmingham Negroes in a better light than the whites and it might possibly mean the loss of some station affiliations in the Deep South. Friendly even had to defend Howard K. Smith's inclusion at the end of the program of a line from Edmund Burke that Smith had felt applied to the majority of whites in Birmingham: "The only thing necessary for the triumph of evil is for good men to do nothing." The C.B.S. brass felt that the line was prejudicial, uncalled for, and presumably anti-good men, and ordered it struck out. As a result of this and other subsequent difficulties, Smith—who has said that he had been unhappy with C.B.S. policy ever since the time of the quiz scandals, when he was forbidden to deliver a strong commentary on the responsibilities of networks—resigned from C.B.S. and went over to A.B.C. as a news commentator.

In spite of these pressures from within and without, Friendly is confident that television will come into its own as a journalistic profession. So far, there seems little doubt that his own biggest contribution toward this end, apart from his talent as a producer, has been his effort to establish some sort of reasonable ethical and artistic standards in a business that has generally managed to get along without them. "This is a whole new tradition we're concerned with," he says.

59

EDGAR MORIN

CHRONICLE OF A FILM (1962)

In December 1959, Jean Rouch and I were jurors together at the first international festival of ethnographic film in Florence. Upon my return, I wrote an article that appeared in January 1960 in *France Observateur*, entitled "For a New *Cinéma-Vérité*." I quote it here because it so clearly conveys the intentions that pushed me to propose to Rouch that he make a film not in Africa this time but in France.

For a New *Cinéma-Vérité*

At this first ethnographic and sociological festival of Florence, the Festival dei Popoli, I got the impression that a new *cinéma-vérité* was possible. I am referring to the so-called documentary film and not to fictional film. Of course, it is through fictional films that the cinema has attained and continues to attain its most profound truths: truths about the relations between lovers, parents, friends; truths about feelings and passions; truths about the emotional needs of the viewer. But there is one truth that cannot be captured by fictional films, and that is the authenticity of life as it is lived.

Soviet cinema of the grande epoque and then films such as *Le voleur de bicyelette* and *La terre tremble* tried their utmost to make certain individuals act out their own lives. But they were still missing that particular irreducible quality that appears in "real life."[1] Taking into account all the ambivalences of the real and of the imaginary, there is in every scene taken from life the introduction of a radically new element in the relationship between viewer and image.

Newscasts present us with life in its Sunday best, official, ritualized, men of State shaking hands, discussions. Once in a while fate, chance, will place in our field of vision a shriveled or a beaming face, an accident, a fragment of truth. This scene taken from life is most often a scene taken from death. As a general rule, the camera is too heavy, it is not mobile enough, the sound equipment can't follow the action, and what is live escapes or closes up. Cinema needs a set, a staged ceremony, a halt to life. And then everyone masquerades—equipped with a supplementary mask on the camera.

Cinema cannot penetrate the depth of daily life as it is really lived. There remains the resource of the "camera-thief," like that of Dziga Vertov, camouflaged in a car and stealing snatches of life from the streets;[2] or like the film *Nice Time*, stealing kisses, smiles, people waiting outside Picadilly Circus. But they can't be seized or caught like scattered snapshots. There remains the resource of camouflaging the camera behind plate glass, as in the Czechoslovakian documentary *Les enfants nous parlent*, but indiscretion seems to halt the filmmaker just as he becomes a spy.

Cinéma-vérité was thus at an impasse if it wanted to capture the truth of human relations in real life. What it could seize were the work and actions in the field or the factory; there was the world of machines and technology, there were the great masses of humanity in motion. It is, in fact, this direction that was chosen by Joris Ivens, for example, or the English documentary school of Grierson.

There were some successful breakthroughs into the peasant world, as in Henri Storck's *La symphonie paysanne* and Georges Rouquier's *Le farrebique*. The filmmaker entered a community and succeeded in revealing something of its life to us. There were some equally extraordinary breakthroughs into the world of the sacred and of ceremonies, for example, Rouquier's *Lourdes* and Jean Rouch's *Les maîtres fous*. But documentary cinema as a whole remained outside human beings, giving up the battle with fictional film over this terrain.

Is there anything new today? We got the impression at Florence that there was a new movement to reinterrogate man by means of cinema, as in *The Lambeth Boys*, a documentary on a youth club in London (awarded a prize at Tours); or *On the Bowery*, a documentary on the drunkards in a section of New York; or *The Hunters*, a documentary on the Bushmen; and, of course, the already well known films of Jean Rouch.

The great merit of Jean Rouch is that he has defined a new type of filmmaker, the "filmmaker-diver," who "plunges" into real-life situations.[3] Ridding himself of the customary technical encumbrances and equipped only with a 16mm camera and a tape recorder slung-actoss his shoulders, Rouch can then infiltrate a community as a *person* and not as the director of a film crew. He accepts the clumsiness, the absence of dimensional sound, the imperfection of the visual image. In accepting the loss of formal aesthetic, he discovers virgin territory, a life that possesses aesthetic secrets within itself. His ethnographer's conscience prevents him from betraying the truth, from embellishing upon it.

What Rouch did in Africa has now begun in our own Western civilization. *On the Bowery* penetrates the real society of drunkards, who are really drunk, and the live location sound recording puts us right in the middle of a live take on what is really happening. Of course, it is relatively easy to film drunken men who are not bothered by the presence of a camera among them. Of course we stay on the margin of real everyday life. But, *The Lambeth Boys* tries to show us what young people really are like at play. This could have been achieved only through participant observation, the integration of the filmmaker into the youth clubs, and at the price of a thousand imperfections, or rather of the abandonment of ordinary framing rules. But this type of reporting opens up a prodigiously difficult new route to us. We have the feeling that the documentary wants to leave the world of production in order to show us the world of consumption, to leave the world of the bizarre or the picturesque in order to research the world of intimacy in human relations, or the essence of our lives.

The new *cinéma-vérité* in search of itself possesses from now on its "camera-pen," which allows an author to draft his film alone (16mm camera and portable tape recorder in hand). It had its pioneers, those who wanted to penetrate beyond appearances, beyond defenses, to enter the unknown world of daily life.

Its true father is doubtless much more Robert Flaherty than Dziga Vertov. *Nanook* revealed, in a certain way, the very bedrock of all civilization: the tenacious battle of man against nature, draining, tragic, but finally victorious. We rediscovered this Flahertian spirit in *The Hunters*, where pre–Iron Age Bushmen chase game that escapes them.[4]

We chose this film for an award not only for its fundamental human truth but also because this truth suddenly revealed to us our inconceivable yet certain kinship with that tough and tenacious humanity, while all other films have shown us its exotic foreignness. The honesty of this ethnographic film makes it a hymn to the human race. Can we now hope for equally human films, about workers, the petite bourgeoisie, the petty bureaucrats, about the men and women of our enormous cities? Must these people remain more foreign to us than Nanook the Eskimo, the fisherman of Aran, or the Bushman hunter? Can't cinema be one of the means of breaking the membrane that isolates each of us from others in the metro, on the street, or on the stairway of the apartment building? The quest for a new *cinéma-vérité* is at the same time a quest for a "cinema of brotherhood."[5]

P.S. Make no mistake. It is not merely a question of giving the camera the lightness of the pen that would allow the filmmaker to mingle in the lives of people. It is at the same time a question of making an effort to see that the subjects of the film will recognize themselves in their own roles. We know that there is a profound kinship between social life and the theater, because our social personalities are made up of roles that we have incorporated within ourselves. It is thus possible, as in a sociodrama, to permit each person to play out his life before the camera.[6] And as in a sociodrama, this game has the value of psychoanalytic truth, that is to say, precisely that which is hidden or repressed comes to the surface in these roles, the very sap of life that we seek everywhere and is, nonetheless, within us. More than in social drama, this psychoanalytic truth is played for the audience, which emerges from its cinematographic catalepsy and awakens to a human message. It is then that we can feel for a moment that truth is that which is hidden within us, beneath our petrified relationships. It is then that modern cinema can realize, and it can only realize it through *cinéma-vérité*, that lucid consciousness of brotherhood where the viewer finds himself to be less alien to his fellow man, less icy and inhuman, less encrusted in a false life.

In Florence I proposed to Rouch that he do a film on love, which would be an antidote to *La Française et l'amour*, in preparation at that time. When we met again in February in Paris, I abandoned this project, as it seemed too difficult, and I suggested this simple theme: "How do you live?" a question that should encompass not only the way of life (housing, work) but also "How do you manage in life?" and "What do you do with your life?"

Rouch accepted. But we had to find a producer. I laid out the idea in two minutes to Anatole Dauman (Argos Films), whom I had recently met. Seduced by the combination of Rouch and "How do you live?" Dauman replied laconically, "I'll buy it." I then wrote the following synopsis for the filming authorization, which we had to request of the CNC (Centre National de la Cinématographie).

This film is research. The context of this research is Paris. It is not a fictional film. This research concerns real life. This is not a documentary film. This research does not aim to describe; it is an experiment lived by its authors and its actors. This is not, strictly speaking, a sociological film. Sociological film researches society. It is an ethnological film in the strong sense of the term: it studies mankind.

It is an experiment in cinematographic interrogation. "How do you live?" That is to say, not only the way of life (housing, work, leisure) but the style of life, the attitude people have toward themselves and toward others, their means of conceiving their most profound problems and the solutions to those problems. This question ranges from the most basic, everyday, practical problems to an investigation of man himself, without wanting, *a priori*, to favor one or the other of these problems. Several lines of questioning stand out: the search for happiness; is one happy or unhappy; the question of well-being and the question of love; equilibrium or lack thereof; stability or instability; revolt or acceptance.

This investigation is carried out with men and women of various ages, of various backgrounds (office workers, laborers, merchants, intellectuals, worldly people, etc.) and will concentrate on a certain number of individuals (six to ten) who are quite different from each other, although none of these individuals could rightly be considered a general "social type."

Considering this approach, we could call this film "two authors in search of six characters." This Pirandellian movement of research will be sensitive and will serve as the dynamic springboard for the film. The authors themselves mingle with the characters; there is not a moat on either side of the camera but free circulation and exchanges. The characters assist in the search, then dissociate themselves, then return to it, and so on. Certain centers of interest are localized (a certain café or group of friends) or are polarized (the problems of couples or of breadwinning).

Our images will no doubt unveil gestures and attitudes in work, in the street, in daily life, but we will try to create a climate of conversation, of spontaneous discussions, which will be familiar and free and in which the profound nature of our characters and their problems will emerge. Our film will not be a matter of scenes acted out or of interviews but of a sort of psychodrama carried out collectively among authors and characters. This is one of the richest and least-exploited universes of cinematographic expression.

At the end of our research, we will gather our characters together; most of them will not yet have met each other; some will have become acquainted partially or by chance. We will show them what has been filmed so far (at a stage in the editing that has not yet been determined) and in doing so attempt the ultimate psychodrama, the ultimate explication. Did each of them learn something about himself or herself? Something about the others? Will we be closer to each other, or will there just be embarrassment, irony, skepticism? Were we able to talk about ourselves? Can we talk to others? Did our faces remain masks? However, whether we reach success or failure in communications during this final confrontation, the success is enough, and the failure is itself a provisional response, as it shows how difficult it is to communicate and in a way enlightens us about the truth we are seeking. In either case, the ambition of this film is that the question that came from the two author-researchers and was incarnated by means of the real individuals throughout the film will project itself on the theater screen, and that each viewer will ask himself the questions "How do you live?" and "What do you do in your life?" There will be no "THE END" but an open "to be continued" for each one.

In the course of subsequent discussions, Dauman, Rouch, and I reach an agreement to proceed with some "trial runs." I propose some dinners in a private home (this will be in Marceline's apartment). The starting principle will be *commensality*, that is, that in the course of excellent meals washed down with good wines, we will entertain a certain number of people from different backgrounds, solicited for the film.[7] The meal brings them together with the film technicians (cameraman, sound recordist, grips) and should create an atmosphere of camaraderie. At a certain given moment, we will start filming. The problem is to lift people's inhibitions, the timidity provoked by the film studio and cold interviews, and to avoid as much as possible the sort of "game" where each person, even if he doesn't play a role determined by someone else, still composes a character for himself. This method aims to make each person's reality emerge. In fact, the *commensality*, bringing together individuals who like and feel camaraderie with each other, in a setting that is not the film studio but a room in an apartment, creates a favorable climate for communication.

Once filming begins, the actors at the table, isolated by the lighting but surrounded by friendly witnesses, feel as though they are in a sort of intimacy. When they allow themselves to be caught up in the questions, they descend progressively and naturally into themselves. It is pretty difficult to analyze what goes on. It is, in a way, the possibility of a confessional but without a confessor, the possibility of a confession to all and to no one, the possibility of *being* a bit of one's self.

This experience also takes on meaning for the person being questioned because it is destined for the cinema, that is to say, for isolated individuals in a dark theater, invisible and anonymous, but present. The prospect of being televised, on the other hand, would not provoke such internal liberation, because then it is no longer a matter of addressing everyone and no one, but a matter of addressing people who are eating, talking.

Of course, no question is prepared in advance. And everything must be improvised. I propose to approach, through a certain number of characters, the problem of work (the laborers), of housing and vacations (the Gabillons), of the difficulty of living (Marceline, Marilou). Rouch chooses the technicians: the cameraman Morillère, who works with him at the Musée de l'Homme, the sound recordist Rophé, the electrician Moineau. We start at the end of May, as soon as Rouch finishes *La pyramide humaine.*

[. . .]

Later on, once the editing had begun, Rouch and I would be interviewed by *France Observateur*. This interview conveys our differences as well as our agreement, as evidenced in the following extract:

What is the importance of the editing of this film, given that you have twenty-five hours of rushes?

ROUCH: There's the crucial point! We are in conflict, Edgar and I—a temporary and fruitful conflict, I hope. My position is the following: The interest of this story is the film; it's the chronology and evolution of the people as a function of the film. The subject itself is not very interesting. It is difficult to bring together the testimonies, because they are often heterogeneous. There are people who cheat a little, others not at all. To bring together their testimonies would be to falsify the truth. I'll take a simple example: we asked people one question, among others, "What do you think of your work?" Most of these people said they were bored in their jobs. The reasons they give are very different: intellectual reasons, sentimental, physical reasons, et cetera. Bringing these reasons together, in my opinion, is less interesting than the individuals themselves and finding out the motives behind their responses. There are some marvelous contradictions in certain scenes of the film; sometimes people contradict themselves in a fantastic way. For example, Angélo, the worker who has been let go by Renault, is talking with Landry, the young African. Landry says to him: "You're at Renault? . . . Ah, it's well known in Africa, the Renault Company! You don't see anything else . . . 1,000 kilos, Dauphines . . ." And all of a sudden Angélo, before even replying, breaks into a smile and says: "Oh yeah? You've heard of the Rénault Company?" It's inimitable!

So from the point of view of editing, my idea is the following: with some rare exceptions, it is almost impossible to upset the filming order. The people evolved in such a way that, if we want to become attached to them, it is necessary to show them as a function of their evolution. In fact, the whole film was conceived that way. That's how I see the film. And that's why I center it on the summer: it begins in spring and ends in autumn. It's the evolution of a certain number of people throughout events that could have been essential but were not. We thought in the spring that the summer of 1960 would be essential for France. It wasn't, but even with this sort of disappointment, this evolution is nonetheless, to my mind, the subject of the film.

So the editing that I am doing at present, which can, of course, be changed, is much more a chronological editing as a function of the filming than editing as a function of the subject or of the different subjects dealt with in the filming.

MORIN: I think that we must try to maintain in the editing a plurality. The great difficulty is that there are in fact many themes. What I would like is to concentrate this collective halo around the characters. In other words, I would not, in the end, like to see everything reduced to purely individual stories, but rather there should be a dimension, not so much of the crowd, but of the global problem of life in Paris, of civilization, and so forth.

What I would like is that at every moment we feel that the characters are neither "film heroes" as in ordinary cinema nor symbols as in a didactic film, but human beings who emerge from their collective life. What I would like is not to situate individualities as we see them in normal films—in classical, fictional narrative films—where there are characters and some story happens to those characters. I would like to talk about the individual characters in order to go on to a more general problem and then come back from the general problem to the individual.

This means doing a sort of *cinéma-vérité* that would overcome the fundamental opposition between fictional and documentary cinema. In fictional cinema, the private problems of individuals are dealt with: love, passion, anger, hatred; in documentary film until now only subjects external to the individual are dealt with: objects, machines, countrysides, social themes.

Jean and I agree at least on one point: that we must make a film that is totally authentic, as true as a documentary, but with the same concepts as fictional film, that is, the contents of subjective life, of people's existence. In the end, this is what fascinates me.

Another thing that fascinates me on the theme of *cinéma-vérité* is not just reviving the ideas of Dziga Vertov or things of that genre, but—and this is what is really new, from the technical point of view, in what Jean has said—it is that *cinéma-vérité* can be an authentic talking cinema. It is perhaps the first time that we will really end up with a sketch of talking cinema. The words burst forth at the very moment when things are seen—which does not occur with postsynchronization.

ROUCH: In the empty Halles, when Marceline is talking about her deportation, she speaks in rhythm with her step; she is influenced by the setting, and the way she is speaking is absolutely inimitable. With postsynchronization and the best artist in the world, you would never be able to achieve that unrelenting rhythm of someone walking in a place like that.

MORIN: In addition, it is a film where there are no fistfights, no revolver shots, not even any kisses, or hardly any. The action, in the end, is the word. Action is conveyed by dialogues, disputes, conversations. What interests me is not a documentary that shows appearances but an active intervention to cut across appearances and extract from them their hidden or dormant truths.

ROUCH: Another extraordinary thing that you've forgotten, and that's understandable, is the poetic discovery of things through the film. For example: a worker, Angélo, leaves the Renault factory, takes the bus to go home, and gets off at Petit-Clamart. To get to his house, he has to climb up a stairway, an unbelievable stairway, and this ascent—after all, it's only a worker on his way home—becomes a sort of poetic drama.

MORIN: Our common base is that neither one of us conceives of this film as merely sociological or merely ethnographic or merely aesthetic, but really like a total and diffuse thing that is at the same time a document, an experience lived by each person, and a research of their contact.

[. . .]

Post-*Chronicle*

Chronicle of a Summer is finished. It is already slipping away from us. Lately we are free to add a postscript, for example, to take the unused film to make one or two supplementary films that could be shown in ciné-clubs. Or maybe we could establish a long version (four hours), again for the ciné-clubs or for private showings. Maybe we will do it, but the film is slipping away from us, that is to say, we must accept it as is.

As for me, I am divided between two contradictory feelings. On the one hand, I feel dissatisfaction in view of what I had ideally hoped for; on the other hand, I feel deep contentment at having lived this experience, adhering to the compromise that such an accomplishment presupposes. Without Rouch, the film would have been impossible for me, not only because it was Rouch's name that convinced the producer to try the adventure, but also and above all because his presence was indispensable for me, and there again not only from the technical point of view but also from the personal point of view. Although intellectually I can distinguish what differentiates us, I cannot practically dissociate this curious pair we formed, like Jerry Lewis-Dean Martin, Erckman-Chatrian, or Roux-Combaluzier.

We must also express our gratitude to Anatole Dauman. Thanks to Argos Film, Rouch and I were able to carry out decisive experiments in our respective researches. It is thus impossible to dissociate the "Argonauts" from *cinéma-vérité*.

This film, which is slipping away from us, now appears before critics and viewers. It presents us once again with problems, indeed with new problems. These are not aesthetic problems but questions more directly related to life. Because unlike other films, the spectator is not so much judging a work as judging other human beings, namely, Angélo, Marceline, Marilou, Jean-Pierre, me, Rouch. They judge us as human beings, but in addition they attach this moral or affective judgment to their aesthetic judgment. For example, if a spectator doesn't like one of us, he will find that person stupid, insincere, a ham; he'll reproach the character for being at the same time a bad actor and an unlikable individual. This confusion of levels at first upsets us but reassures us at the same time, because it expresses the weakness and the virtue of this film. It shows us that, no matter what, though we have been doing cinema, we have also done something else: we have overflowed the bounds of cinéma-spectacle, of cinéma-theater, while at the same time sounding the depths of its possibilities; we are also a part of this confused and jumbled thing called life.

This film is a hybrid, and this hydridness is as much the cause of its infirmity as of its interrogative virtue.

The first contradiction holds in the changeover from real time to cinematographic time. Of course the real time is not the total time, since we were not filming all the time. In other words, there was already a sort of selection in the filming; but the editing obliges us to make a selection, a more difficult composition, more treacherous. We choose the times that we find the most significant or the most powerful; of course, this theatricalizes life. On top of that, the close-up accentuates dramatization. In fact there is more tension in seeing close-ups of Marilou, Marceline, or Jean-Pierre than in being present in the scene itself, because the close-up of the face concentrates, captures, fascinates. But above all we realize that though the editing can improve everything that does not develop through the length of the film, it also weakens and perverts the very substance of what happened in real time (the jetty at Saint Tropez, Marilou unhappy, or Marceline on August 15, for example). Additionally, the compromise that Rouch and I made on the characters works to their detriment. The viewer will not know them well enough, and yet will arrive at a global judgment on their personalities; they are sufficiently (i.e., too) individualized to avoid such judgment. Thus Jean-Pierre, Marilou, Marceline, Angélo, Gabillon will be perceived globally by means of mere fragments of themselves.

These judgments, as in life, will be hasty, superficial, rash. I am amazed that what should inspire esteem for Jean-Pierre or Marilou, namely, their admission of egoism or egocentrism ("egoism" for Jean-Pierre; "I reduce everything to my own terms" for Marilou), will paradoxically produce a pejorative judgment of them. It seems we have underestimated the hypocritical reaction, and as a result, I tell myself that the real comedy, the real hamming, the spectacle, takes place among the petit bourgeois who play at virtue, decency, health, and who pretend to give lessons in truth.

But I must not let myself follow that miserable downslide of the human mind that always transfers blame to others. Errors in judgment of which the characters in the film are victims are provoked because we both over- and underindividualized our characters, because certain tensions whose origins are unclear emerge in the course of the film, because there is a whole submerged dimension that will remain unknown to the public. Without intending to, we have created a projective test. We have only provided a few pieces of a puzzle that is missing most of its parts. Thus each viewer reconstructs a whole as a function of his own projections and identifications.

As a result, while this film was intended to involve the viewer, it involves him in an unforeseen manner. I believed that the viewers would be involved if they asked themselves the question "How do you live?" In fact, the reactions are more diverse, and this diversity is not just the diversity of aesthetic judgments; it is a diversity in *attitudes* toward others, toward truth, toward what one has the right to say, and what one should not say.

This diversity marks our failure as well as our success. Failure, because we did not come away with the sympathy of the majority, because, thinking we were clarifying human problems, we provoked misunderstandings, even obscuring reactions. Success, because to a certain degree Rouch and I gave these characters the chance to speak and because, to a certain degree, we gave the public a liberty of appreciation that is unusual in cinema. We did not merely play the divine role of authors who speak through the mouths of their characters and show the public the sentiments they should feel, their norms of good and bad. It is also because there is this relative freedom, and not only because we filmed under the least cinema-like conditions possible, that we have approached the cinema of life. But in approaching thus we have also approached all the confusion of life.

We have also modified the relationship between actor and spectator, which is like the relationship between an unseen God and a passive communicant. We have emerged from mystery, we have shown ourselves, present, fallible, men among others, and we have provoked the viewer to judge as a human being.

Whether or not we wanted it so, this film is a hybrid, a jumble, and all the errors of judgment have in common the desire to attach a label to this enterprise and to confront it with this label. The label "sociology": is this a film that (a) wants to be sociological, (b) is sociological? Those for whom sociology signifies a survey of public opinion on a cross-section sample of the population, that is to say, those who know nothing about sociology, say: We are being tricked, this isn't a sociological film, the authors are dishonest. But we have in no way presented this film under the label "ethnographic" or "sociological." I also do not see why film critic Louis Marcorelles denounces my "false sociological prestiges." I never introduce myself as a sociologist, neither in the film, nor in real, life, and I have no prestige among sociologists. We have not once, to my knowledge, pronounced the word "sociology" in this film. Our banner has been *cinéma-vérité*, and I'll get to that. Our enterprise is more diffuse, more broadly human.

Let's say to simplify things that we're talking about an enterprise that is both ethnographic and existential: ethnographic in the sense that we try to investigate that which seems to go without saying, that is, daily life; existential in that we knew that each person could be emotionally involved in this research. Any filmmaker could have posed the question "How do you live?", but we wanted this interrogation to be minimally sociological. This minimum is not just an opinion poll, which not only achieves only superficial results when dealing with profound problems but also is totally inadequate for our enterprise. This minimum is first of all a preliminary reflection on the sociology of work and daily life. Next it is an attitude that is engraved in one of the fundamental lines of human sciences since Marx, Max Weber, and Freud. To simplify: for Marx, it is crisis that is revealing, not normal states. For Max Weber, a situation is understood by starting not at a middle ground but with extreme types (which Weber constructed theoretically by the method of utopian realization and named "ideal types"). For Freud, the abnormal reveals the normal as one exacerbates that which exists in the latent or camouflaged state of the other.

If a good part of the film's viewers refuse, reject, or expel from themselves what they consider a "pathological" case that is in no way representative or significant, this indicates not an error in our method but rather the difficulties involved in consciousness of certain fundamental givens of being human. The real question is not whether Marilou, Angélo, Marceline, and Jean-Pierre are rare or exceptional cases but whether they raise profound and general problems, such as job alienation, the difficulty of living, loneliness, the search for faith. The question is to know whether the film poses fundamental questions, subjective and objective, that concern life in our society.

Psychoanalysis, Therapy, Modesty, Risk

I have written that in certain conditions the eye of the camera is psychoanalytical; it looks into the soul. Critics have reproached us for doing false psychoanalysis, that is, of knowing nothing about psychoanalysis. Here we are dealing with a myth of psychoanalysis, just as there is a myth of sociology. Psychoanalysis is a profession and a doctrine with multiple tendencies, all strongly structured. Our venture is foreign to psychoanalysis understood in its professional and structured sense but does go in the direction of the ideas that psychoanalysis has helped to bring into focus. Otherwise we have gambled on the possibility of using cinema as a means of communication, and the therapeutic idea of our plan is that all communication can be liberation. Of course I was aware, and am even more aware since the film has been screened, of all the difficulties of communication, the boomerang risks of malevolent interpretations or of scornful indifference; I know that those

I wanted recognized were sometimes disregarded. I know that if I were to do it again, I would do it differently, but I also know that I would do it. And I reaffirm this principle: things that are hidden, held back, silenced, must be spoken; J. J. Rousseau is worth more than Father Dupanloup; *Lady Chatterley's Lover* is worth more than the censorship that prohibited it. We suffer more from silencing the essential than from speaking.

The need to communicate is one of the greatest needs that ferment in our society; the individual is atomized in what Riesman has called "the lonely crowd." In this film there is an examination of stray, clumsy communication, which our censors have called exhibitionism or shamelessness. But where is the shame? Certainly not in those who make themselves the crude and ostentatious spokesmen of shame: shame does not have such impudence.

But finally one question is asked: do we have the right to drag people into such an enterprise? I will answer that it is first a matter of characterizing this enterprise, that is to say, the risks it involves. Is it an enterprise of vivisection or poisoned psychoanalysis? Or is it, on the contrary, a game of no importance? Does it involve the same sort of risks as taking passengers in a car on vacation roads or leading an expedition into a virgin forest? How can they judge the harmful consequences, those who know neither Marilou, nor Angélo, nor the others? Having thought it all out, I'd say that the greatest risk depends on those who criticize Angélo, Marilou, et cetera; that is to say, their inability to love them. Of course we exposed Angélo, Marilou, Marceline, and Jean-Pierre to this risk because we overestimated the possibilities of friendship. But even in the case of Marilou and of Jean-Pierre, unknown friends are born to them.

In the end, anyone who lives with a woman, has children, recruits adherents to his party, whoever lives and undertakes anything makes others take risks. Each of us risks the destiny of others in the name of their interests and their morals. The ultimate problem is that of each of our own morals.

Bourgeois or Revolutionary Film?

This film is infrapolitical and infrareligious. There is a whole zone left unexplored by the film. If we had been believers, we would not have neglected belief. On the political level, the question is different. We did not want, for example, to present the worker problem at the level of political or union affiliations or of salary claims, because conditions of industrial work should be questioned at a deeper, more radical level. Taking into account this infrapoliticism, we were the only ones in filmmaking to question the war in Algeria and to thus attack the central political problem of the hour.

It was possible to judge this film variously: reactionary or revolutionary, bourgeois or leftist. I don't want to get dragged into defining right now what I understand by reactionary, bourgeois, Left; nor to polemicize with those who find the film reactionary. I would say only that the meaning of the film is clear if one conceives of it as contesting both the reigning values of bourgeois society and Stalinist or pseudo-progressive stereotypes.

Optimism? Pessimism?

It is true that Rouch was naturally carried toward what is cheerful and light and that he was the spokesman of "life is beautiful," while I was naturally carried toward what is sad or sorrowful. The reason for my quest to approach the difficulties of living is not just that happy people have no story to tell but also because there are fundamental problems that are tragic, ponderous, and must be considered. But to confront these problems is not to despair. What disheartens me, on the contrary, is that everyone who is not subjected to the piecework without responsibility or initiative, that is, typical of the laborer or the civil servant, readily takes it for granted. What disheartens me are those people resigned to the artificial, shabby, frivolous life that is given to them well defined. What disheartens me are those who make themselves comfortable in a world where Marceline, Marilou, Jean-Pierre, and Angélo are not happy.

That these may be "my" problems, that my problems should have taken form in this film (at least in an elementary fashion), does not mean that they cease to exist independently of me. That I may have difficulties in life, that I may not really be able to adapt—this does not necessarily mean that I cannot step outside of myself; it may also sensitize me to the problems of others. In any case I drew two "optimistic" lessons from this experience. First, an increased faith in adolescent virtues: denial, struggle, and seeking. In other words, Angélo, Jean-Pierre, Marilou, and Marceline have inspired me to resist the bourgeois life. The second is the conviction that every time it is possible to speak to someone about essential things, consciousness is awakened, man awakens. Everyone, the man in the street, the unknown, hides within himself a poet, a philosopher, a child. In other words, I believe more than ever that we must relentlessly deal with the person, denying something in the person, revealing something in the person.

Cinéma-Vérité?

Finally we come to the problem of *cinéma-vérité*. How do we dare speak of a truth that has been chosen, edited, provoked, oriented, deformed? Where is the truth? Here again the confusion comes from those who take the term *cinéma-vérité* as an affirmation, a guarantee sticker, and not as a research.

Cinéma-vérité: this means that we wanted to eliminate fiction and get closer to life. This means that we wanted to situate ourselves in a lineage dominated by Flaherty and Dziga Vertov. Of course this term *cinéma-vérité* is daring, pretentious; of course there is a profound truth in works of fiction as well as in myths. At the end of the film, the difficulties of truth, which had not been a problem in the beginning, became apparent to me. In other words, I thought that we would start from a basis of truth and that an even greater truth would develop. Now I realize that if we achieved anything, it was to present the problem of the truth. We wanted to get away from comedy, from spectacles, to enter into direct contact with life. But life itself is also a comedy, a spectacle. Better (or worse) yet: each person can only express himself through a mask, and the mask, as in Greek tragedy, both disguises and reveals, becomes the speaker. In the course of the dialogues, each one was able to be more real than in daily life, but at the same time more false.

This means that there is no given truth that can simply be deftly plucked, without withering it (this is, at the most, spontaneity). Truth cannot escape contradictions, since there are truths of the unconscious and truths of the conscious mind; these two truths contradict each other. But just as every victory carries its own defeat, so every failure can bring its own defeat. If the viewer who rejects the film asks himself, "Where is the truth?", then the failure of "How do you live?" is clear; but maybe we have brought out a concern for the truth. No doubt this film is an examination whose emphasis has been misplaced. The fundamental question that we wanted to pose was about the human condition in a given social setting and at a given moment in history. It was a "How do you live?" that we addressed to the viewer. Today the question comes from the viewer who asks, "Where is the truth?" If for a minority of viewers the second question does not follow the first, then we have both supplied something and received something. Something that should be pursued and thoroughly investigated. To live without renouncing something is difficult. Truth is long-suffering.

NOTES

1. The French is *pris sur Je vif.—Ed.*
2. In fact it seems to me that the camera-eye experiments by Dziga Vertov and his friends ran up against equipment that was too heavy and difficult to handle. The camera in the street was visible to those it filmed, and this seemed to the authors to invalidate its result since then both technical manageability and people's reactivity to the camera have evolved considerably. We must also mention Jean Vigo, whose *À propos de Nice* is quite a fascinating endeavor.
3. This image of the filmmaker-diver has always pleased (and flattered) me. The filmmaker with his equipment does indeed look like a deep-sea diver or like an interstellar voyager, but one who navigates in a "non-silent" world.
4. *The Hunters*, produced by the team of the Film Center of the Peabody Museum (Harvard University), comprising John Marshall, Professor Brew, and Robert Gardner.
5. The French is *cinéma de fraternité.—Ed.*
6. This notion of the play of truth and life before the camera, pointed out by Edgar in 1959–1960, is a capital one. Starting, no doubt, at the moment when Edgar sensed it in the drafts presented in Florence, it has been possible to pursue this play, no longer with only men who are alien to our culture (thus brothers to the spectator). From this contact in Florence carne the experience of *Chronicle of a Summer.*
7. At the beginning, this fine meal idea was destined more than anything to satisfy the demonic gourmandise of Morin, thus to get him in the mood for conversation. In fact it allowed a feeling of trust to develop among the actors and the crew, which was indispensable for suppressing inhibitions before the camera (always present and ready to record at any moment).

JONATHAN ROSENBAUM

RADICAL HUMANISM AND THE COEXISTENCE OF FILM AND POETRY IN *THE HOUSE IS BLACK* (2003)

The Iranian New Wave is not one but many potential movements, each one with a somewhat different time frame and honor roll. Although I started hearing this term in the early 1990s, around the same time I first became acquainted with the films of Abbas Kiarostami, it only started kicking in for me as a genuine movement—that is, a discernible tendency in terms of social and political concern, poetics, and overall quality—towards the end of that decade.

Some commentators—including Mehrnaz Saeed-Vafa—have plausibly cited Sohrab Shahid Saless's *A Simple Event* (1973)[1] as a seminal work, and another key founding gesture, pointing to a quite different definition and history, would be Kiarostami's *Close-up* (1990).[2] Other touchstones would include Ebrahim Golestan's remarkable *Brick and Mirror* (1965), Dariush Mehrjui's *The Cow* (1969), Massoud Kimiaï's *Gheyssar* (1969), and Parviz Kimiavi's *The Mongols* (1973). But I'd like to propose a lesser-known short film preceding all of these, Forugh Farrokhzad's *The House Is Black* (1962)—a twenty-two-minute documentary about a leper colony outside Tabriz, the capital of Azerbaijan. For Mohsen Makhmalbaf, it is "the best Iranian film [to have] affected the contemporary Iranian cinema," despite (or maybe because) of the fact that Farrokhzad "never went to a college to study cinema."[3] It is also, to the best of my knowledge, the first Iranian documentary made by a woman. It won a prize at the Oberhausen Film Festival in 1963 and was also shown at the Pesaro Film Festival three years later. For me it is the greatest of all Iranian films, at least among the sixty or seventy that I've seen to date. More than any other Iranian film that comes to mind, it highlights the paradoxical and crucial fact that while Iranians continue to be among the most demonized people on the planet, Iranian cinema is becoming almost universally recognized as the most ethical, as well as the most humanist.

Farrokhzad (1935–67)—widely regarded as the greatest of all Iranian women poets *and* the greatest Iranian poet of the twentieth century, who died in a car accident at thirty-two—made *The House Is Black*, her only film, at twenty-seven, working over twelve days with a crew of three. The following year, in an interview, she "expressed deep personal satisfaction with the project insofar as she had been able to gain the lepers' trust and become their friend while among them."[4] I mainly want to consider it here for its anticipation of "the Iranian New Wave" as I know it. On a more personal level, Mehrnaz Saeed-Vafa and I worked with three others in subtitling *The House Is Black* in English prior to its screening at the New York Film Festival in 1997, on the same program as Kiarostami's *Taste of Cherry*.

Though it was dismissed in a single sentence by the *New York Times*'s reviewer, it clearly made a strong impression on many others who saw it there and in subsequent screenings at the annual Robert Flaherty Seminar and at Chicago's Film Center, before the print was returned to the Swiss Cinémathèque. The same version is what is now being released by Facets Video, and though it doesn't appear to be quite complete—one abrupt edit looks like a censor's cut, and a few stray details visible in some other versions are missing—this is the best version of the film available in North America.[5]

A few relevant facts about the film: its producer, Ebrahim Golestan (born in 1922)—also a pioneering filmmaker in his own right, as I've already noted, as well as a novelist and translator (who translated, among other things, stories by Faulkner, Hemingway, and Chekhov into Persian)—was Farrokhzad's friend and lover for the last eight years of her life, and she worked with him as a film editor before making her own film.[6] Her most notable editing job was on *A Fire*—an account of a 1958 oil well fire near Ahvaz that lasted over two months until an American fire-fighting crew managed to extinguish it. As Michael C. Hillmann accurately describes it, the film juxtaposes the fire with "the sun and moon, flocks of sheep, villagers eating, harvest time, and the like."

Prior to working on *A Fire* in 1959, Farrokhzad studied film production as well as English during a visit to England. Shortly afterwards, she traveled to Khuzestan and worked on films there in several capacities—as actress, producer, assistant, and editor.[7]

According to Karim Emami, a writer and translator who worked for Golestan Films during this period, her first experience in handling a movie camera was shooting streets, oil wells, and petroleum pumps on a handheld super-8 camera in Agha-Jari, shooting from the interior of a touring car—an image that immediately calls to mind Kiarostami, *Taste of Cherry* in particular. She also appeared in the Iranian segments, filmed by Golestan, of an hour-long 1961 National Film Board of Canada TV production, *Courtship*—a discussion of the rites of betrothal in four separate countries—playing the sister of a working-class bridegroom in Tehran. She acted in another Golestan film that was never finished called *The Sea*, and another, in 1961, called *Water and Heat* or *The View of Water and Fire*. She also made one other film after *The House Is Black*—"a short commercial for the classified ads page of *Kayhan* newspaper" which Emami regards as relatively inconsequential.[8] She is also said to have worked on still another Golestan film entitled *Black and White*, and plays an almost invisible cameo in his *Brick and Mirror*—the pivotal part of a young mother who abandons her infant.

In an interview last year, Kiarostami credited Golestan as the first Iranian filmmaker to use direct sound—a common attribution,

I believe. But it's worth noting that *The House Is Black,* which clearly uses direct sound in spots, was made prior to *Brick and Mirror,* raising at least the possibility that Farrokhzad might have been a pioneer in this technique in Iranian cinema.

Defying the standard taboos and protocols concerning lepers—especially the injunction to avoid physical contact with them for her own safety—Forugh Farrokhzad wound up permanently adopting a boy in the colony named Hossein Mansouri, the son of two lepers, who appears in the film's final classroom scene, taking him with her to Tehran to live at her mother's house. Yet some of the film's first viewers criticized it for exploiting the lepers—employing them as metaphors for Iranians under the shah, or more generally using them for her own purposes and interests rather than theirs.

When I first heard about the latter charge I was shocked, for much of the film's primal force resides in what I would call its radical humanism, which goes beyond anything I can think of in Western cinema. It would be fascinating as well as instructive to pair *The House Is Black* with Tod Browning's 1932 fiction feature *Freaks*—which oscillates between empathy and pity for its real-life cast of midgets, pinheads, Siamese twins, and a limbless "human worm," among others, and feelings of disgust and horror that are no less pronounced. By contrast, Farrokhzad's uncanny capacity to regard lepers without morbidity as both beautiful and ordinary, objects of love as well as intense identification, offers very different challenges, pointing to profoundly different spiritual and philosophical assumptions.

At the same time, any attentive reading of the film is obliged to conclude that certain parts of its "documentary realism" (perhaps most obviously, its closing scene in a classroom, as well as the powerful shot of the gates closing, which occurs just before the end)—working, like the subsequent films of the Iranian New Wave, with nonprofessionals in relatively impoverished locations—must have been staged as well as scripted, created rather than simply found, conjuring up a potent blend of actuality and fiction that makes the two register as coterminous rather than as dialectical. (Much more dialectical, on the other hand, is the relation between the film's two alternating narrators—an unidentified male voice, most likely Golestan's, describing leprosy factually and relatively dispassionately, albeit with clear humanist assumptions, and Farrokhzad reciting her own poetry and passages from the Old Testament in a beautiful, dirgelike tone, halfway between multi-denominational prayer and blues lament.)

This kind of mixture is found equally throughout Kiarostami's work, and raises comparable issues about the director's manipulation of and control over his cast members. Yet without broaching the difficult question of authors' intentions, it might also be maintained that the films of both Farrokhzad and Kiarostami propose *inquiries* into the ethics of middle-class artists filming poor people and are not simply or exclusively demonstrations of this practice. In Kiarostami's case, it is often more obviously a critique of the filmmaker's own distance and detachment from his subjects, but in Farrokhzad's case, where the sense of personal commitment clearly runs deeper, the implication of an artist being unworthy of her subject is never entirely absent.

The most obvious parallel to *The House Is Black* in Kiarostami's career is his recent documentary feature *ABC Africa* (2001) about orphans of AIDS victims in Uganda—a film which goes even further than Farrokhzad in emphasizing the everyday joy of children at play in the midst of their apparent devastation, preferring to show us the victims' pleasure over their suffering without in any way minimizing the gravity of their situation.[9] But it's no less important to note that one of Farrokhzad's poems is recited *in toto* during the most important sequence of Kiarostami's most ambitious feature to date, whose title is the same as the poem's, *The Wind Will Carry Us* (2000).

The importance of Farrokhzad in Iranian life and culture—where even today, and in spite of the continuing scandal that she embodies and represents, she's commonly and affectionately referred to by her first name—points to the special status of poetry in Iran, which might even be said to compete with Islam. *The House Is Black* is to my mind one of the very few successful fusions of literary poetry with film poetry—a blend that commonly invites the worst forms of self-consciousness and pretentiousness—and arguably this linkage of cinema with literature is a fundamental trait underlying much of the Iranian new wave.

I hasten to add that "film poetry" is one of the most imprecise terms in film aesthetics, whether it's used to describe Alexander Dovzhenko or Jacques Tati, so a few precisions are in order about why I'm using this term here. Much of what I have in mind is the suspension—or extension—of what we usually mean by "narrative" or "story" so that a certain kind of descriptive presence supersedes any conventional notion of an event. After a leper is seen walking outside beside a wall, pacing back and forth, intermittently hitting the wall lightly with his fingers, we hear Forugh very faintly offscreen reciting the days of the week over this image, the rhythm of her voice sounding a kind of duet with the man's repeated gesture. Two notions of time are being superimposed here so that they become impossible to separate: an event lasting a few seconds and a duration stretching over days (and, by implication, weeks, months, and years).

Similarly, in the film's penultimate sequence, while a one-legged man limps on crutches between two rows of trees towards the camera, we hear Forugh's voice evoke a cluster of other images, some of them with very different time frames, over this single movement: "Alas, for the day is fading, / the evening shadows are stretching. / Our being, like a cage full of birds, / is filled with moans of captivity. / And none among us knows how long / he will last. / The harvest season passed, / the summer season came to an end, / and we did not find deliverance. / Like doves we cry for justice . . . / and there is none. / We wait for light / and darkness reigns." Again there is a kind of duet, ending this time in a kind of rhyme effect as her last two lines give way to the loud, clumping sound of the man's footsteps in the foreground as his dark body directly approaches the camera, dramatically blotting out everything else.

Although the film is mainly framed by two scenes in a classroom, the second of these is briefly interrupted by what can only be called a poetic intrusion—a shot I've already mentioned that is unrelated in narrative terms but enormously powerful in descriptive terms: a crowd of lepers is suddenly seen outdoors, approaching the camera, only to be blocked from us when a gate abruptly closes on them, bearing the words "leper colony" (or more precisely "leper house," tied more directly to the film's title). In narrative terms, this shot has no relation to what precedes and follows it apart from the most obvious thematic connection: lepers. Yet it functions almost exactly like a line in a poem—parenthetically yet dramatically introducing the brutality of our social definition of lepers and how it shuts them away from us—before returning us to the classroom.

That Farrokhzad was the first woman in Persian literature to write about her sexual desire, and that her own volatile and crisis-ridden life (including her sex life) was as central to her legend as her poetry, helps to explain her potency as a political figure who was reviled in the press as a whore and placed outside most official literary canons while still being worshipped as both a goddess and a martyr. Despite her enormous differences (above all, in gender and sexual orientation) from Pier Paolo Pasolini, it probably wouldn't be too outlandish to see her as a somewhat comparable figure in staging heroic and dangerous shotgun marriages between eros and religion, poetry and politics, poverty and privilege—and a figure whose violent death has been the focus of comparable mythic speculations. She and her film remain crucial reference points because of their enormous value as limit cases, as well as artistic models. And as far as I'm concerned, if the Iranian New Wave begins with *The House Is Black*, there's no imagining where it can still lead us.

NOTES

1. See Mehrnaz Saeed-Vafa, "Sohrab Shahid Saless: A Cinema of Exile," in *Life and Art: The New Iranian Cinema*, edited by Rose Issa and Sheila Whitaker (London: National Film Theatre, 1999), 135–44.
2. See Godfrey Cheshire, "Confessions of a Sin-ephile: *Close-Up*," in *Cinema Scope* no. 2 (Winter 2000): 3–8.
3. Mohsen Makhmalbaf, "Makhmalbaf Film House," translated by Babak Mozaffari, in *The Day I Became a Woman* (bilingual edition of screenplay) (Tehran: Rowzaneh Kar, 2000), 5.
4. Michael C. Hillmann, A *Lonely Woman: Forugh Farrokhzad and Her Poetry* (Washington, DC: Three Continents Press/Mage Publishers, 1987), 43.
5. A still better version—with French subtitles, taken mainly from the print shown in Oberhausen, and authorized by producer Ebrahim Golestan—was issued on DVD along with *A Fire* as part of the [then] biannual French magazine *Cinéma* (7 [Printemps 2004]), edited by Bernard Eisenschitz and published by Editions Léo Scheer.
6. See also Mehrnaz Saeed-Vafa, "Ebrahim Golestan: Treasure of Pre-Revolutionary Iranian Cinema," *Rouge* #11, 2007 (www.rouge.com.au/11/golestan.html). [2009]
7. Michael C. Hillmann, op. cit., 42–43.
8. Karim Emami, "Recollections and Afterthoughts" (undated lecture delivered in Austin, Texas), quoted on Forugh Farrokhzad web site, www.forughfarrokhzad.org (unfortunately no longer available at this address).
9. See also Mehrnaz Saeed-Vafa and Jonathan Rosenbaum, *Abbas Kiarostami* (Urbana and Chicago: University of Illinois Press, 2003), 37–40, 83–84, 119–23.

61

JEAN ROUCH WITH DAN GEORGAKAS, UDAYAN GUPTA, AND JUDY JANDA

THE POLITICS OF VISUAL ANTHROPOLOGY (1977)

Dan Georgakas, Udayan Gupta, and Judy Janda interviewed Jean Rouch in English in September 1977 at the Margaret Mead Film Festival at the Museum of Natural History in New York. The questions and responses relate to the seven films by Rouch featured over three evenings at the festival that year: *Les maîtres fous, Moi, un Noir, Chronicle of a Summer, The Lion Hunters, Jaguar, Petit à Petit,* and *Cocorico, Monsieur Poulet.—Ed.*

You are best known in the United States for Chronicle of a Summer. *The more we learn about the film that launched* cinéma-vérité, *the more controversial and intriguing it becomes. For instance, some of your own comments after the screening at the Museum of Natural History raised questions about the fundamental verite of the film. You stated that the secretarial scenes in the film were shot at the offices of* Cahiers du Cinéma. *You also talked at length about the individuals in the film, many of whom went on to become filmmakers, and others like Régis Debray to become prominent Marxist personalities. Rather than the mood of the Parisian "tribe" at the end of the 1950s,* Chronicle of a Summer *actually renders portraits of people in the political and artistic avant-garde. At the same time, there is little footage within the film that demonstrates that these are exceptional people. One minor point is that they never use words like "socialism" or "communism." Could you expand on how the film evolved from an idea to this reality?*

At the beginning, when we first started thinking about such a film, I said to Edgar Morin, my collaborator, that I didn't really know many industrial workers. Edgar said he would arrange for that. I only learned later on that the people he chose all belonged to the same group as Morin, Socialism or Barbarity (*Socialisme ou Barbarie*). This turned out to be critical for the film's development, but it wasn't clear to me at the beginning. I think you are wrong when you say they didn't mention communism. At one point, a worker is unhappy because he is doing nothing, dealing only in papers. Morin says, "Remember when we were militants in the same party? We did something. Now, where are we?" This is a reference to the fact that they had both been in the Communist Party. Morin and the others left the party in disgust after it supported the suppression of the Hungarians.

That doesn't come across so clearly, but you are admitting that it's not about the Parisian tribe after all.

It's a tribe all right, but a specialized tribe [laughter].

Perhaps a subtribe?

Yes, I like that. Fortunately, it was a tribe of substance. In their attitudes, you can see what will explode all over France in May 1968.

There are some troubling implications here for documentary filmmakers, particularly anthropologists. When anyone goes to a foreign place and a guide tells them, "Let me take you to a group of typical workers," or "Let me show you an important ritual," how do we know what we are seeing? Here you were in your own country and working with a dear friend, and in some degree he took you in. He said, "Here are some workers," and they turned out to be of a political tendency whose virtue was that it was not typical at all.

You are absolutely right. Perhaps we should add some subtitles to identify "the party" as the Communist Party.

There's more to it than that.

I would say that it was clear who they are to a French audience. This group was not quite illegal, but it had to be cautious. At that time, the Algerian war was the major political issue, and these people were aiding the revolutionaries. We could not speak to that question because of their own security and the security of the Algerians. The French audience of that time would have no trouble understanding what the speakers represented. Showing it now or in another country, problems emerge which weren't an issue then.

Let's turn to some of the techniques you used. One of the most striking sequences was clearly staged by you as a "director," even though the "actors" didn't know what was coming. We're thinking of the scene where you ask the African students to interpret the meaning of the tattoo on Marceline's wrist.

That was a provocation. When I first saw the film, I noticed that I was smiling a very cruel smile when I intervened. That smile sometimes embarrases me even now. You see, we were having lunch outside the Musée de l'Homme, and the subject came to anti-Semitism. As soon as it began, I knew I would ask the question about the tattoo the Nazis had put on Marceline's wrist because I knew the Africans did not comprehend our concern about anti-Semitism. When I posed the question, the isolation and assumptions of cultures emerged dramatically. It's not quite apparent in the film, but before that moment, people were jovial and laughing. Suddenly the Europeans began to cry, and the Africans were totally perplexed. They had thought the tattoo was an adornment of some kind. All of us were deeply affected. The cameraman, one of the best documentary people around, was so disturbed that the end of the sequence is out of focus. I stopped filming to give everyone a chance to recover. Now, is this a "truthful" moment or a "staged" moment? Does it matter?

The long sequence in which Marceline walks by herself, talking into a tape recorder strapped to her body, is like a cinematic stream of consciousness. There are many such experiments in the film. Where did you get your ideas?

Morin must be given a lot of credit. He proposed to make the first sociological fresco film, a film without the convention of stars or leading performers. He wished to deal with anonymous people as much as possible. I told him this was not possible. When you begin to speak with any person, even a cop, the man is not cops, he is a cop. You can't get around that. So while we can oppose the star system and what it implies, we cannot deny individuals their humanity and personality. We had many discussions on this point. Each day we would project the rushes before doing any new work. We had a lot of give and take between us and the producer Dauman and the people in the film. We had all these ideas we wanted to deal with, more than we ever got in.

For instance, there was a wonderful sequence in which we spent a day with the factory worker Angélo. We couldn't shoot inside the factory because Angélo's politics were well known and both the company and the union were against him. The men who participated had to be secretive. We shot only at the entrance. Then we followed Angélo to his home in a working-class district. There were twenty minutes spent showing him taking a bath. That would be a very good short film in itself, a twenty-five-minute study of a man coming back from his work to his home and a warm bath. But we had to cut it out. Another thing, since making that film, I am not allowed into a factory with my camera. I, too, find myself opposed by both management and the union.

At the museum you indicated that the making of the film involved the simultaneous making of a camera.

Oh yes, that was one of the best parts of making that film. We are now talking about the late fifties, when cameras were heavy and static. I had gone to a film meeting in California where I met Michel Brault, who showed the film *Les raquetteurs*, and he asked me to stop back in Montreal on my way home. I took up the invitation and saw the first films made by the young filmmakers of Quebec. They were using a new type of wide-angle lens. Before then, there had always been the problem of distortion. They had also begun to take the camera from the tripod and go "walking with the camera." I loved that. The cameras were still noisy, but if you wrapped a trenchcoat around them, something could be worked out.

Back in France, Morin approached me about his idea for a film. I began with a very excellent cameraman, but when I wanted him to "walk in the streets," the poor man refused. It was too much of a challenge for him. I then told Dauman, our producer, that the only one who could do what we wanted was Michel Brault. What a comment on the vaunted French cinema! We had to go to Montreal to get a competent person. During the same time I spoke with André Coutant, who was father of the Eclair Cameflex 35mm camera. He said there was a new camera that might interest me. It was a military prototype built for use in a space satellite. That meant it was very light, dependable, and steady. Unfortunately it had a magazine of only three minutes. I asked him if he could build a model with a larger capacity. He said he would try. So we began to make our film with a camera that didn't totally exist. We had a contract with the manufacturer that they would not be responsible for any scratches made on the film, but Coutant agreed that he would personally repair the camera every night. After shooting, Edgar and I would bring it back to him and tell him what problems we had encountered, what new ideas we proposed. The creation of the camera proceeded with the creation of the film. I was overjoyed with the result. It was doubly wonderful because I was in front of these people who were always so serious, and I was joyous at seeing the camera being born. That was one problem I felt about them, especially

Morin. They didn't see the pleasure you could have in life.

One thing that was clear seeing several of your films on three consecutive evenings was that Chronicle *has a very different look than the others. Generally in your African films, we are given long-distance shots of people active in a religious ritual or some other rite involved with nonrationalist values. In* Chronicle *the subjects mainly talk, and they talk about complex philosophical and psychological ideas. The action is generally indoors, and there are many close-up shots.*

Part of the explanation has to do with the camera. When we began the film, the camera was still on its tripod. I thought the effect was much too static, so I began to move it as people spoke. How they looked and what they did with their hands seemed important, so I did close-ups. After a while, we went outdoors and walked in the street. At the end of the film there are no close-ups. Even when we shot the participants viewing what we had completed of the film to that point, there are no close-ups of Marilou, Marceline, or any of them. I don't disagree with the thrust of your question, though. Remember, I didn't know these people personally, and they began to speak of very intimate problems. I was somewhat embarrassed by that. The first Marilou sequence was shot right after I met her for the first time. In the second, we were alone at Marceline's flat after dinner. She was talking so nervously that I had to react. So I took those big close-ups, to try to get inside. I was very upset by that experience. You are right. I never do close-ups like that in other films, but that is true even for other films about France.

It struck us that the film about France emphasizes how the European thinks, while your films on Africa emphasize how the African behaves.

This is an interesting point, and I must say it is the first time the question has been put to me. Normally, I would not see so many films one after the other. As I have said, other films I have done in France do not have so many close-ups. Another thing, at the beginning we shot people at 100 meters, and they did not know we were shooting them. They thought we were a group of people who had a camera. I disliked that very much. We wanted to do something that was spontaneous, but that was more like candid camera, something sneaky. Our caution goes back to the fact that Angelo and his friends had so many enemies that we had to be protective of our subjects. Perhaps the close-ups were a kind of backlash.

That still doesn't explain the African films where nobody ever talks directly to you. How accurate is that, given the strong oral traditions of African culture? What we see in the films is a kind of homage to the primitive, to the past, to the exotic. Aren't Africans as articulate as Europeans? Isn't there a modern African society with elements as creative as the group that called itself Socialism or Barbarity?

You are asking good questions. The explanations come on several levels. One immediate response I have is that I have decided not to make political films about postindependence Africa. After all, these are not my countries. I think it is imperialistic to project your political values onto Africa. That kind of film must be done by Africans. I have been tempted to break my own rule. I had quite good relations with Kwame Nkrumah and started to make a film about him. In *Jaguar* you can see part of the coup d'état. After that coup, everything about Nkrumah was destroyed. I had the idea of doing a film about him while he was in exile. After three months, I saw that it was wrong for him. It would have been impossible to show that film in the one country where it most mattered. And who was I to make such a film? It would be a shame for him and for them.

What about the dialogue in earlier films, during the preindependence era?

At the time we could not do it technically. When we made *Chronicle of a Summer,* the first independence had already taken place in Ghana, three years earlier. I understand what you are trying to get at, but there are terrible problems involved. If I were to do a film now about the political regimes of Africa, it would be a spectacle of disasters, one after the other. It's embarrassing for a European to make a film like that. I don't think it's my own cowardice either, although some people have said I am not courageous. I don't know. I'm censoring myself all the time. In *Cocorico, Monsieur Poulet* we had a sequence where the police bargained up their bribe from two chickens to three. When we saw the rushes, we decided to take it out, even though it was an honest and accurate representation. How to deal with such corruption is a real dilemma for people who make films in Africa, even for the African filmmakers.

Let's take the same issue from a different perspective. What is your conception of the narrative, even in the strictly anthropological film? Your comments on The Burial of the Hogon *and* The Mad Masters *did a great deal to enlighten us about your aims and what the films were all about. When we watched the films beforehand, we were puzzled by many of the images. We were like those Africans who had no way of understanding the tortured history symbolized by that tattoo on Marceline's wrist.*

But the alternative is so boring—to say, "In the village of so-and-so, blah-blah happened." My ideal would be a film that everybody could comprehend without any narration. Language is such a problem. We can't even accurately translate exactly what people are saying in another language. Then, too, I am using more and more feedback. When films are shown to the subjects, narration angers them. Nonetheless I sympathize with your question. It is almost as if the films were still not complete. Something has to be done with them. I have a new film about drumming where I use a different kind of narration. I give a very subjective response to what I am filming.

It's still not clear whether you think narration is good or bad.

My dream is to show in a film what can be understood directly without the aid of narration, to explain everything that needs explanation by filmic devices. But I am perplexed. If people speak, you need to translate. I have one film in which I have created a very precise translation that is on a sound track that is cut in right after they speak. I try to speak the translation in the same way the people speak. That is as close to simultaneous translation on film as you can expect. Stereo would be a better solution. One track could have the original language and the other a translation.

One of your other partial solutions gave us problems. In The Mad Masters, *near the end, you comment that the ritual helps the people to be good workers and to endure colonialism with dignity, that it provides some psychological accommodation. Clearly, one of your aims was to deal with the viewer who would be appalled at seeing people drinking dog's blood. You wanted to show the positive psychic benefits to the individuals involved. Our reaction, though, was that people should not be accommodated to endure colonialism. Is it not far better for anger to explode on the job than to be let off in some harmless religious rite? Is it not better if they were "bad" workers who "accidentally" broke their tools and were "lazy"?*

Quite right. I no longer care for that ending. Originally that commentary was impromptu. I wanted to explain that the ritual was a method that allowed them to function in normal society with less pain. I wanted to make it clear that they were not insane. An important point that got lost was that therapy for the Africans is not a one-to-one private consultation like you have in psychoanalysis and most Western therapies. The therapy we filmed was a public ritual done in the sun. That aspect is one of the most important things we Westerners need to learn. But I can't very well fiddle with the commentary now. The film has existed as is for more than twenty years.

We've come to the conclusion that your body of work is much more excting as cinema than as anthropology. In every film there is some new experiment. Most of the time, as in The Lion Hunters, *there is an imposed dramatic structure. The action builds to a traditional climax. That's effective cinema, but does it describe the tribe accurately? Doesn't a lot get lost for dramatic values?*

This is one point where I disagree with you completely. Good anthropology is not a wide description of everything but a close identification of one technique or ritual. The rituals are supposed to be dramatic. They are creations of the people who want them to be interesting and exciting. In *The Lion Hunters,* twenty minutes have been left out. Those sequences showed the position of the trap, why they use traps, why they hunt in the first place. But you can explain that sort of thing in writing very well. What you can't get in writing is the drama of the ritual. Writing can't have that effect. That's the whole point of visual anthropology.

What about the distortions? For instance, your films exclude the role of women.

If you want to make films about African women, you have to be a woman. A man cannot enter the woman's society. It's just impossible. It is forbidden. Men are not even allowed to have intercourse with their wives when a hunt is about to begin. It is the male society I can be a part of, so that is what I film. There are many things that have to do with women that I could never show.

If you could intervene in The Mad Masters *and show the footage of real colonial officials, why isn't it possible to use similar devices to speak about women?*

That's easier said than done. When I show the water was poured from the well by the wicked women, what visual intervention could be made? Or when we say the poison of the female is stronger than the male poison, more exposition might just confuse matters, because that is not the direct subject of the film. You must understand that there are wonderful women's ceremonies that men are not allowed to view. Obviously they would not allow even a woman to film them if men were to be allowed to see the film afterward. I have one old woman who tells me some things, but she is allowed privileges because of her great age. I have many problems with my students about such matters. I have to explain to women that during their menstruations they are not allowed in some locations. They have to be out of certain villages altogether. What a dilemma for a European woman who wants to work in Africa.

Since we've talked about the different ways people interpret the same images, this might be a good place to talk about the influence your work has had on others. Most people in the United States do not realize that Jean Genet was very affected by seeing The Mad Masters.

Now I am embarrassed in a different way, but Genet's *The Blacks* was directly influenced by *The Mad Masters.* The idea in his play was that the blacks play the masters, as in the ritual. Possession, after all, was the original theater, the idea of catharsis. Genet seized upon the idea of mockery and exchanged identity. That wasn't exactly what the original was all about, but Genet worked the material to his own end.

What do the Africans have in mind when they take part in the ritual?

They insist they are not engaged in mockery or that they have any notion of revenge. I believe that is true, at least on the conscious level. The history of the cult is very complex. It goes back to Africans who went to Mecca. The entire rite, the foaming at the mouth, the sacrifice of the dog, and all the shouting is considered to be the action of spirits which have possessed them. These are powerful new gods who most certainly are not to be mocked. When the cult began, the Islamic priest saw them as heretics and persecuted them. The French administration joined in because they did not like the revival of strong animistic faiths that might turn political. So it was a forbidden cult almost from the start. Many of the original cultists, members of the Hauka, became migratory workers and had to go far from their homelands. Everywhere they were banned, and as usual, the more they were banned, the better it was for the cult. The first compromise was to agree to do it only once a week, on Sunday, at a specific location. Later the cult declined, and the rite took place only once or twice a year. The Hauka movement broke taboos, whether it was eating a dog or modeling behavior on the colonial example. It was like Buñuel's attitude to the church. You cannot feel sacrilegious if you do not respect your opponent. What the Hauka did was very creative and implicitly revolutionary, just as the authorities feared.

I only met Genet twice, but I knew the actors in his play, and we discussed the film quite a bit. Genet was an ex-convict, so he knew about systems within systems and how one resists. I think the film showed him a way to resolve some of his contradictory feelings. What we got on film was one of the last moments of the cult. After independence, there was no more colonial power and thus no model. But there is something extraordinary about that ritual they invented. Every sort of force has attacked them and me for filming them—the colonialists who don't like the portrait, African revolutionaries who don't like the primitivism, antivivisectionists who don't like the sacrificial murder, et cetera, et cetera.

Peter Brook was another person who had a profound reaction to the film.

His response was quite different from Genet's. He saw the film when he was staging *Marat/Sade* and asked all his actors to see the film and model their playing on it. Later we talked together often, and he went with me to Africa. He tried to create a new theater without using any recognizable words. He was fascinated by the Hauka, who had invented an artificial language, part pidgin English, part broken French, part who knows what. Yet people understood the language. I've hypothesized that before this century is over, there will be a movement among blacks in the United States that will use such a language. But Peter Brook was not doing politics. He was interested in theater. His play dealt with a revolutionary period in which power belonged to his subject. He wanted the actors to act as if they were possessed even though they were not. A friend of mine said that if you are moved when you act, you are finished. You have to act to be moved, but not to be moved when you're acting. You have to believe in the roles you are playing. With the Hauka, there is no acting. They believe they are the spirits during the possession. I told Brook that if his actors were too successful in giving up their identity, they might become possessed. Then what would he do? He was not a doctor or a priest. I thought he was playing with fire.

One last thing we should say about the Hauka is that they are no longer in Ghana. They were expelled when they weren't needed as workers. They returned to Niger and took a specific role in each village. Since there is no more colonial power, they have no models and are returning to traditional cultures with an Islamic bent. They and the film I made about them have had a tremendous impact, however. Reaction to that film was one of the sources of my idea to have African anthropologists come to France to film our tribes and rituals.

You've helped a number of Africans begin careers in film. Would you tell us something about them?

Well, there is Oumarou Ganda, the main figure of the film *Moi, un Noir*. He created a narration for the film that works at three levels. The first is a description of what you see, the second is a kind of dialogue, and the third is a statement about his own condition. He's gone on to make films on his own. Another person I've worked with is Moustapha Alassane, who is a kind of renaissance type. I believe some of his films are available in the United States.

We indicated earlier that we thought your films posed very interesting cinematic questions but we were not so certain about their virtue as anthropology. We were thinking in terms of what an anthropological film can and cannot be. Does it just record raw data, or does it interpret? To make a film always involves a selective process and conscious intervention at specific points. That must conflict with an attempt to present anthropological fact.

Most people refuse to recognize that any anthropology must destroy what it investigates. Even if you are making a long-distance observation of breast feeding, you disturb the mother and her infant, even if you don't think so. The fundamental problem in all social science is that the facts are always distorted by the presence of the person who asks questions. You distort the answer simply by posing a question.

If the very presence of the observer causes so much distortion, the presence of a camera must magnify the distortion.

Absolutely! But I think this new distortion can be positive. Let's make a comparison between classical anthropology and visual anthropology. In the first, you take a professional from a prestigious university, and they go to some remote place, where people are usually without a written language. Just by making an investigation, the people of the places are embarrassed and have their routine disturbed. When the survey is completed, the anthropologist goes back to the university, writes the dissertation, and possibly wins distinction in the field. What is the result for those who were surveyed? Nothing. There is no feedback from the disruption the anthropologist has created. The subjects will not read the survey. With a camera, there can be a far more fruitful result. The film can be shown to the subjects. Then they are able to discuss and have access to what has happened to them. They can have reflection even if the film is bad, for however incompetent the film may be, there will be the stimulation of the image you give of them and the chance for them to view themselves from a distance, up there on the screen. Such a distortion changes everything. In the first example given, there can be some reward for the researcher and for science in the abstract. In the second, you can have all that and benefits for the people, too.

There is another problem related to all this, which your readers in particular should appreciate. Six or seven years ago, I attended a conference in Montreal sponsored by the African Section of the American Anthropological Association. That meeting was disrupted by people acquainted with the Black Panther Party. They argued that we were new slave traders. They said that by making a survey of any given tribe and becoming an expert, the anthropologists could gain prominence and teaching posts and writing contracts that would be lucrative for a lifetime. Often, the fieldwork never amounted to more than a few years' work. One American black replied that he was in a different category because he was making a study of workers. The reply was that his work might be even more damaging. It was argued that his reports would be of most value to businessmen and governments who needed data to further exploit and control the workers. I think those arguments were right in one sense, but the solution is not quite as simple as they wanted to make out. Do we stop all research because we cannot control the use of our findings?

Then there is still another kind of exploitation. Some ten years ago, a musicologist recorded a wonderful song of the Watusi. It was published in a very small edition of scientific records. Eventually, the Rolling Stones heard the tune. They liked it so much, they recorded it and made a lot of money. Naturally, the Watusi never earned a cent. They were certainly exploited. The musicologist had made the original recording with good intentions, and the Stones obviously respected the music, but the rip-off occurred. When you record an oral tradition, there are no copyrights and often no original or single creator. This is true for stories, as well. When you are making an anthropological film, the problem is just as severe. The people allow us to film them, but once it is done, the film goes to the West, and the people have no control over what is done with the images of their lives. Often the people who made the film have been given grants or get professional stature. Should the people be paid, too? Or is that another kind of insult?

Once more you address the problem as an artist might, the question of who "owns" a creation.

Well, I've been concerned about this problem a long time. On *Moi, un Noir,* I insisted that 60 percent of the profits go to the actors because they wrote the scenario. They did everything in the film. But even if the contract is observed, we have now created the idea that culture is something to sell or to buy, an idea the Africans never had. This is a long-range distortion that will become increasingly important. Nobody seems to care about this. Consider this possibility: today we make a film in a "backward" region. Ten years from now, the inhabitants of that region may see it on television, perhaps via some orbital satellite. Most likely they will still be poor. What has been the benefit for their culture? And now the African national governments create another distortion. They say if something is done within their borders, it is part of the "national" culture. This is really absurd because a tribe may be cut into three parts, with its people becoming citizens of three separate political states. The people shown in the lion-hunting film have been divided among the states of Upper Volta, Mali, and Niger. The students at each respective national university consider the culture of the tribes in their particular country to be part of their "national" culture. I believe African anthropologists trained in such universities may ultimately prove more destructive than the Europeans.

One solution I propose to this is to train the people with whom you work to be filmmakers. I don't think it's a complete answer, but it has merits in that it leaves the people with something rather than just taking from them. That would mean that anthropologists would have to have training not only as filmmakers but as teachers of filmmaking. Of course, we can't expect miracles. I once had an African student ask me if much money could be made from film. I told him that if I taught someone how to use a pencil, it did not mean they would become Victor Hugo, only that they could write.

This matter of rights has cropped up often in discussions of cinema verite *made in the United States. For example, Fred Wiseman makes a film about welfare recipients and becomes a "hot" television property. What about the desperate people he has filmed? They remain as before. Having helped yet another professional to a successful career.*

That's the problem. Let me go back to *Chronicle of a Summer.* I brought that very problem to Dauman. He solved it as a businessman might, and it was not bad. Marceline, for instance, was paid for six months, and that was how she got her first job in films. Her story had a very happy ending. She stayed in film, married Joris Ivens, and has made films in Cuba and Vietnam. Angélo could not get work because of the film, and Dauman helped him buy a shop because he felt responsible. We did things like that. Next year will be the eighteenth anniversary of that film, and most of the people in it have prospered because of their involvement.

Would you tell us something about the film that had its American premiere at the museum—Cocorico, Monsieur Poulet?

The subject of this film is the "marginals" of Africa. I have come to the conclusion that changes in society are due primarily to those few people who are on the fringe of society, those who see the economic absurdity of the system. I regard them as a kind of populist avant-garde. They have to find some way to make a living without being trapped by the system. They are marginal. The plot deals with how three men go with their car into the countryside to buy chickens for resale in a large city. The three men in the film helped me write and film the story. The car you see belonged to Lam, the main character. He would go in a fifty-mile radius looking for chickens, fish, and millet. That car had no license, no brakes, no lights. I thought it would be most interesting to show the routine of this marginal economy.

In the film the chickens he buys are from a contaminated area. Do you endorse that kind of marginalism?

There was no contamination. That problem happened two years earlier when there was an epidemic. There was a forbidden zone for perhaps a month. The sign in the film was one we made ourselves. We just put it in at the end as a joke.

That created a real problem for those of us unfamiliar with the situation. What we see seems to reinforce basic prejudices against Africa. The women cast evil spells. The police are inept. The merchants have a dangerous car held together with spit and glue. People trade in contaminated chickens. Your idea of showing the "hippies" of Africa doesn't register.

Perhaps this is your own Western prejudice.

That may be true, but Cocorico *is presented as a fiction film, not as anthropology. We are all aware that Africa is in transition, and in this fictional work there doesn't seem to be anything positive going on, concretely or in consciousness.*

From my point of view, it is absolutely positive. Africans have had a history of seeing national and international experts come and tell them that their family life is not good and that they do their work incompetently. Lam and the others had seen many such people come and go. They knew that most of these experts never ask the farmers why they are using a particular technique. I can't see how you can make changes until you learn the habits of the people. I believe there is a prejudice against native African culture. You would think a field had never been planted or that advanced cultures had never thrived. If you want to change African farming methods, you must make a twenty-year commitment at the least. How many engineers, specialists, and experts are prepared to spend so much time in a single African nation? Not many. Most prefer to make a fast survey, write a report, and go home. *Cocorico* shows some of the schemes and strategies used by the common African.

I think the relationship Africans have to their machines is much more positive than the ones in Europe. Lam is a very good mechanic. He can ask anything of his car. It was no problem for him to take the car apart in order to cross the Niger. He did it all by himself. He went to some care about keeping the water from the oil and the cylinder, but he knew what to do. He felt free to rip the car apart because he knew he could put it together with just the simple tools we showed. I could make a film about an African who repairs transistors. He has no formal training, but he has a system with a small loudspeaker like the one in a tape recorder. It is run on a battery and hums when there is a defect in the circuit. This is a spontaneous approach to electronics. You do not have to know the principles of physics to deal with an auto engine or to repair a transistor.

In the film it seemed that the Africans treated their car like the stereotyped "dumb hillbillies" of Appalachia who are used as comic relief in Hollywood films and on American television.

I don't know what the relationship between auto and human is in the United States, but in France, if a car is stuck or if there is a flat tire, there is a catastrophe. In Africa, however, it's a joy because you stay there. A person will say, "Good, we are stuck. Now we can stay a few days and meet people whom we never met before and will never meet again." Back in the early forties, we ran cars on a kind of charcoal gas because there was no petrol. We were stuck all the time. At first I would be furious, but I learned the African way, and now I don't mind such things. I don't even wear a watch. That's the kind of perspective I tried to capture in the film.

What has been the reception of the film in France?

When the film opened in Paris, I happened to be in Africa. So there was no press conference for the film, no publicity of any kind. Still, it opened in three theaters, and in two months there were fifty thousand paid admissions. The only prints of the film were bad 16mm prints without subtitles. One of them was used here. The distributor became ambitious and thought to have the film blown up to 35mm. Five prints were made. Unfortunately the distributor went bankrupt and did not pay the lab. The prints are now blocked, and I am trying to make an arrangement with the laboratory. We are also working to get commercial distribution in Africa.

Earlier you spoke about making a camera while doing Chronicle. *You sounded like Lam dealing with his car. Through the years, your equipment has changed quite a bit, hasn't it?*

I began making films with 16mm because at that time I had no money for 35mm. That was in 1946, when 16mm was strictly amateur. Later I got hold of an old American army newsreel camera with an excellent lens. I shot all my earliest films with that camera. What a time we had. There was no editing table or splicer at that time. You had to cut the film by sticking it with your finger. There was no viewer, so I projected the film with a regular projector and cut and cut. There was no sound except with 35mm. When I completed my second film, I asked some African workers in Paris to play music as they watched a projection. That was a stupid idea, but it gave me genuine African music as an accompaniment, and that was an improvement over nothing.

With the third film, I used the earliest Nagra, the one with a winch. It was supposed to be portable, but there was a handle to turn, and it weighed more than fifty pounds. The film had no sync sound, but there was an attached reel to take up music. Then you had to transfer the sound from the tape to the kind of recording disc used at that time in broadcasting stations. Sometimes I improvised commentary and mixed the sound track. Luckily, television used 16mm equipment, and with the television boom we got major improvements—the first good splicer, the first viewer, the first sound mixer. Still we wanted real sync sound that was portable. We still had equipment that weighed a ton and required a crew of five if we wanted sync sound. We tried all kinds of tricks to get around the problem. One film called *La pyramide humaine* used a technique that really sounds funny now. The camera was put on a tripod in a blimp, and all the people stood around at the same distance so that you could go from one to the other without any problem of focus. You could have people talk with the camera that way. We used that technique more than once, but it was limited. I'm talking of the fifties now. It was when I was editing that film that we decided to shoot *Chronicle of a Summer.*

And that was when you built the Eclair.

Yes I am so pleased to think about that. By the end of the film, Michel went back to Montreal with a new technique, and we all had a new camera. Everyone learned so much from that experience. I learned to "walk" the camera. I learned to use the wide angle. After that film, French cinema was never quite the same. Everyone wanted to walk with the camera, even if they had the camera on a tripod and rolled it in a wagon. We got them to think about what "truth" in film was. Afterward Coutant made further improvements, and we got the small Eclair. Unfortunately, because of deaths, the main engineers left Paris and went back to Grenoble. They started their own company and have built new cameras. Coutant is still a young man, and he's full of new ideas all the time—crazy, wonderful ideas. He works with Godard.

We all feel there are no secrets. Everyone is capable of learning what there is to learn. If you are going to use a camera, you should know how to repair it. The idea with the new cameras is to have you spend at least a day at the factory. You mount it by yourself and dismount it, three or four times until you know it perfectly. You know what you will film. You know how to readjust the camera, how to fix it. You know that there is a machine and it has no magical insides. If something goes wrong, you can change it like you change a flat tire. There are many films still to be made and many improvements in cameras. Coutant has a three-year plan in mind with a technological breakthrough set for each year. He would like to see a camera with the sound quality of Nagra 4, a camera without cables, a focus mike that could connect with the focus on the lens, and a three-zoom lens with a corresponding sound focus. What is important in the kind of work I have done is to record rituals and ways of living that are rapidly disappearing. With the new equipment, we will be able to make much better films, and the people in those films will be able to make them, too. I look forward to more and more of that.

62

RICKY LEACOCK

FOR AN UNCONTROLLED CINEMA (1961)

In 1908 a newsreel was made showing Tolstoy talking to petitioners on the veranda of his home at Yasnaya Polyana. And though it is a remarkable sight, how frustrating that one cannot hear what he is saying to these people! And herein lay the problem. How could you record human relations without that uniquely human means of communication—speech?

The art of the cinema was to develop for a good half of its total life without speech. Four films are reasonably typical of this period: *Potemkin, The Kid, Nanook,* and *The Eternal Triangle* (starring Mary Pickford). Most people will agree that *Potemkin* is fascinating but very odd when one looks at it today; *The Kid* and *Nanook* work perfectly and seem strangely contemporary; and *The Eternal Triangle* appears utterly ludicrous. Yet I think it is the latter film that is the grandmother of what we consider the normal theatrical film of today.

Potemkin represents one of the most exciting developments in the history of film. A film form was developed which was in effect a marvelous visual language. A great amount of attention has been paid to these techniques which came to be called "montage." A body of theory did grow up around montage and it did seem to many that film-making was coming of age and would henceforth have an elegant theoretical base to lean upon. Pudovkin wrote *Film Technique* and Eisenstein wrote *Film Sense* which gave what appeared to be a *general* approach to film-making.

However, when sound-on-film made its appearance, an appalling fact became very evident—one no longer needed a visual substitute for speech. Theories die hard and there are still many film theoreticians who cling to the "golden age of film-making." Perhaps they should look again at Pudovkin's first sound film to see how empty this new situation left him. To quote Roberto Rossellini: ". . . in the silent cinema, montage had a precise meaning, because it represented language. From the silent cinema we have inherited this myth of montage, though it has lost most of its meaning."

There was one ancient art form that lent itself perfectly to the silent cinema and that of course was pantomime (in all its forms, including slapstick). It didn't really matter how the filming was done so long as you could see the pantomime. *The Kid* is still running all over the world. It needs no words and has no "foreign" versions. The pantomime artists of this period achieved a worldwide following that has probably never been equaled.

Ever since the invention of the "talking-picture" it has been blithely assumed that films are an extension of the theatre, a marvelous gadget that allows you to change scenes in an instant, yet retains the fundamental aspect of theatre in that you cause a story to be acted out before an audience (the camera) under controlled conditions. Control is of the essence. The lines are written down and learned by the actors, the actions are rehearsed on carefully selected or constructed sets and these rehearsals are repeated over and over again until the resulting scene conforms with the preconceived conceptions of the director. What horror ... None of this activity has any life of its own. If anything, it has far less "spirit" than a production in a theatre because the tyranny of technique is far greater than in the theatre. True, if you rented an empty theatre nothing would happen of itself ... no play would spontaneously take place ... but as a play is prepared it does seem to take on some life of its own, partly because its form emerges during rehearsals. Whereas a film succumbs to the tyranny of Production Efficiency and is torn to fragments to make things more convenient for the camera. If two utterly unrelated scenes are to be made in the same locale they will be made consecutively even though they will end up at opposite ends of the picture and require completely different emotional responses from the actors.

In a recent interview with the late André Bazin, Jean Renoir complained: "... in the cinema at present the camera has become a sort of God. You have a camera, fixed on its tripod or crane, which is just like a heathen altar; about it are the high priests—the director, cameraman, assistants who bring victims before the camera, like burnt offerings, and cast them in the flames, and the camera is there, immobile—or almost so—and when it does move it follows patterns ordained by the high priests, not by the victims ..." Both theatre and the vast bulk of film-making as we know it are the result of control by these "high priests" and it is not surprising to note that many of our leading film directors divide their time between the theatre and motion picture production.

Many of us have, like Renoir, become "... immensely bored by a great number of contemporary films ...". If we go back to the earliest days of cinema we find a recurrent notion that has never really been realized, a desire to utilize that aspect of film which is uniquely different from theatre: to record aspects of what did actually happen in a real situation. Not what someone thought should or could have happened but what *did* happen in its most absolute sense. From the four examples I gave, *Nanook* comes closest to it, and it is for this reason that it will never outdate. However, it too was limited by the lack of sound.

As far back as 1906 Leo Tolstoy noted: "... It is necessary that the cinema should represent Russian reality in its most varied manifestations. For this purpose Russian life ought to be reproduced as it is by the cinema; it is not necessary to go running after invented subjects ..."

Here is a proposal that has nothing to do with theatre. Tolstoy envisioned the film-maker as an observer and perhaps as a participant capturing the essence of what takes place around him, selecting, arranging but never controlling the event. Here it would be possible for the significance of what is taking place to transcend the conceptions of the film-maker because essentially he is observing that ultimate mystery, the reality. Today, fifty years after Tolstoy's death, we have reached a point in the development of cinema where this proposal is beginning to be realized.

63

BRUCE ELDER

ON THE CANDID-EYE MOVEMENT (1977)

It is a commonplace of the history of documentary film that at the end of the fifties there developed in the United States, France and Canada (including Quebec) a school of cinema known as *cinéma-vérité.* The fact that these allied movements did develop in so many different countries at one particular historical moment no doubt indicates a substantial change in the geological rockbed of cinema—a change which even today continues to affect the course of development of the cinema, turning it towards a greater realism. That all these movements, moreover, attempted to incorporate aspects of the real into the work of art and so share with certain other movements in art (*musique concrète, objet-trouvé, choisisme,* etc.) certain common aspirations clearly must be accounted for, and the willful obscuring or neglect of these similarities could only be accomplished at the expense of understanding why the cinema took this particular course at this particular historical moment.

All of these movements shared certain features in their reaction against the aesthetic of the preceding cinema. The aesthetics which subtended the silent cinema were, for the most part, material-formalist in character; the major innovations of the heroic period of the silent cinema—the fracture of space and time, the use of rigorously formal compositions involving closed forms, the structuration of montage devices on a linguistic model, and the use of an increasingly formal narrative with the concomitant increasing alienation of the cinematic diegeses from the reality—can all be considered in these terms. All of this meant, of course, that the aesthetic value of these works depended upon the rupture between the cinematic object and reality.

During the fifties, allied with those movements in modern art mentioned above, there developed several scattered movements in cinema, the aesthetic of which rested not upon the formal categories opened up by the transcendence of reality, but rather upon the tensions which could be developed in the dialectic between artifice and nature and, more particularly, between fiction and reality.[1] The strategies which characterize the works of these schools—the photographic respect for the integrity of space and time in the use of the long take, the use of more open and less formal compositional devices, the use of non-actors and real locations—were all calculated to integrate the real into the architectonic defined by the dramatic form.[2]

Though this much can readily be admitted, the degree of attention given the similarities among the movements taking place in different countries has resulted in some extremely misleading notions. It is, of course, a commonplace to distinguish between American- and French-style *cinéma-vérité*, usually on the basis of the rejection of interviews in the former (but not in the latter), and the supposedly lesser degree of intervention on the part of the filmmaker in the pro-filmic event, though it seems to me the full measure of the difference between these two schools has not been fully appreciated. As for the Canadian brand of *cinéma-vérité*, it seems to be considered of secondary consequence and derivative of either the American or the French version. According to the usual accounts, the fact that Canada developed the style so close in time to the American and French developments reflects the degree of intimacy between Canadian cinematic culture and that of the United States and France.

The trouble with these accounts is not only that they are historically inaccurate, inasmuch as the developments in Canada actually anticipate those in the United States upon which they supposedly draw,[3] but also that the styles of *cinéma-vérité* developed in these countries differ radically from each other.

The work of Drew Associates, like that of the other allied schools to which we have alluded, usually exploited the tensions inherent in the dramatic form.[4] It is from this use of the dramatic form, in fact, that many of the characteristics which distinguish American *cinéma-vérité* from Canadian Candid-Eye cinema derive.

It has often been commented upon that the Drew films were journalistic in character inasmuch as they depended for their interest on the supposed noteworthiness of the event documented. In fact, the characteristics of the event necessary to sustain the structure on which the vast majority of the Drew films are built can be more precisely specified than this. As Mamber has pointed out,[5] typically these films are based on a contest-type situation. The fact that such a situation is constituted by a struggle between opposing forces—a struggle which by its very nature is decisive inasmuch as it is assured that one of the forces will achieve victory at the expense of another—guarantees that by conducting a simple track on the event, following contours of its external physical development and recording its key incidents, one will arrive at a work structured on the crisis-climax-resolution pattern which constitutes the basis of the dramatic form. The selection of these contest-type situations is therefore largely pragmatic; one can be sure that following such a situation over a specific period of time and recording only its external appearance will result in a workable structure which possesses a measure of dramatic intrigue.[6]

Further evidence of the dramatic quality of American-type *cinéma-vérité* can be found in the nature of its concern with character. The centrality of this concern is seen in the fact that the typical problematic underlying the films can be stated in the form "Will A (the protagonist) succeed in some real contest-type situation?" (e.g., will Hubert Humphrey win the Wisconsin primary? Will Eddie Sacks win in the Indianapolis 500? Will Jane Fonda's initial Broadway appearance be successful? Will Susan Starr win her piano competition?). Typically the introductions to the works in this corpus serve to elicit audience sympathy for the protagonist by showing him engaged in a contest-type situation in which he is strongly motivated to win, since something of very appreciable consequence is shown to be at stake. Thus the conflict situation is calculated to put a stress on the character. The resolution of the film, typically the aftermath of a thwarting of the protagonist's will (consider *Primary, Eddie Sacks, Susan Starr, Jane Fonda,* in all of which the protagonist fails to achieve his goal), portrays the stripping away of his illusions (defined by his ambitious goals) and the emergence of his real character.[7]

Although the sorts of tensions which characterize the dramatic form are imported into the American-type *cinéma-vérité* film, they are, nonetheless, profoundly altered in character; for whereas in an orthodox dramatic work, the actions of the characters are determined by a body of conceptual material which demands that in order for a certain idea to be expressed a certain piece of behaviour must occur, in a *cinéma-vérité* film, the parallel dialectic is transformed into one existing between a person's appearance and his real nature, between his mask and his reality. Thus, in these works, the principle of structuration has shifted from a body of conceptual material to reality.[8]

In the traditional fictional cinema, the factors affecting the articulation of the diegesis are many. If a verisimilitude of reality is desired, as it usually is in conventional cinema, its requirements will be one controlling determinant of the work; competing with this, however, will be other determining factors—those resulting from the nature of the body of conceptual material which constitutes the principle determinant of the structuration of the work and particularly the internal logic of this body of material; those resulting from the aesthetic demands of developing tension, etc. All these factors act to deflect the diegesis away from perfect verisimilitude.

In *cinéma-vérité* films, however, this kind of competition among determing principles is eliminated as the structure of the real event itself substitutes for the logic of the body of conceptual material as the principle of structuration of the work, at the same time guaranteeing the existence of dramatic tensions.

The issue here, then, is not simply one of creating an accurate facsimile of the real. There is a deeper ontological issue involved. The diegesis of the traditional cinema is clearly an artifice, a construct; it is only for this reason that strictly aesthetic categories can be applied when considering its articulation. The representation of the world presented in a *cinéma-vérité* film is not a parallel construct to the real world articulated in accordance with certain aesthetic demands; it is a trace of the real world informed by the same structural principles as the real itself.

This of course profoundly affects the nature of the filmmaker's enterprise. His task is no longer creation but rather revelation. The process of making such a work is not the forging of an imaginative construct through an act of will but rather one of allowing the forms of nature to manifest themselves through an act of attentive submission on the part of the filmmaker; the goal of art is no longer seen as that of producing beauty but rather truth—or perhaps more precisely, truth in beauty.

Having elucidated the formal structures of American-type *cinéma-vérité* films, we are now in a position to grasp the full measure of the difference between the English-Canadian and American versions of "direct cinema," for the history of the Candid-Eye movement can in part be written as a history of the rejection of the dramatic forms. One of the most obvious examples of this rejection occurs in *The Back-Breaking Leaf.* The film begins by establishing a contrast between the well-to-do townspeople who own the prosperous tobacco fields and the itinerant labourers who work the fields in late summer. For a few minutes at the beginning of the film it appears that this contrast will develop dramatically into a conflict between the two groups. So strong is this suggestion that in one remarkable scene we are shown the townspeople practicing archery at their recreation centre. The camera holds for a long time on a tautly drawn bow whose very tension seems to emblemize the tensions between the two groups, while the activity of archery itself is suggestive of the hostilities between them.

The dramatic conflict which this seems to foreshadow indeed appears to be developing as we are shown the labourers in an employment office rallying against exploitative labour practices and unfair wages. This, we sense, is a decisive moment; a show-down between labour and employer is arising which will develop into a crisis-type situation.

Our expectations are thwarted, however, as a remarkable thing occurs: the conflict situation is abruptly abandoned as the film proceeds to document the manner in which tobacco is picked and dried. Indeed, the film concludes as a text on the hazardousness of the enterprise of tobacco-growing.[9]

The contrast between Koenig and Kroitor's *Lonely Boy* and Leacock and Pennebaker's *Jane*, both portraits done in 1962 of young performers at early stages in their careers, is equally illustrative of the point we are considering. Whereas the American film is based on the crisis-type situation of the opening appearance of an actress in her first major role and develops fully the dramatic potential inherent in such a situation, the Canadian film eschews any situations involving conflict, and so lacks any sense of drama whatsoever. It restricts itself to documenting the ordinary day-to-day activities of the young pop star and the factors behind his success.[10]

The reasons for the rigorous stance against the use of dramatic form on the part of the Candid-Eye filmmakers are several. Some of them are related to "end-of-ideology" ideology which was current when this style was forged; others have to do with those colonial attitudes so often found expressed in Canadian arts. But the key reason lies in the particular character of the journalism which provided the basis for the Canadian version of "direct cinema". Both the American and the Canadian versions of "direct cinema" were, as we have seen, essentially journalistic in character; the character of the journalism to which each group was committed, however, differed radically. The American-style of *cinéma-vérité* was, of course, developed under the auspices of Time-Life and the films themselves retained certain features of the Luce-type of journalism which those magazines practiced. Mamber, in his book *Cinema Verite in America*, has demonstrated conclusively the important influence exerted by Robert Drew in the development of cinéma-vérite in the United States, documenting the important role played by Drew's concept of the "key picture"—an image of the moment in which the full drama of a situation emerges—in the formation of the American-type of *cinéma-vérité*. The photojournalism to which the Candid-Eye filmmakers held allegiance, on the other hand, reflects the influence of Henri Cartier-Bresson.[11]

Cartier-Bresson's approach breaks sharply with the traditions of photojournalism, including the Luce type, which prevailed at the time he began working as a photographer. Whereas earlier photojournalists were concerned with the extraordinary event (consider, for example, the subjects of Drew's "key pictures": catastrophes, the photo finish, etc.), Henri Cartier-Bresson captured in his photographs the ordinary and the unexceptional.[12]

One aspect of Cartier-Bresson's work, then, and an aspect which the Candid-Eye doubtless found important, is that it represents a forward step of the demotic tradition in photography. Photography was first called into being when acceleration in the rate of change prompted the recognition of the radical limitations of human vision; it enabled man to capture and freeze a moment within this realm of flux, preserving it for scrutiny in a way that eye sight never could.[13]

Thus, photography was forged to capture the everyday, the ordinary, that which was subject to change. Accordingly, there developed in the early days of photography a genre dealing with the street, for the locus of the acceleration in the rate of change was the city, and the central symbol of the city is the street. Soon, however, an "artistic" approach to photography was developed. In the attempt to elevate photography to the realm of art, a pictorialist style was developed which was based upon strategies in the use of texture, atmosphere, composition and framing which attempted to purge the image of its literalness and worldliness and to raise the subject matter of the photograph to the realm of the transcendental.

By the thirties, a sharp challenge to the pictorialist ambitions of art photography was being posed in the work of Walker Evans, Alfred Steiglitz and Paul Strand. These photographers rejected the use of painterly devices and those strategies designed to elevate the subject matter of the photograph to the transcendental, and took a more literal approach to the photographic image.[14]

This conflict between the pictorialist and literalist approaches to photography rehearsed the conflict between premodernist and modernist concerns[15] in the arts inasmuch as it exemplified a struggle for a modern way of seeing which included the factual, the literal, as a part[16]—a struggle for the right of the real, the everyday, the fleeting and the momentary to occupy a legitimate position in a work of art.

Initially, however, this right was not asserted without reservation, for in the work of these photographers the real found its place only by virtue of a kind of formal appropriation in which the real was transformed to conform to certain formal aesthetic canons. The dialectic between real object and its formal transformation constitutes the major source of tension in an overwhelmingly large proportion of the works of this school.

Once the right of the real to take its place in an art object had been established, on those terms, the struggle became one to allow the real to enter the art-work more on its own terms. The first stage in this struggle was conducted primarily in the field of photojournalism. Certain photojournalists began to develop a style of documentation which precluded the necessity of the real to conform to certain formal canons, thus gaining a victory in the overthrow of those conventions exemplified in the work of Steiglitz, Strand and Evans. Their victory, however, was again qualified in that they took as their subject matter scenes from the underbelly of society. In this way they transformed the document into an image of the exotic, the strange, at times even the bizarre.[17]

Thus, although adherence to formal conventions was markedly reduced in the work of these photojournalists, new conventions arose which derived from the choice of the exotic as subject matter.[18] Full victory in the struggle for the right of the real to enter the work of art had still not been gained for it was only by conformity to certain criteria of the dramatic that the real was allowed to occupy that place.

In the photojournalism of Cartier-Bresson these tendencies towards dramatization were to a considerable degree repudiated. Cartier-Bresson's work does not treat that special class of events (e.g., the catastrophic, the photo-finish), which lent a dramatic quality to the photojournalism which preceded him. His photographs are instead drawn from the everyday. This turn away from the dramatic towards the ordinary is, however, accompanied by a renewed formal interest, for "the decisive moment" approach to photography practiced by Cartier-Bresson consists in selecting from the everyday occurrence precisely that moment in which the pictorial elements in the scene interrelate to form a rigorously composed design.[19] Thus, his works depend upon the tension arising from the dialectical relationship existing between the ordinariness of the occurrences selected for representation and the precision of the formal framework in which these occurences are represented.

In an important sense, therefore, the "decisive moment" approach in photography still rested on the sense of privilege attaching to certain selected fragments of reality by virtue of their conformity to certain formal canons. It is important to note, however, that this conformity obtains in the photographs of Cartier-Bresson in a somewhat different manner than it did in photographs of Steiglitz, Strand, Evans and Weston. In the work of this group the conformity was photographically imposed—it was obtained by using such techniques as the manipulation of depth of focus, of framing, of the control of tones in printing. Cartier-Bresson refuses to impose such a formal framework on the event;[20] rather he discovers it in the event as it runs its natural course.[21]

The Candid-Eye filmmakers in Unit B of the National Film Board followed Cartier-Bresson's lead in rejecting as object matter those special events so valued by the "direct cinema" filmmakers of the American school, and in repudiating the use of dramatic frameworks within which to represent these events. They chose, for the most part, everyday events—tobacco harvesting, the daily round of police activity, days before Christmas, the very ordinary side of the making of a popular music star—and, as did Cartier-Bresson, allowed the formal structure of the work to evolve organically out of the events themselves. Moreover, like Cartier-Bresson, the Candid-Eye filmmakers leaned towards formal rigour rather than dramatic importance in the selection of their images. It is for this reason, I believe, that the Candid-Eye films always have a more polished surface than those of their American counterparts. This refusal to impose forms in the matter being represented and the concomitant desire to allow the forms to evolve organically stem from a particular conception of the photographic image—one which holds that the particular virtue of the photographic essay lies in the character of presenting a detached and objective model of representation.[22]

In keeping with this conception of the virtues of the photographic process, the structures which the Candid-Eye group developed were observational in character; i.e., they are imitative of the acts of an observer witnessing the unfolding of a spectacle. This general character, however, was further specified by two additional conditions: first, in order to remain within the realm of the non-dramatic, the events that were chosen as object matter had to be limited to everyday events; second, in order to remain fully consistent with that quality of photography just described, the structures had to imply a radically detached, non-involved spectator who is neither physically engaged in effecting the course of action of the pro-filmic event nor intellectually active in imposing a preconceived grid on the events. Generally, the most effective sort of structure which evolved to meet these conditions was one whose progression is homologous with the process by which an outsider develops familiarity with an event, character or situation.[23]

The ideological implications of this sort of structure are revealing. The extreme sense of detachment which this suggests and which in the Candid-Eye films often passes over into a kind of self-abandonment in the face of reality implies a form of consciousness which is alienated from the world and whose sole activity is limited to passive observation—a consciousness then which plays no role in the structuring either of reality or of our perception of it. The continual rehearsal of the process of becoming familiar with the everyday things around one suggests the extreme alienation of this consciousness as it tries to come to terms with a world beyond itself. Behind this lies a view of reality which, because it is thought to be beyond the individual's control, appears as mystified and needing continually to be demystified. It is hardly surprising, for it is in keeping with the colonized outlook which all of this embodies, that the structures employed in the Candid-Eye films should suggest that the attempt of the overcoming of this alienation occurs only at a the level of cognition.

In all of this, one is reminded of Frantz Fanon's analysis of the stages of development of colonial art.[24] According to Fanon, the development of national art occurs in three stages: the phase of assimilation of the colonizer's art; a phase of the affirmation of past, native culture but articulated from an external point of view—the view of the colonizer; and finally a fighting phase in which the artist becomes an awakener of the people. The consistently national object matter of the Candid-Eye films situate them within the second phase of Fanon's historical schema.

The benchmarks of this second phase, described by Fanon, precisely characterize the Candid-Eye work. Fanon states that this phase is characterised by an ironic sort of humour. This sense of irony arises from the dialectic inherent in the position of the artist in this period of development: on the one hand he is committed to a national culture, while on the other he views the national culture from a detached, external and hence often amused point of view. The Candid-Eye films frequently exemplify this kind of detached, ironic humour. *Lonely Boy* again is a case in point; the object matter is Canadian but the vantage point taken is a detached one from which the singer is ironically viewed as a kind of amusing, manufactured commodity whose appeal is that of an adolescent curiosity-piece. How far this is from the point of view taken by Leacock and Pennebaker on Jane Fonda's attempt to achieve stardom, which is seen as the stuff of real human drama.

Another contrast between the two films, explainable on Fanon's model, concerns the difference in the degree of rigour of the structures of the two works. The American work employs a very tight structure, as all the incidents of the film relate directly to that one single contest-type situation which provides the central focal point for the entire work. The Canadian film, by comparison, is extremely diffuse and episodic, presenting us with a number of incidents which purport to give us an in-depth portrayal of the man behind the star and of those forces which operate in shaping his stardom.

The effect of this lack of a central focussing event is that the incidents in the film tend to break up into a kind of shower of discrete particulars. Fanon's model would explain this in terms of the artist's grasp of historical realities at this stage in the evolution of national culture. The artist's detachment prevents him from understanding the inner workings of reality or the logic beneath the unfolding of events. As a result, he can see reality as a series of accidental occurrences, that is, only as a kind of assemblage of separate particulars. For this reason, that structure employed in the films of Drew Associates which depends upon a grasp of the homology between the dramatic form and the structure of conflicts which characterize the inner working of reality is not available to the colonized artist of this phase. His work is restricted to presenting merely the surfaces of reality. Thus, what was claimed to be the result of a meritous, willful detachment shows itself, on deeper study, to be a meretricious, alienated lack of understanding. This sort of realism surely deserves the appellation it has sometimes been given—"naive realism."

NOTES

1. Frequently, melodramatic narratives were used in the works of these schools in order to sketch in outline the architectonic of the dramatic form. Thus, the outline of the formal structure of the narrative, to be completed by the integration of the real, is presented almost schematically.
2. On a theoretical level, this tendency was defended by André Bazin in his article, "Montage Interdit." This article presents an argument to the effect that integration of reality and the drama is an essential feature to truly cinematic works.
3. The first fully developed "direct cinema" works in Canada date from 1958 (*Blood and Fire, The*

Back-Breaking Leaf)—anticipating the Drew/Leacock *Primary* by almost two full years—and the roots of the style in Canada can be traced back at least to 1952.

4. On this topic, see Mamber's incisive study of American-type *cinéma-vérité, Cinema Verite in America.*
5. Ibid.
6. Perhaps explaining this idea in another manner would help to clarify it. By basing the films on a contest-type situation, one is guaranteed that there will be a central problematic posed by the film which can be expressed in the form "Will A win over B" and that this question will be answered by following the external course of development of the event. This entails that the course of the unfolding of the physical event is homologous with the form for the drama and thus that a document of the unfolding of the event will possess at least a degree of dramatic intrigue.
7. As an interesting aside to this point, one might note how in these films the conception of a man's real nature is ideologically bound. In every case, man is shown to have the ability to survive under stress, to carry on his struggle despite defeat. As Mamber points out, this is a very American conception of human nature. Mamber compares the depiction of the central protagonist in the Drew films to Hawks's conception of hero. (Though the idea of hero is opposite, I should think the best parallel would be found in the works of Hemingway.) Mamber fails to note, however, how often this depiction of the American is permeated with that strong tone of condescension, even contempt, which is so typical of the eastern American attitude toward the ideals of Middle America. Leacock is most guilty in this regard: *Happy Mother's Day* is thoroughly infected with an attitude of contempt only partially redeemed by his so obvious humane sympathy for Mrs. Fisher. Furthermore, Mamber fails to note how the ambitious, striving American-hero character is consistently depicted in these works as a mask, disguising the underlying essence. The importance of the crisis-type of situation is precisely that it provides the stress to crack open this mask and reveal the real nature of the human character.
8. The fact that this conception of the character's real nature is ideologically determined does nothing to refute the claim that the work derives its structure from reality, for the character's revelation of himself at the moments after the crisis surely admits of something that is undeniably real. What is ideologically determined is the conception that what is revealed in the aftermath of the crisis situation is more basic to the human constitution than what is revealed in the character's choices of his goals. This conception of the unity of truth and beauty, of the affinity between natural and artistic forms (indicated by the use of natural activities to provide the structure by which aesthetic tensions are resolved) and of the organic character of a work of art indicates the allegiance of this kind of cinema (and more generally of the stream of modernism with which it is associated) to the aesthetics of Romanticism.
9. It should go without saying that the ideological implications of this shift in direction in the film are quite profound and disturbing.
10. The examples I have chosen are not isolated cases of the refusal to use dramatic forms for the documentation of situations which have an inherent dramatic potential; indeed, the entire history of the Candid-Eye movement is a succession of crisis-type situations refused, of conflicts not taken into account. Two further examples one could point to are *Blood and Fire* which could have been developed as a drama of the struggle to save souls, and *I Was a 90-Pound Weakling* which could have been a dramatic presentation of individuals striving to overcome their physical limitations.
11. This influence has been attested to by the Candid-Eye filmmakers themselves, for example, Terence Macartney-Filgate in an interview with Sarah Jennings (see "An Interview with Terence Macartney-Filgate" in this book).
12. This approach places the work of Cartier-Bresson within the streams of modernism which eschewed the use of dramatic forms because they tended to privilege certain moments over others. The logical extension of this trend was to repudiate even Cartier-Bresson's "decisive moment" (which will be discussed shortly) and to capture the moments before or after it. This was the step taken by Robert Frank in his important ground-breaking book, *The Americans.*
13. The idea that photography developed when a series of technical innovations made it possible is simply historically false; all the technical components necessary for the development of photography were in existence at least two hundred years prior to its invention.
14. This chronological method of presentation of course oversimplifies and distorts the actual history, for there were at all times literalist as well as pictorialist tendencies co-existing; in fact, at times literalist and pictorialist features co-exist in the work of a single photographer. This chronology does, nonetheless, outline some essential tendencies in the history of photography. (A cogent presentation of the conflict between these two modes of photography is Walker Evans's article in *Hound and Horn* no. 37.)
15. Here I use the term "modernism" not to refer to those tendencies described by Clement Green as defining modernist painting, but to refer to that stream of art flowing from impression.
16. Hence the resemblance between the object matter of much of literalist photography (and of the affinities of photography discussed by Kracauer in his *Theory of Film*) and the object matter of much of impressionist painting.
17. Susan Sontag has described the way in which Surrealism lay close to the heart of the photographic enterprise itself, and showed how those photographs which eschew the

decorative convention introduced by Surrealism into the other arts and cling more nearly to the reproductive process are the most likely to be surreal. An overwhelmingly powerful demonstration of this in films is, of course, Luis Buñuel's *Las Hurdes.* (See Susan Sontag, "Shooting America," *The New York Review of Books*, April 18, 1974.)

18. An alternate approach of the early photojournalist was to deal with the noteworthy, even the spectacular. But here again, the real was allowed to enter the work of art only by virtue of its dramatic qualities.
19. It was not until Robert Frank's publication of *The Americans* that this approach was rejected. Frank refused to select those climactic moments which constituted the object matter of Cartier-Bresson's photographs and instead selected moments precisely on the basis of their ordinariness—of their being typical of the run of events.
20. So extreme is Cartier-Bresson's stance on this matter that he photographs only with a 50mm lens—a lens the angle of acceptance of which most nearly approximates the angle of acceptance of human vision, and he refuses to crop or otherwise manipulate the print in printing.
21. This principle underlying Cartier-Bresson's practice is allied very closely with that principle of non-interference in the pro-filmic event so dear to all practicioners of "direct cinema" in North America. No doubt this accounts in part for the affinity which the Candid-Eye filmmakers felt for his work.
22. This tendency in the practice of photography of this period also finds expression in the theories of photography which evolved contemporaneously. Aestheticians of the time often made claims for the virtues of photograph quality self-effacement. It is noteworthy that these claims for objectivity, for the detached, unmanipulative characteristics of photography, arose only in the mid-fifties.
23. This sort of structure was first used in cinema in the works of Robert Flaherty. It is noteworthy that Flaherty felt compelled to resolve such a structure with a dramatic finale, while the Candid-Eye filmmakers felt no such compulsion.
24. "On National Culture," *The Wretched of the Earth* (New York: Grove Press, 1968).

64

JONAS MEKAS

TO MAYOR LINDSAY / ON FILM JOURNALISM AND NEWSREELS (1966)

To Mayor Lindsay

So the city is clubbing the arts again! So they are burning the books again, so they are tearing apart the little strips of films and the white blood of celluloid is drying in the impersonal and cold-eyed offices of the city.

The whole censorship and licensing business has become so childish by now that it's difficult even to get outraged about it. We all know that any official censorship of art (or life) is doomed, because man has entered into a different, freer, higher stage of consciousness. It's no use wasting much energy on fighting censorship: Censors and licensors are the last craggy symptoms of the old New York. There is a new New York coming! It's almost here! Mayor Lindsay: Please put your ear to the windows, and to the walls, and to the ground, and listen to the new vibrations in the air—and it's not only because it's April! It's a different kind of April that's in the air. Cleaners of the city: Don't put the poor 42nd Street souls and artists in jails: Hire them to paint the subways white and in colors and flowers, and put music in subways, and 8 mm. movie screens so that the uptown and downtown ride will be like really going home, or like really going to see a friend. Oh, there are so many things to do in spring! Dear Mayor Lindsay: Don't let yourself be dragged down by the ghosts of the past!

On Film Journalism and Newsreels

I have been thinking and thinking these last few weeks, and now I should tell you what's bothering me. It's this: There are so many things happening round us, from the ghettos of L.A. to the smoky outskirts of Chicago and all across the country and in Vietnam, and in our own small city—big things, and small things, ugly things, and things like the eyes eaten out by smog, falling out and rolling into the gutters; and how the GIs are dying smiling and happy and in glory like butterflies. Things like that. We see nothing in our movies! And I am not talking about our poets: Our film poets have made the most beautiful poems in the world. I am talking about newsreels and about documentaries and about real life commentaries. With all the new techniques and equipment available to us, with almost weightless and almost invisible cameras, 8 mm. and 16 mm., and with sound, we can go today into any place we want and put everything on film. Why do we neglect film journalism? Eight mm. movies should be secretly shipped from Vietnam; 8 mm. movies should be shipped from the South; 8 mm. movies taken by the ten-year-old Harlem kids armed not with guns but 8 mm. cameras—let's flash them on our theatre screens, our home screens; 8 mm. movies smuggled out of prisons, of insane asylums, everywhere, everywhere. There should be no place on earth not covered by 8 mm. movies, no place without the buzzing of our 8 mm. cameras! Let's show everything, everything. We can do it today. We have to go through this, so that we can go to other things. We have to see everything, to look at everything through our lenses, see everything like for the first time: From a man sleeping, from our own navels, to our more complex daily activities, tragedies, loves, and crimes. Somewhere, we have lost touch with our own reality and the camera eye will help us to make contact again.

Why should we leave all reporting to the press and TV? They are nice people but they are interested in making a living, in money, in many nice things, but not in seeing things. We know that we can never see things as they are, but at least we can come closer to them so that we could feel the warmth of their being or the coldness of their death.

Let's swamp the Cinematheque with newsreels, home-movie newsreels, not the Pathé Bros. newsreels, not the Walter Cronkite reports!

If anyone would ask me what was the most important thing that happened in cinema last week, I would answer that it was Shirley Clarke (who made *The Cool World* and *The Connection*) buying an 8 mm. camera! She is not ashamed of the tiny little 8 mm. camera, she is carrying it everywhere with her, and she is shooting, shooting. I am certain that this marks another big crack in Papa's cinema: That big ship will surely sink. And don't misunderstand me: We like studios and we like 70 mm. and we are going to shoot one million and ten million movies. But we have to do the 8 mm. job too.

The Film-Makers' Cooperative has established the End of Century Newsreel series which will be shipped to colleges, universities, theatres, and whoever wants them. Home-movie-makers all over the world are being asked to film and send to the Co-op whatever happens around the town, this city, country; whatever is exciting, terrible, or beautiful for others to see and to know. We have to start doing this *right now*. Let's record the dying century and the birth of another man. The time is here to change the ways of journalism on this planet Earth. The schools of journalism will soon replace their writing classes with 8 mm. movie-making classes. Let's surround the earth with our cameras, hand in hand, lovingly; our camera is our third eye that will lead us out and in and through. The buzz of our cameras should be louder then the buss of the fuzz. Nothing should be left unshown or unseen, dirty or clean: *Let us see* and go further, out of the swamps and into the sun.

65

JEANNE HALL

REALISM AS A STYLE IN CINEMA-VERITE

A Critical Analysis of *Primary* (1991)

There is a feeling in the air that cinema is only just beginning.

—The editors of Film Culture, awarding Drew Associates the "Independent Film Award" for *Primary* (1960)[1]

Opening a Can of Worms

In March of 1961, Robert Drew announced what *Broadcasting* magazine would dub the "three commandments" of "television's school of storm and stress": "I'm determined to be there when the news happens. I'm determined to be as unobtrusive as possible. And I'm determined not to distort the situation."[2] The name "school of storm and stress" was a glib reference to Drew's preference for subjects wrapped up in their own affairs and apparently oblivious to camera and crew. "I seek people driven by their own forces—forces so strong that they can forget about me," he said.[3] And indeed, in 1960 Drew produced films on the candidates in the Wisconsin Democratic presidential primary, on the winner of the coveted "pole" position in the Indianapolis 500 race, on protestors in Havana's Plaza Civica after Cuba's expulsion from the Organization of American States, and on the parents of students in Louisiana schools during court-ordered desegregation.[4] But the name "school of storm and stress" did not, as it turned out, stick. Neither did "living camera," the title Drew Associates preferred. Their work finally came to be known as "cinema verite," a decidedly pretentious term for which members of the group would endure much abuse, even though they seldom used it themselves.[5] And it could, of course, have been worse: one critic referred to the style as "cinema manqué" and another as "cinema banalité."[6] But cinema verite had as many champions as critics, and the work of Drew Associates inspired a feeling, for some, that cinema was "only just beginning."

"The kind of documentary Mr. Drew describes is the purest documentary of all," declared John Secondari, Executive Producer at ABC-TV in 1963. "When you can tell a story as it unfolds, with your camera and without very much need of words, you have documentary in the palm of your hands."[7] Louis Marcorelles spoke of the work of Drew Associates as part of a "revolution" that would be as important to the future of the cinema as Brecht was to the theater. "Truth no longer lies in seeming to give a 'good performance,' a star turn," he wrote for *Sight & Sound* in 1963, "but in seizing the individual unawares, rather as you may discover the real face of a woman in the early morning on the pillow beside you."[8] With the emergence of cinema verite, something close to a modern religion was born, according to James Blue. "Cinema verite has its orthodoxies, its heresies, its unitarians and its fundamentalists," he wrote for *Film Comment* in 1965. "At no time in the history of film art have mystical and moral considerations been so important in the formation of a film aesthetic."[9] And perhaps, as critics would later allege, some of the cinema verite filmmakers got as caught up in the mystique of their movement as their subjects were wrapped up in their problems. In 1965, Blue described the cinema of Albert Maysles as "one in which ethics and aesthetics are interdependent, where beauty starts with honesty, where a cut or a change in camera angle can become not only a possible aesthetic error but also a 'sin' against Truth."[10] The same year, Richard Leacock admitted, "In a funny sort of way, my hunch is that what we are doing is the most important thing that film can do."[11]

The notion that limiting voice-over narration might render an image "pure," or that the "Truth" might simply reveal itself if a subject were caught unawares—the notion, as Bill Nichols put it, that "the world and its truths exist; they need only be dusted off and reported"[12]—would be the subject of a devastating critique mounted by contemporary film theorists before the end of the 1970s. Stephen Mamber was perhaps the last critic to approach the documentaries of Drew Associates from a classical perspective. In *Cinema Verite in America* (1974), Mamber almost reluctantly acknowledged that the myth of total cinema was finally just that: "Given that no film can ever break down completely the barrier between the real world and the screen world, cinema verite knowingly reaches for unattainable goals."[13] But he insisted that the realism of these documentaries, "the sense of life going on beyond the camera," was more than a function of film style. For Mamber, it was based on cinema verite's unique relation to the real. "This is not a sense expressed through visual metaphor or expressive camera technique," he argued, "but a result of refusing to make events subordinate to filming by means of direct control."[14] Cinema verite "is an attempt to strip away the accumulated conventions of traditional cinema in the hope of rediscovering a reality that eludes other forms of filmmaking," he wrote. As such, there should be "all the difference in the world" between cinema verite and the fictional and traditional documentary film.[15]

"This claim to a new privileged grasp of reality," as Thomas Waugh would write one year later, "appears in retrospect to have been somewhat naive."[16] In 1975, Waugh criticized the filmmakers who, "grouped around Drew Associates, rushed into the streets with their 'caméra-stylos' and discovered, as if for the first time, the vitality of 'unmediated' existence. They talked of honesty, intimacy and above all objectivity, as if these old brickbats of aesthetics had been invented along with the Nagra."[17] While Waugh chided the naïveté of filmmakers like Leacock and Drew, Nichols chided the naïveté of film scholars like Mamber. In *Ideology and the Image* (1981), Nichols wrote: "Stephen Mamber claims that this kind of cinema verite involves 'a faith in unmanipulated reality, a refusal to tamper with life as it presents itself.' The ghost of André Bazin notwithstanding, neither Wiseman nor the others mentioned [Richard Leacock, Donn Alan Pennebaker and Albert Maysles among them] create a neutral or objective style."[18] But the zeal of a handful of "eager young camera wizards" and the enthusiasm of a classical critic could ultimately be overlooked. The most serious liability of the movement, for Waugh, was "its persistent pretense of impartiality."[19] He argued that the 1960s saw a need for more explicit socio-political analysis to support the momentum of alternative politics—a need that cinema verite filmmakers, with their scrupulous objectivity and apolitical anonymity, failed to address. "The failure of Leacock, Wiseman *et al.* was a particularly bitter one" for Waugh, because of their widespread reputation as social critics and because of the potentially activist liberal audience their films addressed.[20] Rather than facilitate social change, they "merely reflected and reinforced a mood which in itself was not enough." Waugh's advocation of "the new documentary of the seventies" (epitomized for him as well as for Nichols by the films of Emile de Antonio) as a radical alternative to the observational strategies of cinema verite was reminiscent of Eisenstein's rejection of Vertov's "kino-eye" in favor of his own "kino-fist."

If cinema verite's claim to "a new privileged grasp of reality" struck post-1968 scholars as naïve, most nonetheless assumed that documentary spectators were naïve enough to be fooled. "In pure cinema verite films, the style seeks to become 'transparent' in the same mode as the classical Hollywood style," Nichols claimed, "capturing people in action and letting the viewer come to conclusions about them unaided by any implicit or explicit commentary."[21] Such "transparency" was seen as treacherous by contemporary documentary theorists. In 1977, for example, Jeanne Allen argued that unless a documentary is flagrantly reflexive, the spectator "apprehends the 'reality' presented by the film as the only one there for the filmmaker to show."[22] And Jay Ruby claimed that cinema verite films, conspicuously lacking in reflexivity, might "foster a dangerous false consciousness" among documentary viewers.[23] One could, of course, argue that cinema verite documentaries drew attention to their own devices a good deal more than most, and that the verite style was anything but transparent, especially in the early 1960s. Ruby in fact admits that some elements of cinema verite films (for example, shots in which the microphone and/or sound person appears) "have been regarded by some audiences as being reflexive."[24] But he discounts all such instances because he doubts that cinema verite filmmakers could have been clever enough to include them intentionally. Similarly, Allen acknowledges that cinema verite's handheld camera might remind viewers of the specific—hence limited—perspective of the filmmaker, but she, too, dismisses such devices because they do not apparently "comment upon themselves within the scope of the film."[25]

And so, like the classical Hollywood cinema (*against* which members of Drew Associates sought to define their form), cinema verite was denounced as a transparent purveyor of ideology. Reflexive documentary filmmakers like Jean Rouch, Jean-Luc Godard, and Emile de Antonio became the darlings of contemporary documentary theory, and indeed, such filmmakers were among the harshest critics of American verite. At the Marché International des Programmes et Equipments de Télévisión, held at Lyon in 1963, for example, Rouch claimed that Leacock accepted "too readily and uncritically" everything he saw.[26] "Nothing will help make an image clear if the intentions are fuzzy," wrote Godard, in reference to both the studied objectivity of cinema verite filmmakers and the blurred, grainy visuals that had come to signify truth.[27] "Cinema verite is first of all a lie and secondly a childish assumption about the nature of film," de Antonio charged. "Cinema verite is a joke. Only people without feelings or convictions could even think of making cinema verite."[28]

Cinema verite, as Noël Carroll quips, "opened a can of worms and then got eaten by them."[29] The rhetoric of the movement quickly fell out of fashion as contemporary film theory called into question the apparently obvious nature of the cinematic sign. Cinema verite filmmakers burst on the scene in 1960 talking of "honesty, intimacy, and above all objectivity"—but by the end of the decade, film studies programs were teaching ideology, interpellation and subjectivity. Cinema verite filmmakers, with their liberal humanism and unabashed empiricism, became easy targets indeed.[30] It is not hard to see why contemporary critics bristled at the rhetoric of the movement. In 1965, Richard Leacock insisted that his work was *more* than just realistic: "And then you've got what we are doing, which has suddenly arisen, which is totally different because this *really* has to do with reality."[31] Documentary scholars were of course right to question such claims. But most simply dismissed cinema verite films for not being "windows on the world" and denounced cinema verite filmmakers for believing or pretending that they were. And many relied upon the rhetoric of the movement for information about the films rather than on the sounds and images of the films themselves.

The rhetoric of the cinema verite movement thus took on a life of its own. Cinema verite filmmakers claimed to have created a cinema in which "the story tells itself through pictures, not through word logic, lecture logic, written logic or interviews."[32] With characteristic audacity, Robert Drew once invited viewers to turn off the sound on their television sets and "follow the logic—even the drama—of the show in what evolves *visually*."[33] Years later, critics would describe cinema verite as "a predominantly visual documentary form,"[34] one whose "address emanates solely from the image track."[35] Others would acknowledge that cinema verite films had soundtracks, but deny they had voice-over narration. One critic, for example, describes the experience of watching the early films of Drew like this: "Deprived of a narrator, the viewer must make the logical connections between shots and scenes. Verbal information is carried not by a carefully scripted narration recorded in a studio, but through sync-sound dialogue recorded 'on the run.' "[36] In fact, all of the early Drew films have "carefully scripted narration recorded in a studio"—and some, like *Yanki No!* (1960) and *Adventures on the New Frontier* (1961), each with well over 2,000 words of it, come remarkably close to delivering the "illustrated lectures" Drew despised.

Cinema verite filmmakers claimed to have created a cinema in which no side was taken and no cause defended. "I think my main feeling about film [is that it] should not lecture," Pennebaker told Gideon Bachmann in 1961.[37] "The moment I sense that I'm being *told* the answer, I tend to start rejecting it," Leacock told James Blue in 1965.[38] Years later, critics would write of cinema verite's "persistent pretense of impartiality"[39] and describe the verite documentarist as "a neutral observer, not a polemicist."[40] In fact, some of the first films of Drew Associates are openly argumentative. *Yanki No!* begins with the announcement, "This is a film editorial," and ends with an impassioned plea for more aid to Latin America.

The Children Were Watching (1960) does not explicitly announce itself as an editorial, but its denunciation of white segregationists is uncompromising. A reviewer for *The New York Times* aptly described the film as "a bold editorial in impressive, often frightening terms," "thirty hard-hitting minutes that were not diluted by trying to please everyone."[41]

Cinema verite filmmakers claimed not to use interviews. "I think even interviewing can establish a control over the subject, or can introduce your propulsion into the subject to such an extent that from then on you won't get what that character would have done without the interview," Drew said in 1963.[42] Years later, critics would claim that "the interview was eschewed as a form of camera-created reality" in American cinema verite films.[43] But a close look at the first films of Drew Associates suggests that the filmmakers routinely conducted interviews—and routinely edited half of each exchange from the finished film. The voters on the streets of Wisconsin in *Primary*, the wife of the race car driver in *On the Pole* (1960), the Soviet seaman in *Yanki No!*, the aviator's secretary in *X-Pilot* (1960), the chief of police in *The Children Were Watching*—all speak directly to the camera, quite clearly in response to a question. Thus, it is not that members of Drew Associates did not conduct interviews, but rather, as *Broadcasting* reported in 1961, that "Mr. Drew's interviewers are for the most part not seen. Even their questions are sometimes not heard by the viewer. From Mr. Drew's point of view, the questions are seldom as important as the answers."[44]

Cinema verite filmmakers claimed to be as unobtrusive as possible, to become like flies on the wall. Drew once insisted that he and his team became "part of the woodwork" in Kennedy's Oval Office "as we did most every place else."[45] Received wisdom has it not that cinema verite filmmakers actually achieved such invisibility, but that all evidence of their inevitable obtrusiveness wound up on the cutting room floor. But in fact, many of the early Drew films feature subjects directly addressing the camera, often referring explicitly to the filmmaking process. "You must go there and take pictures," says the Venezuelan diplomat in *Yanki No!* "I hope for your camera studies that you can get these pictures at night," says the aviator in *X-Pilot*. "Take an old man's picture, son, who's been here and knows about it, and prove what he tells you," says the old man from West Virginia in *Adventures on the New Frontier*, and the camera zooms in on him slightly, punctuating his address to the filmmakers. In *The Children Were Watching*, the screen goes black for several seconds after a protester lashes out at the camera—reminding viewers of the subject's awareness of the filmmaker's presence indeed.

To see the early films of Drew Associates for the first time today is to be amazed at how remotely they resemble their descriptions. True, most of them feature the restless, wandering movements of lightweight, handheld cameras; the dark, grainy images of fast, monochrome film; and the impromptu performances of apparently preoccupied social actors—cinema verite innovations which quickly became conventions. But they also feature (variously) voice-over narration, talking heads, avowed editorials, animated maps, superimpositions, subtitles, nondiegetic music, subjective sequences, matches-on-action—countless conventions of the traditional documentary film and the classical Hollywood cinema that serve to foreground the conventional nature of the realism of cinema verite.

If the first films of Drew Associates failed to fulfill the promises of their makers, contemporary documentary theorists have failed to consider them apart from the hyperbolic rhetoric of the movement. One need not watch these films to know that they do not serve up the "truth at twenty-four frames per second," but one *does* need to watch them in order to understand cinema verite's special brand of realism. The discrepancies between the first films of Drew Associates and the literature that surrounds them suggest that it is time to reopen the can of worms that reportedly devoured cinema verite. We may agree that Drew's "claim to a new privileged grasp of reality appears in retrospect to have been somewhat naive," but what do we know of the films he produced? We may agree that these documentaries do not—indeed, could not—fulfill the stated intentions of their makers, but to what extent do the films themselves even purport or pretend to do so? How do the earliest examples of cinema verite combine recorded sounds and images to construct the illusion of "a reality that eludes other forms of filmmaking"? And how do they combine the conventions of the classical Hollywood cinema and the traditional documentary film with the innovations of cinema verite?

I would like to begin to address these questions with a critical analysis of *Primary*, a film heralded as "a revolutionary step and a breaking point in the recording of reality in cinema"[46] in the early 1960s, and widely regarded as "a landmark film in the aesthetic development of cinema verite"[47] today. *Primary* won the *Film Culture* award for best independent film, the Flaherty award for best documentary, and a blue ribbon at the American Film Festival. In Europe, according to Drew, "*Primary* was received as a kind of documentary second-coming."[48] The film was an inspiration to early critics like Marcorelles, who wrote that "it forces us to look at the cinema in an entirely new way, to redefine it in the way that Leacock, at his best, conceived it."[49] Contemporary critics see *Primary* as "the beginning of a major change in the way human events at all levels were recorded and reported," a film that "would irrevocably change the face of documentary, in America and abroad."[50] But although the importance of the film is generally acknowledged or assumed, very little has actually been written about it. Moreover, the literature that does surround *Primary* provides an excellent example of the way in which the rhetoric of the cinema verite movement set the terms for contemporary discussions of early cinema verite films.

For example, while *Primary* may well represent the "beginning of cinema verite in America," as a catalog published by its distributor claims, it is not "the first completely candid film shot entirely in synchronous sound," as the catalog further suggests. Such claims easily find their way into the popular and trade presses; *Primary* is frequently described as the first documentary "made entirely with location sound and without voice-over narration."[51] Academic critics have been less cavalier with their facts, but I would argue that the way in which the film is discussed in the academic press has nonetheless been determined by the rhetoric of the movement. Thus, Stephen Mamber astutely notes: "For a breakthrough in cinema verite, it is surprising what a small portion of *Primary* was shot with synchronized sound." But he holds the filmmakers to their own cinema verite ideal, rather hastily dismissing non-synch segments as "crude," "ineffective," and "agonizingly artificial."[52] Similarly, Robert Allen writes: "Although *Primary* contained some voice-over narration and considerable nonsynchronous footage (the latter necessitated by equipment problems), it was a documentary unlike anything most Americans had ever seen on television or in movie theaters."[53] Like Mamber, Allen acknowledges a discrepancy between the stated goals of the filmmakers and the formal qualities of their most celebrated film. But he dismisses the importance of the "considerable nonsynchronous footage" in *Primary* with a parenthetical aside, apparently because it was originally necessitated by equipment problems rather than intended by auteurs. Moreover, Allen's focus on cinema verite as an alternative practice—a "full-fledged *avant-garde* aesthetic movement"[54]—leads him to emphasize Drew Associates' *departures* from the conventions of the classical Hollywood cinema and the traditional documentary film, rather than to explore the curious mixture of convention and innovation that the group's early works actually employ.

If we take a step back from the rhetoric of the movement, and drop the assumption that sound—especially non-synch sound—is either nonexistent, inappropriate, or unimportant in cinema verite films, we might better analyze the functions and effects of sound in a film like *Primary*. Moreover, a close analysis of sound-image relations in the film suggests a strategy not apparent upon casual viewing (and certainly not perceptible with the sound turned off). It is, I will argue, a strategy of cinema verite self-validation, and involves the pairing of asynchronous sounds and images for conventionally realistic effects.

Picture Logic in *Primary*: "The Match Game."

The subject of *Primary* is the 1960 Democratic presidential primary in Wisconsin between Senators John F. Kennedy and Hubert H. Humphrey. (Or, as narrator Joseph Julian explains, "Senator John Kennedy, millionaire, Catholic, Easterner from Masachusetts, is challenging Hubert Humphrey, Midwesterner, senator from Minnesota, in his own backyard, the state of Wisconsin.") A handful of scenes from the film have made their way into documentary history: Humphrey nodding off to sleep in a car on the way to Monona, Kennedy kneading his way through the crowd at a rally in Milwaukee. And a handful of stories about the making of the film have found their way into documentary folklore as well: Drew persuading the future president to allow himself to be filmed ("When Kennedy raised an eyebrow I said, 'Trust us or it cannot be done'"[55]); Leacock dropping midgetape recorders in the ashtrays in Kennedy's suite, then sinking into an armchair with the camera in his lap ("I'm quite sure he hadn't the foggiest notion I was shooting"[56]); Pennebaker standing by in a Minneapolis hotel room where he had set up the team's new "portable" editing machine ("It was the size of a ballroom"[57]).

Primary was produced by Time, Inc. in the hope of selling it to a commercial network. Finally, though, the film was aired only on Time-owned stations. Drew believes one reason the networks passed on *Primary* was that its relative lack of voice-over narration was confusing in a time when spoken narration "carpeted" most network documentaries.[58] He tells of showing the finished film to Elmer Lower, then Vice President of NBC News and later President of ABC News: "So I was very proud of the film and took it to Elmer and showed it to him. And his comment was, 'You've got some nice footage there.' But his implication was that, somehow, we didn't pull it all together. And he clearly missed the narration, you know, a lot of narration."[59] *Primary* contains less than 350 words of voiceover narration. The commentary was written by Drew in what *Broadcasting* called a "staccato style, terse and dramatic, almost like a caption for a magazine photograph."[60] It was delivered in what the magazine described as a "low-keyed" voice by Joseph Julian, who reportedly disdained the "voice of doom" narration of March of Time newsreels.[61] But a low-keyed voice is a relative thing, and Julian himself sounds a bit blustery to viewers today—especially speaking Drew's dramatic words:

> The big handshake, the big rally, the wild race across the landscape searching out voters, all repeated endlessly for days and weeks and months, these are the ordeal and the exhiliration of the U.S. presidential candidate. ...

> Now, traveling along with them, hot on the heels of two fast-moving presidential hopefuls, you are about to see a candidate's view of this frantic process, and an intimate view of the candidates themselves: in their cars and busses; behind the scenes in TV studios and hotel rooms; excited, exhausted, and tensely awaiting the verdict of the voters.

Primary delivers on Drew's promise, and there are moments in the film that seem almost embarrassingly intimate: Humphrey watching *The Red Skelton Show* as his early lead disappears, Kennedy sucking on cigarettes and pacing about his suite. Ironically, though, the most celebrated sequence in the film takes place in a public forum rather than "behind the scenes": at the Kennedy rally in Milwaukee. In a crowded meeting hall in the Polish Catholic district of the city, Kennedy supporters await the Senator's late arrival while rally organizers keep them occupied rehearsing the campaign song ("That was much better—you know you've got to put *feeling* into it"). Albert Maysles's camera is with Kennedy when he arrives, weaving its way through the crowd just behind him. It follows him down a long corridor, up a stairway, through a doorway, and out onto a stage—and finds itself, as he does, before a loudly cheering crowd.

After the spectacular tracking shot of the candidate's arrival, Maysles contents himself with pointing out details at the rally. And when the ever-poised Jacqueline Kennedy approaches a microphone to greet the crowd, his camera settles upon her white-gloved hands, fidgeting nervously behind her back as she speaks (Figure 65.1). The shot was controversial among students of verite from the first. Some, like Gideon Bachmann, objected to the close-up itself: "Maybe I would have seen and shown her hat instead of her hands," he told Drew in an interview for *Film Culture* in 1961. Isolating such a detail "created a reality which was not there."[62] Others appreciated the shot itself, but objected to the way it was edited into the scene. The "problem," according to Stephen Mamber, "is that this detail doesn't first become noticeable within a larger context; it needs to be zoomed in on instead of cut to." Subjective details are fine, but only if viewers can "share in a sense of their discovery."[63]

Again Mamber's aesthetic brings to mind André Bazin. Recall the lengthy footnote in

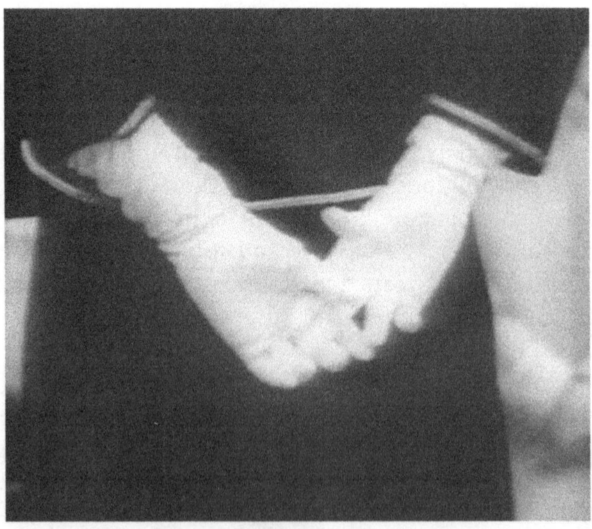

FIGURE 65.1 Screen capture from DVD.

Bazin's "Virtues and Limitations of Montage" essay, in which he describes one unforgettable sequence in an otherwise forgettable English film. The scene involves a young couple, their small child, a lioness and her cub. The child has wandered away from his parents' camp, playfully picked up the cub, and unwittingly alarmed the lioness. Up to this point, as Bazin tells it, everything has been shown in parallel montage. "Then suddenly, to our horror, the director abandons his montage of separate shots that has kept the protagonists apart, and gives us instead parents, child, and lioness all in the same full shot. This single frame in which trickery is out of the question gives immediate and retroactive authenticity to the very banal montage that has preceded it."[64] The scene would have had the same meaning if it had been shot entirely in montage or by process work, Bazin argues, but "in neither event would the scene have unfolded before the camera in its physical and spatial reality . . . [I]t would have had the impact only of a story and not of a real event."[65] For Mamber, the shot of Jacqueline Kennedy's fidgeting fingers in *Primary* has the impact "only of a story and not of a real event" precisely because it is cut to instead of zoomed in on. Indeed, he remarks, "the way the shot appears in the film, it could actually have been photographed days apart from the rest of the scene and simply inserted for dramatic effect."[66]

We need not share Mamber's verite aesthetic in order to appreciate his point: the sound of Jacqueline Kennedy's voice and the image of her hands are paired in a way that is *realistic*, but not necessarily *real*. I want to argue that many of the film's devices function in precisely this way, that *Primary* engages in a sort of "match game" whereby appropriate (if not ontologically linked) images are offered as illustration or explanation for certain sounds. The more likely the sound-image match appears, the more credible the film becomes on its own terms. cinema verite filmmakers probably relinquished more control over the profilmic events they covered than any other documentarists. And yet part of the project of a film like *Primary* is to prove that the filmmakers' diminished control over shooting would ultimately increase spectators' access to the truth. What I've called the "match game" is part of the film's claim to realism; it is an attempt to show that *Primary* can cover not only the planned political drama on stage, but the spontaneous mini-dramas in the audience as well. But the rules of the game are based upon classical conventions of representation rather than cinema verite innovations. Some examples will serve to illustrate this point.

Just before the Kennedys arrive at the rally, a woman announces that cigar and cigarette smoking will be prohibited for the next twenty minutes. Her voice plays over an image of a man lighting up a cigar. As she explains that "there has been some complaint by the women that one of their dresses has been burned by a man smoking a cigar in back of her," we get a close-up of another man, also smoking a cigar, who looks off screen left and continues to puff away (Figure 65.2). As the announcement is completed, drawing jeers and laughter from the crowd, we see a gaunt elderly woman in a feathered hat standing and looking off screen right (Figure 65.3). Although there is no shot establishing spatial proximity between the two—(and indeed, an earlier shot in which the second man appears suggests that he is not seated behind the woman)—the film implies with a neat sound-image juxtaposition and an approximate eyeline match that he is the careless smoker and she the disgruntled owner of a freshly burned dress. Moreover, although the creation of an imaginary relationship between subjects of different shots seems as alien to Drew's aesthetic as the Kuleshov effect to Bazin's, the scene provides a textbook example of the power of juxtaposition. In context, the man appears guilty (although he may well have been photographed before the "no smoking" announcement was made) and the woman

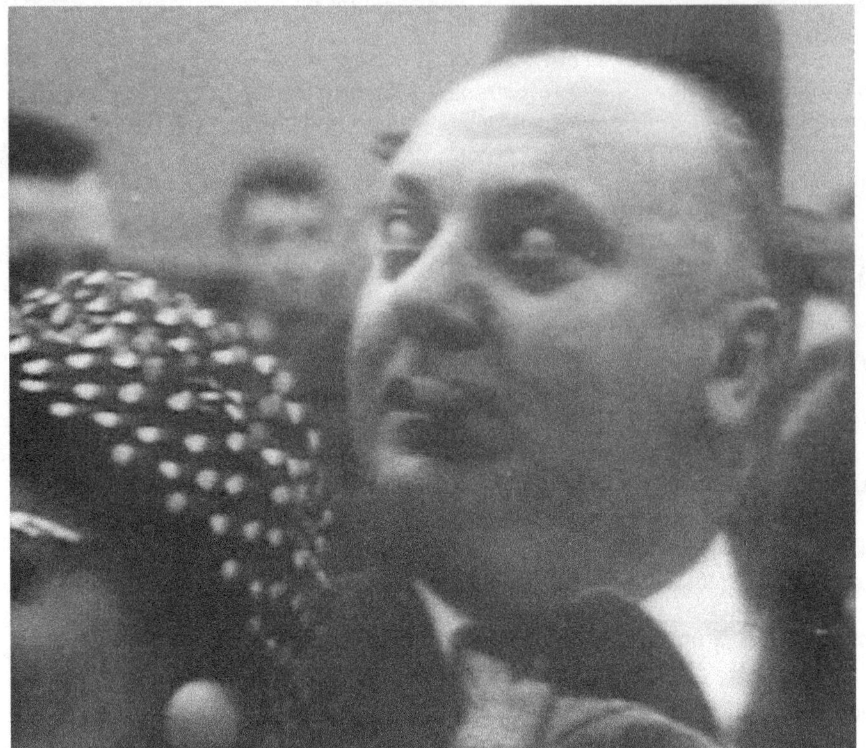

FIGURE 65.2 Screen capture from DVD.

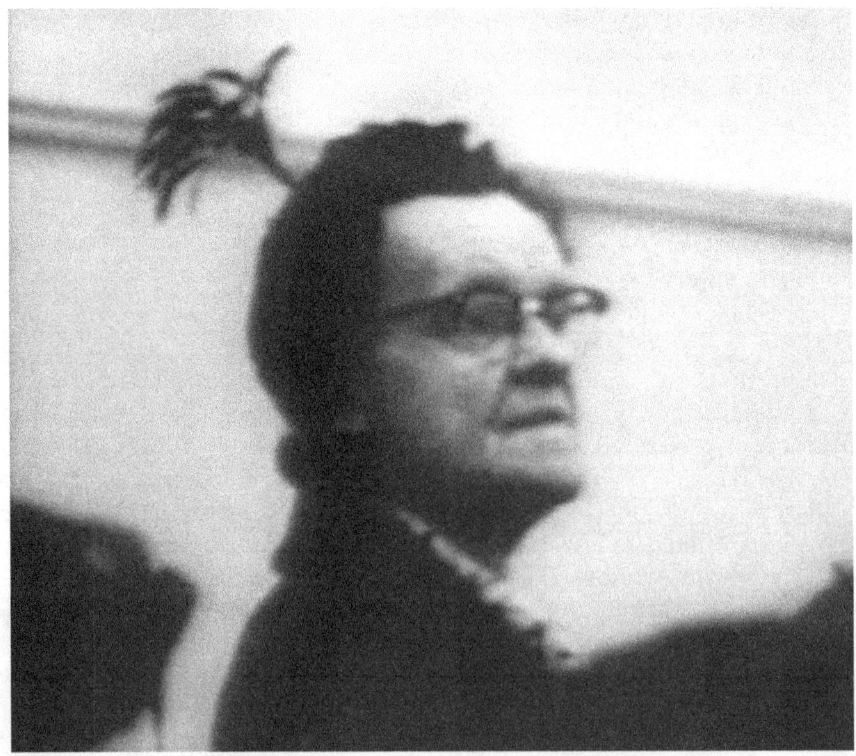

FIGURE 65.3 Screen capture from DVD.

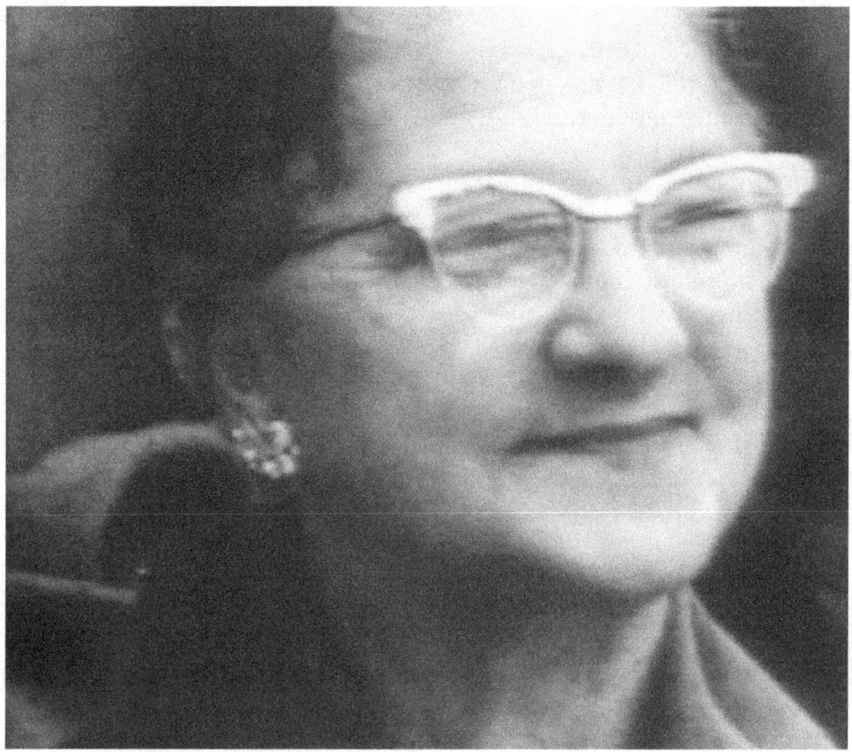

FIGURE 65.4 Screen capture from DVD.

appears angry (although she may simply have been anxious for the Senator to arrive).

A similar sound-image match occurs just as Kennedy reaches the stage. The audience dutifully breaks into the campaign song they've been practicing ("Vote for Kennedy, vote for Kennedy, and you'll end up on top"), and towards the end, the straining voice of an older woman rises high above the rest ("Whoops, there goes the competition, ker-plop"). The camera is fixed upon John and Jacqueline Kennedy standing on the stage, but just as the song ends, we cut to a sweetly smiling elderly woman seated somewhere in the crowd beneath them (Figure 65.4). The cut suggests that she is the enthusiastic crooner, although we never actually see her sing. The scene provides a good example of what Rick Altman calls "the sound hermeneutic": the offscreen sound of the singing voice has an "enigmatic quality which confers upon the image the quality of a response, and thus a certain sense of finality." Like the kitchen scene in *La Règle du jeu* which features the sound of the "Minute Waltz" throughout and ends with a shot of a radio, "the sound asks *where?* and the image responds *here!*"[67]

It is, of course, possible that the individuals who appear on the image track were in fact responsible for the actions attributed to them by the non-synch soundtrack. But it seems more likely that a bit of verite "casting" has occurred in the editing room, and that the "match game" is based upon physical and aural stereotypes: this is the *sort* of man who might be reckless with his ashes, the *type* of old woman who would register a complaint against him, the *kind* of "little old lady" who would sing her heart out, albeit a bit off-key. Based upon traditional conventions of representation, the "matches" are finally rather convincing (imagine switching the "roles" of the two older women about). Verisimilar if not verite, they contribute to our sense that *Primary* is on top of the Kennedy rally—political promises, fidgeting fingers, cigar-burned dresses and all.[68]

A variation of the match game is played again later, and indeed it forms the basis for what Mamber refers to as "a clumsy montage of feet in voting booths"[69] toward the end of the film. "Election day," the narrator announces, "when the voices of the campaign begin to turn into votes." This bit of voice-over commentary suggests an affinity between the opinions expressed in offscreen interviews and the actual votes being cast by the owners of various pairs of feet, which we glimpse under voting booth curtains. (The feet footage, incidentally, was provided by a Wisconsin camera operator; Drew apparently laid the sound on top.)[70] As before, the film relies on our recognition of physical stereotypes as well as regional and class vernaculars. We see the cuffed and pleated trousers of a businessman, the stockings and pumps of a society lady, the dungarees and workboots of a farmer, and the support hose and heavy shoes of an older woman, perhaps a farmer's wife. Frequently (though not always), there are "voices to match."

For example, we hear the mannered voice of a young woman remark, "No, I believe more of the people who are *Republican* will be voting for Humphrey."[71] And as she speaks, we see two shots featuring pairs of feet belonging to two younger women. Both have slender ankles and wear stylish pumps; both rest their weight upon one foot and thrust the other forward in the proper stance for polite women circa 1960 (Figure 65.5). A bit later, we hear the voices of two older women discuss Kennedy's upper-class image in the parlance of common people. ("Just because his *sister's* married to a movie star doesn't make *him* a glamour puss." "He looks like a farmer boy—got a good head of hair on him.") Of the various pairs of feet that pass before us during this conversation, most are older and female, some with support hose stretched over swollen ankles, most wearing heavier, "sensible" shoes, fastened with laces or straps. And most stand with their feet planted squarely beneath them, unlike the "Republican" women seen earlier (Figure 65.6). Several of the voices admit that their vote will be influenced by Kennedy's religion, and it is significant that the voting booth sequence culminates in a shot of what appears to be the gown of a Catholic priest exiting a booth. We can't help but feel that we know how *he* voted—in part because the film encourages us to reason that "anyone who *looks* like this probably *sounds* like this and undoubtedly *votes* like this." The voices of the campaign, as the narrator says, turn into votes indeed.

In his "Rhetoric of the Image" essay, Roland Barthes describes two functions that a linguistic message might serve in relation to an iconic one, functions he terms "anchorage" and "relay." In anchorage, the text delimits the potential meanings of the image, as a caption under a magazine photograph might. In relay, text and image stand in a "complementary relationship" to one another: "The words, in the same way as the images, are fragments of a more general syntagm and the unity of the message is realized at a higher level, that of the story, the anecdote, the diegesis. . . . While rare in the fixed image, this relay-text becomes very important in film, where dialogue functions not simply as elucidation but really does advance the action by setting out, in the sequence of messages, *meanings that are not to be found in the image itself*."[72] Both the rally and voting booth sequences in *Primary* are characterized by this sort of relay; there is nothing in the image of a man smoking a cigar to suggest he has burned a woman's dress, nothing in the image of an older woman's feet to suggest she is voting for Kennedy. This sort of sound-image relationship, whereby an independent meaning is conferred upon an image with sound, is precisely what Drew claimed to avoid by minimizing voice-over

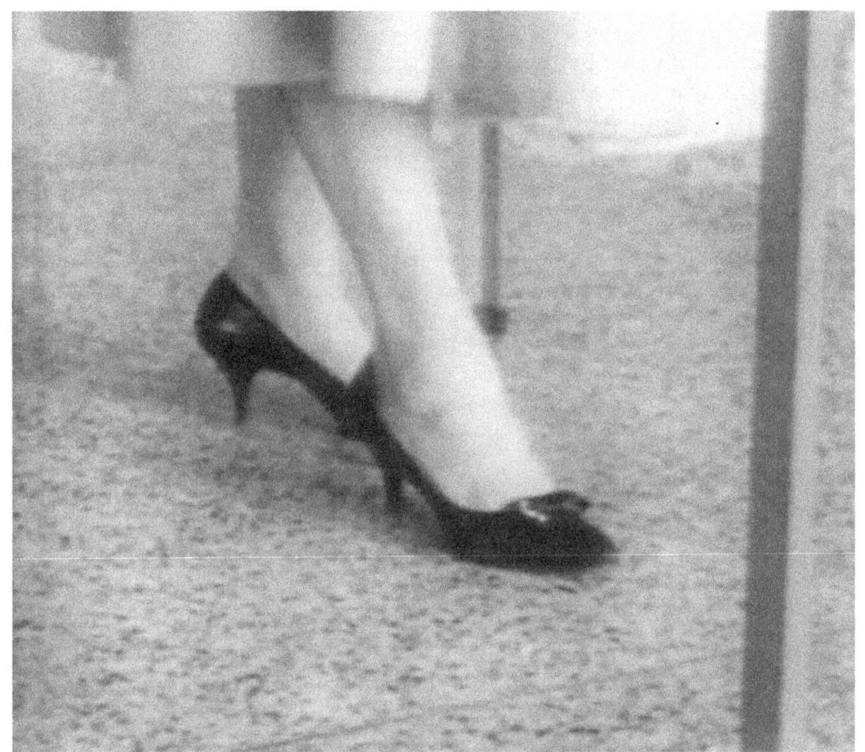

FIGURE 65.5 Screen capture from DVD.

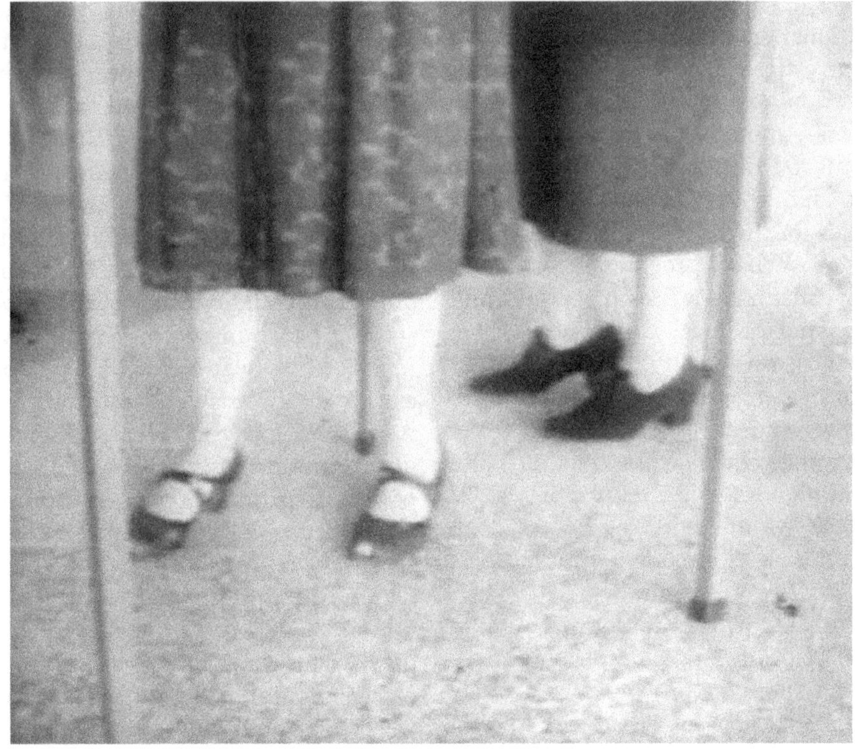

FIGURE 65.6 Screen capture from DVD.

narration in his films. But while Barthes associates the function of relay with dialogue, and Drew attributes a similar function to conventional voiceover narration, the fact is that *any* sound—whether speech, music or noise—can actively shape the way we interpret an image.[73] Sound-image matches in *Primary* are perhaps more subtle than those in the traditional documentaries Drew disdained, but they are finally no less conventional.

Cinema Verite vs. Traditional Documentary: *Primary*'s Critique

I have suggested that part of *Primary's* project is to celebrate cinema verite as a unique source of heretofore privileged information, and that the realism of the film depends in part upon its apparent departure from conventional sound-image relationships in pre-1960 documentaries. I want to argue further that *Primary* foregrounds its comparison of cinema verite and traditional documentary by conducting an open investigation of other documentary media—still photography, television, radio, newspapers—attempting to compromise their claims to truth in the process. *Primary* is, finally, a film about the making of sounds and images for the purpose of political persuasion. As such, it provides information to which consumers of such sounds and images do not ordinarily have access: we *hear* what goes on at a photo session and *see* what goes on at a radio interview. The implication, never spoken, is that cinema verite offers viewers greater access to the truth. Kennedy's photo session, Humphrey's TV and radio shows, and both candidates' dealings with the press provide good examples of this.

In a small portrait studio we find an uncharacteristically awkward John Kennedy, camera and spotlights arranged in a circle around him. The candidate sits in a folding chair, preparing to produce a smile, while the photographer bustles about him, preparing to capture that smile on film. The photographer tinkers with his equipment (adjusting the height of a light), and fusses over his subject (ensuring that the proper amount of cuff peeks out from under his suitcoat sleeves). "Wrap the fingers around just a touch, Senator, just easy-like," he suggests. "Now kind of intertwine the fingers a little. There, that's it. Fine." At one point, Kennedy flashes a toothy campaign grin and holds it for an instant before realizing that, as he says, "It's not time to smile yet, Wally." In the context of *Primary*, Wally seems rather old-fashioned, practicing a form of photography that was necessary, perhaps, before cameras became portable and film stocks fast. Drew once described the portrait session as "a ritual in many small towns," suggesting he found the idea rather quaint. And indeed, the rituals of studio photography, which contrast so strikingly with those of cinema verite, would become a favorite subject of Drew Associates in the years to come. In *Crisis: Behind a Presidential Commitment*, for example, the living camera looks on with bemusement as one of its subjects is carefully posed to have her picture taken for the cover of *Time*.

The photo session scene in *Primary* ends with a cut from Kennedy posing in the studio to a campaign poster of Humphrey plastered on the front of a bus. The sound from the portrait studio bleeds over, and while we see the paper image of Humphrey's smiling face, we hear Kennedy's photographer ask, "Would you swing your body a little bit more to the camera?" Here the sound-image juxtaposition reminds us that Humphrey's polished campaign poster is the product of a similar session: Humphrey, too, has been carefully lit and perfectly posed, perhaps with fingers intertwined "just easy-like" and a quarter-inch of cuff revealed. Moreover, the scene reminds us that the numerous photographs of both candidates that we see throughout the film (hanging on walls, draped across bodies, and mounted on hoods of cars) are carefully constructed campaign images rather than the "candid" shots of the film itself.

Humphrey's television program can be seen as a reversal of the photo session scene, in that this time we see *Humphrey*'s "behind-the-scenes" preparations and cut to *Kennedy*'s "finished product." The scene takes us into the dressing room and onto the set of Humphrey's own TV call-in show, "Ask Senator Humphrey." He plants the first question to be asked of him, tells the camera operator where to focus, and allots his wife, Muriel, exactly thirty seconds to tell the audience what she's been doing all day ("Just say something about 'your husband's been wondering where you've been,' and so on"). The cinema verite camera is positioned behind the studio camera, as it was in the photo session scene ("Leacock relentlessly includes the technical preparations, the anxiety," a reviewer remarked in 1961).[74] And the scene ends with a cut from Humphrey taking a call in the studio to a video image of Kennedy, filmed from a television screen. We are reminded that Kennedy's smooth TV image required technical preparation as well.

This is the sort of parallelism that has led documentary scholars to comment upon the "scrupulous objectivity" of the film. Surely, *Primary* attempts to treat the candidates even-handedly, cutting back and forth between the two throughout, encouraging critics to wonder whether it means to compare or contrast them.[75] Such a structure does not, of course, make the film value-neutral; it is part of the "persistent pretense of impartiality" that characterizes many early cinema verite films, and an appeal to a particular convention of journalistic realism as well: parallel editing as "fair play" in accordance with the "balanced account" provision of the Fairness Doctrine.

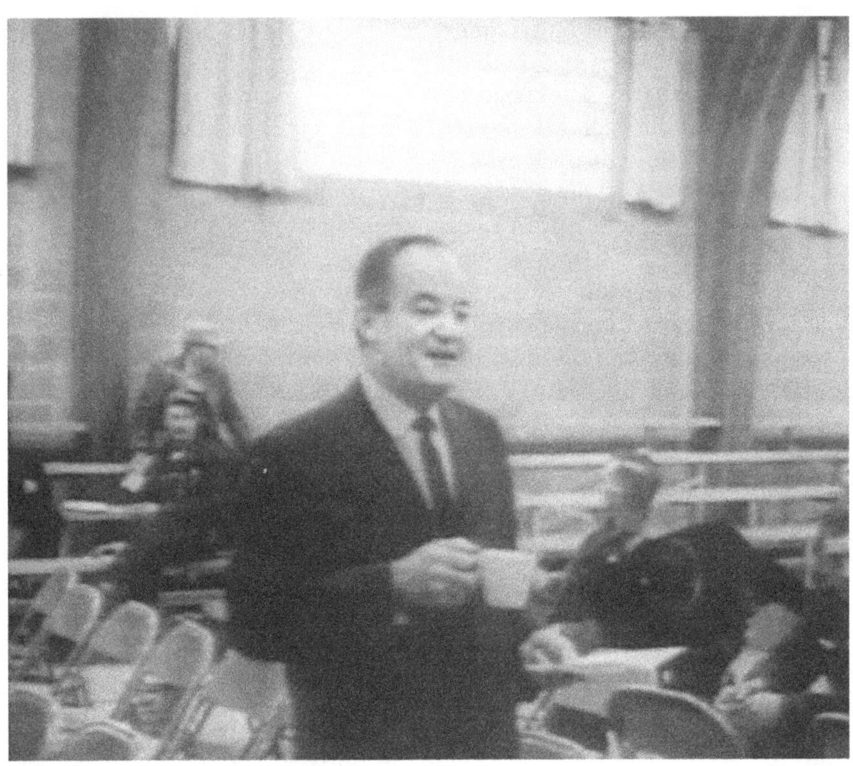

FIGURE 65.7 Screen capture from DVD.

But more important for my argument is that these particular parallel scenes function to remind us that the Drew documentarist does not, apparently, direct his or her subject (as the photographer directs Kennedy in the photo session scene); nor does the subject, apparently, direct the Drew documentarist (as Humphrey directs the camera operator in the television studio scene). And the result, apparently, is "nothing but the truth."

In Humphrey's farm speech scene, we see cinema verite's answer to the tradition of studio portraiture represented in Kennedy's photo session scene. "This is the heart of Senator Humphrey's strength, the farm areas of Wisconsin, close to the border of Minnesota," the narrator announces. "And though he likes to discuss everything from foreign policy to disarmament, here there is only one issue to test the skill of an orator." In a half-empty school auditorium in rural Wisconsin, Humphrey faces the farmers (Figure 65.7). "Not a single candidate in this primary election has paid any attention to the farmer at all—except Hubert Humphrey," he tells them. The speech, Mamber remarks with chagrin, "is shown primarily in long shot and in the faces of the audience so as to hide the obvious lack of synch sound."[76] Actually, the beginning and end of the speech are shown in medium close-up with perfectly synchronized sound. And the faces of the audience, which may serve to hide a lack of synch sound in the middle, surely have other functions in the film as well.

They might best be described as a series of cinematic portraits: medium and close shots of a dozen Wisconsin farmers, seated in bleachers and folding chairs in a space where they probably gather to watch their children perform in school plays or participate in athletic events (there is a small stage with a baby grand piano behind Humphrey, a basketball hoop hanging over his head). Most wear flannel shirts and denim overalls, although some have donned suitcoats over workshirts in honor of the occasion. Skeptical expressions grace weathered faces—faces illuminated only by the stark ceiling lights in the room itself. The images are reminiscent of the portraits of sharecroppers taken by Farm Security Administration (FSA) photographers of the 1930s such as Dorthea Lange and Walker Evans. Lange in fact ran a successful portrait studio before turning her back on the classical tradition and taking her camera to the streets; and indeed, the entire school of American photography exemplified by the work of such artists and championed by magazines like *Life* defined itself in opposition to the tradition of studio portraiture of which we see a remnant in Kennedy's photo session scene. It is worth noting that many of the FSA photographers of the thirties wound up working for *Life* in the forties and fifties, when Robert Drew was a photo editor there. *Primary*'s "portraits," though themselves highly conventional, can be seen as cinema verite's answer to the carefully controlled photography represented in that scene. Here no one is taken out of his world and into a photographer's studio; no one is artificially lit, told where to look or how to position his fingers; no one's cuffs are measured, and there is apparently no danger of anyone smiling too soon—Humphrey works hard to get a laugh and a round of applause from this group.

Of course, the advertised working methods of Drew et al. stood in stark contrast to those of the studio photographer. "I can recall shooting in a situation where a character was in shadow, one inch away from proper light," Drew proudly told colleagues in 1963, "and we were rolling and I knew we wouldn't get anything in that light. Yet I'd rather lose the whole scene and everything that was said than to ask that man to move an inch."[77] Years later, Albert Maysles alluded to *Primary*'s implicit comparison of two schools of photography when he said: "There's a hell of a difference between a photograph by Henri Cartier-Bresson and Richard Avedon. And that's where we stand.

If you'd seen *Primary* at the time that film was made, there was a kind of truth that came on the cinema screen that no one had ever seen before. . . . You knew that all of a sudden something new was born. And I think the newness of it is that it's more truthful. It's like when *Life* magazine carne into being."[78]

Ironically, Humphrey makes some disparaging remarks about *Life* in the course of his talk to the farmers: "Instead of you reading about who you ought to have as president in *Life* magazine, you ought to take a good look at him in the flesh . . . because let me tell you something—*Life, Time, Fortune, Look* and *Newsweek* don't give a hoot about your dairy prices." And perhaps his suspicion of such photo magazines was well founded after all; certainly, the *Life*-like portraits of *Primary* nuance our perception of Humphrey's speech. For example, he opens with a joke about being served only a half cup of coffee because he is "only half Norwegian," and we cut to a shot of an older man deeply inhaling a cigarette, no trace of a smile on his face (Figure 65.8). Throughout the speech, the expressions on the faces of the farmers temper our response to Humphrey's words, as we become aware that his folksy rhetoric reaches only a part of the crowd. Humphrey's speech, like his radio interview, relies mainly on "word logic"; here the "picture logic" of *Primary* works in counterpoint.

The radio interview scene begins with a shot of Humphrey and an announcer sitting behind a glass wall (marked "Studio A," and, significantly, "No Admittance"). "Well, we have a surprise for you this afternoon," the announcer begins, and as he introduces Humphrey to his radio audience we cut to a closer shot of the two, this time inside the glass. As he inquires, "How long do you plan to be in our fair city?" the announcer

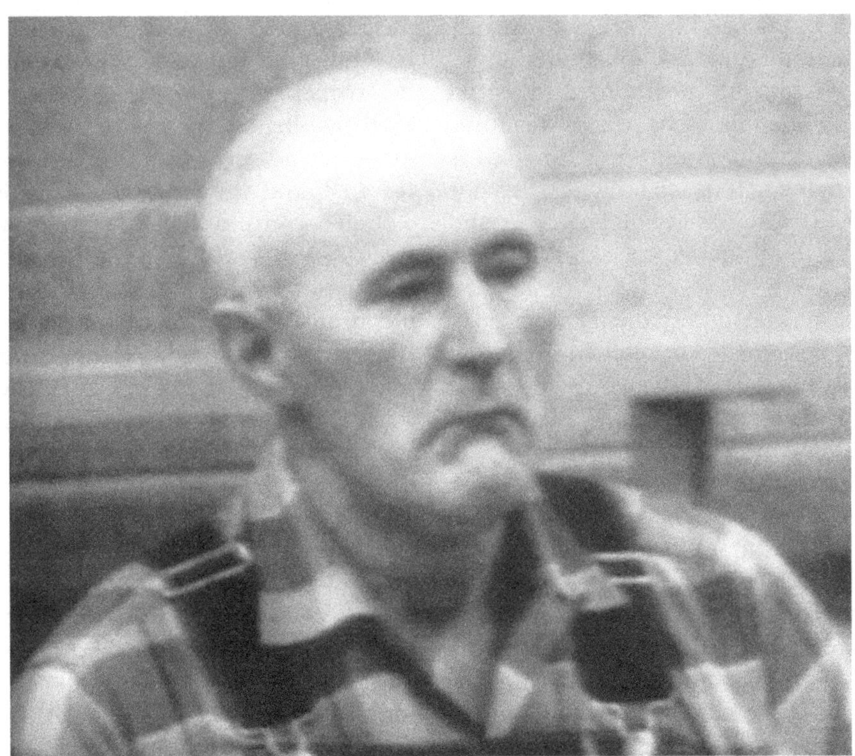

FIGURE 65.8 Screen capture from DVD.

removes a pen from his pocket and jots something down for Humphrey to read. Humphrey nods almost imperceptibly and replies, without skipping a beat, "Well, Tom, I'm not going to be here nearly long enough." The two chat affably until the interview is interrupted by a farm implement commercial, and in the next few shots, the film takes great care to assure us that Humphrey is leaving the station. We see him standing in a foyer with his coat on, descending a staircase, exiting the building, and taking the concrete steps into the street. Curiously, after establishing that Humphrey is well out of earshot, the camera returns to the station, where the announcer apparently speaks to the filmmakers off the air but on the record. "Well, I'll be very frank with you," he begins (and, explicitly acknowledging the invisible interviewer), "The question has been asked me if I think that Senator Kennedy will be out of the election, in other words will not win the election. . . ." He speaks in convoluted sentences ("The answer is yes—I don't believe that he can win"), but finally takes a stand: Kennedy will *not* win the primary in Wisconsin. Then something striking occurs. There is a jumpcut to a slightly closer shot of the announcer as he delivers an absolutely contrary statement: "Senator Hubert Humphrey will be defeated . . . and the Senator John Kennedy of Massachusetts will win."

At best, the announcer appears confused—and the film seems to take delight in the fact that a man who talks for a living cannot put a coherent sentence together. (The jumpcut and probable sound ellipsis between his two conflicting predictions suggest that the scene was edited to emphasize the error.) Moreover, the film stresses that the announcer is literally talking about Humphrey "behind his back" with a final shot of the candidate crossing the street, back to the camera, apparently unaware of the conversation being recorded at the station. The radio listeners of Tomah, of course, never heard this conversation—nor were they admitted "behind the glass" at the radio station. cinema verite, which can let us see the knowing glances passed between interviewer and interviewee (however discreet), and let us hear the interviewer's afterthoughts (however confused), appears to afford its viewers greater access to the truth.

"I consider myself a reporter," Drew often said in the early 1960s, one "working full blast on developing a new kind of journalism."[79] The reliability of the oldest kind of journalism—newspaper reporting—is called into question by *Primary* as well. Early in the film, a group of reporters interview Humphrey on the steps of the capital in Madison. ("Don't you like to talk to reporters, Senator?" one inquires. "I talk to the people that vote," he replies.) They insist on asking him questions about something he professes to know nothing about (the alleged support of the Symington committee for the Humphrey campaign), and then scribble his obligatory answers ("Very fine") in spiral notepads. The exchange is remarkably unrevealing, and its inclusion in the film seems calculated to call into question the validity of the traditional newspaper interview. A similarly hollow exchange between a reporter and a race car driver would serve a similar function in *On the Pole*, and the "unproductive interview" would become another favorite subject of Drew Associates in the years to come.

Later in *Primary*, the possibility that a candidate might be misquoted by a newspaper reporter is raised. The scene is Kennedy's hotel room on the night of the election. The candidate sits slumped in a chair near the phone, frequently dragging himself up to greet campaign workers and occasionally answering calls. "No, that isn't an exact quote," he tells one caller. "I just said I would find it difficult to be nominated—if I lost here I'd find it extremely difficult to be nominated, is what I said." And finally, "I don't care whether they print it or not." The inquiry seems to be in reference to a remark Kennedy made at the rally in Milwaukee—"I've said on many occasions that I didn't think it was possible to be nominated if I were unsuccessful here in Wisconsin, and I must say I mean it"—a remark viewers of *Primary* have already heard in context, since the omnipresent verite cameras and recorders captured it live. But the quotation is apparently subject to both verification ("that isn't an exact quote") and censorship ("I don't care whether they print it or not") before finding its way into print.

"Where we differ from the TV and press is that we are predicated on being there when the things are happening to people that count," Drew said in 1961. "Maybe it is more a journalistic principle than a principle of film-making."[80] He always saw his work as a kind of journalism—but a new and better kind of journalism than had been possible before. *Primary* illustrates this belief by implicitly comparing cinema verite methods with those of still photography, television, radio and newspapers. Years later, the equipment would be far more sophisticated, the budgets higher, and the subjects presidents and prime ministers instead of (merely) senators. But the stakes for Drew would never be quite as high again, the burden of proof for cinema verite never quite so great. In retrospect, *Primary* can be seen as a part of the early discourse on cinema verite, a polemic articulated in the heady rhetoric of the cinema verite movement.[81] It was Drew's own *Man With A Movie Camera*, and it stands today as his manifesto for cinema verite. But the realism of the film finally lies less in any natural relation to the real than in a studied departure from certain conventions of representation (wandering, hand-held cameras replace the still photographer's tripod, voices of "people in the street" replace "voice of doom" narration), and a fall-back reliance upon others (the matching of sounds and images in a conventionally plausible manner, the granting of equal time to opposing points of view). Radically different from classical fiction and traditional documentary films in some ways, *Primary* is remarkably similar to them in others.

Conclusion

That too becomes a cliché.

> Richard Leacock, asked why he didn't more often include shots of microphones, cameras or recorders in his films.[82]

I have argued that *Primary* stakes its own claim to realism in a departure from prevailing conventions of representation, particularly conventional sound-image relations in the documentary film. Kristin Thompson notes that such depar tures often seem most radical at the beginning of a new trend, and indeed, this may account for the "feeling in the air" in the early 1960s that "cinema was only just beginning."[83] After a period of "defamiliarization," however, traits originally perceived as realistic may become "automatized" by repetition; there are those who recall the mid-1960s as "an era when cameramen demanded whether you wanted something shot 'properly' or in 'wobblyscope' and sound recordists audibly queried the acceptability of mumbles."[84] The repetition of the same realistic traits gradually makes their conventional nature apparent; cinema verite's restless, handheld cameras and blurred, grainy visuals no longer seem tied to the real, as such devices are common in Hollywood movies, television commercials and music videos today. Eventually, according to Thompson, other devices may be justified in very different ways as relating to reality, and new kinds of realism appear.[85] This, I think, is the case with cinema verite's fall from grace at the hands of contemporary documentary theorists. Bill Nichols, for example, described the reflexive documentaries of the seventies as having a "more sophisticated grasp of the historical realm" than the cinema verite films of the sixties.[86] And Thomas Waugh argued that the "clear-sighted historical consciousness" of Emile de Antonio's films might take us "beyond verite."[87] De Antonio himself couldn't have agreed more; in 1980 he announced that cinema verite was dead.[88]

In the early 1960s, the films of Drew Associates were said to have revolutionized documentary filmmaking; today they are thought to epitomize American cinema verite. But these films might more accurately be described as hybrid forms. The portable recording equipment that would revolutionize documentary filmmaking was still quite crude in 1960, and Pennebaker recalls that he spent the better part of that year devising "a lot of elegant—and inelegant—solutions" to the team's equipment problems.[89] The early films of Drew Associates bear traces of a struggle between convention and innovation in this transitional period, flaunting innovations that the new technology made possible when it worked, and reverting to established conventions independent of this technology when it did not. Moreover, even when the equipment functioned flawlessly—making innovations such as long, on-site, synch-sound segments possible—the films were often edited and narrated rather conventionally. Ironically, it was Drew himself who insisted on adding extensive voice-over narration to many of the living camera films—much to the chagrin of filmmakers like Leacock and Pennebaker, who eventually quit the team due to disputes over issues such as this. According to Pennebaker, "Ricky and I were making films in which we assumed that everybody was watching closely. But Drew was saying, 'No, they're gonna miss stuff, so you're gonna have to have a narration to explain to them what they miss, and tell them to look at things that are about to happen so they won't miss them.' We found this very redundant, and kind of awkward, and it was the beginning of the problem."[90]

Some original members of Drew Associates did go on to produce "purer" forms of cinema verite—films that depart more decisively from the conventions of the traditional documentary film and the classical Hollywood cinema. At the same time, however, they conventionalized the innovations of cinema verite until "these too became clichés." In *Don't Look Back*, for example, Pennebaker tracks Bob Dylan just as Al Maysles tracked Kennedy in *Primary*: the camera follows the singer as he strolls out of the shadows and onto the stage, into a burst of light and an avalanche of sound. Such shots would become *de rigueur* in rock documentaries produced by Drew expatriots in the years to come—and indeed, would be parodied in Rob Reiner's tribute to such films, *This is Spinal Tap* (1984). (In that film, the camera follows members of a rock band as they make their winding journey through the corridors of an auditorium only to wind up in the boiler room.) Moreover, the unproductive interviews conducted by representatives of more traditional news media in many early Drew films would become the *raison d'être* of *Don't Look Back*; Pennebaker's camera looks on as Dylan savages one reporter after another. (Dylan even denounces *Time*—the filmmaker's former employer—much as Humphrey criticized *Life* in *Primary*.)

The rhetoric of the cinema verite movement can provide an important historical context for the study of cinema verite films—but it cannot provide more than that. All too often, we "remember" the films of Drew Associates in the words of Robert Drew, Richard Leacock, and D. A. Pennebaker; we remember the "three commandments" of "television's school of storm and stress" and we forget how often they were broken. "I'm interested in one approach only," Drew said at a meeting of television documentary producers and directors in 1963, "and that is to convey the excitement and drama and feeling of real life as it actually happens through film. I don't care whether it is thought of as 'artistic.'" John Secondari, Executive Producer of ABC News, replied, "But the presentation of truth as it happens is not the only concern. There must be a beginning, middle and end—organization and a climax. Otherwise it can be truthful but dull."[91] (Or, as David Maysles said two years later, "There is no worth in 'this is the way it was—*exactly*.' Then you'd have people picking their noses and everything else. It could be repulsive."[92]) Perhaps some members of Drew Associates really didn't care whether their films were thought of as artistic—i.e., constructed—or not. (Pennebaker once remarked that aesthetics were "for women and children."[93]) Perhaps they only wanted to capture the "truth at twenty-four frames per second," with Auricon cameras, Perfectone recorders, and Bulova watch tuning forks. Their failure to achieve what Victor Shklovsky saw as an "inadequate goal with inadequate means"—to try to imitate nature in the representational arts—was, of course, inevitable.[94] But the very way in which these filmmakers "failed"—the remarkable means by which they refracted the light passing through cinema verite's "window on the world"—is something about which we have yet much to discover.

NOTES

1. "Third Independent Film Award," *Film Culture* nos. 22–23 (Summer 1961): 11.
2. Quoted in "Television's School of Storm & Stress: Robert Drew's Documentaries Aim at Photographic Realism," *Broadcasting* (6 March 1961): 82.
3. Quoted in A. William Bluem, *Documentary in American Television* (New York: Hastings House, 1965), 259.
4. *Primary, On the Pole, Yanki No!,* and *The Children Were Watching*, respectively. For a filmography, see Stephen Mamber, *Cinema Verite in America: Studies in Uncontrolled Documentary* (Cambridge: The MIT Press, 1974), 265–69.
5. There are very few examples of members of Drew Associates using the term "cinema verite" in the early 1960s. Years later, it was described as "a tag Mr. Drew dislikes but has learned to live with." See Richard Lacayo, "'Why are Documentaries So Dull?'" *The New York Times* (20 February 1983): 29. On the other hand, the term *was* used by early critics to denote both the French and North American schools of the movement. See, for example, "Special Feature on Cinema-Verite: Three Views," *Film Quarterly* 17, no. 4 (Summer 1964): 26–40. Thus, although Erik Barnouw refers to the French school of the movement as "cinema verite" and the North American school as "direct cinema" in his widely used textbook, most documentary scholars (e.g., Robert C. Allen, A. William Bluem, Noël Carroll, Stephen Mamber, Bill Nichols, Thomas Waugh) use "cinema verite" for both schools as well. The term appears in a baffling array of forms in the literature, including not only italics and various quantities of diacritical marks, but also hyphens, capitals, and inverted commas. I have simplified all references herein for convenience and consistency.
6. Stanley Crawford, "From Visionary Gleams to Cinema Verite: One Step Forward, Two Steps Back," *Film* 40 (Summer 1964): 38; William Earle, "Cinema Banalité and Surrealism," *Quarterly Review of Film Studies* 2 (1977): 179–84.
7. Quoted in Bluem, *Documentary*, 259.
8. Louis Marcorelles, "American Diary," *Sight & Sound* 32 (Winter 1962–63): 5.
9. James Blue, "Thoughts on Cinema Verite and a Discussion with the Maysles," *Film Comment* 2, no. 4 (Summer 1965): 22.
10. Ibid., 24.
11. Quoted in Blue, "One Man's Truth: An Interview With Richard Leacock," *Film Comment* 3, no. 2 (Spring 1965): 21.
12. Bill Nichols, "The Voice of Documentary," reprinted in Nichols, ed., *Movies and Methods*, Vol. II (Berkeley: University of California Press, 1985), 261.
13. Mamber, *Cinema Verite*, 250.
14. Ibid., 250.
15. Ibid., 4.
16. Thomas Waugh, "Beyond Verite: Emile de Antonio and the New Documentary of the Seventies," reprinted in Nichols, *Movies and Methods, Vol. II*, 235.
17. Ibid., 234.
18. Bill Nichols, *Ideology and the Image* (Bloomington: Indiana University Press, 1981), 210.
19. Waugh, "Beyond Verite," 235.
20. Ibid., 236.
21. Nichols, "The Voice of Documentary," 260.
22. Jeanne Allen, "Self-Reflexivity in Documentary," *Cine-Tracts* 1, no. 2 (Summer 1977): 38.
23. Jay Ruby, "The Image Mirrored: Reflexivity and the Documentary Film," reprinted in Alan Rosenthal, *New Challenges for Documentary* (Berkeley: University of California Press, 1988), 74.
24. Ibid., 10.
25. Jeanne Allen, "Self-Reflexivity," 39.
26. Marcorelles, "Nothing But the Truth," *Sight & Sound* 32, no. 3 (Summer 1963): 115.
27. Jean-Luc Godard, "*Dictionnaire de 121 Metteurs en Scène*," *Cahiers du Cinema* 25, nos. 150–51 (Dec. 1963–Jan. 1964): 140. My translation.
28. Quoted in Rosenthal, *The Documentary Conscience: A Casebook in Film Making* (Berkeley: University of California Press, 1980): 211.

29. Noël Carroll, "From Real to Reel: Entangled in Nonfiction Film," *Philosophic Exchange* 14 (1983): 7.
30. Waugh criticizes the "Eastern liberalism" of Drew *et al.* in Waugh, "Beyond Verite," 235; Robert Allen discusses the liberal and empiricist roots of cinema verite in "Case Study: The Beginnings of American Cinema Verite," in Robert Allen and Douglas Gomery, *Film History: Theory and Practice* (Alfred A. Knopf, 1985), 233–37.
31. Quoted in Blue, "One Man's Truth," 21. Emphasis in original.
32. Quoted in "Television's School of Storm & Stress," 82.
33. Quoted in Bluem, *Documentary*, 259. Emphasis in original.
34. Waugh, "Beyond Verite," 235.
35. Annette Kuhn, "The Camera I: Observations on Documentary," *Screen* 19, no. 2 (Summer 1978): 73.
36. Robert Allen, *Film History*, 232.
37. Quoted in Gideon Bachmann, "The Frontiers of Realist Cinema: The Work of Ricky Leacock," *Film Culture* 22–23 (Summer 1961): 19.
38. Quoted in Blue, "One Man's Truth," 16.
39. Waugh, "Beyond Verite," 235.
40. Robert Allen, *Film History*, 233.
41. Richard P. Shepard, "School Integration," *The New York Times* (17 February 1961): 54.
42. Quoted in Bluem, *Documentary*, 263.
43. Ed Pincus, "New Possibilities in Film and the University," *Quarterly Review of Film Studies* 2, no. 2 (May 1977): 165. Pincus remarks in a footnote that a "curious exception to this was the car interview," but in fact there were many exceptions. None of the interviews cited in this paragraph, for example, takes place in an automobile.
44. "Television's School of Storm & Stress," 82.
45. Quoted in P. J. O'Connell, "Robert Drew and the Development of Cinema Verite in America: An Innovation in Television Journalism," Ph.D. diss. (Pennsylvania University, 1988): 220. Page numbers here refer to a near-finished draft of the manuscript and may differ slightly from the final version.
46. "Third Independent Film Award," 11.
47. Robert Allen, *Film History*, 224.
48. Robert Drew, "An Independent with the Networks," in Rosenthal, ed., *New Challenges for Documentary*, 396.
49. Marcorelles, *The Living Cinema* (New York: Praeger, 1973), 50.
50. O'Connell, "Robert Drew," 141–43.
51. See, for example, Jim St. Lawrence, "'Leapin' Lizards!' or the Documentary's History," *Videography* (September 1987): 109.
52. Mamber, *Cinema Verite*, 39.
53. Robert Allen, "Case Study," 224.
54. Ibid., 217.
55. Drew, "An Independent," 394.
56. Quoted in Mamber, 37.
57. Drew, "An Independent," 395.
58. Ibid., 396.
59. Quoted in Barbara Hogenson, "Interview with Robert Drew," program, Whitney Museum of American Art (30 March 1982): 4.
60. "Television's School of Storm and Stress," 82.
61. Ibid., 82.
62. Bachmann, "The Frontiers," 20. The example is hypothetical; Jacqueline Kennedy does not wear a hat in this scene.
63. Mamber, *Cinema Verite*, 38.
64. André Bazin, *What is Cinema?*, trans. Hugh Gray (Berkeley: University of California Press, 1971), 49.
65. Ibid., 49.
66. Mamber, *Cinema Verite*, 38.
67. Rick Altman, "Moving Lips: Cinema as Ventriloquism," *Yale French Studies* 60 (1980): 74.
68. Years later, Leacock described the cigar-burned dress sequence as an "outrageous joke": "The whole business about the woman announcing that, 'A lady has objected because . . . a gentleman smoking a cigar has burned her dress.' We found that line, we went through every foot of film, we found a picture of a guy smoking a cigar! And we found a funny-looking lady, we put them together, it makes a joke. Now what's that got to do with the absolute truth?" Quoted in O'Connell, "Robert Drew," 145.
69. Mamber, *Cinema Verite*, 39.
70. Pennebaker recalls that the voting booth section was "provided by a local TV cameraman" and that "Drew was the only sound man, except for some migitape recordings Ricky [Leacock] and I did by ourselves." But Drew remembers recruiting a local sound recorder as well: "We hung a Perfectone on him and showed him how to run it." Robert Farren assisted in editing, but by most accounts Drew was responsible for the final cut. See Donn Alan Pennebaker, "Filmography," in G. Roy Levin, *Documentary Explorations: 15 Interviews with Film-Makers* (Garden City: Doubleday & Company, Inc., 1971), 226 and 256; Drew quoted in Hogenson, "Interview," 3.
71. Wisconsin law permits registered Republicans to "cross over" and vote in Democratic presidential primaries (and vice versa). Later in the film there is a vague reference to Nixon supporters who may have voted for Humphrey because he was less likely than Kennedy to beat Nixon. See Theodore H. White, *The Making of the President 1960* (New York: Giant Cardinal, 1961), 96–97.
72. Roland Barthes, "Rhetoric of the Image," *Image Music Text*, trans. Stephen Heath (New York: Hill and Wang, 1977), 41. My emphasis.
73. See David Bordwell and Kristin Thompson, "Fundamental Aesthetics of Sound in the Cinema," in Elizabeth Weis and John Belton, eds., *Film Sound: Theory and Practice* (New York: Columbia University Press, 1985), 181–99.
74. Ernest Callenbach, "Going Out to the Subject II," *Film Quarterly* 14, no. 3 (Spring 1961): 39.
75. See, for example, Mamber, *Cinema Verite*, 124.
76. Ibid., 39.
77. Quoted in Bluem, *Documentary*, 263.
78. Quoted in Levin, *Documentary Explorations*, 286.
79. Quoted in Bachman, "The Frontiers," 12.
80. Ibid., 18.

81. I am indebted to Murray Smith for this insight. In "Technological Determination, Aesthetic Resistance, or A *Cottage on Dartmoor*: Goat-Gland Talkie or Masterpiece?" Smith argues that an early British talkie can be seen as a part of the "discourse" on sound in the period. See *Wide Angle* 12, no. 3 (July 1990).
82. Quoted in Levin, *Documentary Explorations*, 204.
83. Kristin Thompson, *Breaking the Glass Armor: Neoformalist Film Analysis* (Princeton: Princeton University Press, 1988), 201.
84. Brian Winston, "Documentary: I Think We Are in Trouble," reprinted in Rosenthal, *New Challenges*, 23.
85. Thompson, *Breaking*, 199.
86. Nichols, "The Voice of Documentary," 269. In this essay, Nichols traces the evolution of documentary film style from the "Griersonian direct address" of the thirties and forties to the "cinema verite" of the sixties to the "string of interviews" documentaries of the seventies and eighties. He celebrates the dawning of a "fourth phase," one in which "epistemological and aesthetic assumptions become more visible." According to Nichols: "These new self-reflexive documentaries mix observational passages with interviews, the voiceover of the narrator with intertitles, making patently clear what has been implicit all along: documentaries always were forms of re-presentation, never clear windows onto 'reality'; the film-maker was always a participant-witness and an active fabricator of meaning, the producer of cinematic discourse rather than a neutral or all-knowing reporter of the way things truly are." It is remarkable how closely the early films of Drew Associates seem to fill Nichols's prescription, given that documentaries such as *Primary* and *The Chair* are explicitly excluded from his preferred category.
87. Waugh, "Beyond Verite," 257.
88. Quoted in Rosenthal, *The Documentary Conscience*, 211.
89. Quoted in O'Connell, "Robert Drew," 134.
90. Ibid., 232.
91. Quoted in Bluem, *Documentary*, 258–59.
92. Quoted in Blue, "Thoughts on Cinema Verite and a Discussion with the Maysles Brothers," *Film Comment* 2, no. 4 (Fall 1965): 29.
93. Ibid., 244. For a brief discussion of the role of women in the cinema verite movement, see Jan Rosenberg, *Women's Reflections: The Feminist Film Movement* (Ann Arbor: UMI Research Press, 1983), 34–37. Rosenberg quotes Joyce Chopra as claiming that "the women were all hired for their attractiveness. I was at a conference recently with Pennebaker and he was describing to a group of sociologists how you make a film and he said, 'You know, a cameraman goes out and his girlfriend takes sound.'And that sums up that mentality."
94. Quoted in Thompson, *Breaking*, 19.

66

MARGARET MEAD

AS SIGNIFICANT AS THE INVENTION OF DRAMA OR THE NOVEL (1973)

With *An American Family*, which premieres on PBS Jan. 11, something new has come to television: the first series (12 one-hour episodes) about a real American family, the William C. Louds of Santa Barbara, Cal.

Bill Loud, the head of the family, is the president of his own company, American Western Foundries, which sells replacement parts for the heavy equipment used in strip mining. He is 50 years old. His wife Pat is 45. They have five children: Lance, 20; Kevin, 18; Grant, 17; Delilah, 15; and Michele, 13. For seven months, from May 30, 1971, to Jan. 1, 1972, their day-to-day lives were recorded by New York station WNET camera crews.

This is an age of autobiographies (I have just written one myself) in which people of all sorts share some of their past lives with a large audience, and expose themselves to being critically mauled or exalted. But each person who writes an autobiography is reporting on a known life, a life already lived. He or she can select just those incidents which, remembered, make a point. In *An American Family* nobody knew what was going to happen. The result is certainly not fiction, nor is it the conventional TV documentary, nor the actuality of a moon landing happening as you watch it. It is a new kind of art form.

It is, I believe, as new and as significant as the invention of drama or the novel—a new way in which people can learn to look at life, by seeing the real life of others interpreted by the camera. It is, of course, related to all the current encounter adventures—to group therapy, to the meetings in which one person speaks of his or her own troubles so that others may learn that they are not alone. It is related to a strange new willingness to share one's inner life, to perform on a stage before other concerned eyes. *An American Family* is related to all these manifestations of our contemporary culture, but it is also unique.

Bill and Pat Loud and their five children are neither actors nor public figures going through a public charade. They are members of a real family, deeply concerned with each other, and each concerned with his or her individual, immediate fate. And as the 12-part actualization unrolls, each viewer can experience an intimacy never before present except in the imagination. In the past the imaginative person could reconstruct a scene from another's words, as when your brother or lover, back from Vietnam, told you what it was like that lonely night 10,000 miles away from home. With *An American Family* it is not your imagination but the immediate, the actual, what it is really like, that is there.

The closest television has come to this until now has been the infrequent glimpses it has given us of real life—a father weeping over his son's court-martial, the Kennedy children beside their father's bier, the flickering image of the men who were at that moment on the moon. The historic moment, the poignant moment, the revealing moment, but moments only.

Then there have been documentaries, unreal re-enactments of real events—a carefully staged scene in which real peasants do some extra ploughing—or real events caught by the camera but kept a world away from us because what we see are people from another age: the Tasaday, newly found people of the Stone Age, or African hunters following their quarry through the bush. The viewer is isolated by the knowledge that these people could not know how they would appear in an American living room.

But in *An American Family* the characters are 20th-century people living out their lives in California. They are Bill and Pat Loud trying to face each other, struggling with the problems that separate them from each other and from their children.

When they agreed to let the camera follow their lives, hour by hour, day by day, none of them knew what direction their lives would take. What they did was to agree to lay their as-yet-unlived lives on the line—to share their personal joys and sorrows with millions of other human beings who, months later on TV, would watch that which the Louds had not yet experienced.

In a fiction film the suspense and terror is allayed because, however harrowing the situation, it is, after all, only part of a created screenplay. The viewer knows that the actress who died as Juliet will go out after the scene is shot to drink a Coke or a cocktail, unconcerned with the events that were depicted. If she weeps, it will not be for Romeo, but because the director was rude, or the scene badly shot. It is only as a novel is only a story.

But *An American Family* is not only a story. It is real. And so, to make the suspense bearable, the series has been structured to show the viewer, at the very beginning of the first episode, how the filming ended. The months through which the audience will live with bated breath, with chuckling delight, with exasperation, scorn and acute partisanship—as one lives through life in one's own family—are relieved by this one bit of certainty. Otherwise it might be too much to bear the suspense of one's own life and that of another family's life at the same time.

I do not think *An American Family* should be called a documentary. I think we need a new name for it, a name that would contrast it not only with fiction, but with what we have been exposed to up until now on TV. Whatever that name turns out to be, it will have to include the essential ingredient of trust. The production staff and the family placed their future in each other's hands. They came together in a joint undertaking to produce something quite new.

Poetry has been described as "emotion recollected in tranquility." *An American Family* is emotion experienced in safety, and the actuality of the private life of one family *enhances* the private lives of a million families who are privileged to watch as it unrolls before their eyes.

This is how I see it, set against centuries of ritualistic drama, re-enactments of great plays, the unintended tragedy of moments when publicity tears the veil from the face of a victim of fate. But I had the special experience of watching this form develop when Craig Gilbert (producer of *An American Family*) and his three-man crew went with me to the island of Manus to make my "New Guinea Journal." There I trusted them not to hurt or betray my friends of 40 years, and they trusted me to help them make a picture. But the life we lived in that month on Manus was dedicated to making a film for TV. The life the William C. Loud family lives is its own.

An American Family may well prove to be more controversial than showing open-heart surgery or the birth of a baby on the screen. In an age when so many people are jaded and apathetic, convinced that their own lives are not as interesting or important as those created by writers of fiction, it comes very close to the bone. I think *An American Family* will change their minds.

SECTION V

TALKING BACK

Radical Voices and Visions After 1968

67

JONATHAN KAHANA

INTRODUCTION TO SECTION V

How quickly an avant-garde can become a status quo. In the previous section, we considered the variety of attempts by filmmakers to break the laws of classic documentary, during a decade or so of experiments with subjective, "uncontrolled" approaches to the filming of life. Before long, this dissident aesthetic had established itself as yet another set of conventions that gave filmed reality a familiar appearance. Reviewing one of the first North American works of gay and lesbian documentary to reach a large and general audience, the Mariposa Film Group's feature-length film *Word is Out* (1977), Lee Atwell, writing in the influential cinephile magazine *Film Comment*, distinguishes between the entertainment realm of fiction film and television—where no one would be surprised to encounter the stereotyping of homosexuals as pathetic, marginal individuals—and "the field of documentary or *cinéma-vérité*, where the index of reality is somewhat more reliable. . . ." Within a decade and a half, *cinéma vérité* had become just another way to say non-fiction filmmaking.

This section assembles materials which with to consider what is perhaps the last major revision of the indexical contract documentary film makes between the world and the screen, before basic principles of this relationship—and with it, the enterprise of documentary film as such—were called into question. (Those questions are fleshed out in sections VI and VII.) From roughly the end of the 1960s to the mid-1980s, film- and video-makers around the world take up the traditional struggle to capture "life as it is," as Dziga Vertov liked to say, in a manner that would not just observe and capture the constantly-changing world in all of its quotidian detail, but—as Vertov and his comrades had hoped to do through their "kino-eye"—accelerate those changes with a revolutionary fervor, one matched and, in many cases, explicitly aligned with, movements to change the very structures of social reality. Without abandoning the pursuit of truths captured and revealed that had been central to the very idea of documentary for nearly a century, this oppositional tendency sought to expose, and raise, the stakes of collective reality.

In his essay about the pivotal Argentinian film *The Hour of the Furnaces* (1968), Robert Stam writes that the film stages a "frontal assault on passivity," with images that "fuse with ideas in order to detonate in the minds of the audience." And both the power and originality of *The Hour of the Furnaces* have much to do with its express desire to have material impact on its world, starting with the particular groups that assemble to watch and discuss it. But Stam makes clear that the event-ness of the film—the revolutionary originality intended for every one of its screenings—itself has a long cultural and political history, in Latin America and in cinema. And although it is convenient for us to define radical documentary in this period by dating its impulses to explosive moments in history—"the Sixties," or "1968," for instance—it is important to keep in mind that this explosion has a long fuse, one that stretches across decades and continents. As Pearl Bowser shows in her comprehensive essay "Pioneers of Black Documentary Film," African-American documentary photographers and filmmakers had, for decades, been developing a style and politics of oppositional history for many decades, overlooked or excluded from accounts of "mainstream" (white, Euro-American) documentary history, but equally broad and deep. Similarly, the Latin American filmmakers who lead and inspire developments in radical film practice throughout the First and Third Worlds in the 1960s and 1970s come to their vanguard position through decades of immersion in ongoing international revolutionary cultural and political movements; the essays and statements by Robert Stam, Juan Carlos Espinosa, Santiago Alvarez, and others in this section make clear how, in both personal and collective terms, the development of Argentinian or Cuban social documentary is a transnational and transhistorical program that filmmakers and critics elsewhere in the Americas, and elsewhere in the world, join in progress. The inverse is also true, however: just as tributaries combine to form powerful historical currents, political movements can form doctrinal and practical factions that branch off and irrigate new fields. The internal divisions along racial, ethnic, and gendered lines among progressive American filmmakers in the 1970s and the redefinitions of racial and national, as well as aesthetic, Blackness for young British artists in the 1980s, in Coco Fusco's account of the Sankofa and Black Audio collectives, are two important versions of transnationalism that we find in Latin American radical culture of this period.

It is not untrue, of course, that the commitments of many politically-minded artists in the northern and western hemispheres were forged in the tumultuous year 1968, which saw large street demonstrations and other forms of mass protest disrupt cities and institutions on several continents. The target of these protests, which drew their numbers from labor unions, leftist political groups, war veterans, and university students, were the complex of forces deemed responsible for the war in Vietnam, and for other systemic forms of racism and violence toward the non-white, non-Western "other," as well as toward the Western working classes whose exploited labor kept this "military-industrial complex" going. A number of the filmmaking collectives discussed in this section, including the American radicals of the several Newsreel cadres and offshoots, the Japanese Ogawa Productions group, and various feminist and sexual liberationist circles that took up film and video could trace their membership, their politics, and their methods to the heightening of radical and oppositional consciousness on and around college campuses at the end of the 1960s. And even filmmakers with a less direct link to the street and campus disruptions were in step with the anti-institutional and anti-authoritarian Leftist politics of the period: films produced in 1967–70 by the American documentary *auteurs* Emile de Antonio, Albert and David Maysles, and Frederick Wiseman all subject to critical scrutiny the kinds of governmental and cultural institutions that were the subject of the students' and radicals' outrage. Like the activist and movement films that protest groups made as political interventions, even these *auteurs'* films of this period are at once critiques of institutional violence, and violent in their method. In her ill-tempered review of the Rolling Stones disastrous concert at Altamont Speedway, *Gimme Shelter*—an excellent, if tendentious, summation of late American *cinéma vérité* ethics and aesthetics—Pauline Kael is at pains to prove how volatile the mixture of politics and art could be for middle-class audiences, comparing the Maysles' methods to both Leni Riefenstahl and Roman circuses. In *Gimme Shelter*, Kael bitterly concludes, "the audience and the victims are indistinguishable."

Kael was no fan of radical politics or of *cinéma vérité*, and she could be uncharitable about documentary in general, but she puts her finger on a problem of real urgency for filmmakers in this section: how to breach the line between audience and film? Many of the documentary projects studied here are built around this problem: the direct address to audiences in Latin American Third Cinema described by Stam and Chanan; the consciousness-raising model that Julia Lesage and E. Ann Kaplan discuss in their essays on Anglo-American feminist documentary; the framing, by Jill Godmilow, of independent documentary by in the U.S. *as* a problem of audience and circulation, one to be solved by the filmmaker herself; the community-based filmmaking styles developed with industrial workers in the American South (*Harlan County, U.S.A.*) and aboriginal groups in Australia (*Two Laws*); John Greyson's attention to social pedagogy in AIDS activist video, which recalls the arguments by Espinosa, Fraga, and Pantin for didactic approaches to post-imperial audiences in Latin America. The faces of documentary and its audience were permanently transfigured by what Stam called the "frontal assault" launched in this mode of activist filmmaking.

68

ROBERT STAM

HOUR OF THE FURNACES AND THE TWO AVANT GARDES (1981)

The struggle to seize power from the enemy is the meeting-ground of the political and artistic vanguards engaged in a common task which is enriching to both.

—Fernando Solanas and Ottavio Getino in "Towards a Third Cinema"

If there are two avant-gardes—the formal and the theoretico-political—then *La Hora de los Hornos* (*Hour of the Furnaces*, 1968) surely marks one of the high points of their convergence. Fusing third-world radicalism with artistic innovation, the Solanas-Getino film revives the historical sense of avant-garde as connoting political as well as cultural militancy. It teases to the surface the military metaphor submerged in the very expression "avant-garde"—the image of an advanced contingent reconnoitering unexplored and dangerous territory. It resuscitates the venerable analogy (at least as old as Marey's *fusil photographique*) of camera and gun, charging it with a precise revolutionary signification. Art becomes, as Walter Benjamin said of the Dadaists, "an instrument of ballistics." At the same time, *La Hora*'s experimental language is indissolubly wedded to its political project; the articulation of one with the other generates the film's meaning and secures it relevance.

It is in this exemplary two-fronted struggle, rather than in the historical specificity of its politics, that *La Hora* retains vitality as a model for cinematic practice. Events subsequent to 1968 have, if not wholly discredited, at least relativized the film's analysis. Unmoored and set adrift on the currents of history, *La Hora* has been severed from its original context, as its authors have been exiled from their country. The late sixties were, virtually everywhere, the hour of the furnaces, and *La Hora*, quintessential product of the period, forged the incandescent expression of their glow. Tricontinental revolution, under the symbolic aegis of Frantz Fanon, Che Guevara, and Ho Chi Minh, was deemed imminent, waiting to surprise us around the next bend of the dialectic. But despite salient victories (Viet Nam, Mozambique, Nicaragua), many flames have dwindled into embers, as some of the Third World has settled into the era of diminished expectations. In most of South America, the CIA, multinational corporations, and native ruling elites conspired to install what Noam Chomsky calls "sub-fascist" regimes, i.e., regimes whose politics and practices are fascist but who lack any popular base. In Argentina, class struggle in a relatively liberal context gave way to virtual civil war. Peron—the last hope of the revolutionaries and the bourgeoisie—returned, but only to die. His political heirs veered rightward, defying the hopes of those who returned him to power, until a putsch installed a quasi-fascist regime. Rather than being surprised by revolution, Argentina, and *La Hora* with it, was ambushed by an historical equivocation.

La Hora is structured as a tripartite political essay. The first section, "Neocolonialism and Violence," situates Argentina internationally, revealing it as a palimpsest of European influences: "British gold, Italian hands, French books." A series of "Notes"—"The Daily Violence," "The Oligarchy," "Dependency"—explore the variegated forms of neocolonial oppression. The second section, "An Act for Liberation," is subdivided into a "Chronicle of Peronism," covering Peron's rule from 1945 through his deposition by coup in 1955, and "Chronicle of Resistance," detailing the opposition struggle during the period of Peron's exile. The third section, "Violence and Liberation," consists of an open-ended series of interviews, documents and testimonials concerning the best path to a revolutionary future for Latin America. Much of this section is taken up by two interviews, one with an octogenarian oral archivist of the national memory of resistance, who recounts past combats and predicts imminent socialist revolution, the other with labor organizer Julio Troxler, then living and working underground, who describes mass executions and vows struggle until victory.

While reawakening the military metaphor dormant in "avant-garde," *La Hora* also literalizes the notion of the "underground." Filmed clandestinely in conjunction with militant cadres, it was made in the interstices of the system and against the system. It situates itself on the periphery of the periphery—a kind of off-off-Hollywood—and brashly disputes the hegemony of both the dominant model ("First Cinema") and of Auteurism ("Second Cinema"), proposing instead a "Third Cinema," independent in production, militant in politics, and experimental in language.[1] As a poetic celebration of the Argentine nation, it is "epic" in the classical as well as the Brechtian sense, weaving disparate materials—newsreels, eyewitness reports, TV commercials, photographs—into a splendid historical tapestry. A cinematic summa, with strategies ranging from straightforward didacticism to operatic stylization, borrowing from avant-garde and mainstream, fiction and documentary, *cinéma vérité* and advertising, it inherits and prolongs the work of Eisenstein, Vertov, Joris Ivens, Glauber Rocha, Fernando Birri, Resnais, Buñuel and Godard.

La Hora's most striking feature is its openness. But whereas "openness" in art usually evokes plurisignification, polysemy, the authorization of a plurality of equally legitimate readings, the Solanas-Getino film is not open in this sense: its messages are stridently unequivocal. Its ambiguities, such as they are, derive more from the vicissitudes of history than from the intentions of its authors. The film's openness lies elsewhere, and first of all in its process of production. Coming from the traditional Europeanized left, Solanas and Getino set out to make a socially-minded short documentary about the working class in Argentina. Through the filmmaking experience, however, they evolved toward a left Peronist position. The production process, in other words, inflected their own ideological trajectory in ways that they themselves could not have fully predicted. (One need not endorse the specific nature of this inflection to appreciate the fact of the inflection.) Once aware of the tenuous nature of their initial "certainties," they opened their project to the criticisms and suggestions of the working class. As a result, the film underwent a process of constant mutation, not because of authorial whims (à la *8 1/2*) but under the pressure of proletarian critique. Rather than performing the *mise-en-scène* of preconceived opinions, the film's making entailed inquiry and search. The reformist short became a revolutionary manifesto.[2]

La Hora is open, secondly, in its very structure as a text, operating by what might be called tendentiously aleatory procedures.[3] At key points, the film raises questions—"Why did Peron fall without a struggle? Should he have armed the people?"—and proposes that the audience debate them, interrupting the projection to allow for discussion. Elsewhere, the authors appeal for supplementary material on the theme of violence and liberation, soliciting collaboration in the film's writing. The "end" of the film refuses closure by inviting the audience to prolong the text: "Now it is up to you to draw conclusions, to continue the film. You have the floor." This challenge, more than rhetorical, was concretely taken up by Argentinian audiences, at least until the experiment was cut short by military rule.

Cine-semiologists define the cinema as a system of signification rather than communication, arguing that the gap between the production of the message and its reception, doubled by the gap between the reception and the production of an answering message, allows only for *deferred* communication. *La Hora*, by opening itself up to person-to-person debate, tests and "stretches" this definition to its very limits. In a provocative amalgam of cinema/theatre/political rally, it joins the space of representation to the space of the spectator, thus making "real" and immediate communication possible. The passive cinematic experience, that *rendezvous manqué* between exhibitionist and voyeur, is transformed into a "theatrical" encounter between human beings present in the flesh. The two-dimensional space of the screen gives way to the three-dimensional space of theatre and politics. The film mobilizes, fostering motor and mental activity rather than self-indulgent fantasy. Rather than vibrate to the sensibility of an Auteur, the spectators become the authors of their own destiny. Rather than a mass hero *on the screen*, the protagonists of history are *in the audience*. Rather than a womb to regress in, the cinema becomes a political stage on which to act.

Brecht contrasted artistic innovation easily absorbed by the apparatus with the kind which threatens its very existence. *La Hora* wards off cooptation by a stance of radical interventionism. Rather than being hermetically sealed off from life, the text is permeable to history and praxis, calling for accomplices rather than consumers. The three major sections begin with *ouvertures*—orchestrated quotations, slogans, rallying cries—which suggest that the spectators have come not to enjoy a show but to participate in an action. Each screening is meant to create what the authors call a "liberated space, a decolonized territory." Because of this activist stance, *La Hora* was dangerous to make, to distribute, and, not infrequently, to see. When a repressive situation makes filmgoing a clandestine activity punishable by prison or torture, the mere act of viewing comes to entail political commitment. Cinephilia, at times a surrogate for political action in the United States and Europe, became in Argentina a life-endangering form of praxis, placing the spectator in a booby-trapped space of political commitment. Instead of the mere firecrackers-under-the-seats of the Dadaists, the spectator was faced with the distant possibility of machine-gun fire in the cinema. All the celebrated "attacks on the voyeurism of the spectator" pale in violence next to this threatened initiation into political brutality.

In its frontal assault on passivity, *La Hora* deploys a number of textual strategies. The spoken and written commentary, addressed directly to the spectator, fosters a discursive relationship, the I-You of *discours* rather than the He-She voyeurism of *histoire*. The language, furthermore, is unabashedly partisan, eschewing all factitious "objectivity." Diverse classes, the film reminds us, speak divergent languages. The 1955 putsch, for the elite, is a "liberating revolution," for the people, "the gorilla coup." Everything in the film, from the initial dedication to Che Guevara through the final exhortation to action, obeys the Brechtian injunction to "divide the audience," forcing the audience to "take sides." The Argentinian intellectual must decide to be with the Peronist masses or against them. The American must reject the phrase "Yankee imperialism" or acknowledge that it corresponds, on some level, to the truth. At times, the call for commitment reaches discomfiting extremes for the spectator hoping for a warm bath of escapism. Quoting Fanon's "all spectators are cowards or traitors" (neither option flatters), the film calls at times for virtual readiness for martyrdom—"To choose one's death is to choose one's life"—at which point the lukewarm entertainment-seeker might feel that the demands for commitment have escalated unacceptably.

La Hora also short-circuits passivity by making intense intellectual demands. The written titles and spoken commentary taken together form a more or less continuous essay, one which ranks in rhetorical power with those of the authors it cites—Fanon, Césaire, Sartre. At once broadly discursive and vividly imagistic, abstract and concrete, this essay-text, rather than simply commenting on the images, organizes them and provides their principle of coherence. The essay constitutes the film's control-center, its brain. The images take on meaning in relation to it rather than the reverse. During prolonged periods, the screen becomes an audio-visual blackboard and the spectator a reader of text. The staccato intercutting of black frames and incendiary titles generates a dynamic *ciné-écriture*; the film writes itself. Vertovian titles explode around the screen, rushing toward and retreating from the spectator, their graphic presentation often mimicking their signification. The word "liberation," for example, proliferates and multiplies, in a striking visual and kinetic reminiscence of Che's call for "two, three, many Viet Nams." At other times, in a rude challenge to the sacrosanct "primacy of the visual," the screen remains blank while a disembodied voice addresses us in the darkness.

The commentary participates mightily in the film's work of demystification. As the caption, for Walter Benjamin, could tear photography away from fashionable clichés and grant it "revolutionary use-value," so the commentary shatters the official image of events. An idealized painting celebrating Argentine political independence is undercut by the off-screen account of the financial deals which betrayed *economic* independence. Formal sovereignty is exposed as the facade masking the realities of material subjugation. Shots of the bustling, prosperous port of Buenos Aires, similarly, are accompanied by an analysis of a general systemic poverty: "What characterizes Latin American countries is, first of all, their dependence—economic dependence, political dependence, cultural dependence." The spectator is taught to distrust images, or better, to see through them to their underlying structures. The film strives to enable the spectator to penetrate the veil of appearances, to dispel the mists of ideology through an act of revolutionary decoding.

Much of *La Hora*'s persuasive power derives from its ability to render ideas visual. Abstract concepts are given clear and accessible form. The sociological abstraction "oligarchy" is concretized by shots of the "fifty families" that monopolize much of Argentina's wealth. "Here they are..." says the text; the "oligarchy" comes into focus as the actual faces of real people, recognizable and accountable. "Class society" becomes the image ("quoted" from Birri's *Tire Dié*) of desperate child beggars running alongside trains in hopes of a few pennies from blasé passengers. "Systemic violence" is rendered by images of the state's apparatus of repression—prisons, armored trucks, bombers. The title "No Social Order Commits Suicide" yields to four quick-cut shots of the military. Césaire's depiction of the colonized—"Dispossessed, Marginalized, Condemned"—gives way to shots of workers, up against the wall, undergoing police interrogation. Thus *La Hora* engraves ideas on the mind of the spectator. The images do not explode harmlessly, dissipating their energy. They fuse with ideas in order to detonate in the minds of the audience.

Parody and satire form part of the strategic arsenal of *La Hora de los Hornos*. One sequence, a sight-seeing excursion through Buenos Aires, compares in irreverence to Buñuel's sardonic tour of Rome in *L'Age d'Or*. The images are those customary in travelogues—government buildings, monuments, busy thoroughfares—but the accompanying text is dipped in acid. Rather than exalt the cosmopolitan charm or the bustling energy of Buenos Aires, the commentary disengages its class structure: the highly-placed *comprador* bourgeoisie, the middle class ("eternal in-betweens, both protected and used by the oligarchy") and the petite bourgeoisie, "eternal crybabies, for whom change is necessary, but impossible." Monuments, symbols of national pride, are treated as petrified emblems of servility. As the camera zooms out from an equestrian statue of one of Argentina's founding fathers (Carlos de Alvear), an off-screen voice ironizes: "Here monuments are erected to the man who said: 'These provinces want to belong to Great Britain, to accept its laws, obey its government, live under its powerful influence.'"

Satiric vignettes pinpoint the reactionary nostalgia of the Argentine ruling class. We see them in an antique car acting out their fantasy of *la belle époque*. We see "La Recoleta," their cemetery, baroque testimonial to an atrophied way of life, where the oligarchy tries to "freeze time" and "crystallize history." Just as Vertov destroys (via split screen) the Bolshoi Theatre in *The Man with the Movie Camera*, Solanas-Getino annihilate the cemetary with superimposed lightning-bolts and thunderous sound effects. Using techniques reminiscent of Resnais' art documentaries, they animate the cemetary's neoclassical statues, creating a completely artificial time and space. The statues' "dialogue" in shot/reaction shot to the music of an Argentinian opera whose words ("I shall bring down the rebel flag in blood") remind us of the aristocracy's historical capacity for savage repression. Still another vignette pictures the oligarchy at its annual cattle show in Buenos Aires. The sequence interweaves shots of the crowned heads of the prize bulls with the faces of the aristocracy. The bulls—inert, sluggish, well pedigreed—present a perfect analogue to the oligarchs that breed them. Metonymic contiguity coincides with metaphoric transfer as the auctioneer's phrases describing the bulls ("admire the expression, the bone structure") are yoked, in a stunning cinematic xeugma, to the looks of bovine self-satisfaction on the faces of their owners.

On occasion, Solanas-Getino enlist the unwitting cooperation of their satiric targets by having ruling-class figures condemn themselves by their own discourse. Newsreel footage shows an Argentinian writer, surrounded by jewelry-laden dowagers, at an official reception, as a parodic off-screen voice sets the tone: "And now let's go to the Pepsi Cola Salon, where Manuel Mujica Lainez, member of the Argentine Academy of Letters, is presenting his latest book *Royal Chronicles*." Lainez then boasts, in non-synchronous sound, of his international prizes, his European formation, his "deep sympathy for the Elizabethan spirit." No professional actor could better incarnate the intellectual bankruptcy of the elite, with its fossilized attitudes, its nostalgia for Europe, its hand-me-down culture, and its snide ingratitude toward the country and people that made possible its privileges.

Recorded noises and music also play a discursive and demystificatory role. The sound of a time clock punctuates shots of workers hurrying to their jobs, an aural reminder of the daily violence of "wage slavery." Godardian frontal shots of office buildings with their abstract geometricality are superimposed with sirens; innocuous images take on overtones of urban anxiety. A veritable compendium of musical styles—tango, opera, pop—make mordant comment on the image. A segment on cultural colonialism has Ray Charles singing "I don't need no doctor" as a pop-music junkie nods his head in rhythm in a Buenos Aires record store. A medley of national and party anthems ("La Marseillaise," "The International") lampoons the European allegiances of the traditional left parties. And one of the most poignantly telling sequences shows a small-town prostitute, pubic hair exposed, eating lunch while sad-looking men wait in line for her favors. The musical accompaniment (the patriotic "flag-raising" song) suggests that Argentina has been reduced to exactly this—a hungry prostitute with her joyless clientele.

Solanas-Getino prolong and critically reelaborate the avant-garde heritage. One sequence fuses Eisenstein with Warhol by intercutting scenes from a slaughterhouse with pop-culture advertising icons. The sequence obviously quotes Eisenstein's celebrated non-diegetic metaphor in *Strike*, but also invests it with specifically Argentinian resonances. In Argentina, where livestock is a basic industry, the same workers who can barely afford the meat that they themselves produce are simultaneously encouraged by advertising to consume the useless products of the multinational companies. The livestock metaphor, anticipated in the earlier prize-bull sequence, is subsequently "diegetized" when a shot of the exterior of a slaughterhouse coincides with an account of the police repression of its striking workers. The advertising/slaughter juxtaposition, meanwhile, evokes advertising itself as a kind of slaughter whose numbing effect is imaged by the mallet striking the ox unconscious. The vapid accompanying music by the Swingle Singers (Bach grotesquely metamorphosed into Ray Conniff) counterpoints the brutality of the images, while underlining the shallowly plastic good cheer of the ads.

In *La Hora*, minimalism—the avant-garde esthetic most appropriate to the exigencies of film production in the Third World—reflects practical necessity as well as artistic strategy. Time and again one is struck by the contrast between the poverty of the original materials and the power of the final result. Unpromising footage is transmogrified into art, as the alchemy of montage transforms the base metals of titles, blank frames and percussive sounds into the gold and silver of rhythmic virtuosity. Static two-dimensional images (photos, posters, ads, engravings) are dynamized by editing and camera movement. Still photos and moving images sweep by at such velocity that we lose track of where movement stops and stasis begins. The most striking minimalist image—a close-up of Che Guevara's face in death—is held for a full five minutes. The effect of this inspirational death mask is paradoxical. Through the having-been-there of photography, Che Guevara returns our glance from beyond the grave. His face even in death seems mesmerizingly present, his expression one of defiant undefeat. At the same time, the photo gradually assumes the look of a cracked revolutionary icon. The long contemplation of the photograph demystifies and unmasks: we become conscious of the frame, the technical imperfections, the filmic material itself.[4]

The most iconoclastic sequence, entitled "Models," begins by citing Fanon's call for an authentically third-world culture: "Let us not pay tribute to Europe by creating states, institutions and societies in its mould. Humanity expects more from us than this caricatural and generally obscene imitation." As the commentary derides Europe's "racist humanism," the image track parades the most highly prized artifacts of European high culture: the Parthenon, *Déjeuner sur l'herbe*, Roman frescoes, portraits of Byron and Voltaire. In an attack on the ideological hierarchies of the spectator, haloed art works are inexorably lap-dissolved into meaninglessness. As in the postcard sequence of *Les Carabiniers*, that locus classicus of anti-high-art semioclasm, the most cherished monuments of Western culture are implicitly equated with the commercialized fetishes of consumer society. Classical painting and toothpaste are levelled as two kinds of imperial export. The pretended "universality"of European culture is exposed as a myth masking the fact of domination.

This demolition job on Western culture is not without its ambiguities, however; for Solanas and Getino, like Fanon before them, are imbued with the very culture they so vehemently denigrate. *La Hora* betrays a cultivated familiarity with Flemish painting, Italian opera, French cinema; it alludes to the entire spectrum of highbrow culture. Their attack is also an exorcism, the product of a love-hate relationship to the European parent culture. The same lap-dissolves that obliterate classical art also highlight its beauty. The film's scorn for "culture," furthermore, finds ample precedent within the anti-traditionalist modernism of Europe itself. Mayakovsky asked, even before the revolution, that the classics be "cast from the steamboat of modernity." The dismissal of all antecedent art as simply a waste of time recalls the *antepassatismo* of the futurists. "We must spit each day," said Marinetti "on the altar of art." And both Mayakovsky and Godard have evoked the symbolic destruction of the shrines of high culture. "Make bombardment echo on the museum walls," shouted Mayakovsky, and Godard, in *La Chinoise*, has Véronique call for the bombing of the Louvre and the Comédie Française.

While drawing on a certain avant-garde, *La Hora* critiques what it sees as the apolitical avant-garde. Revolutionary films, in their view, must be esthetically avant-garde—revolutionary art must first of all be revolutionary *as art* (Benjamin)—but avant-garde films are not necessarily revolutionary. *La Hora* eludes what it sees as the vacuity of a certain avant-garde by politicizing what might have been purely formalistic exercises. The ironic pageant of high art images in the "Models" sequence, for example, is accompanied by a discourse on the colonization of third-world culture. Another sequence, superimposing shots of Argentinians lounging at poolside with vapid cocktail dialogue about the prestige value of being familiar with Op art and Pop art, abstract art and concrete art, highlights the bourgeois fondness for a politically innocuous avant-garde which is as much the product of fashion and commodity fetishism as styles in shirts and jeans. In Argentina, its promotion formed part of a pattern of United States cultural intervention in which organizations such as the U.S.I.S. exhibited modernist painting as part of a larger imperialist strategy.

An apolitical avant-garde risks becoming an institutionalized loyal opposition, the progressive wing of establishment art.

Supplying a daily dose of novelty to a satiated society, it generates surface turmoil while leaving the deep structures intact. The artists, as Godard once pointed out, are inmates who bang their dishes against the bars of their prison. Rather than destroy the prison, they merely make a noise which, ultimately, reassures the warden. The noise is then coopted by a mechanism of repressive desublimation and cited as proof of the system's liberality. *La Hora* has nothing to do with such an avant-garde, and to treat it as such would be to trivialize it by detaching it from the revolutionary impulse that drives and informs it.

Embracing elements of this critique of an apolitical avant-garde does not entail endorsing all features of the film's global politics. Without diminishing the directors' achievement or disrespecting the sacrifice of thousands of Argentinians, one feels obliged to point out certain political ambiguities in the film. *La Hora* shares with what one might call the heroic-masochistic avant-garde a vision of itself as engaged in a kind of apocalyptic self-sacrifice in the name of future generations. The artistic avant-garde, as Renato Poggioli and Massimo Bontempelli have suggested, often cultivates the image, and symbolically suffers the fate, of military avant gardes: they serve as advanced cadres "slaughtered" (if only by the critics) to prepare the way for the regular army or the new society. The spirit of self-immolation on the altar of the future ("*Pitié pour nous qui combattons toujours aux frontières/De l'illimité et de l'avenir*") merges in *La Hora* with a quasi-religious subtext which draws on the language and imagery of martyrdom, death and resurrection. One might even posit a subliminal Dantesque structuring which ascends from the *inferno* of neocolonial oppression through the *purgatorio* of revolutionary violence to the *paradiso* of national liberation. Without reviving the facile caricature of Marxism as "secular religion," one can regret the film's occasional confusion of political categories with moral-religious ones. The subsurface millenarianism of the film, while it partially explains the film's power (and its appeal for even some bourgeois critics), in some ways undermines its political integrity.

Equipped with the luxury of retrospective lucidity, one can also better discern the deficiencies of the Fanonian and Guevarist ideas informing the film. *La Hora* is deeply imbued with Fanon's faith in the therapeutic value of violence. But while it is true to say that violence is an effective political language, the key to resistance or the taking of power, it is quite another to value it as therapy for the oppressed. *La Hora* misapplies a theory associated with a specific point in Fanon's ideological trajectory (the point of maximum disenchantment with the European left) and with a precise historical situation (French settler colonialism in Algeria). Solanas and Getino also pay rightful tribute to Che Guevara as model revolutionary. Subsequent events, however, have made it obvious that certain of Che's policies were mistaken. Guevarism in Latin America gave impetus to an ultra-voluntarist strategy which often turned out to be ineffective or even suicidal. One might even link the vestigial machismo of the film's language ("*El Hombre*": Man) to this ideal of the heroic warrior who personally exposes himself to combat.[5] Guerilla strategists often underestimated the repressive power of the governments in place and overestimated the objective and subjective readiness of the local populations for revolution.

As a left Peronist film, *La Hora* also partakes of the historical strengths and weaknesses of that movement.[6] Solanas-Getino rightly identify Peron as a third-world nationalist *avant la lettre* rather than the "fascist dictator" of Eurocentric mythology.[7] ("Peron was a fascist and a dictator detested by all good men . . . except Argentinians," said Dean Acheson, slyly insinuating that Argentinians were not good men.) While *La Hora* does score the failures of Peronism—its refusal to attack the power bases of the oligarchy, its failure to arm the people against right-wing coups, its constant oscillation between "democracy of the people" and the "dictatorship of bureaucracy"—the film-makers see Peron as the man through whom the Argentinian working class became gropingly aware of its collective destiny. Peronism, for them, was "objectively revolutionary," because it embodied this proletarian movement. By breaking the imperial stranglehold on Argentina's economy, Peronism would prepare the way for authentic socialist revolution. The film fails most crucially, however, in not placing Peronism in its most appropriate context—Latin American populism. In this version, populism represents a style of political representation by which certain progressive and nationalist elements of the bourgeoisie enlist the support of the people in order to advance their own interests. Latin American populists, like populists everywhere, flirt with the right with one hand and caress the left with the other, making pacts with God and the Devil. Like the inhabitants of Alphaville, they manage to say yes and no at the same time. As a tactical alliance, Peronism constituted a labyrinthian tangle of contradictions, a fragile mosaic which shattered, not surprisingly, with its leader's disappearance.

Peronism was plagued by at least two major contradictions, both of which are inscribed, to a certain extent, in the film. Wholeheartedly anti-imperialist, Peronism was only half heartedly anti-monopolist since the industrial bourgeoisie allied with it was more frightened of the working class than it was of imperialism. Although Solanas-Getino at one point explicitly call for socialist revolution, there is ambiguity in the film and in the concept of "Third Cinema." The "third," while obviously referring to the "Third World," also echoes Peron's call for a "third way," for an intermediate path between socialism and capitalism. That *La Hora* seems more radical than it in fact is largely derives from its skillful orchestration of what one might call the revolutionary intertext, i.e., its aural and visual evocation of tricontinental revolution. The strategically placed allusions to Che Guevara, Fanon, Ho Chi Minh and Stokely Carmichael create a kind of *effet de radicalité* rather like the *effet de réel* cited by Barthes in connection with the strategic details of classical realist fiction.

Peronism's second major contradiction has to do with its constant swing between democracy and authoritarianism, participation and manipulation. With populism, a plebeian style and personal charisma often mask a deep scorn for the masses. Egalitarian manners create an apparent equality between the representative of the elite and the people who are the object of manipulation. The film, at once manipulative and participatory, strong-armed and egalitarian, shares in this ambiguity. It speaks the language of popular expression ("your ideas are as important as ours") but also resorts to hyperbolic language and sledgehammer persuasion.

La Hora is brilliant in its critique. And history has not shown its authors to be totally failed prophets. It is facile for us, equipped with hindsight and protected by distance, to point up mistaken predictions or failed strategies. The film's indictment of neocolonialism remains shatteringly relevant. The critique of the traditional left, and especially of the Argentine Communist Party, has been borne out as the PCA offers its critical support to a right-wing regime, largely because it concentrates its repression on the non-Stalinist left and makes grain deals with the Soviet Union. The film also accurately points up the ruling class potentiality for violent repression. The current regime, with its horrendous human rights record, its *desapparecidos* and its anti-Semitism, merely reaffirms the capacity for violence of an elite that has "more than once bathed the country in blood."

Despite its occasional ambiguities, *La Hora de los Hornos* remains a seminal contribution to revolutionary cinema. Transcending the narcissistic self-expression of Auteurism, it voices the concerns of a mass movement. By allying itself with a concrete movement, which however "impure" has at least the virtue of being real, it practices a cinematic politics of "dirty hands." If its politics are at times populist, its filmic strategies are not. It assumes that the mass of people are quite capable of grasping the exact meaning of an association of images or of a sound montage; that it is ready, in short, for linguistic experimentation. It respects the people by offering quality, proposing a cinema which is simultaneously a tool for consciousness-raising, an instrument for analysis, and a catalyst for action. *La Hora* provides a model for avant-garde political filmmaking and a treasury of formalist strategies. It is an advanced seminar in the politics of art and the art of politics, a four-hour launching pad for experimentation, an underground guide to revolutionary cinematic praxis.

La Hora is also a key piece in the ongoing debate concerning the two avant-gardes. It would be naive and sentimental to see the two avant-gardes as "naturally" allied. (The mere mention of Ezra Pound or Marinetti refutes such an idea.) The alliance of the two avant-gardes is not natural, it must be forged. The two avant-gardes, yoked by a common impulse of rebellion, concretely need each other. While revolutionary esthetics without revolutionary politics is often futile ("They did away with grammar," said Père Brecht, "but they forgot to do away with capitalism."), revolutionary politics without revolutionary esthetics is equally retrograde, pouring the new wine of revolution into the old bottles of conventional forms, reducing art to a crude instrumentality in the service of a preformed message. *La Hora*, by avoiding the twin traps of an empty iconoclasm on the one hand, and a "correct" but formally nostalgic militancy on the other, constitutes a major step toward the realization of that scandalously utopian and only apparently paradoxical idea—that of a majoritarian avant-garde.

NOTES

1. The idea of "Third Cinema" is fully developed in an essay by Solanas and Getino entitled "Towards a Third Cinema." This essay, anthologized in Bill Nichol's *Movies and Methods*, has been translated into at least a dozen languages and has been highly influential around the world.
2. Solanas and Getino were not historically the first to suggest the combination of film with discussion. In 1933, Béla Balázs proposed that "explanations" be made standard at all screenings: "This does not apply only to our films. We must have critical, satirical analyses of the bourgeois films, expose their reactionary, capitalistic and anti-proletarian ideology, ridicule their philistine narrow-mindedness." Balázs' proposal is, finally, less open than that of Solanas-Getino, since he favors "explanations" rather than "debate," going so far as to suggest that the lecturer record his/her comments on a disc which could accompany the film. More recently, McCall and Tyndall in *Argument* aim to create the preconditions whereby the audience can act on the social situation which the film engages. The film has been shown to small groups followed by discussions with its makers. This experiment too is less audacious than that of Solanas-Getino, since the film is not interrupted, and the debate is only with the filmmakers.
3. Aleatory procedures are, of course, typical of art in the sixties. One need think only of "process art" in which chemical, biological or seasonal forces affect the original materials, or of environmental art, or happenings, mixed media, human-machine-interaction systems, street theatre and the like. The film formed part of a general tendency to erase the boundaries between art and life, but rarely did this erasure take such a highly politicized form.
4. The Argentinian *junta* paid inadvertent tribute to the revolutionary potential of photography when they arrested Che Guevara's mother in 1962, accusing her of having in her possession a "subversive" photograph. The photograph was of her son Che. See *The New York Times*, May 19, 1980, p. A10.
5. Gérard Chaliand, in *Mythes Révolutionnaires du Tiers Monde* (1976), criticizes what he calls the "macho" attitudes of Latin American guerillas which led them to expose themselves to combat even when their presence was not required, thus resulting in the death of most of the guerilla leaders. He contrasts this attitude with the more prudent procedure of the Vietnamese. During fifteen years of war, not one of the fifty members of the central committee of the South Vietnamese National Liberation Front fell into the hands of the enemy.

6. Should there by any doubt about the Peronist allegiances of the film, one need only remember the frequent quotations of Peron, the interviews with Peronist militants, and the critiques of the non-Peronist left. In 1971, Solanas and Getino made a propaganda film for Peron: *Peron: La Revolución Justicialista* (Peron: The Justicialism Revolution). The Cine-Liberacion group which made the film, according to Solanas, served as "the cinematic arm of General Peron." During the Campora administration, Getino accepted a post on the national film board. Upon Peron's death, Solanas and Getino made a public declaration supporting the succession of his wife Isabel. Ironically, the repression unleashed after her ouster was levelled as much against Solanas and Getino as against those who had been more consistently on the left.
7. The simplistic view of Peron as a fascist has been revived in many of the reviews of the Broadway production of *Evita*, with a number of critics comparing the play to the kind of spectacle parodied in Mel Brooks's *The Producers*.

69

JUAN CARLOS ESPINOSA, JORGE FRAGA, ESTRELLA PANTIN

TOWARD A DEFINITION OF THE DIDACTIC DOCUMENTARY

A Paper Presented to the First National Congress of Education and Culture (1978)

Let's begin with this common ground: there is a serious discrepancy between our educational needs and the resources we have at our disposal to satisfy those needs. It is also common knowledge that documentary didactic cinema is one of the most effective means of reducing this discrepancy. There is little merit simply in recognizing this, and the number of documentaries of this type that we have produced in these years of revolution indicates, perhaps, that we do not turn our backs on life's most immediate necessities. But this number is too small in relation to what we need, and it will necessarily have to remain so for some years. We must concern ourselves, then, with working within the limits of what we can do. In order to justify the scarcity legitimately, if that's possible, we must demonstrate the never-ending determination we have to give to the little that we have its greatest effectiveness.

What can we do to increase the educational potential of each didactic documentary? A comparison between the first didactic documentaries that we made eleven years ago, and the more recent ones, indicates the way. It's not the only road, but it seems to us to be one of great interest. Today, we propose to sketch an outline of that road, to map a route, and to invite you to travel along it.

The didactic documentary is, first of all, an auxiliary method of education, an instrument which the professor may use along with text books, maps, and other auxiliary tools. Thus, linked with a particular process of learning, the objectives of the didactic film are the same as those of the teacher.[1]

Since the teacher's goal is to carry out the program, the didactic film takes its content from the program's themes. This content would correspond to that of one class, or to that of all the classes as a whole. In this case, in its scope and in the volume of the ideas and facts it communicates, the didactic film uses the class as a model of the educational unit, and it is within the context of the educational process that the didactic film has its perimeters and fulfills its function. Nothing could be more natural, then, than to base the qualities of the didactic film on the criteria used to define the audience, the program, and the goals of the teacher.

Our first didactic films, even those which weren't destined to be used as teaching aids in the classroom, responded in fact to those criteria.[2] They were illustrations for a learning situation; it didn't matter whether that situation was real or potential. Thus conceived, the didactic film had the advantage, alongside the professor's oral explanation, of improving the possibilities of reception by appealing to more senses, in order to communicate to the student the planned rational content of the program, when it did not exactly coincide with that explanation. It is this initial conception of the didactic film that we would like to discuss, as a result of our own experiences and efforts to take new factors within the educational process into account, under the conditions of our country and according to the goals of the Revolution.

First, the didactic film conceived in this way does not offer the maximum educational efficiency to the class it proposes to aid. Subordinated to the teacher's explanation, its content is limited to the themes of a program set up without the documentary in mind; in short, it is restricted to being the visual illustration of a spoken account. The didactic film necessarily repeats and competes with the role of the teacher and the other teaching aids. Undoubtedly, since they have the same purpose, there must be points of coincidence between different methods of education. But, just as the teacher's effectiveness, and even his existence, are justified because he gives the student something that the book cannot, the role and the effectiveness of the didactic film should not be measured by what it has in common with other educational methods, but by what it has to offer that is unique. The educational process should be considered the union of differing methods, which point towards a common goal, so that each method can attain its maximum effectiveness. So, the didactic film must not take the teacher's exposition as its model and example.

The second reason for our discussing this initial conception of the didactic film goes beyond its basic characteristics as a teaching aid. There is no particular teaching need which is not in some way linked to a general educational need. The most specific problems are tied by a number of links to problems of general interest. It is true that it is not always easy to perceive them, but there is no doubt that these links exist. In the underdeveloped countries, especially if, as in our case, they are undergoing a Revolution, educational needs in particular areas and in general are so pressing that we absolutely must ask ourselves, every time we try to satisfy a specific educational need, if there might not be a way to do so while at the same time satisfying educational needs of a more general nature. Here, the argument for taking the maximum advantage of available methods is the feeblest. The cinema is still an expensive means of cultural communication. Is it legitimate therefore, to make didactic films which serve a particular educational function without satisfying a more general educational need?

But there is a more far-reaching argument than that for the rational use of available methods.[3] We fight underdevelopment, towards a conception of man. We want, for our country and for the world, a unigue culture, stripped of the intellectual and moral inequalities which today lacerate man, free of antagonism between classes and of the social frameworks which, like the cells of a steel beehive, catch men in the trap of the social division of labour. Cultural inequality, social differences, division of labour, all these monuments for the archeologists of the future, which today obstruct the development of all the capacities of all men, cannot be eliminated through the power of the imagination. But if this is our goal, if this is as well the destiny of mankind, shouldn't we ask, starting today and on every occasion, if that which serves to develop a few could not possibly be done in such a way that it would serve to develop everyone? Is there any other way?

If there is a method capable of playing this double role, that method is precisely the cinema. The universality of visual language is natural for eliminating cultural differences, exemplified by, among other factors, the lack of that tendency towards abstraction which verbal language imposes and requires.

We are not proposing a compromise, however. It is not a question of partially sacrificing the particular educational need in order to satisfy, partially as well, the general educational need. We have seen that the didactic film achieves its maximum efficiency through making its particular function distinct from the rest of the educational methods. The possibility of conceiving a kind of didactic documentary which would simultaneously satisfy the specific need and the general need, without prejudicing either, is found precisely in this difference.

But this possibility does not exist simply because of the relationship between the didactic film and the other methods of education. There are at least two more reasons:

The first is this truism: specific educational needs always have essential points in common with the needs of education in general. We will stress two of these areas, in which the didactic documentary can be singularly effective: the nature of the thinking implicit in the teaching, and its motivation.

a) It is no coincidence that serious forms of cultural alienation characteristic of capitalist countries, i.e., gambling, lotteries, and astrology, acquire vast and deeply rooted inroads into the consciousness of the people in underdeveloped countries. The almost non-existent industrial development, and the resulting extremely low level of science and technology, of the socialization of work, and of means of communication and transportation, tools or tracks left by colonial domination, bring about a way of conceiving things, not in their relation to other things, but in themselves. This way of thinking perceives things as results, without considering the processes leading up to them; a way of thinking, in other words, which hearkens back to the magical. After twelve years of revolution, we still find examples of this way of thinking, even in our own communications media, mostly modelled after the tendency to exalt results and omit the process which led up to those results. The cinema, which by nature represents reality in motion, making it extremely useful to demonstrate processes, and through its capacity for revealing relationships between events registered in the most dissimilar conditions of time and place, possesses qualities suitable for education in a rational, concrete, and dialectical way of thinking, as well as immediate effectiveness in communicating knowledge and skills.

b) In general, the specific methods of education are limited to communicating a particular piece of information or a particular skill. They rarely go beyond the framework of their immediate goals. Within the conventional framework of education there is little or no room for establishing relationships between the immediate topic of study and other topics which, without being directly related to the goals in question, could increase the educational effectiveness of the method, developing its motivational value, awakening new interests, bringing to the content of the program new horizons of meaning, and thus stimulating an awareness of their significance. Clearly, a didactic documentary which limited itself to reproducing the method of operation of a certain machine could not contribute much to a course designed to train operators for that machine. This example demonstrates better than others how vain it is to endeavour to substitute for practice itself. But it is equally clear how much more useful a didactic film would be which showed the apprenticing operators the process of the construction of the machine, for example, or the scientific discoveries that have made it possible, or its significance for the development of the economy. With this aim of awakening interests or motivations, or stimulating a sense of responsibility towards that which is being learned, a didactic cinema has before it a wide field of investigation. It is a question of giving education its formative dimension through relations which, in the initial conditions of an underdeveloped country in the throes of revolution, cannot be achieved in the exclusive context of the system of compartmentalized education.

The notion of the documentary which we are outlining here cautions us against an unfortunate characteristic of the genre. It is an error which we ourselves have at times fallen into, and which still appears in world production. A sterile and ahistorical view of the didactic film considers it the genre of "boring" and "dry" topics. But the conventional reaction to this supposed dryness of the so-called "message film" consists of adding enticements to films like sugarcoating a pill—a technique known as the "snare." However, rather than increasing interest in the film, such techniques diminish it, by calling attention to themselves. These "snares," far from raising pedagogical efficiency, are reducing it. Worse still, these "snares" are products of a bourgeois publicity mentality. In fact, the commercial businessman is only interested in the act of selling, and the profit that he can obtain thereby. He is not interested in the concrete qualities of the product he offers. For him, everything, even ideas and feelings, are nothing more than values of exchange. On perceiving the product he sells, the businessman cannot know the qualities of that product; it is impossible to see a thing as an exchangeable unit and perceive its condition as a use-value at the same time. And, since it is characteristic of the bourgeois to think that everyone thinks as he does, he appeals to stimuli which have nothing to do with the nature of the product, in order to create more demand for it or stimulate the interest of the consumer; sex, the desire for recognition and prestige, feelings of inferiority—everything besides the actual demonstration of the concrete properties of the object. Even though, because of their content, the "snares" on occasion are not obvious expressions of commercial zeal, the fact of considering their use is in itself bourgeois. The didactic documentary must break once and for all with this retrogressive tradition, and integrate into its philosophy the principle that no themes are "dry" or "boring," and to suspect that when interest is lacking in the result, most times, or perhaps always, it is because interest is lacking in whoever has brought it about. The greatest interest of a theme lies in the theme itself, in its content, its history, and in its ties with the urgencies of life. The formal techniques must be derived from the theme and put at its service. It's the old moral demand for a unity between form and content.

We were saying that the concept of the didactic documentary, which we are presenting, warns against this error. And, in fact, aside from considerations of an ideological nature, or along with them, the temptation of using "snares" arises when the didactic film is relegated to being the illustration of what the teacher has explained. In other words, when it is repetitive, it can be tiring, and one therefore searches for other foci of attention. The previous explanation given the student by the teacher detracts from what the student would have to discover for himself. The result is inevitably colourless.

Conclusions

To sum up the foregoing, we could say that the critical analysis of our own experience brings us to a number of ideas which point towards a definition of the docuinentary genre, which consist in seeing it as an auxiliary educational method, and in defining its function and efficiency in terms of how it may be distinguished from the other methods. Thus conceived, the didactic film can at the same time satisfy general educational needs, and in doing so, make each particular method more effective, by bringing to it the dimensions of interest and incentive.

NOTES

1. For further information about Cuba's educational system, see Nelson P. Valdes, "The Radical Transformation of Cuban Education," in *Cuba in Revolution*, ed. Rolando E. Bonachea and Nelson P. Valdes (New York: Doubleday, Anchor Original, 1972) pp. 422–455.
2. At the I.C.A.I.C. in 1961 and 1962, during the Education Year, film makers produced two series of didactic films: *Enciclopedia Popular* and *Documentales Cientifico-Populares*. All these films were used in classrooms in order to illustrate social and health reforms organized by the Revolutionary Government.
3. Ché Guevara's main ideological contributions to the Cuban Revolution can be divided into two political methods. The first is guerrilla warfare in the war of Revolution. The second is the establishment of socialism, through man's conscious decision to control his environment for the benefit of all humanity. Thus the "creation of a new man." See George Lowan, ed. *Ché Guevara Speaks: Selected Speeches and Writings* (New York, 1967) and particularly *Notes on Man and Socialism in Cuba*.

NORM FRUCHTER, MARILYN BUCK, KAREN ROSS, ROBERT KRAMER

NEWSREEL (1969)

During the past year, young American film-makers and radicals have been banding together into a new organization, NEWSREEL, with a program markedly different from that of earlier documentaries—different from the British or New Deal films of the thirties (and their successors, the TV documentaries) and different from the cinéma-vérité documentaries of the sixties. NEWSREEL film-makers wish to use film as a revolutionary weapon; and the consequences of this basic orientation are being worked out by a growing band of film-makers, on both east and west coasts. In order to present something of the flavor of this work, we present below a montage of programmatic comments by NEWSREEL film-makers, followed by more detached comments from a critic not associated with the group.

Norm Fruchter, NY Newsreel

Newsreel, for me, is the constant challenge of facing choices which are at once, and indissolubly film-making choices, political choices, activist choices, aesthetic choices. None of us are satisfied with the blend that emerges . . . how to make what we want? Films as weapons? (Historical phrase—badly weathered.) Bullets kill, and some films get into people's heads, to shock, stun, arrest, horrify, depress, sadden, probe, demand. We want that kind of engagement—films people can't walk away from, with "Oh yes, I saw a filmshow last night, sort of political."

Who doubts, any more, that this country is so monstrously damaging, to both its domestic and foreign captive populations, that revolution is essential? The problem is how: what forces we're building, what this multifaceted thing we call the Movement will grow into, what real organizations we're making out of all the disaffection this country breeds. Not that armageddon is coming, or apocalypse—but in small ways the streets explode, and the fabric of consent which sociologists once celebrated shreds visibly on the TV. Who knows what's happening to this country? So our films have to attack, they come out of as close as we can get to the activity we value. Getting deeper, harsher, more corrosive, more inflammatory—those are our problems.

We should hate a lot more. Let it out. Let it dissolve the insufferable smugness which protects everybody. The media. None of us are old enough to have any illusions about infiltrating the major media to reach mass consciousness and change it—we grew up on TV and fifties Hollywood....

Marilyn Buck and Karen Ross, San Francisco Newsreel

This society is one of spectators, who live and perceive through the news media, particularly the visual media. People's lives revolve around the assumptions which are made by which channel they watch or what movie they choose to see. And all the TV channels and American films speak from the same mouth of control and power. We looked around ... and Newsreel was conceived and born. A way for film-makers and radical organizer-agitators to break into the consciousness of people. A chance to say something different... to say that people don't have to be spectator-puppets.

In our hands film is not an anesthetic, a sterile, smooth-talking apparatus of control. It is a weapon to counter, to talk back to and to crack the facade of the lying media of capitalism.

The radicals who have become involved in San Francisco Newsreel had previously participated in the development of the left political movement. Yet some of these experiences resulted in alienation. A disappointment and frustration with the forms of the left. Creative action was lacking. Newsreel has offered a definite medium in which to work; a weapon to destroy the established forms of control and power over people. We have had to overcome our lack of technical knowledge of film-making. Moreover, we must realize our political responsibility within our chosen form.

Many others who came to Newsreel as filmmakers and artists had isolated themselves in their own work and private political fantasies. Newsreel has become an outlet for real political expression in a medium familiar to them. Their political fantasies were exposed. They had to begin relating to more active participation in the movement. They were political but it was necessary to combine the political content with form.

Fruchter

Easier to define than make the films we want. We're tied to events, and we shouldn't be: Pentagon, Columbia, Chicago, the Haight. Where should we begin? Most instincts are particular: narrow it down—this group, this action. Follow the officers of the Hanna Company in their jaunts through Brazil? Follow a Peace Corps volunteer? But why document the obvious—none of the people we make films for need *that* bad joke exposed, they've lived with (and often worked within) the reality. The varieties of domestic and external pacification deserve burlesque, no more. New forms? But how much will time, limited energies, finance, and the wearing pressure of events, the race to stay responsible, limit us?

Buck & Ross

Newsreel is a collective rather than a cooperative; we are not together merely to help each other out as film-makers but we are working together for a common purpose: to make films which shatter the image and reality of fragmentation and exploitation in this society. Yet there are problems in developing and maintaining this collective form. These lie in the question of assimilation. Assimilation of the film-maker and the radical, assimilation of the individual into the collective. In making films together which reflect a collective, a movement of ideas and actions rather than the individuality of the artist, we must develop new values, forms, new criteria for individual interaction. Differences in techniques and analysis of content must be worked out collectively. The body must endorse the resulting film or it cannot be distributed through Newsreel.

Fruchter

Responsibility. There's no revolutionary party yet, only fledgling forms of various undergrounds. No coherent strategy, no discipline to stay hewed to, so we make our politics (our films) on the hoof; our discussions often threaten to become interminable. How transcend this transition stage? What's our response, for instance, if we think that sabotage is only marginally effective and yet guys are going to jail for it? What's our response to the police ambush in Cleveland, who among us has doubts about why black men are moved to shoot police? Newsreel is a jumping-off point. Or are we kidding ourselves? In '42, '43, '44 in Italy, what did Zavattini and Rossellini and the rest say to themselves? Were the partisan units a real alternative? What were the terms on which they said, "But we must fight as film-makers"? What historical stage are we in, what categories can we use to decide what we must do?

Robert Kramer, New York Newsreel

We began by trying to bridge the gap between the states of mind and ways of working that we were accustomed to as film-makers, and the engagement/daily involvement/commitments of our political analysis and political activity. This had immediate implications—not only for our film-making, but for interpretations of what, as film-makers, as people engaged in a struggle against established forms of power and control, against established media of all forces, we had to do with or without cameras.

In regard to our films. I think we argue a different hierarchy of values. Not traditional canons of "what is professional," what is "comprehensive and intelligent reportage," what is "acceptable quality and range of material." No. Nor do we accept a more sophisticated argument about propaganda in general: that if the product isn't sold well, if the surface of the film (grainy, troublesome sound, soft-focus, a wide range of maladies that come up when you are filming under stress) alienates, then the subject population never even gets to your "message" about the product—they just say, "Fuck that, I'm not watching that shit."

The subject population in this society, bombarded by and totally immersed in complex, ostensibly "free" media, has learned to absorb all facts/information relatively easily. Within the formats now popularized by the television documentary, you can lodge almost any material, no matter how implicitly explosive, with the confidence that it will neither haunt the subject population, nor push them to move—in the streets, in their communities, in their heads. You see Cleaver or Seale on a panel show, and they don't scare you or impress you or make you think as they would if you met them on the street. Why? Because they can't get their hands on you? Partly, sure. (Fear and committed thought exist in terms of the threat that power will be used against you—in terms of the absolute necessity of figuring out what has to be done —not in terms of some vague decision to "think it through" in isolation.) But also, because their words are absorbed by the format of the "panel show," rational (note well: ostensibly rational) discussion about issues that we all agree are important and pressing, and that we (all good liberal viewers) are committed to analyzing. Well: bullshit. The illusion of the commitment to analyze. The illusion of real dissent. The illusion of even understanding the issues. Rather, the commitment to pretend that we're engaging reality.

OK. At the point when you have considered this argument then you start to make films with different priorities, with shapes justified in a different way. You want to make films that unnerve, that shake assumptions, that threaten, that do not soft-sell, but hopefully (an impossible ideal) explode like grenades in peoples' faces, or open minds up like a good can opener. We say: "The things you see in these films are happening at this moment, they are our 'news,' they are important to us and do not represent the droppings of a few freaks, but the activity of a growing wave of people, your children who were fighting the pigs at Columbia, your brothers who walked out of this high school, your sons who deserted the army, your former slaves who will not now accept your insufficient reparations, etc., etc. You know this reality. You know enough to know that this is real—now deal with it, because soon it's going to come to deal with you, in one way or another." The effect of our films is more like seeing 250 Black Panthers around the Oakland Court House, or Columbia students carrying on the business of revolt at Kirk's desk, or Free Men occupying the streets of Berkeley, than listening to what some reporter tells us about what these people might have said, and how we can understand "rebellion" psychologically. We strive for confrontation, we prefer disgust/violent disagreement/painful recognition/jolts—all these to slow liberal head-nodding and general wonderment at the complexity of these times and their being out of joint.

We want a form of propaganda that polarizes, angers, excites, for the purpose of discussion—a way of getting at people, not by making concessions to where they are, but by showing them where you are and then forcing them to deal with that, bringing out all their assumptions, their prejudices, their imperfect perceptions.

Buck & Ross

Some viewers make the whole choice to see Newsreels. They are aware of what they are going to see, and the films thus reinforce their conceptions—or they may shake these viewers back into radical action and analysis. Most importantly, Newsreels must be weapons: they must confront people who are not motivated to go see them. Newsreel must make half the decisions for them. Street projection is the first answer we've come up with so far. We take the films into the street, we stop people on the street, and confront them with our films. Involve them as participants. They're not home glued to their TVs, where if subjected to action they merely sit and absorb it in some unconscious place in their heads. The truck, mobile, produces live action on the street. Motion within motion. It has come to them during a walk down the street, they've stumbled upon it. Newsreel has forced itself into their consciousness. They have been confronted. The decision to watch, to register disgust or interest is now theirs. We have the opportunity to talk with them about their reactions, between films. To those inquisitive, we explain more. To those objecting, we can try to break their arguments. We have our confrontation as people, Newsreel has its confrontation through film.

Newsreel can evaluate the effectiveness of its films by looking at its audiences and their responses to the films. Many of our showings have been very discouraging: not many people or no reaction to the films at all. Others have been elating: lots of people who react vigorously to the films, asking questions or arguing about the validity of the films. And the difference in the showings may be only the audience. Middleclass neighborhood groups may feel that the straight documentary sync-sound film on draft resistance is very good to see: informative, encouraging, and perhaps even motivating. But when the same film is shown to young chicanos, it's absolutely useless. The guys walk out, hiss, and ask "When are you going to show us some action?" And so, we run the Haight riot film, a five-minute street film with a lot of action set to contemporary rock music. And they dig it. We show *Garbage*, a cultural exchange between the Motherfuckers of New York and Lincoln Center, a fast-moving film also, thinking this might also turn the guys on, and they are bored by it and finally walk out. But college and ex-college radicals say, "Far out, those guys are doing some good things—I like their style." And the older, middleclass people in the audience may not dislike it, but don't quite see the point . . . or register confusion or a polite distaste for the obscene language and people of the film.

Kramer

We shoot as best we can—but we shoot what's important to us, what meets our perceptions of our lived reality; we cut according to our priorities, our ideologies, not "to make it plain and simple to them." Not to present a "line." Not to present the lived reality as less complex than it really is. Not to enter into that sterile game: modulating our emotions and intensities and intelligences in some vain hope that by speaking your language your way we can persuade you. No, we know the effective outcome of that: only the acceptance of another of the subtle forms of domination and control. Now we move according to our own priorities, and we are justified in this by objective conditions. Five years ago, for example, such a decision would have been suicidal. Our movement was only emerging—few people knew anything about it—few people were involved. But now, all our audiences (and our audiences represent the full spectrum of the society) know the essence of what we're talking about. They read it every day in every paper digested and shaped to their preconceptions. So now we present it to them in its nakedness, in our true understanding of it, not vitiated by analyses and "in-depth studies" that we do not accept, but just exactly what counts from our point of view. The established media have done the job of popularizing: now we must specify and make immediate; convert our audiences or neutralize them; threaten.

Buck & Ross

The Columbia film, about the seizure of Columbia and the politics of that seizure, is an important film to college students. It was shown to students at the University of California, Santa Cruz, on the eve of a scheduled protest against the board of regents which was meeting on campus the next day. The film helped to bolster enthusiasm for the students' action and create a mood in which the protest could take place and be successful. The film on the Black Panther Party turns people's heads around, aweing them with the strength and the nature of the Panthers of which they may not have previously conceived. We think the film is politically and visually exciting—it demands that people react to it, and not pass it off. It is a film that evokes response with the most diverse kinds of audiences—liberals on their way to the film festival, students at the universities, the black community in the streets.

Kramer

Our films remind some people of battle footage: grainy, camera weaving around trying to get the material and still not get beaten/ trapped. Well, we, and many others are at war. We not only document that war, but try to find ways to bring that war to places which have managed so far to buy themselves isolation from it.

So, to return to the issue of propaganda. Our propaganda is one of confrontation. Using film—using our voices with and after films—using our bodies with and without cameras—to provoke confrontation. Changing minds, altering consciousness, seems to us to come through confrontations, not out of sweet/ reasonable conversations that are one of the society's modes of absorbing and disarming dissent and movement, of giving that illusion that indeed we are dealing with "the issues." Therefore we keep moving. We keep hacking out films, as quickly as we can, in whatever way we can.

To all film-makers who accept the limited, socially determined rules of clarity, of exposition, who think that films must use the accepted vocabulary to "convince," we say essentially: you only work, whatever your reasons, whatever your presumed "content" to support and bolster this society: you are a part of the mechanisms which maintain stability through re-integration; your films are helping to hold it all together, and finally, whatever your descriptions, you have already chosen sides. Dig: your sense of form and order is already a political choice—don't talk to me about "content"—but if you do, I will tell you that you cannot encompass our "content" with those legislated and approved senses, that you do not understand it if you treat it that way. There is no such thing as revolutionary content, revolutionary spirit, laid out for inspection and sale on the bargain basement counter.

71

FREDERICK WISEMAN WITH ALAN WESTIN

"YOU START OFF WITH A BROMIDE"

Conversation with Film Maker Frederick Wiseman (1974)

[. . .]

CLR: How do you decide which particular school, hospital, police force, or other institutions to go to?

WISEMAN: The standards I use in selection are first, that I can get permission to film, and second, that it's a place that is considered a reasonably good or even superior institution of its kind and is not a sitting-duck institution. There must be some sense that people are making a genuine effort, however short of some ideal standard that may fall. I have no way of determining what's typical, normal, average, standard, or whatever. I don't pretend to be an expert in any of these fields.

CLR: Do you do much research before you film?

WISEMAN: I don't believe in doing very much research before going in to shoot. The shooting of the film is the research. The editing is like writing the book. The research instead of being on 3-by-5 cards is on film. The final film is the product of studying and thinking about how you are going to structure, order, and find a form for the chaotic raw material of the research. In this process 100,000 feet of film are reduced to 3,000 feet, and the film emerges.

In *High School* I went to what was regarded as a fine middle-class school, and I didn't know what to anticipate. Then after a short time the boredom of the school began to get to me. The school grounds looked like a General Motors assembly plant, the playground like a huge parking lot. The last day of shooting I got a sequence that put together some of the feelings I'd had after being in the school for a month. At a faculty meeting the principal read a letter from a recent graduate, a boy on an aircraft carrier off Vietnam. The boy said he was making the school the beneficiary of his GI insurance in case he got killed. He wrote, "I have been trying to become a Big Brother in Vietnam, but it is very hard to do. . . . Am I wrong? . . . If I do my best and believe that what I do is right—that is all I can do. . . . I am only a body doing a job." The principal thought he was an excellent product. After reading the letter she said, "Now when you get a letter like this, to me it means that we are very successful at Northeast High School." This boy wanted to show his appreciation to the school for all it had done to teach him about duty, authority, and self. His uncritical, unthinking acceptance made him just like a Chevrolet rolling off the GM line.

CLR: Does this mean that you sometimes don't know how you are going to portray an institution until you get there?

WISEMAN: That's right, and that's one of the things that interests me about making a film. You start off with a little bromide or stereotype about how prison guards are supposed to behave or what cops are really like. You find that they don't match up to that image, that they're a lot more complicated. And the point of each film is to make that discovery. Before the film the tendency is to simplify. The discovery is that the actuality is much more complicated and interesting. The effort in editing is to have the completed film reflect that discovery.

CLR: Is there a film in which that discovery was particularly surprising to you?

WISEMAN: It's been true in all of them. *Law and Order* is a good example, however. I went to shoot *Law and Order* right after the police rioted at the 1968 Democratic Convention in Chicago. It seemed to me a golden opportunity to "get" the cops by showing how they behaved like "pigs." But after I rode around in police cars for a few days (and eventually for more than 400 hours), I realized what a simpleminded, naive view that was. The police are no different from the rest of us. The film dealt more with what people do to each other, the behavior that makes police necessary. Police brutality is shown as part of a more generally shared violence and not something isolated or unique.

Something of the same thing happened when I went to film at Metropolitan Hospital. I expected to find a lot of bureaucratic callousness and a hardened staff, indifferent to the problems of the poor. What I generally found, though, were a lot of doctors, nurses, and hospital personnel who really cared, trying to deal with the medical consequences of bad housing, illiteracy, no jobs, malnutrition, and so on.

CLR: Does this explain the ambiguity that many reviewers have noticed about your films, that one person can see a Wiseman film and come away appalled at what that institution is doing, and another person will conclude that the officials are doing a relatively good job under trying conditions?

WISEMAN: I think all the films have a well-defined point of view. My point of view toward the material is reflected in the structure of the film—the relationship of the sequences to each other and the themes that are developed by this particular order. However, a person's reaction to the film in part depends on his values and experience. Since the reality is complex, contradictory, and ambiguous, people with different values or experience respond differently. I think that there should be enough room in the film for other people to find support for their views while understanding what mine are. Otherwise I'd be in the propaganda business.

CLR: Let's talk about what your films reveal of civil liberties issues, particularly the question of how the rights of individuals are—or should be—treated in public institutions. As you probably know, the American Civil Liberties Union has recently sponsored a series of handbooks on the rights of various groups in American society—teachers, students, mental patients, prisoners, women, etc.

The main premise of many of these books is that it would be better for American society if the rights of individuals caught up in its institutions, many of them involuntarily, could be more fully defined and protected. In general, do you share that view?

WISEMAN: Of course. But, in a way, saying that is like coming out in favor of motherhood when that was popular. What intrigues me is the discrepancy between ideological statements like that and what actually goes on.

CLR: Let's apply what you just said to *Law and Order*. You have some striking sequences that show the use of excessive police force. For example, there's the black youth who's being arrested for stealing a car. The way he's thrown down on the automobile hood by the policeman, although he's manacled and poses no physical threat, is quite shocking. He was cursing the police, of course, but didn't pose any physical threat to the two officers there.

WISEMAN: Right. There was certainly no reason to beat that kid's head against the car, and I'm sure the policemen knew it. But a situation in which somebody's calling you a motherfucker and saying, "I'm gonna get you," is intense. It's not surprising that in those situations police like the rest of us sometimes lose control. How do you train a cop or anybody else not to react harshly to that kind of provocation?

CLR: But the policeman is an officer of the law, invested with a gun, and we do expect him to control the way he responds. Not to do so degrades the system of law the police are sworn to uphold.

WISEMAN: Yes; of course; we expect him to be that way. That's the ideology. But we've also got to recognize that we're asking him to exercise more restraint and control than most of us are capable of. Which is not in any way to excuse or forgive police brutality, but it suggests that the cop is not alone in having those kinds of aggressive or wild responses.

CLR: That brings us back to the question of whether more defined rights for people would improve the situation. I gather that you have some doubts about that.

WISEMAN: Take the situation in *High School*. Even if the law were to declare that students had more defined rights, I wonder whether it would make a great difference. I saw lots of passive, indifferent students at Northeast High. The only activists at the school that I met, really, were some kids in a human-relations discussion group shown in a sequence toward the end of the film, and everyone in that group was on the verge of flunking out for one reason or another.

Furthermore, it's a question of what values the kids are being taught at home, and whether they would want to challenge parental authority. Several of the sequences in the film showed the parents expressing the same kinds of values the school officials were enforcing. In one sequence a mother is talking to the guidance counselor about an incident in which her daughter has been accused of a disrespectful act toward her teacher. And the mother says to the guidance counselor, "The main thing in our home has always been respect for an adult. I was brought up that way; my husband was. And we have been trying to teach our children the same thing. To me, I think, one of the worst offenses is being disrespectful to an older person. Irregardless of what the condition may be." That's almost word for word what the dean of discipline tells the kid in an earlier sequence, to take his punishment and obey orders without dispute. What comes through is that this school is a perfect expression of the values of the people in this community. They wouldn't think in terms of rights and authoritarianism. It would be a matter of learning to do the right thing—regardless of what the condition may be. There are discipline sequences in *Basic Training* that are almost word for word from *High School*.

CLR: Didn't you find any form of student protest in Northeast High?

WISEMAN: No. A few days after Martin Luther King, Jr. was killed, there was a two-hour meeting of the student council. And a very serious debate about whether to send fruit or flowers to Mrs. King. The decision was made in favor of fruit.

CLR: Where does that leave you in terms of deciding whether the expansion of student rights would make schools like Northeast more democratic?

WISEMAN: Well, it makes me somewhat pessimistic about how much difference it would make. It would make *some*, and therefore expanding student rights is worth the effort. But a theme in almost all the films is that there is already a gap between the formal ideology and actual practice, between the rules and the way they are applied. In almost all these institutions, the officials talk as though they believed people have some rights. In practice, they do whatever they think is necessary to carry out their jobs, acting all the time out of a belief, often quite sincere, that this is the best way to help those they are teaching and guiding.

In *High School* the ideology of the school is revealed in the daily bulletin, the signs on the walls. There's one that says: "The mind is like a parachute, it functions best when open." The announced values are democracy, trust, sensitivity, understanding, openness, innovation—all the wonderful words we all subscribe to. But the practice is rigidity, authoritarianism, obedience, do as you're told, don't challenge.

CLR: And from the standpoint of what you thought would be fair and democratic, how did you react to the way the dean of discipline conducted himself?

WISEMAN: In one sense I was appalled; in another I thought I was watching a television situation comedy. But most situations aren't that clear-cut. Their strength as film sequences lies in their ambiguity and the expression of conflicting values. A rigid ideological approach to some of these questions can diminish the film by making it one-dimensional. For example, in *Titicut Follies* the young patient-inmate, Vladimir, is shown making a perfectly accurate critique of Bridgewater—that he isn't getting any real treatment, that his psychiatric sessions are a farce, and that he wants to go back to a regular prison where he can get better treatment. You see him appearing before a review board consisting of a psychiatrist, a psychologist, and several social workers who hear out his complaints, mumble a lot of parody psychiatry, and conclude that Vladimir can't be transferred, but rather his drug dosage should be increased. No one responds to Vladimir's needs. Vladimir really is sick; he keeps saying that he thinks his thorax has been poisoned by the food. The situation is complex because Vladimir's critique is accurate and he is also quite sick. Once the label paranoid schizophrenic is attached to him the staff is satisfied. The fact that he has problems or has been convicted of a crime doesn't mean that he should be subjected to the kind of "treatment" he's getting. The film doesn't say what the alternative should be, but I believe it says clearly that alternatives are needed.

CLR: Did you find that problem with formal rights in other institutions? How about *Juvenile Court*?

WISEMAN: People's reaction to *Juvenile Court* and their assessment of the court depends on how much they know about the law and how much they believe formal rights must be observed. The more they know about the law, the more critical they are of some of the procedures shown in the film. The less they know about the law, the more impressed they are with the humanitarianism and the practical solutions to difficult problems that are arrived at. *Juvenile Court* shows people of good will trying hard to deal decently with very complex problems, many of which are totally insoluble by any known or existing therapies. The question is whether more rigid application of due process standards would result in any better dispositions of the cases.

CLR: It's interesting that what you stress in your answer is "better dispositions," because that's different from the average civil libertarian's key question: Are people's rights violated? Am I characterizing fairly what you said?

WISEMAN: I'm sure that's a fair comment on what I've said. I guess, in part, I'm a little leery of a kind of professional civil libertarian view that can be just as pompous and as rigid as some of the formal ideologies that are being mocked in *High School*.

CLR: Is it rigid to believe that we should extend more legally-enforceable rights—of privacy, due process, and free expression—to people who are subject today to almost unchecked authority in so many of these institutions?

WISEMAN: I don't have any difficulty agreeing with your rhetoric. It's that I have doubts about the capacity to have such rights administered on a large scale in these types of institutions. I don't see the signs that people want such rights granted and then would be willing to support their enforcement in practice. Consider the massive effort that it took to make the American people think about the Vietnam War, or about integration, or any other major social problem. I come away with doubts about the capacity to motivate people to what is usually called large-scale social change.

CLR: Did you start off in 1967 with such pessimism?

WISEMAN: No, it's developed as I've made more films. I no longer have the view that I had in the beginning that there might be some direct relationship between what I was able to show in these films and the achievement of social change. Nor have I observed any particularly successful strategies of change, as they're called.

CLR: But millions of people are seeing your films; don't you expect or at least hope that they will be spurred to seek changes in public schools, prisons, hospitals, the army?

WISEMAN: Of course, but it's not for me to say what the change should be. What the films do is give people some information. Hopefully on the basis of this and other information people will be able to make more informed decisions about what, if any, change they would like to have take place. It's not my wish to impose solutions; that would be presumptuous.

CLR: In what sense? You're a trained lawyer, you're sensitive to issues of social justice, you've gotten inside half a dozen major institutions as a film maker; why aren't you entitled to draw up some prescriptions?

WISEMAN: I'm not a pharmacist. I've had an opportunity to observe how middle-class reformers play the social change game. I guess I've gone very far away from the liberal clichés and bromides that I started with, especially the simple-minded social-work view of help and intervention.

I was once involved with what was called a social science consulting firm in Cambridge, and it was a grand boondoggle. And this was only an aspect of the larger consulting game, which was in turn made available through a variety of federal programs where millions of dollars at the federal level got pissed away on nothing. It went to middle-class professionals who were just sitting around in rooms, speculating about experiences they knew nothing about.

Then I go out to work on a film and see all this misery and there just doesn't seem any relationship between the talk and what you observe in people's lives. I suppose it's one of the sad conclusions of the experience of making the films that a lot of the solutions seem grandiose and the change agents, as they call themselves, full of pious goodwill.

CLR: Is that what you concluded in your latest film?

WISEMAN: *Juvenile Court* is concerned with the limits of intervention. The court has to deal with problems of incest, murder, rape, child abuse, and parental neglect, to name only some. The judge and his staff work hard and ably to cope with the suffering they have to deal with on a daily basis.

Competent people from medicine, social science, and social work are available to the court. There is no way of knowing whether the interventions are useful, preventative, therapeutic, inconsequential, or harmful.

CLR: There's one thing that troubles me a bit, in terms of my experiences with some of these institutions. In all your films, we see confrontations and encounters between individuals and authorities. But there are no professionals there directly representing the individuals, such as lawyers in the Kansas City police stations, or any organized groups pressing the claims of their members, such as student groups, racial groups, welfare-rights groups, patient-rights groups. Why are these groups absent from your films?

WISEMAN: In the six weeks in Kansas City I rarely saw a lawyer either at the precinct or headquarters. It wasn't that those sequences were cut out; they just didn't exist. I had the same experience with the other films. At Northeast High there was no student protest or activist organization. At Fort Knox most of the trainees seemed to enjoy basic training. There had been a coffeehouse which was a center of anti-war activity, but the local authorities had closed it down some months before the film was shot. In the month in Memphis I was in the courtroom every day and no representatives of the sorts of organizations you have in mind were present. In 1967 there were no prisoners' rights groups that came to the defense of *Titicut Follies*, nor were they active inside Bridgewater.

CLR: Yet the very clear message of your films is that the individual has no intermediate institutions between himself and the authorities in these public organizations—no groups to protect his interests and assert his rights. And that contradicts what we know is happening in many institutions of the type you have filmed.

WISEMAN: At the times and places the films were made, these intermediate institutions weren't there. Their absence makes me wonder whether such civil liberties and civil rights groups are covering their turf as well as they should.

CLR: You're quoted in many interviews as saying it's still remarkable to you how much people are willing to reveal about themselves while you're filming them. Have you given any more thought to why that's so? Why do people talk about the most private kinds of things—sex, drugs, alcohol use, personal relationships—right in front of you and for the public to see later?

WISEMAN: A combination of reasons: pleased that they're in a film, passivity, a sense that it's important that others know about their work, and indifference.

CLR: As you know, your work has raised questions about invasion of privacy. Anyone watching your films is impressed almost immediately by the realization that these are not actors but real people—being stripped nude and inspected at Bridgewater, discussing their sexual misconduct with a psychiatrist, admitting to all kinds of anti-social behavior before probation officers in juvenile court, and so on. We see parents talking intimately to their children, ministers counseling kids, doctors talking to patients and about patients. This raises some issues about the boundary lines between publicity and privacy that you've been involved with since your first film. What are your thoughts on the ethical and legal aspects of this?

WISEMAN: These are films about public institutions, supported by public money, taxpayers' money, and the public has a right to know what goes on in them.

CLR: But the privacy issue involves the individual people who are caught up in such public institutions, not the privacy of the state.

WISEMAN: That's right. Film technology now allows us to look at the relationship between the individual and the state in these publicly-supported institutions in a way that wasn't possible twenty years ago. Each sequence describes a relationship between private citizens not on the public payroll and other people who are state employees:

doctors, policemen, nurses, school teachers, drill sergeants, judges, social workers, etc. One way of asking the question is: What are the limits to be placed on the technology that makes the documentary film form possible and, by setting those limits, what kinds of information unique to the documentary form do you prevent the public from having? I think it comes down to a pragmatic consideration: At what point does the individual's right of privacy bend to a more general need to share that information with other people? Documentary films are just as valid news as newspaper stories about the same events.

CLR: How do you deal with the individual's own right to decide what he reveals about himself, which is the conventional definition of the right to privacy?

WISEMAN: I don't get written releases, but I do get consents. Either before the sequence is shot or just after, I explain to the participants that I'm making a film that's going to be shown on television and generally to the public both nationally and in the community where the film is made. I ask whether they object to my using the sequence in the film. And I tape record the question and the answer. Also before the shooting begins there are announcements on bulletin boards, and stories in local newspapers, and institutional newsletters explaining the film and its uses.

CLR: Do they ever object?

WISEMAN: Very rarely. And if they do object, I don't use the sequence. But the objection has to be registered at that time. In other words, I don't go back and look for people a year after the film is edited and ask permission then.

CLR: I know that there have been threats of invasion-of-privacy suits, and trouble over showings in some communities with several of your films, but none has produced the epic battle that *Titicut Follies* stirred. Could we go into this?

WISEMAN: Ever since I began to take law classes to Bridgewater I'd wanted to do a film there. The superintendent at Bridgewater approved the idea, but permission had been denied by the state commissioner of corrections. Then a friend of mine who was a state legislator arranged for me to see Elliott Richardson, who was then lieutenant governor and had health, education, welfare, and correctional institutions under his jurisdiction. I saw Richardson, explained what I wanted to do, and he called the commissioner of corrections in my presence, endorsing the idea. A few weeks later the commissioner of corrections wrote that I could go ahead if I got the permission of the state attorney general, then Edward Brooke. Brooke's office issued an advisory opinion saying a film could be made in Bridgewater if I had the permission of the superintendent, and pictures were taken of "consenting" inmates.

Since I had the permission of the superintendent, I went ahead and made the film. Richardson was one of the first persons I showed the completed film to, in a screening room along with the superintendent of Bridgewater and Richardson's driver. Richardson thought the film was great. He understood it, understood what I was trying to do with it, and congratulated me warmly. The superintendent asked him whether I should show it to anybody else in state government, and Richardson said no, not even the governor, who was then John Volpe. The conversation took place in a sound studio. Unfortunately, it wasn't recorded.

That was in June of 1967. In the fall of '67 the film was about to be shown publicly, and it had begun to be reviewed. A former social worker wrote to the governor saying how dreadful it was that a film showing naked men could be shown publicly. Then some state legislators decided to hold public hearings, not about the dreadful conditions at Bridgewater that the film showed, but rather about how I had gotten permission to film there. I was attacked viciously in the press, the *Boston Herald*, for example, for exploiting the poor inmates at

Bridgewater and trying to make money off their misery.

Richardson—who had then shifted from lieutenant governor to state attorney general—was in trouble because he had not told his advisors that he had been instrumental in getting me permission to make the film. When he told them, I think he was advised that he had better move actively against the film to protect himself. So he got a temporary restraining order from a superior court judge against showing the film in Massachusetts. That's what started the proceedings.

CLR: Did you ever have any contact with him about his change in position?

WISEMAN: We had a meeting in his office before he got the restraining order. Richardson said he always had liked the film, but he now expressed concern, for the first time, about the privacy of the inmates. Then, in his capacity as attorney general, claiming to be the legal guardian of incompetent persons in state institutions, he hired two special assistant attorney generals from his former law firm to pursue the film in court. Their tactical position was that the film was an obscene document.

CLR: What was the trial based on?

WISEMAN: Actually, there were three allegations made by the state. One was that I had breached an oral contract giving the attorney general, the commissioner of corrections, and the superintendent at Bridgewater the right to exercise final censorship over the film. Secondly, they charged the film was an invasion of the privacy of one of the inmates. This man is taken naked from his cell, is slapped by the guards, shaved by them while they banter about his past as a school teacher, taunted about why he doesn't keep his cell clean, and then returned naked to his cell. The third claim was that all receipts from the film should be held in trust for the inmates.

At the trial, the Judge found that I had breached an oral contract and had violated the inmate's privacy, but he rejected the trust requirement. He ruled that the film could not be shown to the general public in Massachusetts, and that all prints and negatives should be destroyed. He said that there were no First Amendment issues, and that the film was "a nightmare of ghoulish obscenities."

CLR: Richardson wrote a letter to *The New Republic* defending his action against the film, stating:

> It would seem that a decent regard for the dignity and privacy of those who happen to be patients at Bridgewater State Hospital could easily have been reconciled with the announced intention of the film and the conditions at the institution honestly depicted without violating the rights of individuals.

How do you react to that?

WISEMAN: It's a high-winded pomposity. There was no way of making a real film about Bridgewater without shooting people's faces and becoming involved in the intimate aspects of the daily routine there. Richardson certainly knew that, and certainly approved of the film as it was made. There was no evidence introduced at the trial that the film was not an honest portrayal of the conditions. There is some question about whether the inmates had any privacy to begin with. If Richardson and the other politicians in Massachusetts were genuinely concerned about the privacy and dignity of the inmates of Bridgewater, they would not have allowed the conditions that are shown in the film to exist. They were more concerned about the film and its effect on their reputations than they were about Bridgewater. The superintendent of Bridgewater certainly originally wanted the film made because he was fed up. He couldn't get any support from the legislature or the politicians to bring about any changes there. At that time there was neither a statutory nor a common law right of privacy in Massachusetts. If the public in Massachusetts had seen the film, some voters might wonder about their elected officials. Instead, the state acted as a censor and prevented people from learning about Bridgewater. So that I think that Richardson's concern about privacy, while sounding very good, was essentially a fake issue in terms of the realities of Bridgewater.

CLR: The Civil Liberties Union of Massachusetts was involved in the case, wasn't it?

WISEMAN: My experience with the civil liberties union illustrates the discrepancy between ideology and practice I've been discussing. My first lawyer in the case was then the chairman of the CLUM. One day, a cartoon appeared in the *Boston Herald* showing two white horses going in opposite directions, one labeled "Titicut Follies" and the other "Massachusetts Civil Liberties Union," and my lawyer, Gerald Berlin, was shown astride them. That same day he told me that he could no longer represent me because the CLUM would lose contributions if he did so, and besides he now thought that I didn't have a good case and suggested that I give it up. I left the office furious because his primary obligation was to me, his client, and not to CLUM. I then retained other lawyers who were not professional civil libertarians.

Despite Berlin's prior involvement, CLUM took a position in the case against the film. On appeal to the Massachusetts Supreme Court they filed an amicus brief written by five people who, to my knowledge, had never seen the film or read the trial transcript. They came up with the Solomon-like solution that I should cut out the faces of the inmates, and that the film should only be seen by audiences made up of limited groups, such as social workers and medical professionals. The latter was essentially what the Massachusetts Supreme Judicial Court decided, and remains the rule for showings in that state. The conditions under which I can show the *Follies* are so restrictive that I have not shown the film rather than comply with the terms of the restraining order. The moral insensitivity and cowardice of CLUM and its chairman were for me the worst part of the *Follies* case. The response of Richardson and most members of the Massachusetts legislature was at least consistent with their general public political behavior.

The national ACLU stayed out of the case. All I could get at the New York office were a few stale ironies from the staff general counsel. Fortunately, other organizations did not react with the same muted interest. The American Sociological Association and the American Orthopsychiatric Association filed amicus briefs in support of the film, arguing strongly that it was fully protected by the First Amendment. At the present time the *Follies* is the only film in American constitutional history (other than those dealing in obscenity) that has court-approved restrictions on its use.

CLR: Do you have any parting thoughts on any aspect of your film work and civil liberties?

WISEMAN: I hope that if I were to do a film on the Civil Liberties Union I would be as surprised as I was with the police.

DAVID MACDOUGALL

BEYOND OBSERVATIONAL CINEMA (1975)

Truth is not a Holy Grail to be won: it is a shuttle which moves ceaselessly between the observer and the observed, between science and reality.

—Edgar Morin[1]

[. . .]

The classical voice of the fiction film is the third person: the camera observes the actions of the characters not as a participant but as an invisible presence, capable of assuming a variety of positions. To approximate such an approach in the nonfiction film, filmmakers must find ways of making themselves privy to human events without disturbing them. This is relatively easy when the event attracts more attention than the camera—what Edgar Morin has called "intensive sociality" (de Heusch 1962:4). It becomes more difficult when a few people are interacting in an informal situation. Yet documentary filmmakers have been so successful in achieving a sense of unobtrusiveness that scenes of the most intimate nature have been recorded without apparent embarrassment or pretense on the part of the subjects. The usual practice is to spend so much time with one's subjects that they lose interest in the camera. They must finally go on with their lives, and they tend to do so in their accustomed ways. This may seem improbable to those who have not witnessed it, yet to filmmakers it is a familiar phenomenon.

I have often been struck in my own work by the readiness of people to accept being filmed, even in societies where one might expect a camera to be particularly threatening. This acceptance is of course aided by de-emphasizing the actual process of filming, in both one's manner and one's technique. While making *To Live with Herds* (1972) among the

Jie of Uganda, I used a camera brace that allowed me to keep the camera in the filming position for twelve or more hours a day, over a period of many weeks. I lived looking through the viewfinder. Because the camera ran noiselessly, my subjects soon gave up trying to decide when I was filming and when I was not. As far as they were concemed I was always filming, an assumption that no doubt contributed to their confidence that their lives were being seen fully and fairly. When, at the end of my stay, I took out a still camera, everyone began posing—a clear sign that they recognized this as essentially different from cinema.

I would suggest that at times people can behave more naturally while being filmed than in the presence of other kinds of observers. A person with a camera has an obvious job to do, which is to film. The subjects understand this and leave the filmmaker to it. The filmmaker remains occupied, half-hidden behind the camera, satisfied to be left alone. But as an unencumbered visitor, he or she would have to be entertained, whether as a guest or as a friend. In this, I think, lies both the strength and the weakness of the observational method.

The purpose behind this curiously lonely approach of observational cinema is arguably to film things that would have occurred if one had not been there. It is a desire for the invisibility of the imagination found in literature combined with the aseptic touch of the surgeon's glove—in some cases a legitimation, in the name of art or science, of the voyeur's peephole. It has even been reduced to a formula for anthropology. Walter Goldschmidt defined ethnographic film as "film which endeavors to interpret the behavior of people of one culture to persons of another culture by using shots of people doing precisely what they would have been doing if the camera were not there" (1972: 1).

Invisibility and omniscience. From this desire it is not a great leap to begin viewing the camera as a secret weapon in the pursuit of knowledge. One's self-effacement as a filmmaker begins to efface the limitations of one's own physicality. The filmmaker and the camera are imperceptibly attributed with the power to witness the *totality* of an event. Indeed, they are expected to. Omniscience and omnipotence.

It is an approach that has produced some remarkable films. And for many filmmakers it has in practice a comforting lack of ambiguity. The filmmaker establishes a role that demands no social response from the subjects, and he or she then disappears into the woodwork. Allan King's *Warrendale* (1966) and *A Married Couple* (1969) make the audience witness to scenes of private emotional anguish without reference to the presence of the film crew. In the film *At the Winter Sea-Ice Camp, Part 3* (1968), from the Netsilik Eskimo series, the Inuit subjects seem altogether oblivious of Robert Young's camera, and in Frederick Wiseman's *Essene* (1972), a study of people striving painfully to live communally in a religious order, one sometimes has the curious sense of being the eye of God.

When films like these are functioning at their best, the people in them seem bearers of the immeasurable wealth and effort of human experience. Their lives have a weight that makes the film that caught but a fragment of it seem trivial, and we sit in a kind of awe of our own privileged observation of them. That emotion helps us accept the subjects' disregard of the filmmaker. For them to notice the filmmaker would amount almost to a sacrilege—a shattering of the horizons of their lives, which by all rights should not include someone making a film about them. In the same way, some scholars resist descriptions in which anthropologists are acknowledged as instruments of cultural contact and change.

Audiences are thus accomplices in the filmmaker's voluntary absence from the film—what Richard Leacock called "the pretense of our not being there" (Levin 1971: 204). From a scientific standpoint, the priorities of research also de-emphasize the filmmaker, because to pay attention to the observer is to draw valuable attention away from the subject at hand. Finally, the literature and films we have grown up with have shaped our expectations: Aeneas is unaware of Virgil; the couple on the bed ignores the production crew of twenty standing round. Even in home movies people are often told not to look at the camera.

Filmmakers begin as members of an audience and carry part of that attitude with them. But the act of filming tends to interpose its own barriers between the observer and the observed. For one thing, it is difficult for filmmakers to photograph themselves as an element in the phenomenon they are examining unless, like Jean Rouch and Edgar Morin in *Chronique d'un été* (1961), they becomes "actors" before the camera. More often it is through their voices and the responses of the subjects that we feel their presence.

Perhaps more important, filmmakers exhaust most of their energy making the camera respond to what is before it. This concentration induces a certain passivity from which it is difficult to rouse oneself. Active participation with the subjects suggests an altogether different psychic state. This may partly explain the successes of cinema as a contemplative art.

Among ethnographic filmmakers, another restraint is the special reverence that surrounds the study of isolated groups. The fragility of these societies and the rarity of filming them turns the filmmaker into a recording instrument of history—an obligation which, if accepted or even felt, must necessarily weigh down efforts to pursue more specific fines of inquiry.

This distancing view is often reinforced by an identification with the audience that may cause a filmmaker to mimic, consciously or otherwise, their impotence. As members of an audience we readily accept the illusion of entering into the world of a film. But we do so in complete safety, because our own world is as close as the nearest light switch. We observe the people in the film without being seen, assured that they can make no claims upon us. The corollary of this, however, is our inability to reach through the screen and affect *their* lives. Thus our situation combines a sense of immediacy with an absolute separation. Only when we try to invade the world of the film do we discover the insubstantiality of its illusion of reality.

In their attempt to make us into witnesses, observational filmmakers often think in terms of the image on the screen rather than their own presence in the setting where the events are occurring. They become no more than the eye of the audience, frozen into their passivity, unable to bridge the separation between themselves and their subjects.

Finally, however, it is scientific objectives that have placed the severest strictures on ethnographic film. Inevitably, the extraordinary precision of the camera-eye as a descriptive aid has influenced conceptions of the uses to which film should be put, with the result that for years anthropologists have considered film preeminently a tool for gathering data. And because film deals so overwhelmingly with the specific rather than the abstract, it is often considered incapable of serious intellectual articulation.

Certainly there are enough ethnographic films containing crude or dubious interpretations to explain, if not justify, such a conclusion. Films risking more legitimate, if more difficult, kinds of analysis are often flawed in the attempt. Still others receive no credit because their contribution exists in a form that cannot be assessed in the terms of conventional anthropology. Each of these factors adds weight to a widespread view among anthropologists that attempts to use film as an original medium of anthropology are simply pretexts for self-indulgence. What is more, each attempt that fails can be viewed as one more opportunity lost to add to the fund of "responsible" ethnography.

With data-gathering as the objective, there is of course no real need for the making of films, but merely for the collection of footage upon which a variety of studies can later be based. Indeed, E. Richard Sorenson (1967) suggested that footage might be collected with only this broad objective in view. Yet much bad anthropological writing is a similar gathering and cataloguing of information, deficient in thought or analysis. This is not far from the criticism that Evans-Pritchard levels at Malinowski:

> The theme is no more than a descriptive synthesis of events. It is not a theoretical integration, . . . There is consequently no real standard of relevance, since everything has a time and space relationship in cultural reality to everything else, and from whatever point one starts one spreads oneself over the same ground. (1962: 95)

The same criticism could be made of many existing ethnographic films. If this is a valid criticism—if ethnographic film is to become anything more than a form of anthropological note-taking—then attempts must continue to make it a medium of ideas. There will inevitably be more failures. But it seems probable that the great films of anthropology, as distinct from ethnography, are still to be made.

Curiously, it is the survival of the data within the context of thought, inescapable in the cinema, that is responsible for the impatience of many social scientists with film as a medium for anthropology. The glimpse gained of the original field situation may be so immediate and evocative that it proves tantalizing to those who would like to see more, and infuriating to those whose specific theoretical interests are not being served. Thus an ecological determinist may well dismiss as shallow a film in which the study of social relationships takes precedence over ecology.

Films prove to be poor encyclopedias because of their emphasis upon specific and delimited events viewed from finite perspectives. Yet surprisingly, it is often the supposed potency of film to record everything that has led to its disparagement. At first glance, film seems to offer an escape from the inadequacies of human perception and a factual check on the capriciousness of human interpretation. The precision of the photographic image leads to an uncritical faith in the camera's power to capture, not the images of events, but the events themselves—as Ruskin once said of some photographs of Venice, "as if a magician had reduced reality to be carried away into an enchanted land" (1887). So persuasive is this belief in the magic of photography that it is assumed by scholars who in the rest of their research would challenge far more circumspect assumptions. When disillusionment comes, it is therefore profound.

The magical fallacy of the camera parallels the fallacy of omniscient observation. It may result from a tendency in viewing films to define what has been photographed by what one is seeing. The film image impresses us with its completeness, partly because of its precise rendering of detail, but even more because it represents a continuum of reality that extends beyond the edges of the frame and which therefore, paradoxically, seems not to be excluded. A few images create a world. We ignore the images that could have been, but weren't. In most cases we have no conception of what they might have been.

It is possible that the sense of completeness created by a film also lies in the richness of ambiguity of the photographic image. Images begin to become signs of the objects they represent; yet unlike words or even pictographs, they share in the physical identity of the objects, having been produced as a kind of photochemical imprint of them. The image thus continually asserts the presence of the concrete world within the framework of a communicative system that imposes meaning.

The viewfinder of the camera, one might say, has a function opposite to that of the gunsight that a soldier levels at an enemy. The latter frames an image for annihilation; the former frames an image for preservation, thereby annihilating the surrounding multitude of images that could have been formed at that precise point in time and space. The image becomes a piece of evidence, like a potsherd. It also becomes, through the denial of all other possible images, a reflection of thought. In that double nature is the magic that can so easily dazzle us.

Observational cinema is based upon a process of selection. The filmmaker is limited to that which occurs naturally and spontaneously in front of the camera. The richness of human behavior and the propensity of people to talk about their affairs, past and present, are what allow this method of inquiry to succeed.

It is nevertheless a method that is quite foreign to the usual practice of anthropology or, for that matter, most other disciplines. (Two exceptions are history and astronomy, which time and distance require to function in the same way.) Most anthropological fieldwork involves, in addition to observation, an active search for information among informants. In the laboratory sciences, knowledge comes primarily from events that the scientist provokes. Thus observational filmmakers find themselves cut off from many of the channels that normally characterize human inquiry. They are dependent for their understanding (or for the understanding of the audience) upon the unprovoked ways in which their subjects manifest the patterns of their lives while they are being filmed. They are denied access to anything their subjects know but take for granted, anything latent in their culture that events do not bring to the surface.

The same methodological asceticism that causes filmmakers to exclude themselves from the world of their subjects also excludes the subjects from the world of the film. Here the implications are ethical as well as practical. By asking nothing of the subjects beyond permission to film them, the filmmaker adopts an inherently secretive position. There is no need for further explanation, no need to communicate with the subjects on the basis of the thinking that organizes the work. There is, in fact, some reason for the filmmaker not to do so for fear it may influence their behavior. In this insularity, the filmmaker withholds the very openness that is being asked of the subjects in order to film them.

In refusing to give the film subjects access to the film, filmmakers are also refusing them access to themselves, for this is clearly their most important activity when they are among them. In denying a part of their own humanity, they deny a part of their subjects'. If not in their own personal demeanor, then in the significance of their working method, they inevitably reaffirm the colonial origins of anthropology. It was once the European who decided what was worth knowing about "primitive" peoples and what they in turn should be taught. The shadow of that attitude falls across the observational film, giving it a distinctively Western parochialism. The traditions of science and narrative art combine in this instance to dehumanize the study of humanity. It is a form in which the observer and the observed exist in separate worlds, and it produces films that are monologues.

What is finally disappointing in the ideal of filming "as if the camera were not there" is not that observation in itself is unimportant, but that as a governing approach it remains far less interesting than exploring the situation that actually exists. The camera *is* there, and it is held by a representative of one culture encountering another. Beside such an extraordinary event, the search for isolation and invisibility seems a curiously irrelevant ambition. No ethnographic film is merely a record of another society; it is always a record of the meeting between a filmmaker and that society. If ethnographic films are to break through the limitations inherent in their present idealism, they must propose to deal with that encounter. Until now they have rarely acknowledged that an encounter has taken place.

The main achievement of observational cinema was that it has once again taught the camera how to watch. Its failings lie precisely in the attitude of watching—the reticence and analytical inertia it induces in filmmakers, some of whom feel themselves agents of a universal truth, others of whom comment only slyly or by indirection from behind their material. In either case, the relationship between the observer, the observed, and the viewer has a kind of numbness.

Beyond observational cinema lies the possibility of a *participatory cinema,* bearing witness to the "event" of the film and making strengths of what most films are at pains to conceal. Here the filmmaker acknowledges his or her entry upon the world of the subjects and yet asks them to imprint directly upon the film aspects of their own culture. This should not imply a relaxation of purposefulness, nor should it cause filmmakers to abandon the perspective that an outsider can bring to another culture. But by revealing their role, filmmakers enhance the value of the material as evidence. By entering actively into the world of their subjects, they can provoke a greater flow of information about them. By giving them access to the film, they make possible the corrections, additions, and illuminations that only the subjects' response to the material can elicit. Through such an exchange a film can begin to reflect the ways in which its subjects perceive the world.

[. . .]

NOTES

This essay was written for the International Conference on Visual Anthropology held in Chicago in 1973 as part of the IXth International Congress of Anthropological and Ethnological Sciences. It first appeared in *Principles of Visual Anthropology*, edited by Paul Hockings (The Hague: Mouton, 1975).

1. From his preface to *The Cinema and Social Science* by Luc de Heusch (1962: 5).

73

PAULINE KAEL

BEYOND PIRANDELLO (1970)

The young movie audience will want to see Altamont on film, because even if it went bad it's still their scene. They will go to *Gimme Shelter* for Mick Jagger—the most incredible of all rock stars, the man you hate to love—and death on film. The cinematography is highily variable, but it's good enough to show what is going on. The editing of the images to the music is very good, but the film's structure is a bit confusing. The filmmakers, Albert and David Maysles and Charlotte Zwerin, obviously wanted the suspense factor of the violence to come at Altamont but also wanted to use their best stuff on Jagger from earlier concerts, so after you've been prepared to expect Altamont they've thrown numbers in without telling you where they were performed. However, you don't expect clarity in this kind of film, and you don't think to worry about where you are when you get tough little Jagger in a silvery Uncle Sam hat, or with a Marlene Dietrich-style breeze rippling his shining hair and his draperies. His effects are brilliantly insolent. Jagger's new form of show-biz can seem anti-show-biz because it's so openly corrupt it appears incorruptible. And what other movie has dozens of freak-outs and a death?

But how does one review this picture? It's like reviewing the footage of President Kennedy's assassination or of Lee Harvey Oswald's murder. This movie is into complications and sleight-of-hand beyond Pirandello, since the filmed death at Altamont—although, of course, unexpected—was part of a *cinéma-vérité* spectacular. The free concert was staged and lighted to be photographed, and the three hundred thousand people who attended it were the unpaid cast of thousands. The violence and murder weren't scheduled, but the Maysles brothers hit the *cinéma-vérité* jackpot.

If events are created to be photographed, is the movie that records them a documentary, or does it function in a twilight zone? Is it the cinema of fact when the facts are manufactured for the cinema? The Nazi rally at Nuremberg in 1934 was architecturally designed so that Leni Riefenstahl could get the great footage that resulted in *Triumph of the Will*; in order to shoot *A Time for Burning*, William C. Jersey instigated a racial confrontation that split an Omaha church; the Maysles brothers recruited Paul Brennan, who was in the roof-and-siding business, to play a Bible salesman for the "direct-cinema" *Salesman*. It is said to be a "law" that the fact of observation alters the phenomenon that is observed—but how can one prove it? More likely, observation sometimes alters the phenomenon and sometimes doesn't. In Gerald Temaner's and Gordon Quinn's *Home for Life*, the principal character—a woman entering a home for the aged—is so disoriented that she may accept the camera as just one more factor in her confused situation; in parts of Fred Wiseman's *Law and Order*, the police are in such routine but taxing situations that they may go on doing what they usually do. There is no reason to think the freaked-out people in *Gimme Shelter* paid much attention to the camera crews, but would the event itself have taken place without those crews? With modern documentarians, as with many TV news cameramen, it's impossible to draw a clear line between catching actual events and arranging events to be caught; a documentarian may ask people to reenact events, while a TV journalist may argue that it was only by precipitating some events that he was able to clarify issues for the public—that is, that he needed to fake a little, but for justifiable reasons. There are no simple ethical standards to apply, and because the situations are so fluid and variable, one has to be fairly knowledgeable not to get suckered into reacting to motion-picture footage that appears to be documentary as if it were the simple truth.

A *cinéma-vérité* sham that appeals to an audience by showing it what it wants to believe may be taken as corroboration of its beliefs, and as an illumination. Would audiences react to the Arthur Miller-Eugene O'Neill overtones in *Salesman* the same way if they understood how much of it was set up and that the principals were playacting? One should be alert to the questionablc ethics in *Gimme Shelter*, to what is designed not to reveal the situation but to conceal certain elements of that situation. *Gimme Shelter* plays the game of trying to mythologize the event (Altamont) and to clear the participants (the Rolling Stones and the filmmakers) of any cognizance of how it came about.

When Mick Jagger is seen in *Gimme Shelter* pensively looking at the Altamont footage—run for him by the Maysles brothers—and wondering how it all happened, this is disingenuous moviemaking. One wants to say: Drop the Miss Innocence act and tell us the straight story of the background to the events. What isn't explained is that, four months after Woodstock, Stone Promotions asked the Maysles brothers to shoot the Stones at Madison Square Garden. The Maysles brothers had done a film on an American tour by the Beatles, and Albert Maysles had shot part of *Monterey Pop*. When, as a climax to their American tour, the Stones decided on a filmed free concert in the San Francisco area, the Maysles brothers made a deal with them to film it and rounded up a large crew. Melvin Belli's bordello-style law office and his negotiations for a concert site are in the film, but it isn't explained that Porter Bibb, the producer of *Salesman*, was the person who brought in Belli, or that Bibb became involved in producing the concert at Altamont in order to produce the Maysles film. The sequence in Belli's office omits the detail that the concert had to be hurriedly moved to Altamont because the owners of the previously scheduled site wanted distribution rights of the film. *Gimme Shelter* has been shaped so as to whitewash the Rolling Stones and the filmmakers for the thoughtless, careless way the concert was arranged, and especially for the cut-rate approach to keeping order. The Hell's Angels, known for their violence, but cheap and photogenic, were hired as guards for five hundred dollars' worth of beer. This took less time and trouble than arranging for unarmed marshals, and the Hell's Angels must have seemed the appropriate guards for Their Satanic Majesties the Stones. In the film, the primary concern of the Angels appears to be to keep the stage clear and guard the Stones.

The Hell's Angels, whose rigid, scary faces are already familiar movie faces from the wheelers—a genre they inspired and appear in—are made the villains in *Gimme Shelter*, and though I don't wish to suggest that the Hell's Angels should have been made the heroes, the fact is that the Angels—who don't have any share in the profits of the film—are made the patsies, while those who hired them are photographed all bland and sweet, wondering how it happened. When the self-centered, mercenary movie queen of *Singin' in the Rain* talked about bringing joy into the humdrum lives of the public, we laughed. Should we also laugh at Melvin Belli's talk in *Gimme Shelter* about a "free concert" for "the people" and at the talk about the Stones' not wanting money when the concert is being shot for *Gimme Shelter* and the Rolling Stones and the Maysles brothers divide the profits from the picture? One of the jokes of *cinéma-vérité* is that practically the only way to attract an audience is to use big stars, but since the big stars cooperate only if they get financial—and, generally, artistic—control of the film, the *cinéma-vérité* techniques are used to give the look of "caught" footage to the image the stars are selling.

Mick Jagger, the most polymorphous-perverse star since Marilyn Monroe, is hypercharged and narcissistic; when he performs he's close to sadistic in the way he holds audiences and dominates them. Even those who loathe him—and it is said that many young girls do—acknowledge that he's a spellbinder. One half expects him to be sacrificed to the audience at the end of the concert. Offstage, he seems tranquillized and wan and pale. A hip, Mod zombie, he pouts prettily, and smiles with the meaningless sweetness of an earlier type of popular singer—not unlike the skinny young Sinatra, whom he resembles. In this movie, as in *Performance*, when Jagger is offstage it's as if he were offscreen; he doesn't have an actor's presence—he becomes a private, non-communicative person. It makes sense that someone who performs so totally burns himself out onstage, but the near-catatonic figure of Mick Jagger wearing saucy little hats and mumbling mild platitudes gives plausibility to the view of him as demon-possessed when he sings in that harsh, abrasive voice and prances like a witch doctor.

This film has caught his feral intensity as a performer (which, oddly, Godard never captured in *One Plus One*, maybe because he dealt with a rehearsal-recording session, without an audience). It has also captured his teasing, taunting relationship to the audience: he can finish a frenzied number and say to the audience, "You don't want my trousers to fall down now, do you?" His toughness is itself provocative, and since rock performers are accepted by the young as their own spokesmen, the conventional barriers between performer and audience have been pushed over. From the start of *Gimme Shelter*, our knowledge of the horror to come makes us see the Rolling Stones' numbers not as we might in an ordinary festival film but as the preparations for, and the possible cause of, disaster. We begin to suspect that Mick Jagger's musical style leads to violence, as he himself suggests in a naïve and dissociated way when he complains—somewhat pettishly, but with a flicker of pride—to the crowd that there seems to be trouble every time he starts to sing "Sympathy for the Devil." He may not fully understand the response he works for and gets.

The film has a very disturbing pathos, because everybody seems so helpless. Many of the people at Altamont are blank or frightened but are in thrall to the music, or perhaps just to being there; some twitch and jerk to the beat in an apocalyptic parody of dancing; others strip, or crawl on the heads of the crowd; and we can see tormented trippers' faces, close to the stage, near the angry Angels. When Grace Slick and then Jagger appeal to the audience to cool it, to "keep our bodies off each other unless you intend love," and to "get yourselves together," they are saying all they know how to say, but the situation is way past that. They don't seem to connect what they're into with the results. Mick Jagger symbolizes the rejection of the values that he then appeals to. Asking stoned and freaked-out people to control themselves is pathetic, and since the most dangerous violence is obviously from the Hell's Angels, who are trying to keep their idea of order by stomping dazed, bewildered kids, Jagger's saying "Brothers and sisters, why are we fighting?" is pitifully beside the point. Musically, Jagger has no way to cool it, because his orgiastic kind of music has only one way to go—higher, until everyone is knocked out.

Mick Jagger's performing style is a form of aggression not just against the straight world but against his own young audience, and this appeals to them, because it proves he hasn't sold out and gone soft. But when all this aggression is released, who can handle it? The violence he provokes is well known: fans have pulled him off a platform, thrown a chair at him. He's greeted with a punch in the face when he arrives at Altamont. What the film doesn't deal with is the fact that Jagger attracts this volatile audience, that he magnetizes disintegrating people. This is, of course, an ingredient of the whole rock scene, but it is seen at its most extreme in the San Francisco-Berkeley audience that gathers for the Rolling Stones at Altamont. Everyone—the people who came and the people who planned it—must have wanted a big Dionysian freak-out. The movie includes smiling talk about San Francisco as the place for the concert, and we all understand that it's the place for the concert because it's the farthest-out place; it's the mother city of the drug culture. It's where things are already wildly out of control. The film shows part of what happened when Marty Balin, of the Jefferson Airplane, jumped off the stage to stop the Angels from beating a black man and was himself punched unconscious. After that, according to reporters, no one tried to stop the Angels from beating the crazed girls and boys who climbed onstage or didn't follow instructions; they were hit with leaded pool cues and with fists while the show went on and the three dozen cameramen and soundmen went on working. There were four deaths at Altamont, and a cameraman caught one. You see the Angel's knife flashing high in the air before he stabs a black boy, who has a gun in his hand. You see it at normal speed, see it again slowed down, and then in a frozen frame. But is it simply a news event. In the bright stage lights, surrounded by cameras, Mick Jagger is the apotheosis of star. He's the new Mr. Show Business—a moth sizzling in his flames. However, the Maysles brothers' approach to moviemaking is much too callow to cope with the phenomenon of people who are drawn to Mick Jagger's music in order to lose control—except at the level of attracting them and then exploiting the disastrous consequences.

It's impossible to say how much moviemaking itself is responsible for those consequences, but it is a factor, and with the commercial success of this kind of film it's going to be a bigger factor. Antonioni dickered with black groups to find out what actions they were planning, so that he could include some confrontations in "Zabriskie Point." M-G-M's lawyers must have taken a dim view of this. A smaller company, with much to gain and little to lose, might have encouraged him. Movie studios are closing, but, increasingly, public events are designed to take place on what are essentially movie stages. And with movie-production money getting tight, provoked events can be a cheap source of spectacles. The accidents that happen may be more acceptable to audiences than the choreographed battles of older directors, since for those who grew up with TV careful staging can look arch and stale. It doesn't look so fraudulent if a director excites people to commit violent acts on camera, and the event becomes free publicity for the film. The public will want to see the results, so there is big money to deodorize everyone concerned. What we're getting in the movies is "total theatre." Altamont, in *Gimme Shelter*, is like a Roman circus, with a difference: the audience and the victims are indistinguishable.

74

PEARL BOWSER

PIONEERS OF BLACK DOCUMENTARY FILM (1999)

The first half of this century witnessed the mass exodus of African Americans from the south.[1] Lured by stories of educational opportunities and employment, individuals, families, and sometimes whole groups abandoned their homes, leaving the fields of the deep south for the Promised Land—the industrial areas up-south and farther north.[2] Communities and individuals whose lives had occupied the margins of American life and history emerged abruptly at the center of changes that would resonate throughout the nation, crossing the color line and unraveling a once-sturdy web of segregation, disenfranchisement, and intimidation.

The dispersion of blacks among the growing metropolises of Detroit, Philadelphia, Chicago, New York, Indianapolis energized these cities, and spurred the growth of a black middle class. Despite rigid segregation and an oppressive legal environment, a similar transformation occurred in Southern cities like Memphis, Tennessee, and Jackson, Mississippi, that drew black migrants from more rural areas. In all of these places, a new class of wage earners clamored for services, and African American entrepreneurs and investors helped to fill this demand, erecting apartment buildings, establishing banks, hotels, and insurance companies. They established newspapers and schools; they designed and built churches, theaters, and movie houses.

The Contributions of Black Photographers

The great migration brought in its wake affirming stories of ordinary and extraordinary lives, captured by black artists in a variety of media. As early as 1900, black photographers documented their communities in the act of self-transformation and renewal. Working in the field and in their studios, these men and women chronicled growth and change in individual lives and in the lives of their communities, at once personalizing and historicizing the great social and economic changes that were taking place.

A study of the black documentary rightfully begins with these community photographers. They created portraits of shopkeepers in their places of business; laborers, skilled and unskilled, digging the subways or paving the streets; artists and entertainers; participants in all areas of community life. They recorded the parades, celebrations, and other activities of the churches and schools, clubs and other community institutions. In thousands of photographs, they captured moments in family histories that graced the walls in the homes of field hands and merchants, domestics and professionals.

Today many of these portraits and life scenes, preserved in libraries, museums, and private collections, are testimonials to the desire to establish one's own identity and, by extension, a group identity. The images speak to us knowingly of a particular time and culture, and constitute a vital part of the historical record of that culture. Indeed, some images will stand as the primary text for lost segments of that history.

The work and careers of these black photographers constitute an important chapter in the history of African American documentary film production. Like the first film documentaries, their photographs were signifiers of uplift and achievement, images that reflected the dreams and ambitions of their subjects. Indeed, among the subjects were some who were determined to record their dreams: a family poses in the front yard of their own home; a woman frames two portraits of herself side by side, one in a maid's uniform, the other in satin and lace.[3]

The contributions of black photographers to early cinema have long been unrecognized. Most accounts would have us believe the craft and technology of photography and cinema were created exclusively for and by whites. The guiding assumption has been that the face behind the camera was naturally white and male. Only in the last decade has this assumption been re-examined by such scholars as Deborah Willis-Thomas, whose seminal research project, *Black Photographers, 1840–1940: An Illustrated Bio-bibliography*, was published in 1985, and Jeanne Moutoussamy-Ashe's *Viewfinders: Black Women Photographers*, one of the first studies to document the history of black women photographers, appeared in 1986.

Primary sources from as early as 1900 tell the story.[4] The history of black photography follows a trail of entrepreneurs through local business directories and census listings, proceedings of National Negro Business League meetings, archives of the War Department and foreign governments, diary and journal entries by black writers, and personal scrapbooks.

Census data, for example, confirm that African Americans, although few in number, were among the ranks of the nation's professional photographers in the century's early decades. In 1910, the year of the first census, blacks made up about eleven percent of the total population, but accounted for just over one percent of professional photographers. Where occupational records were kept, 404 blacks were listed as photographers.[5] By 1920 the number of black professional photographers had increased to 608, including 101 women.[6] Because occupational data were not consistently collected or kept, these figures certainly underestimate the actual number of black photographers, but serve to document their existence.

The names and experiences behind these numbers are occasionally preserved in newspaper ads and local business directories that listed photographic services and occasionally offered information on the photographer's background or training. Some who opened studios on Main Street or in the heart of the community were self-taught; others, such as Peter P. Jones in Chicago and Jennie Toussaint Welcome in New York, were highly trained in art and photography and well educated in other disciplines as well. Elise Forrest Harleston and her husband opened the Harleston Studio in Charleston in the early 1920s. Elise Harleston had taken graduate courses in photography at Tuskegee Institute under C. M. Battey, distinguished photo-documentarian and head of the Institute's photography department.

[. . .]

Black Documentaries of the Silent Era

Newspaper accounts, diary entries, and other such sources are even more vital to the history of black film documentary than black still photography. So little footage remains from these early films produced by African Americans that the history is fragmented; information about the people who took part in these productions is incomplete. However, the emergence of narrative films by and about African Americans—known as race films—provided a measure of opportunity, creating a training ground for still photographers who wanted to make the transition to cinematic photography.

We know, from advertisements, accounts, and occasional reviews in the black press, that one- and three-reel films were screened for public audiences in the early decades of the century. References to these early works generally identify them only by title and length, giving little sense of their form or structure. To what extent did these early works adhere to, or advance, evolving conventions of the film documentary? In the absence of actual footage, it is difficult to know. However, the few on-screen images that remain do offer a view of the American experience that is often obscured or left out of local histories: ordinary citizens, people of little renown, whose stories are rarely reflected in the modern interpretive texts that purport to represent the African American experience.

Community events filmed on location, such as parades, conventions or special celebrations, provided the texts for early newsreels and documentary short subjects. Carlton Moss, documentary filmmaker and educator, referred to these unedited, unrehearsed moments lifted from life as "actualities," adding that early filmmakers "shot whatever they saw—because it was moving."[7] The recorded moments ranged from commonplace doings to moments of pomp and ceremony.

The rudiments of story emerged out of activities or events that sparked recognition or pride: people at church; students at work on a black college campus; black soldiers training or going off to war. Early footage captures baseball games and boxing matches; social clubs; gatherings of the Negro club women's movement; a black state fair; conferences; and the activities of prominent political and cultural figures. More than a few African American film companies produced short subjects depicting blacks in the workplace, particularly in government jobs. They showed the first black postal worker, for example, officials of an all-black incorporated town, or blacks serving in the armed forces. The subject matter of these documentaries was often unplanned and spontaneous with an apparent local focus, but they reflected shared areas of interest and experience for a wider audience of African Americans hungry for their own image.

Some documentaries called attention to the progress and pride of ordinary citizens. Two such films were screened at the State Theater in Chicago: *A Day in the Magic City,* described by a reviewer as "an extraordinary picture of colored people of Birmingham, Alabama," and a screen story entitled *Youth Pride and Achievement of Colored People of Atlanta, Georgia.* In these films, communities celebrated themselves and told their own stories. The State Theater promoted these films as "a new type of production—featuring the progress and pride of colored people in motion pictures."[8]

Movie houses that catered to African Americans—race theaters—provided ready audiences for these natural scenes of black life. In the beginning there were no formal distribution networks for documentaries aimed at the African American spectator. Some prints were sold outright, while others followed a prescribed distribution Circuit of towns and cities mapped out by showmen[9] or the filmmakers themselves. Often they served as fillers in mixed programs of vaudeville and film. Many of the companies responsible for short subjects also produced comedies and later dramatic pieces.

Sometimes comic or dramatic skits were incorporated into the short subject, adding a story line to the captured moments of community life. These embellishments helped to create a mirror through which the audience might view itself as participants in their own culture and contributors to the larger tapestry of American life.

Advertisements suggest that the typical program shown in race theaters of this period might include newsreels, several short subjects (documentaries), and the ever-popular Western serials.[10] But the arrival in town of a black film of any length was treated as an occasion; the film was often featured prominently on the marquee, and ads were placed in the local paper by the theater owner or the production company.

When they added local flavor to the fare at race movie houses, short subjects proved to be highly effective marketing tools. Owners of race theaters in rural towns along the Delta commonly offered prizes and used a variety of gimmicks to increase their box office, but images of the patrons proved to be the most powerful draw. In Ruell, Mississippi, for example, one theater owner would film patrons gathered in front of his establishment on a Saturday, capturing images of country people who had come to town for a little relaxation. He exploited the vanity of his subjects, promising to display their images, larger than life, on the silver screen the following week. This form of advertisement became a common and effective way to ensure repeat business. Footage from his camera in the Jackson, Mississippi, archives reveals a group of people in front of his theater, including a black teenager carrying a white baby on her hip. Ironically, the theater marquee in the background announces an Oscar Micheaux movie called *God's Step Children.*[11]

While geared to small towns, the practice spread to urban theaters as well. In Chicago, the Magic Motion Picture Company ran an ad in the *Chicago Defender* announcing something new for Chicago and its citizens—a "Picture Making Exhibition and Grand Ball." The copy read, "Have you seen the movie picture cameraman in your neighborhood? Well He Got a Picture of You and it will be shown at this moving picture exhibition and hall so don't miss coming and seeing it."[12] The pictures were to be shown at the 8th Regiment Armory—the same space where in 1919, Oscar Micheaux had shown his first feature, *The Homesteader*—the longest black film of that time.

The subjects of black shorts were both entertaining and educational, connecting the lives of people in disparate communities to larger events. Many of the documentaries and newsreels shown in commercial venues were also used in educational programs run by churches, schools, lodges, and other community organizations at the forefront of the race consciousness movement.

Among early black documentaries were race movies promoting and documenting economic and political movements and organizations, such as Booker T. Washington's National Negro Business League (NNBL) and Marcus Garvey's United Negro Improvement Association (UNIA). Washington commissioned and inspired the first black documentary, which is discussed below. The UNIA not only published its own newspaper, *The Negro World,* but also established its own film company to publicize the movement and its leader, who proclaimed himself "The Provisional President of Africa." Garvey carried his message of Negro improvement into black communities across thirty-eight states, attracting thousands of new members along the way. Photographer James Van Der Zee, among others, made portraits of Garvey's elite guard in dress uniform with their families. He recorded the August, 1920 parade of fifty thousand Garveyites on Harlem's wide boulevard, and covered UNIA conventions and rallies.

African American camera operators working for the UNIA film company captured movement activities on film, including the "Garvey fleet"—a ship of the "Black Star Line" with its black captain Hugh Mulzac and crew—steaming up the Hudson. Purchased with money raised by Garvey's followers, the ship promoted the return of blacks to their African homeland and publicized commerce between the Garvey movement and Africa.

As chroniclers of their people's culture, life styles, hopes, and dreams, African American photographers and filmmakers—amateur and professional alike—reinforced the sense that they were presenting slices of reality in moving pictures by giving their work such prosaic titles as *A Day with the Tenth Cavalry* or *A Day in Birmingham, The Magic City.* The kinds of everyday, untold stories that black photographers across the nation had been documenting in their communities and in their studios were now subjects for films.

Researching Early Black Documentaries

Most if not all of these early films are lost to us. Our knowledge of them comes largely from newspapers of the time—information mentioned in reviews and ads; buried in the stories of veteran reporters such as D. Irland Thomas of the *Chicago Defender* or St. Clair T. Bourne of the *Amsterdam News;* or wedged between announcements from J. A. Jackson's rolltop desk in *Billboard* and the *Defender;* or noted in unsigned columns and stories in the *Indianapolis Freeman, New York Age, Norfolk Journal and Guide* or other newspapers and magazines of the period.

These sources are not sufficient, however, to allow us to gauge the audiences that these films reached, or their impact on various communities. The films were not advertised or reviewed every time they played in a theater or became part of a larger program. More often than not, the producer was his or her own distributor, and made films available not only to commercial theaters, but also to lodge halls, neighborood churches, and club groups. Sometimes the films found their way into the baggage of individual showmen who took to the road with projection equipment. These showmen brought a personal style of presentation and an eclectic mix of programs to whatever public space could be found in small towns in the deep south that lacked movie theaters but had an enthusiasm for the "picture show."[13]

Other documentaries were never intended for public viewing, but nevertheless figure in the history of black filmmaking. These include promotional and training films made by businesses in the first half of this century. For example, the Walker Manufacturing Company of Indianapolis, Indiana, produced its own films showing the development and production of an array of beauty and hair products and promoting the "Walker System of Beauty." Long before the age of television, Madame C. J. Walker's products, and the beauty culture she developed, were being marketed as far away as South Africa. The company used films to train women in beauty techniques (how to apply makeup, care of the skin, hair styles, etc.) and to prepare them to go into business for themselves.

The sections that follow describe these films and filmmakers, placing them in historical context. Perhaps the best known of these was the film that is generally considered the first black documentary—*A Day at Tuskegee.*

The First Black Documentary

The silent era produced a host of newsreels and short subjects, but none was as widely seen or as influential as *A Day at Tuskegee.* The moving force behind this project was Booker T. Washington, the first president of Tuskegee Institute in Alabama.

A passionate advocate of industrial education for Negroes, and a fiery orator, Washington attracted the support of many wealthy and powerful white businessmen and politicians, including former President Theodore Roosevelt. Welcoming his accommodationist views, many of these individuals provided the financial support that helped Washington to pursue his long-range goal of an economically self-reliant and independent black workforce. In 1900, he established the National Negro Business League to foster his program and to encourage, by example and shared information, the growth of black enterprises. Annual meetings, located in a different region each year, encouraged new black enterprises around the country. Indeed, one such meeting held during an NNBL convention was filmed and screened for the general public at a nearby theater. This experiment proved successful, and was repeated at other NNBL conventions. While informational, such films were also objects of race pride; they permitted the general audience to take part in events at the NNBL convention meeting that was taking place in their town. At the same time, they promoted participants' individual businesses by associating them with the larger national organization wherever the film was screened.

Recognizing the persuasive power of film, Booker T. Washington commissioned George W. Broome to make a short film about Tuskegee Institute that would help to promote his industrial education program. This project resulted in *A Day at Tuskegee.* Broome and a group of NNBL businessmen in Boston formed a production company, and shot the film on the Institute's 2,400-acre grounds and in buildings erected with student labor.

In December, 1909, a private screening in Boston exhibited some 43 scenes shot at the Alabama school, depicting the industrial education of young men and women. Emmett J. Scott, Dr. Washington's assistant at Tuskegee, attended the screening at the Crescent Theater and commented favorably on the film. A reporter for the *Defender* promised to make every effort to bring the film to Chicago and noted, "Booker T. was way ahead of the game.... [The film] will show our would-be leaders what makes Booker T. so great."[14]

The film opened at a public meeting in New York's Carnegie Hall on January 24,1910. The press reported that an audience of two thousand (black and white) attended the meeting, which was chaired by New York's former mayor, Seth Low. Speakers included President Finley of City College, Dr. B. F. Riley of Alabama, and Dr. Booker T. Washington.

Producer George W. Broome had previously spoken at an NNBL meeting about the importance of the motion picture as an instrument of communication capable of delivering information to African American communities a thousand miles away. The black press reviewing the film reported, "People could see what the school was doing and what an industrial education, as Booker T. Washington conceives it, means." The *New York Age* maintained that critics of Tuskegee have usually been "those who know the least about it." The Broome company announced its intention to produce similar films showing the progress of the Negro along industrial lines for Shaw Institute in North Carolina, Hampton Institute in Virginia, and Fisk Institute in Tennessee.[15]

Washington's industrial education program did not escape criticism, however.

Two factions emerged in the debate over the development of trade schools. One group of black intellectuals and educators, including W. E. B. Du Bois, put the education of black professionals at the top of their agenda. Du Bois was the author of *The Souls of Black Folk*—an essay collection that was to shape the course of the emerging civil rights movement, and one of Washington's staunchest critics. Du Bois believed that it was essential to develop leadership among young men and women through a college education steeped in the arts, sciences, history, and literature; he asserted that the realization of full citizenship would be hastened through the development of an intellectual elite—or "Talented Tenth." On the other side of the debate was the powerful machine built by Washington at Tuskegee with the backing of northern industrialists and southern segregationists. Washington described his critics as "artificial" men—"graduates of New England colleges" who did not represent the masses of black people.[16] His comments did not name, but referred to, not only Du Bois, but also Monroe Trotter, publisher of the *Guardian*.

Washington was confident that he not only had the total support of blacks, but would also be listened to by whites in high places. But his access to the White House and his association with white industrialists sparked controversy when President Theodore Roosevelt disastrously mishandled two key events: the Brownsville raid of 1905 and the brutal outbreak of violence against blacks in Atlanta in 1906. In the first case, Roosevelt summarily and unfairly discharged and disgraced the famous black 25th Texas Regiment, which had taken part in the charge up San Juan Hill.[17] In the second, the president belatedly ordered the use of federal troops to quell the mob.

In the aftermath of these events, the rock-solid support Washington had enjoyed showed signs of erosion. He weathered the storm, however, and over the next decade Tuskegee Institute became the focus of a number of films shown in churches, schools, and theaters. These films helped to shape the public discourse of the day concerning Washington's accommodationist views and Du Bois's more progressive stance on education and leadership. Long after his death in 1915, Booker T. Washington's industrial education program, his bootstrap approach, and identification with the greater mass of the working class proved to have seductive power. His image and his influence have pervaded popular culture through portraits, statuary, and film; his name has become synonymous with self-reliance (a bootstrap approach to the progress of the race) and African American entrepreneurship.

The images that filled *A Day at Tuskegee* became symbols of what could be achieved: not only the stately buildings that graced the campus, but also the images of students at work in the classroom and in the fields. By 1915 the school was not only a monument to its founder, but also a symbol of progress and race pride. Films about Tuskegee and the controversial educational experiment continued to have an audience as late as 1923.[18]

What role did Washington play in making *A Day at Tuskegee* beyond commissioning the Broome company? Was he in a position to suggest or encourage black camera operators to participate in the project? Press reports indicate only that Washington's assistant, Emmett J. Scott, attended the preview screening of the film prior to the New York public event. There appears to be no mention of anyone else from the Institute staff taking part in the project. Some years earlier, Tuskegee students had participated in a "parade of 100 wagons" exhibiting the various activities of the school before a reviewing stand occupied by former President Theodore Roosevelt and his party. The documentation on film of the school's vocational studies program was indeed a novel idea in 1909—a time when print dominated communication.[19] Washington apparently recognized that film could be not only a powerful educational tool, but also an effective fund-raising instrument, and he used it when he approached white industrialists and educators in the north for support. On January 10, the *New York Age* provided a detailed description of the film's content and named George Broome as the manager, but provided no other credits. Three years later *A Day at Tuskegee* was picked up by another company, the Anderson Watkins Film Company.[20]

A final word about *A Day at Tuskegee.*[21] While Booker T. Washington launched this project, others deserve credit for the production itself, and for the technical quality of the film. But who these individuals were remains a mystery, in spite of the attention the film enjoyed in the black press. Tuskegee certainly had a professional photographer on staff.

The Peter P. Jones Photoplay Ltd.

The Peter P. Jones Photoplay Ltd. was one of the few early race companies with an identified professional camera operator. Jones scripted, shot, and edited his own films. He began his career as a photographer in 1900 in a small studio on State Street capturing images of Chicago's African American community, including portraits of leading figures in sports, the arts, and business. He was also commissioned to photograph buildings designed by African American architects, in particular Chicago's black churches. In 1914, with the backing of South American investors, Jones established the Peter P. Jones Photoplay Ltd. to make short films focusing on the black community. The company's first production, reported in the *Chicago Defender,* recorded a Shriners parade in Chicago:

> The march of the Mystic Shriners Sunday is to be perpetuated in moving pictures and incidentally Jones, former State Street photographer again comes into the limelight in this new scientific fad. He was the operator of the machine and strange to say it was set up in front of the first place on State Street that he did his photographic work. This is the first moving picture ever taken of the Shriners and marks the beginning of a series [on] our marching organizations and other features of race life that will encourage and uplift.[22]

The Freeman: A National Illustrated Colored Newspaper in Indianapolis praised Jones's work for setting new standards for race pictures, noting that in addition to his work in motion pictures, he was a prize-winning commercial photographer and colorist, and a member of the American Photographers Association. *The Freeman* also reported that Jones's productions would be shown in Brazil and other South American countries before opening in the United States. No records of such screenings exist; we do know, however, that the films Jones created with South American backing were shown in the United States in 1914.

An ad for *The Dawn of Truth,* a Peter P. Jones Photoplay production, listed titled sections that incorporated the company's earlier films in a "movie spectacle."[23] The program contained scenes from the *Lincoln Jubilee* (Chicago, August–September 1915), including *Gorgeous Elks Parade; Historie National Baptist Convention* (two reels); *Negro Soldiers Fighting for Uncle Sam* (three reels); *Progress of the Negro: Facts from Farm, Factory, and Fireside; Tuskegee and Its Builder; Mound Bayou, Miss.: A Negro City Built by a Former Slave; Prime Factors in the Re-birth of a Nation.* This complex grid of images was produced, directed, and edited by Jones. The final documentary contained footage acquired from the War Department and other agencies, a compilation of materials from Jones's earlier films, newsreel footage (probably from his own camera), and added interludes of drama and comedy. The program also included scenes of other cities' celebrations of the Half Century Anniversary Exposition and the Lincoln Jubilee. Under the headline, "Featuring Negro Progress in Moving Pictures," one reviewer referred to scenes of troops embarking for Cuba (*On to Cuba*) followed by

> a pleasing little drama which was supposed to have been enacted on that soil. In this playlet were included all the little turns known to the moving picture art. . . . The colonel's daughter, "Lucy," the captain who courted her and the major who failed in his suit was realistic leaving an impression on the memory owing to the faithfulness to the ways of men. It is a rare thing to see one of the race, depicted by the race, as a rascal or a scoundrel. As the story goes Major Duplex was that, because worsted in his love by Captain Smith, who wins "Miss Lucy." The plot was clean cut, holding through in spite of the spirit of war that enveloped all. One gets a real war glimpse with all of its possible horror.[24]

The heading of Jones's ad for the program—"1865 to 1915" framed by broken slave chains and shackles—cites the fiftieth anniversary of freedom from slavery. A review appearing in the *Freeman* describes Peter P. Jones as an artist whose photographs have been exhibited at galleries at home and abroad, and refers specifically to Jones's long-time relationship with the Victor George Galleries. The reviewer was particularly impressed with one segment of the film:

> Beyond all of this almost matchless experience is the grand work which was thrown on the screen to the view of the curious throngs. As for things that stand for the real and enduring, and the monumental growth of the race perhaps, the splendid buildings and spacious well-kept grounds of Tuskegee are the most inspiring. One thinks of all this as the ingenuity of a member of the race and occupied by the race. Nothing like these scenes have been seen here before. The art triumph of the presentation is decidedly the 8th Regiment scene . . . where the troops are being reviewed by Governor Dunne of Illinois, Col. Dennison and his staff of officers. Here the artist and his subjects seem to have been at their best. The most exacting military martinet and the purest art critic would have been convinced and satisfied.[25]

This description suggests that footage from Jones's 1914 documentary, *For the Honor of the 8th Illinois Regiment* was incorporated into *The Dawn of Truth*. It is quite possible that Jones recycled scenes from this documentary as well as footage of a number of other events that he had filmed earlier. But more importantly, Jones's title, *Rebirth of a Nation,* appearing in the ad as part of the special program, embodied the spirit of the African American celebration of fifty years of freedom and achievement since Lincoln's signing of the Emancipation Proclamation. That anniversary was widely celebrated and Jones's "movie spectacle," according to the reviewer, included documentation of these festivities in other cities. The reviewer commented:

> The management of the production speaks of it as re-birth of a nation, somewhat in answer to that orgy of contempt and reflection known as the "Birth of a Nation." These pictures are the true birth of a nation as it concerns the Negro race. They

> tell the story of the ascent from life's hovel to where the Negroes fused and became one with other people in the great melting pot of the nation. They do not show the ugly past: it is known well enough. The victories are the subject, leaving it to the dead past to bury the dead.[26]

In the absence of the actual film, we can only speculate about how Jones may have handled the making of *The Dawn of Truth*. Many questions remain. Did the audience see the program as one long documentary or as a series of short pieces tied together under a single title? Did Jones draw upon footage from earlier films to create an entirely new piece, or did he assemble earlier shorts as chapters of a longer work? The former appears more likely, based on Jones's years of experience as a studio photographer and photo documentarian, his considerable darkroom and editing skills, and his experiments with natural light in architectural photographs. The lengthy review that ran in *The Freeman* following the Washington Theater screening in Indianapolis, alludes to the quality of Jones's images: "The fine art of making motion pictures has not been confined to a special people. This fact was proven when the splendid pictures by the Peter P. Jones Film Company of Chicago were shown at the Washington Theater."[27]

Today, much more is known about Jones's career and his artistry with both still and motion picture cameras than about most of his contemporaries in the field. His photographs frequently appeared in newspaper ads, and the *Chicago Defender* followed his career, running stories about his projects. He was lauded for his portraits of famous people (Booker T. Washington, Henry O. Tanner, Bert Williams, Henry Bannerchek, Ada Overton Walker, and others), and reproductions of these works were marketed by William Foster, an African American producer and distributor. His portraits of well known actresses and performers such as Anita Bush, founder of the Lafayette Players, were used in ads for various black businesses promoting hair products, cosmetics, and personal instruction.[28] Jones clearly saw his work as a celebration of black life and an homage to black identity. His company was founded to film the first in a series of marching organizations and others germane to the African American community.

Jones seems to have had few competitors—at least in Chicago, where he spent the better part of his professional career from 1908 to 1922. To be sure, there were other African American commercial photographers producing films or at least working as camera operators during this period. Several photographs survive showing camera operators with the tools of their trade: one is a portrait of Arthur Bedou, who had himself photographed walking with his camera in the center of a crowd; another is Richard Samuel Roberts's photograph entitled "Man with a Movie Camera."[29] But there is little mention of these professionals in the press.

Jones was already well known in the field and had recently released his third film, a short comedy called *The Slacker,* when he went to work for the Selznick Film Laboratories in 1917. He quickly gained a reputation as the industry's most skilled still photographer. He was praised in the company paper for the quality of his photographs and his work as a colorist, and for his shrewd selection of scenes to be photographed and used on lobby cards advertising a film.[30]

Other Early Production Companies

During the silent era, the number of venues open to producers of race movies was severely limited. Nevertheless, over time a number of commercial African American production companies came into being. In addition to Peter P. Jones Photoplay Ltd., there were Foster Photoplay Company (1913), Afro-American Film Company, Haynes Photoplay (1914), Lincoln Motion Picture Company (1916), Whipper's Reel Negro News (1921), Dunbar Films, Monumental Pictures Corporation (1921) organized solely for the production of newsreels, Turpin Film Company, and others. Each produced one or more newsreels or documentaries as well as short narratives, and each developed its own strategies for dealing with the tough challenge of promoting and distributing its work.

While we know that these companies were in business in the 1910s and 1920s, relatively little is known about their personnel, production process, or technical capacities. This is one of the frustrating facts of life for scholars of early black cinema: there tend to be few details available about a production or its crew unless the information happened to be included in a release, review, or newspaper ad of the time. For films which are known to have been made, but for which no copies remain, production details are particularly elusive. Fortunately, some records were kept. For example, George P. Johnson, general manager of the Lincoln Motion Picture Company, kept extensive clipping files on his company's productions and on the race movies of other producers. (This collection is now housed at the University of California at Los Angeles.) However, Lincoln used the same white camera operator, Harry Grant, on all of its films from 1916 until it ceased production in 1922; Johnson did not record the names of technical staff (such as camera operators) working for other companies.[31]

Among the first black companies to produce or distribute shorts subjects was the Afro-American Film Company. Based in New York City, the company announced plans to produce films recording the activities of prominent Negro leaders. In 1913, it produced coverage of a regional meeting, convened in Philadelphia, of the National Negro Business League (NNBL), the organization Washington helped to establish in 1900. In 1914, it filmed the regional NNBL meeting in Muskogee, Oklahoma, and in the same year, it produced scenes of the incorporated all-black town of Boley, Oklahoma.[32]

At the same time, other companies were also documenting life in black communities. The Haynes Company filmed the Odd Fellows convention in Boston in 1914, and in 1916 it documented notable Negro enterprises that were developing in the eastern part of the country. The Foster Photoplay Company, run by William Foster, a producer of short comedies, also produced at least one newsreel, *YWCA Parade,* which was shown along with his comedies *The Pullman Porter* and *The Butler* in 1913.[33] He also attempted to establish himself as a distributor, listing Peter P. Jones's documentary *For the Honor of the 8th . . .*,[34] and briefly handled sales of photographs, suitable for framing, of well known figures such as Booker T. Washington and Paul Laurence Dunbar. Other companies in various parts of the nation were filming blacks at work in fields and factories, the proceedings of conventions, activities of local dignitaries, or the work of renowned figures such as Marcus Garvey and the United Negro Improvement Association.[35] Since much of this work has been lost, we can only speculate about the aesthetic that these artist/photographers brought to the film documents they created.

World War I and the Post-War Years

Black soldiers in battle was a dominant theme of documentaries and newsreels, as well race movies, during the silent era. While the press may not have had camera operators in the trenches or on the battlefield, there were writers who shared their personal stories with black newspapers, and news of the states' black regiments was eagerly followed in the papers. *The Chicago Defender,* the *Pittsburgh Courier,* papers with national black readership, more than likely had journalists in the field. In *This Is Our War* (1945), Carl Murphy writes that, "*The Afro-American* sent none of its writers abroad to cover World War I. As a weekly newspaper with its influence then limited mainly to Baltimore, it depended altogether on letters from service men abroad, on occasional interviews with returned soldiers and on War Department handouts."[36] There were some efforts to document blacks' contributions to the war effort on film. In 1916, for example, Jennie Louise and Ernest Toussaint Welcome made *Doing Their Bit* (1916), a twelve-part series shown in two-reel segments focusing on "the military and economic role played by all races in the War of Nations both 'Over Here' and 'Over There.'" But the most memorable documentary efforts of the World War I era focused on an earlier generation of black soldiers, recalling their exploits in Cuba and Mexico.

Heroic black soldiers were also the subject of a lithograph by Jennie Louise Toussaint Welcome and Ernest Toussaint Welcome. The lithograph, displayed in many black homes, depicted members of the 369th Colored Infantry fighting the Germans in hand-to-hand combat in a French forest. The soldiers' faces were painted from photographs—a common practice that avoided long studio sessions, and each soldier was identified by name. The 369th and the 371st regiments were awarded the Croix de Guerre, and individual soldiers were cited for bravery.

In 1914, Peter P. Jones Photoplay Ltd., the era's most prominent producer of documentaries, made a three-reel film called *For the Honor of the Fighting 8th Illinois Regiment,* which included scenes of the 8th Illinois in dress parade; being reviewed by the governor; marching in Cuba during the Spanish-American War; being attacked and later repulsing the enemy on a bridge in Cuba with a thousand soldiers engaging in battle; taking a block house on San Juan Hill; firing cannons; and the victory celebration.[37] By combining newsreel footage of the 8th Illinois in battle with his own footage of their triumphal return, Jones created an historical record that directly addressed the black spectator. This documentary did not survive, and one can only imagine the historical and cultural insights it might have provided.

Two years later, in 1916, Jones's company produced *The Colored Soldiers Fighting in Mexico,* which also featured the 8th Illinois Regiment. Soldiers in training and battle—this period's recurring theme—brought home to audiences African Americans' contributions to the nation's security and their role in its history.

One of the most successful films of the military genre, and the first to garner national exposure in the decade of World War I, was Lincoln Motion Pictures' dramatic re-enactment of the Negro soldiers of the Tenth Cavalry at the battle of Carrizal along the U.S.-Mexican border. *Trooper of Company K* (1916) was a story of individual acts of heroism that caught the attention of the general public and was seen by both black and white audiences, according to the production company's general manager, George P. Johnson.[38]

Trooper might be considered an early "docudrama." It owed much of its popularity to its re-creation of the historic battle and the heroism of troopers in the face of the enemy's superior firing power with the Gatling gun. The Lincoln Motion Picture Company restaged the battle with a cast of three hundred, including former Ninth and Tenth Cavalry troopers and Mexican cowboys. The film's most affecting moment, which created a momentary bond between the races, depicted the rescue of the Tenth Cavalry's white commanding officer. Lobby cards and posters for the film showed the unknown trooper of Company K (played by

Noble Johnson) carrying the wounded officer to safety.

Lincoln Motion Pictures invested in multiple prints to meet exhibitors' demands, but the film's initial success was not sustained. *Trooper of Company K* could not match the enduring popularity of the 1910 documentary, *A Day at Tuskegee*. The George Broome documentary or some version of it was still in distribution as late as 1922. Like most early black documentaries, *Trooper* was forgotten; once they had completed their initial run, they were ignored by critics and other journalists, and disappeared from advertisements.

Several factors may have contributed to the demise of these early documentaries: the lack of distribution outlets; the small number of commercial venues; and limited advertising budgets. It is also possible that the films had a longer life as educational material, and were shown in schools and local clubs. They may have been exhibited by showmen in small theaters which changed their programs on a daily basis and rarely advertised specific titles in the papers.

In the years following World War I, black documentarians continued to pursue military themes, focusing on black soldiers' heroism in Europe. Initially, the U.S. government encouraged this effort. The Frederick Douglass Film Company produced the documentary *Heroic Negro Soldiers of the World War* (1919), showing black regiments as they trained for war, embarked for overseas, fought in battle, and triumphantly returned home. The *New York Age* printed a glowing review of the film and its producers, praising the quality of the screen images, saying:

> There is no doubt about this being the best and most attractive motion picture made of the Negro soldier in the World War. The company is owned and controlled by Negroes, whose aim is to present the better side of Negro life, and to use the screen as a means of bringing about a better feeling between the races. In most pictures the Negro only appears in menial positions or in a degrading role, but the Frederick Douglass Film Company shows the race at its best. Dr. W. S. Smith, the director, has given much time and study to photographing the negro and has become an expert in making the features clear and distinct under all conditions. This picture measures up to the standards of motion picture requirements, and is a credit to Dr. Smith's ability as a director.[39]

One might be led, from the description in the *Age*, to believe that Dr. Smith was the camera operator as well as director. It was important for the audience to be able to identify their loved ones, and the critic for the *Age* took pains to inform the audience of the director's sensitivity and skill in representing on screen the physical appearance of the Negro.

In 1921, the Lincoln Motion Pictures Company produced *A Day with the Tenth Cavalry at Fort Huachaca, Arizona* (1921), a one-reel pictorial of 33 scenes showing the black cavalry training at the fort. For black audiences, such scenes sustained public memory of African Americans' loyalty and patriotism, and inspired them to continue to press for the rights of citizenship. After 1922, *A Day with the Tenth Cavalry* attracted little attention in the press. The use of such images in race propaganda or efforts to resurrect and recycle footage of blacks in the military seemed to wane.

In the years after World War I, the political climate had become more contentious. Racial tensions ran high in 1919, as reports of lynchings made front-page headlines in the black press. Films of heroism and sacrifice in battle, shown not only in theaters, but also in community churches and lodge halls, helped to strengthen African

American resolve to fight against the prejudice, hatred, and oppression they faced at home. At the same time, images of heroic black soldiers taking up arms to defend their homes, neighbors, or towns, and defeating the enemy in hand-to-hand combat, challenged notions of racial inferiority and threatened white domination. It was becoming all too clear that these black documentaries, which had initially been accepted as an effort to stir patriotism against a foreign enemy, were also capable of uniting blacks in the struggle for democracy at home. Images of heroism were a great source of pride, and each individual act of valor in the war to "make the world safe for democracy" held the promise of victory at home.

"The Man Behind the Movie Shorts"

By the mid-1920s, race movies were on the decline. They had always been undercapitalized, but now fewer venues and smaller profits plagued the field's veterans and made the enterprise less attractive for newcomers. In the years that preceded the advent of sound and the collapse of the stock market, Hollywood was actively developing theater chains and squeezing out the smaller independent movie houses. In that atmosphere there were fewer and fewer new black production companies, and among the veterans in the field only Oscar Micheaux successfully negotiated the transition into the era of sound. As sound took over the next decade, the market for short films focusing on black music was dominated by Hollywood and by white independent filmmakers. It was against this backdrop that a talented young cameraman, Edward Lewis, ventured forth with a novel idea—an all-sports African American newsreel.

An article in the *Amsterdam News,* under the headline "The Man behind the Movie Shorts," profiled 26-year-old Edward Lewis, producer of two popular series that were making the rounds nationally: *The Colored Champions of Sports* and *Colored America on Parade.* The article described Lewis as "the youngest motion picture producer in America and the only one who does his own camera work and script writing."[40] In 1938, Lewis purchased his own movie camera and left a promising career as photographer for the *New York Daily News* to start over as an independent filmmaker.

As an experienced news photographer Lewis knew how to tell a story with pictures, and in 1938, he set out to create a series of documentary shorts joined by a common theme. This series, *Life in Harlem,* followed a day in the lives of Harlem residents. Working as a one-man production company—scripting, shooting, and editing his own material—Lewis produced twelve documentary shorts in 1939 which were released by Million Dollar Productions.

Lewis followed up with a second series that capitalized on the popularity of African American sports figures. His *Colored Champions of Sports* brought to the screens of neighborhood theaters the players most viewers had only read about in the entertainment sections of black newspapers. Shown in ten-minute segments along with regular programs, the series featured World Heavyweight Champion Joe Louis at his training camp or socializing in the community; Josh Gibson of the Grays, the heaviest-hitting catcher in the colored league; Smokey Joe Williams, one of the oldest and best pitchers in colored baseball; and boxer Henry Armstrong, who held both the lightweight and welter-weight titles.[41]

Sitting in their local movie houses, audiences could watch the Black Yankees play, or witness young athletes representing the U.S. abroad at Olympic competitions. Segments on athletes like track star Jesse Owens or Negro League pitcher Satchel Paige could be seen at the Loew's Theaters in Harlem, for example, and often these short pieces were as big an attraction (if not bigger) than the Hollywood features sharing the marquee.

Despite his substantial accomplishments, Edward Lewis never achieved prominence as a filmmaker. While he was well known in Harlem for his documentaries, audiences outside New York City seldom knew his name or realized that he was African American. The expense of producing his documentaries made his operation unprofitable. The value to black audiences of the short films he made far exceeded the small monetary returns the filmmaker realized in his all too brief career.

Lewis was not the only journalist to contribute to documentary filmmaking. For example, veteran reporter St. Clair T. Bourne was often called upon to write a script for one of *Lewis's Colored Champion of Sports* reels or for William Alexander's *All American Newsreels.* A versatile writer, Bourne reported on both domestic and international news, sports, and entertainment. He contributed film reviews and wrote for the society pages. Bourne says that black reporters had to be ready for anything: they could expect to be sent by an editor to Washington one week to cover the activities of a half-dozen federal agencies, and then to the deep south the next week to report on segregation, jobs, race relations, or other issues of the day. Such broad experience made journalists like Bourne a valuable asset for independent filmmakers like Lewis, who were always short staffed and strapped for funds.[42]

In the years leading up to World War II, a number of other black filmmakers were devoting themselves to producing newsreels and documentaries. In the 1930s, Gordon Parks was beginning to shape a career in photography. A high school dropout from Kansas, Parks was a self-taught, multi-talented artist who developed his craft in the field, first as a commercial photographer and then as a cinema photographer. With the advent of war, Gordon Parks and his contemporaries, Carlton Moss and William Alexander, seized the opportunity to broaden their experience as cameramen and journalists in the military, and to bring to public attention black participation in the war effort at every level. They wanted to bring home the sacrifices made by blacks despite the bigotry and oppression they experienced at home.

This goal proved very difficult for Parks to pursue. African American pilots and their segregated units were assigned to escort the big bombers making raids on German strongholds in World War II. The black pilot's job was to divert anti-aircraft guns and enemy fighter planes from the bombers. The government was not eager to publicize this strategy, or the success of the African American pilots—this was an issue of racism, not military secrets. When documentaries appeared recently about the "Tuskegee Airmen," they ended a half-century of suppression of images of these men in combat. For the most part, war correspondents representing the black press had to rely on interviews conducted on the ground and handouts provided by the govemment. Papers with small circulations had to make use of letters from returning soldiers or interviews that took place stateside.[43] Images of black troops in combat were systematically suppressed, edited out of mainstream media in the U.S.

Gordon Parks set out to document the experience of the black airmen. Although he held the rank of first lieutenant in the Office of War Information (OWI), his efforts to carry out an assignment to follow the 332nd fighter pilots into action were thwarted. The experience ended in bitter disappointment, and his formidable skills as a photo-documentarian went unrealized.

Parks went on to become a fashion photographer and photojournalist for *Life* magazine and the first African American producer, director, writer, and composer to make his mark in Hollywood. (He filled all of these roles in his first feature film, *The Learning Tree,* 1969.) *Diary of a Harlem*

Family, a 20-minute short made for television in 1968, was Parks's first film documentary and sought to give poverty in America a human face. Parks spent the winter moftths of 1968 getting to know the family and winning their trust by talking to them about what he was trying to do. The project grew out of a photo essay entitled *Flavio* that Parks had previously published in *Life*. *Flavio* depicted poverty in São Paulo, Brazil, by telling the story of a teenage boy who tries to hold his family together in the face of poverty, illiteracy, and unemployment. It also showed individuals and communities reaching out to help the boy and his family. The strong emotional impact that *Flavio* had on the magazine's large readership moved Parks to undertake *Diary of a Harlem Family*, this time capturing the family's experience on film. Another documentary made nearly two decades later, *Moments without Proper Names* (1987), brought to the screen a brilliant visualization of the filmmaker's life—his travels, the films he produced, and the people he knew. Covering nearly 40 years, the film is impressionistic and lyrical, employing Parks's artistry not only as a filmmaker, but also as a photographer, writer, and musician.

Near the end of World War II, Parks's contemporaries, Carlton Moss and William Alexander, were more successful in their wartime filmmaking efforts. Moss's *The Negro Soldier* (1944) and Alexander's *A Call to Duty* (1946), depicting blacks in the navy, were part of the war effort to boost civilian morale and patriotism. Both films resurrected the theme of black soldiers' heroism, as earlier documentaries had done in the World War I era.

The Films of William Alexander

The early pioneers of the black documentary, like George Broome and Peter P. Jones, were dedicated men with a mission. They were motivated by the desire to break new ground, to burst through the color line, and in the process to make names for themselves. Others continued in their footsteps in the decades that followed. Oscar Micheaux (1884–1951) certainly had their pioneering spirit and commitment to individualism. A producer, writer, and director, Micheaux was determined to go it alone right up to the end of his 30-year career.

While Micheaux is credited with being the most prolific black feature filmmaker of his time, William H. Alexander has an equally strong claim as producer of documentaries. Compared with Micheaux, Alexander kept a lower profile. He tended to be a team player who surrounded himself with top professionals—the best talent he could find. For example, Alexander engaged working journalists to write scripts for some of his projects. Veteran reporter St. Clair T. Bourne wrote and narrated scripts for a number of his documentaries.[44] Alexander was always on the lookout for ways to improve the quality of his productions, and would seize any opportunity that would help meet his goals. In 1973 a Paramount Pictures press biography described Alexander as the "consummate producer" and offered this account of his career: "For more than a quarter of a century, Colorado-born William Alexander has been roaming the world performing minor miracles of communication through filmmaking. . . . A man of boundless energy, close associates have known him as a daring self-starter, full of original ideas, with the aggressiveness to set the domino theory in motion and effect its ultimate results."[45]

Alexander grew up in Colorado, where he attended Greeley High School and Colorado State College of Education before spending several years studying at Chicago State University. He moved to Washington, D.C:, where he ran a radio show inferviewing blacks in government and generally covering the social life of the African American middle class in the nation's capital.

Like Moss, Alexander's career was deeply affected by his work with the Office of War Information during World War II. Headed by Elmer Davis, OWI played a key role in boosting Negro morale around the country through press releases sent out to black newspapers. Planning and carrying out this effort was the work of a group of men sometimes known as the "Black Brain Trust" who fed the black press with stories and pictures. In addition to Alexander, information specialist and chief of the black press section, the group included William Bryant, an organization analyst attached to the Bureau of Intelligence, and Charles Austen, staff cartoonist.

Recognizing the power of film, Alexander's group at OWI went beyond the print media and formed a production company. In an interview given after the war, Alexander explained it this way:

> We were very concerned about the morale of "minority groups"—whatever that meant. They worked in war industries, but when people went to the cinema, it looked like a white man's war. We formed the All American Newsreel Company and used to take OSS film crews and shoot stuff all over the world. One of the most interesting stories was on Willa Brown Coffee, the second black woman aviator (Bessie Coleman was the first). She trained all the instructors for the black 99th Pursuit Squadron at her Coffee School of Aeronautics outside Chicago. Although the releases were made in a government agency, the documentaries were privately filmed. Two of our shorts were on blacks in the Army and Navy: *The Highest Tradition,* narrated by Fredric March, and *Call to Duty,* narrated by Walter Huston.[46]

The All American Newsreel Company, under Alexander's direction, produced more than 250 newsreels. This collection has survived, and was recently purchased from a private collector by the Columbia Broadcasting System (CBS).

After the war, in 1945, Alexander moved to New York taking with him a wealth of experience and contacts acquired in his work for OWI. There he established the Associated Film Producers of Negro Motion Pictures, Inc., and started producing short musical films and features for theatrical release. Like Edward Lewis, Alexander leased these shorts to theaters. He then found a new market for his work, taking three-to-five minute performance segments from the shorts and selling them as soundies that played in coin-operated jukeboxes in restaurants, bars, and cafes.

These short performance pieces had very simple stories or plot lines. They were cheap to produce and easy to sell, according to Haryette Miller Barton, Alexander's production assistant and one of the few African American women working in the film industry behind the camera. She explains:

> Mr. Alexander's shorts were sometimes made just to give a group of musicians work, making up the story as they went along or using the lyrics of a song for plot. Sometimes we shot in donated spaces—a barber shop after hours or on a Sunday. But for top performers like Billy Eckstine and his band, the Sweet Hearts of Rhythm, and Dizzy Gillespie's band, we worked with larger budgets, in a studio with a hired union (usually white) crew. Soundies and shorts were quick, easy to set up, and required little or no costuming. The plus was . . . they helped to pay the rent and salaries.[47]

In 1950 Alexander moved to London and established the Blue Nile Production Company. With London as his base he traveled to Africa where he produced a series of documentaries for and about the newly independent countries of the Sub-Sahara. These films, many commissioned by individual states, reflected life after independence and were used for public relations purposes and to record the historic changes that were taking place.

Alexander's films reflected life in the newly emerging African nations. The documentaries were used by individual states for public relations purposes and to record the historic changes that were taking place. He often worked with heads of state, and in two cases took on an official capacity: Alexander became the official film producer for the Republic of Liberia, and subsequently served in the same post for the government of Ethiopia. The documentaries produced by Alexander in these capacities received critical acclaim around the world. *The Village of Hope,* about a leper colony in Liberia, won a prize for the Best Short Film at the 1964 Cannes Film Festival. At the Venice Film Festival the following year, Alexander won a prize for his *Portrait of Ethiopia,* and in 1967 he received the United Nations Award at the International Festival in Madrid for *Wealth in Wood.*

Alexander spent nearly 18 years working in Africa and Europe. Relatively little of the work he produced during the African period has surfaced so far. The scope of his work is well documented, however.

Alexander filmed some of the first conferences of the Organization of African States. He helped bring television equipment to Liberia and Ethiopia, and assisted in developing TV programming in those countries. He received awards or decorations from heads of states in all of the 22 countries where he worked, including Liberia, Ethiopia, the Sudan, Morocco, the United Arab Republic, Zaire, Kenya, Senegal, Ghana, Algeria, Malagasy, Dahomey, Togo, Malawi, Sierra Leone, Tanzania, Zambia, French Congo, the Ivory Coast, Guinea, and the General African Republic. (His work was also recognized by the government of Singapore.)[48]

The films Alexander produced between the mid-1950s and 1973 constitute a sizeable body of work. Despite the awards he received abroad, his contribution as filmmaker and visionary at a critical juncture in Africa's history has yet to be fully acknowledged at home. Scholars have yet to address key questions about his work. What contributions did his documentaries make to each nation's development? How was his perspective and approach influenced by the heads of state who hired him, including such leaders and thinkers as Sékou Touré, Julius Nyerere, Jomo Kenyatta, Gamal Abdul Nasser, and Léopold Senghor? Answers to some of these questions must await the recovery of Alexander's historically important footage of the African independence movements, shot inside the former colonies. This footage would provide an invaluable resource for historians and film scholars alike.

Bridging the Generations

Alexander remained active into the early 1970s, when he undertook an ambitious project to produce a film version of William Bradford Huie's novel, *The Klansman.* He acquired the screen rights to the novel and then, according to the Paramount Pictures press biography, traveled more than 300,000 miles to acquire financial backing ($4.5 million), engage a top director and crew, and attract a cast that included Richard Burton, Lee Marvin, O. J. Simpson, and Lola Falana. His expansive filmmaking career bridged a gap between the first generation of black documentary filmmakers that had all but disappeared by the 1950s, and a new generation of more strident, independent voices that emerged in the 1960s and helped to shape and record the civil rights struggle.

In the tradition of Peter P. Jones, Jennie Toussaint Welcome, Addison N. Scurlock, and other pioneers of black documentary filmmaking, these new chroniclers of African American history and culture used film to capture events as they were happening, and to empower their community by offering a deeper, stronger sense of its own identity and history, and ultimately to effect change. Their call to action helped to break the iron circle of segregation, racism, and containment, and to bring about a new era of race consciousness and renewal. While the media brought film clips and sound bites of the revolution in the streets to a national audience, African American filmmakers challenged viewers with a fuller, more textured sense of black culture and history, providing a context for the scenes of protest that were appearing more and more often on the evening news.

Today, as one generation reaches out to the next, the list of African American filmmakers is steadily growing. Foremost among them is William Greaves, who became executive producer of the public affairs program *Black Journal* in 1969. Greaves's work in network television created crucial new outlets for black documentarians. He helped to usher in a new era of filmmaking not only through his own work, but also through his efforts to mentor and support other filmmakers. William Miles, Louis Massiah, St. Clair Bourne, Julie Dash, Stan Lathan, Michelle Parkerson, Yvonne Smith, Stanley Nelson, Carroll Parrott Blue, Gil Noble, Henry Hampton, Charles Hobson, S. Pearl Sharp, Carol Munday Lawrence, Orlando Bagwell, Ayoka Chenzira, and (the late) Jackie Shearer and Toni Cade Bambara—these documentarians, and many others, are helping to light our way into the next century.

Looking ahead, many challenges await not only filmmakers, but also film historians. Many questions remain unanswered. Photographers' contributions in the century's early decades have yet to be fully explored.[49] The recovery of information about individual photographers and filmmakers may help to expand and clarify what is known about early motion picture technology. And more filmmakers need to be rescued from anonymity: what names might we attach to footage of African American soldiers in battle during the First World War? Or in Cuba during the Spanish American War?[50] A great deal of footage remains to be found. Many early filmmaking efforts are no doubt lost forever, but the whereabouts of later films are more puzzling. Where, for example, are the missing documentaries of William Alexander?

To be sure, current documentary techniques and approaches are light years away from those of the early pioneers, but for the most part, today's black filmmakers share the commitments of their forerunners: recording the highs and lows of ordinary folk, as well as extraordinary moments in black history and culture as seen from within. From the 1910 Tuskegee footage to Jones's marching bands and regiments to Alexander's newsreels, to today's commentaries—each has contributed to bringing to life the great canvas of African American experience.

NOTES

1. Nicholas Lemann, *The Promised Land: The Great Black Migration and How It Changed America* (New York: Knopf, 1991).
2. Ibid.
3. Thomas L. Johnson and Philip C. Dunn, eds., *A True Likeness: The Black South of Richard Samuel Roberts, 1920–1936* (Columbia, S.C.: Bruccoli Clark; and Chapel Hill, N.C.: Algonquin Books of Chapel Hill, 1986), 107.
4. See *Negro History Week*, February 10, 1935, 15.
5. The 1910 census listed 3,257 white photographers.
6. Jeanne Moutoussamy-Ashe, *Viewfinders: Black Women Photographers* (New York: Dodd, Mead, 1986).
7. Carlton Moss interview conducted by Pearl Bowser, 1987; Carlton Moss interview for *Midnight Ramble*, conducted by Pearl Bowser and Saundra Sharp 1991.
8. *Chicago Whip*, July 16, 1921.
9. Sherman H. Dudley, Robert T. Motts, and others contributed to the development of a circuit

of theaters for black vaudeville and films. Sherman Dudley owned several theaters which were part of the substructure already in place for race movies. Showmen with packaged material worked the churches and lodge halls and set up tent shows. Before 1910, C. E. Hawk was exhibiting footage of the famous black Ninth Cavalry in the Inaugural Parade being applauded by President Theodore Roosevelt. The Ninth Cavalry served in Cuba under Roosevelt during the Spanish American War. Who shot the footage? Where did Hawk purchase this and other films he traveled with? Were black camera operators among the groups of freelance photographers selling to distributors or showmen before 1910? These are among the questions that remain unanswered.

10. Noble Johnson, African American actor and founder of Lincoln Motion Pictures, played in one such serial, *Bulls Eye*, produced by the Lubin Company. The black press advertised this serial as if Johnson were the star instead of white actor Eddie Polo. Johnson was under contract with the Lubin Company and ultimately had to choose between his own company and a steady job with a Hollywood studio. He chose Hollywood and a career that rewarded him with more than one hundred character roles in mainstream cinema.
11. Footage in the Jackson, Mississippi, Archives about 1940. The theater marquee displayed the race movie *God's Step Children*, an Oscar Micheaux film.
12. *Chicago Defender*, September 22, 1923.
13. *Deep South Showman Versie Lee Lawrence: A Reflection Book* (New York: Carlton Press, 1962). Henry Sampson in *Blacks in Black and White*, p. 2, cites touring black companies and showmen before 1910 exhibiting films for black audiences in schools, parks, and churches, including C. E. Hawk's *Electrical Display of Life Motion Pictures* (1905) and Royston's *Chicago Moving Picture Show* (as early as 1899.)
14. *Chicago Defender*, December 31, 1910.
15. Ibid.
16. David Levering Lewis, *W. E. B. Du Bois: Biography of a Race, 1868–1919* (New York: Henry Holt and Company, 1993), 301.
17. The Brownsville raid occurred in 1905 when a group of black soldiers was accused of starting a gunfight and "shooting up" the town. Soldiers in the famous black 25th Texas Regiment, though innocent, were summarily discharged by order of President Theodore Roosevelt, without a trial or court martial. This was the same regiment that had fought with Roosevelt in Cuba in the taking of San Juan Hill. Now, by his order, its members were disgraced and discharged from the military without pay or benefits. The President, who had claimed to be a friend of the Negro and Washington, refused to rescind the order even though he knew the regiment was innocent. Roosevelt's popularity among African American voters was further eroded after the bloody riot in Atlanta in 1906. Federal troops had been sent in by Roosevelt's order.
18. *Booker T. Washington's Great Industrial School at Tuskegee, Alabama*, shown on February 3, 1910 (*New York Age*); A Trip to Tuskegee (*New York Age*, August 11, 1910); *A Tuskegee Pilgrimage* (Reol Productions, 1922); *Tuskegee Finds a Way Out* (Crusader Films, 1923).
19. *New York Age*, January 10, 1910.
20. Henry T. Sampson, *Blacks in Black and White: A Source Book on Black Films* (Metuchen, N.J.: Scarecrow Press, 1995), 584.
21. A personal note about *A Day at Tuskegee*. Reflecting on the history of the black documentary, seemingly small and prosaic in its beginnings, the author is struck by the tenacity of details so familiar they seem like only yesterday—a part of my immediate experience and not incidents nearly a century old. In the early 1970s, I was invited to Tuskegee Institute by the South Carolina Arts Council. At that time, there were still hints of the architectural grandeur described in reviews of the film.
22. *Chicago Defender*, May 1914.
23. *The Freeman, an Illustrated Colored Newspaper*, April 1, 1916. Jones probably designed this ad himself. The ad indicates the *Dawn of Truth* had been a part of the special movie spectacle in 1915, the year before this announcement of the availability of the film for bookings. It is also conceivable, based on the dates in the ad, that in 1914 the films were shown first abroad in South America and Brazil. Sampson refers to this as newsreel coverage of the August 21–September 16, 1915, celebration.
24. Ibid.
25. Ibid.
26. Ibid.
27. Ibid.
28. Anita Bush starred in two black silent Westerns: *The Crimson Skull* (1921) and *The Bull-Dogger* (1923). She is credited with founding one of the first African American dramatic stock companies, The Anita Bush Stock Company, in 1915, which included such notable actors as Dooley Wilson, Charles Gilpin, Andrew Bishop, and Carlotta Freeman.
29. See photographs of unknown camera operators in Johnson and Dunn, *A True Likeness*, 90; and on the set of an outdoor stage on Wisconsin-Ebony Pictures promotional/stock offering material, George P. Johnson Collection.
30. Sampson, *Blacks in Black and White*, 184.
31. Harry Grant, the George P. Johnson Collection, University of California Archives, Los Angeles.
32. Sampson, *Blacks in Black and White*.
33. *Chicago Defender*, July 26,1913.
34. Ibid.
35. *The Negro News Reel*, 1923, produced by William Herman, *The Negro Rice Farmer*, 1921. Dunbar Film and Theatrical Company documentary: Negroes at work in the rice fields in Louisiana.
36. *This Is Our War: Selected Stories of Six War Correspondents—Six Who Were Sent Overseas by the Afro-American Newspapers* (Baltimore, Washington, Philadelphia, Richmond, and Newark: The Afro-American Company, 1945). Introduction

by Carl Murphy (Baltimore: The Afro-American Company, December 15, 1944), 7.

37. Sampson, *Blacks in Black and White,* 588.
38. George P. Johnson interview conducted by Pearl Bowser, Los Angeles, 1969.
39. *New York Age,* May 24, 1919.
40. *Afro-American,* March 1939.
41. Handbill for Loew's Victoria and Loew's 116th Street theater, January 5–9,1938.
42. St. Clair T. Bourne telephone interview conducted by Pearl Bowser, September 11, 1997.
43. *This Is Our War,* 7.
44. St. Clair T. Bourne telephone interview.
45. *By Line,* biography of William Alexander.
46. Newspaper article provided by Harryette Miller Barton, undated.
47. Harryette Miller Barton interview conducted by Pearl Bowser, 1990.
48. Based on an interview conducted by William Greaves with William Alexander a week before Alexander's death on November 20, 1991. William Greaves starred in Alexander's *The Fight Never Ends* (1947) and *Souls of Sin* (1949).
49. Examples of unanswered questions include: Who might have used Macbeth's daylight screen? What year was it invented? Did showmen such as Royston, Hawks, or Professor A. A. Moncret, who were exhibiting moving pictures before 1910, show their programs in parks as well as churches and schools?
50. Henry Sampson attributes images from the war in Cuba to Lubin Ceneographs, which a black company, Royston's Chicago Moving Picture Show, included in its tour of Virginia's black churches, schools, etc. See Sampson, *Blacks in Black and White,* 2nd ed., 2.

75

MICHAEL CHANAN

REDISCOVERING DOCUMENTARY

Cultural Context and Intentionality (1990)

For more than twenty-five years a new cinema has been developing in Latin America, carving out spaces for itself even under the most inimical circumstances, a cinema devoted to the denunciation of misery and the celebration of protest. When these diverse films first began to arrive in Europe and North America in the 1960s, they challenged many of the norms of established film narrative, unequivocally announcing the existence of a new avant-garde in world cinema: Nelson Pereira dos Santos and Glauber Rocha in Brazil, Tomás Gutiérrez Alea and Humberto Solás in Cuba, Miguel Littín in Chile, Jorge Sanjinés in Bolivia, and many others.

Among these films were several eye-opening documentaries. From Cuba, a number of explosive short films by Santiago Alvarez—among them *Now* (1965) and *LBJ* (1968), with their biting satire and sense of urgency—seemed to reinvent the concept of agit-prop. From Uruguay Mario Handler's *Me gustan los estudiantes* (*I Like Students,* 1967), another modest masterpiece of agit-prop, captured the explosive energy of the national student movement. From Argentina, a mammoth four-hour film in three parts, *La hora de los hornos* (*The Hour of the Furnaces*, 1968), made by Fernando Solanas and Octavio Getino, described by its makers as "an act of liberation," caused a sensation at its European premiere in Pesaro, Italy. From Colombia, *Chircales* (*Brickmakers*) by Jorge Silva and Marta Rodríguez, extended ethnography into systematic political analysis.

These were only isolated examples of a growing mass of films and filmmakers throughout Latin America. In this burgeoning movement that would become known as the New Latin American Cinema, documentary held a central position. Part of the originality of numerous fiction films derived from their incorporation of documentary techniques and styles.

The question has been asked whether all this activity really amounts to an artistic movement, whether these characteristics are concrete and specific enough to give a sense of unity to the extremely diverse ways in which they are employed. This is a question, however, as much about the forms of cultural development in Latin America as about cinema per se. First of all, not all artistic movements have the same kind of logic. There are significant differences among, for example, impressionism, fauvism, futurism, surrealism, and so forth. Second, we should not assume that artistic movements work the same way in Latin America, Africa, or Asia. Is it not possible that the basic concepts of cultural history enlisted to identify broad cultural movements like Renaissance humanism, classicism, or modernism are quintessentially European?

The New Latin American Cinema, whether or not it is thought of as a movement, certainly possesses a bewildering diversity of styles and forms. Cuban filmmakers are given to observe that the idea of socialist realism is an empty one if it can be taken to include both a Bondarchuk and a Tarkovsky. What should we say of the contrast between Rocha and dos Santos, or Sanjinés and Antonio Equino, his former cameraman? Or between the vastly different works of other directors? What do Latin American filmmakers mean by the New Latin American Cinema, a term they themselves often greet with suspicion? Is it, perhaps a piece of bravura?

The paradigmatic role of documentary cinema can shed light on these complex questions. Nowhere can documentary's importance be observed more vividly than in Cuba. As a kind of testing laboratory for the New Latin American Cinema, Cuba has produced the most fascinating and contradictory findings. Before the 1959 revolution, Cuba had been a leading Latin American producer of commercial radio and television and a leading consumer of Hollywood movies. The chronic absence or distortion of images of national life in films before 1959 helps explain why documentary would carry such weight in Cuba's postrevolutionary film production.

The historical moment of the Cuban revolution was also, by coincidence, a period of aesthetic revolution in documentary cinema. Within the space of a few years, 16mm, previously regarded as a substandard format like 8mm or half-inch video today, became viable. Technical developments, inspired by the needs of space technology as well as television, stimulated the production of high-quality 16mm cameras light enough to be raised on the shoulder and equipped with fast lenses and film stocks that reduced or even eliminated the need for artificial lighting. Portable tape recorders and improved microphones provided synchronous sound, allowing the sound technician a mobility commensurate to that of the camera operator. No longer forced to shoot with bulky 35mm equipment that restricted them to studios or prepared locations, documentarists felt as if reborn. New-style documentary filmmakers sprung up on both sides of the Atlantic. In Europe the style became known as cinema verité, in the United States as direct cinema.

[. . .]

It would be natural to suppose that the Cubans eagerly took up the revolution in documentary occurring at the same moment as their own political and social revolution. Watching the documentaries of the revolution's early years, however, one rapidly discovers that this was not the case. Sometimes, indeed, the styles and forms of cinema verité are most noticeable by virtue of their absence. One reason is that the first task of the new film institute, ICAIC, was to set up operations in 35mm. By the time this was accomplished, the U.S. blockade had been imposed and there were no longer funds available for developing 16mm. One is tempted to ask, would it have been any different if there had been? Examination of the evidence both on and off screen leads to the conclusion that it would not.[1]

The rapid expansion of ICAIC's documentary output, from four films in 1959 to twenty-one the following year and forty in 1965, makes it a hopeless task to attempt to survey these films individually without looking for a way to categorize them. This exercise is fraught with the most thorny problems. Any system of classification is liable to backfire, through imposing a conceptual scheme foreign to the material it is trying to classify. Caution therefore urges that we look first at systems of classification the Cubans themselves have employed.

In an interview published in 1971, Julio García Espinosa was asked how nonfiction output was classified.[2] He cited four categories: popularizing documentaries (*documentales de divulgación*), scientific subjects for popular consumption, newsreels, and cartoons. These divisions correspond to the way production in ICAIC was organized. The first is a general category; the second refers to specifically didactic films. (A department for didactic documentaries was set up in 1960, and though the catalogue classification under this heading came to an end in 1970, the types of films it included continued to be made. There was also a series entitled *Popular Encyclopedia* for which thirty-one films were produced during 1961–1962.)[3] The last two categories refer to the departments of newsreel and animation headed by Santiago Alvarez and Juan Padrón, respectively, which continued to function as separate units within ICAIC through the 1980s because their specific organizational requirements remained distinct.

Clearly these categories do not have any great aesthetic relevance. It would be more useful to look for a system of classification according to subject or theme, which might at least tell us something about the relative weight the Cubans have given to different fields of interest and could also serve as a starting point for more detailed analysis. A group of students under Mario Piedra, using ICAIC's own Cuban-assembled computer, have analyzed the institute's documentary output over the years 1959–1982.[4] Using thirty-three categories, they made a simple count of the numbers in nine broad thematic groups, and arrived at the following percentages:

working-class themes (*tematica social-obrera*): 24.27
artistic or cultural topics: 20.38
international topics: 15.25
didactic topics: 13.45
educational topics: 7.35
historical topics: 6.38
sports: 5.68
problems in the construction of socialist society: 4.02
other: 3.19

This kind of typology, though it seems to offer a fair guide to the range of subjects treated by Cuban documentary, is not a satisfactory classification system because it gives no idea of stylistic variety. Certain films elude confinement to a single category; many films fall under one heading or another only ambiguously or incompletely. Themes that are less often treated are not necessarily less important. Finally, some films reveal the extent of their importance only over time, like the modest six-minute montage experiment made by Santiago Alvarez in 1965 called *Now*, widely regarded as a classic of social protest.

Another question raised by this classification system involves defining exactly what a didactic film is. Within a set of terms referring to subject areas, the category seems anomalous, for it delimits not so much subject as treatment. It really belongs to a different set of terms altogether, the set which rather than dealing with subject matter, identifies the intention with which the film is made. Though it does not constitute a systematic classification scheme, the categorization of documentary according to intention represents the way documentary is thought of in Latin America, because it arises directly from the conditions under which filmmakers at the receiving end of imperialism have to operate. These terms are far more aesthetically compelling than the previous schema. In addition to *cine didáctico*, they include:

cine celebrativo—celebrational cinema
cine de combate—the combat film
cine denuncia—the protest film
cine encuesta—investigative documentary
cine ensayo—the film essay
cine reportaje—reportage (overlaps with *cine encuesta*)
cine rescate—films that "rescue" aspects of national or regional history or culture
cine testimonio—the testimonial film

This list is neither exhaustive nor definitive. There is no single source from which it is drawn. These are only the most frequently used of a series of terms that occur across the whole range of literature about Cuban and radical Latin American film, writings that express the preoccupations and objectives of the New Latin American Cinema movement. They can be found in film journals from several countries, including Peru (*Hablemos de Cine*), Venezuela (*Cine al Día*), Chile (*Primer Plano*), Mexico (*Octubre*), and Cuba (*Cine Cubano*), to cite only the most important.

The distinctive feature of all the terms listed is precisely their intentional character. They indicate a variety of purposes: to teach, to offer testimony, to denounce, to investigate, to bring history alive, to celebrate revolutionary achievement, to provide space for reflection, to report, to express solidarity, to militate for a cause. These are all needs of revolutionary struggle, both before and after the conquest of power, when they become part of the process of consolidating, deepening, and extending the revolution.

An unsympathetic critic from the metropolis would quite likely dismiss the entire list with a single term: propaganda. Bourgeois ideologies have always equated propaganda with mere rhetoric, the selective use of evidence to persuade. (Or, as a Cambridge professor once put it, "a branch of the art of lying which consists in very nearly deceiving your friends while not quite deceiving your enemies.") Propaganda and didacticism are usually considered incompatible. Every revolutionary aesthetic finds this a false and mendacious antinomy. Revolutionary propaganda is the creative use of demonstration and example to teach revolutionary principles, and of dialectical argument to mobilize intelligence toward self-liberation. It seeks—and when it hits its target it gets—an active not a passive response from the spectator. As the Argentinian filmmakers Fernando Solanas and Octavio Getino put it, "Revolutionary cinema does not illustrate, document or establish a situation passively; it attempts instead to intervene in that situation as a way of providing impetus towards its correction."[5] There is obviously a didactic element in this, but there's a difference: the aim of teaching is not immediately to inspire action, but to impart the means for the acquisition of more and better knowledge upon which action may be premised. Accordingly, there's a practical difference in revolutionary aesthetics, too, between the propaganda film and the didactic film.

Ten years before Solanas and Getino made *The Hour of the Furnaces*, another Argentinian, Fernando Birri, set up the film school at the Universidad del Litoral in his native Santa Fe. He based the idea of the kind of cinema he was aiming for on two main sources: Italian neorealism, and the idea of the social documentary associated with John Grierson. Both precedents are conventionally dominated by a naive realist aesthetic, so it is not surprising to find Colombian filmmaker Jorge Silva saying in an interview a few years later, "At the inception of the militant film movement, it was said that the essential thing was simply to capture reality and nothing more, and to make reality manifest. Afterwards this formulation began to seem insufficient."[6]

However, it was not as if Birri or anyone else involved meant these paradigms to be accepted uncritically. The way Birri saw it, to apply the humanistic ideas behind neorealism and the social documentary to the context of underdevelopment immediately gave them a dialectical edge. In an interview in *Cine Cubano* in 1963, he explained the function of the documentary in Latin America by means of a play on the word *underdevelopment*—in Spanish, *subdesarrollo*. In opposition to the false images of Latin American commercial cinema, documentary was called to present an image of authentic reality as it was and could not in all conscience otherwise be shown. It would thus bear critical witness by showing itself to be a subreality (*subrealidad*), that is to say, a reality suppressed and full of misfortune. In doing this, says Birri, "*it denies it* [reality as conventionally depicted]. It disowns it, judges it, criticises it, dissects it: because it shows things as they irrefutably are, not as we would like them to be (or how they would have us, in good or bad faith, believe that they are)." At the same time, "as a balance to this function of negation, realist cinema fulfills another, one of affirming the positive values in the society: the values of the people, their reserves of strength, their labours, their joys, their struggles, their dreams." Hence the motivation and the consequence of the social documentary, says Birri, is knowledge of reality and the grasp of awareness of it—*toma de conciencia* in Spanish, *prise de conscience* in French. (What Brecht wanted his theater to be.) Birri summarizes: "Problematic: The change from sub-life to life." In practical terms: "To place oneself in front of the reality with a camera and film this reality, film it critically, film underdevelopment with a popular optic." Otherwise, you get a cinema that becomes the accomplice of underdevelopment, which is to say, a subcinema (*subcine*, like *subdesarrollo*).[7]

[. . .]

Cine testimonio, or testimonial cinema, is another central category, one with two distinct strands. One of them is well represented by the Mexican documentarist Eduardo Maldonado, founder in 1969 of a group which took the term itself as its name: Grupo Cine Testimonio. According to Maldonado, *cine testimonio* is concerned to put cinema at the service of social groups which lack access to the means of mass communication, in order to make their point of view public. In the process, he says, the film collaborates in the *concientización* of the group concerned. At the same time, the filmmaker's awareness is directed towards the process of the film. The process of shooting becomes one of investigation and discovery which reaches, he believes, its final and highest stage in the editing. The film thus embodies "the aesthetic approach to *concientización*."[8]

The style which attracted Maldonado as most appropriate to these purposes was that of direct cinema. "We're not interested in propagandistic documentary work," he said, "because we find it very boring. Nor are we interested in fictional filmmaking with big stars and big screens. Instead, what we're after is a kind of direct cinema, a way of making films quickly like cinema verité, which seeks to film events in the flesh, with the people who are the protagonists of real occurrences. This type of cinema tries to penetrate reality, to find the internal and external contradictions in order finally to discover the meaning behind things." He continues:

> Observation and analysis are the basis for this kind of film making, both as the means of capturing reality and of finding the particular dialectical interpretation in each instance.
>
> We do not wish to impose our blueprints or mental categories on reality. To do this would only mean that our films would become tracts. And that would be meaningless when compared to the standards of truth and interpretation to which the people being filmed are exposed.

> The basis of our films is our personal testimony, so we have to respect what people think about their own circumstances. Do we want to know how the subjects of the film live and how they think? Then we have to let the facts speak for themselves.[9]

Although Maldonado falls back into the language of empirical subjectivism, it's not as if these ideas are those of naive realism any more than Birri's, only that the formulation is careless. At the same time, it may appear that in distancing the aims of the group from propaganda and in disparaging the film-tract, Maldonado is explaining the position of filmmakers who were not party militants. There are, however, a good many filmmakers in Latin America who, though they are indeed party militants, would substantially agree with Maldonado. They would agree with the search for a dialectical interpretation of reality, with the reluctance to impose alien blueprints and mental categories on the popular classes, and with the need to respect what people think about their own circumstances. Above all, Latin American filmmakers from across a broad spectrum of political affiliations would agree that in confronting the ruling elite, a film has to struggle against standards of truth that are no truth at all.

The other strand of *cine testimonio* is literary in origin and particularly strong in Cuba. The earliest paradigms are found in the *literatura de campaña* ("campaign literature") of the nineteenth-century Cuban wars of independence: the memoirs, chronicles, and diaries of Máximo Gómez, Manuel de Céspedes, José Martí, and others. These are the accounts of participants writing in the heat and haste of events, aware of their necessarily partial but privileged perspective. Che Guevara followed the same imperatives in his accounts of the Cuban revolutionary war in the 1950s and the Bolivian campaign of the 1960s. Cuban documentarist Víctor Casaus has traced this testimonial genre through Cuban journalists of the 1930s, particularly Pablo de la Torriente Brau.[10] Numerous writers of the 1970s and 1980s—the Argentinian Rodolfo Walsh, the Salvadorean Roque Dalton, the Uruguayan Eduardo Galeano, the Nicaraguan Omar Cabezas—continue to cultivate the genre.

Filmmakers have also developed their own testimonial subgenres, according to Casaus. The ICAIC newsreel was the first of these because its character as a week-by-week chronicle is not a simple piecemeal record of the events but, under the guidance of Santiago Alvarez, became their interpretative analysis. It is obviously essential to the idea of the testimonial that it convey a sense of lived history. This means, in cinema, that the camera is not to be a passive witness. The newsreel learned how to insert itself into the events it recorded by breaking the conventional structure of the newsreel form and converting itself into a laboratory for the development of filmic language. This influenced the whole field of documentary, with its already obvious affinities to testimonial literature.

Casaus specifies four characteristics of *cine testimonio*: first, rapid and flexible filming of unfolding reality without subjecting it to a preplanned narrative *mise-en-scène*; second, choosing themes of broad national importance; third, employing an audacious and intuitive style of montage, of which the outstanding exponent is Santiago Alvarez; and last, using directly filmed interviews both for the narrative functions they are able to fulfill and because they provide the means of bringing popular speech to the screen. (This was the last of Casaus's four principles actually to be incorporated into the Cuban documentary, since the Cubans initially lacked the technical capacity for direct sound filming.)

What Casaus seems to be arguing is that the vocation of documentary is testimonial, though in a sense this is an a priori argument that cannot explain the different kinds of film which have appeared. At the same time, the Cubans have given a great deal of thought to the question of *cine didáctico*, a form that becomes particularly important after a revolution reaches power. What changes in cinema with the accession to power is not just that militant filmmakers are no longer forced to work clandestinely or semiclandestinely, but that the whole emphasis of their art is altered. The tasks for which films are intended qualitatively shift, and nowhere is this more marked than in the scope that opens up for didactic cinema. As Pastor Vega explained in an article dating from 1970 entitled "Didactic Cinema and Tactics," when ICAIC set up a didactic films department in 1960, dealing with a whole range of scientific and technical subjects, not all the necessary conditions for such a project existed, "but it wasn't possible to wait for them; . . . the demands of a revolution which alters the dynamic of history in all its dimensions leave no alternative."[11] ICAIC recognized that it was necessary to create a whole new batch of filmmakers without having the time to give them proper training. They would have to learn on the job, jumping in at the deep end. The didactic film has to become didactic in more ways than one; the films would educate their makers in the process of attempting to educate their audiences. What the filmmaker has to learn takes on a double aspect—there is the subject on which the film is to be made, and at the same time, learning how to make this kind of film. Formally speaking, these are two separate functions, but in the circumstances they get completely intertwined. *Cine didáctico* thus becomes a paradigm for new ways of thinking about film.

The new documentary becomes the essential training ground in Cuban cinema because the filmmaker has to learn to treat reality by engaging with the people the film is for. *Cine didáctico* teaches that the value of communication is of paramount concern because the film would achieve nothing if it didn't succeed in its primary function, which is instruction (in the broadest sense). This theme was taken up in a paper presented jointly to the National Congress of Culture and Education in 1971 by Jorge Fraga, Estrella Pantín, and Julio García Espinosa, "Toward a Definition of the Didactic Documentary."[12]

The authors discuss the idea of the didactic documentary in light of the preoccupations that had been animating their work over the previous decade. Their line of argument is itself eminently didactic. Much of what they say is philosophically grounded in the analysis of commodity fetishism and alienation, but they appeal in equal measure to more accessible concepts and ideas. They argue that a cultural heritage distorted by imperialism produces a way of thinking that perceives things in a dissociated way, that sees things only as results, without grasping the processes that create them. Underdeveloped thinking comes to be ruled by a sense of contingency and fatalism, which harkens back to the magical (but the magical now shorn of most of its previous cultural legitimacy). They observe, "After twelve years of revolution, we still find examples of this way of thinking even in our own communications media, mostly modelled after the tendency to exalt results and omit the process which led up to those results."[13]

But, they continue, cinema possesses the very qualities needed not only to communicate knowledge and skills effectively, but also to educate for a rational, concrete, and dialectical way of thinking—because it is capable of reproducing reality in motion and therefore of demonstrating processes and, further, because it's capable of revealing relationships between elements that come from the most dissimilar conditions of time and place. Utilitarian conceptions of the didactic documentary limit its potential: the result is sterile and ahistorical. Capitalist cinema conventionally deals with the problem of the genre's dryness by adding enticements to the treatment of the film, sugar-coating the pill—a technique known from advertising as "the snare." Advertising "appeals to stimuli which have nothing to do with the nature of the product in order to create more demand for it or stimulate the consumer's interest: sex, desire for recognition and prestige, fear of feelings of inferiority—anything apart from concrete demonstration of the actual properties of the object." This mentality that thinks only in terms of selling becomes all-pervasive, and everything, including ideas and feelings, is reduced to bundles of exchange values. To fall in with all this was obviously hardly acceptable. The didactic documentary, they argue, must break once and for all with this retrogressive tradition; it must link itself with the urgency of its subjects and themes. The formal techniques employed "must be derived from the theme and put at its service. It's the old moral demand for unity between form and content."[14]

Pastor Vega's account of the didactic film has the same moral emphasis, and his arguments are similarly built on an historical materialist analysis. The socio-economic transformation created by the revolution, he explains, has propelled the newly literate peasant from the Middle Ages into the second half of the twentieth century where he becomes an operator of tractors and agricultural machinery. This accelerated passage through multiple stages of development involved in the sudden acquisition of the products of modern science and technology, requires a qualitative leap in the process of mass education. The didactic film must be transformed accordingly, throwing off the molds of the form as it originated in the developed countries and going in search of the originality that arises from very different socialist patterns of development. The filmmaker must acquire new perspectives and seek a different filmic language than the archetypes of the documentary tradition. The didactic film must be seen as a new aesthetic category in which the artist and the pedagogue meet.

[. . .]

NOTES

1. The reasons for this are examined at length in the book from which these paragraphs are taken. In the paragraphs that follow, I present some of the findings.
2. Julio García Espinosa, "El cine documental cubano," *Pensamiento crítico*, no. 40 (July 1970), 81–87.
3. Today films for strictly educational use are made primarily by the film section of the Ministry of Education, while a range of military instructional films and television programs are made by the film section of the armed forces.
4. Mario Piedra, "El documental cubano a mil carácteres por minuto," *Cine cubano*, no. 108 (1984), 43–49.
5. Fernando Solanas and Octavio Getino, "Hacia un tercer cine," *Tricontinental*, no. 13 (October 1969); rpt. in Solanas and Getino, *Cine, cultura y descolonización* (Mexico City: Siglo Veintiuno Editores, 1973). An English translation by Michael Chanan and Julianne Burton, "Towards a Third Cinema," appears in *Twenty-Five Years of the New Latin American Cinema*, ed. Chanan (London: British Film Institute and Channel Four Television, 1983), pp. 17–27.
6. Interview with Jorge Silva and Marta Rodríguez by Andrés Caicedo and Luis Ospina, *Ojo al cine*, no. 1 (1974), 35–43. An excerpted translation appears in *Cinema and Social Change in Latin America: Conversations with Filmmakers*, ed. Julianne Burton (Austin: University of Texas Press, 1986).
7. "Cinema and Underdevelopment, An Interview with Fernando Birri," *Cine cubano*, nos. 42–44 (1963), 13–21; translated in *Twenty-Five Years of the New Latin American Cinema*, ed. Chanan, pp. 9–12.
8. Interview with Eduardo Maldonado by Andrés de Luna and Susana Chaurand, *Otro cine*, no. 6 (April–June 1976); unpublished translation by Julianne Burton.
9. Ibid.
10. Victor Casaus, "El género testimonio en el cine cubano," *Cine cubano*, no. 101 (1982), 116–25.
11. Pastor Vega, "El documental didáctico y la táctica," *Pensamiento crítico*, no. 42 (July 1970), 99–103.
12. Fraga, Pantín, García Espinosa, "El cine didáctico," *Cine cubano*, nos. 69–70, translated as "Toward a Definition of the Didactic Documentary," in *Latin American Film Makers and the Third Cinema*, ed. Zuzana Pick (Ottawa: Carleton University Film Studies Program, 1978), p. 200.
13. Ibid., p. 206.
14. Ibid.

SANTIAGO ALVAREZ WITH THE EDITORS OF *CINEASTE*

"5 FRAMES ARE 5 FRAMES, NOT 6, BUT 5"

An Interview with Santiago Alvarez (1975)

[. . .]

Q: *We'd like to begin with a little personal history about yourself—what you did before the Revolution, how you came to work in the cinema, and so on.*

A: Before the Revolution I was just a film buff, just a spectator like any other spectator from any other part of the world. I belonged to a cultural society Nuestro Tiempo [Our Times], which had a cine-club where we saw and theoretically discussed the film classics. Other comrades who today work at ICAIC—Alfredo Guevara, Julio Garcia Espinosa, Tomas Gutierrez Alea—also belonged to that cine-club. We also screened some of the classic revolutionary films from the Soviet Union. There was a distributor of Soviet films for Cuba and Mexico and we used to rent them and show them in a small movie house on Sunday mornings. We would get together to show the films and discuss them but it was also a pretext to recruit leftist people and talk about social problems.

Before that, in 1939, I lived in the United States, working as a dishwasher and working in the coal mines in Pennsylvania. It was here in the United States that I started to become politically conscious and when I went back to Cuba I became a communist. American imperialism is the greatest promoter of communism in the world. In fact, it was my experiences here that form the roots of NOW, my film against racial discrimination in the U.S. That film grew directly out of my experiences here. It all came back to me one day when I was listening to a song called "Now" sung by Lena Horne—it's a melody based on an old Hebrew song by an anonymous author. When I started to work on the film at ICAIC, that background, that experience, helped me—I used all the hate I had felt against discrimination and brutality.

I really started learning about the cinema in 1959. After the revolution when the film institute was created—it was the first law about cultural matters that Fidel signed—I started making a newsreel of the first trip that President Dorticos made throughout Latin America. That was the first issue of ICAIC's "Noticiero Latinoamericano." The day that the Moviola arrived at ICAIC so we could do the work it was a cause for celebration. It was a Moviola with only a viewing screen and no sound head, but I still have it and work with it. Every piece of equipment then, like the little pins where you hang the takes in the editing room, was something new for us. We had all talked about the cinema but we didn't know how to make it. Behind all our ignorance about equipment, though, there was a tremendous desire to move ahead, to fight the reactionary capitalist newsreels that were still being made and disseminating counter-revolutionary propaganda during that period in Cuba.

In 1959–60 there were still three newsreels in Cuba—El Nacional, El Noticiero America, and one more, I can't remember the name—which were transmitting news in a subversive, counter-revolutionary way about what was happening in Cuba. This was when Manuel Urrutia was President of Cuba. At that time, the Revolution hadn't stabilized its power yet, there were still conflicts going on, there was much mass agitation, the people were restless, and the right was putting the Revolution in peril. It was then that we decided at ICAIC that we had to create a revolutionary newsreel that would promote the revolutionary policies and counteract the influence of the reactionary newsreels.

Q: *As time went on, was there any noticeable evolution in the style of the newsreels? It seems to me that there are a lot of similarities between your films and those of the Soviet film-maker, Dziga Vertov.*

A: Actually, the first newsreels that we made were influenced by traditional newsreels. They were not revolutionary in a formal sense but the content was revolutionary. After we had completed about 20 of them, we started to look for new, expressive cinematic forms for the newsreel.

As for Dziga Vertov, that is a question I'm asked in every interview but I must say that there is absolutely no influence of Vertov in my films. In fact, when I first started making films I hadn't seen any films by Vertov. It is true that the reality Vertov experienced is similar to the one we have experienced and it is this reality, perhaps, which is the common denominator of our films.

In this regard, I think it is important to point out the importance of the Revolution as a powerful motivating force for us—the revolutionary process in Cuba has been the main inspirational muse of all our work. Before the Revolution there was no cinematic expression in Cuba. Every four or five years a North American producer would come to the country and make a psuedo-folkloric or musical film, utilizing exotic elements of our culture in a superficial manner. Sometimes they would use a few Cuban technicians, maybe borrowed from the TV studios, but only a few. So in order for us to begin making films there had to be a revolutionary will, a revolutionary inspiration.

In other words, I became a film-maker, and other comrades in Cuba became professionally involved in things they never thought they would do, because the revolutionary will and the social needs *forced* us to become what we did. The people in the Sierra Maestra or on the Granma expedition had never been professional soldiers, had never studied in a military academy like West Point, and yet they won against an institutional army with North American advisors schooled in military theory. The guerilla isn't a professional soldier but someone compelled by a desire to smash an unjust structure, motivated by a revolutionary will which enables him to take up a gun and learn how to use it. No one is born a revolutionary, it is the needs of society which makes revolutionaries. Likewise, I didn't go to any school to learn cinema, I became a film-maker by making films. Before I had only fooled around with a 16mm camera like any amateur but I was possessed of this revolutionary will. I think anyone can make films—the only problem is to have the motivation, like any other activity.

I don't think one is born a creator, one becomes a creator. The creative element can be found in every human being and in any profession—engineer, pilot, lawyer, truck driver, whatever. In any human being there is this creative element and it is circumstances, the world one lives in, that stimulates or frustrates this element. How many young people before the Revolution in Cuba were frustrated because the society they lived in didn't give them the means or the chance to become what they wanted? And how many frustrated minds there must be here, how many creative minds that are working in radio and TV and who are not able to produce what they want? How many frustrations there must be accumulated!

[. . .]

Q: *When making a film, what are your relations to other members of the crew?*

A: In the newsreel department we have a group of cameramen and I have worked with all of them but there are a few I have worked with many times and, when circumstances permit, I prefer to work with one of the cameramen I know and get along best with. I think teamwork, collective work, is very important. Many times I have worked with two to five cameramen at one time.

The part of making a film I like best is the editing. My work in the editing room is completely different from that of the other comrades at ICAIC. Many times editors don't want to work with me because they're used to having an easy time with directors who just supervise and let them do the work. But I do all the work myself—I myself break up the material, I don't let the assistant editor do it, I myself hang up the takes in order to see what each sequence is all about. I look at it and look at it and look at it. And I am meticulous, I even choose the exact frame where I want to cut—five frames are five, frames, not six, but five. Then, while I am looking at the footage and doing the editing, I start thinking about editing the sound. When I transfer to mag-track, I'm still doing the editing of the sequences because I'm searching for the music at the same time that I'm doing the montage. When I'm listening to the sound I'm thinking about the structure of the sequence and when I'm editing the image I'm always thinking of what sound will go with it. As I'm putting it together and it begins to take on a certain rhythm, I think about what effects, what sound, what music, will go with that image. 50% of the value of a film is in the soundtrack.

Q: *A controversial topic in political film circles these days is whether or not new, revolutionary forms are needed to express revolutionary content. That is, some people say it is absolutely impossible to make a revolutionary or radical film that employs traditional narrative techniques. What has been the experience of Cuban film-makers in this regard?*

A: A good example is a recent film, *El Hombre de Maisinicu*, which has been a big success. It is a film which tells the story of people from the Ministry of the Interior who infiltrate behind the lines of the counter-revolutionaries and it is a film which has, let us say, a conventional structure. But the success of this film tells us that we don't always have to use *new* forms to express revolutionary values, we can use traditional techniques to do it. Traditional cultural elements have a value at a certain point; we don't have to catalog or label and say that the conventional can never be used. Innovation results from making traditional forms valuable, by revitalizing them. Methods of construction in our country, for example, employ both traditional methods and new methods and by mixing the two we obtain revolutionary results. Likewise, the Beatles have innovated and revolutionized music by using traditional elements, they have been great innovators of the traditional.

Q: *How successful have Cuban film-makers been in improving public taste? Do Cuban audiences still prefer "entertainment" films to "political" films?*

A: We *are* the public, film-makers *are* the public. We start from the basis that we belong to the social reality of our country, we are not foreigners, we are part of the people and our films grow out of a shared reality. If we thought we were a privileged group above the people, then we would probably make films that communicated only with a minority or an elite group. But we are not a group of poets producing abstract or bizarre poetry. One can only be a revolutionary artist by being with the people and by communicating with them.

It has been a challenge for us but we have been successful to some extent in breaking public movie-going habits. Due to the influence of capitalism, even in socialist countries, it has always been the custom to show documentaries only as supplementary material with a feature-length fiction film with actors as the main attraction. But we have been able to show documentaries as the main attraction in theatres. For example, *De America Soy Hijo* which lasts 3 hours and 15 minutes and which features as its main character Fidel on a trip, was released simultaneously in 7 theatres and there were still long lines of people and they had full houses for two months. Another documentary *Y el Cielo Fue Tomado por Asalto*, which lasts 2 hours and 8 minutes, was similarly successful.

[. . .]

Q: *How many directors are there at ICAIC?*

A: Unfortunately, we don't have many film directors in Cuba. We are limited by our lack of resources—we don't have many cameras or much sound equipment or big labs. Everything that's related to film in Cuba, from grease pencils to raw stock, is imported. So we have to set priorities in our film production. Our goals for 1974, for instance, consisted of 8 feature films, 41 documentaries, 52 newsreels and 10 animation films. By comparison, Japan produces 500 films per year. We do everything, the shooting, the sound, everything except the lab work. By May or June of 1975, however, we'll have our own color lab installed in Cuba and it will be one of the best labs in Latin America.

[. . .]

Q: *Are there many women film-makers in Cuba?*

A: We don't have many women film-makers but there are some who work as film editors and in the labs. It's not that we've planned it this way, it's just that women film-makers haven't appeared. There are four or five young women students now at ICAIC and maybe they'll become directors.

Q: *In conclusion, any thoughts about the future?*

A: I think that in 20 years the cinema is going to disappear, there will be another technology to replace it. There will be new developments in electronic techniques which will completely change the traditional method of making films, not only in Cuba but everywhere. Technology is going to absolutely change everything and the means of communication—for the painter, the musician, the film-maker—will change radically.

I think the individualistic conception of art will change completely and we will no longer continue the practice of the museum or private exhibition of art works as we do now. The creators, the artists in society, will put their energies into making not just one painting but into creating mass art works, into beautifying shoes, homes, factories, everything, the total environment. It will be an anti-individualistic conception of artistic creation where everything will be for the benefit of all humanity.

77

ABÉ MARK NORNES

THE POSTWAR DOCUMENTARY TRACE

Groping in the Dark (2002*)

The 1998 Yamagata International Documentary Film Festival featured a major retrospective of Japanese documentary films from the 1980s and 1990s. This was the last installment in a biennial series that painstakingly covered the one-hundred-year history of nonfiction filmmaking in Japan. Previous retrospectives confidently displayed a national heritage and its sure but steady growth, but the title of the 1998 edition suggested a less than optimistic attitude: "The Groping in the Dark: Japanese Documentary in the 1980s and Beyond" ["Nihon Dokyumentar no Mosaku: 1980 Nendai Ikō"]. Nowhere was the cautious uncertainty more evident than in the accompanying symposium. On the stage were four filmmakers representing various generations in Japanese film history. In the middle sat Kanai Katsu (who started filming in the 1960s) and Ise Shin'ichi (from the 1980s). On either end were Iizuka Toshio (1960) and Kawase Naomi (1990s). Iizuka served as assistant director to the late Ogawa Shinsuke from the 1960s until Ogawa's death in 1992 and has since become a director in his own right. Kawase had recently returned from the Cannes International Film Festival, where her first feature (shot, incidentally, by Ogawa's cameraman Tamura Masaki) surprised everyone by taking a special jury prize. The media—of which a sizable contingent sat at Kawase's feet in Yamagata—was calling the Cannes coup for *Suzaku* [*Moe no suzaku*] an indication that a new generation of filmmakers had attained international recognition and that Japanese cinema had entered a new era. This claim has far more to do with Japan's anxiety about its place in global cultural production than with any sense of film history. However, as I hope to demonstrate, it is right on the mark, at least from a certain perspective.

The seating arrangement at Yamagata was a piece of history writing in and of itself. It did not take long before the generational structure bared itself onstage.

*Revised 2015.

Any "groping" that evening would be between those on either end of the platform. Iizuka and Kawase would have it out over the question posed by moderator Yamane Sadao, one of Japan's finest critics. Taking a cue from Fukuda Katsuhiko (an ex–Ogawa Productions member who stayed in Sanrizuka after the collective left), Yamane suggested that in the mid-1970s something happened that transformed Japanese documentary, leaving it in its present, seemingly precarious state. As in any serious discussion of documentary in Japan, the words *shutai* (subject) and *taishō* (object) constantly came up. They are rarely, if ever, defined, yet they are repeated like the mantra of postwar documentary; functionally they generally demarcate historical articulations of difference to construct a periodization for postwar documentary. The artists onstage quickly staked out the territory. Iizuka laid out the generally accepted view that the filmmakers of the 1960s and early 1970s had a political commitment and took their engagement with the world seriously. They assumed a subject (*shutai*) that was thoroughly social, one that required visible expression on film and at the same time acknowledged its delicate relationship to the object (*taishō*) of the filming. Younger filmmakers, argued Iizuka (in an obvious critical swipe at Kawase), are too wrapped up in their own little world. They focus on either themselves or their family without reference to society, without engaging any political position or social stance. Kawase responded defensively, though perhaps not convincingly, that her own documentaries about her aunt and the search for her lost father had the kind of social resonance Iizuka claimed for his own work. In the end the two offered only implicit criticism of each other. For all the groping, which included contributions from the floor by Tsuchimoto Noriaki (the Minamata Series) and Fukuda, almost everyone felt they had been left in the dark, especially on the question, "What happened to the exhilaration and passionate engagement of the Japanese documentary world of the 1960s?"

This essay provisionally accepts Fukuda and Yamane's periodization. Following the filmmaking of the 1960s and early 1970s, which was spectacular in both quality and quantity, something *did* happen, and the Japanese documentary went into a steady decline. At the very least, all historians accept that the sheer number of stirring, creative documentaries in that earlier period was unprecedented, that the present situation pales in comparison, and that the popular support that made these documentaries possible in the first place has evaporated. And how ironic that of all the art forms to experience decay in the 1980s bubble economy—in the age of *jōhōshihonshugi* (information capitalism)—documentary would lose its confidence and end up groping in the critical darkness for a toehold in Yamagata at the close of the 1990s. Few films today are as compelling or as daring as the prodigious work straddling the year 1970. Today's films and videos in Japan represent a turn to the self, a movement that appears strikingly similar to developments in Euro-American film and video making. However, the latter is rigorously political and theoretically informed, while its Japanese counterpart documents the self from a vaguely apolitical place. That is to say, the intertwining histories of documentary and its conceptualization largely took their own course in Japan. They developed with relative autonomy vis-à-vis Euro-American nonfiction film. Japanese writers and directors were aware of vérité, direct cinema, third cinema, and developments in the Western avant-garde but remained resistant to slavish imitation. As will soon become clear, this independence has been a correlate of the vigor of ongoing debates in the field, the innovation of the filmmakers, and the perception that the local social and political stakes were high. Tracking the transformations in debates over *shutaisei* (subjectivity), this essay will grope for the "something" that did happen, the thing that seems to divide the filmmaking group shooting other groups and the camera-toting individual documenting the self, the public and the private, the *shutai* and its *taishō*—the 1960s and the present day.

The Fifties: Problematizing Realism

As a form of filmmaking, documentary has been attractive to persons at both ends of the political spectrum since the 1920s. This, one can argue, is due to several qualities specific to the medium. First, by the early years of the Shōwa era the infrastructure for the movies had developed sufficiently enough to allow quick distribution of images to masses of people scattered across vast distances. This gave cinema an easy national, even international (colonial) reach. A further reason lies in the indexical quality of cinematic representation. The on-screen image is an index in the Piercian sense, like a fingerprint or a thermometer. It possesses a striking spatial and temporal immediacy to its indexed object, a quality that documentary filmmaking uses to set itself far apart from the fictive film. Exploiting this seemingly privileged link to reality, filmmakers with a sense of social commitment developed an arsenal of rhetorical devices to move those newly formed masses of moviegoers. These special qualities were initially evident to filmmakers involved in primary education and the proletarian culture movement in the late 1920s and early 1930s. However, these two tendencies—pedagogy and sociopolitical enlightenment—converged as Japan went to war; at the same time differences between left and right became increasingly ambiguous. However, with the end of the conflict, independence for filmmakers meant new possibilities for deploying cinema as an oppositional force in society. Leftist activists, particularly those aligned with the Japan Communist Party, gravitated toward the documentary form, which became a powerful force within the organizations devoted to documentary and the educational film. Like their predecessors in the prewar and wartime eras, these leftist filmmakers were strongly attracted to the possibility of a medium based on an indexical representation of the public arena; through this newly democratized apparatus they intended to construct an alternative space of the nation, one capable of *moving* people in every sense.

The critical push came from a rebellious, certainly audacious young filmmaker named Matsumoto Toshio, whose contributions to the critical discourse were as influential as his filmmaking. He started publishing missives and manifestos, contributing to a critical turbulence that would shake the foundations of the film world in the next decade. Matsumoto and others critiqued the approaches of old and renovated documentary practice by turning the term *shutai* against the grain. We must approach the translation of *shutai* with considerable caution. Its meaning varies depending on the context of the utterance or inscription. Every field treats it differently, making any easy correspondence to the English word *subject*, a tricky word itself, impossible. The term *shutai* appeared in film theory of the prewar period in essays by philosophers such as Nakai Masakazu and in debates over the scientific or artistic merits of nonfiction film. However, it was during the Occupation that it entered film discourse in an engaged way and apparently then toed the Japan Communist Party (JCP) line. Film critics borrowed the terms of the debate over war responsibility raging within the left and transposed them to the film world.[1] However, in the December 1957 issue of *Kaihō*, the newsletter of the Kyōiku Eiga Sakka Kyōkai (Association of Education Filmmakers), the primary organization of nonfiction filmmakers that was decidedly leftist, Matsumoto published "On the Subject of the Filmmaker" ["Sakka no Shutai to Iu Koto"]. It was the first essay in a decade-long series of political and aesthetic critiques by Matsumoto. It also stood as a declaration of generational difference. Matsumoto began this initial dispatch with the following words:

> During the war, [documentary filmmakers] uncritically produced films collaborating with the war, changing course because of absolutely external power and transitively switching directions without any serious internal criticism. In that period of political promotion they quickly and hysterically, in the manner of a fast-spreading disease among children, engaged in a biased practice that subordinated art to politics. Lacking principles, they subsequently adapted to the PR film industry in a period of retreat. Here, consistent from start to finish, there are only slavish craftsmen lacking subjectivity. One might say that, from the beginning, there were no artists here.[2]

The furor that followed the publication of "On the Subject of the Filmmaker" contributed to the shake-up of the organization. The members changed their name from Kyōiku Eiga Sakka Kyōkai to Kiroku Eiga Sakka Kyōkai (Association of Documentary Filmmakers), indicating a broadening of practice, and established *Kiroku Eiga* [Documentary film] as their monthly journal. This would become their "movement magazine," the site where the conceptualization of the future of documentary would be worked out. Matsumoto's criticism was the lightning rod for a backlash led by the organization's leader, Yoshimi Tai. In a series of articles published in the first three issues of *Kiroku Eiga* he defended the work of filmmakers whose careers straddled 1945.

> On the one hand, we use film production as a weapon of citizens' movements—in other words, we widely disseminated the idea of making film belonging to the people, and the results from this experience have been epochal. It is also extremely meaningful that we have uncovered this route for making works featuring independent planning and independent expression. Moreover, for artists in particular, the experience gained from this period has been precious. The majority of artists, through the pursuit of both realism and a creative method, were certainly able to accumulate practice.[3]

However, it was precisely this continuing commitment to realism that bothered Matsumoto, partly because of its continuity with wartime approaches to documentary but also because of the suppression of the artists' subjectivity that it implied. A cinematic style that presents itself as a privileged referential representation of the lived world ultimately rests on a set of conventions. These conventional constructions hide the work demanded by realist styles, and this amounts to a suppression of the subjective procedures at the heart of filmmaking. For Matsumoto this was both irresponsible and dangerous because it inevitably involves a veiling of politics as well. The realist agenda of nonfiction filmmaking "for the people" hid an authoritarianism Matsumoto associated with a Stalinism at the heart of the JCP. He vigorously attacked these older leftist filmmakers in a series of articles, the most famous of which was an essay on Alain Resnais's *Guernica*. This was a short documentary on the Picasso painting, and in this—both the film and the painting—Matsumoto found traces of what he believed to be missing in Japanese films:

> Internal consciousness is the decisive disengagement of the subject and the external world of today, the idolatry of the relationship between the two. It is the consciousness established upon recognition of the collapse of the classical human image. Naturalists should bear in mind that capitalist alienation exists, more than anywhere, in the process of materializing one's internal self and dismantling the subject. When they rely easily on the outer world without an awareness of their own internal world, then they cannot but grasp matter itself through attributes and atmosphere. They end up drying up their imaginative power and developing a pattern of helpless emotion. The documentarists who capture the *taishō* with an unemotional eye cannot gain a total grasp of reality without using an inner document as a medium. Sharply confronted with avant-garde art, to which at first giance they have no connection, they fail to aim for a higher realism as an opportunity to negate the self. This is because of the artists' own lack of subject-consciousness.[4]

Attacking the highly lauded realism of 1950s "Golden Age" cinema by advancing a theoretical critique grounded in subject relations, this declaration is a kind of statement of principles for the emerging battle between Old and New Left filmmakers. When Matsumoto's writings were collected in *Eizō no Hakken*, they quickly became a bible for the new cohort of artists. Matsumoto supported his written critiques with some fascinating filmmaking. In works such as *Poem of Stones* [*Ishi no uta*] (1959) and *Security Treaty* [*Anpo jōyaku*] (1960) he blurred any easy distinction between documentary and the avant-garde, bringing the realism of nonfiction film together with moments of shocking surrealism. For example, *Security Treaty* is a collage film combining found footage, documentary imagery, photographs, and drawings related to the 1960 security treaty between Japan and the United States. Rather than simply presenting the images in a matter-of-fact fashion (as you would see in a television documentary, for example), Matsumoto mutilated still photographs of Japan's leaders and literally spit on the projected, moving image of a U.S. soldier and a prostitute. This was aggressiveiy experimental filmmaking that politicized film style itseif. It caused an uproar.

By early 1959 the power on the editorial board of *Kiroku Eiga* had shifted to Matsumoto and his supporters, most notably Noda Shinkichi. They began publishing work by strong writers outside the organization, creating alliances with intellectuals in other fields who opposed the Stalinist mainstream of the left. These contributors included Satō Tadao, Hanada Kiyoteru, Uriu Tadao, and others. This was a turning point for documentary in Japan. The field was experiencing a growth as explosive as that of the late 1930s. In 1959 documentary short production was about to surpass 900 films a year, marking a growth of nearly 500 percent over the course of the decade.[5] Made-for-television education productions constituted another 900 films a year, up from none at the beginning of the 1950s.[6] Within this healthy industry Matsumoto's pressure to innovate, through both critical attacks and artistic examples, met massive institutional weight and its inertia from those working within established organizations. The ultimate solution for reformers was independence—whatever that might come to mean in 1960.

The So-Called Sixties

This decade, so extraordinary in so many societies across the globe, represents ten years marked by public passion, the spectacle of governments struggling to contain their people's energies, and the shifts in consciousness that lead to new approaches to artistic expression. In Japan historians have the convenient bookends of the U.S. security treaty renewals, but for our purposes we must place "the sixties" in scare quotes. The (early) 1970s are also "the sixties"—after all, that was when *something happened.* The second Anpo was not an ending.

Documentary film is one of the most fascinating artistic fields because of the claims it makes to represent our world. Its easy alliance with centers of power and its national, even global reach make it a crucial ground for contestation in times of pressure. Within this complex of forces bearing down on the cinema was precisely where Matsumoto and company positioned themselves in the late 1950s. By their reasoning, the realism espoused by the older generation of filmmakers was a sham. It was deeply implicated in the propaganda of the government and the public relations of industry; it was a specious realism aligned with oppressive forms of power. The editorial board of *Kiroku Eiga* announced a new direction for their efforts in 1960, a reconfiguration premised on three intertwining agendas: (1) the logical interrogation (*ronrika*) of the relation of the setting and the filmmaker's subjectivity, (2) the logical interrogation of representation and the filmmaker's subjectivity, and finally (3) the logical interrogation of the deep correspondence between subject/setting and subject/representation. Upon these three pillars they would attempt to revolutionize nonfiction film. At the seventh general assembly in December 1960 they changed their name to Kiroku Eiga Sakka Kyōkai, sloughing off the word *education* and emphasizing their identity as documentarists. In 1961 their journal cover was printed in color, and they began thinking about selling *Kiroku Eiga* on newsstands, thanks to thoughtful writing by authors such as film critic Satō Tadao and philosopher Hanada Kiyoteru, as well as contributions from high-profile filmmakers such as Teshigawara Hiroshi, Ōshima Nagisa, Atsugi Taka, Kuroki Kazuo, and Yoshida Yoshishige.

The critical buttressing of their filmmaking remained the debate over subjectivity. This term initially entered film discourse during the Occupation. Marxism in general engaged in a lengthy and complicated debate over its meaning in the context of war responsibility. Matsumoto, Noda, and others attempted to turn the vocabulary in a new direction, apparently ignoring previous debates in their assertion of new definitions. This is one of the most striking aspects of this discourse: its fragmentary quality and lack of development. Writers freely changed the character of subjectivity, switching contexts with little regard to previous incarnations, within or outside Japan.

Directors Masumura Yasuzō and Ōshima Nagisa, for example, were discussing *shutaisei* in articles about feature film. However, this seems strikingly disconnected from what was going on in documentary circles. One of the few links between mainstream fiction filmmaking and nonfiction discourses is Ōshima's "What Is a Shot?" ["Shotto to wa nanika?"] in the November 1960 issue of *Kiroku Eiga*. Ōshima argues for a recognition of authorial subjectivity built into the temporal limits of the shot.[7] Most other writers emphasized montage when thinking about authorial intervention in filmmaking (in fact, *Kiroku Eiga* had published a special issue on editing just months earlier). Matsumoto worked in similar territory, but his activities signaled the direction the documentary discourse would take in the 1960s. In what is probably the most intriguing of his articles, he drew on psychoanalysis and Freud's essay on the uncanny (*unheimlich*). "Record of the Hidden World" ["Kakusareta sekai no kiroku"] was published in the June 1960 issue of *Kiroku Eiga*. Here Matsumoto attempted to turn the debate surrounding documentary toward the very existence of the *mono* (thing) recorded by the filmmaker:

> The existence of the *taishō* is, finally, nothing other than a *heimlich* (intimate) thing. There, the estranged facts of reality are suppressed by the stereotypes of everyday consciousness and become *heimlich* (concealed) things. Rather, precisely because of that, the existence of the *taishō*—what could be thought of as everyday consciousness or as the law of causality—is powerfully negated by the non-everyday, hidden reality that our consciousness still cannot grasp. It is overturned by the world reproduced [*utsusu in hiragana,* thus it could mean *remove* or *film* and/or *project*] as something nonexistent in our everyday consciousness. When this happens, our consciousness, touched for the first time by that kind of reality we have never experienced directly, dismantles its balance with the outside world. We take it as strange, or as an *unheimlich* (unearthly) thing.[8]

It was with the untapped energy of the hidden world that we must resist the very structures that hide, that oppress through veiling apparatuses like cinematic realism. Thus while feature filmmakers like Ōshima and Masumura were concerned with the subjective expression of the artist in fiction forms, as a documentarist Matsumoto naturally wanted to account for the existential force of the real people he was dealing with. While Matsumoto never developed these ideas further in print and no one else picked up where he left off, his 1960 essay held the promise of inserting psychoanalysis into the debate. It is both surprising and unfortunate that this was another route abandoned.

While the specifics of Matsumoto's essay went undeveloped, we can see how it expressed the transformation that the nonfiction film was undertaking. It signaled a new emphasis on the *taishō* in the debate on *shutaisei*. This part of the equation was largely missing from previous theorization. Its significance lies in the conceptualization of the documentary image as a *document of a relationship* between the filmmaker and the object; this latter term is usually referred to as the "subject of the film" in English-language film criticism. This would have wide-ranging effects on documentary practice in the following decades. At the same time, Matsumoto's impulse to draw on psychoanalysis would also prove important, if only because the move went nowhere. It meant a discourse on subjectivity that did not take into account the most important and richest body of thought exploring the contours of the human mind. The implications of this omission were multiple and varied. The fact that various writers and artists did not share a common language and conceptual framework meant the *shutaiseiron* would inevitably splinter into many directions at once. From the distance afforded by time we can look back and see a seemingly endless variety of positions, with people deploying words like *shutai* and *taishō* to significantly different ends. Without the substantial buttressing from an external body of theory, there was no need or pressure to engage in pointed arguments to advance a common line of thought. This dearth of structure enabled a popular conception of *shutaiseiron* to circulate in the documentary world—a malleable version that ironically may have been more productive than a "high theory" comprehensible primarily to specialists. Most importantly, we might speculate that the fact that psychoanalysis was so swiftly raised and dropped from the equation would contribute to the *something* that happened in the 1970s. But we would be getting ahead of ourselves.

As with so many endeavors grouped around the pivot of the 1960 Anpo, *Kiroku Eiga* began losing energy in the first few years of the decade. The organization was dismantled in March 1964 but quickly reformed in June as Eizō Geijutsu (Image Arts), a group of some eighty members that suffered some of the same structural problems as the previous organization. An atomization of individual interests interfered with any attempt at sustained debate. The focus widened with the introduction of the Euro-American avant-garde by individuals such as Iimura Takahiko, who wrote about what was happening on the New York film scene. In one sense the dissipation of the group had to do with the success of the members. Their issues became normalized, so they no longer felt a need for organization.

Indeed, the production side was getting interesting, thanks in large part to the legacy of Iwanami Productions. In the 1950s the film department quickly became a hotbed of creative filmmaking in the wake of Hani's innovations. Building room to maneuver within the structure of what was essentially a public relations firm, Iwanami allowed its filmmakers the (relative) freedom to stretch the limits of the public relations (PR) film. Within this atmosphere a group coalesced in 1961 to explore these conventional boundaries of the sponsored documentary. Its membership reads like a roster of the best directors and cinematographers in Japan: Ogawa Shinsuke, Tsuchimoto Noriaki, Kuroki Kazuo, Higashi Yōichi, Tamura Masaki, Suzuki Tatsuo, and others. Calling themselves the Blue Group (Ao no Kai), they regularly performed experiments, read and discussed criticism and theory, and previewed cuts of their film projects for feedback. They would gather at a bar, drink, eat, and hold intense discussions through the night. Their efforts brought the PR film to unusually spectacular levels, deploying interesting montage, narration, and even 35mm cinemascope color photography. Nevertheless their subject matter was restricted to steel factories and construction sites—a limit on their ambitions that would soon intersect with other pressures.

Working within an industrial context forced the filmmakers to aestheticize the human-made, industrial spaces created by the high-growth economy. But riding the coattails of the spectacular rise of economic power proved problematic for this group of filmmakers because of their sympathies with those social elements bringing capital and government under critique. While Iwanami filmmakers made industrial-strength commercials for some of the most corrupt, polluting corporations in Japan, social movements of every sort were taking to the streets. Chafing under the weight of these contradictions, the members of the Blue Group abandoned Iwanami for a politicized, independent documentary.

Kuroki left in 1961; Tsuchimoto, Higashi, and Ogawa went independent in 1964. They helped pioneer a new independent cinema aligned with the New Left, joining others such as Noda, Matsumoto, and Ōshima Nagisa. Compared with where they had learned their craft, the former Blue Group members located their independent practice in the most contrary space imaginable: the student movement. Higashi made films in U.S.-occupied Okinawa. Ogawa shot *Sea of Youth* [*Seishun no umi*] (1966), a documentary about the dilemma of correspondence students and their contentious relationship with the school administration—at the same school where he had made a PR film for Iwanami some years before. He followed this with *Forest of Pressure* [*Assatsu no mori*] (1967), which described the noisy protests at Takaseki University from behind the barricades. That same year Ogawa directed a documentary about the massive protests that attempted to interrupt Prime Minister Sato's departure for the United States: *Report from Haneda* [*Gennin hōkpku: Haneda tōsō no kiroku*] (1967). Ogawa also produced Tsuchimoto's radical film *Prehistory of the Partisan Party* [*Paruchizan zenshi*] (1969), which detailed the inner workings of the ultraradical student group that had taken over a building at Kyoto University. All of these films rejected the rhetoric of objective reportage used by the television news documentary to veil its alliance with the government and big business. Ogawa and Tsuchimoto's films documented the thrill of independence, of crossing barricade lines and taking sides. This bold move attracted the burgeoning student movement, making the filmmakers cultural heroes on the left. At this stage the radical students formed both their subject matter and their audiences, which made their next move appear quite ambitious. In 1965 Tsuchimoto went to Kyushu and started a series of films on mercury poisoning in the villages ringing Minamata Bay; Ogawa moved his operation to a village outside Tokyo where the government was attempting to evict farmers for a new international airport. The films made in these new sites—Tsuchimoto's Minamata Series and Ogawa's Sanrizuka Series—remain monuments of postwar Japanese cinema.

Their filmmaking was swept up in larger political movements, electrifying audiences and inspiring considerable debate on the role of cinema in society. The films were produced through a combination of rental fees, donations, and loans from labor unions and individuals. Once completed, they were shown across Japan in both urban and rural areas, in labor union meetings, citizen movements, independent theaters, universities, and even a surprising number of high schools. The filmmakers themselves would often travel across the countryside, film under arm, and arrange screenings anywhere they could. For obvious reasons the films were never shown in regular movie theaters or on broadcast television.

Of the two, the Sanrizuka Series is the more innovative and theoretically interesting, despite the fact that Tsuchimoto was and remains the intellectual leader of Japanese documentary. However, Ogawa's films, as well as the way he produced and exhibited them, are more relevant to our concerns. His constant innovation points to new modes of nonfiction filmmaking, and this involved nothing less than carving out local, public spaces that resonated with the struggles and latent contradictions of other localities, or of the nation itself. For example, villagers in *any* part of Japan easily could identify with films about the farmers' face-off with the central government. Later Ogawa would attempt to create a nationwide network of offices that would exhibit independent documentaries while producing and sharing their own films on local problems. While these are later developments, key features of Ogawa's creative manipulation of the nonfiction image are evident early.

After the release of *Report from Haneda* in 1968, Ogawa's group took the name Ogawa Productions and could finally be described as a collective. The crew had started to live together part time and work together, and they slowly began extending their collaboration to the people being filmed as well. In 1968 they moved to the construction site of the airport, taking over a house in Sanrizuka and turning it into their home base. In all they produced seven films over nine years, a total of twelve and a half hours of film that views the power of the state through farmers' eyes. The filmmakers lived with the farmers and made films while fighting for their cause. They were not alone. Perceived as one more abusive government project, this time with connections to the war in Vietnam, the airport plan attracted the attention of the student movement and other political groups committed to environmental and social causes. The construction site became a war zone with the addition of these groups, and this figured into how Ogawa Pro approached their subject matter. The camera crews modified their equipment to withstand abuse, and they themselves wore helmets and protective gear. Judging from the hand-to-hand combat shown in the films, they needed such precautions. At one point cameraman Ōtsu Kōshirō and Matsumoto Takeaki were even arrested, an incident caught on film in *Summer in Sanrizuka* [*Nihon kaihō sensen: Sanrizuka no natsu*] (1968).

Ogawa Pro's first films reflected the willingness of the filmmakers to sacrifice body and freedom. The fights over fallow fields were massive and violent. The police outnumbered the farmers and put up an intimidating front in their riot gear and helicopters. The collective shot the first film from April to July 1968 as survey teams investigated the lands protected by riot police. In this initial stage the farmers watched the soil of their livelihood mapped out as a prelude to being obliterated. For the first time they found themselves confronting raw state power—a police force fully armed—while the farmers themselves had little more than rocks and sticks. By this time the students had arrived in Sanrizuka with various factions of the student movement who perceived the battleground of rice paddies and fallow fields as a new, pure, political landscape on which to confront the state. *Summer in Sanrizuka* is rough in both photography and editing and focuses on the confrontations between airport employees, their police escorts, and protesters. Ogawa called it an "action film" along the lines of a John Ford western, with the epic proportions of a violent confrontation between representatives of national power and local residents fighting for their ancestral lands—but with the documentary difference.

In July and October 1970 Ogawa Pro released two more films from Sanrizuka. *Winter in Sanrizuka* [*Nihon kaihō sensen: Sanrizuka*] and *The Three-Day War in Narita* [*Sanrizuka: Daisanji kyōsei sokuryō soshi tōsō*] have significant similarities to and differences from the collective's earlier films. Both films have the spectacle of peasants battling the repressive apparatuses of the state, as seen in the first film of the series. However, these scenes of violence begin to alternate with sequences in which the farmers reflect upon their situation. *Winter in Sanrizuka* opens with the image of farmers stubbornly sitting in front of a massive bulldozer. Shot over a six-month period after the airport authorities began breaking ground, it shows the growing fear of the farmers as their fields come under attack. During the skirmishes many farmers are arrested. At the same time the filmmakers also stop to listen to and record the farmers' own thoughts about what they were experiencing. Put simply, the relationship between filmmaker and *taishō* was undergoing a subtle but deep transformation. *The Three-Day War in Narita* uses a similar structure, the difference being that it was a creditless, agit-prop cinetract shot over the course of three days. As the forced survey pushed into its final phase, the farmers and students undertook a massive attempt to obstruct its progress. This film records those days of combat between twenty-five hundred protesters and sixty-five hundred riot police. School had even been let out so that children could participate. Nevertheless, as cameraman Tamura Masaki often recalls, Ogawa began sending the crews out with instructions to shoot butterflies in long, thirty-second takes in the midst of a massive social struggle. Such unusual instructions indicate the new path Ogawa Pro was embarking on.

Their next effort, *Sanrizuka: Peasants of the Second Fortress* [*Sanrizuka: Dai ni toride no hitobito*] (1971), marks a turning point hinted at in the previous year's films—one significant for both Ogawa Pro and Japanese documentary film. The determination displayed by both sides was escalating the struggle into civil-war-like proportions. The farmers and their entire families built fortresses that they defended with bamboo spears. Students pitched Molotov cocktails from behind the walls. Out in the fields various groups—from the student-led Zengakuren to housewives' associations—lined up and battled police. The violence the filmmakers captured was shocking. Of course by now the fights were regularly captured by television news crews, but these filmmakers kept their distance and remained behind the police lines in every sense. Ogawa's crews, now led by former Blue Group cinematographer Tamura Masaki, traversed the barricades freely and literally dove into the clashes. The spectacle had grown to epic scale, a standoff between a reported twenty thousand protesters facing thirty thousand police. Some of the scenes are heart wrenching; women confront a long wall of riot police, grab their shields, and scream, "Can't you see you're killing us? What would your mothers think?!?" When police storm the fortresses, they beat people and rip away mothers and children who have chained themselves to their trees.

Amid this cinematic spectacle, familiar from previous films but now considerably larger and more violent, something very different is going on. In *Peasants of the Second Fortress* there are occasional moments when the action of the film grinds to a halt and people simply talk. While the students were once Ogawa's focus, they now haunt the background of the film. They appear only occasionally to clash with mobs of riot police. In their stead the farmers take center stage, and in the most awkward style. Their speech is halting, filled with pauses and repetition. Where the typical filmmaker would search out the most articulate conversations and speakers (usually male leaders) and give them voice, Ogawa photographed unexceptional discussions and strategy sessions in long takes. The breaks, silences, sidetracks, and repetitions were left untouched by editing. As the farmers' comprehension of their own situation deepened, so did Ogawa Pro's understanding of the farmers themselves. This is particularly evident in one scene shot under the earth. One of the strategies of the farmers was to burrow underground—under *their ground*—and build catacombs of basements under their fortresses. Groups would rotate duty, living in the tunnels to make eviction and construction impossible. When the Ogawa Pro cameras tour the tunnels, their guide stops at a small hole designed for ventilation. After briefly describing how it works, the farmer holds a candle up to the hole: "See, when I put the flame near the hole, the fresh air nearly blows it out." He repeats this action for several minutes. The point is clear the first time, after which the typical documentarist would cut to the next scene; but this ventilation hole is important to the farmers. It allows them to survive under the earth, and Ogawa refuses to interrupt the demonstration. This is paradigmatic of a new attitude toward documentary forming within Ogawa Pro. It becomes the predominant stance in the rest of their work.

Moreover, this approach became generalized throughout the discourse on documentary, in part because Ogawa Pro was closely watched by everyone interested in the relationship between film and politics. For example, in 1969 a group of filmmakers including Oshima, Wakamatsu, Matsumoto, and Adachi Masao helped bring back *Eiga Hihyō*, once an important forum for film theory in the era surrounding the previous Anpo. The writers of the new *Eiga Hihyō* attempted to theorize the contours of a "movement cinema" (*undō no eiga*). To this end they resurrected the *shutaiseiron*, although with apparently little regard for the actual genealogy of the term. (Indeed, they also had little sense of their own history, since the theorists of the Proletarian film movement [Prokino] laid the groundwork for a movement cinema in the early 1930s but are not mentioned.) For example, in a typical debate from 1970 the writers discuss the complex relationship between the "conscious subject," "image," and "conditions." The image came to be perceived as a record stamped by the assertive hand of the filmmaker—that conscious, active subject—in the midst of the volatile conditions of the world. This world hid enemies and was structured by powerful institutions handed down from the past. As the new *Eiga Hihyō* group saw it, the quality of that relationship had implications for a politicized aesthetics. In the next few years the writing on Ogawa Pro and Tsuchimoto developed such ideas, focusing on the nature of *shutai/taishō* relations. It must be said that while we can certainly find continuity with earlier discourses on nonfiction filmmaking, the new discussions about *shutaisei* have none of the rigor or intertwining engagement typical of other moments in film theory. They reintroduce a protean *shutaiseiron*, the very vagueness of which may have made it more aesthetically productive in actual practice. For example, we sense only distant echoes of Matsumoto's *Eizō no Hakken* when Ōshima Nagisa writes that Ogawa's method "returns to the original intention of documentary, realizing the principle of documentary. What are the principles and original intention of documentary? First it is a love toward the object documented, a strong admiration and attachment, and it is carrying this first principle over a long period of time. Nearly all the films considered masterpieces fulfill these two conditions."[9]

By the early 1970s it was hard not to describe the films of Ogawa and Tsuchimoto, indeed of most independent documentary filmmakers as well, in these rather vague terms. In 1973 these tendencies arrived at their natural conclusion with Ogawa's *Heta Village* [*Heta Buraku*]. Now the protests had faded into the film's background, and the world of the villagers became the exclusive focus. In incredibly long takes the peasants discuss their everyday life and the ancient history of the village. In terms of style *Heta Village* is the inverse of the rough, action-packed *Summer in Narita*. The airport struggle remains, but our access to it is mediated entirely by its traces on village life and the villagers' consciousness. Now the axis of the film is situated completely, deeply within the world of the villagers. The elders are disturbed when their communal graveyard falls into the hands of the airport authorities; the young people share their fear of arrest after three policemen are killed. All of this is shown in a series of calm, lengthy sequence shots. This approach starts from the position of the filmed "object" and ends there, too. It is described variously as "letting the *taishō* enter the *shutai*," "going with the *taishō*," "betting on" or "depending on the *taishō*," or becoming "wrapped up in the *taishō*." Suzuki Shiroyasu, who will soon figure prominently in this developing story, described this approach in the following manner:

> I think that "symbiosis" (*kyōseikan*), as a goal or aim for the documentary, first came into parlance with Tsuchimoto. . . . The filmmaker tries to take in and accept all the troubles, the conflicts, really the whole existence of the object being filmed. That's fundamentally different from the Western style of filmmaking. In the West, the object is never anything more than an element of the work, a particular work that is being made by a given filmmaker for him- or herself. I think you can also see the effects of the Japanese attempts at a "symbiotic relationship" in the way the objects of the film are treated, or in the way the director refers to them. For example, Tsuchimoto doesn't call those suffering from Minamata disease simply *kanja* (victim), but he adds the polite suffix *-san: Kanja-san* (victim-*san*). Ogawa refers to the farmers in his films with the honorific expression "*nōmin no katagata.*" They elevate the object of the film to their own level, or are treating the relationship with their objects and the objects themselves with a degree of respect.[10]

By way of contrast, Western theory since the poststructuralist intervention has theorized the documentary in terms of subject and representation, putting the referent (*taishō*) in brackets and only reticently discussing it. This is to say, Western documentary film theory focuses on the relationship of signified and signifier raked by the subjectivities of producer and spectators.

Japanese theoretical and popular discourses do not suffer from this linguistic confusion between subject and object. In post-1960 film theory and filmmaking it is precisely the relationship between the subject and the referent that produces the sign. Where the American filmmaker creates a sign from a referent in the world, the Japanese filmmaker's intimate interaction with the referent leaves a signifying trace we call a documentary film. It is a subtle but decisive difference in emphasis that one can find in virtually every discussion of nonfiction film in Japan, a difference one would have difficulty articulating with the critical tools of contemporary documentary theory outside Japan.[11]

Furthermore, it is significant that this orientation to production also informs Japanese filmmakers' often remarkable approaches to distribution and exhibition. Tsuchimoto and Ogawa worked to elevate local struggles onto the national public stage. At the same time they attempted to negotiate a borderline between public and private spheres, territory generally mapped out by the state and by capital on their own terms. In the high-growth economy after the Occupation, public space increasingly became privatized and nationalized. In the film industry a handful of heavily capitalized studios controlled "mainstream" spaces for cinema production and exhibition. Thus mainstream theaters—those deceptive places that pose as public spaces—would not touch the work of dissident filmmakers. As one kind of media the movie theater could provide an arena for shaking the hegemony of the *keiretsu* system, as the short-lived New Wave attempted to do at Shochiku Studios. Significantly, these feature filmmakers went independent; many also made documentaries. Cultural critic Ikui Eikō points out that it is more appropriate to think of the cinema underground of the 1960s and early 1970s as functioning well above ground. This is a measure of their success in carving out a space for public discourse unmediated by state and capital—a place like a park, where strangers could meet and shake up one another's worlds. In the case of these filmmakers this public exchange occurred within a dynamic between the local, regional, and national levels.

Ogawa Pro was far more aggressive at constituting an alternative sphere for public discourse. Beginning with their independence from Iwanami they were forced to distribute their films alone. Their own records, which include distribution schedules and reports filled out at the screenings, reveal that in the late 1960s and early 1970s their films were shown virtually every day of the week somewhere in Japan. When a film was new, the members themselves would organize screenings by traveling across the countryside with their prints and posters. Ogawa would give them only enough money to go to a region, where they would move from one village or town to another, showing the films wherever they could. When people found out they were from Ogawa Pro, they were always offered somewhere to stay for free in village halls or dorm rooms.

Most of the screenings, however, were organized at the local level. Rental prints went to unions, universities, and citizens' movements of every kind. A surprising number of the screenings were organized by high school students and teachers. At each screening the organizers would do their best to collect donations to send back to Ogawa Pro with the rental receipts and profits from selling posters and programs. These showings were often accompanied by speeches, songs, and cat calls when police came on-screen. The members also began to transform the spaces where they showed their films, staging photo and art exhibitions in the lobbies. They displayed a famous photographer's images of Sanrizuka or student art projects about the airport struggles, the equipment the film was shot with, or even a portrait of every villager (mixed in with the film collective). They decked the entranceways with bamboo and agitprop banners, and there were always discussions after the films. Eventually they codified their network into branch offices in Tohoku, Hokkaido, Kansai, and Kyushu. While acting as distribution hubs for the Sanrizuka films, the branches were to engage local issues through production of their own documentaries. The public envisioned by Ogawa Pro was a collection of localities connected by cinema, not a homogenized national space based on a collective defense, an imperial symbol system, or a corporate network of production and consumption.

But something happened. . . .

"Something Happened"

In the early 1970s documentary was peaking. The National Film Center held major retrospectives of pre- and postwar documentary in 1973 and 1974. The leaders of documentary filmmaking were producing the finest films of their careers. Ogawa Pro released *Heta Village* in 1973. Tsuchimoto made two master works in the same year; *Shiranui Sea* [*Shiranuikai*] (1975) was probably his best film. His interview techniques with the victims of Minamata disease were by this time refined into a powerful tool. He patiently listened to them talk about their joys and anxieties, often with the sea—that source of life and harbinger of death—as sparkling backdrop. He revisited familiar personalities from previous films in the series and traveled to far-off islands where new victims are still being discovered. *Shiranui Sea* was Tsuchimoto's last attempt at a comprehensive survey of the Minamata situation.

As Tsuchimoto and Ogawa were approaching the pinnacles of their careers, quite a few other filmmakers were also producing fine films: Yamatani Tetsuo's *Living: Twenty-five Years after the Mass Suicide on Tokashiki Island, Okinawa* [*Ikiru: Okinawa Tokashikijima shūdan jiketsu kara nijūgonen*] (1971) and *Miyako* (1974); Hara Masato's First Emperor [*Hatsukuni Shirasumera no Mikoto*] (1973); the NDU collective's *Onikko: A Record of the Struggle of Youth Laborers* [*Onikko: Tatakau seinenrōdōsha no kiroku*] (1970) and *Motoshinkakurannu* (1971); Jōnouchi Motoharu's *Going Down into Shinjuku Station* [*Chika ni oriru Shinjuku Suteshon*] (1974); Yamamura Nobuki's *Tokyo Chrome Desert* [*Tokyo kuromu sabaku*] (1978); and Haneda Sumiko's *My View of the Cherry Tree with Grey Blossoms* [*Usuzumi no sakura*] (1978).

It is, however, in retrospect that we see these filmmakers peaking because we know what followed. After the efflorescence of the early 1970s, the conditions of the documentary slumped, or at least the conditions the filmmakers aspired to were slipping into the impossible. In the next few years most of these filmmakers migrated to television and PR film or simply took up unrelated careers. Others settled into academia. Higashi and Kuroki basically became feature film directors, apparently giving up on documentary, even though they continue to appear in public forums on the subject. The filmmakers who attempted to remain independent struggled and quickly lost their artistic and political edge, while their audiences disappeared. While Tsuchimoto moved to smaller, less ambitious projects, he always engaged politically controversial subjects, such as Hiroshima, Afghanistan, and a few other Minamata-related topics; but none of these films are as compelling or innovative as his previous work. Ogawa Pro began transforming during the production of *Heta Village*. In 1972 the Tohoku branch dissolved; then in rapid order the Hokkaido and Kansai branches followed suit. The

Kyushu branch survived until 1975, but by then Ogawa Pro had left Sanrizuka. The distribution of *Heta Village* had been the most creative to that point, with projection teams, tickets made of branded wood, decorated theaters, lobby exhibitions, and the like. Nevertheless, the collective found it difficult to attract audiences. The times were clearly changing. The airport was nearing completion, and the student movement was in disarray. In northern Japan, however, a local culture movement came out in droves for the film and then issued an invitation. If the collective moved to Yamagata, they could borrow a house and some land to make rice—and films. The members accepted, but they produced only two major films in the next fifteen years. Granted they were spectacularly good films, but by the time of Ogawa's death in 1992 the Ogawa Pro collective had dwindled to a handful of people (the only longtime members were producer Fuseya Hiroo; Ogawa's wife, Shiraishi Yōko; and Iizuka Toshio).

Amid the apparent dissolution of the support structures of the documentary world, two figures arrived on the scene to signal what would become a new direction, a path Japanese documentary has followed to the present day. Hara Kazuo and Suzuki Shirōyasu are the pioneers of what has come to be called private film (*puraibeto firumu*) in Japan, a new production mode based on the solitary work of a singular filmmaking subject. In this thoroughly artisanal mode, the lone filmmaker oversees the initial conceptualization, the photography, the editing, and even the distribution of his or her work. It is significant that the term *private film*—used as it is to signify a historical difference—implicitly posits the work of Ogawa and Tsuchimoto as public film. And once again the *shutai/taishō* dyad maps this transformation.

Hara burst onto the documentary scene in 1974 with *Extreme Private Eros: Love Song 1974* [*Kyokushiteki erosu: Renka 1974*] (1974). The film lays the filmmaker's personal relationships out for the world to see. Having left his rather abusive wife (Takeda Miyuki) and taken up with a new woman (Kobayashi Sachiko, his present wife and producer), Hara decides to make a film to, as he explains in the opening voice-over, come to terms with his ex. This indulgence in the personal, this extremely public exposure of the private, proved earth shaking in the context of a documentary world whose values were formed by films like *Heta Village* and the Minamata Series.

Hara's emergence was followed by the arrival of Suzuki, an NHK television cameraman and prominent poet. Considering this combination of vocations it should not be surprising that the contradictions between producing corporate and personal representations proved stifling. Inspired by Jonas Mekas, Suzuki began producing diary films. His *Impressions of a Sunset* [*Nichibotsu no inshō*] (1974) and the 320-minute *Harvesting Shadows of Grass* [*Kusa no kage o karu*] (1977) recorded the mundane events of daily life, the details of the physical spaces he moved through, and his fetishistic fascination with the camera.

Thus the early to mid-1970s seem to constitute a break, with new filmmakers rejecting the dominant conception of documentary practice in which films were produced within organizations of people, whether collectives, companies, political parties, or the military. However, to perceive this shift only as a break would conceal important continuities that can help us answer the question, "What happened?" Hara and Suzuki are the most important figures in this narrative for more than their timing. Both are simultaneously fascinated and repulsed by the collective approach to filmmaking represented by Ogawa and Tsuchimoto, yet they still locate themselves in that territory through their films, writings, lectures, and interviews. Indeed, they can hardly avoid this since they both have a strong historical consciousness, a sense of where they have come from or an identification with a long-running documentary heritage within the context of their own national cinema.

Moreover, both Hara and Suzuki have continued to place their work within the discourse of *shutaisei*. We have already seen signs of this in a quote from Suzuki, but it is easy to find Hara speaking the same language. For example, in an interview with Laura Marks at the Flaherty Seminar, Hara described his approach in familiar terms that are difficult to gauge without contextualization in the Japanese postwar discourse on nonfiction filmmaking: "As a filmmaker I try to understand what I want to do, not so much by *confronting* my object, but by trying to become 'empty inside myself' and letting my object enter me. The object becomes my opponent and I become the receiver of the opponent's action and development."[12]

Readers unfamiliar with the previous discourses on subjectivity in documentary will key in on words like *confronting* and *opponent* (or possibly make comparisons to a Zen-like "emptying of the self"). However, Hara is actually staking out territory in relation to and within the theoretical heritage that has been handed down to him. This complex relationship to the past is also what sets Hara and Suzuki apart from the general turn to the individual that they helped create. If we use the *shutai/taishō* pair to sketch the shape of this shift, we could say that if the previous generation of documentarists strove to "go with" or "sympathize with" the *taishō*, the new generation of documentarists folded the *taishō* into the *shutai*. This is to say, the *shutai became the taishō*. The subject matter now centers on the self or the family and often with very personal concerns and obsessions. More often than not the private film lacks any significant engagement with others outside the family and reveals a reticence to set out into the public world like the previous generation. Many of these young filmmakers, particularly those emerging in the 1990s, were students of Hara and Suzuki. Thus while the two are often seen as epitomizing the private film, it is far better to see them as transitional figures with feet in both camps.

At their best these Japanese documentarists who mine the self for subject matter can create moving portraits of emotional life. Kawase Naomi's *Embracing* [*Nitsutsumarete*] (1992) is an 8mm record of her traumatic search for a father who abandoned her; it is a beautifully crafted film that ends on a deeply moving note when she finally decides to phone her father. But most of these films and videos disappoint. On the opposite end of the spectrum of quality are the so-called self-nudes, which are produced exclusively by young women who turn the camera on their own bodies. Examples include Kamioka Fumie's *Sunday Evening* [*Nichiyōbi no yūgata*] (1992); Wada Junko's *Claustromania* [*Heisho shikosho*] (1993) and *Peach Baby Oil* [*Momoiro no bebi oiru*] (1995); and Utagawa Keiko's *Water in My Ears* [*Mimi no naka no mizu*] (1993). This has been done in Western video art, but the Japanese variety has little of the self-conscious inquiry into problems of representation as does, for example, early video art such as *Birthday Suit: Complete with Scars and Defects* (1975).

There is something ironic about the moniker private film, considering that even such a film is, by design, meant for public viewing. Probably anything named private implies a specularization of itself, as in Hara's *Extreme Private Eros*. However, quite unlike Hara, what we have here is a retreat from the world, leaving the moving image a singular conduit connecting the private self with a vague, inscrutable public. In the 1990s the vector originally taken by Hara's and Suzuki's rejection of collective film practice intersected with the culture of the *otaku*. The stereotypical image of this 1990s icon is the dysfunctional cyborg youth, safely ensconced in the wired bedroom where all social communication becomes mediated through electronic gear such as fax machines, computers, and phone networks. This turn inward is topologically equivalent to the artists of the private film who too often cut themselves off from social connection and interaction, that referential stuff of the documentary form. The *shutaiseiron* Matsumoto initiated cannot hope to account for the subjectivity of an *otaku*, a measure of the historical specificity of this theory and perhaps its philosophical poverty.

Onstage at the Yamagata Film Festival, Ogawa Pro's Iizuka Toshio directed this very critique at Kawase Naomi, the de facto representative of the private film. She insisted vigorously that her films *did* have the *shakaisei* (sociality) Iizuka felt was missing. I have suggested this is probably the case; however, Iizuka does have a point. Private films are often creative works, but they nearly always disappoint in terms of conceptualization. The artists seem unable to articulate what they are doing or to comprehend the political and social implications of their work in representing the world. They present a politics of public exposure strikingly naive about the relationship between subjectivity and representation; theirs is a politics devoid of politics. Like Hara, they are standing at the front door of the public world with countless people and issues to engage; unlike Hara, who chooses to move through that public space as an individual, the private filmmakers only retreat to the family rooms and bedrooms.

So what *did* happen to documentary representations of the world in the mid-1970s?

What Happened

Since the 1970s there has been no shortage of brilliant films available for inspiration. The best work from around the world is regularly shown at forums such as Image Forum, Scan Gallery, and various museums, festivals, and minitheaters across Japan. The generation that seemed to fall apart in the early 1970s managed the occasional film. In fact, the latter work of Ogawa Pro and Hara is particularly impressive. So why the sense of devolution? Why the need to "grope" at Yamagata near the end of the 1990s? Perhaps it is nothing more than a premature millennialism. In any case, panel members could not produce an adequate answer to Yamane's query, "What happened?"

So I would like to hazard a guess... or two. First, of course, the New Left energy and its student movement dissolved. Just as clear for the case of Ogawa Pro is the completion of Narita Airport. Since these citizen and student movements constituted both the audience and the source for production monies for the movement filmmakers, reliable new venues and fund-raising sources have yet to emerge in the wake of the 1970s. We could also chalk up the current situation to the hyperconsumerism of late capitalism, which does after all encourage self-absorption and retreat from the social imperatives of the 1950s to 1970s. However, do we not also find some form of that capitalism and consumerism in, for example, the United States? Perhaps it is an even more intense variety than Japan's in New York, San Francisco, Los Angeles, and other centers of the U.S. personal documentary. Clearly the most succinct response to Yamane is, "It's overdetermined." However, I would like to suggest a less obvious explanation for what happened.

As we have seen, there has historically been a productive relationship between film criticism, theory, and practice, a relation traceable back to the 1910s. However, this relationship also seemed to unravel at the same time that documentary declined. Comparison to the U.S. situation is instructive. At the same time the independent film world in Japan experienced its shift, film theory and criticism in the West took a turn that would ultimately provide the theoretical ground for the Western work about subjectivity and identity politics. This is the innovation brought by feminist theory. In the post-1968 scene, as semiotic and

Marxist applications of nonfilmic theoretical discourse began to play out, feminism provided the field for the poststructuralist synthesis of thinkers as diverse as Marx, Freud, Jacques Lacan, Ferdinand Saussure, Jacques Derrida, and Michel Foucault. These developments coincided with our problematic moment in Japan. In 1972, the year Ogawa Pro's branch offices started closing, *Women and Film* began publishing and major women's film festivals were held in New York and Edinburgh. Laura Mulvey presented "Visual Pleasure and Narrative Cinema" in 1973, the year *Heta Village* was released, publishing it the year of *Shiranui Sea* (1975). Audiences were watching *Impressions of a Sunset* when the first issue of *Camera Obscura* came out in 1976. This feminist synthesis of poststructuralist theory has been remarkably productive for film theory and constitutes a complex, long-running debate continuing into the present. More recent inquiries into identity politics, in both print and moving image, owe much to feminism if only because it enabled a shift from discussions about positive images/negative images to questions about the apparatus of representation itself.

In Japan, however, while Japanese feminism proved a potent agent for social reform and protest on many fronts, the discussions occurring in the film world did not respond to the feminist challenge. Although Japanese filmmakers and theorists paid close attention to Jean-Luc Godard's Dziga Vertov Group and the Third Cinema theories from Latin America of the same era, Mulvey's article was not translated until 1997, and then by a scholar trained at a U.S. film school. Japanese film semiotics was generally emptied of politics and never served as the petri dish for the cross-fertilization of diverse theories or for keeping theory socially and politically engaged. Considering this, it should come as no surprise that a self-consciously feminist film and videomaker such as Idemitsu Mako always faced severe criticism in her struggle for legitimacy. Or that the women in the Ogawa Pro collective were restricted to "supporting roles" like shopping and doing housework. Or that Kawase is virtually the only aspiring young female director to work in 35mm. Many of the most powerful women in the Japanese film world are in programming and distribution of primarily independent work (Nakano Rie of Pandora, Kamiyama Katsue of Image Forum, Kitano Etsuko of the National Film Center, and Ono Seiko and Fujioka Asako of the Yamagata International Documentary Film Festival).

The point of this comparison has not been to imperiously suggest that feminism was a necessary or natural—and thus missing—stage in the development of Japanese film (although the film world's imperviousness to it has had material implications for women interested in careers in film). Rather, this comparison reveals a deep, dogged authoritarianism, patriarchal in inclination, that carried over from the Old to the New Left. Reflecting on his generation's deep antagonism for the older independent filmmakers, Ogawa's cameraman Tamura Masaki suggests, "You don't attack someone so harshly unless you are very close. Why else would you care? How else would you establish your difference?" In retrospect it would appear that the critics of the Old Left, though honestly attempting to renovate the relationship between art and politics, never substantially rethought social politics. Indeed, if we look at the way Ogawa Productions actually functioned, it was obviously an autarchy. For all the rhetoric about collective production, there was a crystal-clear hierarchy with Ogawa Shinsuke in the unquestioned seat of power. Those who could not keep up with the debate were swiftly purged. This structure may also be seen as an analog of the nation-state itself. The authoritarianism that all these factors point to may have left Japanese critical theory and documentary filmmaking of the early 1970s an inflexible discourse incapable of meeting the challenges of a social world undergoing massive change.

Furthermore, this authoritarianism used its own historical prestige to disallow other conceptualizations and theorizations of power and politics. The legacy of the movement politics generation hamstrings both itself and the artists following in its wake. For example, one of the most interesting documentaries at the end of the twentieth century was Matsue Tetsuaki's private film *Annyong-Kimchi*, which premiered at the 1999 Yamagata International Documentary Film Festival. It is, not surprisingly, about his own family. However, what sets this apart from other private productions is the fact that Matsue films from the point of view of a third-generation Korean living in Japan, and he therefore has a relationship to Korea very different from that of either his parents or his grandfather. The energy driving this charming film's production is Matsue's feeling of guilt for not being a good grandson to his first-generation grandfather. Along the way he maps out the identities of the different generations vis-à-vis "home": one aunt living in the United States has left both Korea and Japan behind, another aunt seems split between Korea and Japan, his grandmother thoroughly identifies with Korea, and he and his sister basically consider themselves Japanese. But what of his grandfather? He remains a cipher that pushes the film along because he seemed to suppress his Korean heritage all the way to the grave (which has the Matsue name on it). In the course of filmmaking, Matsue nervously decides to reveal his racial difference to his best friends, who do not know his real roots, and shoot the scene with a hidden camera. They respond, "Yeah, so what?" Of course Matsue's film is profoundly political, ranging deftly across subjects such as generation gaps, North versus South Korea, World War II, forced labor, racial discrimination, imperialism, national and racial identity, immigration, and exile. However, over long conversations Matsue firmly asserted that his film was *non-pori* (no-policy) because he was a third-generation Korean living in Japan. In other words, he refused to perceive his own work as political in any sense. When I mentioned this conversation to Hara Kazuo, who was at Yamagata for an event centered on mentoring young filmmakers, he shook his head and compared it to an allergic reaction. Matsue's conflation of policy and politics, his fervent desire to avoid looking political, and his inability to acknowledge the politicalness of his own doing reveal the depth to which the earlier generation has impoverished younger filmmakers. They set the terms, which have not been transformed along with the social world. By irrevocably linking political documentary to movement cinema, they have problematized movement through public space and contact with the other—the very foundation of documentary itself.[13]

Historiographic Caveat

Up to this point I have focused on the generational differences represented onstage at Yamagata by Iizuka and Kawase Naomi. However, it is crucial not to neglect the fact that there were two other filmmakers on that stage, Ise Shin'ichi and Kanai Katsu. Ise makes very fine, very conventional documentaries; Kanai is known for his wildly experimental films that also have a documentary touch. As the other two filmmakers argued over Yamane's provocation about the generational split on group versus individual, Ise and Kanai looked on, slightly puzzled, wondering what it had to do with them. They said as much. Their existence cannot be accounted for in this topology of self and other. They point to two large areas of practice, the conventional documentary, often made for television, and the avant-garde, that are largely excluded from the Japanese historiography of postwar nonfiction film in Japan. In other words, what we have here in these discourses surrounding *shutaisei* is a historical narration that suppresses vast areas of practice while offering a powerful explanation for others with more prestige.

This essay has presented the strong version of postwar Japanese documentary history, but this rhetorical strength is precisely what makes it useful for present-day observers. If such tropes of discourse thin out our sense of history, they are also unavoidable because they attained such cogent powers of explanation *and affect*. Produced here by the pressures of postwar politics, they provide a measure for the filmmaking identity. The artists that emerged in the late 1950s and 1960s transformed their art in reaction to the authoritarianism of both the war and the high-growth economy. They searched for a form of representation that did not involve an imperial or technocratic signification that overpowered and dominated the referential world. In theory, and especially in practice, they accomplished what appears to be a radical democratization of the relationship between *shutai* and *taishō*. Often inserting an equals sign between the words *film* and *movement*, they started with the assumption that such a public art form—so easily reproduced and presented to masses of strangers—was so rooted in the world that it could not but affect the world. Clearly, it possessed the power to complicate a public sphere.

That there are lessons to be learned that are concealed in this story is Hara Kazuo's sense as well. Recently he signaled a turn from the private film by forming a nascent collective of his own. His office bustles with the energy of young people who have gathered around him. Together they conduct miniseminars Hara calls Cinema Juku (which could be translated as "cinema cram schools"). These are short courses held in various parts of Japan to investigate historical and aesthetic questions like the ones raised in this essay. Visitors include famous directors, cinematographers, and actors, and they recently released their first documentary film project, *My Mishima* [*Watashi no Mishima*] (1999).[14] As part of this ongoing investigation of Japanese cinema, Cinema Juku has undertaken a long-term study of and possible book project about Ogawa Pro. Hara senses that the future for artists of the documentary lies in the interstices between the individual and the collective, between fiction and documentary, between the extremely private and the extremely public.

NOTES

1. J. Victor Koschmann provides a useful sketch of this larger debate in *Revolution and Subjectivity in Postwar Japan* (Chicago: University of Chicago Press, 1996). Joanne Izbicki writes about the situation within film circles in "Scorched Cityscapes and Silver Screens: Negotiating Defeat and Democracy through Cinema in Occupied Japan" (Ph.D. diss., Cornell University, 1997).
2. Quoted in Matsumoto Toshio, "*Kiroku Eiga* no oboegaki" [*Documentary Film* memo], *Eiga Hihyō*, March 1971, 95. By "transitively switching directions" Matsumoto is referring to *tenkō*. This is often translated as *ideological apostasy* and refers to the great numbers of left-leaning intellectuals, artists, and activists in the 1930s who—for a wide variety of reasons—caved in to political pressure and renounced their political positions. Some filmmakers who underwent *tenkō* gave up filmmaking, but most became the producers of wartime propaganda films. They also formed the generation of postwar documentarists Matsumoto's generation attacked.
3. Ibid., 96.
4. Matsumoto Toshio, "Zen'ei kiroku eigaron" [On avant-garde film], in *Eizō no Hakken* [Discovering the image] (Tokyo: Sanichi Shobō, 1963), 54.
5. Data from Eikyo, quoted in Tanaka Jun'ichiro, *Nihon kyōiku eiga no hattatsu-shi* [History of the development of Japanese education film] (Tokyo: Kagyūsha, 1977), 227.
6. Ibid., 248.
7. Ōshima Nagisa, "Shotto to wa nanika?" *Kiroku Eiga* 3, no. II (November 1960): 6–8 Also see Ōshima Nagisa, "Sakka no suijaku: Watakushi no kiroku eigaron" [The weakness of the auteur: My theory of documentary film], *Kiroku Eiga* 3, no. 5 (May 1960) 26–28
8. Matsumoto Toshio, "Kakusareta sekai no kiroku," in *Eizō no Hakken*, 86.
9. Ōshima Nagisa, "Ogawa Shinsuke: Tōsō to datsuraku" [Ogawa Shinsuke: Struggle and loss], *Eiga Hihyō*, December 1970, 17.

10. Abé Mark Nornes, "Documentarists of Japan: An Interview with Suzuki Shirōyasu," *Documentary Box II*, April 1993, 14–15.
11. This is not to suggest that subjectivity in Euro-American film is complex while in Japan it is simple. The conceptualization of subjectivity in Japanese film theory is what is problematic. One reason for the difference has to do with the filmmaking itself, which was conceptualizing documentary practice and the relationship between filmmaker and filmed along different lines. Another has to do with the lack of serious, critical engagement between all the scholars, critics, and filmmakers deploying the ideas. Thus there was consensus on the meaning of terms such as *shutai, taishō, shutaisei*, and the like.
12. Laura Marks,"Naked Truths: Hara Kazuo's Iconoclastic Obsessions," *Independent* 15, no. 10 (1992): 26.
13. One factor in my coming to this conclusion was Aaron Gerow's presentation "The Image of the Self: Women Personal Filmmakers in the Early Nineties" (Japanese Women Filmmakers Conference, 5 October 2000, University of Colorado, Boulder). Gerow's reading of the 1990s personal film by women filmmakers—the self-nudes in particular—finds a hint of critique within the form. While granting they may lack complexity, he suggests their explorations of personal identity, sexuality, and the body do engage the central problematics of their generation's relationship between self and other. His readings have convinced me there is an impulse to break out of the private spaces and recognize how the public penetrates the private (something I believe I missed on my own viewings because my taste has been constructed by both the Japanese movement cinema and the Euro-American documentary). At the same time, he also shows how that impulse is consistently checked, precisely the dynamic I am examining in this article.
14. Hara premiered this film at the 1999 Yamagata International Documentary Film Festival. The event featured the work of Cinema Juku and Full Shot, a youthful documentary collective from Taiwan. It was a fascinating scene. The Taiwanese filmmakers criticized the Japanese for being too nostalgic for a nonproblematic past and avoiding any political aspects of their subject (people leaving rural Japan for life in the big city). Hara continually expressed his frustration with his own students over the issues discussed in this essay. Both sides struggled to understand each other, and the missing ingredient seemed to be a historical consciousness that could help explain their different conceptions of self and other, individual and the world, private and public.

78

EMILE DE ANTONIO WITH TANYA NEUFELD

AN INTERVIEW WITH EMILE DE ANTONIO (1973)

[Tanya Neufeld:] *Why have your films always been political in nature?*

[Emile de Antonio:] I have always looked upon documentary as belonging to politics as much as to art. Those documentary films which have survived, which have had meaning, which have been artistically interesting, have been political. These include Eisenstein's reconstructions, the work of Shub and Vertov, and the documentaries made by Americans in the thirties, such as *The Plow That Broke the Plains* and *The River*.

In 1948, Robert Flaherty made his last film, *Louisiana Story*. It was the first American documentary film to be shown in theaters after World War II until *Point of Order*. I would like to attack Flaherty and the principles of his work, and *Louisiana Story* is exactly the opposite of everything that I have aspired to do in film—in the way it was made, in intention, and the way it was financed. *Louisiana Story* was financed by a $285,000 grant from Humble Oil Company. $285,000 in 1948 is like $500,000 today. It becomes one of the costliest documentaries ever made. It was a repudiation of the tradition of dissent and of such films as *The Plow That Broke the Plains,* made in the days of the New Deal, that questioned the rape of our country. That's what *The Plow That Broke the Plains* is about, the creation of the dust bowl. It was how the insane and insulting abuse of the earth created an emptiness in the center of America that forced people to go westward. But *Louisiana Story* is finally an accommodation between the oil map and the people of the bayou.

When you make a film like *Louisiana Story*, the film of a young Cajun boy confronted by the drilling rigs in Louisiana, and you've been commissioned to make this film by an oil company, you are already compromised. One of the reasons this film played so widely is because Humble Oil gave it away to theaters all over the country. Each time we look at anything, we change it. Seen today, Flaherty seems to stand for shallow aestheticism, a search for the artificially exotic. Flaherty's staged conflicts between man and nature were, in the first place, false, and in the second place, because of the brilliant execution and personal devotion, they deflected documentary into hopeless and unrewarding motions. The enemy out there isn't ice or the sea, but man. The Flaherty line leads directly to cinema verité. A line dead, blank, and empty.

At the time of *Louisiana Story* we were already in the Cold War, which is what my life in film is all about, including *Painters Painting*. What you had in that period was silence. The silent fifties. But the fifties weren't silent on the part of the United States government. The government in its various forms produced Richard Nixon and the House Un-American Activities Committee; it produced Joseph McCarthy; it produced a thousand films through the U.S. Information Agency supporting Korea and the Cold War. What you had was silence on the part of the people. There were very few documentary films, mainly those made by television, which were links of sausage, not films. Most of them sought after that illusory concept—objectivity—which is pure bullshit and in reality means no offense to advertisers.

[Tanya Neufeld:] *Do you feel that the politically oriented film can serve an essential function to the community in much the same way that an annual theater festival in fifth-century Athens combined politics, religion, and entertainment into a single integral community event?*

[Emile de Antonio:] The theater of Aeschylus, Sophocles, and Euripides is essentially a theater of celebration. Even including the disharmony within the Athenian state, from what we know of it, and I have the most serious doubts about the validity of history as an idea, but from what we know of it, it always took place at a certain time of year under the auspices of the state. So even if Euripides was thought of as a subversive, the plays were nonetheless put on by the state in a state-operated and state-trained theater. In our time, the film documentary is the art of opposition. My films have been against the chief assumptions of the American state, and I think my films have succeeded in making a new kind of art form in film out of political material. This is precisely the problem that interested me. My films were made alone, outside the structure, opposed to the structure, opposed to specific activities of the United States government. When you put my films together, they constitute the history of the United States in the days of the Cold War.

Point of Order deals with witch-hunts in the broadest sense, and with McCarthyism, which was the dominant idea of domestic politics in the United States in the fifties. *Rush to Judgment* is not about the death of President Kennedy, nothing could interest me less. Nothing could bore me more than those USIA films like *Years of Lightning, Day of Drums* with Kennedy's coffin and weeping Jackie. What was of interest to me was the suppression of evidence and the elevation of the police to a superpower within the United States. That was the consequence of the death of Kennedy. The FBI and the Secret Service and the Dallas police had at the very least been remiss. They were covered up by a government commission of most august people. The film I made was out of outrage at the police and judicial conspiracy. One result of the Warren Report is that we are now living in a form of police state. *In the Year of the Pig* is a cry of outrage against our war in Vietnam. After Kent State and Cambodia, I stopped work on *Painters Painting* to make *Millhouse*.

Millhouse is historical in approach. It begins with Nixon's career and traces it throughout as comedy, as satire. Nixon is the Tartuffe of the Cold War from its beginnings to its most refined development in 1972. One of the things that happened from 1945 to 1970, the years covered in *Painters Painting*, is that the United States, in some curious way, for the first time confronting the whole problem of abstraction, produced a new kind of painting. It was the painting with which I grew up. I knew a good many of the artists personally, and it introduced me to a problem which lay in the back of my mind as I was doing all my other films, which is the relationship between art and politics.

The inconsistency of having left-wing politics, as I do, and liking the paintings of Jackson Pollock, Jasper Johns, and Frank Stella, is not to me contradictory. The film is largely supportive of what I consider the chief lines of American painting from 1945 to the present in the days of the Cold War. This is painting that is apolitical, that is concerned with painting, not with politics. This is painting that was concerned with paint, canvas, and objects. There seems to be an apparent schizophrenic separation between what I was doing on the one hand and what these people were doing on the other. It's a question I raise myself and there is no answer to it.

Could the art of the forties, fifties, and sixties have been produced without the political and economic structure that supported it?

That's the key question that has been worrying me all these years. This is why I go out of my way in *Painters Painting* to separate the painters from the collectors, the dealers, and the people who create the market, although they are an intrinsic part of the world.

What do you see for the future of painting?

One of the reasons *Artforum* is writing so much about film is that the fantastic movement that was going on in American painting has come to an end. I think the thing that worries the best young painters we have, like Stella, is that there is nobody behind them. They don't hear that herd of hoofbeats, that compression that you had with abstract expressionism followed by Johns and Rauschenberg, followed by Stella and Noland, followed by pop art, all these ideas, movements, ferments, one right after the other, bang, bang, bang. Suddenly, where are the guys twenty-five years old? I don't see them.

Aren't there more people making art today than ever before?

That's right, but most of it is not good art. And this is the key to the whole thing, quality. One of the reasons I made *Painters Painting* is that I was alive in the middle of this extraordinary period which was a kind of rush of talent, of ambition, of energy. Abstract expressionism, when Rauschenberg and Johns came on the scene, was exhausted. The second-generation abstract expressionists were for the most part very, very second-generation. One night I was playing poker with several of them in East Hampton and they were saying, "What are you doing going around with people like Johns and Rauschenberg? Are you some sort of fucking anarchist? They're not artists, they're antiart." I said, "Precisely, that is the point."

I'm not equating art with fashion. There was a compression of energy, one thing following another, but it stopped—by the time you get to Stella and Poons, it's over.

I think that one of the reasons *Artforum* is in such a coy, arty, and academic way searching out all kinds of crap in film is that most of the filmmakers you are dealing with are failed painters or filmmakers who think like painters or aspire to a painting "scene." People like Hollis Frampton and the people who seem to amuse Annette Michelson and film fleas like Jonas Mekas are essentially failed painters. They were choked off and cast aside into the development of another art form and came to film out of desperation. They are the tail end, and they have all the same feeling toward visual material that the painters had who succeeded in their art. They tried to translate their failure on canvas into some kind of cinematic existence; what they do doesn't work in film. When Jasper Johns paints letters it's art; Hollis Frampton's A, B, C, D film is something else. The idea of literally transposing exhausted painting ideas into film is a boring idea and most of the people doing this are painters *manqués*. These are the people who seem to interest art critics, which is one of the reasons why art magazines are devoting so much time to this sort of work. An issue of *Artforum* on Brakhage!

What of the young artists today who are putting their energies into other media such as videotape, Conceptual art, etc.?

When I began work on *Painters Painting* I went to Henry Geldzahler and got permission to film his show *American Painting 1940–1970* at the Metropolitan Museum. The camera crew and I spent ten nights there filming those canvases. Nobody will ever film those works again. Nobody will ever again bring together such a collection. First of all, modern painting is much more fragile than the old masterpieces. A Rembrandt holds up much better than a Rauschenberg. They were painted with better paint on better canvas. Then there are the present-day problems of shipping and insurance. Henry's intuition behind the choice of time span for his show was similar to mine for *Painters Painting*. No matter how many good paintings these artists go on to make, the original source of that information is finished for me. The younger artists are into nonpainting activity, which I regard as another world that is not necessarily a new world or an interesting world. Conceptual art is a symbol of exhaustion.

What motivated you to make Painters Painting?

As much as I distrust history, I live in it and I work in it. One of the things I wanted to do in *Painters Painting* was to make something, rather than doing a film about it as TV does it. TV uses a narrator to explain it, to tell you what it was about. I wanted to make a film which would be a thing in itself, which would reflect what happened in those twenty-five years in which I lived, what I thought was important, what generated it. I wanted it in the words of the people who did it, rather than making a film *about* it, and I wanted to define who did it in the widest possible sense. The film includes the promoters, the dealers, the collectors, as well as the people who make the art.

It is perfectly obvious that when you have a man like Barnett Newman who was so extraordinarily articulate, whose work I happen to like tremendously, who had such a sense of the pertinent anecdote, and was able to tie that pertinent anecdote to a genuine point in the development of his art and to abstract art in America, you tend to use more of Barney than you do of many others in the film. This suggests one of the limitations in the kind of film I made—you were in a sense trapped by the projective capacity of those you film. There is an extraordinary sweet expressiveness about de Kooning; there's a steely passion in Stella; there's a fantastic ability to articulate and an intellectuality in Newman; there's an iron, logical precision, and a gift for speech, in Jasper Johns which are overwhelming. So you tend to be more interested in them because you are dealing with films as well as painting.

Would you have included more artists in Painters Painting *if time had allowed?*

I made the film as long as I wanted it. One thing about making the films I make is that I'm not responsible to anybody. I could have made the film eight hours long if I had wanted to.

I find that there is no written overall history of the art of this period which covers the field as thoroughly as *Painters Painting*. As I read the written history of American Painting in the twentieth century, I find remarkable shallowness that is highly journalistic rather than revealing.

In Painters Painting, *was the end result similar to your original intent?*

One of the reasons the film works is that most of the painters are articulate people. One thing about the birth of abstract expressionism, one thing about beginning at the bottom, being born in despair without acceptance the way modern American painting began, is that it created verbal expressiveness as defense. It forced an artist to become a theorist to defend his position. This is one reason artists, particularly like Newman, became brilliant at rhetoric. A question I asked during the interviews was, "How old were you when you had your first one-man show?" Willem de Kooning was forty-four, Barnett Newman was forty-five. Hans Hofmann was over sixty. Painters of the next generation were having their first shows in their twenties.

Do you feel that the decline in the quality of art is due to the partial elimination of the struggle, since there is now more money, more galleries, more public and private support than ever before?

The struggle was eliminated by the time Stella and Johns appeared. There are more galleries, but the successful galleries throughout the country are selling the work of these same artists.

A big point of argument between Phil Leider and myself was that he thought that Earthworks and Conceptual art had a special social meaning. Originally, I did an interview with Phil about that but decided to substitute a later interview in the film. For me their social meaning was negative.

I wasn't interested in Smithson's *Spiral Jetty*. Some post-Stella artists were tired of the whole gallery setup, which they considered bourgeois and proprietary, and they were trying to move their art out of the galleries. They started by having exhibits in their studios, which was not very different really than having an exhibit in a gallery. They still put up the pictures and had somebody come in and buy them. Some people will argue that the artists who moved art out into the landscape, like Michael Heizer and Robert Smithson, destroyed the buying and selling concept. How? You still had to have a patron: you had to go back and have a Holy Roman Catholic Church pay the bill or a Bob Scull.

How old were you when you made your first film?

I was forty years old when I started work on my first film, *Point of Order*, twelve years ago. Before that my life had been a sort of stew. How does an intellectual survive when he doesn't have anything that he really wants to do?

The first job I had after I got out of college was as a translator, then as a longshoreman in Baltimore, and then into the army. After the army I went to graduate school at Columbia and was a barge captain at the same time. A barge captain is the only job for an unemployed intellectual because you have absolutely nothing to do. I used to read all day and get paid for it. But I was bored by everything.

I saw an ad in the paper once that said "Wanted: economist with graduate degree," so I called up and said, "I'm an economist." All they did was check to see that I had a degree, but not in what subject.

Then I taught at the College of William and Mary and at CCNY [City College of New York]. But that was never a completely engrossing activity. The interesting problem in teaching was to teach something for the first time, when you weren't sure of the material yourself, when you had to get up on your tightrope, and something about the excitement of that made you a good teacher. The second time it was already flat.

After teaching I flopped around into different things and then I became a combination peddler and idea man. It was very uninspiring but lucrative. I put people together who weren't very logical together. My first relationship with Andy Warhol was commercial. I got him a job painting a Puerto Rican theater in Spanish Harlem. Andy went to the theater owner and told him to paint it Puerto Rican colors, pink and gaudy. The man did and Andy got a fee for saying that and I took a piece of Andy's fee. It was kind of a joke. I was always astounded at how silly businesspeople were. At that time I never went to the movies, I really disliked the medium.

What finally got you interested in making a film?

I saw a film in 1958–59 which had a great deal to do with the art world called *Pull My Daisy*. There was a new spirit in the air—we were emerging from the '50s and there was a new questioning that meshed with my own mood. I'd been a radical at the age of sixteen, then I became quiet. *Pull My Daisy* was shot by Alfred Leslie and Robert Frank. Allen Ginsberg and Larry Rivers were in it. It was the most brilliant text that Jack Kerouac had ever done. I liked the film because it was a very grubby little film, very cheaply made. It was a very alive film and it had a great sense of black and white which I liked. I was suddenly looking at films, looking at films I should have seen before, and I was excited by them.

What motivated you to make Point of Order*?*

There was a hole, something that had to be filled. Dan Talbot and I talked about his problem of getting new films to show in his theater. He hadn't at that time been able to procure all the old films and start the great classic series that he did. So originally he had the idea of taking the footage from the Army-McCarthy hearings and showing it at his theater. That's the point at which suddenly something went click in my head, which was "No. We shouldn't do that—we should make a film. It should be an imposition of order over chaos. It should be something different."

Did you have any training in filmmaking at all?

No. I'd never seen a piece of film, I'd never seen an editing machine. I started from scratch. It's a brutal way to learn things, but a very good way to find out everything for yourself.

The sociological aspect of all this that I find entertaining is that my life is a reversal of the American Dream, which is that you work your ass off to make a lot of money and when you're forty you retire. I gambled with my life. I spent all my time doing all the things that people who wanted to retire hoped to do when they retired, but didn't have the energy to do. I knew a lot of women, drank a lot, played very hard. That's what I did when I was young. When I reached middle age I started working very hard, nonstop. Right now I'm in a state of exhaustion and boredom. So I'm about to strike out in a new direction. It's not the subject alone, it's not the fact that I've looked upon documentary as a way to right wrong, as a way to cry out against injustice, as a way to attack the social system: I still feel that all those problems remain and that films should be made about them. But I've done everything I can. I can't say anything else with force in the documentary that I haven't said before.

This is something that happens to everyone in every art form. "What are you going to do next?" You can't fall back on earlier ideas. They're boring. The crack of that whip is very loud indeed and it prevents you from going back.

Richard Roud, whom I call Richard Rude, the director of the New York Film Festival, thought *Point of Order* was very good but not a film. It was just far enough ahead of its time that a festival director was too blind to see it. Dan Talbot's New Yorker is a better festival than Roud ever promoted.

A film is anything that goes through a projector. I'd been saying that for ten years before I read it in *Artforum*. I heard it in defense of a film by Peter Kubelka in which he simply ran white leader through the projector. My definition of film is anything that passes through a projector and produces a filmic response in people. It doesn't matter where the material comes from. But the audience is part of it.

Point of Order was shot with two absolutely fixed cameras. It's lucky that all I had to work with was those two fixed cameras grinding away remorselessly for 188 hours.

The film worked better because there were no tricks in it. It was stripped down to where it really mattered. The aesthetics in that film was the politics, it was the character, it was the tone and the voice, it was America. That's what film is about, not beautiful shots.

What interests me more than anything else in film is structure. The Army-McCarthy hearings themselves were untrue, as the historical present usually is. What I did was make them true because what appeared to be the truth, that which actually happened, included all the efforts to sweep it under the rug, included that weaselly little ending in which everyone wanted to run away and not acknowledge what had been let loose in the land. When I changed it all around, it became not only a new kind of documentary, but also the truth.

Will you define structure?

The Swedes in reviewing *Millhouse* said it was the best portrait of a statesman since Charlie Chaplin's *The Great Dictator*. I think it's different than fiction, but it is made up in a sense. What I wanted to do in *Millhouse* was to create a portrait of a political figure, to make it very clear that I wasn't being objective, to make Nixon as round as he could be on film, to make him as round as a figure in Molière, to have certain sympathy for him, to understand this poor boy from the lower middle classes with the burning desire and energy to have the whole piece of cake. Who wanted to eat the whole thing and got to eat the whole thing no matter how many Asian peasants were to die for it. Everybody who wrote about it missed the Horatio Alger structure. *Millhouse* starts with Nixon in 1962, defeated for the governorship of California, after already losing a shot at the presidency. To put that together in such a way on film, the Vietnam War and everything else, and not to make it strictly chronological but to have theme and subtheme . . . it's a wholly different experience in documentary. Structure is all.

All my films are collage films and I've wondered if there was any relationship between what I was doing and the fact that I did know these painters who were doing collage before I ever made films. *Millhouse* is cut from millions of options; it's the marriage of all kinds of elements. I use collage in film to make a political point because it's a shorthand to the truth of the documents.

Is there anyone today making films that, in your opinion, are superior or significant?

Not too many. One of the great problems of being an American is that you are driven mad by all the technical garbage that goes on around you, and you become inordinately impressed with the significance of technique and technical things. Lots of people have gone that route.

What about Andy Warhol's films?

What Andy was doing, which nobody picked up on, was reproducing the whole history of film from the beginning. His first films were silent; Andy didn't know how to use sound. He didn't know how to deal with motion. His films were static. One of his first films was *Sleep*—about a guy lying on a couch. Another was a transvestite eating a banana. It was exactly like the beginning of film. Then Andy learned how to move the camera, so you got a little more action. Then he learned how to do sync sound. Although Andy didn't do much of this himself, there would be no Warhol films without Warhol. Without Andy, I doubt if the people around him could exist. Andy is the organizing force and intelligence. Whether he actually handles the camera himself isn't important. As he has moved closer to conventional film, the films are less interesting.

I was the subject of a film by Warhol so I saw him work, what I could remember of it. He made a seventy-minute film of me getting drunk. I drank a quart of whiskey in twenty minutes—that's very hard to do and stay alive. I noticed his technique was primitive (this was early in his film life). It was refreshing. That "Look, Ma, no hands" aspect of Andy's work was always the most interesting part of his work, whether it was in painting or in film. Again, it was the necessary and proper rebellion against the million-handed Hollywood monster. How else could you begin except the way Andy began or the way I began, if you were going to make serious films? He didn't cut anything. His films were just rolls of film spliced together. It was like he invented cutting as Porter and Griffith did. Andy got it reduced to a pre-modern minimum. What you saw in his life, taking place about every three months, was the whole history of film being redone.

What sort of material do you consider to be documents for your films?

My films are made with documents, whether I film the document or whether the document exists. The structure, the technique, everything else is invented. There are no actors employed.

An aspect of all this that I find interesting is the films of mine that have been commercial failures, like *Rush to Judgment*, 1966, which was the first film that began with a collage of events, newsreels, and interviews. A film that I really dislike, *The Sorrow and the Pity*, is an absolute imitation of my film, and is financially one of the most successful documentaries ever made. *Rush to Judgment* was seen in France by all the people in the film world. It had a run there before it ran here, and it was the first film made like that. *The Sorrow and the Pity* is the same film, sentimentally done and badly structured. It's more sentimental for New Yorkers because it emphasizes the Jewish question under the Nazis, and because we're already nostalgic about Hitler, World War II, and the Resistance. Also it doesn't offend anybody. It's very safe to talk about the Resistance and to take the mealymouthed position Anthony Eden does in that film. A liberal film. It's easy to get up and talk about the fall of France, or the Resistance, because it's all so alien to our culture or to English culture at this point, and it's so dim in the past. Hitler is dead and buried. But to talk about the assassination of John F. Kennedy in Dallas right now is still dangerous.

Are your films being rereleased now?

Yes. The American Film Institute did a retrospective of my films two years ago and since that time different countries have been doing it, the Swedes, the Danes, the Finns, the Norwegians, now the University of Wisconsin. No film of mine has ever been on television in the United States in its original version. Every film of mine has played television in Holland, Belgium, Sweden, England, West Germany, and at the commercial rates.

Annette Michelson replies

It is, of course, because Emile de Antonio's work in film has so many qualities of interest and of urgency that we are pleased to have him speak for us on film-making, and because of them, as well, that we are discouraged by his lack of interest in his lack of sympathy with, those younger men, working in considerable difficulty, who might be regarded as his fellows in independence and integrity. The impulse behind the glacial and categorical rejection no doubt spurs the assumption that one's own concerns are serious, while those of one's interlocutor take place on the level of irresponsible amusement.

Inscribed within de Antonio's hostility toward *Artforum*'s present concern with film are questions about film's relation to painting and to other fine arts, to the tradition we know as modernist, the manner in which film solicits our particular critical and theoretical attention. As to the question of iconographic sources, no one would take seriously the double claim that Jasper Johns' use of numbers and letters derived from Cubist sources and could be, therefore, no more than derivative. So Hollis Frampton's use of the alphabet in a major filmic work, *Zorns Lemma,* has a function, structural, semantic, that can simply not begin to be accounted for by the very loose, lazy rhetoric of de Antonio's art-historical free associations.

The real, by no means academic question of the nature of current filmic aspirations and their relation to older art, has already been posed, in a more than tentative manner, in the first of our special issues devoted to film (*Artforum,* September 1971). Because that issue is now out of print, I offer the following excerpts from its foreword:

> This present issue of *Artforum* is, then, designed to evoke—largely through the work of younger critics—for some of the artists, critics, and their audiences who compose a visually literate public here and abroad, the urgency of recognition for an achievement whose importance will eventually be seen as comparable to that of American painting in the 1950s and onwards.
>
> That achievement is radically indebted to the disciplined energy, generosity and prescience of men like Jonas Mekas—a statement which is no sooner made than it forces remembrance that there is indeed none like him.
>
> Advanced film-making in this country demands to be studied in relation to the growing constriction of pictorial and sculptural energies and the inflation of an economy which has reactivated, through the desperate polarity of "conceptual" and "body" art, the esthetic syndrome of that ancient, obstinate malady, philosophical dualism.
>
> The critical task is going to be redefined by those for whom both reading and writing serve the medium, by those, above all, in whom cinematic consciousness has been heightened by the disciplined readjustment of the perceptive processes which film requires of artist and audience. New critics are demanding a situation in which that cinematic consciousness can develop with a rigor no totally disjoined from generosity. It is time for a transvaluation of values; only then will conventions perpetuated in the disingenuous rhetoric of intellectual pathos and personal coquetry be dissolved.

Artforum's increasing concern with film-making and film criticism in its most advanced aspects quite naturally elicits pained reactions for those with vested interests in the art of the recent past, just as it tends to provoke discomfort in those official and largely journalistic film-critical milieus who have responded with enthusiasm to de Antonio's own work. Thus, the recent attempt to examine through a comparative study of Eisenstein and Brakhage the montage tradition upon which de Antonio is largely dependent, was designed to call into question a number of historical, formal, theoretical conventions. We shall continue in this direction, directing our attention to areas of film still waiting their inscription into critical discourse—and to those ill-served by a rhetoric now outworn.

79

BILL NICHOLS

THE VOICE OF DOCUMENTARY (1983)

It is worth insisting that the strategies and styles deployed in documentary, like those of narrative film, change; they have a history. And they have changed for much the same reasons: the dominant modes of expository discourse change; the arena of ideological contestation shifts. The comfortably accepted realism of one generation seems like artifice to the next. New strategies must constantly be fabricated to represent "things as they are" and still others to contest this very representation.

In the history of documentary we can identify at least four major styles, each with distinctive formal and ideological qualities.[1] In this article I propose to examine the limitations and strengths of these strategies, with particular attention to one that is both the newest and in some ways the oldest of them all.[2]

The direct-address style of the Griersonian tradition (or, in its most excessive form, the March of Time's "voice of God") was the first thoroughly worked-out mode of documentary. As befitted a school whose purposes were overwhelmingly didactic, it employed a supposedly authoritative yet often presumptuous off-screen narration. In many cases this narration effectively dominated the visuals, though it could be, in films like *Night Mail* or *Listen to Britain*, poetic and evocative.

After World War II, the Griersonian mode fell into disfavor (for reasons I will come back to later) and it has little contemporary currency—except for television news, game and talk shows, ads and documentary specials.

Its successor, *cinéma vérité*, promised an increase in the "reality effect" with its directness, immediacy, and impression of capturing untampered events in the everyday lives of particular people. Films like *Chronicle of a Summer, Le Joli Mai, Lonely Boy, Back-Breaking Leaf, Primary* and *The Chair* built on the new technical possibilities offered by portable cameras and sound recorders which could produce synchronous dialogue under location conditions. In pure *cinéma vérité* films, the style seeks to become "transparent" in the same mode as the classical Hollywood style—capturing people in action, and letting the viewer come to conclusions about them unaided by any implicit or explicit commentary.

Sometimes mesmerizing, frequently perplexing, such films seldom offered the sense of history, context or perspective that viewers seek. And so in the past decade we have seen a third style which incorporates direct address (characters or narrator speaking directly to the viewer), usually in the form of the interview. In a host of political and feminist films, witness-participants step before the camera to tell their story. Sometimes profoundly revealing, sometimes fragmented and incomplete, such films have provided the central model for contemporary documentary. But as a strategy and a form, the interview-oriented film has problems of its own.

More recently, a fourth phase seems to have begun, with films moving toward more complex forms where epistemological and aesthetic assumptions become more visible. These new self-reflexive documentaries mix observational passages with interviews, the voice-over of the film-maker with intertitles, making patently clear what has been implicit all along: documentaries always were forms of re-presentation, never clear windows onto "reality"; the film-maker was always a participant-witness and an active fabricator of meaning, a producer of cinematic discourse rather than a neutral or all-knowing reporter of the way things truly are.

Ironically, film theory has been of little help in this recent evolution, despite the enormous contribution of recent theory to questions of the production of meaning in narrative forms. In documentary the most advanced, modernist work draws its inspiration less from post-structuralist models of discourse than from the working procedures of documentation and validation practiced by ethnographic film-makers. And as far as the influence of film history goes, the figure of Dziga Vertov now looms much larger than those of either Flaherty or Grierson.

I do not intend to argue that self-reflexive documentary represents a pinnacle or solution in any ultimate sense. It is, however, in the process of evolving alternatives that seem, in our present historical context, less obviously problematic than the strategies of commentary, *vérité,* or the interview. These new forms may, like their predecessors, come to seem more "natural" or even "realistic" for a time. But the success of every form breeds its own overthrow: it limits, omits, disavows, represses (as well as represents). In time, new necessities bring new formal inventions.

As suggested above, in the evolution of documentary the contestation among forms has centered on the question of "voice." By "voice" I mean something narrower than style: that which conveys to us a sense of a text's social point of view, of how it is speaking to us and how it is organizing the materials it is presenting to us. In this sense "voice" is not restricted to any one code or feature such as dialogue or spoken commentary. Voice is perhaps akin to that intangible, moiré-like pattern formed by the unique interaction of all a film's codes, and it applies to all modes of documentary.

Far too many contemporary film-makers appear to have lost their voice. Politically, they forfeit their own voice for that of others (usually characters recruited to the film and interviewed). Formally, they disavow the complexities of voice, and discourse, for the apparent simplicities of faithful observation or respectful representation, the treacherous simplicities of an unquestioned empiricism (the world and its truths exist; they need only be dusted off and reported). Many documentarists would appear to believe what fiction film-makers only feign to believe, or openly question: that film-making creates an objective representation of the way things really are. Such documentaries use the magical template of verisimilitude without the story teller's open resort to artifice.

Very few seem prepared to admit through the very tissue and texture of their work that all film-making is a form of discourse fabricating its effects, impressions, and point of view.

Yet it especially behooves the documentary film-maker to acknowledge what she/he is actually doing. Not in order to be accepted as modernist for the sake of being modernist, but to fashion documentaries that may more closely correspond to a contemporary understanding of our position within the world so that effective political/formal strategies for describing and challenging that position can emerge. Strategies and techniques for doing so already exist. In documentary they seem to derive most directly from *The Man with a Movie Camera* and *Chronicle of a Summer* and are vividly exemplified in David and Judith MacDougall's Turkana trilogy (*Lorang's Way, Wedding Camels, A Wife Among Wives*). But before discussing this tendency further, we should first examine the strengths and limitations of *cinéma vérité* and the interview-based film. They are well-represented by two recent and highly successful films: *Soldier Girls* and *Rosie the Riveter*.

Soldier Girls presents a contemporary situation: basic army training as experienced by women volunteers. Purely indirect or observational, *Soldier Girls* provides no spoken commentary, no interviews or titles, and like Fred Wiseman's films, it arouses considerable controversy about its point of view. One viewer at Filmex interjected, "How on earth did they get the Army to let them make such an incredibly anti-Army film?" What struck that viewer as powerful criticism, though, may strike another as an honest portrayal of the tough-minded discipline necessary to learn to defend oneself, to survive in harsh environments, to kill. As in Wiseman's films, organizational strategies establish a preferred reading—in this case, one that favors the personal over the political, that seeks out and celebrates the irruptions of individual feeling and conscience in the face of institutional constraint, that re-writes historical process as the expression of an indomitable human essence whatever the circumstance. But these strategies, complex and subtle like those of realist fiction, tend to ascribe to the historical material itself meanings that in fact are an effect of the film's style or voice, just as fiction's strategies invite us to believe that "life" is like the imaginary world inhabited by its characters.

A pre-credit sequence of training exercises which follows three women volunteers ends with a freeze-frame and iris-in to isolate the face of each woman. Similar to classic Hollywood-style vignettes used to identify key actors, this sequence inaugurates a set of strategies that links *Soldier Girls* with a large part of American *cinéma vérité* (*Primary, Salesman, An American Family*, the *Middletown Series*). It is characterized by a romantic individualism and a dramatic, fiction-like structure, but employing "found" stories rather than the wholly invented ones of Hollywood. Scenes in which Private Hall oversees punishment for Private Alvarez and in which the women recruits are awakened and prepare their beds for Drill Sergeant Abing's inspection prompt an impression of looking in on a world unmarked by our, or the camera's, act of gazing. And those rare moments in which the camera or person behind it is acknowledged certify more forcefully that other moments of "pure observation" capture the social presentation of self we too would have witnessed had we actually been there to see for ourselves. When *Soldier Girls'* narrative-like tale culminates in a shattering moment of character revelation, it seems to be a happy coincidence of dramatic structure and historical events unfolding. In as extraordinary an epiphany as any in all of *vérité*, tough-minded Drill Sergeant Abing breaks down and confesses to Private Hall how much of his own humanity and soul has been destroyed by his experience in Vietnam. By such means, the film transcends the social and political categories which it shows but refuses to name. Instead of the personal becoming political, the political becomes personal.

We never hear the voice of the film-maker or a narrator trying to persuade us of this romantic humanism. Instead, the film's structure relies heavily on classical narrative procedures, among them: (1) a chronology of apparent causality which reveals how each of the three women recruits resolves the conflict between a sense of her own individuality and army discipline; (2) shots organized into dramatically revelatory scenes that only acknowledge the camera as participant-observer near the film's end, when one of the recruits embraces the film-makers as she leaves the training base, discharged for her "failure" to fit in; and (3) excellent performances from characters who "play themselves" without any inhibiting self-consciousness. (The phenomenon of filming individuals who play themselves in a manner strongly reminiscent of the performances of professional actors in fiction could be the subject of an extended study in its own right.) These procedures allow purely observational documentaries to asymptotically narrow the gap between a fabricated realism and the apparent capture of reality itself which so fascinated André Bazin.

This gap may also be looked at as a gap between evidence and argument.[3] One of the peculiar fascinations of film is precisely that it so easily conflates the two. Documentary displays a tension arising from the attempt to make statements about life which are quite general, while necessarily using sounds and images that bear the inescapable trace of their particular historical origins. These sounds and images come to function as signs; they bear meaning, though the meaning is not really inherent in them but rather conferred upon them by their function within the text as a whole. We may think we hear history or reality speaking to us through a film, but what we actually hear is the voice of the text, even when that voice tries to efface itself.

This is not only a matter of semiotics but of historical process. Those who confer meaning (individuals, social classes, the media and other institutions) exist within history itself rather than at the periphery, looking in like gods. Hence, paradoxically, self-referentiality is an inevitable communicational category. A class cannot be a member of itself, the law of logical typing tells us, and yet in human communication this law is necessarily violated. Those who confer meaning are themselves members of the class of conferred meanings (history). For a film to fail to acknowledge this and pretend to omniscience—whether by voice-of-God commentary or by claims of "objective knowledge"—is to deny its own complicity with a production of knowledge that rests on no firmer bedrock than the very act of production. (What then becomes vital are the assumptions, values, and purposes motivating this production, the underpinnings which some modernist strategies attempt to make more clear.)[4]

Observational documentary appears to leave the driving to us. No one tells us about the sights we pass or what they mean. Even those obvious marks of documentary textuality—muddy sound, blurred or racked focus, the grainy, poorly lit figures of social actors caught on the run—function paradoxically. Their presence testifies to an apparently more basic absence: such films sacrifice conventional, polished artistic expression in order to bring back, as best they can, the actual texture of history in the making. If the camera gyrates wildly or ceases functioning, this is not an expression of personal style. It is a signifier of personal danger, as in *Harlan County, U. S. A*, or even death, as in the street scene from *The Battle of Chile* when the camera man records the moment of his own death.

This shift from artistic expressiveness to historical revelation contributes mightily to the phenomenological effect of the observational film. *Soldier Girls, They Call Us Misfits*, its sequel, *A Respectable Life*, and Fred Wiseman's most recent film, *Models*, propose revelations about the real not as a result of direct argument, but on the basis of inferences we draw from historical evidence itself. For example, Stefan Jarl's remarkable film, *They Call Us Misfits*, contains a purely observational scene of its two 17-year-old misfits—who have left home for a life of booze, drugs and a good time in Stockholm—getting up in the morning. Kenta washes his long hair, dries it, and then meticulously combs every hair into place. Stoffe doesn't bother with his hair at all. Instead, he boils water and then makes tea by pouring it over a tea bag that is still inside its paper wrapper! We rejoin the boys in *A Respectable Life*, shot ten years later, and learn that Stoffe has nearly died on three occasions from heroin overdoses whereas Kenta has sworn off hard drugs and begun a career of sorts as a singer. At this point we may retroactively grant a denser tissue of meaning to those little morning rituals recorded a decade earlier. If so, we take them as evidence of historical determinations rather than artistic vision—even though they are only available to us as a result of textual strategies. More generally, the aural and visual evidence of what ten years of hard living do to the alert, mischievous appearance of two boys—the ruddy skin, the dark, extinguished eyes, the slurred and garbled speech, especially of Stoffe—bear meaning precisely because the films invite retroactive comparison. The films produce the structure in which "facts" themselves take on meaning precisely because they belong to a coherent series of differences. Yet, though powerful, this construction of differences remains insufficient. A simplistic line of historical progression prevails, centered as it is in *Soldier Girls* on the trope of romantic individualism. (Instead of the Great Man theory we have the Unfortunate Victim theory of history—inadequate, but compellingly presented.) And where observational cinema shifts from an individual to an institutional focus, and from a metonymic narrative model to a metaphoric one, as in the highly innovative work of Fred Wiseman, there may still be only a weak sense of constructed meaning, of a textual voice addressing us. A vigorous, active and retroactive reading is necessary before we can hear the voice of the textual system as a level distinct from the sounds and images of the evidence it adduces, while questions of adequacy remain. Wiseman's sense of context and of meaning as a function of the text itself remains weak, too easily engulfed by the fascination that allows us to mistake film for reality, the impression of the real for the experience of it. The risk of reading *Soldier Girls* or Wiseman's *Models* like a Rorshach test may require stronger counter-measures than the subtleties their complex editing and *mise-en-scène* provide.

Prompted, it would seem, by these limitations to *cinéma vérité* or observational cinema, many film-makers during the past decade have reinstituted direct address. For the most part this has meant social actors addressing us in interviews rather than a return to the voice-of-authority evidenced by a narrator. *Rosie the Riveter*, for example, tells us about the blatant hypocrisy with which women were recruited to the factories and assembly lines during World War II. A series of five women witnesses tell us how they were denied the respect granted men, told to put up with hazardous conditions "like a man," paid less, and pitted against one another racially. *Rosie* makes short shrift of the noble icon of the woman worker as seen in forties newsreels. Those films celebrated her heroic contribution to the great effort to preserve the free world from fascist dictatorship. *Rosie* destroys this myth of deeply appreciated, fully rewarded contribution without in any way undercutting the genuine fortitude, courage, and political awareness of women who experienced continual frustration in their struggles for dignified working conditions and a permanent place in the American labor force.

Using interviews, but no commentator, together with a weave of compilation footage as images of illustration, director Connie Field tells a story many of us may think we've heard, only to realize we've never heard the whole of it before.

The organization of the film depends heavily on its set of extensive interviews with former "Rosies." Their selection follows the direct-cinema tradition of filming ordinary people. But *Rosie the Riveter* broadens that tradition, as *Union Maids, The Wobblies* and *With Babies and Banners* have also done, to retrieve the memory of an "invisible" (suppressed more than forgotten) history of labor struggle. The five interviewees remember a past the film's inserted historical images reconstruct but in counterpoint: their recollection of adversity and struggle contrasts with old newsreels of women "doing their part" cheerfully.

This strategy complicates the voice of the film in an interesting way. It adds a contemporary, personal resonance to the historical, compilation footage without challenging the assumptions of that footage explicitly, as a voice-over commentary might do. We ourselves become engaged in determining how the women witnesses counterpoint these historical "documents" as well as how they articulate their own present and past consciousness in political, ethical, and feminist dimensions.

We are encouraged to believe that these voices carry less the authority of historical judgment than that of personal testimony—they are, after all, the words of apparently "ordinary women" remembering the past. As in many films that advance issues raised by the women's movement, there is an emphasis on individual but politically significant experience. *Rosie* demonstrates the power of the act of naming—the ability to find the words that render the personal political. This reliance on oral history to reconstruct the past places *Rosie the Riveter* within what is probably the predominant mode of documentary filmmaking today—films built around a string of interviews—where we also find *A Wives' Tale, With Babies and Banners, Controlling Interest, The Day After Trinity, The Trials of Alger Hiss, Rape, Word is Out, P4W: Prison for Women, Not a Love Story, Nuove Frontieras (Looking for Better Dreams),* and *The Wobblies.*

This reinstitution of direct address through the interview has successfully avoided some of the central problems of voice-over narration, namely authoritative omniscience or didactic reductionism. There is no longer the dubious claim that things are as the film presents them, organized by the commentary of an all-knowing subject. Such attempts to stand above history and explain it create a Paradox. Any attempt by a speaker to vouch for his or her own validity reminds us of the Cretan paradox: "Epimenides was a Cretan who said, 'Cretans always lie.' Was Epimenides telling the truth?" The nagging sense of a self-referential claim that can't be proven reaches greatest intensity with the most forceful assertions, which may be why viewers are often most suspicious of what an apparently omniscient Voice of Authority asserts most fervently. The emergence of so many recent documentaries built around strings of interviews strikes me as a strategic response to the recognition that neither can events speak for themselves nor can a single voice speak with ultimate authority. Interviews diffuse authority. A gap remains between the voice of a social actor recruited to the film and the voice of the film.

Not compelled to vouch for their own validity, the voices of interviewees may well arouse less suspicion. Yet a larger, constraining voice may remain to provide, or withhold, validation. In *The Sad Song of Yellow Skin, The Wilmar 8, Harlan County, U.S.A, Not a Love Story,* or *Who Killed the Fourth Ward?,* among others, the literal voice of the film-maker enters into dialogue but without the self-validating, authoritative tone of a previous tradition. (These are also voices without the self-reflexive quality found in Vertov's, Rouch's or the MacDougalls' work.) Diary-like and uncertain in *Yellow Skin*; often directed toward the women strikers as though by a fellow participant and observer in *Wilmar 8* and *Harlan County*; sharing personal reactions to pornography with a companion in *Not a Love Story*; and adopting a mock ironic tone reminiscent of Peter Falk's Columbo in *Fourth Ward*—these voices of potentially imaginary assurance instead share doubts and emotional reactions with other characters and us. As a result they seem to refuse a privileged position in relation to other characters. Of course, these less assertive authorial voices remain complicit with the controlling voice of the textual system itself, but the effect upon a viewer is distinctly different.

Still, interviews pose problems. Their occurrence is remarkably widespread—from *The Hour of the Wolf* to *The MacNeil/Lehrer Report* and from *Housing Problems* (1935) to *Harlan County, U.S.A.* The greatest problem, at least in recent documentary, has been to retain that sense of a gap between the voice of interviewees and the voice of the text as a whole. It is most obviously a problem when the interviewees display conceptual inadequacy on the issue but remain unchallenged by the film. *The Day After Trinity*, for example, traces Robert F. Oppenheimer's career but restricts itself to a Great Man theory of history. The string of interviews clearly identify Oppenheimer's role in the race to build the nuclear bomb, and his equivocations, but it never places the bomb or Oppenheimer within that larger constellation of government policies and political calculations that determined its specific use or continuing threat—even though the interviews took place in the last few years. The text not only appears to lack a voice or perspective of its own, the perspective of its character-witnesses is patently inadequate.

In documentary, when the voice of the text disappears behind characters who speak to us, we confront a specific strategy of no less ideological importance than its equivalent in fiction films. When we no longer sense that a governing voice actively provides or withholds the imprimatur of veracity according to its own purposes and assumptions, its own canons of validation, we may also sense the return of the paradox and suspicion interviews should help us escape: the word of witnesses, uncritically accepted, must provide its own validation. Meanwhile, the film becomes a rubber stamp. To varying degree this diminution of a governing voice occurs through parts of *Word is Out, The Wobblies, With Babies and Banners,* and *Prison for Women*. The sense of a hierarchy of voices becomes lost.[5] Ideally this hierarchy would uphold correct logical typing at one level (the voice of the text remains of a higher, controlling type than the voices of interviewees) without denying the inevitable collapse of logical types at another (the voice of the text is not above history but part of the very historical process upon which it confers meaning). But at present a less complex and less adequate sidetracking of paradox prevails. The film says, in effect, "Interviewees never lie." Interviewees say, "What I am telling you is the truth." We then ask, "Is the interviewee telling the truth?" but find no acknowledgement in the film of the possibility, let alone the necessity, of entertaining this question as one inescapable in all communication and signifcation.

As much as anyone, Emile de Antonio, who pioneered the use of interviews and compilation footage to organize complex historical arguments without a narrator, has also provided clear signposts for avoiding the inherent dangers of interviews.

Unfortunately, most of the film-makers adopting his basic approach have failed to heed them.

De Antonio demonstrates a sophisticated understanding of the category of the personal. He does not invariably accept the word of witnesses, nor does he adopt rhetorical strategies (Great Man theories, for example) that limit historical understanding to the personal. Something exceeds this category, and in *Point of Order, In the Year of the Pig, Millhouse: A White Comedy*, and *Underground*, among others, this excess is carried by a distinct textual voice that clearly judges the validity of what witnesses say. Just as the voice of John Huston in *The Battle of San Pietro* contests one line of argument with another (that of General Mark Clark, who claims the costs of battle were not excessive, with that of Huston, who suggests they were), so the textual voice of de Antonio contests and places the statements made by its embedded interviews, but without speaking to us directly. (In de Antonio and in his followers, there is no narrator, only the direct address of witnesses.)

This contestation is not simply the express support of some witnesses over others, for left against right. It is a systematic effect of placement that retains the gaps between levels of different logical type. De Antonio's overall expository strategy in *In the Year of the Pig*, for example, makes it clear that no one witness tells the whole truth. De Antonio's voice (unspoken but controlling) makes witnesses contend with one another to yield a point of view more distinctive to the film than to any of its witnesses (since it includes this very strategy of contention). (Similarly, the unspoken voice of *The Atomic Cafe*—evident in the extraordinarily skillful editing of government nuclear weapons propaganda films from the fifties—governs a preferred reading of the footage it compiles.) But particularly in de Antonio's work, different points of view appear. History is not a monolith, its density and outline given from the outset. On the contrary, *In the Year of the Pig*, for example, constructs perspective and historical understanding, and does so right before our eyes.

We see and hear, for example, US government spokesmen explaining their strategy and conception of the "Communist menace," whereas we do not see and hear Ho Chi Minh explain his strategy and vision. Instead, an interviewee, Paul Mus, introduces us to Ho Chi Minh descriptively while de Antonio's cutaways to Vietnamese countryside evoke an affiliation between Ho and his land and people that is absent from the words and images of American spokesmen. Ho remains an uncontained figure whose full meaning must be conferred, and inferred, from available materials as they are brought together by de Antonio. Such construction is a textual, and cinematic, act evident in the choice of supporting or ironic images to accompany interviews, in the actual juxtaposition of interviews, and even in the still images that form a pre-credit sequence inasmuch as they unmistakably refer to the American Civil War (an analogy sharply at odds with US government accounts of Communist invasion). By juxtaposing silhouettes of Civil War soldiers with GIs in Vietnam, the pre-credit sequence obliquely but clearly offers an interpretation for the events we are about to see. De Antonio does not subordinate his own voice to the way things are, to the sounds and images that are evidence of war. He acknowledges that the meaning of these images must be conferred upon them and goes about doing so in a readily understood though indirect manner.

De Antonio's hierarchy of levels and reservation of ultimate validation to the highest level (the textual system or film as a whole) differs radically from other approaches. John Lowenthal's *The Trials of Alger Hiss*, for example, is a totally subservient endorsement of Hiss's legalistic strategies. Similarly, *Hollywood on Trial* shows no independence from the perhaps politically expedient but disingenuous line adopted by the Hollywood 10 over thirty years ago—that HUAC's pattern of subpoenas to friendly and unfriendly witnesses primarily threatened the civil liberties of ordinary citizens (though it certainly did so) rather than posing a more specific threat to the CPUSA and American left (where it clearly did the greatest damage). By contrast, even in *Painters Painting* and *Underground*, where de Antonio seems unusually close to validating uncritically what interviewees say, the subtle voice of his *mise-en-scène* preserves the gap, conveying a strong sense of the distance between the sensibilities or politics of those interviewed and those of the larger public to whom they speak.

De Antonio's films produce a world of dense complexity: they embody a sense of constraint and over-determination. Not everyone can be believed. Not everything is true. Characters do not emerge as the autonomous shapers of a personal destiny. De Antonio proposes ways and means by which to reconstruct the past dialectically, as Fred Wiseman reconstructs the present dialectically.[6] Rather than appearing to collapse itself into the consciousness of character witnesses, the film retains an independent consciousness, a voice of its own. The film's own consciousness (surrogate for ours) probes, remembers, substantiates, doubts. It questions and believes, including itself. It assumes the voice of personal consciousness at the same time as it examines the very category of the personal. Neither omniscient deity nor obedient mouthpiece, de Antonio's rhetorical voice seduces us by embodying those qualities of insight, skepticism, judgment and independence we would like to appropriate for our own. Nonetheless, though he is closer to a modernist, self-reflexive strategy than any other documentary film-maker in America—with the possible exception of the more experimental feminist film-maker, Jo Ann Elam—de Antonio remains clearly apart from this tendency. He is more a Newtonian than an Einsteinian observer of events; he insists on the activity of fixing meaning, but it is meaning that does, finally, appear to reside "out there" rather than insisting on the activity of producing that "fix" from which meaning itself derives.

There are lessons here we would think de Antonio's successors would be quick to learn. But, most frequently, they have not. The interview remains a problem. Subjectivity, consciousness, argumentative form and voice remain unquestioned in documentary theory and practice. Often, film-makers simply choose to interview characters with whom they agree. A weaker sense of skepticism, a diminished self-awareness of the film-maker as producer of meaning or history prevails, yielding a flatter, less dialectical sense of history and a simpler, more idealized sense of character. Characters threaten to emerge as stars—flashpoints of inspiring, and imaginary, coherence contradictory to their ostensible status as ordinary people.[7]

These problems emerge in three of the best history films we have (and in the pioneering gay film, *Word is Out*), undermining their great importance on other levels. *Union Maids, With Babies and Banners*, and *The Wobblies* flounder on the axis of personal respect and historical recall. The films simply suppose that things were as the participant-witnesses recall them, and lest we doubt, the film-makers respectfully find images of illustration to substantiate the claim. (The resonance set up in *Rosie the Riveter* between interviews and compilation footage establishes a perceptible sense of a textual voice that makes this film a more sophisticated, though not self-reflexive, version of the interview-based documentary.) What characters omit to say, so do these films, most noticeably regarding the role of the CPUSA in *Union Maids* and *With Babies and Banners. Banners*, for example, contains one instance when a witness mentions the helpful knowledge she gained from Communist Party members. Immediately, though, the film cuts to unrelated footage of a violent attack on workers by a goon squad. It is as if the textual voice, rather than provide independent assessment, must go so far as to find diversionary material to offset presumably harmful comments by witnesses themselves!

These films naively endorse limited, selective recall. The tactic flattens witnesses into a series of imaginary puppets conforming to a line. Their recall becomes distinguishable more by differences in force of personality than by differences in perspective. Backgrounds loaded with iconographic meanings transform witnesses further into stereotypes (shipyards, farms, union halls abound, or for the gays and lesbians in *Word is Out*, bedrooms and the bucolic out-of-doors). We sense a great relief when characters step out of these closed, iconographic frames and into more open-ended ones, but such "release" usually occurs only at the end of the films where it also signals the achievement of expository closure—another kind of frame. We return to the simple claim, "Things were as these witnesses describe them, why contest them?"—a claim which is a dissimulation and a disservice to both film theory and political praxis. On the contrary, as de Antonio and Wiseman demonstrate quite differently, Things signify, but only if we make them comprehensible.[8]

Documentaries with a more sophisticated grasp of the historical realm establish a preferred reading by a textual system that asserts its own voice in contrast to the voices it recruits or observes. Such films confront us with an alternative to our own hypotheses about what kind of things populate the world, what relations they sustain, and what meanings they bear for us. The film operates as an autonomous whole, as we do. It is greater than its parts and orchestrates them: (1) the recruited voices, the recruited sounds and images; (2) the textual "voice" spoken by the style of the film as a whole (how its multiplicity of codes, including those pertaining to recruited voices are orchestrated into a singular, controlling pattern); and (3) the surrounding historical context, including the viewing event itself, which the textual voice cannot successfully rise above or fully control. The film is thus a simulacrum or external trace of the production of meaning we undertake ourselves every day, every moment. We see not an image of imaginary unchanging coherence, magically represented on a screen, but the evidence of an historically rooted act of making things meaningful comparable to our own historically situated acts of comprehension.

With de Antonio's films, *The Atomic Cafe, Rape*, or *Rosie the Riveter* the active counter-pointing of the text reminds us that its meaning is produced. This foregrounding of an active production of meaning by a textual system may also heighten our conscious sense of self as something also produced by codes that extend beyond ourselves. An exaggerated claim, perhaps, but still suggestive of the difference in effect of different documentary strategies and an indication of the importance of the self-reflexive strategy itself.

Self-reflexiveness can easily lead to an endless regression. It can prove highly appealing to an intelligentsia more interested in "good form" than in social change. Yet interest in self-reflexive forms is not purely an academic question. *Cinéma vérité* and its variants sought to address certain limitations in the voice-of-god tradition. The interview-oriented film sought to address limitations apparent in the bulk of *cinéma vérité*, and the self-reflexive documentary addresses the limitations of assuming that subjectivity and both the social and textual positioning of the self (as film-maker or viewer) are ultimately not problematic.

Modernist thought in general challenges this assumption. A few documentary film-makers, going as far back as Dziga Vertov and certainly including Jean Rouch, and the hard-to-categorize Jean-Luc Godard, adopt the basic epistemological assumption in their work that knowledge and the position of the self in relation to the mediator of knowledge, a given text, are socially and formally constructed and should be shown to be so. Rather than inviting paralysis before a centerless labyrinth, however, such a perspective restores the dialectic between self and other: neither the "out there" nor the "in here" contains its own inherent meaning. The *process* of constructing meaning overshadows constructed meanings. And at a time when modernist experimentation is old-hat within the avant-garde and a fair amount of fiction film-making, it remains almost totally unheard of among documentary film-makers, especially in North America. It is not political documentarists who have been the leading innovators. Instead it is a handful of ethnographic film-makers like Timothy Asch (*The Ax Fight*), John Marshall (*N!ai*) and David and Judith MacDougall who, in their meditations on scientific method and visual communication, have done the most provocative experimentation.

Take the MacDougalls' *Wedding Camels* (part of the Turkana trilogy), for example. The film, set in Northern Kenya, explores the preparations for a Turkana wedding in day-to-day detail. It mixes direct and indirect address to form a complex whole made up of two levels of historical reference—evidence and argument—and two levels of textual structure—observation and exposition.

Though *Wedding Camels* is frequently observational and very strongly rooted in the texture of everyday life, the film-makers' presence receives far more frequent acknowledgment than it does in *Soldier Girls*, or Wiseman's films, or most other observational work. Lorang, the bride's father and central figure in the dowry negotiations, says at one point, with clear acknowledgment of the film-makers' presence, "They [Europeans] never marry our daughters. They always hold back their animals." At other moments we hear David MacDougall ask questions of Lorang or others off-camera much as we do in *The Wilmar 8* or *In the Year of the Pig*. (This contrasts with *The Wobblies, Union Maids* and *With Babies and Banners* where the questions to which participant witnesses respond are not heard.) Sometimes these queries invite characters to reflect on events we observe in detail, like the dowry arrangements themselves. On these occasions they introduce a vivid level of self-reflexiveness into the characters' performance as well as into the film's structure, something that is impossible in interview-based films that give us no sense of a character's present but only use his or her words as testimony about the past.

Wedding Camels also makes frequent use of intertitles which mark off one scene from another to develop a mosaic structure that necessarily admits to its own lack of completeness even as individual facets appear to exhaust a given encounter. This sense of both incompleteness and exhaustion, as well as the radical shift of perceptual space involved in going from apparently three-dimensional images to two-dimensional graphics that comment on or frame the image, generates a strong sense of a hierarchical and self-referential ordering.

For example, in one scene Naingoro, sister to the bride's mother, says, "Our daughters are not our own. They are born to be given out." The implicit lack of completeness to individual identity apart from social exchange then receives elaboration through an interview sequence with Akai, the bride. The film poses questions by means of intertitles and sandwiches Akai's responses, briefly, between them. One intertitle, for example, phrases its question more or less as follows, "We asked Akai whether a Turkana woman chooses her husband or if her parents choose for her." Such phrasing brings the film-maker's intervention strongly into the foreground.

The structure of this passage suggests some of the virtues of a hybrid style: the titles serve as another indicator of a textual voice apart from that of the characters represented. They also differ from most documentary titles which, since the silent days of *Nanook*, have worked like a graphic "voice" of authority. In *Wedding Camels* the titles, in their mock-interactive structure, remain closely aligned with the particulars of person and place rather than appearing to issue from an omniscient consciousness. They show clear awareness of how a particular meaning is being produced by a particular act of intervention. This is not presented as a grand revelation but as a simple truth that is only remarkable for its rarity in documentary film. These particular titles also display both a wry sense of humor and a clear perception of the meaning an individual's marriage has for him or her as well as for others (a vital means of countering, among other things, the temptation of an ethnocentric reading or judgment). By "violating" the coherence of a social actor's diegetic space, intertitles also lessen the tendency for the interviewee to inflate to the proportions of a star-witness. By acting self-reflexively such strategies call the status of the interview itself into question and diminish its tacit claim to tell the whole truth. Other signifying choices, which function like Brechtian distancing devices, would include the separate "spaces" of image and intertitle for question/response; the highly structured and abbreviated question/answer format; the close up, portrait-like framing of a social actor that pries her away from a matrix of on-going activities or a stereotypical background, and the clear acknowledgment that such fabrications exist to serve the purposes of the film rather than to capture an unaffected reality.

Though modest in tone, *Wedding Camels* demonstrates a structural sophistication well beyond that of almost any other documentary film work today. Whether its modernist strategies can be yoked to a more explicitly political perspective (without restricting itself to the small avant-garde audience that exists for the Godards and Chantal Akermans), is less a question than a challenge still haunting us, considering the limitations of most interview-based films.

Changes in documentary strategy bear a complex relation to history. Self-reflexive strategies seem to have a particularly complex historical relation to documentary form since they are far less peculiar to it than the voice-of-god, *cinéma vérité* or interview-based strategies. Although they have been available to documentary (as to narrative) since the 'teens, they have never been as popular in North America as in Europe or in other regions (save among an avant-garde). Why they have recently made an effective appearance within the documentary domain is a matter requiring further exploration. I suspect we are dealing with more than a reaction to the limitations of the currently dominant interview-based farm. Large cultural preferences concerning the voicing of dramatic as well as documentary material seem to be changing. In any event, the most recent appearances of self-reflexive strategies correspond very clearly to deficiencies in attempts to translate highly ideological, written anthropological practices into a proscriptive agenda for a visual anthropology (neutrality, descriptiveness, objectivity, "just the facts" and so on). It is very heartening to see that the realm of the possible for documentary film has now expanded to include strategies of reflexivity that may eventually serve political as well as scientific ends.

NOTES

1. Many of the distinctive characteristics of documentary are examined broadly in *Ideology and the Image* (Bloomington: Indiana University Press, 1981), pp. 170–284. Here I shall concentrate on more recent films and some of the particular problems they pose.
2. Films referred to in the article or instrumental in formulating the issues of self-reflexive documentary form include: *The Atomic Cafe* (USA, Kevin Rafferty, Jayne Loader, Pierce Rafferty, 1982), *Controlling Interest* (USA, SF Newsreel, 1978), *The Day After Trinity* (USA, Jon Else, 1980), *Harlan County, U.S.A* (USA, Barbara Kopple, 1976), *Hollywood on Trial* (USA, David Halpern, Jr., 1976), *Models* (USA, Fred Wiseman, 1981), *Nuove Frontiera (Looking for Better Dreams)* (Switzerland,

Remo Legnazzi, 1981), *On Company Business* (USA, Allan Francovich, 1981), *P4W: Prison for Women* (Canada, Janice Cole, Holly Dale, 1981), *Rape* (USA, JoAnn Elam, 1977), *A Respectable Life* (Sweden, Stefan Jarl, 1980), *Rosie the Riveter* (USA, Connie Field, 1980); *The Sad Song of Yellow Skin* (Canada, NFB—Michael Rubbo, 1970), *Soldier Girls* (USA, Nick Broomfield, Joan Churchill, 1981); *They Call Us Misfits* (Sweden, Jan Lindquist, Stefan Jarl, c. 1969), *Not a Love Story* (Canada, NFB—Bonnie Klein, 1981, *The Trials of Alger Hiss* (USA, John Lowenthal, 1980), *Union Maids* (USA, Jim Klein, Julia Reichert, Miles Mogulescu, 1976), *Who Killed the Fourth Ward?* (USA, James Blue, 1978), The Wilmar 8 (USA, Lee Grant, 1980), *With Babies and Banners* (USA, Women's Labor History Film Project, 1978), *A Wives' Tale* (Canada, Sophie Bissonnette, Martin Duckworth, Joyce Rock, 1980), *The Wobblies* (USA, Stuart Bird, Deborah Shaffer, 1979), *Word is Out* (USA, Mariposa Collective, 1977).

3. Perhaps the farthest extremes of evidence and argument occur with pornography and propaganda: what would pornography be without its evidence, what would propaganda be without its arguments?
4. Without models of documentary strategy that invite us to reflect on the construction of social reality, we have only a corrective act of negation ("this is not reality, it is neither omniscient nor objective") rather than an affirmative act of comprehension ("this is a text, these are its assumptions, this is the meaning it produces"). The lack of an invitation to assume a positive stance handicaps us in our efforts to understand the position we occupy; refusing a position proffered to us is far from affirming a position we actively construct. It is similar to the difference between refusing to "buy" the messages conveyed by advertising, at least entirely, while still lacking any alternative non-fetishistic presentation of commodities that can help us gain a different "purchase" on their relative use- and exchange-value. In many ways, this problem of moving from refusal to affirmation, from protest at the way things are to the construction of durable alternatives, is precisely the problem of the American left. Modernist strategies have something to contribute to the resolution of this problem.
5. After completing this article, I read Jeffrey Youdelman's "Narration, Invention and History" (*Cineaste*, 12:2, pp. 8–15) which makes a similar point with a somewhat different set of examples. His discussion of imaginative, lyrical uses of commentary in the thirties and forties is particularly instructive.
6. Details of de Antonio's approach are explored in Tom Waugh's "Emile de Antonio and the New Documentary of the Seventies," *Jump Cut*, no. 10/11 (1976), pp. 33–39 and of Wiseman's in my *Ideology and the Image*, pp. 208–236.
7. An informative discussion of the contradiction between character witnesses with unusual abilities and the rhetorical attempt to make them signifiers of ordinary workers, particularly in *Union Maids*, occur in Noel King's "Recent 'Political' Documentary—Notes on *Union Maids* and *Harlan County, USA*," *Screen*, vol. 22, no. 2 (1981), pp. 7–18.
8. In this vein, Noel King comments "So in the case of these documentaries (*Union Maids, With Babies and Banners, Harlan County, U.S.A*) we might notice the way a discourse of morals or ethics suppresses one of politics and the way a discourse of a subject's individual responsibility suppresses any notion of a discourse on the social and linguistic formation of subjects" ("Recent 'Political' Documentary," p. 11). But we might also say, as the film-makers seem to, "This is how the participants saw their struggle and it is well-worth preserving" even though we may wish they did not do so slavishly. There is a difference between criticizing films because they fail to demonstrate the theoretical sophistication of certain analytic methodologies and criticizing them because their textual organization is inadequate to the phenomena they describe.

JAMES ROY MACBEAN

TWO LAWS FROM AUSTRALIA, ONE WHITE, ONE BLACK

The Recent Past and the Challenging Future of Ethnographic Film (1983)

Recently, a new documentary film dealing with Australian Aboriginal peoples and their historical struggles to preserve (or win back) their traditional lands has been screened in the US, mostly on the West Coast but also in New York City, where it was presented in October at the 1982 Margaret Mead Film Festival. Completed in 1981, *Two Laws* is a feature-length documentary that succeeds both in being informative and in undercutting many of our expectations regarding ethnographic films in particular, and documentary films in general.

Already hailed in Australia, where its subject matter—Aboriginal land rights—is considered politically controversial, *Two Laws* was nominated for (although it did not win) the Australian Film Institute's 1982 award for best documentary. At a running time of two hours and ten minutes, *Two Laws* is an ambitious, complex, problematic film that was made *collectively* (and I mean this word quite literally and rigorously) by two white Australian film-makers, Alessandro Cavadini and Carolyn Strachan, and the Borroloola Aboriginal community from the remote Gulf of Carpentaria region of Australia's Northern Territory.

The questions raised by *Two Laws* will have to be taken seriously in ethnographic film circles, and elsewhere as well, if for no other reason (but there are others) than the fact that this is a film, unlike 99.9% of ethnographic films,[1] in which the traditional (or tribal) peoples themselves collectively controlled the decision-making processes of what to film and how to film it—even down to what lens to use on the camera. That the results, cinematically, look so different from what we are accustomed to seeing in even the "best" ethnographic films up to now, certainly causes us to sit up and take notice, and to raise questions (and doubts) about how ethnographic film-makers have been proceeding.

International Ethnographic Film Conference 1978, Canberra, Australia

In addition to raising important questions, *Two Laws* may also provide at least a tentative answer to a question posed in 1978 at the International Ethnographic Film Conference, which I attended, in Canberra, Australia. This conference was a major event in ethnographic film circles; it had strong participation from—and reverberations among—Australia's Aboriginal peoples; and several of the individuals who subsequently went on to collaborate on the film *Two Laws* participated in this conference; so it seems important to offer, by way of background, a summary of the way various issues in ethnographic film were discussed at this lively and seminal conference.

One conference participant, Roger Sandall (himself an ethnographic film-maker in Australia) reported in *Sight and Sound* (Autumn 1978) on the remarkable and volatile mix of people gathered from around the globe at this conference—a mix that included not only ethnographic film-makers and anthropologists but also, for a change, various representatives of the traditional peoples the ethnographers usually study. Of course, most conferences, as Colin Young (who featured prominently in this one) has recently pointed out, are really about *power*. Young, head of Britain's National Film School, puts the issues this way:

> Go to most conferences and the subject, no matter what is on the agenda, is power. Which methodology is going to win out? People invest in their methods to the exclusion of others. The method defines you, and you it. If I criticize your method I harm you. It's a way of saying that I don't like you. . . . Supporters of a methodology are racist with respect to all others.[2]

At the 1978 conference, *power* was certainly very much at issue. Indeed, it was even placed on the official agenda by the conference convenors, David and Judith MacDougall—eminent ethnographic film-makers themselves, and resident directors of the Film Unit of the Australian Institute of Aboriginal Studies, which hosted the conference. Sympathetic with Aboriginal peoples' increasingly vociferous demands to be provided access to the media and to the means of film and television *production*, the MacDougalls had scheduled a session in the conference agenda to explore these issues. However, the amount of time allotted was not considered sufficient by many invited participants, who requested, and were granted, a session on these issues, which was scheduled for the final day of the conference.

Before that final day, the struggle for power was carried out in the territory staked out by Colin Young—that of rival documentary film methodologies. As the conference's senior statesman, Young presented the opening salvo, offering his own summary of documentary film history. Young spoke of the accomplishments, but mainly of the dangers and limitations of the Grierson approach ("too polemical and didactic"); of the virtues of the Flaherty approach ("he got close to his subjects"); of the fundamental flaws in Robert Gardner's filmic strategies in *Dead Birds* ("he *tells* us on the sound track information not substantiated by the image"); and of the refreshingly participatory filmic strategies of Jean Rouch ("in *Turou et Bitti* the film-maker almost functions as the combustion element in a ritual leading to trance").

In addition, Young turned over the podium briefly to Timothy Asch, who delivered homage to John Marshall for his longstanding dedication to filming the !Kung Bushmen of the Kalahari. (Asch, a former associate of Marshall's, has gone on to make a number of important films on the Yanomamo of the Orinoco Basin in collaboration with anthropologist Napoleon Chagnon.) Finally, Young also spoke of the breakthroughs made in the early sixties by the practitioners, mostly French, Canadian and American, of *cinéma vérité*.

All this could be taken as uncontroversial documentary film "history"; but there was also a tendentious side to Young's presentation. As he toted up the assets and liabilities of each documentary approach, Young wove a clearly discernible thread of apparent historical "progress" into the chaotic fabric of documentary film history, in such a way that, in his account, it would seem to reach some at-least-for-the-present optimum realization of its potential (and, implicitly, of its "realist vocation") in the contemporary methodology of what Young calls "observational cinema."

This approach consists of a refined version of *cinéma vérité*'s ability to use light-weight, unobtrusive equipment and a minimal crew (often only two persons) to film long takes in synchronous sound of the ordinary interactions and conversations of people going about their regular daily lives. It is demonstrated, Young asserted, in the films of David and Judith MacDougall as well as in the *Vermont Conversations* series by Hancock and DiGioia (and in their film *Naim and Jabar* for the *Faces of Change* project), and in Roger Graef's studies of decision-making for the two British television series, *The Space Between Words* and *Decision*.

As Colin Young would be the first to admit, there is a decidedly "incestuous" cast to the lineup he proposes under the rubric of observational cinema. The MacDougalls, Hancock and DiGioia all got their start in film as students in the ethnographic film program started by Young (and Walter Goldschmidt) at UCLA in the late sixties. Of course, the community of film-makers, anthropologists, and other scholars involved in the world of ethnographic film is a fairly small community in any case. We have all known one another from way back. I have known the MacDougalls as close friends for about twenty years; and I have known Colin Young (through the MacDougalls) nearly as long. Friendship notwithstanding, I would have no hesitation in picking the MacDougalls' films (from their first, *To Live With Herds*, right up to their latest films dealing with Australian Aboriginal peoples) as representing the best of contemporary tendencies in ethnographic film. However, I must take issue with Colin Young on one point, because I am not convinced (nor was I at the 1978 conference) that the complex filmic strategies employed by the MacDougalls are done justice by the term "observational cinema." (I shall deal with these issues in the following section of this essay.)

Where Young's historical survey of documentary film at the conference is concerned, Bill Nichols pointed out in his remarks to the conference that while Young's presentation had been interesting as a personal account of how Young, and presumably others, had found their own path through the thicket of documentary methodologies, the thicket itself had not really been cleared for cultivation on solid theoretical ground; and the discussions were strangely devoid of recourse to recent developments in film theory, communications theory or anthropology itself.

Indeed, it became clear in ensuing days that what was being presented was a low-keyed, disarmingly attractive yet tendentious version of both the history and the present situation of ethnographic film—as seen by proponents of one particular school of documentary methodology. The morning after Young's opening presentation, the mantle was passed to James Blue, a long-time friend and associate of both Young and the MacDougalls, who announced that his contribution would be to demonstrate in more detail, and with specific illustrations, the general line set out by Young's opening talk. Blue's presentation emphasized the virtues of Robert Flaherty's filmic strategies, exemplified by a seal-hunting sequence from Flaherty's *Nanook*, which was projected side-by-side with a sequence (also showing seal-hunting) from Asen Balikci's Netsilik Eskimo series of films.

Blue's argument was that Balikci, although one of our contemporary ethnographic filmmakers, had reverted to an older, anachronistic and more "didactic" style of shooting and editing ethnographic film. Blue's comparison of the two sequences was all to the favor of Flaherty, who was credited with simply letting the action unfold in front of the camera instead of breaking the action up into different edited pieces shot from different camera angles.

The only trouble—and Blue, sensing this, got off to an awkward and somewhat nervous start—was that the morning's audience wasn't ready to buy this praise of Flaherty, at least partly because the previous evening's conference event had turned into a tumultuous debate touched off by a screening of Flaherty's 1934 film *Man of Aran*, followed by George Stoney's just-completed documentary exploration of *Robert Flaherty's "Man of Aran": How The Myth Was Made*. Stoney's film, while appreciative of Flaherty's genius for poetic imagery, had popped the lid off all the distortions and omissions in Flaherty's highly romanticized depiction of life on the Aran Islands off Ireland.

Many in the audience at the conference's première screening of Stoney's revelatory documentary had been incensed at what they now saw to be Flaherty's falsification of the life he had purported to be documenting. Particularly troublesome was Flaherty's total lack of interest in the actual sociopolitical affairs of the Islanders, who, in his film, are represented by only three people—significantly, a nuclear family of man, wife and son—whose highly romanticized struggle for survival in an awesomely inhospitable Nature becomes the "whole" picture.

On this issue Stoney's film effectively documents how distorted—and *politically* skewed—is Flaherty's depiction of the allegedly arid and inhospitable soil of the Aran Islands. Showing us the very same rugged, rocky terrain that Flaherty had filmed, Stoney then makes a small pan with his camera to show that with this simple camera movement one can see the lush, fertile agricultural land-holdings that were in Flaherty's day and still are in the hands of a few absentee landlords. The richest of these, Stoney observes, had in fact turned over his baronial house, the largest on the islands, to the Flahertys, where the film-maker and his wife Frances had enjoyed a quasi-feudal relationship to the impoverished Islanders during their stay.

Such revelations as these had made their points with the conference audience. In Flaherty's retreat from the realities of the contemporary situation in favor of a highly romanticized vision of ways of life no longer practiced, many conference participants saw a betrayal of documentary film's mission to "show it like it is." Small wonder, then, that James Blue (whose subsequent death in 1980 is a loss to us all) met with such resistance when he valiantly went ahead with his presentation of the virtues of Flaherty's filmic strategies. He prefaced his remarks with an account of how he too, like others in the audience, had been influenced by his years studying film in the heady political milieu of Paris; how he too had gone through a phase of politicization during which he sought to root out all traces of "fascist" film style from his film-making repertory; and how he too had wanted, indeed still wanted, to make films that were politically constructive. But gradually he had discovered, he told us, that Flaherty's way of letting the camera simply observe what was happening had seemed to him the most honest and direct way to get at the larger truth and complexity of a situation.

It was all very affably, albeit defensively put by Blue; and there was much to consider in what he said. And yet, to many in the audience, Blue's championing of Flaherty, and his treatment of his own "politicized phase" as if it were merely a childhood stage one outgrew, smacked of an attempt to take the edge off any politically activist approach to documentary film-making. At least this is how it was "read" by many of the young Australian documentary film-makers present, who also construed it as a pitch to tone down the political element in their films to make them more acceptable to the potential television market, which, according to both Young and Blue, was ready to open its doors to ethnographic film.

The possibility of television distribution, however, was perceived by the Australians to be the proverbial carrot held out in front of the horse who allows himself to be fitted with blinders. The modest success in Great Britain of Brian Moser's "Disappearing World" series of ethnographic films for Granada Television was hardly persuasive, especially when Granada's representatives to the Canberra Conference acknowledged that very few of the "Disappearing World" films had taken up in any way the vital *political* issues of why so many (but not all) tribal or traditional societies are in danger of "disappearing" in today's world.

To many conference participants, the singleminded emphasis on an "observational" camera-style (coupled with an apparent insensitivity to the political dynamics of ethnographic film-making) began to wear very thin; and a current of reaction set in against the "house style" proposed by Young and Blue. Filmmakers Cavadini and Strachan, for example, later expressed their frustration with the apolitical approach that dominated the early days of the conference.

> We've been amazed at the way ethnographic film-makers deny that their films are political. This denial is enforced by a claim that the camera in particular is neutral and observational; but what is in fact produced are visions of the exotic or the romantic. This came out very strongly at the Canberra Conference. There is an explicit lack of theorising about the politics of going into and disrupting a community, or taking information and images from one society to be exploited by another.[3]

Moreover, there were problems, many of us at the conference felt, with the argument James Blue developed in his comparison of the Flaherty and Balikci footage. To present an alternative view, I pointed out that one could argue that Balikci's way of breaking a complicated process (of seal-hunting) into different shots taken from different camera angles at least had the merits of (1) revealing details of the action that might not be visible or noticed from one single camera position; and, (2) openly acknowledging the filmmaking process—of selecting camera angles, of shooting, of editing, etc.—at the same time as it explored the Eskimo's process of seal-hunting. In short, Balikci's filmic strategies (including his avoidance of omniscient narration on the sound track) could be credited with being both *process-oriented* and *self-reflexive*.

By contrast, I observed, Flaherty's filmic strategies in the seal-hunting sequence from *Nanook* could be seen as mystifying the processes both of seal-hunting and of filming. Flaherty sets up his camera in advance at a small hole in the ice towards which Nanook is seen to make his way from the distant background, as if searching the ice-flow for telltale signs of the presence of a seal's airhole. Thus, in effect, Flaherty gives the camera the classic, privileged narrator's point of view that implies—but does not openly acknowledge—the godlike omniscience of the film-maker while reinforcing the seemingly unimpeachable authority of the information provided by the image. Such an "impression of reality" was especially problematic, I argued, in the case of Flaherty. After all, in *Nanook* as in *Man of*

Aran, the apparent "reality" being filmed is an extremely contrived re-enactment of ways of life that were never quite as romantic as Flaherty makes them out to be, and which are *not*, in any case, the ways of life of the contemporary people he is actually filming.

Moreover, even if the viewer does not notice that Flaherty's camera has been set up in advance at the very spot Nanook eventually "discovers," there is ample evidence to tip off the fact that this entire sequence is staged for the camera. At Flaherty's urging, no doubt, Nanook hams up his demonstration of the process of spearing a seal through the breathing hole in the ice. In fact, the scene is turned into slapstick comedy, with Nanook ostensibly being tugged this way and that by the not yet visible seal beneath the ice. Finally, when the seal is ultimately hauled up through the ice, it is so obviously long-dead—and apparently frozen solid—that the entire sequence becomes ridiculous.

At the Canberra conference, the appearance of the dead seal was greeted with great hoots of laughter. Jokes were made of "the observational style of filming a frozen-seal hunt." Soon nearly everyone was taking pot shots at "observational cinema" and at Flaherty—with Blue and Young still valiantly attempting to defend their position. Finally, the session was adjourned, but many participants kept right on arguing the issues, moving in for the kill, wielding their small personal tape recorders like weapons as they endeavored to pin down, for the record, their respective antagonists. At this point, the event was laughingly dubbed "the battle of the tape recorders"—a battle of ritual warfare enacted by a strange and exotic tribe of academics and media professionals. In a verbal play on the title of James Blue's own latest film, *Who Killed The Fourth Ward?* (about redevelopment in Houston, Texas), it was jocularly suggested that a sequel to the conference be planned, under the prospective title, "Who Killed Observational Cinema?"

This is the question I alluded to at the beginning of this article—the question to which the 1981 film *Two Laws* provides at least a tentative answer. Of course, one film, even such a probing and forceful film as *Two Laws*, does not by itself bring about the imminent demise of "observational cinema." Nor would I wish for its demise. I am confident that there will continue to be a place (or, rather, certain types of ethnographic and documentary situations) where the filmic strategies associated with observational cinema will still be fruitfully employed. However, what *Two Laws* may be instrumental in laying to rest is a notion of observational cinema as a panacea that could cure all the infirmities of ethnographic or documentary film-making.

[. . .]

Two Laws: The Theory and Practice of Ethnographic Film

Having voiced their demands loud and clear at the 1978 Canberra Conference, and having obtained from the Institute of Aboriginal Studies a strengthened commitment to proceed faster in providing Aboriginal peoples access to equipment and to film-making instruction, Australia's Aboriginal peoples also intensified their efforts to enlist some of Australia's white documentary film-makers to work with the black communities in making films that would *express* rather than merely *observe* Aboriginal culture. Many Aboriginal communities initiated requests for films to be made, and many of these requests were directed to David and Judith MacDougall in their roles as Director and Assistant Director of the Film Unit of the Institute of Aboriginal Studies.

Already heavily involved in making a series of films requested by the Aurukun Aboriginal community (which has been in the center of Australia's most controversial political struggles over land rights, mining rights, and conflicts of federal and state jurisdiction), the MacDougalls and their staff simply couldn't handle all the requests for films coming from various Aboriginal communities.

However, the Borroloola people were determined that they wanted to make a film dealing with the history of their community. Leo Finlay had seen *Protected*, a film on the Palm Island Aboriginal community made collectively by two white Australian film-makers, Alessandro Cavadini and Carolyn Strachan, in collaboration with the Palm Island community. *Protected* was a very impressive film; so Leo Finlay paid a visit to Cavadini and Strachan in Sydney and asked them for help in making a film on the Borroloola community. Cavadini and Strachan accepted the invitation, went to Borroloola, and spent the first two months traveling from one Aboriginal settlement or camp to another, learning their proper "skin" or kinship relation within the Borroloola Aboriginal society, and discussing what sort of film the Aboriginal peoples wanted to make.

From the beginning, it was clear what the general outline of the film was to be. The Borroloola community wanted to provide a historical background to their insistence that their Aboriginal system of law was, in fact, just that—a system of law which regulated their interactions with one another and with land and property. This was important, they felt, because preliminary hearings in land rights cases during the seventies had demonstrated that white judges tended to discount Aboriginal land claims based on Aboriginal tradition whenever they were in conflict with land claims based on leases, titles and contracts recognized by white law.

Even before commencing filming, Cavadini and Strachan found that the Aboriginal sense of "law" pervaded everything the Borroloola community did. When Cavadini and Strachan arranged evening screenings of films dealing with land rights issues, the next morning there would be a formal meeting, according to Aboriginal law, where the community would collectively discuss the previous night's films, debate their strengths and weaknesses, and explore their potential use, to them and to their film, of this or that stylistic approach. Gradually, in this way, the community collectively planned what it wanted to film and how it wanted to film it.

Cavadini and Strachan gradually realized that this traditional collective decision-making process was itself a fundamental feature of Aboriginal law, that "leaders" were only ceremonial figures; and that correlatively, the formal community meeting could provide the structural base of the film. Once this was decided, it became obvious how these formal meetings were to be filmed. As Cavadini and Strachan explain it,

> Because there isn't any television and few films had been seen, the people were unfamiliar with the whole of Western film culture, so their ideas came largely from Aboriginal structure. For instance, when we got down to filming there was automatically only one position for the camera and one position for the sound recordist—because everyone has their place in a highly structured spatial arrangement. Men sit in one position, women in another, and each individual sits with particular relatives. So the determinations had to do with the tribal structure into which the film fitted as opposed to being outside it.[4]

Moreover, as Cavadini and Strachan point out, not only camera and sound positions were engendered by Aboriginal sense of law and structure, but also even the choice of what lens to use on the camera was engendered this way.

> During those first two months we did do a number of tests to try out different ideas, and the choice was made to shoot the entire film with a wide-angle lens. It was the one that people responded to and liked. With a wide-angle lens you can include much more in the shot than with a standard lens, but it's not so appropriate for close-ups. If someone wants to make a statement, others have to be present to make that statement possible—to confirm or contradict it. Sometimes there was disagreement between people but it's presented as a group discussion as opposed to one individual being the authority.[5]

The title, it was decided, should be *Two Laws*; and the film should begin with a shot of a formal meeting where Leo Finlay introduces Cavadini and Strachan by saying simply "I think you know these two, Alessandro and Carolyn; they're going to help us make a film, and it's our film so let's make a good film." The camera, with its wide-angle lens, pans right to left across the seated community at the formal meeting, men on one side, women on another; and as the camera completes its pan we even see the sound recordist—a woman, Carolyn—in her designated place alongside the Borroloola women.

The film overall is divided into four parts, arranged chronologically (although with some overlaps) into sections called "Police Times," "Welfare Times," "Struggle for Our Land," and "Living with Two Laws." "Police Times" deals with the situation in the thirties, a period still vividly remembered by a few older members of the Borroloola community but largely unknown by most younger community members, who only learned of these times and events in the process of making the film.

Although "Police Times" focuses on one particular event that happened in 1933, especially as this event is recalled—and reenacted—by people who participated in it, there is a sense in which the present community's effort to grasp an understanding of their past is far more important than a reconstituting of the past. As Cavadini and Strachan explain it,

> The way Aboriginal people approach history is very different from the way we see history as located firmly in the past. People talk about history in the present tense, use the first person, employ dialogue, re-enact events. In everyday life people tell stories that happened yesterday or happened one hundred years ago.[6]

The task of re-telling the past—specifically, the events of 1933, as characteristic of those times—is carried out in a complex, sophisticated combination of oral history (story-telling) and re-enactment *plus analytical commentary* on both the telling and the acting-out of history. Moreover, the re-enactment includes its own *self-reflexive* component of *analysis*, for the re-enactment is presented in a way that emphasizes the group process of play-acting. Aboriginal community members sit in rows on the ground as the camera pans or tracks to pause as each one introduces himself by saying "my name is X, and I'm playing the part of Dolly . . . or Doris . . ." and so on.

Furthermore, although they filmed enough re-enactment footage to comprise a 90-minute drama film, the Borroloola community decided not to go that route, preferring, for political reasons, to emphasize the overall *context* of events rather than the events themselves. Finally, the 1933 events—a forced march of Aboriginal peoples who were rounded up by one Constable Stott, who beat them into a forced confession of killing and eating a bullock (steer) owned by a white rancher—were judged too brutal in their depiction of violence to be used in the finished film. So it was decided

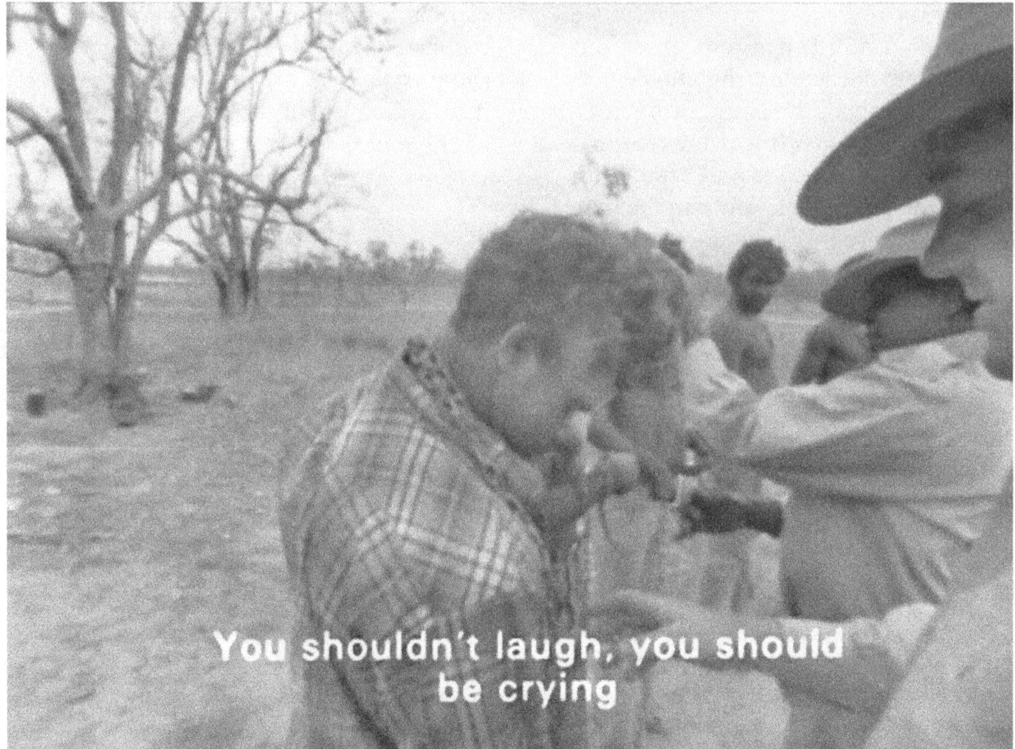

FIGURE 80.1 Shooting the "Police Times" section of *Two Laws*. Screen capture from DVD.

instead to emphasize the acting-out strategy, to film stylized and symbolic expressions of the violence enacted upon Aboriginal peoples. Thus, there are scenes where the white actor "playing" Constable Stott symbolically lowers his stick slowly across the back of an Aboriginal man instead of bashing him with it, or slowly applies his stick first to one side of an Aboriginal woman then to the other to indicate the brutal beating which resulted in her death. And, in another scene, an old Aboriginal man describes how he was beaten across the back, first one way then another; then he grabs a stick and proceeds to demonstrate how he was beaten by bashing a tree first this way then another. "Finally," he says, "I was forced to confess. 'Yep,' I told him, 'I ate that bullock, ate the whole thing!' "

The Aboriginal peoples' sense of humor is evident in many moments of *Two Laws*, as they laugh in retrospect about what they had to endure in the past and as they revel in the chance now to recall and act out what they have experienced. This is most evident in the second part, "Welfare Times," where a group of Aboriginal women discuss with a white woman how the latter should play her part as a welfare administrator. Rehearsing a scene where the Aboriginal women have to present themselves for inspection, they coach the white woman on the lines the welfare administrator should speak. Running through the scene, the welfare woman speaks her lines in an impressively convincing way; and the Aboriginal women remark, "Yes, that's just the way they would talk to us; and we would just stand there and look down at our feet, not daring to speak a word."

But immediately after this remark there is a cut to another take of this same scene, with the Aboriginal women presenting themselves for inspection and the white woman saying "Good morning, have you all washed today? If you're nice and clean and if your children are nice and clean then you'll get a pretty dress for being good girls. And you'll get clothes for the children too. But if you're not clean or if your hair is untidy then you'll not get anything until you've fixed yourself up properly." And here, in this take, the Aboriginal women are shown laughing at the whole scene, dramatizing, in effect, both what used to happen to them and the distance they have come in asserting themselves.

The welfare system, as they see it, was blatantly assimilationist. By way of introducing "Welfare Times," one Aboriginal woman reads a passage from the Government's submission to the Land Claims Court, which reads as follows: "The year 1953 was the beginning of the Welfare Ordinance. Its aim was to direct and encourage the re-establishment of the Aborigenes, that they would eventually be assimilated as an integral part of the Australian community." To which, the Aboriginal woman adds, looking directly into the camera, "Which means that they wanted us to be like white people."

While assimilation was certainly the Australian government's long-term plan for the Aboriginal population (paralleling the US government position on Native Americans), at least as important was the short-term urgency of getting the Aboriginal peoples out of the way of the white mining interests that wanted access to the country's vast mineral deposits. In *Two Laws*, the Borroloola Aboriginal community recounts—and re-enacts—how they were suddenly told that their welfare station and the entire Aboriginal community would have to move to Robinson River, several hours away by truck. There was no consultation involved; they were just told to pack their things, and a government truck was provided to carry them and their possessions. Only later did they find out that large mining interests had obtained a lease on huge tracts of

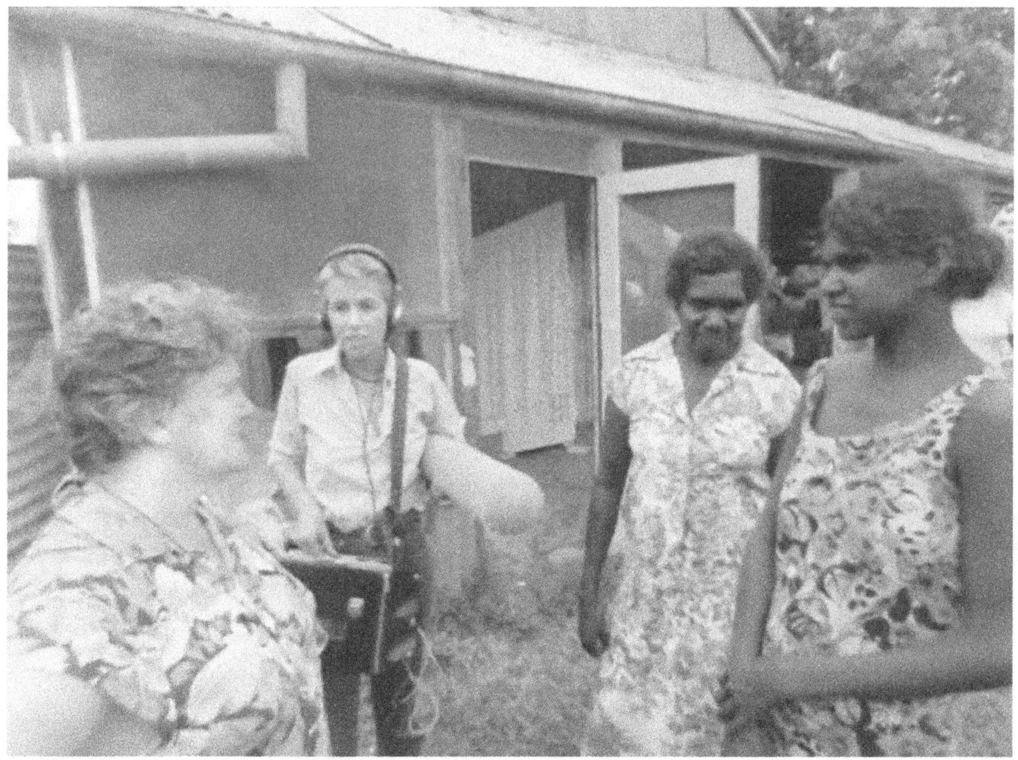

FIGURE 80.2 Shooting the "Welfare Times" section of *Two Laws*. Screen capture from DVD.

land around Borroloola and had insisted on the Aboriginal community's removal to make way for the vast Mt. Isa Mines operations.

The notion of two different legal concepts of land tenure (one black, one white) is best brought out by the third part of the film, "Struggle for Our Land." Interestingly, there is one sequence in this section which is filmed utilizing what might be called an observational approach. It involves a conversation between a white Australian laborer (a recent immigrant from Yugoslavia) and an Aboriginal man who is protesting that the white laborer, by razing hundreds of trees along a dirt roadway, has both diminished the Aboriginal food supply (they eat the fruit of this particular tree) and, more importantly, desecrated a sacred site which had been entrusted, ceremonially, to his particular custodianship, or *djunkai*.

The conversation is filmed in synch sound and long takes, and since both men are speaking English, there is no need for subtitling of dialogue. The white laborer questions the black man's ability to prove his "ownership" of the land. "Do you have a title to the land?" he asks. The Aboriginal man responds that when the white men came they just took the land and didn't bother with titles. The white laborer then retorts that land wasn't always just taken, that sometimes blacks actually sold land to the whites. "Can you prove," he asks, "that your father, or his father, didn't sell that land to the whites?"

Pausing for a moment, the white laborer then continues, "And if that land was sold to the whites, then what would happen now if the government or the land claims court decided to give that land back to the blacks? Who would pay back the money to the whites that they had originally paid the blacks for that land?" The Aboriginal man reflects on these questions for several minutes, then shakes his head stoically, observing that "You're still just thinking in white peoples' terms about all this."

The point is well taken, although it would be nice if the Aboriginal terms of communal land tenure—as opposed to private property—had been spelled out more explicitly. Apparently this is exactly what happens when the finished film is shown to audiences of other Aboriginal communities throughout Australia: they actually leap to their feet at this moment in the film and start discussing loudly exactly what *they* would have said to that white laborer. And even within the film we see the way the film-making process offers material for further work and reflection, as we later see several Aboriginal women activists listening, with ear phones, to the sound tape of that particular conversation—which stirs them to compose a letter offering *their* response to the white laborer. In short, even the observational sequence is clearly and firmly placed in the overall context of a process initiated and carried through by the Aboriginal community themselves—a process that involves them in making a film in the first place because they are above all involved in a political struggle to retain—or to regain—their traditional land.

Keeping the political context in mind, the Aboriginal community is able to incorporate into *Two Laws* some footage of traditional rituals and ceremonial dances, but in such a way that does not allow this material to fall into the trap of the exotic—where the Aboriginal is depicted as the mysterious other. Instead, by delaying any treatment of ritual until the fourth and final part of *Two Laws*, and by including footage of rituals involving some of the men, and, especially, some of the women we have come to know somewhat through the first three parts of the film, the Aboriginal community is able to provide the audience with a sense of the inter-relatedness of all these activities and of their articulation within the overall context of their ongoing lives and struggles.

All in all, the film *Two Laws* is a breakthrough of major significance in ethnographic film. It may not provide the kind of drama and action we are used to in the cinema, even in the "observational cinema"; but it provides much more important things. Above all, *Two Laws* provides the ethnographic "subjects"—in this case, the Australian Aboriginal community of Borroloola—the opportunity to express what they want to express about their lives and their culture and their struggles, and to express all this in filmic terms of their own choosing. In doing so, they may have made that "disappearing world" a bit more visible and audible again, to the benefit of all of us.

NOTES

1. There have been a few experiments set up by white American academics to investigate whether minority sub-cultures (Navajo Indians, lower-class urban black children), given some rudimentary training with film equipment, might be able to express, in original and indigenous imagery, certain essential characteristics of their cultures. The work with Navajos by Sol Worth and John Adair resulted in a number of short pieces (of several minutes duration) of "subject-generated" film-imagery, only one example of which was thought to express genuinely "Navajo" imagery. Similar results were obtained in work with lower-class urban black children by Richard Chalfen.
2. Colin Young, "MacDougall Conversations," *Royal Anthropological Institute News*, June 1982.
3. Quoted from an interview with Cavadini and Strachan conducted by Charles Merewether and Lesley Stern, published in *Filmnews*, Sydney Filmmakers' Cooperative, April 1982, p. 8.
4. Quoted from Cavadini and Strachan interview cited in footnote 3 above, p. 9.
5. Ibid., p. 9.
6. Ibid., p. 9.

81

LEE ATWELL

REVIEW OF *WORD IS OUT* (1979)

Historically the cinematic image of the homosexual, which has only come into focus within the last decade, has consistently suffered from stereotypical distortion, derision, and condescension. As minority members who have never been in control of their public image, gays have witnessed in narrative fiction film an almost systematic attempt to devalue, while giving token recognition to, their lives and feelings. If television responds on occasion with a sympathetic episode, movies are largely content with liberal notions of obvious "fairies" for humorous relief, or worse, unhappy psychopathic villains, reinforcing ignorance and prejudice among what Christopher Isherwood terms "the heterosexual dictatorship."

In the field of documentary or *cinéma-vérité,* where the index of reality is somewhat more reliable, and where we at least have the advantage of experiencing not actors impersonating gay types, but the real thing, isolated examples failed to have any significant impact. In *The Queen,* Frank Simon penetrates behind the facade of male drags participating in a beauty contest, while at another extreme, Rosa von Praunheim's *It Is Not the Homosexual Who is Not Perverse but the Society in Which He Lives* offers a cynical, candid glimpse into the S&M/motorcycle/leather faction of the macho gay world; and Shirley Clarke's feature-length interview with a black male prostitute, *Portrait of Jason,* conveys an unsparing, albeit unpleasant confessional vision.

Diverse and positive images of gay persons were not forthcoming for two basic reasons. In spite of the clarion call of "Out of the Closets" by liberationists, large segments of the gay populace feared any sort of public exposure that might mean loss of jobs, friends and/or family support. Simply getting an openly gay woman or man to appear before a camera was a primary difficulty. And secondly, the difficulties in financing a nonsensational (noncommercial) treatment of the subject was virtually insurmountable.

The first work reflecting the otherwise extremely vocal politics of Gay Liberation was a highly professional student production, *Some of Your Best Friends* by Ken Robinson of the University of Southern California. Employing a *cinéma-vérité* format, Robinson captured the spirited genesis of the movement in New York and Los Angeles, interviewing up-front participants about feelings and experiences of oppression and freedom. Especially memorable is a Los Angeles man walking through Griffith Park, relating how he was entrapped by a local vice officer and his plans to defend himself in a court trial (which he subsequently won). A gay contingent is seen confronting a psychiatric convention, challenging its oppressive advocacy of aversion therapy with a rousing debate. Representatives of a New York homophile organization are shrouded in shadow to protect their identity while the bright, shining faces of the street folk project pride, prominently including women as well as men.

Six years were to pass, however, before other gay film-makers were to significantly take up the direct-cinema approach begun by Robinson. Though financial support was still virtually nonexistent for pro-gay films, the rising tide of anti-gay propaganda, spearheaded by Anita Bryant's Bible-thumping crusade, provoked social consciousness and a revitalization of a movement throughout the land. A highly sophisticated quality gay news medium began to unite divergent forces into political cohesiveness and at the same time the awareness of a need to communicate prompted socially conscious film-makers to action. Their efforts resulted in two unique and exceptional human documents, *Gay USA* and *Word is Out: Stories of Some of Our Lives.* Both films employ the interview as a fundamental technique but their production circumstances and organization of material differ distinctly in spite of occasional parallels.

In 1975, Peter Adair, then a producer for San Francisco's KQED, had become dissatisfied with the quality of his work there. "I felt that I needed to make films that were of value to me . . . I wanted to get into some sort of social film-making. I started with the issue that concerned me most—that was rights for gay people." He envisioned a short film to be used as a teaching aid for college and professional groups, made of interviews with diverse individuals. In spite of two years of perseverence, Adair discovered foundations were unresponsive to such a project and finally resorted, like the makers of *Gay USA,* to private and individual investors. He joined forces with his sister Nancy, assistant cameraman Andrew Brown, sound editor Veronica Selver, New York film-maker Lucy Massie Phenix, and Rob Epstein, and the Mariposa Film Group came into existence. With the expansion of the group came the decision to enlarge the scope of the work. What had begun as a modest presentation of positive role models for gay people became a much larger sampling of the vast range of America's gay population.

Every attempt was made to engage film-makers and participants in a collective expression, decentralizing all procedures from shooting to editing. In preparation, the members "pre-interviewed" 200 persons from varied sections of the country on videotape. The team then collectively viewed this material and selected 26 women and men whom they returned to film. As Teresa Kennett notes in *The Reel Thing,* certain ground rules were agreed on by the Mariposa Group. "The setting for every interview was worked out very carefully between subject and film-maker. Choice of location and 'props'—photographs, pets, clothing, etc.—was made on the basis not only of what looked good visually, but of what was meaningful to the interviewee. Making the subject feel at ease was of utmost importance; to this end a stationary camera setup was decided upon, thus eliminating any extra distraction. And since whoever operated the camera also conducted the interview (usually with only one other person on sound) it was possible to develop real unbroken communication between interviewer and interviewee." In addition to the interview material, several hours of *vérité* footage were filmed, depicting working and living situations of the subjects, and songs performed by Trish Nugent and the gay rock band Buena Vista.

Four of the Mariposa Group spent over a year editing various cuts down from approximately 50 hours of material. From time to time cuts were screened for predominantly gay audiences, with responses solicited in questionnaire form. Thus, the larger community was able to participate in determining the actual final content of the film. In this process it soon became evident that the large amount of cutaway material detracted from rather than amplified the succession of interviews, and in the final 135-minute version, its presence is minimal. And this undoubtedly accounts for the strength of the film's emotional and psychological impact, as well as for its structural and conceptual weaknesses.

Word is Out is divided into three broad sections; "The Early Years," "Growing Up," and "From Now On." The rather vague nature of these arbitrary categories becomes evident as each section unravels, prefaced by an introductory montage of the personalities included in each segment. Although the interviewees have been carefully chosen to display a richly diverse and contrasting series of views and lifestyles, no apparent structural pattern emerges in the editing scheme. Individual interviews are broken up and reappear from time to time, often being used in more than one section, as remarks seem generally relevant to the broad category.

The static stationary camera angle is consistently a frontal medium-close to close shot, giving the impression of a talking portrait in which the subject directly addresses the camera/audience, creating an intimate, engrossing and often emotionally charged rapport between subject and viewer. However, in a film of a two-hour-plus duration, variety and contrast are essential to retain the viewer's interest, regardless of how riveting the interview material is assumed to be. In the final analysis, though each individual shot has its own mood, composition, and dynamic center, it is an isolated unit that only marginally relates to the other units that make up the framework.

In addition to the gay musicians, who are seen at random intervals in studio and in concert performances, three sequences deviate significantly from the armchair-interview format, giving a much-needed variation in the cinematic space. Elsa Gidlow, 79, the eldest member of the cast, is seen talking with three young women in her Northern California home about lesbian politics and her feelings about appearing in the film. Suddenly, for the first time we see the faces of interviewer(s) and interviewee in the same space, engaged in a conversational exchange, while the hand-held camera freely moves from face to face. Similarly, after we have become familiar with a blond lesbian named Whitey, who lives in a Northern California cabin, we see an early morning excursion in which she and her friends saw off a section of a giant tree that is threatening her domicile. The operation, shot from a variety of angles, is successful and audiences invariably cheer and applaud this rustic interlude. Following interviews separately and together with lesbian mothers Pam Jackson and Rusty Millington, we see a beautifully filmed sequence in which the two women play touch football with Rusty's children on a beach and serve a picnic supper, during which one of the children is interviewed. Other cutaway material, such as the film's self-proclaimed drag queen, Tede Mathews, frolicking with children at a playground, or the middle-aged couple Harry Hay and John Burnside picking berries together in the countryside, displays a charm that is more poignant than their speech.

In spite of its diversity of ethnic and sexual types, it would be a mistake to draw anything other than superficial sociological arguments from *Word is Out*, which is only a bare suggestion of the variety of gay lifestyles. Brooklyn professor Betty Powell, one of the film's most articulate speakers, emphasizes, for instance, that she should not be taken as in any sense representative of black lesbian feminists (though she is in fact the only one to appear in the film).

Nevertheless, certain patterns begin to emerge in the selection of material that assert a strongly middle-class value structure. The large number of stable couples suggests an ideal of traditional matrimonial bliss. Only one character speaks up for the single, casual-sex status that characterizes vast numbers of gay people. Although only one speaker, a vice-president of a New York corporation, defines himself as a conservative ("I feel that radicals are necessary and I feel that we are necessary") the majority of persons interviewed can be categorized as politically conservative, especially those whose formative years preceded the sixties and Gay Liberation. Comedienne Pat Bond, a middle-aged ex-WAC who talks of communal, role-defined lesbian life in postwar years and recounts the terrors of the Army's inquisition during the McCarthy period (which resulted in 500 dishonorable discharges) is nevertheless nostalgic about the past. Although she sees the necessity of gays coming out publicly now and finding a new sense of identity, she misses the butch/femme role dichotomy and the secrecy of "the Little Orphan Annie decoding society" in her early years.

The film's final section, "From Now On," tends to focus on the more radical dimension of gay politics and its most eloquent and persuasive arguments are presented by lesbian feminists Betty Powell and Sally Gearhart. Powell, who is a member of the National Gay Task Force, tells of coming out of a heterosexual marriage and realizing her love for a woman through the women's movement. Her assertion that "lesbians and gay men have a great deal to offer in terms of restructuring the world culture," is more fully articulated by Sally Gearhart, who asserts that all humans are born with a bisexual potential, but from the moment they are born they are made half-persons by society's strict programming of appropriate gender behavior and attitudes. Gays tend, on the other hand, more toward a natural balance of male and female in one person. This is, of course, an ideal and the film's inclusion of stereotypical dykes such as Pat Bond (who quaintly classifies herself as "femme") and effeminate men like Roger Harkenrider (who honestly admits to archetypal "faggoty" behavior) suggests the infinite complexity of sexual role-playing in the gay world. On the other hand, there are typically male models present in Donald Hackett, a black truck driver, and female models in Linda Marco, a pretty, former "American dream daughter," both of whom came out from heterosexual marriages (another significant pattern in the cast). It is also interesting to note that while the film's most cogent intellectual arguments come from women, its strongest emotional moments emerge from men. Probably the most memorable is George Mendenhall's tearful reminiscence of a male opera singer named José encouraging men in a gay bar to sing "God Save Us Nellie Queens" in the fifties when San Francisco police mercilessly harrassed gays. More deeply touching is the confession of young David Gillon: "In high school thought I was just one of those people who could never love anybody. When I fell in love with Henry, it meant I had incredibly deep emotions—it meant I was human."

[. . .]

JULIA LESAGE

THE POLITICAL AESTHETICS OF THE FEMINIST DOCUMENTARY FILM (1978)

Feminist documentary filmmaking is a cinematic genre congruent with a political movement, the contemporary women's movement.[1] One of that movement's key forms of organization is the affinity group. In the late 1960s and early 1970s in the United States, women's consciousness-raising groups, reading groups, and task-oriented groups were emerging from and often superseded the organizations of the antiwar New Left. Women who had learned filmmaking in the antiwar movement and previously "uncommitted" women filmmakers began to make self-consciously Feminist films, and other women began to learn filmmaking specifically to contribute to the movement.[2] The films these people made came out of the same ethos as the consciousness-raising groups and had the same goals.

Clearly the cinematic sophistication and quality of political analysis vary from film to film, but aside from an in-depth discussion of *Self Health,* which I value both cinematically and politically, to explore such differences would be beyond the scope of this article.[3] Here I shall describe the emergence of the Feminist documentary as a genre, the aesthetics, use, and importance of this genre, and its relation to the movement from which it sprang—a discussion important to any consideration of the aesthetics of political films.

Many of the first Feminist documentaries used a simple format to present to audiences (presumably composed primarily of women) a picture of the ordinary details of women's lives, their thoughts—told directly by the protagonists to the camera—and their frustrated but sometimes successful attempts to enter and deal with the public world of work and power. Among these films, which now have a wide circulation in libraries and schools, are *Growing Up Female* by Julia Reichert and Jim Klein, *Janie's Janie* by Geri Ashur, and *The Woman's Film* by the women of San Francisco Newsreel.

Other films dealing with women talking about their lives include Kate Millet's *Three Lives,* Joyce Chopra's *Joyce at 34,* Donna Deitch's *Woman to Woman,* and Deborah Schaffer and Bonnie Friedman's *Chris and Bernie.* Some films deal with pride in the acquisition of skills, such as Bonnie Friedman's film about a girl's track team, *The Flashettes,* or Michelle Citron's study of her sister learning the concert violin from a woman teacher, *Parthenogenesis.* Others have more political analysis and are often collective productions that provide a Feminist analysis of women's experience with the following: (a) prison (*Like a Rose* by Tomato Productions, *We're Alive* by California Institute for Women Video and UCLA Women's Film Workshop); (b) the health care system (*Self Health* by San Francisco Women's Health Collective, *Taking Our Bodies Back* by Margaret Lazarus, Renner Wunderlich, and Joan Fink, *The Chicago Maternity Center Story* by Kartemquin Films, and *Healthcaring* by Denise Bostrom and Jane Warrenbrand); and (c) rape (*Rape* by JoAnn Elam).

It is no coincidence that films about working-class women show their subjects as the most confident and militant about their rights in the public sector, and their willingness to fight for those rights. Yet even these films, from Madeline Anderson's *I Am Somebody* to Barbara Kopple's *Harlan County, U.S.A,* focus on problems of identity in the private sphere—how one strike-leader's husband views her union organizing unenthusiastically, or how miners' wives reach a new solidarity only by overcoming sexual suspicions and jealousies. As Feminist films explicitly demand that a new space be opened up for women in women's terms, the collective and social act of Feminist filmmaking has often led to entirely new demands in the areas of health care, welfare, poverty programs, work, and law (especially rape), and in the cultural sphere proper in the areas of art, education, and the mass media.

And if the Feminist filmmakers deliberately used a traditional "realist" documentary structure, it is because they saw making these films as an urgent public act and wished to enter the 16mm circuit of educational films especially through libraries, schools, churches, unions, and YWCAs to bring Feminist analysis to many women it might otherwise never reach.

Biography, simplicity, trust between woman filmmaker and woman subject, a linear narrative structure, little self-consciousness about the flexibility of the cinematic medium—these are what characterize the Feminist documentaries of the 1970s. The films' form and their widespread use raise certain questions. Why are they patterned in so similar a way? Why are these films the first ones thought of whenever a group of women decide they want to "start learning something about women" and set up showings in churches, public libraries, high schools, Girl Scout meetings, union caucuses, or rallies for the ERA? Why do activists in the women's movement use the same films over and over again? What is the films' appeal? These films often show women in the private sphere getting together to define/redefine their experiences and to elaborate a strategy for making inroads on the public sphere. Either the filmmaker senses that it is socially necessary to name women's experience, or women together within the film do so, or a "strong" woman is filmed who shares her stance with the filmmaker and, by extension, with the women who see the film. Conversations in these films are not merely examples of female introspection; the filmmakers choose not to explore the corners of women's psyches (as in Romantic art). Rather, the women's very redefining of experience is intended to challenge all the previously accepted indices of "male superiority" and of women's supposedly "natural" roles. Women's personal explorations establish a structure for social and psychological change and are filmed specifically to combat patriarchy. The filmmaker's and her subjects' intent is political. Yet the films' very strength, the emphasis on the experiential, can sometimes be a political limitation, especially when the film limits itself to the individual and offers little or no analysis of sense of collective process leading to social change.[4]

Example: *Self Health*

Among Feminist documentaries, *Self Health* is an exemplary film in terms of its cinematic style, the knowledge it conveys, and the self-confidence and understanding it gives women about themselves. The film presents women in a group situation, collectively learning to do vaginal self-exams with a speculum, breast exams, and vaginal bimanual exams. Such groups have been conducted over the past five or six years by women who are part of an informal "self-help" or "self-health" movement in the United States; sometimes their work is connected with the home-birth movement and sometimes with pregnancy testing and abortion referral services. As the health care industry grows like a mushroom under capitalism, the general North American public has become more and more aware of the poor quality of the expensive services offered to them. The women in the self-health movement form part of a large, often informally constituted radical movement to improve health care delivery for the masses of people instead of for an elite.

The place where such a self-health session takes place is usually someone's home or a women's center, rather than a medical clinic. In the film *Self Health,* the locale is a sunny apartment or informal women's meeting place. Although we see two women giving most of the explanations and demonstrations, no one is distinguished as nurse or doctor. As important to the film as the conveying of anatomical information is the fact that all the women discuss together their feelings about and experiences with their bodies and their sexuality, and that they very naturally look at and feel each others' bodies. To gain knowledge by looking at and feeling each other is acknowledged perhaps for the first time as woman's right.

Such a film attacks both the artistic and medical tradition of viewing women's bodies. These traditions, as well as the mass media's use of women's image to sell consumer goods, have robbed most women of a real knowledge of both their own and other women's bodies. Furthermore, many women have little personal sense of rightfully possessing their own bodies, little sense of what's "normal" for themselves physically, and little sense of what sexuality on their terms or on women's terms in general might mean.

Toward the end of the film, one of the women puts on a rubber glove to demonstrate how to do a bimanual vaginal exam. The subject is a woman lying on a table in a sunny room with a flowered pillow under head and a green fern near her. The "teacher" inserts two lubricated fingers into the vagina and pushes up underneath the cervix. First she shows the woman being examined and then the other women gathered around the table, how to press down hard on the abdomen to ascertain the size and location of the uterus and then the ovaries. "Why does it always hurt when the doctor does it?" they ask. They also express surprise about the size and location of the uterus ("about the size of a walnut") and the ovaries ("feels like a Mexican jumping bean").

Women watching the film usually find this information about the uterus completely new. Medical textbook drawings have traditionally shown the uterus as big and near the navel, with large fallopian tubes winding around prominent ovaries. The clitoris, until Masters and Johnson's studies, was not "taught" in medical school as women's organ of sexual sensation. Although

I was raised in a doctor's family, I faced similar ignorance, for I learned only three years ago—after having a vaginal cyst cauterized without any local anesthesia—what was to me a startling fact, that the vagina has relatively little sensation because there are few nerve endings there. Why, women are asking, has such ignorance about women's sexuality been promoted in our society—especially since both pornography and modern medicine pretend to be so liberal about sex?

Doctors, male lovers, photographers, artists, and filmmakers have taken woman's nude body as their "turf," especially as an *object* of study. John Berger, in his film series and book, *Ways of Seeing,* has described the tradition of female nudity in oil painting and the presentation of women's bodies in advertising. He understands how the fact that women are "an object of vision, a sight," has affected women's view of themselves: women constantly "survey" themselves to judge how they appear, to try to gain some kind of control over how they might be treated in a circumscribed, patriarchal world.

> In the art-form of the European nude, the painters and spectator-owners were usually men, the persons treated as objects, women.... The essential way of seeing women, the essential use of which images are put, has not changed.[5]

In the film *Self Health,* one of the instructors relates how she attacked the depersonalization a woman feels when her body is an "object," especially as she experienced it during a gynecological exam:

> This summer I went to have the regular pap smear and pelvic exam. As soon as I got into the stirrups, the whole feeling came back. I really remembered it and felt completely vulnerable and terrified. There was like this miner's cap sticking up, and finally I said, "OK. I have to deal with this some way," and I just took the curtain and tore it off and threw it into the garbage can. It really blew his mind. He said, "You know, I never thought how ominous it is to see the head of this person, and this part of you divided, not yours."

That so much of the basic physical information conveyed by the film is very new for women viewers (e.g., the film lets us see the cervix and the os, or the normal sebaceous secretion from the nipple) indicates just how colonized a space women's bodies still are. *Self Health* goes a long way toward reconquering that space.

Cinematically, the film is characterized by its presentation of women in a collective situation sharing new knowledge about their physical sexuality. About fifteen young women are gathered in a friendly, mundane environment rather than in a clinical white office where the woman patient is completely isolated from her ordinary social context. As the group does breast self-examinations together, they sit around in a circle in what might be a living room; hanging on the wall we see a Toulouse-Lautrec reproduction of a woman. Warm brown-red and pink tones predominate. As the women remove their tops, we notice them as individuals—some with rings and other jewels, some with glasses, many with different hairstyles. The group is young, they look like students or young working-women in flowered peasant blouses and dresses, shirts and jeans. In sum, the colors and the *mise-en-scène* create a sense of warmth, intimacy, and friendliness.

Even more important to the *mise-en-scène* is the women's collectivity. Women look at and touch each other; they all see their own sexual organs and those of others, probably for the first time. They learn the variety of physical types and the range of "normality" in sexual organs in look, color, texture, and feel. The fact that almost any woman would feel shy and embarrassed about doing such an overt exploration is mitigated by these women's doing it in a group where everyone feels the same way. The women realize that their fears and doubts about their bodies do not originate from their individual situation as much as from women's physical and psychological "colonization" under patriarchy. Too often, women have experienced as degrading getting contraception information, having a gynecological exam, and having a baby. Certainly at those moments, women's ignorance about their bodies was rarely dispelled. But this collective process gives them the self-confidence to demand answers from doctors face to face and to demand a different kind of health care overall. That such a film does not provide an institutional analysis of the health-care industry, as does *The Chicago Maternity Center Story*, limits how much this one film can achieve in directly promoting a different kind of health care for women; yet, because of the wide range of discussion and kinds of challenges to the established order it encourages women to formulate, it is useful in a wide range of women's struggles.

Visually and in terms of its overall structure, the film moves as far away as you can get from pornography, yet the cinematography also captures that kind of nervous tension and excitement of discovery which the women themselves undoubtedly felt. The film opens on a close up of naked skin, the surface moving to the rhythm of a woman's breathing; there is a pan to a breast and a shot of either pubic or axillary hair in close up. As it starts out, the film could be porn. For most women audience members, the initial sequence provides a moment of tension—"Do we dare to or want to look at this?" The voice over assures us of what we want to hear: "We're learning from our bodies, teaching ourselves and each other how each of us is unique . . . and the same . . . We see it as reclaiming lost territory that belonged to our doctors, our husbands, everyone but us." As the title comes on, we hear the excited voices of women speaking all at once, a device also used at the end of the film over the credits. The voices of discovery, talking in a simultaneous outburst or sharing observations, needs and experiences—these are the tension-breaking devices, the part of the film that an audience unfamiliar with such a situation first identifies with. And these voices imply an outburst of discussion that cannot be contained, that begs to be continued after the film is seen.

In an early sequence, a woman lying on a table is surrounded by other women as she talks about and demonstrates the external genitalia, using her own body as a model. Various women talk here about their sense of being at a distance from their own sexual parts, of feeling squeamish about them. Alternating shots show close ups of the demonstration of faces looking intently at what they are being shown. When the woman on the table demonstrates the use of the speculum and inserts it into her vagina, one woman's voice exclaims, "Oh, God!" which elicits nervous laughter in the audience and expresses the group's tension. As the woman inserts the speculum and shines the light inside it, the camera cuts to another angle and zooms in to show her cervix and its opening, the os, that which the doctor always "examines" but which we never see. Laughter and sounds of excitement are heard as the onlooking women comment and ask questions about what they see.

After this sequence, a high-angle long shot shows three women lying on the floor against pillows and sleeping bags propped up against the wall. Their legs are spread apart and they are all doing vaginal self-exams with speculum, flashlight, and mirror. A pan shot shows the whole group of women on the floor, lined up along the wall, doing the same thing with some women looking at or helping each other. A mixture of voices exclaim and comment on what they see, especially on the variety and uniqueness of the genitalia. This sequence is a first in narrative cinema. It decolonizes women's sexuality. Women occupy the whole space of the frame as subjects in a collective act of mutual, tangible self-exploration. As one of my students said of this sequence, "It has none of the 'Wow!' of *Candid Camera* and none of the distance of medical or so-called sex education films." Particularly in this one section of *Self Health,* women filmmakers have found a way to show and define women's sexuality on their terms—not with the thrill of possession and not with objectification, but with the excitement of coming to knowledge.

Later, as the film shows the women doing breast self-exams together, they and we notice and let ourselves deliberately look at the variety of women's breasts. The women themselves feel each others' breasts to learn what normal breast tissue is like. Although the Cancer Society promotes breast self-examination, women's breast tissue is fibrous and also varies with the menstrual cycle and the individual. As a result, women often do not know what is normal or what a "lump" might be. A doctor can spot such phenomena from having had the opportunity to feel many women's breasts. Why should such knowledge not be made available to, or seized by, women themselves?

The anatomy lesson, the sharing of feelings, and the learning about others are all part of the self-health experience and all have equal importance in the film. Close-ups demonstrate specific examination techniques or show individuals talking and listening; long shots convey the sense of a communal experience in the self-health group. No woman is filmed as an object; everyone is a subject who combines and presents physical, emotional, intellectual, and political selves. The women filmed have an amazing spontaneity and lack of self-consciousness about the camera, particularly given the close range at which the filming was done.

Self-health groups and this film itself both function in an explicitly political way. Reclaiming "the lost territory" of women's bodies and health care is a personal act that has a strong effect on women's identity, emotional life, and sense of control. This film also directly attacks the medical establishment. Women who see the film immediately want to talk about two things—sex education and health care—mainly in terms of what patriarchal society lacks.

In one sense, the film is utopian. It shows a new, collective form of women learning together. It would be an ideal film, for example, to show in high schools. But when I showed the film on the university level to women's studies classes and to film students, both sets of students agreed that the idea of such a collective form of learning about sexuality would have been viewed as "pornography" in their high schools by the teachers, the school boards, and many of the parents. In cinematic terms, the film's vision of women's sexuality, of their being total subjects to one another and to the audience, is also utopian. Women's very physical presence is defined here in women's terms, collectively. And some might ask, in referring to documentary film alone, why haven't these images and these concepts of women's united physical and intellectual selves been presented by filmmakers before?

Feminist Documentaries and the Consciousness-Raising Group

Cinéma vérité documentary filmmaking had features that made it an attractive and useful mode of artistic and political expression for women learning filmmaking in the late 1960s. It not only demanded less mastery of the medium than Hollywood or experimental film, but also the very documentary recording of women's real environments. Their stories immediately established and valorized a new order of cinematic iconography, connotations, and range of subject matter in the portrayal of women's lives. Furthermore, contemporary Feminist filmmakers, often making biographical or autobiographical films, have used *cinéma vérité* in a new and different way. They often identify personally with their subjects. Their relation to that subject while filming often is collaborative, with both subject and filmmaker sharing the political goals of the project. The Feminist documentarist uses the film medium to convey a new and heightened sense of what *woman* means or can mean in our society—this new sense of female identity being expressed both through the subject's story and through the tangible details of the subject's milieu.

Yet why do so many Feminist filmmakers choose to film the same thing? Film after film shows a woman telling her story to the camera. It is usually a woman struggling to deal with the public world. It seems that these Feminist documentarists just plug in different speakers and show a certain variation in milieu—especially in class terms—from the aristocratic home of *Nana, Mom, and Me* by Amalie Rothschild to the union organizers' photos of their younger days in *Union Maids* by Julia Reichert and Jim Klein. In fact, the Feminist documentaries have as a narrative structure a pattern that is as satisfying for activists in the contemporary women's movement to watch as it is for women just wanting to learn more about women. That is, these films evince a consistent organization of narrative materials that functions much like a deep structure, the details of the individual women's lives providing the surface structure of these films.[6]

Such an organization serves a specific social and psychological function at this juncture in history. It is the artistic analogue of the structure and function of the consciouness-raising group. Furthermore, it indicates to the filmmaker a certain reason to be making the film, a certain relation to her subject matter and to the medium, and a certain sense of the function of the film once released. The narrative deep structure sets the filmmaker in a mutual, nonhierarchical relation with her subject (such filming is not seen as the male artist's act of "seizing" the subject and then presenting one's "creation") and indicates what she hopes her relation to her audience will be.[7]

The major political tool of the contemporary women's movement has been the consciousness-raising group. Self-consciously, a group of about a dozen women would reevaluate any and all areas of their past experiences in terms of how that experience defined or illuminated what it meant to be a woman in our culture. It was an act of naming previously unarticulated knowledge, of seeing that knowledge as political (i.e., as a way of beginning to change power relations), and of understanding that the power of this knowledge was that it was arrived at collectively. This collective process served to break down a sense of guilt for one's own problems and provided a sense of mutual support and of the collective's united strength and potential for action. It was and is a political act carried out in the private sphere.

Initially, there is a healing in the very act of naming and understanding women's general oppression in collectively creating this new knowledge and identity. Then, the group usually elaborates specific strategies to make inroads on, help its individual members enter, and change power relations in the public sphere. They may, for example, discuss tactics for helping one of their members to say no to making coffee at work or to demand that the department hire a woman in an executive position. They may strive to get gynecological services at a school clinic. They may help a member of the group insist at work that no more clerical staff be hired and that all women be upgraded, which would mean that everyone in the office do both writing and typing. But consciousness-raising groups cannot be idealized as revolutionary structures. Their problems have been well analyzed by women who have used them and learned how much more organization and economic power is needed to make major changes in the public sphere.[8]

In many ways—for Feminists and all the rest of the women in the United States—the private sector of society is uniquely women's space. In that private space, the home, women of my mother's generation were systematically robbed of their sense of being the possessors of their own bodies. Throughout patriarchy, women have been men's possession and the reflection of men's desires in the sexual act, especially in marriage. Mothers are the child-bearers and self-sacrificers, which is the constant theme of soap operas and domestic melodramas in film. The sense of self for women under capitalism has traditionally had to come from their children, their house, their jewelry, and their clothes. All the physical, peripheral extensions of themselves that they've been allowed to "possess" has been a mock analog of the real patriarchal possession of themselves, their families, and the sources of economic power that they and their families have had to depend on.[9]

In testimony to the psychological condition of living out one's life in a state of mental colonization and in a sphere where one's labor is not valorized socially by either a salary or public power, many women's narratives are about identity, madness, and the fluidity or fragmentation of woman's ego. Yet the very act of writing a diary, of writing poems, or of consulting a neighbor woman about how to get along when times are hard—all these are testimonies to the struggle women wage to create a language, to formulate a stable sense of self, and to survive economic dependency on men. Just as women's domestic labor and way of relating to each other are disdained, so too their forms of resistance in that sphere tend to go unnoticed and unvalorized in a world where the hegemonic male culture, the public culture, has established the socially acknowledged "rules," appropriated women's bodies, and institutionalized the modes of discourse, especially through the Church, education, literature, the medical profession, the law, and the state.

Because women's identity is shaped and sustained in a sphere where men are largely absent, and because girls grow up in an emotional continuum with their mothers and the other women in their intimate environment (unlike a boy's Oedipal development), their emotional ties are deep to other women.[10] Women have traditionally constantly consulted with each other about domestic matters. One of the functions of the consciousness-raising group of the contemporary women's movement is to use an older form of subcultural resistance, women's conversation, in a new way. There is a knowledge that is already there about domestic life, but it has not necessarily been spoken in uncolonized, women-identified terms. Women's art, especially the Feminist documentary films, like consciousness-raising groups, strive to find a new way of speaking about what we have collectively known to be really there in the domestic sphere and to wrest back our identity there in women's terms.

A Shift in Iconography

Much has been lost in women's iconography as it has been purveyed in films, advertising, and television. We have, in fact, maintained a rich photographic history of women over the last hundred years, yet this source is not tapped in its richness and variety in patriarchal narrative film. For example, the women that Dorothea Lange photographed do not "speak" to us either visually or verbally in mainstream cinema. In the United States in the early 1900s, many strikes were led by workingwomen dressed in their best clothes and striding down city streets arm in arm. Why did that iconography get lost?

In the cinematic portrayal of contemporary life, we must question how the details of childrearing, women's crafts, and women's intellectual endeavors are or are not presented in films, news, or ads. We rarely see media images that match the variety of clothes that women wear in daily life, women's varieties of weight and age and tone of voice or accent, and women's varieties of gesture according to their mood and the specific moment in their lives. The patriarchal visual iconography of female figures in film includes the following; mother, child, virago, granny (variant: old maid), ingenue, good wife, and siren. Good wives are blonde, sirens dark haired; erotically eligible figures of both sexes are slender and not yet old. An occasional comic figure escapes the classification by body type. Women's gestures in cinema are rigidly codified, and women's *mise-en-scène* predetermined by the connotative requirements of a previously established narrative scheme.

There are both psychological and economic reasons why the domestic world is devalued in our culture.[11] It is rarely seen or interpreted by hegemonic patriarchal culture for what it is and contains, and its elements are named and defined primarily within the context of a seemingly powerless women's subculture. The domestic sphere, except in melodrama, is rarely depicted in film as an interesting place or the locus of socially significant, multiple, interpersonal relationships. Rather, the domestic sphere is the place where a woman is possessed and a man possesses a woman, a man's castle, a place that the woman clings to. Feature films often judge the woman in the home as narrow, as having a stance morally inferior to the male protagonist's commitment to public duty; or home may become the projection backward to the security and presumed moral strength of the mother, regained through an alliance with a good wife. The home is out of history; cinematic heroes go out into the public sphere to do whatever it is that makes them the hero.

Connotative elements in cinema—here the connotative aspect of film's portrayal of the domestic sphere—are shaped both according to a film's narrative and to what people already know and have seen and experienced.[12] What the elements of the domestic sphere suggest is already conventionalized, already thought about before it gets in a film. But traditional filmmaking has drawn very narrowly even from the pool of conventional knowledge about domestic life.

One of the self-appointed tasks of contemporary Feminist art is to articulate, expand, and comment on women's own subcultural codification of the connotations of those visual elements and icons familiar to them in their private sphere. Thus, painter Judy Chicago paints "cunt" flowers, and other artists, notably sculptors, have elaborated sculptures or artifacts of paper crafts, sewing, quilting, feathers, enclosed spaces and cubicles, and family photos, such materials being used for the suggestive value they bear from the domestic sphere.

For Feminist writers and filmmakers, autobiography and biography provide an essential tool for looking in a self-conscious way at women's subculture, their role in or exclusion from the public sphere, their fantasy life, their sense of "embeddedness" in a certain object world. In other words, they become the way both back and forward toward naming and describing what woman really is, in that political and artistic act that Adrienne Rich calls "diving into the wreck."

Feminist films look at familiar women's elements to define them in a new, uncolonized way. Among the connotative elements to which Feminist documentaries draw our attention and give an added complexity are the visual cues that define womanliness in film. The women characters' gestures, clothes, age, weight, sexual preference, race, class, embeddedness in a specific social milieu elicit our reflection on both the specificity of the subjects' and our own lives, and on the difference between these cinematic representations and those of dominant cinema. As a result of these films, a much broader range of and more forceful and complex women characters now engage our interest as cinematic subjects, and they are shown doing a wider range of activities in greater detail than ever before in narrative cinema. The biographical documentary serves as a critique of and antidote to past cinematic depictions of women's lives and women's space.

In the film *Self Health*, two whole areas of visual imagery are challenged: the portrayal of women's sexuality and nudity, and health care. Domestic space in this film becomes the locus for a collective coming to knowledge about women's bodies and simultaneously the locus for a new kind of health care delivery. *The Chicago Maternity Center Story*, contrasting home delivery with hospital care, valorizes the same iconic contrasts: health care at home is more "human."

Talking Heads/New Rules of the Game

The visual portrayal of the women in Feminist documentaries is often criticized for its transparency (film's capturing reality) or for the visual dullness of talking heads. Yet the stories that the filmed women tell are not just "slices of experience." These stories serve a function aesthetically in reorganizing women viewers' expectations derived from patriarchal narratives and in initiating a critique of those narratives. The female figures talking to us on the screen in *Janie's Janie, Joyce at 34, Union Maids, Three Lives, The Woman's Film*, and *We're Alive* are not just characters whom we encounter as real-life individuals. Rather, the filmmakers have clearly valorized their subjects' words and edited their discourse. In all the Feminist documentaries, the sound track, usually told in the subjects' own words, serves the function of rephrasing, criticizing, or articulating for the first time the rules of the game as they have been and as they should be for women.

The sound track of the Feminist documentary film often consists almost entirely of women's self-conscious, heightened, intellectual discussion of role and sexual politics. The film gives voice to that which had in the media been spoken for women by patriarchy. Received notions about women give way to an outpouring of real desires, contradictions, decisions, and social analyses. After I showed Kate Millet's *Three Lives* to an introductory film class in 1972, a woman student came up to me gratefully after class and commented, "I'll bet that's the first time a lot of those guys have had to sit and listen uninterruptedly to women talking for ninety minutes. I wonder what it means to them to listen to women without having the chance to butt in and have their say."

More than what it means for men to listen to women's self-consciously told "stories," what has it meant for us women in the course of the contemporary women's movement—what have we learned? We have learned what our sexuality is, how mothers can hate and need and love their children, how we can tell a boss or a lover or a friend or a sexist fool off, how "It's not our fault," and where our personal struggles are located in and contribute to and are supported by the larger forces that define our historical period. These films both depict and encourage a politicized "conversation" among women; and in these films, the self-conscious act of telling one's story as a woman in a politicized yet personal way gives the older tool of women's subcultural resistance, conversation, a new social force as a tool for liberation.

Contribution to Public Struggle

The Feminist documentaries speak to working women, encourage them in their public struggles, and broaden their horizons to make demands in other spheres as well. To define structures of patriarchy is as important to women workers as to define structures of capitalism. An existential or gut-level militancy becomes refined by a political movement that offers an analysis of and provides a way for seeing both the parameters and details of the struggle as a whole. Yet because of male competitiveness, agressiveness and bluff are not skills women learn as children (and many women do not, necessarily want to learn these tactics as adults either); the women's movement seeks to create new structures to facilitate women's entry into the public sphere of work and power, and to make that public sphere one they would want to inhabit.

Clearly, the powerless will want power, especially once they specifically define the ways they have systematically been robbed of it. But women also want to imagine what that power would be if executed in a form commensurate with Feminist goals. Although it is seemingly filmed in domestic space, *Self Health* is a powerful public document in the model for sex education and the vision of collective, community control that it presents. And its sense of women together, coming to (creating, seizing) knowledge is subversive. As one of my women students said, in a single-sex discussion we had after the film and which became an outpouring of women's concerns," My mother is a liberal and thinks children and adolescents should have sex education. But where she'd accept a film showing a nurse or doctor examining a woman, she'd be horrified to see this one where women are doing it in a group."

JoAnn Elam's *Rape* represents perhaps a new trend in Feminist documentaries.[13] Coming out of an experimental film tradition, Elam uses both Brechtian intertitles and a symbolic iconography intercut with a video transfer of a conversation she taped with rape victims one night in one of the women's apartment. The women's conversation forms the sound track of the film, and Elam both heightens and comments wittily on their points by repeating some of their lines in the intertitles. The film is an angry one that elaborates a whole new film style adequate to treating the subject of rape with neither titillation nor pathos. The women filmed are impassioned and intellectual. They are discussing their experiences with the group's support and within the security of domestic space; most of them are political activists in organizations against rape, and all saw the making of this film as an explicitly public act. The Feminist documentary films articulate a vision, in part being realized now, of what the shift in relations in the public sphere would be and how power would be enacted if women were to gain and use power in a Feminist way.

The Feminist documentaries represent a use of, yet a shift in, the aesthetics of *cinéma vérité* due to the filmmakers' close identification with their subjects, participation in the women's movement, and sense of the films' intended effect. The structure of the consciousness-raising group becomes the deep structure repeated over and over in these films. Within such a narrative structure, either a single woman tells her story to the filmmaker or a group of women are filmed sharing experiences in a politicized way. They are filmed in domestic space, and their words serve to redefine that space in a new, "woman-identified" way. Either the stance of the people filmed or the stance of the film as a whole reflects a commitment to changing the public sphere as well; and for this reason, these filmmakers have used an accessible documentary form. In the "surface structure" of the films, a new iconography of women's bodies and women's space emerges that implicitly challenges the general visual depiction of women in capitalist society, perhaps in many socialist ones, too. The sound tracks have women's voices speaking continuously; and the films' appeal lies not only in having strong women tell about their lives but even more in our hearing and having demonstrated that some women have deliberately altered the rules of the game of sexual politics. All *cinéma vérité* is not the same, and much of the current discussion of and attack on cinematic realism dismisses the kind of documentary film style that most people are used to. If one looks closely at the relation of this politicized genre to the movement it is most intimately related to, we can see how both the exigencies and forms of organization of an ongoing political movement can affect the aesthetics of documentary film.

NOTES

1. This article is part of a book-length project on the presentation of women's bodies and women's space in contemporary documentary film.
2. Many of the Feminist documentaries (I have given only a representative list of them) are described briefly in Linda Artel's and Susan Wengraf's *Positive Images: Non-Sexist Films for Young People* (San Francisco: Booklegger Press, 1976). Interviews with Feminist filmmakers often appear alongside reviews of their films in *Jump Cut.*
3. Experimental filmmaking techniques or an innovative "stretching" of the *cinéma vérité* form are particularly well used in JoAnn Elam's *Rape,* Michelle Citron's *Parthenogenesis,* and the collectively produced *We're Alive.*
4. An activist in health care struggles criticizes the political analyses offered in Feminist health care films in Marcia Rothenberg's "Good Vibes *vs.* Preventive Medicine: Healthcaring From our End of the Speculum," *Jump Cut,* No. 17 (April, 1978), p. 3.
5. John Berger, *Ways of Seeing* (New York: The Viking Press, 1973), pp. 63–64.
6. Such an idea loosely derives from the work of Claude Lévi-Strauss in *Structural Anthropology,* trans. C. Jacobson and B. G. Schoepf (Garden City, N.Y.: Doubleday Anchor, 1967).
7. *Cinéma vérité* films in the United States made by male filmmakers are characized precisely by the film's ironic distance from the subject and the filmmaker's presentation of his vision of the subject as his "creation." Films by Frederick Wiseman, Richard Leacock, David Pennebaker, Tom Palazzolo, and the Haysles brothers fall in this category.
8. For an extended discussion of consciousness-raising groups, see Jo Freeman, *The Politics of Women's Liberation* (New York: David McKay, 1975).
9. For a consideration of these issues—women's "dispossession," their loss of a sense of self, and their role in the domestic sphere—see the following: Susan Brown miller. *Against Our Will: Men, Women, and Rape* (New York: Bantam, 1975); TiGrace Atkinson, "The Institution of Sexual Intercourse," *Amazon Odyssey* (NewYork: Links Books, 1971); Charles Kleinhans, "Notes on Melodrama and the Family under Capitalism" (contains useful bibliography). *Film Reader,* No. 3 (1978); Laura Mulvey, "Douglas Sirk and Melodrama," and Geoffrey Nowell-Smith, "Minelll and Melodrama," *The Australian Journal of Film Theory,* No. 3 (1977).
10. Nancy Chodorow, "Mothering, Object-Relations and the Female Oedipal Configuration," *Feminist Studies,* 4, No. 1, (February 1978); "Family Structure and Feminine Personality," *Woman, Culture and Society,* Michelle Rosaldo and Lois Lamphere, eds. (Stanford: Stanford University Press, 1974); "Oedipal Assymetries and Heterosexual Knots," *Social Problems,* 23, No. 4 (April 1976).
11. Sheila Rowbotham, *Woman's Consciousness, Man's World* (Baltimore: Penguin, 1973); Eli Zaretsky, *Capitalism, the Family, and Personal Life* (New York: Harper, 1976); Juliet Mitchell, *Woman's Estate* (New York: Pantheon, 1971).
12. Lesage, *"S/Z* and *Rules of the Game," Jump Cut,* No. 12/13 (1976).
13. This discussion is drawn from a paper on the film *Rape,* which I delivered at the 1978 Purdue Conference on Film Studies and which will be published in a forth-coming issue of *Jump Cut.*

83

E. ANN KAPLAN

THEORIES AND STRATEGIES OF THE FEMINIST DOCUMENTARY (1983)

Over the past decade, a large number of women's independent films have been produced internationally; they reflect a wide variety of styles and genres (from realism to animation, from the non-narrative abstract film to fiction films), a broad range of subjects, and a wide spectrum of ideological perspectives. Women interested in bringing about change, however (I reserve the word "feminist" for such women), have been involved in the question of strategies in two important ways: first, ever since the publication in 1973 of Claire Johnston's essay, "Women's Cinema as Counter-Cinema," filmmakers and critics have been involved in an often heated debate about the most effective strategies to be used *within* film texts; second, and more recently, they have been concerned with the question of strategies of production, exhibition, and distribution of independent feminist films. Both of these involve the positioning of the spectator, but in the first, focus is on how a text positions the spectator (if, indeed, we agree that texts monolithically do this); while in the second, the focus is on how the *institutional context* of a film's production and reception affect the way the spectator "reads" the film.

In structuring my discussion around the issues of strategies for bringing about change, I realize that I am entering the slippery terrain where theory and practice overlap. This is dangerous on two levels: there is first the danger of alienating both theorists and those involved in practice; and second, there is the danger of slippage of terms as one moves from one discourse to another.

But in the case of feminism in particular the bridging of discourses seems crucial: feminism, as it has always defined itself historically, is a social and political movement; it has risen out of the realm of the social, that is, out of women's dissatisfaction with their political and social positioning. It is thus particularly inappropriate for feminist thought to remain locked into a theoretical discourse unrelated to practice. This is not to say that feminists should not develop theory—far from it. For if theory needs a practice to which it relates, practice without theory is equally empty.

In this first part of the essay, concerned with the debate about the most effective cinematic strategies, I will first, demonstrate that the attack on women's realist documentary was part of an attack on realism in general and that it involved a related attack on "essentialism," or the assumption that there existed a specific female power in the body of individual women. Second, I will discuss two well-known early women's documentaries in order to show that these criticisms have a certain validity while at the same time exploring some of the problems with the theory out of which the criticisms emerge; and finally, I will analyze and evaluate some alternative cinematic strategies that arose specifically out of the theoretical problems with realism.

In the second (shorter) part of the essay, I will deal with the strategies of production, exhibition and reception, and raise a number of questions about work that needs to be done as we look back at the enterprise of the last decade—an enterprise that reveals a shift from the essentially didactic and propagandistic strategies of early activists and bourgeois feminists, to the focus on signifying practices, that is, on representation and the cinematic apparatus, which are now seen as crucial concerns in any effort to bring about change.

Part I

First, the objection against realism and *cinema verité*: In her essay, Claire Johnston argued that *cinema verité* or the "cinema of non-intervention," was dangerous for feminists since it used a realist aesthetic developed specifically out of Capitalist notions of representation. *Verité* films do not break the illusion of realism. Since the "truth" of our oppression cannot be captured on celluloid by means of an "innocent" camera, for feminist cinema to be effective, she argued, it must be a counter-cinema.

> Any revolutionary must challenge the depiction of reality; it is not enough to discuss the oppression of women within the text of the film; the language of the cinema/depiction of reality must also be interrogated, so that a break between ideology and text is affected.[1]

Feminist filmmakers, that is, must confront within their films the accepted representations of reality so as to expose their falseness. Realism as a style is unable to change consciousness because it does not depart from the forms that embody the old consciousness. Thus, prevailing realist codes—of camera, lighting, sound, editing, *mise-en-scène*—must be abandoned and the cinematic apparatus used in a new way so as to challenge audiences' expectations and assumptions about life.

Noel King argues something very similar in a recent *Screen* article on two political feminist documentaries—*Union Maids* and *Harlan County U.S.A.* (which belong in the category of historical/retrospective films). He elaborates on points that Johnston, given her brief essay, was unable to develop, and attempts to "read these documentaries against the grain, to refuse the reading it is the work of their textual systems to secure."[2] In doing this, he is applying the same critical categories that have been used to decode Hollywood films, making essentially no distinction between the realist techniques used in the classical Hollywood tradition and those being used in the new feminist documentary. (He is here building on work done by Stephen Neale on the '30's Populist films and Nazi propaganda films.)[3] King points, for example, to the way the films' strategies work to suppress any discourse on the social construction of the subjects being interviewed in the interests of asserting the individual's responsibility for bringing about change through a moral insight into injustice:

> In this sense, the politics in *Union Maids* might be termed a "redemptive politics": that is to say . . . a system where questions of individual responsibility are paramount. It is a politics articulated by textual mechanisms which fix the individual subject as responsible, as either fulfilling, or not fulfilling a morally given imperative and this in turn results in a notion of triumph or guilt.[4]

Second, he talks of the films' strategies as essentially narrative ones: they use, he says "a series of sub-forms of narratives: biography, autobiography and popular narrative history." These, King shows, all follow a cause-effect relationship, the origin always containing the end. Through the linking of archival footage, the anecdotal reminiscences constructed in the interviews, and the bridging voice-over narration (spoken by the three women) talking about America in the 1930's, *Union Maids* produces a " 'discourse of continuity' which results not in 'the past' but in the effect of the past."[5] What King is ultimately objecting to is the way the narrative in *Union Maids* and *Harlan County U.S.A.* produces a "syntagmatic flow of events, an easy diachronic progression which ensures a working out of all problems, guarantees an increase in knowledge on the reader's part, promises containment and completion."[6] This kind of suturing is, of course, the traditional device of the classic Hollywood film in its arm to smooth over possible contradictions, incoherences, and eruptions that might reflect a reality far less ordered, coherent, or continuous than Hollywood wants to admit or to know. Like Claire Johnston, King concludes by asserting the necessity of creating a different type of text, one that resists the rhetorical conventions of populist cultural history that "depicts its own strategies and practices, and which does not provide a complete, unified representation of class and collectivity."[7]

The second overall objection to women's realist films is summarized by the charge of essentialism. In their discussion of several textual strategies employed by women artists, Sandy Flitterman and Judith Barry argue that female creators of all kinds must avoid claiming a specific female power which could find expression if allowed to be explored freely. They realize that the impulse toward this notion is understandable for the way it seeks "to reinforce satisfaction in being a woman in a culture that does the opposite"[8] and to encourage solidarity amongst women through emotional appeal. But, they argue, this form of feminist art harbors a danger by not taking into account "the social contradictions involved in 'femininity.' " They suggest that "a more theoretically informed art can contribute to enduring changes by addressing itself to structural and deep-seated causes of women's oppression rather than its effects. A radical feminist art would include an understanding of how women are constructed through social practices in culture."[9] They argue ultimately for "an aesthetic designed to subvert the production of 'woman' as commodity," much as Claire Johnston had earlier stated that to be feminist, a cinema had to be a counter-cinema.

Before analyzing the validity of these positions on realist women's documentaries, it is important to understand the theoretical sources for such arguments. Although Russian Formalism and Brecht had some place in their development, by far the most important influence on new film criticism generally came from the fields of semiology, structuralism and psychoanalysis as they were developed in France in the '50's and '60's by writers such as Lévi-Strauss, Lacan, Metz, Barthes, Kristeva and Althusser. They found their way into British film criticism in the '70's and shortly afterwards, into the work of American graduate students who studied at the French Cinema School organized in part by Metz and Bellour. The combined influence of the French and British film theory produced a new body of theory in America that has far-reaching implications in relation to the underlying view of the human subject and of women in society, as is evident from the attack on realism.

[...]

Realism as an artistic style is designed to perpetuate this illusion of a stable world; and within realism it is of course the *verité* documentary that seems most confidently "a window through which . . . (the) world is clearly visible," and "where the signifiers appear to point directly and confidently to the signifieds."[10] The realist aesthetic semiologists were in opposition to was developed in the post-war period, stimulated in part by the Italian neo-realist movement. Theorists Kracauer and Bazin argued for the cinema "as the redemption of physical reality," and for the belief that realist techniques allowed us to perceive actuality for ourselves, unmediated by the distortions produced through other cinematic techniques. The realism outside of the commercial cinema, stimulated by World War II, whether documentary or fiction, took as its aim the capturing on film of the daily experiences of ordinary people. Directors saw their closer relationship to lived *experience* as arising from (a) their use of working class people and issues for their subjects (i.e. this class, and its concerns, are somehow more "real" than the middle classes); (b) their basing of their films on real life rather than fictional events; (c) their use of on-location shooting rather than artificial studio sets: (d) finally, their use of cinematic techniques, such as the long-take, which were assumed to prevent the meddling with actuality that was characteristic, in their view, with montage.

The first independent women's films that I will discuss situated themselves essentially in the kind of realist tradition which is anathema to the semiologists. The immediate influence was primarily the British Free Cinema movement and the work of the National Film Board of Canada, but the French New Wave was also important. Particularly influential for women's documentaries, in the midst of this complex interaction affecting film generally, was the work of the American Newsreel collective, started in 1962 and largely inspired by Norm Fruchter after working in England. Newsreel's aims (partly influenced by Vertov's weekly newsreel of events from the War front) were explicitly propagandistic; i.e. to publicize the many political events that '60's radicals were involved in, including civil rights, community organizing, black power, the Vietnam movement, strikes and sit-ins, the take-over of educational institutions, and finally, the women's movement. They used the, by this time familiar, verité techniques (that originated in the French New Wave) of fast film stock (with its grey, grainy tones), handheld camera, interviews, voice-over (not necessarily commentary), editing both for shock effect and to develop a specific interpretation of political events. Made on a very low budget, and in a collective mode, the films are necessarily rough, often sloppy: but this reflects merely the overriding aim not to produce aesthetic objects but to create powerful organizing tools. It is precisely their validity as organizing tools that the new theory questions. For according to the theory, the films draw on codes that cannot change consciousness.

This is expressed most strongly by Eileen McGarry in her article on "Documentary, Realism and Women's Cinema." She points out that long before the filmmakers arrive at the scene, reality itself is coded "first in the infrastructure of the social formation (human economic practice) and secondly by the superstructure of politics and ideology."[11] The filmmaker, then, is "not dealing with reality, but with that which has become the pro-filmic event: that which exists and happens in front of the camera."[12] She argues that to ignore the "manner in which the dominant ideology and cinematic traditions encode the pro-filmic event is to hide the fact that reality is selected and altered by the presence of the film workers, and the demands of the equipment."[13]

While this is true to a certain extent (obviously any screen image is the result of a great deal of selection, both in terms of what footage to show, which shot to place next to which, the angle and distance from the subject, what words to use, etc.), as we will see, the documentarist neither has total control over the referent nor is she totally controlled by signifiying practices. Paradoxically, what she does have more control over is precisely ideology. For I cannot even begin a discussion of the films without differentiating them according to ideological perspective—i.e. their feminist politics—and this is a distinction that the theory does not allow for, given its high level of abstraction. All the early films used the same cinematic strategies, but the ends to which these strategies were directed fell into two broad camps: there were first, films like the pioneering Newsreel's *Woman's Film* that exhibited a clear leftist-activist politics; and films like Reichert/Klein's *Growing Up Female* that reflected a more liberal-bourgeois stance, showing how sex-roles in our society were clearly demarcated so as to privilege men, but not analysing the underlying reasons for gender-typing or dealing with class and economic relations. The Newsreel film aimed to raise consciousness explicitly and exclusively on the matter of exploitation of working-class women by a capitalist system geared to support private enterprise, and the accumulation of individual wealth; while the second film urged women to try to free themselves from the sex-roles that limited their opportunities for a rich, fulfilling, challenging, individual life. Yet, the cinematic devices in the two films were identical.

Let us now look at two early films, *Joyce at 34* and *Janie's Janie* (made shortly after those already mentioned) in order to assess the degree to which some of the semiological theoretical criticisms are indeed valid, and the degree to which they are clearly inadequate: (a) to explain concrete differences between the films in terms of their ideology: (b) in terms of the conception of the cinematic apparatus; so that fiction and documentary are seen as essentially the same; (c) in terms of the conception of the positioning of the spectator as "fixed," by the codes of the signifying practices.

First, let me summarize the degree to which this criticism of realism is valid for aspects of both *Joyce at 34* and *Janie's Janie.* To begin with, the cinematic strategies of both films are indeed such as to establish an unwelcome imbalance between author and spectator. The authors in each case assume the position of the one in possession of knowledge, while the spectators are forced into the position of passive consumers of this knowledge. The filmic processes leave us with no work to do, so that we sit passively and receive the message in the first film about how marriage, family, and career can together function harmoniously, and in the second, about how, with some determination, a woman on welfare can organize her community for needed changes. There is a classic resolution in each case, since both heroines arrive at some destination, leaving us with a sense of completion, as though there were nothing left for us to do.

Second, the direct mode of address in both films encourages us to relate to the images of Joyce and Janie as "real" women, as if we could know them. Yet, in fact both figures are constructed in the film by the processes of camera, lighting, sound, editing. They have no other ontological status than that of representations.

Third, the reason we do not realize that each female figure is a representation is that, neither film draws attention to itself as film, or makes us aware that we are watching a film. Neither film, thus, breaks our usual habits of passive viewing in the commercial cinema.

Fourth, underlying all of the above is the key notion of the unified self that characterizes pre-semiological thought. Both Joyce and Janie, as subjects, are seen in the autobiographical mode, as having essences that have persisted through time and whose personal growth or change is autonomous, outside the influence of social structures, economic relations, or psychoanalytic laws. The use of both home movies and old photographs is crucial as a device that establishes continuity through time and that reflects the fiction-making urge that, as Metz and Heath have shown, pervades even the documentary. Used as unproblematic representations, the past images function to seal individual change instead of providing evidence of the way women and their bodies are constructed by the signifying practices of both the social and psychological institutions in which they are embedded. (Interestingly enough, this construction makes a main theme in Michelle Citron's *Daughter Rite* [1978] where the slowing down of home movies enables us to see that the representations are far from an "innocent recording," that the process of making the movies in itself functions to construct the place for the female children.)

But this is as far as the similarities in the realist mode go; the differences rise out of the different relationship to class issues on the part of the filmmakers. In *Joyce at 34*, all mention of class and of economic relations is suppressed, so that we are never allowed to focus on the privileged situation that Joyce enjoys with her freelancing writer husband (he can be at home much of the time) nor the support of her comfortably middle-class parents. The cinematic strategies here work to suture over conflicts and contradictions as in a Hollywood film. Joyce's voice-over, with its "metaphysic of presence" keeps the spectator believing in Joyce as a person. It guides us and makes coherent what would otherwise be a disoriented, disconnected, chaotic world, a series of shots with no necessary connection. Her voice alone makes a comfortably reassuring world where the signifiers respond to an apparently solid signified. And as representation, Joyce does not in herself threaten accepted norms, while her unusually handsome husband adds a gloss to Joyce's environment which, in any case, fits the bourgeois model of commercial representations.

The structure of *Joyce at 34*, thus, perpetuates the bourgeois illusions of the possibility of the individual to effect change and of the individual's transcendence of the symbolic and other social institutions in which he/she lives. In fact, reading the film against the grain, one can see how Joyce is very much at the mercy of the structures that shaped her! *Janie's Janie*, on the other hand, shows a woman who is aware of the economic and class structures that formed her and who has made a deliberate, and decisive, break with those structures. She speaks of her awareness of her position as Other to the two men in her life—father and husband—without blaming them personally for the oppression she suffered at their hands. They are also victims of the symbolic organization of things.

Second, Janie's image itself violates normal codes. As a working class figure (one that is rarely treated without condescension in visual representation or without being seen as co-optable by reform or charity—as are the figures in Grierson's and Jennings' work), who speaks roughly and is not elegantly turned out, Janie's image is subversive. As an unabashedly militant, determined woman who is ready to fight, Janie resists dominant female placing.

Third, in contrast to *Joyce at 34*, the traditional apparatus of the "gaze" does not come into play in *Janie's Janie*. Janie is not placed as object of the male look (although she cannot avoid the look of the camera or of the male audience). Within the diegesis, she is never looked upon by men or set up for their gaze as in commercial cinema.

Finally, the cinematic strategies are not as boringly realist as are those in *Joyce at 34*.

There are soft superimpositions (Janie's face in the kitchen window superimposed on the street and house outside), darkly-lit shots (to suggest Janie's loneliness before starting community organizing, a poignant music track, odd angles of filming, and suggestive shots of washing blowing in the wind. There is, thus, a nice "before" and "after" division. This is a realist film which, given its parameters, manages to achieve much both ideologically and visually.

This comparison of *Joyce at 34* and *Janie's Janie* has, I think, shown that while criticisms of the realist *verité* film are to a degree entirely valid, their monolithic, abstract formulation is a problem. When one looks closely at individual realist films, one realizes the weakness of the large generalizations. Realist films, that is, are far more heterogenous and complex in their strategies than the theoretical critique can allow for. We need a theory that will permit/accept different positionings toward class and economic issues in the realist mode, and that, while not mitigating any of the semiological problems, especially around the overall positioning of the spectator as passive recipient of knowledge, at least grants a limited area of resistance to hegemonic codes in certain examples of the form.

It is at this point important to explore the implications of the position from which the critique of realism emerged, particularly in relation first, to the concept of the human subject in society as well as in film (i.e. is the theory of knowledge underlying the objection to realism valid?); and second, in relation to the theory of the cinematic apparatus, and the way that it functions.

First, realism is objected to because semiology denies that there is any knowable reality outside discourse, that is, outside signifying practices. If the eighteenth-century neo-classical critics went wrong in demanding that the discrepancy between poetry and reality be eliminated (i.e. in asking that poetry imitate the external world as it is, keeping to "the *kinds* of objects that we know to exist, and the *kinds* of events that we know to be possible, on the basis of an empirical knowledge of nature and nature's laws");[14] and if the Romantic critics who followed went wrong in asserting a privileged poetic discourse that reflected not external reality but the spontaneous overflow of feelings (i.e. the poet's mind as it transformed, by intense emotional excitement, external nature and put forth images, that corresponded to nothing outside of the poet);[15] then semiology goes wrong (in some applications) in conceiving of art and life as equally "constructed" by the signifying practices that define and limit each sphere.

The documentary filmmakers were misguided in returning to the eighteenth-century notion of art as capable of simply imitating life, as if through a transparent glass, and in believing that representation could affect behaviour directly (i.e. that an image of a poor woman would immediately bring political awareness of the need to distribute wealth more fairly). But there are problems also in making the signifier material in the sense that it is all there is to know. Discussing semiology in relation to Marxism, Terry Eagleton points out the dangers of this way of seeing for a Marxist view of history. History evaporates in the new scheme; since the signified can never be grasped, we cannot talk about our reality as human subjects. But, as he goes on to show, more than the signified is at stake: "It is also," he says, "a question of the referent (i.e. social actuality), which we all long ago bracketed out of being. In rematerializing the sign, we are in imminent danger of dematerializing its referent; a linguistic materialism gradually reverts itself into a linguistic idealism."[16]

Eagleton no doubt overstates the case when he talks about "sliding away from the referent," since neither Saussure nor Althusser denied that there was a referent. But it is true that while semiologists talk about the eruption of "the real" (i.e. accidents, death, revolution), on a daily basis they see life as dominated by the prevailing signifying practices of a culture, i.e., as refracted through those discourses which define "reality" for people. While I have no quarrel with this concern with the discourses which define and limit our notions of "reality" and agree that these discourses are essentially controlled by the classes that are in power, it seems important to allow for a level of experience that differs from discourse, or that is not only discourse. Where semiology and post-structuralism are most useful is in finally ridding us of the notion of a privileged aesthetic discourse—a notion that has only perpetuated a hampering dualism between art and science (broadly conceived). But if we want to create art that will bring about change in the quality of people's daily lives in the social formation, we need a theory that takes account of the level now usually referred to scornfully as "naively materialistic."[17]

But before leaving the attack on realism as a cinematic strategy, I want to deal briefly with two assumptions about the cinematic apparatus that appear in the theory. First, how valid is it to apply the same criticism to realist practices used in the commercial, narrative cinema and to those used in the independent documentary form? I would rather loosen up the theory, and argue that the same realist signifying practices can indeed be used for different ends, as we have already seen in comparing *Janie's Janie* and *Joyce at 34*. Realism in the commercial cinema may indeed be a form analogous to the nineteenth century novel, in which a class-bound, bourgeois notion of the world is made to seem "natural" and "unproblematic." But *Janie's Janie* is not *An Unmarried Woman;* while *Joyce at 34* does come close to the form as used in Mazursky's work.

Johnston's and King's attack on realism is confused by their assumption that the realist cinematic mode in *itself* raises problems about the relation of representation to lived experience. The problems reside rather in either the filmmaker's or the audience's assumptions about this relation. But taken simply as a cinematic style that can be used in different genres (i.e. documentary or fictional), realism does not insist on any special relation to the social formation.[18] As Metz has noted, it is "the *impression of reality* experienced by the spectator . . . the feeling that we are witnessing an almost real spectacle. . . ." that causes the problems.[19] It is, Metz continues, the fact "that films have the *appeal* of presence and of a proximity that strikes the masses and fills the movie theaters."[20]

In fact, as Metz goes on to show, the crucial difference is not between cinematic modes (illusion of realism versus anti-illusionism), but between an event in the here and now, and a *narrated* event. As soon as we have the process of telling, the real is unrealized (or the unreal is realized, as he sometimes puts it).[21] Thus, even the documentary or the live television coverage, in *narrating* the event creates the distance that affects unrealization. "Realism," Metz notes, "is not reality. . . . [it] affects the organization of the contents, not narration as a status."[22]

Thus, despite the fact that documentary and fiction films begin with different material (the one actors in a studio, the other actual people in their environment), once this material becomes a strip of film to be edited as the author wishes, to be constructed in whatever way he/she wishes, the difference almost evaporates. Both fiction and non-fiction tend to create fiction, as we've seen—often in the family romance mode. And indeed, if we go along with McGarry, we have seen that even before the filming starts, the pro-filmic event is heavily coded by the cultural assumptions people bring to the process of making a film. So the documentary ends up as much a "narrative" in a certain sense, as an explicitly fiction film. Working from the opposite direction, in addition, one can argue (as has Michael Ryan) that all fiction films are really "documentaries" in that all of us watching know, on one level, that everything has been enacted, that we are watching a star playing at being someone, at actions manipulated in a studio to look like real events.[23]

Yet, on two fundamental levels, one that affects the filmmakers and one that involves the spectator, documentary and fiction *are* different. As regards the filmmakers, there is clearly a degree more control in the fiction film than in the documentary. Documentary filmmaking may permit more or less control depending on the project (i.e. a retrospective film, relying on real footage, allows more reconstruction of actual events through montage in the manner of narrative films), than, say, does a documentary about a demonstration when the filmmakers on the scene have little idea of how things will work out.) But what happens in fiction is only controlled if one is working within certain genres, or within institutions, like Hollywood, that permit only certain things to happen. Otherwise, fiction has the potential for representing imaginative possibility—(e.g. models for change)—once the Oedipal mode is broken.

My aim in asserting a difference between fiction and documentary from the perspective of the filmmakers is to avoid the unsatisfactory alternatives of (1) a fixed, binary opposition between fiction and documentary; or (2) annihilating *all* difference through the assertion that all cinematic discourse is controlled by the same signifying practices that define and limit what can be represented. While Metz's broad distinction between an event and a *narrated* event obviously holds, it works only on a very abstract and general level. In fact, we need to make distinctions between different genres in the "narrated" category, recognizing that there is a broad spectrum of film types—from narrations limited by their reliance (to a degree) on the physical world, to those that use everyday logic but construct their environments, to those that use the supernatural (what Metz calls a "non-human logic"). The problems that the filmmakers face in each case are different and each film-type has certain dangers, certain advantages.

Second, as regards the spectator: audiences are clearly positioned differently in fictional and in documentary films, as may be seen from the betrayal spectators experience in films like Mitchell Block's *No Lies* or Michelle Citron's more recent *Daughter Rite*. In both cases, the directors use *verité* techniques, deluding us into thinking we are watching non-actors while in fact at the end we learn that everything was scripted, with actors playing the roles. The anger that audiences experience must mean that a different identification process takes place in the two situations, and this may well have implications for calculating the ultimate effect on the spectator.

Any discussion of these effects must, unfortunately, be entirely speculative, given the lack of reliable research into this area. If I may descend into totally non-scientific evidence for a moment, some responses by students lead me to believe that it's true (as Mulvey has argued) that the identification with stars in a fiction film involves a return to the world of the Imaginary (i.e. some evocation of an ego-ideal that, in Lacan's system, predated the entry into the Symbolic); whereas the documentary involves a relating to images that is *analogous* to, i.e. *not* the same as (this was the error of the neo-classical movement) the way we respond to people in our daily lives. Although on one level the documentary realist strategies do indeed construct the spectator as passive recipient of the "knowledge" the authors hold, on another level, the spectator may be making judgements about the screen-image woman that indeed have to do with the codes of signifying practice, but which result from the sociological and political positioning of the spectator, i.e. his/her class, race, gender, educational background, as this affects experiences with signification.[24] For instance, some students react quite hostilely to Janie, criticizing the way she treats her children (she is too rough on them, she does not dress them well, she does not love them enough, she does not educate them properly); some may object to the way she looks, to the fact that she wears a wig or dyes her hair different colors, etc.

Two things may be happening here: a Barthesian answer is that the spectator is applying to the screen image the codes through which we learn to perceive reality in the outside world; but in addition, the spectator may be resisting being presented with an unconventional image, one which violates his/her expectations, given commercial representations. In other words, much more may be taking place as people watch such documentaries than we know about (the representations may bore, shock, please, or inform, depending on the class, race and background of the spectator), but an *active* response is being evoked, one that has potential for (a) challenging assumptions about what we expect from cinema and (b) adding to what we know about the world.

However, as specific organizing strategies, the films may very well not work. If semiologists were wrong in denying that realism can produce an effect leading to change, then leftist-activists were wrong in assuming that merely showing something is an argument in its own right. The authors of *Janie's Janie* evidently assumed that any spectator would automatically side with Janie because they had set her up as a figure to be admired, presented her change as an exemplary one. They did not seem aware of the possibility that Janie as *image* would appear in another light than Janie as the real woman they knew, and thus would be shocked by the kinds of readings my students gave.

[. . .]

I have tried to show that the debate about realism is in some sense a false debate, premised first on an unnecessarily rigid theory about the relationship between form and content; and second on a theory of knowledge which, while it illuminates our contemporary system of relationships (particularly the relationship of the individual to language and the other social structures in which he/she lives) is nevertheless inadequate when applied to a practice intent upon bringing about concrete change in the daily lives of women.[25]

[. . .]

The exposing of the decentered, problematic self through semiology and psychoanalysis (I am not now questioning its validity) has not been followed by sufficient study of its political and social implications. So much concern has been given to undermining bourgeois modes of thought and perception that we have failed to consider the problem of where this leaves us. Women critics and filmmakers have been placed in a position of negativity—in strategies subverting rather than positing. The dangers of undermining the notion of the unified self and of a world of essences are relativism and despair.

At this point, then, we must use what we have learned in the past ten years to move theoretically beyond deconstruction to reconstruction. While it is essential for feminist film critics to examine signifying processes carefully in order to understand the way in which women have been constructed in language and in film, it is equally important not to lose sight of the material world in which we live, and in which our oppression takes concrete, often painful, forms. We need films that will show us how, having once mastered (i.e. understood fully) the existing discourses that oppress us, we stand in a different position in relation to those discourses. Knowledge is, in that sense, power. We need to know how to manipulate the recognized, dominating, discourses so as to begin to free ourselves *through* rather than beyond them (for what is there "beyond"?).

It should be clear that I am far from advocating a return to realism as the best or only viable cinematic strategy for bringing about change, and it should also be clear that I am excited by (and have in fact been one of the main promoters of) the new theory-films. On the level of theory, I am arguing for a less dogmatic approach to cinematic practice, one that would allow directors to see realism as a possible mode, given that we now know more about the way it operates, are aware of its limitations, and understand it as a system of representation, not truth. And meanwhile theorists should continue to push the limits of cinematic practice, to see what different techniques can yield.

Part II

I want to turn, finally, to the strategies of reception, the importance of which has become increasingly evident. The problem is that the debate that I have followed has taken place mainly on an abstract, theoretical level, divorced from the concrete situation of production, exhibition, and reception. We have been so concerned with figuring out the "correct" theoretical position, the "correct" strategies *theoretically*, that we have forgotten to pay attention first, to the way subjects "receive" (read) films; and second, to the contexts of production and reception, particularly as these affect what films can be made and how films are read.[26]

That criticism is finally turning to this area may be seen from a reading of recent articles in *Screen*, and elsewhere[27] as well as Willemen/McPherson in *British Independence* which looks back at the '30's in order to discover how production, exhibition and distribution practices shaped, or influenced, certain documentary forms.[28] Although it is hard to grasp the implications of practices as one is living them, the Willemen/McPherson book shows the importance of attempting to understand the ways in which *apparently* independent practice is in fact formed by the social institutions in which it is inevitably embedded. Total independent cinematic practice is a utopian myth.

Let me substantiate this last statement by looking briefly at some of the contradictions which have dominated alternate practices of all kinds during the very years when critics have been debating cinematic strategy:

a) Filmmakers have had to rely for funding on the very system they oppose;
b) In the case of the anti-illusionist films, directors have been using cinematic strategies that are difficult for the majority of people raised on narrative and commercial films;
c) Having made the films, directors have not had any mechanism for the distribution and exhibition of their films on a large scale (screenings have been by necessity limited to small art cinemas in a few large cities and to college campuses. It is important to note that things are rather different, and slightly better in Europe).
d) The culminating contradiction is that filmmakers whose whole purpose was to change people's ways of seeing, believing and behaving, have only been able to reach an audience already committed to their values.

Thus critics (hopefully increasingly together with independent filmmakers) need to discuss cinematic strategies not only in terms of the most correct theory, but also in relation to the contradictions outlined above. We have to re-examine together (as a unit, that is) our theory, our cinematic strategies and the strategies of reception as they affect the way a film is "read." But even before doing this, we need to look carefully at the economic base for film production and at the possible influence that funding agencies have had on the very shape of alternate practice.

[...]

It is essential for both feminist film theorists and feminist filmmakers to focus on these central questions if we are to move beyond the impasse that I think we have reached after ten years of intensive, varied, and exciting work. We must begin to create institutions in which feminist theorists and filmmakers can work together for the mutual benefit of both groups. As I've shown, at least in Britain, an apparently beneficial collaboration between filmmakers and theorists has resulted in a group of interesting and innovative films. Such a collaboration is just beginning over here (cf., for example, Michelle Citron's *Daughter Rite,* which shows the influence of the new theories on her filmmaking practice in her attempt to bridge the gap between the early realist-*verité* films and the new anti-illusionist ones). Such collaboration will, I think, produce some interesting work in the near future. Let us use what we have learned from the work of the past decade to overcome divisions between filmmakers and film theorists, and between people with differing theoretical conceptions in each group, so that we can challenge and change dominant discourses and secure ourselves a powerful and permanent voice.

NOTES

1. Claire Johnston, "Women's Cinema as Counter-Cinema," in Johnston, ed., *Notes on Women's Cinema* (SEFT: London, 1973) p. 28.
2. Noel King, "Recent 'Political' Documentary—Notes on *Union Maids* and *Harlan County, USA,"* Screen, Vol. 22, No. 2 (1981), p. 9.
3. Cf. Steve Neale, "Propaganda," *Screen*, Vol. 18, No. 3 (1977), p. 25.
4. King, op. cit., p. 12.
5. Ibid., p. 5.
6. Ibid., p. 17.
7. Ibid., p. 18.
8. Sandy Flitterman and Judith Barry, "Textual Strategies: The Politics of Art Making," *Screen*, Vol. 21, No. 2 (Summer, 1980), p. 37.
9. Ibid., p. 36.
10. Ibid., p. 143.
11. Eileen McGarry, "Documentary Realism and Women's Cinema," in *Women in Film* Vol. 2, No. 7 (Summer, 1975), p. 50.
12. Ibid., p. 50,
13. Ibid., p. 51.
14. M.H. Abrams, *The Mirror and the Lamp. Romantic Theory and the Critical Tradition* (London: Oxford University Press, 1953), p. 267. The whole of this chapter (10) explores the issues of "truth to nature."
15. Ibid., Chapters V and VI on the development of the Romantic theory of poetry.
16. Terry Eagleton, "Aesthetics and Politics," *New Left Review* No. 107 (Jan.-Feb., 1978), p. 22.
17. What I have in mind here is the danger of a theory that ignores the need for emotional identification with people suffering oppression. We may be able to explain the situation of a strike, for example, in terms of dominant versus minority discourses: the dominant discourse in the factory is that of the owners who construct the position of the workers to suit their (the bosses') own interests. One of the few reactions to domination available to the oppressed group is that of striking, although it is clear that this position is very much a defensive one, constructed by the dominant discourse and causing the workers themselves a lot of hardship. The workers, thus, are on a basic material level in need of support (food, clothing), and on the psychological level, in need of emotional support. The level of abstraction on which the theory functions often makes it seem as if these other levels are unimportant or not worth mentioning. That Metz is one of the few critics who retains constant awareness of the level of the social formation is evident not only in his discussion of realism in *Film Language* (see below), but also in an interview in *Discourse* (paradoxically, his statements here prompted Noel King's article referred to above), where he supports the "naively" realist documentary, like *Harlan County U.S.A.* Asked if he thinks a documentary of a strike could be misleading "insofar as it assumes that knowledge is unproblematic, and on the surface," replies Metz: "If the film has a very precise, political and immediate aim; if the filmmakers shoot a film in order to support given strike . . . what could I say? Of course, it's o.k." Talking specifically about *Harlan County,* Metz continues:

    > It is the kind of film that has nothing really new on the level of primary/secondary identification, but it's a very good film . . . It is unfair, in a sense, to call a film into question on terms which are not within the filmmaker's purpose. She intended to . . . support the strike and she did it. It's a marvelous film and I support it.

    "The Cinematic Apparatus as Social Institution—An Interview with Christian Metz," in *Discourse*, No. 1 (Fall, 1979), p. 30.
18. Cf. Dana Polan, "Discourses of Rationality and the Rationality of Discourse in Avant-Garde Political Film Culture," Ohio University Film Conference, April, 1982.
19. Christian Metz, *Film Language: A Semiotics of the Cinema*. Trans. Michael Taylor. (New York: Oxford University Press, 1974), p. 4.
20. Ibid., p. 5.
21. Ibid., p. 22.
22. Ibid., pp. 21–22.
23. Cf. Michael Ryan, "Militant Documentary: Mai 68 Par Lui," in *Ciné-tracts*, No. 7/8.
24. For further discussion of this problem, see Gledhill, op. cit., pp. 469-473.

25. For a full discussion of realist theories of knowledge and society, together with a critique of Althusserian theories, see Terry Lovell, *Pictures of Reality* (London: The British Film Institute, 1980).
26. Julia Lesage began to think about problems of production, exhibition and distribution in a 1974 article, "Feminist Film Criticism: Theory and Practice," *Women and Film*, Vol. 1, Nos. 5-6, pp. 12–20; and in general the journal *Jump Cut* focussed more than others on matters of the social and political context for feminist films. Julia Lesage's article is reprinted in slightly revised version in Patricia Erens, ed., *Sexual Stratagems: The World of Women in Film* (New York: Horizon Press, 1979) pp. 156–167.
27. Cf. for example, Marc Karlin, et al. "Problems of Independent Cinema," *Screen*, Vol. 21, No. 4 (1980/81), pp. 19–43; John Hill, "Ideology, Economy and British Cinema," in *Ideology* and Cultural Production, Michael Barrett, et al., eds. (London: Billings and Sons, Ltd., 1979); Anthony McCall and Andrew Tyndall, "Sixteen Working Statements," *Millennium Film Journal*, Vol. 1, No. 2 (Spring/Summer, 1978), pp. 29–37; Steve Neale, "Oppositional Exhibition: Notes and Problems," *Screen*, Vol. 21, No. 3 (1980), pp. 45–56; Michael O'Pray, "Authorship and Independent Film Exhibition," *Screen*, Vol. 21, No. 2 (Summer 1980), pp. 73–78; Susan Clayton and Jonathan Curling, "Feminist History and *The Song of the Shirt*," *Camera Obscura*, No. 7 (Spring, 1981), pp. 111–127; and their "On Authorship," *Screen*, Vol. 20, No. 1 (Spring 1979), pp. 35–61; John Caughie, "*Because I am King* and Independent Cinema," *Screen*, Vol. 21, No. 4 (1980/81), pp. 9–18; Steve Neale, "Art Cinema as Institution," *Screen*, Vol. 22, No. 1 (1981), pp. 11–41.
28. Don Macpherson, ed. *Traditions of Independence* (London: British Film Institute, 1980); cf. especially, Claire Johnston "'Independence and the Thirties—Ideologies in History: An Introduction," pp. 9–23; and Annette Kuhn, "British Documentary in the 1930's and 'Independence'—Recontextualizing a Film Movement," pp. 24–35.

84

JILL GODMILOW

PAYING DUES

A Personal Experience with Theatrical Distribution (1977*)

Let me assume that I'm speaking basically to the kind of filmmaker who makes a film because it's one that he or she needs and wants desperately to make (it will become obvious very soon that my remarks do not apply to filmmakers who make a "product" because it has a defined market and, therefore, will surely generate a great deal of money). In essence, my theatrical experience has been this:

I took a good, entertaining, one-hour, color documentary about a woman symphony orchestra conductor and tried to get a good theatrical run for it in as many cities as possible. I've only done it once, so I'm hardly an expert, I don't recommend it for every documentary or for every filmmaker since it required and truly brought out in me the most compulsive aspects of my personality. It took six full months out of my life, and I don't regret a minute of it; but I also don't think it would work for all films or for all people.

Whatever intelligence there was in my campaign had a lot to do with the support of another filmmaker, Jerry Bruck, Jr. He had gone through approximately the same process one year before with his excellent documentary *I. F. Stone's Weekly*, and he had developed certain techniques and ideas. He advised me and encouraged me; and when I was ready to quit, he was there to remind me why I had undertaken this project in the first place. I often forgot because of sheer exhaustion. It was his plan and his technique—a technique that he had developed—so I will defer to him for most of the technical explanations about how to do it. What I can tell you are the reasons *why* I did it and suggest that some of them might apply to other filmmakers and other films.

This I have learned: no product finds its market and is successful in that market without being pushed or shoved or promoted or publicized or sold by somebody. Hits don't "just happen" in any field. The success of *Antonia* had a great deal to do with Jerry and myself going out there and doing that intensive six months of work. I'm not saying that the film would have been unsuccessful

*Revised 2015.

without that work, but it would have had the normal (very limited) educational distribution that most documentaries get, instead of the national attention and excitement that drew all shapes, sizes, and varieties of audiences to the theater, to church auditoriums, to classrooms, and to their television sets to see this film. It just wouldn't have happened if I hadn't done the work myself, and it is my sincere belief that there is no one, professional, or otherwise, who could have or would have done the same job for this film.[1]

In the summer of 1973, Judy Collins (who co-directed the film with me) and I were sitting around New York with this perfectly wonderful, one-hour documentary which nobody wanted. No one had ever heard of Antonia Brico and, in fact, that's what most people said to me when I went to them for help: "No one has ever heard of her—how can we put it on television?" or "How can I put it in a theater? No one's ever heard of Antonia Brico!" The film had cost about $60,000, and had been made with the vague illusion that if you created something good enough, that wasn't politically or sexually offensive to anyone, you could sell it to commercial television and at least make your costs back that way. To us it seemed that the rest of the distribution, whatever that was going to be—and we didn't think about it very often—would just flow from that commercial television sale. As it turned out, it just wasn't so.[2]

Judy and I had wonderful connections in the networks and were able to get in and see people, but it took two months to find out that commercial television doesn't buy any independent product. Everywhere I went, producers and vice-presidents in charge of this and that told me they loved it. Sometimes they cried during the screening and sometimes they asked if they could borrow the print because they thought their wives should see it. But, they said, it was impossible to "program" it. (I am still searching for a definition of that word.) And that turned out to be a constant problem both in this country and in the European market. So much for television.

The non-theatrical distributors were also bubbling over with excitement when they saw it. I would estimate that four out of five major companies whom I dealt with reminded me to be sure to get in touch with them if I ever cut a 26-minute version. But they were unwilling to take on the hour-long film. They told me that there was a problem with "programming" it, since it was a 60-minute film and most classroom sessions were 40 minutes. The couple of distributors who were interested in the film were offering very little: no advances, no promotion, no particular skill in distributing this kind of film, and the average 25% of the gross, which would mean that a film like *Antonia* would have to gross about $240,000 before production costs would be paid back. These distributors also offered next-to-nothing in the way of hope for profits. Somehow, none of that seemed like enough.

That's the main reason why I got involved in the theatrical effort. The idea was to make the film a hot enough property so that I could make a better deal with non-theatrical distributors and with television. The idea was to make it "special" through the theatrical distribution so that it would be well-reviewed, talked about everywhere as new and original, and so that we could create an image of the film that would make it in demand, a "must-see" film. Then, I could go out and do an outrageously wonderful job in the non-theatrical market. Basically, it worked. The success of *Antonia* in all other market areas—including print sales, community and educational rentals, large, paid-admission show dates, and U.S. and international television—was all made possible by the outstanding pedigree the film acquired during its theatrical runs.

Looking back now, I can cite a few other good reasons to try it. The incredible experience I acquired as a businesswoman I now consider to be basic dues paid for the rest of my life as an independent filmmaker and a woman. What I learned about dealing with business people, making deals, when to give, when not to give, is essential—not just for making films but for life—as far as I'm concerned. I don't see how you can be an independent filmmaker without that knowledge or some of that experience, and I encourage everyone to get as much of that experience as they can. It's a real world out there, and I didn't know about it. I feel much more capable of taking care of myself now, having survived and succeeded in that deadly arena.

There's another major reason why I got involved in the theatrical distribution to the extent that I did. Judy and I had made what was considered essentially a woman's film, or at least it seemed to be a film that women's groups wanted to see. A lot of them needed a product that they could use for fundraising events, whether for a lesbian newspaper or for an Episcopal women's auxiliary that was trying to raise money for scholarships. There was a movement to plug my film into, and I did a lot of opening night, theatrical benefits with groups like these.

The groups were able to make serious money for their effort with a "class product" and a good image, and I got my share from the major promotion effort these women were able to do in their own communities, which I could never have pulled off from New York City. They would go out and hustle and put up posters in places where I couldn't have gotten to, and they could get me on local television and radio shows. They could make the media contacts I could have never made from my home base. I find it unlikely that any traditional non-theatrical distributor would have sought out or gotten deeply involved with groups like these, and I consider that it was a very important part of my distribution campaign.

I also cared very much about the subject of the film, Antonia Brico. Without going into great detail, I think the theatrical distribution of this film helped Antonia enormously and the cause of women musicians in general. Antonia emerged from all of this with a rather full second career. She's conducting all over the country again, and I don't think much of that would have happened without the special attention the film got in theatrical realms.

The other big reason for getting involved in the theatrical mess is ego, and that I found has been really important. The experience of watching your own film actually run in a theater—well, there is nothing like it, nor any better place for a film to communicate best with its audience. There's something about the lights going out, a very big screen, a good sound system, people who've come because they've heard about the film, and who hire baby-sitters, park their cars, and pay money to go into that theater that makes their viewing experience much better than anywhere else. The film is better received and the excitement level is higher; there's a communication among the audience. As a result, the ideas and emotions that you've put in the film are communicated best in that theatrical situation. Beyond all that, it's beautiful just to see your name up there in lights, and this is *really* important. If you're going to go out and spend the next year raising money to make your next film, and the year after that making it, you're going to need every minute of that glory and every minute of that excitement to go out and do it again.

For all of the above reasons (none of which were too consciously formulated at the outset), I sought my low-cost, high-yield, "smash hit," New York opening and subsequent runs. The Whitney Museum's New American Filmmakers' series provided that opportunity in many ways:

1. They offer the filmmaker a real "run." The Whitney offered me two full weeks with three shows a day. You need a successful run so that you can get real box-office and attendance figures to convince theater bookers that your film

will draw on a continuous basis. Flashy, one-night premieres, like the New York Film Festival, can be terrific for getting press (although reviews of our "lesser" films often get buried under the mountain of articles about "important" films in the same festival), but these one-nighters don't provide the realistic evidence that your film can generate word-of-mouth and keep people coming, which is the basic ingredient of a successful financial run.

2. The timing with the Whitney was perfect. We opened in early September, two weeks before the New York Film Festival started, so that local and national critics weren't swamped with other work and had space in their newspapers and magazines to print their reviews of *Antonia*.
3. The Whitney had some money in its budget for paid advertising. In fact, *Antonia* was designated to open the Fall series and, as a result, got more paid space in the *Village Voice* and *The New York Times* than most other films in the series. The Whitney also had a staff person at that time, Terry Kemper, who had maintained excellent relationships with the press. He was a blessing. Terry and I coordinated our contacts and ran two major press screenings and many individual ones for those critics with "special needs." We provoked, and we prodded, and we pushed our materials around to every radio, TV, newspaper, and magazine film critic in the city—from *Time Magazine* and "The Today Show" all the way down to the 40 or 50 college newspapers and radio stations in the New York area.

These were the important elements. Because of the coordinated reviews and appearances on radio and television, *Antonia* burst upon the New York scene in September of 1974 looking like it had a lot of energy and money behind it, and that kept a lot of people talking about it for a long time. The Whitney sold out three and four shows a day for two weeks, which was exactly what Jerry Bruck (with *I. F. Stone's Weekly*) and I needed to move into the first theatrical situation.[3]

With only a week's interruption in the run (and even that week was detrimental and should have been avoided), we opened our double bill at the Quad Theater in Greenwich Village. The Quad is a four-screen, multiple theater which is helpful for a film like *Antonia*, because audiences at the other three films notice that your film is there; so it becomes a kind of advertising which you can't get any other way. The theater is in Greenwich Village which was also an intelligent choice because it was very close to New York University and also to the kind of "downtown" people who might be looking for something unusual and would take a chance on two documentaries.

Our theater was small, about 250 seats, which was also a good idea. First, because it's cheaper than a large house (and you know from the outset that you could never fill a theater that has 600 or 700 seats). It always feels better for you, for the exhibitor, and for the audience to be in a full house in a small theater than in a half-empty house in a large theater. I should also mention that the management and owner of the Quad had an unusual associate in the person of Mort Hoch, who runs the advertising agency that has the Quad's account. He is an adventurer par excellence with years of experience in the "biz." I dedicate this to Mort. It was he who convinced the Quad's owners to take a chance on our two films. Without that first run, the whole theatrical thing would never have gotten started.

And on it went. We did six pretty decent weeks at the Quad, trailed off badly through two more terrible ones, but managed to convince Larry Jackson, of the Orson Welles Cinema in Cambridge, Massachusetts, to give us a try, where *Antonia* eventually ran 15 weeks with a half-hour short by Elliott Erwitt, *Beauty*

Knows No Pain. A year from then, *Antonia* had played in theaters in about 20 cities, mostly on the East and West Coasts with varying lengths of time and with varying financial success. We never lost money (Los Angeles was the worst, but even there we came out with $87, and Boston was the best—about $10,000 net profit for the filmmakers).

Each situation was different, but each was the same in that it required exhausting, 20-hours-a-day, 8-days-a-week energy, and each paid back with gratifying audience response, excruciating lessons in business and pain, and hundreds of high-profit, paid admission, non-theatrical bookings. I calculate very roughly that the gross for both films in the theatrical situations was about $30,000, and that the costs were about $8,500. The profit was there, although it wasn't huge; but beyond that, the effort was well worth it in that *Antonia* has done exceedingly well in all other market areas. I have no regrets.

Ed. note: *Following its theatrical run, the producers of* Antonia*...signed a contract with a commercial distribution company for non-theatrical release of the film.*

NOTES

1. In 1973, Jerry Bruck had pioneered theatrical distribution with his excellent 60-minute, 16mm documentary, *I. F. Stone's Weekly*. In 1974, seeking a second run for his film, we paired up *Antonia* and *I. F. Stone's Weekly* to make a two hour program. Then he taught me all he had learned: how to cut a deal with an exhibitor; how to make newspaper ads and posters; how to produce a 1/4-inch tape of "sound bites" for radio interviews and 16mm film clips for TV interviews. (Of course this was way before 3/4-inch videotape and way, way before the internet or anything digital.)
2. Previously, distribution of independently-made documentaries consisted only of print sales to public and university libraries, college classroom rentals, and sometimes broadcast on European television networks (rarely on American public television and never on American commercial networks).
3. *Antonia* was reviewed in *The New York Times*, *The New Yorker*, *New York*, *Time*, *Newsday*, *New York Post*, *Village Voice*, *Cue*, and *Variety*.

85

COCO FUSCO

A BLACK AVANT-GARDE?

Notes on Black Audio Film Collective and Sankofa (1988)

One of the crucial things about media education in Britain is that you're involved in very Eurocentric theories, and if you have any sort of Black consciousness you begin to wonder where there might be room for your experience within these theories. In Roland Barthes' *Mythologies,* one of the key texts for students of semiology, the only reference to anybody Black is to the soldier on the cover of *Paris Match.* The very superficial critique of colonialism found in such texts really isn't enough.

As we began to think about images and about our politics, we realized that the history of independent film and Black images was pretty dry politically speaking. And political films were also really dry stylistically, mostly straight documentary. And there is always the problem that there hasn't been much space for Black filmmakers in Britain. In terms of political film also, there wasn't much room for pleasure.

—Martina Attille, Sankofa[1]

In the winter of 1986, two films from the British workshops opened at downtown London's Metro Cinema.[2] One was a multilayered dramatic feature, and the other a nonnarrative, impressionistic documentary—formats usually considered to be too difficult for the theatrical market. While it was highly unusual for low budget "experimental" films to find their way to commercial venues, what made these runs even more unusual was that the films, *The Passion of Remembrance* (1986) and *Handsworth Songs* (1986), were produced by the London-based Black workshops Sankofa and Black Audio Film Collective. Those theatrical screenings were firsts for local Black film collectives, and are one of the many signs that the Black workshops are effecting radical changes in British independent cinema.[3]

Sankofa and Black Audio's intervention in British media institutions seems to have touched several raw nerves. Their insistence on shifting the terms of avant-garde film theory and practice to include an ongoing engagement with the politics of race sets them apart from longstanding traditions of documentary realism in British and Black film cultures. Black Audio's *Handsworth Songs* is a collage of reflections on the race riots that have shaken Thatcherite England, and the inadequacy of all institutional explanations of them—particularly those of the mass media. The filmmakers weave archival footage with reportage, interior monologue, and evocative music to create a gracefully orchestrated panoply of signs and sounds that evoke Black British experiences. Sankofa's *The Passion of Remembrance* is the story of Maggie Baptiste, a young woman grappling with the problematic legacy of a Black radicalism that foreclosed discussion of sexual politics and with the differences between her vision of the world and that of her family and friends. Public and private memory reverberate through interconnected stories that take different forms: dramatic narrative, allegorical monologues, and film within film.

Critical attention to *Handsworth* and *Passion* has outstripped the response to other workshop films of the same scale. The films are at the center of polemical debates in the mainstream and Black popular press that often do little more than bespeak critical assumptions about which filmic strategies are "appropriate" for Blacks. At its best, institutional recognition takes the form of the John Grierson Award, which Black Audio received in 1987 for *Handsworth Songs*; the more common version, however, is the constant scrutiny to which the entire Black workshop sector is subjected.[4] All the Black workshops contend that they must conform much more consistently and closely to the laws that regulate them than their white counterparts.

As filmmakers and media activists, Sankofa and Black Audio question Black representation in British media from mainstream television to such bastions of liberal enlightenment as the British Film Institute (BFI), and academic film journals such as *Screen* and *Framework*. They are interrogating "radical" film theory's cursory treatment of race-related issues, and subverting the all too familiar division of independent film labor between first-world avant-garde and third-worldist activism. Sankofa and Black Audio are also concerned with mainstream images of Black identity, preconceived notions of Black entertainment, and the terminology and mythologies they inherit from the '60s-based cultural nationalism that remains allied with a realist tradition. Sankofa's reflections on the psychosexual dynamics and differences within Black British communities, and Black Audio's deconstruction of British colonial and postcolonial historiography are groundbreaking attempts to render racial identities as effects of social and political formations and processes, to represent Black identities as products of diasporic history. While these workshops are not the first or only Black filmmakers in Britain, they are among the first Black British film artists to recast the question of Black cultures' relations to modernity as an inextricably aesthetic and political issue.

Although racism is not a problem specific to Britain, the English version has its own immediate history. The existence of the Black British workshops and the nature of their production are due to the 1981 Brixton riots and the institutional responses that gave the filmmakers access to funding.[5] The newly established workshops provided the infrastructure that, combined with racially sensitive cultural policies, created conditions for them to explore and question theoretical issues. Though the chronologies of events that inform *Passion* and *Handsworth Songs* are specific to Britain, institutionalized racism, its attitudes, arguments and historical trajectories are not. In addition to institutionalized racism, we in America share the legacy of cultural nationalism, its ahistorical logic, anachronistic terms, and the scleroticizing danger of separatism. The U.S. psycho-social dilemma of belonging, which harshly affects people of color, might be offset slightly by melting pot myths and a longer history of Black American presence. But the massive influx of peoples from Latin America and the Caribbean since World War II (not to mention the abundance of mixed-race Americans) is both evidence of a similar plurality of Black cultures here and a symptom of the U.S. neocolonialist projects. The contemporary U.S. situation, then, exceeds any monolithic discourse on race, calling for strategic recognition and articulation of a plurality of racial differences. The British use of "black" as a political term for all U.K. residents of African, Afro-Caribbean, and Asian origin expresses a common social, political, and economic experience of race that cuts across original cultures, and works against politically devisive moves that would fragment them into more easily controlled ethnic minorities. As mainstream American media constitute new markets by race (the heralding of the new Hispanic moviegoer with the opening of *La Bamba* is one recent example) and as critical reflection on media culture hovers around the question of colonialism, treating it at times as if it were a phenomenon that exists "elsewhere"—we must continue a systematic, ongoing analysis of the homogenizing tendencies of both the mass media and post-structuralism, as well as the contrived segregation of post- and neocolonial subjects into folklorically infused, ahistorical, ethnic groups. Recognizing nationality's problematic relationship to the diasporic phenomenon, I will, in this article, examine the work of Black Audio and Sankofa as an instance in the development of a necessarily international critical study of race and representation.

Given the two Black workshops' stress on how multiple histories shape their presence/present, it is appropriate to begin by outlining events that led to their practice. Sankofa's and Black Audio's members are first-generation immigrants, largely from West Indian families that arrived in Britain in the 1950s and '60s. The combination of an expanding post-World War II economy in England, changing immigration laws and chronic economic hardship in newly independent colonies resulted in rapid growth of the British-based Black population into the mid-70s, when economic decline and stringent immigration policies began to close the doors. Most of the first generation of Black British subjects reached adolescence in the '70s, with little hope for decent employment, a minimal political voice, and virtually no access to media. This atmosphere of dispair and foreboding was sensitively portrayed by Black British independent pioneer Horace Ove in his first feature, *Pressure* (1975), focusing on the frustrations of Black youth, and later addressed by Menelik Shabazz in his 1982 feature *Burning An Illusion*.

Britain in the last years of the Labor government before Margaret Thatcher saw the rise of neofascist groups and racially motivated attacks against Afro-Caribbean and Asian peoples, coupled with changes in policing tactics now aimed at containing the Black population. Public gatherings within the Black community, such as carnivals, were increasingly perceived and constituted as sites of criminality.[6] The Brixton riots of 1981 were not the first violent response by Blacks to their situation, but the ensuing spread of civil disturbances throughout the country generated enough fear and media coverage to prevent the explosive situation from being ignored by the government. Despite statistics indicating that the Brixton riots resulted in the arrests of more whites than Blacks, the mass media and adjunct power mechanisms had already succeeded in constituting a new Black Threat, with a new Black, male youth as its archetypal protagonist.

The independents and the Association of Cinematograph Television and Allied Technicians (ACTT) directed many of their efforts toward the establishment of Channel 4 as a commissioning resource and television outlet for British films.[7] Its charter affirms the channel's commitment to multicultural programming. Those interest groups' lobbying, together with support from Channel 4 and the BFI, also led to the Workshop Declaration of 1981, giving nonprofit media-production units with at least four salaried members the right to be franchised and eligible for production and operating monies as nonprofit companies. Workshops are expected to engage in ongoing interaction with their local communities through educational programs and training, and at the same time produce innovative media that could not be found in the commercial sector.

1981 was also a crucial year for the Greater London Council (GLC), as the beginning of its governing Labor party's six year effort at social engineering through politically progressive cultural policy.[8] This project ended with Thatcher's abolishing the council by decree in 1986. A race relations unit and Ethnic Minorities Committee were instituted largely in response to the 1981 riots and sociological studies that followed. Within the Ethnic Minorities Committee was the Black Arts Division, which, under the supervision of Parminder Vir, slated monies for Black cultural activity, particularly those areas such as film and video that had previously been inaccessible due to high costs. The future members of Sankofa and Black Audio had, at this time, just completed their academic and technical training—Sankofa's members were primarily from arts- and communications-theory backgrounds, and Black Audio's members had studied sociology.[9] Funding from organizations such as the GLC and local borough councils financed their first works and made them eligible for workshop status.

By the time Sankofa and Black Audio began to work collectively, a race-relations industry had developed not only in the nonprofit cultural institutions, but in academia as well. Those theoretical debates on colonialism and postcolonialism, in which Black Audio and Sankofa actively participate, draw extensively on the work of Homi Bhabha, Stuart Hall, and Paul Gilroy.[10] Bhabha's writings combines a Lacanian perspective on the linguistic construction of subjectivity, with Fanon's investigations of racism as a complex psychic effect of colonial history.[11] These ideas provide a theoretical framework from which to investigate the unconscious dimensions of the colonial legacy, to understand racism as a dialectical encounter in which victim and oppressor internalize aspects of the other, at both the level of the individual and the social.

Passion's concern with sexual conservatism in contemporary Black communities and *Handsworth*'s poignant resurrection of the '50s immigrants' innocent faith in the "motherland" resonate with these psychological dilemmas in an expressive manner that transcends didactic illustration. They suggest alternatives to predominant forms of representation that posit the colonized as helpless victim (the liberal view) or as salvagable only through a return to an original precolonial identity (the underlying assumption of cultural nationalism). They also undermine the liberal assumption that racism is an aberration from democratic ideals of the nation-state, by bringing out their historical inextricability. In other words, the development of capitalism and the rise of the British Empire were contingent on colonial exploitation and racism—the colonial fantasy, as Bhabha puts it—is nationalism's unconscious, its dialectical negation. Black Audio's stunning reassemblage of archival images from the British colonial pantheon—*Expeditions* (1983)—is a critical reinterpretation of the fantasies that give rise to both the imperial project and its documentation.

Also influential to Sankofa's and Black Audio's aesthetics are the writings of Paul Gilroy and Stuart Hall. The two social theorists bring Foucauldian methods of institutional critique to the issue of race and the constitution of the Black subject. In their analyses of racism's many mechanisms and manifestations, they are acutely sensative to the significance of the media and image production as means of transmitting ideas about nationality and nationalist prejudice.[12] Gilroy's interpretations of Black British culture (particularly music) as a synthesis of modern technologically influenced aesthetics and Black oral traditions theorize cultural dynamics in the Black diaspora, significantly shifting the terms of contemporary debates on postmodern eclecticism. While Hall employs Gramscian theories of hegemony to comprehend the complex power relations between institutions and the "resistance" of specific groups, he is particularly sensitive to the danger of imputing radicalism to all forms of popular expression, tempering widespread tendencies of cultural nationalism to project resistance as a leitmotif onto all popular history. The character Maggie's search for new ways of approaching past and present desires in *Passion* evokes the condition these writers address. Like them, she seeks a more nuanced political vocabulary to approach a range of subjective and collective concerns.

Before Maggie's passions, and Handsworth's songs, however, came the two workshop's earlier, more esoteric endeavors: Black Audio's *Expeditions* and Sankofa's *Territories* (1985). *Expeditions* is a two-part tape/slide show, subheaded *Signs of Empire* and *Images of Nationality*, in which archeological metaphors organize an aestheticized, ideologically charged enquiry. Drawing on images from high colonial portraiture, ethnographic photography, and contemporary reportage, Black Audio uses them as raw materials in a choreographed audiovisual performance. Over images of the past are inscribed philosophical phrases of the present. Between images of present conflict are "expeditions" that open onto a past seen through the representational genres that elide the violence of the orders with which they collude. From this new angle, maps become measurements of both distance and domination, and placid portraits take on a sinister cast. As a majestic male voice claiming that Blacks "don't know who they are or what they are," repeats over and over, it becomes a stutter-like symbol for the speaker's own incapacity to comprehend the Other's identity. Ambient sounds and manipulated voices resonate forcefully, unearthing the deep structural meanings that bind the signs together. *Expeditions* is a decidely antirealist document; instead its makers struggle with every possible formal means of achieving a vision both poetically allusive and lucidly interpretive.

Sankofa's *Territories* also uses formal experimentation as a means of decentering thematic and structural traditions. Their first collectively produced film was made after founding member Isaac Julien's video documentary, *Who Killed Colin Roach?* (1983) about the mysterious death of a Black male youth—a case similar to that of American grafittist Michael Stewart. It is a self-conscious return to the most visible Afro-Caribbean stereotype—the carnival—examining its places and displacements within British society. Charting the intensification of policing practices over three decades, *Territories* represents carnival as a barometer of institutional attitudes. Interconnected with these political and historical developments is a critique of ethnographic representations of carnival, which reify it as a sign of "original culture," masking its evolving sociopolitical significance. The two strategies bespeak the colonialist presupposition that carnival, as an archetype of Black expression, is by nature eruptive (savage) and erotic (dangerously pleasurable and potentially explosive), and therefore calls for order imposed from without. The film's second half, a surreal collage of gay couples dancing over riots, bobbies and burning flags, is a formal rendering of that very threat of chaos, a site of excess that mocks attempts at discursive and institutional control. The film, however, not unlike the carnivalesque, is somewhat limited by its own idiom, falling back on an all too familiar avant-garde conflation of all forms of realism and narrative to add strength to its counternarrative's assertions.

This issue, however, was not central to the film's critical reception in Britain. Like *Expeditions, Territories* was deemed by many to be too intellectual and inaccessible. According to the filmmakers, the doubts about both works often came from white media producers who had surfaced after a decade of immersion in structuralist stylistics with a zealous new concern for "the popular." Also participating were proponents of the "positive image" thesis who argue that positive representation of Black characters is the answer to racist misrepresentation. They faulted the two workshops for, in a sense, missing the point. The ironic result of this sort of social engineering is that, despite its sensitivity to media and its attempts to create new spaces, it imposes limitations that eschew any psychological complexity. As Julian Henriques puts it in his article, "Realism and the New Language,"

> The danger of this type of approach is that it denies the role of art altogether. Rather than appreciating works of art as the products of various traditions and techniques with their own distinct language, art and the media are reduced to a brand of political rhetoric.[13]

What is at stake in all these arguments, and what explains Sankofa's and Black Audio's notoriety is that their works implicitly disrupt assumptions about what kinds of films the workshops should make and about what constitutes a "proper" reflection of the underrepresented communities from which they speak. As BFI Ethnic Affairs Advisor Jim Pines put it, the overriding assumption of the debates is that Black filmmaking is a form of social work, or rather that aesthetically self-conscious film practice is too highbrow and superfluous.[14]

Clearly, there are also economic imperatives operating here. As many more established British independents gain international acclaim, arguments in support of a more commercially viable product gain momentum. And for the burgeoning collectives, the production costs of dramatic narrative are prohibitive. But the problem for the workshops remains that the combined effect of the arguments is to restrict the space they need to develop a critical voice and vision, to experiment with a variety of ready-made materials and discourses in order to "tell stories of our experiences in a way that took into account the rhythm and mood of that experience."[15]

Confronting the positive image as a problem rather than a given and defining relations to trends beyond the traditional parameters of "black communities" are issues that figure prominently in *The Passion of Remembrance*. Its dialogues are filled with questions about the images of Black identity that surround the characters and inform their behavior. The allegorical Black radical woman rebukes the allegorical radical Black man for the latent sexism in his Black Power ideology; Maggie and her family evaluate the Black couples on a prime-time TV game show; she and her brother attack one another's visions of political struggle; Maggie faces her peers' accusations that her interest in sexuality and sympathy for gay rights are not really Black concerns. Contradictions between self-image and prescribed images, between desired ones and painful ones, are repeated in the film's different generic sites, or levels. In the dramatic narrative devoted to the Baptiste family, identity conflicts are articulated as generational and cultural. The immigrant father's skills are no longer applicable in the labor market. As if to protect himself, he holds onto an outdated image of both England and the West Indies, while his son's grass-roots radicalism fossilizes into romantic nostalgia. When Maggie and her friend get ready for a night on the town, the conflicts between the men's world view and Maggie's are beautifully underscored by vivid intercutting of calypso and pop music. Indeed, what stands out most in *Passion* is the soundtrack, rich in music, poetic excerpts and charged verbal exchange. At times the filmmakers rely a bit too heavily on dialogue to carry the film's ideas, rather than exploiting the possibilities of its visual material. But even if *Passion* suffers at moments from a lack of formal cohesiveness, its intellectual strength comes from its insistence on the multiplicity of elements and images that shape Black consciousness.

Perspicacity of this sort appeared to be beyond the capacities of mainstream documentation of the 1985 Handsworth and Broadwater Farm riots.[16] In response to this conceptual lacunae came Black Audio's first film, *Handsworth Songs,* which shatters the reductivism of previous media coverage. Countering the desire of the nameless journalist for a riot "story" is the film's most often quoted line, "There are no stories in the riots, only the ghosts of other stories." In the place of monological explication are delicately interwoven visual fragments from the past and present, evoking larger histories and myths. Among the images are familiar scenes from previous riots, such as the attack of nearly a dozen policemen on one fleeing dreadlocked youth from the Brixton uprisings. With the shots of news clips, they remind us that by the time of the 1985 riots, an established and limited visual vocabulary about Blacks in Britain was in place. These references to a "riot" iconography form the synchronic dimension of Black Audio's poetic analysis of the representation of "racial" events.

The film uses archival cut-aways to reveal an uneasy relationship between camera and subject. At one point, an Asian woman turns, after having been followed by the camera, and swings her handbag at the lens; at another, the camera swoops dizzily into a school yard, holding for several seconds on children's faces, nearly distorting them. This dreamlike movement is repeated in the filmed installations of family portraits, wedding pictures and nursery school scenes, which, combined with clips from dances and other festivities, become images of the "happy past" that are a precious part of the Black immigrants' collective memory. Juxtaposed against the violence and frustrations of the present, these "happy memories" brim over with pathos, but they are also set against other images from the past which betray their innocence. Newsreel images highlight the earnestness and timidity of the immigrants, while voice-overs belie the hostile attitudes expressed at their arrival. The film depicts how a Black Threat was perceived to be transforming the needs of British industry into the desires of an unwanted foreign mass. These judgemental voices are confronted by newer ones, which offer no direct explanations or responses. Refining the style they developed in *Expeditions,* the filmmakers achieve such an integration of image and sound that the voices seem as if to arise from within the scenes. We hear poems, letters, an eye witness account of Cynthia Jarrett's death by her daughter, introspective reflections, which together create a voice-over marked by lyrical intimacy rather than omnipresence. That sense of intimacy shines throughout both *Passion of Remembrance* and *Handsworth Songs.* Rarely do such formally self-conscious projects express comparable sympathetic bonds with their characters, maintaining a delicate balance between a critique of liberal humanism and a compassion for the spiritual integrity of their subjects.

Some British critics have attempted to identify specific avant-garde influences in Sankofa and Black Audio's works, citing Sergei Eisenstein and Jean-Luc Godard as predecessors. While these assertions have doubtlessly helped to legitimate the filmmakers in the eyes of some, Sankofa and Black Audio's direct concern with current media trends and with rethinking Black aesthetics compel us to look elsewhere. The two groups, while well schooled in Eurocentric avant-garde cinema, are surrounded by and acutely aware of "popular" media forms. They can draw on the experiences of a cultural environment in which musical performance can function as a laboratory for experimenting with ready made technologically (re)produced materials.[17] They also produce films in an environment where television is the archetypical viewing experience. The fast-pace editing and nonnarrative structures found in advertising and music video—not to mention the effect of frequently flipping channels—have already sensitized television audiences to "unconventional" representation, upsetting the hegemony of the classic realist text.

The filmmakers are also concerned with how to develop an aesthetic from diasporic experiences common to Black peoples. This involves rethinking the relationship between a common language and a people, between ideas of history and nation. Paul Gilroy has pointed out that modern concepts of national identity and culture have invoked a German philosophical tradition which associates a "true" people with a place.[18] Access to historical identity as a people with a common voice is bound to the idea of a singular written language and of place. Yet centuries of capitalist and colonial development have literally displaced Black populations. Their cultures have evolved through synthesis with others as much as through preservation and resistance, forging an ongoing dialectic of linguistic and cultural transmutation. While I am wary of labelling this process a kind of proto-postmodernism, I cannot avoid noting the formal resemblances. What seems more important than ascribing terms to diasporic cultural dynamics is to be aware of the ways in which Black Audio and Sankofa have taken this dynamic into account.

> Our task was to find a structure and a form which would allow us the space to deconstruct the hegemonic voice of the British TV newsreels. That was absolutely crucial if we were to succeed in articulating those spacial and temporal states of belonging and displacement differently. In order to bring emotions, uncertainties and anxieties alive we had to poeticize that which was captured through the lenses of the BBC and other newsreel units—by poeticizing every image we were able to succeed in recasting the binary of myth and history, of imagination and experiential states of occasional violence.[19]

Sankofa and Black Audio speak from Britain, with a clear focus on the conditions of racism in a country where their right to full participation in civic society is more obviously complicated by legal questions of citizenship. Given our own immigration dilemmas and chronic inequities of Black American participation in the political process, however, parallels are far from contrived. The Black British filmmakers are keenly aware of their spiritual kinship with Black American cultures, though their actual connections are primarily textual. They clearly see themselves as heirs to developments that have roots in this country, evidenced by *Handsworths*'s poignant passage devoted to Malcolm X's visit to Birmingham, and Sankofa's acknowledgement that their critique of sexual politics in Black communities draws on Black American feminist writings of the '70s and '80s. The same GLC policy-makers who funded their first works also organized Black Cinema exhibitions, introducing audiences to the cinematic endeavors of Julia Dash and Ayoka Chenzira, Haile Gerima, and Charles Burnett.

Nonetheless, there are certain distinctions between the American and British conditions for Black independents.

Institutional structures such as the workshops and ACTT grant-aided division, while far from ideal, do not work against notions of shared interests the way that America's individualized, project-specific funding procedures can. And competition with the more monied, auterist ventures of Britain's more mainstream independents is a far cry from the economic and philosophic chasms that divide marginalized independent experiments from high-budget production in the U.S. But Britain specifically, and Western Europe in general, is involved in a larger postcolonial crisis that has forced them to rethink national and cultural identity; the dilemmas touched on by Black Audio, Sankofa and others are part of that crisis. Theirs is a poetics of an era in which racial, cultural, and political transitions intersect. It is no surprise then, that their works contain references to sources as varied as Ralph Ellison and Louis Althusser, June Jordan and Jean-Luc Godard, Edward Braithwaite and C.L.R. James. On this very sensitive point I must insist that this is not a rejection of the goals of Black consciousness. This "eclecticism," aimed at theorizing the specificity of race, reflects the mixed cultural, historical, and intellectual heritage that shapes life in the Black diaspora. The sad truth is that many Blacks must live that biculturalism, while few others seek to do so. If dominant cultures' relation to Black cultures is to go beyond tokenism, exoticizing fascination or racial violence, the complexities and differences which these film artists address must be understood. Sankofa, Black Audio and many other Black media producers in Britain are mapping out new terrains in a struggle for recognition and understanding.

I would like to thank the following individuals for their invaluable assistance in providing information for this article: Julian Henriques, Parminder Vir, June Givanni, Fred D'Aguiar, Colin McCabe, Jim Pines, Stephen Philip, Dhianaraj Chetti, and of course, the filmmakers of Sankofa Film/Video Collective and Black Audio Film Collective.

NOTES

1. Martina Attille, interview with the author, in "Young, British and Black: The Sankofa Film and Video Collective," *Black Film Review* 3, no. 1 (Winter 1986-87), p.12.
2. The Metro Cinema occupies a place analogous to that of the Film Forum in New York City.
3. Menelik Shabazz was the first Black British independent filmmaker to screen his film commercially in London. *Burning An Illusion* opened in 1982.
4. I have chosen to limit my discussion of the Black workshops to Black Audio and Sankofa because of the debates around them and their filmic strategies set them apart from the rest of the Black workshop sector. Other Black workshops in England are: Cardiff, Macro, Star, Retake, and Ceddo. The last two are also London based, and I conducted interviews with their members as part of my research. I should mention here that Ceddo also produced a documentary about racially motivated riots, entitled *The People's Account* (1986). It was commissioned by Channel 4, but has not yet been aired, due to an unresolved conflict involving Channel 4 and the Independent Broadcasting Authority (IBA). The IBA found the original version of the documentary unacceptable for its accusations against the British state, even after Channel 4 lawyers had submitted requests for minor changes and had them attended to. When I was conducting research for this article last summer, the IBA was insisting on a balancing program to accompany the documentary, and on the right to cancel the airing of both if they did not approve of the balancing program.
5. Although there had been outbreaks of violence in the '70s and earlier in protest of harassment by police and right-wing groups, and in protest of the state's strategic neglect of racial injustice, the riots that took place in 1981 mark a watershed moment in the history of British race relations. The first disturbances in Britain were immediately related to the suspicious deaths of three Black youths. But what began in the Brixton area of London spread to urban ghettos in most of the industrial centers of London, lasting an entire summer. The scale of the protests, as I mention later in the article, made it impossible for the government and the media to ignore the situation. Sociological investigations into the conditions of Blacks in Britain, such as the Scarman Report, were a direct governmental response to these events. The cultural policies of the GLC and new attention to race in many British cultural institutions were other responses.
6. For an in-depth discussion of this, see Paul Gilroy, *There Ain't No Black in the Union Jack: The Cultural Politics of Race and Nation* (London: Century Hutchinson Ltd., 1987), chap. 3; also Cecil Gutzmore, "Capital, 'Black Youth' and Crime" in *Race & Class* XXV, no. 2 (Autumn 1983), pp. 13–30; and Lee

Bridges, "Policing the Urban Wasteland" in the same issue, pp. 31–48.

7. Channel 4 started broadcasting in 1982. It is government subsidized but funded by a number of sources, including advertising and subscription payments. When it was set up it was supposed to commission and air a variety of voices, including ethnic minorities, the independent filmmaking sector, foreign programming, and nontraditional formats. The actual percentage of airtime and monies allocated to the independent sector has been exaggerated in the U.S. Most of what would be considered innovative programming is shown on two one-hour weekly slots ("Eleventh Hour" and "People to People") at off-peak hours.
8. For an in-depth discussion of this, see Franco Bianchini, "GLC R.I.P.: Cultural Policies in London, 1981–1986," in *New Formations* (Summer 1987), pp. 103–117.
9. Sociology departments in the more progressive British Polytechnics (such as Portsmouth, Middlesex, and South Bank) have a quite different course of study from their American counterparts. Theory and Research Methods are distinct branches of study, and it was within the theory rubric that Black Audio members John Akomfrah, Reese Auguiste, Lina Gopaul, and Avril Johnson encountered the critical writings that would later inform their creative work.
10. This list is not exhaustive. The work of Birmingham's Center for Contemporary Cultural Studies and London's Institute for Race Relations is also extremely important. The filmmakers are also interested in the work of many Black American essayists, particularly June Jordan.
11. For more about Bhabha's relation to Lacan and Fanon, see "Of Mimicry and Man: The Ambivalence of Colonial Discourse," in *October*, no. 28 (Spring 1984), pp. 118–124. Also see Frantz Fanon, *Black Skin, White Masks*, Charles Lam Markman, trans. (New York: Grove Press, 1967).
12. See Gilroy, *There Ain't No Black in the Union Jack*, and *The Empire Strikes Back* (London: Hutchinson, 1982).
13. Julian Henriques, "Realism and the New Language," *Artrage*, no. 13 (Summer 1986), pp. 32–37.
14. Jim Pines, interview with the author, London, July 1987.
15. Attille, "Young, British and Black," p. 14.
16. In 1985, riots in Handsworth and Broadwater Farm were set off by the deaths of Cynthia Jarrett and Cheryl Groce. Police entered the Jarrett home and began to question Ms. Jarrett, who suffered from a heart condition and began to feel ill when she was questioned. The police did not respond to the oncoming heart attack. She died shortly thereafter. Ms. Groce was shot by police who were supposedly searching for someone else. The Broadwater Farm riot gained infamy from the killing of a policeman by rioters on the first night.
17. See Gilroy, *There Ain't No Black in the Union Jack*, chap. 5.
18. Ibid., chap. 6, p. 69.
19. "*Handsworth Songs:* Some Background Notes," an unpublished paper by the Black Audio Film Collective, 1987, p. 4.

JOHN GREYSON

STRATEGIC COMPROMISES

AIDS and Alternative Video Practices (1990)

> AIDS is a war. Perhaps it didn't have to be—we'll never know. AIDS is a plague of government indifference, medical negligence and right-wing opportunism. AIDS is an epidemic of sexual intolerance. Like most wars, AIDS has been turned into megabucks by the multinational media industry, who exploit paranoia and ignorance with every new cover story and "in-depth report." Like most wars, AIDS was made into a war by those who consider that whole (disenfranchised) sectors of the population are expendable. Like most wars, these same opportunists shed public tears for the tens of thousands of those dead (whose dignity they irrevocably deny). Like most wars, these same opportunists ignore the needs of the hundreds of thousands who are fighting to stay alive.
>
> These are unsubtle words, because AIDS is a war, not only of politics and medicine, but also of representations. While the mass media's response to the health crisis has been anything but uniform, the results have nevertheless (in spite of "good intentions") been lethal. In stark contrast, a subculture of alternate media is fighting back. From the front lines of the battlefield, artists, community activists, and cable producers have launched a counteroffensive against such deadly discourses.

These "unsubtle words" are excerpted from the program notes I wrote for a six-night exhibition of AIDS tapes[1] by independent producers and artists, that was presented in Toronto in October, 1988.[2] These words express polemically and schematically an opposition common to left cultural criticism, an opposition that (ex)poses the "lies" of the commercial mass media against the "truth" of oppositional media practices.[3] They claim that alternate media can be used by "the people" to transform society. As media critic Hans Magnus Enzensberger says, "The open secret of the electronic media, the decisive political factor . . . is their mobilizing power."[4] These words serve to place the groundswell of independent videotapes addressing AIDS shown in the exhibition within a rich history of social change media and the "committed documentary,"[5] one that dates back to the Bolshevik revolution, one that has born witness to the many other wars for social justice.

Polemically insisting on the vitality of these tapes as effective weapons for social change, such simplifications are perhaps defensible in activist terms. However, such optimistic expressions end up erasing the complexities and contradictions of how such tapes are produced and experienced, creating the illusion of a unified, uncomplicated field of alternate media. But when each tape is examined in depth (interrogating the varied representational practices used, the funding sources that shaped its script, the type of community it came out of and/or is intended for, etc.), it becomes clear that easy generalizations about the praxis of such AIDS tapes (and indeed, of any social change media) are elusive, to say the least.

Media producers are dangerously closer to the belly of their particular beast (the film industry) than other visual artists. Caught between two mythologies (that of the artist, whose individual "vision" is supposed remain pure, unfettered by responsibility to audience, and that of the commercial film/TV producer, whose hierarchical yet collaborative industrial production mode constantly compromises vision in favor of reaching the audience) they must care about both vision and audience. They therefore learn the necessity of strategic compromises.

Over the past year, I've previewed 150 AIDS tapes (for the exhibition and also for a sixty-minute compilation of clips from AIDS tapes for Deep Dish TV, an alternate satellite network).[6] They included the following:

1. Cable access talk shows addressing such topics as discrimination experienced by PLWAs (persons living with AIDS) and lesbian efforts against AIDS
2. Documents of performances and plays addressing AIDS
3. Documentary (memorial) portraits of PLWAs, most of whom had died by the time the tapes were completed
4. Experimental works by artists deconstructing mass media hysteria, lies and omissions
5. Educational tapes on transmission of and protection against the HIV virus, designed for specific community audiences (women, Blacks, Latinos, youth, prisoners), often commissioned by AIDS groups
6. Documentaries portraying the vast range of AIDS service organizations and support groups that have sprung up around the country
7. Safer-sex tapes, that adapt the conventions of porn to teach their bi (bisexual), straight, and gay audiences the eroticization of safer sex
8. Activist tapes, which document the demonstrations and protests of an increasingly militant AIDS activist movement
9. A growing handful of tapes for PLWAs, outlining issues of alternate treatments for HIV infection and AIDS-related diseases

Such categories are immediately suspect. For instance, which of these tapes would not be "educational," given that they all seek to comment on some aspect of the AIDS crisis? What definition of "activist" are we using—are "activist" tapes defined solely by the inclusion of street demo footage? What constitutes enough formal innovation to qualify for the moniker "experimental?"

Certainly useful to programmers organizing screenings, these expedient categories nevertheless do little to elaborate the complexity of the work they seek to contain.

Generalizations about how these tapes differ from mass media offerings similarly collapse when put to the test. For instance, it's often claimed that independent tapes address issues that the mainstream media has generally ignored or misrepresented. However, any survey of network television AIDS coverage in the past year (dramas, sitcom episodes, documentaries, news updates) must conclude that the dominant media shift and shimmy much faster than any media critique can allow. Compare the appalling morbid sentimentality of the made-for-TV melodrama *An Early Frost* (1986), chronicling the return-of-the-dying-yuppie-fag-prodigal-son-to-the-bosom-of-his-impossibly-middle-class-family with the (relatively) more sophisticated recent offering *The Ryan White Story* (1986), based on America's favorite PWA, the working-class kid from Kokomo who successfully fought to attend school and is cheating the AIDS-is-always-fatal prophecy five years after his diagnosis. (All right, the show was appalling in its own right—but its representational practices reflected a very different agenda than its predecessor, with its story focused on the struggle of a PLWA to combat discrimination and live a full self-determined life.)

News coverage similarly has been transformed in some instances, primarily through the efforts of the AIDS activist movement, who have created *new* news through demonstrations, successfully zapped mass media offenders for journalistic AIDS crimes such as irresponsible reporting, and also worked to educate reporters and editors about issues that have been ignored or suppressed.

One material reason that the mass media have been somewhat responsive, and that some AIDS representations have not remained as hysterical and fear-mongering as they once were, is that some of their producers have *personally* been affected by the epidemic, much more so that their counterparts workings on issues like the homeless or Nicaragua. After all, a *New York Times* reporter rarely hangs out with a Sandinista or a street person, but they may well have a friend of a friend who has AIDS.

However relatively horrendous mainstream media representations continue to be, they are always moving, attempting to keep pace with the shifts (both reactionary and progressive) in dominant and oppositional discourses of AIDS, be they scientific, bureaucratic, governmental, or grassroots. Any theory of the mass media that sees such AIDS representations as monolithic misses the daily contradictions and slippages.

However, it's not overstating the case to note that the dominant representational clichés the networks and studios cling to for dear life (the suffocating conventions of dramas and sitcoms, documentaries and news updates) severely contain, indeed cripple, the sort of messages that are allowed to be broadcast. Information *must* be linear. Narratives *must* have closure. Authority *must* be constituted by an "expert." Television always speaks about AIDS from its mythical "outside" position of objectivity—even its so-called sensitive dramas about gay PWAs somehow always manage to erase any sense of being *inside* a community. It's perhaps here that the greatest claims can be made for an "us" versus "them" position, if one maintains that what most characterizes independent media production is their confident insiders vernacular, and the formal challenges that such a perspective suggests.

However, the range of the independent tapes previewed includes many that embrace conventional representational practices. Some cling to tried-and-true methods of documentary authority. Others prioritize "education" of a target group with inevitable simplifications and distortions. Some embrace formal tropes that are embarrassingly clichéd (didactic, too sentimental, you name it). These users of mainstream conventions are sometimes motivated by a desire to be politically effective, to communicate to as broad an audience as possible through the reassuring use of familiar constructions. In other cases, the producers thoughtlessly reproduce these conventions because they have no gripe with the mainstream and its messages—their independence is more determined for them by the lack of a CBS freelance contract.

Similarly, many of the tapes were made in collaboration with AIDS service organizations, reflecting to a greater or lesser degree the politics of the sponsor. What does this do to notions of "independence?" Artists choosing work this way have done so for diverse reasons—sometimes as a political choice, deciding to be answerable to/ engaged with their community; and sometimes as a "straight" commission that pays the rent. How do such material conditions impact on questions of autonomy, of intentionality?

Contemporary media critics, especially those engaged in the post-structuralist/ feminist/semiotic/psychoanalytic debates concerning theories of representation, have rightly insisted that all film/video constructions are texts that speak on several simultaneous levels. Regardless of the producer's stated intentions, these texts are dependent more on the codes and conventions (the signifying practices) they utilize and the social context determining their reception by an audience. For instance, a producer may set out to make an AIDS education tape that speaks sympathetically to gay teenagers in their own language. However, the conventions she or he may adopt may reproduce typical pedagogical authority (lecturing) which the target teens would probably reject. Similarly, any typical classroom situation has so much homophobia built into it that a closeted gay teenager might end up feeling vulnerable and threatened by such a screening, and be forced to reject it publicly through peer pressure.

As a result, intentionality is commonly a discredited concept in media criticism, yet for any video artist making social change media (and certainly for the majority of these AIDS producers), it is a central issue. Tape after tape exhibits the active desire to communicate its particular urgent message. These dozens of dozens of producers continue to negotiate (sometimes consciously, sometimes unconsciously) a host of contradictory agendas. Form, for instance: Deconstructive strategies may capture the terrifying ambience of the AIDS culture we live in better than traditional realist practices, but will they alienate/ mystify the intended audience? Politics: An activist script may be appropriate, but will the local AIDS committee (for whom the tape is intended) feel threatened by such rhetoric and not use it? Focus: Connecting various issues (like AIDS homophobia, AIDS sexism, and AIDS racism) may seem vital, yet will it make the tape too broad, too general, so it ends up simply being a token (Trotskyist) shopping list of progressive issues? Funding: Will the state arts council support a didactic documentary? Will the Red Cross support an esoteric arts tape? Guilt: Should I continue to produce experimental works that win awards on the arts circuit but never reach the AIDS community, or should I be responsible and throw all my efforts into a collective, community cable access AIDS show? And so on. . . . This continual jousting with that many-headed hydra called "effectiveness" is paramount in this AIDS war. How do we communicate our (very varied) agendas without being marginalized, and on whose terms? How do our efforts intervene and interrupt dominant discourses? How do we prevent our tapes from being neutralized and recontained within a complacent status quo?

Compromise is a term that the left righteously (indeed religiously) rejects. Yet the strategic compromises outlined above (always difficult, never completely satisfactory) are exactly the ones that makes these AIDS tapes so vital, so exciting. In order to pursue this theme, I've constructed the following "case studies" which schematically juxtapose pairs of tapes that superficially share similar subjects. In some cases, I have talked with the producers at length; in others, I'm making assumptions based on brief conversations and the tapes themselves. In all cases, due to lack of space, I've simplified and generalized some aspects of the productions.

'Til Death Do Us Part and *Another Man*

In a culture where school prayer is more acceptable than sex education, it's not surprising that the plenitude of AIDS tapes for youth are having a hard time finding an audience.[7] That is, there's megabucks in the AIDS education market—every school board wants an AIDS tape. They just want it to say what *they* believe about AIDS. It's also not surprising that the tapes have been organized around one agenda: prevention. Prevention, of course, is the cornerstone of the Reagan/Bush administration's recent and begrudging response to AIDS, which has criminally ignored every other aspect of the health crisis. In other words, it is assumed that today's youth have no interest in how teenagers cope with *having* AIDS, no interest in the politics of medicine, no interest in the interconnections between health care and poverty. . . . The political and social are erased, leaving only the personal: how to protect yourself. It should go without saying that this is vital information that every youth must get (and is still not getting). It should also go without saying that "prevention" agendas run the gamut from naive appeals for celibacy, to murderously inaccurate endorsements of monogamy, to nonjudgmental advice on condoms and cleaning your needles. An excellent critique of several of these tapes appeared in *AIDS: Cultural Analysis, Cultural Activism* (issue 43 of the theoretical journal *October*), which has become a veritable "red book" for activists working on issues of AIDS and representation.[8]

While most of these tapes talk down to kids in a traditional pedagogical fashion, *'Til Death Do Us Part* attempts to subvert this condescension by turning over the means of production to youth themselves. Or at least, halfway. This twenty-minute film is adapted from the Washington-based Black Youth Theatre Ensemble's collectively-produced play about AIDS. A freewheeling mix of rap, skits, gospel, and dramatic scenarios sketch out the social impact of AIDS, as written and performed by a talented group of teenagers. On paper it sounds terrific. The fact that it's also one of the only productions to target Black audiences makes it even more promising, given the fact that twenty-five percent of all PLWAs in the U.S. are Black and Latino.

The rap songs are vibrant: "This is Alvin on the mike, when I talk I talk it right. . . . So take my advice and have safe sex, don't share needles—yeah, I think that's best." Their take-offs on TV ads, satirizing the commodification of sex (edible underwear, toothpaste for added sex appeal) are humorous. An all-too-familiar implicit message begins to assert itself, however. The (bad) sexual marketplace has perverted the (good) institution of sexual love within marriage—and when you succumb to its sinful pleasures, the result is AIDS. In a similar conflation, a mimed needle-sharing scene (again, premised on selfish pleasure) results in retribution. Thus, sex and drugs *cause* AIDS. The last half revolves around an embarrassingly clichéd representation of Death, voraciously seducing and claiming the entire cast, including a gratuitous baby doll wrapped in a blanket. Despite the rap songs' realistic advice, the overall message is distinctly Catholic: sin will condemn you to the everlasting fires of hell.

I showed the tape to several members of the Toronto-based Black CAP (Coalition for AIDS Prevention), who reluctantly admitted they couldn't use it in their outreach to the Black community. Beyond the offensive moralism and scare tactics, it never *once* mentions gay men or youth.

It's unclear how "excerpted" the film is from the original production, and who made the editorial choices—filmmaker Ginny Durrin or the Theatre Ensemble (who have the script credit). I suspect that what happened is an all-too-common problem: that in putting the piece together, dominant political agendas (from facilitators, TV, educators, "authorities") were internalized and reproduced by the Ensemble. Many media projects, attempting to empower the disenfranchised by giving them the means of production, have run into the same problems—those "enfranchised" end up denying their own experiences, their own authority, and say instead what they think people (usually the facilitators) want them to say. And they are certainly sincere, to the point of not recognizing their complicity in this hegemonic process.

At the same time, such an analysis runs the risk of extreme condescension, suggesting that the theatre group capitulated completely to the demands of dominant ideologies. Looking at it another way, the tape is a good example of compromised strategies going way too far. Perhaps the ensemble were consciously calculating what they thought they could get away with, not only with their authorities, but also with their peers. "Queer" content or realistic drug scenarios might jeopardize both their funding and their image. As a result, *'Til Death Do Us Part* (despite its moments of street smarts) comes off like a wannabe *Cosby* episode.[9] Politics are erased, poverty and AIDS are ignored, and ultimately the Bush/Reagan agenda is validated by the very people (Black youth) that could arguably suffer the most from the administration's murderous policies.

In stark contrast *Another Man* is a lively safe-sex music video that in five short minutes takes aim at the politics of AIDS and scores a bull's eye. Like *'Til Death Do Us Part,* it was collectively written by a group of "youth." However in this case there was no "adult" supervision, and they directed, produced, and edited it themselves (okay, some of them were in their twenties). Variously called the Mr. Tim Collective or the Anarchist Queer Collective, an ad hoc group of straight/bi/gay punks-about-town, they recruited friends at a local Toronto art college and co-op post production facility to help out with the technical aspects, and produced it on a three-figure budget. Scenes of straight and gay interracial couples under the bed covers are superimposed with the directives: "Use a condom" and "Use your imagination." Two punks make out in a bus shelter, framed by one of the forbidding just-say-no-type city-sponsored AIDS info posters. Jerry Falwell is shown spewing forth some sort of homophobic gibberish; his image is frozen and a superimposed condom is pulled over his head. A woman talks about how Canadian customs routinely censors lists of safer-sex practices featured in American gay magazines. The song which unites these disparate elements is upbeat, celebratory, and decidedly defiant.

Used in a classroom setting, this tape could instigate far-reaching discussions about safer-sex practices, homophobia, and youth sexuality. Two predictable blockades will prevent this in all but the most exemplary circumstances. School boards have never been remotely interested in independent art tapes, especially those that use the word "fuck" (once) and that adopt a freely associative, nonprescriptive (and therefore threatening) form. Secondly, even if *Another Man* ever finds its way into a classroom, all sorts of students, socialized by a homophobic and conformist culture, could easily turn against such queer anarchy, especially if the teacher was unsympathetic to the tape and the issues raised. By remaining true to its origins, the tape will be kept out of the schoolyard, where

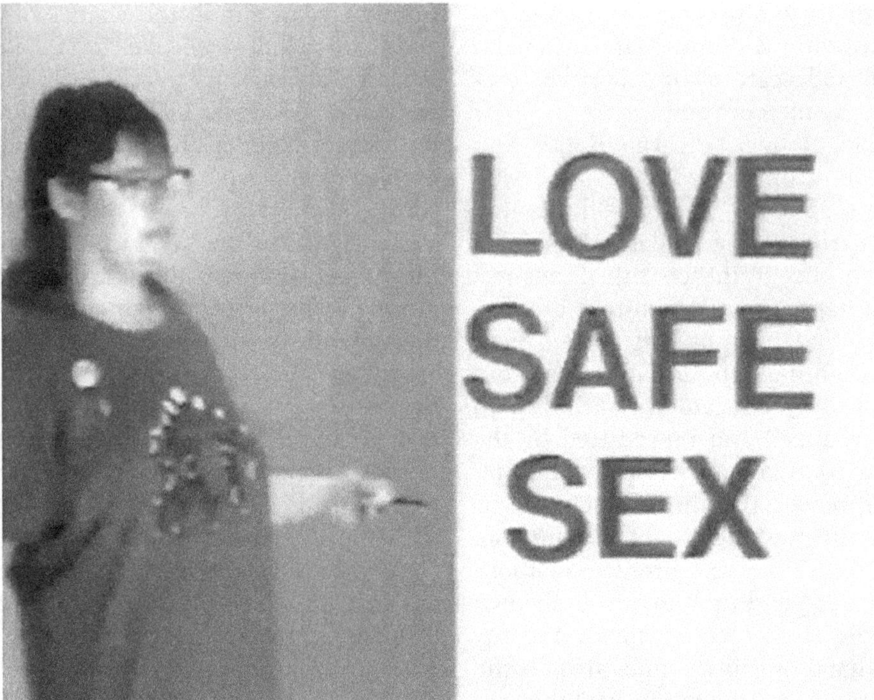

FIGURE 86.1 *Another Man* (Youth Against Monsterz, 1988). Screen capture from digital file.

it is needed most. However, it is enjoying an active distribution life on the art circuit and through various AIDS distribution projects.

Chuck Solomon: Coming of Age and *Danny*

> The mass media has allowed PLWAs (with few exceptions) several severely proscribed roles, as Simon Watney has noted: the self-hating "queer" dying pitifully in a hospital bed, abandoned by the world; the dangerous "carrier" whose "irresponsibility" is hysterically condemned; and the "innocent victim" (usually a child or woman) who was "infected" by a transfusion or "carrier."[10]

Alternate portrait tapes of PWAs constitute a significant political statement unto themselves, endowing their subjects with a dignity that the mainstream (with a few exceptions) has summarily denied them. Moreover, because these tributes are often requiems, they perform a vital pedagogical function, implicitly teaching audiences a language for processing loss that our death-phobic culture has denied most of us. Diametrically opposed to the broadcast obituaries for deceased celebrities which coldly isolate the individual according to outstanding achievements, these portraits capture the subtler details that matter most to friends, families, and lovers.

Chuck Solomon: Coming of Age is perhaps typical of this genre of tapes, produced mostly within the gay community. Initially conceived simply as a document of Chuck's fortieth birthday party by independent producers Wendy Dallas and Marc Huestis, the tape cuts back and forth between the cabaret performances and moving interviews with the performers—Chuck's collaborators and friends. The founder of Theatre Rhinoceros, San Francisco's premiere gay

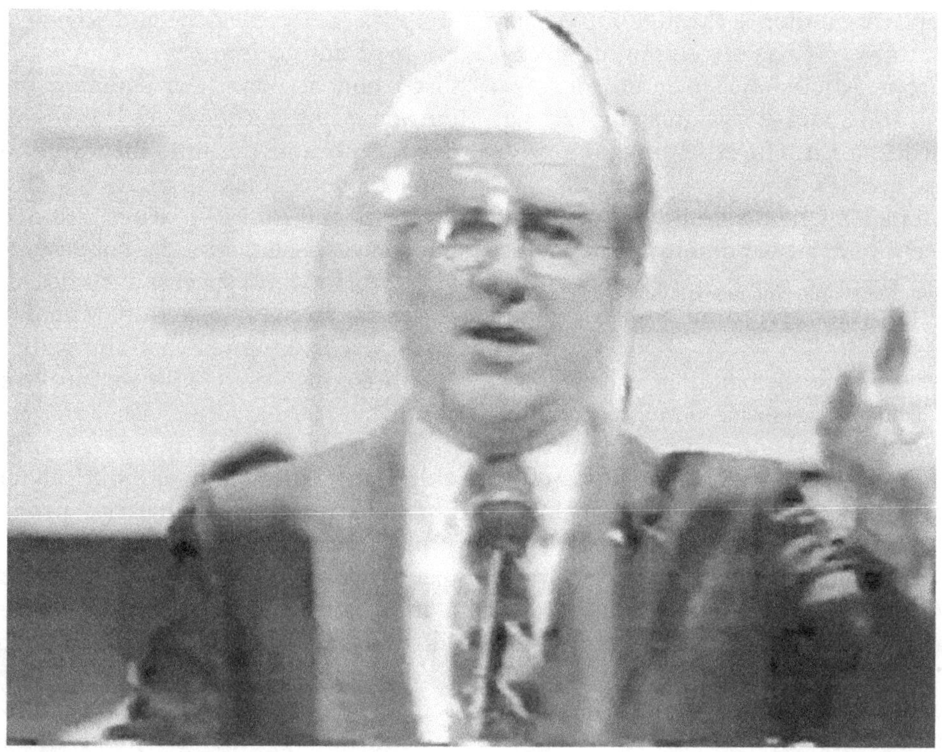

FIGURE 86.2 *Another Man* (Youth Against Monsterz, 1988). Screen capture from digital file.

theater company, Solomon himself speaks with vitality of his life and work, and the difficulty of coping with the AIDS-related deaths of both his lover and brother. The huge outpouring of love and affection from the 350 assembled is extremely moving, as is Solomon's invitation to them all to attend his fiftieth birthday party. He died nine months later.

Executed from within the close personal networks of Solomon's life, this is more an intimate home-movie tribute than an "objective" (and therefore distanced) portrait. While this captures the inside of a community beautifully, it also means there are no warts showing. Bitterness, fear, and anger are all absent, despite the fact that he was one of San Francisco's more outspoken activists. Capturing his warmth, wit, and dignity, the tape memorializes the legacy he left to the city's theater community. It's impossible not to be moved by this unabashedly sentimental tribute, even though it tends to elevate him to the status of gay sainthood.

I can't quibble with the urgent collective need we all have to "honor" our dead, especially in a culture that can't deal with death. However, is it perhaps unfair that Solomon should be singled out for such a tribute when so many of the other 60,000-plus AIDS-related deaths passed unheralded? Doesn't this tribute have a responsibility to condemn the government and medical establishment for allowing Solomon and the others to die from their homophobic neglect? Obviously no one tape can bear the burden of everything that needs to be said, and these are questions that the culture, as much as the tape, must answer. By insisting on its roots as a home movie, a celebration of this alternate family supporting one another, the tape is somewhat vindicated in its tight focus and sincerity, and has found an appreciative audience throughout the gay community.[11] It has also enjoyed success in Europe, where it has been broadcast on British and Spanish TV, but so far PBS has refused to air it. Huestis thinks the problem is that it's "too gay." That PBS feels threatened by this incredibly sweet and innocent portrait of Solomon is shocking, but no surprise when you consider their appalling track record on both AIDS and gay issues.[12]

A far more demanding experimental tape, *Danny,* has so far remained marginalized on the video art circuit. Structured as an impressionistic requiem, it reconstructs a sketchy portrait of an unapologetically flagrant disco queen through layers of slides, landscapes and processed imagery. Originally Danny and producer Stashu Kybartas had planned to collaborate on a tape about his experiences with Kaposi's sarcoma, a disfiguring cancer that sometimes accompanies AIDS. However, he became sick, and moved back to his parents' home in Ohio, where he died. The tape pieces back together the fragments of what they did shoot (mostly slides), organized by Kybartas's voice-over, which speaks directly to the dead Danny.

Of all the portrait tapes I've seen, this is one of the only ones that refuses to make a narrative out of the subject's life. It refuses to justify choices, to explain Danny's lifestyle, to make effects have causes. No attempt is made by either man to sum up, to make sense of, to "understand" AIDS or death. Instead, glimpses of a "gay" lifestyle that is now almost taboo in terms of representation are offered, with a refusal of anything approaching moralism.

Danny at one point catalogues a typical weekend in his heyday: the beach, the discos, the packaging of his crotch in button-fly jeans for a night out, the drugs, the sex, the cruising. Tinged with nostalgia, this brief reminiscence subverts the traditional judgment of such "hedonism." His lifestyle, far from being the "cause" of his illness, was simply a fact, the way he and so many others lived and continue to live. A recurring disco punctuation: "I'm standing on the outside of the inside where I want to be. " Stashu recounts the time they were in the studio together, taking slides of Danny's lesions, and they touched—something happened—again, with the subtlest of gestures and the most specific of stories, desire is reintroduced, into a story where traditionally it is assumed that automatic celibacy accompanies the HIV seropositive test result.

These fragments never editorialize, either in sentimental or political terms, and it is this refusal that has prompted some unease among some straight *and* gay viewers. They would seem to prefer a more streamlined narrative, where the "dirty" ambivalences of the gay ghetto were sanitarily summed up by a safe, prescriptive conclusion. If Solomon becomes a saint, Danny remains a Judas, betraying the "respectable" gay community (wherever that is) with his kiss.

Coming of Age chose to compromise the complexity of Solomon's life, in part because it was made as a collaboration with him—not only as a celebration of his achievements and his community, but also as a way he could make a record of his thanks. *Danny* started as a collaboration between subject and producer, and became Kybartas' complicated response to the untimely death of his friend, thereby compromising its potential for a broad, popular audience. Both choices grew out of the specific lives (and deaths) of their title subjects, demonstrating a formal, political, and personal responsiveness that the mainstream media (with its unshakeable conventions) finds impossible. Both *Danny* and *Coming of Age,* as disparate as they are, speak from direct gay experience, without apology and without generalization. It is in their specific words, of sorrow, confusion, and tribute, that we begin to find our own.

Testing the Limits and *Fighting for Our Lives*

Collectively produced and released in 1987, *Testing the Limits* signaled a definitive turning point in representations of AIDS resistance. Born out of the crucible of the early ACT UP meetings (AIDS Coalition To Unleash Power, a group dedicated to fight for the social, medical and political rights of PLWAs), the tape is a freewheeling collage capturing various battlefields in the AIDS war. In its fast-packed twenty-eight minutes, it explicitly attempts a rewriting of AIDS agendas, insisting on an analysis that refuses to patiently explain or pacify. Having no time for polite requests, it passionately demands.

The speaking subjects are often on the street, in the middle of demonstrations, shouting to be heard above the chants. A rapid-fire progression of AIDS activist issues is sketched out: testing; quarantine; educating drug users to clean their works; the politics of safer sex education for target audiences; condemnations of the U.S. health care system; demands for the immediate release of promising treatments and drugs for PLWAs; and denunciations of how racism, sexism, homophobia and poverty have shaped official responses to the AIDS crisis.

Several formal strategies make *Testing the Limits* distinct from solidarity tapes of other struggles. For starters, the tape's purposefully rough look and rapid-fire pace make for a breathless viewing experience, much faster than most activist documentaries. Secondly, the collective foregrounds their active participation in the movement, both through their intimate camera angles and their rapport with their subjects. One quibble: there is an unfortunate reliance throughout on *New York Times* headlines to "prove" or "illustrate" verbal points made, despite the fact that the tape explicitly condemns mainstream coverage of the epidemic. This contradiction is never adequately addressed.

What's not apparent on the first viewing is the careful and calculated progression of issues, leading viewers through a complicated analytic framework that insists on connections but doesn't foreclose them. The tape is disturbing because it refuses to "explain" anything thoroughly, at least by the conventions of broadcast TV. Instead, its rapid succession of issues and agendas, speakers and crowds, delivers an effective and incendiary message: "Where are you in this war?" By refusing to contain any one issue through closure, *Testing the Limits* forces viewers to position themselves, picturing themselves finally (however uncomfortably) in the midst of this groundswell.

Fighting for Our Lives, by Ellen Seidler and Patrick Dunah, operates from the opposite end of the formal spectrum. Adopting the tried-and-true conventions of broadcast documentaries, it sets out to capture the range of San Francisco's response to the AIDS crisis. Linda Hunt (of *The Year of Living Dangerously* fame) serves as interpretive BBC-type narrator, conferring a disquieting respectability on the subject. In fact, the documentary's tone is at distinct odds with its content. It talks frankly from within the gay community about political tensions between AIDS service groups, the vital role of lesbians in AIDS work, and the racism that has characterized funding and hindered the vital outreach that needs to be done in the city's Black and Latino communities. While this narrative acknowledges some contradictions, it also—by its very form—must erase or streamline others.

For instance, there is an interview with Randy Shilts, the conservative and controversial gay author of the bestselling *And the Band Played On,* an extremely egotistical and partisan version of the epidemic's history that equally blames the government, the medical establishment, *and* the gay movement for the health crisis. Shilts is allowed to speak "objectively" about the closure of the gay baths, despite his hysterical anti-sex views on the subject.[13]

We are presented with the "story" of San Francisco's response to the AIDS crisis. We are introduced to some of the issues and efforts, which are then recontained and summed up in a neat package at the "story's" conclusion. Linda Hunt assures us that they are fighting for their lives, and the *they* is very important. An inevitable result of such representational practices, it means *we* are never implicated, never involved, except as voyeurs.

This very palatable form allowed it to be broadcast as part of a series of AIDS tapes on KCET (the Los Angeles PBS affiliate) while *Testing the Limits* was rejected, despite intensive lobbying efforts on the part of the programmer. Now (and I'm not necessarily playing devil's advocate): Does this make *Fighting for Our Lives* more subversive (and hence more effective) than the latter, since its reassuring form probably encouraged straight suburban viewers to watch it, and therefore see the gay community portrayed (however voyeuristically) with some degree of subtlety and dynamism? *Testing the Limits* would no doubt alienate those same viewers—its passionate militancy would be all too easily dismissed, and switched off. Indeed, depressingly large sectors of the gay community would probably respond in the same way. The thousands of white, middle-class gay men who have achieved some measure of comfort and security would no doubt feel even more threatened than their straight counterparts by the tape's images of a multiracial grassroots movement that has taken to the streets, because the tape implicates them directly. In contrast, Linda Hunt implicitly reassures her viewers that sit-ins are only one option in a menu of choices, that all efforts are equally important. Her reassuring mediation (compromising important political issues in the process) has perhaps spurred many apolitical gays and straights to get involved in a nonradical AIDS service organization—and who's going to say that's a bad thing?

An opposite argument can also be made. *Testing the Limits* should be broadcast all over the country, precisely because it will upset and not pacify. It has in fact since been broadcast on WNET, the PBS affiliate in New York. AIDS is *very* upsetting and *very* present—arguably (polemically), any documentary that isn't as upsetting as the crisis is shouldn't be broadcast. Secondly, there is a large audience desperate for these very taboo images of activism—gays and straights of all ages and races who would be immensely empowered and politicized by such incendiary representations. Conservative gay men *should* feel threatened, and *should* be shaken out of their complacency. Thirdly, broadcast distribution is hardly the ultimate outlet. Community screenings around the country may not deliver the same numbers, but their social status as communal events makes for another vital sort of "effectiveness." At a recent Toronto AIDS forum, organized by AIDS Action Now, *Testing the Limits* began the evening, followed by speakers on a variety of subjects. In the ensuing public discussion, audience members repeatedly referred to the tape: "I really agree with what that woman said about dental dams. . . ." It became clear that for much of the audience, the tape constituted the same direct authority as the live speakers, addressing issues that would otherwise not have been raised.

Effectiveness and Strategic Compromise

This recurring question of effectiveness is obviously and most importantly contextual, dependent not just on audiences and their politics, but also on their response to media form. For instance, youth may intuitively respond more positively to the anarchic sensibility of *Another Man*, than the conventional histrionics of *'Til Death Do Us Part*. However, conditioned to validate didactic object lessons in what to think (especially around issues of gender roles and sexual preference), they might (at least, in front of their peers) claim to prefer the conservative politics of the latter. Gay audiences addicted to *Dynasty* are no doubt more comfortable with the sentimental narrative of *Coming of Age* than the disjunctive subtexts of *Danny*. AIDS organizers, even those involved in the issues that ACT UP champions, have at times complained that *Testing the Limits* is too fragmented, too inconclusive, that it doesn't tell a story, and have programmed something more conventional (like *Fighting for Our Lives*) instead.

Each of the above choices, opting for the reassuring tape over the demanding one, presumes that audiences prefer to be passively entertained instead of challenged. This condescending truism is rampant in production and distribution circles (partly because of conservatism, partly because it contains a grain of truth), and AIDS artists who want to reach audiences take it very seriously. Two contradictory polemics express the poles of this debate: "AIDS is a war, there's no time for artsy debates about formal issues. We have to make clear, effective propaganda that reaches as many people as possible!" versus "AIDS is a war, not just of medicine and politics but of representations—we must reject dominant media discourses and forms in favor of a radical new vocabulary that deconstructs their agendas and reconstructs ours!"

Most artists, consciously or unconsciously, negotiate their way between these two positions, attempting to meet audiences halfway. Each of the six tapes in these "case studies" made a series of strategic compromises, negotiating the difficult terrain of "effectiveness" in six different ways, each according to their particular context. *Danny* and *Chuck Solomon: Coming of Age* prioritized the very personal voices of their subjects over other concerns, and ended up making works that speak to audiences who never knew the title characters. *Another Man* and *Testing the Limits* used inventive versions of seductive media tactics to "sell" their radical political agendas, and succeeded in reinventing how we imagine representations of safer sex and activism respectively. *'Til Death Do Us Part* and *Fighting for Our Lives* prioritized conventional moralism and conventional documentary values respectively in an effort to reach larger audiences, and ended up selling out their subjects—which in turn accounts for their relative distribution success.

The desperate need for alternare AIDS media images remains as pressing today as it was in 1981. Whole subjects and issues have still not been addressed. At the same time, the rich and energetic video subculture has laid a firm foundation for (hopefully) hundreds of new tapes. Each of these artists will in turn have to negotiate their own set of strategic compromises, each interrogating their own aesthetic and political responses to this question of "effectiveness." Our critical response must be even more tough *and* flexible, responding in detail to the particular context that each tape comes from, refusing the temptation of any single programmatic prescription. Like current wisdom concerning treatments for HIV infection and the opportunistic diseases that can accompany AIDS, we must recognize that this representational war will only be won when we select and combine, appropriate to each case and context, a variety of "cures."

NOTES

1. For a complete list of alternate tapes and films on AIDS, contact: The Media Network, 121 Fulton St., New York, NY 10038 (212-619-3455).
2. Throughout this essay I will sometimes use "tapes" and "video" as a short form for speaking about both video and film—a bit of revenge against decades of thoughtless critics who say "film" when they mean both video and film. This "festival" of twenty-five tapes was presented at A Space, 183 Bathurst St., Toronto, Canada M5T 2R7 (416-363-3227). A modest program is available.
3. For an excellent critique of representations of AIDS in the mass media, see: Simon Watney, *Policing Desire: Pornography, AIDS and the*

Media (Minneapolis: University of Minnesota Press, 1987).

4. Hans Magnus Enzensberger, "Constituents of a Theory of the Media," *Video Culture* (Rochester: Visual Studies Workshop, 1986), 97.
5. Phrase coined by Tom Waugh. See Tom Waugh, ed., *Show Us Life* (Metuchen: Scarecrow Press, 1984), xiv.
6. This 60-minute compilation, *Angry Initiatives, Defiant Strategies,* was one of sixteen weekly specials satellite delivered to over 300 cable access stations around the U.S. in the spring of 1988. Other subjects included Central America, Latino images, and disarmament. For more information: Deep Dish TV, 339 Lafayette St., New York, NY 10012 (212-420-9045).
7. AIDS education tapes for youth audiences include: *AIDS in Your School, The AIDS Movie, AIDS-Wise, No Lies, AIDS: Answers for Young People, AIDS: Can I Get It?, AIDS: Changing the Rule, AIDS: Everything You and Your Family Need to Know, AIDS: Questions and Answers, AIDS: The Classroom Conflict, AIDS: The Facts of Life, All of Us and AIDS, Condom Education in Grad Schools, Sex, Drugs & AIDS*. . . . The list goes on and on.
8. See especially: Martha Gever, "Pictures of Sickness: Stuart Marshall's *Bright Eyes*," and Douglas Crimp, "How to Have Promiscuity in an Epidemic," in *AIDS: Cultural Analysis, Cultural Activism, October*, issue 43 (Cambridge: MIT Press, 1987), 109, 237.
9. *The HIV Anti-Body Test for the Black Community,* designed as an educational tape for anonymous HIV test sites in San Francisco's Black community, similarly uses a dramatic form, but its content is completely nonjudgmental about both sex and drugs. The information is clear and engaging, especially when it stresses the politics of testing—unfortunately, it too assumes a straight audience, and never once mentions gay sex.
10. Simon Watney, "Common Knowledge," *Art and Crisis: AIDS and the Gay Politic, High Performance*, issue 36 (Los Angeles: 1986), 44.
11. Huestis and Dallas organized a forty-two-city tour of the film and four others in the summer of 1988, accompanying the already legendary Names Project, a quilt commemorating those who have died.
12. Gevet, "Pictures of Sickness," 111–12.
13. For a summation of Shilts's conservative, anti-sex views, see Crimp, "Promiscuity in an Epidemic," *October*, 238–246.

SECTION VI

TRUTH NOT GUARANTEED

Reflections, Revisions, and Returns

87

JONATHAN KAHANA

INTRODUCTION TO SECTION VI

Who knows if *Shoah* is good for you?

—J. Hoberman, "*Shoah*: The Being of Nothingness"

Different dates define the epoch covered in this section, which takes its title from a remark by filmmaker Errol Morris, a leading figure of what could be called a post-modern documentary cinema. 1989, the year that Morris's crucial film *The Thin Blue Line* gained wide public and critical attention, would be one suitable place to begin. As he demonstrates in his interview with the magazine *Cineaste*, Morris defied conventional wisdom about non-fiction filmmaking. In *The Thin Blue Line*, Morris reinvested traditional, even obsolete, methods with currency and curiosity. In a manner that was soon imitated widely, Morris embraced cinematic artifice, incorporating techniques of performance, of cinematography and *mise-en-scène*, of musical scoring, and of editing that were anathema to the reportorial ethos of *cinéma vérité*, the observational style that remained, even in the late 1980s, a badge of authenticity and seriousness among filmmakers in parts of the world where the *vérité* styles had once been the mark of independence and innovation. (The universality of this stylistic code is a subject of debate in section seven as well, where a number of selections examine local and continental variations, beyond North America and Western Europe, on the ideals of spontaneity, immediacy, and directness.) *The Thin Blue Line* and other "blockbuster" documentaries of the next several years made a controversial splash, the impact of which was amplified when they were passed over for Academy Awards, despite their success with audiences and critics.

This popular phenomenon had its parallel in the academic realm: at the end of the 1980s, scholars were not only making their peace with the notion that documentary film might be (as Robert Sklar presciently observed) more artifice than artifact, but systematically applying methods borrowed from literary studies and the semiotic analysis of fiction film to prove that documentary film had a poetics, a narrative structure, and a set of genre conventions, just like any expressive language a writer or artist might use. In fact, the academic subfield of documentary film studies that emerges in the 1990s follows patterns identified by Sklar a decade and a half prior, in his 1975 review of two notable books on what he called the "documentary motive in mass communications media," William Stott's *Documentary Expression and Thirties America* (1973) and Erik Barnouw's *Documentary: A History of the Non-Fiction Film* (1974). Sklar was himself a professional historian in 1975—he had not yet moved to the department of Cinema Studies at New York University—and his interest in these two important studies of documentary media is galvanized by their attention to artifice, in both senses: making and faking. Stott's and Barnouw's are among the first book-length works of criticism to concentrate, at the scale of an entire documentary culture, on the lengths to which producers and audiences will go in crafting the suspension of disbelief that had, for decades, made documentary film a popular and effective form of history, social research, and civic advocacy.

Although Stott and Barnouw might not have intended to do so, their books helped establish a comprehensive revaluation of documentary film's "first principles" and of what Sklar called its "service of truth," a rethinking of documentary privileges, priorities, and protocols, by critics and practitioners alike, that continues to this day. The topics of this reconsideration included:

- documentary ethics, and the moral economies of reform-minded filmmaking (a problem Brian Winston encapsulates as the "tradition of the victim" in social documentary);
- documentary evidence, or the ontological nature of recordings that made photographs, moving images, and audiotape seem like irrefutable testimony from past and present reality (a concerned aired in and around films by Trinh T. Minh-ha, Claude Lanzmann, and Michael Moore, among others in this period, and by such prominent American critics as Vivian Sobchack, Michael Renov, Linda Williams, and Paul Arthur);
- the priority of staged over unstaged action, a lingering effect of the fascination with direct cinema that was challenged by film- and video-makers who, like Morris and Moore, or the Berkeley-based scholar and artist Marlon Riggs, incorporated performance and choreography into what would otherwise have been traditionally journalistic or investigative documentary; likewise, theorists like Thomas Waugh challenged critical readers to recall the other times and places in which "acting to play oneself," in Waugh's terms, was a perfectly acceptable documentary technique;
- the documentary value of publicness, objectivity, and disinterestedness, leading to the thorough interrogation by both filmmakers and critics of what Philip Brian Harper called the "subjective position" in documentary, as well as the mainstreaming of what was once (by Jonas Mekas and others) called a "diary film," and the revelation on very public screens of deeply personal and self-interested material: a development foreseen by Sklar in his closing distinction between documentaries and "documents," and elaborated here in apologia for the personal essay, auto-ethnography and home video by Mekas, Chick Strand, and Marsha and Devin Orgeron;
- the very idea—perhaps fundamental to the "documentary motive" itself—of documentary as a way of being serious about the world and its problems, rather than, as Waugh put it, "playing"

with the real: if narrative, staging, and spectacle made a return to documentary, so too did the generic structures and pleasures of comedy and drama. As Paula Rabinowitz argues here in writing about popular laborist documentaries, even topics as grim as the class struggle could serve as material for melodrama in films no less properly documentary because they inflamed the emotions of both their characters and their viewers.

Viewed in historical or historiographic terms—that is, as a story about the past built from a collection of cultural high points, or as a way to understand how that story got written—this section might be confusing, since the reader will find in it ideas about documentary that contradict each other, or that seem to retard the project of getting inexorably closer to essential truths about society, the self, or nature. Sometimes the work being done by writers in this section looks like a retooling of documentary film, a return to the origins of the artform with the aim of keeping it relevant. Sometimes it seems more like a rejection of the very idea of documentary film. One can hear these competing tendencies in what Errol Morris has to say about his ideals and his methods in "Truth Not Guaranteed," as well as in the dialogue with Claude Lanzmann, "Site and Speech: An Interview with Claude Lanzmann about *Shoah*," and in J. Hoberman's two reflections on *Shoah*, one of which defends the film against a viciously skeptical review by his New York colleague Pauline Kael. By contrast with Kael's stubbornly literal approach to *Shoah*, Hoberman's position is quintessentially post-modern: *Shoah* tells a profound truth about the Holocaust because of what it *doesn't* and *can't* show, and because of the pictures this absence generates in the head of the viewer, not because of actual pictures the viewer confronts on the screen.

On the one hand, documentary—a term that fell into disfavor among commercially-oriented filmmakers and film distributors in the 1980s and 1990s—seemed to be a faith losing its true believers, a naïve and old-fashioned hobby in an ironic and endlessly "reflexive" age. On the other hand, forms of reality-based art and entertainment were proliferating. By the late 1990s, it seemed that one could not step into a multiplex theater, turn on a television, or enter an art gallery without confronting something that resembled, at least superficially, one of the many styles of documentary that had graced a page, stage or screen over the past hundred years. On the one hand, the study of documentary film—which had, for a long time, consisted mainly of either comprehensive theories about the entire enterprise of documentary or the criticism of individual films, the accuracy of their representation, and their contextual effects—was starting to look like any other field of research: increasingly sophisticated, generating more, and more specialized, research, publications, conferences, classes, and students. On the other hand, making a documentary has never seemed to require so little qualification: widely distributed access and nearly compulsory uptake of personal sound and image communication and recording technologies, and the networks of distribution on which their data travels, has seemed to make it easier for inhabitants of consumer societies—which now nearly blanket the globe—to record one's own life, community, or culture. At times it feels like *everyone* is making a documentary. (Perhaps you are making one right now.)

For the student of documentary film history, it can be difficult to reconcile these dichotomies. Is it more correct to say that, in this post-modern age, documentary as we have known it is being reinvented or becoming obsolete? Does the vast menu from which filmmakers can today choose a style or technology to film the real make it easier or harder for viewers to credit a recording with "authenticity"? When the "document" appears everywhere, what makes the "documentary" continue to matter?

88

ROBERT SKLAR

DOCUMENTARY

Artifice in the Service of Truth (1975)

Erik Barnouw. *Documentary: A History of the Non-Fiction Film.* New York: Oxford University Press, 1974. vii + 332 pp. Illustrations, afterword, source notes, bibliography, and index. $10.95.

William Stott. *Documentary Expression and Thirties America.* New York: Oxford University Press, 1973. xvi + 361 pp. Illustrations, bibliography, and index. $12.50.

The revival of historical studies on popular culture and mass communications presents scholars with the opportunity—and the complex challenge—of integrating a broad range of nontraditional evidence into their field of vision. Television and radio programs, motion pictures, photographs, advertisements, oral testimony, design in furnishings and clothes: these are among the documents taking a place alongside the book, newspaper, private letter, probate record, census tract. Large claims have been made for what such material can reveal about the culture that produced them, yet there exists no clear consensus, and little theoretical exploration, on how they may be studied and understood.

One frequently voiced view holds that the products of mass communication and mass consumption are "mirrors" which accurately reflect their culture, or "artifacts," representative cultural documents which may be studied as objects-in-themselves, without reference to the circumstances of their production. The two studies under review serve, in separate ways, as useful correctives to that inadequate perspective. They focus on what may be called the documentary motive in mass communications media, and they suggest paradoxically that in nonfiction communication—as in fiction—the operative word may not be artifact but *artifice.* The urge to document is the urge to tell the truth, to present a vision of reality, yet opinions differ as to what is true or real. We are accustomed to taking such differences into account in studying written and oral evidence, but less practiced with the still or moving picture document. These studies make clear that the visual document, far from being a mirror or artifact to be interpreted by the scholar, itself comprises an interpretation. Therein lies its principal methodological challenge.

William Stott describes his book as a work both of mass communications theory and of cultural history, and it is as the latter that historians will primarily appreciate it. In many respects it serves as a model of a "new" cultural history emerging from the grid where intellectual and social history, literary and art criticism, and American Studies overlap and intersect: in its transcendence of the high culture/popular culture conflict and its capacity to move with assurance across the spectrum of communications and the arts, taking in, among other subjects, radio, photography, reportage, social science field work, fiction, and ballet; in the sensitivity and penetration of its analysis of cultural productions at all levels of intention and accomplishment; in the breadth of its curiosity and interest, its ability in some measure to comprehend American society and culture, in Raymond Williams's term, as "a whole way of life"; above all in its grasp of technique (particularly in photography), of the processes whereby choices are made and effects created.

What enables Stott to unite American society and culture of the 1930s within a single field of vision is his conviction that the documentary genre played a pervasive role in cultural expression during the period. He devotes fully a fifth of his text to defining what documentary is, though his generally helpful discussion sometimes bogs down in a blurring of nomenclature. Thus he is at pains to distinguish between two different kinds of documentary, the "human" and the "social": the human document is essentially a factual report (for example, an account of a natural disaster which evokes feelings such as awe or pity in the observer); the social document is deliberately intended to provoke specific feelings about an "unimagined existence," unimagined at least by the audience to which it is addressed, to persuade and convince, to serve as catalyst for social amelioration or change. In a confusing way, the social document ends up in Stott's language as more "human" than the human document. It is also synonymous with propaganda, though in suggesting the similiarity between a neutral term and one which we normally use invidiously, Stott knows he risks our condemning social documentary simply as falsehood.

Indeed the basic ambiguity in documentary lies in distinguishing the false from the true. Radio was the paradigmatic medium of documentary in the 1930s for Stott, because it combined what he describes as the two methods of documentary—the direct and the vicarious, the unmediated experience and the interpretative commentary—and often in simultaneous juxtaposition. You could hear the sounds of warfare, but you needed the correspondent's voice to tell you which were bombs, which antiaircraft shells. Would it have produced the same emotions if you knew the sounds were studio sound effects? Many of us as children avidly followed baseball on radio, knowing full well the sounds came not from the ballpark but were created in the studio from Western Union wire reports. Thousands of listeners believed soap opera characters were as real as Edward R. Murrow, and the panic created by Orson Welles's *War of the Worlds* is legendary. The form of the medium made its communication seem real even when it was not. Perhaps the crucial aspect is the willingness of audiences to believe, or suspend disbelief, attitudes which change with time and technology.

Stott is at his best in explicating the truth and falsity of photographs. Perhaps we tend to think that photographs are more real and trustworthy than written descriptions, because they are direct rather than vicarious documents—it's a picture, that's what the thing looks like. But Stott shows us the photographer's mediating presence at work: selecting the angle and lighting, posing the subject, choosing one negative from among many, cropping the print, all steps which impose the photographer's interpretation of the subject on the viewer. Arthur Rothstein, a Farm Security Administration photographer, embroiled the FSA in controversy when a Republican newspaper accused him of faking a drought photograph by creating a scene of a steer skull on parched ground (for details on the episode see F. Jack Hurley, *Portrait of a Decade: Roy Stryker and the Development of Documentary Photography in the Thirties* [1972], pp. 86–92). Stott's point, however, is that no photograph can escape being in some sense a manipulation.

Ultimately Stott's attitude toward documentary is a reflection of the genre's ambiguous nature. He is clearly sympathetic with the documentary impulse to portray the "unimagined existence" of the poor and neglected in American society, yet he is skeptical of the results in the depression decade, both as expression and as social policy. On the one hand, the instrumental purpose of social documentary led its practitioners in the 1930s to adopt stock language and portray formulaic experience, the better to achieve a desired response from audiences; the result is a vast body of books, articles, photographs, and other documents of historical interest, but lacking lasting merit. On the other hand, the very act of calling attention to "unimagined existences" could be turned, as Stott says, from criticism to celebration, an homage to the common man, the lowly, the obscure, as sources of the vital energy and unifying cement of American democracy. Stott's book debunks the documentary as it pays tribute to it.

For Stott himself is impelled by an instrumental motive: "Whether certain ways [to describe actuality and the socially disadvantaged] aren't *ultimately* better . . . is a question that haunts these pages," he writes (p. 144, his italics). And he finds an answer which itself is ambiguous in the way that art is. The classic work of documentary expression in the 1930s, for Stott, is *Let Us Now Praise Famous Men*—James Agee's text and Walker Evans's photographs on the lives of three Alabama sharecropper families. The book's task, as Agee said in another context, was "to perceive the aesthetic reality within the actual world"—to show the beauty that was in the sharecroppers' lives and not merely in the eyes of their beholders. The art of Agee and Evans does not merely culminate, it explodes social documentary. "That the world can be improved and yet must be celebrated as it is are contradictions," Stott concludes. "The beginning of maturity may be the recognition that both are true" (p. 314). Fine as these words are, they do not say whether both enterprises can be combined in a single act.

Stott's bias toward art is evident from the fact that his cultural history is almost entirely cultural criticism. He is interested in the cultural product and the aesthetic strategies and social motives of its creator. The social and cultural relations of the people who make cultural productions occupy him hardly at all. This gap ultimately makes his book less than a fully satisfactory model for the "new" cultural history. The men and women whose works he studies were with few exceptions employees of the federal government or of private corporations; only with Agee and Evans are the implications of such facts explored. The constraints and demands of employers, the commercial as well as the social motive, the pressures of the social and economic context are essential aspects of cultural communication. The "new" cultural history needs to be aware not only of the process of cultural creation but also of the process of cultural production.

That artistry, though a necessary standard, is by itself an insufficient one for cultural analysis of mass communications is made clear by the example of Robert Flaherty's famous documentary film *Louisiana Story* (1948), as Erik Barnouw presents it in his survey of the nonfiction film. This film, on oil exploration in the Louisiana bayous, the last in Flaherty's distinguished career as an independent filmmaker, was financed by the Standard Oil Company of New Jersey at a cost of more than a quarter of a million dollars. Yet the company did not interfere in production, gave Flaherty ownership and distribution rights, and insisted that its name not be mentioned in screen credits.

Why such corporate altruism? The answer, Barnouw suggests, is that the company recognized that the pervading aesthetic of Flaherty's films would serve its own interests—and more effectively as art than as public relations. In *Nanook of the North* (1922), *Moana* (1926), *Man of Aran* (1934), and other documentaries Flaherty had shown people of traditional cultures, Eskimos, Samoans, Aran Islanders, living in intimate relation with the forces of nature. "Standard Oil," Barnouw writes, "could expect that Flaherty would make precisely the kind of film he had always made, and of which *Louisiana Story* became another example: an expression of his love for the unspoiled wilderness and its life. By focusing on this—and de-emphasizing oil—the film had the message: have no fear, the wilderness is safe. This became in subsequent years—despite oil slicks in bayou, stream, and sea, or perhaps because of them—the recurring theme of countless oil-sponsored films and television commercials" (pp. 218–19). Here is art that celebrates the world as it is and yet says it can be improved—and the beginning of maturity is to explore, as Barnouw does, the circumstances of its production.[1]

One learns very little about art in Barnouw's book. In a text of under 300 pages, densely illustrated by stills and photographs, he surveys the world history of nonfiction films from the 1890s to the present, and skims over scores of films and filmmakers with no more than a few sentences for most. Of necessity it is a superficial book but it is also often a shrewd one. Barnouw organizes his theme within the larger framework of political, economic, and technological change. Documentary for him, as for Stott, is a genre able "to open our eyes to worlds available to us but, for one reason or another, not perceived" (p. 3). Because film presents more complex technical and aesthetic problems than most of the media Stott discusses, Barnouw makes even more clear how central a role artifice plays in fulfilling the documentary aim.

Again it is a question of how much audiences are willing to suspend disbelief. In the early days of cinema, film companies faked films of Spanish-American war scenes and the San Francisco earthquake. Staged actions, or miniature sets, may have provided viewers with scenes more accurately fulfilling their expectations of events than the actual events themselves. Some of the famous War Department *Why We Fight* documentaries used footage from Hollywood features. Hollywood, moreover, had accustomed viewers to a rich variety of simultaneous perspectives in film construction—cuts from medium shots to close-ups, reverse shots showing first one viewpoint, then its opposite. To achieve similar effects documentary filmmakers often had to re-enact scenes, with the cooperation of the subjects, or if that was not possible, with actors. Voice-over narration, sound track music, special effects—all contributed to make the motion picture documentary a vicarious, mediated, interpreted experience of the actual. Henry Luce described *The March of Time* newsreel style as "fakery in allegiance to the truth."

The tradition of tolerance for manipulation in nonfiction films made it easier for audiences to accept the rapid rise of corporate-sponsored films to dominate the documentary field in the United States after World War II. Barnouw is at his most trenchant in discussing this trend. The decline of short (as well as feature) film production in Hollywood, the emerging practice of selling television time to sponsors, the new ideological needs of multinational corporations, the purge of dissident viewpoints from the communications media through blacklists, all these factors combined to concentrate production of documentary films in the hands of business corporations and the major networks. Cold War political and economic perspectives dominated the visual mass media more completely than any other form of communication—and in 1959 the networks adopted a policy of rejecting any documentary footage produced outside their news departments that was likely to be "opinion-influencing." Barnouw shows how this network policy, along with vigorous United States government efforts to keep foreign-made documentary films from entering the country, deprived American audiences of significant information about the Indochina war.

The technical innovations that corporations fostered, however, helped to break their control over documentary production. Small 16mm cameras, videotape portapacks, portable sound recorders made possible new kinds of immediacy and authenticity in documentary filmmaking. There was no longer a need for voice-over narrations or studio sound effects or reenacted scenes when the moving camera could be part of the action, when every sound could be directly recorded. Indeed there was no longer a need for interpretation or mediation at all: equipment is simple enough that anyone can learn to operate it. Some filmmakers put cameras in the hands of the people they were filming and gave them a chance to record their own vision of their lives. It is premature to guess how widespread such use of visual media may become, but historians may yet have available visual documents that, whatever artifice they contain, are unmediated by outside interpreters: documents, not documentaries.

NOTE

1. The idea that Flaherty's art would serve the company's interest came from Roy Stryker, who joined the public relations staff of Standard Oil in 1943 after resigning as head of the FSA historical section, where he had directed the famous New Deal efforts in documentary photography. See Arthur Calder-Marshall, *The Innocent Eye: The Life of Robert J. Flaherty* (London: W. H. Allen & Co., 1963), Pelican edition, p. 211; and F. Jack Hurley, *Portrait of a Decade: Roy Stryker and the Development of Documentary Photography in the Thirties* (Baton Raton: Louisiana State University Press, 1972), pp. 170–72.

89

CHICK STRAND

NOTES ON ETHNOGRAPHIC FILM BY A FILM ARTIST (1978)

I first began studying anthropology seriously at the University of California at Berkeley in the mid-Fifties. I was captivated by the idea of learning about people different from ourselves, living in small cohesive cultures which appeared to be stable in comparison with our own. A growing civil rights movement made my generation aware of the necessity of learning about other cultures which were disappearing. The field of anthropology was the most popular social science because we believed that through the study of other cultures we would learn something valuable about the human condition. The information we gathered would potentially lead to understanding and problem-solving in terms of dealing with the rapid acculturation of indigenous cultures, and would also give us insights into problems in our own changing society. With the knowledge that these small cultures were being destroyed by the tide of nationalistic and technological societies, we were anxious to get out into the field and assume our role as scientific observers in order to study, analyze and preserve our knowledge about them by documentation. We were idealistic and humanistic. We thought that our work would be used as a reference in intelligent and humane decision-making on the part of the policy-makers having authority over the people in the cultures that we studied.

Of course this didn't happen. Doors were not opened to us, and usually there was no policy-making except that of economic, technical and material progress. Acculturation became like a giant glacier, uncontrollable, unceasing and unchangeable, picking up and dropping people and their traditions, mixing them up almost at random, moving them from their land, slaughtering them and gouging out huge wounds, forever unmendable. The cultures changed so much that they melted one into the other to form a gigantic stew of faceless men and women. The lives of individuals existing in remote and alien cultures became unimportant to most people in view of unsolvable world problems, technological progress and the question of our own survival.

In the Fifties we thought there was a possibility of easing the acculturation process for the people we studied and loved, and that we could both adhere to the ethics of our profession and act upon the dictates of our hearts as private people. We were naive and felt the fervor of the call.

I loved anthropology. I loved reading about the cultures and various approaches to study, and the possibility of doing something really meaningful beyond the study, beyond the documentation. Most of all, I was thrilled at the chance of getting to know these people on their own terms, of getting to know them as human beings. But the ethnographies were very disappointing. It was only rarely that the people of the culture came to life because they were not presented as reachable and accessible human beings. I thought that perhaps in graduate school I would somehow be given the golden key to unlock the door into their inner lives and feelings so that I could understand their culture in depth. I wanted to know what it was like for Balinese dancers to prepare and go into a trance, what it meant to them personally. I wanted to know and feel what it was like for a young girl to approach and pass through fertility rites. With the material I was given, I could easily imagine the ceremonies as a general event, but what was it like to be a part of it? How did the people feel about it? What part did it play in their lives? What were their dreams and fears? What did they talk about?

I wasn't given the key and after a year in graduate school became disenchanted because anthropologists really didn't pay much attention to the heart and soul of a culture which is manifested in the people themselves. Anthropology, after all, is the study of *Homo-sapiens*. To leave the individuals out as they contribute to, take from and function in their culture negates the whole idea of anthropology. More and more I felt that the profession was mainly a battle between the inflated egos, the insensitive, inflexible personalities, the rigid perspectives and sensibilities of the anthropologists themselves. There was no excitement and enthusiasm leading to new discoveries. Anthropologists believed that they had found their techniques and methodology, closed themselves up and called themselves scientists. Safe and secure in their university positions, they allowed the field to become stagnant and dry. No longer were they the mavericks, the crazy people who spent years in the field trying to sort out the wealth of information they encountered for the joy of it, the love of it. Their method became one of getting into and out of the field as rapidly as possible in order to come back, organize their material and publish it.

I was at the point in my life where I had to make a decision about how I wanted to use my creative energies. I left anthropology because I could see that it was a dead end and became involved in the avantgarde film movement. I wanted to make personal experimental films. In order to learn film techniques, I entered UCLA as a graduate student in film. Even though I thought of myself by that time as a film artist using the film medium as an art form, I still was involved in anthropology, and when I learned that the university was offering an ethnographic film program, I enrolled in the classes and began watching ethnographic films. I sat in the dark squirming with anger and frustration. With very few exceptions these films present the people with the same lack of involvement and insensitivity as the ethnographies, like animals in a zoo, like cultures prepared on a slide for observation under a microscope, with an invisible shield placed between them and the viewer by the anthropologist. The films are made with cold indifference to living, breathing people. They are fragmented and abstract because they rarely show the whole person, the individual relating within his society. They present people as masses, unfathomable as individuals and as lacking in dimension as puppets in a Javanese shadow play. People are shown participating in the culture, usually in a super-event, as one of many clones.

Just as I doubt that an alien would learn much about the complexities of our culture by seeing the ritual of a Christmas Mass on film, I doubt if we really learn much in depth when we see a ritual from another culture, even though we are able to relate it to other events and various social structures within the culture. We need to be able to relate to the individuals involved in the event. We get no feeling for the culture because we are given no clues to the actual lives and inner thoughts of the people. These films aren't objective, truthful or holistic because they make everyone seem the same. In a scientific attempt to present what is perceived only by what the anthropologist sees, all nuances, sensibilities, aesthetics, emotions and human drama in the culture are lost. Insights into their art of living, uniqueness of spirit, complex variety of motivations and individual actions and reactions are impossible. It is the people of a culture rather than how many hops in a dance step or how they weave their baskets that will leave the biggest, darkest, most barren and mourned empty space in our world when the culture is forever lost to us.

In the written ethnography the inner life is studied in terms of generalities and never in individual terms. This is one way to learn how the entire culture is structured and works within its environment. But film is another ballgame because it is a medium of intimacy and immediacy, and we are able for the first time to *see* and *feel* the culture and its people and relate to them. But anthropologists have used film in the same way and to the same ends that they use the written material, and thus they have restricted their field of study, passing by the richness in individual human experience in favor of mass behavior patterns and a sort of generalized personality that we must assume holds true for all individuals in the society because we are not told otherwise. This is a separatist and racial presentation. Much information is lost because it is ignored and a one-sided picture is shown.

I wonder which is more scientific, presenting all the information or withholding some? I wonder which is more important to the anthropologists, science or the human beings they swore above all else to protect? The anthropologist always presents them from his own perspective, never from their perspective. This is neither honest nor scientific. The people can reveal their culture in new and exciting ways if only they are allowed to speak for themselves. What can we learn about a culture from the texture of the lives of human beings, the way they move through their culture, the way they relate and react on a daily basis with their family, friends and colleagues? What can we learn from the casual way that their tools are arranged and the rhythm of their bodies as they use them, what they do with their hands during leisure at home or while discussing a planned ritual with their age group, how they relate to their children, how feelings of affection or dislike are manifested?

In a novel, we are forced to make up the images of the people and their environment. We form a mental picture from the clues given in the description by the author. We make an image in our minds, invent an entire landscape and the physical/psychological being of the characters and take ourselves there. As we read the entire novel, these images keep flashing across our minds and form our own private spectacular film. If we read the book again years later, we form the same images, and it is like visiting a place we once knew very well, reacquainting ourselves with familiar places, things and people. The ethnography does not let us relate to people, places and things, because in the need to be scientific, the anthropologist often neglects giving us the description to put us there and practically never gives us clues so that we can imagine what it is *like* to be there, what it is *like* to be a member of the society. I'm not saying that the ethnography should read like a novel, but I don't think that the anthropologist's role is merely to give us a dry run-down of the culture; it is to give life to it as well.

When we are presented with a film, we are no longer expected to form our own images; we are presented with the actual places with people moving through them, things with people handling and using them, and the people themselves moving in space and time, behaving and relating and going about their daily lives. By looking at a film we can relate to the place and things. But in most ethnographic films, the people are presented in groups, acting out a ritual as a mass—faceless, nameless, all the same, all appearing to act and react in the same manner. We see events that happen only once in a while in the culture, and not what goes on daily. Even when a few people are separated out, we only get to see them in the most formal or fragmented behavior as it pertains to the event, and we know nothing else about them, except what the anthropologist chooses to tell us. Rarely are their own words used, even in translation. An uncaring and uninvolved voice of a narrator tells us what is going on. The films are like textbooks and not true film documents of a people.

Where are the people in these films? To leave out the spirit of the people presents a thin tapestry of the culture, easy to rent, lacking in strength and depth. I want to know really what it is like to be a breathing, talking, moving, emotional, relating individual in the society. The films lack intimacy, dimension, heart and soul and most of all they are artless. The people are presented as bit actors in a culture play. An alien interpretation is superimposed over the lives of the people. The films only show what the anthropology feels is important to show, not what the people feels important to their lives. And the only way to find what is really important is to let them speak for themselves. How much are we missing? How much by their silence and indifference are anthropologist contributing to the destruction of humans and their cultures?

Anthropologists have been reluctant to deal with the inner person in film because they haven't yet accepted the techniques, already discovered by film artists, to present it in such a way that would be acceptable under scientific scrutiny. Anthropologists see film as a way to emphasize parts of a written ethnography as a restatement of it. They do not understand that film can open doorways to knowledge and discovery as a way to present material that cannot be presented some way in the ethnography with a few photographs. Film is a four-dimensional medium. It makes people bigger than life and there is no way to avoid this. Why not use it? It can go around, and we have learned, as we learned as infants to make the upside down image in our retinas seem right side up, to perceive the dimension on a flat surface, the screen. A film also has the fourth dimension of time. It can be made to distort and curve time by editing and can be complicated by the ability to show actual time and compressed time in the same film. Things are not only omitted in time, but several things happening at once have to be shown in a continuum. Just as we have learned to "see" the third dimension of depth, we have learned as movie-goers to deal with "film" time. We have learned to see film time and place it in real time in our minds. A closeup of someone talking and then a cut to another person reacting is easily understood as happening at the same time. Added to this is the sound, which can be related one to one with the picture or presented in counterpoint or fugue with the information conveyed by the image.

The language of film is easily understood by intelligent people who go to the movies. Ethnographic filmmakers should not hesitate to use cinematic techniques because they think they are not presenting events in context. If presented correctly, the viewer can put events in context. When there is a choice in ethnographic filmmaking between ethnographicness and artfulness many anthropologists feel that ethnographic consideration must come first and art must be sacrificed. I can't imagine a situation where one must make a choice. It is always possible to present material artfully.

The above mentioned physical attributes are the basis for the development of the language of the film medium. But there are also psychological aspects, the ability to put us there. Film is an immediate, intimate and revealing tool in terms of trying to understand human experience. But anthropologists are unwilling to use it to full potential. "No closeups please," they say. "It is not the normal way of seeing." But it is normal for an infant to be close to the face of the mother, normal for a lover to be close to the body of the beloved, normal to face a friend eye-to-eye a foot away and talk intimately and normal for that person to see only the face of the friend and not his or her own face. "No fragments of movement," they say. But it is normal for a child sitting beside women grinding corn to see only their hand movements, normal to catch fragments of the costume of the person dancing next to you out of the corner of your eye, normal to see only the flank of a cow when you are milking her. Maybe it is normal for the anthropologist to be so far removed, but not for the people living in the culture. "No small talk," they say. "It doesn't go anywhere." What *do* the people talk about in ordinary situations? Who knows? We haven't been told.

To see a film, the viewer sits in a darkened room, a captive audience for its duration. There is little possibility of making the projector go back and show a part of the film over again. All information must be assimilated in one or two viewings. As images flow and sounds weave in and out, we react immediately to the visual and audio information and try to relate to the people in the film. While watching ethnographic films, we are frustrated and bored because we cannot relate. Anthropologists don't see a need for their audiences to relate, or that it is the role of anthropologists to present a film that the audience can relate to.

Who reads an ethnography? With rare exceptions they are read only by anthropology students and professors. Who sees a film about other cultures? Usually a much larger group with varied motivations sees them. Even more would see them if the films were better, more artful, more interesting and more informative. No one I have ever met, anthropologist or not, has really liked most ethnographic films. Not only have they not liked them, but they feel that the films convey very little important information and contribute very little to the understanding of the cultures involved. Anthropologists as filmmakers have been miserable failures. My conclusion is to take the cameras out of the hands of the anthropologists and let artists make the films.

My approach to ethnographic film has been liberal and radical in terms of the accepted methods of anthropology. I prefer to assume that the written ethnography can stand by itself as a general outline of the culture. It provides the cultural context; I think that film should be used on another level to explore new ways for gathering information through the individuals who live their lives in the culture. I like to make films about one person or one family or two people from two cultures in an acculturation process. In examining personal lives in detail, I am able to get a microscopic view of one of the threads that make up the tapestry of the whole culture. With several films, I begin to see how the threads are woven together, how they split apart and how they are mended.

I wonder if there isn't such a thing as too much preparation for the field, if there aren't too many preconceptions of what to look for and how to limit and present information. I want to feel like Bronislaw Malinowski must have felt when he went into the field, free, open to anything, not knowing what to expect or what would be found or how to present it once it was found. Too much preparation for an artist limits the eye, tires the mind, puts boundaries on perception and worst of all diminishes the possibility to be open to new and different revelations. I don't want to know too much beforehand about the film I'm going to make. My films evolve in the field. I try not to have too many preconceptions of what I am going to show in the film or the kinds of events I'll film. Once in the field, I am then able to go after the very best that is presented to me, and I am not blinded to what *is* really important by a preconceived notion of what *will* be important. Artists are recorders of life and their perception of the human condition is keen. Good artists want and need to be hit hard with their own experience and that of others, and they can accept it without judging it. With a little help they can focus their observations in an objective way without making their own social statements. Their expert knowledge of the tools and techniques of film, their heightened perceptibility, awareness and creative processes can get them beyond the place where ethnographers stop, where they can't imagine going. Ethnographic films can and should be works of art, symphonies about the fabric of a people, celebrations of the tenacity and uniqueness of the human spirit.

90

JONAS MEKAS

THE DIARY FILM

A Lecture on *Reminiscences of a Journey to Lithuania* (1972)

Reminiscences falls into the form of a notebook, or a diary, a form into which most of my later work seems to fall. I did not come to this form by calculation but from desperation. During the last fifteen years I got so entangled with the independently made film that I didn't have any time left for myself, for my own film-making—between Film-Makers' Cooperative, Film-Makers Cinematheque, *Film Culture* magazine, and now Anthology Film Archives. I mean, I didn't have any long stretches of time to prepare a script, then to take months to shoot, then to edit, etc. I had only bits of time which allowed me to shoot only bits of film. All my personal work became like notes. I thought I should do whatever I can today, because if I don't, I may not find any other free time for weeks. If I can film one minute—I film one minute. If I can film ten seconds—I film ten seconds. I take what I can, from desperation. But for a long time I didn't look at the footage I was collecting that way. I thought what I was actually doing was practising. I was preparing myself, or trying to keep in touch with my camera, so that when the day would come when I'll have time, then I would make a "real" film.

The second week after I arrived here in 1949, I borrowed some money from people I knew who came before me, and I bought my first Bolex. I started practising, filming, and I thought I was learning. Around 1961 or 1962 I looked for the first time at all the footage that I had collected during all that time. As I was looking at that old footage, I noticed that there were various connections in it. The footage that I thought was totally disconnected suddenly began to look like a notebook with many uniting threads, even in that unorganized shape. One thing that struck me was that there were things in this footage that kept coming back again and again. I thought that each time I filmed something different, I filmed completely something else. But it wasn't so. It wasn't always "something else." I kept coming back to the same subjects, the same images or image sources. Like, for example, the snow. There is practically no snow in

New York; all my New York notebooks are filled with snow. Or trees. How many trees do you see in the streets of New York? As I was studying this footage and thinking about it, I became conscious of the form of a diary film and, of course, this began to affect my way of filming, my style. And in a sense it helped me to gain some peace of mind. I said to myself: "Fine, very fine—if I don't have time to devote six or seven months to making a film, I won't break my heart about it; I'll film short notes, from day to day, every day."

I have thought about other forms of *diary*, in other arts. When you write a diary, for example, you sit down, in the evening, by yourself, and you reflect upon your day, you look back. But in the filming, in keeping a notebook with the camera, the main challenge became how to react with the camera right now, as it's happening; how to react to it in such a way that the footage would reflect what I feel that very moment. If I choose to film a certain detail, as I go through my life, there must be good reasons why I single out this specific detail from thousands of other details. Be it in the park, or in the street, or in a gathering of friends—there are reasons why I choose to film a certain detail. I thought that I was keeping a quite objective diary of my life in New York. But my friends who saw the first edition of *Diaries, Notes, & Sketches (Walden)*, said to me: "But this is not *my* New York! My New York is different. In your New York I'd like to live. But my New York is bleak, depressing. . . ." It's then that I began to see that, really, I was not keeping an *objective* notebook. When I started looking at my film diaries again, I noticed that they contained everything that New York *didn't have*. . . . It was the opposite from what I originally thought I was doing. . . . In truth, I am filming my childhood, not New York. It's a fantasy New York—fiction.

I realized something else. At first I thought that there was a basic difference between the written diary which one writes in the evening, and which is a reflective process, and the filmed diary. In my film diary, I thought, I was doing something different: I was capturing life, bits of it, as it happens. But I realized very soon that it wasn't that different at all. When I am filming, I am also reflecting. I was thinking that I was only reacting to the actual reality. I do not have much control over reality at all, and everything is determined by my memory, my past. So that this "direct" filming becomes also a mode of reflection. Same way, I came to realize, that writing a diary is not merely reflecting, looking back. Your day, as it comes back to you during the moment of writing, is measured, sorted out, accepted, refused, and re-evaluated by what and how one is at the moment when one writes it all down. It's all happening again, and what one writes down is more true to what one is when one writes than to the events and emotions of the day that are past and gone. Therefore, I no longer see such big differences between a written diary and the filmed diary, as far as the processes go.

By the time I decided to look at my ten years of early footage, I had used up three Bolexes. That was a time when the liberation of the independent film-maker was taking place, when the attitudes to filming were changing radically. Like many others, during the years 1950–1960, I wanted to be a "real" film-maker and make "real" films, and be a "professional" film-maker. I was very much caught in the inherited film-making conventions. I was always carrying a tripod. . . . But then I looked through all my footage, and I said: "The park scene, and the city scene, and the tree—it's all there, on film—but it's not what I saw the moment I was filming it! The image is there, but there is something very essential missing." I got the surface, but I missed the essence.

At that time I began to understand that what was missing from my footage was *myself*: my attitude, my thoughts, my feelings the moment I was looking at the reality that I was filming. That reality, that specific detail, in the first place, attracted my attention because of my memories, my past. I singled out that specific detail with my total being, with my total past. The challenge now is to capture that reality, that detail, that very objective physical fragment of reality as closely as possible to how my Self is seeing it. Of course, what I faced was the old problem of all artists: to merge Reality and Self, to come up with the third thing. I had to liberate the camera from the tripod, and to embrace all the subjective film-making techniques and procedures that were either already available, or were just coming into existence. It was an acceptance and recognition of the achievements of the avant-garde film of the last fifty years. It affected my exposures, movements, the pacing, everything. I had to throw out the academic notions of "normal" exposure, "normal" movement, or normal and proper this and normal and proper that. I had to put myself into it, to merge myself with the reality I was filming, to put myself into it indirectly, by means of pacing, lighting, exposures, movements.

Before we go further, I'd like to say something about this thing of "reality." Reality . . . New York is there, it's "real." The street is there. The snow is falling. I don't know how, but it's there. It leads its own life, of course. Same with Lithuania. So, now, I come into the picture. And with the camera. As I walk with my camera, something falls into my eyes. When I walk through the city, I don't lead my eyes consciously from that to that or that. Rather, I walk and my eyes are like open windows, and I see things, the things fall in. If I hear a sound, of course, I look towards the direction of the sound. The ear becomes active, and it directs the eye; the eye is searching for that thing that makes that noise. But most of the time things keep falling in—images, smells, sounds, and they are being sorted out in my head. Some things that fall in strike some notes maybe with their color, with what they represent, and I begin to look at them, I begin to respond to this or that detail. Of course, the mind is not a computer. But still, it works something like a computer, and everything that falls in, is measured, corresponds to the memories, to the realities that have been registered in the brain, or wherever, and it's all very real.

The tree in the street is reality. But here, I singled it out, I eliminated all the other reality surrounding it, and I picked up only that specific tree. And I filmed it. And if I now begin to look through my footage, that I have collected, I have a collection of many such singled-out details, and in each case they fell in, I didn't seek them out, they chose me, and I reacted to them, for very personal reasons, and that's why they all tie in together, for me, for one or another reason. They all mean something to me, even if I don't understand why. My film is a reality that is sorted out through me by way of this very complex process, and, of course, to one who can "read" it, this footage tells a lot about me—actually, more about me than about the city in which I film this footage: you don't see the city, you see only these singled-out details. Therefore, if one knows how to "read" them, even if one doesn't see me speaking or walking, one can tell everything about me. As far as the city goes, of course, you could say something also about the city, from my *Diaries*—but only indirectly. Still, I walk through this actual, representational reality, and these images are all records of actual reality, even if only in fragments. No matter how I film, fast or slow, how I expose, the film represents a certain actual, historical period. But as a group of images, it tells more about my own subjective reality, or you can call it my objective reality, than any other reality.

I used the process of elimination, cutting out parts that didn't work, the badly "written" parts, and leaving in those parts that worked, practically without any changes. Which means I was not editing the individual sequences. I left in those parts which, I felt, captured something, meant something to me, and didn't offend me technically and formally. Even if some parts caught something of essence but bothered me formally, I threw them out. I have this joke, that Rimbaud had *Illuminations,* and I have only eliminations.

I spend much time figuring out, trying out how this detail or that one, this note or this sketch works in the totality of the reel. It was a lesser problem in *Reminiscences,* but with *Diaries, Notes, & Sketches (Walden)* I really had to work hard and long. After you sit for two hours, watching a movie, it's important what comes during the third hour. The question of repetition comes in. Sometimes I have to eliminate even parts which I like, because too much of something is too much. In this case, in the case of *Reminiscences,* the editing was very fast. Hans Brecht of Norddeutscher Television helped me to pay for the film stock and Bolex in return for the rights to show it on German television. But then I came back, and I completely forgot about Hans Brecht. And he forgot about me. But then, on Christmas day he called me. "Is it ready? I need it on January twentieth." "January twentieth? Why didn't you tell me this earlier?" I went to my editing table and I stared at it. After I came back from Lithuania, I kept thinking: "How am I going to edit it?" This footage was very very close to me. I had no perspective to it of any kind. And even now, today, I have little perspective to it. I had about twice as much footage as you see in the film. So now I stood there and I said to myself: "Fine, very fine. This emergency will help me to make decisions." For two or three days I didn't touch the footage, I thought about the form, the structure of the film. Once I decided upon the structure, I just spliced it, very fast, in one day. I knew that this was the only way I could come to grips with this footage: by working with it totally mechanically. Another way would have been to work very very long on it, and either to come up with a completely different film, or destroy the footage in the process.

I have shifted the time sequence only on a few occasions. In *Reminiscences* I kept the time sequence. In *Diaries, Notes, & Sketches (Walden)* in a few places, when I had two long sketches side by side, I pushed one of them further in time, or back in time, for structural reasons.

Those of you who have seen the first edition of *Diaries, Notes, & Sketches (Walden),* and now *Reminiscences,* will see the difference between the two. The basis of *Walden* is the single frame. There is a lot of density there. And when I was going to Lithuania I thought I would bring back material in the same style. But, somehow, when I was there, I just couldn't work in the style of *Walden,* there. The longer I stayed in Lithuania the more it changed me, and it pulled me into a completely different style. There were feelings, states, faces that I couldn't treat too abstractly. Certain realities can be presented in cinema only through certain durations of images. Each subject, each reality, each emotion affects the style in which you film. The style that I used in *Reminiscences* wasn't the most perfect style for it. It is a compromise style. I'll explain why. For instance, I made one bad mistake which I'll never make again. My third Bolex died just before I had to go on this trip. I had fixed it several times, but this time I just couldn't fix it any more. So I bought a new Bolex. The Lithuanian footage was the first footage that I shot with this new Bolex. But even if two Bolexes were totally identical, just the very fact that you never held the new one in your hands effects you. You have to get used to every new camera so that during the filming it responds to you, and you know its weaknesses and its caprices. Because, later, when I started filming, I discovered that my new Bolex wasn't identical with the old one at all. It was, actually, defective, never kept a constant speed. I set it on 24 frames, and after three or four shots it's on 32 frames. You have constantly to look at the speed meter, because the speeds of frames-per-second affect the lighting, exposure. And when I finally realized that there was no way of fixing it or locking it—I decided to accept it and incorporate the defect as one of the stylistic devices, to use the changes of light as structural means.

As soon as I noticed that the speeds were changing constantly (especially when I filmed in short takes, brief spurts) I knew that I wouldn't be able to control the exposures. I don't exactly mean that I wanted to have "normal," "balanced" lighting. No, I don't believe in that. But I can work within my irregularities, within my style of clashing light values, only when I have complete control, or at least "normal" control over my tools. But here that control was slipping. The only way to control it was to embrace it and use it as part of my way of filming. To use the over-exposures as punctuations; to use them in order to reveal reality in, literally, a different light; to use them in order to imbue reality with a certain distance; to compound reality.

When I went to Lithuania, I was offered a team of cameramen, and cameras, and I could have used them. But I didn't. I knew that although the images recorded by these technicians, following my instructions, would have been "better" professionally, they would have destroyed the very subject I was going after. When you go home, for the first time in twenty-five years, you know, somehow, that the official film crews just do not belong there. Thus I chose my Bolex. My filming had to remain totally private, personal, and "unprofessional." For instance, I never checked my lens opening before taking a shot. I took my chances. I knew that the truth will have to hang on and around all those "imperfections." The truth which I caught, whatever I caught, had to hang on me and my Bolex. When you shoot with a Bolex, you hold it somewhere, not exactly where your brain is, a little bit lower, and not exactly where your heart is—it's slightly higher. . . . And then, you wind the spring up, you give it an artificial life. . . . You live continuously, within the situation, in one time continuum, but you shoot only in spurts, as much as the spring allows. . . . You interrupt your filmed reality constantly. . . . You resume it again. . . .

[. . .]

([Robert Flaherty] International Film Seminar, August 26, 1972)

91

MICHAEL RENOV

TOWARD A POETICS OF DOCUMENTARY (1993)

Poetics will have to study not the already existing literary forms but, starting from them, a sum of possible forms: what literature *can* be rather than what it *is*.

—Tzvetan Todorov
"Poetics and Criticism"[1]

I don't have aesthetic objectives. I have aesthetic *means* at my disposal, which are necessary for me to be able to say what I want to say about the things I see. And the thing I see is something *outside* of myself—always.

—Paul Strand
"Look to the Things Around You"[2]

The notion of poetics has been a contested one from the beginning. Indeed, Aristotle's founding treatise, the starting point for all subsequent studies in the West, has long been understood as a defense against Plato's banishment of the poets from his *Republic*. With a rigor and systematicity that has tended to characterize the myriad efforts that followed, Aristotle's *Poetics* set out to show "what poetry is and what it can do"; its opening lines set forth as the field of inquiry "[t]he art of poetic composition in general and its various species, the function and effect of each of them."[3] According to Lubomír Doležel, Occidental poetics has since evolved through several stages: the *logical* (inaugurated by Aristotle's divination of the universal "essences" of poetic art), the *morphological* (the Romantic/organic model issuing from Goethe's analytical focus on "the structure, the formation and the transformations of organic bodies"[4]), and the *semiotic* (from the Prague School through the structuralism of Barthes and Todorov, the study of literary communication within a general science of signs).[5]

[. . .] The attitude of inquiry provided by a poetics is particularly apropos for the documentary insofar as poetics has, as we shall see, occupied an unstable position at the juncture of science and aesthetics, structure and value, truth and beauty. Documentary film is itself the site of much equivocation around similar axes given nonfiction's too-frequently-presumed debt to the signified at the expense of the signifier's play. It is the "film of fact," "nonfiction," the realm of information and exposition rather than diegetic employment or imagination—in short, at a remove from the creative core of the cinematic art. I shall be at pains to contradict these inherited strictures by way of an analysis of documentary's constitutive modalities—its conditions of existence—to more fully articulate a sense of documentary's discursive field and function, aesthetic as well as expository. I will argue that four modalities are constitutive of documentary.

It is an analysis that must be speculative. For if, as Tzvetan Todorov has claimed, poetics is still "in its early stages," even after 2500 years, these initial efforts toward a poetics of the documentary can be little more than first steps. It will be necessary first to trace a preliminary genealogy of poetics to situate its most recent, hybrid manifestations in the social and human sciences, then to attend, in broad strokes, to an elaboration of the discursive modalities of the documentary in film and video.[6]

The Question of Science

Since Aristotle, poeticians have been intent on minimizing the mingling of normative or even interpretive aims with descriptive considerations.[7] The most ambitious projects for a "scientific criticism" have sought to banish interpretation outright, a task not so easily accomplished. Todorov has argued that pure description—the hallmark of science as objective discourse—can only be what Derrida has called a "theoretical fiction": "One of the dreams of positivism in the human sciences is the distinction, even the opposition, between interpretation—subjective, vulnerable, ultimately arbitrary—and description, a certain and definitve activity."[8] It is important to recognize the limits of a method borrowed from the natural sciences applied to aesthetic forms. It is equally essential that a new poetics acknowledges the historical effects of the valorization of science within the humanities.

In Roland Barthes's "The Return of the Poetician," a 1972 paean to the work of Gerard Genette, a description/interpretation dichotomy (and implicit hierarchy) is assumed: "When he [*sic*] sits down in front of the literary work, the poetician does not ask himself: What does this mean? Where does this come from? What does it connect to? But, more simply and more arduously: *How is this made?*"[9] This heuristic angle to the study of aesthetic forms—the attention to the "simple" and "arduous"—bears a much-remarked upon resemblance to the inductive methods of science.[10] Poetics, frequently understood to be the "science of literature," might, thus, be seen as an intrinsically chiasmatic site of inquiry. Coleridge's organicist formulation of the poem as "that species of composition which is opposed to works of science by proposing for its immediate object pleasure, not truth" would suggest poetics as the science of anti-science.[11] To risk a poetics of documentary is to up the stakes yet again, since it is commonly supposed that the aim and effect of documentary practices must be (to return to the Coleridgean opposition) truth and only secondarily, if at all, pleasure. A documentary poetics would, thus, be the science of a scientistic anti-science! [. . .]

In what follows I shall attempt to outline some fundamental principles governing function and effect for documentary work in film and video within an historical frame through an examination of discursive modality. This effort, though preliminary, will essay the parameters and potentialities of documentary discourse with the ultimate goal the enrichment of the documentary film, that least discussed and explored of cinematic realms. A stunted popular awareness of the breadth and dynamism of the documentary past, the scarcity of distribution outlets for the independent documentarist and the relative critical neglect of nonfiction forms have combined to hamper the growth and development of the documentary.[12]

All of which contributes to the relative impoverishment of a *documentary film culture*, an energized climate of ideas and creative activities fueled by debate and public participation. Such an environment may once have existed in the Soviet Union in the twenties or in this country during the late thirties or early sixties. But, with the consolidation and economic streamlining of commercial television networks (with their preference for "reality programming" over even in-house documentary) and the virtual lockout of the independent from public television series formats such as *Frontline*, such an environment exists no more. While recent Congressional action creating an Independent Television Service to support and showcase the work of independent producers resulted from the concerted lobbying efforts of a coalition of independent producers, educators, and concerned citizenry, those gains are being seriously threatened by conservative forces in the Congress. Indeed, the very survival of independently produced, state-supported art in the United States remains in question, a circumstance best illustrated by the continuing drama surrounding the National Endowment of the Arts.[13] If political activism is to remain possible in the early nineties, then it behooves us to remain equally attentive to the sharpening of the conceptual tools required to enhance the development of a viable film culture for the documentary.

The Four Fundamental Tendencies of Documentary

What I wish to consider here in the context of a nascent poetics of the documentary—those principles of construction, function, and effect specific to nonfiction film and video—concerns what I take to be the four fundamental tendencies or rhetorical/aesthetic functions attributable to documentary practice.[14] These categories are not intended to be exclusive or airtight; the friction, overlaps—even mutual determination—discernible among them testify to the richness and historical variability of nonfiction forms in the visual arts. At some moments and in the work of certain practitioners, one or another of these characteristics has frequently been over- or under-favored. I state the four tendencies in the active voice appropriate to their role in a "poesis," an "active making":

1. to record, reveal, or preserve
2. to persuade or promote
3. to analyze or interrogate
4. to express.

I do not intend to suggest that the most meritorious work necessarily strikes an ideal balance among these tendencies or even integrates them in a particular way. Rather I hope to show the constitutive character of each, the creative and rhetorical possibilities engendered by these several modalities. My not-so-hidden agenda is to point to and perhaps valorize certain of the less-frequently explored documentary tendencies in the hopes of furthering the kind of "basic research" in the arts that makes for better culture just as surely as it does better science. This notion of "basic research" is fundamental to a poetics of any sort. In the case of documentary, however, there has been little research of any sort which can shed light on the governing discursive conditions which give rise to what is branded "nonfiction." It is to be hoped that the interrogation of these several documentary modalities can begin to dislodge the sense of historical inevitability attached to whatever (im)balance may obtain within the field of current practices (e.g., the rhetorical function overshadowing the analytical) in order to engage with the wider potential, repressed but available.

The Four Functions as Modalities of Desire

These four functions operate as modalities of desire, impulsions which fuel documentary discourse. As such, the record/reveal/preserve mode might be understood as the mimetic drive common to all of cinema, intensified by the documentary signifier's ontological status—its presumed power to capture "the imponderable movement of the real." Writing in the late 1930s, Hans Richter described the historical demand for filmic preservation with great eloquence: "Our age demands the documented fact.... The modern reproductive technology of the cinematograph was uniquely responsive to the need for factual sustenance.... The camera created a reservoir of human observation in the simplest possible way."[15] As early as 1901, the cinema was recruited to the service of cultural preservation with Baldwin Spencer's filming of aboriginal ceremonies.[16] Anthropology, in its zeal for the salvaging of "endangered authenticities" [a trope which has drawn fire from many quarters of ["The Totalizing Quest For Meaning," chapter 5 of *Theorizing Documentary*, ed. Michael Renov], has seized upon the camera eye as a faithful ally.

One of the crucial texts for a discussion of the desire underpinning the documentary impulse must surely be André Bazin's classic "The Ontology of the Photographic Image." As the essay reaches its affective crescendo, any notion of the image's asymptotic relationship to the real is discarded in favor of an account by which the indexical sign becomes identical to the referent. In the following pronouncement, one feels the force of desire (historical? authorial?) as it transforms a discussion about the ontological status of the photographic image into a statement about semiosis itself.

> Only a photographic lens can give us the kind of image of the object that is capable of satisfying the deep need man has to substitute for it something more than a mere approximation, a kind of decal or transfer. The photographic image is the object itself, the object freed from the conditions of time and space that govern it. No matter how fuzzy, distorted, or discolored, no matter how lacking in documentary value the image may be, it shares, by virtue of the very process of its becoming, the being of the model of which it is the reproduction; it *is* the model.[17]

Bazin's position moves beyond the construction of a scene of absolute self-presence for the documentary sign, suggesting instead an outright immateriality arising from its utter absorption by the historical referent.[18]

There are, to be sure, historical contingencies which temper any claims for "modalities of desire" as eternal or innate. The documentative drive may be transhistorical, but it is far from being untouched by history. While Bazin may have alerted us to such categorical matters as a photographic ontology, he was also attentive to the variable effects which history exercises over audiences and their responses to filmic expression.

In his "Cinema and Exploration," Bazin discusses the relative merits of some films which take up the visual reconstruction of scientific expeditions. His preference is for a film such as *Kon-Tiki* (Thor Heyerdahl's documentation of a 4500-mile sea voyage) in which only a very little footage—poorly shot, frequently underexposed 16mm blown up to 35mm—provides an authoritative rendering of experience: "For it remains true that this film is not made up only of what we see—its faults are equally witness to its authenticity. The missing documents are the negative imprints of the expedition—its inscription chiselled deep."[19] This predilection for the real at any cost is rendered historical in Bazin's account: "Since World War II we have witnessed a definite retum to documentary authenticity.... Today the public demands that what it sees shall be believable, a faith that can be tested by the other media of information, namely, radio, books, and the daily press.... the prevalence of objective reporting following World War II defined once and for all what it is that we require from such reports."[20] Four decades later—in the wake of countless TV ads which trade on their documentary "look" (shaky camera, grainy black-and-white)—the technically flawed depiction of a purported reality no longer suffices as visual guarantee of authenticity. It is simply understood as yet another artifice. I would thus argue that while the instinct for cultural self-preservation remains constant, the markers of documentary authenticity are historically variable.

As for the category of promotion and persuasion, one might understand the rhetorical function of film as a facilitator of desire in its most rationalist aspect. Given Aristotle's fundamental insight on the necessity of rhetorical proofs to effect change ("Before some audiences not even the possession of the exactest knowledge will make it easy for what we say to produce conviction"[21]), persuasive techniques are a prerequisite for achieving personal or social goals. We may advisedly associate certain historical personages with this tendency of the documentary film (e.g., John Grierson's camera hammering rather than mirroring society). But the promotional impulse—selling products or values, rallying support for social movements, or solidifying subcultural identities—is a crucial documentative instinct to which nonfiction film and video continue to respond.

We might say that the "analyze or interrogate" mode is a response to cognitive requirements, an extension of the psychological activities which, according to Constructivist psychologists, allow humans to organize sensory data, make inferences, and construct schemata.[22] While much attention has been given the role of perceptual and cognitive processes in story comprehension, relatively little has been written on a documentary-based heuristics of cognition or analytics. As Bill Nichols has argued, Frederick Wiseman's films (to name a notable example) deploy "the codes of actions and enigmas that usually pose and subsequently resolve puzzles or mysteries by means of the characters' activities."[23] Moreover, these documentary presentations "imply a theory of the events they describe" by virtue of a sophisticated structuring of the profilmic into an overall ensemble Nichols describes as "mosaic" (each sequence, a semiautonomous, temporally explicit unit in itself, contributing to an overall but non-narrative depiction of the filmed institution). In this instance, the organizational strategy bears with it an epistemological agenda, for such a schema of filmed segments "assumes that social events have multiple causes and must be analyzed as webs of interconnecting influences and patterns."[24] This parameter of documentary discourse is thus tied up with deep-seated cognitive functions as well as a strictly informational imperative; the documentary film addresses issues of seeing and knowing in a manner quite apart from its more frequently discussed fictional counterpart.

The last of the four documentary tendencies encompasses the aesthetic function. It has frequently been presumed that the creation of beautiful forms and documentary's task of historical representation are altogether irreconcilable. Near the beginning of *Of Great Events and Ordinary People* (1979), Raoul Ruiz quotes Grierson to that effect. "Grierson says: 'The trouble with realism is that it deals not in beauty but in truth.' " It then becomes the work of the film to confound that pronouncement, to produce a "pleasure of the text" capable of merging intellectual inquiry and aesthetic value.

The pitting of "truth" against "beauty" is the product of a regrettable (Western) dualism that accounts for the rift between science and art, mind and body. Raymond Williams traces the hardening of the art/science distinction to the 18th century, the moment at which *experience* (i.e., "feeling" and "inner life") began to be defined against *experiment*.[25] Hans Richter's account of cinematic development offers an illustration of the effects of this presumed binarism and its contribution to a kind of documentary anti-aesthetic: "It became clear that a fact did not really remain a 'fact' if it appeared in too beautiful a light. The accent shifted, for a 'beautiful' image could not normally be obtained *except at the expense of its closeness to reality*. Something essential had to be suppressed in order to provide a beautiful appearance [emphasis added]."[26] And yet, despite the limitations of these presumptions, it will become clear that the aesthetic function has maintained an historically specific relationship with the documentary since the Lumières.

It now remains to work through each of the four modalities of the documentary in some detail and through recourse to specific texts in order to trace the contours of a poetics of documentary. What becomes immediately clear is the extent to which individual works slip the traces of any circumscribed taxonomy. Indeed, any poetics of value, despite the explanatory power it might mobilize through an elaboration of conceptually discrete modalities, must be willing to acknowledge transgressiveness as the very *condition* of textual potency. As desire is put into play, documentary discourse may realize historical discursivity *through and against* pleasurable surface, may engage in self-reflection *in the service of* moral suasion. As metacritical paradigms, the four functions of the documentary text may be provisionally discrete; as specific textual operations, they rarely are.

I. To Record, Reveal, or Preserve

This is perhaps the most elemental of documentary functions, familiar since the Lumières' "actualités," traceable to the photographic antecedent. The emphasis here is on the replication of the historical real, the creation of a second-order reality cut to the measure of our desire—to cheat death, stop time, restore loss. Here, ethnography and the home movie meet insofar as both seek what Roland Barthes has termed "that rather terrible thing which is there in every photograph: the return of the dead."[27]

Documentary has most often been motivated by the wish to exploit the camera's revelatory powers, an impulse only rarely coupled with an acknowledgment of the processes through which the real is transfigured. At times, as with Flaherty, the desire to retain the trace of the fleeting or already absent phenomenon has led the nonfiction artist to supplement behavior or event-in-history with its imagined counterpart—the traditional walrus hunt of the Inuit which was restaged for the camera, for example.[28]

An interesting format to consider in this regard is the electronic or filmed diary (e.g., the work of Jonas Mekas, George Kuchar, Lynn Hershman, or Vanalyne Green) which reflects on the lived experience of the artist. In the case of these four artists, the interest lies not so much in recovering time past or in simply chronicling daily life—there is little illusion of a pristine retrieval—as in seizing the opportunity to *rework* experience at the level of sound and image. Whether it is Mekas's street scenes of New York with his world-weary narration voiced-over from many years' remove or Hershman's image overlays which couple self-portraiture with archival footage of concentration camp survivors, these diary efforts exceed the bounds of self-preservation.

The duplication of the world, even of what we know most intimately—ourselves—can never be unproblematic. We know as much from the writings of Michel de Montaigne, 16th-century man of letters, who writes of his attempt to portray not *being* but *passing*. Throughout three volumes of *Essays*, Montaigne remains vigilant to the flux which constitutes us all. He writes near the beginning of his "Of Repentance" (III:2, 610): "The world is but a perennial movement. All things in it are in constant motion—the earth, the rock of the Caucasus, the pyramids of Egypt—both with the common motion and with their own. Stability itself is nothing but a more languid motion." It does not take a post-structuralist to divine the inadequacy of reflection theories of art, those positions which would have us believe that mimesis (even as photographic representation) means producing simulacra which are the equivalent of their historical counter-parts. Signifying systems bear with them the weight of their own history and materiality; Freud reminds us that even language, the most insubstantial of signifying systems, has a material existence in the unconscious. When watching the most "verité" of films, we should recall, with Magritte, that this too is not a pipe. Given the truth claim which persists within documentary discourse as a defining condition ("what you see and hear is of the world"), the collapse of sign and historical referent is a matter of particular concern.

Our attempts to "fix" on celluloid what lies before the camera—ourselves or members of other cultures—are fragile if not altogether insincere efforts. Always issues of selection intrude (which angle, take, camera stock will best serve); the results are indeed *mediated*, the result of multiple interventions that necessarily *come between* the cinematic sign (what we see on the screen) and its referent (what existed in the world).[29]

It is not only the ethnographic film that depends so crucially on this fabled ability of the moving image form to preserve the fleeting moment. Think only of the myriad history films so popular in the seventies and eighties that offered revisionist versions of the Wobblies or riveting Rosies. These pieces were predicated on the necessity of offering corrective visions, alternatives to the dominant historical discourse which had scanted the struggles of labor, women, the underclasses, and the marginalized. All too frequently, however, the interest in the visual document—interview footage intercut with archival material—outpaced the historian's obligation to interrogate rather than simply serve up the visible evidence. These were honest, warm, sometimes charismatic people much like ourselves or (even more troubling) as we wished we could be.[30] The kinds of emotional investments and narrative enticements which keep us riveted to our seats during the melodramas of the silver screen were thus mobilized. Problems arose when historical analysis, mindful of contradiction and complexity within and across documents (e.g., competing versions of texts or social phenomena as well as questions raised by translation from one language or vernacular usage to another), was displaced by anecdote and personal memory.

But public history cannot simply be an aggregate of private histories strung together or nimbly intercut. These oral histories remain valuable for their ability to bring to public notice the submerged accounts of people and social movements.

But their favoring of preservation over interrogation detracts from their power as vehicles of understanding. Delegating the enunciative function to a series of interview subjects cannot, in the end, bolster a truth claim for historical discourse; the enunciator, the one who "voices" the text, is the film or videomaker functioning as historiographer. Although a thorough discussion of the self-reflexive gesture cannot be undertaken here, it is worth citing Roland Barthes's incisive pronouncements on the discursive status of all documentative utterances:

> At the level of discourse, objectivity, or the absence of any clues to the narrator, turns out to be a particular form of fiction, the result of what might be called the referential illusion, where the historian tries to give the impression that the referent is speaking for itself. This illusion is not confined to historical discourse: novelists galore, in the days of realism, considered themselves "objective" because they had suppressed all traces of the *I* in their text. Nowadays linguistics and psychoanalysis unite to make us much more lucid towards such ascetic modes of utterance: we know that the absence of a sign can be significant too. . . . Historical discourse does not follow reality, it only signifies it; it asserts at every moment: *this happened*, but the meaning conveyed is only that someone is making that assertion.[31]

Art historian John Tagg has written what may be the definitive account of the historically contingent character of documentary representation as evidence (the preservational condition, par excellence) in his introductory essay to *The Burden of Representation: Essays on Photographies and Histories*. Taking as his starting point a critique of Barthes's blissfully personal treatment of the documentary image in *Camera Lucida*, Tagg argues that the indexical character of the photograph can guarantee nothing.

> At every stage, chance effects, purposeful interventions, choices and variations produce meaning, whatever skill is applied and whatever division of labour the process is subject to. This is not the inflection of a prior (though irretrievable) reality, as Barthes would have us believe, but the production of a new and specific reality. . . . The photograph is not a magical "emanation" but a material product of a material apparatus set to work in specific contexts, by specific forces, for more or less defined purposes. It requires, therefore, not an alchemy but a history. . . . That a photograph can come to stand as *evidence*, for example, rests not on a natural or existential fact, but on a social, semiotic process. . . . It will be a central argument of this book that what Barthes calls "evidential force" is a complex historical outcome and is exercised by photographs only within certain institutional practices and within particular historical relations. . . . The very idea of what constitutes evidence has a history. . . . The problem is historical, not existential.[32]

II. To Persuade or Promote

We would do well at this stage of the argument to review a crucial condition of this study, namely, the paradoxical mutuality of the four documentary functions. For although I am attempting to distinguish among the several modalities of the documentary, the better to understand their effectivity, such an effort must fail if a discrete separability is posed. Over the years, efforts have been made to map the nonfiction firmament through recourse to generic labeling (e.g., "the social documentary"), the determination of documentary types whose exemplars are meant to embody particular attributes (e.g., a social change orientation).

In such instances, one soon runs head-on into the logical paradox of all genre designations best described by Derrida in his "The Law of Genre": "In the code of set theories, if I may use it at least figuratively, I would speak of a sort of participation without belonging—a taking part in without being part of, without having membership in a set." Derrida further challenges the stability of boundaries erected in the name of genre.

> And suppose for a moment that it were impossible not to mix genres. What if there were, lodged within the heart of the law itself, a law of impurity or a principie of contamination? And suppose the condition for the possibility of the law were the a priori of a counterlaw, an axiom of impossibility that would confound its sense, order, and reason?[33]

How can we account for a sluice gate of nomination capable of exclusion (the setting of limits) yet infinitely susceptible to expansion? How are we to understand a designation of difference that remains viable only on condition of its potentiality for the violation of its closure (the genre as"dynamic" or transformational)? What is the precise principle of difference that thus obtains? Such, at least, are Derrida's musings on the simultaneous purity and impurity of genre's status. In the present instance, the positing of the efficacy of a nominal isolation of *functional* difference exists concurrently with an equally insistent claim for the mutual interpenetration of regimes at the level of the textual instance. For, of course, one crucial parameter of persuasion in documentary could not occur were it not for the veridical stamp of documentary's indexical sign-status, itself a condition of the record/preserve mode understood as the first documentary function. Nor can we reasonably suppose that the expressive domain is altogether separable from a discussion of persuasive powers. So, in fact, these paradigms of a documentary poetics, though capable of mobilizing explanatory power—at the level of metacriticism—along a vertical axis of historically precise meaning, are never, in fact, encountered vertically. There is no ontological purity at stake.

Persuasion is the dominant trope for nonfiction films in the tradition of John Grierson, the man alleged to have first coined the term "documentary." Polemicist and social activist, Grierson left his mark on the film cultures of Britain, Canada, the United State, indeed the world. For this son of a Calvinist minister, the screen was a pulpit, the film a hammer to be used in shaping the destiny of nations. The promotional urgency which characterized the work of Britain's Empire Marketing Board under Grierson's tutelage in the thirties [e.g., *Night Mail* (1936), *Housing Problems* (1935)] has been equaled both before and since in many state-supported contexts, ranging from Dziga Vertov's exuberant *Man With a Movie Camera* (1929) in the Soviet Union to Cuban Santiago Alvarez's formal as well as political radicalism in such works as *Now!* (1965) and *79 Springtimes of Ho Chi Minh* (1969).

As was the case with the preservational modality, documentary persuasion must be understood as an effect of history within precise discursive conditions. Tagg has written that the effectiveness of much New Deal photography as a tool for mobilizing popular support for governmental policy can only be accounted for within a broadly drawn context of historical forces.

> The very years in which the liberal, statist measures of the New Deal were being enacted and fought for,

> witnessed a crucial historical "rendezvous" of means, rhetoric and social strategy. Only in this conjuncture could the documentary mode take on its particular force, command identification, and exert a power, not as the evocation of a pristine truth but as a politically mobilized rhetoric of Truth, a strategy of signification, a cultural intervention aimed at resealing social unity and structures of belief at a time of far-reaching crisis and conflict.[34]

While persuasion is most frequently identified with projects exhibiting a singularity of purpose and tone—the stridency of Frank Capra's *Why We Fight* series from the World War II years or Leni Riefenstahl's infamous paean to National Socialism, *Triumph of the Will*—we would do well to consider the greater diversity of the promotional impetus and the complexity of its presentational forms. Do we not, after all, in the instance of Alain Resnais's *Night and Fog*, find ourselves persuaded (moved toward a certain comprehension of the incommensurable) through the starkness of Resnais's iconic choices (a mountain of eyeglasses), the poetic character of Jean Cayrol's writing, or the stateliness of the camera's inexorable tracking across and through time and space? Expressivity—the modulated play of the documentary signifier here isolated as the fourth documentary function—can give rise to persuasion as the concrete instantiation of the signified (rhetorical figures, logical proofs, the structuration of argument at the level of sound and image).

In his *Ideology and the Image*, Bill Nichols recalls for us the Aristotelian triad of proofs operative in the documentary: ethical, emotional, and demonstrative. We can be persuaded by the ethical status of the filmmaker or interview subject, by the tug of heartstrings, or by a barrage of bar graphs. Edward R. Murrow's very presence accounted for much of the social impact of *Harvest of Shame* just as the handicapped veteran interviewed in *Hearts and Minds* moves us more deeply than could all the bona fide experts. The documentary "truth claim" (which says, at the very least: "Believe me, I'm of the world") is the baseline of persuasion for all of nonfiction, from propaganda to rock doc.

One could argue for the relative merits of, say, emotional versus demonstrative proofs—photographs of the suffering versus expert witnesses. Certainly ethical considerations arise within the context of such a discussion; yet I am not concerned here to weigh the value or appropriateness of any particular persuasive approach. More to the point for me is the claim that the persuasive or promotional modality is intrinsic to all documentary forms and demands to be considered in relation to the other rhetorical/aesthetic functions.

III. To Analyze or Interrogate

Analysis, in this context, can be considered as the cerebral reflex of the record/reveal/preserve modality; it is revelation interrogated. Too few documentarists share the critical attitude held by anthropologist Clifford Geertz when he writes: "I have never gotten anywhere near to the bottom of anything I have ever written about.... Cultural analysis is intrinsically incomplete. And, worse than that, the more deeply it goes the less complete it is."[35] If this is true for the scholar able to devote years to fieldwork, how much truer might this be for the media artist whose in-depth explorations of topics must be contoured to the requirements of the cultural marketplace and a capital-intensive mode of production?

This documentary impetus transforms the unacknowledged questions that lie beneath all nonfictional forms into potential subject matter: that is, on what basis does the spectator invest belief in the representation, what are the codes which ensure that belief, what material processes are involved in the production of this "spectacle of the real" and to what extent are these processes to be rendered visible or knowable to the spectator?[36] While many of these questions are familiar from the debates around reflexivity and the so-called Brechtian cinema, applicable to fiction and nonfiction alike (the films of Vertov, Godard, and Straub/Huillet have most frequently inspired these debates), their urgency is particularly great for documentary works, which can be said to bear a direct, ontological tie to the real. That is, every documentary claims for itself an anchorage in history; the referent of the nonfiction sign is meant to be a piece of the world (albeit a privileged because a visible and/or audible one) and, thus, was once available to experience in the everyday.

The analytical documentary is likely to acknowledge that mediational structures are formative rather than mere embellishments. In *The Man with a Movie Camera*, the flow of images is repeatedly arrested or reframed as the filmic fact is revealed to be a labor-intensive social process which engages cameramen, editors, projectionists, musicians, and audience members. Motion pictures are represented as photographic images in motion, variable as to their projected speed, duration, or screen direction: galloping horses are capable of being halted mid-stride, water can run upstream, smiling children can be transformed into bits of celluloid to be inspected at the editor Svilova's work bench. This is not to say that every documentary must reinvent the wheel or leave in the occasional slate to remind the audience that this is, after all, only a film. What is being suggested here is that presentation is not automatically interrogation and that the latter can be a valuable ingredient for any nonfiction piece. Brecht polemicized that art's real success could be measured by its ability to activate its audience. The flow of communication always ought to be reversible; the teacher ever willing to become the pupil.

Much has been said about empowerment in recent years. The bottom line is that the artwork should encourage inquiry, offer space for judgment, and provide the tools for evaluation and further action—in short, encourage an active response. The film or videotape that considers its own processes rather than seals over every gap of a never-seamless discourse is more likely to engender the healthy skepticism that begets knowledge, offering itself as a model.

Allow me to offer a few exemplary instances of the analytical impulse in the documentary film. In the sound era, the breach between image and its audio counterpart has rarely been acknowledged; synchronized sound, narration, or music is meant to reinforce or fuse with the image rather than question its status. Such is not the case with *Night and Fog* with its airy pizzicatti accompanying the most oppressive imagery of Holocaust atrocities; affective counterpoint underscores the horror. Chris Marker's *Letter From Siberia* (1958) is another departure from the norm. The connotative power of nonlinguistic audial elements (music, vocal inflection) is confirmed by the repetition of an otherwise banal sequence; the sequencing of images and the narration remain unchanged while the accompanying music and tonal values of the narrating voice create differing semantic effects. Every viewer is forced to confront the malleability of meaning and the ideological impact of authorial or stylistic choices that typically go unnoticed. In Jean-Marie Straub and Danielle Huillet's *Introduction to "An Accompaniment for a Cinematographic Scene"* (1972), a musical composition, Arnold Schoenberg's Opus 34, is "illustrated" by the recitation of Schoenberg's correspondence as well as by his drawings, photographs (of the composer and of slain Paris Communards), archival footage of American bombing runs over Vietnam, and the imaging of a newspaper clipping about the release of accused Nazi concentration camp architects. A process of interrogation is thus undertaken through the layering and resonance of heterogeneous elements. Schoenberg's music, the work of a self-professed apolitical artist, becomes the expressive vehicle for an outrage whose moral and intellectual dimensions exceed the parochial bounds of politics proper. Yet the collective coherence of the filmic elements remains to be constructed by a thinking audience. The analytical impulse is not so much enacted by the filmmakers as encouraged for the viewer.

In a culture that valorizes consumption—and the disposable culture responsive to that imperative—it may well be crucial for documentarists to consider the stakes of an intervention: to challenge and activate audiences even in the process of instruction or entertainment. In this regard, analysis remains the documentarist's most crucial support.

IV. To Express

The expressive is the aesthetic function that has consistently been undervalued within the nonfiction domain; it is, nevertheless, amply represented in the history of the documentary enterprise. While the Lumières's actualities may have set the stage for nonfiction film's emphasis on the signified, an historically conditioned taste for dynamic if not pictorialist photographic composition accounts for the diagonal verve of the train station's rendering at la Ciotat. Most sources agree that Robert Flaherty was the documentary film's first poet as well as itinerant ethnographer. Flaherty's expressivity was verbal as well as imagistic in origin; to the compositions in depth of trackless snowscapes in *Nanook of the North* (1922), one must consider as well the flare for poetic language ("the sun a brass ball in the sky"). The cycle of "city symphony" films of the 1920s [*The Man with a Movie Camera, Berlin: Symphony of a Great City* (1927), *A Propos de Nice* (1930)] declared their allegiance in varying degrees to the powers of expressivity in the service of historical representation. The artfulness of the work as a function of its purely photographic properties was now allied with the possibilities of editing to create explosive effects—cerebral as well as visceral. The early films of the documentary polemicist Joris Ivens [*The Bridge* (1928), *Rain* (1929)] evidence the attraction felt for the cinema's aesthetic potential, even for those motivated by strong political beliefs.

And yet, the historical fact of a repression of the formal or expressive domain within the documentary tradition is inescapable. Such a circumstance arises, however, more from an institutionalization of the art/science opposition than from an inherent limitation. By way of visible proof and case study, we might consider the photographic work of Paul Strand in whom a dual emphasis, perhaps along the very lines of the "experience/experiment" division posed by Williams, was always distinguishable. Attention was paid to the inexhaustible subject matter of the world around him ("What exists outside the artist is much more important than his imagination. The world outside is inexhaustible."[37]), but equally to its organization by the artist. A palpable tension can thus be said to animate Strand's work in both film and photography, arising from seemingly irreconcilable requirements: for objectivity—an attitude toward his subject matter which his one-time mentor Alfred Stieglitz termed "brutally direct"—and, with an equal level of insistence, for the free play of the subjective self.

The work of Paul Strand reminds us that the documenting eye is necessarily transformational in a thousand ways; Strand's mutations of the visible world simply foreground the singularity of his vision as against the familiarity of his object source. Under scrutiny, the Griersonian definition of documentary—the creative treatment of actuality—appears to be a kind of oxymoron, the site of an irreconcilable union between invention on the one hand and mechanical reproduction on the other. And, as with the figure of the oxymoron in its literary context, this collision can be the occasion of an explosive, often poetic effect. So much can be said, at least, for the work of Paul Strand.

Take, for example, certain of Strand's early photographs from 1915 or 1916 ("Abstraction—Bowls," Connecticut, 1915 and "White Fence," 1916) in which everyday objects or landscapes are naturally lit and composed for the camera in such a way as to urge their reception as wholly constructed artifacts, sculptural or collaged. Strand here enforces a kind of retinal tension between the two-dimensional image surface (forcefully restated by the aggressive frontality of the white picket fence) and the three-dimensionality implied by chiaroscuro or deep-focus photography. There is, at the same moment, a tension of another sort that arises in our apperception of such compositions—that which is occasioned by a clash between a perceived sense of the everyday (objects or vistas that one might encounter casually) and of the wholly formal ensemble (that which has been taken causally, fabricated, for its aesthetic value).

Consider further in this regard Strand's treatment of architectural motifs, tightly framed or nestled in a landscape of competing geometrical and tonal motifs. Is it simply a special case that allows what might be termed the "competent reader" of the photograph to see "Mondrian" with and against the documentary image in one instance ("Basque Facade," Arbonnes in the Pyrennes, 1951) or, in another, a dazzling white arrow pointed heavenward rather than a simple frame structure in a cluster of other dwellings ("White Shed," the Gaspé, 1929)? One of Strand's truly emblematic images, his rendering of Wall Street shot from the steps of the Subtreasury Building, transforms the fact of scale—the monumentality of the Morgan Building and its darkened windows looming over insect-sized humans—into a moral statement. The close-up of the latch of a door in Vermont, made in 1944, performs an inverse operation; distance is replaced by proximity. An unexpected display of scale here alters a realist detail into a textural field intensified by the play between the natural (the swirl of grain) and the man-made (the horizontals and verticals of carpentry). It is, in fact, the photographic artist's discovery of the unanticipated—his ability to unleash the visual epiphany—that wrenches the image free of its purely preservational moorings. As a study of Strand's work and that of other accomplished documentary artists reveals, there need be no exclusionary relations between documentation and artfulness.

It is important to expand the received boundaries of the documentary form to consider work traditionally regarded as of the avant-garde. Films such as Stan Brakhage's "Pittsburgh Trilogy" (three films made in the early seventies—one shot in a morgue, another in a hospital, the third from the back seat of a police car) or Peter Kubelka's *Unsere Afrikareise* share with mainstream documentary a commitment to the representation of the historical real. Significantly, the focus of pieces such as these typically remains the impression of the world on the artist's sensorium and his or her interpretation of that datum (Brakhage's tremulous handheld camera as he witnesses open-heart surgery in *Deus Ex*) or the radical reworking of the documentary material to create sound/image relationships unavailable in nature (Kubelka's "synch event"). For indeed, the realm of filmic nonfiction is a continuum along which can be ranged work of great expressive variability—from that which attends little to the vehicle of expression (the not-so-distant apotheosis of cinema verité—surveillance technology—might serve as the limit case) to that which emphasizes the filtering of the represented object through the eye and mind of the artist. Manny Karchkeimer's *Stations of the Elevated*, for instance, is a film about New York subways and the graffiti that covers them that includes not a single spoken word. It is the composition of images and their orchestration in relation to a dynamic jazz score that accounts for the film's effectiveness.

That a work undertaking some manner of historical documentation renders that representation in a challenging or innovative manner should in no way disqualify it as nonfiction because the question of expressivity is, in all events, a matter of degree. All such renderings require a series of authorial choices, none neutral, some of which may appear more "artful" or purely expressive than others. There can be little doubt that our critical valuations and categories ("artful documentary" or "documentary art") depend on various protocols of reading which are historically conditioned. Moreover, the ability to evoke emotional response or induce pleasure in the spectator by formal means, to generate lyric power through shadings of sound and image in a manner exclusive of verbalization, or to engage with the musical or poetic qualities of language itself must not be seen as mere distractions from the main event. Documentary culture is clearly the worse for such aesthetic straitjacketing. Indeed, the communicative aim is frequently enhanced by attention to the expressive dimension; the artful film or tape can be said to utilize more effectively the potentialities of its chosen medium to convey ideas and feelings. In the end, the aesthetic function can never be wholly divorced from the didactic one insofar as the aim remains "pleasurable learning."

Conclusion

I have, in these remarks, attempted to sketch out the epistemological, rhetorical, and aesthetic terrain within which the documentary enterprise has historically arisen. My purpose has been to clarify and enrich—to clarify certain key issues implicit to our shared pursuits in order to enrich the critical and creative activities that arise out of that commitment. By invoking the model of a poetics for the documentary through the elaboration of four discursive functions—those of preservation, persuasion, analysis, and expressivity—I have hoped to introduce into these considerations a measure of critical stringency capable of encompassing historical and political determinations. By a progressive focus on first one then another of what I take to be the most fundamental functions of documentary discourse, I have attempted to judge their historical contingency, textual efficacy, and mutually defining character. Such a study is necessarily open-ended and demands extension in several directions, not the least of which might be the evaluation of the specific effects of video rather than film practices within each of the functional categories.

As a writer and teacher, I benefit from work which challenges my critical preconceptions and takes the occasional risk. It is my hope that the practitioner can likewise draw upon my research as a basis for an ongoing process of self-examination and boundary-testing. For in the cultural context in which lively debate gives way entirely to survival techniques or business as usual, all pay a price. If a vital, self-sustaining documentary film culture is, indeed, our shared goal, we cannot afford to fail.

Acknowledgment

An earlier version of this essay was delivered as the keynote address to the Twelfth Annual Ohio University Conference in November 1990. I am grateful to Bill Nichols, Chuck Wolfe, and Edward Branigan for their careful reading and for suggestions which have greatly benefited this text.

NOTES

1. Tzvetan Todorov, *The Poetics of Prose*, trans. Richard Howard (Ithaca: Cornell University Press, 1977), 33.
2. Quoted in Calvin Tomkins, "Look to the Things Around You," *The New Yorker*, 16 September 1974, 90.

3. Aristotle, *Poetics*, trans. Gerald F. Else (Ann Arbor: The University of Michigan Press, 1967), 4, 15.
4. Lubomír Doležel, *Occidental Poetics: Tradition and Progress* (Lincoln: University of Nebraska Press, 1990), 56.
5. Despite the historical limitations of Doležel's account of the evolution of Occidental poetics—he ends in 1945, prior to the postwar effloration of inquiry in France—the book offers a useful periodization of poetics in the West and a sense of the rich ancestry of contemporary manifestations.
6. I will insist on including video in the discussion of documentary film even while noting that the two media forms are irreducibly distinct. It is my sense that the four modalities of documentary discourse traced here obtain for both film and video but manifest themselves differently and within distinguishable historical contexts. One brief example must suffice by way of illustration. It might be said that video has emerged as a discursive field with a particular relationship to preservation, the first documentary function. Videotape was developed in 1956 as a storage system for an electronic signal and has been deeply enmeshed with surveillance technologies ever since. For unlike the Lumières' cinematic apparatus which, from the first, could double as a camera and a projector, television—a medium of transmission dating to the 1930s and earlier—required another technology to effectuate the preservation of the sounds and images it produced. Video is, among other things, television's preservational other. On purely historical grounds, it would simply be a mistake to conceptualize the preservational dimension of documentary video as identical to that of its filmic counterpart. The case could be made in similar ways for each of the four modalities of documentary discursivity for video. Such a working through is much deserved but must await another occasion.
7. Tzvetan Todorov, *Introduction to Poetics*, trans. Richard Howard (Minneapolis: University of Minnestoa Press, 1981), 4–5. Todorov does not entirely discount the possibility that there could be a substantive separation of interpretation and science (hence, poetics) because the latter is neither entirely descriptive nor interpretive but instead works for "the establishment of general laws of which this particular text is the product" (6). Todorov does not so much critique science (as the scholar's dream discourse) as indemnify it against its potential detractors. That critique will be Foucault's.
8. Roland Barthes, "The Return of the Poetician," *The Rustle of Language*, trans. Richard Howard (Berkeley: University of California Press, 1989), 172.
9. Barthes' position in the question of the separability of interpretation and description is, as ever, complex. In his 1977 "Inaugural Lecture" at the College de France, Barthes argued that, in regard to the presumed opposition between the sciences and letters, "it is possible that this opposition will appear one day to be a historical myth" [*A Barthes Reader*, ed. Susan Sontag (New York: Hill and Wang, 1982), 464], The statement is equivocal: It could mean that, in the manner of Todorov, there is no description without interpretation (thus, all science is, to a degree, "artful") or simply that literary studies is capable of being undertaken with the rigor of science (thus, some aesthetic inquiry is the epistemological equal of science). The statement could also be understood as a statement about Barthes's own intellectual history, his journey from the painstaking semiological treatises of the 1960s to the essayistic writings of the late 1970s. The art/science split has certainly been the subject of much debate (see, for example, the classic exposition of the problem in C. P. Snow's *Two Cultures* or Raymond Williams' entry on science in *Keywords*). Of all branches of aesthetic inquiry, poetics confronts the question most vigorously.
10. From Coleridge's *Biographia Literaria* (1817), as cited in Doležel (87).
11. It is gratifying to note that the critical tide is now beginning to turn; judging by the number and quality of recent conference presentations and books recently completed or underway, considerably more attention now seems to be accorded nonfiction work. But in relative terms, theoretical considerations of the documentary lag far behind.
12. Much has been written about the uncertain status of the peer panel review process for NEA grants in the spring and summer of 1992. Under the leadership of a Bush appointee, Anne-Imelda Radice, the National Endowment of the Arts has rescinded a handful of grants for art works whose subject matter was deemed erotic.
13. Long after fashioning this fourfold typology for documentary discursivity (which has evolved in my teaching over a decade), I noted the possible relationship to Hayden White's discussion of the four "master tropes" (metaphor, metonymy, synecdoche, irony) which reappear in critical thought from Freud to Piaget to E. P. Thompson. White attributes to Vico the notion that this diataxis of discourse "not only mirrored the processes of consciousness but in fact underlay and informed all efforts of human beings to endow their world with meaning" [Hayden White, *Tropics of Discourse: Essays in Cultural Criticism* (Baltimore: The Johns Hopkins University Press, 1978), 5].
14. Hans Richter, *The Struggle for the Film*, trans. Ben Brewster (New York: St. Martin's Press, 1986), 42–44.
15. Karl G. Heider, *Ethnographic Film* (Austin: University of Texas Press, 1976), 19.
16. André Bazin, "The Ontology of the Photographic Image," *What Is Cinema?*, trans. Hugh Gray (Berkeley: University of California Press, 1967), 14.
17. Some years later, Derrida reminded us that all writing places memory and forgetfulness in tension. The creation of a documentary image may be a memorializing gesture but it equally implies an acknowledgment of the radical alterity of the sign, defined as the place where "the completely other is announced as such—without

any simplicity, any identity, any resemblance or continuity—in that which is not it" [Jacques Derrida, *Of Grammatology*, trans. Gayatri Chakravorty Spivak (Baltimore: The Johns Hopkins University Press, 1974), 47]. Writing is "at once mnemotechnique and the power of forgetting" (Derrida, *Of Grammatology*, 24]. From this perspective, one might say that the documentative desire responds both to the pleasure principle and its beyond.

18. Andre Bazin, *What Is Cinema?*, trans. Hugh Gray (Berkeley: University of California Press, 1967), 162.
19. Ibid., 155, 158.
20. Aristotle, *Rhetoric*, trans. W. Rhys Roberts (New York: Random House, 1954), 22.
21. For a brief account of the cognitivist paradigm and its relation to matters of filmic narration, see David Bordwell, Narration in the Fiction Film (Madison, WI: University of Wisconsin Press, 1985), 29–47. See, generally, Bordwell's "A Case for Cognitivism" in a special issue of *Iris* devoted to "Cinema and Cognitive Psychology," Vol. 5, No. 2 (1989), 11–40.
22. Bill Nichols, *Ideology and the Image: Social Representation in the Cinema and Other Media* (Bloomington: Indiana University Press, 1981), 210.
23. Ibid., 211–212.
24. Raymond Williams, *Keywords: A Vocabulary of Culture and Society* (London: Flamingo, 1976), 278.
25. Richter, *The Struggle for the Film*, 46.
26. Roland Barthes, *Camera Lucida*, trans. Richard Howard (New York: Hill and Wang, 1981), 9.
27. The threshold of audience acceptance for documentary reconstruction or reenactment remains volatile; it is dependent both on historical moment and subject matter. "Preenactments" (visions of what *could be*, presented in a documentary format) have proven to be most controversial when the future vision they offer is apocalyptic. Both Peter Watkins' *The War Game* (1966) and Ed Zwick's *SpecialBulletin* (1983)—two films about nuclear disaster—proved plausible enough for contemporary audiences to foster political battles (the BBC refused to screen Watkins's film as planned) or public dismay (the media coverage following the *Special Bulletin* broadcast offered testimony to the panic caused despite the disclaimers which accompanied the broadcast). The controversies which swirl around the question of documentary reconstruction/ reenactment—"post-enactments"—seem inescapable insofar as they address a core issue for all documentary—veracity. Most attacks against *The Thin Blue Line* or *Roger and Me*, for example, have been based upon the presumption that authorial liberties taken toward the presentation of the "facts" have vitiated the films' possible claims to authenticity. (Question: Can documentary truth ever afford to be stylized?) The popular attachment to truth in cinema suggests that the erosion of referentials associated with the postmodern is being resisted in some quarters with great intensity.
28. See Michael Renov, "Re-Thinking Documentary: Toward a Taxonomy of Mediation," *Wide Angle*,Vol. 8, Nos. 3 and 4, 1986, 71–77.
29. For a detailed discussion of the psychosocial dynamic engaged through an idealization of the "other" in documentary film practices, see my "Imaging the Other: Representations of Vietnam in Sixties Political Documentary," *From Hanoi to Hollywood: The Vietnam War in American Film*, Linda Dittmar and Gene Michand, eds. (New Brunswick, N.J.: Rutgers University Press, 1990), 255–268.
30. Roland Barthes, "Historical Discourse," *Introduction to Structuralism*, ed. Michael Lane (New York: Basic Books, Inc., 1970), 149, 154.
31. John Tagg, *The Burden of Representation: Essays on Photographies and Histories* (Amherst: The University of Massachusetts Press, 1988), 3–5.
32. Jacques Derrida, "The Law of Genre," Glyph 7 (Spring 1980), 204.
33. Tagg, *The Burden of Representation*, 13.
34. Clifford Geertz, "Thick Description: Toward an Interpretive Theory of Culture," *The Interpretation of Cultures* (New York: Basic Books, 1973), 29.
35. My discussion of the analyze/interrogate modality would suggest that documentary interrogation necessarily entails reflexivity. This is certainly not the case as any retum to the historical roots of the analytical impulse of documentary cinema will testify. Whether one considers the earliest Muybridge experiments in animal locomotion, Vertov's belief in the perfectibility of the kino eye, or the interrogation of visible action in Timothy Asch's *The Ax Fight* which essays social-scientific explanation over simple description, it is clear that the *interrogation* (here distinguished from the *observation*) of social reality via camera and recorder has been one of the documentarist's chief concerns. My own preference is to focus on instances of the analytical function which include an additional metacritical level of interrogation insofar as they, in taking their own discursive operations as a crucial component of analysis, provide an ideal model for study. This is not to suggest that the analytical impulse in documentary is excluded from all but the most reflexive instances. Rather, it is my sense that the reflexive text constitutes a kind of limit case or crisis of documentary analytics which can illustrate the functional grouping most vividly.
36. See Earl Miner's *Comparative Poetics: An Intercultural Essay on Theories of Literature* (Princeton, NJ: Princeton University Press, 1990), particularly his introductory chapter, "Comparative Poetics" (12–33). Quoted in Calvin Tomkins, "Look to the Things Around You," *The New Yorker*, 16 September 1974, 45.

92

TRINH T. MINH-HA

MECHANICAL EYE, ELECTRONIC EAR AND THE LURE OF AUTHENTICITY (1984)

In the quest for a scientific use of film, there is, typically, a tendency to validate certain technical strategies, in order to ensure the defense of the ideological neutrality of the image. The purposeful, object-oriented camera eye does not allow any filmed event to simply be fortuitous. Everything must be bathed with meaning. Translated or scientifically interpreted. Contrary to what many writers on documentary films have said, the striving for verisimilitude and for that "authentic" contact with "lived" reality is precisely that which links "factual" ("direct and concrete" according to another classification) films to studio-made films and blurs their line of distinction. Both types perpetuate the myth of cinematic "naturalness," even though one tries its best to *imitate* life while the other claims to *duplicate* it. THIS IS HOW IT IS. Or was. The unfolding scene is captured, not only by an individual, but also by a mechanical device. The mechanical bears testimony to its true existence and is a guarantee of objectivity. "Seeing is believing." The formula, dear to both fictional and factual films, assumes that cinema's role remains that of hypnotizing and propagandizing. The more sophisticated the recording technology, the closer to the real the film practice is said to be. (Documentary) films that appeal to the objective, scientific mind are those eager to "tie cinematic language to scientific rigor." With the development of an increasing, unobtrusive technology, the human eye is expected to identify with the camera eye and its mechanical neutrality. The filmmaker/camera-operator should either remain as absent as possible from the work, masking thereby the constructed meaning under the appearance of the naturally given meaning, or appear in person in the film so as to guarantee the authenticity of the observation. Such a boldness or a concession (depending on how you interpret it) denotes less a need to acknowledge the subjectivity of an individual's point of view (if it does, it is bound to be a very simplistic way to solve the problem), than a desire to marry impersonal observation and personal participation. This happy synthesis of the "universal scientific" and the "personal humanist" is thought to result in a greater humanity and at the same time a greater objectivity. In the progression toward Truth, it seems clear that one can only gain, never lose. First, conform to scientific demands, then show scientists are also human beings. The order is irreversible. And the ideology adopted is no other than that of *capturing* the movement (objects) of *life* or restituting it (them) in a raw manner, and revealing the authentic reality by a neutral camera as well as a neutral cineaste, whose role is to interfere/participate as little as possible, therefore to hide technologically as much as feasible. Human interventions in the filming and editing process are carried out "scientifically" and reduced to a minimum.

> *Some call it Documentary. i call it No Art, No Experiment, No Fiction, No Documentary. To say something, no thing, and allow reality to enter. Capture me. This, i feel, is no surrender. Contraries meet and mate and i work best at the limits of all categories.*

> *Reassemblage. From silences to silences, the fragile essence of each fragment sparks across the screen, subsides and takes flight. Almost there, half named.*

There is no hidden unity to be grasped. Yours. Perhaps a plural moment of meeting or a single significant note, on the run. To seize it as substance is to mistake the footprints made by the shoes for the shoes themselves. To fix it as pure moment pure note is to restore it to the void.

The nature of many questions asked leads inescapably to intention-oriented answers . On the frontline, every single intervention on my side has its reason of being. True. But the truth of reason is not necessarily the reality of the lived. Filming supposes as much premeditation as submission. Intentionally unintentional then?

> *The fools are interesting people, a film says. And i look outside. Can't do without rest. Can't the fools be fools too?*

> *We all see differently. How can it be other wise when images no longer illutstrate words and words no longer explain images? Which progression? Which folding?*

The cineaste still selects the framing, lighting (be it natural or artificial), focus, speed, but s/he should follow validated technical strategies and avoid all montage—regarded as an artifice likely to compromise the authenticity of the work. The question at issue is that of greater or lesser falsification. Although the selection and treatment of the material being filmed already indicate the side s/he chooses (with its ideological bias and constraints), *lesser* falsification—such as editing in the camera [*sic*] or exposing cuts as black spaces in the structure of the film—often implies *no* falsification. At least, this is what one senses through many documentary filmmakers' discourse and what their works connote. For despite "their denial of conventional notions of objectivity and contempt for romantic naturalism, they continue to ask: how can we be more objective? better *capture the essence?* "see them as they see each other?" and "*let them speak for themselves?*" Among the validated strategies that reflect such a yearning and state of mind are: the long take, hand-held camera, sync sound (authentic sound) overlaid with omniscient commentary (the *human science* rationale), wide-angle lens, and anti-aestheticism (the natural versus the beautiful, or the real/native versus the fictional/foreign). To value the long take as an attempt at eliminating distortions is, in a way, to say that life is a continuous process with no ruptures, no blanks, no blackouts. The longer, the truer. Hollywoodian montage also aims at the same: building up the illusion of continuity and immortality. For death strolls between images and what advanced technology holds out to us are the prospects of longer and longer life. The fusing of real time and film time may denote an intent to challenge the codes of cinematic tricks as well as a rigor in working with limitations. But the long take is rarely used as a principle of construction in itself, involving not only the length but also the quality and structure of the shot. In most cases, it is defended on the grounds of its temporal *realism*, and the goal pursued remains chiefly that of preventing reality from being falsely interpreted or deformed through the removal of expressive editing techniques. The same may be said of the hand-held camera.

> *What self expression? i mis-express myself more than it mis-expresses me. Impresses itself on me. Until it enters. Penetrates. Ensnares. Now i see and hear myself decensoring.*
>
> *Jump cuts; jerky, unfinished, insignificant pans; split faces, bodies, actions, events; rhythms, rhythmized images, slightly off the beat, discord; irregular colors, vibrant, saturated or too bright; framing and reframing, hesitations; sentences on sentences, looped phrases, snatches of conversations, cuts, broken lines, words; repetitions; silences; chasing camera; squatting position; a look for a look; questions, returned questions; silences.*

For many of us, the best way to be neutral and objective is to copy reality meticulously. Repeated.

> *Discontinuity begins with non- cleavages. Inside/outside, personal/impersonal, subjectivity/objectivity.*

They can't do without cleavages. i always blink when i look. Yet they pretend to gaze at it for you ten minutes, half an hour without blinking. And i often take back what i've just shown, for i wish i had made a better choice. How do you go about framing life? We linger on, believing everything we show is worth showing. "Worth?"

Emphasis, here again, is laid on coherence of cinematic space, not on discontinuity (the hand-held camera can be used precisely to deny and shatter that coherence). The travelling shot gives the image a touch of authenticity: the movements of the person filming and those of the camera intermingle, even though nothing in the result yielded seems to suggest a radical departure from the conventional realist account of an action. Walking about with the camera does provide the camera operator with greater freedom of movement, hence greater ability to catch people either unaware or acting naturally, that is to say while they are still "alive." The camera changes situations, especially when it remains static on a tripod, and when the operator has to move from one "observation post" to another. But what so often goes unchallenged here—in the tripod as well as hand-held camera—is the assumed need to offer several views of the same subject/object from different angles, to follow or circle him/her/it; and the exigency for an identification between the camera's eye and the spectator's eye, as well as for a "perfect balance" between the movements of the camera/operator and those of the subjects being filmed. Omniscience.The synchronous recording of image and sound further reinforces the authentic contact with the lived and living reality. Given the present state of technology, the use of sync sound has become almost mandatory in all factual films. So has the practice of translating and subtitling the words of the informants. There is a certain veneration for the real sound of the film (an electronic sound that is often spoken of as if it is "real life" sound) and for the oral testimony of the people filmed. There is also a tendeney to apprehend language exclusively as Meaning. IT HAS TO MAKE SENSE. WE

WANT TO KNOW WHAT THEY THINK AND HOW THEY FEEL. Making a film on/about the "others" consists of allowing them paternalistically "to speak for themselves" and, since this proves insufficient in most cases, of completing their speech with the insertion of a commentary that will objectively describe/interpret the images according to a scientific-humanistic rationale.

That's not imposing, that's sharing. i frequently accept similar formulas . . . sometimes, i think, i should hes-i-tate more.

"Breaking rules" still refers to rules.

On the lookout for "messages" that may be wrested from the objects of observation.

Music is the opium of cinema.

Why not put in some natural sounds instead of silences? someone asks.

Images. Not only images, but images and words that defy words and commentary.

A sliding relation between ear and eye. Repetitions are never identical.

Language as voice and music—grain, tone, inflections, pauses, silences, repetitions—goes underground. Instead, people from remote parts of the world are made accesible through dubbing/subtitling, transformed into English-speaking elements and brought into conformity with a definite mentality. This is astutely called "giving voice"—literally meaning that those who are/need to be *given* an opportunity to speak up never had a voice before. Without their benefactors, they are bound to remain non-admitted, non-incorporated, therefore, unheard. One of the strategies that has been gaining ground in ethnographic cinema is the extensive if not exclusive use of the wide angle. Here again, the wide angle is favored for its ability to reduce false interpretations and is particularly valued by filmmakers concerned with, for example, indigenous peoples' complex kinship structures and their notions of the community, the group or the family. This time, the creed is: the wider, the truer. Closeups are too partial; the camera that focuses on an individual or a group proves to be heavily biased, for it fails to relate that person's or that group's activities to those of their kin. So goes the reasoning, as if a larger frame (one that contains more) is less of a frame, as if the wide angle does not, like the closeup, cut off life. Moreover, the wide angle is known to distort images.Thus, when it is used exclusively and unquestionably throughout a film, even in instances where there is only one person in front of the camera, it involuntarily deforms the figures of the subjects, giving the spectator the impression of looking constantly through an aquarium. Some filmmakers will not hesitate to answer to this that the aesthetic quality of the visuals is of secondary importance. No Art here. A beautiful shot is apt to lie, while a bad shot "is a guarantee of authenticity," one that loses in attractiveness but gains in truth. Which truth, finally? And which reality, when "life" and "art" are perceived dualistically as two mutually exclusive poles? When *dead,* shallow, un-imag-inative images are validated on pretext of their "capturing *life* directly?" It is, perhaps, precisely the claim to catch life in its motion and show it "as it is" that has led a great number of "documentarians" not only to present "bad shots," but also to make us believe that life is as dull as the images they project on the screen. Beauty for beauty's sake sounds hopelessly sterile in today's context of filmmaking. However, between a film that is not slick—that is to say not concerned with aestheticism per se—one that wallows in natural romanticism, and one that mechanically or lifelessly records the seen, there are differences. And differences, I believe, never offer two absolute oppositions.

To say nothing, no thing and shut that spinning verbal top.
Or shatter that outer, inner speech, which fills in every time space, allowing me to exist as a crystallized I.

Hear with that mechanical eye and see with that electronic ear. The text is not meant to duplicate or strengthen the verisimilitude of the images. It can, at best, strip them of their usual chatter.

The tyranny of the camera goes unchallenged. Instead of alleviating it and acknowledging it, many declare it arrogant and walk on unpressured.

Surely, "there is more to Art than the straightness of lines and the perfection of images." Similarly, there must be more to Life than analogy and accumulation of the real.

A fiction of security.

When i spoke about relationships i was immediately asked: "between what?" i have always thought "within what?" For "between" can be endless, starting from you are me camera/filmmaker/spectator/events/persons filmed/images/sound/silence/music/language/color/texture/links/cuts/sequences/

The very effort will kill it.

They only speak their own language and when they hear foreign sounds—no language to their ear—they walk off warily, saying: "It's not deep enough, we haven't learned anything."

93

BRIAN WINSTON

THE TRADITION OF THE VICTIM IN GRIERSONIAN DOCUMENTARY (1988*)

You know this film (*Children at School*) was made in 1937. The other thing is that this film shows up the appalling conditions in the schools in Britain in 1937 which are identical with the ones which came out on television the night before last: over-crowded classes, schoolrooms falling down, and so on. It's the same story. That is really terrible, isn't it?

—Basil Wright, 1974

One

A. J. Liebling once remarked that it was difficult for the cub reporter to remember that his (or her) great story was somebody else's disastrous fire. Much the same could be said of the impulse to social amelioration, which is a central element in Grierson's rhetoric and which, therefore, has become over this past half-century a major part of the great documentary tradition. Documentary found its subject in the first decade of sound, and by the late thirties the now familiar parade of those of the disadvantaged whose deviance was sufficiently interesting to attract and hold our attention had been established. It was not yet dominant and World War II was to distract from its importance, but it was there. Each successive generation of socially concerned film-makers since the war has found, on both sides of the Atlantic, in housing and

*Revised 2015.

education, labor and nutrition, health and welfare an unflagging source of material. For the most prestigious publicly funded documentarist as well as the least effective of local news teams, the victim of society is ready and waiting to be the media's 'victim' too.

This "victim," however, does not figure much in the theoretical or public discussion of documentary. There an agenda has been set which concentrates on issues of transparency and narratology, on the morality of mediation and reconstruction, on the development of style, and on the effects of new equipment. The people whose co-operation is crucial to documentarists have as little place in that discussion as they do (usually) in the making of the films and tapes in which they star. Indeed documentarists by and large take an aggrieved view of this issue, should it be raised. Frederick Wiseman:

> Sometimes after films are completed people feel retrospectively that they had a right of censorship, but there are never any written documents to support that view. I couldn't make a film which gave somebody else the right to control the final print.[1]

Wiseman's attitude is, I would argue, the typical one. Interference of any kind is a clear breach of the film-makers' freedom of speech and, as such, is to be resisted. But given the "tradition of the victim," the filmmakers' freedoms often seem like nothing so much as abridgements of the rights of their subjects, rights which, for all that they are less than well defined, are nevertheless of importance in a free society.

The persistence of the social problems that these texts are, at a fundamental level, supposed to be ameliorating is never discussed. But if it is the case that housing problems are unaffected by fifty years of documentary effort, what justification can there be for continuing to make such films and tapes? Grierson's purpose was clearly enunciated: "To command, and cumulatively command, the mind of a generation.... The documentary film was conceived and developed as an instrument of public use."[2] There was nothing, though, in this ambition (shared by the entire documentary movement) to be the propagandists for a better and more just society which would inevitably lead to the constant, repetitive, and ultimately pointless exposure of the same set of social problems on the televisions of the West night after night. How this came to be the case is the subject of this paper.

The Griersonian tradition cannot be contained by referencing the practice of one small group of British film-makers during two decades of activity. For good or ill, it is here assumed, that Grierson's direct and indirect influence have affected documentary film production worldwide. In particular, it is suggested that in North America the influence has been strong and obvious, both as to the institutional framework seen to be appropriate for documentary production and in the topics documentarists choose to make films about. Thus the argument of this paper will criss-cross the Atlantic. First a crucial shift in the documentary subject will be isolated as having taken place in Britain in the mid-thirties. This, the discovery of the "victim of society" as a suitable subject, raises a number of essentially ethical questions for Grierson and his successors, questions which confront contemporary documentary practice on both sides of the Atlantic. These will be addressed in the third section below. Since there is little debate in documentary circles about the implications of these practices in the final sections we shall turn to the courts for guidance, situating these ethical questions in the traditions of the common law and its approaches to the issue of privacy. Most of our evidence here comes from the United States, so we will conclude by concentrating, perforce, on American legal precedents.

But we shall begin half a century ago in the U.K., confident in the belief that Grierson's practice has directly influenced contemporary film-makers in many countries, including the U.S.; and that it is his benchmarks which have been established for all subsequent documentary work both in film and television for the entire English-speaking world and beyond.

Two

From 1929 to 1937 Grierson synthesised two distinct elements. Firstly he focused the general social concern of his time into a program of state-supported film-making. Such were conditions during the Great Depression that even on the Right in Britain the need for measures of state intervention in many fields was accepted. Indeed the generation of young Conservatives whose political philosophy was formed at this time were exactly those post-war leaders who agreed to the Welfare State and thereby established the consensus which is only now being destroyed. I mention this simply because it is easy to treat the group around Grierson as dilettantes. (Wright speaks of his "slight private income"[3]; Rotha writes of his parents as "far from well-off" who, nevertheless, managed to send him to thirteen private schools in as many years[4]; Watt states: "I came from a normal middle-class background. My father was a member of Parliament."[5]) To modern eyes the films they made, virtually all of them stilted and condescending, tend to reinforce the unfortunate impression that, as a group, they were nothing but poseurs, clutching their double firsts from Cambridge. There is no reason, though, to doubt the sincerity of their impulse to "get the British workmen on the screen" or indeed to help the working class in other ways.[6] "To start with we were left wing to a man. Not many of us were communists, but we were all socialists."[7] Grierson's first job, lecturing on philosophy at the Durham University outpost in Newcastle-upon-Tyne, allowed him time to work, and work seriously, in that city's slums.[8]

In its day, the social attitude of Grierson's colleagues was genuine and to be expected; and their achievement on the screen was not inconsiderable. Grierson claims that "the workers' portraits in *Industrial Britain* were cheered in the West End of London. The strange fact was that the West End had never seen workmen's portraits before—certainly not on the screen."[9]

> [The films] were revolutionary because they were putting on the screen for the first time in British films—and very nearly in world films—a workingman's face and a workingman's hands and the way the worker lived and worked. It's very hard with television nowadays and everything, to realise how revolutionary this was, that British films, as such, were photographed plays, that any working class people in British films were the comics.[10]

This emerging iconography, a contrast to the parade of Noel Coward servants that was the norm, did not, at first, concentrate on the lower classes as victims.

On the contrary, the second element influencing the movement ensured that this would not be the case. Robert Flaherty's powerful example moved the desire to document the realities of working life into the realm of the poetic. Flaherty was responsible for *Industrial Britain* although the film was finished by Grierson (and ruined by the distributor who added the "West End" voice and overblown commentary). Grierson's group admired Flaherty's approach enormously. Their primary aesthetic allegiance was the Soviet silent cinema which meshed well with their socialist rhetoric, but they were also susceptible to Flaherty's poeticism despite the fact that it eschewed the social responsibilities they embraced. Grierson was dismissive of what he called Flaherty's emphasis of "man against the sky," preferring films "of industrial and social function, where man is more likely to be in the bowels of the earth."[11]

> There wasn't any serious attempt at characterisation of the kind you find in Flaherty because we regarded this as a bit romantic. We were all pretty serious-minded chaps then, you know, and we believed, like the Russians, that you should use individuals in your film in a not exactly dehumanized way but a sort of symbolic way.[12]

Edgar Anstey encapsulates the group's view, but nevertheless Flaherty's insistence on using the individual as the centerpiece of his narratives was to prove as seductive as the poeticism of his camera style. Flaherty's contribution to the notion of the documentary (the individual as subject and the romantic style) when mixed with Grieson's (social concern and propaganda) leads directly to privileging "victims" as subject matter. For the working class can be heroes only in the abstract sense that Anstey describes.

> The early school of documentary was divorced from people. It showed people in a problem, but you never got to know them, and you never felt they were talking to each other. You never heard how they felt and thought and spoke to each other, relaxed. You were looking from a high point of view at them.[13]

Examining the individual worker, given the predelictions of these filmmakers, meant moving from the heroic to the alienated. Hence victims, and the emergence of a sub-school of film-makers who

> wanted to lay on what the problems were for Britain so that we should see and learn and do something about it. But you don't do something unless you feel some sort of empathy and concern with the problem, and the cold commentary voice doesn't really excite you very much.[13]

The competition between Grierson's line and the splinter group was short-lived. Grierson's attempt to reconstruct the landscape of industrial Britain in terms of Flaherty's exoticism (and Eisenstein's editing methods) withered on the vine.

> We worked together [explains Grierson] and produced a kind of film that gave great promise of very high development of the poetic documentary. But for some reason or another, there has been no great development of that in recent times. I think it's partly because we ourselves got caught up in social propaganda. We ourselves got caught up in the problems of housing and health, the question of pollution (we were on to that long ago). We got on to the social problems of the world, and we ourselves deviated from the poetic line.[14]

Grierson is being a little self-serving here for the group as a whole did not get "on to the social problems of the time" and, in fact, it split apart on the issue. Arthur Calder-Marshall, ever the most perceptive of Grierson's contemporary critics, summed up the problem. Commenting on the failure of the G.P.O. film unit to document the unrest of postal workers, he wrote:

> Mr. Grierson is not paid to tell the truth but to make more people use the parcel post. Mr. Grierson may like to talk about social education surpliced in self-importance and social benignity. Other people may like hearing him. But even if it sounds like a sermon, a sales talk is a sales talk.[15]

Grierson's autocratic grip on documentary production in Britain was loosened and the "serious-minded chaps" established a measure of distance and independence from him. What is more significant is that they also established the way forward, a way that the "poets" themselves came to in a few years.

Rotha, partly because of personality clashes but more on principle, had quit to set up his own unit. Now Anstey and Elton, although still disciples, also left. In the films these men made in the mid-thirties can be plotted the shift from worker-as-hero to worker-as-victim.

In *Shipyard*, a typical Griersonian project about the building of a ship, Rotha (commissioned by the shipping line and working for a subsidiary of Gaumont-British) injected an understanding of how the shipbuilders would be once more idle when the work was completed. Out of material collected on his journeys to and from the yard, he also made, for the electricity generating industry, *Face of Britain* which, inter alia, contained the first material on the slums of the industrial heartland. That same year, 1935, Elton was making *Workers and Jobs*, a film with synchronous sound about Labour Exchanges for the Ministry of Labour. With Anstey he worked on the crucial *Housing Problems* for the gas industry. This too employed synchronous sound.

In *Housing Problems*, Cockney slum dwellers address the camera directly to explicate the living conditions the film depicts. This was the first time that the working class had been interviewed on film *in situ*. Giving them a voice by obtaining location sound with the bulky studio optical recording systems of the day was an exercise in technological audacity as great as any in the history of the cinema. Sound had come slowly. In 1934 Grierson was promising, "If we are showing workmen at work, we get the workmen to do their own commentary, with idiom and accent complete. It makes for intimacy and authenticity, and nothing we could do would be half as good."[16] Rotha had used a shipworker to do the commentary on *Shipyard* but for synchronous sound it was necessary to go into the studio, building sets and duplicating all the procedures of the fiction film. It is no accident that the first of their synchronous sound productions was *BBC: The Voice of Britain*, for the locations were studios, albeit designed for radio. In *Night Mail* technological limitations meant all the train interiors being shot on a sound stage. The desire to add the worker's voice to an authentic location image was easier to announce than to achieve.

But *Housing Problems* was much more than an early solution to a major technical problem. In making the film, Elton and Anstey had rethought much of the artistic rhetoric that Grierson had imported from Flaherty. Anstey:

> Nobody had thought of the idea which we had of letting slum dwellers simply talk for themselves, make their own film. . . . we felt that the camera must remain sort of four feet above the ground and dead on, because it wasn't our film.[17]

Because Elton and Anstey eschewed the usual proprietary artistic attitude, the people in *Housing Problems* are all named, allowed the dignity of their best clothes and the luxury of their own words (albeit somewhat stiltedly expressed for the gentlemen of the production unit). Of course, this claim of non-intervention ("it wasn't our film") cannot be taken too seriously, since the interviewees were chosen and coached by the team and the results edited without consultation. But it did represent a new theme in the group's thinking about the function of the documentary director, one which was unfortunately not to be heard again for three decades.

What was immediately influential was Anstey's view of his interviewees. Instead of heroic representatives of the proletariat, he thought of them but as "poor, suffering characters"—victims. The films were moving in topic from romanticized work through unemployment to the realities of domestic conditions.

In the years to come Anstey's view of his role, that of enabler rather than creator, and the courtesies he afforded his interviewees would disappear. The victim would stand revealed as the central subject of the documentary, anonymous and pathetic, and the director of victim documentaries would be as much of an "artist" as any other film-maker.

Before the war, Anstey was to make *Enough to Eat* about malnutrition and for *March of Time* he was to cover a bitter strike in the Welsh coal fields—rather than the titanic miner at work who was the earlier icon of the industry. Watt was to do a number of exposés for *March of Time* on the scandal of church tithes and the riches of football pools (a soccer-based commercial lottery) promoters. Wright, the most poetic of them all, made *Children at School*.

It is with some justice that these men claim that all current documentary practice can be traced back to their activities in the thirties. The most potent of their legacies, however, is this tradition of the victim.

Factual television cements the tradition into place. It affords a way of apparently dealing with the world while, as Calder-Marshall said of Grierson's *Drifters*, "running away from its social meaning." For it substitutes empathy for analysis, it privileges effect over cause, and it, therefore, seldom results in any spin-offs in the real world—that is, actions taken in society as a result of the program to ameliorate the conditions depicted. So although the majority of television documentaries and news features deal with victims, normally as types of deviance, such treatment scarcely diminishes the number of victims left in the world as potential subjects.

Independent documentary production is in like case. The rise of direct cinema produced, by the early sixties, the currently dominant style of "crisis structure" documentary. Robert Drew, whose position in these developments is not unlike Grierson's thirty years before, describes the goal of such work:

> What makes us different from other reporting and other documentary film-making, is that in each of these stories there is a time when a man comes against moments of tension, and pressure, and revelation, and decision. It's these moments that interest us most. Where we differ from TV and press is that we're predicated on being there when things are happening to people that count.[18]

But where the direct cinema practitioners turned out to be the same was in their choice of the people they would witness in such situations. Of course, they could and did observe presidents and movie tycoons but, as in the thirties, the more fruitful strand turned out to be not the powerful but the powerless. And, more than that, direct cinema gave the victim tradition the technology that allowed a degree of intrusion into ordinary people's lives which was not previously possible.

Direct cinema and *cinéma vérité* were the outcome of a concerted effort, culminating in the late fifties, to develop a particular technology—a lightweight, hand-holdable, synchronous sound film camera. The demand for this had come directly out of the Griersonian experience, where any sort of synchronous shooting required enormous intervention, if not reconstruction, on the part of the film-makers. In the years after the war it seemed to many that without such portable equipment, documentary film would never deliver on its promise to offer un- (or minimally) mediated pictures of reality. It can be argued that this was entirely the wrong agenda because reconstruction was not the real issue, since mediation occurs in far subtler and more or less unavoidable ways whatever the techniques used. The argument was nevertheless deployed and the equipment developed.

Television had already begun to use 16mm for news gathering purposes, forcing the creation of ever more sensitive film stocks. The equipment the industry used for this work formed the basis of the direct cinema experiments. In turn, the broadcasters took up the adaptations the direct cinema practitioners made and thereby created a market for the manufacture of custom-designed self-blimped cameras and hi-fidelity battery-driven tape recorders. The possibility of events being more important than were the processes of filming them now existed for the first time. No door, especially the door behind which the disadvantaged were to be found, need or could be closed to the film-makers.

Aesthetic as well as technical trends also favored the victim as subject. It is received opinion that television demands close-ups, but it is no part of professionalisation, in my experience, to stress any such thing. The industry tends to avoid the big scene because of the expense such shots involve rather than because they are considered unreadable by the audience, which, palpably, they are not. A number of other factors lead to the close-up—against light backgrounds, receiver tubes (for at least twenty years after the war) tended to over-modulate and reduce all darker areas to silhouette. By moving into the face this could be avoided. The very small eyepieces of 16mm reflex cameras (and, latterly, lightweight video equipment) again encourage the close-up as being more easily focused than longer shots. The prevalence of the 10:1 zoom lens, which can only be properly focused at the long (i.e. close-up) end of its range, has the same effect. All these technological constraints result in the close-up emerging at the dominant shot in the documentary.

(There was an early period when the direct cinema style encouraged the use of a wide-angle lens to simplify focusing problems. This lens has been largely abandoned because the variable shot size possible with the zoom lens better serves the needs of transparent editing. It also avoids distortions, again serving the needs of transparency. And, because it is much more difficult to use than a wide-angle, the mysterium of the cameraperson's craft is more effectively maintained.)

The documentary tradition begins with the individual heroic Inuit, "against the sky" in long shot. Currently it most often displays the private inadequacies of the urban under-class, "in the bowels of the earth" in close-up. The line that enabled this to happen can be traced from Flaherty's exotic individuals, through Grierson's romanticized and heroic workers to Anstey's victims caught in Drew's crisis structures. The line was an easy one to follow because technological developments, journalistic predelictions, and ideological imperatives all played a role in facilitating it.

But there is one major concomitant problem involved in the emergence of the victim tradition which has never received the attention it demands. By choosing victims, documentarists abandoned the part supposedly played by those who comment publicly on society (the watchdogs of the guardians of power). Instead, in almost any documentary situation, they are always the more powerful partner. The moral and ethical implications of this development are not only ignored; they are dismissed as infringements of film-makers' freedoms.

Three

> A monstrous, giant, smouldering slagheap towering over a shabby

> street of slum houses, hovels fallen into ruin with one lavatory for fifty persons. But inhabited. Rent for a house was 25 shillings per week. All the property belonged to the company that owned the mine. Few men were in work. I watched the rent collectors at their disgusting job; wringing a few shillings from women some of whose men were bloodying hands and shoulders in the earth hundreds of feet below where we stood, or standing on the street corners. From some petty cash I had with me, I paid the rent for some families and bought beer in the pub for some of the miners. It gave me pleasure that the profits of Gaumont-British should be so used. How I justified it in my accounts when I got back to London is neither remembered nor important. So this was Britain in the 1930s.[19]

Rotha went to the village of East Shottom in Durham because J. B. Priestley had reported on it in a series of newspaper articles which became the book *English Journey*. This perfectly describes the normal relationship between the print and audio-visual media, but I quote the diary because it is one of the few references to a film-maker's relationship with a subject that I can find in the literature on documentary film. For instance Joris Ivens, the most overtly political of the great documentarists, in his memoir of four decades of film-making (*The Camera and I*) details only one non-unidimensional relationship.[20] Normally film-makers regard contact with their subjects as too uninteresting to report. In consequence the literature tends to contain only references to what are considered deviant encounters, usually where the film-maker has to resort to subterfuge to get the material needed.

> While I was waiting outside with the film crew . . . a truck pulled up in front of us and a burly guy clambered out and started yelling, "What the hell are you guys doing here. You're trespassing, and get the hell off my property." This was Chudiak, president of the farmers' co-op, but I didn't know it at the time and had to figure out, first, who is this guy; second, what do I say to prevent the whole show from disappearing then and there; third, how can I prevent him from learning what I'm really doing but still tell him a sufficient amount so that I won't feel forever guilty of having lied; and fourth, how can I keep the trust of the migrants, the crew chief, and gain the confidence of this guy, all at the same time.[21]

A film-maker's lot is clearly not a happy one—but it is, arguably, less unhappy than that of the migrant workers, the subjects of the above documentary. Film-makers do worry about lying—to exploiting farmers or the like. This sort of worry can be traced back to the thirties. Watt described conning vicars while making his *March of Time* about church tithes:

> Being film people, we'd take advantage. We used to go to sweet vicars living in a twenty room house and with a congregation of ten, mostly old women. And I'd say, "What a beautiful house and beautiful church. May I photograph?" Of course, I was showing that he was living in this enormous house and having ten parishioners. The church was very annoyed about the whole thing, but it was just what *March of Time* wanted.[22]

With all due respect to these film-makers, such worries are easy. They reveal the film-maker in a traditional journalistic role as protector of the powerless and fearless confronter of the powerful. The more vexed moral issue is raised not by the need to misrepresent oneself before the farmer but rather by the necessity of remaining silent, as to the reality of their situation, in the presence of the migrant workers. It is not the fabrication of intention for the vicar but the easy assumption that the film-maker and the film production company know better than the church established what the society best needs. And it is these issues that are not addressed. There are film-makers who bring a high-degree of sensitivity to their work. In the seventies, some like George Stoney, actively began exploring other roles for themselves. Others created what almost amounted to a subclass of films in which the documentarist dealt with their own families, as in *Best Boy.* It is, though, our contention that these were exceptions and that the potential for documentarists they represent is still attenuated. The victim tradition dominates.

The victim tradition makes it all too easy to itemize, almost at random, a wide range of problems.

First, when dealing with the powerless what does the legally required consent mean? Since for most people the consequences of media exposure are unknown, how can one be expected to evaluate such consequences? For some people, as with the mentally ill in Wiseman's banned *Titicut Follies,* there is a question of whether or not consent can be given in any circumstances. The same would apply to the male child prostitutes appearing in the videotape *Third Avenue, Only the Strong Survive.*

In this same text is raised a second question, that of complicity. The crew reconstructed a car heist and then filmed one of the protagonists in prison subsequent to another robbery of the same kind. All films about deviant activities place the film-makers in, at best, quasi-accessory positions.

Beyond the illegal there is the dangerous. Flaherty paid the men of Aran £5 to risk their lives by taking a canoe out into a heavy sea. (There is some quite infuriatingly stupid comment about this sequence suggesting that the men were in no danger because of the peculiarities of the waters round Aran. Any who believe this have simply failed to look at the film.) Or there can be more specific danger as in a student project which took a man recovering from compulsive gambling to the track to see how well he was doing and to provide the film with a climax.

A more unexpected problem arises when the subject desires media exposure, as in a BBC documentary about an exhibitionist trans-sexual shot in the most voyeuristic manner consistent with public exhibition. In another British television film, *Sixty Seconds of Hatred,* a man's murder of his wife was examined. I was invited to screen the movie, on the eve of transmission, and found, also among the critics, the murderer and the teenage son of the marriage who was a child when the crime was committed. There was no doubt that the man was eager to relive the incident; but, beyond a careful decision not to include him in the film, nobody had further considered what such a public retelling of the tale might do to the boy.

These are not, in my view, abstract concerns affecting only the subjects of documentaries. The problems also redound to the filmmakers. In a British television documentary, *Goodbye, Longfellow Road,* the film crew documented a woman's descent into pneumonia. The crew interviewed the doctor as he was rushing her stretcher to the ambulance and ascertained that it was indeed the result of her living in a hovel that had caused her condition. As a television producer, I would find it extremely difficult to comfort myself with the thought that I had contributed to the public's right to know when I could have, for a pittance, provided my victim with a roof, however temporary. Of course, I would have needed another subject for my film.

Other problems arise from the fact that these texts have extended and perhaps nearly indefinite lives. Paul, the failed "salesman" in the Maysles film of that name, is constantly exposed as such wherever documentary film classes are taught or Maysles retrospectives are held. The anonymous Midwestern boy who spews his heart up as a result of a drug overdose in Wiseman's *Hospital,* spews away every time the film is screened. Should it be played in the community where he is now, one hopes, a stable and respectable citizen there is nothing he can do about it. For the film is not a lie; is not maliciously designed to bring him into either hatred, ridicule, or contempt; and, therefore, he has no action for libel. And the film was taken with his consent, presumably obtained subsequent to his recovery.

And this consent is, indeed, all that the law requires. The question must be asked, is it enough? The answer is to be culled largely from American experience.

Four

In 1909 two steamships collided in Long Island Sound. On board one of them, a radio operator, John R. Binns, successfully (and for the first time anywhere) used his machine to call for help. As a result of his C.D.Q. only six of the seventeen hundred passengers on board drowned. Binns was a hero. The Vitagraph Company, after the fashion of the day, made a "documentary" about the incident, entirely reconstructed and using an actor to impersonate Binns. Binns, the actor, was shown as lounging about and winking at the passengers at the moment of the collision. Binns, the hero, sued—not only for libel but also for invasion of privacy. He won on both counts. But the privacy decision was to prove exceptional.[23]

The courts over the years, according to the account given by Pember in *Privacy and the Press,* were to take the basic view that any filmed event, if not reconstructed, was protected by the First Amendment.[24]

The only line of exceptions to this arose, both for films and the press, out of a series of decisions about the unauthorized use of images in advertisements, the earliest being heard in the English Court of Chancery in 1888. By 1903, New York State had a privacy statute on the books specifically limited to such unauthorized uses for advertising or "trade purposes." The courts were to be very restrictive in defining "trade purposes" and again and again privacy actions failed if the commerce involved was simply the commerce of the news business, whatever the medium. In such cases the conflict is seen as being between the public's right to know and the private citizen's right to privacy, and the former normally prevails.

The courts were happy to distinguish between advertising and news; and the above exceptions were based upon the distinction. For, despite the terminology used, the cases turn on some sense of property, upon the idea that another should not profit *directly* out of the use of one's image. Other arguments have been advanced suggesting that persons should be protected from exploitation by the news media because they are private individuals. These have been, by and large, as unsuccessful as the attempts to extend the concept of commercial exploitation. The idea of the "public man" goes back to 1893 and was extended in the twenties.[25] The right to privacy was then defined as:

> The right to live one's life in seclusion, without being subjected to unwarranted and undesired publicity. In short it is the right to be left alone ... There are times, however, when one, whether willing or not, becomes an actor in an occurrence of public or general interest. When this takes place he emerges from his

> seclusion, and it is not an invasion of his right of privacy to publish his photograph with an account of such occurrence.[26]

One can become an "involuntary public figure" by giving birth to a child at twelve years of age, being held hostage by a gunman, having one's skirts blown above one's head in public.[27] And becoming an "involuntary public figure" was no temporary thing. A boy prodigy could not prevent the press pursuing him and removing the cloak of obscurity he had sought.[28] Neither, since the common law has never acknowledged distress as a ground of action, could parents prevent the publication of pictures of the dead bodies of their children.[29] Nor can the victims of rape, for the same reason, keep their names from the media, unless statute orders otherwise, which it does in some states.

Consent, equally, has never been developed as a concept, except that it was deemed to be unobtainable from minors. In *Commonwealth of Massachusetts v. Wiseman* it was further held that consent was not obtained from the participants in the film *Titicut Follies*. Of the sixty-two mental patients seen in the film, most were not competent to sign releases and only twelve such forms were completed.[30] (The need for written consent had been established in a case where CBS was successfully sued by a person who was represented in a dramatic reconstruction of a real-life incident which had been made with his consent and advice but without written permission.[31]) Wiseman's account of the *Titicut Follies* case is in rather different terms:

> I had permission from the superintendent. I had permission from the commissioner of correction. I had an advisory opinion from the attorney general of Massachusetts, and I had the strong support of the then lieutenant governor. However, some of these men turned against me when the film was finished, with most of the trouble starting two or three months after the superintendent and the attorney general had seen the film.[32]

Wiseman, in this interview, claims "this was the first time in American constitutional history ... whereby publication of any sort which has not been judged to be obscene has been banned from public viewing." Rather it was the first time that an injunction was obtained on the grounds that there was a failure to obtain consent outside of advertising. The case, although therefore important, still does not acknowledge the existence of a right of privacy in any well-defined way. It joins *Binns* and *Vitagraph Co.* among the few precedents which go against the interests of the press and which, almost all, turn on consent issues.

One understands and sympathizes with the emotions stirred by the First Amendment, but it is an eighteenth-century device addressing eighteenth-century situations. Insisting that what was conceived of as a virtual private right should attach to any legal entity in the society however large; insisting that no technological advance in communications has affected the basic essence of privacy and reputation; insisting that these freedoms are so fragile only a domino-theory approach can protect them—all of these things must be abandoned if the real dangers of the late twentieth century are to be faced. The point is that, traditionally, media have been considered as not just the representatives of the general public but the general public itself. Such a view, while understandable in eighteenth-century terms, fails to distinguish present-day realities where the media are far from being the general public but are instead a special interest dominated by an oligopolistically arranged group of international conglomerates. The commonly held view that the freedoms of expression demanded by such entities must be protected because identical individual freedoms will be at stake if they are not is, I would submit, simply false. The individual's right of free speech is now separated from the media's right of the same name by an abyss of technology. They can and should be treated differently.

Five

For film and video-makers caught in the Griersonian tradition of seeking social amelioriation through the documentation of societies' victims, the law, given the amplification of message possible with current technologies, allows too much latitude. Documentarists, by and large, do not libel and, by and large, do not "steal" images. Yet they are working with people who, in matters of information, are normally their inferiors—who know less than they do about the ramifications of the film-making process.

Instead of the crude "consent" we now have, more refined consideration would be needed. Such refinements already exist in the area of medical and social-science research procedures developed, mainly without the pressure of law, by many professional bodies. Among the most comprehensive of these was the Nuremburg Code.

> The voluntary consent of the human subject is absolutely essential. This means that the person involved should have legal capacity to give consent; should be so situated as to be able to exercise the free power of choice, without the intervention of any element of force, fraud, deceit, duress, over-reaching, or other ulterior form of constraint or coercion; and should have sufficient knowledge and comprehension of the elements of the subject matter involved as to enable him to make an understanding and enlightened decision. This latter element requires that before acceptance of an affirmative decision by the experimental subject there should be made known to him the nature, duration and purpose of the experiment; the method and means by which it is to be conducted; all inconveniences and hazards reasonably to be expected; and the effects upon his health or person which may possibly come from his participation in the experiment.[33]

Substitute "film" for "experiment" and "experimental" in the above and a fair definition of a film-maker's duty of care results. Film-makers will argue that this would massively reduce access to subjects. So be it. Since the fifty-year parade of the halt and the lame has patently done more good to the documentarists than it has to the victims, I see no cause to mourn a diminution of these texts.

NOTES

1. A. Rosenthal, *New Documentary in Action* (Los Angeles: Univ. of California Press, 1971), 71.
2. H. F. Hardy (ed.), Grierson on Documentary (London: Faber, 1979), 48, 188.
3. E. Sussex, *The Rise and Fall of British Documentary* (Los Angeles: Univ. of California Press, 1975), 21.
4. P. Rotha, *Documentary Diary* (New York: Hill & Wang, 1973), 1.
5. Sussex, *Rise and Fall*, 29.
6. Rotha, *Documentary Diary*, 49.
7. Sussex, *Rise and Fall*, 77.
8. Hardy (ed.), *Grierson on Documentary*, 29.
9. Ibid., 77.
10. Sussex, *Rise and Fall*, 76.
11. Hardy (ed.), *Grierson on Documentary*, 64.
12. Sussex, *Rise and Fall*, 18.
13. Ibid., 76.
14. Ibid., 79.
15. A. Calder-Marshall, *The Changing Scene* (London: Chapman and Hall, 1937).
16. "The G.P.O. Gets Sound" in *Cinema Quarterly*, London, 1934.
17. Sussex, *Rise and Fall*, 62.
18. In S. Mamber, *Cinéma Vérité in America* (Cambridge, Mass.: MIT Press, 1974), 118.
19. Rotha, *Documentary Diary*, 104.

20. (New York: International Publishers, 1974), 193–204.
21. Rosenthal, *New Documentary in Action,* 108.
22. Sussex, *Rise and Fall,* 89.
23. *Binns v. Vitagraph Co.,* 210 N.Y. 51 (1913).
24. (Seattle: Washington University Press, 1972).
25. *Corliss v. E. W. Waler and Co.* Fed. Rep. 280 (1894).
26. *Jones v. Herald Post Co.,* 230 Ky. 227 (1929).
27. *Meetze v. AP,* 95 S.E. 2nd 606 (1956).
28. *Sidis v. New Yorker* 133 Fed. 2nd 806 (1940).
29. *Kelly v. Post Publishing Co.,* 327 Mass. 275 (1951).
30. Pember op. cit., 224 et seq.
31. *Durgom v. CBS,* 214 NYS 2nd 1008 (1961).
32. Rosenthal, *New Documentary in Action,* 68 et seq.
33. In P. D. Reynolds, *Ethics and Social Science Research* (Englewood Cliffs, N.J.: Prentice-Hall, 1982), 143.

94

J. HOBERMAN

SHOAH

The Being of Nothingness (1985–86)

Claude Lanzmann's *Shoah* is not simply the most ambitious film ever attempted on the extermination of the Jews; it's a work that treats the problem of representation so scrupulously it could have been inspired by the Old Testament injunction against graven images. "The Holocaust is unique in that it creates a circle of flames around itself, a limit which cannot be crossed because a certain absolute horror cannot be transmitted," Lanzmann wrote in a 1979 essay, ostensibly about the mini-series *Holocaust*. "Pretending to cross that line is a grave transgression."

Shoah, which takes its title from the Hebrew word for "annihilation," doesn't cross that line, it defines it. For much of its nine and a half hours, the film seems formless and repetitive. Moving back and forth from the general to the specific, circling around certain themes, *Shoah* overwhelms the audience with details. For those who demand linear progression, Lanzmann's method may seem perverse—the film's development is not a temporal one. "The six million Jews did not die in their own time, and that is why any work that today wants to render justice to the Holocaust must take as its first principle the fracturing of chronology," Lanzmann has written. Although *Shoah* is structured by internal corroborations, in the end you have to supply the connections yourself. This film throws you upon your own resources. It compels you to imagine the unimaginable.

Length aside, *Shoah* is notable for the rigor of Lanzmann's method: the eschewing of archival footage and narration in favor of contemporary landscapes and long interviews (shown mainly in real time) with those who, in one form or another, experienced the Holocaust. "The film had to be made from traces of traces of traces," Lanzmann told one interviewer. Like the Swedish *Chaim Rumkowski and the Jews of Lodz* or the Hungarian *Package Tour,* two recent documentaries with less global perspectives on the war against the Jews, *Shoah* embodies a powerful and principled restraint. Like Syberberg's *Hitler, a Film from Germany,* it refuses to "reconstruct" the past, thus thwarting a conventional response and directing one to the source of one's own fascination.

Lanzmann, however, is scarcely as theatrical as Syberberg. In some respects, his strategy resembles that employed by Jean-Marie Straub and Danièle Huillet. The Straubs' 1976 *Fortini-Cani,* for example, punctuates readings by the Italian-Jewish-Communist poet Franco Fortini with long ruminations upon sylvan vistas where, 30-odd years earlier, the Nazis massacred a group of Italian partisans. Lanzmann shares the same conviction that the past surrounds us, that history is inscribed (if only through its erasure) on the present. In his *Holocaust* piece, he approvingly quotes the philosopher Emil Fackenheim: "The European Jews massacred are not just of the past, they are the *presence of an absence.*" This is why, while the vast Auschwitz complex has come to epitomize the Nazi death machine, *Shoah* emphasizes Treblinka—a camp built solely to exterminate Jews, a back-countrysite razed and plowed under by the Nazis themselves in an attempt to conceal all physical evidence of 800,000 murders.

The landscapes in *Shoah* are no less tranquil than those of *Fortini-Cani,* but they are haunted beyond the mind's capacity to take them in: Piney woods and marshy fields cover mass graves, a brackish lake is silted with the ashes of hundreds of thousands of victims. The camera gazes at the overgrown railroad tracks, end of the line, site of a ramp where a quarter of a million Jews were unloaded then hurried along with whips to their doom; it considers the postcard town of Chelmno where, one day after Pearl Harbor, the first Jews were gassed in mobile vans, using engine exhaust. What can be more peaceful than the ruins of Birkenau's snow-covered cremos and gas chambers? Of course, not every vista is so scenic. In one unforgettable camera movement, Lanzmann slowly pans down to the brown winter grass covering the rusty spoons and personal detritus that still constitute the soil of Auschwitz.

What binds these landscapes together are the trains that chug through Europe bound for Poland and the east. Lanzmann even managed to find an engineer who drove the Jewish transports. One of the film's recurring images is that of a train crossing the Polish countryside or pulling up in Treblinka station, with this very engineer, now wizened and bony as some medieval Death, looking back towards his invisible freight. In the argument of *Shoah,* these trains underscore the extent of bureaucratic organization needed to commit genocide, the blatant obviousness of the transports, and, finally, the existential terror of the journey. While the Jews were systematically deprived of water, the railroad crew was plied with drink. Through a translator, the former engineer tells Lanzmann the run was so harrowing the Germans were forced to pay a bonus in vodka. "He drank every drop he got because without liquor he couldn't stand the stench," the translator explains. "They even bought more liquor on their own ..."

If landscapes give *Shoah* its weight, interviews provide its drama. Over and against these images of present-day Poland and Germany is the testimony of witnesses ranging from Jewish survivors to Polish onlookers to Nazi commandants. But the film is as filled with silence as with talk. Nine hours' worth of subtitles barely make a comfortably margined 200-page book. Pauses, hesitations, are often more eloquent than words. The evident torment with which Jan Karski, a onetime courier for the Polish government, recalls two clandestine tours of the Warsaw Ghetto carries an expressive charge far beyond his pained halting description. Indeed, his face gray with agony, Karski breaks down and bolts off camera before he can even start.

Moreover, words are belied by expressions. Among the most scandalous aspects of *Shoah* are Lanzmann's interviews with the Polish residents of Chelmno and Treblinka. Although there are exceptions, their blandly volunteered memories and perfunctorily offered concern ("it was sad to watch—nothing to be cheery about") are almost more damning than the casual anti-Semitism ("all Poland was in the Jews' hands") the interviewer has little difficulty in provoking. Real malice only surfaces in tales of "fat" foreign Jews "dressed in white shirts" riding to their death in passenger cars where "they could drink and walk around" and even play cards. "We'd gesture that they'd be killed," one peasant adds, passing his finger across his throat in demonstration. His buddies assent, as if this macabre signal was itself an act of guerrilla warfare directed at the Germans.

If the sequence induces the unbearable mental image of trains run by drunken crews, packed to overflowing with a dazed, weeping human cargo, careening through a countryside areek with the stench of gas and burning bodies, jeered at by peasants standing by the tracks, this and more are corroborated by the surviving Jews: "Most of the people, not only the majority, but 99 per cent of the Polish people when they saw the train going through—we looked really like animals in that wagon, just our eyes looked outside—they were laughing, they had a joy, because they took the Jewish people away."

As for the Nazis, it's hard to know which is worse, the pathetic evasions of the avuncular Franz Grassler, onetime deputy commissioner of the Warsaw Ghetto, insisting that the Jews knew more about the final solution than did their jailers, or the affable, expansive Franz Suchomel, an SS *Unterscharführer* at Treblinka, expressing a grotesque camaraderie with the people he was killing. Among other things, *Shoah* precisely details the means by which the Jews were compelled to participate in their own destruction. Meanwhile, the testimony of Suchomel and others, such as the former head of Reich Railways Department 33, demonstrates that genocide—by which the Nazis proposed to have the Jewish vanish *without a trace*—posed incredible logistical difficulties, solvable only by a modern, mobilized bureaucracy. It is here that the language of problem-solving takes on a hallucinative unreality. Suchomel allows that at its peak, Treblinka "processed" 12,000 to 15,000 Jews each day ("we had to spend half the night at it"), a train-load of victims going "up the funnel" in two or three hours. Unlike at Auschwitz, prisoners at Treblinka were gassed with engine exhaust. "Auschwitz was a factory!" Suchomel explains. "Treblinka was a primitive but efficient production line of death."

You watch this in a state of moral nausea so strong it makes your head swim. Nor does Lanzmann ease you into the flow. *Shoah* opens at the site of the Chelmno death camp, with one of the film's few narrative voice-overs observing that of the 400,000 Jews who were sent there only two survived. (Later we meet them.) The film's second part begins with another sort of horror, Suchomel singing the Treblinka anthem:

Looking squarely ahead, brave and
joyous,
At the world,
The squads march to work.
All that matters to us now is Treblinka.
It is our destiny.
That's why we've become one with
Treblinka
In no time at all.
We know only the word of our
commander,
We know only obedience and duty,
We want to serve, to go on serving,
Until a little luck ends it all.
Hurray!

Each morning, he explains, the newly arrived Jews selected for slave labor were taught the song: "By evening they had to be able to sing along with it." (Even now I can't get this idiotic martial melody out of my head. In Jean-François Steiner's *Treblinka,* it is reported that, after the day's work, Jewish laborers were compelled to stand at attention and repeat these words for hours—as well as sing the anthem as they marched.)

Lanzmann's most detailed interviews are with former members of the Sondercommando—the Jews who were kept alive at Treblinka and Auschwitz to stoke the annihilation machine. "We were the workers in the Treblinka factory, and our lives depended on the whole manufacturing process, that is, the slaughtering process at Treblinka," one explains. Only the naive or the pitiless can call them collaborators. In a sense, these men hyperbolize the dilemma of Jewish survivors in general—it is one of the Holocaust's cruelties that every Jew who survived is somehow tainted. One woman who managed to weather the war hiding in Berlin describes her feelings on the day that the last Jews in the city were rounded up for deportation: "I felt very guilty that I didn't go myself and I tried to escape fate that the others could not escape. There was no more warmth around, no more soul . . . [only] this feeling of being terribly alone. . . . What made us do this? To escape [the] fate that was really our destiny or the destiny of our people." A terrible fate, an absolute isolation are ideas that recur in *Shoah* again and again.

If the Nazis are all too human, the survivors are as mysterious as extraterrestrials. What is one to make of the urbane, ironic Rudolf Vrba smiling as he describes cleaning the bodies out of the gas chamber, or the beseeching eyes of Filip Müller, survivor of five liquidations of the Auschwitz special detail? (His relentless discourse—an account of undressing corpses, shoveling them into the cremo, witnessing the last moments of thousands of Jews, some knowing, some not—is delivered in a tone of perpetual amazement, as though always for the first time: "It was like a blow on the head, as if I'd been stunned.") Unlike other accounts of the Holocaust, *Shoah* deliberately minimizes acts of individual heroism—to have been a Jew in Hitler's Europe was to have had the most appalling kind of heroism thrust upon you. "I began drinking after the war," the grim, noble-looking Itzhak Zuckerman, second-in-command of the Warsaw Ghetto's Jewish Combat Organization, tells Lanzmann. "It was very difficult. Claude, you asked for my impression. If you could lick my heart, it would poison you."

People have been asking me, with a guilty curiosity I can well understand, whether *Shoah* really has to be seen. A sense of moral obligation is unavoidably attached to such a film. Who knows if *Shoah* is good for you? (One hopes, probably in vain, that reviewers will declare a moratorium on the already debased currency of movie-ad hype.) There were many times during the screening that I regarded it as a chore and yet, weeks later, I find myself still mulling over landscapes, facial expressions, vocal inflections—the very stuff of cinema—and even wanting to see it again. The published text can in no way substitute for the film itself; the "text" of *Shoah* can only be experienced on the screen. On the other hand, the book is quite helpful in grasping Lanzmann's structure. For, if at first, *Shoah* seems porous and inflated, this is a film that expands in one's memory, its intricate cross-references and monumental form only gradually becoming apparent. One resists regarding *Shoah* as art—and, as artful as it is, one should.

This movie transfixes you, it numbs you, and finally—with infinite solicitude—it scars you. There are moments when you simply can't bear to look at another human being; *Shoah* is something that you experience alone. (If it teaches us anything, it's the meaning of the word "inconsolable.") The film ends in Israel—as it has to—with a member of the Jewish Combat Organization describing his fantasy, while searching the empty ruins of the Warsaw Ghetto, of being "the last Jew." (After he finishes comes a coda of trains implacably rolling on . . .)

Leaving the theater, you may recall one survivor's account of a secret mission out of the Ghetto to "Aryan" Warsaw: "We suddenly emerged into a street in broad daylight, stunned to find ourselves among normal people. [It was as if] we'd come from another planet." The horror of it is, that planet is ours.

* * *

I first heard the bitter pun "there's no business like *shoah* business" while working at YIVO, an institution almost exclusively staffed by Holocaust survivors or their children. The joke acknowledged the seemingly limitless appetite for Holocaust materials, mainly as fund-raising tools within the Jewish community, but also as a source of identity—even a perverse ethnic pride—as well as the antidote to the fascination with Nazism.

The joke also observes that nothing in this world is beyond recuperation. Elie Wiesel has dedicated himself to keeping the Holocaust pure, so to speak, and untrivialized. In doing so, his insistence has become so official and automatic that he himself has become a mass-culture cliché—the gaunt, tragic-eyed Holocaust survivor. On the surface, Claude Lanzmann's *Shoah* would seem to be another candidate for this sort of recuperation. But the film's nine-and-a-half-hour length, among other things, helps it to resist easy assimilation despite the extravagant reviews I quoted several weeks ago.

Shoah is the latest example of an epic genre, born with *The Sorrow and the Pity,* but also including the TV miniseries *Holocaust* and *The Winds of War,* Fassbinder's *Berlin Alexanderplatz,* Edgar Reitz's *Heimat,* and Syberberg's *Our Hitler,* which attempts to elevate memory to the level of myth (or antimyth), to lay bare the central event of the century before it vanishes from living history. Whether confronting the events of World War II or the origin of barbarism in the heart of western civilization, these films are susceptible to a nostalgic appetite for eternal verities—cooking up the past into a digestible narrative complete with ending. With the exception of the Syberberg film, *Shoah* is the only one of these to refuse this closure and rethink the problem of representation.

That so advanced and lucid a filmmaker as Ernie Gehr would independently develop strategies parallel to *Shoah*'s (with his recent *Signal—Germany on the Air*) is a kind of backhanded acknowledgment of Lanzmann's formal intelligence. There's a sense—mainly in its use of real time and existential drama—in which *Shoah* has as much in common with *The Chelsea Girls* as *The Sorrow and the Pity.* It's even closer to Jean-Marie Straub and Danièle Huillet's *History Lessons,* in which the camera dramatizes the search for historical verity by circling around a central absence, and their *Fortini-Cani* or *Too Early, Too Late,* both of which interrogate now-peaceful landscapes, the sites of past atrocities, for what a believer might call the silence of God.

Documentary is a tricky concept, made even more so by celluloid halls of mirrors like *The Atomic Café* and *One Man's War*—films that "document" earlier films. Archival footage carries its own baggage. But although *Shoah* is largely oral history, Lanzmann's eschewal of illustration triggers a primitive response to the photographic image. Looking at a photograph, one sees *through* the composition and imagines what has been pictured. Hence, Lanzmann's fanatical attention to detail; this is a film which can only unfold in the mind's eye. The question that underlies *Shoah* is, how did the Holocaust happen? Lanzmann sets out to answer this both in terms of practical logistics and human sensations. How was it done, how did it feel?

Much of what has been written about *Shoah* glosses over the film's provocations—its repetitions, its absences, its Talmudic system of cross-references. Review after review contains a flash of recognition—to experience the Holocaust onscreen is still, on some level, to experience the Holocaust—followed by a movement to put the film at arm's length. "If this isn't the best film of 1985, what does that category mean?" one well-known TV critic asked his partner. (What *does* that category mean? Less than a month later, he answered his own question with *The Color Purple,* an altogether more upbeat film about brutality and oppression.) In light of the extravagant praise *Shoah* has received, Pauline Kael's notorious negative appraisal in *The New Yorker*—which reportedly held her copy several weeks before tacking it onto the December 30 reviews of *Out of Africa* and *The Color Purple*—would seem particularly nervy. But Kael's response is something more complex than a personal distaste.

If *The New Yorker*'s review has convinced some people that *Shoah* isn't worth seeing, one could also sense a backlash at the meeting of the National Society of Film Critics this year. *Shoah* was not above criticism after all. Sitting through it may even have been, as Kael suggested, "a form of self-punishment." There was a free-floating embarrassment among some of Lanzmann's partisans, complemented by a revisionist line that the film's significance was historical (or documentary) rather than cinematic, and even by a certain amount of open hostility. During the three ballots necessary to arrive at a best picture, *Shoah* was always in the running (it finished fourth). At strategic intervals throughout the process, one critic kept petulently pointing out that we *would* be voting a best documentary while, during the voting for that category (which *Shoah* easily won), another gaggle of reviewers indicated their disdain by ostentatiously casting ballots for *Pee-Wee's Big Adventure.*

If there has been very little written so far about *Shoah* from a formal point of view, there has been an undercurrent of criticism which I've heard expressed in conversation but, until Kael's piece, hadn't seen surface in the press. Basically, this critique involves the notions that Lanzmann treated the Polish peasants unfairly and that his aggressive interviewing techniques violate the boundaries of propriety.

The charge that the film is anti-Polish was leveled by the Polish government soon after *Shoah* opened in Paris. (Later tactics shifted and the film was acquired by Polish TV, which followed telecast excerpts with a round-table denunciation of Lanzmann and, according to a report published in *Variety,* the suggestion that the film was fictional.) The basis for this is Lanzmann's interviews with the peasants who lived near the death camps at Chelmno and Treblinka. These eyewitnesses express various degrees of ordinary anti-Semitism, more an indication of indifference than hatred, a cultural climate rather than an ideology, but no less startling for that. One would have imagined that the extermination of their Jewish neighbors would have left a more thoughtful residue. In this, *Shoah* reveals a syndrome touched on in *Now . . . After All These Years,* a West German documentary about a town that had once been half Jewish. The older inhabitants remembered the Third Reich as an embarrassing drunken spree in which otherwise good people acted as perhaps they shouldn't have, but that was a long time ago, and in any case, they'd been punished for it by the war; there seemed to be no empathy for the Nazis' victims, as though the centuries-long Jewish presence in Germany was transitory—certainly no great loss.

While *Shoah* documents that anti-Semitic attitudes persist in the very place where millions of Jews were sent, as the Nazis put it, "up the chimney," it has been observed that Lanzmann interviews only one Pole who seems to have helped the Jews. But just as the subject of the film is the Jews who were exterminated, not the handful who survived (hence the absence of escape stories), *Shoah* necessarily focuses on prevailing attitudes rather than exceptional deeds. (In her recently published *When Light Pierced the Darkness: Christian Rescue of Jews in Nazi-Occupied Poland,* Nechama Tec points out that the Polish Gentiles most apt to risk their lives to help Jews were almost invariably—albeit in wildly different ways—extraordinary, nonconforming individuals, and, in group terms, peasants were the class least likely to offer assistance.

Anyone familiar with the history of pre-World War II Poland knows that, during the 1930s, traditional anti-Semitism was elevated to a quasi-official policy. Anyone familiar with the history of postwar Poland knows that 1968 saw a quasi-sanctioned anti-Semitic campaign resulting in the emigration of some 30,000 remaining Polish Jews (most of them assimilated, many of them Communists). And anyone who followed developments during the 18 months of Solidarity is aware that—even in the absence of a Jewish community—anti-Semitic rhetoric surfaced in both the union and the party. Yet, according to *Variety,* representatives of Polish TV collected the peasants interviewed and had them confess that they were paid by Lanzmann to make up their anti-Semitic remarks.

Kael is only a few steps behind this assertion that *Shoah* is a fabrication. In one of the most remarkable passages in her review, she implies that, "eager to seize on signs of ignorance and prejudice," Lanzmann is somehow responsible for what he has uncovered. Obviously the Polish authorities were embarrassed that Lanzmann could stand outside a church in which, 40-odd years before, the town Jews were rounded up, beaten, and then transported to nearby gas chambers, and find a large crowd of worshipers ready to characterize that event as punishment for the Jews' murder of Christ. But why would an American critic find this excessive, even phony—an attempt to con the audience with, as Kael puts it, "Woody Allen's convention of village idiots"? (And why, one might well ask, Woody Allen?)

The essential question here is one of identification. If one doesn't identify with the Jews in *Shoah,* one is left with the Poles—stand-ins for the rest of the world, which was not, after all, unduly preoccupied with the fate of European Jewry at the hands of the Nazis. Indeed, in its structure *Shoah* encourages the viewer to identify with the victims. As Timothy Garton Ash wrote in *The New York Review of Books* in a piece that's extremely well-informed on precisely the issue of Polish anti-Semitism and *Shoah*'s representation of it: "This deadly repetition, this exhaustion, this *having* to sit through it, is an essential part of Lanzmann's creation. He deliberately uses the dictatorial powers of the director to lock you in a cattle wagon and send you for nine and a half hours down the line to Auschwitz." (The implications of this can return in the least-expected contexts. Watching the latest, sub-Spielberg remake of *King Solomon's Mines*—a succession of death-defying, exhilaratingly narrow escapes—I was suddenly reminded of *Shoah,* a film about death in which, over and over, no one ever escapes.)

This may contribute to the objections I've heard about Lanzmann himself, his "arrogance" and "self-indulgence." Yes, he is single-minded, relentless, and sometimes abrasive. So are many filmmakers, but Lanzmann has the guts to show himself thus on the screen—it's necessary to his method. (Marcel Ophuls—who called *Shoah* "the greatest documentary on contemporary history ever made"—writes, "for a Jewish filmmaker to ingratiate himself in this particular context would have been akin to the frantic, laughable, and eventually unsuccessful attempts of so many of our elders to blend into the landscape.")

When people refer to Lanzmann as tasteless or pushy, as a fetishist or a ghoul, who do they really mean? In the wake of Bitburg, it should be evident that Jews, Jewish suffering, Jewish moral indignation are no longer fashionable. On the contrary. You can read the boredom in

Richard Corliss's glib lead in *Time*: "Why is this holocaust different from all other holocausts?" Although Corliss eventually gets around to fashioning a sort of answer to the question, his first suggestion is that the distinguishing factor may simply be publicity—"in raw nightmare numbers, the Nazi extermination of the Jews ranks below the Soviet Union's systematic starvation of the rebellious Ukraine in 1932–33 [10 million by Stalin's count] . . ." Typically, Kael is a lot more blunt. "*Shoah* is a long moan," she wrotes. "It's saying 'We've always been oppressed, and we'll be oppressed again.'"

If Kael misses Lanzmann's carefully constructed point about the uniqueness of the Holocaust (in Jewish as well as world history), her profoundly hostile reaction—perceiving the film as a stand-in for paranoid Jews wallowing in self-pity—suggests a view of the Holocaust I believe more widespread than generally acknowledged. On one hand, the Jews are faulted for passively going to their doom; on the other, for making themselves tiresome by refusing to shut up about it. Both charges blame the victim; both have a dialectical engagement with what could be termed the Gentile world's indifference. Dwelling on the minutiae of genocide, the nexus of events (including—does one really have to say it?—European anti-Semitism) that made the Final Solution possible, *Shoah* is the most ambitious attempt ever to make the extermination of the Jews tangible. For Lanzmann, the Holocaust was an impossible, perhaps incomprehensible event—requiring time and effort and a multitude of facts to begin to understand it. For Kael, his entire enterprise can be reduced to "a Jew's pointing a finger at the Gentile world and crying, 'You low-lifes—you want to kill us!'"

Given her contempt for *Shoah*'s "lack of moral complexity," the coarseness of Kael's own formulations are astonishing. "If you set him loose," she writes of Lanzmann, "he could probably find anti-Semitism anywhere." Imagine, he actually found anti-Semitism at Treblinka. Who knows, if he's not tied up again, he might even find it in *The New Yorker.*

95

CLAUDE LANZMANN WITH MARC CHEVRIE AND HERVÉ LE ROUX

SITE AND SPEECH

An Interview with Claude Lanzmann about *Shoah* (1985)

Claude Lanzmann: I have already said many things about *Shoah,* but I would very much like to talk about it as a film. Certain people have irritated me a lot: it is as if, having discovered things that took place yesterday, they are so over-whelmed by the horror that they develop a kind of sacred and religious attitude toward it and do not see the film itself. One has to understand why and how this horror is transmitted. In truth, I myself have difficulty in speaking about this because I can talk about it only in a circular fashion, as the film itself is constructed that way, and it remains in many respects opaque and mysterious. I will explain *Shoah,* using examples from *Shoah,* in a book I will write. Above all to tell the story of these ten years, in truth more than ten years since I began to work on it in 1974.

1. To See and to Know

Cahiers: *How did the project come about? From what starting point?*

C. Lanzmann: I began by reading, for a year, every book of history that I could find on the subject, everything to be found by going through the archives—the written archives, not the photo archives. And I assessed the extent of my ignorance. Today Jews who do not want to go see the film say, "We know all about this." They make me laugh. They know nothing; they know only one thing: that six million Jews were killed, that's all. That is not interesting!

I did not know at all how I was going to proceed. I was obliged to make up budgets in order to get the money, and they always asked me, "What is your conception [of the film]?" That was the most absurd question: *I did not have any conception.* I knew that there would not be any archival materials in it. I had some personal obsessions, and I knew from the very moment I began that it would be difficult to make me let go of it. But the question about my conception was an abstract question, a historian's question, one that was meaningless. I therefore began by accumulating a great deal of bookish, theoretical knowledge. Afterward, armed with this knowledge that was not my own, this secondhand knowledge, and quaking a bit, I started to look for, to seek out witnesses. And I did not want just any witnesses. There are many deportees. There are swarms of them, as an anti-Semite would say. But I wanted very specific types—those who had been in the very charnel houses of the extermination, direct witnesses of the death of their people: the people of the "special squads."[1] I began to meet them.

I was like someone who has little talent for dancing but who takes lessons—as I did twenty years ago—and then tries and does not make it. There is an absolute gap between the bookish knowledge I had acquired and what these people told me. I understood nothing. First of all, it was difficult getting them to speak. Not that they refused to speak. Some were crazy and incapable of conveying anything. They had lived through experiences so extreme that they could not communicate anything. The first time I saw Srebnik, the survivor of Chelmno, who was thirteen during the period—these were very young people—he gave me an account that was so extraordinarily confused that I understood nothing at all. He had lived through so much horror that it had destroyed him. I therefore proceeded by trial and error. I went to the places, alone, and I perceived that one had to combine things. One must know and see, and one must see in order to know. These two aspects can't be separated. If you go to Auschwitz without knowing anything about Auschwitz and the history of the camp, you will see nothing, you will understand nothing. In the same way, if you know without having been there, you will also not understand anything. It therefore requires a combination of the two. That is why the issue of the site is so important. I did not make an idealist film; it is not a film with grand metaphysical or theological reflections about why all this happened to the Jews, why they killed them. This is a film from the ground up, a topographical film, a geographical film.

Cahiers: *Yes, there are very precise notions of place, for example what the Nazi says about the narrow passageway at Treblinka,*[2] *and at the same time an absence of traces.*

C. Lanzmann: That's where I made the film. The sites I saw were disfigured, effaced. They were "non-sites" of memory [*non-lieux de mémoire*].[3] The places no longer resembled what they had been. I had shots (for example, those of Treblinka). And I had models (for example, the plaster model of the people descending into the gas chamber). I therefore made a film with the landscapes of today, with the present-day shots and models. A film in which one moves from a shot of a contemporary landscape, from a speech sounding over a contemporary landscape, to the model of a gas chamber, which often imbues it with an extraordinary power, and which is derived from the extreme internal sense of urgency I felt to understand and to imagine it all. These extremely detailed questions make the film powerful and vital.

Cahiers: *The film was made from a will to know and to communicate, all the while knowing that there will always be a part that . . .*

C. Lanzmann: . . . cannot be conveyed. Absolutely! That is why the American series *Holocaust* was rubbish in every respect.[4] Fictionalizing such a history is the most serious sort of transgression: it shows the Jews entering the gas chambers, arm in arm, stoically, as if they were Romans. It's

Socrates drinking the hemlock. These are idealist images that permit all kinds of reassuring identifications. *Shoah*, however, is anything but reassuring.

Cahiers: *What's very powerful about the film is how it was made in the face of its own impossibility.*

C. Lanzmann: That's a very accurate observation about the film, because I started precisely with the impossibility of recounting this history. I placed this impossibility at the very beginning of my work. When I started the film, I had to deal with, on the one hand, the disappearance of the traces: there was nothing at all, sheer nothingness, and I had to make a film on the basis of this nothingness. And on the other hand, with the impossibility of telling this story even by the survivors themselves; the impossibility of speaking, the difficulty—which can be seen throughout the film—of giving birth to and the impossibility of naming it: its unnameable character. That is why I had so much trouble finding a title. Over the years, I thought of different titles. I had one that I liked a lot but it was a bit abstract: *Site and Speech*. There was a provisional title that I did not come upon myself because the film did not have one, but I was obliged to name it for the CNC:[5] *Death in the Fields*. I remember when I first said that I was going to tackle this project, a very dear friend who is now dead, Gershom Scholem in Jerusalem—a great Kabbalist—said, "It is impossible to make this film." He even believed to a certain extent that it should not be made. And in truth, yes, it was impossible and highly improbable to produce it and to succeed in doing so.

2. The Absence of Archives

Cahiers: *Was the absence of archival images foreseen from the beginning?*

C. Lanzmann: What do we have as archival material? There are two periods. The period between 1933 and 1939, during which the Jews in Germany were persecuted, not killed, but persecuted. There are photographs: of Nazis burning books, of the Storm Troopers, of *Kristallnacht* in 1938. And suddenly the war. One no longer knew anything about the people under German control; they were cut off from the world. For this period there are two or three little propaganda films shot by the Nazis themselves, the PK—the Propaganda Companies of the German army and the [Nazi] party—in the Warsaw Ghetto, where they had opened phony cabarets and forced the women to wear makeup, where they staged scenes in order to show that life was all right and that the Jews were hedonists. Other than this and some photographs of the Warsaw cemetery with handcarts transporting the cadavers, there is nothing. About the extermination strictly speaking there is *nothing*. For a very simple reason: it was categorically forbidden. The Nazis kept the extermination secret, so much so that Himmler formed a special squad, Commando 1005, composed of young Jews selected because they were sturdier than the others from among the death convoys that arrived. They made them open the trenches and erect gigantic pyres that burned for days, as the film says, in order to make the traces disappear. The problem of getting rid of the traces was therefore crucial in every respect.

The only thing I found—and I really saw everything—was a little film lasting a minute and a half by a German soldier named Wiener (whom I located and spoke to). It is the execution of Jews at Liepaja in Latvia. In it one sees—it is silent—a truck arrive, a group of Jews get out and run to an antitank ditch, where they are shot by a machine gun. It is nothing at all. Like such a film, Nazi images of the ghetto (that have since been combined with all kinds of sauces; one always sees the same ones without any indication that they are propaganda images) are not intended to say anything; in a certain sense, one sees such things every day. I call these "images without imagination." They are just images that have no power.

There were therefore no archival images. And even if there had been some, I don't much like montages of archival images. I don't like the voice-over commenting on the images or photographs as if it were the voice of institutionalized knowledge. One can say whatever one wants, the voice-over imposes a knowledge that does not surge directly from what one sees; and one does not have the right to explain to the spectator what he must understand. The structure of a film must itself determine its own intelligibility. That is why I knew and decided very early on that there would be no archival documents in the film. I have them: I have a mass of photos that come from the Institute for the Second World War in Warsaw. They do not mean anything. One had to make a film from life, exclusively in the present tense.

Cahiers: *Exactly, the film is made entirely of words and gestures around a kind of blind spot that is the absence of the images it speaks about.*

C. Lanzmann: Absolutely. But as a result, it is more thoroughly evocative and powerful than everything else. It so happens that I have met people who are convinced they saw images in the film, ones they hallucinated. The film forces the imagination to work. Someone wrote to me and, moreover, did so magnificently: "It was the first time I heard the cry of an infant in a gas chamber." That is how powerfully the sensation was evoked by the words.

Cahiers: *How were the interviews one sees in the film produced? Over what length of time?*

C. Lanzmann: There are three kinds of characters in the film: the Jews, the Nazis, and the witnesses (the Poles). Insofar as the Nazis are concerned, that is a story in itself. The presence of each Nazi in the film is a miracle. For the others, the primary difficulty—which meant that the interviews had to be very long, much longer than those in the film—was that the people had trouble speaking. One can see this in the scene with the barber who cut the hair of women arriving at the gas chamber. At the start, his discourse is sort of neutral and flat. He communicates things, but he does so poorly—first of all because it was very painful for him and he only conveyed things intellectually. He evaded my questions. When I said to him, "What was your first impression when you saw all these naked women and children coming for the first time?" he turned away and did not respond. It became interesting the moment when, in the second part of the interview, he repeated the same thing but in a different way, when I placed him in the situation and said to him, "How did you do it? Imitate the gestures that you made." He grabbed his customer's hair (whose hair would have been cut long before if the barber had really been cutting his hair, since the scene lasts twenty minutes!). And from this moment on, truth became incarnate, and as he relived the scene, his knowledge became carnal. It is a film about the incarnation of truth. That's a cinematic scene. Because in reality he wasn't a barber any longer: he was retired. I rented a hairdressing salon and told him, "We're going to shoot there." I found him in New York and I filmed him in Israel because he had left New York and now lived there. I knew that it would be difficult and I wanted to place him once again in a situation where his *gestures* would be identical. Every expression of feeling demonstrates something, and conversely, every proof of this sort is itself a form of emotion.

3. To Frame Is to Excavate

Cahiers: Mise-en-scène *therefore plays a role. That means that truth cannot emerge from archival images, but from restaging.*

C. Lanzmann: There are a lot of staged scenes in the film. It is not a documentary. The locomotive at Treblinka is *my* locomotive. I rented it at Polish Railways, which was not so easy to do, just as it was not a simple matter to insert it into the traffic schedule.

Cahiers: *Exactly. In the structure of the film there are pivotal elements: images of trains, of freight trains. There is the idea of retracing not only the gestures but also the routes, the journeys.*

C. Lanzmann: I wanted to do so at all cost. Treblinka is a triage station: there are trains, the boxcars—the *same* ones—are there, and it's shocking to see them. I filmed them from top to bottom; I got up into the trains and we filmed, filmed without exactly knowing what I was going to do with the material.

Cahiers: *You even filmed from the interior of the boxcars, from the point of view of the Jews arriving in Treblinka. You crossed the line with a very violent cinematic act.*

C. Lanzmann: It's one of the things that I have trouble understanding today. It was the middle of winter. I said, "Let's get into the boxcar and film the sign for Treblinka." The distance between past and present was abolished, and everything became real for me. The real is opaque; it is the true configuration of the impossible. What does it mean to film reality? Making images from reality is to dig holes in reality. Framing a scene involves excavating it. The problem of the image is to create a hollow space within a full image. I had another terrible time at Birkenau: the cameraman trembled as he executed a handheld tracking shot while descending the steps into the crematorium, and he fell and smashed his face. I reshot what he had done. I was petrified by the truth and the pain. The first time I went to Treblinka, I did not yet have in my head a conception of the film and I said to myself, "What's the point of filming all this?" Then, since I am not very imaginative and have little gift for fictionalizing, I could not shoot anything but the reality before me. I went back there and filmed the stones like a madman.

Cahiers: *About the train: there was also the idea of having the driver play his former role and to make the terrifying gesture of cutting his throat. I had the impression that he did so on his own.*

C. Lanzmann: Exactly. I found him by chance. It was in winter, in Treblinka. Night had already fallen, and I was going around the farms looking for witnesses. It was the first time that I had come to Poland. At the beginning, I did not want to come. I thought much like one of the women in the film who, when I asked her, "Haven't you ever returned to Poland?" responded, "What would I see there? Nothing is left." I thought that the destruction of Judaism in Eastern Europe was like the destruction of a forest. Once a forest is destroyed, the climatic conditions are altered for kilometers around. I said to myself that Poland is a non-site of memory and that this history had been "diasporized," that one could recount it anywhere—in Paris, New York, or Corfu. Poland had become a sort of eye of the hurricane where I could not go.

Then I arrived at Treblinka, and I saw the camp and these symbolic commemorative stones. I discovered that there was a train station and a village called Treblinka. The sign for "Treblinka" on the road, the very act of naming it, was an incredible shock for me. Suddenly, it all became true. These places have become so charged with horror that they have become "legendary." Right then and there I went beyond my theoretical knowledge of the legends that could exist only in my own imagination, and into a confrontation with the real. In going to the farms, I noticed that when given the opportunity, the Poles began to speak about this history as a kind of legendary experience. I perceived that it was very alive in their consciousness, that scars had not yet formed. They spoke to me about the conductor of a locomotive. I arrived at his house at ten o'clock at night, at a farm 10 kilometers from Treblinka, where he lived with his wife. There were crucifixes all around. He received me with an extreme gentleness, he hid nothing from me, and I set about speaking with him without giving everything away in advance.

Cahiers: *Have you always adopted such an approach: so as not to give away in advance what is to go on in front of the camera?*

C. *Lanzmann*: Absolutely. When I had the locomotive and came back to film him, I said to him, "You are to get up into the locomotive and we are going to film the arrival at Treblinka." I said nothing else. We arrived at the station; he was there, leaning out, and on his own, he made this unbelievable gesture at his throat while looking at the imaginary boxcars (behind the locomotive, of course, there were no boxcars). Compared to this image, archival photographs become unbearable. This image has become what is true. Subsequently, when I filmed the peasants, they all made this gesture, which they said was a warning, but it was really a sadistic gesture.

Cahiers: *Did you ask that they do so?*

C. *Lanzmann:* It was a collective gesture. I induced them to make it and they did so voluntarily. We learn about it via a detour, by returning to the survivor, Glazar, who witnessed it—they had made it to him—and to other Polish witnesses who made the gesture. At this moment everything becomes clear: the film is based on corroboration, hence its length: the truth is constantly attested to at different levels; one must dig for it. At the same time, correspondences emerge because I always posed the same questions. The circularity of the film is derived from the obsessional character of my questions, my personal obsessions: the cold, the fear of the East (the West for me is human; the East scares the hell out of me). I became aware that I asked everyone these questions: about the cold, always the cold, the idea that these people waited for death in this passageway, that they drove them on with lashes of the whip.

But to return to this idea of drilling [for truth], of archaeology, and of its importance for the editing: there is a tracking shot in a car through the little village of Wlodawa where the guy, very gently and quietly, explains that there was a Jewish home here, and over there a Jewish shop. I had to be satisfied with this. And one day, during my second "Polish campaign," while going to Chelmno I saw a sign: Grabów. I had read in Poliakov's book[6] the letter of the rabbi of Grabów that I read in the film. I stopped and I decided to return to film there. This scene seemed to come from a real Western: the wooden houses, the types of people sitting on their front doorsteps, the women looking out from behind the curtains. The fact that I arrived there with a camera and a team must have made me look something like a lawman coming to demand justice. They experienced it that way. In comparison with Wlodawa, where the guy took me around and showed me the Jewish houses, it was the same story, except that here I questioned those who lived in the houses: I got into greater depth. And the old medieval Christian anti-Semitism of the Polish peasants became blatant. If I had placed this scene at the beginning, the film would have been polemical, violent, aggressive, but such things needed to be discovered gradually.

Cahiers: *That is also what differentiates the staging from the "reassuring"* mise-en-scène *of* Holocaust.

C. *Lanzmann*: Yes. *Shoah* is a fiction rooted in reality [*fiction du réel*], which is something entirely different.

4. The Paradox of Character

Cahiers: *The first sentence—it is written—in the film is: "The action begins . . ." and further on, a subtitle describes one of the people interviewed as the "next character," that is, in fictional terms.*

C. *Lanzmann:* Fictional, yes, or theatrical. It is as if saying, "by order of appearance on stage."

Cahiers: *Yes, even while refusing a fiction of the* Holocaust *variety, you describe a person who is there, in front of us, who has experienced certain events, as if he were a character.*

C. *Lanzmann:* They are the protagonists of the film.

Cahiers: *The characters of History?*

C. *Lanzmann:* Yes, not the characters in a reconstruction [of the past], because the film is not one, but in a certain way these people had to be transformed into actors. They recount their own history. But just retelling it is not enough.They had to act it out, that is, they had to give themselves over [*irréalisent*] to it.

That's what defines imagination: it de-realizes. That's what the entire paradox of the actor is about. They have to be put into a certain state of mind but also into a certain physical disposition. Not in order to make them speak, but so that their speech can suddenly communicate, become charged with an extra dimension.

The film is not made out of memories, I knew that right away. Memory horrifies me: recollections are weak. The film is the abolition of all distance between past and present; I relive this history in the present. One sees memories every day on television: the guys with ties behind their desks who talk about things. Nothing is more annoying. It is through staging that they become characters. I found a guy from the *Sonderkommando* at Auschwitz, a Hungarian Jew who arrived there in 1944 and who was immediately led to the crematorium at a moment when there was a glut of traffic since they had to kill 450,000 Jews in two and a half months, and instead of burning the Jews in the ovens, they burned them in immense pits. This guy arrived there from a ghetto. You can imagine the shock. Terrifying. When I found him, he was a butcher in a little town in Israel. He was the most taciturn, the most silent man I have ever known. I came to see him many times and we spoke about present-day matters. I finally dragged out of him that the only thing he really liked to do was to go to the seashore and fish. I also like to fish, and I said to myself, "When I come back to film him, I will take a fishing pole and we'll go fishing together and try to talk." I could not do so because he was dead before I could return. But it was precisely through such a maneuver, by fishing together today, above all because it no longer involved remembering, that he would have become a character.

The barber also became a character because he was no longer a barber. The simple fact of filming in the present allows these people to pass from the status of witnesses to History to that of actors. When I conducted the interview with Filip Müller, who tells the story of the massacre of the Czech family camp in the second part of the film, it was very difficult. At first he did not want to speak. I filmed with him over the course of three days, and presenting the discussion as it occurred was out of the question. But I edited his words, his voice, setting them over the contemporary landscapes, constantly moving back and forth from synch-sound to voice-over. When I used voice-over, the difficulty was to preserve the interior rhythm of the voice even as I refined it. The transition from on- to off-screen sound is fundamental to the film: the voice exists over the landscape and they reinforce each other. The landscape lends the words an entirely different dimension, and the words reanimate the landscape.With Filip Müller I did not stage anything; it was impossible: I placed him on his sofa and began to film. But the staging is created by the editing.

5. Montage: The Method and Its Object

Cahiers: *Did you know very quickly that the film would be so long?*

C. Lanzmann: I did not know how much time I would need to do it, but very quickly it seemed to me that it would be no less than six hours long. There were content requirements—there were some fundamental things that I had to say—and formal requirements, architectural considerations that made it so long. It could have been longer: I shot 350 hours of footage. Of these 350 hours, roughly speaking, about 100 had to be jettisoned: silent shots, the beginnings of the interviews, things that were ruined. But there were also magnificent things. It broke my heart not to use them in the editing, yet at the same time, not so much. The film took shape as I made it, and an underlying form shaped all that followed. Even if it was something very important, abandoning some things did not make me suffer too much, since the general architecture compelled me to do so. I was absolutely driven crazy during the editing by problems of length. I said to myself, "If it's too long, who will go to see it?" I was reluctant to make three films, each three hours long, since I said to myself, "No, the film is round, a circular film, and it must end as it began." The end of the first film is a gas van traveling, a contemporary Saurer[7] van. And the second film ends the same way, except that it is no longer a van but a train.

Cahiers: *How did the architecture of the film emerge from the enormous quantity of material you had?*

C. Lanzmann: That was terrifying. It took five and a half years to edit. It was like being on the north face of a peak and having to invent a way up, to devise a route to the top. I had to invent both the method and the object. I had first of all to internalize this immense amount of material. I started by deciphering and typing all the speeches, everything that was said: 5,000 or 6,000 pages of text. And I had to learn the images. I began by shutting myself up for a month in a house with one of the women who worked with me, and then with the principal editor in order to develop a tentative structure. I constructed a film of four and a half hours exclusively about Chelmno. Now, the film had to be a structure encompassing everything. At the same time, all these attempts and mistakes were a way to learn the material: I had to go through this process. After I constructed the first half hour, the form emerged and hinted at the rest that was virtually present. But I had to make progress, to go forward. The construction is a symphonic construction with themes that are initiated and then shift at pivotal moments that I will tell about in the book. These led me to make a lot of progress. For example, the history of the Jewish cemetery at Auschwitz: two million Jews were killed there, and the only thing that remains is the cemetery of the Jews who formerly lived there. All the attempts at theoretical constructions were absurd and failed. I did not immediately come upon the idea to end the first film by returning to the beginning, with the first survivor of Chelmno, or to put the ghetto at the end. I was obliged to make the film with what I had: there were wonderful scenes that constituted pivot points around which I had to construct the film—for example, the massacre of the family camp when Filip Müller breaks down and cries. It is a major story because it incarnates what for me are a lot of fundamental issues: knowledge and ignorance, deceit, violence, resistance. The same for the ghetto: I had this Pole[8] who visited it and I had to integrate this part. When I say that I constructed the film with what I had, this means that the film is not a product or derivative of the Holocaust; it is not a historical film: it is a sort of original event, since I filmed it in the present and I myself had to construct it with traces of traces, with what was powerful in what I had shot. The structure is rooted in several complicated logics.

The difficulty was that there is no concessive proposition in cinema: you cannot say "although." You can say that in a book, via a detour in a sentence, but if you want to say it in a film, what you want to *insert* immediately becomes a kind of absolute, killing what precedes it and determining what will follow.

Cahiers: *That becomes a major proposition.*

C. Lanzmann: Yes, and I confronted this difficulty during the entire time it took to edit. I had to preserve the general architecture of the film and, once the sequence was edited, I had to reproject everything that preceded it to see how it connected. At times I discovered that the sequence was too linear, that it became boring or intolerable, and that I had to interrupt it by inserting something else. For example, when I questioned the peasants at Treblinka, I asked the fat guy—this guy was a pig—if he remembered the first convoy of Jews coming from Warsaw on the 22nd of July 1942. He said that he remembered it very well and then forgot that we were speaking about the first convoy and placed it in the routine course of the extermination, among the convoys that he saw arrive every day. And, moreover, there is the guy from the station at Sobibor who speaks of the silence ("the ideal silence") after the arrival of the first convoy. Logically, I should have placed it at the end. I tried to do so but the difference between the manner of the two men's accounts was too large: they did not come together at all. The fat guy put himself into the logic of routine while the other, by his comment about the silence, suddenly became conscious of having been a witness to an unprecedented event. He takes on this almost legendary tone I was speaking about a moment ago. I was keen that he be in the film, but I did not know where to put him. It was only further on that I placed him, after listening to the Nazis who explained the urgency of beginning the extermination, the fact that there were too many bodies they did not know what to do with and too many living people who had not yet been killed. It is a parenthesis in the logic of the film, but it is very important that it does not come immediately after the fat guy's statements. It was also important to place the ghetto at the end, after one knows how radical and total death was, in order to show that the logic of the ghettos, where one starved to death, was part of the extermination process.

There was another reason: in order for there to be a tragedy, and also in order for there to be suspense, you have to know the end at the beginning. You have to know what will happen, all the while having the feeling that this should not happen. That's what Sartre called "the defeatist tone" in American crime films like *Double Indemnity*[9] after the war. The structure was also dictated by questions of morality. I did not have the right to bring about a meeting between characters. It was out of the question that the Nazis would meet with the Jews—not that I would have gotten them to meet physically, which would have been more than obscene, but even that I would make them meet through the editing. These are not former combatants who meet forty years later on television for a virile handshake. That is why the first Nazi enters only after two hours have gone by. No one encounters anyone else in the film. Neither do Jews and Poles, except the survivor of Chelmno.[10] At the church he is there, silent; he understands everything and he is terrorized by them, as he was as a child. And then he is alone in the forest clearing. He is split: he does not even meet himself.

Cahiers: *How did you think about the audience and the extent of its knowledge when you were constntcting the film?*

C. Lanzmann: That's a real question, and one that increasingly imposed itself since I refused all commentary. The film is absolutely historically rigorous. You can say to me, "You have not dealt with this or that." I know. But one cannot take me to task. There are a thousand things that I dealt with and filmed but did not edit into the film. And there are some things that I did not deal with for the simple reason that, in certain cases, the destruction succeeded and there are entire episodes where there is no one, not a single witness, nothing. But it is an important question: What does the audience know? What does it not know? Up to what point may one preserve the mystery? Finally I said to myself that I did not have to say everything, that people ought to ask questions. The film is made so that the people continue to work at it—during the screening, but also afterward. The massacre of the family camp (why did they keep them for six months before killing them?), even if one roughly knows the reasons, remains mysterious. One must preserve the mystery and make the imagination work: one does not have to explain everything.

NOTES

1. Lanzmann is referring to the so-called *Sonderkommandos*, composed of Jewish prisoners who were forced to operate the crematoria, instruct the victims about "the showers," then clear and incinerate the bodies, etc.–Tr.
2. This passageway was also known as the *Schlauch* or *Himmelfahrtsweg* and is discussed in *Shoah* by Suchomel, a German guard at Treblinka, as well as by former prisoners Abraham Bomba and Richard Glazar. –Tr.
3. Lanzmann is referring to the famous collective historical project on national memorial sites in France, *Les Lieuxde mémoire*, edited by the French historian Pierre Nora (Paris: Éditions Gallimard, 1984). –Tr.
4. The television series *Holocaust*, written by Gerald Greene and directed by Marvin Chomsky, aired in 1978 in the United States and provoked an enormous response in West Germany and other European countries. –Tr.
5. Le Centre National de la Cinématographie. –Tr.
6. French historian Léon Poliakov wrote *Bréviaire de la haine: le IIIe Reich et les Juifs*, preface by François Mauriac (Paris: Calmann-Lévy, 1951), among many other books. –Tr.
7. The German firm Saurer made the gas vans used in Chelmno and elsewhere. –Tr.
8. Lanzmann is referring to Jan Karski, a courier of the Polish Underground Army who was charged by Jewish leaders in the Warsaw Ghetto to report his eyewitness accounts of ghetto conditions and the facts of the extermination camps when, in late 1942, Karski managed to travel clandestinely to the West. His discussions with Churchill, Eden, Roosevelt, and Frankfurter, among others, proved fruitless. These are recounted in his classic *Story of a Secret State* (Boston: Houghton Mifflin, 1944), pp. 320ff. –Tr.
9. Directed by the German Jewish refugee Billy Wilder and released in the United States in 1944, *Double Indemnity* starred Fred MacMurray, Barbara Stanwyck, and Edward G. Robinson. –Tr.
10. Lanzmann is referring to Simon Srebnik, the boy singer of Chelmno, the first survivor we meet in *Shoah*. –Tr.

LINDA WILLIAMS

MIRRORS WITHOUT MEMORIES

Truth, History, and the New Documentary (1993)

The August 12th, 1990 Arts and Leisure section of *The New York Times* carried a lead article with a rather arresting photograph of Franklin Roosevelt flanked by Winston Churchill and Groucho Marx. Standing behind them was a taut-faced Sylvester Stallone in his Rambo garb. The photo illustrated the major point of the accompanying article by Andy Grundberg: that the photograph—and by implication the moving picture as well—is no longer, as Oliver Wendell Holmes once put it, a "mirror with a memory" illustrating the visual truth of objects, persons, and events but a manipulated construction. In an era of electronic and computer-generated images, the camera, the article sensationally proclaims, "can lie."

In this photo, the anachronistic flattening out of historical referents, the trivialization of history itself, with the popular culture icons of Groucho and Rambo rubbing up against Roosevelt and Churchill, serves almost as a caricature of the state of representation some critics have chosen to call postmodern. In a key statement, Fredric Jameson has described the "cultural logic of postmodernism" as a "new depthlessness, which finds its prolongation both in contemporary 'theory' and in a whole new culture of the image or the simulacrum" (Jameson, 1984, 58). To Jameson, the effect of this image culture is a weakening of historicity. Lamenting the loss of the grand narratives of modernity, which he believes once made possible the political actions of individuals representing the interests of social classes, Jameson argues that it no longer seems possible to represent the "real" interests of a people or a class against the ultimate ground of social and economic determinations.

While not all theorists of postmodernity are as disturbed as Jameson by the apparent loss of the referent, by the undecidabilities of representation accompanied by an apparent paralysis of the will to change, many theorists do share a sense that the enlightenment projects of truth and reason are definitively over. And if representations, whether visual or verbal, no longer refer to a truth or referent "out there," as Trinh T. Minh-ha has put it, for us "in here" (Trinh, 83), then we seem to be plunged into a permanent state of the self-reflexive crisis of representation. What was once a "mirror with a memory" can now only reflect another mirror.

Perhaps because so much faith was once placed in the ability of the camera to reflect objective truths of some fundamental social referent—often construed by the socially relevant documentary film as records of injustice or exploitation of powerless common people—the loss of faith in the objectivity of the image seems to point, nihilistically, like the impossible memory of the meeting of the fictional Rambo and the real Roosevelt, to the brute and cynical disregard of ultimate truths.

Yet at the very same time, as any television viewer and moviegoer knows, we also exist in an era in which there is a remarkable hunger for documentary images of the real. These images proliferate in the *vérité* of on-the-scene cops programs in which the camera eye merges with the eye of the law to observe the violence citizens do to one another. Violence becomes the very emblem of the real in these programs. Interestingly, violent trauma has become the emblem of the real in the new *vérité* genre of the independent amateur video, which, in the case of George Holliday's tape of the Rodney King beating by L.A. police, functioned to contradict the eye of the law and to intervene in the "cops'" official version of King's arrest. This home video might be taken to represent the other side of the postmodern distrust of the image: here the camera tells the truth in a remarkable moment of *cinema vérité* which then becomes valuable (though not conclusive) evidence in accusations against the L.A. Police Department's discriminatory violence against minority offenders.

The contradictions are rich: on the one hand the postmodern deluge of images seems to suggest that there can be no a priori truth of the referent to which the image refers; on the other hand, in this same deluge, it is still the moving image that has the power to move audiences to a new appreciation of previously unknown truth.

In a recent book on postwar West German cinema and its representations of that country's past, Anton Kaes has written that "[T]he sheer mass of historical images transmitted by today's media weakens the link between public memory and personal experience. The past is in danger of becoming a rapidly expanding collection of images, easily retrievable but isolated from time and space, available in an etemal present by pushing a button on the remote control. History thus retums forever—as film" (Kaes, 198). Recently, the example of history that has been most insistently returning "as film" to American viewers is the assassination of John F. Kennedy as simulated by film-maker Oliver Stone.

Stone's *JFK* might seem a good example of Jameson's and Kaes's worst-case scenarios of the ultimate loss of historical truth amid the postmodern hall of mirrors. While laudably obsessed with exposing the manifest contradictions of the Warren Commission's official version of the Kennedy assassination, Stone's film has been severely criticized for constructing a "countermyth" to the Warren Commission's explanation of what happened. Indeed, Stone's images offer a kind of tragic counter-part to the comic mélange of the *New York Times* photo of Groucho and Roosevelt. Integrating his own reconstruction of the assassination with the famous Zapruder film, whose "objective" reflection of the event is offered as the narrative (if not the legal) clincher in Jim Garrison's argument against the lone assassin theory, Stone mixes Zapruder's real *vérité* with his own simulated *vérité* to construct a grandiose paranoid countermyth of a vast conspiracy by Lyndon Johnson, the C.I.A., and the Joint Chiefs of Staff to carry out a *coup d'état*. With Little hard evidence to back him up, Stone would seem to be a perfect symptom of a postmodern negativity and nihilism toward truth, as if to say:

"We know the Warren Commission made up a story, well, here's another even more dramatic and entertaining story. Since we can't know the truth, let's make up a grand paranoid fiction."

It is not my purpose here to attack Oliver Stone's remarkably effective deployment of paranoia and megalomania; the press has already done a thorough job of debunking his unlikely fiction of a Kennedy who was about to end the Cold War and withdraw from Vietnam.[1] What interests me however, is the positive side of this megalomania: Stone's belief that it is possible to intervene in the process by which truth is constructed; his very real accomplishment in shaking up public perception of an official truth that closed down, rather than opened up, investigation; his acute awareness of how images enter into the production of knowledge. However much Stone may finally betray the spirit of his own investigation into the multiple, contingent, and constructed nature of the representation of history by asking us to believe in too tidy a conspiracy, his *JFK* needs to be taken seriously for its renewal of interest in one of the major traumas of our country's past.

So rather than berate Stone, I would like to contrast this multimillion-dollar historical fiction film borrowing many aspects of the form of documentary to what we might call the low-budget postmodern documentary borrowing many features of the fiction film. My goal in what follows is to get beyond the much remarked self-reflexivity and flamboyant auteurism of these documentaries, which might seem, Rashomon-like, to abandon the pursuit of truth, to what seems to me their remarkable engagement with a newer, more contingent, relative, postmodern truth—a truth which, far from being abandoned, still operates powerfully as the receding horizon of the documentary tradition.

When we survey the field of recent documentary films two things stand out: first, their unprecedented popularity among general audiences, who now line up for documentaries as eagerly as for fiction films; second, their willingness to tackle often grim, historically complex subjects. Errol Morris's *The Thin Blue Line* (1987), about the murder of a police officer and the near execution of the "wrong man," Michael Moore's *Roger and Me* (1989), about the dire effects of General Motors' plant closings, and Ken Burns' 11-hour *The Civil War* (1990), (watched on PBS by 39 million Americans) were especially popular documentaries about uncommonly serious political and social realities. Even more difficult and challenging, though not quite as popular, were *Our Hitler* (Hans-Jürgen Syberberg, 1980), *Shoah* (Claude Lanzmann, 1985), *Hotel Terminus: The Life and Times of KlausBarbie* (Marcel Ophuls, 1987) and *Who Killed Vincent Chin?* (Chris Choy and Renee Tajima, 1988). And in 1991 the list of both critically successful and popular documentary features *not* nominated for Academy Awards—*Paris Is Burning* (Jennie Livingston), *Hearts of Darkness: A Filmmaker's Apocalypse* (Fax Bahr and George Hickenlooper), *35 Up* (Michael Apted), *Truth or Dare* (Alex Keshishian)—was viewed by many as an embarrassment to the Academy. *Village Voice* critic Amy Taubin notes that 1991 was a year in which four or five documentaries made it onto the *Variety* charts; documentaries now mattered in a new way (Taubin, 62).

Though diverse, all the above works participate in a new hunger for reality on the part of a public seemingly saturated with Hollywood fiction. Jennie Livingston, director of *Paris Is Burning*, the remarkably popular documentary about gay drag subcultures in New York, notes that the out-of-touch documentaries honored by the Academy all share an old-fashioned earnestness toward their subjects, while the new, more popular documentaries share a more ironic stance toward theirs. Coincident with the hunger for documentary truth is the clear sense that this truth is subject to manipulation and construction by docu-auteurs who, whether on camera (Lanzmann in *Shoah,* Michael Moore in *Roger and Me)* or behind, are forcefully calling the shots.[2]

It is this paradox of the intrusive manipulation of documentary truth, combined with a serious quest to reveal some ultimate truths, that I would like to isolate within a subset of the above films. What interests me particularly is the way a special few of these documentaries handle the problem of figuring traumatic historical truths inaccessible to representation by any simple or single "mirror with a memory," and how this mirror nevertheless operates in complicated and indirect refractions. For while traumatic events of the past are not available for representation by any simple or single "mirror with a memory"—in the *vérité* sense of capturing events as they happen—they do constitute a multifaceted receding horizon which these films powerfully evoke.

I would like to offer Errol Morris's *The Thin Blue Line* as a prime example of this postmodern documentary approach to the trauma of an inaccessible past because of its spectacular success in intervening in the truths known about this past. Morris's film was instrumental in exonerating a man wrongfully accused of murder. In 1976, Dallas police officer Robert Wood was murdered, apparently by a 28-year-old drifter named Randall Adams. Like Stone's *JFK, The Thin Blue Line* is a film about a November murder in Dallas. Like *JFK,* the film argues that the wrong man was set up by a state conspiracy with an interest in convicting an easy scapegoat rather than prosecuting the real murderer. The film—the "true" story of Randall Adams, the man convicted of the murder of Officer Wood, and his accuser David Harris, the young hitchhiker whom Adams picked up the night of the murder—ends with Harris's cryptic but dramatic confession to the murder in a phone conversation with Errol Morris.

Stylistically, *The Thin Blue Line* has been most remarked for its film-noirish beauty, its apparent abandonment of *cinéma-vérité* realism for studied, often slow-motion, and highly expressionistic reenactments of different witnesses' versions of the murder to the tune of Philip Glass's hypnotic score. Like a great many recent documentaries obsessed with traumatic events of the past, *The Thin Blue Line* is self-reflexive. Like many of these new documentaries, it is acutely aware that the individuals whose lives are caught up in events are not so much self- coherent and consistent identities as they are actors in competing narratives. As in *Roger and Me, Shoah,* and, to a certain extent, *Who Killed Vincent Chin?,* the documentarian's role in constructing and staging these competing narratives thus becomes paramount.[3] In place of the self-obscuring voyeur of *vérité* realism, we encounter, in these and other films, a new presence in the persona of the documentarian.

For example, in one scene, David Harris, the charming young accuser whose testimony placed Randall Adams on death row and who has been giving his side of the story in alternate sections of the film from Adams, scratches his head while recounting an unimportant incident from his past. In this small gesture, Morris dramatically reveals information withheld until this moment: Harris's hands are handcuffed. He, like Adams, is in prison. The interviews with him are now subject to reinterpretation since, as we soon learn, he, too, stands accused of murder. For he has committed a senseless murder not unlike the one he accused Adams of committing. At this climactic moment Morris finally brings in the hard evidence against Harris previously withheld: he is a violent psychopath who invaded a man's house, murdered him, and abducted his girlfriend. On top of this Morris adds the local cop's attempt to explain Harris's personal pathology; in the end we hear Harris's own near-confession—in an audio interview—to the murder for which Adams has been convicted. Thus Morris captures a truth, elicits a confession, in the best *vérité* tradition, but only in the context of a film that is manifestly staged and temporally manipulated by the docu-auteur.

It would seem that in Morris's abandonment of voyeuristic objectivity he achieves something more useful to the production of truth. His interviews get the interested parties talking in a special way. In a key statement in defense of his intrusive, self-reflexive style, Morris has attacked the hallowed tradition of *cinéma vérité*: "There is no reason why documentaries can't be as personal as fiction filmmaking and bear the imprint of those who made them. Truth isn't guaranteed by style or expression. It isn't guaranteed by anything" (Morris, 17).

The "personal" in this statement has been taken to refer to the personal, self-reflexive style of the docu-auteur: Morris's hypnotic pace, Glass's music, the vivid colors and slow motion of the multiple reenactments. Yet the interviews too bear this personal imprint of the auteur. Each person who speaks to the camera in *The Thin Blue Line* does so in a confessional, "talking-cure" mode. James Shamus has pointed out that this rambling, free-associating discourse ultimately collides with, and is sacrificed to, the juridical narrative producing the truth of who, finally, is guilty. And Charles Musser also points out that what is sacrificed is the psychological complexity of the man the film finds innocent. Thus the film foregoes investigation into what Adams might have been up to that night taking a 16-year-old hitchhiker to a drive-in movie.[4]

Morris gives us some truths and withholds others. His approach to truth is altogether strategic. Truth exists for Morris because lies exist; if lies are to be exposed, truths must be strategically deployed against them. His strategy in the pursuit of this relative, hierarchized, and contingent truth is thus to find guilty those speakers whom he draws most deeply into the explorations of their past. Harris, the prosecutor Mulder, the false witness Emily Miller, all cozy up to the camera to remember incidents from their past which serve to indict them in the present. In contrast, the man found innocent by the film remains a cipher, we leam almost nothing of his past, and this lack of knowledge appears necessary to the investigation of the official lies. What Morris does, in effect, is partially close down the representation of Adams' own story, the accumulation of narratives from his past, in order to show how convenient a scapegoat he was to the overdetermining pasts of all the other false witnesses. Thus, instead of using fictionalizing techniques to show us the truth of what happened, Morris scrupulously sticks to stylized and silent docudrama reenactments that show only what each witness claims happened.

In contrast, we might consider Oliver Stone's very different use of docudrama reenactments to reveal the "truth" of the existence of several assassins and the plot that orchestrated their activity, in the murder of JFK. Stone has Garrison introduce the Zapruder film in the trial of Clay Shaw as hallowed *vérité* evidence that there had to be more than one assassin. Garrison's examination of the magic bullet's trajectory does a fine dramatic job of challenging the official version of the lone assassin. But in his zealous pursuit of the truth of "who dunnit," Stone matches the *vérité* style of the Zapruder film with a *vérité* simulation which, although hypothesis, has none of the stylized, hypothetical visual marking of Morris's simulations and which therefore commands a greater component of belief. Morris, on the other hand, working in a documentary form that now eschews *vérité* as a style, stylizes his hypothetical reenactments and never offers any of them as an image of what actually happened.

In the discussions surrounding the truth claims of many contemporary documentaries, attention has centered upon the self-reflexive challenge to once hallowed techniques of *vérité*. It has become an axiom of the new documentary that films cannot reveal the truth of events, but only the ideologies and consciousness that construct competing truths—the fictional master narratives by which we make sense of events. Yet too often this way of thinking has led to a forgetting of the way in which these films still are, as Stone's film isn't, documentaries—films with a special interest in the relation to the real, the "truths" which matter in people's lives but which cannot be transparently represented.

One reason for this forgetting has been the erection of a too simple dichotomy between, on the one hand, a naïve faith in the truth of what the documentary image reveals—*vérité's* discredited claim to capturing events while they happen—and on the other, the embrace of fictional manipulation. Of course, even in its heyday no one ever fully believed in an absolute truth of *cinéma vérité*. There are, moreover, many gradations of fictionalized manipulation ranging from the controversial manipulation of temporal sequence in Michael Moore's *Roger and Me* to Errol Morris's scrupulous reconstructions of the subjective truths of events as viewed from many different points of view.

Truth is "not guaranteed" and cannot be transparently reflected by a mirror with a memory, yet some kinds of partial and contingent truths are nevertheless the always receding goal of the documentary tradition. Instead of careening between idealistic faith in documentary truth and cynical recourse to fiction, we do better to define documentary not as an essence of truth but as a set of strategies designed to choose from among a horizon of relative and contingent truths. The advantage, and the difficulty, of the definition is that it holds on to the concept of the real—indeed of a "real" at all—even in the face of tendencies to assimilate documentary entirely into the rules and norms of fiction.

As *The Thin Blue Line* shows, the recognition that documentary access to this real is strategic and contingent does not require a retreat to a Rashomon universe of undecidabilities. This recognition can lead, rather, to a remarkable awareness of the conditions under which it is possible to intervene in the political and cultural construction of truths which, while not guaranteed, nevertheless matter as the narratives by which we live. To better explain this point I would like to further consider the confessional, talking-cure strategy of *The Thin Blue Line* as it relates to Claude Lanzmann's *Shoah*. While I am aware of the incommensurability of a film about the state of Texas's near-execution of an innocent man with the German state's achieved extermination of six million, I want to pursue the comparison because both films are, in very different ways, striking examples of postmodern documentaries whose passionate desire is to intervene in the construction of truths whose totality is ultimately unfathomable.

In both of these films, the truth of the past is traumatic, violent, and unrepresentable in images. It is obscured by official lies masking the responsibility of individual agents in a gross miscarriage of justice. We may recall that Jameson's argument about the postmodern is that it is a loss of a sense of history, of a collective or individual past, and the knowledge of how the past determines the present: "the past as 'referent' finds itself gradually bracketed, and then effaced altogether, leaving us with nothing but texts" (Jameson, 1984, 64). That so many well-known and popular documentary films have taken up the task of remembering the past—indeed that so much popular debate about the "truth" of the past has been engendered by both fiction and documentary films about the past—could therefore be attributed to another of Jameson's points about the postmodern condition: the intensified nostalgia for a past that is already lost.

However, I would argue instead that, certainly in these two films and partially in a range of others, the postmodern suspicion of over-abundant images of an unfolding, present "real" (*vérité*'s commitment to film "it" as "it" happens) has contributed not to new fictionalizations but to paradoxically new historicizations. These historicizations are fascinated by an inaccessible, ever receding, yet newly important past which does have depth.[5] History, in Jameson's sense of traces of the past, of an absent cause which "hurts" (Jameson, 1981, 102), would seem, almost by definition, to be inaccessible to the *vérité* documentary form aimed at capturing action in its unfolding. The recourse to talking-heads interviews, to people remembering the past—whether the collective history of a nation or city, the personal history of individuals, or the criminal event which crucially determines the present—is, in these anti-*vérité* documentaries, an attempt to overturn this commitment to realistically record "life as it is" in favor of a deeper investigation of how it became as it is.

Thus, while there is very little running after the action, there is considerable provocation of action. Even though Morris and Lanzmann have certainly done their legwork to pursue actors in the events they are concerned to represent, their preferred technique is to set up a situation in which the action will come to them. In these privileged moments of *vérité* (for there finally are moments of relative *vérité*) the past repeats. We thus see the power of the past not simply by dramatizing it, or reenacting it, or talking about it obsessively (though these films do all this), but finally by finding its traces, in repetitions and resistances, in the present. It is thus the contextualization of the present with the past that is the most effective representational strategy in these two remarkable films.

Each of these documentaries digs toward an impossible archeology, picking at the scabs of lies which have covered over the inaccessible originary event. The film-makers ask questions, probe circumstances, draw maps, interview historians, witnesses, jurors, judges, police, bureaucrats, and survivors. These diverse investigatory processes augment the single method of the *vérité* camera. They seek to uncover a past the knowledge of which will produce new truths of guilt and innocence in the present. Randall Adams is now free at least partly because of the evidence of Morris's film; the Holocaust comes alive not as some alien horror foreign to all humanity but as something that is, perhaps for the first time on film, understandable as an absolutely banal incremental logic and logistics of train schedules and human silence. The past events examined in these films are not offered as complete, totalizable, apprehensible. They are fragments, pieces of the past invoked by memory, not unitary representable truths but, as Freud once referred to the psychic mechanism of memory, a palimpsest, described succinctly by Mary Ann Doane as "the sum total of its rewritings through time." The "event" remembered is never whole, never fully represented, never isolated in the past alone but only accessible through a memory which resides, as Doane has put it, "in the reverberations between events" (Doane, 58).

This image of the palimpsest of memory seems a particularly apt evocation of how these two films approach the problem of representing the inaccessible trauma of the past. When Errol Morris fictionally reenacts the murder of Officer Wood as differently remembered by David Harris, Randall Adams, the officer's partner, and the various witnesses who claimed to have seen the murder, he turns his film into a temporally elaborated palimpsest, discrediting some versions more than others but refusing to ever fix one as *the* truth. It is precisely Morris's refusal to fix the final truth, to go on seeking reverberations and repetitions that, I argue, gives this film its exceptional power of truth.

This strategic and relative truth is often a by-product of other investigations into many stories of self-justification and reverberating memories told to the camera. For example, Morris never set out to tell the story of Randall Adams' innocence. He was interested initially in the story of "Dr. Death," the psychiatrist whose testimony about the sanity of numerous accused murderers had resulted in a remarkable number of death sentences. It would seem that the more directly and singlemindedly a film pursues a single truth, the less chance it has of producing the kind of "reverberations between events" that will effect meaning in the present. This is the problem with *Roger and Me* and, to stretch matters, even with *JFK:* both go after a single target too narrowly, opposing a singular (fictionalized) truth to a singular official lie.

The much publicized argument between Harlan Jacobson and Michael Moore regarding the imposition of a false chronology in Moore's documentary about the closing of General Motors' plant in Flint, Michigan, is an example. At stake in this argument is whether Moore's documentation of the decline of the city of Flint in the wake of the plant closing entailed an obligation to represent events in the sequence in which they actually occurred. Jacobson argues that Moore betrays his journalist/documentarian's commitment to the objective portrayal of historical fact when he implies that events that occurred prior to the major layoffs at the plant were the effect of these layoffs. Others have criticized Moore's self-promoting placement of himself at the center of the film.[6]

In response, Moore argues that as a resident of Flint he has a place in the film and should not attempt to play the role of objective observer but of partisan investigator. This point is quite credible and consistent with the postmodern awareness that there is no objective observation of truth but always an interested participation in its construction. But when he argues that his documentary is "in essence" true to what happened to Flint in the 1980s, only that these events are "told with a narrative style" that omits details and condenses events of a decade into a palatable "movie" (Jacobson, 22), Moore behaves too much like Oliver Stone, abandoning the commitment to multiple contingent truths in favor of a unitary, paranoid view of history.

The argument between Moore and Jacobson seems to be about where documentarians should draw the line in manipulating the historical sequence of their material. But rather than determining appropriate strategies for the representation of the meaning of events, the argument becomes a question of a commitment to objectivity versus a commitment to fiction. Moore says, in effect, that his first commitment is to entertain and that this entertainment is faithful to the essence of the history. But Moore betrays the cause and effect reverberation between events by this reordering. The real lesson of this debate would seem to be that Moore did not trust his audience to learn about the past in any other way than through the *vérité* capture of it. He assumed that if he didn't have footage from the historical period prior to his filming in Flint he couldn't show it. But the choice needn't be, as Moore implies, between boring, laborious fact and entertaining fiction true to the "essence," but not the detail, of historical events. The opposition poses a false contrast between a naïve faith in the documentary truth of photographic and filmic images and the cynical awareness of fictional manipulation.

What animates Morris and Lanzmann, by contrast, is not the opposition between absolute truth and absolute fiction but the awareness of the final inaccessibility of a moment of crime, violence, trauma, irretrievably located in the past. Through the curiosity, ingenuity, irony, and obsessiveness of "obtrusive" investigators, Morris and Lanzmann do not so much represent this past as they reactivate it in images of the present. This is their distinctive postmodern feature as documentarians. For in revealing the fabrications, the myths, the frequent moments of scapegoating when easy fictional explanations of trauma, violence, crime were substituted for more difficult ones, these documentaries do not simply play off truth against lie, nor do they play off one fabrication against another; rather, they show how lies function as partial truths to both the agents and witnesses of history's trauma.

For example, in one of the most discussed moments of *Shoah*, Lanzmann stages a scene of homecoming in Chelmno, Poland, by Simon Srebnik, a Polish Jew who had, as a child, worked in the death camp near that town, running errands for the Nazis and forced to sing while doing so. Now, many years later, in the present tense of Lanzmann's film, the elderly yet still vigorous Srebnik is surrounded on the steps of the Catholic church by an even older, friendly group of Poles who remembered him as a child in chains who sang by the river. They are happy he has survived and returned to visit. But as Lanzmann asks them how much they knew and understood about the fate of the Jews who were carried away from the church in gas vans, the group engages in a kind of free association to explain the unexplainable.

> [Lanzmann] Why do they think all this happened to the Jews?
>
> [A Pole] Because they were the richest! Many Poles were also exterminated. Even priests.
>
> [Another Pole] Mr. Kantarowski will tell us what a friend told him. It happened in Myndjewyce, near Warsaw.
>
> [Lanzmann] Go on.
>
> [Mr. Kantarowski] The Jews there were gathered in a square. The rabbi asked an SS man: "Can I talk to them?" The SS man said yes. So the rabbi said that around two thousand years ago the Jews condemned the innocent Christ to death. And when they did that, they cried out: "Let his blood fall on our heads and on our sons' heads." The rabbi told them: "Perhaps the time has come for that, so let us do nothing, let us go, let us do as we're asked."
>
> [Lanzmann] He thinks the Jews expiated the death of Christ?
>
> [The first? Pole] He doesn't think so, or even that Christ sought revenge. He didn't say that. The rabbi said it. It was God's will, that's all!
>
> [Lanzmann, referring to an untranslated comment] What'd she say?
>
> [A Polish woman] So Pilate washed his hands and said: "Christ is innocent," and he sent Barabbas. But the Jews cried out: "Let his blood fall on our heads!"
>
> [Another Pole] That's all; now you know! (*Shoah*, 100).[7]

As critic Shoshana Felman has pointed out, this scene on the church steps in Chelmno shows the Poles replacing one memory of their own witness of the persecution of the Jews with another (false) memory, an auto-mystification, produced by Mr. Kantarowski, of the Jews' willing acceptance of their persecution as scapegoats for the death of Christ. This fantasy, meant to assuage the Poles' guilt for their complicity in the extermination of the Jews, actually repeats the Poles' crime of the past in the present.

Felman argues that the strategy of Lanzmann's film is not to challenge this false testimony but to dramatize its effects: we see Simon Srebnik suddenly silenced among the chatty Poles, whose victim he becomes all over again. Thus the film does not so much give us a memory as an action, here and now, of the Poles' silencing and crucifixion of Srebnik, whom they obliterate and forget even as he stands in their midst (Felman, 120–128).

It is this repetition in the present of the crime of the past that is key to the documentary process of Lanzmann's film. Success, in the film's terms, is the ability not only to assign guilt in the past, to reveal and fix a truth of the day-to-day operation of the machinery of extermination, but also to deepen the understanding of the many ways in which the Holocaust continues to live in the present. The truth of the Holocaust thus does not exist in any totalizing narrative, but only, as Felman notes and Lanzmann shows, as a collection of fragments. While the process of scapegoating, of achieving premature narrative closure by assigning guilt to convenient victims, is illuminated, the events of the past—in this case the totality of the Holocaust—register not in any fixed moment of past or present but rather, as in Freud's description of the palimpsest, as the sum total of its rewritings through time, not in a single event but in the "reverberations" between.

It is important in the above example to note that while *cinéma vérité* is deployed in this scene on the steps, as well as in the interviews throughout the film, this form of *vérité* no longer has a fetish function of demanding belief as the whole. In place of a truth that is "guaranteed," the *vérité* of catching events as they happen is here embedded in a history, placed in relation to the past, given a new power, not of absolute truth but of repetition.

Although it is a very different sort of documentary dealing with a trauma whose horror cannot be compared to the Holocaust, Errol Morris's *The Thin Blue Line* also offers its own rich palimpsest of reverberations between events. At the beginning of the film, convicted murderer Randall Adams mulls over the fateful events of the night of 1976 when he ran out of gas, was picked up by David Harris, went to a drive-in movie, refused to allow Harris to come home with him, and later found himself accused of killing a cop with a gun that Harris had stolen. He muses: "Why did I meet this kid? Why did I run out of gas? But it happened, it happened." The film probes this "Why?" And its discovery "out of the past" is not simply some fate-laden accident but, rather, a reverberation between events that reaches much further back into the past than that cold November night in Dallas.

Toward the end, after Morris has amassed a great deal of evidence attesting to the false witness born by three people who testified to seeing Randall Adams in the car with David Harris, but before playing the audio tape in which Harris all but confesses to the crime, the film takes a different turn—away from the events of November and into the childhood of David Harris. The film thus moves both forward and back in time: to events following and preceding the night of November, 1976, when the police officer was shot. Moving forward, we learn of a murder, in which David broke into the home of a man who had, he felt, stolen his girlfriend. When the man defended himself, David shot him. This repetition of wanton violence is the clincher in the film's "case" against David. But instead of stopping there, the film goes back in time as well.

A kindly, baby-faced cop from David's home town, who has told us much of David's story already, searches for the cause of his behavior and hits upon a childhood trauma: a four-year-old brother who drowned when David was only three. Morris then cuts to David speaking of this incident: "My Dad was supposed to be watching us.... I guess that might have been some kind of traumatic experience for me.... I guess I reminded him ... it was hard for me to get any acceptance from him after that. ... A lot of the things I did as a young kid was an attempt to get back at him."

In itself, this "getting-back-at-the-father" motive is something of a cliché for explaining violent male behavior. But coupled as it is with the final "confession" scene in which Harris repeats this getting-back-at-the-father motive in his relation to Adams, the explanation gains resonance, exposing another layer in the palimpsest of the past. As we watch the tape recording of this last unfilmed interview play, we hear Morris ask Harris if he thinks Adams is a "pretty unlucky fellow?" Harris answers, "Definitely," specifying the nature of this bad luck: "Like I told you a while ago about the guy who didn't have no place to stay . . . if he'd had a place to stay, he'd never had no place to go, right?" Morris decodes this question with his own rephrasing, continuing to speak of Harris in the third person: "You mean if he'd stayed at the hotel that night this never would have happened?" (That is, if Adams had invited Harris into his hotel to stay with him as Harris had indicated earlier in the film he expected, then Harris would not have committed the murder he later pinned on Adams.) Harris: "Good possibility, good possibility. . . . You ever hear of the proverbial scapegoat? There probably been thousands of innocent people convicted. . . ."

Morris presses: "What do you think about whether he's innocent?" Harris: "I'm sure he is." Morris again: "How can you be sure?" Harris: "I'm the one who knows. . . . After all was said and done it was pretty unbelievable. I've always thought if you could say why there's a reason that Randall Adams is in jail it might be because he didn't have a place for somebody to stay that helped him that night. It might be the only reason why he's at where he's at."

What emerges forcefully in this near-confession is much more than the clinching evidence in Morris's portrait of a gross miscarriage of justice. For in not simply probing the "wrong man" story, in probing the reverberations between events of David Harris's personal history, Morris's film discovers an underlying layer in the palimpsest of the past: how the older Randall Adams played an unwitting role in the psychic history of the 16-year-old David Harris, a role which repeated an earlier trauma in Harris's life: of the father who rejected him, whose approval he could not win, and upon whom David then revenged himself.

Harris's revealing comments do more than clinch his guilt. Like the Poles who surround Srebnik on the steps of the church and proclaim pity for the innocent child who suffered so much even as they repeat the crime of scapegoating Jews, so David Harris proclaims the innocence of the man he has personally condemned, patiently explaining the process of scapegoating that the Dallas county legal system has so obligingly helped him accomplish. *Cinéma vérité* in both these films is an important vehicle of documentary truth. We witness in the present an event of simultaneous confession and condemnation on the part of historical actors who repeat their crimes from the past. Individual guilt is both palpably manifest and viewed in a larger context of personal and social history. For even as we catch David Harris and the Poles of Chelmno in the act of scapegoating innocent victims for crimes they have not committed, these acts are revealed as part of larger processes, reverberating with the past.

I think it is important to hold on to this idea of truth as a fragmentary shard, perhaps especially at the moment we as a culture have begun to realize, along with Morris, and along with the supposed depthlessness of our postmodern condition, that it is not guaranteed. For some form of truth is the always receding goal of documentary film. But the truth figured by documentary cannot be a simple unmasking or reflection. It is a careful construction, an intervention in the politics and the semiotics of representation.

An overly simplified dichotomy between truth and fiction is at the root of our difficulty in thinking about the truth in documentary. The choice is not between two entirely separate regimes of truth and fiction. The choice, rather, is in strategies of fiction for the approach to relative truths. Documentary is not fiction and should not be conflated with it. But documentary can and should use all the strategies of fictional construction to get at truths. What we see in *The Thin Blue Line* and *Shoah*, and to some degree in the other documentaries I have mentioned, is an interest in constructing truths to dispel pernicious fictions, even though these truths are only relative and contingent. While never absolute and never fixed, this under-construction, fragmented horizon of truth is one important means of combating the pernicious scapegoating fictions that can put the wrong man on death row and enable the extermination of a whole people.

The lesson that I would like to draw from these two exemplary postmodern documentaries is thus not at all that postmodern representation inevitably succumbs to a depthlessness of the simulacrum, or that it gives up on truth to wallow in the undecidabilities of representation. The lesson, rather, is that there can be historical depth to the notion of truth—not the depth of unearthing a coherent and unitary past, but the depth of the past's reverberation with the present. If the authoritative means to the truth of the past does not exist, if photographs and moving images are not mirrors with memories, if they are more, as Baudrillard has suggested, like a hall of mirrors, then our best response to this crisis of representation might be to do what Lanzmann and Morris do: to deploy the many facets of these mirrors to reveal the seduction of lies.

Acknowledgment

I owe thanks to Anne Friedberg, Mark Poster, Nancy Salzer, Marita Sturken, Charles Musser, James Shamus, B. Ruby Rich, and Marianne Hirsch for helping me, one way or another, to formulate the ideas in this article. I also thank my colleagues on the *Film Quarterly* editorial board, whose friendly criticisms I have not entirely answered.

NOTES

1. See, for example: Janet Maslin, "Oliver Stone Manipulates His Puppet," *The New York Times* (Sunday, January 5, 1992), p. 13; "Twisted History," *Newsweek* (December 23,1991), pp. 46–54; Alexander Cockbum, "J.F.K. and *J.F.K.*," *The Nation* (January 6–13, 1992), pp. 6–8.
2. Livingston's own film is an excellent example of the irony she cites, not so much in her directorial attitude toward her subject—drag-queen ball competitions—but in her subjects' attitudes toward the construction of the illusion of gender.
3. In this article I will not discuss *Who Killed Vincent Chin?* or *Roger and Me at* much length. Although both of these films resemble *The Thin Blue Line* and *Shoah* in their urge to reveal truths about crimes, I do not believe these films succeeded as spectacularly as Lanzmann's and Morris's in respecting the complexity of these truths. In *Vincent Chin*, the truth pursued is the racial motives animating Roger Ebans, a disgruntled, unemployed auto worker who killed Vincent Chin in a fight following a brawl in a strip joint. Ebans was convicted of manslaughter but only paid a small fine. He was then acquitted of a subsequent civil rights charge that failed to convince a jury of his racial motives. The film, however, convincingly pursues evidence that Ebans' animosity towards Chin was motivated by his anger at the Japanese for stealing jobs from Americans (Ebans assumed Chin was Japanese). In recounting the two trials, the story of the "Justice for Vincent" Committee, and the suffering of Vincent's mother, the film attempts to retry the case showing evidence of Ebans' racial motives.

   Film-makers Choy and Tajima gamble that their camera will capture, in interviews with Ebans, what the civil rights case did not capture for the jury: the racist attitudes that motivated the crime. They seek, in a way, what all of these documentaries seek: evidence of the truth of past events through their repetition in the present. This is also, in a more satirical vein, what Michael Moore seeks when he repeatedly attempts to interview the elusive Roger Smith, head of General Motors, about the layoffs in Flint, Michigan: Smith's avoidance of Moore repeats this avoidance of responsibility toward the town of Flint. This is also what Claude Lanzmann seeks when he interviews the ex-Nazis and witnesses of the Holocaust, and it is what Errol Morris seeks when he interviews David Harris, the boy who put Randall Adams on death row. Each of these films succeeds in its goal to a certain extent. But the singlemindedness of *Vincent Chin*'s pursuit of the singular truth of Ebans' guilt, and his culture's resentment of Asians, limits the film. Since Ebans never does show himself in the present to be a blatant racist, but only an insensitive working-class guy, the film interestingly fails on its own terms, though it is eloquent testimony to the pain and suffering of the scapegoated Chin's mother.
4. Shamus, Musser, and I delivered papers on *The Thin Blue Line* at a panel devoted to the film at a conference sponsored by New York University, "The State of Representation: Representation and the State," October 26–28, 1990. B. Ruby Rich was a respondent. Musser's paper argued the point, seconded by Rich's comments, that the prosecution and the police saw Adams as a homosexual. Their eagerness to prosecute Adams, rather than the underage Harris, seems to have much to do with this perception, entirely suppressed by the film.
5. Consider, for example, the way Ross McElwee's *Sherman's March*, on one level a narcissistic self-portrait of an eccentric Southerner's rambling

attempts to discover his identity while traveling through the South, also plays off against the historical General Sherman's devastating march. Or consider the way Ken Burns' *The Civil War* is as much about what the Civil War is to us today as it is about the objective truth of the past.

6. Laurence Jarvik, for example, argued that Moore's self-portrayal of himself as a "naïve, quixotic 'rebel with a mike'" is not an authentic image but one Moore has promoted as a fiction (quoted in Tajima, 30).
7. I have quoted this dialogue from the published version of the *Shoah* script but I have added the attribution of who is speaking in brackets. It is important to note, however, that the script is a condensation of a prolonged scene that appears to be constructed out of two different interviews with Lanzmann, the Poles, and Simon Srebnik before the church. In the first segment, Mr. Kantarowski is not present; in the second he is. When the old woman says "So Pilate washed his hands . . . " Mr. Kantarowski makes the gesture of washing his hands.

WORKS CITED

Baudrillard, Jean. 1988. "Simulacra and Simulations." In Mark Poster, ed., *Jean Baudrillard: Selected Writings.* Stanford, CA: Stanford University Press.

Doane, Mary Ann. 1990. "Remembering Women: Physical and Historical Constructions in Film Theory." In E. Ann Kaplan, ed., *Psychoanalysis and Cinema.* New York: Routledge.

Felman, Shoshana. 1990. "A L'Age du temoignage: *Shoah* de Claude Lanzmann." In *Au sujet de* Shoah: *le film de Claude Lanzmann.* Paris: Editions Belin.

Grundberg, Andy. 1990. "Ask It No Questions: The Camera Can Lie." *The New York Times,* Arts and Leisure. Sunday, August 12, pp. 1, 29.

Jacobson, Harlan. 1989. "Michael and Me." *Film Comment,* vol. 25, no. 6 (November–December), pp. 16–26.

Jameson, Fredric, 1984. "Postmodernism or the Cultural Logic of Late Capitalism." *New Left Review* 146 (July–August).

______. 1981 .*The Political Unconscious: Narrative as a Socially Symbolic Act.* Ithaca, N.Y.: Cornell University Press.

Kaes, Anton. 1989. *From Hitler to Heimat: The Return of History as Film.* Cambridge: Harvard University Press.

Lanzmann, Claude. 1985. Shoah: *An Oral History of the Holocaust.* New York: Pantheon.

Lyotard, Jean-François. 1984. *The Postmodern Condition: A Report on Knowledge.* Minneapolis: University of Minnesota Press.

Morris, Errol. 1989. "Truth Not Guaranteed: An Interview with Errol Morris." *Cineaste* 17, pp. 16–17.

Musser, Charles. 1990. Unpublished paper. "Film Truth: From 'Kino Pravda' to *Who Killed Vincent Chin?* and *The Thin Blue Line.*"

Shamus, James. 1990. Unpublished paper. "Optioning Time: Writing *The Thin Blue Line.*"

Tajima, Renee. 1990. "The Perils of Popularity." *The Independent* (June).

Taubin, Amy. 1992. "Oscar's Docudrama." *The Village Voice.* March 31, p. 62.

Trinh T., Minh-ha. 1990. "Documentary Is/Not a Name" *October* 52 (Spring), pp. 77–98.

97

ERROL MORRIS WITH PETER BATES

TRUTH NOT GUARANTEED

An Interview with Errol Morris (1989)

Errol Morris performs two jobs in his documentary film The Thin Blue Line: *as a filmmaker who injects a personal, unorthodox style into the work and as offscreen detective who ends up influencing events. The detective role is not unusual for him, because he has done investigative work in the past. Before he could support himself as a filmmaker, he worked as a Wall Street private eye, investigating cases involving bonds and government securities.*

Morris did not intend to make The Thin Blue Line. *He slipped into it inadvertently, while trying to develop a completely different film about self-deception and violence. He is now back working on that film, a pastiche of several stories whose characters include Dr. Grigson (the psychiatrist in the Adams case), a lion tamer, scientists working on animal behavior, etc. He is also concurrently working on another project, a film about a dog accused of murder.*

With minimal advertising, the film opened nationwide to favorable reviews (including one in the Dallas Times Herald). For a controversial documentary, it has received very little negative publicity. "It's kind of disappointing, really." said Morris. "I thought the film would have created some degree of antagonism. That makes me suspicious. Can it really be any good?" Errol Morris was interviewed for Cineaste *by Peter Bates.*

Cineaste: *What has happened in the Randall Adams case since the release of* The Thin Blue Line?

Errol Morris: A date was set in Dallas state court to hear arguments on why the 1977 trial should be disallowed. Of course these hearings have happened before. The previous one lasted two years and the only thing we proved was that the judge should have disallowed himself from the case. This case has a lot of layers; it's still an ongoing investigation. We're uncovering new facts all the time. David Harris's cellmate recently came forward and said that Harris confessed the crime repeatedly to him. Together they called Adams "the unlucky fucker." Harris's mother produced a letter he wrote from death row, indicating he was responsible for the murder. She turned it over to Adams's defense attorneys, and I guess that produced a rift between mother and son. There is no doubt that Randall Adams didn't receive a fair trial. They concocted evidence by editing testimony, suppressing significant documents; really, manufacturing a case that didn't exist.

Cineaste: *Why didn't you put Doug Mulder, the district attorney in this case, on film?*

Morris: I didn't put him on film because the interview with him was boring. He didn't say anything interesting. He refused to speak of the details of the case, preferring instead to speak in generalities. He was beyond cautious: he was non-responsive. Also, I interviewed him at an early stage in the filming, at a time when I didn't have that much information about the role he had played at trial.

Cineaste: *You couldn't even get a damning "no comment" from him?*

Morris: I don't put that kind of stuff in my film. There's no attempt to catch people in lies, to get them to sweat nervously in response to a difficult question.

Cineaste: *What kind of resistance did you meet while filming* The Thin Blue Line?

Morris: I met resistance everywhere, all along the way. I found that generally people were not necessarily enthusiastic about appearing on film. A lot of them didn't even want to talk about this case. It took a lot of coaxing and cajoling to get them to agree to appear. That was the hardest part. Once they agreed, most people enjoyed talking into the camera.

Cineaste: *Did you find similar reasons for their reluctance?*

Morris: Not really. Maybe a lot of them knew they had somehow been involved in a miscarriage of justice, but I don't think so. There could have been some suspicion about my motives for doing this thing, and they probably wondered if I shared their conviction that Adams was guilty.

Cineaste: *For example, the police officers?*

Morris: Possibly. Of course, I didn't indicate my opinion one way or another. I let them all speak and tell me what they believed in their own words.

Cineaste: *Are they any documentary filmmakers for whom you feel an affinity? People from whom you've learned things?*

Morris: Well, Frederick Wiseman, the king of misanthropic cinema. He's produced an extraordinary body of work. I like his films because they embody something of his own vision or ideas; they're very personal and idiosyncratic. His content interests me, even though his style is the polar opposite of mine. All of my films break with the basic tenets of *cinéma-vérité*: No handheld camera or shooting with available light, no running after the action, no trying to remain as unobtrusive as possible.

Quite the opposite, I try to be as obtrusive as possible. All my interviews are staged for the camera with the same lighting and poses. I believe *cinéma-vérité* set back documentary filmmaking twenty or thirty years. It sees documentary filmmaking as a sub-species of journalism. My films are a return to an older idea of how films should be put together, *more* than journalism rather than less. There's no reason why documentaries can't be as personal as fiction filmmaking and bear the imprint of those who made them. Truth isn't guaranteed by style or expression. It isn't guaranteed by anything.

I admire some documentaries created by directors more known for their other work, like Herzog, Bunuel. Herzog produced *Land of Silence and Darkness* (1971), *The Great Ecstacy of the Sculptor Steiner* (1974), *Fata Morgana* (1970); Bunuel, *Land Without Bread* (1932). I can't name many documentary filmmakers today whose films have this sort of individual imprint.

Cineaste: *Music plays an important role in* The Thin Blue Line. *Why did you choose to use Philip Glass's music?*

Morris: I had used portions of his previously-recorded music in the editing of this film. It worked so well, I thought, why not hire Philip Glass? Commission him to write an original score. I think it gives the film an underlying feeling of inexorability, of inevitability, which is part of the film noir aspect of the story. You know, there's a chance meeting on a roadway and it's the beginning of a headlong trip to the Texas Department of Correction's Eastham Unit. No matter what Randall Adams did, he got further entangled. This feeling of doom and desperation is underlined by Glass's music. I've been told that it is the best use of his music in any film.

Cineaste: *Do you think this particular case is emblematic of the American Justice system? Are there many other such cases still behind bars?*

Morris: Most of the people in jail are guilty. I interviewed thirty-five inmates who had been sentenced to death and I believe they were all guilty—with the exception of Randall Adams. My film is not an argument for the innocence of people in jail, nor a story about how the American justice system produces unfair convictions and puts the wrong people in jail. I'm not in a position to make any sweeping generalization about American justice and I wouldn't do it.

The Thin Blue Line is a story about how easy it is to deceive ourselves that we have some privileged access to the truth. It is a story about how the American justice system failed because of the people practicing it. People who broke the rules, suppressed evidence, put perjured evidence on the stand. They broke the rules, because somehow they felt that the end justified the means, that if Randall Adams was truly guilty, then it's okay; whatever we did was justified. After all, we helped put a cop killer in the electric chair. The only trouble is they had the wrong man.

Cineaste: *What impressions do you want your audiences to leave with?*

Morris: Well, outrage, that's certainly one of them. It is hard to feel that Randall Adams was not denied a fair trial in 1977 and not to have serious questions, even on the simplest level, about the reliability of the prosecution's "eyewitness testimony." I don't think anyone could come away from the movie and feel that their three surprise eyewitnesses—Emily and R. L. Miller, and Michael Randall—have any credibility at all. I sometimes think of them as evil clowns [laughs]. You know. R. L. Miller has seen the film. I was told that afterwards he was so afraid to show his face, he had to slink out of the theater.

I'd also like to give the impression that our perch in life is not as secure as we might like to think. I want people to feel, it happened to him, it could happen to me. It's about slipping through the cracks, being incorrectly observed by the people around you (or not at all), and getting caught in some gigantic lie from which there is no escape. The scary part is that our desire to seek the truth is a lot weaker than our desire to tell ourselves what we want to hear, to perpetuate our own beliefs. The truth is not like that, it's not something that comes to us at our convenience.

98

MICHAEL MOORE WITH HARLAN JACOBSON

MICHAEL & ME (1989)

[. . .]

When I started making appointments with Moore—who was crazed with making personal appearances and cutting a distribution deal in the most dizzying round of talks any independent filmmaker has ever undertaken (culminating in a deal with Warners for some $3 million for all rights and requiring it to buy four houses for evicted families plus give away 20,000 tickets to the unemployed)—I was hardly surprised when either he, or I for that matter, broke the dates. Sometimes Michael wouldn't show up, sometimes I'd show up too late to accomplish an interview inside the hour he had cut me. Once, he met me on the steps of St. Patrick's Cathedral—along with his mom and two associates—and wanted them along for the interview over lunch. Well, we had a nice lunch. Around the *Film Comment* basement, our dance became known as Michael & Me.

Michael always called me, always stayed in touch. Eventually, we sat down one night in the office of his lawyers (who were busy not only doing the deal but thinking their way through the thicket of threatened lawsuits, not the least of which was Bob Eubanks'). And had at it.

[. . .]

[Jacobson:] *Since you have shown your film in Toronto, and now New York, what has been Roger Smith's response to date?*

[Moore:] First week it was no comment, the second week it was a one paragraph prepared statement. Which was "We have no comment."

The third week he came out and said, I haven't seen the film but I know I don't like it. The fourth week they went on a p.r. binge and had an early opening of this engineering center in Flint.

The Great Lakes Technological Centre.

Right, which does not create one new job in the city of Flint. It merely transfers a thousand engineers from Detroit to Flint.

And then Smith said. . . .

"We have no empty facilities in Flint." Because they tore it down [laughs]. Although it's still not a true statement. There are three empty or semi-empty factories, [including] one where one of the two lines has been mothballed.

Would you call it a manipulation of the facts. . . ?

I call it a lie. Just a lie. It's printed as fact because the media generally accepts what a corporation says as fact. It accepts what the government says as fact: "Unemployment is at five percent;" it's printed that way, as fact. Michael Moore says it cost $160,000 to make his movie, the article reads "According to Moore . . ."; or "Moore claims . . ."; or "Moore says that his movie cost him $160,000."

They're even opening up AutoWorld for six weekends at the holidays to coincide with the opening of the film there. I don't know why they think that is a smart p.r. move; it'll just reinforce my point and the point of the movie.

Which is?

Which is how ridiculous it was to build this thing in the middle of the devastated area and think that a million tourists a year were going to come. See, people could only go on my word or on the few images I give of it in the film. Now, they'll actually be able to see this monstrosity.

Let's talk about that. When did it open originally?

Auto World opened July 4, 1984.

And it closed?

Ahh, it closed January 6, 1985.

And the Hyatt?

The Hyatt opened in 1982, I think.

And did not close but. . . .

Hasn't closed. It's up for sale.

The underwriter foreclosed.

Foreclosed, right.

And Water Street Pavilion opened when?

Water Street opened December of 1985. And just recently last week it was announced that all the stores would be closed and turned into offices. Or so they hope.

The truck plant in Flint was shut when?

May of 1987.

And Fisher #1?

December of 1987.

And there were a total of eleven plants that were idled.

What's happened to the plant has taken place over a ten-year period.

Or longer?

It's all connected, everything is connected. There were terrible depressions in the '50s and '60s in those plants.

Net loss of 32,000 jobs since 1974.

Right, give or take a couple thousand.

In the November '86 reduction, a total of something like 10,0000.

Roughly.

How far back was AutoWorld a discussion?

A couple of years before maybe, I think. I don't know. The first I heard of it was probably, oh, the year before . . .'83 . . . they announced it and started building it.

If I said that it went back in the discussion as far as 1970, would that make sense to you?

No. I wouldn't know that. I know what they *say*, that Harding Mott said at one time he was watching TV, and they were burying a car, and he got all upset and wanted to build some monument to the automobile that would set the country right about the contribution of the GM automobile. I wasn't privy to any discussions back in 1970.

There was money put into it for architecture and design as early as '78 and '79, through a combination of UDAG grants, the Mott Foundation and CRI?

Is that true?

I never heard of it in 1978. I never heard of it until just a year or two before it actually opened.

Let's take one or two possible scenarios with respect to that whole development: it was not developed piece by piece but as a concept, a unity. AutoWorld was meant to bring in, as you said, a million tourists a year supported by a hotel and a place to spend money at the retail level, Water Street Pavilion.

No, there was never a plan that had all three of those things connected.

Granted, Flint was totally in a stranglehold by GM, but when GM began relocating, or laying off by attrition or outright in the late '60s, was this three-part complex a legitimate government response to help?

No, you can't take away jobs that are paying people a decent wage, where they can buy a home, a car and raise a family, and replace them with minimum wage jobs. . . .

Who built them?

Auto workers did not build these buildings.

Why was that not a local issue?

Well, that's a good question. In fact, they hired a contractor to come in from Indiana. They brought in people from out of state. People who were laid off were not given jobs to build these things.

[. . .]

If AutoWorld opened up in '84, and it was preceded by the Hyatt in '82, these things had to be on the planning stage under Democratic administrations before.

No.

How do you open something up in 1982 . . .

You can open up a hotel pretty quick. You don't need years of planning—that's bullshit. I don't know why you want to get into UDAG, the Mott Foundation, or CRI. I don't know what this has to do with the movie.

The impression that one has from the movie is that there was a single felling blow, directed at Fisher Plant #1, which cut loose 30,000 people from employment, resulting in immediate and massive devastation to which the local government responded with fantasy projects. There is no mention that those projects existed on the boards back to 1970. . . . maybe/maybe not; back to 1978 . . . maybe/maybe not; but certainly no mention that they opened up, ran their course, and closed prior to the cutbacks which form the spine of your movie.

Right. Well, first of all the movie never says that 30,000 jobs . . . that this one announcement eliminated 30,000 jobs in Flint. The movie is about essentially what has happened to this town during the 1980s. I wasn't filming in 1982 . . . so everything that happened happened. As far as I'm concerned, a period of seven or eight years . . . is pretty immediate and pretty devastating.

You may be right in spirit but you're playing fast and loose with sequence—which viewers don't understand is happening.

I don't think so.

Why?

I just don't think so. I think it's a document about a town that died in the 1980s, and this is what happened.

I think that's true. And I think that it is incredibly powerful and makes its point.

Good.

It is unquestionably true that you made a film about a town that died in the 1980s, a town that was in one company's hip pocket, just like all of the towns that have ever been in one company's hip pocket back to the railroads which built company shacks and company stores. But I think that its also useful to address the question of the sequencing.

What would you rather have me do? Should I have maybe begun the movie with a Roger Smith or GM announcement of 1979 or 1980 for the first round of layoffs that devastated the town, which then led to starting these projects, after which maybe things pick up a little bit in the mid '80s, and then *boom* in '86 there's another announcement, and then tell that whole story?

Where now there are Son of AutoWorld and the Great Lakes Technology Centre and all these things I call "Dance Bands on the Titanic," the diversions, the distractions, the things that are used to tell the town "See, we're gonna come back, things are going to get better"? Then it's a three hour movie. It's a *movie*, you know; you can't do everything. I was true to what happened. Everything that happened in the movie happened. It happened in the same order that it happened throughout the '80s. If you want to nit-pick on some of those specific things, fine but. . . .

It's not a nit-pick, and I'll tell you why I don't think it's a nit-pick. You call it a movie; it has the form of documentary. We all know that documentaries have points of view . . . what goes into the documentary, even down to the camera angle, has a bias. But we expect that what we are seeing there happened, in the way in which it happened, in the way in which we are told it happened. We all know the doubt that arises and the actions that come from the reporting of an event in which the sequence is screwed around with. You and I are both old enough to remember the Gulf of Tonkin—we were told by a president that we had been attacked. . . .

That's an insulting thing to say. That's really insulting. That's an insulting comparison. What that lie of Johnson's did to this country, to people in our generation, people we know that died. That's really insulting, Harlan.

I'm sorry you feel that way.

Yeah, well, I don't think you are sorry. Think of a different example of how you have to sometimes deal with chronology and order, when you are trying to make a movie.

Are we talking about a fiction film or a documentary?

Then why didn't I deal with the Japanese? Why didn't I deal with the oil embargo? Why didn't I deal with all the other factors that aren't in the movie? Did I tell a true story by not telling those parts of the story?

You've bought into their bullshit, to their lie about UDAG grants in '78.

I haven't bought any. . . .

Yeah, you have. The whole basis of your argument here with me is that you have bought these things as fact.

I didn't talk to Roger Smith. Roger Smith wouldn't talk to me.

No, I'm talking about the people of Flint that you talked to. This bullshit about 1970 is total bullshit. I don't know where you got that, that's a Mott Foundation lie. That's Harding Mott sitting in his chair watching a TV show. It was an '80s response to the declining auto industry in Flint. Tell me why you think Hyatt, AutoWorld, and Water Street were built?

I came here to ask you that, because you're probably a far better observer of the local scene than I am.

They were built for the very reasons I stated in the film: as the layoffs began in the late '70s and early '80s, the city turned toward these goofy ideas as a means to divert public attention from the real issue.

[. . .]

I don't think that you should be angry with me when I question your methodology—it's going to come up sooner or later—because you are dealing with people's perception of truth. You and I are both journalists—that's the only thing that we take into the marketplace. That's why you function as a co-equal to Roger Smith.

Okay, so you can say that the chronology skips around a bit. That's why I don't use dates in the film. I just didn't want to [deal with] how to compact eight years into the two-and-a-half years that we were filming.

So I don't say, "Well, this opened in '86, but that happened in '87." The point is that at the end of the Carter administration factories started to close, and jobs started to be eliminated. You would be happy if I had said in broadcast voice "In 1979 . . ." If I had said something like that.

I think you could have established that with an insert or a crawl, that there wasn't a single blow. . . .

As far as I'm concerned, everything that took place in the '80s was a single blow. We are talking about an 80-year history of this company and during the Reagan years this was a single blow. . . . If you're using the Gulf of Tonkin as a metaphor, then you're really hung up with this. . . .

That's what happens when one manipulates sequence . . . and that's the core credibility of the documentary.

All art, listen, every piece of journalism manipulates sequence and things. Just the fact that you edit, that certain things get taken out or put back in. That's just a ridiculous statement.

It goes back to the issue of the belief in the integrity of the information.

Uh-huh, yeah, sure.

Do you see a problem with the inclusion of the Reverend Schuller footage, which happened in 1982, and the impression you give that it was done post-1986?

I didn't say it was done post-1986. . . . It happened during the same decade, when after thousands of people were laid off, they brought in Reverend Schuller.

You are trying to hold me to a different standard than you would another film . . . as if I were writing some kind of college essay. . . .

No, I hold you to documentary film standards.

Because you see this primarily as a documentary.

It's not in any category I know as fiction.

It's not fiction. But what if we say it's a documentary told with a narrative style. I tried to tell a documentary in a way they don't usually get told. The reason why people don't watch documentaries is they are so bogged down with "Now in 1980 . . . then in '82 five thousand were called back . . . in '84 ten thousand were laid off . . . but then in '86 three thousand were called back . . .but later in '86 ten thousand more were laid off." If you want to tell the Flint story, there's the Flint story.

I'm not against documentaries having a bias. They don't have to remain "objective." . . .

We are not talking about objectivity. We are talking about a *style* that you don't seem to like.

Let's go to where this leads. . . . If GM has sold out America, how do you see the '90s?

Well, I hope that people will respond. In what way? [Maybe] politically.

Is that what you wanted from the film?

Yeah.

To galvanize people?

Yeah. Well, that's asking a lot from a film. But maybe people could think about it just a little bit, you know, instead of just passing it by when they see the unemployment figures in the newspapers . . . or the line in the TV news.

Do you think that your film functions as a political manifesto?

No, not really.

Do you think of it as a documentary?

No, I think of it as a movie, an entertaining movie.

That's being coy.

No, I don't think so. It's an entertaining movie that hopefully will get people to think a little bit about what is going on.

An entertaining movie like K-9?

An entertaining movie like *Sophie's Choice.*

Like Sophie's Choice?

An entertaining movie like any Charlie Chaplin film that dealt with social commentary, the problems of the day, but also [let] a lot of people laugh a little bit, [and did] not numb them, [did] not totally depress them.

Do you think that the response to Chaplin's little dictator was that people were supposed to go home and laugh about Hitler tossing the globe up into the air and playing with it? Or do you think that it was meant to galvanize public opinion?

It's not one or the other. You can't separate them. People can not be galvanized without being allowed to laugh and to feel the humanity of it.

We do want to laugh, we do want to feel the humanity. But I can't believe that you would separate yourself from the political content of your own film.

No, you're trying to say it's a political manifesto, or whatever.

I'm trying to get from you how you see it.

How do you see it?

That your film is essentially an extraordinarily angry film . . . that uses humor coupled with anger—those two qualities do go together—about the political selling-out of the working class of America. [You] mean to lay the platform for a basis of thinking about governmental and corporate actions that says "Stop! Stop right here." That is the reaction that went to sleep in the '70s and '80s, and it was not the reaction that you and I grew up with in the '60s. Maybe it's where we're headed in the '90s . . .

Well, that would be nice.

I know where I live. I live in the United States of America . . . okay? A nation that's been numbed. Whatever happens is going to happen with just a few people. I guess you can say that is the course of most history . . . I don't see people rising up to march in the streets.

[. . .]

99

THOMAS WAUGH

"ACTING TO PLAY ONESELF"

Notes on Performance in Documentary (1990)

In 1940, Joris Ivens, in the midst of finishing *Power and the Land* for Pare Lorentz's U.S. Film Service, wrote an essay on "Collaboration in Documentary." It was time to summarize much of what he had learned in the first fifteen years of his career. Much of the resulting manual of the classical documentary concerns the challenge of working with nonprofessional subjects in "re-enactment," one of documentary's "wide variety of styles." As a lead-in to my reflection on the presence of performance within the documentary film tradition, it is worth excerpting this text at length:

> . . . We come to the problem that has attracted and sometimes baffled us for many years: the handling of non-actors. In re-enacting a situation with a group of extremely pleasant persons, who for your purposes have become actors, the danger of letting them do what they like, of falling back on pleasant, easy naturalism, is even greater. And as your location work progresses, the non-actors become the central figures in your group, creating problems that temporarily force all the other problems out of your consciousness. . . .
>
> Our farm film presented material that seemed to demand re-enactments. . . . In choosing the people who were to play the roles (of themselves—the farmer as the farmer, his sons as the farmer's sons, etc.), the first visual impression is very important. Casting has its own difficulties too. A father and a son may work well separately, but not at all well when they're together in a scene. To get close enough to these people, to work with them, the director must be sensitive to these relationships. In general, I feel a knowledge of psychology is demanded of every member of the group, for all must watch and sense delicate situations.
>
> The writer must employ his imagination to manipulate the real personal characteristics of the new actors—searching them with seemingly careless observations. He

must learn thereby, for example that the farmer takes a special pride in the sharpness of his tool blades, and therefore suggest a toolshed scene which will make use of that fact. The key to this approach, I think, is that a real person, acting to play himself, will be more expressive if his actions are based on his real characteristics.

My experience has been that directives to non-actors who are playing together would usually be given them separately, so that a certain amount of unrehearsed reaction can be counted upon. To get natural reactions we played tricks similar to those Pudovkin has recorded, and some of them worked. For example: the father was filmed receiving a notification from the dairy that his milk is sour; he expected to unfold and pretend to read a blank piece of paper. But he read instead a startling message from me, complaining about his sour milk in no uncertain terms.

In general my method was to give precise directions to these non-actors but not to do it for them—simply to tell them what has to be done. . . . The farmer will have his special way of doing it, whether it is entering a room or moving a chair, and it is usually a very good way.

I have come to believe it is best to have as few retakes as possible. Repetition seems to have a deadening effect on the non-actor. If rehearsals are necessary, allow some time to elapse between rehearsals, and shooting. Use yourself or anybody as stand-ins—to keep the non-actor from exhaustion or self-consciousness. On the other hand, if the period of filming a re-enactment is short or very rushed, there can be less care in humoring him, depending more on the camera's ability to break up the action into useful close-ups.

The cameraman has to understand the special difficulties in working with non-actors ("What good is all this fooling with lights?") to render the length of time during light and camera adjustment tolerable to the non-actor. I don't believe in having long conferences before takes, while the non-actor waits. Keep discussions away from him. He begins to feel that these long, visible, but inaudible conversations are about himself and his acting—and he is usually right. We learned to use a code. Whenever a cameraman said, after a shot, "Very good" I knew he meant, "It's not so hot, try some other way." . . .

The surest way to avoid loss of time with re-takes is to know and anticipate the real movements of the man, to catch the regular rhythm of his normal action (which is far from re-enactment). The whole action should be watched (away from the camera) before breaking it up for filming. And the breaking up, and covering shots, should absolutely include beginnings of an action, endings of an action, and the places where the worker rests—not just other angles of the most exciting sections of his movement. Thus you get material for good human editing. . . .

Overcoming self-consciousness is of course the greatest problem with the non-actor, no matter what his background. If you work for months with the same group of persons, you can gradually expect to find more consciousness of themselves as actors. They become more flexible and adaptable and greater demands can be made of them. They can even be taught something of the film's technique. When the father in the farm film couldn't understand why

> he had to repeat an action more than once while the camera was shifted about, I took him to see a Cagney movie at the local theatre and pointed out how an action in a finished film was made out of long shots, medium shots and close-ups. From then on he understood our continuity problems and gave very useful assistance in this way. But I don't think it wise to show them their own rushes. I waited until the last few days before showing our farm family themselves on the screen.
>
> I advise not to fool with a man's professional pride. Don't ask a farmer to milk an empty cow, even though it's just for a close-up of the farmer's face. He fights such an idea because to him it is false—until he has been with the film group for a long time.
>
> Even as simple a rule as "Don't look at the camera" is bound up with the man himself. But this is such a basic necessity for the quality of your film that you must enforce the rule even though it hurts you to.[1]

Ivens goes on to illustrate this last point with an anecdote from his Chinese shoot a few years earlier *(The Four Hundred Million)* where he had had to force himself to impose the rule of not looking at the camera on traumatized stretcher-bearers in a battle scene.

Acting Naturally in the Classical Documentary

Documentary film, in everyday commonsense parlance, implies the absence of elements of performance, acting, staging, directing, etc., criteria which presumably distinguish the documentary form from the narrative fiction film. Ivens' text helps focus a discussion of performance in documentary because it challenges the common understanding. It reveals how basic the ingredients of performance and direction are within the documentary tradition—certainly within the classical documentary as reflected in this 1940 document, but also, as I will argue, in the modern *vérité* and post-*vérité* documentary as well.

For Ivens and his generation, the notion of performance as an element of documentary filmmaking was something to be taken for granted. Towards the end of the thirties, as documentarists yearned to get out of the basements and into the theaters, semi-fictive characterization, or "personalization," as Ivens called it, seemed to be the means for the documentary to attain artistic maturity and mass audiences. Social actors,[2] real people, became documentary film performers, playing themselves and their social roles before the camera.

The decade's prevailing notion of documentary performance is reflected most in Ivens' terminology with its echoes of narrative studio-based filmmaking: "roles," "re-take," "continuity," "covering shots," "rehearsals," "casting," etc. His directing techniques, significantly, are borrowed from Pudovkin, a director notable for his work with professional dramatic actors. Documentary performers "act" in much the same way as their dramatic counterparts except that they are cast for their social representativity as well as for their cinematic qualities, and their roles are composites of their own social roles and the dramatic requirements of the film.

Ivens' term "natural" indicates a problematical concept and practice for the classical (pre-*vérité*) documentarist. By "naturalism" Ivens means a cinematography characterized not by "content value" (a concept he uses elsewhere in the article) but by a spontaneous textural or behavioral quality, a quality which the later *vérité* generation would transform into an aesthetic gospel. But he also refers to "acting naturally," in reference to not looking at the camera, the code of illusion by which both extras, such as the Chinese stretcher bearers, and principal (non-) actors should "perform" unawareness of the camera. This clearly artificial code of acting naturally is so rooted in our cinematic culture, then as now, that Ivens posits it unquestioningly as a basic axiom of "quality" cinema. The *vérité* school, in its American observational incarnation (Leacock, Wiseman), would share this axiom with Ivens and his generation however much they would repudiate the didacticism of the principie of "content value."

But the concept and the practice of acting naturally are far more complex than either generation realized, and the familiar concepts of "representational" and "presentational" discourse are of some help. Let us use "representational" to refer to Ivens' "acting naturally," the documentary code of narrative illusion borrowed from the dominant fiction cinema. When subjects perform "not looking at the camera," when they represent their lives or roles, the image looks natural, as if the camera were invisible, as if the subject were unaware of being filmed. This performance convention is by no means inherent in the documentary mode. Certainly, in documentary still photography it is considerably less unanimous, for from August Sander to the Farm Security Administration to Diane Arbus, from Wilhelm von Gloeden to Robert Mapplethorpe, the convention of posing is much more the dominant tradition. In contrast, the convention of representation as found in, say, Henri Cartier-Bresson, (whose influence on the *cinema-vérité* is of course not without interest), informs a vigorous but secondary counter-current. The convention of performing an awareness of the camera rather than a nonawareness, of presenting oneself explicitly for the camera—the convention the documentary cinema absorbed from its elder sibling photography—we shall call "presentational" performance.

Although posing, the presentational convention of acknowledging the camera, never became the standard convention in classical documentary cinema, it did become an important secondary variant of documentary cinematic practice, particularly in the sound era. Whereas Flaherty's silent Nanook was depicted performing presentationally a few times—posing for the camera with a grin or a look—he for the most part performed naturalistically, "acting" or representing his daily life for the camera without explicitly acknowledging its presence. *Moana* similarly displayed some engaging moments of presentation—a subject displaying a captured tortoise to the camera, for example—but by and large Flaherty succeeded in getting his Samoan social actors to perform according to the codes of representation. By the time of his later features, *Man of Aran* and *Louisiana Story,* Flaherty was following the codes of representation obsessively—to the extent that they become abstract mytho-narrative meditations on exotic landscapes rather than social narratives rooted in the daily cultural contexts of those landscapes' inhabitants. These latter films are no longer able to bear, for contemporary eyes at least, the slightest pretension to ethnographic veracity, nor even, my students would say, the least claim to the documentary mantle at all—a point whose significance I will take up later.

Not all sound documentarists followed Flaherty's lead. During the sound era, the countercurrent of presentational performance in fact became quite visible—or rather audible. Inspired in part by radio, aural presentational conventions like the interview, the monologue, even choral speech, were experimented with in the thirties by Vertov, by Grierson's British school, by Frontier Films, and even by Flaherty himself in his project for the U.S. Film Service (slightly later than Ivens'), *The Land.* Traumatized by the devastation he "discovered" in his own backyard on this latter project, Flaherty somehow let go of the representational style he'd perfected on Aran. Prominent in the film are curious silent/non-sync variations of aural presentational performances as well as several moments of silent presentational posing clearly inspired by Flaherty's fellow Federal employees in the still photography business. For his part, Ivens was accustomed of course to "representing" far more traumatic devastation than nonelectrified farming in Ohio, as his Chinese anecdote reminds us. In *Power and the Land,* then, his representational skills were thus honed to their finest point, and the performances that spurred the writings excerpted at the outset of this article became milestones in documentary representation.

It is interesting that the two traditions intersect in the career of a single editor, Helen van Dongen. Ivens' long-time collaborator and a principal pioneer in the perfection of representational documentary editing, Van Dongen edited both *The Land* and *Power and the Land.* I have always found odd her complaint about the staged quality of Flaherty's most intricate representational scene, in which a black farmhand moves about a deserted plantation and rings the plantation bell. In practice, Van Dongen sculpted this scene with all the representational precision and smoothness which she had just brought to *Power and the Land* and would later bring to *Louisiana Story.*[3] Flaherty's uncharacteristic posing shots, however, were never brought up in her published notes about the editing, though they clearly disturbed the seamless continuum that was Van Dongen's professional pride. The FSA-style posing shots she treated with an anomalous awkwardness, cutting them off with abrupt, haunting fadeouts before the intrinsic rhythm of the shot and the dynamic of the spectator's encounter with the performers are fulfilled.

As for Flaherty's and Ivens' British contemporaries (and admirers), they pushed the cumbersome sound technology of the day much further than the Americans in the direction of both presentational and representational performances, achieving unintentional self-parody with the latter in *Night Mail* and groundbreaking revelation with the former in the legendary interviews and monologues of *Housing Problems.* In the Soviet context, such experimentation appeared even earlier. As early as 1931, the only Soviet documentarist of the sound period whose work is available in the West, Dziga Vertov, incorporated short production pledges delivered as monologues by shock workers in *Enthusiasm,* the film that must be considered his manifesto of the possibilities of documentary sound, despite the stilted and self-conscious effect of these first attempts. Three years later, *Three Songs of Lenin* offered vivid and personalized portraits of Soviet citizens by virtue of a more developed use of monologue performances: two of the portraits feature a woman shock worker who shyly describes how she averted an accident with some concrete tubs in a construction project, and a woman Kolkhoz worker who chats with amazing informality and dramatic gestures about the role of women on her farm. The possibility of Vertov's influence on his Western European counterparts is a strong one since the Grierson group knew his work.

Yet, despite the inspiration occasioned by Grierson's rat-plagued housewife holding forth to the camera, and by Vertov's vivid portraits, the presentational style predominated only in the documentary vernacular of the commercial newsreel (as later in its descendent, television journalism), or in specialized forms like the still rare campaign film (such as Renoir's *La Vie est à Nous,* which incorporates Party oratory along with a range of representational sketches). Ivens' representational style of naturalistic acting and *mise-en-scène* was never edged from its hegemony within the hybrid repertory of the so-called artistic documentary of the period.

In summary, now that we have returned to Ivens, performance—the self-expression of documentary subjects for the camera in collaboration with filmmaker/director—was the basic ingredient of the classical documentary. Most directors relied principally on naturalistic, representational performance style borrowed from fiction, which some varied from time to time with presentational elements akin to the conventions of still photography and radio. The difference between representation and presentation is not that one uses performance and the other doesn't, but that the former disavows and hides its performance components through such conventions as not looking at the camera, whereas the latter openly acknowledges and exploits its performance components. This difference must be explored.

Presenting Versus Representing

The distinction between representational and presentational performance is a very useful one for looking diachronically at documentary history. The pendulum of fashion and usage has swung back and forth between the two conventions, from one period to another, from one culture to another, and from the margin to the mainstream within one particular period and culture. I have already mentioned, for example, that presentational performance became visible, though not predominant, during the latter half of the thirties, during the first maturity of the sound documentary. At the same time proponents of the predominant representational element of the period's hybrid form often went even further than Ivens in availing themselves of the resources of fictional cinema: the use of studio sets *(Night Mail)* and professional actors *(Native Land)* during the thirties as a means of both overcoming technological difficulties and deepening social perspective did not attract any notice at the time, but would become anathema thirty years later during the heyday of *vérité*. During the Second World War *(Fires Were Started)*, and especially during the postwar decade, the representational convention evolved so much that the resulting "docudrama" format *(Quiet One, Strange Victory, Mental Mechanisms Series)* seemed the unanimous style on the eve of the *vérité* breakthrough, although voiceover narrations by subjects sometimes superimposed a presentational patina *(Paul Tomkowicz Street-Railway Switchman, All My Babies)* on representational films from those years.

The first wave of *vérité* or direct technology, cresting in the early sixties, continued the representational mode of performance. At the same time, *vérité* radically revised its execution. The new technology was often able to dispense with *mise-en-scène*, though not with performance, to follow an event or performance without "setting it up." While much of the studio paraphernalia of rehearsals and retakes, etc. was no longer necessary, the code of not looking at the camera, whether implicit or explicit, was still in force—at least in the United States. The classical American *vérité* filmmakers systematically snipped out all looks at the camera in order to preserve the representational illusion. It didn't matter that even the most noninterventionist camera instigated palpable performance on the part of subjects, tacitly understood and enacted as part of the representational code: has anyone seen hospital workers or high school teachers as conscientious, flamboyant, and downright cinematic as those who performed their daily jobs for Wiseman? The subject in a Wiseman film, consenting to continue daily activity, to act naturally, and to perform the pretense that there is no camera or crew, consenting to show the putative audience his or her life, is performing at a most basic level. The pretense, the disavowal of performance on the part of filmmakers, editors, and subjects is at the heart of the basic contradiction of *cinéma-vérité*—the contradiction between the aspiration to observational objectivity and its actual subjectively representational artifice. Small wonder that the best moments in Wiseman often involve highly histrionic individuals such as *Hospital's* black "schizophrenic" hustler, fighting the system for his self-reliance while flirting with the camera operator, or the bad-tripping art student, who waxes melodramatic indeed ("I don't want to die") amid the floods of vomit and the most attentive audience he has ever had. These social actors become such memorable film actors because their clearly inscribed awareness of the camera amplifies their performance and transcends the representational pretense of *vérité* observation.

Small wonder also that two important genres of *vérité* have outshone Wiseman's cold observational eye in the marketplace to this day, genres that by their subject matter bypass and compensate for *vérité*'s disavowal of performance:

(1) films whose crews have or establish intimate relationships with subjects, such as *Warrendale, Grey Gardens, Harlan County U.S.A., Best Boy, Soldier Girls, Seventeen,* leading to on-camera performances that are clearly enabled by, addressed to, and improvised enactments of that relationship, despite token adherence to the "don't look at the camera" code; and

(2) films about subjects whose extra-filmic social role consists of public performance, including entertainers (*Jane, Burroughs, Comedian, Eye of the Mask*), musicians (from *Lonely Boy* to *Woodstock* and *Stop Making Sense* via *Antonia: A Portrait of the Woman*), prostitutes (*Chicken Ranch, Hookers on Davie*), politicians (*Primary, Milhouse, The Right Candidate for Rosedale*), transsexual people (*The Queens, What Sex Am I?, Hookers on Davie*), sexual performers (*Not a Love Story, Striptease*), guerillas (*Underground, When the Mountains Tremble*), bodybuilders (*Pumping Iron I* and *II*), artists (*Painters Painting, Portrait of the Artist—As an Old Lady*), teachers (*High School*), street kids (*Streetwise*), salespeople (*Salesman, The Store*), crusaders (*If You Love This Planet*), and clergy (*Marjoe*). In this group of films, special scrutiny is usually given to the dialectic of public and private, the subject's identity expressed by means of an onstage-offstage intercutting. The genre offers as one of the pleasures of the text the deciphering of borders between social performance, film performance, and so-called private behavior, and the discovery that the borders are both culturally encoded and imaginary.

Interviews and Beyond

Now, of course, within North American documentary, we have been back in a phase since the early seventies where presentational forms of performance are very much in vogue. The seventies revived the interview in the documentary, thanks largely to the feminists, the New Left, and such individual pioneers as Emile de Antonio. The eighties have witnessed a flourishing wave of hybrid experimentation with these presentational modes as well as with stylizations of representational modes, including dramatization, a wave that has been termed, not surprisingly, "post-documentary."[4] The current repertory includes a whole spectrum of performance elements, usually incorporated within hybrid works, as often as not alongside vestiges of earlier styles, from voice-of-God direct address narration, to observational *vérité*, to interview/compilation conventions of the seventies.

[. . .]

A timely intervention by Bill Nichols has pointed out a central problem of authority and voice arising from the seventies current of interview films, namely those mostly historiographical projects reacting against *vérité* discourses, building on the de Antonio model, and addressing Feminist or New Left constituencies.[5] The model is very familiar: representative subjects offer interview performances of personal reminiscences or present experiences that figure large in a documentary investigation of a politically apt topic. Nichols' criticism is directed at those documentaries in which the authority of the filmmaker is diffused through, or uncritically hidden behind, the voices of the subjects. The best known example of this risk is New Day Films' *Union Maids,* in which the evasions and nostalgias of the subjects' oral histories become the liabilities of the film as a whole. "Interviews diffuse authority." Nichols argues,

> A gap remains between the voice of a social actor recruited to the film and the voice of the film.... The greatest problem has been to retain that sense of a gap between the voice of interviewees and the voice of the text as a whole ... [In *The Day After Trinity,*] the text not only appears to lack a voice or perspective of its own, the perspective of its character-witnesses is patently inadequate ... the voice of the text disappears behind characters who speak to us ... we no longer sense that a governing voice actively provides or withholds the imprimatur of veracity according to its own purposes and assumptions, its own canons of validation ... the film becomes a rubber stamp.... The sense of hierarchy of voices becomes lost.

The problem of the disappearing voice, however, is not intrinsic to the interview performance mode—it may just as well be a condition of state funding for most of the films in question. In any case, it would be extremely foolish to disparage the tremendous advances in popular social history and the political enfranchisement enabled by the interview genre, nor to disallow filmmakers' choices to mute their individual voices in favor of providing a forum for voices that have been suppressed, forgotten, or denied media access. Nichols points to several films—such as *Rosie the Riveter* and de Antonio's works—in which the self-reflexive contextualization of interviews allows the filmmaker's analytic perspective to complement and coexist with, without drowning out, the voices of subjects. The disappearance of the voice derives less from the interview format than from a lack of focus in conceptualization, research, and goals, or from a self-censorship triggered by Public Broadcasting or NFB or NEH funding. It has also derived from a fuzzy and sentimental populism leading to what Jeffrey Youdelman has described as an abdication of political leadership on the part of media intellectuals, and to the absence of historical contextualization with which both Youdelman and Chuck Kleinhans have taxed *The War at Home.*[6] Ethics also enters into the picture, whether it is a question of responsibility to the subject or to the spectator. The latter is certainly not served by the camouflage of the terms of the construction of the discourse: does the spectator not have the right to know who is speaking, what the author's political relationship to the speaker is, and how, to whom, and to what end the film is addressed?

Nichols diagnoses this latter problem by focusing on corrective self-reflexive tendencies in some of the best recent films. However, it is more pertinent to this article to focus on evolving performance styles in the same work, particularly on the very promising excursions into the presentational mode (which in any case have much in common with Nichols' prescription of self-reflexivity). For the most visible and innovative pattern in the current decade is in fact the expansion of performance input by social actors which goes beyond the oral history format of the seventies to experiment with dramatic performance modes, both presentational and representational. The new visibility of dramatized and semifictional performance components constitutes a reaction against the "string-of-interview" orthodoxy. Dramatization is clearly a useful means of fleshing out the gaps left by the interview format, gaps of a technical or ideological nature, or gaps due simply to uncontrollable factors (as in *Michael, a Gay Son,* in which a very tense "coming out" encounter with the protagonist's hostile family is conveyed through fictionalized role-playing). It is not surprising that the new "dramatized" documentaries, (or "docudramas," as they are called in some quarters, misleadingly I think, since the term is used most commonly and aptly for fictionalized reconstructions like the United States television films *The Missiles of October* or *The Atlanta Child Murders*)[7] may be divided like all their forebears into: (a) those whose emphasis or context is presentational *(In the King of Prussia, Far from Poland, The Kid Who Couldn't Miss, Two Laws, Not Crazy Like You Think, Quel Numéro/What Number*—in fact films Nichols would call self-reflexive) and (b) those whose primary address is representational *(Michael, a Gay Son, What You Take for Granted, Journal Inachevé, Democracy on Trial,* the historical episodes of *When the Mountains Tremble, Le Dernier Glacier, Caffé Italia, The Masculine Mystique).* Needless to say, the new expansion of the repertory into the terrain of dramatization has greatly multiplied the importance of performance in documentary as a whole and greatly expanded the opportunities for social actors to "perform" their lives in every format from semifictional improvisation to didactic sketches.

The eclecticism of the expanded hybrid repertory sharpens our sense of our bearings in relation to our documentary past. One useful observation is that the more presentational of these new formats is most in keeping with the traditional documentary genius for incorporating the presence and performance of social actors into the cinematic text. The more representational films seem inclined more towards a long tradition of "docu-flavoured" fiction (de Sica/ Rossellini, Cassavetes, McBride, Loach/ Garnett). From another point of view, the new repertory removes us yet another step away from the sixties: the small amount of work still appearing in an unadulterated *vérité* style *(Middletown, The Store)* seems purist indeed, even classical, and reminds us that the sixties are no longer the definitive crucible for today's documentarists, but more and more just another period style available for postmodern recycling. On the other hand, the new work looks back in a very vivid way to the years of the Popular Front, in particular to the "wide variety of styles" that characterized such late-thirties hybrid films as *Spanish Earth* and *Native Land.*

It is not surprising that the thirties are evoked more than any other period by the present work. For Ivens and his contemporaries were no strangers to several contextual conditions that have influenced today's alignment of a hybrid performance-based documentary style with an atmosphere of increasing political polarization and crisis, and of cultural attrition:

(1) Economic factors may have been predominant: after the late seventies and the arts funding crisis of the Reagan-Thatcher-Mulroney era, very few independents other than Wiseman, the National Film Board, and a handful of TV-funded artists have been able to afford the high-ratio budget of representational *vérité* (except perhaps in video). Sustaining representational illusion is too expensive for the austerity of the eighties, and presentational elements offer filmmakers and subjects alike more control over the pro-filmic event and the budget. In the pre-war period, for similar reasons, it was no accident that it was with the (relatively) luxurious state-supplied budget of *Power and the Land* that Ivens left behind the off-the-cuff hybridity of his earlier films for the graceful representational coherence of that film.

(2) The fact that the new presentational performance modes were pioneered by political filmmakers, whether feminists or other progressives, is highly pertinent. In this regard, we've arrived once more back

at Ivens, the Old Left grandfather of New Left political documentarists and their contemporaries. For Ivens, the proto-*vérité* style that he called "easy naturalism" precluded the organized communication of "content value," that is, the psychological dynamic or atmospheric texturing obscured the social text. Social documentarists generations later came independently to the same conclusion: pure representational *vérité* was often a medium of aestheticist psychologism that by itself often precluded the political explorations that such filmmakers sought to produce.

(3) Other factors in the post-*vérité* configuration must not be discounted, though they are decidedly minor. First, the critical acceptance of the presentational performance style was encouraged by the currency of Brechtian theory in film culture persisting since 1968. There may also have occurred a certain cross-fertilization with a presentational counter-tradition outside of Anglo-Saxon culture that predates the current phenomenon by a whole generation. This tradition, originating in France (Rouch and Marker) and in Quebec (Pierre Perrault and a national documentary tradition known as "*le direct*"), has never had any commitment to representational illusion. Since the late fifties, this tradition has accumulated a rich repertory of presentational elements, elevating verbal and interactional performances to a degree of exceptional expressiveness. Although Rouch is a household word among documentarists (and Perrault would be were he from Paris rather than Montreal), this possible cross-fertilization remains a subject for future research since the cross-linguistic circulation of this cinema has been greatly hampered by its privileging of speech and oral culture. Finally, the postmodernist absorption and recycling of the presentational television vernacular is surely as important as it is hard to quantify as an element of the new post-documentary performance style.

Performance and Collaboration

"Collaboration in Documentary": Ivens' title is more than just a literal description of the relationship engendered by the *mise-en-scène* of subject performance by filmmaker. "Collaboration" also embodies a perennial ideal of the documentary tradition, the goal of a changed, democratized relationship between artist and subject. The subject' s performance for the camera becomes a collaboration, a stake in and a contribution to the authorship of the work of art. Performance becomes a gauge of the ethical and political accountability of the filmmaker's relationship with subject.

Although Ivens' respect for the integrity of his cast is obvious, his distance from the democratic ideal of collaborative performance is problematical. He admits quite openly to manipulating and tricking his "performers" into performing, and of keeping them in the dark as to film techniques and as to the results of their own performance. These less-than-egalitarian terms of the collaboration were necessary, he claims (not unlike some Method director who has terrorized his leading lady) to preserve elements of freshness in the performance. Unwittingly, Ivens points to an ethical liability of the representational mode during its classical phase, a problem which surfaces perhaps even more acutely in the work of Ivens' contemporary, Flaherty.

I mentioned earlier the dichotomy in Flaherty's work between his two silent ethnographic features with their presentational elements and his later mytho-narrative features based exclusively on representational performances. The issue of collaboration seems to be the crux of this dichotomy. The absence of presentational elements in *Man of Aran* and *Louisiana Story* is surely an index of the films' minimization of the input of the subjects and of their virtual embargo on the cultural textures and social realities of the Aran (West Irish) and Cajun communities respectively. It is true that in both films rudimentary voice-tracks gently ruffle the surface of the seamless representational unity: in the former, the performers improvise semi-synchronized dialogue-commentary over the edited film, and in the latter, Flaherty's voice-over commentary is interpolated by a few awkward and static direct sound sequences of an expository nature. But the verbal performances of the actors in either case do not constitute a qualitative heightening of their collaborative input—especially in *Louisiana,* with the heavily scripted and heavily rehearsed feel of the dialogue. The representational web is ultimately as intact as the hegemony of authorial vision and control over ethnographic mission and subject input. The legendary contribution of "Nanook" to the film that bears his name is by now a distant memory and inoperative ideal.

A decade after *Louisiana,* the introduction of direct sound technology into the documentary arena transformed the potential for subject collaboration as surely as it transformed the nature of subject performance. *Vérité,* as I have stated, failed to push this potential as far as it would go by retaining the representational mode of documentary performance. By the time the *vérité* movement had consolidated direct sound as the everyday vocabulary of the documentary, grassroots political movements were beginning to arise to profit from the hitherto untapped political potential of the new apparatus. The New Left of the late sixties, and especially the women's movement a few years later, embraced speech and intercommunication as a political process, favored participatory and collaborative cultural forms, and privileged oral history as an essential means of political and cultural empowerment. It is not surprising then that their documentary cinema featured presentational performance elements ranging from the simple interview and group discussion formats[8] of the early years to the more complex formats I have listed. Incorporating vocal performances into a film was a crucial strategy for an artist who wished to share creative and political control with subjects/social actors. Whereas *vérité* had by and large retained the Flahertian mystique of authorial control, the presentational modes of the New Left and the women's movement dissipated that mystique and permitted varying degrees of subject input into the finished documentary, of subject responsibility for his or her image and speech. The ideal to which such filmmakers subscribed, to greater or lesser degree, was of the documentarist as resource person, technician or facilitator, and of the subject-performer as real steward of creative responsibility.

Such a prescriptive distinction between the political and ethical advantages of a specific formal strategy of course runs the risk of aesthetic idealism and political naivete, not to mention a technological fallacy: the power of the filmmaker is such that ultimately no strategy is the automatic guarantee of collaborative process. Even the most presentational, collaborative performance is subject to ethical abuse in the editing room or exhibition context. Ultimately, the creative and political accountability of the artist is clearly the final guarantor against political and ethical abuses. However, this caveat having been registered, a concluding glimpse at two recent Canadian documentaries that focus on a similar subject clarifies the political dimension of the distinction between presentational and representational modes that I would like to insist on as a general guideline to the artist's accountability to subject performance and collaboration.

Bonnie Klein's National Film Board of Canada feature, *Not a Love Story, A Film about Pornography,* and Kay Armatage's independent short, *Striptease,* consider aspects of the sex industry through predominantly representational and presentational approaches respectively. With *Not a Love Story,* the relationship between the on-screen filmmaker persona, embarked on her voyage of discovery of the pornographic night, and her guide, ex-stripper

Linda Lee Tracy, is conveyed representationally through traditional *vérité*. Much of the criticism of the film centered on the manipulative appearance of this relationship between artist and collaborator. The narrative thread of the relationship includes two sex performance interludes set in representational frames (Tracy as stripper on location in a Montreal club, Tracy as centerfold model in the studio of a *Hustler* photographer) and an ultimate conversion denouement, in which filmmaker and stripper discuss the latter's re(-)formed vision of her past and future. This thread is intercut with interviews with feminist authorities on the subject. Caught up in the emotional charge of the subject, the audience may not notice that the distribution of representational and presentational roles in the film follows a certain hierarchy. The sex worker, Tracy, is caught in a representational role, performing her ongoing life in the service of the film, while the recruited intellectuals perform their role of analysis and polemics within the presentational interview formats. It is not difficult to conclude that the democratic ideals of feminism are being sacrificed in the process—are sex workers themselves less entitled than intellectuals to verbalize directly about the sex industry? Furthermore, the specter of voyeurism and visual pleasure is unavoidably raised by the strong construction of observational discourse in Tracy's two principal scenes of sexual performance, with their assault on conventional notions of tact and their inescapable flirtation with the "pornographic" discourse that is the target of the film. To compare the *Hustler* posing session, for example, with its scandalous aura of brutality and complicity (the female photographer applies "pussy juice" before the take), with, say, the similar scenes from the improvised but fictional *Prostitute,* where the sexual performance scenes are lucid, controlled, and self-reflexive, demonstrates the clear shortcomings of representational *vérité* in the domain of sexual politics.

Armatage's *Striptease* has surprisingly more clarity and complexity than *Not a Love Story* despite its infinitely more modest means: strippers and other sex industry workers present themselves in interviews and monologues, and present their work in erotic dance-performances constructed solely for the camera (in *Prostitute,* at the other end of the scale, they perform semifictional dramatizations within a self-reflexive narrative, collaboratively scripted, to a similar effect). In *Striptease,* the sex industry is not validated, but its workers are: subject-generated performance, sharpened by its presentational mode, ensures that the dignity and subjectivity of the subjects are respected along with their right to present themselves, to define their images and their lives. As for the problem of voyeurism, I suspect that the visual pleasure of the spectator is compromised by the explicit aura of control that characterizes the sexual performance. It is no coincidence that Armatage enables glimpses of a collective political solution (unionization) that makes Klein's ambiguous individual moral solution all the more superficial.

Voice and First-Person Performance

Not a Love Story has been criticized also for the autobiographical presence within the diegesis of author Bonnie Klein. The first-person performance seemed ineffectual in terms of cinematic charisma presumably, but more importantly in terms also of the issue of authorial voice. As Nichols puts it, such authorial presence lacks both the "self-validating, authoritative tone of a previous [voice-of-God] tradition" and "seem[s] to refuse a privileged position in relation to other characters."[9] Submitting both to the authoritative testimony of the stellar lineup of expert witnesses and to the grandstanding of her representational protagonist

Tracy, the diegetic Klein serves rather as a timid, inconclusive, perhaps *faux-naif* guide throughout the pornographic nightmare. Similar problems are arguably posed by the whole tradition of autobiographical performance, from the first-person narrations of Flaherty (*The Land*) and John Huston (*The Battle of San Pietro*) in the forties to the Me-Decade's self-presentations of everyone from Werner Herzog (*La Soufrière*) to Michael Rubbo (*Waiting for Fidel*, etc.). It seems to me that the first-person format too often limits social-issue documentary to the exploratory phase, pegs it at the level of political evasion, bewildering empiricism, and individual moral or metaphysical floundering. Even where it is rigorously self-reflexive, as with Jill Godmilow, the personal is perhaps shown to be political, but the political often fails to rise above the personal level. While the first-person performance does undeniably provide a manageable dramatic entry to the enormously complex subjects of pornography, solidarity (*Far from Poland*), and the Holocaust (*Dark Lullabies, Shoah*), it does not necessarily serve the political dissection of these subjects. It may be argued that the strategy seems best suited for properly individual, autobiographical subjects such as intrafamily relationships (*Best Boy, Coming Home*), or for the feminist genre that connects individual socialization to broader political forces (*Daughter Rite, Joyce at 34, Home Movie*).

Ultimately, while the problems of authorial voice can be addressed in part by the strategy of first-person performance, and while authorial presence can signal a refreshingly self-reflexive honesty, more often than not the authorial performance—whether representational in such films as *Not a Love Story*, or presentational and self-reflexive in such films as *Far from Poland*—raises as many issues as it solves. In any case, a whole range of other questions are raised by autobiographical performance in documentary—from ethics to narcissism to the demographic representativity of the media worker—but these are beyond the scope of this paper and are receiving due critical attention.[10]

Conclusion: The Right to Play Oneself

I have offered a historical overview of the presence of performance in documentary. I have discerned alternating and simultaneous impulses toward presentational and representational performance throughout the documentary tradition, then briefly engaged the current debate about voice in political documentary, and finally only touched on the distinct subcategory of autobiographical performance. All of this has led to a global assertion of the special aptness of the presentational mode in the present context, alongside both an insistence on the continuing relevance of the interview format of oral history popularized in the seventies and an enthusiastic welcoming of the current experimentation with hybrid performance modes, including dramatization. Subject performance, affirmed and enriched as a presentational element of documentary film, remains a means by which the most committed of documentary filmmakers can aspire to the realization of their democratic ideals. Collaboration between artist and subject, as elaborated by Joris Ivens at the end of the thirties, remains a meaningful political ideal as well as an artistic strategy, but the terms he set out have been somewhat transformed. "Acting to play oneself " is still the key, but, "Don't look at the camera" is replaced by, "Look at the camera" as a "basic necessity" of documentary collaboration. In the same decade, Walter Benjamin spoke of "modern man's legitimate claim to be reproduced";[11] might we not add that the individual has now established the claim also to construct that reproduction, the right to play oneself?

NOTES

1. This text excerpted from the periodical *Films*, vol. 1, no. 2 (Spring 1940), pp. 30–42, appears in a later modified form in Ivens' autobiographical *The Camera and I* (New York and Berlin: International Publishers, 1968), pp. 187–206.
2. The term "social actors" designating real-life characters playing their own social roles in nonfiction film and presumably having an extratextual autonomy has been standard usage in documentary studies since Bill Nichols' influential *Ideology and the Image: Social Representation in the Cinema and Other Media* (Bloomington, Ind., 1981) cf., pp. 181–85.
3. Helen van Dongen, "Robert J. Flaherty, 1884–1951," *Film Quarterly*, vol. XVIII, no. 4 (Summer 1965), p. 4.
4. See for example Geoff Pevere, "Projections: Assessing Canada's Films of '85," *The Canadian Forum*, vol. LXV, no. 755 (March 1986), p. 39.
5. Bill Nichols, 'The Voice of Documentary," *Film Quarterly*, vol. 36, no. 3 (Spring 1983); rpt. in Nichols, ed., *Movies and Methods, Volume II* (Berkeley, 1985), pp. 265–6.
6. Jeffrey Youdelman, "Narration, Invention, and History: A Documentary Dilemma," *Cineaste*, vol. XII, no. 2, 1982, pp. 8–15; Chuck Kleinhans, "Forms, Politics, Makers, and Contexts: Basic Issues for a Theory of Radical Political Documentary," in Thomas Waugh, ed., *Show Us Life: Toward a History and Aesthetics of the Committed Documentary* (Metuchen, N.J.: Scarecrow Press, 1984), pp. 318–42.
7. For example, the scope of a 1986 McGill University symposium on docudrama included a range of NFB productions: a TV-movie style fictionalized reconstruction *(Canada's Sweetheart: The Saga of Hal C. Banks)* anarchival compilation interpolated with cabaret-style theatrical sketches *(The Kid Who Couldn't Miss)*, several documentarles incorporating fictional episodes *(Mourir A Tue-Tete, Le Dernier Glacier, Passiflora)*, and a scripted fiction feature constructed on improvisational performances by nonprofessional actors *(Ninety Days)*. Cf., the author's "Thunder over the Docudrama: Symposium Highlights NFB's World-Class Role," *Cinema Canada*, no. 128 (March 1986), p. 26.
8. Julia Lesage has often discussed the importance of consciousness raising as a deep structure of feminist discourse in documentary, most recently in *"Feminist Documentary: Aesthetics and Politics,"* in Waugh, op. cit., pp. 223–51.
9. Nichols, op. cit., p. 265.
10. See for example a recent installment of the ongoing discussion of autobiographical documentary: David Schwartz, "First Person Singular: Autobiography in Film," *The Independent*, vol. 9, no. 4, pp. 12–15. The author of one of the most elaborate studies of documentary autobiography is John Stuart Katz, e.g., Katz, ed., *Autobiography: Film/Video/Photography* (Toronto: Art Gallery of Ontario, 1978). Katz's more recent work and much other material relevant to this article appears in Larry Gross and Jay Ruby, eds., *Image Ethics: The Moral and Legal Rights of Subjects in Documentary Film and Television* (Philadelphia, 1988).
11. Walter Benjamin, "The Work of Art in the Age of Mechanical Reproduction," in Hannah Arendt, ed., *Illuminations* (New York: 1969), p. 232.

100

PHILLIP BRIAN HARPER

MARLON RIGGS

The Subjective Position of Documentary Video (1995)

It is probably true that, in the United States at least, the museum is the cultural institution that has been most directly challenged by the video art of the last thirty years. From the early installations of Nam June Paik and Peter Campus, which disrupted conventional ideas of what *media* were suitable for gallery display, to the narrative pieces of such artists as Cecilia Condit, which have raised the slightly different question of what representational *modes* might be featured in exhibition, serious videowork has consistently interrogated the criteria by which the museum defines "art," if only so that it could, paradoxically, itself accede to that privileged status.[1]

The work of Marlon Riggs, on the other hand, is less self-consciously concerned with the parameters of art than with the bounds of *video* in a more conventional sense. Prior to the emergence of video as a high-art medium—and before the term itself became synonymous with MTV's pop-music film shorts—"video" was most widely invoked in its function as the visual component of standard broadcast television, usually in the context of picture failure: "We have temporarily lost the video portion of our broadcast," an announcer would intone over a test pattern or station-identification screen; "please stand by." In this sense video was neither a specific artistic medium nor a particular representational genre; and while it was always implicitly paired with the *audio* portion of the television broadcast, the latter was also clearly subordinated to it because it was, after all, specifically the video element that made television what it was.

Of course, to invoke what television was (or *is*) is to suggest that broadcast TV, no less than the museum itself, constitutes a relatively discrete culture characterized not only by the manifestation of various distinctive features, but, conversely, by the *exclusion* of certain elements whose eventual admission to the realm must figure as a significant intervention. Museum and television cultures, varying as they do, will register such interventions in different ways. As the citation of an extensive electronic infrastructure, for instance, the video installation jars in the museum context precisely because it contrasts with the latter's traditional investment in an art defined by individualized craft and signature technique. Broadcast television, on the other hand, is actually *constituted through* its extensive range and *predicated on* installation, and any effective challenge to its norms will thus register not primarily as "art," but as an innovation in the *programming* that defines the televisual project. Begun as a version of standard television documentary, Riggs's work can be understood as precisely such an innovation.

One reason for this is that most of Riggs's work has actually been presented in national telecast. Three of his four feature-length productions have been shown by PBS, though the controversy surrounding one of the broadcasts seems to have indicated as much about the risks taken by videomakers in pursuing PBS distribution as it did about the degree to which Riggs's work itself challenged television's generic boundaries; at the same time, however, those risks—stemming from PBS's reliance on the government-funded Corporation for Public Broadcasting and the tenuousness of congressional support for the latter since the Reagan-Bush era—suggest the extent to which Riggs troubled broadcast convention, seen as implicitly under attack in the presentation of his work.

There is very little, if any, indication of such a challenge in Riggs's first professional feature documentary, *Ethnic Notions* (Figure 100.1), which was produced in association with public television station KQED in San Francisco. This work, which examines the caricature of black people in U.S. popular culture of the late nineteenth and early twentieth centuries, presents a standard set of contemporary talking-head interviews

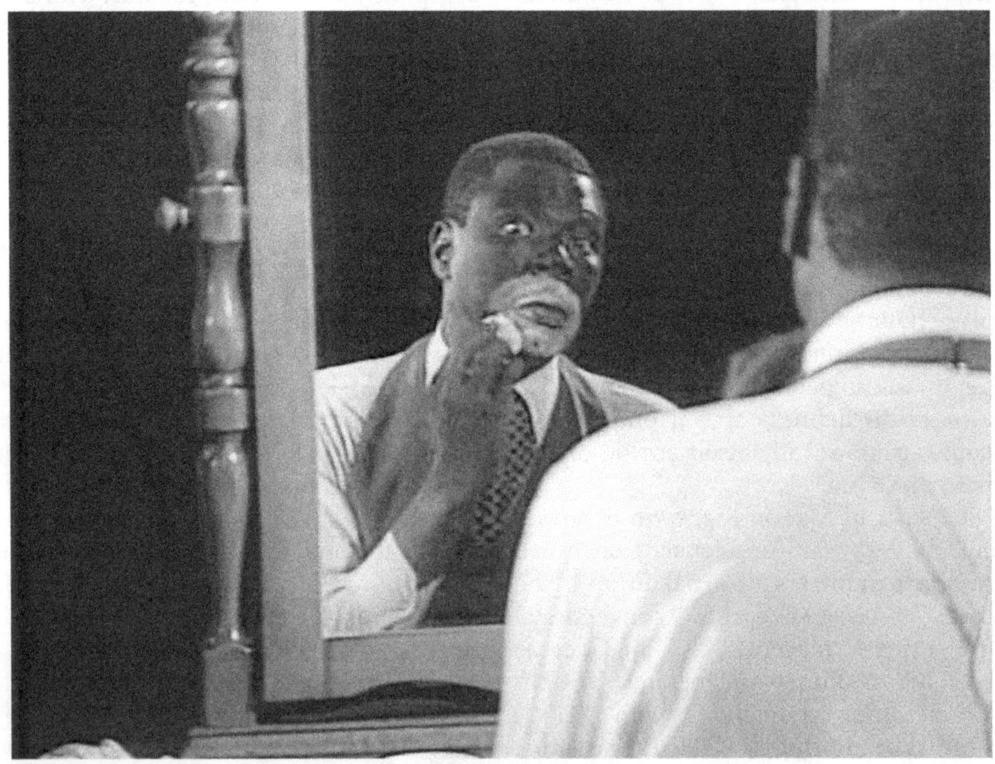

FIGURE 100.1 *Ethnic Notions* (Marlon Riggs, 1987). Screen capture from DVD.

with "expert" commentators (cultural critic Barbara Christian, performance historian and choreographer Leni Sloan, historian George Fredrickson, among others) intercut with historical stills and film footage documenting the cultural stereotyping under consideration. In both its format and its fairly conventional liberal-pluralist critique, *Ethnic Notions* largely exemplifies the mode of documentary exploration long familiar to PBS audiences. Still, its subject matter is striking, incorporating materials whose blatant racism is so alien in the late twentieth century as to startle greatly most viewers. Ranging from product names and mascots like Aunt Jemima, Uncle Remus, and Nigger Head; through such household items as caricature cookie jars, "pickaninny" joke cards, and Parker Brothers' *Ten Little Niggers* game; to entertainments like vaudevillian minstrelsy, the films *Birth of a Nation* and *The Jazz Singer,* and a cartoon featuring Bugs Bunny and Elmer Fudd performing in blackface, the objects of *Ethnic Notions'* immediate critique are many and varied, indicating the depth and pervasiveness of U.S. cultural racism. The point of Riggs's piece, however, is not merely to expose the widespread invocation of offensive stereotype, but, beyond this, to suggest such invocation's detrimental consequences. In a strikingly didactic concluding sequence, boldface intertitles declare that the artifacts examined in the video confirm popular ideas of blacks as ugly, savage, and happy in servitude. Christian sums up the effect of racist caricature in household knickknacks in the statement that gives the piece its name, asserting that stereotyping "notions in the home" lead to derogatory "notions in the mind."

The forthrightness of this proclamation comprises a critical element of Riggs's larger videographic project. Specifically, in presenting such unabashed judgment as to the social effect of racist artifacts, the piece veers from the putative norms of cultural documentary to which it otherwise adheres in its formal structure. At the same time, the authoritative significances of that structure—derived largely from the dual factors of the talking-head interview format and the unenhanced visual presentation of the historical materials—work to dissemble the questionable character of the judgment itself; for, even granting that racist representations can foster racist sentiment, the complexities of representation are such that it is altogether unclear exactly *how* they might do so.

It is not at all necessary that such videowork as this, with its evident documentary function, present, for the sake of that function, a fully substantiated cultural analysis, as opposed to *Ethnic Notions'* properly hypothetical proposition. There is, however, a formal tension in the piece that raises the question of whether it best represents the type of sociocultural interrogation that the medium can sustain. It is the tension between the generalized seat of authority—represented by the interview sequences in *Ethnic Notions*—and such necessary and powerful speculative judgment as that which the piece asserts regarding the effects of racist caricature. Precisely because the strength of such judgment lies substantially *in* its speculative character—so alien a quality amid the classic instances of talking-head reportage that imbue the form with its authoritative significance—its most productive figuration would seem to be one that questioned, rather than depended upon, traditional modes for the assertion of cultural authority.

This point becomes clearer, perhaps, when we consider another standard element of documentary television that *Ethnic Notions* incorporates—the narrative voice-over. This feature—provided by African American actor Esther Rolle, and running almost without interruption throughout the production—enhances the authoritative effect of the piece in a way similar to that of the "experts'" pronouncements: seemingly emanating from the experience of overarching surveillance that it imaginatively conjures up, the voice-over formally bespeaks an apparently omniscient perspective from which the work can make proclamations that are consequently registered as general and universal. This generality and universality are quickly problematized, however, within the first few minutes of the piece, when the narrator—whose voice easily registers as "black" even if it isn't recognized as that of Rolle—invokes the meaning in "our" lives of the various racist caricatures collected in "our" homes during the period under examination. These invocations, which occur amid claims as to the onetime currency of such caricatures throughout the country, seem meant to connote a genericized "American" citizenry; but the narrator's discernible blackness, coupled with the fact that it is specifically caricatures *of* blacks that are under consideration, render such a reference problematic at best, and this in a way that confuses—rather than productively complicating—the subjective position of the work.

By the time of his follow-up to *Ethnic Notions*—the 1991 piece *Color Adjustment*, which focuses specifically on images of blacks in U.S. television from the mid-1940s through the 1980s—Riggs seemed to have become much more certain of exactly how the subjectivities informing the work could best be formally engaged. While the two videos share basic elements of structure and format, they differ significantly in the ways they use those elements to establish critical perspective; two points in particular are noteworthy.

First of all, though *Color Adjustment* maintains the focus on individual authorities that characterizes *Ethnic Notions*, its interviewees represent many more *types* of authority than are admitted in the earlier work. Indeed, not only does *Color Adjustment* temper the credentialed academicism that it reprises from *Ethnic Notions* with the different (yet equally professionalized) considerations of television actors, directors, and producers, but it also supplements the professional assessments of *all* the interviewees with their *personal* reflections on blacks' televisual depictions. Thus, not only do the star and the producer of the 1960s sitcom *Julia*—Diahann Carroll and Hal Kanter—discuss the import of the show in its historical moment, but Rolle (an interviewee in this video, rather than the narrator) recounts her own reaction to the program during its run. Similarly, Carroll and producer Steve Bochco speak of the impact on them, *as viewers*, of Nat "King" Cole's short-lived variety show of the late 1950s. By the same token, cultural commentators Henry Louis Gates, Jr., and Patricia Turner not only analyze the significances of such programs as *Good Times* and *The Cosby Show*, but they also recall their personal responses to television appearances by blacks during the relatively recent period when these were still rare. In other words, the judgments made in *Color Adjustment*, rather than seeming to issue from a putative neutral zone conjured in the relation between expert testimony and omniscient narration, are clearly grounded in the subjective experiences *and* the considered deliberations of those chosen by Riggs to undertake the cultural criticism implicated in the piece.

Second, Riggs does not shy away in *Color Adjustment* from positing the video itself as representing a subjective viewpoint—a specifically African American perspective. Most pointedly, while *Ethnic Notions* deploys a voice-over narrative whose conjuration of generalized "universality" runs athwart the evidently *interested* character of the producing subject, the narration for *Color Adjustment*, supplied by Ruby Dee, unequivocally references its invocations of a collective "we" to a specifically African American constituency from which the guiding subjectivity of the video itself clearly emerges. *Color Adjustment* differs significantly, then, from its forerunner. Like the earlier work, it oversimplifies the relation between representation and social fact, suggesting, for instance, that *The Cosby Show* of the 1980s and early 1990s affirmed the ideology of the Reagan-Bush era without considering how it might also have challenged Reaganist thinking. This aside, however, the later piece represents a much more confident and sophisticated engagement with issues of critical subjectivity than is evident in the earlier one, which suggests that the five years separating the two works was a period of profound development in Riggs's theory of video production.

What happened during that period, of course, is that Riggs produced *Tongues Untied* (Figure 100.2), the piece for which he is probably most widely known, and as a result of which he became pegged as a controversial figure. Representing the complete abandonment of the conventional documentary technique in which he was trained and that he adapted in *Ethnic Notions, Tongues Untied* can be considered specifically a *meditation* on the life experiences of gay-identified African American men at the time of the work's production. Insofar as it depicts those lived experiences, *Tongues Untied* is no less "documentary," in the broad sense of the term, than Riggs's more conventional early piece. The *modes* of that figuration, however, are very different from the ways that *Ethnic Notions* registers the import of the material that it engages.

For instance, there are no conventional interview scenes in *Tongues Untied*. Rather, the work presents an array of short ensemble performances, monologues, poetry readings, and musical presentations interwoven with footage documenting various moments in the lives of black gay men. There is no unitary thesis in the work, but several interrelated thematic lines run throughout, addressing black gay men's alienation from much of African American society ("I cannot go home as who I am," one refrain line declares), the need for black gay men to break silence regarding their sexuality (referenced in the title of the piece), and the urgency of black men's loving support for one another (signaled in the video's effective slogan: "Black men loving black men is *the* revolutionary act"). Further—and most significantly—*Tongues Untied* incorporates two fundamental revisions in documentary subjectivity, which it posits together in such a way as to confer that subjectivity with a potency rarely found in the genre. On the one hand, Riggs himself appears in the piece as a full participant in (and often the guiding consciousness behind) the performances presented on tape; on the other hand, those same performances are profoundly collective, not only being executed by an ensemble of black gay men, as I have already indicated, but incorporating the creative work (music, prose reflections, verse poetry) of such men, in *addition* to that of Riggs, as primary materials. Thus *Tongues Untied,* insofar as it admits of Riggs's own meditative reflections (on, among other things, his childhood sexuality, his experience of racism from white gay men, his HIV-positive status), veers from conventional documentary into creative expression. At the same time, by incorporating the imaginative contributions of men other than Riggs, the work extends beyond narrowly personal individualism. Finally, inasmuch as all the contributions are based on the reality of lived experience, the piece remains as "factual" as traditional documentary itself.

This expansive amalgam of documentary and expressive modes and of individual and collective voices is *Tongues Untied's* most notable achievement, in light of which the debate over the video's celebration of homoeroticism (cited by numerous PBS affiliates across the country as sufficient reason not to air the show) appears as the grossest Philistinism.[2] It is Riggs's expert realization of such polyvalent subjectivity, moreover, that carries over from *Tongues Untied* back to the more recognizable documentary format of *Color Adjustment* in 1991.

Not that Riggs did not continue to work in the more expansive mode that *Tongues Untied* exemplifies. The short 1990 piece *Affirmations* combines three sections in a whole that achieves the same type

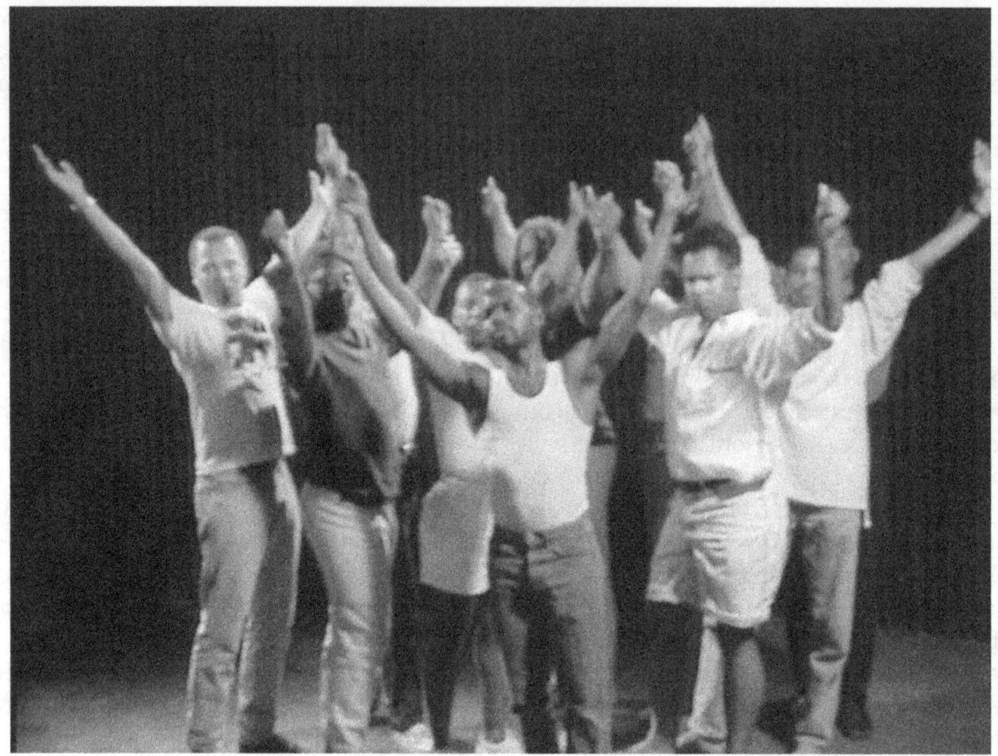

FIGURE 100.2 *Tongues Untied* (Marlon Riggs, 1989). Screen capture from DVD.

of complexity as the longer 1989 work. Segueing from a monologic coming-out story by black gay writer Reginald T. Jackson, to footage of the group Gay Men of African Descent marching in a Harlem African American Freedom Day parade, to various black gay men's recitations—over reprised march footage and a freedom song sound track—of their "wishes" for the future, *Affirmations* recapitulates the synthesizing effect of *Tongues Untied* in such a way as to become its effective coda—brief, eloquent, eminently moving.

The 1995 release *Black Is . . . Black Ain't*—left unfinished by Riggs at the time of his AIDS-related death in April 1994 and completed by his colleagues Nicole Atkinson and Christiane Badgley—takes on the overwhelming topic of black identity itself, which, with its myriad contradictions and overdeterminations, is in many ways perfectly suited for the expansive mode Riggs developed in *Tongues Untied*. Perhaps because the question of what constitutes "blackness" *is* so big, however (the video zips at breakneck speed through considerations of religion, skin color politics, sexuality, gender difference, and class stratification, to name just a few of the issues it tackles), *Black Is . . . Black Ain't* is less successful than *Tongues Untied, as a videographic piece*. Based loosely on a metaphorical conceptualization of African American life as a type of gumbo, the work closes by considering what constitutes the *roux* that binds together the disparate ingredients of blackness. It settles on no answer to this question, and the video itself similarly lacks a unifying element. This could have been provided by the leitmotif footage—much of it intensely moving—of Riggs in his hospital bed during one of his final illnesses, reflecting on his life, his work, his coming death, his blackness. This personal experience of

AIDS is never collectivized, however, in the way that the individual histories presented in *Tongues Untied* are, resulting in a less fully realized work than one imagines Riggs envisioned when he first conceived the piece.

It is a testament to the level of Riggs's accomplishment that his own work provides the best standard against which this last project can be measured. His interventions in the definition of documentary video have altered not only our sense of what constitutes viable television broadcast, but the terms of what counts as "creative development" in that traditional realm of video production.

NOTES

1. For documentation of the work of Nam June Paik, see Toni Stooss and Thomas Kellein, eds., *Nam June Paik: Video Time—Video Space* (New York: Harry N. Abrams, 1993); for Peter Campus, see his *Video-Installationen, Foto-Installationen, Fotos, Videobanden*, exh. cat. (Cologne: Kölnischer Kunstverein, 1979). On Cecilia Condit, see Patricia Mellencamp, "Uncanny Feminism," in *Indiscretions: Avant-Garde Film, Video, and Feminism* (Bloomington: Indiana University Press, 1990), 126–39.
2. For a contemporaneous account of the controversy, see Frank J. Prial, "TV Film about Gay Black Men Is under Attack," *The New York Times*, June 25, 1991, C13. For commentary about it, see John J. O'Connor, "Critic's Notebook: Counting Casualties of Attacks on PBS," *The New York Times*, August 6, 1991, C11.

101

PAULA RABINOWITZ

MELODRAMA/MALE DRAMA

The Sentimental Contract of American Labor Films (2002)

"Do not ask me to write of the strike and the terror. I am on a battlefield.... But I hunch over the typewriter and behind the smoke, the days whirl, confused as dreams," declared the young Tillie Lerner (Olsen) during the 1934 San Francisco general strike.[1] In this classic example of reportage, the division between observation and participation, between fact and fantasy, has broken down. "I am on a battlefield," not merely as a war correspondent but as one of the combatants. In Florence Reece's ballad trumpeting the news of the 1934 Kentucky coal strikes in bloody Harlan County, one must decide "Which Side Are You On?": "if you go to Harlan County/there is no neutral there, you'll either be a union man/or a thug for J. H. Blair."[2] The labor struggles of the 1930s had clearly defined battle lines, and everyone sympathetic to workers knew which side was right; yet the engaged writer, knowing she was on a battlefield, was left "behind the smoke ... confused as dreams" by her double duty—to march and to type. Contemporary labor documentaries owe much to the literary genre of reportage, especially as practiced in the 1930s by committed journalists and worker correspondents. This form collapses distinctions between reader and participant by placing the observer/writer in the midst of the action as it happens; and because the two poles are clearly marked—you either are a union man or a thug—sentiment lodges on the side of labor. Florence Reece and the other balladeers could march *and* sing, but writers eventually left the line to tell the story. By leaving the line, the writer momentarily escaped the conflict, confusing her class allegiance; however, an either/or situation demands that both reporter and reader must choose sides within a dichotomous class structure. In reportage, documenters serve not only to witness, but to fight, like Frederick Douglass, who stresses that his indoctrination into the "hell of slavery" began when he recognized his role as "a witness and a participant" and ended only after he battled the overseer Covey, vowing never to be whipped again.

During the 1930s, many writers forged these sentimental contracts as they journeyed in search of "the trouble" befalling a nation suffering through extreme economic crisis.[3] In many ways, reportage mediated the feminized stance of the novelist—whether male or female, the writer was viewed by the Left as effete, bourgeois—and that of the hard-boiled reporter, as tough masculine worker, because these writers did not simply report from the sidelines; they put their bodies on the line. In modern times, radical intellectuals often have romanticized the industrial worker as the authentic vehicle of revolution. Moving into workers' homes to march with them became a standard activity of radical journalists following the strikes in coal, rubber, and steel during the 1930s. For instance, in 1934, a young Smith College graduate, Harriet Woodbridge, writing as Lauren Gilfillan, traveled to the coal fields of western Pennsylvania to report on the strikes there. She entered the struggle only to be reminded that she was an outsider. *I Went to Pit College* described her position as radical journalist within a mining community, riven by rival unions, political enmity, class conflict, and racial, ethnic, and religious divisions, which at least coalesced around a mutual suspicion of outsiders, especially those sporting linen dresses. Her book, widely reviewed and often denounced as sentimental tripe and a melodramatic portrayal of middle-class feminine thrill-seeking, was also praised for a willingness to bare herself as a voyeur and explore these class confusions, as it provided a vivid portrait of a community torn apart by labor strife.[4] Reportage, "in no way content simply to depict facts," risked sentimentality, according to Georg Lukács, because it "does indeed appeal to our feelings, both in its depiction of the facts and in the call to action."[5] Too much investment in one side of the battle, too much detail, a fetishistic "portrayal" of the victims of capitalism, however, got in the way of clear-sighted "scientific" analyses of the prevailing economic and political crisis. Because it opens the way for tears, reportage treads a fine political line, locating sentiment in the house of labor.

Sentimentality emerges in eighteenth-century England under curious and contradictory conditions. On the one hand, discussions about the proper use of tears were linked to a long history of antirational conservatism, starting with the embarrassingly sentimentalized male philosophers, such as Edmund Burke, resisting the Enlightenment revolutions in France. Claudia Johnson argues persuasively that "the welfare of the nation and the tearfulness of private citizens—actual as well as fictional—were understood in the 1790s to be urgently interconnected."[6] I would add that this was no less true of the 1990s. On the other hand, the rise of the bourgeois state required a break with the teary-eyed men who maintained a chivalric honor unnecessary under a new democratic regime. Men's tears are throwbacks to an era when the spectacle of men crying could be understood as part of the workings of an aristocratic order of "sentimentality [under which] the prestige of suffering belongs to men" (17). Within the culture of middle-class sensibilities, women became the vessels of feelings. The new forms of gendered subjectivity developing within bourgeois culture, feminist literary historians such as Nancy Armstrong, Cathy Davidson, and Jane Tompkins argue, require the "cultural work" of women's sentimentality to establish the modern subject, a being drenched in emotion and encased in privacy during the age of revolution and after. Sentiment became private because its public expression threatened social order. According to Raymond Williams, what Burke resisted was the incursion of the rational state into zones previously cordoned off as civil society. Emotions publicly displayed by citizens of a democracy led to the frightening spectacle of mobs and masses in the streets.[7] Bourgeois culture thus contained sentimentality within women's domain.

Its leakage into "the methods of science" appropriate to journalism,[8] especially in the service of that most melodramatic public staging—the strike—threatened to undo political authority. That would seem a good thing if one's goals, like those of the literary radicals of the 1930s, were to overthrow a failed capitalism.

However, in the rhetoric of both the Left and modernism, bourgeois culture as a whole had taken on the sentimentalized characteristics of feminized, aristocratic decadence—an image repeated in IWW iconography, socialist cartoons, Thorsten Veblen's *Theory of the Leisure Class*, communist pamphlets, modernist manifestoes, and even in Teddy Roosevelt's speeches.[9] Only the heroic workers (or modernist poets, but that's another story) standing shoulder-to-shoulder in solidarity could break with sentimentality and usher in a new world. The working stiff, like the freelancing detective and the mobile femme fatale, offers a tough resistance to the decay of modern life. This picture of masculine triumph had its own sentimental logic that also dates from the eighteenth century. "The first great tribune of the industrial proletariat," William Cobbett, declared, according to Raymond Williams, collective action to be "a movement of the *people's* own," a concerted response to the "masters [who] combine against them;" leaving them barely able to feed themselves and their families (*Culture and Society*, 3, 17). If a strike provides a stirring, emotionally-saturated, political tableau, its visual economy owing much to melodrama, where the forces of good and evil are decisively separate, that is because since the late eighteenth century, the working class has been cast in heroic and victimized poses.[10]

In twentieth-century America, the most powerful icons of this dual image of the working class have been found within the traditions of the documentary photography inaugurated by Lewis Hine. Hine's 1932 children's book, a photographic record called *Men at Work*, subtitled "Photographic Studies of Modern Men and Machines," offers a vision of labor poles apart from his earlier images of children dwarfed by massive looms. This volume carefully integrates the male body into the machinery of modern construction (many of the images are from Hine's on-location photographs of the Empire State Building rising from the streets of Manhattan as it was built). The scale of the masculine body establishes the size of the machine it works. Some of the "men of courage, skill, daring and imagination" are "heroes," says Hine paraphrasing Marx in his introduction, "the spirit of industry." Heroes because "cities do not build themselves; machines do not make machines.... [R]eal men make and direct them."[11] Hine shoots individual men intimately curled over and around their tools, but he also provides a vision of collective labor in shots showing how modern work requires cooperation among many men on the job.[12] This highly erotic, actually homoerotic, vision of men and machinery became a staple of documentary, culminating in Robert Flaherty's 1948 *Louisiana Story*, where the arrival of the enormous oil derrick moves the young boy to explore the world of machinery as he had once covered the natural landscape. The boy, embraced (literally) by this all-male world, ultimately integrates nature and machine and his body in the penultimate shot as he curls himself around the "christmas tree," the capped oil pipes, left standing in the bayou. Flaherty's film was hardly a left-wing celebration of machinery and labor; Standard Oil footed the bill for this "fantasy," as Flaherty referred to it.

Hine's 1932 photographs initiated a visual rhetoric of sentimentality that cloaked workers bodies and gigantic machinery in a celebration of the collective labors required to build America. In this, his images were visual updates of Melville's ecstatic whale-rendering scenes in *Moby-Dick*. This new sentimentality contrasted with Hine's earlier portraits of America's working victims suffering under capitalism's brutality. The recourse to sentiment among labor's documenters is tied to confusing gender codes, which have historically dictated who can and who cannot cry, and to conflicting class and national allegiances, which also involve delegating the proper expression of sentiment. Modern national allegiance requires tears—one need only watch any athletic segment or any commercial during NBC's broadcast of the 1996 or 2000 Olympics to get a shorthand lesson in the centrality of tears to national identity. We watch as athletes cry in victory or sob in defeat; we cry with them at home, our living rooms linked mysteriously through the flowing tears. Like nations, class formations, precisely because they require imaginative communities linked through ideas and sentiments, resemble these emotion-laden fantasies. Class codings can be made invisible with proper grooming and elocution, so says Henry Higgins to Elizabeth Doolittle in *My Fair Lady*, because unlike sexual or racial differences, they are not inscribed on the bodies' surfaces. For this reason, class is a slippery analytic category, even among feminists otherwise sensitive to nuanced gender, sexual, and racial differences. In the differing views of Burke and Cobbett, workers combined, either sinisterly as a mass or rationally as a class, in response to the workings of the capitalist state, a state formed in the interests of one class, the bourgeoisie, in part by cordoning off sentiment. This is also why the rhetoric of sentimentality—so crucial to modern national and class formations—still circulates within labor documentaries, even those questioning the form of documentary itself.

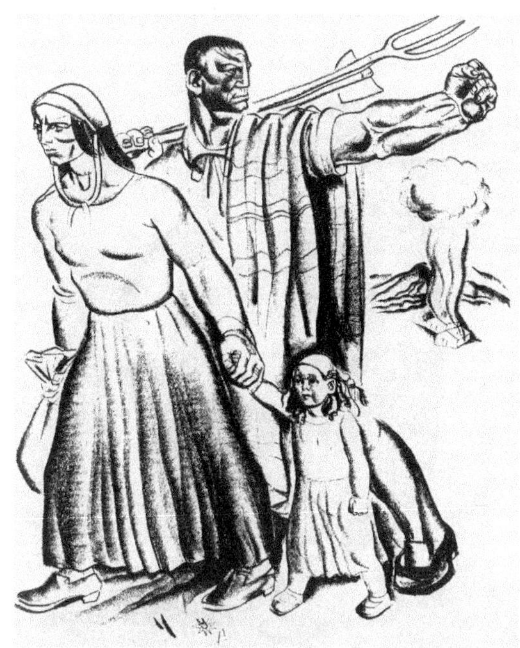

FIGURE 101.1 "Primary Accumulation: The Expropriation Whereby the Countryfolk Were Divorced From the Land," in Hugo Gellert, *Karl Marx' 'Capital' in Lithographs* (New York: Ray Long & Richard R. Smith, 1934).

Roger & Me(n)

In differing ways, Michael Moore's *Roger & Me* (1989) and Barbara Kopple's *American Dream* (1990) tap this long-standing tradition of figuring class conflict through gendered discourses of sentimentality.[13] *Roger & Me*, ever ironic about documentary, General Motors, and government policies that favor corporate greed over human need, cannot escape its heritage. In the 1930s, Hugo Gellert, a cartoonist for the left-wing journal *New Masses*, illustrated a selection of writings from Karl Marx's *Capital* with his drawings of solidly muscled workers.[14] The butt of in-jokes within the Left, these heroic figments of radical imagination were fantasies of excessive virility.[15] A strong working class could overcome both the crisis of capitalism and the malaise the lost generation was suffering after the First World War. A heavy load to bear—making the revolution and saving American masculinity at once—this construction of the manly worker occluded a vision of the working-class woman, who, in Gellert's drawings, bulge with hefts of

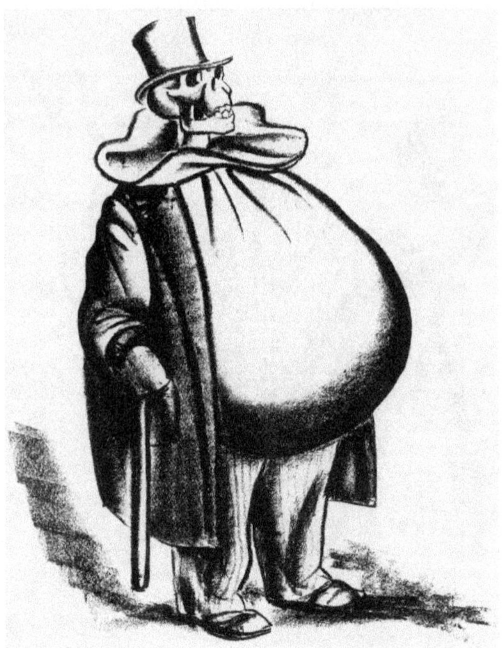

FIGURE 101.2 "The Working Day: Struggle For a Normal Working Day; Laws to Enforce the Extension of the Working Day, Passed From the Middle of the Fourteenth to the End of the Seventeenth Century," in Hugo Gellert, *Karl Marx' 'Capital' in Lithographs* (New York: Ray Long & Richard R. Smith, 1934).

muscle and a muscled breast nourishing her buffed-out baby boy, the kind of "revolutionary girl" celebrated in proletarian poems by such forgotten poets as H. H. Lewis. By contrast the bourgeoisie was a feminized and decadent class: corpulent men stuffed into top hats and tails, like the banker on the Monopoly game, sucking the vitality from the labor of others; or desiccated spinsters whose dried up lives were doomed to disappear once the new working-class family took possession of its rightful place.

It was a ludicrous picture then, when at least a quarter of the work force was female. In the 1980s, it should have been trotted out only as parody; yet *Roger & Me* returns to these stock types with a straight face to cast its saga of deindustrialization. Almost all the scenes with women target the lavish lifestyles of the rich and infamous of Flint, Michigan, and feature chiffon-dressed women sounding like Marie Antoinette before the revolution. The one exception—the lonely rabbit breeder whose uncanny pragmatism (pets or meat) seems demented at best, vicious at worst—clearly survives outside the economy of contemporary American late capitalist relations. She is a holdover from another era and another place, perhaps the mountains of Kentucky from which many autoworkers migrated during and after the Second World War, like a character out of Harriet Arnow's 1954 novel, *The Dollmaker*, devastated by city life and industrial work discipline.[16] Moore is drawn to this odd woman; she reappears as the star of his short sequel, *Pets or Meat: The Return to Flint* (1993), which also aired on PBS stations.[17]

Sentimentality requires a hero, just as melodrama demands clearly defined sides. Moore is a contemporary (anti-)hero, a goofy guy who has shed his class origins just barely because his skills lie in intellectual labor—the production of words and images—not the backbreaking assembly work of his father's generation.[18] His film unveils "an anti-aesthetics of failure in contemporary documentary,"[19] an absence that looms large in this story of contemporary labor: no strikes; no "men at work." What *Roger & Me* finds instead is lack: the lack of union militancy; the lack of work, as thousands of autoworkers have been laid off; the lack of industry, as plants close and move their operations overseas. Flint, Michigan, stands as an emblem of militant union organizing; site of the 1936 sit-down strike, the most effective use of the strategy in American history, whose stirring images of men curled amid their tools and machinery asleep on the shop floor galvanized generations of organizers. Josephine Herbst had caught this scene, connecting it to the rise of "the worker-writer," when she closes her 1939 novel, *Rope of Gold*, with a striking autoworker penning his autobiography.[20]

As a fantasy melding industry with aesthetics, like a bridge girder or a poured concrete dam, this quintessential modernist figure—an idle worker sprawled across the plant floor recording the details of the strike for the *Daily Worker*—has no place in a deindustrializing economy. Even the sit-down strike is ineffective against plant closures. The story has shifted elsewhere to the corporate and financial boardrooms where the flows of capital not productivity (which requires bodies) are key to profits.

Without the bodies of workers at their machines or the masses on the picket line, Moore's saga comes down to a lone quest for an elusive figure, General Motors CEO Roger Smith. Smith's continual absence is one more hole in the fabric of American industry; a boss can no longer be embodied either. The rotund cigar-smoking capitalist who lorded over a semifeudal "industrial valley" has also been displaced.[21] For example, in the new world order of virtual strikebreaking, to combat striking unions at Detroit's two largest newspapers, *The Detroit News* and *The Detroit Free Press* no longer needed to hire thugs. They set up home pages on the World Wide Web denouncing union tactics on the picket lines and praising those who cross the lines, including stories about the terrific food served to those who show up for work.[22] Moore fails to get close to the real boss—Roger Smith—so he goes for the cheap shot, the vacuous country club wives of Chevy's middle managers who declare Flint a wonderful city and wonder why everyone is complaining.

If the CEO cannot be located, neither can the worker; he is neither on the picket line nor on the assembly line. Charlie Chaplin's working-tramp represented the modern anti-hero of labor—dwarfed by the machine, encompassed by the masses. The counterpart to the Tramp's incorporation into the machine of capital is Chaplin's wonderful overhead crane shot, which offers a visual joke on working-class unity as the Tramp, after picking up a red flag that has fallen off the back of a carriage, unknowingly leads a demonstration of protesting workers only to find himself beaten and jailed by the police. Instead, Moore finds his postmodern worker-tramp in Ben Hamper, a contemporary Midwestern worker-writer, in the tradition of Jack Conroy, the "rivethead" whose column had previously appeared in Moore's alternative newspaper, *The Flint Voice*, now a novelist. Hamper explains, while aimlessly shooting hoops, that he was laid off with a medical disability because he had cracked up on the shop floor. He feels like a fraud compared to the women he met in the hospital—suicidal and depressed—whose mental illnesses were somehow more real, caused as they were by domestic, personal troubles. The public world of work is not supposed to cause mental breakdowns, but without the masses to provide a collective shelter for the worker, his psyche becomes as fragile as a housewife's.[23] Moore empathizes with his high-school buddy; they share history, each with a middle-aged, working-class inelegance that has no place, despite their new roles as intellectuals, circulating language and images.[24]

Moore's film, picked up and distributed by Time-Warner, sparked a major debate within corporate boardrooms and across business and industry pages;[25] his wry humor showed up GM as callous, the Flint Chamber of Commerce and Mayor's Office in the pockets of GM, and a citizenry suffering from delusions and privation so extreme that "recovery" appears unlikely.[26] Moreover, his decision to tamper with history, revising chronology to suit his narrative, caused a minor stir.[27] Moore's recourse to staged melodrama—placing Ronald Reagan in Flint in the midst of the shut down—gave ammunition to GM, which wanted to defuse the film's effects.[28] But Moore's manipulations came from a long tradition of documentary filmmaking. As he remarked: "With nonfiction, you have no idea when you go out to shoot what's going to happen, and you have to figure it all out once you're in the editing room."[29] Dziga Vertov's scissors cutting celluloid in *The Man With a Movie Camera* had foregrounded the editing process as crucial to *Kino-Pravda*—a job requiring the hands of his female assistant editor, Yelizaveta Svilova. With absence—no jobs, no organization, no boss—as capital flows elsewhere and workers sit idle, its central feature, Moore's postmodern portrait of labor still rests on the prehistory of modern male worker's melodramas, embodied by the two forces—Roger, endlessly beyond the camera, and M(oor)e, endlessly performing for it.[30]

Spam's Home

American Dream follows Kopple's magisterial view of worker solidarity in *Harlan County, U.S.A.* (1976) with a darker vision of the contradictions and complexities of contemporary union organizing in the heartland. Despite the ostensibly amiable atmosphere of Garrison Keillor's Lake Wobegone, Austin, Minnesota's, Hormel plant, and the efforts of meat packers at Local P-9 of the United Food and Commercial Workers (UFCW) to maintain union solidarity, *American Dream* presents a wretched scene. Anticipating the gruesomeness of *Fargo,* it lends bloody Harlan County a nostalgic glow. Kopple's complex gesture in *American Dream* traces the present conditions for union militancy in a typically Midwestern industry—hog processing—during this era of multinational corporate flight; its story of the multiple forces working at odds complicates the melodrama of union men vs. scabs staged in *Harlan County, U.S.A.* The 1984–85 strike against the Hormel plant dramatized how the arena has been complicated with a proliferating cast whose allegiances and identities are not so easily coded as good or bad. This corrective seems in part a response to critiques of her earlier film as overly humanistic; perhaps deindustrialization forces another cinema as much as another politics.

American Dream begins with shots of the hog kill room, which Kopple was able to film with a hidden camera by posing as a New York high-school student doing a report on the meat industry. The process of turning pigs into bacon is dangerous and disgusting work; the work site and work process, which are not central to the film's story, focusing as it does on the intricacies of local and international organizing, bargaining, and the strike and its aftermath, establishes the source of the action. If the establishing shot of the typing pool on the bottom floor of the Pacific All-Risk Insurance Company in *Double Indemnity* reminds us of the repetitive boredom of white-collar office work that contributes to film noir, the assembly line at Hormel presents pure horror and exploitation. In the brief encapsulated history the film provides, we hear Reagan's "off-the-cuff" remark about the economy: "I'm prepared to tell you it's a hell of a mess." Jesse Jackson then tells a packed crowd in 1986, "[W]hat Selma was to the civil rights movement, Austin is to the movement for workers' rights." The scene shifts two years earlier and follows two men past a playground where children swing and climb and slide to the front door of a large house where the wife of a Hormel executive lectures the men to be grateful they now receive $8.75 an hour: "When we were your age . . ." she begins, but the men cut her off: "Give us a fair shake, like you got." Although a town like Austin represses its class structure, visible evidence lies everywhere. In Austin, 22,000 people live in "a little world by ourselves," Hormel counsel Nyberg explains, echoing the boosterism found at the town's border: "Enjoy Austin, where the good life is here to stay." To some extent this civic hype rings true; as the Hormel promotional film Kopple inserts into hers outlines, the social contract the corporation struck with its workers decades ago guaranteed good wages, lifetime benefits, and profit sharing. But the ragged years of recession, corporate mergers, and wholesale assault on unions fostered by Reagan's administration have taken their toll. "Let us live in our house," pleads one woman stuffing envelops at the union hall, "our $32,000 house." The company that makes that quintessential American product, Spam, staple of United States Army K-rations during World War II, now expresses "the mood of the industry," as CEO Knowlton declares; despite record 29.5 million dollar profits in 1984, Hormel workers receive a 23 percent wage cut.

Thus the stage is set for the nightmare to unfold; a dark romance Kopple scripts around the struggle of a "new family," as the striking P-9ers describe their changed relationships to each other and to their formerly paternalistic employer, to come to terms with the betrayal by the new "father," Jay Hormel, son of the corporation founder who instituted the "social consciousness" of the company. But the real battle in Kopple's eyes involves a conflict waged by outsiders, distant cousins arriving to contest the company's will: on the one hand, Ray Rodgers, New Yorker and vegetarian head of Corporate Campaign whose successful national boycott of J. P. Stevens Co. finally resulted in union recognition in many southern textile plants; and, on the other, Lewie Andersen, hard-bitten vice-president of UFCW, former hog butcher and tough negotiator, who has finally accepted the UFCW's strategy of across-the-board contracts to bring up the wage floor in nonunion meat-packing plants. These giants battle on a grand scale for the hearts and minds of the P-9ers; their personalities are so charismatic that they seem to be determining the action, sweeping the quieter, restrained Minnesotans along with them. Yet the determination of the strikers and their families is the real story: they keep on with the strike even after P-9 has been decertified by the UFCW; they keep gaining support from unions around the country even after the AFL-CIO, America's central union organization, discourages its affiliates from offering solidarity; they keep showing up at the picket lines even after the National Guard has been called out and some local members defy the strike. Playing out against the bleak snow-covered landscape is the new "American dream" of community and family and their fracture, with brother turned against brother, another civil war with the inevitable result.[31]

Kopple's fascination with grand melodramatic historical epics owes as much to D. W. Griffith as the fragile voice of Hazel Dickens's ballads in *Harlan County, U.S.A.;* but in Austin the heroes are less pure and villains less obvious, if more devious. Unlike the coal miners' strike in Kentucky, where "you either are a union man or a thug for D. H. Blair," the complexities of fighting on three fronts—against the corporation, against the state, and against the union's international—complicate the dichotomized narration of melodrama. However, this multiplying set of powerful forces allied against the tiny P-9 local does not automatically call up greater sympathy for the strikers. Instead, those who gave up and crossed the picket line in the face of community censure invoke the rhetoric of sentimentality. Shedding tears is central to the labor documentary—Lawrence Jones's martyred body and his mother's wailing marked the turning point for the United Mine Workers in *Harlan County, U.S.A.*—but in *American Dream* it is the scabs who mourn themselves as outcasts. The question is: Do we care about these crying men?

American Dream had its public debut in Minneapolis (following its premiere in Austin) as a fundraiser for the Pittston miners' strike. The stage was crowded with Kopple, Senator Paul Wellstone, author of the Replacement Worker Bill barring the hiring of permanent replacements for strikers, and striking miners from Pittstown, West Virginia, as well as the remaining striking P-9ers, still out of work yet offering donations to the strikers in West Virginia. The entire audience was moved to tears by the spectacle of solidarity, suggesting that Kopple's interpretation of the dream came from a textured vision of class in contemporary America as deeply contradictory and overdetermined. Many local union activists and P-9 supporters, however, condemned the film; they felt it to be a betrayal for failing to capture the culture that grew during the strike. Her conclusions question P-9's tactics, even blame them for losing the strike; but evidence to the contrary remained on the cutting room floor. (Actually unused footage for *American Dream* is housed in University of Wisconsin's archives.) The picture is complicated because the politics is complex, but also because the profound shift in the economy has dislodged the melodramatic form of this battlefield and its representation.

An inheritance from the CPUSA's 1930s Popular Front attempt to meld communists (overwhelmingly urban and immigrant and Jewish) into the People, the sentimental invocation of "family," "movement," "community," and "culture" can insidiously repress conflicts and differences within America's class and racial structure. In 1938, General Secretary of the CPUSA Earl Browder outlined *The People's Front* as a program whose "first consideration in promoting new forces is to find native Americans" to lead its organizations, because the Communist Party was "destined to carry on and complete the work begun by Tom Paine, George Washington, Thomas Jefferson, and Abraham Lincoln."[32] To an extent, *Harlan County, U.S.A.* participated in this "archaic aesthetic," as Jesse Lemisch calls it,[33] and Kopple received a series of critiques for her "conventional" portrayal of social events from a position of "knowledge" available to the outsider.[34] The postmodern condition of labor in the 1980s demanded another sort of story; Kopple responds by exaggerating the rhetoric of sentimentality until its claims collapse. Kopple manipulates the codes of sentimentality to the point that our tears seem to merge the viewer with the scabs and against the strikers.

This direction comes in part because the situation in Austin, unlike that in Harlan County, is multiply fractured. Kopple may just be doing her job as a documentary filmmaker by presenting a comprehensive picture of strikers, scabs, and international representatives; or she may be paying a debt to the many locals and internationals that contributed funding for the film; or she may be attempting to enter the action, much as she did in Harlan County, at the picket line, by witnessing the sense of emptiness and hostility of those who break ranks. In Kentucky, her presence at the daily "sunrise revivals" became a factor in the escalating violence during the strike. At times it appeared that Kopple's crew egged on the scabs and company goons; at others, the camera clearly helped avert violence. In Austin, when she shows the scabbing P-9ers (the P-10ers, as they were derisively called) crying as they decide to cross their union's picket line, Kopple would seem to be siding with their unpopular decision. Yet the scene is filled with bathos, its emotional timbre highly suspect as the men cry on cue about how hard it is when you can't feed your family. Their tears are supposed to elicit our sympathy; but clearly their actions do not. Which side are we, the viewers, supposed to be on?

Unlike me, most critics of the film—such as Peter Rachleff, who wrote *Hard-Pressed in the Heartland* in part to counter Kopple's Academy Award–winning portrait of the Hormel strike—consider Kopple a sell-out because she provides a forum for these men, who from the first worked hand-in-hand with the UFCW leadership to undermine the strike and now run the trusteeship union that replaced P-9.[35] Rachleff refers to the local treasurer, John Williams, as her "star" because he gets so much screen time to anguish over his actions.[36] Maintaining a nostalgia for working-class authenticity and community characteristic of America's Left since the Popular Front, Rachleff fails to register the squeamishly maudlin and trite picture being painted. Kopple is relying on the left-wing conventions of picturing the scab as feminized (a scab, like a thug, is not a union *man*) that would seem to reinforce Rachleff's position, but the men's tears are powerful visual cues calling forth audience sympathies. So the picture is confusing, but this seems to be precisely the point: in the era of deindustrialization, it is not so easy to distinguish the union man from the scab.

While the strikers are presented as full of conviction—perhaps a bit naïve in their faith in Ray Rodgers—they are still proud and angry folks, even if their militance includes media-savvy campaigns. The scabs snivel about their lost manhood and the betrayal they feel: they hate to cross a line; the union has driven them to it. Lewie Andersen may steal the screen with his hard-nosed cynicism about P-9, but the UFCW comes off as retrograde and suspect, especially after UFCW President Wynn storms into a meeting shouting that he will make the P-9 local sign the contract: "[A]ll it takes is a few good men, oh and some women too," he nods to "the little lady there with the camera." Perhaps because Kopple's style is so consistently illusionistic—she appears to offer a pure vision of the struggle in Harlan County and a balanced version of the strike in Austin—the excesses in *American Dream* don't read as critique; but I think they should—not necessarily of the P-10ers but of the aesthetics and politics lodged in the sentimental itself as much as in the paradox of union politics in deindustrializing America.

Although correcting Kopple's film served as one impetus for both of the book-length accounts of the Hormel strike, neither does more than mention Kopple's presence in Austin.[37] Her authority is implicitly challenged by the reports of these partisan insiders who were active in the support systems—either Corporate Campaign (Hardy Green) or Twin Cities Support for P-9 (Peter Rachleff); Kopple remained an outsider. Falling for the charismatic Lewie Andersen, she failed to see the transformative effects the strike had on the lives of the union members and their families as she had in *Harlan County*. This transformation from alienated labor to a "movement culture" requires the creation of the alternative "prefigurative" institutions through which working people can galvanize into a collective agent for social and economic change.[38] To understand this process, outsiders need to get inside the homes, churches, and meeting halls of the strikers, but Kopple's up-close-and-personal moments more often come between her and the P-10ers or Andersen. Rachleff provides a prehistory of P-9 through analyses of its earlier incarnation in a consumer and producer union, which had achieved wall-to-wall unionization in Austin during the 1930s, establishing the base for the militancy and solidarity of the 1984–85 strike, the first against Hormel in fifty-two years. The two books also explain the changes in the meat-packing industry as a whole since the 1970s and in the contracts at Hormel that led Hormel to slash wages by 23 percent after promising to maintain them. What had been a locally owned, paternalistic company in a homogenous town in southern Minnesota became a lean and mean corporation with national and international subsidiaries linked to other major corporations during the era of mergers and buy-outs. Kopple fails to give this kind of background from the point of view of Austin; instead of letting the strikers speak, as she had in Harlan, where old-timers recounted the bloody days of the 1930s strikes for her through memories, songs, and photographs, she leaves it to Andersen to fill in the background.

Rachleff accuses Kopple of turning the P-9ers into "victims" rather than seeing them as victimized by the collusion of business unionism, state and local police, and corporate conglomerates, all working in tandem to destroy a renegade local that had taken on enormous symbolic significance in the antiunion climate of Reagan's America. Yet the only ones to appear as victims, in the classic melodramatic sense, are the P-10ers who sob before the camera after deciding to cross their union's picket line: "A person takes a lot of pride in being a breadwinner," says Ron Bergstrom. Since the eighteenth century, sentimentality, argues Robert Markley, has served as a "theatrics of virtue" for the display of feminized emotions; within the sentimental, the "passive victim" is always female, and it is up to the sensitive male to sympathize with her.[39] This is a class politics of bourgeois affects, thus hardly the virile profile of labor militancy so crucial to left-wing romance; the P-10ers vamp as hero(in)es. Kopple positions her camera with the men who do cross the line and, with them, gets barraged with insults from neighbors, friends, even brothers, such as R. G. Bergstrom, who is a firm supporter of the strike. He lives outside Austin on a 4 3/4-acre farm with his wife and three kids and explains that he goes to the picket line to watch his brother cross it as much as to perform strike duty. R. G.'s brother, Ron Bergstrom, by contrast, has accepted the logic of Hormel and 1980s corporate concessions for workers: "If you want a job," he tells Kopple, "you're going to have to take it." Ron Bergstrom becomes one of the original seven local members to return to work after twenty weeks on strike. In a telling scene later on, these seven watch themselves crossing the picket line and being jeered on the television news that evening: "The minute we crossed that line," remarks one, "we left them, left that organization."

Political Tears

Because the union itself, Hormel's policies, and the subsequent reconstructions of the events have turned on the familial make-up of the town, its work force, and its organizations, the act of scabbing is more than a betrayal of a lifetime of working-class upbringing and consciousness; it is also a divorce, a disownment, a severance of all family ties. These men have placed themselves outside the gates of the city when they reenter the factory gates. Their overly melodramatic responses to their own acts fail to exculpate them however: they may have been forced by circumstances to return, yet the circumstances are outdated, based on an ideal of the male breadwinner providing fully for his family. In both working-class and middle-class American homes, the family wage has failed to provide adequately since the 1970s. These men are victims as much of a passé vision of masculinity as of an outmoded form of unionism that is apparently ineffective against vicious corporations, although they do all right for themselves. Lewie Andersen has predicted from the start that the P-9 strike will fail, and it appears—though not so clearly in the film as in the written accounts of the strike—that the UFCW has actually worked to ensure failure, in part by courting these few dissident critics of the Corporate Campaign. In a reversal of fortune reminiscent of melodrama, these men assume leadership of the local after it is put into trusteeship.

If the P-10ers are pathetic, even bathetic, the P-9ers occasionally appear misguided. Lacking strategy, lacking a program, they are a bit too smitten with the New Age self-esteem assertiveness-training mentality that Ray Rodgers trumpets with quotations from Bruce Springsteen. Yet when one of the women leaves the "war department" (the office in the union hall for strike committee meetings) after a meeting with Lewie Andersen, she explains, "I want a union for the 1980s." The strikers are trying to explain to Andersen that something more than wages is at stake in this strike. In part, they have bought Ray Rodgers's theory that traditional organizing tactics are ineffective under current corporate structures with easy flows of capital allowing quick relocation. Unions must use intensive media campaigns to dishonor companies by targeting investors and stockholders. More important, however, is the alteration of the community's social fabric. P-9 President Jim Guyette and many others describe how the union hall became a "fun place to be" where people "did what they liked to do," fixing cars, carpentry, cooking, in an informal bartering economy set up during the strike. Vying for the power inherent in its sentimental invocation, they claim that "a whole new family" was formed through their union activism. This is especially true of the women's support network, which both Hardy and Rachleff contend accounts for the widespread "movement culture" P-9 was able to create. That Austin is an extremely homogenous and insular small town with a paternalistic company that stably employed generations contributed to the ease with which a "new family" could be formed within and through the union, but it also explains the sense of betrayal the Hormel workers felt at the concessions demanded of them by both the company and the UFCW, which set the stage for rupturing Local P-9. But this (women's) story does not grab Kopple as it did in Harlan County; she's watching the men cry this time.

This feel of intimacy is a modern feature characterizing both oral history and documentary. Kopple had moved in with the miners' families in Harlan County. Her attendance at meetings and on the picket lines and road blocks happened because of her connections with the strikers, even though she came from the outside. The presence of her camera became central to some of the action that happened. When Kopple is asked by the coal company thug for her press pass after she comes up to him with camera and tape recorder to ascertain his opinion of the strike, she turns the question on him, demanding to see his identification. They come to a testy truce, after each refuses to produce these documents of identity. The camera watches as he turns his pick-up truck around and leaves, averting violence. When a miner's wife pulls a revolver from her bodice, she directly addresses the camera, daring her viewers to judge how violence escalates. The media contribute to its eruption, heightening the rhetoric and action of the strikers, even as it may rein in its actual expression. The camera's presence sometimes provokes confrontation and violence, as when the armed thugs single out the camera as if it were a body to be beaten. Like the infamous scene in *The Battle of Chile,* in which cameraman Leonardo Henricksen filmed his own murder at the hands of Pinochet's army, this scene suggests that despite a legacy of bloody confrontations, the filmmaker's presence may be provoking violence. However, Lawrence Jones's death occurs off-screen, leaving us to wonder whether he might still be alive if the crew had ventured out that morning. Instead, Kopple films the emotion of the funeral, lingering on Jones's mother's anguished cries, tracking her collapsing body as it is carried from the church. The raw feeling spilling out inappropriately for public consumption accentuates the keenly divided world of victims—strikers—and tyrants—mine owners and their goons.

Watching *Harlan County, U.S.A.* still moves me to tears, despite my recognition of the discourses of sentimentality at work; the carved worn-down faces of the old timers and the incredible youth and poverty of the others, the violence and fear, the haunting ballads pull at the heart strings just as any tearjerker out of Hollywood might. Yet the tough talking women, the humorous encounter between the miner picketing the Wall Street offices of Brookside's parent corporation and the New York City cop comparing benefits, wages, and working conditions, the old miners—black and white—suffering from black lung joking that, although when they entered the mines each day they were different colors, when they left they were all "soul brothers" temper the pathos with humor. It gives *Harlan County, U.S.A.* the feel of solidarity. The escalating crisis and its violence are offset by the heady sense of power gained through collective actions. The sheer brutality of the labor miners perform pales compared to the degree to which companies will go to keep workers from improving their lives. In the United States, in the mid-1970s, citizens who worked full time in a major industry still lived without plumbing, without heat, in rickety shacks. Mines are not metaphors for hell; they are hell. Despite her obvious differences as a young, single New York Jew with a camera, she entered the privacy of the miners' lives. Unlike Lauren Gilfillan's more ambivalent attempt in 1934, Kopple's move had opened a hidden world of exploitation to public view and garnered tremendous support for the mineworkers. A strike still looked noble in 1976, especially when it was clear which side one was on.

American Dream, unlike *Harlan County,* slips the veil of sentimentality over the wrong faces. When Peter Rachleff refers to the P-10ers as the "stars" of Kopple's film, is it because they get too much screen time? Or is it because they get to explain their decision more fully than those who remain on the line? Or because in their explanation, they resort to emotional outbursts of tears, rather than the anger expressed by R. G. Bergstrom at his brother's betrayal, and so appear conventionally sympathetic? Kopple's grim tone, set early in the film and accentuated by the bleak, blanc noir, Minnesota winterscapes of Austin, the tacky interiors of meeting rooms and negotiating suites in hotels, the gruesome images from inside the Hormel plant, offer none of the elevating and alleviating humor, hope, warmth, or sarcasm that occasionally lightened *Harlan County, U.S.A.* The miners' pineboard shacks nestled in the hollows of West Virginia conveyed the picturesque, aestheticizing poverty in a way that James Agee deplored, even as he lyricized the perfect symmetry of the tenants' housing he found in Hale County, Alabama, in *Let Us Now Praise Famous Men.*[40] Nothing of the sort exists in Austin, a tidy middle American town of postwar tract housing. The spirit of possibility following the democratization of the United Mine Workers is also missing from *American Dream.* It seems the dream of solidarity is over too—another casualty of Reaganomics. If Moore undermined the heroic male worker through satire, Kopple finished off his image as the one who will lead us from the brutality of capitalism through united movements of militant solidarity. The American dream of the 1930s Left, that the male working class holds the keys to revolution, rests on modernist economic relations and their melodramatic stagings. It served as the background for the dilemmas of the noir hero caught in a cruel and overdetermined world ruled by rank corruption and uncontrollable desire. The film noirs of the 1940s and 1950s appeared as cynical antidotes to both the melodramatic romance of the 1930s working stiff and the nostalgic portrait of the 1930s migrant mother. But the power of genre is such that labor's sentimental contract persists. Kopple undercuts the rhetoric of the labor documentary by thoroughly inscribing the sentimental. Obsessively observing the contract to the letter, she uses men's tears against their modern origins to tell a postmodern tale still unfolding around us.

NOTES

1. Tillie Lerner, "The Strike," *Partisan Review* 1 (November 1936). Reprinted in Charlotte Nekola and Paula Rabinowitz, eds., *Writing Red: An Anthology of American Women Writers, 1930–1940* (New York: The Feminist Press, 1987), 245.
2. Florence Reece, "Which Side Are You On?," in Nekola and Rabinowitz, *Writing Red,* 182.
3. See Ruth McKenney, *Industrial Valley* (1939; reprint, Ithaca: Cornell University Press, 1992; Martha Gellhorn, *The Trouble I've Seen* (New York: William Morrow, 1936); Lallah Davidson, *South of Joplin*

(New York: W. W. Norton, 1939); and selections in *Writing Red.*

4. Lauren Gilfillan, *I Went to Pit College* (New York: Literary Guild, 1934). For a detailed discussion of this book, see Paula Rabinowitz, *Labor and Desire: Women's Revolutionary Fiction in Depresion America* (Chapel Hill: University of North Carolina Press, 1991), chapter 4.
5. Georg Lukács, "Reportage or Portrayal?" [1932] in Rodney Livingstone, ed., *Essays on Realism*, trans. David Fernbach (Cambridge, Mass.: MIT Press, 1981), 49.
6. Claudia L. Johnson, *Equivocal Beings: Politics, Gender and Sentimentality in the 1790s: Wollstonecraft, Radcliffe, Burney, Austen* (Chicago: University of Chicago Press, 1995), 2.
7. See Raymond Williams, *Culture and Society: 1780–1950* (1953; reprint, New York: Columbia University Press, 1983), 3–12.
8. Lukács, "Reportage or Portrayal?," 50.
9. On the complicated refusal of femininity in the rejection by modernism of sentimentality, see Rey Chow, *Women and Chinese Modernity: The Politics of Reading Between East and West* (Minneapolis: University of Minnesota Press, 1991), and Suzanne Clark, *Sentimental Modernism: Women Writers and the Revolution of the Word* (Bloomington: Indiana University Press, 1991). On the gendered iconography of the Left, see Rebecca Zurier, *Art for the Masses: A Radical Magazine and its Graphics, 1911–1917* (Philadelphia: Temple University Press, 1988); Barbara Melosh, *Engendering Culture: Manhood and Womanhood in New Deal Theater and Art* (Washington, D.C.: Smithsonian Institute Press, 1991); Elizabeth Faue, *Community of Suffering and Struggle: Men, Women and Labor in Minneapolis, 1915–1945* (Chapel Hill: University of North Carolina Press, 1991).
10. For critical analyses of melodrama as a debased form that allowed marginalized peoples, especially women and the working class, a popular platform for resistance within generic and social containment, see Martha Vicinus, "Helpless and Unfriended: Nineteenth-Century Domestic Melodrama," *New Literary History* 13 (Autumn 1981); Jackie Byars, *All That Hollywood Allows: Re-Reading Gender in 1950s Melodrama* (Chapel Hill: University of North Carolina Press, 1991); Christine Gledhill, "The Melodramatic Field: An Investigation," in *Home Is Where the Heart Is: Studies in Melodrama and the Woman's Film* (London: British Film Institute, 1987); Lynn Hunt, *The Family Romance of the French Revolution* (Berkeley: University of California Press, 1992); Ien Ang, *Watching Dallas: Soap Opera and the Melodramatic Imagination* (London: Routledge, 1989); Michael Denning *Mechanic Accents: Dime Novels and Working-Class Culture in America* (London: Verso, 1987). The standard theoretical work on the mechanics of melodrama is Peter Brooks, *The Melodramatic Imagination: Balzac, Henry James, Melodrama and the Mode of Excess* (New Haven, Conn.: Yale University Press, 1976).
11. Lewis W. Hine, *Men At Work: Photographic Studies of Modern Men and Machines* (1932) (New York: Dover Publications, Inc., 1977).
12. Terry Smith, *Making the Modern: Industry, Art and Design in America* (Chicago: University of Chicago Press, 1993), analyzes the way in which 1930s celebrations of machines enabled the rise of a corporate state. See also Michael Szalay, *New Deal Modernism: American Literature and the Invention of the Welfare State* (Durham, N.C.: Duke University Press, 2000). Left-wing filmmakers, such as Leo Hurwitz, however, celebrated the "machine itself, as an instrument for the transformation of labor and material into what people need." Michael and Jill Klein, "Native Land: An Interview with Leo Hurwitz," *Cineaste* 6 (1974): 7. The aesthetics of streamlining, Raymond Loewy, one of its most creative designers, told *Life*, meant "that society could be industrialized without becoming ugly." Quoted in Jane N. Law, "Designing the Dream," in Fania Weingartner, ed., *Streamlining America*, (Dearborn, Mich.: Henry Ford Museum and Greenfield Village, 1986), 21.
13. See Joan W. Scott's critique of Gareth Stedman Jones's reading of the Chartist's political claims in *The Language of Class*in *Gender and the Politics of History* (New York: Columbia University Press, 1988); Elizabeth Faue, *Community of Suffering and Struggle* on women's organizing during the 1930s Minneapolis Truckers' Strike, and Rabinowitz, *Labor and Desire* on the gendered iconography of class in proletarian novels of the 1930s.
14. Hugo Gellert, *Karl Marx's "Capital" in Lithographs* (New York: Ray Long and Richard Smith, 1934).
15. But there is some truth to it. In an interview with Carol Brightman, "Mary, Still Contrary," *The Nation* (May 19, 1984): 611–20, Mary McCarthy describes the faces of the men in the Gdansk shipyard as familiar, like those of the workers in this country she watched picket the great industries during her youth in the 1930s; their supple muscles and slender figures assuming the heroic poses Hine pictured. "Those young workers [in Solidarity]," she says, "I've never seen such handsome men. . . . You know, we haven't had a worker in this country that looked like that in fifty years." The bodies of 1930s American workers photographed by Hine have Renaissance proportions in stark contrast to the physiques of late twentieth-century workers pictured by Milton Rogovin, in Rogovin and Michael Frisch, *Portraits in Steel* (Ithaca, N.Y.: Cornell University Press, 1993). However, "brawny, heroic, manly men . . . are back," as heroes since September 11, 2001, according to Patricia Leigh Brown, "Heavy Lifting Required: The Return of Manly Men," *The New York Times*, News of the Week in Review (October 28, 2001), 5. Brown quotes "conservative social critic" Camille Paglia's echo of Mary McCarthy: "I can't help noticing how robustly, dreamily masculine the faces of the firefighters are. These are working-class men, stoical, patriotic."

16. See Harriet Arnow, *The Dollmaker* (1954; reprint, New York: Avon Books, 1972). This story had been a staple of 1930s proletarian fiction. The many novels about the Gastonia, North Carolina, strike centered on the transition from folk culture to a culture of capitalist exploitation and the especially difficult time women, as repositories of family lore and tradition, had adjusting to the changes. See Joseph Urgo, "Proletarian Literature and Feminism: The Gastonia Novels and Feminist Protest," *Minnesota Review* 24 (Spring 1985): 64–84.
17. While the Corporation for Public Broadcasting has been a primary funder for many documentaries, including those investigating class relations in America, its audience is decidedly middle class. In *Pets or Meat*, Moore may have been working out a certain ambivalence toward PBS, which funded his films but which does not "bring the working class of this country into its network. . . . [T]hey don't ever seem to speak to people like us." Jay Bobbin, "Moore Moves 'Nation' to Fox," *Glens Falls Post-Star*, July 20, 1995, D8.
18. Speaking of *TV Nation*, Moore comments, "[I]t's very bizarre and rare that a group of people such as me and my friends would be able to come from Flint, Mich., and have a network TV show." Bobbin, D8.
19. Paul Arthur, "Jargons of Authenticity (Three American Moments)," in Michael Renov, ed., *Theorizing Documentary* (New York: Routledge, 1993), 104.
20. This is Douglas Wixson's name for those Midwestern proletariat authors, such as Jack Conroy, who came out of the working class, see *The Worker-Writer in the Midwest* (Urbana: University of Illinois Press, 1993). In the late 1920s, Mike Gold's editorials in the *New Masses* often called for a new movement of worker-correspondents to "Tell us your story . . . in the form of a letter. . . . Write as you talk. Write." Michael Gold, "A Letter to Workers' Art Groups," *New Masses* 5 (September 1929): 16.
21. In *Industrial Valley*, her reportage novel about the United Rubber-workers Union strike in Akron, Ohio, McKenney remarks on the geography of the company town in which the heights are reserved for the ruling families, with managers situated midway between them and the vast working-class neighborhoods spread around the plants in the valley.
22. Walter R. Baranger, "On Line, Management Also on Picket Line," *The New York Times*, July 24, 1995, D6. This tactic has been employed as well by cyberspace corporations: "a section on Amazon[.com]'s internal Web site gives supervisors antiunion material to pass on to employees" and alerts managers of tell-tale warning signs that a union is trying to organize. Be wary of " 'hushed conversations when you approach which have not occurred before' and 'small group huddles breaking up in silence on the approach of the supervisor.' " Steven Greenhouse, "Amazon.com Is Using the Web to Block Union's Effort to Organize," *The New York Times*, November 29, 2000, C1–2. At the same time, however, organizing efforts have been carried out in cyberspace. In 1996, the University Faculty Alliance and the AAUP at the University of Minnesota successfully fought a Board of Regents' effort to revise the tenure code by effectively using e-mail to communicate with the more than three thousand faculty members.
23. See Ben Hamper, *Rivethead: Tales from the Assembly Line* (New York: Warner Books, 1992), for a full accounting of Hamper's fascinating gendering of mental illnesses. Thanks to Carol Mason for bringing this to my attention. The effects of unemployment are among the most devastating chronicles of work life in late twentieth-century America. The stories of displaced workers are full of alcoholism, depression, suicide, abuse, and so forth. The alienation of labor Marx detailed seems even more exacerbated by the loss of self accompanying loss of work. See the interviews in *Portraits of Steel* conducted by oral historian Michael Frisch for moving accounts of the psychic wreckage caused by plant closures.
24. Jay Bobbin, columnist for the Tribune Media Services, quotes Moore's remarks on "one of a series of really wonderful ironies" that his television show, *TV Nation*, which often scrutinized corporate America, aired in 1994 on NBC, moved in 1995 to Fox, owned by international media tycoon, Rupert Murdoch, CEO of the News Corporation, which owns Fox among many other tabloids. Glens Falls *Post-Star* July 20, 1995, D8.
25. "Warner Acquires 'Roger' Docu for World Distribution," *Variety* 337 (November 1, 1989): 12.
26. See Chester Burger, "What Michael Didn't Say About Roger," *Public Relations Journals* 46 (April 1990): 40–42; Susan Duffy, "The Real Villain in *Roger & Me*? Big Business," *Business Week* (January 8, 1990): 42–45; David C. Smith, "Michael & Roger: GM Critic's Film Makes No Pretense at Fairness," *Ward's Auto World* 25 (November 1989): 5.
27. See Carl Plantinga, "Roger and History and Irony and Me," *Michigan Academician* 24 (Spring 1992): 511–20; and Carley Cohan and Gary Crowdus, "Reflections on *Roger & Me*, Michael Moore and His Critics," *Cineaste* 17:4 (1990): 25–30.
28. This controversy was played out in the pages of *The New York Times* among other widely read national media venues and took on new life after it was learned that the film was not nominated for an academy award: on January 19, 1990, D. P. Levin reported that "Maker of Documentary That Attacks GM Alienates His Allies," C12; then on February 1, 1990, Richard Bernstein asked "*Roger & Me:* Documentary? Satire? Or Both?," C20; on March 2, 1990, D. Bensman contributed an op-ed piece stating: "*Roger & Me*: Narrow, Simplistic, Wrong," A33; on March 26, 1990, V. J. Dimidjian responded

in a letter to the editor, "*Roger & Me*," A16. In the midst of this, *Newsweek* asked "Will GM Retaliate?" (February 26, 1990): 4.

29. Bobbin, "Moore Moves 'Nation' to Fox," D8.
30. In *The Family Romance of the French Revolution* (Berkeley: University of California Press, 1993), historian Lynn Hunt argues that melodrama was a key factor in the decision to behead royalty because this popular theatrical form securely differentiated between the righteous and evil ones, and applauded ridding the stage of evil power. Moore is hardly advocating Roger's death; but his ability to collapse the situation into a struggle between himself and his adversary—richer, more powerful, more deceitful—recalls this plot.
31. Of course, the title *American Dream* refers to the post–World War II promise, which film noir undercuts and exposes, made to the white working class of a home, a car, a stable job, and so forth earned at the expense of militant unions and through the build-up of a militarized federal budget. But I also think that because of the way the film portrays family conflicts, it is not entirely wrong to sit Freud before this dream and put his analytic powers to work.
32. Earl Browder, *The People's Front* (New York: International Publishers, 1938), 56, 235.
33. For a devastating critique of the vestiges of Popular Front culture lurking within left-wing expressions of solidarity with the working class, see Jesse Lemisch, "I Dreamed I Saw MTV Last Night," *The Nation* (October 18, 1986): cover, 374–76.
34. Anthony McCall and Andrew Tyndal, "Sixteen Working Statements," *Millennium Film Journal* 1 (Spring/Summer 1978), 36. See also Noel King, "Recent 'Political' Documentary: Notes on *Union Maids* and *Harlan County, USA*," *Screen* 22, no. 2 (1981): 7–18.
35. Peter Rachleff, review of *American Dream, The Oral History Review* 20 (Spring/Fall 1992): 94–96.
36. Peter Rachleff, *Hardpressed in the Heartland* (Boston: South End Press, 1993), details the history of the UFCW in Austin, as well as offers a completely different picture of the effects of the P-9 strike for the U.S. labor movement. A labor historian at Macalester College in St. Paul, Minnesota, Rachleff was instrumental in establishing the Twin Cities Support for P-9. Rachleff alerted me to the footage stored in Wisconsin's archives. (Personal communication, April 21, 1996). Tim Leland, business agent for the building trades union in Minnesota, voiced a great deal of criticism of the P-9ers, echoing Andersen that the strike was hopelessly doomed and thus resulted in hundreds of Hormel workers in Austin and Owatonna, Minn., losing their jobs. (Personal interview, November 10, 1994).
37. Rachleff's book is one of the two; the other is Hardy Green, *On Strike at Hormel: The Struggle for a Democratic Labor Movement* (Philadelphia: Temple University Press, 1990).
38. See Wini Breines, *Community and Organization in the New Left, 1962–1968: The Great Refusal* (New York: Praeger; South Hadley, Mass.: J. F. Bergin, 1982), on the 1960s movements' adoption of this model for organizing. I will take this up at length in chapter 8.
39. Robert Markley, "Sentimentality as Performance: Shaftesbury, Sterne and the Theatrics of Virtue," in Felicity Nussbaum and Laura Brown, eds., *The New Eighteenth Century* (New York: Methuen, 1987), 211–12.
40. James Agee and Walker Evans, *Let Us Now Praise Famous Men* (Boston: Houghton-Mifflin, 1941).

102

MARSHA ORGERON AND DEVIN ORGERON

FAMILIAL PURSUITS, EDITORIAL ACTS

Documentaries after the Age of Home Video (2007)

I think it's going to be very interesting . . . to see what happens with this digital generation of parents who have recorded their kids' every footstep. . . . People can just go back to the data bank and see exactly how little Jimmy spooned his peas into his mouth at age four. There'll be a record of it.

—Ross McElwee, quoted in Lawrence F. Rhu, "Home Movies and Personal Documentaries"

Since the 1990s a significant number of documentaries have been produced that rely heavily upon primary footage taken by the subject(s) of the documentaries over the course of their purportedly predocumentary lives. In films like *Tarnation* (Jonathan Caouette, 2003) the film's subject and director are the same. More often, as in *Capturing the Friedmans* (Andrew Jarecki, 2003) and *Grizzly Man* (Werner Herzog, 2005), the film's director employs footage that was taken by and of the documentary subject(s). In so doing, the documentary director assumes the role of editor and interpreter of a prerecorded, personal moving image archive that has already been edited, always conceptually and sometimes literally. This extensive use of home movies—home videos would be the more accurate term in most recent cases—signals a shift in recent documentary production, one that compels us to consider the implications of using home videos as narrational and illustrative tools, as conduits to history and memory.[1] The representational and ethical ramifications of this recent spate of documentaries that rely on home video have yet to be assessed. What follows considers these issues by focusing on the current generation of obsessive self-documentarians and the 35mm, feature-length, theatrically released documentary films that have been made, at least partly, out of their autobiographical video records.

A close but selective engagement with the aforementioned early-twenty-first-century films will aid in our understanding of this phenomenon of lives lived seemingly in preparation for documentary exploration. As McElwee seems to suggest in the epigraph above, the prevalence, ease, and affordability of home video equipment have made it possible for people to create an expansive library of moving image material with which to illustrate their lives. Personal memory is made tangible—it is, in essence, authorized—when a visual record appears to substantiate it. However, as we suggest, the availability of these video records also informs the shape and scope of the histories and memories these documentaries represent. In other words, home videographers have already made a preemptive directorial intervention by virtue of their representational decisions, inclusions as well as exclusions, and these decisions impact the nature of the documentaries that employ this footage. The home video cameras' presence not only affects the moment of recording (perhaps especially so when the subjects document themselves) but also provides seemingly irreplaceable evidence of that moment. These moments are, of course, partly dictated by the videographer's intentions, which guide the expenditure and focus of the primary video footage. The documentary filmmaker working with extant biographical or autobiographical video material performs, then, a kind of secondary editorial role in which relevant video footage is assembled before the commercial cinematic product is even undertaken.

McElwee's observations above also point, however obliquely, to a central concern arising in these films with regard to the state of the American family. Where he envisions a generation of parents with a "data bank" of video material documenting their children's lives, these recent films suggest a shift away from parents as the *producers* of photographic records to "children" as videographers who often take parents and parenthood as their *subjects*.[2] Considered alongside each other, the films investigated here present a provocatively destabilized image of the contemporary American family and its organizing structure: from the nuclear (*Capturing the Friedmans*), to the extended and re-created (*Tarnation*), to the "families we choose" or invent (*Grizzly Man*).[3] This article, then, is also an attempt to confront a thematic convergence around the subject of family—both literal and constructed, traditional and alternative—in these at first seemingly disparate documentaries. The quest to understand or to achieve a sense of family pervades, indeed motivates, all of the amateur videographers examined here. The availability of these preconceived video materials also facilitates the narration of the domestically centered melodramas unfolding within each subsequently constructed documentary.

Where home *movies* have been characterized as providing highly selective, idealized glimpses of family life, as Patricia Zimmermann and Richard Chalfen demonstrate in their respective studies, home *videos*, particularly as they operate in these three films, provide an archival representation that goes beyond the iconography of picture-perfect birthday parties and Christmas mornings. This is not to make a technologically determinist argument, for clearly there are important cultural, ideological, and individual reasons for the video revelations we encounter in these documentaries. It is, however, crucial to acknowledge that the technology of the video age, which facilitates the core content of these recent documentaries, also makes possible some of these historically unconventional representational tendencies. In *There's No Place Like Home Video,* James Moran, who painstakingly lays out his theoretical rejection of essentialist arguments about medium specificity, argues that "home video continues a tradition of ideal family representation" (xiv). As the following pages demonstrate, we are less certain about this contention. Though no less performative, no less the product of authorial invention and intention, the home videos used in these three documentaries expose the family in various states of decay and dissolution, capturing the antithesis of domestic harmony in sometimes astonishingly clinical detail and in a fashion that undoes the myth of "ideal family representation" associated with home movies. What follows, then, focuses on the circulation and status of home video images in recent documentary practice, which first requires some consideration of the foundational, material object central to each of these documentaries: home videos.

From Home Movies to Home Videos

> In our lexicon a mediocre movie is one that only your family can enjoy. A good movie can entertain an audience that doesn't know the actors.
>
> —Roy Pinney, "Better Home Movies," in *Parents Magazine,* May 1955

Although it is unlikely that *Parents Magazine* could have predicted the way that home movies would be seen by mass audiences in the context of documentaries made fifty years after it published its evaluative criteria, it is worth taking a moment to consider the public/private nature of home movies and the way this concept has shifted in the home video age. By the post World War II era, home movie making was a significant hobby for American families, especially for those experiencing the nation's overall prosperity. Marketing strategies employed by major equipment producers as resources (equipment as well as film) were made available again in the postwar period pitched home movies as the ideal tool for parents seeking to document their family and their children in particular, a message that resonated with the baby boom generation.[4]

Working within the predetermined limits of three minutes' worth of 8mm or Super 8mm, this generation of home filmmaker required adequate lighting for proper film exposure (especially indoors) and incurred the additional expense and wait-time involved in film processing. As home movie scholars such as Patricia Zimmermann and Richard Chalfen have indicated, this resulted in a necessarily selective filmmaking practice typical of the prevideo age. These particular, technologically rooted challenges were eradicated after the proliferation of home *video* technology, which surfaced in earnest during the 1980s, became more affordable over the course of the next decade, required no processing, was forgiving in less-than-ideal lighting conditions, and eventually benefited from user-friendly home computer editing programs.[5] By the 1980s and 1990s the skills—indeed, even the resources—needed to film and edit no longer appeared the exclusive province of adults, the former gatekeepers of the family iconography. Even kids could use a video camera, and a new generation of videographers was able to move outside of the parentally controlled patterns that dominated the home movie age.[6] We find evidence of this shift in the documentaries under discussion here, which support our claim that home videography lends itself to capturing the family in ways that are not consonant with earlier conventions of home filmmaking, earlier conventions, in fact, that occasionally appear, often by way of contrast, in these recent documentary films.

This is a significant change, for it begins to speak to the often unruly, invasive, and subversive nature of the home video footage surfacing in this crop of recent documentaries. Discussing the climate for home movie making in the 1950s, Zimmermann contends that "with leisure-time expansion, the nuclear family's most important recreation was itself. Home movies conscripted 'togetherness,' family harmony, children, and travel into a performance of familialism ... [H]ome movies preserved and evoked a residual social formation of families as important cultural and social agents through idealizing, indeed worshipping, its cloistered interactions" (133). Zimmermann's thesis is supported not only by surviving home movie footage but also by several decades of industrial and hobbyist publications focused squarely on the family as an idealized amateur cinematic subject. Three-minute memories were created to capture moments of social and familial value, depicting an almost always positive conception of family and community.[7]

The video age carries over some of the same rhetoric (early video manuals hardly advise operators to *waste* tape and still instruct users in the basics of good composition), but the mechanics of the situation are fundamentally different, a selling point not lost on home video users. Although James Moran patently rejects a technologically determinist argument, "which confers upon a medium some autonomous and immanent force of inevitable social change," when he turns to defining the differences between film and video he inevitably encounters those material differences: affordability, ease of use, widespread availability, and, perhaps most critically, the comparatively enormous capacity of video, all of which conspired to allow a new generation of videographers to venture beyond the conventions established during the amateur film era (xv).[8] This is not to argue that home video changed the nature of the family but rather that home video made posible a new, seemingly more "complete"—or at least more complex—and perhaps more critical way of capturing the family. Moran explains:

> The basic differences of operation [between film and video] will precipitate differences of production and reception, which in turn may extend home videos' range of content and space for interpretation beyond the limitations of home movies.... [R]ather than expose random moments from everyday life, which would require a much greater financial investment, home moviemakers generally film only the highlighted moments of ritual events wherein participants could be posed and conventions controlled in advance of shooting. (41)

Moran gets to the core of some crucial material facts: videotape was not only cheap but also rerecordable, and the time, cost, and inconvenience of processing had become, in the video age, the hurdles of a bygone era. Moran is right to point to these differences, as he is to tread carefully when suggesting the degree of influence these technological changes inspired in the realm of representation. What we mean to suggest in the following pages, then, is that these videographic records, marked by the tendencies and possibilities we've been discussing, offer both a representational gift and an equally important challenge for the documentary director opting to work with these primary materials. An awareness of the different layers of representation and indeed of argumentation at work here—the initial videographed moments and the selective use of these moments in the documentary that enfolds and recontextualizes this footage—suggests the ways in which authorship is complicated by this recent generation of mainstream feature documentaries.

Video footage in *Tarnation, Capturing the Friedmans,* and, in a different fashion, *Grizzly Man* functions to *unprotect* the family, thereby challenging the domestic idealization prevalent in the representational tropes of the prevideo age. "Togetherness" is not abandoned by this generation; rather, it is problematized, largely for its frustrating elusiveness. Moran insightfully argues that "home video reveals that families have always been more complex and contradictory than home movies have generally portrayed them . . . [representing] the fuller range of domestic ideologies already present in the culture, well before the arrival of home video" (43). The medium does not, in other words, determine the message so much as it allows the message to be recorded and revealed. Indeed, the films under discussion here capture and accentuate the gaps that Zimmermann suggests lurked in the *off-screen* space of a previous generation's moving documents. These fissures, present in and sometimes the focus of the original materials, are made visible by the initial representational decisions made by these particular videographers and are thereby accessible to the documentary director working with these initial renderings.

Paul Arthur has described this phenomenon as "the revenge of the home movie" ("Feel the Pain" 47), claiming that "in an age when practically no one is outside the media loop, every life is understood as intrinsically a production-in-the-making whose idioms are shaped by a spectrum of documentary practices from eyewitness news to cell phone cameras to 'candid' sex videos" ("Extreme Makeover" 19).[9] Ross McElwee offers the following, related diagnosis of this state of affairs:

> This notion of constantly wanting to capture reality as much as humanly possible is a kind of neurosis. It's also one that's perhaps more pervasive than it ever has been. We have a proliferation of readily available digital, and now computer-based and web-based technology, where making movies has become much easier than writing a novel or a poem. Now, technically speaking, almost anybody can make a movie. It's interesting to think about the pathological aspects of this addiction to filming, this desire to interact with reality by filming it. (Rhu 10)

Indeed, the pervasive mediation of experience McElwee identifies and, to some degree, participates in has produced a generation of individuals whose every move might be captured on film (though less frequently now) or video and shared via easy-to-execute duplication on VHS or DVD as well as via the Internet (think of portals such as youtube.com). Cell phones with moving and still photographic capabilities can store and transmit these documents of the moment, fostering a kind of pandocumentary culture for whom the recorded event has become a dominant form of communication.

Indeed, by returning to the epigraph with which we began this section we might posit that this recent documentary activity enacts both an inversion as well as a confirmation of *Parents Magazine*'s formula for judging the mediocrity or goodness of a home movie. This trilogy of films could hardly be "enjoyable" for the families depicted in them, divulging as they do so many elements of trauma, embarrassment, and untoward frankness, precisely that which—at least until fairly recently—has been considered the province of the private and not the public sphere. However, we must also acknowledge that the allure of these films partly hinges on their promise of a glimpse beyond the surface, an invitation to see the unlovely elements typically concealed by the curtain drawn on private lives, and that these elements are made visible especially through the documentary director's use of primary home video footage. These documentaries function as not just introductions to but intrusions, however welcome, *into* the lives of these unfamiliar "actors," to use *Parents Magazine*'s language; these intrusions, however, are made possible by the video footage that the film's subjects have, willingly or unknowingly, provided.

Fly in the Face: *Capturing the Friedmans*

All of the films under consideration here turn to the idea of self-documentation because of something happening within the domestic universe, and all parade an array of disharmonies that are antithetical to the self-representation of family in the pre-video age. Of these three films, *Capturing the Friedmans* is the least reliant on home video for its overall visual content. In it the creation of home video footage is inspired by a dramatic familial rupture; in fact, the presence of the home video camera and its primary operator are motivated by and may even play a role in the further disturbance of the already-fragile Friedman family. Whereas fly-on-the-wall cinematography became the hallmark of the direct cinema movement, home video in *Capturing the Friedmans* might better be understood in terms of its "fly-in-the-face" politics, as both the video camera and its operator harass, provoke, and interrogate those on the receiving end of its gaze.

Directed by Andrew Jarecki, who came upon the Friedmans' saga while making a short documentary about clown entertainers in New York City, the film tells the story of a Long Island family whose lives are radically disrupted when the father, Arnold, and one of the sons, Jesse, are arrested and charged with child molestation. The film employs a number of media in the telling of its story: contemporary footage shot by Jarecki's crew, news footage, home movies (which introduce us to the members of the Friedman family under the credit sequence), and home videos (shot largely by one of the Friedman sons, David). In fact, the film is as much about access and recording as it is about anything (one need only think of the film's multivalent title), from the fact that the first time cameras are permitted in a Nassau County courtroom is for the Friedmans' indictment, to the eldest son David's decision to get a video camera at a certain point in all of this chaos to document the unraveling of his own family and of himself.

The use of home movies and videos in *Capturing the Friedmans* supports the representational dichotomy discussed above. The home movies in *Capturing the Friedmans*—of birthday parties, children growing up—are typical of the genre: their visual register of cheerful familial togetherness offers a stark contrast to the contemporary images of this family captured by the video camera. Only Jarecki's editorial intervention in this home movie footage—both in terms of juxtaposition and narration—resignifies the seemingly "innocent" home movie images. At one such moment, an interview with Elaine Friedman is intercut with home movie footage and still images of herself with one of her babies, as she explains, "I wasn't the most well balanced person myself." Jarecki's editorial act here—adding Elaine's present-day commentary to the otherwise innocuous home movie footage—questions the otherwise "innocent" image, implicitly casting some blame on the mother for the current state of the family.

Casting blame on Elaine Freidman is also the driving force behind the home video footage taken, primarily by David, during Arnold's and Jesse's trials and convictions. Indeed, it seems as if David's home video is made with the aim of proclaiming—perhaps

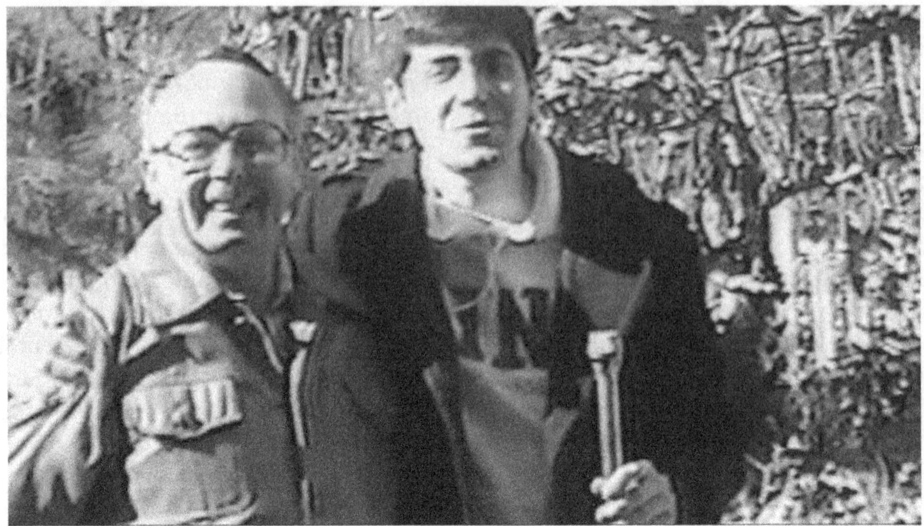

FIGURE 102.1 Home video footage in *Capturing the Friedmans* (Andrew Jarecki, 2003). Screen capture from DVD.

somehow proving—his father's innocence and his mother's monstrosity. Paul Arthur discusses the scene in which the sons argue about their father's innocence and mother's culpability, writing that it presents "the hideous flipside of those picnic-y exhibitions of middle-class satisfaction" that predominate home movies of an earlier period ("True Confessions" 5). While this is certainly true, more important is the fact that David's videography enables a certain interpretation of the family and its dynamics that is, at times, both provocative and sensational. As the recorder of these home video segments, David is aggressive, if not outwardly hostile, especially toward his mother. At several points he harangues his father about his mother, telling Arnold that he doesn't trust her. When he is on-camera David often seems on the verge of becoming unhinged. Arnold, on the other hand, usually appears overwhelmed by the video camera, sometimes staring away from its gaze or blankly out at the audience that was, at that point, only his son. David's desire to envision—and, one may presume, to eventually present—his family in this fashion is articulated by these moments in which the family performs at least partly in response to David and his camera's often-combative presence.

David's videography presents us with footage of two important familial meals, a Thanksgiving dinner and a Passover Seder. An unusual presence at the dining table, the camera appears to be autorecording from a stationary position just behind one of the chairs at the table, capturing at one point an ongoing argument as Arnold interrupts to declare what has, for the film's audience, become obvious: "Things are deteriorating here." That video is uniquely capable of rolling long enough to capture the deterioration is key, as is David's position as director. David's privileged access to this ostensibly private moment, the tacit trust between the cinematographer and his subjects, renders this scene of communal consumption and eruption all the more shocking for its exposure, for its unprotecting affect on the already-fragile family structure. David provides Jarecki with an infrequently realized view of intimate family life at a critical moment of crisis. This shift from celebration to crisis as a motivating factor for the home videographer, a shift that is also marked by a move away from the camera as "portrait-producer" to live-action video-journal, suggests the pivot between the film and video age.

Lauren Rabinovitz has noted the degree to which "documentary *vérité* seeks the spontaneous outburst that reveals the private person behind its public face.... If emotions are real ... then film-makers must 'move in' with their subjects, must see them every day at home to know them" (136). David's videography makes this seamless inhabiting of the Friedman universe possible; he and his camera are both an integrated part of this domestic scene and an affecting element. When Elaine begs to find out why nobody in the family supports her, Arnold tries to quiet the yelling family, however ineffectually, and the scene devolves into chaos. At moments such as this one has to wonder how much this display of disharmony was inspired by David's desire to capture and perhaps to provoke just this kind of domestic scene.

Jarecki's use of this video footage also begins to demonstrate the ways that contemporary self-documenters can shape their own eventual third-person presentations. David Friedman, for instance, provided Jarecki with seemingly intimate footage he took of himself in 1988, his "video diary" as the film terms it. Jarecki uses this footage at two key moments, the first of which finds David, at a point fairly early in the film, presenting a monologue in his underwear. Preceded by a video blue screen with a "play" icon in the lower left side of the frame, this scene alerts us to the complexity of both the Friedmans' home video record and Jarecki's film: "[sighs] Well, this is private, so if you're not me then you really shouldn't be watching this because this is supposed to be a private situation between me and me. This is between me now and me of the future, so turn it off, don't watch this, this is private. If you're the fucking ... oh god, the cops. If you're the fucking cops go fuck yourselves, go fuck yourselves because you're full of shit."

David's definition of privacy is curious here. Clearly, Jarecki could not have obtained this footage without David's assistance, alerting us to either the seemingly disingenuous nature of David's videoed privacy claim or the impermanence of the idea of privacy in the video age. What purpose does this declaration—or its absence—serve (both David Friedman and Andrew Jarecki)? And why does David anticipate an audience, instructing them to turn the video off? There are, we would argue, no private situations in the presence of the video camera. In the context of videography, privacy is always a shifting conceptualization, one that can easily be invalidated. David's interrogational techniques, evidenced elsewhere in the film, seem to support the camera's deprivatizing capacities, even when he locates himself on the receiving end.

This scene also raises a larger ethical question, which will come to the fore in our discussion of *Grizzly Man:* what boundaries might exist for the home videographer, and how, if at all, do they extend to the documentary filmmaker? Does David's presumably exhibitionist desires—to share this footage, to "entertain" an audience by clowning, or to tell his family's story—make him a masochistic subject in need of protection from himself? His willingness to display himself at his most abject suggests, at minimum, a real insincerity to the idea of privacy in the modern media age. But there is also the larger question concerning Jarecki's decision to convey such a moment to a commercial moviegoing audience. Why record a moment if not to share it with others? And, more critically, to what end might this sharing be put? To some degree, of course, Jarecki's film offers a possible answer by involving the viewer in the drama of the Friedman family but ultimately refusing to take a clear stand on Arnold's or Jesse's guilt or innocence. Intimacy, in other words, is Jarecki's goal, and his film seeks proximity more than it does any notion of truth or justice. David's suggestion that the footage is private, in other words, is used by Jarecki as a deliberately placed teaser, drawing the spectator into this immensely intimate view.

Toward the end of the film, David offers two explanations for his introduction of the video camera into his family at this particular moment in their history. At one point he says, "Maybe I shot the videotape so that I wouldn't have to remember it myself," and later, in response to video footage of Jesse clowning around on the courthouse steps on the day of his plea bargain, David claims, "I think it was about distracting ourselves." There is a valid point to be made regarding the camera's ability to enable distance at moments of problematic proximity (one thinks of Margaret Bourke-White's well-known articulation of this in the context of her concentration camp liberation photography at the close of World War II). David's footage, in spite of his words to the contrary, functions differently. Bringing himself, the camera, and the disavowed but always implied viewer closer to the trauma, David's video acts effectively disturb the various parts of the familial unit, factionalizing the group and, perhaps as a consequence, the audience as well. Although joking about David's close-ups at one point, Arnold's statement, "I feel like I'm being dissected here," seems especially to apply to Elaine, who at one point is shown getting angry about being videotaped. Elaine seems cognizant of the fact, as she implies in an interview with Jarecki's crew, that what David and her other sons really wanted was to capture her on video proclaiming her husband's innocence, something she refuses to do. Aggressive, confrontational, and propagandistic at the microscopic level, David's videography teases out familial chaos in search of an affirmation of his own beliefs. Where Jarecki's film obliquely examines the video camera's implication within a family about to disintegrate, Jonathan Caouette's *Tarnation* purports, especially in its later segments, to use video to reconnect the dissolved family. The layers of performance in Caouette's film, however, are even more complex.

A Self-Made Man in the Video Age: *Tarnation*

Though interestingly performative themselves, one of the defining characteristics of the Friedman family is their father's highly mediated and much publicized desire to look, perhaps inappropriately. Video intrudes rather late in the family's history, tipping the group in the direction of their divided destiny and providing a highly charged document of this process. Jonathan Caouette's *Tarnation* is guided by another, though certainly related, impulse. Motivated more by a need to "show" (as opposed to the need to "see," although the two concepts are linked), the footage at the center of *Tarnation* is clinically exhibitionist, helmed by a lifelong filmmaker operating under the assumption that his own cathartic self-exhibition will be as healing to those around him as it has been to him. Like David Friedman's lens, Caouette's is similarly drawn to the recording of familial crises.

We might situate *Tarnation* within Jim Lane's category of the self-portrait documentary, which "directly confronts the status of individuality in its attempt to show others why the self is the way it is" (120). The film, whose legendary microbudget of around two hundred dollars and iMovie provenance provided plenty of marketing fodder for its post-Sundance life, consists largely of a dizzying imagistic and sonic montage primarily captured by Jonathan Caouette of himself and of his family: home movies, video, news footage, photographs, and answering machine and tape recordings. Caouette bills himself in the credit sequence as editor, producer, and director (in this order), and his long-term obsessive self-documenting combined with his often quite poetic, avant-garde use of this footage results in a complex and haunting portrait of a family—one far from the traditional, nuclear family of *Capturing the Friedmans*—that seems to exist almost in spite of itself. In fact, it is hard at times to draw the line in this film between the home videographer and the documentary filmmaker. In some ways, the commercial film we're watching has been in production since Caouette first got access to a video camera.[10] *Tarnation* is a necessarily narcissistic venture, although Caouette's decision to display his family and his own life in this fashion might lead us to understand this narcissism as a kind of therapeutic response to instability and disorder, especially of the mental variety.[11]

Where *Capturing the Friedmans* uses home video that was itself produced to document and perhaps even to exacerbate ruptures in the family structure, *Tarnation* employs home video in a palpably desperate attempt to understand and, ostensibly at least, to heal. Indeed, Jonathan's (first names refer to the "characters" in the film, although this gets complicated at times) video footage seems motivated by a desire to create a space away from the instability of his family; to document their eccentricities, their varying degrees of self-awareness; and to try to understand how and why his family turned out the way it did. One might argue that the film we know as *Tarnation* is the culmination of Jonathan's lifelong attempt to understand, aestheticize, and find his own place within this unconventional family. Jonathan's footage, in other words, appears to be organized around an attempt at *resolution*.

Caouette, whose mother, Renee, sustained an injury as a child that led to years of shock therapy and hospitalizations, explains—entirely in intertitles—that he was raised in and out of often-abusive foster care as well as by his grandparents, Adolph and Rosemary. Like his mother, Jonathan would also attempt suicide and be hospitalized on a number of occasions. But where Renee's life is depicted as a haphazard collection of barely successful attempts to survive, Caouette depicts himself as struggling to create order in the chaos of his situation. Throughout the film Jonathan exhibits an unusual awareness regarding the performative nature of video documentation and uses this knowledge to reinvent himself. In fact, the first sustained video segment in *Tarnation* is of Jonathan at age eleven, apparently taping himself. Jonathan performs this scene in the guise of a lower-class woman, wearing make-up and a headscarf. "She" speaks in a heavy southern accent about her traumatic family life leading up to the moment she killed her abusive husband, theatrically gesturing while talking with tears in her eyes as if appearing on a daytime television talk show. At this early point in the film, Caouette seems to be offering a kind of lesson on his modus operandi. Jonathan, already aware that he can transform himself on video, is here escaping from his all-too-immediate surroundings (faint voices are heard occasionally in the background throughout the scene), if only momentarily.

This scene and several others like it throughout the film affirm the degree to which the self might be both performed and transformed, a nice and perhaps necessary fantasy for someone surrounded by considerable unhappiness and confusion. Jonathan's recording impulse, pulled as it is both toward the "fictional" and the "factual," is also a critical response to a generation of familial silence and denial. Jonathan nurtures the urge to perform in all of his family members (even Rosemary is asked to do her Bette Davis imitation after she's suffered a stroke), but this is especially evident in footage featuring Renee. Renee at various points pretends to be wearing Elizabeth Taylor's old earrings, to be talking to someone nonexistent on a new phone, as well as to dance (throughout) and lip-synch (another recurrent mode of performance employed both by her and by Jonathan). However, Renee also *seems* to lack the awareness exhibited by Jonathan in the sequence just discussed. What becomes clear over the course of the film is that Caouette is curating these performances, allowing the subject—especially himself—to escape *into* actorly moments. Theatricality seems to be a kind of substitution for a painfully absent sense of normality, which the film never makes mention of but which seems always to be the elusive referent. Outrageous as they often are, these unsettling performances also remind us of a previous generation's attempts to display and perform its *normality* before the home movie camera.

Renee seems, for the most part, comfortable with this mode of interaction with the video camera; she typically exhibits a gleeful abandon whenever she gets the chance to perform in these situations, sometimes to our embarrassment. Indeed, at a point late in the film—after Renee has overdosed on lithium and returned to her father's disheveled Texas home—Caouette provides his audience with an excruciating long take of one of these performances gone wrong. Renee, who no longer seems to be simply playing along in an effort to please her camera-obsessed son, appears to have lost touch with reality. She rambles, sings nonsense songs about pumpkins and dolls, straightens pillows, picks up props to play with, laughs hysterically, and seems trapped in this off-kilter performative mode. With her father glimpsed occasionally in the deep field sitting at a table and ignoring her entirely, Renee is revealed here as damaged, probably irreparably. Caouette's decision to subject viewers to a significant duration of this unedited footage, unlike earlier moments, which are always presented in a montage of other images, suggests his desire to create of this collection of sounds and images something approximating a narrative: Renee's tragic, postoverdose performance is this film's climax.

Renee's lack of self-awareness in this scene is painful to watch, in part because it seems that her performance is encouraged by the presence of her son's camera. Elsewhere in the film Renee demonstrates significant resistance to being in front of the camera when it appears to seek "the truth," which has become impossible for Renee to bear. On a visit to New York, Renee is interviewed by Jonathan about her past. This is the first time Caouette includes footage of this nature, rather than the heavily edited glimpses at Renee's more playful, if disturbing, behavior. Here Renee talks about being abused as a child by Adolph and Rosemary, saying earnestly that she hopes she "didn't bring over any of the abuse to my children." When Jonathan asks her about her childhood accident, however, she gets up from the seat in which she is being interviewed. Caouette cuts to another question he asks her about being hospitalized, and Renee again gets upset and walks away from the camera. After spinning his camera around the room, Jonathan shoots her from a distance as he tries to bring her back into the interview, pleading "talk to me" as he zooms in on Renee, who seeks refuge in the other room. Caouette then cuts to footage of Renee, presumably having returned to the conversation, talking about Jonathan's biological father. Again, Renee walks away, scolding Jonathan for bringing up the past on camera, refusing to participate not in the conversation per se but in the *recording* of the conversation. Jonathan's response to Renee's refusals is frankly self-interested: "Please help me with my stupid film. . . . I'd like to find out a few things about myself, too."

While purportedly intent upon investigating the history of his mother's neurosis, the film ends up exposing Jonathan's, suggesting throughout that video has become his primary way of knowing, interacting, understanding, and finding out. It is not just home video but video intended—now perhaps even produced—for public consumption. Fed up with the interrogation, Renee tells Jonathan, quite coherently, quite logically, "We can talk, Jon, we don't need it on film." The act of filming or of being filmed, watching films, and quoting films has overtaken familial interactions for Jonathan. Realizing this or not, the most painful moments in the film find Jonathan attempting to impose this inanimate surrogate family member on his literal family.

We would argue, then, that like the video footage used in *Capturing the Friedmans,* home video footage in *Tarnation* represents an attempt by the videographer to control and order the family. Jonathan, recognizing the disorder that surrounds him, attempts to aestheticize it, to (in the clinical language the film rehearses) *depersonalize* it. Nowhere is this more evident than in the literal reunion Jonathan stages between his mother, his father, and himself. Renee is restless and uncomfortable in this scene of domestic rehabilitation; she repeatedly gets up and walks out of the frame. At this point it becomes clear that Jonathan has decided to live his life on camera. The camera's intrusion on this reunion (as the intertitle tells us, "It was the first time all three had been together . . . in 30 years") is palpable; there is no illusion that everyone is acting as they would without their knowledge of its presence. Renee's occasional discomfort—both here and in the interrogation scene just discussed—reminds us that Jonathan's desire to record might also interfere with his other family members' desires not to be recorded.

The opening and closing of the film offer a curious framework for the extensive visual archive that exists in between. In the opening sequence, shot in March 2002 in New York, Caouette assembles footage of his partner, David, coming into their apartment, turning off a snowy television, and waking up Jonathan, who begins to talk about a dream he's just had about his mother. Like the other performative footage in which Jonathan pretends to be someone other than he is (such as the southern murderess discussed above), this seems a highly staged and unspontaneous re-creation of something that *might* have happened without the camera's presence. Here Jonathan seems to be trying to order his 2002 life in a way that his actual home life never was. The shot is perfectly framed and timed; it is narratively sensible. Caouette is effectively creating a new family history for himself, one characterized by stability and order even in the midst of the inescapable chaos of his past. More critically, this and the film's other staged moments—captured on video, viewable *ad infinitum,* capable of being reorganized, edited, enhanced—become tangible, consumable, comprehensible objects. This is true for the viewer, certainly, but more critically for Jonathan, for whom the domestic images captured seem to make little sense prior to the act of capturing and ordering them.

This pattern is repeated at the end of *Tarnation,* during which a camera seems always to be waiting for Jonathan to appear. There is a shot of a video camera that Jonathan is preparing to shoot himself with, making it certain that at least two cameras are being employed to capture this moment. Jonathan tells us that he has closed himself in a bathroom at 5:00 AM, takes things off the walls behind him, and confesses that he "wanted this scene to kind of be in the dark like it was when I was younger with the light, and the sun's about to come up so I have to hurry up and do this." This formal staging—an attempt to re-create the mood of the past at the moment of the film's closure, even Jonathan's verbal acknowledgment that he is creating "a scene"—is a fascinating glimpse into the director's process. His reliance upon video to maintain or imitate self-awareness reminds us of the degree to which even these acts can be performed and controlled.

In this fashion, Jonathan's on-camera monologue in this scene resonates oddly with the earlier weepy disclosures of the characters he inhabited in his teenage role playing. With tears in his eyes he swears and states, "I don't ever want to turn out like my mother and I'm scared because, um, when I was little and she was my age that I am now, which is 31, um, she seemed a lot better than she does now. I love my mother so much, as fucked up as it is. I can't escape her. She lives inside me; she's in my hair; she's behind my eyes; she's under my skin; she's downstairs [Jonathan laughs]." Here Jonathan moves toward the camera, saying, "I can't do this," and presumably turns it off, concluding in a fashion that pinpoints most painfully the real subject of and motivation for his project. The curious and at times frustrating textual overload of the film's first half—which consists largely of a constant barrage of titles that try to narrate, however insufficiently, his mother's early life, accompanied by a rapidly moving, at times repetitive swarm of still and moving images—is answered by this comparatively minimalist monologue. In trying to unlock the mystery of his mother's fate Jonathan seems frustrated by the lack of *comprehensible* images and information, the revelatory magic footage that might answer his questions. At least partly, Jonathan appears careful not to repeat this state of affairs in his own life story. To record is to control, or at least to attempt to.

Capturing it all on video; re-creating what was not caught; inventing scenarios for the camera; cataloging, organizing, restructuring, and ultimately sharing this footage—Jonathan, who is everywhere in the film worried about his genetic history, ensures that his own mental processes will be documented, will be caught on video. Walking delicately along the line separating self-obsession and self-confirmation, Caouette's footage shares much in common with Timothy Treadwell's. Werner Herzog's *Grizzly Man* similarly documents the life of a man whose quest for an alternative family sets him filming. Unlike Caouette, however, Treadwell is not afforded the luxury of final cut.

"Any idiot could make a film out of it": *Grizzly Man*

Werner Herzog's *Grizzly Man*, which at first seems to share little with the more overtly domestic narratives of *Capturing the Friedmans* and *Tarnation*, ends up being equally about both family and the desire to document its instability.[12] In place of a traditional family, however, in *Grizzly Man* we find Timothy Treadwell's admittedly eccentric, substitutive attempts to create a family outside the species. James Moran has convincingly argued, "In our contemporary era of families we choose, for whom traditions and conventions may be in continual flux, the home mode [of videotaping] offers an important tool for tracing common roots no longer nourished only by blood" (60). Along these lines, *Grizzly Man* is about a man who constructs—both through deed and through video—an alternative family out of the bears and foxes he tries to protect in the Alaskan wilderness. Similar to both David Friedman and Jonathan Caouette's video footage, Treadwell's is focused on familial crisis, though here the crisis expresses itself in the shape of Treadwell's apparent isolation from this and all human communities and his problematic attempts to situate himself as not only the author of his surrogate family but also its patriarch and protector. Though video allows Treadwell the liberty to shoot for hours upon end (much of the footage Herzog uses might best be thought of as Treadwell's "outtakes"), of particular interest are his desperate attempts to capture the illusion of *harmony* he has assembled for himself in the wilderness.

Treadwell lived among the grizzlies in the Alaskan wilderness for part of each year, worked as an activist on their behalf, recorded his experiences, and gave classroom lectures based upon them. When he and a female companion, Amie Huguenard, were killed by a bear in 2003, he left behind an extraordinary video record of his experiences (over one hundred hours of video footage, according to Herzog), which constitutes a large part of *Grizzly Man*. Although Herzog is no doubt being cagey when he claims that any idiot could make a film from this exceptional footage, his point is well taken: as a director, Herzog is working with another filmmaker's material, something that he freely acknowledges, functioning in large part as an editor of what Treadwell had already chosen to record.[13]

Although living among the grizzlies might seem an invasive approach to protecting and studying the species, Treadwell considered himself an integrated part of their community. The opening sequence of *Grizzly Man,* in fact, addresses this element of Treadwell's life, showing self-taken video footage of Treadwell explaining his process: "I am like a fly on the wall, observing, noncommittal, noninvasive in any way." This is a curious fantasy, a rehearsal of the language of *vérité* that runs counter to the evidence his footage provides. Direct address and direct involvement are Treadwell's preferred modes, constituting a significant portion of the video program he created in which he attempts to make an argument about his relationship with his animal family, not merely his observation of their activity.

Treadwell defines himself as "different," as loving "these bears enough to do it right." His self-perceived exceptionalism emerges both in his visual methodology and verbally. At one point he dares his imaginary spectator to try to do what he does; his rhetorical response: "You will die here. You will fuckin' die here. They will get you." Treadwell's favorite composition affirms his self-perceived connection to the bears. In it, the bears are in the deep (and sometimes not-so-deep) field and he is in the foreground, remaining in the frame while he narrates. This compositional tendency indicates the shifting nature of Treadwell's purported subject, which is as much the bears as it is himself. Treadwell also seems willing—perhaps eager—to make himself vulnerable, reaching out toward a bear or coming just close enough that he has to assert himself in order to escape from harm. He documents these moments of borderline danger, it seems, in large part to suggest his privileged status among the bears, whom he affectionately refers to by name throughout the film.

If Treadwell isn't quite the fly on the wall he imagines, neither is Herzog, despite his temporal distance from the original moment of Treadwell's videography (Herzog came to the project after Treadwell's death). Herzog does not refrain from entering the world of *Grizzly Man* at a number of points in the film, both visually and through voice-over narration. Herzog offers his interpretations throughout, inserting himself and his ideas into what has already been captured on video prior to his involvement in the project. Herzog is perpetually aware of these insinuative decisions, beginning the film by crediting Treadwell with shooting all of the footage in an act of citation that suggests the degree to which Herzog wants to foreground the parasitic elements inherent in a project of this nature. Herzog appears to deeply admire what Treadwell has achieved in his videography, interrupting Treadwell's story on occasion to praise his compositional choices and accidentally magical moments. Herzog's passions, which find expression throughout his storied career, also run toward the *apparently* accidental. His is a sort of home movie aesthetic, and elsewhere he has stated, in a manner strangely appropriate to our concerns here, that "there is no independent cinema, with the exception of the home movie made for the family album" (Cronin 202). Never entirely public or private, Treadwell's footage complicates the definition of *home* video by focusing on his own attempts to reorganize the very concept of a symbolic home in the wilderness.[14]

The relationship between the public and private elements of Treadwell's footage, especially as it is filtered through Herzog's intervention, resonates with the other films under discussion here. Clearly, Treadwell understood some of this footage as having a potential for eventual public consumption. Herzog tells us that Treadwell often repeated takes, some up to fifteen times, and he provides us with some of these duplicate stagings where we see Treadwell redoing a "scene" to make it more adventuresome, exciting, or professional. Herzog also includes footage of Treadwell at one point commenting that "this stuff could be cut into a show later on." Much of Treadwell's footage, then, is inherently different from what we think of as home video, and not just because Treadwell's "home" is an unconventional one. Rather, it is also conceived of as a presentation of Treadwell's performances, as a document meant to represent his bear family and his relationship with them to the outside world.

It is worth considering, then, the ethical implications of Herzog's use of some of the more private moments of Treadwell's footage. Treadwell, who made many of these trips alone, often appears to treat the camera as a companion, a family member, occasionally even as a god. Early in the film Herzog gives the viewer a glimpse of this relationship, showing Treadwell goofily interacting with the camera: "Give it to me baby, that's what I'm talking about." Elsewhere he converses with the camera about his fears of being hurt by a bear; wonders why he can't develop long-term relationships with women; curses out a fox who has stolen his hat ("where's that fucking hat, that hat is so friggin' valuable for this trip"); rants about the Park Service; and ruminates on the existence of God, speaking directly to the camera ("thank you"), as if it was the deity he sought to convene with. In what might be the most transgressive moment in his footage, Treadwell marvels over a fresh pile of bear feces first feeling the heat from it and then touching it while saying how amazing it is to commune with something that was just inside one of his bears. "I know it may seem weird that I touched her poop," Treadwell says. But to whom is Treadwell speaking? And why did Herzog deem these moments essential to the telling of Treadwell's story?

If Treadwell often treats the camera as if it was a confidante, interspersing his potentially public recordings with footage he surely never imagined would reach the public, then we also have to ask why he left the camera running on occasions that seem to defy the logic of self-documentation in the context of the public image he was attempting to construct. Like David Friedman's video diary and Jonathan Caouette's lifelong self-documenting project, Treadwell seems to be seeking a dialogue with himself. He might have been more directorially selective, less revealing, but instead opts to undergo a kind of self-scrutinizing record keeping that transcends the heroic, public self he was simultaneously constructing. Treadwell, like the subjects of the previous films under investigation here, seems to lose track of his existence outside of the camera's presence, needing it as a witness to these intimate moments, even the flawed moments with his unconventional, interspecies family, moments not entirely unlike those we witness in *Capturing the Friedmans* and *Tarnation*.

The relationship between Treadwell as the maker of his own documentary image, however dualistic, and Herzog as the distributor of that image is equally fascinating. Herzog clearly feels an obligation to Treadwell and his vision of himself, even as he explains his take on Treadwell's self-delusions to his film's audience and includes moments that undermine Treadwell's vision of himself. Treadwell's death and Herzog's handling of it bring these representational and ethical issues to the foreground. When Treadwell and Amie are attacked by a bear (they will die during the attack), Treadwell is unable to remove the lens cap on his camera, leaving only an audio recording. Unlike the rest of the film, then, there is no visual counterpart for this part of Treadwell's story. Herzog first introduces us to the sound portion of the videotape when he interviews the coroner, who narrates what is on the tape: "We can hear the sounds of Amie screaming," etc. The coroner acts as an interpreter of the recording, distancing the film's audience from the original content and offering his take on the attack: it occurred quickly, and Amie was faithful and brave, staying with Timothy while they tried to fend off the bear for a full six minutes.

Herzog ends this scene by backing the camera away from the coroner but does not otherwise articulate his own interpretation of or feelings about the tape, this snuff film *sans image*. The second time *Grizzly Man* addresses the subject of the imageless video, immediately following this scene, Herzog enters the visual landscape of the film for the first time, appearing on camera with Jewel, a friend of Treadwell who is in possession of this audio remnant. On-screen with headphones, Herzog listens to the tape that Jewel has never allowed herself to hear. He is shot from behind, in profile, holding his eyes as he selectively narrates what he hears. He then stops, choked up, and we get a shot of Jewel with tears in her eyes, inspired by what she can only imagine. Herzog tells her, "Jewel, you must never listen to this . . . and you must never look at the photos that I've seen at the coroner's office . . . You should destroy it [the tape] . . . because it will be the white elephant in your room all your life."

As if to confer the recording of Treadwell's death with the official status of the repressed, this tape surfaces for a third time toward the end of the film when Herzog returns us to footage of the coroner describing the audiotape. The coroner's descriptions are more explicit here, giving the spectator a sense of the gruesomeness of Timothy's and Amie's deaths. This kind of detail—"All of a sudden the intensity of Amie's screaming reached a new height. . . . These horrifying screams were punctuated by Timothy saying, 'Go away, leave me,'" etc.—is all the more surprising given Herzog's earlier prohibition. His decision to absent this audio from his film and yet to spin around it like the center of a whirlpool creates a spectacle out of that which he refuses to include. Who is Herzog protecting here? His audience? Jewel? Treadwell? The bears? It is also worth remembering that Herzog offers this prohibition—that neither Jewel nor, it turns out, his audience will hear this tape—while also emphasizing his privileged access both to it and to the photographs that he chooses not to show. It is, we might argue, the elephant in his own film.

All of this has to do, more or less, with the politicized idea of the gaze and its auditory counterpart. Bill Nichols, in *Representing Reality*, suggests:

> Mulvey's concern with the eroticization of the gaze and the gender hierarchy that classic (Hollywood) narrative imposes does not translate directly into the terms and conditions of documentary production. (Although it is hardly alien either.) The institutional discourse of documentary does not support it, the structure of documentary texts does not reward it, and the audience expectations do not revolve around it. Voyeurism, fetishism, and narcissism are present but seldom occupy the central position they have in classic narrative. (76)[15]

Nichols's project in the early 1990s was to acknowledge what had been a dominant critical discourse in film studies, one he felt needed to be retooled when applied to documentary practice. Quoting Mulvey and then reshaping her logic to fit what he takes to be the largely different enterprise of documentary production and reception, Nichols presents us with terms appropriate to our present investigation: "One way to give further consideration to this shift in problematics from narrative to documentary would be to address the specific qualities of the documentary gaze and its object of desire: the world it brings into sight" (77).

Herzog, perhaps more obviously than our other filmmakers but very much in keeping with their course as well, frustrates Nichols's suggestion by concentrating attention around that which is not shown, the world both he and Treadwell refuse or are unable to bring into sight. In *Grizzly Man* that world includes both the taboo footage (refused at Herzog's much-discussed discretion) and, perhaps even more critically, the world (familial, social, romantic) beyond that which Treadwell had created for himself (ignored, we are led to believe, at Treadwell's own videographic discretion). This absence becomes a critical trigger for spectatorial desire, casting Treadwell's none-too-romantic solitary existence in relief and marking his failed patriarchal dominion over the bears as a tragic response to a similarly failed familial existence. Herzog's decision to flirt with the ethical boundaries he has imposed upon himself reminds us of the degree to which Nichols's trifecta—voyeurism, fetishism, and narcissism—has become, in recent years, not just a central but an essential part of the documentary project. This is all the more the case in films centering on home video footage, which is so suited to bringing the most personal, and vulnerable, of worlds "into sight."

The unseen, the unavailable, the unfilmed are equally critical elements within Jarecki's and Caouette's films. All three of these films make plain that, as raw material, personal video footage imposes certain representational boundaries upon the documentary filmmaker, even as it opens up others. Bearing the video age imprimatur of authenticity, these at times starkly exposed moments of self-revelation are moments twice chosen, first at the moment of filming and again at the moment of editing. In the context of a discussion about autobiographical film and video, Michael Renov argues that if "memory is, like history, always revision, translation, the gap between experience (the moment of filming) and secondary revision (the moment of editing) produces an ineradicably split diaristic subject" ("The Subject in History" 6). Within the context of the documentary films under investigation here, the referent of the "split" is doubly significant. Using Caouette's borrowed psychoanalytic language, we are certainly faced here with a range of "depersonalized" subjects. We are also faced, however, with a range of "defamiliarized" families. In both cases the critical rupture seems to occur somewhere in the gap between the desire to represent and record and the desire to contain and control. In the video age memory *appears* to come cheaply. Family, these films argue, does not.

NOTES

1. In suggesting that this is a new trend, we are also quite aware that there is a significant history of cinematic self-documentation that precedes this current generation of home videocentric documentaries. There is, of course, a legacy of self-documentation to be found in home movies themselves; in avant-garde cinema, especially the work of Jonas Mekas and Stan Brakhage; as well as in documentary filmmaking. For more on this history see Lane; see also Chalfen, whose *Snapshot Versions of Life* was written on the precipice of the shift from home movies being primarily shot on film to home movies being primarily shot on video. In addition to the experimental films made by Mekas and Brakhage, Chalfen briefly discusses a group of 1970s films that exemplify an earlier burst of activity involving the use of home *movies:* Sandy Wilson's *Growing Up at Paradise* (1977), Frederick Becker's *Heroes* (1974), Barry Levine's *Procession* (1978), Victor Faccinto's *Sweet and Sour* (1976), Jerome Hill's *Family Portrait* (1971), Martha Coolidge's *Old-Fashioned Woman* (1976), Jan Oxenberg's *Home Movie* (1973), Alfred Guzzetti's *Family Portrait Sittings* (1975), Amalie Rothschild's *Nana, Mama, and Me* (1974), and Don and Sue Rundstrom's *Uprooted! A Japanese American Family's*

Experience (1978). Renov addresses the related idea of the essayistic, autobiographical film in "The Subject in History."

2. The case of *Grizzly Man* is more complicated, since the film does not concern a conventional human family (except the one its protagonist absents himself from) but rather a man and his surrogate animal family, as will be discussed in the final section of this essay.
3. The phrase "families we choose," coined by Kath Weston, is used by Moran in *There's No Place Like Home Video* to address the fact that "the nuclear family has increasingly diminished statistically over the last three decades, replaced by alternatives ranging from single parenthood and gay marriage to 'families we choose' among relatives, friends, and colleagues" (xvii).
4. For more on this see Zimmermann (112–42). Zimmermann notes that in the 1950s there were even home movie editing services, which would "transform the jumble of unconnected frames into a coherent and interesting story of a family's life" (127). Originally published by Harry Kursch and Harold Mehling, "Your Life on Film: Ralph Eno, Amateur Editor," *American Mercury* (November 1956): 69.
5. Zimmermann cites a number of trade and popular publications that attest to some of the essential differences between home movies and home videos. Drukker trots out a list of pros and cons in his essay "The Video Difference." At the time video equipment was still clunky and pricey, but videotape was "dirt cheap and reusable," requiring no development and allowing you to record "for hours" as opposed to three minutes at a time (Drukker 90). In the early 1980s complaints were still circulating about battery power and editing capabilities for video technology, but these issues would be resolved over the course of the next decade.
6. Adam Shell and Darren Stein's *Put the Camera on Me* (2003) supports this thesis about the shift toward children as the producers of home video. However, the emphasis in this documentary is on the degree to which these kids, guided by their precocious leader, created alternative videographic worlds for themselves, some of which would be shared with their parents and some of which seemed to be for their own consumption.
7. For more on this see Zimmermann; she discusses the degree to which "images of family, children, and travel coalesced into the ideology of togetherness" (135).
8. Moran discusses the differences between film and video throughout his first three chapters, especially pages 40–42.
9. The phrase "revenge of the home movie" is used in a discussion of explicitly autobiographical documentaries such as *Tarnation*. Elsewhere Arthur notes that the phenomenon of directors intentionally and regularly appearing in their own documentaries is also relatively recent, dating back to Ross McElwee's *Sherman's March* (1986) and Michael Moore's *Roger and Me* (1989) ("Feel the Pain" 47–50).
10. This is simplifying things somewhat, since Caouette uses video, film, and still photography throughout.
11. Bonastia posits that a number of recent films, *Tarnation* among them, function as "exercises in self-help" more "than as expressions of artistic vision with the intention of connecting with an audience" (20). Although we don't agree with the latter part of Bonastia's assertion, it seems true that Caouette, David Friedman, and, as we shall see in *Grizzly Man*, Timothy Treadwell all find the act of filming themselves and their families on video to be cathartic, a form of self-administered therapy. Bonastia, a sociologist, has concerns about this tendency both in documentary filmmaking and in the recent "flood of memoirs" (22), positing that "the urge to share your every musing with the world is contagious" (24).
12. The quote in the subhead is from Werner Herzog, talking about the process of working with Timothy Treadwell's footage for the making of *Grizzly Man* (Garcia 16).
13. Joe Bini, in fact, edited *Grizzly Man* and has worked with Herzog on a number of films. We intend the idea of editing to be understood here in a conceptual fashion as much as a literal one.
14. Moran makes a point about the conception of family and home that is relevant here: "While usually thought of as geographic, home may be photographic as well, unconfined to a specific place, but transportable within the space of imagination" (61).
15. See also Mulvey. In *The Subject of Documentary* Renov critically reconsiders the terms of Nichols's argument by attempting to articulate documentary's own erotic patterns of desire.

WORKS CITED

Arthur, Paul. "Extreme Makeover: The Changing Face of Documentary." *Cineaste* 30.3 (2005): 18–23.

________. "Feel the Pain." *Film Comment* 40.5 (2004): 47–50.

________. "True Confessions, Sort Of." *Cineaste* 28.4 (2003): 4–7.

Bonastia, Christopher. "Is Documentary the New Memoir? A Sociologist's View from the Couch." *Independent: A Magazine for Video and Filmmakers* 28.10 (2005): 20–24.

Bourke-White, Margaret. *Portrait of Myself.* New York: Simon and Schuster, 1963.

Chalfen, Richard. *Snapshot Versions of Life.* Bowling Green: Popular P, 1987.

Cronin, Paul, ed. *Herzog on Herzog.* New York: Faber and Faber, 2002.

Drukker, Leendert. "The Video Difference: Taping vs. Filming." *Popular Photography.* May 1981: 90–91, 191–92.

Garcia, Maria. "Grizzly Tale: Werner Herzog Chronicles Life of Ill-Fated Naturalist." *Film Journal International* 108.8 (2005): 14–16.

Lane, Jim. *The Autobiographical Documentary in America.* Madison: U of Wisconsin P, 2002.

Moran, James. *There's No Place Like Home Video.* Minneapolis: U of Minnesota P, 2002.

Mulvey, Laura. "Visual Pleasure and Narrative Cinema." *Movies and Methods*, vol. 2. Ed. Bill Nichols. Berkeley: U of California P, 1985.

Nichols, Bill. *Representing Reality.* Bloomington: Indiana UP, 1991.

Pinney, Roy. "Better Home Movies." *Parents' Magazine* May 1955: 126.

Rabinovitz, Lauren. *They Must Be Represented: The Politics of Documentary.* New York: Verso, 1994.

Renov, Michael. "The Subject in History: The New Autobiography in Film and Video." *Afterimage* 17.1 (1989): 4–7.

———. *The Subject of Documentary.* Minneapolis: U of Minnesota P, 2004.

Rhu, Lawrence F. "Home Movies and Personal Documentaries, an Interview with Ross McElwee." *Cineaste* 29.3 (2004): 6–12.

Zimmermann, Patricia. *Reel Families: A Social History of Amateur Film.* Bloomington: Indiana UP, 1995.

103

VIVIAN SOBCHACK

INSCRIBING ETHICAL SPACE

10 Propositions on Death, Representation, and Documentary (1984)

Always concerned with the subversive capacity of cinema to show us what we may not wish to see, critic Amos Vogel has frequently commented on the medium's tendency to avert its eyes before the sight of actual death. He writes:

> Now that sex is available to us in hard-core porno films, death remains the one last taboo in cinema. However ubiquitous death is—we all ultimately suffer from it—it calls into question the social order and its value systems; it attacks our mad scramble for power, our simplistic rationalism and our unacknowledged, child-like belief in immortality.[1]

Death, Vogel suggests, possesses a "ferocious reality" which exceeds attempts to repress it or culturally contain it. Indeed, semiotically speaking, we can say that death presents a special problem in representation.

What follows is best identified as a semiotic phenomenology of death as it is represented and made significant for us through the medium and tropes of documentary film. Such a phenomenology of representation attempts to describe, thematize, and interpret death as it appears on the screen and is experienced by us as indexically real, rather than iconically or symbolically fictive. As well, given that representation is the object of its scrutiny (and, indeed, the means of its description), such a phenomenology is necessarily culturally informed and historicized. It is not transcendentally removed from the cultural and historical situation in which it was carried out. My essay's aim, therefore, is less to arrive at universal, "essential," and proscriptive categories, than to address the "thickness" of one particular mode of visual representation as it richly and radically entails a crucial aspect of human existence and our present attitudes in the sight of it. To that end, after a general historical situation of death and its representation in our culture, I will pose ten propositions as a way to focus on and semiotically describe some of the problematic relations which exist between death and its cinematic representation. Further, thematizing and interpreting these relations will lead to an exploration of the ethical stances which existentially (but always also culturally and historically) ground certain "codes" of documentary vision in its specular engagement with death and dying.

Historicizing Death and Representation

Let us first consider the particular threat death presents to representation in our current culture. Its present force has been succinctly historicized in Philippe Ariès' *Western Attitudes toward Death.*[2] Ariès takes us from the Middle Ages to the present, pointing out how the social significance of death and dying has radically changed over the centuries. Initially a social and public event, death has become an anti-social and private experience—all the more shocking when we are publicly confronted with the sight of it. Ariès charts a course from the public space of the Medieval bedchamber and a natural, "tamed" and socially speakable event to the private and anti-social space of the individual bedroom, where—from the 16th through the 18th century—the parallel paroxysms of sex and death condense to form a major iconography, one which stresses the "undomesticated" and "irrational" behavior of the body as culturally disruptive.

[. . .]

Experiences and attitudes changed in the 20th century. Encounters with natural death became less common. Natural death became less "natural"—on the one hand, less part of daily life, and on the other, more attributed to "foreign" causes that had exotic medical names. Increasingly institutionalized, medicalized, and technologized, natural death was displaced not in elaborate representation, but in physical space. The event of death was moved from its site in the home and bedroom to a regulated hospital room or mortuary where the dying and the dead could be "overseen" by professionals and "overlooked" by family and community. Removed from sight and common experience, from a site integral with cultural activity, natural death in our culture became, Ariès tells us, a "technical phenomenon," one "dissected, cut to bits by a series of little steps, which finally makes it impossible to know which step was the real death, the one in which consciousness was lost, or the one in which breathing stopped."[3] If impossible to prevent, natural death became possible to efface.

Given the public "disappearance" of natural death, and concurrently the increasing public emphasis on sexuality, our 20th-century culture has rejected what Ariès calls the 19th century's "eloquent decor of death."[4] Breaking with the excesses of Romanticism and the sexual prudery of the Victorians, and opting for the social goal of a prosaic "collective happiness," 20th-century culture finds poetic and aristocratic expressions of "melancholy nostalgia" repugnant and embarrassing.[5] Such excess untinged with the slightest irony is seen as self-indulgent, even masturbatory. There is no need for it when its "cause" is displaced from public sight. Thus, as Ariès concludes (paralleling Amos Vogel's words which began this essay), "death has become a taboo . . . and . . . in the twentieth century it has replaced sex as the principal forbidden subject." Citing social anthropologist Geoffrey Gorer's influential 1955 article "The Pornography of Death," Ariès summarizes:

> The more society was liberated from the Victorian constraints concerning sex, the more it rejected things having to do with death. Along with the interdict appears the transgression: the mixture of eroticism and death so sought after from the sixteenth to the eighteenth century

> reappears in our sadistic literature and in violent death in our daily life.[6]

The point to be emphasized here is that by removing the event of natural death from everyday sight so that its exoticism and strangeness continue intact, and by diminishing, making shameful, and rejecting the excessive displacements of death found in the social representations of the 19th century, 20th-century Western culture has effectively made natural death a "taboo" subject for public discourse and severely limited the conditions for its representation. Removing natural death from public space and discourse leaves only violent death in public sites and conversation. This leads to Gorer's "pornography of death"—that is, representation obsessed with and limited to the sensational activity of a body-object abstracted from the latter's simultaneous existence as a sensing and intentional body-subject.

[. . .]

If anything, our exposure to violent death has increased since Gorer wrote his essay in 1955. Assassinations, snipings, mass murders, civil violence, terrorism—all bring death into public sight and mark its significant representation as violent. As Lawrence Langer points out in his *The Age of Atrocity*, death in our current culture is generally regarded as "a sudden and discontinuous experience," as always "inappropriate," as an "atrocity."[7] It is in our cinematic fictions that "sudden," "discontinuous," "violent," "inappropriate," and "atrocious" deaths find their current representation. Safely contained by narrative, in iconic and symbolic signs and structures, they titillate and offer a mediated view which softens their threat and real ferocity. Our documentary films, on the other hand, avoid the representation of death. Indexical in code and function, they observe the social taboos surrounding "real" death and generally avoid reference to it.

The Semiotics of Death

Thus, in our present culture, we have limited representations of death. A taboo subject, it titillates us in our fictions as a "pornography" of death while it remains "unnatural" and "unnamable" in our real social relations, and in those forms of representation which most indexically point to those social relations. Indeed, if, as Vogel suggests, the "ferocious reality" of death in our present culture calls into question our "social order and its value systems," then it also radically calls into question that culture's semiotic systems. That is, the event of death as it is perceived in our culture points to and interrogates the very limits of representation in all its present forms—including, of course, the cinematic.

Certainly, death is not the only "ferocious reality" to make the camera avert its gaze or despair of representing the existential reality of both human and social being. Vogel points out in his *Film as a Subversive Art* that "the periodic transformation of matter from one state into another continues to evoke all the superstitious alarms and taboos of pre-history."[8] These superstitions and taboos, many of them cross-cultural, all have to do with the ultimately uncontrollable and therefore mysterious and often frightening semiosis of the body. Difficult to contain in cultural vision, such acts of human bodily transformation include excretion, sexual union, and birth, as well as the event of death. In addition, the visual taboos surrounding these transformations of the animate body often extend to those particular bodily signs which indexically point to and foreground the essential mystery of bodily being and nonbeing. For example, always in some way treated as sacred—either through the observance of ritual or ritual nonobservance—the deformed living body and the human corpse serve as radical signs of human "matter" transformed "from one state into another." The body is thus the primary indexical sign of what Langer calls "the universal dilemma of dealing with one's 'creatureliness'—of living critically and self-consciously while so vulnerable to the physical cruelties of men, nature, and science."[9]

Nonetheless, of all transformations of the lived body in our culture, the event of death seems particularly privileged in its threat to representation. Indeed, it so challenges our notion of representation that it seems unrepresentable. Birth in our culture, for example, involves a bodily transformation which interrogates conventional systems of representation with its radical originality, but it also affirmatively signifies an entrance into conventional culture, into social order and value systems, into a representable world and a world of representation. Birth, for us (and possibly for all cultures), is the sign to begin all signs. Death, however, is a sign that ends all signs. In our culture, it is perceived as the last, the ultimate act of semiosis. It is always original, unconventional, and shocking, its event always simultaneously representing both the process of sign production and the end of representation. Thus, while birth and death are each processes and representations of liminal moments of bodily transformation which threaten the stability of cultural codes and conventions with their radical originality, in our present culture death is the more subversive transformation of the two.

Hence, we come to my ten propositions about death and its current cinematic representation. Each proposition, while certainly open to argument, is offered as a focal point for thought about the significance and signification of death in our cinematic culture. Thus, all the propositions are limited in their claims, even as they are couched in assertive language, and may, in fact, contain descriptive force which crosses cultural boundaries. Additionally, their focus is primarily on the nature and experience of indexical representation.

1. *The representation of the event of death is an indexical sign of that which is always in excess of representation, and beyond the limits of coding and culture: Death confounds all codes.* That is, we do not see death on the screen, nor understand its visible momentum or contours. While being can be visibly represented in its inscription of intentional behavior (the "having of being" concretely articulated in a visible world), nonbeing is not visible. It lies over the threshold of visibility and representation. Thus, it can only be pointed to, the terminus of its indexical sign forever off-screen, forever out of sight. Within the technological culture we inhabit, the cinematic representation of death is inscribed and understood as a "technical phenomenon" rather than a lived-body experience. What Ariès says of death in our current culture holds true and is parallel to its indexical representation. The classic structure of the dissection of death into a series of "little steps" which "finally make it impossible to know which step was the real death" is paralleled by the recording of death by the film moving through camera and projector in twenty-four "little steps" per second. The classic "proof" of the excess of death over its indexical representation was the fascination exerted by the Zapruder film of John Kennedy's assassination; played again and again, slowed down, stopped frame by frame, the momentum of death escaped each moment of its representation. Indeed, in *Report*, Bruce Conner loops this footage and, through repetition, ironically comments upon (among other things) the impossibility of our "really" seeing Kennedy's death. This excess of death over visibility and representation is felt most acutely in our encounter with images which are primarily indexical. Fictive death primarily represented by iconic and symbolic signs does not move us to inspect it, to seek out a visibility we feel—in seeing it—it lacks. Even without the slow motion ballet of death made paradigmatic by Sam Peckinpah in

The Wild Bunch, fictive death is experienced as visible. Referring significantly only to themselves, representations of death in fiction film tend to satisfy us—indeed, in some films, to sate us, or to overwhelm us so that we cover our eyes rather than *strain* to see. Thus, while death is generally experienced in fiction films as representable and often excessively visible, in documentary films it is experienced as confounding representation, as exceeding visibility.

2. *It is the visible mortification of or violence to the existential, intentional, and representable lived-body which stands as the index of dying, and the visible cessation of the body's intentional behavior which stands as the index of death.* Dying and death, particularly in documentary film, cannot be represented and made visible on the screen with an exactitude experienced as "fullness." The transformation of a being into nonbeing, its location at what T.S. Eliot in "Burnt Norton" describes as the "still point of the turning world" where being is "neither flesh nor fleshless," is only perceptible by way of contrast with what is representable. That is, the moment of death can only be represented in a visible and vigorous contrast between two states of the physical body: the body as lived-body, intentional and animated—and the body as corpse, as flesh unintended, inanimate, static.

In this regard, the corpse is not so much an indexical sign of "death" as it is of the "dead." It signifies not a *process* of transformation, but a *thing*. This is not to say that we do not respond to the sight of a corpse on the screen, but rather that we respond to it always as "other" than we are, as an "object." Thus, the corpse is not perceived as a subject—although it confronts us and reminds us of subjectivity and its objective limits. [...] The corpse, then, exists with paradoxical semiotic force. It is a significant bodily sign of the body which has no power to signify. It engages our sympathy as an *object which is* an index of a *subject who was*.

But as an object, the corpse is also alienated from human being. It may have been a subject, but it is not now a subject. Thus, as John Fraser points out in his *Violence in the Arts*, "the very thing that cries out for the deepest sympathy serves in some measure to inhibit that sympathy, namely the conversion of the sufferers into 'monsters.'"[10] Our sympathy for the subject who was is mitigated by our alienation from the object that is. We are not dead and cannot imagine what it would be like to "be" so (that is, to "not be"). Thus, the corpse becomes an object for scrutiny, a way of releasing and fulfilling our natural curiosity about a taboo cultural object. We are fascinated and fearful, filled with what Vogel indicates is "the thrilling guilt of the voyeur/transgressor (to see what one has no right to see), coupled with the fear of punishment. How delicious when it does not come and the forbidden ... image can continue to be viewed."[11]

The corpse visibly provides the premises for visual reflection upon being and not-being, between the subjective lived-body and the body-object. But it does not necessarily so quicken us in our own lived-bodies as does the active inscription of the process of mortification on another lived-body. The corpse as a body-object is physically passive, semiotically impassive. It can be offered to a devouring scrutiny, or embalmed with the richest symbolism. It can be *used*, offering no resistance to the willful viewer—either filmmaker or spectator. And, as Fraser points out:

> In general, passivity does not invite empathy. What does invite it ... is anything that permits one to see the other as an agent. ... two of the most important factors making for empathy are a sense of the individual as engaged in work, and a sense of the physicality of the body.[12]

Although the corpse is the most physical of bodies, it is so because it is just a physical body. It does not "work"; it is not lived. As such, death cannot be inscribed upon it in an *activity* of transformation that signifies the passage between being and not being, between the being of a body-subject and merely objective existence. Thus, it is the lived body which is the primary signatory field for indexically signifying "dying" and "death," while the corpse is the primary iconic and symbolic sign for the "dead." From this need to signify the active transformation that death visits upon the physical body as a representation of a vigorously perceived contrast between two extreme states of visible existence, a third proposition emerges.

3. *The most effective cinematic signifier of death in our present culture is violent action inscribed on the visible lived-body*. This proposition is perhaps the most controversial thus far. Although it is descriptive rather than prescriptive, it still moves us to an ethical response. For if we abhor violence and its rupture of both the social and fleshly fabric of culture and individual human life, it is difficult to acknowledge that it is the best signifier of death in visual representation. However, as has been earlier indicated, our present culture's primary relationship to death is one marked by the now natural "unnaturalness" of violence. Given our current social relations to the event of death (the visible presence of death as externally and violently caused and the "structuring absence" of natural death), it is hardly surprising that violent action is the most effective sign-vehicle to signify the transformation of being to not-being. The sign function of violence is aptly described by Langer:

> In an age of private violence and public slaughter, which threatens to make atrocity socially respectable, inappropriate death has become an issue which we can no longer consider an aberration from the normal rhythms of experience. Sudden violent death is now a fact of our imaginative existence, crowding out the serene metaphors. . . . More recently the mushroom cloud has been displaced in our national consciousness by a personal act of aggression gradually approaching the status of metaphor—assassination.[13]

Consider how, in our cinematic culture, violence gives death a perceptible form, and signifies its ultimate violation of the lived-body. The objectively visible, usually externally caused, and violent end to animate and intentional activity is particularly and personally shocking seen on the screen—for the film medium, in its inherent representation and presentation of movement is life-giving, life-sustaining, and life-affirming. Thus, the violent cessation of movement and animation in a lived-body subject visibly and spatially emphasizes the temporal contrast between animate and inanimate—between the living and the dead. It visually transforms the cinematic present into a visible past tense, and an embodied subject into a body-object. In relation to this transformation, a fourth proposition is suggested.

4. *The most effective cinematic representation of death in our present cinematic culture is inscribed on the lived-body in action that is abrupt*. Ironically, although we have little to actually do with "natural death" in our current culture, the idea of natural death is comforting insofar as it is perceived as gradual and easeful. For example, the notion of dying in one's sleep significantly returns us to the bedchamber and a "tame" death, one not usually associated with pain or bodily humiliation. The latter, insupportably subversive of our culture's myth of process as progress, has led to the spatial displacement of lived-bodies undergoing the process of decay. As Ariès notes, by the late Middle Ages, decomposition of the body has become the sign of Man's failure, but by our time, that failure has become

transformed into something shamefully personal.[14] Except in the case of the sudden, fatal heart attack, we do not customarily think of natural death in the binary terms that violence inscribes. Indeed, the analogic qualities of natural death mark not the sudden end to the body's representation, nor a single dramatically significant moment of bodily transformation. Rather, they mark a process. The slow and primarily imperceptible transformation of the animate into the inanimate, of the lived-body into a corpse, does not signify our more usual contemporary experience of death as a "break," a "rupture." Rather, natural death sets up its own expectations and fulfills them over a perceived *durée*. In regard to its visual representation, it exists in temporal equivalence to the present-tense process of the film medium, marking little or no contrast between movement and stillness, between presence as an embodied being and a merely present body. Visualized as a gradual rather than abrupt process, then, the transformation of animate subject into inanimate object does not so much represent dying and death as it does the *living* of the process of dying. Thus, referring to Michael Roemer's *Dying* (which documents three people dying of various forms of cancer and interviews with the widow of a fourth), reviewers can truthfully tell us: "Theirs is a lesson about living," or "shock it will, not because it is painful to watch but because it isn't. . . . it is an unabashed plea for death as ritual."[15] These comments echo Ernest Becker's in *The Denial of Death*, when, after asking "Are images of dying and farewell as deep as the real feeling that one has absolutely no power to oppose death?", he points out that "disease and dying are still *living* processes in which one is engaged. But to fade away, leave a gap in the world, disappear into oblivion—that is quite another matter."[16]

Abruptness does not allow for the temporal experience of process, ritual, formal analgesics. The abrupt transformation of the animated body into an inanimate corpse denies formal reason and connotatively signs the "irrationality," "arbitrariness," and "unfairness" of death. Abruptness is itself a structure of what we perceive as violence, and it may well be that, in our present culture, both abruptness and violence best articulate death so that its binary marking of existence can be felt viscerally and personally by those who view its signs. Indeed, it could be said that the analogic representation and *durée* of dying on the screen serves as a sign of a third-person death—whereas the abrupt binary representation of death through a violently sudden transformation signs a first-person death and can be appreciated, to at least some extent, as "mine" because it always appears "untimely." In *A Very Easy Death*, Simone de Beauvoir writes:

> There is no such thing as a natural death: nothing that happens to a man is ever natural, since his presence calls the world into question. All men must die: but for every man his death is an accident and, even if he knows it and consents to it, an unjustifiable violation.[17]

Beauvoir's existential assertions are, of course, situated historically and socially in 20th-century experience, one dominated by images of massive discontinuity and upheaval. Robert Jay Lifton more particularly locates the emergence of attitudes toward death as "accident" and "violation" in the social discontinuities and upheavals caused by the wars we have experienced since the early part of the century. He tells us: "Without a cultural context in which life has continuity and boundaries, death seems premature whenever it comes. Whatever the age and circumstances, it is always 'untimely.'"[18] Thus, abruptness correlated with violence most effectively serves to signify death in our time. As Langer puts it:

> Atrocity, with its emphasis on the grotesqueness of abrupt and violent death, intensifies man's latent apprehension that dying is an unmanageable event; it erodes culture's carefully nurtured positions for withstanding this threat, and leaves man with the options of terror or awareness.[19]

Linked with atrocity, violence, abruptness, it is no wonder that in today's culture, death has replaced sex as a visual taboo.

The subversive action death performs upon and in culture and visual representation, its excess and its primary articulation as violence on a lived-body subject, in part explains the particular ethical problems its event poses for the cinema. If death is kept from cultural sight except when it violently breaks into a public site, how is a visual medium to deal with its representation without breaking a cultural taboo? Here Langer is apposite (as he quotes from Avery Wiseman's *On Death and Denying*):

> Men are reluctant to speak about death because "words have a primitive equivalence with the underlying reality to which they allude." To speak about *real* death, therefore, as opposed to death in the *abstract*, "puts us in the role of someone who violates a taboo. . . ."[20]

In the cinema, it seems the narrative representation of death is experienced as a visualization in the abstract, whereas the documentary representation of death seems experienced as a visualization of the real. Therefore, although primarily expressed in the limited tropes and obsessions which Gorer identifies as pornographic, the excessive visual attention lavished on violent death in the narrative film seems culturally tolerated—if often criticized. Conversely, documentary film is marked by an excessive visual avoidance of death, and when death is represented, the representation seems to demand ethical justification. Thus, when death is represented as fictive rather than real, when its signs are structured and stressed so as to function iconically and symbolically, it is understood that only the *simulacrum* of a visual taboo is being violated. However, when death is represented as real, when its signs are structured and inflected so as to function indexically, a visual taboo is violated, and the representation must find ways to justify the violation.

Narrative, then, only plays with visual taboo, containing death in a range of formal and ritual simulations, and also often boldly viewing it with unethical and prurient interest, as if, thus simulated, it simply "doesn't count." The audience generally responds in kind. That is, it is less ethically squeamish about looking at narrative death, and also less stringent in its judgment of the film's "objective" curiosity. Documentary, on the other hand, unable to "play" in the fields of simulation, tends to avoid the visually taboo—in most instances constituting its dread and violent images of the dying and the dead accidentally, or at personal risk to the filmmakers. Caught so nearly "unawares," or facing his or her own mortality, the filmmaker and camera are less vulnerable to possible charges of prurience, of unethical behavior, from an audience who morally judges their represented gaze at death as an inscription of their humanity and moral responsiveness to a social world *shared* by filmmaker and audience.

Perhaps this reluctance to face judgment accounts for why, according to Vogel,

> there are so few film records of individuals dying of natural causes; it is rather war deaths or executions that have been caught on film. Even these are rarely shown except on ceremonial occasions at which an audience gathers in guilt, remorse, or solemn, ineffectual vows never to forget.[21]

Certainly, as we have seen, what is here called "natural death" is the least "natural" and commonplace in the public sight of our culture. Thus, we are less able to deal with it, to encounter it. Its very temporality is threatening. Gradual, "natural" death allows time and space for the ill-mannered "stare" to develop and objectify the dying. The filmmaker's ethical relation to the event of death, the function of his or her look, is open to slow scrutiny. Thus, as the filmmaker watches the dying, we watch the filmmaker watching, and judge the nature and quality of his or her interest. Less potentially problematic, the abruptness of, for example, a war death or an assassination leaves no time or space for the stare, either the filmmaker's or our own. Alternatively, the incredibly painful anticipatory gaze which waits for and records an execution is, however horrific, always partially sanctioned by its political service, either for or against the executioners. These observations lead to the next propositions.

5. *The visible representation of vision inscribes sight as moral insight; as well, sight visibly inscribes its own concrete situation—or site—in a social world which "incites" its visual activity.*[22] In the indexical representations of documentary, the very act of vision which makes the representation of death possible is itself subject to moral scrutiny. The vision must visibly respond to the fact that it has broken a visual taboo and looked at death. It must justify its cultural transgression and make the justification itself visible. Thus, although perhaps once spontaneously responsive to contingent situations, the visual behavior made visible in documented visions of death has come to inscribe itself in relatively conventional ways so as to justify its vision. It has, to a certain extent, become codified—commuting, as codes do, an existential confrontation with an excessive event into a morally framed vision that marks and contains not only a visible death, but also the visible situation of the filmmaker.

Such signs of the filmmaker's situation are, for example, inscribed in and visibly represented by the camera's stability or movement in relation to the situation which it perceives, in the framing of the object of its vision, in the distance that separates it from the event, in the persistence or reluctance of its gaze. And, as discussed previously, because death always so forcefully exceeds and subverts its indexical representation, it is the act of dealing with its exorbitance by means of human and technological vision that documentary cinema most fully documents, most effectively represents. Thus, those visual "signifiers" which make death seemingly visible on the screen most significantly signify the manner in which the immediate viewer—the filmmaker with camera—physically mediates his or her own confrontation with death, the way s/he ethically inhabits a social world, visually behaves in it and charges it with a moral meaning visible to others. As well, such signifiers are the means by which the mediate viewer—the spectator of the film—immediately and ethically inhabits the theater and visually behaves in it. (Do we shrink in our seats or lean forward? Do we cover our eyes—or peek through the frame of our fingers? Do we stare at the vision before us or watch from the corners of our eyes?)

6. *Before the event of an unsimulated death, the viewer's very act of looking is ethically charged and is, itself, the object of ethical judgment when it is viewed: The viewer is held ethically responsible for his or her visible visual response.* The cinematic signs of the act of viewing death provide the bases upon which the spectator judges not only the filmmaker's ethical behavior in response to death, but also his or her *own* ethical response to the visible visual activity represented on the screen. Two viewers are ethically implicated in their relations with the viewed event, be it the event of death or the event of the film which makes death visible. Thus, responsibility for the representation of death by

means of the inscribed vision of cinema lies with both filmmaker and spectator.

It is the codification of visual behavior as it acts to circumscribe the sight of death and bear (bare) its traces that allows both filmmaker and spectator to overcome, or at least to circumvent, the transgression of what in our present culture is a visual taboo. It allows both filmmaker and spectator to view death's "ferocious reality," if not from a comfortable position, then from an ethical one. Such codification inscribes in the film text what Roger Poole in *Towards Deep Subjectivity* has called an "ethical space"—that is, the visible representation or sign of the viewers's subjective, lived, and moral relationship with the viewed.[23] Thus, even though documentary often represents death in visual activity initiated less by conscious moral concerns than by the technical necessity and specific contingencies of the pro-filmic event, this activity has been codified and used to inscribe the text within the contours of an ethical viewing. This activity constitutes a *moral conduct*: the conventionally agreed upon manner and means by which a visually taboo, excessive, and essentially unrepresentable event can be viewed, contained, pointed to, and opened to a scrutiny that is culturally sanctioned.

At this point, the difference between the documentary and narrative representation of death must be readdressed. I have already made some distinctions between the sign-functions of both genres; documentary is primarily indexical, narrative primarily iconic and symbolic. As well, it has been observed that the criteria for "ethical vision" in narrative are not commonly so stringent as they are for documentary. There appears to be more ethical room in the iconic and symbolic space of the "imagined" than in the indexical space of the "looked at." (This is not to say that narrative vision does not also have to meet at least a certain minimum set of ethical criteria to find cultural sanction.) Thus, physical mortification, violence, and death are much the stuff that narrative is visually made of. Narrative death draws the camera to its representation. Narrative films inspect death in detail, with the casual observation of "realism," with undisguised prurient interest, or with formal reverence, the latter ritualized in slow motion or stately montage rhythms. For reasons previously suggested, death in our narrative films is a commonplace—rather than taboo—visual event. The emotions we feel as viewers in the face of it, the values we risk in looking at it, the ethical significance we find in our encounter with it, differ in kind as well as degree from the way we respond to death in the documentary.

These differences are problematized in the film that generated this inquiry: Jean Renoir's classic humanist narrative, *Rules of the Game*. There are two instances of death in the film, and although both are seemingly homogenized by their equivalent mode of cinematic representation and their mutual containment in a single narrative's boundaries, each differs radically and problematically from the other. The first to die in the film is a rabbit. The second is a human character. I have chosen my words here so as to make the point that the rabbit is not perceived by us solely as a character in the narrative. Rather, it dies in the service of the narrative and for the fiction. On the other hand, the human character who dies does so only in the fiction. Even though they eventually survive the actor, both his character and the narrative are immediately survived by him. We cannot, however, say the same of the rabbit. What is important to note here is that the knowledge which informs our distinction between the fate of the actor and rabbit is primarily *extra-cinematic* and *intertextual*. That is, the cinema-specific codes of representation are the same for both actor and rabbit, and each of their deaths serves a similar function in the narrative. Nonetheless, a distinction is made between them. Indeed, the textual moment of the rabbit's death gains its particular force from a cultural knowledge which contextualizes and exceeds the representation's sign-function as narrative. This brings us to the next proposition.

7. *The intertextuality provided by cultural knowledge contextualizes and informs any textual representation of death.* That is, a sign-function is only so functional within a text as it is not challenged or subverted by extra-textual knowledge. Watching *Rules of the Game,* we know that it is easier to kill a rabbit than to teach it to play dead. We also know it is easier to teach a man to play dead than to kill him. What is meant by "easier" in the ethical context of our culture and the economic context of cinema is "faster," "cheaper," and "less morally problematic." Rabbits are slow learners, bad actors, and their lives expendable. A filmmaker will not be sent to jail for killing even the cutest rabbit, but he may lose his life for killing even the worst actor.

Cultural and ethical knowledge contextualizes both deaths in Renoir's films, and momentarily fractures the classical coherence of its narrative representation, introducing the off-screen and unrepresented space in which the viewer lives, acts, and makes distinctions as an ethical social being. Thus, watching *Rules of the Game,* we know—above and beyond cinematic codes—that André Jureau's murder is merely represented, while the rabbit's death is both represented and presented. The senselessness and shock generated by the earnest young aviator's death make narrative sense and satisfy, rather than surprise and subvert, narrative expectations. His death is not merely contained by the codes governing the narrative, but is, in fact, constituted and determined by them. The rabbit's death, however, exceeds the narrative code which communicates it. It ruptures and interrogates the boundaries of narrative representation. It thus has a "ferocious reality" which the character's death does not. It stands as an indexical sign in an otherwise iconic/symbolic representation. That is, it functions to point beyond its function as a narrative representation, to an extratextual referent executed not only by, but also for, the representation. The rabbit's death violently, abruptly, punctuates narrative space with documentary space.

Documentary space is thus of a different order than narrative space which confines itself to the screen, or, at most, extends off-screen into an imagined world. Its constitution, however, is dependent upon an extra-textual knowledge which contextualizes the sign-functions of the representation within a social world and an ethical framework. (This, indeed, is a process problematized by the titillating ambiguity of the "snuff" film in which signs of death "tease" the viewer by offering themselves as indexical against the context of a known and powerful extra-textual interdict which suggests that the signs must "really" be iconic and symbolic. The great moral problem which must emerge in watching such a representation and making a judgment regarding its sign-functions also tests the ground between documentary and narrative space.) The world into which documentary space extends and to which its indexical signification points is perceived as the concrete and inter-subjective world of the viewer. That is, as much as documentary space points off-screen to the viewer's world, it is a space also "pointed to" by the viewer who recognizes and grasps that space as, in some way, contiguous with his or her own. There is an existential—and thus particularly ethical—bond between documentary space and the space inhabited by the viewer.

8. *Documentary space is indexically constituted as the perceived conjunction of the viewer's life-world and the visible space represented in the text; the agency of this conjunction is the viewer's gaze, informed by cultural and ethical knowledge, and inscribed as ethical and subjective action.* Given that the constitution of documentary space, to whatever degree it may be conventionally constructed, is finally dependent not merely upon codes of textual representation, but also upon extra-textual

knowledge and judgment, the viewer (both as filmmaker and spectator) bears particular subjective responsibility for the action marked by—and in—his or her vision. Thus, even that vision which inscribes its action as "objective" is judged on its ethical appropriateness in the context of the event at which it gazes.

9. *Documentary space is constituted and inscribed as ethical space; it is the objectively visible totalization of subjective visual responsiveness and responsibility toward a world shared with other human subjects.* The vision inscribed in and as documentary space is therefore never seen as a space alternative to or transcendental to the viewer's life-world. As well, it reflexively points to a lived-body occupying concrete space and shaping it with others in concrete social relations which describe a moral structure. Vision is both subjectively situated and objectively visible to the ethical scrutiny and judgment of other embodied and intentional viewing subjects who are to use Alfred Schutz's terms, "consociates," "contemporaries," or "predecessors."[24]

10. *While death itself confounds and exceeds its indexical representation in documentary space, the viewer's ethical behavoir does not.* Whether by necessity, accident, or design, the documentary filmmaker represents—and thus encodes—his or her act of vision as a sign of an ethical stance toward the event of death s/he witnesses. Given, however, that our present culture has made death visually taboo, has attempted to remove it from public sight and sites, how may the filmmaker visually confront its event and visibly represent it so that the representation is justifiable in its viewing of the "forbidden"? It seems that in all cases, the inscription of the filmmaker's visual activity must visibly indicate that it is in no way party to the death it views (again, the immorality of the "snuff" film comes to mind here). As well, it must visibly indicate that its visual activity in no way substitutes for a possible intervention in the event, that is, it must indicate that watching the event of death is not more important than preventing it.

Documentary Ethics

To meet these two conditions which attest to the ethical behavior of the filmmaker encountering the event of death, five "forms" of visual activity emerge across a wide range of documentary films and "raw footage." Each is constituted in visible behavior which is encoded in the representation to signify the particular embodied situation of the filmmaker, and thus his or her capacity to affect the events before the camera lens. These visual forms can be thematized as the "accidental gaze," the "helpless gaze," the "endangered gaze," the "interventional gaze," and the "ethical" or "humane stare." In addition, there is a sixth visual form which is ethically ambiguous and suspect, presenting problems in judgment to both filmmaker and spectator alike. This form, unsure of its ethical grounding and allegiance, can be called the "professional gaze."

Inscribed as the least ethically suspect in its encounter with the event of death, the "accidental gaze" is cinematically coded in marks of technical and physical *unpreparedness*. The film gives visual evidence that death was not the filmmaker's initial object of scrutiny, that it happened before the camera suddenly, randomly, and unexpectedly, surprising the filmmaker's vision and disallowing any possibility of complicity or intervention. Unpreparedness is signified by the camera's unselective vision in relation to the death, by its conceptual and often literal "oversight": its lack of focus and attention on the fatal spot and event, its intentional interest clearly located elsewhere. Examples of the accidental gaze include, at one extreme, the previously mentioned "amateur" Zapruder footage of the Dallas motorcade in which

JFK was assassinated, and at the other, a film like the Maysles' *Gimme Shelter*, which "unwittingly" films a murder at the Rolling Stones concert in Altamont. In the latter film, although the death is seen, the spectator (and the camera) literally has no insight into it, doesn't know where to look in the huge crowd it sees, until the film inspects its own footage to find the death for itself and for us. In both of these representations, the breaking of visual taboo is cinematically coded as unintentional. Indeed, the wonder and fascination generated by such films is that a death happens, is visible, and yet is somehow not seen, that it is attended to by the camera rather than by the filmmaker or spectator. Thus, there is a desire to stop-frame the film so as to see the death attentively, intentionally, as if that would somehow make the representation clearer, its signification more precise. This, in fact, is what is done *in* the Maysles' film and *with* the Zapruder footage; in both instances, viewing and reviewing the film increases our focus and direction, but never finally overcomes the accidental oversight of the immediate visual encounter with mortality (and the excess of the death over its representation).

The "helpless gaze" before death is coded in marks of technical and physical *distance* from the event. The distance may be extremely great—in which case physical intervention on the part of the filmmaker is visibly perceived as impossible. In some other instances, particularly when the death is a legal execution, the filmmaker may be technically and physically closer to it, but is legislatively distanced and prevented from intervening. Distance, and the helplessness it confers, are signified not only by the long shot, but by the frequent use of the zoom lens. The death is brought closer in view and attention, but not in actual physical proximity. Additionally, although the gaze is often stable (that is, technically fixed on a tripod so that the frame is not marked by abrupt physical agitation), it does not maintain the cool fixity of a stare, but rather covers the figured space as if to shift its attention: panning as if to seek visual escape, zooming out as well as in toward the event, contextualizing the event of death in a space which absolves the gazer from active intervention. This marked visual movement and discomfort is to be distinguished from both the "humane stare" and the ethically ambiguous "professional gaze," both of which will be described shortly.

The "endangered gaze," as differentiated from the "helpless gaze," is coded in terms not of distance but of *proximity* to the events of violence and death. It is inscribed by signs which indexically and reflexively point to the mortal danger faced by the filmmaker, point to a physical and embodied presence behind the camera and present at the scene. The representation is marked by the relative instability of its framing—the camera shaken, for example, by nearby explosions, or hand-held over rough terrain (pointing, of course, to a concrete body, to a vulnerable human operator). Endangered vision is frequently obstructed, marking its need for protection, inscribing its fragile yet concerned relation to the horrors of mortality it grasps. Parts of vehicles and buildings, foliage, rubble, and the like partially hide the object of vision, but also hide, while indexically pointing to, the filmmaker as the mortal subject of vision. Thus, looking at death with an endangered gaze is an ethical tradeoff for breaking a visual taboo: the filmmaker inscribes the risk to his own life as s/he represents the death of another.

In his *Theory of the Film*, Béla Balázs discusses the endangered gaze in relation to war documentaries dedicated to cameramen killed during the films' shooting. He writes:

> This fate of the creative artist is . . . a new phenomenon in cultural history and is specific to film art. . . .

> This presentation of reality by means of motion pictures differs essentially from all other modes of presentation in that the reality being presented is not yet completed; it is itself still in the making while the presentation is being prepared. The creative artist . . . is present at the happening itself and participates in it.
>
> . . . The cameraman is himself in the dangerous situation we see in his shot and is by no means certain that he will survive the birth of his picture. Until the strip has been run to its end we cannot know whether it will be completed at all. It is this tangible being-present that gives the documentary the peculiar tension no other art can produce.[25]

This personal peril, so long as it is visibly encoded in the film, absolves the filmmaker from seeking out and gazing at the death of others.

The rarest, and usually the most poignant, ethical representation of a visual encounter with death is the "interventional gaze." Moving beyond the endangered gaze, it literally comes out of hiding; its vision is confrontive. It is more than visually active in its engagement with the event at which it looks. It is often marked with the urgent physical activity of the camera, and often the filmmaker's voice—usually repressed or suppressed—adds spatial and physical dimension to the inscription of bodily presence and involvement. In its extreme instance, the interventional gaze represents not only the death of another, but also its own. Balázs describes the breaking off of a sequence in a French documentary (similar to one in *The Battle of Chile*):

> It darkens and the camera wobbles. It is like an eye glazing in death. The director did not cut out this "spoilt" bit—it shows where the camera was overturned and the cameraman killed, while the automatic mechanism ran on. . . .
>
> Yes, it is a new form of consciousness that was born out of the union of man and camera. For as long as these men do not lose consciousness, their eye looks through the lens and reports and renders conscious their situation. . . .
>
> . . . The internal processes of presence of mind and observation are here projected outwards into the bodily action of operating the camera. . . . The psychological process is inverted—the cameraman does not shoot as long as he is conscious—he is conscious as long as he is shooting.[26]

Thus, it is the visible image which inscribes the loss of the human intentional behavior which informs it, vision becoming random in relation to its objects and fading to black.

The act of looking at death may also be performed not as a gaze, but as a "humane stare." The humane stare struggles to encode itself subjectively; for, as mentioned earlier, the fixed look tends to objectify that at which it gazes, and announces its technical and human readiness to break a cultural taboo, to accept without "blinking" or "flinching" the event of death which occurs before it. Thus, dependent upon the event's nature, the humane stare takes one of two forms. It may fix itself as shock and disbelief, its gaze "hypnotized" by the horror it observes. Atrocity usually generates this response as exemplified in the famous footage of a South Vietnamese officer executing a suspected North Vietnamese terrorist in the middle of a Saigon street. In a sense, the frozen quality of the stare, the bodily paralysis and inertia it represents, suggests a recognition that there is no tolerable point of view from which to gaze at such a death.

The humane stare may settle, rather than fix, itself, engaging its gaze with the gaze of human others, inscribing the intimacy and respect and sympathy it feels with those who die in its vision. The rare documenting of gradual death usually generates this response—exemplified most comfortingly by the aforementioned film, *Dying*. Here, there is complicity between the filmmaker and the dying subject who has "invited" the former to watch and unblinkingly record the subject's death (which the filmmaker cannot prevent). What is stared at is "a ritual organized by the dying person himself," one who presides over it and knows its "protocol."[27]

In both instances of the humane stare, however, the image is inscribed by the mark of a steady camera, placed in a generally measured distance from its visual object, and by smooth technical and physical activity. When zooms occur, they are controlled and steady. Vision is purposefully framed and clearly focused. However, what seems most of interest about the humane stare is that its identification as such is so dependent upon the nature of the death before it. That is, the spectator's judgment about the stare's humanity is determined by the magnitude or quality of the event which prompts it. "Shock," "paralysis," and "disbelief" cannot be ascribed to the filmmaker's every fixed gaze—for example, to the stare that watched a young man ignite a match and set fire to himself to protest unemployment. Although the event was horrific, it was comprehensible in human terms and, as well, the filmmakers might have prevented it. The frozen an hypnotized gaze is generated by the incredibly inhumane and incomprehensible, by a disbelief that what one is seeing is existentially possible. Representation is transfixed, at a loss in the presence of such an excessive referent.

In the ascription of humanity to the stare which inspects gradual death, however, the event invites human interest. The possibility of planned exploitation of human beings, of ghoulishness, of a cold voyeurism, is belied by the dying subject's openness to the probity of the gaze, by a collaboration with its interest, by a frequent address to the stare which inscribes the off-screen presence and intimate acceptance of the filmmaker. In a regression from the social conditions of death in the 20th century as noted by Ariès, the bedchamber again becomes a space for public ceremony, a space organized, in part, by the dying subject. Under the dying person's self-direction, the filmmaker's stare becomes ethically simplified. Death occurs before the latter's gaze "in a ceremonial manner, yes, but with no theatrics, with no great show of emotion."[28]

These are the inscriptions of documentary vision signified as ethical in the face of death, an event which charges the act of looking at it with moral significance. There is, however, yet another visual "form" which addresses death, one which problematically straddles the already relatively ambiguous border that separates ethical from unethical activity. This problematic form is the "professional gaze." It is always in the service of two masters, each with differing, but equally arguable, ethical claims on the filmmaker's vision. An article in *TV Guide* concisely popularizes the issue on its title page. Headed by the announcement "Reporters' Dilemma," bold letters ask "*SAVE A LIFE OR GET THE STORY?*" A smaller insert sums up: "The camera's whirring . . . someone's in trouble . . . and TV journalists must decide where their duty lies."[29] The article, which begins by referring to the aforementioned "invitational" self-immolation of a young man protesting unemployment goes on to ask the crucial ethical question which is posed but never answered in the footage of such events: "When the values of good journalism and humanitarianism collide, what should a journalist do?"[30]

The entire piece, somewhat sensationally but also appropriately, presents the voices of filmmakers and their employers in ambiguous but revealing debate which can be thematized as one about ethical responsibility to the human moment or to the forging of historical consciousness. One filmmaker (indeed, the one whose Vietnam footage mentioned earlier did contribute to altering American perceptions about the nature of the war) tells us his "professional" philosophy: "I always disregarded the events that I was covering. I was there just to record events, not to think about them."[31] Another says: "You have to remove your feelings as a human being when you're shooting something gruesome. You have to psych yourself up to cover the news and turn off your personal feelings."[32] Alternatively, an ABC official cautiously suggests: "Journalists are observers, not participants. But where life is at stake, there may be an exception."[33] Another journalist is much stronger: "I have always maintained that the journalist owes his duty to humanity. When there's a conflict between being a journalist and a human being, I'll always hope I'll be a human being. It's a grave error for reporters to set themselves aside from humanity."[34]

If it is visibly inscribed at all then (the camera not abandoned completely or turned to the service of the earlier-described "interventional gaze"), the professional gaze is marked by ethical ambiguity, by technical and machine-like competence in the face of an event which seems to call for further and human response. "You don't show your tripod" when you're a professional, says Fred Friendly. "By being a good Samaritan, we get in the way of our lenses. It makes it impossible for us to do our job well. We blur the image of the job we're trying to do: explain complex issues."[35] The concern for getting a clear and unobstructed image, and the belief that it is possible to strip that image, that representation, of human bias and perspective and ethicality so that it is "objective," indelibly marks the inscriptions of the professional gaze with their own problematic ethical perspective in the face of both human mortality and visual taboo.

In sum, the physical and social event of death in our culture poses a moral question to vision and challenges representation. What eventually gets on the screen and is judged by those of us who view it in the audience is the visible constitution and inscription of an "ethical space" which subtends both filmmaker and spectator alike. It is a space which takes on the contours of the events which occur within it and the actions which make it visible. It is both a space of immediate encounter and mediate action. Within the constraints of this present exploration, I have focused on the radical origins and articulations of this space. I have not, however, addressed its secondary articulations, those entailed in the editorial practices of filmmaking which take the original and visible representations of violence and death and further contain them in what may be called a secondary and "reflective" ethical vision. A few comments would seem to be in order, at the very least to suggest the additional complexity and dimension of the issues in question.

Certainly, the least shaped and structured films of death are experienced as the most immediate and shocking in terms of a directly visceral, unprepared, and unintellectual confrontation with the abrupt violence which currently signifies human mortality in our culture. These films are often not even considered "documentaries," but seem to exist in some "realer" (i.e., more indexical) state as "documents." The Zapruder footage, the Vietnamese being shot in the head—to quote W.H. Auden: "These are events which arouse such simple and obvious emotions . . . poetic comment is impossible."[36] While this may be an exaggeration or, more precisely, need specific elaboration, we do experience "single-shot" and "raw" footage as representing the event of death more "immediately": as unshaped, uncooked (to use a pertinent metaphor from structuralism). No ritual or art intervenes. However, once that footage is incorporated into a shaped film, or merely juxtaposed with other footage, although the intellectual impact of the death may be enhanced and its significance enlarged with rational, poetic, symbolic meaning, such shaping will also be in some ways always reductive. Thus, the raw footage of the Vietnamese street execution incorporated into Peter Davis's *Hearts and Minds* gains an ironic dimension as it is juxtaposed with other images, but it also loses the force of its essential and violent unspeakability and partially submits to the containments of form. The most shaped and structured films of death tend to be poetic elegies which speak less of the deaths they contain than of death's unspeakability. They aestheticize the space that exists as "visual silence." Moving us less viscerally and directly than the "raw" footage, they move us emotionally by removing us from such direct contact. Death becomes the object of mediated contemplation in such films as Georges Franju's powerful *Blood of the Beasts* and Alain Resnais' *Night and Fog*. Their contemplation of death is ritually formalized as a moral consideration of the mortal conditions of the body, of the fragility of life, of the end of representation that death represents.

The conjunction of death, representation, and documentary foregrounds what is true of all vision as it engages a world and others. Certainly, this is because death in our culture is among the least expressible and least malleable of subjects available to a filmmaker. Any intentional camera angle or camera movement or editorial juxtaposition will comment upon what is essentially a moment of unspeakable transformation and chaos, and will inscribe it in an act of human vision which makes visible a moral insight. As Roger Poole forcefully points out:

> There can be no flaccid action, no action which is not immediately imbued with an ethical ballast, filled in from our point of view in the world of perspectives. . . . Acts in space are embodied intentions.[37]

The event of death may finally exceed and confound all indexical representation and documentary codings, but it also generates the most visible and morally charged acts of visual representation.

NOTES

1. Amos Vogel, "Grim Death," Film Comment 16, No. 2 (March-April 1980), p. 78.
2. Philippe Ariès, *Western Attitudes toward Death: From the Middle Ages to the Present*, trans. Patricia M. Ranum (Baltimore: The John Hopkins University Press, 1974).
3. Ibid., pp. 88–89.
4. Ibid., p. 106.
5. Ibid., pp. 93–94.
6. Ibid., p. 93.
7. Lawrence L. Langer, *The Age of Atrocity: Death in Modern Literature* (Boston: Beacon Press, 1978), pp. xii–xiii.
8. Amos Vogel, *Film as a Subversive Art* (New York: Random House, 1974), p. 263.
9. Langer, p. 63.
10. John Fraser, *Violence in the Arts* (London: Cambridge University Press, 1974), p. 59.
11. Vogel, *Film as a Subversive Art*, p. 201.
12. Fraser, p. 61.
13. Langer, p. 6.
14. Ariès, pp. 39–46.
15. David Dempsey, "The Dying Speak For Themselves on a TV Special," *The New York Times*, 25 April 1976, Section 2, p. 29.
16. Ernest Becker, *The Denial of Death* (New York: The Free Press, 1973), p. 104.
17. Simone de Beauvoir, *A Very Easy Death*, trans. Patrick O'Brien (New York: Warner Paperback Library, 1973), p. 123.
18. Robert Jay Lifton and Eric Olson, *Living and Dying* (New York: Praeger, 1974), p. 28.
19. Langer, p. 64.
20. Langer, pp. 14–15. Langer cites from Avery Weisman, *On Dying and Denying: A Psychiatric Study of Terminality* (New York: Behavioral Press, 1972), pp. 16, 26.
21. Vogel, *Film as a Subversive Art*, p. 266.
22. These four homonymic terms were inspired by Larry Crawford in "Looking, Film, Painting: The Trickster's In Site/In Sight/Insight/Incite," *Wide Angle* 5, No. 3 (1983), 64–69.

23. Roger Poole, *Towards Deep Subjectivity* (London: The Penguin Press, 1972).
24. Alfred Schutz, *The Phenomenology of the Social World*, trans. George Walsh & Frederick Lehnert (Evanston, Ill.: Northwestern University Press, 1967), pp. 163–214.
25. Béla Balázs, *Theory of the Film: Character and Growth of a New Art*, trans. Edith Bone (New York: Dover Publications, 1970), pp. 170–171.
26. Ibid., pp. 171–172.
27. Ariès, p. 11.
28. Ibid., pp. 12–13.
29. Howard Polskin, "Save a Life or Get the Story?" *TV Guide*, 23 July 1983, p. 4.
30. Ibid., p. 5.
31. Ibid., p. 6.
32. Ibid.
33. Ibid.
34. Ibid.
35. Ibid., p. 8.
36. W.H. Auden quoted in William Stott, *Documentary Expression in Thirties America* (New York: Oxford University Press, 1973), p. 13.
37. Poole, p. 6.

PAUL ARTHUR

JARGONS OF AUTHENTICITY (THREE AMERICAN MOMENTS) (1993)

By now it is, or should be, standard wisdom that documentaries and Hollywood narratives do not issue from separate and pristine worlds but have over the course of their histories maintained a tangled reciprocity—by turns technological, thematic, political—in which each has, in part, defined its purview through cultural myths of what the other is not.[1] Predictably, the results of this interpenetration have historically been neither constant nor symmetrical. Whether approached as cohesive movements, as nexuses of formal practice, ideological weapons, or vehicles of the status quo, American documentaries have never marshalled a serious challenge to the hegemony of fiction film in the representation of social reality. And this is so despite the demonstrable status of nonfiction genres in popular literature and television.

However, two prominent moments of documentary production—New Deal sponsorship in the late thirties and the surge of cinema verité-activated theatrical features in the late sixties—exhibit features crucial to any popular contestation of the regime of studio fiction.[2] The unexpected notoriety around a cluster of nonfiction films released in the last few years provides an occasion to reexamine consistent dynamics in documentary's desultory vision of mainstream intervention and the claims of heightened epistemic authority which undergird that vision.[3] If the territory consigned to documentary historiography has often resembled a frozen tundra, the search for *noncontingent* templates is a project akin to Nanook's igloo: a half-built shelter maintaining the illusion of closure yet exposed to all the elements.

A number of factors tend to converge during documentary's interludes of high visibility. Technological breakthroughs such as sound recording or the lightweight sync-sound rig open production processes to new representational options. Reception garnered by individual films—*The River* (1937), *Monterey Pop* (1967), *Roger and Me* (1989)—stimulate public interest and with it a climate for viable distribution. There is as well the cyclical revival of debate over the moral probity of dominant film practices, their escapism or sensationalism or "irrelevance" to glaring social problems. At the height of the Depression, in the cauldron of late sixties' rebellion, and in the throes of Reagan's disastrous economic policies, joumalistic assaults on Hollywood's irresponsibility have directed normally myopic media attention to nonfiction's promise of greater verisimilitude.[4] This translates into the traditional notion that documentary flourishes in the midst of crisis. The crisis scenario, however, must be ballasted by recognition that moments of prominence are also co-extensive with major consolidations in the motion picture industries. Social documentaries of the 1930s developed within and against the growing strength of Hollywood's major studio monopolies. Direct cinema and its theatrical offshoots emerged with the sovereignty of prime-time television, while the recent wave of documentary releases follows the precipitous rise of home video and cable TV and is contemporaneous with an onslaught of "reality-based" programming.[5] In each case, transient cultural leverage has been fueled by, and in tum amplifies, other nonfiction discourses found in literary, art, theatrical, advertising, and other arenas.

This chapter is concerned with several interlocking elements of mainstream documentary as situated at particular historical junctures: the formal embedding of truth claims, guarantees of authenticity, and hierarchies of knowledge; the imaging or textual projection of technology in relation to issues of social power and authority; and the intramural valorization, via allegories of production, of documentary as an alternative and politically progressive cinematic program. My assumption is that regardless of the events or personalities presented, or the ideological forces with which films are aligned—almost exclusively, the undulations of American liberalism—commercial documentaries enact polemical dialogues both with previous nonfiction styles and with reigning codes of dominant cinema. Further, succeeding styles tend to repudiate the methods of earlier periods from the same perspective of realist epistemology attending the nineteenth-century bourgeois novel's "attempt to use language to get beyond language," the absolute desire to discover a truth untainted by institutional forms of rhetoric.[6] Or as Brian Winston suggests of the cinematic conventions inevitably arising from this effort: "The need for structure implicitly contradicts the notion of unstructured reality" and documentary movements are sustained by "ignoring" this contradiction.[7] Each new contender will generate recognizable, perhaps even self-conscious, figures through which to signify the spontaneous, the anticonventional, the refusal of mediating process.

Analyzing structures and visual patterns in New Deal and direct cinema documentaries requires that certain established critical axioms be jettisoned; principally, that films of the thirties offer a totally unproblematized declaration of authority—textual as well as social—and that direct cinema, since it expunges any hint of "metaphor and pattern,"[8] is uniquely and universally descriptive (rather than prescriptive). Against this backdrop, recent works can be construed as acknowledging false claims implicit in earlier styles while fashioning determinate conventions under a contemporary rubric of decentered subjectivity and the inadequacy of cinema's cognitive tools.

Pluralism, Technocracy, and Naturalization

> Who shall be master, things or men?
>
> *The City*

> Technics can by itself promote authoritarianism as well as liberty, scarcity as well as abundance, the extension as well as the abolition of toil.
>
> Herbert Marcuse[9]

Freighted with unprecedented cultural significance, *The Plow That Broke the Plains* (1936), *The River, The City* (1939), and a few other sponsored documentaries were honed by the imperatives of two historical conditions: widespread mobilization of nonfiction practices as instruments in the expression and propagation of liberal democratic social philosophy; and the increased validity of nonfiction production under terms of economic scarcity. Like its European counterparts, American social documentaries conspired in a public belief that it was advantageous to address pressing needs through a discourse purporting to offer the highest quotient of immediacy, responsiveness, clarity, and verisimilitude. Such epithets were commonly ascribed by politicians and journalists to a variety of remedial government activities from FDR's "Fireside Chats" to the WPA State Guides. Similar virtues were located in the popular reception of radio, weekly news magazines, political theater as "living newspaper," and the first versions of public opinion polls.

The embodiment of approved *political* values as properties of filmic structure and iconography directs an understanding of how this truncated film movement served as an armature of New Deal policy and ideological contestation while advancing a heuristic model of progressive cinema. An initial strategy can be referred to as stylistic fragmentation and multiplicity, a concatenation of discrete segments containing disparate visual and aural cues yet bracketed by a unifying theme and narrational logic. *The City* is the most conspicuous example although *The River* marks a similar preference for mixed materials; for instance, the sandwiching of original footage with maps, archival shots, intertitles, and other graphics presented over a soundtrack combining original music and voice-overs with diegetic voices or sound effects. The division in *The City* into semiautonomous sections has prompted critiques that cite a "crucial weakness [in] placement and tone."[10] In this view, the film loses focus and sacrifices potency due to insufficient structural balance, stylistic unity, or transparency. Its claims to truth, therefore, are vitiated.

The problem with this reproach is it discounts the role of aesthetic alterity in establishing preeminence over competing modes of realism. A brief gloss of *The City*'s ordering principles confirms the impression of disparity as it invites other possible readings. Sections vary in length from two minutes to over fifteen minutes. Visually, the opening "Colonial" sequence is characterized by static long shots, even lighting, lyrical tracking, and panning movements and circular object motifs. By contrast, the "megalopolis" section features jarring rhythmic montage, extreme camera angles, dislocations of scale, and the absence of eyeline matches. The concluding "Green Belt" section employs narrativized editing of action, a profusion of centered medium shots, and wipes and other soft transitions. In addition, the music track, while developing a consistent set of melodic phrases and motifs, dominates during the "megalopolis" section but retreats to the background in favor of spoken narration for the "Green Belt" segment. The voice-over itself frequently shifts in tone, tense, and mode of address, juxtaposing a hortatory second-person with first- and third-person plural comments.

The polemical thrust of successive tropes is readily apparent. Depersonalization in the metropolis is figured as a disorienting clash of graphic elements, whereas the humanizing appeal of the planned community is reified in familiar Hollywood conventions of spatio-temporal harmony and continuity. The alleviation of urban disorder by social engineering is argued verbally and demonstrated visually. Spoken narration is not the sole or leading repository of the film's "message," as many contend. Visual metaphor and pastiche may prompt abstract ideas not readily conveyed by verbal speech while serving other channels of argumentation. As the reflexive index of a politically ratified method of production, stylistic heterogeneity inscribes a discontinuous, multiple process of creativity onto the film's surface. Shot in different locations by different cameramen, written and edited in successive stages by a loose-knit group—a necessary expedient for documentaries of the period—*The City* invokes, through its structure, a signifier of plural authorship, a trope of individual freedom embedded within a unifying consensus of social directives.

Admittedly, the film's overarching analysis *cum* solution is unfrayed by this symbolic plurality. Yet the lodging of presentational authority in a foregrounded play of difference metaphorically links the process of production—and by extension that of viewing—to the social remedies proposed. That is, the rationalized urban planning advocated by the film reconstitutes *gemeinschaft* concepts of individual autonomy in contradistinction to then-rampant conservative attacks on the state's purported authoritarian suppression of individual (municipal, state, regional) liberties.

Additionally, the text's refusal to subsume formal gaps and disparities proffers in its historical context a higher guarantee of verisimilitude. As Alfred Kazin remarked of Christopher Isherwood's contemporaneous *Berlin Stories:*

> If the accumulation of visual scenes seemed only a collection of "mutually repellent particles," as Emerson said of his sentences, was not *that* discontinuity, that havoc of pictorial sensations, just the truth of what the documentary mind saw before it in the thirties?[11]
>
> From this perspective, formal elements appear immiscible because they are ordered by extenal and unmanipulated properties of daily life. Like instances of literary production such as Dos Passos's *U.S.A.* trilogy or the theatrical wave of "living newspapers," *The City* (and to a lesser degree *The River, And So They Live* [1940]) displays heterogeneity and imbalance as realist tropes, as more concerted obeisance to the textures of lived reality, and, in *The City*, as a demonstration of the unequal parameters of urban growth and decay.

Undoubtedly, cinematic provenance for this mixed presentation derives from the newsreel.[12] Despite the newsreel's alliance with conservative Republican politics, its professed spontaneity helped legitimize an essaylike discursivity, lending *The City* a cloak of provisionality and openendedness belied by the vehemence of its verbal brief. Yet, if social documentaries tapped the well of authenticity inherent in the newsreel tradition, they also maintained a requisite distance from it through the absorption of avant-garde impulses pioneered by Cavalcanti, Ruttmann, Leger, and especially by Soviet cinema. As Grierson himself was quick to note, emphasis on the "creative treatment" of reality works to blunt the charge of propaganda.[13] Truth and Beauty exist in inverse proportion to one another. The former can be signified through a negation of "classical" codes, while the latter acts to counter assertions of political manipulation. This tightrope of rhetorical artifice and directness toiled to ensure filmic fidelity as well as relative autonomy.

The precedent of Soviet cinema offered other weapons for an aesthetic arsenal. A matter of frequent debate in thirties documentary circles, Soviet films were admired for their experimental rigor and challenged on grounds of political servitude. Along with montage editing and themes such as the mass hero, American documentaries imported for their own purposes the self-conscious thematization of industrial technology exemplified in the work of Dziga Vertov. Given the tenor of New Deal politics, it is no surprise that films uncritically valorized the role of technology in progressive social change: for instance, *The River* espouses benefits of hydroelectric dams, while *Power and the Land* (1940) lobbies for agricultural modernization. Yet, the bureaucratic machinery required to rationally implant and control mechanical devices posed a more serious representational dilemma. Liberal documentaries were faced with the unenviable task of reconciling the idea of centralized government power to viewers fed on obdurate tenets of individualism, free enterprise, and states rights. Patterns of machine imagery took on a pivotal role in this partisan polemic.

With direct support from government agencies or indirect support from liberal foundations, documentaries were virtually obliged to show the historical advance of capitalist technology and the social relations it enforced as a natural process: organic, not simply dependent on but co-extensive with the utilization of natural resources. There is a central myth rehearsed iconographically and augmented by spoken narration that goes something like this. In an Edenic, preindustrialized past there existed a balance between man and nature, between individual and communal sustenance. Without intended malice (to say nothing of class interest), uncontrolled economic growth upset the balance. Although growth is inherently beneficial, a lack of rationalized limits produces aberrations such as floods, ecological pillage, and uninhabitable cities. The founding harmony can be restored by judicious application of technology in federal programs: Good (i.e., natural) tools placed in the hands of benevolent craftsmen.

Marcuse observes—in an essay written just two years after *The City* and indebted to that film's philosophical mentor, Lewis Mumford:

> Technology, as a mode of production, as the totality of instruments, devices and contrivances which characterize the machine age is thus at the same time a mode of organizing and perpetuating (or changing) social relationships, a manifestation of prevalent thought and behavior patterns, an instrument for control and domination.[14]

Although Marcuse's critique is directed at the technocratic rationalization of fascist regimes, it is equally pertinent to New Deal advocacy of social engineering. He defends the concept of a democratically constituted "public bureaucracy," but perceives the danger in policies underwritten by the "natural law" of, say, Frederick Taylor's "scientific" theories of industrial management. Technology can never be merely a neutral (natural) framework of social organization. Simply stated, Marcuse's position is that machines produce or enforce their own debased axioms of human need in social formations that grant them a paramount role in the alleviation of oppression.

Unable or unwilling, due to constraints of sponsorship or mass appeal, to directly confront the contradictions of a capitalist political economy, documentaries visualize *power* as an abstraction. They routinely conflate idealist properties of advanced technology, human and natural resources, and centralized planning. The linchpin in this metaphoric equation is the fusing of technology—as reified image of federal policy—with elements such as water, forestation, crop growth, and other forms of natural productivity. Bureaucratic solutions are thus figured as technological interventions equipped with the stamp of natural process. It takes a river to harness a river. Further, it was ideologically useful to represent liberal remedies as a return to rather than a divergence from a prelapsarian unity of nature, society, and individual. Real and imagined threats to New Deal philosophy by entrenched conservative interests were rhetorically vanquished or deflected through association of the New Deal with a version of history placing it as the culmination of an authentic, innate process.

Urban overcrowding, like the flooding of the Mississippi or the deracination of the environment, are excesses of ineluctable socioeconomic development. Central government acts to refocus not the social ends but the "techniques." If the river of American historical development overflows its banks and creates human misery, then the well-oiled machine of New Deal policy can step in to resolve privation, restore the course. The narrator at the end of *The City* tells us "a different day begins." This new day, the implementation of federal controls, the promise of a New City, is given symbolic expression in images of children at play. The "rebirth" of *gemeinschaft* society is exemplified by kids sliding down a playground chute, an image then compared with the rush of water over a sluice—creating a small visual epiphany melding machine, childhood, and nature. Cities and forces that govern their growth are confected as organic shapes: A small housing tract and an urban street scene are match cut to the vertical profile of forests; the New York skyline is rhymed in a single composition with a field of weeds.[15]

In *The River*, the Roosevelt administration is described implicitly as a formal mirror of the Mississippi, its branches and tributaries stretching across the nation's continental limits, offering cohesion to the disorderly flow of regional and local conflicts. Similarly, in *Power and the Land*, the collective purchase of electrical power through the Rural Electrification Project is analogized to the communal harvesting of crops. Displacing conflict, competition, capitalism's distorted human license onto images of cooperation, sponsored documentaries enlist montage not as the dialectical forum imagined by Soviet filmmakers but as a device for reconciling otherwise troubling discrepancies of wealth and privilege.[16]

A final plank in the documentary agenda ties images of technology to the apparatus of film production via the argument over control of resources. The narrator of *The City* challenges: "You decide. Both are real, both are possible." We the citizen-viewers can retain the excesses of the present system of fulfilling human needs or choose what is arguably the next historical stage. There the question "Who shall be master, things or men?" generates the answer: "At last man will take over." What is meant by "man" is open to several readings. Given the polemical stance taken against Hollywood by documentarists of the period,[17] the studio system with its assembly-line manufacture and its profit motive are, by implication, aligned with the uncontrolled forces of private industry and urban growth. Given models such as *The Man with the Movie Camera* (1929) and Leger's *Ballet Mecanique* (1924), the identification between machinery and the mechanics of film production is an inclusive means of celebrating the liberatory potential of advanced technology.

If the charge against American capitalism in thirties' documentaries, meager as it is, concerns a lack of regulation, the failure to employ resources to spread enough benefit to enough people, the same complaint was lodged against Hollywood. The era of a variegated market stocked by small corporate competitors was over; the major studios exerted sovereign control through vertical integration, the star system, and streamlined narrative formulas. If documentaries argued the best method for regulating industrial/natural resources—the efflorescence of private capital or federal controls—the same choice might apply to cinema as industry and social institution. Intent on challenging the domination of fiction film and infused with a heady faith in the cinema apparatus as a progressive instrument for change, engaged artists welcomed government and foundation sponsorship as the promise of an alternative system of production. Funding was inadequate and precarious at best; yet by consciously aligning their fate with New Deal policy, filmmakers acted out of both civic responsibility and self-interest. A majority of creative personnel on these films received their training during the early thirties in radical newsreel and agit-prop groups such as the Film and Photo League. They had grown disenchanted with limitations on production and distribution and sought a wider audience and a larger aesthetic vehicle through which to participate in the struggle for social change.[18]

Despite justifiable misgivings over sponsorship, liberal-left documentarists hoped to build a "third term" of film production, one which retained the human-scaled collaborative ethos of their former radical projects while enhancing the ability to affect public opinion. The modest popular success of *The River* and *The City* created a tiny aperture through which a challenge to Hollywood's stranglehold could be envisioned. Promotion of New Deal ideology provided a foundation from which to allegorize the role of documentary in a naturalized landscape of cinema.

Performance, Authority, and Direct Cinema

> The period is charged with its stupid issuelessness as with an explosive.
>
> Erich Auerbach[19]

Thirty years removed from the Great Depression, a new generation of documentarists forged a loose-knit coalition whose aesthetic philosophy was primed by resistance to the same common enemy, Hollywood, yet was as vehemently opposed to the methods of *The City* and its cohort. An extensive body of interviews conducted in the late sixties and early seventies forms a collective text that remains the best theoretical account of direct cinema. A set of shared assumptions precipitate around issues of technology, immediacy, and mediation; disputes surface over ethical procedures and, particularly, the chimera of objectivity. There is, however, general agreement that New Deal documentaries and films share a premeditated, even authoritarian, vision of social representation that is no longer tenable. The verbal articulation, in Stephen Mamber's phrase, of an "uncontrolled cinema" is rife with a familiar privileging of phenomenal experience over artifice accompanied, as in realist doctrines of the previous century, by abject denials of fixed tropes or rhetorical structuration. Without invoking the spectre of a cinema verité political unconscious, it is possible to locate in the denial of conventionality a textual crisis of authority, a twinned symptom of fulsome speech and reticence, an ambivalence toward what has been called the "documentary voice."[20]

Much has already been written in reproof of the movement's idealist faith in neutral, noninterventionist recording and editorial reconstruction. In its *ad hoc* polemics, an ethical imperative weds the sync-sound rig to an aesthetic of unscripted, handheld long takes ordered solely by response to profilmic "stimuli." Thomas Waugh correctly scores the "fetishization of the image" and suggests it is driven by a "gospel of inarticulacy."[21] Bill Nichols similarly disdains the "magical template of verisimilitude" fashioned to disguise the work of standard continuities and rhetorical effects.[22] Unquestionably, refinements in lightweight camera and sound equipment increased speed, mobility, and representational purview as it simplified the process of production. However, an almost transcendant faith in equipment defers intentionality as it creates, in the minds of many filmmakers, a virtual metaphysics of presence.

In pragmatic terms, all traditional *a priori* activities, such as research, scripting, rehearsal, and various *posteriori* stages, such as narration, musical scoring, and analytical editing, are either eliminated or collapsed onto the moment of recording. The crucial, if not the only, labor takes place in the confrontation of camera/sound operator and event or social actor. An analogous moment of "focus" occurs as spectators apprehend the image on the screen. Spontaneous, aleatory signification caught in the synapse of recording is unsealed in its phenomenal freshness during the act of reception. As Frederick Wiseman puts it:

> The way I try to make a documentary is that there's no separation between the audience watching the film and the events in the film. It's like the business of getting rid of the proscenium arch in the theater . . .[23]

Behind the curtain of such verbal positioning stands a tableau of glaring contradictions in which the dynamics of "pure observation" are undercut by textual markers guaranteeing the same order of truth enacted in the partisan structures of thirties films. Albeit in a different register, direct cinema inscribes self-validating diegetic figures invested with the movement's own philosophical qualities. There is as well a corresponding reciprocity between filmic rhetoric and the context of liberal ideological discourse, now in decline rather than ascendency. Direct cinema is as much a product of and participant in a popular discourse of social renovation as its predecessor.

The cornerstone of direct cinema's rejection of previous approaches is voice-over narration, engendering the contrary demand to "show" instead of "tell"; a preference for the particular instance over the abstract and, by extension, the holistic (image or human presence) over the fragmentary. By 1960, Robert Drew was promoting a style that would allow filmmakers to "stop talking and let the action within the frame tell the story."[24] Numerous statements follow Drew's lead by connecting the "freedom" (Richard Leacock's term) afforded by the apparatus with the refusal of didacticism or "manipulative" meaning in any form. D. A. Pennebaker takes solace in not having to "label" events,[25] whereas Wiseman wants to avoid the temptation to "formalize" meaning "as a series of rational statements."[26] The implied aversion to language in its ordering, or depleting, of sensory impressions is a pervasive—and quite powerful—facet of the antiauthoritarian program of sixties countercultural and political opposition.[27]

A lesson gleaned from the triumphs and limitations of thirties activism was an abiding mistrust of top-down solutions—at its political extremes a mistrust of social theory *tout court*—expressed in cinema as a complete abandonment of extratextual appeals to authority, the refusal of history as causal explanation, and the disavowal of preconceived agendas and concrete social prescriptions. Albert Maysles provides a striking summary: "I don't see frankly, trying to make a film to create better understanding. Our motivations for making films aren't intellectual ones."[28] Wiseman avers: "I personally have a horror of producing propaganda to fit any kind of ideology other than my own view. . . ."[29] This "horror" is quite palpable, it undergirds the movement's entire aesthetic philosophy. Just as Wiseman "doubts the capacity to motivate people to large-scale social change,"[30] he and his cohort envision the production process as a form of value-free "research" (a term employed by several makers) in which the goal is, as Wiseman again phrases it, "to find out what my own attitude is towards the material that's the subject of my film."[31]

It is possible to extrapolate from these statements the wish to exchange one brand of social science methodology for another. Sponsored documentaries display an obvious debt to reformist sociology, particularly the Chicago School and related theorists such as Mumford. Direct cinema, many of whose adherents came from social science and physical science backgrounds, adopts methodological as well as ethical principles which mirror data-based empirical methods aligned with a corporate liberal fixation on "disinterested" science.[32] Documentary's version of pure observation intersects a sociology of the status quo in which social inequities are simultaneously privatized and made an object of nonapprobatory study. The filmic project becomes, in Wiseman's words, a "natural history" of American life all the more valuable because it "refuses to take sides, cast blame, or offer solutions."[33] The finished works can then be understood as "unanalyzed data," the accretions of a "statistical survey," with filmmakers cast in the role of field workers "with a camera instead of a notebook."[34]

Unlike earlier documentaries in which the presentation of evidence, argument, and scenic displays of collective social transformation govern formal construction, direct cinema insists on decontextualization. Because its "findings" are unfalsifiable, it cedes to itself an imminent freedom from contradiction. Whereas thirties films were construed as overburdened by the general, direct cinema hews to the particular, refraining from classifying individuals as types or social interactions as symptomatic of any larger pattern (although titles such as *Salesman, Showman, High School*, and *Law and Order* suggest otherwise). Judgment is thrust in the lap, or mind, of the individual spectator. Makers and supporters alike subscribe to traditional realist metaphors[35] in claiming a more active, more pluralistic, "democratic" spectatorship arising from the ambiguity of (in theory) unassimilated scenes and/or the lack of mediation through which they are presented. As Nöel Carroll points out, liberal doctrine of the period was transposed cinematically as a space where multiple viewpoints were entertained, a Bazinian principle of perceptual freedom adduced as "an expressive emblem of egalitarianism."[36] In the arena of circulation, a stance of noncontrol neatly attached itself to the demands of the FCC's Fairness Doctrine by which controversial issues were to be presented devoid of "untruthful" partisanship.[37]

One function then of direct cinema's intense specificity is to deny not only the onus of explanation but potential disagreement, relegating knowledge claims to an intersubjective plane, Leacock's "one man's truth." If part of documentary's continual need to guarantee fidelity to the Real entails a sign of openness or plurality, direct cinema attempts to displace the New Deal's formal tropes of heterogeneity onto presumably symmetrical, equivalent acts of recording and reception (the myth of filmmaker as "naive" viewer). Whereas in an earlier period, argumentative mastery or the ability to coherently assemble fragments of reality signaled an objective reckoning of historical process, here nonclosure or simplicity of design are equated with unbiased access or a "multiple consciousness of opposing perspectives."[38]

In league with the movement's confusion of textual "authority" with the "authoritarian," there is a linkage between the privileging of technology as a marker of neutrality and the assertion of individual over technocratic or collective social solutions. Resisting general propositions as a framework through which to understand society, the "personal" is mobilized not, in the jargon of sixties counterculture, as "political" but, to borrow Erich Auerbach's wonderful description of Flaubert, as charged with an explosive issuelessness. Visually as well as philosophically, direct cinema is predisposed toward intimacy, physical proximity, an isolated focus on "personality" struggling for self definition in a web of institutional pressures. This is, in essence, the master narrative at the heart of Robert Drew's celebrated "crisis structure." If one could isolate for thirties films the most characteristic image category, it would probably be groups of people in exterior long shots. In direct cinema's brief commercial foray of the late sixties, the typical configuration is most likely an interior facial close-up.

This formal shift, determined in part by technological advances, social science allegiances, and enveloping humanist discourses, can be retraced at several textual levels. Whereas thirties documentary expressed the quotidian through contrastive editing—as a shared, historically grounded condition—direct cinema constructs everyday life as a temporally distended preserve of idiosyncratic behavior. Refitting a cinematic construct of duration, the long take, to the expression of personhood, immediacy and authenticity are signaled by tropes of uneventfulness within the image, by awkward gaps and silences, the seemingly haphazard trajectories of handheld movements. This visual array conforms to what Roland Barthes locates in literature as "the realistic effect," grounded in the adumbration of "non-signifying detail"; events, gestures, objects seemingly absolved of coded meaning.[39] In direct cinema, social history is transposed into a kind of portraiture; dramatization of social process replaced by dramatization of the camera recording process. The value of concerted action as theme and formal logic gives way to stasis, the individual entrapped by circumstance, as a measure of commitment to the present.

Extrapolated from interviews and films, this schema helps to illuminate direct cinema's central and obsessive attachment to subjects under public scrutiny, to performers in one guise or another, as it clarifies the movement's agenda of self-realization. In the early Drew Associates "Living Camera" productions, network broadcasting dictated a concentration on famous or newsworthy people. Yet it is not simply Kennedy, Nehru, Jane Fonda, Marion Brando, and the Beatles who are shown navigating among predictable role-playing, humanizing improvisation, and breakdown. It is also racecar driver Eddie Sachs, the salesmen who peddle bibles door-to-door, guards and inmates in *Titicut Follies* (1967), and teachers and administrators in *High School* (1968). Due to self-imposed methodological constraints and the positive program proclaimed for spontaneous observation, direct cinema virtually required preestablished identities or role expectations behind which filmmakers could mask their intervention and against which they could define a heightened authenticity and insight into character.[40]

Significantly, the existential locus of performance provides implicit justification for the camera's presence. Far from exhibiting the flux of spontaneous behavior, what occurs on direct cinema's makeshift stage is already mediated, learned, in greater or lesser degree intended for visual/auditory consumption. Compare the self-conscious, direct-address "routines" of even an inexperienced performer such as the young female English teacher in *High School* to the indirect and cognitively unsettling images of share croppers' cabins in *The River*. For various reasons, the latter sequence required the imposition of fourth-wall theatrical conventions of invisibility, in context a protective shield for social actors and an inadvertent sign of the camera's estrangement. A constant theme of direct cinema is the blurring and remapping of lines between mandated roles and autonomous expressions of personal identity. Designation of celebrity helps maintain the fiction that camera observation is part of a natural landscape of behavior.[41] Whether the camera is addressed directly or buffered by a profilmic audience or interrogator, it is there because of an inherent complicity by which one's "image" or personal identity is a mutual construct of performer and receiver.

It is of little consequence whether a subject is filmed in a public, semipublic, or "intimate" setting. In films such as *Meet Marlon Brando* (1965) and *Don't Look Back* (1966), the narrating posture of image and sound maintains a seemingly discreet neutrality hinged precisely on diegetic figures such as newspaper and magazine reporters who ask the questions and conduct the interviews eschewed by filmmakers on ethicoaesthetic grounds. Thus, an unspoken drive to reveal through verbal language a hidden or more truthful facet of personality is projected onto others. These unwitting go-betweens, in their misguided fealty to rational speech as benchmark of communication (in contrast to direct cinema's faith in the unfettered image) elicit patently unconvincing responses, confirming the probity of an observational style. What can be known of an individual and his or her social surround emanates from the compact of behavioral freedom from artifice struck between camera and subject. Foregrounding of performance can thus paradoxically "defuse it as a threat to its claims for truth."[42] In *Don't Look Back*, Bob Dylan dismisses a reporter's attempt to encode meaning in language: "The truth? The truth is a plain *picture* of a tramp vomiting into the sewer."

Separate films or directorial choices pose diverse enactments of this structuring relationship. In privatized settings such as the working class homes in *Salesman* (1969), the film's ostensible objects—the door-to-door vendors—become surrogates in the interviewing process, drawing out intimate details of clients lives in the course of their sales pitch. The interactions of salesman and client are bracketed, placed in quotes, by recognition of (and endless dialogue about) performance skills: an example of how direct cinema often subcontracts the task of intervention, sometimes commentary and analysis, to central or peripheral players in the profilmic. In *Titicut Follies*, guards are more than willing—when they are not engaged in singing, telling jokes, and reciting anecdotes—to "perform" their mentally deranged charges, eliciting for the camera the most antic, disoriented routines which are set against literal stage acts. Wiseman elaborates parallels between guards and inmates, sane and insane, as he extends a theatrical metaphor in multiple scenes of "public" performance: His "follies" include inmates singing, dancing, delivering long speeches, and playing musical instruments.[43] In Wiseman's and Leacock's films, the gesture of zooming from medium shot to close-up serves as formal correlative of the desire to delve into inner, psychological states while clinging to a facade of unguided attention.

Acute interest in performance leads, finally, to another source of anxiety over the problematic of power and textual authority. Just as social actors are recruited for their ability or failure to direct their own images, the filmmaking process is often allegorized—through the mediation of a performer—as a techno-physical contest and/or an existential quest. An inkling of this self-serving stake in performance appears when filmmakers criticize their previous work or the work of a colleague on grounds of failing to relinquish enough control over meaning—commiting the error of, say, creating a metaphoric relation through editing or visually isolating a potentially symbolic object.[44] At the same time, they freely endorse intricate means by which to suppress the viewer's perception of spatiotemporal discontinuity. From this perspective, if one could command the equipment and physically negotiate the field with absolute fluidity and perceptual acumen, the breach between life and representation might be healed. Recording becomes an arena of personal testing on both sides of the camera. David Maysles speaks of "raw material that doesn't want to be shaped"; Leacock and Pennebaker refer to "challenges" and "confrontations" arising from the recording situation.[45]

Direct cinema's stipulation of transparency and noncontrol as a paradigm of authenticity is at once futile and disingenuous. Even at a technological level, the search for a degree-zero mode of recording is endless. Just as documentarists in the sixties criticized the ponderous production methods of thirties films, Joel DeMott and Jeff Kreines rebuke direct cinema for its reliance on three-person crews:

> Shooting one-person restores the possibility of kinship. The filmmaker doesn't carry on with "his people" in front of "his subjects." The dichotomy those labels reveal, in the filmmaker himself, is gone along with the crew.... The filmmaker becomes another human being in the room.[46]

The next step might be remote control or implanted mini-cams, *roboverité*. Clearly, the bone of contention here is not neutrality but *mastery*: how to realize the ideal performance for image/sound recorders in the theatricalized role of "pure observer." There are in fact plenty of textual models, in particular the grace-under-pressure narrative spun for direct cinema's roster of artists, sports heroes, politicians, and commonplace eccentrics. Among the most concise declarations occurs in *Man Who Dances: Edward Villella* (1970) as the dancer—choreographer states in direct address his "perfect vision of a great performance." It is "easy, smooth . . . linear . . . possessing freshness, honesty ... quickness, lightness"—in short the very qualities of structure and camera-handling most cherished by direct cinema practitioners.

Nehru (1962), made for television by Drew Associates in advance of the commercial flowering of documentary features, is a remarkable example of recorder–subject interaction as a contest of skill and wit. It constitutes a kind of inventory of possible hurdles and small triumphs registered in the act of filming. According to Stephen Mamber, the film is "an almost open admission of failure,"[47] yet, from another angle, it allows unique access to a powerful subtext in the movement as a whole. Leacock and soundman Greg Shuker admit that the decision to include extensive voice-over commentary, as well as visual references to the recording process, stemmed from the producer's desire to pump up audience interest in footage that ultimately fell short of the convulsive drama suggested in the opening narration: "It was a time of foreboding in India; of war, invasion, signs in the heavens."

As Nehru calmly conducts quotidian affairs of state, the filmmakers fabricate a "crisis" of production. They strike a bargain with the Prime Minister: "He would ignore our presence; we for our part would do nothing to interfere with what was going on . . . ask no questions, simply observe." The progress of the film turns on which party will best serve the bargain. Actually, the subject seems to have little trouble keeping his end, but the filmmakers lurch and stumble, barely able to refrain from probing interview questions they mutter behind the scenes. Shuker gets his equipment caught in a moving jeep transporting Nehru from a frenzied rally and his agile escape from danger is duly recorded and applauded in voice-over. The added commentary reproduces a running phenomenological report on the filming process: "I decide to move my mike in closer"; "Nehru sees something and I pan over to see what it is"; "Now Nehru has noticed us, a slip on his side of the bargain"; "With my camera still moving I'm trying to force my way forward." From an almost Godardian prologue—where the camera equipment is introduced directly to the viewer—to a jitterbug performed by camera and feisty dog at a family dinner, *Nehru* exposes anxiety about not only "seeing" but identifying with, and being *seen* by, the object of the camera's "detached" gaze. The agreement, or more accurately the complicity, inherent in documentary's social intervention is here centered and calibrated in its, often comic, vicissitudes.

Leacock and Shuker discover a diegetic trope for their own professed cinematic philosophy, the Indian concept of *darsham*: an aura of intense but impersonal and unobtrusive witnessing. Nehru is said to embody this state and so, by extension, do the filmmakers. Yet the textual evidence symptomatically suggests a founding ambivalence that is played out in an improvised scenario of presence and absence, where the supposed baggage of a shaping (analytic, polemical, authoritative) ego is tactically withdrawn only to be reinvested in the performative treatment of exemplary personalities. The movement's rhetoric is bonded to its public figures in a mutual validation of agency, the inscription of vocational competence—or, in Wiseman's institutional critiques, malfeasance.

The assertion that direct cinema utilizes its social actors as a relay for or projection of its own cinematic program—encoding specific political and ideological assumptions (including the reification of a patently masculinist performance ethos)—can be placed within sporadic efforts to re-read the movement's contradictions under a rubric of modernist reflexivity.[48] However, in several notable appraisals, failure to acknowledge the hardening of figuration into tropic patterns results in much the same metaphysical morass opened by the filmmakers' own *ad hoc* theorizing. The conventional nature of direct cinema is denied by Gianfranco Bettetini, for instance, when he revalues the documentary sequence shot as foregrounding processes by which scenes are "manufactured." He compares an inferred constructedness of mobile-camera long takes to Brecht's prescriptions for epic theater, yet adopts a familiar recourse to claims of renewed fidelity to the Real:

> In the sequence-shot, reality is revealed according to parameters that appear to be rather more its own, and less invented, than is the case in narrative situations codified by classical editing.[49]

In his formulation, the sequence shot is an ideal format for a kind of "research" from which the "fortuitous, aleatory and accidental elements . . . find room to expand naturally."[50]

In a similar vein, Jean-Louis Comolli, in an article that confusingly melds related strategies in documentary and the French New Wave, notes how an emphasis on theatrical performance can endow reality with "a new lease of meaning and coherence . . . its truth reinforced by and because of this detour through the 'fictitious.'"[51] He proposes that direct cinema has inherent "political value" because it circumvents a "triple ideological dependency: capital-intensive production, spectacle, and rhetorical convention." It seems to me that this is hardly an improvement on the idealist assertions made by filmmakers on behalf of a heightened authenticity. In effect, this approach disdains documentary's fiction of truth only to install something like the truth of fiction.

Against a backdrop of repeated calls for a more overt, discontinuous, and demystifying set of nonfiction film practices[52] and following more than a decade of political documentaries mixing interviews with archival footage—*The Murder of Fred Hampton* (1971), *Hearts and Minds* (1974), *Union Maids* (1976), *With Babies and Banners* (1977)—some recent mainstream films attempt to revitalize previous practices through a cultural discourse befitting the postmodern moment.[53]

Gilding the Ashes: Toward an Aesthetics of Failure

> My success seemed dependent on the failure of others.
>
> Tony Buba
> *Lightning Over Braddock*

There is currently more popular interest in nonfiction cinema than at any time since the late sixties. This renewal has been spurred by, among other factors, wholesale incorporation of *verité* techniques in TV advertising, the continuing strength of nonfiction genres in the publishing industry, and the onslaught of prime-time dramatic and news series such as "America's Most Wanted" and "Cops" which deploy an array of fictional and direct cinema strategies around tabloid stories. What the recent body of theatrical films—*Sherman's March* (1987), *Lightning Over Braddock* (1988), *Roger and Me* (1989), *Driving Me Crazy* (1990), and *The Thin Blue Line* (1990)—shares with other cultural phenomena is a perhaps unprecedented degree of hybridization. Materials, techniques, and modes of address are borrowed not only from earlier documentary styles but from the American avant-garde and from Hollywood as well. Voice-over narration, found footage, interviews, reenactments, and printed texts mingle in a pastiche that implicitly rejects the boundary distinctions of prior filmic modes. However, unlike related media and literary practices, the new documentary's most salient quality is an explicit centering of the filmmaking process and a heavily ironized inscription of the filmmaker as (unstable) subject, an anti-hero for our times.

As a group the new films do not manifest, or not yet, the coherent polemics, social ambit, or ideological fealties which define New Deal or direct cinema documentaries as part of a movement. In occasional interviews or writings, filmmakers predictably denounce the aesthetic assumptions and impact of earlier styles. Errol Morris says bluntly:

> I believe cinema verité set back documentary filmmaking twenty or thirty years. It sees documentary as a sub-species of journalism. . . . There's no reason why documentaries can't be as personal as fiction filmmaking and bear the imprint of those who made them. Truth isn't guaranteed by style or expression. It isn't guaranteed by anything.[54]

If Morris and company dismiss one type of formal truth claim, their films are organized around a set of strategies in which authority and verisimilitude are rhetorically embedded in a negative register of denial, mockery, and collapse. By inference, the social ideals of bureaucratic control in New Deal films, or spontaneous individual performance in direct cinema, are no longer able to support an edifice of documentary truth.

Indeed, the prospect for completion of a straightforward documentary project of any stripe may be under interrogation. In each case cited above—and in *Demon Lover Diary* (1980), a cogent if little known anticipation of the current style—*failure* to adequately represent the person, event, or social situation stated as the film's explicit task functions as an inverted guarantee of authenticity. The new works are textual parasites, fragments or residues of other works which for one reason or another became impossible to realize.[55] One ramification of postmodern aesthetics, precipitated in part by the anti-metaphysical bent of poststructuralist theory, is that certain types of artistic mastery are culturally suspect. The epistemic ambition to speak from a totalizing framework of knowledge about some fully intelligible reality is anathema. The proscription of unified subjectivity is perhaps especially severe for (politically conscious) white male filmmakers working at the margins of mass culture. Although it is too soon to make any decisive judgment, it is tempting to posit a documentary "aesthetics of failure" that grafts a protean cultural agenda onto traditional problems of authority.[56]

Operating under sanctions of what did *not* happen—an interview with General Motors Chairman Roger Smith; an account of General Sherman's attack on the Confederacy; a collection of filmic portraits of a depressed steel town; a behind-the-scenes promotional trailer for a Broadway musical—filmmakers assume an active presence as diegetic characters and/or voice-over narrators (either spontaneous with the flow of recording or indirect). This presence is marked by a studied self-deprecatory distance and a resultant celebration of formal disjuncture and disorientation. The displacement of textual (non) authority into the profilmic allows as well a return of analytic commentary, discursive sequencing, and associative or metaphoric editing patterns while maintaining some of direct cinema's myth of immediacy. Operating under this libertarian ethos, it is required that filmmakers peel away the off-screen cloak of anonymity and, emerging into the light, make light of their power and dominion.

At once recognizing and missing the point entirely, Gary Crowdus remarks that "*Roger and Me* might have acquired a little more political bite if it had focused a little more on 'Roger' and somewhat less on 'Me.'"[57] In truth, it is precisely Moore's confection of an ineffectual, uncertain journalistic self that lends an Everyman quality to his social analysis. The assertion in all of these films of the recorder's central, albeit amusingly out-of-control, position in the representational process is reminiscent of Jean Rouch's cinema verité self-implication in *Chronicle of a Summer* (1961) and other films. But a willingness to actually take apart and examine the conventions by which authority is inscribed—as opposed to making sport of them—is largely absent.[58] As distinct from Rouch's work, an unrealized or "impossible" project disguises mechanisms of internal validation which are as immunized against contradiction as direct cinema's allegories of performance.

Thirties social documentaries annex cinematic authority in iconographic identification with industrial technology and the power of central government symbolized in this motif, and direct cinema exhibits diegetic figures as mirrors for an ideal of filmic performance. The new films affirm a vested, and ultimately naturalized, stake in the inadequacy of *any* representational system to capture lived reality. *Sherman's March* starts with a brief invocation of common materials out of which historical documentaries are fashioned: maps, still photos, voice-over recitation of facts. It veers quickly into a diaristic account of the filmmaker's journey south and his visits with family and friends. A counterthematic is proposed: "A meditation on the possibility of Romantic love in the South during an era of nuclear weapons proliferation." Although there are occasional metonymic connections among Sherman, romance, and weaponry, what ensues is scarcely a "meditation." In short order, even the ancillary focus becomes a front for the work of self-absorbed disconnection, the externalized crisis of making a "commitment."

At one point, director Ross McElwee's sister tells him, "You have an instant rapport with people because you have a camera." Indeed, the documentary camera is a derisive, but unmistakably useful, weapon and defensive shield. Most of McElwee's filmed adventures revolve around antiquated, silly projections of masculinity. He frequently compares himself to Sherman (even donning a Civil War uniform in one shot), yet stresses his inability to conquer any of the targets, female or filmic, in his path. At a Scottish picnic, he watches passively "as men compete in various events of strength and virility." A succession of aspiring performers are interviewed: the women as potential love objects, the men as alter egos or distorted versions of his own doubts and desires. A Burt Reynolds impersonator, and then Reynolds himself, are simultaneously addressed and chided as embodiments of assertive qualities he ambivalently lacks.

McElwee has qualms about the digression from the Sherman project: "I keep thinking I should return to my original plan . . . but I can't stop filming Pat"; "it's all very confusing . . . I can't figure out what to do next." He imagines "a sort of creeping psychosexual despair" that is then echoed in myriad malfunctions. The car breaks down; he forgets to turn on the tape recorder for an important encounter; an amusement park train ride runs into technical difficulties; he cannot frame or adequately follow certain subjects with the camera. Constant self-effacement and irresolution assume the shape of a dramatic device, intended to minimize and deflect the grotesque ambition of finding a love life through *cinema verité* interaction. What the device certifies through negative mastery is finally the sincerity and truth of the filmmaker's observations about himself, women, and social attitudes. In a telling twist of the traditional realist promotion of a "styleless style," *Sherman's March* parades a narrative of introspective abasement as the very sign of unvarnished reflection.

Despite profound differences in approach and aspiration, *Roger and Me* steers an analogous course. Here, the ostensible, unrealized goal is modest and politically pointed: trapping GM's Roger Smith into a spontaneous reckoning of the disastrous human effects of his corporate policies. This scenario is not doomed from the outset. Unlike McElwee, Moore is at pains to demonstrate good faith in meeting his announced goal. There is a gradual awareness, however, that the desired interview would be unilluminating and ambiguous. Lacking the requisite subject–recorder complicity, the filmmaker redirects his failure to engage Smith as proof of his own honorable political sympathies and of corporate America's malfeasance.

Once again ironic citations of misconnection and confusion pile up as the measure of a heightened authenticity. In a humorous prelude devoted to Moore's childhood perceptions of General Motors, he states: "My heroes were people who got out of Flint." He then relates a painful professional experience in San Francisco where, after losing a job as a magazine editor ("California and I were a mismatch"), he returns to Michigan in the same sort of rented truck featured in later scenes of laidoff workers. His new job as filmmaker is consistently identified with the conditions of the (often eccentric) unemployed workers; and it is predicated on their mutual failure to make the system work. Like the ex-worker who breeds rabbits to sell as either meat or pets, the filmmaker demonstrates improvisatory skill by seeming to readjust the shape of his movie as he goes along. That is, unlike *Roger and Me*'s corporate nemesis, the film text cannot be constructed like an assembly-line product. Moore's social solidarity is grounded in a trope of technical awkwardness, a feigned inadequacy and victimization defined against the ruthless instrumentality of General Motors—and, by extension, Hollywood.

Stalking the aloof chairman, he invents fake identities: "My friends and I decided to pose as a TV crew from Toledo. . . . I wasn't sure what a TV crew from Toledo looked like but apparently the ruse worked." Just then, Moore and his crew are unceremoniously escorted from the building. Found footage from Hollywood movies and industrial advertisements are cobbled together with interviews and observational sequences while popular songs (for example, the Beach Boys' "Wouldn't It Be Nice") impose a flat irony over scenes of economic privation. Prevented from obtaining access to GM headquarters, Moore typically remarks: "I was getting the big blow-off once again." Smith's refusal of contact is dramatized directly and also displaced onto other forms of technical miscarriage. A "Nightline" broadcast from Flint is cancelled when the engineering truck is stolen. Various schemes to rejuvenate the local economy end in collapse. Officials issuing on-screen corporate excuses or cheery prognostications are later fired. When Moore invades the annual GM stockholders' meeting to confront Smith face-to-face, his microphone is turned off. A textual array of breakdowns and exposed limitations presents the filmmaking process as a series of inadequate gestures at empowerment by which fidelity to the Real is simultaneously derided as a goal and instated.

Parallels between documentary process and productive (and nonproductive) labor are even more extensive and politically incisive in *Lightning Over Braddock*. Buttressed by the same autobiographical impulse found in *Sherman's March* and *Roger and Me*, the film interweaves personal history with social history toward a highly subjective account of the depleted fortunes of a Pennsylvania milltown. It opens on a TV interview with Tony Buba, whose previous films on the local economy garnered (for himself and for Braddock) some useful publicity. This gambit leads to a recapitulation in direct speech, voice-over exposition, and film excerpts, of Buba's college life and initiation into documentary filming. Shifting easily between tenses, levels of presentation, and epistemic frameworks, the film issues a kind of metadiscourse that undercuts every spontaneous gesture and sincere mimetic intention.

Present as a muted concern in other films, here the intricate slippage in roles from recorder to social actor to scripted fictional character to commentator provides a structuring logic formalized in an extreme concatenation of materials. There are collisions of video footage and film fragments shot in different gauges; actual and faked interviews and observational sequences; enacted flashbacks and ramshackle Hollywood fantasies such as the local staging of Ghandi's assassination. One can never be sure of the director's interpersonal ties with the featured characters, all unemployed denizens of Braddock. They seem, in turn, autonomous subjects and willing conspirators earning a modest payday before the camera; yet, in sequences with cranky "Sweet Sal" Carulo, a feeling of genuine antagonism creeps in. At an early stage, Buba informs us that the project planned as "Lightning Over Braddock" is under constant revision and that the original scheme of a sweeping portrait of the town must be abandoned.

Toward the end, we are told that grant money ran out before many sequences were finished. The screen goes black (as it does at several points), then forges ahead with new ideas and ambitions—including blowing up (which?) *Lightning* into 35mm for mass distribution and other partially realized projects such as a "steel mill musical." Buba says he is unclear about what he is doing and inserts demands by collaborators that he simply "quit." Later, he renounces his commitment to social documentary altogether and plots to "sell out" to Hollywood, a vocation for which the fictional sequences are to presumably serve as advertisement.

An anarchic pattern of technical struggle, breakdown, and recuperation is directly linked to economic conditions. The film both demonstrates and refuses the "real irony" that "as the layoffs increase, his fortunes rise." Yet power is thwarted by vivid limitations. Buba exploits the inability to use sound for a performance of "Jumping Jack Flash" by a worker scrounging cash as a club entertainer; rights to the song cost $15,000 "three times the per capita income of a Braddock resident." "Hey," he reminds us, "this isn't a Hollywood feature we're making here." The singer's silently moving lips—like the failed business ventures of another figure, Jimmy Ray, and the unfathomable acting career of "Sweet Sal"—binds film and subject in a concordance of nonfulfillment. And here, as elsewhere, it is exactly the open admission of, indeed a central obsession with, inadequacy emblazoned by formal disjunction and underwritten by dramatic displays of nontotalized knowledge—patriarchal mastery in disarray—which performs the labor of signifying authenticity and documentary truth.

In a recent essay, filmmaker–theorist Trinh Minh-ha, following a cogent dissection of documentary myths of verisimilitude, proposes a new nonfiction epistemology based on challenging filmic patterns of authority rather than merely replacing one unacknowledged source of authority with another:

> To compose is not always synonymous with ordering-so-as-to-persuade, and to give the. . . Meaning can therefore be political only when it does not let itself be easily stabilized, and when it does not rely on a single source of authority but, rather empties or decentralizes it.[59]

She advocates a practice in which the subject is constantly "in process," where documentary "displays its own formal properties or its own constitution as work" and where the expression of identity or subjective agency is one in which

> the self vacillates and loses its assurance. The paradox of such a process lies in its fundamental instability; an instability that brings forth the disorder inherent in every order.[60]

Trinh's prescriptions are nuanced and ardently progressive. And she intends her remarks for, and produces her own work within, a cinematic order largely unconstrained by commercial demands for topicality, familiarity, and identification. She would thus appear to have little interest or faith in the transformation of mainstream cinematic genres. Keeping this in mind, it is odd to find her notions—of defeating the "establishment of totality" by creating "a space in which meaning remains fascinated by what escapes and exceeds it"—at least partially tested by recent filmic practice. One explanation for this unexpected convergence lies in the popular translation in multiple fora of poststructuralism's critique of Western metaphysics. For instance, the unavoidable multiplicity of subjecthood and the constructedness of historical truth prop up recent controversies over multicultural education in the United States and the ramifications of the film *JFK* (1991).

It is doubly ironic, then, that the strategies found in these fashionable, mainstream postmodern documentaries remain wedded to the same principles of authenticity, if not the same rhetorical codings, as earlier styles. As I hope is now apparent, *Roger and Me* and its ilk substitute reflexive abnegation for New Deal and direct cinema paradigms of authority. There have been, and will continue to be, versions of the quest for documentary truth which develop different orders of structuration or manage to obviate the most self-contradictory tensions in the opposition of lived reality and tropes of presentation. The three moments of production considered here are yoked in a formal tradition that defines itself according to both Hollywood fictional codes and competing documentary styles. Despite affinities, the individual movements are embedded in and determined by particular historical and cultural assumptions about appropriate expressions of truth, and by corollary discourses that shape available options for representing social reality.

Technology and its imbrication with power is thematized in each instance according to the changing political dynamics of liberalism: in the first, iconographic identification with industrial technology and its ability to rectify social affliction; in the second, an incorporation and masking of the apparatus as an extension of individual cognitive acuity and physical skill; and in recent films, disavowal or technical proficiency as guarantee of non-omniscience and metaphoric link with disenfranchised profilmic subjects. Thus, the role of authorial agency in its manifest relation to technology moves from a stance of partisan intervention to one of neutral, transparent observation to a slippery ambivalence in which the instrument of cinema is a necessarily visible but confoundingly inadequate mediator.

Finally, all three sketch implicit cinematic programs for an exemplary nonfiction treatment of reality. Each construes its values and functions in opposition to Hollywood domination while adhering to certain of that institution's most ingrained effects of knowledge, coherence, and closure. In a sense, what succeeding documentary styles *refuse* of the formulas of narrative fiction bespeak their designated areas of social impact. Sponsored documentaries of the thirties eschew the establishing of strong individualized characters and the attendent possibility of viewer identification while providing familiar cues for dramatic expectation and closure. Direct cinema and, with some readjustment, recent films withhold or actively undermine closure and distend—if not abolish—prospects for dramatic development while offering compensation in the form of diegetic intimacy with sympathetic characters (including the filmmakers themselves). It is highly unlikely that the realist windmills of authority and transparency against which American documentaries have been tilting for fifty years will suddenly disappear or be demolished by postmodern allegories. The quiddity of the form will, for better or worse, continue to pivot on historically specific legitimations of authenticity.

I wish to thank Amy Taubin, Dana Polan, Ivone Margulies, and members of the Columbia University Seminar of Cinema and Interdisciplinary Interpretation for their valuable comments during the preparation of this chapter.

NOTES

1. The imbrication of documentary and fiction modes is a formidable topic but, contrary to indications, it is not central to my concerns. Nonetheless, what I have in mind ranges from fiction film's recourse to extratextual authority (e.g., the opening of *Psycho*), direct incorporation of nonfiction footage (as in *Reds*) to the miming of formal strategies such as direct cinema's handheld sequence shots (*Medium Cool*); on the other side of the ledger, documentaries from Flaherty on adapt coherence effects of continuity editing. Parker Tyler, in a 1949 essay, lays a critical foundation for further discussion [in *The Documentary Tradition*, ed. Lewis Jacobs (New York: Hopkinson and Blake, 1971), 251–266]. I note a tendency among recent commentators to discuss nonfiction's signs of transparency as mirroring those of the classical Hollywood. See, for example: Jeanne Hall, "Realism as Style in Cinema Verite: A Critical Analysis of *Primary*," *Cinema Journal* Vol. 30, No. 4 (1991), 29; Bill Nichols, "The Voice of Documentary," *Movies and Methods Vol. II*, ed. Bill Nichols (Berkeley: University of California, 1985), 260; E. Ann Kaplan, "Theories and Strategies of the Feminist Documentary," *Millennium Film Journal*, 12 (1982–83), 81. Nöel Carroll assails the blurring of fiction/documentary distinctions in "From Real to Reel: Entangled in Nonfiction Film," *Philosophic Exchange* 14 (1983), 5–15.
2. It should be clear that by "challenge" I mean the rather nebulous arena of cultural perception, not box-office. The quite different economic desiderata of TV, however, make parity a plausible condition. As to the scope of impact, direct cinema, at the apex of its commercial success in 1967–1968, circulated more than a dozen features with varying degrees of mass appeal, including *Don't Look Back, Monterey Pop, Warrendale, The Endless Summer, Portrait of Jason, A Face of War, Rush to Judgement*, and *Years of Lightning, Day of Drums*.
3. An objection can be raised that my easy periodization performed suppresses the reality of continual diachronic shifts and that an account of such shifts is especially crucial to the historicization of nonstudio modes. A similar objection is that isolation of American films masks a complex interdetermination with European documentary (to say nothing of Neo-Realist and New Wave movements). In response, my aim is to establish continuities among movements often addressed as antipodal. And that while recognizing the mesh of transnational and transgeneric exchanges, it is useful to see how *primary* allegiances in social documentaries are welded to discourses of national self-interest.
4. The case for heightened effectivity in nonfiction cultural production during the thirties is discussed at length in William Stott, *Documentary Representation and Thirties America* (New York: Oxford University, 1973) 65–141. John Hallowell, in *Fact and Fiction* (Chapel Hill: University of North Carolina, 1977), sketches a confluence of social anxieties and cultural

demands as contributory to the revaluation of nonfiction and rise of New Joumalism during the sixties. That period's manifold critique of Hollywood and the centrality of TV's war reporting were two obvious conditions of possibility for commercial documentary.

5. *TV Guide* (November 9, 1991; p. 3) reported that the fall 1991 roster of prime-time series included *eighteen* news and nonfiction hybrids, a fivefold increase from 1989. Relations between theatrical documentaries and their enveloping industrial contexts is a forceful, if gnarled, topic somewhat tangential to this essay.
6. George Levine, *The Realist Imagination* (Chicago: University of Chicago Press, 1981), 12.
7. Brian Winston, "Documentary: I Think We are in Trouble," *New Challenges For Documentary*, ed. Alan Rosenthal (Berkeley: University of California Press, 1988), 21.
8. Richard M. Barsam, "American Direct Cinema: The *Re*-presentation of Reality," *Persistence of Vision*, Nos. 3/4 (Summer 1986), 132.
9. Herbert Marcuse, "Some Social Implications of Modern Technology," *The Essential Frankfort School Reader*, ed. Andrew Arato and Eike Gebhardt (New York: Continuum, 1985), 139.
10. William Alexander, *Film on the Left* (Princeton, NJ: Princeton University Press, 1981), 254. In the same section, Alexander cites identical charges by contemporaneous writers such as Richard Griffith and James Arthur.
11. Cited in Stott, *Documentary Representation and Thirties America*, 77.
12. It should be recalled that at the height of their popularity newsreels were not only a staple of film exhibition, there were theaters devoted entirely to the showing of nonfiction short subjects.
13. Among several versions of Grierson's cagey equivocation, see Forsyth Hardy, ed., *Grierson on Documentary* (New York: Praeger, 1971), 237–248.
14. Marcuse, "Some Social Implications of Modern Technology," 138.
15. Similar iconographic patterns of naturalization are found in British films of the same period such as *Night Mail* (1936), *Housing Problems* (1935), and *The Line to the Tschierva Hut* (1937) in which, for instance, a locomotive is compared both metonymically and through editing to clouds, mountain tops, flights of birds, etc.
16. This notion of montage as reconciliation is taken from William Guynn excellent essay, "Politics of British Documentary," *Jump Cut* 8 (March–April 1975), 27. A similar tendency to use Soviet-style montage as an instrument of conceptual blurring is displayed in Riefenstahl's *The Triumph of the Will* (1934).
17. There are numerous examples from every point on the political compass. Grierson's influential stance can be found in Hardy, *Grierson on Documentary*, 146–147.
18. For an overview of the development of radical documentary groups in the early thirties, see Alexander, *Film on the Left*, 3–113.
19. Erich Auerbach, *Mimesis*, trans. Willard Trask (Princeton, NJ: Princeton University Press, 1953), 491.
20. Bill Nichols, "The Voice of Documentary," 261.
21. Thomas Waugh, "Beyond *Verité*: Emile de Antonio and the New Documentary of the Seventies," *Movies and Methods* Vol. *II*, 242, 235, respectively.
22. Nichols, "The Voice of Documentary," p. 261. See also Hall, "Realism as Style in Cinema Verite," for a rehearsal of related objections.
23. Thomas R. Atkins, *Frederick Wiseman* (New York: Monarch Books, 1976), 44.
24. Cited in Robert C. Allen and Douglas Gomery, *Film History: Theory and Practice* (New York: Knopf, 1985), 224.
25. G. Roy Levin, *Documentary Explorations* (Garden City, NY: Doubleday, 1971), 235.
26. Atkins, *Frederick Wiseman*, 43.
27. Anthropologist Victor Turner offers lively discussion of the counterculture's case against verbal language in *Dramas, Fields, and Metaphors* (Ithaca, NY: Cornell University Press, 1974), 262–266. In terms of both film practice and theory, Stan Brakhage exemplifies the American avant-garde's parallel revolt against socially regulated, hence morally and artistically bankrupt, language.
28. Levin, *Documentary Explorations*, 280.
29. Atkins, *Frederick Wiseman*, 56.
30. Ibid., 56.
31. Levin, *Documentary Explorations*, 315.
32. Allen and Gomery make a similar point in *Film History*, pp. 233–234. For a critique of the empiricism sweeping the American academy in the late fifties and early sixties, see Frankfort Institute for Social Research, *Aspects of Sociology*, trans. John Viertel (Boston: Beacon Press, 1956).
33. Atkins, *Frederick Wiseman*, 29.
34. Stephen Mamber, *Cinema Verite in America* (Cambridge, MA: MIT Press, 1974), 221, 152, 3, respectively.
35. Early pronouncements on the ethical superiority of the nineteenth-century realist novel by Taine, Saint-Beuve, George Eliot, and others mobilize nearly identical aesthetic–political metaphors. See George J. Becker's *Documents of Modern Literary Realism* (Princeton, NJ: Princeton University Press, 1963).
36. Carroll, "From Real to Reel," 23.
37. Allen and Gomery, *Film History*, 231.
38. Atkins, *Frederick Wiseman*, p. 4. In *Telling the Truth* (Ithaca, NY: Cornell University Press, 1986), Barbara Foley describes the changing historical character of literary mimesis and rehearses orthodox arguments for the separation of factual and fictional literature on the basis on nonclosure versus closure, "correspondence" rather than "coherence," and so on (74–84).
39. Roland Barthes, "The Realistic Effect," trans. Gerald Mead, *Film Reader* 3 (1978), 133–135.
40. Two types of resistance to the lure of celebrity are evident in direct cinema: Wiseman's diffused focus on institutional roles as opposed to individual identity; and the poignant noncompliance in the

recorder–actor agreement in *Happy Mothers Day* (1963).

41. Mamber, in *Cinema Verite in America*, recognizes the importance of public personality to direct cinema but draws a rather different set of conclusions; see pp. 90 and 183.
42. Michael Renov, "Re-Thinking Documentary," *Wide Angle* Vol. 8, No. 3/4 (1986), 73.
43. Wiseman traces his horror at the Bridgewater mental hospital to field trips taken with his law students. It should be pointed out that 1967 was a ripe year for the trope of mental illness as political theater/performance with, to cite two examples, Peter Brook's wildly popular staging of Peter Weiss' *Marat/Sade* and psychiatrist R.D. Laing's bestselling book *The Politics of Experience* (NY: Ballantine, 1967), on madness as a liberatory response to modern life.
44. For examples of this occasionally humorous internecine critique, see Levin, *Documentary Explorations*, 219, 285.
45. Ibid., 277, 182–183, 198, respectively.
46. Cited in David Schwartz, "Documentary Meets the Avant-Garde," *Independent America: New Film 1978–1988* (Astoria, NY: American Museum of the Moving Image, 1988), 28.
47. Mamber, *Cinema Verite in America*, 85.
48. Two alternative, and I think largely compatible, readings of direct cinema's textual legitimation are provided by Hall, "Realism as Style in Cinema Verite" (pp. 38–39) and Allen and Gomery, *Film History* (235). Both concern the manner in which TV documentaries of the early sixties embed direct demonstrations or hints of their own superiority over competing cinematic or joumalistic types of representation.
49. Gianfranco Bettetini, *Realism and the Cinema*, ed. Christopher Williams (London: Routledge and Kegan Paul, 1980), 222–223.
50. Ibid.
51. Jean-Louis Comolli, *Realism and the Cinema*, 226.
52. For a selection of demands for the revision of documentary along materially reflexive lines, see Kaplan, "Theories and Strategies of the Feminist Documentary," (p. 80), Renov, "Re-Thinking Documentary" (p. 75), Nichols, "The Voice of Documentary" (p. 263), and Jay Ruby, "The Image Mirrored," *New Challenges for Documentary*, ed. Alan Rosenthal (Berkeley: University of California Press, 1988), 64–77.
53. The mention here of an intervening group of films posing an alternative to direct cinema may seem a bit misleading, raising a further problem of periodization. Unquestionably, documentaries of the past few years owe a considerable debt to the methodological "break" of the seventies discussed in Waugh, "Beyond *Verite*," and in Nichols, "The Voice of Documentary" (pp. 268–271). Nonetheless, my feeling is that recent work is no more comfortable with the rhetorical certainties of seventies films than they are with those of direct cinema. More to the point, the group of films I cite avoid the self-valorizing tactics whose historical pattern I chart.
54. Cited in Carl Plantinga, "The Mirror Framed: A Case for Expression in Documentary," *Wide Angle*, Vol. 13, No. 2 (1991), 51. In a related show of defiance, Michael Moore claims that his intention in *Roger and Me* was never to make a "straight documentary" and has little sympathy with classical conventions: Harlan Jacobson, "Michael and Me," *Film Comment*, Vol. 25, No. 6 (November 1989), 24.
55. *The Thin Blue Line* is slightly different; the set of images for which it is a self-conscious substitute is not another film but the actual murder it kaleidoscopically reenacts.
56. It is unclear to me whether the tropes ascribed to recent films have broader application. That said, I intrepidly adduce a brief art review by Kim Levin in *The Village Voice* (February 4, 1992; p. 71): "Curator Ralph Rugoff explores the new aesthetic of the hopelessly pathetic in this display of deliberately shabby, awkward, flawed, idiotic or otherwise impaired art objects. Sad, funny, inept, and absolutely right for right now. . . ." Among the artists included in the show were Mike Kelley, Jeffrey Vallance, Cady Noland, and Jim Shaw.
57. Gary Crowdus, "Reflections on *Roger and Me*: Michael Moore and his Critics," *Cineaste*, Vol. 17, No. 4 (1990), 30.
58. I want to stress a divergence between the recent documentary style and the venerable history of what might be called anti-documentaries, from Bunuel to Straub/Huillet to Welles and Ruiz. The brittle irony found in the new American revival does little to subvert the "naturalness" of documentary's *dispositif*.
59. Trinh T. Minh-ha, "Documentary Is/Not a Name," *October*, Vol. 52 (Spring 1990), 89.
60. Ibid., 95. She argues against superficial modernist gestures of reflexivity, exposure of the apparatus or anti-illusionist markers of materiality, endorsed somewhat ambiguously by Jay Ruby in "The Image Mirrored" and other essays.

SECTION VII

DOCUMENTARY TRANSFORMED

Transnational and Transmedial Crossings

105

JONATHAN KAHANA

INTRODUCTION TO SECTION VII

The Chinese filmmaker and producer Wu Wenguang, one of the foremost names in international documentary at the turn of the last century, helps us chart the distance that documentary has traveled over the course of this anthology when he narrates a series of important professional discoveries, revelations no less significant for their source in banal personal rituals, in his essay "DV: Individual Filmmaking." Wu—who has gained prominence on the national and world stage in the past two decades as a leader of the Chinese digital video documentary movement—found himself, in the early 1990s, at a crossroads. "At that time," he writes,

> I was surrounded by a group of people using the medium of film to make documentaries, reasoning that only in this way could a work be considered a "professional documentary film." . . . Once I started thinking this way I began to disdain video; I then had excellent reason to lie around in bed and talk about how, once I found the money, I'd make one of those soul-stirring documentaries that would also circulate widely.

But a trip to the United States in 1997 and a long visit with the independent filmmaker Frederick Wiseman at his home convinced Wu that he was on the wrong track, and that new video technologies that were then starting to reach consumers around the globe might offer a way out of his rut. From that point on, as Wu tells it, he not only left behind the idea that film was the essential documentary medium, but left behind as well his notion of what a documentary film was, and how to make one. Where he would once pursue "like a hunter, a single aim," he now let himself ramble, following his camera. And it frequently took him into the wilderness:

> Getting up in the mornings, I'd pull on my shoes, walk out of the tent, and take a piss in the wilderness, the air incomparably clear and fresh and perfectly silent. A young roadie would be squatting not far off, taking a shit; we'd greet each other: "You're up." At times like these, Beijing

felt really far away. All that modern art—really far away.

The metrics Wu uses to measure his independence—his distance from the city, from the art world, from other people and their bodies—would hardly have been reasonable, or even imaginable, as ways for an earlier generation of filmmakers to map out a future for documentary. It would not have occurred to Joris Ivens, or many of the filmmakers inspired by the example he set with his long career, to compose a manifesto for the documentary avant-garde that rejected urban life, professionalism, and the institutions of modern art. "Professional documentary filmmaker" was not an occupational category in the 1930s, and is still about as reliable a career path as "professional explorer" or "professional magician." Nor would Ivens' sponsors in industry, party political movements, or the agencies of the welfare state have had much interest in a filmmaker who proposed to locate the independent spirit of documentary at a makeshift toilet in the woods of rural China—or, for that matter, at the home of a comfortably bourgeois filmmaker from Boston. But Wu's perverse method for finding a literally grass-roots position from which to declare documentary independence—by being rigorously personal, and submitting physically to the technological apparatus—is nonetheless consistent with at least one credo of the documentary filmmaker: rethink received wisdom. Or, to use critical jargon: *deconstruct.*

Describing the work of political documentarists in India, filming the ruins of sectarian violence fostered by a neo-fascist religious state, Geeta Kapur asks us to notice an "unstated correspondence between the 'deconstructed' technology of the video-medium and what is now perceived and debated to be the already disassembled nation."[1] Artists like Amar Kanwar exemplify, Kapur argues, a new kind of political documentary practice, one that advances a "politics of place" by refusing, and refuting, the "leveling effects of the no-history, no-nation, no-place phenomenon promoted by globalized exhibition and market circuits."[2] On a parallel critical track, Rachel Gabara, writing about the mode of autobiography in African documentary, suggests that the idea of the individual central to this centuries-old literary practice is not a universal principle, and does not translate into African cinematic dialects quite so easily. For the authors and artists collected in this final section, the imperative to deconstruct the documentary and its aesthetic, ideological, and critical premises means various things.

This is not to say that documentary studies of non-Western "others" operate as merely personal, local knowledge, reducible to untheorized empiricism. One can see and hear the effects of unsettled continental intellectual and cultural histories in biographical and autobiographical documentary by filmmakers in the African diaspora, like the British multi-disciplinary artist Isaac Julien and the masterful French-Cameroonian essayist Jean-Marie Teno. Julien's video portrait of Frantz Fanon, *Frantz Fanon: Black Skin, White Mask* (1996)—a film which polymorphously embodies the "subjective position" Phillip Brian Harper describes, in the previous section, in the work of Marlon Riggs—threads a path between memoir, historical legend, psychoanalytic theory, and fantasy to give Fanon's life and thought an appropriately queer form, one we might call un-documentary. Teno similarly uses the basic tools of documentary recording to reframe and look awry at some well-trodden terrain. In "Writing On Walls," Teno searches for metaphors for the culture of African documentary video in the neighborhoods of Ouagadougou overlooked by visitors to that city who come just to see the official selections at FESPACO, the Pan-African film festival. Along with other filmmakers represented in this section, these artists operate in what some would call a transnational space of documentary.[3] Like their work, which can be playful, complex, and obscure, these artists are hard to pin down, and for some of them the term "filmmaker" no longer seems singularly appropriate: many work, often quite literally, in an off-the-wall way, installing serial or multiple versions of a project on television, in art galleries or on the internet. A member of the "post-socialist" generation of Chinese documentary artists Chris Berry discusses in "Getting Real," Wang Bing, makes films so long and slow—his 2008 film *Crude Oil* runs fourteen hours—that very few venues where they might otherwise have found audiences will or can show them, and very few viewers who have encountered them can be said to have fully seen them. Some, like the well-known director Werner Herzog, whom Barbara Klinger discusses in an essay on the documentary frontiers brought into view by 3D, use new technologies to unfold very old problems of realism, ones that date back to the earliest gallery walls. Like Wu, who has largely given up making his own films to promote community-based video documentation, some eschew the notion of individual authorship for documentary. (Some literally take pains to deform themselves and transform their identities through the documentary process, like the documentary prankster Morgan Spurlock, who gains weight and makes himself sick on a month-long diet of fast food in *Supersize Me* (2004), or the masochists of MTV's "Jackass" series of programs and films.) In *What Farocki Taught* (1998), the film she discusses here with Harun Farocki, Jennifer Horne, and me, Jill Godmilow simply remakes an earlier film by Farocki against the Vietnam War, producing the uncanny situation of an American documentary film in which American actors in the 1990s playing German actors from the 1960s playing American scientists and bureaucrats pretending that they are not producing napalm. Self-criticism is often central to this work, which contests modern myths of progress—liberal democratic universalism and financial-technological globalization—while complicating the national and individual identities on which oppositional filmmakers might once have relied for their counter-histories and alternative truths.

One could argue, of course, that documentary film has always operated at in the borderlands between fiction and nonfiction, theory and history, art and politics; but Teno, Julien, Wu, Kanwar and many other documentary makers do so now with a heightened sensitivity to the mobile character of the (self-)image, and to all the ways identity has been set adrift from its foundations. And these developments are not limited to inhabitants of other—Third, non-Western, diasporic—places. We are just as likely to see the sovereign self pixilated in the documentary work of filmmakers from overdeveloped nation-states like Germany, the United States or Israel, where filmmakers like Herzog, Farocki, Godmilow, Michael Moore, and Avi Mograbi have applied techniques of abstraction, satire, self-parody, and digital dispersion to challenge the integrity of imperial consciousness. Though we have traveled some distance from the conception of the documentary film with which we began this anthology, we find ourselves again forming the question occasioned its beginnings: what do we know from pictures that move and talk?

NOTES

1. Geeta Kapur, "Tracking: The Politics of Place," in *Experiments With Truth*, ed. Mark Nash (Philadelphia: Fabric Workshop and Museum, 2004), 109.
2. Kapur, "Tracking: The Politics of Place," 105.
3. See, for instance, John Hess and Patricia Zimmermann, "Transnational Documentaries: A Manifesto," *Afterimage* 24, no. 4 (January/February 1997): 10–14.

HARUN FAROCKI AND JILL GODMILOW WITH JENNIFER HORNE AND JONATHAN KAHANA

A PERFECT REPLICA

An Interview with Harun Farocki and Jill Godmilow (1998)

The questions were posed and answered by e-mail and fax; Harun Farocki responded from Berlin and Berkeley, CA, where he lives and works; Jill Godmilow, who teaches at the University of Notre Dame, responded from New York City. This seemed appropriate, given the feeling of spatial and temporal dislocation that pervades *Inextinguishable Fire,* Farocki's 1969 film about the research and development of napalm, and Godmilow's 1998 remake, *What Farocki Taught.* We asked both filmmakers to discuss the historical and cultural context of the films—how politics shaped their aesthetics, and vice versa. (Farocki's responses were translated from the German by Anne Bilek.)

Q: Harun Farocki, tell us about the context in which you were working when you made *Inextinguishable Fire.*

Farocki: In 1968 I, along with seventeen others, fled the film academy in West Berlin. We were engaged in a constant political struggle with the directors of the academy and in May of 1968, we occupied the academy. We even renamed it "Dziga Vertov Academy." This happened concurrently with a nation-wide campaign against welfare laws. Not only that but my daughters had just been born and I had to earn money—to make films that weren't simply exercises. In our circles at that time collectivity meant a lot and it was almost a crime

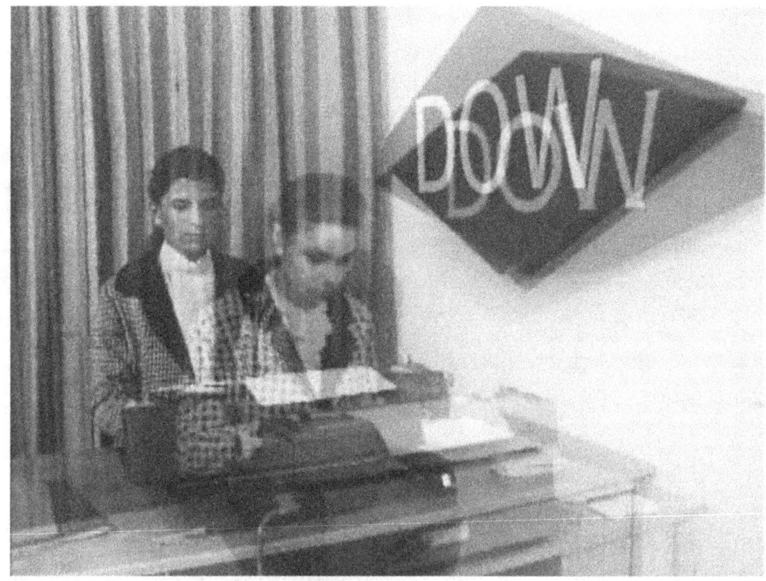

FIGURE 106.1 *What Farocki Taught* (Jill Godmilow, 1998). Screen capture from DVD.

if the impetus for a film came from a single person. Probably for this reason I sought out an area in which no one other than myself worked. I called it the agitation of technical expertise. I appointed myself Propaganda Minister for Engineers.

Q: *Inextinguishable Fire* is about the American production of the deadly chemical weapon napalm. Why did you choose napalm rather than one of the other weapons used during the war in Vietnam?

Farocki: Auschwitz has become the symbol for all concentration camps because so many types of camps were collected into one and because there were survivors who could tell their stories. In the Vietnam war there were many terrible weapons. The herbicides that were used to poison the water did not show their effects until years later. Napalm is a pre-modern weapon. Napalm stirs the imagination because it reminds us of when wars had a ritual and magical aspect.

Q: How was *Inextinguishable Fire* received upon its initial release?

Farocki: In the fall of 1969 I showed the film at a festival in Mannheim. There were some criticisms of the technical quality of the film but otherwise the reaction was positive. Although one newspaper wrote that I would achieve nothing with the film, the writer mentioned that one *could* achieve something with a film and that even the aim (*das Anliegen*) of the filmmaker may be justifiable. The film was shown several times on television in Germany and I received continued encouragement, especially from people who had up until then found the student movement to be nonsense. Only recently did it occur to me that the film spoke of Hiroshima and Vietnam, but didn't mention Auschwitz. It had to do with the participation of the scientists and technical people in the crime; and the fact that the Nazi concentration camps were highly organized factories of death. My omission made me think that the terrible war the United States waged in Vietnam not only horrified the Germans, but unburdened them as well—we are not the only barbarians.

The film and television industry in Germany recognized that my film was different than what they had made. There was a short period in which I was invited to a screening of *Inextinguishable Fire* by studio producers. They treated me as if I could teach them something! But that didn't last very long, and soon it was impossible to make such a film. Many people in the political movement were devotees of Socialist Realism and found my punk aesthetic unbearable. I believe that the ugliness of the pictures taken with an extreme 10.5mm wide angle lens let loose more horror than the scenes of the burning of a dead rat.

Q: Jill Godmilow, to the extent that *What Farocki Taught* is about the Vietnam War, why remake a film about Vietnam now? Why change the title?

Godmilow: If you don't want anymore Vietnams, you have to understand how Vietnam came about—actually, and materially. Farocki's film offered significant information. He shows how the war was made in the laboratories of Dow Chemical and how the people participated in the war. The structure of labor relationships at the research corporations of America is one good place to look at the Vietnam war, and by projection, a good place to look for the source of all the pollutants, poisons, waste products, useless products and wasted labor we live with today.

Q: *What Farocki Taught* doesn't follow the most typical approach to the remake. How did you decide to remake the film without significantly changing or updating it?

Godmilow: The idea was to "show" Farocki's film itself, its precision and its exact, deadly, logical structure, the largest meaning-making system in the film. To add to or change it would not have been to the point. It was that simple . . . I wanted to call attention to what Farocki had done, *then,* and to the plain fact that we should have been able to see his film back then and learn from it. Structures of distribution made it hard then, and in some ways even harder now. How many 29-year-old German documentaries are playing at the Film Forum in New York, on public television or in college film series today? None. Certainly it might have been possible to put out a video version of Farocki's film, but who would see it? So few people in this country know his work. It seemed obvious that the gesture of the perfect replica, in color and in English, would draw attention to *Inextinguishable Fire* and Farocki's work in general, and it has.

I should add that it was also an opportunity to extend certain theoretical questions about the original and the copy, the real and the fake (how they are the same or not, how the two are valued differently) into non-fiction cinema, a practice that takes authenticity and actuality for its pedigree.

In that way, I never set out to make a film about wars, or weapons. I saw a film in 1991 that I wished I had seen many years before. *Inextinguishable Fire* was very provocative in terms of non-fiction strategies because it successfully circumvented, and simultaneously marked out all of the classical documentary dilemmas and offered some solutions. It is a film that is useful to non-filmmakers and filmmakers alike. I wanted to show it to everybody because I felt that in this country what is called the left-liberal documentary is unexamined and out of touch. But it was impossible to start showing Farocki's film after I first viewed it in 1991. There is only one print left and he is not well known. So I remade Farocki's film, copied it exactly, thinking that maybe this somewhat outlandish, perhaps obscene, gesture of replication would bring some attention to it. So it's accurate to say that I set out to make a film about Farocki's filmmaking.

Q: Dow is a company fresh in the minds of many women as a producer of silicone breast implants. Did you consider broadening Farocki's critique to incorporate, so to speak, bodies of women? Is the end of *Inextinguishable Fire,* where we are presented with the potential coalition of the (male) factory workers and the (male) students, a place where the question of gender in oppositional politics might have been added to the film?

Godmilow: Yes, for a second I thought about that, but just for a second. There was a defensive, slightly self-conscious moment when it seemed I had to make this film more *mine*, by adding a particular feminist perspective, or updating it. Finally I shook off the compulsion and decided that my job was to re-make the film, exactly. My film speaks about film history by producing a perfect replica of an antique object but leaving it, hopefully, an intact and complete artifact, but also a new, useful and available object. Because of this, critics sometimes refer to my film as an homage. Certainly it can be seen that way, but that wasn't the point.

Secondly, Farocki's film was not about "getting Dow," as many American anti-war documentaries were. Dow itself, that nasty corporation in Midland, Michigan, simply stands in—just as the actors stand in—for any/every research corporation. Moving on to breast implants was not the point. The point was to understand the structures of capitalism that produce both napalm and breast implants, as well as useful building materials and useful pesticides. However, I did update it a little; not in the replica of Farocki's film, but in the epilogue.

Q: You appear before the camera yourself answering questions about the relationship between Farocki's critique and yours, which had to be updated.

Godmilow: The concept of the "military-industrial establishment" as the generator of all corporate evil had to be revised, since so much has changed since 1969. In the full-tilt transnational corporate mode we are in today one has to identify other sites of production. In fact, I chose to identify a site of consumption—the huge discount stores like K-Mart and Best Buy—to point out the place where we all participate in the production cycle. The poisons, and the wasted labor that produce them, are dispersed now, and available to everybody.

Q: The images we see on the television screens when the Dow employees watch the news have the appearance of stock footage: they're scratched, spliced and otherwise marked as "used." At the same time, this is the only actuality footage in *Inextinguishable Fire*, and perhaps the only "documentary" reference to the Vietnam War. How does this footage work in terms of the reality effect of the film?

Farocki: That was really the founding idea of my film: in the evenings there are pictures on TV that have the taste of the real and the true. What we don't understand, however, is how we consume these pictures. Our own life, our own experience, doesn't appear to be presentable to us. We see images from the war in Vietnam, but what binds us to these images? We see people suffer, and as emotional beings, we can empathize with the victims. But what we can't understand from these images is that we also are or could be the perpetrators.

Godmilow: Farocki's use of that series of nineteen very short shots of newsreel footage is one of the things I like most in his film. First, it was bold and brave of him to dare to include actuality footage in a film whose whole premise is that you can't understand napalm—that is, take it in with all its weight and meaning—by looking at newsreel footage from the war. In his film, Farocki asks the audience: "How can we show you the use of napalm in action? First you'll close your eyes to the pictures, then to the memory, then to the facts, then you'll close your eyes to the whole story. If we show you napalm burns, we'll hurt your feelings. If we hurt your feelings, you'll feel we've tried out napalm on you and at your expense. We can give you but a weak show of napalm's effects." I disagree with Farocki here. In newsreel footage of the war, you can only find excitement: the pornography of war, the horror-show. Audiences don't turn away from it or feel any guilt; rather, we seem programmed to enjoy that kind of horror by other kinds of experiences in the cinema.

But when Farocki uses Vietnam newsreel material, he doesn't produce pornography. He does something extraordinary, draining the shots of excitement by running this very formal sequence of newsreel shots that seem to mark off the progression of daily destruction. First there are two shots of generals walking around and a shot of a jeep passing by. Then there is an explosion and fire, bare trees; and children are seen praying. A bomber swoops down on a village, helicopters land and peasants flee. Two quick shots of napalm burns on human skin and then suddenly you're looking at the shot of the burned rat again, and the tweezers are tugging at the scar. Farocki is connecting the dots. The shots are the dots: taking the napalm burns back to the lab and to the people who discovered that a polystyrene developed for rubber shoe soles was the perfect ingredient to get napalm to stick to human skin. The sequence is also a formal review or prod to remember how we watched the war, night after night, on television, not to reproduce that experience but to remind us of our experience watching it. Farocki shows the aforementioned sequence twice in the film. The Dow scientists need to watch TV to study the results of their work in the field, that is, in the rice paddies of Vietnam. That's how the two newsreel sequences are rationalized in the film. The blond chemist has said earlier, "What works in experiments won't always work in reality." Then she watches the news on the television to see if it does.

I made a mistake in making *What Farocki Taught* that I now regret. I asked Farocki if somehow the cut newsreel sequence had survived the intervening twenty-nine years. It had not. So I had to reproduce the sequence as perfectly as I could by going through maybe thirty or forty videotape documentaries about Vietnam, looking for matching shots. (I found all but one: I faked the two children crossing themselves with the children of a friend, a Chinese restaurant owner in South Bend, Indiana). Some of the shots I found were in color and some in black and white (the war years marked the period of transition). I converted all the color shots to black and white on Avid to make them consistent with each other. I should have done the reverse, "painted" in the black and white shots, because now, as a series of black and white newsreel shots on a television in a color film, they are marked too much as historical, made archival by their difference from the rest of the color film. In *Inextinguishable Fire* they exist concurrently with the rest of the black and white film. In my film, they end up being too much about "that war then," and don't sit well enough in the present tense of the film's diagetic plane.

Q: So *Inextinguishable Fire* and *What Farocki Taught* should not necessarily be classified as documentary films?

Farocki: At the time I made the film I found documentaries very suspicious. Because Marxism teaches us that history's laws of effect are invisible, that what is evident is untrue. (In any case, the truth must reveal itself in revolution, kind of the way it is with God.) For this reason I wanted above all else to portray the construction of thought or ideas the way a photo montage does. Today I'm more interested in less obvious constructions.

Godmilow: The word "documentary" is problematic for me. Everybody thinks they know what they mean by it but I don't. It's a term that masks or clouds the realities of film experience, seeming to deny that fiction can tell useful sober truths and affirming that documentary can do nothing but. When I teach documentary, I use a substitute term, "films of edification," because I think the best way to describe this group of films is by their stance. All non-fiction films claim to edify. (Whether they do or not is another matter.)

But as I say in *What Farocki Taught*, we need another term, a sub-category of the edifying film, for Farocki's *Inextinguishable Fire* and others like it. Clearly it's not bourgeois melodrama, but its strategies also put it outside the domain of the "documentary" as it's practiced and understood in this country. In my film I call it "agit-prop": *Inextinguishable Fire* has a clear political analysis that it puts forward very directly. The film is punctuated by inter-titles that speak direct political statements to the viewer about what to do. It takes responsibility for its thesis, something 99% of documentaries never do.

Q: The Kodachrome also distinguishes your film from a traditional documentary look.

Godmilow: Well, I thought of my replication or re-enactment of Farocki's film as a period piece, so I had to find costumes, sets and props from the late '60s. I even asked the male actors to let their sideburns grow if the character they were duplicating had long sideburns in Farocki's film. But how to get a period look to the filmmaking itself? The obvious choice was to replicate the film in black and white, but that presented a dilemma: I disagree with the film convention of using black and white to represent "the historical," *Schindler's List*-style. And I wanted to clearly separate Farocki's black and white film from mine. I looked for a color way to go and ended up picking Kodachrome, one of the reversal stocks from the '60s and '70s, to get the right feel and look. There was also a technical and economic reason: I planned to superimpose certain scenes from *Inextinguishable Fire* onto my color scenes. That is much cheaper to do with reversal than with color negative stocks, because you can avoid making expensive optical negatives.

Q: You talk in front of the camera in your film. What does it mean to you to appear in front of the lens as you do in the self-reflexive epilogue?

Godmilow: Perhaps it's for lack of a better idea, but there were some things—simple things, I hope—that I wanted to say about Farocki's film and I couldn't think of a better way than just to stand up and say them. Because I could never have performed that much text in one take, I broke my thoughts up into a series of questions and answers. I was pretty sure I could answer questions on camera. I had my production manager ask the questions. Later I re-dubbed the questions with a very flat, youngish "studenty" kind of voice to mark the pedagogical nature of the sequence. A collaborator of mine, Gloria Jean Masciarotte, thought some of my answers were a little high-handed, so I interrupted my answers here and there with black film, which gave me time to explain what I "really meant" by what I was saying. At first I was fearful of how I would appear by doing this—perhaps lacking in authority, or just silly. Now I like the "corrections"—they seem to critique the viewer's expectations of finding perfect expression and clarity of meaning in the performance of an on-camera author. But also because *it was scary*. I went ahead. In my experience, that's been the source of everything fresh I've had to say in my films. *Far From Poland* (1984) was much scarier—making a film about current events in Poland without going there. What would legitimate my right to speak about such things, except *vérité* footage from Poland? A friend said, make a film called *Far From Poland*. With weak knees and nightmares I tried it. Everything was different, everything had to be reinvented, and those are the most interesting things about the film. I think that you have to put yourself in the face of big problems to make something worth looking at in art, or you can't invent anything at all. That's how filmmaking goes for me—solving real problems as fearlessly and as well as you can.

Q: *Inextinguishable Fire* is a film that is clearly quite critical of the military-industrial complex and of a specific corporate entity within that complex. The film also raises questions about the place or role of cinema in capitalism, as a technology of reproduction, and also as a product.

Farocki: I wasn't very critical of technology in this film. However, the scene at the end with the vacuum cleaner and the machine guns expresses something like if the producers could control production, the world would be saved. A democracy of production could end the production of weaponry. Not only that, the film calls into question how people should appear in films. I am stylistically indebted to the early Brecht: his idea of "man is man." It has to do with the fact that Man himself is not that great, he is the raw material to be constructed. Both Brecht, in his play on British colonialism, and I, in my film on Vietnam, abhor the abuses that took place, but we also find that there are possibilities hiding in those situations. Look at how Marxists talk about industry: it's terrible at the moment, but you can't go back anyway, so you might as well develop it further. By the way, it was the producer who was afraid that the film would look too much like a bad film and not like an intentional deviation. I had each dialogue dubbed. We did that with very long loops so that the tone was never quite synchronized.

Godmilow: Certainly film is an industrialized process, although less so the small independent production with a crew of six and a budget of $10,000 than a major motion picture with a crew of 200 and a budget of $600 million. I remember being in France, in about the third week of production on *Waiting for the Moon* [Godmilow's 1987 feature about Gertrude Stein and Alice B. Toklas]. One day I looked around at the crew of forty-five and was struck by the disheartening thought that filmmaking was the ultimate capitalist process. I was squeezing labor out of forty-five people for six weeks, and the juice out of $950,000 of materials and goods, all of which would flow through me and my ideas to end up spread on a thin piece of celluloid with sprocket holes, weighing about forty pounds, that could be endlessly reproduced into hundreds of copies, all of which could be running simultaneously in front of audiences watching it on sixty-foot screens, and listening to it through huge speakers all over the world. This is advanced capitalist production of the highest order. You have to be morally responsible, and conscious of the experience you produce when you make a film.

Q: You are talking about ethical limits.

Godmilow: Yes, one could argue that the crew and cast had all read the script of my film before they signed on to the project, whereas most of the scientists and engineers who developed napalm could not have known what would come of their labors. And one can say that the two products operate very differently in the material world. Serious cultural products—and a good film is one of these—are objects of contemplation. You can't wear them, or eat them or kill anybody with them—at least not directly. They are for perception only, designed to open minds. (They can close minds too, and misrepresent, and raise violent emotions and stupid fears that result in destruction.) Napalm, on the other hand, was designed only to produce fear and terror, to drive Vietnamese peasants from their villages into American camps where they could be watched, controlled, and supposedly "protected from their oppressors," the Vietcong.

Q: Is *Inextinguishable Fire* addressed to a national public or an international one?

Farocki: I believe that the film appeals to anyone who saw the pictures from Vietnam on television every night. It has to do with the lifestyle, with consumerism and with the people in North America and Europe above all. It was never really meant as a criticism of the U.S. We criticized political and economic power—just as we did our own government. West Germany didn't participate in the Vietnam war, but the politicians and most of the media vehemently supported the U.S. Even Chancellor Willy

Brandt expressly advocated the U.S. in the war. In this sense we were "internationalists," since the war was the opposition. We tried to make the war our issue.

Godmilow: Because *Inextinguishable Fire* speaks to its German audience very rationally about a specific war they are not responsible for, it creates an unusual space for American audiences—who are or were responsible for the war—to watch it with some distance, exactly because they are not the designated audience of the film. I think some of this space (and perhaps the unusual *frisson* generated by watching German actors take American roles) is lost for American audiences in *What Farocki Taught*, because of the translation into English and the use of American performers. Yet I'd argue that *What Farocki Taught* speaks to an international audience as well because of the analysis it offers, which is pertinent to people in any industrialized country in the world, whether they are engaged in a war or not.

Q: What sorts of directions did you give your actors?

Farocki: I was constantly telling them: "Don't do it that way, not that way! Separate the plot from the words! Separate the acting from your showmanship!" They didn't understand me. The resistance to my directions was at any rate occasionally very interesting. I made two feature-length films with actors: *Between Two Wars* in 1977 and *Before Your Eyes—Vietnam* in 1981. The actors once again rebelled and I understood that not only did they not understand me, but I also didn't have enough to say. You can only develop this kind of acting method over a period of years with a theater company—it's as difficult as learning Chinese mask theater or Javanese dance.

Godmilow: I used non-actors—mostly friends and university colleagues, as did Farocki—to play the parts. When I was shooting, I wasn't sure whether or not I would eventually dub all the film's speeches, so I tried to get performances from these folks that matched Farocki's dubbed speech. It's hard even for professional actors to disavow emotional values when they're speaking lines like these. My actors, after lots of coaching and rehearsals, did well enough, but the complete "alienation effect" was not there, perhaps simply because of the effect of sync sound. Actors opened their mouths and perfectly synchronized speech came out. They became "people" and lost the aspect of just "standing-in" for others. So in the end, I dubbed all the on-camera dialogue, as Farocki had done, and made sure that the dubbed speech appeared to be dubbed, often slipping it a frame or two to move it out of sync just enough to achieve the right effect.

Q: The issue of place seems important to both *Inextinguishable Fire* and *What Farocki Taught*. Did you think that what you were doing was an attempt to have viewers understand their own social, historical or geographical place differently?

Farocki: The issue is interesting and has often occupied my daydreams. How unjust it is that some people are at the right place at the right time and others are not.

Godmilow: Ideologically, I think the first "location" you have to occupy, in order to oppose national policy, is an understanding of where your own labor goes. Who uses it and what is it used for? You have to cut through misinformation, as do the students, who are sure the vacuum cleaner plant they work in is making automatic weapons for the Portuguese, and the self-inflation, as does the female chemist, who asks, "I'm a chemist—what should I do?" Then you have to move your labor out of a system that produces napalm, or even, if you are a university professor, out of misinformation itself. So yes, it's always an individual matter first, requiring self-alienation from systems of thought and production. The film actively encourages audiences to think about their own labor.

107

RACHEL GABARA

MIXING IMPOSSIBLE GENRES

David Achkar and African Autobiographical Documentary (2003*)

David Achkar's 1991 film *Allah Tantou* [God's will] contains autobiographical, biographical and historical (both national and international) layers and first, second and third-person narratives.[1] Documentary material, including photographs, newspapers, newsreels, and home movies, is combined with fictional reenactments as Achkar slips back and forth between personal and historical narrative, telling a piece of the history of a postcolonial West African nation through the story of his father, Marof Achkar, ambassador of newly independent Guinea to the United Nations until his imprisonment in 1968 by President Sékou Touré's government. Achkar's film not only mixes genres, but interrogates its genres and genre itself, exploring the nature of historical narrative, the relationship of autobiography to biography and of both to history. *Allah Tantou* provides us with a new vantage point from which to examine recent theories of genre within three academic fields—literary history and theory (including the study of autobiography), African and postcolonial studies, and film history and theory (including the study of documentary). I will read the film for two generic aspects that scholars in these domains have deemed theoretically impossible, as an African autobiography and as an autobiographical film, focusing on Achkar's use of different voices and visual evidence of the past in his fragmented revision of history.

I have chosen a single film as the subject of this essay, yet *Allah Tantou* is representative of a group of 1990s francophone West African films that are innovative personal as well as historical documentaries.[2] I do not wish to argue, however, for the presence of a *new* genre epitomized by this film, but rather hope to create space within autobiography for works of self-presentation from

*Revised 2015.

many regions of the world and in different media. European and North American academics have excluded, as we shall see, both African autobiography and autobiographical film from the genre of autobiography. More strikingly, both have also been proscribed by theorists of a revolutionary African cinema, working against Hollywood and European art films in the tradition of 1960s Latin American political "Third Cinema." Alastair Fowler proposed that we think about genres as not classes but families, whose "individual members are related in various ways, without necessarily having any single feature shared in common by all."[3] After examining the arguments behind the exclusion of a work such as *Allah Tantou* from the category of autobiography, I will show what we gain when we add it to the family.

The genre of autobiography has been a troubled one in the West at least since Rousseau, yet its difficulties threatened to become overwhelming during the second half of the twentieth century as we learned that the author is dead, the self is hopelessly (or hopefully) fragmentary, and autobiography is therefore uncomfortably indistinguishable from fiction. Critical discussions of autobiography in the 1970s tended to rely nonetheless on the inherent recognizability of the members of the genre. Philippe Lejeune, perhaps the most prolific of all theorists of autobiography, asserted the impossibility of autobiographical hybrids that would be difficult to classify—"autobiography is not a question of degree; it is all or nothing."[4] A multitude of debates about the autobiographicalness of various texts, however, belies both of these assertions. To add to the confusion, many of the same European and North American writers of fiction and theory who had proclaimed either the end or the impossibility of autobiography, including virtually all of the French New Novelists, Roland Barthes, and Jacques Derrida, went on in the 1980s and '90s to write their autobiographies. These unexpected autobiographers and their literary critics sought to extract themselves from the impasse of autobiography by insisting that their work differed from "traditional" life-stories, replacing "autobiography" with terms such as "new autobiography," "autofiction," *romanesque, autobiographique*, "autobiographics," "pseudo-autobiography," and "fictography."

I would like to investigate what happens when we do *not* inherently recognize autobiography, when a text is not just "new" or "pseudo-autobiography," but from a different narrative tradition and in a different form. I will not, however, subdivide "new" from "old" autobiography nor further qualify or yet again rename the genre. Derrida's now famous "counter-law of genre" reminds us that just as a conception of genre must always exist, genres cannot ever have been other than mixed: "A text cannot belong to no genre. Every text participates in one or several genres, there is no genreless text; there is always some genre and always some genres, yet this participation is never a belonging. . . . Marking itself with genre, a text demarcates itself."[5]

Autobiography is always a locus of contact among many genres, at once representation and invention, non-fiction and fiction, in the present and in the past and in the first and third persons. Much contemporary art, whether fiction or non-fiction, exhibits what Ihab Hassan has called a postmodern hybridization of genres,[6] and *Allah Tantou* will be no exception. Achkar's film marks itself off as autobiography, biography, documentary, historical and fictional narrative, participating in genres on all sides of the conventional boundaries of autobiography, but most importantly forcing the spectator to reflect upon these boundaries themselves. It is a postmodern film in the sense that, to quote Thomas Beebee, "the effect that many identify as postmodern is produced by defeating the generic expectations of the reader."[7] An African autobiographical film, however, bears a particular and very peculiar burden of generic expectation.

Avrom Fleishman has noted, using the examples of Arabic, Japanese, and Chinese texts, that a viewpoint he calls "Autobiography as a Distinctive Phenomenon of Western Culture" relies on the invention of various reasons to exclude the many and varied examples of non-Western self-writing from the genre of autobiography.[8] And, in fact, non-African theorists have consistently denied Africans the privilege of autobiography, of telling individual stories. In 1956, in a widely-read article that marked the beginning of a renewed critical interest in the study of autobiography, Georges Gusdorf claimed that the concept of individual identity was uniquely Western, "expresse[d] a concern particular to Western man," and that therefore "authentic" non-Western autobiography was impossible.[9] Paul John Eakin has also maintained, thirty years after Gusdorf and without much additional explanation, that "the very idea of African autobiography sounds paradoxical, and so it is."[10]

In the early 1970s, James Olney claimed, following Gusdorf's lead, that African autobiography is "less as an individual phenomenon than . . . a social one," since an African subject, as opposed to a Western one, is not individually, but rather socially determined.[11] Olney, who in his extensive work on Western autobiography always affirmed the existence of a generic boundary between autobiography and fiction, argued that in Africa autobiography and fiction were one and the same. The novels of Nigerian Chinua Achebe were "something like a supra-personal, multi-generational autobiography of the Ibo people" and Malian Yambo Ouologuem's *Bound to Violence* was "a symbolic autobiography of the entire continent and community of Africa." (*TA* 17) Either Africans cannot write autobiography (or biography), since they cannot write about an individual as distinct from a collective, or they can only write collective autobiography, even when they say they are writing fiction. [. . .] Fredric Jameson has similarly maintained that all "third-world" texts "necessarily project a political dimension in the form of national allegory: *the story of the private individual destiny is always an allegory of the embattled situation of the public third-world culture and society.*"[12] Olney calls all African texts autobiographies and Jameson calls them all national allegories, but both in fact argue the impossibility of African self-writing.

The same contrast between the Western individual and the African collective reappears in theoretical discussions about the nature of African film, more specifically a revolutionary and anticolonial African Third Cinema. Clyde Taylor strictly opposes the Cartesian "I think, therefore I am" to the Xhosa proverb "A person is a person only because of other people" and characterizes African Cinema as a "hero-less narrative."[13] Tahar Cheriaa states that "the main character in African films is always the group, the collective, and that is what is essential,"[14] while Elizabeth Malkmus and Roy Armes agree that there can be no individual hero in African cinema since "an emphasis on a broad issue (such as the anti-colonial struggle) as the primary set of a narrative . . . shifts focus away from the individual (who would be helpless in such a struggle) to the collectivity (which alone has the potential to embody power or to offer viable resistance)."[15] If an individual African life cannot be narrated, whether in fiction or non-fiction, in fictional or documentary film, then neither biography nor autobiography, neither biographical film nor autobiographical film, can exist. Teshome Gabriel, one of the foremost theorists of African cinema, does allow for autobiographical film, although he curiously rejoins Olney by excluding the possibility of *individual* autobiographical film. He warns that: "I do not mean autobiography in its usual Western sense of a narrative by and about a single subject. Rather, I am speaking of a multi-generational and trans-individual autobiography, i.e. a symbolic autobiography where the *collective* subject is the focus ... (perhaps hetero-biography)."[16] It is quite astonishing to discover so many differently situated theorists in agreement that there is no place for postcolonial narration in or of the singular, at the same time that we find a group of African filmmakers who disagree, mixing autobiography and biography, articulating the individual, the personal, the singular, the first person, into history. Furthermore, despite their efforts to reject Western cinematic models and theories, the above theorists of African film in fact continue a Western tradition of denying the possibility of personal history in filmic form.

The study of film was on its way to establishing itself as an academic discipline toward the end of the 1950s when Gusdorf's essay renewed critical interest in the genre of autobiography. It is surprising then, that the question of autobiographical documentary film has rarely been addressed. The earliest reference I have located to a "first-person" voice in film appears in a 1947 article by Jean-Pierre Chartier, in which he discusses not autobiographical film but first-person narration, which he calls interior monologue, in fiction film.[17] The only discussions of autobiography and film in the 1950s and 60s grew out of French *auteur* theory. In a 1959 review of François Truffaut's *400 Blows* in *Cahiers du cinéma*, for example, Fereydoun Hoveyda asserted that "every film is in some sense autobiographical. For better or for worse, film absorbs and reflects the personality of the *auteur*."[18] Annette Insdorf similarly pointed to filmic allusions within Truffaut's entire *oeuvre*, not claiming any one of Truffaut's films as an autobiography but judging that "many ... characters, themes, techniques, and structures are intimate reflections of François Truffaut."[19] Arguing, like Hoveyda (and much like Olney about African texts), that every film is in some sense an autobiography of its *auteur*, Insdorf leaves us with no framework for the analysis of a specific autobiographical film as opposed to the entire body of work of a filmmaker. Nor, more importantly, can we distinguish between a fictional film about a filmmaker making a film, such as Truffaut's *Day for Night* or Federico Fellini's *8 1/2*, and a documentary in which a filmmaker attempts to recount his or her life.

These distinctions were made by Elizabeth Bruss and Philippe Lejeune in articles about autobiographical film published in the 1980s, yet both declared its impossibility based on the untranslatability of the concept of autobiography from written to filmic narrative. Bruss argued not only that autobiographical film cannot exist, but that its existence would threaten the existence of autobiography altogether: "If film and video do come to replace writing as our chief means of recording, informing, and entertaining, and if (as I hope to show) there is no real cinematic equivalent for autobiography, then the autobiographical act as we have known it for the past four hundred years could indeed become more and more recondite, and eventually extinct."[20] Lejeune began his brief consideration of autobiographical film with a series of questions: "Can the 'I' express itself in the cinema? Can a film be autobiographical? Why not? But is it the same thing as when we speak of literary autobiography? ... Is autobiography possible in the cinema?"[21] He ultimately, like Bruss, answered in the negative, since "It is not possible to be on both sides of the camera at the same time, in front of it and behind it" (CA 8).

Several scholars of film have hinted at other ways of thinking about autobiography in film, which will allow me to begin my reading of *Allah Tantou*. In his analysis of avant-garde diary films from the 1960s and '70s, P. Adams Sitney drew a parallel, rather than Bruss and Lejeune's stark contrast, between literary and filmic autobiography. Sitney maintained, remembering instead of trying to forget the difficulties of self-narration in writing, that "filmmakers resemble the literary autobiographers who dwell upon, and find their most powerful and enigmatic metaphors for, the very aporias, the contradictions, the gaps, the failures involved in trying to make language (or film) substitute for experience and memory."[22] Michael Renov, who has been interested in films that construct "subjectivity as a site of instability—flux, drift, perpetual revision—rather than coherence," reminds us that artifice is a necessary component of autobiographical narration in any medium.[23] Jim Lane notes that the autobiographical documentary always contains at least two voices, always "bears the mark of personal, actual events and a consciousness that bears witness to, and forms an opinion about, these events through documentary representation."[24] Filmic autobiography, with its material, visible split between director or filmer and actor or filmed self bemoaned by Bruss and Lejeune, troubles our conventional notions of coherent identity and provides us with new forms in which to explore and represent fragmented subjectivity.

No analytic framework has been established, however, for a study of autobiographical film. Very little work has been done on genre in film in general, and what has been done has been surprisingly limited. Alan Williams pointed out almost twenty years ago that virtually all critical studies of filmic genre have dealt exclusively with North American films.[25] This is still the case, not only for the considerations of autobiography and film above but also for the essays collected in Nick Browne's *Refiguring American Film Genres*, those in the second edition of Barry Keith Grant's *Film Genre Reader*, for Steve Neale's *Genre*, and Rick Altman's recent *Film/Genre*.[26] All of the genre categories discussed by these critics are therefore derived from North American film history, and most often from Hollywood studio films. Canonical Western European films occasionally make a brief appearance, but the Latin American, East Asian, and African cinemas are notably absent from the debate. Moreover, scholars have overwhelmingly chosen to study the "genre film" rather than the ways in which ideas of genre circulate in film. Grant's "comprehensive bibliography" is thus divided into the following generic subsections: comedy films, crime films, disaster films, epic films, erotic films, film noir, gangster films, horror films, melodrama, musical films, science fiction films, sports films, war films, western films, and miscellaneous. Judith Hess Wright limits herself to the western, science fiction, horror, and gangster films.[27] These categories are of very little use to the study of African film, especially of African documentary. Williams suggests that we classify cinematic texts within only three, more broadly construed genres—narrative film, experimental/avant-garde film, and documentary (the second two of which have no place at all in Grant's long list)—that would accommodate a wider range of films from all over the world (RGC 121). But even this system will not provide an easy place for Achkar's film, which contains aspects of all three.

Allah Tantou begins with a dedication in white letters against a black background—"To my father, and to all of the prisoners of Camp Boiro and elsewhere"—followed by 8mm home movie footage of a family decorating their Christmas tree. These images, which then shift to footage of a father picking up and holding his young son, are accompanied by David Achkar's first-person voice-over, stating that "Many sons admire their fathers. I hardly knew my father. What I know of him, I know from what my mother or his friends have told me. But also from what he wrote to us." The title credits to the film quickly follow, over an image of a man writing while sitting on the floor of a prison cell. We gather from the credits and subsequent narration that this is an actor, Michel Montanary, playing the role of the filmmaker's father Marof Achkar, who died in 1971, and that the boy in the home movies is his son David. The next images are of the letters that Marof Achkar wrote to his family from prison, which are then replaced by more 8mm footage, now of a government ceremony. We hear another voice-over, but this time it is "Marof Achkar," that is to say, the actor playing the role of David Achkar's father, who speaks in the first person and in the present tense.[28] He tells us of the hero's welcome he received upon his return from abroad, just before his arrest and imprisonment at Camp Boiro during one of Sékou Touré's purges of his own government. Achkar then cuts from the 8mm footage to a series of photographs of Marof Achkar in his official capacity at the U.N. and newspaper headlines from articles about him: "Achkar Calling Tune," "That New African Bombshell," "Africa's Clark Gable Warns Denmark."

I have as yet described only the first three minutes of *Allah Tantou*, but the fragmented and polyphonic nature of this unconventional documentary is already evident. David Achkar, Marof Achkar's son, speaks in a first-person autobiographical voice-over in the film, sometimes addressing the spectator and at other times addressing his father. "Marof Achkar" also uses the first person, both in voice-overs and in diegetic dialogue within the scenes that reenact his time in prison. Third-person narration within David Achkar's voice-over and the incorporated newsreel footage is occasionally joined to the two first-person voices. These layered voices together narrate the story of Marof Achkar's political career: the son provides both personal and historical information; the "father" tells his personal and political experiences and realizations while in prison, from the inside; the newspapers and newsreels document his political life prior to his imprisonment, from the outside. Achkar combines elements of the fictional narrative, the experimental/avant-garde, and the documentary genres, in a film that forces us to question our preconceptions about genre. He tells an autobiographical and biographical story of two individuals, challenging the impossibility of African autobiography, and tells it in filmic form, challenging the impossibility of autobiographical film.

"Marof Achkar"'s voice-over continues as Achkar cuts to another scene, during which Montanary is sitting on a stool in an large, empty cell. As the camera circles over "Achkar"'s head, we learn that it has been "197 days since my arrest on October 17, 1968," and that he still does not know the charges brought against him by a special court, composed of President Sékou Touré's friends and family. As the voice-over progresses, the reenactment images are replaced by 8mm documentary footage of crowds cheering at the side of a road, welcoming Marof Achkar home. "Achkar"'s voice-over is then replaced by that of the filmmaker, who accompanies more home movie footage with "it is here in Coyah," a village fifty-four kilometers from Conakry, "that you were born." Achkar then jumps to the beginning of his father's political career:

> 1958. Guinea, your country, led by Sékou Touré, your president, says "no" to the constitution proposed by General de Gaulle, becoming the first independent francophone African country. Sékou Touré becomes a myth, Africa's providential man. A singer and dancer with the Ballets Africains, you, like so many others, put yourself at the service of your country and begin a brilliant career at the U.N.

Speaking to us of his father, he at the same time speaks *to* his father, apostrophizes him, bringing him to life in and by means of his film.

Achkar further traces his father's political trajectory via newsreel footage of him speaking about human rights in South Africa in his role as ambassador to the United Nations. The narrator of the newsreel identifies "Achkar Marof, of Guinea, chairman of the United Nations Special Committee on the policies of apartheid in South Africa," and provides information both about apartheid in South Africa and the ways in which the U.N. was working against it, mentioning a special meeting of this U.N. committee in Stockholm. The members of the committee, including Marof Achkar, are listed for us as we see footage of him shaking hands with other dignitaries in Sweden. Achkar then cuts abruptly to a reenactment scene showing "Marof Achkar" asleep on the floor of his prison cell. This strategy of juxtaposition emphasizes the cruel shock of Marof Achkar's fall from international renown to miserable isolation and imprisonment. Achkar stresses the irony of his father's transition from investigator of human rights violations in apartheid South Africa to political prisoner of the black African government of his own country.

David Achkar reflexively manipulates, then, the multiple visual media, still and moving pictures, documentary evidence and fictional reenactments, that make up *Allah Tantou*. He links the different image-fragments that make up his narrative through both conjunctive and disjunctive uses of sound. The dialogue and voice-overs often overlap or bleed over from one type of image to another, continuing over a cut, for example, from a reenactment to 8mm home movie footage. This mixing of diegetic levels serves various purposes. The conjunction of a reenactment voice-over with images from home movies often produces an effect of focalization as a result of which the footage seems to constitute the memories of "Marof Achkar." This could function to add depth to his character, to make him seem more lifelike, yet Achkar consistently juxtaposes the documentary photographs and footage of Marof Achkar with the "Marof Achkar" of the reenactments. Since the two quite simply look like two different people, it is impossible for the viewer to "believe in" the character. [29] No attempt has been made to trick the spectator into confusing father and actor and believing that this is an "unmediated recording of reality;" Achkar explained that "I shot [the film] with my cousin. He doesn't really look like my father—he's my mother's nephew. He didn't even see the home movies."[30] At the same time, however, the transitions back from reenactment to footage clearly marked as documentary remind us that Marof Achkar and his son David had off-camera lives. The film rejects generic categorization either as only documentary or only fiction.

The mainstream documentary tradition has been one of coherent third-person narration (the infamous "voice of God") rather than of Achkar's fragmented first person. When Achkar went to Amnesty International and requested funding to finish his film, "they said I shouldn't have made a film about my father. I thought that was nonsense" (MH 112). An Amnesty human rights film should speak in the third person and not the first, about a group or collective and not an individual, and especially not about a member of one's family. Bill Nichols has pointed out that, according to convention, "subjectivity, rather than enhancing the impact of a documentary, may actually jeopardize its credibility."[31] Hayden White argues that the insertion of the first-person voice into historical narrative constitutes the difference between narration and narrativization, between "a discourse that openly adopts a perspective that looks out on the world and reports it and a discourse that feigns to make the world speak itself and speak itself as a story."[32] Both Nichols and White draw on the work of Roland Barthes, who wrote that the "objective" historian eliminates all traces of an "I" from his discourse, so that "the (hi)story seems to recount itself."[33] Achkar does not want history to seem to tell itself, but instead makes us aware of the fact that it is being told, using not just one but two first-person voices in his biographical and historical narrative.

Achkar complicates conventional documentary narration not just by his use of the first person, but also by drawing attention to the fact that any history is a narrative (re)construction of the past. We know that "Marof Achkar"'s words are either drawn directly from his letters and prison writings or scripted by his son based on what his mother and his father's friends have told him, but Achkar keeps us off balance, nowhere specifying whether, or when, he is citing a source as opposed to extrapolating or imagining. Achkar has imagined and then reenacted his father's time in prison since no documentary images of this period of his life exist. These reenactments do not belong to any recognizable filmic genre, are neither realistically documentary nor realistically fictional, and disconcert the spectator. The camerawork is heavily stylized and does not attempt to convey documentary authenticity; Achkar said that "for the mise-en-scene of this drama, I decided to stay away from any realism."[34] In several of the reenactments, we simultaneously hear "Marof Achkar" participate in dialogue and speak in a voice-over and are jolted into remembering that the scene, as we are watching and hearing it, could not possibly have taken place. The scenes that recreate "Marof Achkar"'s torture in prison are the starkest of the film; we see him hanging on a bar suspended from the ceiling, hands and feet tied, alone against a black background that cloaks even the walls of the cell. The most crucial reenactment scene, however, is that of the confession that this torture was designed to extract. In December of 1969, after seven months in prison, "Marof Achkar" finally learns that the charges against him are of financial mismanagement and his captors type a confession for him to read as they record his statement. They tell him to read with conviction—"You were an actor. You know the routine." The spectator knows not only that Marof Achkar was an actor and dancer by training, but that "Marof Achkar" is here being played by an actor, as are his captors. These words have been scripted by the filmmaker for ironic effect, and our awareness of this reflexivity blocks the creation of any "reality effect" in a scene that could have easily been written and filmed to grip the spectator through identification and suspense.

"Marof Achkar" then continues, "My name is Marof Achkar. Born in 1930 in Coyah, son of Moustapha Achkar and Damaë Camara. Married, four legitimate children, artist, ex-Ambassador." This first-person autobiographical narrative is followed by the false confession that has been scripted for him, in which he claims to have been part of a French colonial network and a traitor to his country. In another reflexive voice-over, "Marof Achkar" states that "It's a script, a bad script" and Achkar cuts from the reenactment to a series of photographs of Marof Achkar in Paris and on a world tour with the Ballets Africains in the 1950s. These documentary images combine with the preceding scene and the voice-over to inform the spectator that this, in fact, is what Marof Achkar had been doing in Europe, to remind us once again of the ridiculous nature of the concocted confession. Achkar then cuts back to the prison reenactment scene, to "Marof Achkar"'s confession that in 1964, when he became Ambassador, he went on the C.I.A. payroll and recruited other Guineans to betray their country. He reads that he received $10,000 for his treasonous acts, at which point his captors stop him and ask him to change this sum to $500,000, since "It's a much more serious sum . . . The People must think that you earned a lot." An elderly Imam who has been watching the proceedings tells "Marof Achkar" to be sure to include his participation in Nazi networks as well. The script, written by those who imprisoned Achkar and rewritten by his son for this reenactment, has gone from ridiculous to patently ludicrous. Not only is Marof Achkar's innocence affirmed without a doubt in the mind of the spectator, but Touré's strategy of deceiving "the People" for their own good is unmasked in all of its hypocrisy. David Achkar sets *Allah Tantou* as a document against the confession represented within it, rewriting its false rewriting of his father's political work and commitment.

Nichols observes that another "risk of credibility" is involved in the use of reenactments in documentary film; the supposedly indexical bond between image and reality is "ruptured," since the spectator knows that "what occurred occurred *for* the camera" and is thus an "imaginary event" (*RR* 21). He draws on White's work to remind us, however, that this is a false problem, since all history depends on reenactment; "History . . . is always a matter of story telling: our reconstruction of events must impose meaning and order on them."[35] Written nonfiction also often "reenacts," attaching invented dialogue to historical accounts, in order to acquire more, and not less, credibility for its narrative. The difference is that writing, unlike film, is not "burdened with the problem of an actual actor who would approximate without being the historical personage" (*RR* 22). David Achkar not only bears but brandishes the burden of the need for a "stand-in" for his father in his autobiographical documentary. As a result of the obvious inauthenticity of these reenactments, the spectator is never allowed to forget that "Marof Achkar" is not and cannot be Marof Achkar, since Marof Achkar was shot and killed, was permanently taken away from his son after suffering for many years in prison.

Analyzing suture, the knitting of the spectator into the film he or she is watching through a process of identification and desire, Kaja Silverman has noted that classic film narrative works not only to "activate the viewer's desire and transform one shot into a signifier for the next, but . . . to deflect attention away from the level of enunciation to that of the fiction."[36] Like fiction film, the documentary genre has its own narrative conventions that shift attention away from the level of enunciation in order to convince us that it is simply presenting the world "as it is." Nichols has described the reflexive mode of documentary film, however, as that in which "the representation of the historical world becomes, itself, the topic of cinematic meditation," the filmmaker engages in "metacommentary" and speaks about "the process of representation itself" (*RR* 56).[37] Whereas conventional documentary realism "provides unproblematic access to the world," in reflexive documentary "realist access to the world, the ability to provide persuasive evidence, the possible of indisputable argument, the unbreakable bond between an indexical image and that which it represents—all these notions prove suspect" (*RR* 57, 60). In *Allah Tantou*, Achkar uses juxtaposition to teach the spectator how to read, never telling us what to think but forcing us to interpret the fragments with which we are presented. He refuses to give us what we expect from documentary, never letting the images of history seem to tell their own story. The film's reflexivity breaks the illusion that classical Hollywood cinema maintains by means of invisible editing; Achkar refuses to let the spectator be drawn into identification with either character or camera.

Allah Tantou makes evident the extent to which Marof Achkar's life, both as a dancer and a politician, was publicly recorded. Yet even with all of this visual evidence, a public hero can be "rewritten" and disgraced or forgotten. How can his son use the images of his father that have survived him? How can he connect them to resurrect his father both for himself and in the public mind and eye? How can Achkar accomplish the biographical documentary of a dead man—a man, moreover, that he barely knew? Oliver Lovesey has claimed that despite the problems with Jameson's formulation of *all* "third-world" literature as national allegory, the genre of the prison diary is "one of the defining genres of African literature and one of the best examples of 'national allegory.' "[38] As written by Wole Soyinka, Ngugi wa Thiong'o and Kwame Nkrumah, among others, the African prison diary is a reflexive genre, which "brushes against the grain of official histories of the prisoner's activities; it rewrites official 'master narratives' of national history" (APD 214). In *Allah Tantou*, David Achkar films his father's prison diary for him, in his absence, telling his father's untold story and re-establishing his "good name" against the false confession, part of Touré's master narrative, that had been his official biography. He then reflects upon the link between his father's story and his nation's history. Over 8mm footage of Marof Achkar speaking at a government congress, "Marof Achkar"'s voice-over from his prison cell continues:

> My son. Insults are the weapons that remain at the disposition of the weak when it seems that nothing more is to be gained with a conciliatory attitude. I was so well integrated into his regime that I was not able to sense what was about to happen. I saw things as if a student; I could neither see nor understand what was hiding behind each of their attitudes, each of their words. I will never be so naive again.

Addressing his son, the "father" recounts, from beyond the grave, the realization of having participated in a government to whose crimes he had been blind. In 8mm footage from another congress, a banner proclaims that "The Revolution is Exigency," quoting the title of a poem published by Touré in 1978, which begins "Let us resolutely destroy/Any betrayer of the nation." The filmmaker then reciprocates his father's address in another voice-over:

> Victim of a purge. Every three or four years, politically weak governments that have experienced failures must accuse and condemn some of their members in order to justify themselves. You were among the first. Your voice and your personality, which had become too strong abroad, frightened them. Once the Revolutionary Committee got what it wanted, a signed, recorded, and filed deposition, it could be used at any moment. This was how the regime functioned. No-one was safe from it.

We hear overlapping and fragmentary meditations on the past, present, and future of Africa: "Illusion, deception, realism, efficiency, these are the stages the young African diplomat goes through;" "It is too early to judge the evolution of democracy in Africa"; "Marxist theory, which is a leftist ideology. . . ." Over newsreel footage of Cuba, juxtaposed with footage of African women dancing and then footage of Nelson Mandela giving a speech, different voices claim that African countries are too weak and too underdeveloped, that Marxism encourages a cult of personality as evidenced by Stalin, Mao, and Castro, that the colonized still need their ex-colonizers, that colonization was a crime against humanity. These chaotic theories and images present but do not resolve the dilemmas facing not just Guinea, but all postcolonial African nations—democracy versus socialism, Christianity versus Islam, tradition versus modernity.

In a very real sense, then, Marof Achkar's story *is* shown to be a national allegory; his tragedy is not only the tragedy of other Guineans, but of innumerable other Africans. We must examine, however, the way that David Achkar concludes the story of his father's odyssey through politics in the reenactment of his time in prison. "Marof Achkar" physically and mentally deteriorates into blindness and delirium, considering suicide before reaching a state of calm resolve. As he writes in his cell, he says that:

> I hope that I will learn more, since I hope to find freedom and personal

> fulfillment through this ordeal . . . I have never felt as free as I do now. Of course it is difficult to be in prison, but this is only physical subjugation. My mind has never been as free as it is now. Because I know exactly who I am and what I want, where I am going and why. I know precisely my ideal. . . . I hope to be able to begin everything again very soon. I regret having participated in this government.

This personal resolution stands in stark contrast to the non-resolution of the collage of images and quotations that allegorized Marof Achkar's experience. "Marof Achkar" has come to certain realizations as an individual and not as a participant in a national collective. David Achkar then takes over the voice-over, providing most, but not all, of the last chapter of his father's story. We learn that, after a pact was signed between Touré and Amilcar Cabral, "On November 22, 1970, a commando unit of the Portuguese army, then involved in a colonial war with Guinea Bissau, the neighboring country, landed in Conakry" to liberate their citizens from Camp Boiro. Marof Achkar was free for a few hours but was then easily recaptured because of his blindness. In the following years, Touré accused half of his population and nine tenths of his government of treason; there were hangings in Conakry, "but no news of you." We see photographs of other Camp Boiro prisoners, one by one, in silence. In 1971, David Achkar and his mother were sent into exile and in 1984, after Touré's death, the camp was opened following a military coup. Not until 1985 did Achkar and his mother receive a death certificate, of which we see a close-up, that stated that Marof Achkar had been shot on January 26, 1971. The last words of the film, however, are in "Marof Achkar"'s voice, over 8mm footage of cars traveling along a dirt road; "It was on a morning such as this, on a road like this one, that I was shot, in January 1971." Achkar cuts to white and then fades in to the image of a handwritten letter signed by Marof Achkar, its last words "Dedicated to my son F.M. David Achkar on his tenth birthday." Through the medium of film, in another joltingly reflexive moment, David Achkar has allowed his father to pronounce an impossible autobiographical statement—"I was shot." The film ends in a first-person voice passed from son to father; the dedication from son to father that began the film has reciprocated the one in this last letter.

Olney praised those African autobiographies in which the individual presents himself as "representative" of African experience (*TA* 37) and Jameson, responding to the criticism of Aijaz Ahmad, once again defined national allegory as "the coincidence of the personal story and the 'tale of the tribe.'"[39] Yet neither David nor Marof Achkar's history "coincides" with that of Guinea; an essential aspect of the tragic death of Achkar's father is that his murderer was the leader of Guinea and a hero of African independence. Marof Achkar's political trajectory was one of an individual destroyed in the name of a collective, of a People's revolution, and his son has used a formally reflexive text that combines first-person autobiography and biography in the second and third person, to resist his father's erasure from Touré's version of Guinean history.

Touré himself, moreover, linked what he considered to be an un-African individualism to an un-socialist realist art: "Africa is essentially "communocratic." Collective life and social solidarity provide its customs with a humanist basis that many peoples could envy . . . Yet who has not observed the progression of personal egoism in the social circles contaminated by the spirit of the colonizers? Who has not heard the defense of the theory of art for art's sake . . . the theory of every man for himself?"[40] He believed that the cinema should never be anything but "an instrument, a means, a tool put to the use of the Revolution;" it should not create, but rather be an "adaptation of what has existed."[41] It is therefore not surprising that David Achkar would choose to address the relationship between his father as an individual and Touré's repressive collectivism in a film that, although not a purely formalist work of "art for art's sake," does reject formulaic realism. Yet a tension with regard to the political value of formal experimentation has pervaded theories of African Third Cinema. This is evident within the work of Teshome Gabriel, who has praised, like Touré, radical content in conventionally realist narrative, claiming that "Third Cinema film-makers rarely move their camera and sets unless the story calls for it" (TC 60). Gabriel has also stated, however, that anticolonial films "try to expand the boundaries of cinematic language and devise new stylistic approaches appropriate to their revolutionary goals," that revolutionary filmmakers seek "the demystification of representational practices as part of the process of liberation."[42] *Allah Tantou* has been open to criticism for *how* it tells its story, both for an excessive concern with form and for a focus on the individual. Yet it is Achkar's innovative style and use of a first-person autobiographical and biographical voice, his many subversions of our generic expectations, that enable the fashioning of a historical narrative asserting an African perspective not only on colonization and decolonization, but on the complications and crimes of African post-independence politics as well.

In "Marof Achkar"'s voice-over following his discovery of inner peace while in prison, he says that he loves his wife and children and that "We want to be continued after our children. Who wants to be forgotten, afterwards?" What can save one from being forgotten? Raw documentary evidence is not enough, not if it is denied by a dictator or lies hidden in archives, and in any case, no one life can ever be completely recorded. David Achkar has made meaning from a combination of evidence and artifice, from the public documentary images of his father and from reenactments based on the letters, books, and memoirs his father wrote in prison. By doing so, he has not only "continued" Marof Achkar, saved him from "*l'oubli*," but has also been one of the first to denounce Touré's reign of terror in Guinea. And, at the same time, Achkar has told a story that is his own, saying of *Allah Tantou* that "I felt I would only exist once I had finished the film" (MH 112). Intertwining private story and history, the personal and the historical, he has placed his family at the center of national and international, colonial and postcolonial, history. Filmmaker Raoul Peck has claimed that the autobiographical elements of his 1992 documentary, *Lumumba: Death of the Prophet*, were designed to draw the viewer into the story.[43] Though this may be part of the case, it is also true that Peck, like Achkar, is drawn into History by his film, as both have drawn History into their stories.

Achkar has made a film that in some ways resembles the introspective avant-garde diary films discussed by Sitney, yet unlike Jerome Hill and Stan Brakhage he looks outward rather than inward in his reflexive exploration of personal identity and history. I have stressed the autobiographical aspect of the film, but it is clear that *Allah Tantou* is as much biography as autobiography. I would argue, however, that the biographical neither dilutes nor destroys the autobiographical. Achkar shows us that stories of self and other(s) are necessarily interwoven. He structures his film around his relationships to an individual hero, his father, whose story is inextricably linked to the stories of the communities and nations within which both have lived and acted, achieving an imbrication of the personal within the historical without any dissolution or deprecation of the individual. The individual is in fact glorified and memorialized in connection with his role in a collective struggle. *Allah Tantou* places an emphasis on the individual that cannot and should not be allegorized away; not only is the personal political, but the political personal. Individual here in no way implies the stereotypical Enlightenment model of the unitary, coherent subject; the complex narrative construction of the film precludes any risk of such an understanding.

Both African autobiography and autobiographical film are not only possible, but have much to teach African and non-African scholars of fictional and documentary literature and film. Declarations of the impossibility of African autobiography deny African writers and filmmakers the individuality previously denied them by colonial powers. Declarations of the impossibility of autobiographical film ignore the global proliferation of autobiographical films and videos. In order to escape the critical impasse that results from a restrictive model of autobiography, we must instead choose to conceptualize a genre that has flexible and porous borders, one that includes rather than excludes works such as Achkar's. These new members of the family of autobiographical texts offer innovative possibilities for the interrelation of autobiography, biography, and history, expanding the boundaries of what has been considered first-person narration. *Allah Tantou*, impossible to theorize according to our existing generic frameworks for understanding autobiographical as well as African narratives, shows us our shortcomings and dares us to account for it.

NOTES

1. *Allah Tantou*, dir. David Achkar, perf. Michel Montanary, Archibald Films, 1991. All translations mine. Achkar died suddenly in 1998 at the age of 38, having completed a second film, *Kiti: Justice in Guinea* (1996), but leaving a third unfinished.
2. Other examples include Jean-Marie Teno's *Africa, I Will Fleece You* and *Vacation in the Country* (1992 and 2000, Cameroon), Raoul Peck's *Lumumba: Death of the Prophet* (1992, Haiti/Congo), Mweze Ngangura's *The King, the Cow, and the Banana Tree* (1994, Congo), Samba Félix Ndiaye's *Letter to Senghor* (1997, Senegal), and Abderrahmane Sissako's *Rostov-Luanda* (1997, Mauritania).
3. Alastair Fowler, *Kinds of Literature* (Cambridge: Harvard Univ. Press, 1982) 41.
4. Philippe Lejeune, *Le pacte autobiographique* (Paris: Seuil, 1975) 25. My translation.
5. Jacques Derrida, "The Law of Genre," trans. Avital Ronell, *Glyph* 7 (1980): 212. I have slightly modified Ronell's translation.
6. Ihab Hassan, *The Postmodern Turn* (Ohio State Univ. Press, 1987) 170.
7. Thomas Beebee, *The Ideology of Genre* (University Park: Pennsylvania State Univ. Press, 1994) 9.
8. Avrom Fleishman, *Figures of Autobiography: The Language of Self-Writing in Victorian and Modern England* (Berkeley: Univ. of California Press, 1983) 472.
9. Georges Gusdorf, "Conditions and Limits of Autobiography," *Autobiography: Essays Theoretical and Critical*, ed. James Olney (Princeton: Princeton University Press, 1980) 29.
10. Paul John Eakin, *Fictions in Autobiography* (Princeton: Princeton Univ. Press, 1985) 200.
11. James Olney, *Tell Me Africa* (Princeton: Princeton Univ. Press, 1973) viii; hereafter cited in text as *TA*.
12. Fredric Jameson, "Third-World Literature in the Era of Multinational Capitalism," *Social Text* 15 (1986): 69.
13. Clyde Taylor, "Black Cinema in the Post-aesthetic Era," *Questions of Third Cinema*, ed. Jim Pines and Paul Willemen (London: British Film Institute, 1989) 90, 106.
14. Tahar Cheriaa, "Le groupe et le héros," *Camera nigra: Le discours du film africain*, ed. Victor Bachy (Paris: L'Harmattan, 1984) 109. My translation.
15. Elizabeth Malkmus and Roy Armes, *Arab and African Film Making* (London: Zed Books, 1991) 210.
16. Teshome Gabriel, "Third Cinema as Guardian of Popular Memory: Towards a Third Aesthetics," *Questions of Third Cinema* 58; hereafter cited in text as TC.
17. Jean-Pierre Chartier, "Les 'films à la première personne' et l'illusion de réalité au cinéma," *La revue du cinéma* 1.4 (1947): 32.
18. Fereydoun Hoveyda, "The First Person Plural," *Cahiers du cinéma, the 1950s: Neo-realism, Hollywood, New Wave*, ed. Jim Hillier (Cambridge: Harvard Univ. Press, 1985) 55.
19. Annette Insdorf, *François Truffaut* (New York: Cambridge Univ. Press, 1994) 173.
20. Elizabeth Bruss, "Eye for I: Unmaking Autobiography in Film," *Autobiography: Essays Theoretical and Critical* 296-7.
21. Lejeune, "Cinéma et autobiographie: problèmes de vocabulaire," *Revue belge du cinéma* (1986): 7–8. My translation; hereafter cited in text as CA.
22. P. Adams Sitney, "Autobiography in Avant-Garde Film," *Millenium Film Journal* 1.1 (1977–8): 61. Jay Ruby has similarly found "personal art films" to be the filmic equivalent of literary autobiography. ["The Image Mirrored: Reflexivity and the Documentary Film," *New Challenges for Documentary*, ed. Alan Rosenthal (Berkeley: Univ. of California Press, 1988) 72.]

23. Michael Renov, "The Subject in History: The New Autobiography in Film and Video," *Afterimage* 17.1 (1989): 5.
24. Jim Lane, "Notes on Theory and the Autobiographical Documentary Film in America," *Wide Angle* 15.3 (1993): 32.
25. Alan Williams, "Is a Radical Genre Criticism Possible?" *Quarterly Review of Film Studies* 9.2 (Spring 1984): 122; hereafter cited in text as RGC.
26. Barry Keith Grant, ed., *Film Genre Reader II* (Austin: University of Texas Press, 1995); Nick Brown, ed., *Refiguring American Film Genres: History and Theory* (Berkeley: Univ. of California Press, 1998); Steve Neale, *Genre* (London: British Film Institute, 1980); Rick Altman, *Film/Genre* (London: BFI, 1999).
27. Judith Hess Wright, "Genre Films and the Status Quo," *Film Genre Reader II* 41.
28. I will use quotation marks when referring to David Achkar's father as imagined or reenacted in his son's film in order to distinguish between "Marof Achkar" as acted by Montanary and the real Marof Achkar as represented in photographs, newsreels, and home movies. Without a first name, Achkar will always refer to the filmmaker, David Achkar.
29. It is interesting that several critics, including Frank Ukadike and Stephen Holden, have incorrectly asserted that David Achkar himself is playing the role of his father, either not noticing or resisting Achkar's reflexive strategy in an overly autobiographizing reading of the film. See N. Frank Ukadike, "The Other Voices of Documentary: *Allah Tantou* and *Afrique, je te plumerai*," *Iris* 18 (1995): 81; Ukadike, "African Cinematic Reality: The Documentary Tradition as an Emerging Trend," *Research in African Literatures* 26.3 (1995): 88–96; Stephen Holden, "Independence in Africa and Death in High Places," *New York Times* 30 Sept. 1992: C18.
30. Pat Aufderheide, "Memory and History in Subsaharan African Cinema: An Interview with David Achkar," *Visual Anthropology Review* 9.2 (Fall 1993): 112; hereafter cited in text as MH.
31. Bill Nichols, *Representing Reality* (Bloomington: Indiana University Press, 1991) 29–30; hereafter cited in text as *RR*.
32. Hayden White, *The Content of the Form* (Baltimore: Johns Hopkins University Press, 1987) 2.
33. Roland Barthes, "Le discours de l'histoire," (1967) *Le bruissement de la langue* (Paris: Seuil [Points], 1984) 168. My translation.
34. "Allah Tantou," *Le film africain* 2 (Mai 1991). My translation.
35. Bill Nichols, *Blurred Boundaries: Questions of Meaning in Contemporary Culture* (Bloomington: Indiana University Press, 1994) 32.
36. Kaja Silverman, *The Subject of Semiotics* (New York, 1983), p. 214.
37. Ukadike has briefly examined *Allah Tantou* and Teno's *Africa, I Will Fleece You* in relation to Nichols' category of reflexive documentary. See "African Cinematic Reality: The Documentary Tradition as an Emerging Trend."
38. Oliver Lovesey, "The African Prison Diary as 'National Allegory,'" *Nationalism vs. Internationalism* (Tübingen: Stauffenberg, 1996) 210; hereafter cited in text as APD.
39. Fredric Jameson, "A Brief Response," *Social Text* 17 (1987): 26.
40. Ahmed Sékou Touré, *L'Afrique en marche, t. X* (Conakry: Imprimerie nationale Patrice Lumumba, 1967) 520. My translation.
41. Ahmed Sékou Touré, *La révolution culturelle* (Conakry: Imprimerie nationale Patrice Lumumba, 1969) 360, 364. My translation.
42. Teshome Gabriel, *Third Cinema in the Third World: An Aesthetics of Liberation* (Ann Arbor: UMI Research Press, 1982) 24, 95.
43. Response to a question from the author after a screening of the film at the Margaret Mead Film and Video Festival, American Museum of Natural History, November 1998.

108

JEAN-MARIE TENO

WRITING ON WALLS

The Future of African Documentary Cinema (2010)

In following the issues and day-to-day workings of a neighbourhood video-club in Ouagadougou, home of the FESPACO and capital of African cinema, my latest work, Sacred Places, *allowed me to question my own work as a filmmaker in Africa, and to consider the direction that cinema is taking on the continent.*

Offering a personal reading of both past and present documentary filmmaking in Africa, this article aims to continue that reflection, raising one of today's most salient questions: that of transmission. As the visionary Abbo reminds us in Sacred Places: *"In the beginning was the word . . ." But who is speaking? And to say what to whom?*

When I arrived in Ouagadougou for my first FESPACO in 1983, I was struck by the intensity and abundance of debates about African film. In the endless discussions to define African cinema and its future, one of the points that kept coming up was the impression that the first films by African filmmakers were either documentary in style or of documentary value.

This overriding view apparently emerged as most of these first films—*Afrique sur Seine, Contras' City, Borom Sarret,* to name but a few—took place in urban settings, with characters often playing their real-life roles. Moreover, the content of these stories, often rooted in the social and political context of the time, led many people somewhat disparagingly to equate these films with documentaries, at a time when documentary film had not achieved the levels of popularity it has gained in recent years with the films of Michael Moore and other European and American directors.

If realism in African cinema led critics to associate narrative films with documentaries at a time when documentary did not have the appeal of fiction film, who can blame African filmmakers for turning their backs on realistic stories set in African cities to embrace stories set in the imagined and idealized village, giving rise to what became referred to as "calabash cinema" in the Eighties?

Along with Idrissa Ouedraogo and his award-winning films *Yaaba* and *Tilai,* the most striking example of this to my mind is Souleymane Cissé, who first made *Den Muso*, then went on to make what I consider to be one of the masterpieces of African cinema: *Baara*. Released in 1978, *Baara* is a well-crafted film that has barely aged and can be seen as an example of an African cinema that is both challenging and popular. Cissé went on to make *Finye*, before completing *Yeelen*, one of African cinema's most mysterious, complex and sophisticated films, bringing him the international recognition he deserved and encouraging him to embark on the strange adventure of the film *Waati*, a multi-headed monster that almost sunk his career.

Before Cissé, the very first wave of African filmmakers had successfully appropriated the film medium in their efforts to accompany the social and political struggles of the early years of African independence. Their works directly and indirectly challenged colonial discourse and offered African audiences representations that promoted dignity and gave them the hope, strength and confidence to embark on the task of inventing a future in a turbulent and changing world.

The Sixties saw the emergence of masters such as Mustapha Alassane, who went from narrative, to documentary, to animation to address issues that were relevant at that time, and which remain relevant today, fifty years later. One fully appreciates the talent of this man when working, as I currently am, with young avant-garde filmmakers in the US, who still use 16mm today to reinvent, create and propose daring metaphors about their lives. In his 1966 film *Le Retour d'un aventurier*, Alassane did just that and more in his little village in Niger, creating a parody of the western to brilliantly and metaphorically address the intrusion of colonial culture in African societies. This is another example of what popular culture can be at its best: inventive, funny and relevant to the contemporary socio-political situation.

By reappropriating ethnographic codes and blending them with elements of oral tradition, and specifically the griot's narrative style, Beninese filmmaker Richard de Meideros' short film *Teke, Hymne au Borgou* (1974) paved a path we are still following many years later.

Both Mustapha Alassane and Richard de Medeiros shared a legitimate concern: how to find ways to represent African realities in an accessible form, incorporating African narrative approaches and European aesthetics, but reframing these to serve new purposes. This strategy worked in other art forms too, such as the visual arts and music in particular, with musicians like Manu Dibango or Fela Anikulapo Kuti and Afro jazz. By blending African and Western music styles into what would become the new modern African music, they durably changed African music and found a way to impose it internationally without losing their souls.

Almost ten years older than me, Samba Felix Ndiaye followed in the footsteps of these two pioneering filmmakers, while at the same time developing his own personal style.

Unlike Mustapha Alassane's popular approach to film, however, the late Samba Felix Ndiaye saw himself more as a painter, an artist looking at society, bringing elements together for everyone to see, irrespective of whether the majority of the audience was able to read the relevant connections between them or not.

Samba felt that cinema could stand only for what it was, nothing more. This gave him the ability, the freedom, to step back and achieve a distance that allowed him to make films that I considered observational and at times even a little "bourgeois," as I felt they sometimes lacked political edge at a time when I personally considered this crucial in the fight for democracy in Africa.

In all fairness, Senegal in the Eighties was in a far better political situation than many other African countries, even if the situation has since declined. In April 1984, we had a mini civil war in Cameroon; Paul

Biya came to power in 1982, and we thought that the 25-year-long nightmare of Ahidjo was over and that the country would move towards democracy. We were deluding ourselves, sadly, and we slid deeper and deeper into the mire. It was in this context of a totalitarian society that I started and continued to make documentary films. One of the goals I set out to achieve was to decomplexify life around me and to present the social and political situation in Cameroon in a comprehensive manner. That is why I choose to narrate my films. In 1992, in *Afrique, je te plumerai* I adopted first-person narrative for the first time and I have continued to use it to bring viewers, wherever they are, to look at the world through my eyes, through the eyes of an African. My latest film *Sacred Places* took me into St Leon, a neighbourhood of Ouagadougou, the "capital of African cinema," to meet Bouba, the videoclub operator, Jules-Cesar, the djembe-maker who sees the djembe as the ancestor of cinema, and Abbo who writes philosophical statements on the neighbourhood walls for everyone to see. Together, these three characters are a metaphor for African film: Jules-Cesar incarnates sound and film's creative aspects; Bouba the image and its constraints; and Abbo is like the filmmaker, writing on the "walls" of his neighbourhood, hoping for people to come by and read his words.

Many other filmmakers choose to use first person narrative like Zeka Laplaine in *Kinshasa Palace* adding another dimension of complexity by incorporating themselves in the film as another fictional character. A way of blurring the boundaries of fictional documentary or an attempt to confuse the viewer and leave him wandering where the truth lies in the story unfolding in front of him. The visual presence of self in films as a narrator and as a character was also present in Mahamat Saleh Haroun's film *Bye Bye Africa* and in Abdherramane Sissako's *La Vie sur terre.*

Samba Felix and I often ran into each other at film festivals, or in Paris, where we discussed our work avidly. He repeatedly told me to pay more attention to the form. In retrospect, I realize that my work kept unconsciously answering: "forget the form, as long as I truthfully represent my perception of African reality without loosing my audience." Personally, my main concern was to improve my filmic structures and make my narration as poetic, funny and engaging as possible without compromising the content.

Samba studied his classics in film school and was fascinated by a Dutch filmmaker, Johan Van der Keuken, whom we both knew. In Berlin in 2000, a year before his death, Van der Keuken told me that he was fortunate to have been born in a place where the basic issues of democracy had been resolved, and that he was not sure he would have made the same films if he had been born in some of the places he had filmed. This was a kind way of acknowledging my work, even if it was totally different in its approach to his, and I remain grateful to him for that.

Samba Felix Ndiaye and Johan Van der Keuken belong to the family of great filmmakers whose empathy for the people in front of their cameras transpires clearly in their films. They also showed the same empathy to their peers, and especially their younger colleagues, for whom their time and advice was precious. Their absence will leave a long and lasting void.

Despite the disdain for African documentary film that has prevailed up to this date, there are reasons to be cautiously hopeful: 2009 confirmed both the increase in the number of documentary films produced by first-time filmmakers and the number of festivals on the African continent dedicated to documentary film. At the same time, it also saw European cultural institutes, such as The Goethe Institute and the French Cultural Centers, and organizations, such as Africadoc, vying to offer training to young African filmmakers.

This latter situation brought back to mind the words of one African professor from Cheik Anta Diop University in Dakar, whom I met after a screening of *Afrique, je te plumerai*. He commented: "Your film ends with the affirmation that education is one of the solutions for the future of Africa, but the question is, what education?"

Indeed, one of the recurring problems of cinema on the continent is the absence of transmission from one generation to the next, partly due to the lack of local policies to support film. In such a context, filmmakers rarely have time for anything other than their own daily struggle to create and survive. This does not nurture filiations or long-time collaboration between filmmakers of different generations. Each generation is thus left to fend for itself and each new generation acts like it thinks it has reinvented the wheel!

With the exception of a few institutions such as Gaston Kabore's Imagine in Burkina Faso, which offers training to African filmmakers from all over the continent, today's training schemes seem to perpetuate a paradigm not dissimilar to the colonial era's civilizing mission: the globalizing mission. Today, for example, the Goethe Institute brings young German filmmakers to Africa to train African filmmakers, as if there were not enough trained filmmakers on the continent to transmit their knowledge to their younger peers. Europeans training Africans to look at and represent themselves raises certain questions, especially if one considers many of these teachers' lack of awareness and sometimes lack of interest in the history of the continent, and particularly the history of African representation.

Isn't it ironic that, fifty years after the first generation of African filmmakers began the struggle to challenge and rectify colonial representations of Africa, Europeans are back to train our youth to look at and represent themselves, often taking as examples and references the ethnographic images they are familiar with, rather than the works of other African filmmakers?

When European organizations such as Africadoc claim to be initiating documentary filmmaking in Africa, what message do they send to their trainees about the legacy of the pioneering documentary filmmakers working on the continent before them?

Have African artists and filmmakers been struggling to introduce elements of complexity in the representation of Africa, to challenge simplistic and essentializing colonial representations, simply to see the return of a new form of cultural colonization fifty years on, in the name of globalization?

Despite the situation I have just described, there is hope. Amidst the numerous productions flourishing all over the continent, some real talents are emerging and their works are opening up encouraging perspectives for the future. Katy Lena Ndiaye (Senegal), for example, whose aesthetic approach is a pure pleasure for the senses, can no doubt be classed as a descendant of the director Samba Felix Ndiaye.

Nourished by her solid journalistic background and a fearless approach to injustice, Cameroonian director Oswalde Lewat has successfully managed in her three films to remind us all that the fight for democracy and change in Africa is still the responsibility of the artist.

In South Africa, the new individual voices of Khalo Matabene and Dumissani Pakhati are embracing and addressing the complexity of the new South Africa in audacious styles that complement the observational approach of experienced filmmakers such as Francis Webster.

In *From a Whisper*, a sort of fictional documentary that puts some of the realities facing the African continent at the centre of the creative cinematic process, another impressive woman filmmaker, Kenyan Wanjiri Kanui, took a real event—the bombing of the American embassy—and created fictional characters to address the full complexity of Islamic fundamentalism and terrorism. This successful reconciliation of narrative and documentary echoed the approach of pioneering Mustapha Alassane.

Finally, I would like to cite the work of Moussa Toure, who worked as a technician on many of the classics of African cinema before directing his own 35mm features *Toubab-Bi* and *TGV*. In 2000, Toure took a video camera and started travelling the continent, shooting *Poussière de ville* (2001), a film about street children in Congo after the war, followed by the poignant *Nous sommes nombreuses* (2003) on rape as instrument of war and its consequences. Moussa Toure has since gone on to deal with immigration and environmental issues in his neighbourhood in Dakar.

Moussa Toure's work is interesting not only for his relatively atypical cinematic path from narrative film to documentary; his work also raises important ethical questions. When, while shooting *Poussière de ville*, for example, Moussa went looking for the families of his characters, the street kids, he was going beyond the habitual role of the filmmaker *vis-à-vis* his subject by assigning himself the duty, the responsibility of taking the kids back to their relatives. At the same time, Moussa's films remain difficult to find internationally, even if he does screen them locally: in a sense, it is as if Moussa were writing on walls like Abbo in *Sacred Places*, as most of us are in our local communities.

For me, these two points raise the following key questions, on which I would like to conclude: can the filmmaker, as an artist, allow him/herself to be defined by others who have the means to manipulate and orientate the reading of his/her work, or should he/she be writing on the walls like Moussa in his neighbourhood, at the risk of not being seen further afield?

Are those who choose to write meaningful things on the walls, for their communities, more likely to survive in the long run, to make a more lasting impact, than those who run after the mirage of a global recognition?

Whilst the walls cannot be moved, today's new forms of internet technology do make it possible to relay those messages, offering a diversity of voices to challenge the standardizing tendencies of globalization. So, ultimately, the question still remains: what messages are we choosing to write on the walls?

109

CHRIS BERRY

GETTING REAL

Chinese Documentary, Chinese Postsocialism (2007)

Since 1989 innovative documentary has been one of the hallmarks of Chinese film and video. Most of the documentary makers associated with this new direction have professional backgrounds completely separate from the Urban or Sixth Generation of young feature filmmakers. They usually shoot on video and come from the world of television, which has its own training institutions and regulations that are apart from those of film. However, there are also notable similarities between their works and those of the Urban or Sixth Generation. In this essay I examine the new documentaries within a comparative framework, arguing that the new documentary and feature filmmakers both operate under the imperative to "get real."

"Getting real" has two meanings here. On the one hand, it indicates the drive to represent the "real" behind both the new documentaries and the feature films. On the other hand, it also refers to the slang phrase "get real," meaning "wise up" or "stop dreaming." In the People's Republic since 1989, this has meant developing a new understanding of the limits of the emergent public sphere and the possibilities of social transformation after, on the one hand, the Tiananmen Square massacre (or "incident," as the regime prefers to call it) and, on the other, the negative example of the former Soviet Union's fragmentation and decline following the transition to democracy and capitalism in the 1990s. In a nutshell, "getting real" is the condition of contemporary postsocialist cinema in China. There is no doubt that these two senses of "getting real" work together as a productive tension, or overdetermining contradiction, that conditions the new Chinese documentary. A more difficult question is whether the new documentary participates in the maintenance of Chinese postsocialism or disturbs it.

I specify "Chinese postsocialism" here for two reasons. First, I wrote this essay out of the conviction that the new documentary in China can only be understood in this locally specific context. By way of comparison, Bérénice Reynaud has introduced some of the work considered here in a survey essay that bristles with wonderful insights and provocations by placing the work along with a range of other critical and independent Chinese videos from the period before 1989, from Hong Kong, from Taiwan, and from the diaspora, including the United States. Reynaud links this material with the framework of response to the experience of colonialism and a general progressive politics of critical intervention.[1] While I do not challenge broad (and detailed) takes such as Reynaud's, in this essay I supplement them with an emphasis on the local specificity that makes independent documentary distinctive in post-1989 China. For example, many of the new documentary makers have drawn upon the cinema verité of Fred Wiseman and Ogawa Shinsuke's socially engaged documentary modes. But beyond the formal similarities, both the appeal and the significance of these modes in post-1989 China is quite different from that in 1960s United States and Japan, as well as that in Taiwan and South Korea, where Ogawa's mode has also been appropriated.

The second reason stems from the fact that postsocialism is at once a condition shared across many different countries and experienced in locally specific ways. The term "postsocialism" has been used colloquially to mean simply "after the end of socialism." This makes sense in the countries that have appeared after the break-up of the Soviet Union, for instance. In the People's Republic of China, however, postsocialism has more parallels with Lyotard's postmodernism, where the forms and structures of the modern (in this case socialism) persist long after faith in the grand narrative that authorizes it has been lost.[2] Furthermore, the general postsocialist condition has also been felt among the forces in the West of what was the Left, where the fall of the Berlin Wall in 1989 has forced the remaining diehards to confront not only a declining faith in liberal capitalist democracy but also the absence of any "actually existing" alternative. In other words, I write this essay not with a neo-cold war hope that China may one day join the "free world," but out of a shared interest in the question of tactical responses to having to work in the globalizing territory of what de Certeau calls "the space of the Other" at a time when the absence of visible and viable outside space threatens the meaningfulness of the very phrase.[3]

Who, then, are the new documentary makers in the People's Republic? What characterizes their work, and when did it begin? Probably the best-known Chinese documentary internationally and the one many would assume initiated the new documentary form is *River Elegy* (Heshang, a.k.a. *Death Song of the River,* 1988; dir. Xia Jun). This polemic on cultural isolationism and the persistence of feudalism aired on the national state television network China Central Television (CCTV) in the months prior to the 1989 Tiananmen Square massacre, and in its wake placed the show's producers among China's most-wanted fugitives.[4] However, although its message was challenging, in other ways it followed existing paradigms. All Chinese documentaries made prior to 1989 took the form of the pre-scripted illustrated lecture. For the most part they were known as *zhuanti pian* (literally, "special topic films") as opposed to newsreels *(xinwen pian)*, which cover a range of topics in short reports. With the benefit of hindsight, the criticism is often made that the "cultural fever" and "democracy spring" of the late eighties were events isolated from ordinary people. And indeed, the continued use of the illustrated lecture format in *River Elegy* implies that its arguments are part of disputations among the governing elite. It belies both the Maoist rhetoric of going down among the people to learn from them and the newer participatory rhetoric of democracy, suggesting that the ordinary people *(laobaixing)* are not involved in the process of determining the future of their society but are waiting to be educated about the decisions made above and about them through documentaries such as *River Elegy* and other pedagogical materials.[5] Therefore, *River Elegy* cannot be considered the beginning of new documentary in China; the defining feature of the new documentary is a more spontaneous format.

Furthermore, the first Chinese documentary to move away from the illustrated lecture format and toward spontaneity was made outside the state-run system. Wu Wenguang's *Bumming in Beijing: The Last Dreamers* (*Liulang Beijing*, 1990; dir. Wu Wenguang) was first shown outside China at the Hong Kong Film Festival in 1991, after which it traveled the world. It has, of course, never been broadcast in China. *Bumming In Beijing* provoked the same excited response that the feature film *Yellow Earth* (Huang tudi, 1984, dir. Chen Kaige) did when it screened in Hong Kong in 1985.[6] Bérénice Reynaud speaks of "the feeling that a new chapter of the history of representation was being written in front of my eyes."[7] Lu Xinyu, author of *The New Documentary Film Movement in China*, also traces to *Yellow Earth* the first manifestations of that "movement."[8]

Four main characteristics, all shared with the other new documentaries that began to appear in China at this time, made *Bumming in Beijing* so striking. These characteristics also provide a framework for comparing the film to the new feature filmmaking and for situating both forms within contemporary Chinese postsocialism. First, the experience and memory of June 4th (*liusi*) 1989 is a crucial structuring absence. Second, the focus is directly on contemporary city life in China among educated people like the documentary makers and the filmmakers themselves. Third, as mentioned above, the illustrated lecture format is abandoned for more spontaneous shooting. And fourth, production within the state-owned system is eschewed for independent production. All of these characteristics change over time. The first fades as the immediate possibility of redress and political change also fades. The second increasingly comes to mean a focus on ordinary people in China today rather than on the educated elite. The third undergoes a shift from more experimental to more mainstream modes of spontaneous documentary shot on more lightweight technology, including digital video. And the fourth is increasingly imbricated with television, making it more difficult to draw lines between independence, government direction, and determination by the market in a manner following the broader social and economic direction of postsocialist China, where it is harder and harder to draw a clear line between the state and private enterprise.

To start with the issue of June 4th, *Bumming in Beijing* consists of four vignettes about four artists living in Beijing and working, like Wu Wenguang himself, outside the state-run system. Shooting began in mid-1988 and ended in late 1990.[9] In the film we observe the independent artists' difficult living conditions along with their depression. With one exception, by the end of the documentary all but one of the artists have married foreigners and are preparing to leave or have left China.[10] Although the documentary does not directly address the 1989 Tiananmen Square massacre and the associated dashing of ideals, it resonates with its absent presence; without any other reason offered for the overwhelming atmosphere of hopelessness and the desire to leave the country the Tiananmen event is most likely understood as accounting for both. Indeed, the lack of discussion of the event may imply that it is too dangerous to mention and thus effectively communicates the conditions producing the mood of the interviewees and the documentary itself.

The June 4th issue is also the structuring absence at the heart of other relatively early new documentaries. Shi Jian, who together with his colleagues ran a documentary-making team known as

Structure, Wave, Youth and Cinema (a.k.a. the SWYC Group), is another pioneer of the new Chinese documentary. The film *I Graduated!* (Wo biyele, 1992; dir. SWYC Group) was screened at the Hong Kong International Film Festival in 1993. Also based on interviews, it focuses on members of the graduating class of Beijing University. There is much handheld camera work, possibly because, as we see in the film itself, the equipment has to be smuggled onto campus in sports bags. Also, these soon-to-graduate students are not at all ebullient. Instead, they worry about their job assignments and mention other students that they miss.[11] Eventually, viewers may recall that this campus and this class of students were very active in the 1989 democracy movement. That is why the campus is so strictly guarded, why they miss friends (shot? arrested? executed?) and why their futures are so uncertain. As the documentary develops, the interviewees allude more and more to the events that haunt them. In the years before and after 1989, SWYC also made an eight-part series called *Tiananmen Square* (Tiananmen, 1991; dir. SWYC Group), which also was marked by an absence of the events of 1989 themselves. An important later documentary film that also seems overdetermined by the taboo on June 4th is the feature-length documentary *The Square* (Guangchang, 1994; dir. Zhang Yuan and Duan Jinchuan). As a cinema verité portrait of the various daily activities and power plays that occur on the stagelike square, no one in the film addresses the event, precisely because it is taboo.

This structuring absence of June 4th also lies at the heart of two of the earlier examples of the new feature filmmaking of the 1990s, *Red Beads* (Xuanlian, 1993; dir. He Jianjun), and *The Days* (Dongchun de rizi, 1993; dir. Wang Xiaoshuai). The title of the first film refers to bloodshed, and the narrative centers on post-traumatic mental illness. The second film, like *Bumming in Beijing,* focuses on alienated artists and the question of whether or not to go overseas. Here it seems important to note that whereas documentary filmmaking played little or no role in the wave of new Chinese cinema associated with the Fifth Generation directors in the 1980s, it seems to have been central to post-1989 cinema, as well as possibly to set the tone for feature filmmaking.

Both the new documentaries and feature films allude to politically sensitive topics indirectly, as the Fifth Generation also did. But where Fifth Generation films like *Raise the Red Lantern* (Da hong denglong gao gao gua, 1991; dir. Zhang Yimou), *Yellow Earth,* and *Horse Thief* (Daoma zei, 1986; Tian Zhuang-zhuang) use historical and/or geographically remote settings as allegories for the present, the new documentaries and feature films focus squarely on contemporary life. This second characteristic has continued, even after the triggering event of 1989 receded into the background with the passing of time, new economic growth, and the negative example of democratic change accompanied by social chaos in the former Soviet Union. But where the new features have the reputation for focusing on urban youth—earned through features ranging from *Beijing Bastards* (Beijing zazhong, 1991; dir. Zhang Yuan) to *Beijing Bicycle* (Shiqi sui de danche, 2001; dir. Wang Xiaoshuai)—the documentaries have diversified more within the common focus on contemporary life.

Initially, documentaries like *Bumming in Beijing* and *I Graduated!* examined the lives of young, urban, educated people who are similar to the filmmakers themselves. Wu Wenguang continued this trend in, for example, his follow-up to *Bumming in Beijing, At Home in the World* (Sihai rujia, 1995), where he interviews the same subjects in their new homes around the world, as well as in 1966, *My Time in the Red Guards* (1966, Wo de hongweibing shidai, 1993), where he interviews former Red Guards, including the Fifth Generation filmmaker Tian Zhuangzhuang. But other filmmakers have moved out to cover everyday life outside of the major cities and as experienced by more ordinary people, with such notable examples as Duan Jinchuan's trilogy of films about Tibet (discussed further below); Lu Wangping's video about a traveling rural opera troupe, *The Story of Wang Laobai* (Wang Laobai de gushi, 1996; dir. Lu Wangping); and Wen Pulin's various videos about his own involvement in contemporary Tibetan Buddhism, such as *The Living Buddha of Kangba* (Kangba huofu, 1991), *The Nuns of Minqiong* (Minqiongan de ninü, 1992), *The Secret Site of Asceticism* (Qingpu, 1992; codirected with Duan Jinchuan), and *Pa-dga' Living Buddha* (Bajia huofu, 1993).

The interest of many documentary filmmakers in "minority nationalities" and the far-flung border regions of China is a feature shared more with the Fifth Generation of feature filmmakers than with the Sixth or Urban Generation that forms the primary framework in which the documentaries are considered here. This link can be traced to the mid-1980s fascination with these regions and peoples as some kind of "others" within China. By virtue of that paradoxical status, they could express the sense of alienation and distance from their own culture felt by many educated Chinese amid the disillusion of the post-Mao era.[12] At this time, feature filmmakers went to shoot in these areas, and many who in the future would become independent documentary makers went to visit, live, or work in these areas. For Wen Pulin, Tibet is clearly an appealing place of refuge from the failure of modern materialist culture, whereas Duan Jinchuan seems to approach life in contemporary Tibet as one aspect of life in the People's Republic as a whole.

In the process of recording scenes of contemporary Chinese life, many documentaries have inevitably also touched on contemporary Chinese postsocialism's turn to the market economy for economic growth under the overall umbrella of the state-run system. In some cases, this effort is clearly deliberate. For example, *Diary of Tai Fu Xiang* (Taifuxiang riji, 1998; dir. Lin Xudong) details the efforts to put ownership of a bankrupt state-owned department store in Shijiazhuang into the hands of its employees, including the difficulties that many of those employees have in finding the funds to invest in this dubious venture. *Out of Phoenix Bridge* (Huidao fenghuangqiao, 1997; dir. Li Hong) follows a group of young women who as undocumented workers from the village of Phoenix Bridge in Anhui province have come to Beijing to seek employment as maids, a phenomenon that could not have occurred before the new mixed economic and social structure. And the DV (digital video) documentary *Jiang Hu: Life on the Road* (Jianghu, 1999; dir. Wu Wenguang), follows the efforts of an entertainment troupe to find forms that will appeal to the market. This diversification in subject matter means the new documentary is no longer a phenomenon among the educated elite.

But even more significant in this broadening of the new documentary is how the films and videos are made, both stylistically and institutionally, as well as their wide appeal. For not only do these new documentaries regularly "go down among the people" but they also give (or appear to give) the ordinary people a direct voice, which enables (or appears to enable) them to speak directly to other ordinary people and resonates with the economic agency that the development of a market sector gives (or appears to give) them.

Stylistically, this giving of a voice is centered in unscripted spontaneity. This was also one of the most immediately striking features of *Bumming in Beijing*, and of all the other new documentaries that have followed it. In Chinese, the most frequently used term in publications to describe this filmmaking mode is "on-the-spot realism" (*jishizhuyi*). In practice, in terms of documentary it refers to a spontaneous and unscripted quality that is a fundamental and defining characteristic distinguishing them from the old scripted realism of the "special topic" documentaries. It is frequently accentuated by handheld camera work and technical lapses and flaws characteristic of uncontrolled situations. The documentaries often also highlight events that conspicuously signify spontaneity and a lack of script. The most obvious example in *Bumming in Beijing* would be the nervous breakdown suffered on camera by the painter Zhang Xiaping. In *I Graduated!* the cracked voices and tears of the interviewees function in the same way.

This drive to produce a new vision of the real is one aspect of the "getting real" referred to above. The political significance of this change should not be sidestepped by invoking the rhetoric of emerging Chinese pluralism (*duo-yuanhua*), but at the same time it must be acknowledged that its precise political significance is difficult to determine in an environment where economic liberalization has been accompanied by tighter political and ideological control. At a minimum it suggests the old realism is out of touch with China today and needs to be updated. But it may also be read as suggesting implicit contestation and challenge to the authority and legitimacy of those associated with the older pedagogical mode, appropriate to a structure where agency and leadership is concentrated in the state apparatus and its functionaries.

The same term used to describe the new documentary, *jishizhuyi* or "on-the-spot realism," is often also used to describe the contemporary urban films made by the younger generation of feature filmmakers. However, whereas for documentary makers "on-the-spot realism" is distinguished from the scripted quality of the old "special topic" or *zhuanti* films, "on-the-spot realism" distinguishes the new features from two older stylistic traditions. One is the realism associated with "socialist realism," which is expressed in Chinese using a different term, *xianshizhuyi*, which means representational realism. With the decline of faith in socialism, *xianshizhuyi* has come into disrepute. Where once it simply meant "realism," these days it seems to carry a connotation of fakery or at best reality as the authorities wish it were. This disrepute has prevailed for twenty years now, and indeed the Fifth Generation directors also saw many of the key characteristics of their work as reclaiming the real from *xianshizhuyi*. The use of locations as opposed to sets; of natural light or darkness rather than artificial lights and blue filters; and of unknown actors rather than stars are all examples that can be readily observed in foundational Fifth Generation works like *One and Eight* (Yige he bage, 1984; dir. Zhang Junzhao) and *Yellow Earth*. However, the use of "on-the-spot realism" or *jishizhuyi* to describe the new trend of the nineties in feature films also distinguishes it from the art film stylizations and historical allegory of much Fifth Generation work, where it pursues instead an unadorned contemporary look that is the fictional counterpart of the new documentary's spontaneous style.[13]

Deleuze's ideas on the "movement-image" versus the "time-image" present perhaps one framework in which to consider the shift from the more conventional structures of the illustrated lecture format documentaries, socialist realist feature films, and even some of the more dramatic Fifth Generation films, on the one hand, and the new documentaries and Sixth or Urban Generation films on the other. For Deleuze, the movement-image refers to the regime most commonly associated with Hollywood studio filmmaking. Here, time appears indirectly as a regime of movement, where framing, cutting, and the like follow movement as a marker of change and therefore of time. The rational, step-by-step logic of the documentary lecture also fits this logic.[14] By contrast, when the rational cause-and-effect subtending these linear structures disappears and it becomes less possible to predict when the cut will come, how the next shot will be linked to the last, or how long the shot will last, Deleuze believes that a more direct access to time as duration opens up.[15]

On occasion, this seems like a quest for some sort of transcendent truth. But the prime examples of the cinema of the time-image are for Deleuze more historically and socially grounded. They are drawn from European art films, and he links them to the collapse of faith in the grand narratives of modernity following Nazism and World War II; the same environment that laid the groundwork for the kind of postmodernity discussed by Lyotard. I have already indicated that the Chinese postsocialist environment and culture bear comparison to this phenomenon. Some of the independent documentaries and Urban or Sixth Generation features also break away from the logic of the "movement-image" toward a distended form in which shots continue beyond any movement logic either in the literal sense or in the sense of narrative development. Both Jia Zhangke's feature films and Wu Wenguang's documentaries seem to follow this pattern, dwelling on time passing in a seemingly uncontrolled manner. (Perhaps it is not a pure coincidence that Jia's second feature, *Platform* (Zhantai, 1999), followed an entertainment troupe, as does Wu's *Jiang Hu: Life on the Road.* Although this sense of time passing is not the philosophical sense of "duration" invoked by Deleuze in reference to the time-image, this distended form does loosen the structure of the films. The relation between shots never becomes completely unpredictable, and although chronology is followed (in not quite the condition of what Deleuze calls "anyspace-whatever") it becomes hard to have a sense of teleology or progress as interviewees ramble verbally in Wu's films and characters ramble literally in Jia's. One loses any sense of knowing when a shot will end or exactly what it will cut to, and this is quite different from the certain sense of progress invoked by the ideologies of modernity, be it driven by the socialist command economy or the alleged socialist market economy of the new era. Instead, the certainty of progress is replaced by a contingent life in which characters react and respond rather than initiate, looking for ways to get by rather than having a clear sense of purpose.

Both Duan Jinchuan and Wu Wenguang have told me that their preference for unscripted work, handheld cameras, and events that signal spontaneity can be traced back to their encounters with the foreign television crews that started coming to shoot in China at the stations where they worked in the eighties. This preference for spontaneity also helps to explain why they and other new documentary makers were drawn to cinema verité, be it in the French interview style associated with Jean Rouch and his classic film *Chronicle of a Summer* (Chronique d'un été, 1961) that is echoed in the interview films of Wu, or the American observational style associated with filmmakers such as Fred Wiseman that is evoked in some of the films of Duan. After some of the early independent works were screened in Hong Kong and elsewhere, documentary makers such as Wu and Duan were invited to attend Asia's leading documentary film festival at Yamagata. There, in 1993, a special retrospective of Wiseman's work was held. The most direct evidence of the impact of this event can be seen in two films that Duan directed after the Yamagata festival: *The Square* (codirected with Zhang Yuan) and *No. 16 Barkhor Street South* (Bakuonanjie shiliuhao, 1996), part of his trilogy of Tibetan works. Both of these films scrupulously follow Wiseman's formula of pure observational work with no interviews or arranged scenes, no extra-diegetic music, and complete dependence on editing to bring the material together into a coherent whole through "mosaic structures."[16] *Barkhor Street* also followed Wiseman's well-known interest in social institutions, for the address that gives the film its title is that of the neighborhood office on Barkhor Street in central Lhasa where pilgrims circumambulate and protestors sometimes gather. Duan's own residence of eight years in Lhasa in the 1980s, and his links with local Tibetan audio-visual and cultural groups, put him in a unique position to carry out this project. The result is also unique in that it comprises an unscripted record of the workings of the Chinese government at the grassroots level and a picture of daily life in Tibet not written according to the ideological requirements of either Beijing or Dharamsala. For this film, Duan won the 1996 Prix du Réel in France, the first major international prize awarded to a Chinese documentary film.[17]

The appeal of cinema verité and other more spontaneous documentary techniques because of their ability to reclaim the authority of realism from the increasingly devalued "special topic" films can be understood as an example of cultural translation. Most theorists of cultural translation emphasize incommensurability and the idea that everything is somewhat changed in the process of translation. Lydia Liu, in her essay "Translingual Practice," recognizes not only how the direction and impact of translation may be conditioned by power but also the idea that whatever may enter a culture or society from overseas can only be made sense of in terms of the existing local cultural conditions and conventions. She therefore emphasizes the role of local agency in this process.[18] Given this, some additional local factors should be borne in mind in accounting for the appeal and significance of spontaneous documentary techniques in the nineties.

First, in an environment saturated by institutional and self-censorship, spontaneous documentary techniques have a distinct advantage. For example, it is impossible for the authorities to require that a script be submitted. Also, it is difficult to blame the documentary makers for what subjects say or do if they are not being told what to say or do by the documentary maker. Furthermore, if the subjects are the ordinary people revered by socialism, it is difficult for the censors to complain if the people say things that they do not want to hear.

Second, these spontaneous documentary techniques seem like an extension of the well-established and very popular local genre of reportage literature (*baogao wenxue*, also known more recently as *jishi wenxue*). Reportage also derives a certain authority and ability to withstand censorship from its claim to veracity. Although this fact has not always exempted reportage writers from trouble with the authorities after publishing accounts of events the authorities wish had not happened, it has made reportage a powerful site of resistance within China.[19]

Third, by giving voice to ordinary people, spontaneous documentary also taps into the longstanding practice of seeking out a public space for airing otherwise unresolved grievances. Most famously, this practice was co-opted by the communists in the tradition of "speaking bitterness" (*suku*), where public meetings were held after a community was liberated and the local poor were encouraged to speak out about their sufferings at the hands of the local rich and powerful as a prelude to punishment. This pattern is less relevant regarding the spontaneous documentaries made by individual filmmakers and given little circulation within China, but the spontaneous techniques of the new documentary have spread like wildfire. In addition to all manner of home movie documentaries produced by complete amateurs with access to digital video cameras and no training or idea of broadcast standards—but often with an eye for remarkable materials—the spontaneous documentary has become a television staple. It appears most famously in magazine shows such as *Oriental Moment* (Dongfang shikong) and *Life Space* (Shenghuo kongjian), both aired by the national state-run station CCTV, and the successors to these shows, but it has also been taken up by all manner of local stations and programs. The resulting shows have been extremely popular, most likely at least in part because of the refreshing nature of seeing ordinary people speaking relatively openly and without rehearsal.[20] However, although there may be no kindly Party Secretary "uncle" *(shushu)* on-screen to guide what happens, television broadcasting does raise issues relating to commercial sponsorship, television station "gatekeepers" who self-censor, and government censorship itself.

That brings us finally to the original distinguishing characteristic of the new documentary; independence. As indicated by the increasing appearance of television programs that take on many of the characteristics of the early new documentary films, independent production may no longer be such a hallmark. But at the beginning of both the new documentary and the new feature films of the nineties, this was a very notable characteristic. In a country where any form of production of anything outside the state-owned system was for many years frowned upon as "capitalist roading," such independence was very striking indeed. Furthermore, it seems that after the many difficult negotiations with the government censors experienced by feature filmmakers in the late eighties, and the specter of much tighter control in the wake of the events of 1989, the decision to pioneer independent production was a common and distinguishing feature of both new documentary and new feature filmmaking. All the early films that won attention as new documentaries, such as *Bumming in Beijing* and *I Graduated!*, as well as many of the early feature films of the younger Urban Generation of directors, such as *The Days, Beijing Bastards,* and *Red Beads,* were made independently.

However, what does "independence" mean for documentary makers in postsocialist China? There are two aspects that need to be addressed to answer this question. First, there is the difference between independence for feature filmmakers and for documentary makers that is the result of their different places in the administrative structures of the state and the different regulations and laws applying to them. Second, there is the issue of what independence means under contemporary Chinese postsocialist conditions. In many ways, independent production is the film- and video-making equivalent of the broader appearance of a market sector of the economy within the overall state-planned socialist framework, which is one of the defining hallmarks of Chinese postsocialism. The market sector is not only licensed by the state but also as a smaller sector of the overall socioeconomic structure. It is thus dependent upon and has to work with the state-owned sector regardless of tension, frictions, and disjunctures.

The implications of independent status for the documentary makers and for the feature filmmakers are quite different. Both China's independent documentary and feature filmmakers resist the label "underground" and insist that independence does not necessarily equate opposition to the state, the Party or the government. However, film and television historically have been two separate worlds in China, where until the mid-nineties each was administered by separate offices and thus governed by very different regulations. Filmmakers and television program makers train in different institutes and there are few connections between them. While many connections can be seen among the documentary makers—in codirection, for example, none of them have made feature films. There is, however, one notable exception to this pattern. Zhang Yuan is a member of the so-called Sixth Generation of feature filmmakers who graduated from Beijing Film Academy in 1989. But he has also shown a strong interest in documentary since his first feature, *Mama* (Mama, 1990)—a film about the mother of a disabled child, which includes documentary sequences of interviews with real-life mothers of disabled children. Although since then Zhang has continued to make both features and documentaries, he is the only one to do so,[21] and despite similar aesthetic strategies and thematic interests, feature film and documentary makers are two separate groups operating in separate worlds.

The most serious consequence of this concerns the possibility of independent production in the sense of production outside the state system. When the separate regulations designed to monitor and control television and film production were drawn up many years ago, they could not and did not envisage the physical and organizational possibility of independent production. The equipment was too expensive and there was no independent sector.

Within the state-run film system, various proactive and reactive local and national censorship regulations have been in place at different times, insisting on script approval prior to production as well as approval of completed films prior to release. Throughout the nineties, the government has actively intervened to close any loopholes enabling filmmakers to avoid scrutiny—loopholes such as investment from overseas, editing overseas, sending films to film festivals prior to submitting them for approval for release, and so forth. Finally, in July 1996 the government passed a new film law that explicitly made illegal any film production other than that done within the state-owned studio system.[22] This means that although would-be independent feature filmmakers might not think of themselves as underground or subversive, they have been defined as such by the government.

Within the state-run television system, however, the situation is significantly different. The regulation is of television stations and what they air, not the production of materials on video. Furthermore, unlike film, the production of video materials can be achieved with ever cheaper and more accessible equipment, so it is not viable to attempt to gain proactive control over video production. In these circumstances, although many new documentaries have not been aired and may never be aired, so far there have not been any regulatory or legal interventions against the makers of these independent documentaries. In other words, unlike their film colleagues, video makers can be independent without being forced into a position of seeming underground or subversive.

However, this does not mean that the new documentary makers feel free to make whatever kinds of films they might like. An example of this issue is how the highly influential mode of production associated with the late Japanese documentary maker Ogawa Shinsuke has been taken up in China. The Yamagata International Documentary Film Festival was initiated by Ogawa and his associates, and thus it is perhaps not surprising that Ogawa's impact has been felt among the independent Chinese documentary makers who have attended the festival.[23] Ogawa's filmmaking has two main features. First, Ogawa is socially and politically engaged rather than a detached observer; possibly his most famous films compose the "Fortress Narita" series (referring to *Narita: The Peasants of the Second Fortress* [Sanrizuka: Dainitoride no hitobito, 1971]), which were made in the late sixties and early seventies as part of the resistance to the forced selling of land for the building of Tokyo's Narita Airport. Second, he lives and works among his subjects, relating to them not as an outsider but as a friend and colleague. For the Chinese new documentary makers, being socially and politically engaged has never been an option because such movements are ruthlessly suppressed in the People's Republic. But Ogawa's quality of relating to his subjects has been shared by the Chinese from the first. Wu Wenguang's *Bumming in Beijing* is about people the filmmaker knows well and relates to as friends. Lu Wangping spent a year traveling around with the opera troupe he documents in *The Story of Wang Laobai,* and Li Hong spent two years befriending, living with, and returning home with the young women whose story she tells in *Out of Phoenix Bridge.*

This apparent self-censorship (conscious or unconscious) raises the other side of the question of working independently within postsocialism. Just as the market sector is dependent on the state sector in the economy as a whole, the independent documentary makers cannot operate without reference to the state sector. Indeed, for the most part they were trained within and worked within the state-owned television sector for years. Further, many of them continue to do so by making independent documentaries on the side while they earn their income in a television station. Shi Jian of the SWYC Group has been a powerful figure at CCTV all along, where he initiated the program *Oriental Moment* in 1992. Li Hong made *Phoenix Bridge* while moonlighting from CCTV and by borrowing station equipment.[24] Even those who, like Duan Jinchuan, have set up their own independent production companies continue to depend on the state-owned sector to some degree because there are no privately owned television stations in China and thus no other way to air their works. Duan studied at the Beijing Broadcasting Institute and then went to work at Lhasa Television Station for eight years in the 1980s before returning to Beijing. Even though all of his films in the 1990s were made independently, the main investor in *No. 16 Barkor Street South* was CCTV (which at the time of my last inquiry had not yet aired it) with a Tibetan company as a smaller financial partner. And the boom in television programming featuring the new documentary styles has given the new documentary makers opportunities for work that they have not passed up. Lin Xudong's *Diary of Tai Fu Xiang* and Lu Wangping's *The Story of Wang Laobai* were both made for CCTV. In addition, Jiang Yue of *The Other Bank* has since made a video for CCTV called *A River Is Stilled* (Jingzhi de He, 1998) about the building of the Three Gorges dam from the perspective of the workers on the project.

This mutual implication of the "independent" documentaries and the state-owned television sector raises some complex questions. Put simply, what is the relation of these documentaries to the state? Are they a challenge or are they complicit? If the relation is not to be considered in such a binary way, do they function as a supplement that changes the system or as a co-opted token that props it up? These questions are impossible to answer in an absolute and generally applicable way. It is even difficult to give a simple answer in regard to any individual film. For example, *Crazy English* (Fengkuang Yingyu, 1999; dir. Zhang Yuan) is a cinema verité film that follows the celebrity Li Yang as he moves along the circuit of his mass English-teaching rallies. Mixing pedagogy and demagogy, Li yells out in English nationalistic business slogans about making money and outdoing the West, which the crowd then yells back at him in response. Li has been accepted by the authorities as a patriotic paradigm, and it seems that they also have accepted Zhang's film as a eulogy to this popular national hero. However, as I watched the film I could not avoid thinking that Li's mass teachings seemed deeply demagogic like perverse postsocialist mutations of Mao rallies. Given the use of the cinema verité mode, it is difficult if not impossible to detect the filmmaker's own attitude.

Questions surrounding television broadcasting illustrate how difficult it is to make clear-cut judgments about these issues. We need to ask if the television documentaries really do provide a voice for the ordinary people to speak back to power. Or does the fact that they are made within conditions of government control and censorship mean that actually they act as a way of fooling the people into speaking their minds, or of getting good information about public opinion for the government whose own officials ordinary people would be wary of? And if the latter is true, is this necessarily a bad thing? Does it promote positive government change or prop up the existing system and its problems?

Many more difficult questions can be posed as such, but the fundamentally unstable, tense, and ambivalent Gramscian hegemony that is postsocialism makes it impossible to provide definitive answers. Instead, only future developments and more research will determine how this period and these documentary makers are seen in hindsight as contributors to a struggle for gradual transformation from within or to the containment of tensions that later surfaced.

NOTES

1. Bérénice Reynaud, "New Visions/New Chinas: Video-Art, Documentation, and the Chinese Modernity in Question," in *Resolutions: Contemporary Video Practices*, ed. Michael Renov and Erika Suderburg (Minneapolis: University of Minnesota Press, 1996), 229–57.
2. For further discussion of the different uses of the term in the Chinese context and why I draw on Lyotard as opposed to some of the other usages, see Chris Berry, "Seeking Truth from Fiction: Feature Films as Historiography in Deng's China," Film History 7, no. 1 (1995): 95.
3. Michel de Certeau, *The Practice of Everyday Life* (Berkeley: University of California Press, 1984), 36–37.
4. Su Xiaokang and Wang Luxiang, *Deathsong of the River: A Reader's Guide to the Chinese TV Series "Heshang,"* trans. Richard W. Bodman and P. Wan (Ithaca, N.Y.: East Asia Program, Cornell University, 1991). Currently residing in the United States, Su has recently published his memoirs, *A History of Misfortune*, trans. Zhu Hong (New York: Knopf, 2001).
5. Many of the essays composing the Chinese debate about *River Elegy* have been translated into English and published in *Chinese Sociology and Anthropology* 24, no. 4, and 25, no. 1 (1992). For a critical analysis of the documentary's argument, see Jing Wang, "*Heshang* and the Paradoxes of the Chinese Enlightenment," in *High Culture Fever: Politics, Aesthetics, and Ideology in Deng's China* (Berkeley: University of California Press, 1996), 118–36.
6. According to Tony Rayns, the occasion, which he finds "tempting" to date as the birth of the "New Chinese Cinema," "was received with something like collective rapture" ("Chinese Vocabulary: An Introduction to *King of the Children* and the New Chinese Cinema," in *King of the Children and the New Chinese Cinema*, ed. Chen Kaige and Tony Rayns (London: Faber and Faber, 1989), 1.
7. Reynaud, "New Visions/New Chinas," 235.
8. Lu Xinyu, *Zhongguo Xin Jilupian Yundong* [The New Documentary Film Movement in China] (Shanghai: Shanghai Wenyi Chubanshe, 2003). I thank Professor Lu for sharing her ideas and parts of her manuscript with me.
9. Wu Wenguang, "*Bumming in Beijing—The Last Dreamers*," in *The Twentieth Hong Kong International Film Festival*, ed. Urban Council (Hong Kong: Urban Council, 1996), 130.
10. The remaining subject, a theater director called Mou Sen, was the focus of another early documentary, *The Other Bank* (Bi'an, 1995) by Jiang Yue. The video follows Mou Sen's eponymous workshop, which attracts youngsters from around the country but neglects to offer any practical help beyond the experience of the modernist and experimental workshop itself. Lu Xinyu opens her book with an extended discussion of this film, which she sees as representative of the fall away from utopianism and self-criticism among the former avant-garde at the heart of new documentary.
11. Regarding job assignments, at this time students were on graduation still assigned work by the state.
12. For different opinions on this phenomenon in feature filmmaking, see Chris Berry, "Race (*Minzu*): Chinese Film and the Politics of Nationalism," *Cinema Journal* 31, no. 2 (1992): 45–58; Hu Ke, "The Relationship between the Minority Nationalities and the Han in the Cinema," in Chinese National Minorities Films [Lun Zhongguo shaoshu minzu dianying], ed. Gao Honghu et al. (Beijing: China Film Press [*Zhongguo Dianying Chubanshe*], 1997), 205–11; Zhang Yingjin, "From 'Minority Film' to 'Minority Discourse': Questions of Nationhood and Ethnicity in Chinese Cinema," in *Transnational Chinese Cinemas: Identity, Nationhood, Gender*, ed. Sheldon Hsiao-Peng Lu (Honolulu: University of Hawaii Press, 1997), 81–104; Dru C. Gladney, "Representing Nationality in China: Refiguring Majority/Minority Identities," *Journal of Asian Studies* 53, no. 1 (1994): 92–123; Esther C. M. Yau, "Is China the End of Hermeneutics? Or, Political and Cultural Usage of Non-Han Women in Mainland Chinese Films," *Discourse* 11, no. 2 (1989): 115–38; and Stephanie Donald, "Women Reading Chinese Films: Between Orientalism and Silence," *Screen* 36, no. 4 (1995): 325–40.
13. Here, I have noted the mimetic realist qualities found in some Fifth Generation films. For an interpretation that sees the non-mimetic qualities of these films as a form of "expressive realism" (or *xieshizhuyi*) also distinct from socialist realism's representational realism or *xianshizhuyi*, see Chris Berry and Mary Ann Farquhar, "Post-Socialist Strategies: An Analysis of *Yellow Earth* and *Black Cannon Incident*," in *Cinematic Landscapes: Observations on the Visual Arts and Cinema of China and Japan*, ed. Linda C. Ehrlich and David Desser (Austin: University of Texas Press, 1994), 81–116.

14. Gilles Deleuze, *Cinema 1: The Movement Image*, trans. Hugh Tomlinson (Minneapolis: University of Minnesota Press, 1986).
15. Gilles Deleuze, *Cinema 2: The Time Image*, trans. Hugh Tomlinson and Robert Galeta (Minneapolis: University of Minnesota Press, 1989).
16. As Bill Nichols notes: "In a conventional mosaic, the *tesserae* (facets) merge to yield a coherent whole when seen from a distance . . . The *tesserae* or sequences of a Wiseman film are already coherent and do not merge into one impression or one narrative tale so much as supplement each other. The whole of a mosaic is almost invariably embedded in a larger architectural whole but such a larger whole is absent in Wiseman's case . . . the films . . . offer little overt acknowledgment that the institutions under study directly relate to a larger social context" (Nichols, "Frederick Wiseman's Documentaries: Theory and Structure," in *Ideology and the Image* [Bloomington: University of Indiana Press, 1981], 211). Much the same could be said of Duan's film.
17. For more on Duan, *The Square*, and *No. 16 Barkhor Street*, see Chris Berry, "Interview with Duan Jinchuan," *Metro* 113/114 (1998): 88–89.
18. Lydia H. Liu, "Translingual Practice: The Discourse of Individualism between China and the West," *positions* 1, no. 1 (1993): 160–93.
19. On reportage as resistance, see Yingjin Zhang, "Narrative, Ideology, Subjectivity: Defining a Subversive Discourse in Chinese Reportage," in *Politics, Ideology and Literary Discourse in Modern China: Theoretical Interventions and Cultural Studies*, ed. Liu Kang and Xiaobing Tang (Durham, N.C.: Duke University 1993), 211–42.
20. In addition to the spontaneous documentaries, nationalistic documentaries the "special topic" *zhuanti* mode have also found new audiences on television even in the movie theaters, where in 1996 the film *Test of Strength* about the Korean War, known in China as the War to Resist U.S. Aggression and Aid Korea, was an unprecedented box office hit in the cities. See Ye Lou, "Popular Docmentary Films," *Beijing Review* 41, no. 26 (1998): 28–29.
21. For a more detailed discussion of Zhang Yuan's films focused on *East Palace, West Palace*, see Chris Berry, "*East Palace, West Palace*: Staging Gay Life in China," *Jump Cut*, no. 42 (1998): 84–89.
22. Although some may object to the statement that fewer films than ever are made directly by the studios, my understanding at the time of this writing is that the law requires that, at least nominally, films are made within the studio system and in conformity with the attendant censorship practices. This often involves "buying a studio logo" (*mai yige changbiao*) or paying a studio a fee nominal supervision.
23. Barbara Hammer's documentary *Devotion: A Film about Ogawa Productions* (2000) not only gives a useful background to Ogawa but also features his footage of foreign documentary makers listening to the great Ogawa expound during a lecture. Among the attentive listeners is Wu Wenguang. Also noteworthy is the decision made by Ogawa's widow to invite the Chinese Fifth Generation feature filmmaker Peng Xiaolian to finish his final work, *Manzan Benigaki*, which was shown at the 2001 Yamagata festival.
24. Chris Berry, "Crossing the Wall," *Dox*, no. 13 (1997): 14–15.

110

WU WENGUANG

DV

Individual Filmmaking (2006)

Two years ago, in May 1999, in a place in Shanxi Province called Guxian, I spent some time with a traveling performance troupe called the Far & Wide Song and Dance Troupe. This was a group of itinerant entertainers that traveled around from place to place, performing under the big tent they carted around with them. The boss, a fifty-ish man named Liu, came from a small village in the Pingdingshan region of Henan Province. His two sons, their girlfriends, and some of his nieces and nephews were all in the troupe. Counting all the actors and crewmembers, there were probably around thirty people, all of them around twenty years old and most of them from rural Henan. I'd been spending time with this group since the previous year; I had first met them when they were performing on the streets outside the South Fourth Ring Road in Beijing. Ever since then I had been tagging along with them from time to time as they performed in suburban Beijing and Hebei and Shanxi provinces, filming them with a small digital video camera. Here I don't want to talk about what material I filmed or what I discovered about the "lower rungs" or that kind of thing; instead, I'd like to talk about how the feel of this project was totally different from the very "professional" kind of documentary filmmaking I had done before. With this project I just carried the DV camera around with me like a pen and hung out with the members of the troupe. Every day my ears were filled with the rough sounds of Henan dialect; in the evenings, lying on the stage under the big tent, I was surrounded by the sleeping forms of the roadies, and the air was filled with the stink of feet and the smells of the wilderness while the stars glittered through the holes and cracks in the tent's roof. Getting up in the mornings, I'd pull on my shoes, walk out of the tent, and take a piss in the wilderness, the air incomparably clear and fresh and perfectly silent. A young roadie would be squatting not far off, taking a shit; we'd greet each other: "You're up." At times like these, Beijing felt really far away. All that modern art—really far away.

Before that, for me documentary filmmaking wasn't such a casual, individual activity. It was the kind of thing that involved a bunch of people carrying big machines on their shoulders—very conspicuous, even from a long way off. But in 1995, after I finished *At Home in the World* (Sihai Wei Jia), I felt I had some serious problems. The problems were not just with that film itself; I felt that all my documentaries were caught in a fundamental dilemma. This dilemma was that, on the one hand, in making documentaries I was working from individual motivations: I would shoot whatever I wanted and do whatever I wanted with what I shot, rather than conforming to the dictates of television or distribution networks. But on the other hand, the filming and production techniques I was using were the usual ones, techniques that required money. At the very least, before even beginning to film you had to have a little money to rent the camera equipment. But the resulting films usually had very little commercial appeal. This approach, of "taking money to play with ideas," meant that even the people who were interested in giving you money soon stopped daring to play along with you, and your own wallet was never thick enough to support you, so it was hard to sustain for long. Then I thought that maybe "use film, not video" was the way to go. At that time I was surrounded by a group of people talking about using the medium of film to make documentaries, reasoning that only in this way could a work be considered a "professional documentary film." I was an enthusiast of this approach, and my experiences at film festivals had led me privately to feel that using film instead of video would also allow me access to more competitions, awards, art house cinemas, and distribution networks. Once I started thinking this way I began to disdain video; I then had excellent reason to lie around in bed and talk about how, once I found the money, I'd make one of those soul-stirring documentaries that would also circulate widely.

This was my way of thinking in 1995. At the time I felt that this was perhaps the right way to go, but other people who thought this way were already having problems. So I decided to stop completely and do nothing at all. Then in 1997 I spent some time in the United States. During that trip I spent two weeks in Boston, in Frederick Wiseman's studio. Of all the documentary filmmakers of that generation, Wiseman is the one I respect the most. For more than thirty years he has been using his own unique style to document all different levels of American society. And he's made a film every year without interruption—something unheard of not only in the United States but anywhere in the world. While all the other documentary filmmakers in the world talk about how incomparably difficult it is to make documentaries, there is this guy just making them, one after another. I found this really puzzling. In the space of two weeks, I didn't manage to solve this puzzle, but I did discover the source of my problems. During that time Wiseman and I spent day and night together in his Boston home. In the daytime I sat behind him in his studio as he worked at the editing board cutting his new film *Belfast, Maine*, and occasionally he would turn around and chat briefly with me. In the evenings we would make dinner together at his house, talking while we ate, and then after dinner we would usually take a walk for an hour or so. The next morning at nine, when I was just getting up, Wiseman would already be in the studio. Most of the time our conversations had nothing to do with documentary filmmaking; we talked about family, friends, hobbies, what kinds of novels we liked, and so on, but as I came one step closer to understanding the simple, everyday life of this giant in the world of documentary filmmaking, I felt that what I saw in Wiseman resembled an author far more than any of the film people I was familiar with. This discovery came upon me suddenly one day as I sat behind him, watching him spooling back and forth through foot after foot of film, like he always did. I believe this was the most important discovery I made in the four years I have known this man: not some easily learned documentary approach or technique, but the spirit hidden behind this approach. It's impossible to articulate what this spirit is; it can only be intuited. The most direct way to express this intuition is: now I know what it is that I most sorely lack.

Through the years that I've been getting to know documentary film two people have directly inspired me in this way. The first was Japan's Ogawa Shinsuke, who, in the course of film screenings and discussions in his studio in 1991, led me to understand that documentary should not be simply about film or art—it should have a direct relationship with the reality that we live in every day, a relationship with social work. From this it follows that one person making a documentary film is not important; what is important is many people working together for its sake. In 1997 in Wiseman's studio I discovered that there is no direct relationship between the word "independent" and video or film; it is a way of life, something that runs in your veins. I was very fortunate that, soon after I made these discoveries, small digital video recorders became available; or perhaps it was that the changes I had undergone had primed me to be able to grasp almost immediately the advantages of this format. Then I took one in my hands and followed it, allowing it to change me into the way I am today: I have abandoned the notions of themes and plotlines, abandoned the idea of pursuing, like a hunter, a single aim; instead, I ramble around by myself, minicam in hand, distancing myself ever more from professional filmmakers.

Sometimes I ask myself exactly what it is that I am doing. Other people ask me this question too. Once in a small town in Shanxi Province, the troupe was accused of "performing obscene material." The local police closed down the big tent, hauled the boss and all the actors down to the station for questioning, and then fined them for having a "substandard performance license." I was there for the whole thing (though of course I couldn't film any of it), and I was also questioned as to what I was doing. The two answers I could come up with—"I'm making a documentary film" and "I'm an author"—sounded strange even to me, and did nothing to dispel the suspicions of my interrogator. Three days later, everything that had been confiscated from the tent was returned to the troupe; they loaded it all onto the truck and moved to another small town, reassembled the tent and the stage, and the sound of music and singing once again filled the air. That day, in order to celebrate and because the troupe members hadn't seen a piece of meat in days (the wok had gone all rusty), I went to the butcher's shop in town and bought ten catties of pork, came back, picked up a ladle, and cooked up a big wokful of my specialty, *hongshao* braised pork. The cook stove was right next to the stage where a performance was in full swing, so the aroma of braised pork wafted out into an atmosphere already full of song and dance. Everyone backstage crowded around the stove; as the actors finished their parts and came offstage they made straight for the wok, and when it was their turn to go back onstage they went directly from stove-side to center stage; the songs being sung onstage were echoed back offstage. It really felt like a festival; everyone was in high spirits. In my right hand I held the ladle and in my left the DV camera, kidding around and randomly recording stuff; after awhile someone else took the camera, and then countless hands snatched it back and forth, everyone filming each other.

It's been two years since then, and there are a lot of people and things I've forgotten, but those days I spent with the troupe stay with me. Now, even though the film *Jianghu: Life on the Road* and the book *Report from the Jianghu* (Jianghu Baogao) are long since done and published, I still can't leave the "big tent." What I mean is that I'm no longer able to disappear from the scene as soon as the filming is done, like the "professional documentary filmmaker" I used to be. I can't stop myself from keeping in touch with members of the troupe. Some of them have left the troupe and joined other troupes, and some new people have joined. From time to time I go stay with them in the tent or in their home villages, and each time I go I bring along my DV camera, filming now and again as the mood strikes. I don't know if this material will ever be used, and at the moment I'm not particularly worried about it. I'm just following my own sensibilities. Following life itself.

In the three years since I began filming *Jianghu* I've roamed around in other places with my DV camera as well. I have two DV cameras, one big and one small. The big one is a Canon XL-1, with interchangeable lenses, and the small one is a Sony 100E Handycam; which one I use depends on the environment and what I want to film. One after another people and events enter my lens. I don't go looking for them with the idea of making a film; they just naturally happen in the course of my life. For example, a young guy from rural Shandong brought me a script he wrote about his struggles to fulfill his dreams of becoming a filmmaker in Beijing, wanting me to make it into a film. I didn't make his film; what I did do was follow him around with my DV camera as he talked to all kinds of production companies, investors, and directors, which ended up drawing out all kinds of people and issues related to film. For another example, I videotaped the wedding of some friends of mine from Shanghai that later developed into the possibility of a poignant love story. An art exhibit, a rock concert, a dinner party with friends, a stroll down the street—all kinds of people and events crowd together onto the DV tapes, entirely without theme, intention, or plot. After two or three years, maybe some of this material could be worked into a long film, some of it could make a ten-minute short, some of it might be worked into multimedia material I've made for theater or dance performances. Of course most of it consists of "paragraphs" or fragments of everyday life, which may not have any connection to great plots or profound meanings, and will forever be just a series of digital frames and sounds recorded on tape; but it is all still a part of my "diary of images."

I'd like to talk a bit now about the editing of my films. To match my style of DV filming, I've set up an "individual non-linear workstation" that is actually just a regular personal computer with a video card and a big hard drive. It cost a total of 20,000 RMB [approximately U.S. $2,500], but it allows me to work comfortably and freely at home. "Just five steps from bed to computer editing board"—that pretty well describes how personal my approach to filmmaking is. I am very happy not to have anything to do with the kind of post-production that goes on in editing rooms, and not to have a voice from behind me telling me to do this or not to do that.

Having removed myself from the usual orbit of "a bunch of people eating, drinking and working together for a film," I've become an individual with a DV camera, filming as I please whatever happens to be in my line of vision, whether or not it has anything to do with a "theme"; I then edit the material as I please, cutting out whatever is irrelevant to my own intentions; and finally, when the film is finished, I have a few screenings and discussions in universities, bars, film festivals, libraries and so on. Because this approach doesn't cost much money I don't really care whether or not it turns a profit. Maybe this is what is meant by "individual filmmaking." The result of this way of doing things is that I've moved farther and farther away from "professionalism," television, film festival competitions and awards, but I find that I've moved closer and closer to myself, my own inner world. As a result, I have finally come to understand that "independent filmmaking" and "free cinema" are not just "stances" that can be achieved through "manifestoes" or "position statements" or the attitude that one or two films can sustain you for the rest of your life. Given the "investigative" and commercial imperatives that filmmakers are surrounded by these days, if I boast emptily about "independence," you can be sure that it's just hot air. So today, when talking about my relationship to documentary film, I can only speak about DV. I also must say that I want to thank DV: it was DV that saved me, that allowed me to maintain the kind of personal relationship to documentary filmmaking I have today, and made it far more than just a status.

111

RICHARD PORTON

WEAPON OF MASS INSTRUCTION

Michael Moore's *Fahrenheit 9/11* (2004)

Since the American release of *Fahrenheit 9/11*, Michael Moore has been hailed by the left as the new Tom Paine, denounced by his right-wing opponents as the incarnation of Joseph Goebbels and Leni Riefenstahl, and compared by film critics to such disparate figures as Sergei Eisenstein and Kenneth Anger. Moore has become a lightning rod for hyperbolic praise and disgust, and the vigorous, and unusually vehement, responses to his bracingly sardonic anti-Bush salvo are probably as much aligned with the polarization produced by this unsavory administration's invasion and occupation of Iraq as with the persona of its—to invoke the ubiquitous and perhaps inevitable cliché—"controversial" director. For those of us who initially viewed the film at Cannes with nary a Bush supporter in sight, the eventual *Palme d'or* winner was one film (and one documentary, if the many other nonfiction films screened out of competition are included) among many; speculation concerning *Fahrenheit*'s potential to influence the upcoming American elections was of course rife but there was also an opportunity to discuss its esthetic strengths and weaknesses in a relatively dispassionate fashion. On its home turf, as op-ed columnists who rarely comment on movies chimed in with their often stale "takes," *Fahrenheit* became a full-fledged media event with both supporters and naysayers assuming a virtually take-no-prisoners attitude as the actual film became a mere pretext for sets of liberal or conservative "talking points."

The assault on Moore's film from assorted attack dogs at Fox, MSNBC, and David Horowitz's website FrontpageMagazine.com has only been instructive for letting us know that these pundits don't believe that their *bête noire* has made a documentary; after all, it has a "point of view," is less neutral than a *National Geographic* special, and might well be "propaganda." Unwittingly throwing decades of documentary history down the collective memory hole, Joe Scarborough, Bill O'Reilly, and their cohorts inadvertently demonstrate the necessity of some sort of antidote to the noxious "spin" and outright lies disseminated by the Bush Administration over the last three-and-a-half years. (Listeners to New York's NPR station, WNYC, were also treated to a film professor's startling revelation that we should be wary of Moore's cinematic sleight of hand since voice-over commentary can transform an audience's perceptions of meticulously edited images—Gee, hold the presses!) As the pseudonymous "Vern," an on-line, self-proclaimed "outlaw" critic, fulminated, "If the American news media had been doing their job, there would be nothing new to report. So you fucks in the media, stop complaining about this movie. It's your fault it even exists."

However highly leftists might esteem Noam Chomsky, Robert McChesney, Alexander Cockburn, and other eviscerators of the mainstream media, these mainstays of *Z* and *The Nation* have been—if not precisely "preaching to the converted" on all occasions—instructing a much smaller audience than the populist Moore. As a popularizer, Moore compresses and synthesizes a large chunk of research and invective that surfaced in the alternative press as well as a hit parade of post-9/11 best sellers—Greg Palast's painstaking inventory of official deceit in Florida before and after the 2000 election, journalist Ahmed Rashid's incisive history of the Taliban's rise to power, Craig Unger's insistence on casting a cold eye on the affinities between the House of Saud and "the House of Bush," as well as the contributions of lesser Internet luminaries featured in postings on, among others, MoveOn.org, TomPaine.com., and *CounterPunch.*

It's easy to empathize with left-of-center critics who are distraught that their lack of enthusiasm for Moore's shameless self-infatuation and freewheeling polemical style will be falsely construed as de facto conservatism. On the other hand, there's something slightly prissy and myopic in the refusal of Moore's critics to acknowledge that his wildly popular meld of humor, media critique, and anti-Establishment ire implicitly skewers the self-delusions of many esthetes (I don't exclude myself) who tend to equate popular appeal with selling out. To wit, while *Fahrenheit* is arguably the most straightforward and rhetorically effective film the Big Guy has yet made, the source of its considerable verve as ad hoc political rabble-rousing—as well as its sporadic annoyances—can be traced to a clever fusion of the documentary-essay tradition (a genre that, from the erudite radicalism of Chris Marker and the muckraking of Emile de Antonio to the kitschier realm of *The Atomic Café,* has often employed found footage for didactic purposes) with a host of other nonfiction genres: adversarial campaign commercials as well as the newer, even less intellectually respectable terrain of rock videos and reality television.

Moore's own forays into political pranksterism—*TV Nation* and *The Awful Truth*—were pioneering attempts to wed political satire and Reality TV. A faint echo of Moore's fondness for ambushing the complacent and powerful can even be discerned in the thoroughly apolitical *Punk'd,* a show that refuses, according to the MTV website to "kiss major celebrity butt." *New York* magazine went as far to compare *Fahrenheit*'s urge to underline its jabs at Dubya with a steady barrage of rock tunes to *Pop Up Video* and the wall-to-wall music that provides commentary on Jessica Simpson and Nick Lachey's marital entanglements during the MTV mega-hit *Newlyweds: Nick and Jessica.* As an entertainer who is now part of pop culture himself, Moore's decision to deploy—if you'll excuse the phrase—any means necessary to construct his arguments has undoubtedly alienated some on the left as well as the right. Even while Moore's argument is unified by common motifs and an overweening hostility to Bush, his minions, and the rationale and conduct for the invasion and occupation of Iraq, its stylistic eclecticism no doubt accounts for the elderly historian (and former *Vogue* film critic) Arthur Schlesinger, Jr.'s observation that *Fahrenheit* "could have been more effective if it had any perceptible structure" and the general uneasiness some viewers have had with the documentary's sudden shifts in tone. It has become commonplace to praise a film by, say, Mike Leigh or Atom Egoyan for its effective oscillations between humor and pathos. Moore's analogous alternation of righteous outrage with concerted smarminess has nevertheless proved irksome as well as unsettling for many who feel reluctant to jump on the *Fahrenheit* bandwagon.

That being said, this lavishly praised (and vigorously maligned) movie's precredits sequence is probably the most accomplished, even moving piece of filmmaking in Moore's corpus. The plangent tone of the opening sequence, recapitulating the 2000 election debacle in Jeb Bush's Florida, is uncharacteristically lyrical (Jeff Gibbs's creepily resonant, Philip Glass-like music certainly helps) for Moore, and (dare I say it?) almost approaches the spirit of Marker's rueful ironies. Given the now-common propensity to divide recent American history into a far from Edenic but nevertheless more "normal" pre-9/11 phase and a politically and morally hellish postlapsarian post-9/11 era, Moore's voice-over proclaiming, "Was it all just a dream?," as Ben Affleck, Robert De Niro, and Stevie Wonder celebrate a chimerical Gore victory, succinctly sums up the chasm between then and now. After the mood turns increasingly sour, the sadly ineffectual efforts of members of the House of Representatives, including many members of the Congressional Black Caucus, to recruit at least one senator to prevent certification of a Bush victory, reminds even readers of *The Nation* and regular visitors to MoveOn.org that some slices of history have been skillfully buried. Greg Palast titled the introduction to *The Best Democracy Money Can Buy*, which chronicles Jeb Bush's spectacular success in purging 57,000 people from the Florida voter roles (the majority "guilty of being Black"), "Who Gives a Shit?" Once the brouhaha of 2000 subsided, few outside of the usual dissident organs appeared to give a shit; it is the great merit of this prelude to Moore's scathing assessment of the Bush presidency that a largely quiescent electorate now has the opportunity to share the black representatives' agony. Perhaps Gore's stone-faced repose during this mournful session—one that he presides over in his capacity as President of the Senate—is the most infuriatingly paradoxical moment in the film. His seeming obliviousness to his own fate nearly confirms many disgruntled voters' conclusion that, after waging a lackluster, thoroughly uninspired campaign, the Vice President almost deserved to lose.

Once the credits unfurl, the political vaudeville for which *Fahrenheit* has been both celebrated and reviled, kicks in. Some dainty souls insist that the satellite news "feeds" of Republican luminaries acting foolish when they believed the cameras were off—the decidedly nauseating sight of neoconservative honcho Paul Wolfowitz garnishing his comb with saliva and President Bush's almost Pee Wee Hermanish eye-rolling—are undignified cheap shots. Nevertheless, without drawing any hyperbolic comparisons, it's clear that satirists—from Jonathan Swift to the practitioners of political cabaret in Munich and Berlin during the Twenties, as well as the bravura comic riffs of Mort Sahl and Lenny Bruce during the Cold War Fifties—have always relished the detonation of cannily aimed, no doubt necessary, cheap shots. Moore is a lesser, more erratic wit than Bruce, and certainly Swift, but left-liberal whining about cheap shots goes a long way to demonstrate why the loyal, or perhaps craven, opposition is often derided as ridiculously genteel.

Fahrenheit's by-now-legendary chronicle of the seven, seemingly interminable minutes during which Bush continued to read *My Pet Goat* (or, according to a "Talk of the Town" piece in *The New Yorker, The Pet Goat*) to a second-grade class in Sarasota, Florida, while Americans endured the shock of attacks on the World Trade Center and the Pentagon, has even been dismissed as a facile satirical jape (that might even enrage those vacillating "undecided" voters in "swing" states) by an assortment of nominally liberal columnists. Yet perhaps no other footage of our hapless leader better conveys his status as a befuddled, clueless cipher who is powerless, and literally voiceless, without his handlers. Admittedly, a few of Moore's other comic interludes resemble throwaway sketches on an off night of *Late Night With David Letterman.* An attempt to skewer the ineffectuality of the Bushites' half-hearted efforts to root out al Qaeda in Afghanistan is tepidly lampooned with a *Bonanza* parody featuring Blair, Bush, Cheney, and Rumsfeld as less glamorous incarnations of the Cartwright family. Similarly, the much-vaunted, if in fact ragtag "Coalition of the Willing" is parodied with ludicrous stock footage deriding the minuscule troops proffered by Palau and Romania, while managing to omit the pivotal participation of Great Britain, for the sake of a few less than hearty laughs. Still, there are times when Moore's blend of rock-video esthetics and smart-ass humor hits its target brilliantly; as Bush's notorious military records come on the screen, for example, a few bars of Eric Clapton's "Cocaine" are heard on the sound track. The allusion is so fleeting and apt that it seems nearly subliminal.

By now, few readers will have to be informed that the extended sequence probing the Bush family's economic ties with Saudi Arabia has elicited more overwrought carping from Moore haters than any other aspect of the film. While the film's accretion of accusations is occasionally poorly focused, this can be attributed to an entirely different set of problems than those raised by the Republican talking heads who are eager to yell conspiracy theory—as if the case formulated by Moore was somehow akin to *The Protocols of the Elders of Zion* or an old John Birch Society pamphlet. In fact, Moore's delineation of the "special relationship" between the Bushes and the Saudi Royal family (culled from sources such as Unger and Rashid's books and refashioning its modus operandi from the first chapter of Moore's own *Dude, Where's My Country?*) has the salutary result of at least providing a provisional dossier of ways in which the current administration's foreign policy might well be compromised and sullied by a convoluted web of investments and murky alliances. Unfortunately, the breathless Cook's Tour of Bush *père*'s willingness to shill for the Carlyle Group, with its well-documented links to the bin Laden family (which resembles the Cliff Notes version of *Exposed: The Carlyle Group,* a documentary produced by the Dutch television network VPRO, available on-line at www.informationclearinghouse.info/article3995.htm) and the amusing tidbit, familiar to readers of Unger's book, that the Bush family christened Prince Bandar, the Saudi ambassador to the U.S., "Bandar Bush," personify the weaknesses of Moore's scattershot indictment.

It is not that the barrage of accusations aren't rooted in tangible research or that most of us can't help but relish Moore's loaded rhetorical question to a GW deeply indebted to his Saudi pals: "Who's your daddy?" It's more to the point that our gleeful *schadenfreude* is not complemented by even a sketchy account of how the Bush family's sordid history mirrors the systemic rot of American foreign policy that, far from sui generis, began in earnest with the blunders of the Reagan and Clinton Administrations. Steve Coll, for example, in his magisterial *Ghost Wars: The Secret History of the CIA, Afghanistan, and Bin Laden, From the Soviet Invasion to September 10, 2001,* gloomily concludes that both Reagan and Clinton "typically coddled undemocratic and corrupt Muslim governments, even as these countries' frustrated middle classes looked increasingly to conservative interpretations of Islam for social values and political ideas. In this way America unnecessarily made easier, to at least a small extent, the work of al-Qaeda." Coll's assiduous inventory of American hubris dovetails nicely with Chalmers Johnson's concept of "blow-back"—"the unintended consequences of the U.S.'s international activities that have been kept secret from the American people."

Moore prefers to focus on intriguing minutiae such as the probable allure of a proposed trans-Afghan pipeline spearheaded by Unocal and Hallibuton for Cheney and Bush, who appeared relatively unperturbed by Osama bin Laden or al Qaeda and obsessed by the phantom threat of Saddam Hussein's Iraq. Perversely enough, Rumsfeld himself was on smashing terms with Hussein during the Reagan Administration, a fact driven home by a 1983 photograph of the two men that Moore cleverly inserts into the film as Bush assumes the demeanor of a dazed rabbit during his awkward sojourn at the Sarasota elementary school. Yet, while acknowledging that a film made for a mass audience cannot include the cinematic equivalent of footnotes and appendices or rival the book-length analyses of Coll and Johnson, it might have been nice for audiences to have known that Rumsfeld's newfound rage towards an old friend was complemented, and reinforced, by Wolfowitz and fellow neocon Richard Perle's support for both the Likud Party's attack on Palestinian rights *and* their belief that the goals of the Israeli far right could be best facilitated by regime change in Iraq. Or we could have had an indication that the neoconservatives, among them Rumsfeld and Wolfowitz, who urged President Clinton to wage "preventive war" against Hussein in 1998 view the current conflagration as something of a continuation of the Cold War by other means in another historical context; as Robert Fisk pointed out a year after the war broke out, "Condoleezza Rice, Bush's specialist on threats and terror, warned us about a 'mushroom cloud'—the Russian version, presumably, rather than Hiroshima and Nagasaki."

At the end of the revised edition of his classic study, *The First Casualty: The War Correspondent as Hero and Myth-Maker from the Crimea to Kosovo*, Phillip Knightley muses that, in an era where TV viewers decry "images of bomb victims and battle casualties " as "too upsetting," it's likely that "spin doctors, propagandists, and military commanders will find further justification for managing the media in wartime and that the Gulf and Kosovo will become the pattern for all future wars." In certain respects, Moore's focus on the Iraqi invasion and occupation in the latter half of *Fahrenheit 9/11* is a conscious attempt to counteract most journalists' escape from responsibility as they willingly agree to be muzzled by the White House and the Pentagon. It's true that the shock cuts employed to contrast the official consensus on Iraq with the carnage and collateral damage that have gone unreported represent the triumph of sledgehammer editing. Sadly, the use of a subtler approach would probably have been ineffective in an era when a leisurely pace is equated with boredom. For this reason, the images of heavy metal-crazed airmen preparing their targets, the juxtaposition of a traumatized Iraqi woman surveying the destruction of her home with Britney Spears's air-headed support for Bush, and the clash between Rumsfeld's homage to "humane" antipersonnel weapons and the actual damage they inflict are unsubtle but effective jabs at the somnolent U.S. media.

Some of Moore's critics, including some liberals, have chastised him for supposedly emphasizing American misconduct at the expense of any mention of Saddam Hussein's crimes. But, even if many of us disagreed with, say, Paul Berman's provisional support of the war, there is nothing in *Fahrenheit 9/11* that is not congruent with his "challenge" in the June 28, 2004 issue of *The New Republic:* "to rage at Saddam and other enemies, and at the same time, to rage in a somewhat different register at Bush, and to keep those two responses in proportion to one another." Of course, while it is uncertain whether Berman would consider *Fahrenheit*'s rage against Bush appropriately Solomonic, Moore's strategic emphasis on American transgressions is once more intended to offset the cheerleading for a war that has gone terribly awry in ways that were predicted by commentators with more prescience than the staff of *The New Republic.* The film's footage of Katie Couric gushing over Navy SEALs (who apparently "rock"), and Dan Rather pledging eternal allegiance to any wars his country might engage in, reflect the jingoistic distortion of patriotism that has infected this country during the current administration's reign of error. Footage obtained by Moore depicting sexual and verbal abuse of Iraqis by American soldiers that is startlingly reminiscent of the shocking revelations from Abu Ghraib is preceded by his pronouncement that "immoral behavior" breeds more immoral behavior. This sequence is a more powerful admonishment of Berman and Christopher Hitchens's hawkish rhetoric than any verbal argument: the superficial "altruism" of the prowar camp is countered by evidence that the U.S. has not set an example for Iraqis oppressed for years by Hussein but instead mimics the regime it excoriates.

If the Fourth Estate is cheerfully complicit with its own silencing, it is no surprise that the bulk of the public proved equally happy to embrace, to the extent that they were even aware of them, the most repressive provisions of the U.S.A.-Patriot Act. Moore's cagey interview with Rep. John Conyers highlights the world-weariness that plagues even the best-intentioned politicians, and *Fahrenheit*'s slightly tongue-in-cheek chronicle of how the unthreatening dissidents of Peace Fresno become infiltrated by a police spy, and the odd tale of a bodybuilder whose denunciation of Bush inspires a fellow gym rat to report him to the FBI, provide a cautionary glimpse of the creeping authoritarianism that has marked the post 9/11 era. (The absence of any discussion of how a large number of Muslims, especially those granted temporary visas, have been detained and harassed by U.S. immigration authorities is one of the film's glaring omissions. Fortunately, a string of documentaries that almost form a new subgenre are tackling this much-ignored scandal. These films are at least partially designed as grass-roots activist tools.[1])

In order to offset this mood of gloom, Moore offers us several moving conversion narratives. Sgt. Abdul Henderson of the Marine Corps announces that he won't return to Iraq; a once devoutly Republican veteran announces he'll campaign for the Democrats. The film's portrait of Lila Lipscomb of Flint, Michigan, however, might well be a pivotal sequence for those almost mythic "undecided" voters who are so beloved by panelists on Sunday morning political chat shows. Moore's working-class roots notwithstanding, his work has occasionally treated so-called "ordinary people" with grating condescension (e.g., the comic relief of "The Rabbit Lady" in *Roger & Me* and *Pets or Meat*). Lipscomb, who describes her family "as part of the backbone of America," is far from a figure of fun. A self-described conservative Democrat who once had nothing but contempt for antiwar protestors, Lipscomb's account of her son's death in a helicopter accident in Iraq reportedly brought tears to Moore's eyes. Facile irony does not rear its head at all when the newly antiwar Lipscomb and the burly filmmaker agree that the U.S. is a "great country." Without attempting overly strained comparisons, the mood is slightly reminiscent of a near-forgotten time in American history during the Popular Front when patriotism was a left-wing priority as well as a right-wing shibboleth, of a moment in American popular culture when a conservative populist director such as Frank Capra and a left-wing populist screenwriter such as Sidney Buchman could join forces on a movie as wonderfully contradictory as *Mr. Smith Goes to Washington* (1939)—the convergence of cornball, but thoroughly earnest, patriotism with anguished disdain for political malfeasance. Moore also drops his smart-alecky façade when confronting the problems of African Americans. Whether detailing the predatory tactics of military recruiters eager to recruit black youth threatened with unemployment, the Flint kids who compare their devastated neighborhood with bomb-scarred Iraq, or the moral crisis plaguing Sgt. Henderson, Moore is never less than completely empathetic when depicting the raw deal dealt America's African American citizens.

The film is also attuned to affinities between the overt injuries of class and the indignities of racism. In a sequence leading up to the recruiters' search for likely prospects, a working-class resident of Flint remarks that he once wrote G.W. Bush about his community's plight and, unsurprisingly, never heard back. Towards the end of the film, in one of the most revelatory archival clips unearthed by Moore, Bush tells a well-heeled audience of Republican donors that while "some people call you the elite, I call you my base." And, as we know, members of this base can easily exempt themselves from wars that they expect the less fortunate members of society to fight on their behalf. One of the many anti-Moore web sites (www.bowling-fortruth.com) charges the supposedly duplicitous director with "unfair and inconsistent attacks on the U.S. armed forces," a theme apparent in many of the impromptu conservative "blogs" which have mushroomed in the wake of *Fahrenheit*'s box-office success. What the angry bloggers fail to mention is that Moore, although quite willing to mock the pretensions of the military establishment, has nothing but respect for the poor, black, and disenfranchised Americans who serve in the military without asking for any favors in return.

It is an open secret (exhaustively researched in David L. Robb's *Operation Hollywood: How the Pentagon Shapes and Censors the Movies,* Prometheus Books, 2004) that the American military brass routinely vets scripts of Hollywood films in return for access to their equipment and personnel. Tributes to a glamorized military elite are often the result; Tony Scott's Tom Cruise vehicle, *Top Gun* (1986), is one of the archetypal examples. Robb quotes Taylor Hackford's observation that [producer] "Don [Simpson] got huge cooperation from the Department of Defense for *Top Gun* . . . He made a lot of money on *Top Gun*, and he made it the way the military wanted it. He told them it would show off their planes and show their guys as dashing young men." In a rather pathetic attempt to duplicate the Hollywood panache of his idol Ronald Reagan, Bush arrived in *Top Gun* regalia on the USS *Abraham Lincoln* during a rather premature 2003 victory celebration that Moore derides as a hubris-laden "party on a boat." The once-AWOL Bush assuming the mantle of Tom Cruise—and subsequently forced to live down a banner reading "Mission Accomplished" that became a conspicuous part of the photo-op—is the polar opposite of the Flint youths captured by Moore's camera (certainly not part of the President's 'base') who consider the military their ticket out of unemployment and hopelessness.

The Irish stand-up comic Dylan Moran maintains that G.W. Bush is bad for comedians: the President always gets to the punch lines first and the poor comics feel that they're picking on the slowest kid in the class. The Bush portrayed as a charming, if dimwitted, frat boy in Alexandra Pelosi's HBO documentary *Journeys with George* comes off in *Fahrenheit* as a man with a malicious sense of humor that reveals his profound sense of entitlement. The now-notorious satellite feed of the President initially denouncing terrorist killers and then instructing reporters to admire his golf swing ("Now, watch this drive.") might be as intrinsically "unfair" as some of the film's critics maintain. But it is an unfairness that has its origins in a deep sense of outrage towards Bush's own unfairness and general incompetence. In fact, many of us who found *The Fog of War*'s supposed "fairness" exasperating find ourselves pleased by a documentary that doesn't mince words.

Fahrenheit may be an on-target guided missile aimed at Bush, but each viewer must nevertheless formulate an interpretation of its multifaceted agenda. As a case in point, a predictably hostile reviewer in *National Review* takes Moore to task for supposedly implying (with the inclusion of a fragment from a Halliburton promotional film) that the war is being fought solely for the sake of Dick Cheney's favorite corporation. But *Fahrenheit,* however unnuanced at times, never reduces the outbreak of war to a single cause (even though economic priorities loom large) and never denies that wars have multiple causes. It would be silly to ignore the spectacularly obvious fact that the U.S. wants hegemony in the Middle East in order to control its oil reserves. The horrible duplicity of the Iraq invasion recalls Brecht's argument in *Mother Courage and Her Children* that "war is a continuation of business by other means, making the human virtues fatal to those who exercise them." Corporate greed is, without doubt, an important component of Bush's military folly, but there are countless other ideological reasons for his administration's endorsement of "preventive war."

Chalmers Johnson's recent book, *The Sorrows of Empire: Militarism, Secrecy, and the End of the Republic,* makes the claim that the war in Iraq "is irrational in terms of any cost-benefit analysis . . . given the widespread political unrest [in the Middle East] and a strong revival of militant Islam, the United States seems inexplicably intent on providing future enemies with enough grievances to do us considerable damage." Johnson can only ascribe this irrationality to the ideal of an imperial "New Rome" endorsed by Bush and his neoconservative cronies. By portraying Bush primarily as a buffoon (while conveniently ignoring his born-again Christian missionary zeal),[2] Moore's movie obviously focuses on individual villainy rather than the entire spectrum of reasons that have brought us to our current crisis. Nevertheless, he does a brilliant job in stripping the wannabe emperor (and, by extension, the all-too-real empire) of his/its new clothes.

Given the opportunity to design the ideal artist to satirize the current administration's mendacity, we would probably request some currently unrealizable combination of Brecht, Eisenstein, Chaplin, Georg Grosz, and Goya. Michael Moore is, alas, all we have and he is good enough, and perhaps all we really deserve, for these dark times. In any case, David Denby's strange assertion that Moore "has never known how to change anyone's politics" seems patently false. If my anecdotal, thoroughly unscientific findings have any merit, *Fahrenheit* is stirring up debate (of an often quite ferocious variety) at dinner parties, multiplexes, office water coolers, and public meetings. Whether you love, loath, or feel ambivalent about Michael Moore, it's obvious that more than a few minds have been changed.

NOTES

1. Among the most notable of these documentaries are *Persons of Interest* (distributed by First Run/Icarus Films, www.frif.com), *Point of Attack* (The Cinema Guild, www.cinemaguild.com), *Out of Status* (www.chaibreak.com), *Lest We Forget*, and *Everything is Gonna Be Alright.*
2. William Karel's less playful, but in certain respects more informative, *Le monde selon Bush* (*The World According to Bush*, 2004), explores the right-wing radicalism of neocons such as Perle and Wolfowitz, as well as the President's affection for fundamentalist Christianity.

SCOTT MACDONALD

UP CLOSE AND POLITICAL

Three Short Ruminations on Ideology in the Nature Film (2006*)

A few months ago I saw a film on TV, one of the *Nova* series, I think, about spiders. I've never see anything more fascinating, or more visual. How can you possibly ignore such work? I'm delighted it's there, and I've always wanted to show it. And it's always worked very well, in terms of audiences.

—Amos Vogel[1]

Probably no substantial dimension of film history that is so widely admired by a public audience and so frequently utilized in academic contexts has been so thoroughly ignored by film critics, historians, and theorists as the nature film (or, to use the current, more widely accepted term, the "wildlife film"): those films and videos that purport to reveal the lives of other species.[2] Indeed, the recent appearance of Gregg Mitman's *Reel Nature: America's Romance with Wildlife on Film* (1999); Derek Bousé's *Wildlife Films* (2000), currently the definitive exploration of American wildlife cinema; and the beautiful book on the French nature-film pioneer, Jean Painlevé, *Science Is Fiction: The Films of Jean Painlevé* (2000), edited by Andy Masaki Bellows and Marina McDougall, with Brigitte Berg, are the exceptions that prove the rule. Until the appearance of these books, there had been a dearth of writing about nature film, at least within the annals of American film scholarship.[3] My guess is that while their

*Revised 2015.

colleagues in the sciences may show nature films, most academic film studies professionals barely consider nature film a part of film history. There are few better indications of the educationally counterproductive gap between the humanities and the sciences.

While one can hope that the three volumes mentioned above—along with the remarkable recent successes of *Winged Migration* (Jacques Cluzaud and Jacques Perrin, 2001), *Deep Blue* (Andy Byatt and Alastair Fothergill, 2003), and especially *March of the Penguins* (Luc Jacquet, 2005)—will instigate further exploration and exhibition of this neglected genre, the general attitude of film historians and scholars currently makes such a revival less than certain. The obvious location for serious thinking about the nature film, at least within academic film studies, would seem to be within the history and theory of documentary film. In fact, in the popular mind, few forms of filmmaking are more obvious instances of documentary than the nature film. But historians of documentary routinely ignore the nature film, for reasons articulated by Bill Nichols.[4] For Nichols, the capacity of the photographic image to generate indexical representations of the world makes it valuable for scientific imaging, but cinema's very usefulness to science "depends heavily on minimizing the degree to which the image, be it a fingerprint or X-ray, exhibits any sense of perspective or point of view distinctive to its individual maker. A strict code of objectivity, or institutional perspective, applies. The voice of science demands silence, or near silence, from documentarian or photographer."[5] Since documentary requires a "voice of its own," according to Nichols—"voice of its own" meaning a clear or at least identifiable ideological position—nature film is by definition not part of documentary history.[6]

There are several problems with this position, and they grow increasingly evident the more fully modern society comes to terms with the many dimensions of the evolving environmental crisis. Of course it is true, as Nichols suggests, that nature films (science films in general) have historically pretended to objectivity. There are a variety of reasons for this. Since science is our cultural attempt to find out what aspects of the physical world can be known through observation and experimentation (that is, those aspects of the physical world that are verifiable regardless of ideology or belief), it is hardly surprising that scientific films have an aura of objectivity that is confirmed by the cinema's ability to make indexical, seemingly objective, records of sensory phenomena. But the moment a nature filmmaker begins to construct a particular film, there is no escaping point of view: filmmakers must choose what to show us and determine a filmic structure that exhibits a particular set of conclusions, whether they are those of an individual scientist, a group of scientists, or science-interested laypeople. The presumption of objectivity in science film is simply a particular instance of the aura of objectivity that documentary nearly always carries with it, and which, as Nichols has so often made clear in other contexts, must be qualified by the point of view that is explicit/implicit within any specific documentary.

A second reason for the widely held position that nature films are not really documentaries, and therefore not worth serious investigation within a film studies context, is historical, in at least two senses. First, until Mitman and Bousé, no American scholar had described a history of nature film or made an attempt to identify its pivotal moments and landmark contributions; even the valuable chronology of the wildlife film Bousé includes in *Wildlife Films* is limited in significant ways.[7] It is hard to take a genre seriously if one has no sense of it *as a genre*—and especially since nature films are rarely exhibited as instances of an evolving history. Second, since research into natural phenomena, and other species in particular, is ongoing, and since it is in the nature of new research to make previous research outmoded, nature films that may have seemed state-of-the-art at one point can seem outdated in a few years. This tendency is exacerbated by the fact that a good many nature films, especially those designed for use in primary and secondary schools, use strategies that may seem educational to one generation, but hopelessly corny to the next: Bruce Conner's recycling of material from outdated educational films in surreal montages (e.g., *Mongoloid,* 1978) has the impact it does because those older educational films now seem to reveal more about the absurdities of their era than about scientific information.

This essay makes no pretense of providing anything like a definitive sense of the nature film. I hope, however, that it usefully references a few of the important historical contributions to the genre as a way of foregrounding some of the issues raised in nature films and some aspects of their value in a film studies context. The nature film has, of course, a long prehistory and history that arguably begin with the dawn of the photographic motion picture: Eadweard Muybridge's breakthrough animal locomotion photographs and Zoopraxiscope demonstrations and Etienne-Jules Marey's chronophotographs used a variety of animal species as their primary subject matter. During the first decades of film history, there was a minor tradition of "animal fight films" that included *A Fight Between Spider and Scorpion* (Biograph, 1900) and *A Fight Between Wild Animals* (Kalem, 1912).[8] Films about wildlife, especially hunting films, were important early contributions to the development of the cinema audience. *Roosevelt in Africa* (1910), shot by Cherry Kearton during Theodore Roosevelt's African expedition in 1909, and the more melodramatic and popular fictionalized version of Roosevelt's hunting adventures, *Hunting Big Game in Africa* (1909) by Colonel Selig, instigated a genre of "bring 'em back alive" films that included *Paul Rainey's African Hunt* (1912), William Douglas Burden's footage of the Komodo dragon, and Martin and Osa Johnson's *Trailing African Wild Animals* (1923) and *Simba* (1927).[9] And, of course, exotic animals play pivotal roles in such early proto- or pseudo-ethnographic documentaries as Robert Flaherty's *Nanook of the North* (1921) and *Moana* (1926), and Ernest Schoedsack and Meriam C. Cooper's *Grass* (1925) and *Chang* (1927). The mythic version of these early films is, of course, *King Kong* (1933), produced by Cooper and Schoedsack and based on their own and others' adventures filming in the wild.[10]

While the early films about hunting exotic wild animals and the symbiotic relationships between non-industrialized peoples and animals provoked, and continue to provoke, widespread debate about what is science and what is showmanship, there were also, at least from the 1910s on, attempts to use cinema to focus on the life cycles of other species, apart from their interaction with human society. Two particularly significant contributions to this history are the series of short films made by Jean Painlevé, beginning with *The Octopus (La Pieuvre)* in 1928 and concluding with *Acera, or the Witches' Dance (Acéra, ou le bal des sorcières)* in 1972; and the Walt Disney Studio's True-Life Adventures (in particular, those directed by James Algar), beginning with *Seal Island* (1948), *Beaver Valley* (1950), and *Nature's Half Acre* (1951), and culminating in a series of features, including the commercial breakthroughs *The Living Desert* (1953) and *The Vanishing Prairie* (1954). The Painlevé films and the Disney films could hardly be more different, especially in their exemplification of two very different attitudes with regard to the representation of other species in cinema.

Disney versus Painlevé

Painlevé's pioneering efforts to demonstrate the potential of cinema in scientific experiment and to establish the nature film as a form that combines good science with entertainment and aesthetic awareness precede Disney's True-Life Adventure films by two decades. In the United States there is almost no awareness of Painlevé's contributions, while the Disney films are not only well known, but were formative for several generations of American children—and important for a good many adults as well. Independent filmmaker Nathaniel Dorsky, for example, counts the early True-Life Adventures as one of the primary influences on his work:

> I had started to make films with an 8mm camera when I was around ten or eleven. I was very influenced by the Disney True-Life Adventure series, like *Beaver Valley* and *Nature's Half Acre*. They were the first time I saw, for instance, flowers growing in time-lapse—very photographic films, held together with music and narration. Both films went through the four seasons, and for some reason, I was very taken with that.[11]

I do not remember precisely when or where I first saw the early True-Life Adventures, but such characteristic elements as Winston Hibler's narrating voice, the use of an animated paint brush to introduce films, and the overall tenor remain deeply familiar artifacts of childhood.

Disney began producing wildlife films as a way of dealing with the financial problems created by the high cost of animation. While the series of animated features the Disney studio released during the 1940s were, and remain, immensely popular—*Pinocchio* (1940), *Fantasia* (1940), *Bambi* (1942), *Song of the South* (1946), and *Cinderella* (1949) were the five most popular films of that decade, according to the 2005 *New York Times Almanac*—the considerable cost of these features made them, at first, economically tenuous at best. During this financially strained moment, the comparatively low cost of a nature film—even a feature nature film—allowed this new Disney product to be a financial success. While *Bambi* cost \$2 million, and lost \$1 million during its first run, *The Vanishing Desert* cost around \$350,000, and grossed \$4 million.[12]

Furthermore, the True-Life Adventure films were, like the animations, durable: neither the animations nor the nature films aged as quickly as most live-action films tend to. Over the decades, the Disney animated features have done quite well and continue to be successful in re-release. While the nature films fell prey to changing science and an evolving social awareness (the opening narration of *The Vanishing Prairie,* for example, is patronizing to Native America in ways that have come to seem quite problematic), they too endured to become popular television entertainment during the years when Disney was a major force in television programming. The True-Life Adventures were also inevitable parts of school libraries across the country during the decades when school districts routinely bought 16mm prints of educational films. Several of the feature-length True-Life Adventures can still be found in video rental outlets.

The popularity of the Disney films was the result of their combination of first-rate nature photography with forms of narrative entertainment developed by the Disney Studio during the decades that preceded the release of *Seal Island.* True, Disney nature photographers were sent into the field without a script and were supposed to capture the most interesting imagery they could find, and ideally, according to James Algar, "those unexpected and unpredictable happenings that cannot possibly be written into a story ahead of time."[13] But Disney made sure that the films that developed out of this cinematic research were as carefully constructed and entertainment-driven as any film produced by a Hollywood studio. While the Disney nature films may have seemed to their first audiences as devoid of politics or ideology as the early Silly Symphony cartoons, these films promoted not only particular attitudes toward family life and gender, but a deep complacency about the history of Manifest Destiny and modern middle-class life. Indeed, for all their charm and beauty, the True-Life Adventures can seem as ideologically motivated as *Animal Farm* to a contemporary viewer.

In *The Vanishing Prairie,* as in so many Disney films, the focus is on the nuclear family, especially on the bond between mothers and children and on moments within the lives of animals that seem to mirror middle-class American mores (and in one way or another confirm the gender politics of the time). The film begins with birds migrating—beautiful shots that retrospectively seem like premonitions of *Fly Away Home* (Carroll Ballard, 1996) and *Winged Migration* (Jacques Perrin, 2002). It then moves through various avian courtship rituals and focuses on an amusing moment in the domestic life of a pair of grebes: a piebilled grebe father looks after grebe eggs while the mother grebe is searching for food for several chicks. He does not see that one of the eggs has gotten caught in his feathers and inadvertently moves it out of the nest when he steps out. The narrator comments, "Like most males, he's rather careless about domestic chores!" and then mouths the thoughts of the mother grebe when she returns: "Well, that's typical! Perhaps if he had to *lay* these eggs, he'd be more careful. I declare, these husbands—always leaving things for someone else to pick up!" The fact that the male grebe is tending to the children and the female grebe is out looking for food runs counter to white middle-class gender roles in the 1950s, but the possible impact of this moment is quickly suppressed in favor of humorous banter that locates the grebes within conventional family patterns.[14]

A sequence of amusing mating rituals among grouse leads to a passage on buffalo, punctuated by the birth of a buffalo calf, the mother's care of the calf, and the calf's first attempts to nurse. Then it's on to a passage on prong-horned antelope and big-horned sheep; then to a long segment about a mother mountain lion caring for and training her cubs; then to a complex passage focusing primarily on a community of prairie dogs and their amusing attempts to deal with interlopers (including a mother coyote searching for food for her pups and a male badger who meets a female and falls in love). The climax of *The Vanishing Prairie* is a sequence that begins with buffalo in mating season (no actual mating is shown), followed by a lightning storm that starts a prairie fire, which is put out by heavy rain and a flood. The well-known and much-imitated finale takes us to mountains in winter, where male big-horned sheep battle to the music of "The Anvil Chorus." The film concludes with the narrator's assurance that "Nature preserves her own and teaches them how to cope with time and the unaccountable ways of man. Mankind, in turn, beginning to understand Nature's pattern, is helping her to replenish and rebuild so that the vanishing pageant of the past may become the enduring pageant of the future."

It is, of course, a pageant that Disney provides in *The Vanishing Prairie, The Living Desert,* and in the other True-Life Adventure films. In the completed films, we are sutured into the Disney vision by the continual presence of the narrator; by the music, which is carefully and continuously synched with the action so as to create particular, interpretive cinematic moods; and by the film's visual and textual framing of the "adventures" of the animals. Not only do these films create animal characters that are meant to lure children, mothers, and fathers into emotional identification in much the same way as Disney's animated features do, but individual sequences are often fabricated to suggest that the animals, like the spectators in the theater, are interested observers of what is occurring onscreen. In *The Living Desert* an owl "watches" a burrowing snake, a courtship ritual of tarantulas, and a scorpion mating dance. And, when ground squirrel "Skinny," the "kid from across the way," confronts a Gila monster and chases it away by kicking sand in its eyes, the heroic exploits of the little guy are watched and admired by the neighborhood ground squirrels, who realize they have underestimated Skinny (at the end of the sequence, Skinny rides off into the sunset on the back of a desert tortoise). In other words, in these films—as in any other Hollywood melodrama—we enjoy the pleasure of gazing at the private lives of characters we can identify with, and we share the characters' gazes at each other.

Originally, the True-Life Adventures provided a new, exotic form of entertainment (after half a century, at least judging from a recent class on the history of documentary I taught at Bard College, the entertainment value of *The Living Desert* is still considerable for film students); they combined the conventional pleasures of entertainment film with sense that the audience was learning something. Of course, the True-Life Adventures create an expanded sense of the animals that inhabit particular regions, combined with an emotional residue of pleasant nostalgia for the innocent past and an implicit acceptance of the inevitable progress of civilization. The True-Life Adventures may have created in their first audiences a greater awareness of the natural environment, but it was an awareness qualified by a deep complacency. The natural world is valuable and admirable, the Disney films suggest, precisely to the degree it can be understood to reflect and confirm the ideology of contemporary American middle-class family life.

When one comes to the Painlevé films having first experienced the Disney nature films as a formative childhood influence, it is difficult not to feel that they are transformative, at least in terms of what we assume a nature film can be. While the True-Life Adventures were instigated by financial concerns, Painlevé's nature films were an attempt to demonstrate the value of cinema for science (a highly controversial idea for French scientists of the 1920s), and to produce both good science and good cinema.[15] In a sense, the pageantry of the Disney films reflects their origins in the studio system: many of the True-Life Adventures were elaborate feature-length extravaganzas, produced within a hierarchical studio system involving many people. The Painlevé films are generally eight to fifteen minutes long, and were relatively humble productions, often collaborations with Painlevé's wife, Geneviève Hamon, in which Painlevé—working with technology he himself invented for filming underwater—did his own cinematography or worked with a single cameraperson (usually either Andre Ramond or Eli Lotar). Like the Disney films, Painlevé's nature films were shot in 35mm and were shown in public theaters. Indeed, one of these films, *The Seahorse (L'Hippocampe,* 1934) was successful enough to support a spin-off: a line of seahorse jewelry designed by Hamon and displayed "in chic boutiques alongside aquariums filled with live sea-horses."[16] But *The Seahorse* was the only Painlevé nature film to break even (and, unfortunately, the profits from the seahorse jewelry were stolen). Painlevé was, throughout his life, more a scientist and educator than a capitalist, and his energies were generally directed toward the promotion of science films as an educational tool.

Not surprisingly, given their production process and purpose, the scope and underlying ideology of the Painlevé nature films are very different from the Disney films. The second of Painlevé's "Ten Commandments" for filmmakers is "You will refuse to direct a film if your convictions are not expressed."[17] Each Painlevé film tends to focus on a single organism, usually a single sea creature. Each film presents, clearly and concisely, the crucial moments in the life cycle of the chosen organism, often acknowledging that this particular organism might not at first seem worthy of being the focus of a film. In general, Painlevé's commitment is to the wonder and the beauty of organisms that some would consider beneath our notice (the sea urchin, for instance, or the acera, a tiny mollusk). And he is drawn to organisms, or aspects of organisms, that some would find disgusting: the South American vampire bat in *The Vampire (Le Vampire,* 1945), for example, and the love life of the "cephalopod, horrifying animal" in *The Love Life of the Octopus (Les Amours de la pieuvre,* 1965). Though the body of each film offers in-close examinations of the organisms, Painlevé often makes clear how the organism he has chosen to focus on relates to human society—in a simple practical sense. *The Vampire,* for example, begins with a brief reminder of the pervasiveness of vampires in our imaginations and in the arts—a shot from Murnau's *Nosferatu* (1922) is included; and *Shrimp Stories (Histoires des crevettes)* begins with imagery of men and women fishing for shrimp in ocean shallows.

While the True-Life Adventures tend to be live-action confirmations of attitudes and ideas evident in Disney's early animated features and cartoons, the Painlevé films can be seen, at least in part, as related to Painlevé's interest in art, particularly Surrealism. Painlevé (the son of distinguished mathematician and onetime French prime minister Paul Painlevé) studied mathematics, then medicine, then biology and zoology. In 1923, at the age of 21, he coauthored a scientific paper with one of his professors and presented it to the Académie des Sciences. In 1924, he graduated from the Sorbonne with a degree in physics, chemistry, and biology. By the time he finished university, he had become fascinated with the then-thriving French avant-garde art scene in Paris. Soon, he was friendly with a number of the Surrealists; he was one of the publishers of, and a contributor to, the single issue of the journal *Surréalisme.*[18] Painlevé also became involved with the ciné-club movement that was sweeping through France and the rest of Europe and making available a wide variety of forms of cinema not regularly screened in commercial theaters. Through ciné-club activity, he became close friends with Jean Vigo and in 1927 he finished his own short Surrealist film, *Methuselah,* which is particularly reminiscent of René Clair's *Entr'acte* (1924).[19] Painlevé's engagement with Surrealism would continue; for example, he supplied the remarkable text for the narration of Georges Franju's *The Blood of the Beasts (Le Sang des bêtes,* 1949).

The defiance of social convention implicit in Painlevé's early movement between the worlds of science and Surrealism is frequently evident in his nature films, especially in his (usually implicit, but clearly evident) reasons for focusing on particular organisms. While the Disney nature films focus on animals whose activities can be seen as analogous to, or sentimentally reminiscent of, the activities of the largely middle-class families who were their primary audience, Painlevé's choices often seem, at least in part, a function of the ways in which particular organisms offer a challenge to conventional societal assumptions and values. For example, in an unpublished conversation with Brigitte Berg, Painlevé makes clear that one of the reasons for his early choice of the seahorse as subject was the way the male and female seahorses collaborate on child-raising: the female lays her eggs in the male's abdominal pouch; once the eggs are fertilized, the male nourishes the eggs and, in time, gives birth to the baby seahorses. As Painlevé explained to Berg, "The seahorse was for me a splendid way of promoting the kindness and virtue of the father while at the same time underlining the necessity of the mother. In other words, I wanted to re-establish the balance between male and female."[20] Rather than using the seahorses to reconfirm conventional middle-class American family patterns, Painlevé uses his cinematic report on seahorses to do what he sees as progressive gender politics; he wants us to learn not only *about,* but *from* this strange fish.

Painlevé's interest in the acera mollusks in *Acera, or the Witches' Dance* seems to have two motivations: one of them obvious and the other more subtle. Of obvious interest is the acera's way of finding a mate; as suggested by the film's title, the acera do a kind of ballet, during which the cloaks that encircle their bodies fly open, evoking tutus. A substantial portion of the film is devoted to shots of this dance, which is fascinating and lovely—and reminiscent of moments from Oskar Fischinger films and Disney's *Fantasia* (1940). But once the acera have found mates, we learn that their means of sexual reproduction could not be further from anything implied in a Disney film: each acera is bisexual and can function sexually as either male or female, or, as is demonstrated in *Acera, or the Witches' Dance,* simultaneously as male *and* female. At one point, we see a chain of five acera in which each of the three middle partners fertilizes the eggs of another while, at the same time, having its own eggs fertilized. For Painlevé, the beauty of the acera does not depend on the way it mimics conventional Western assumptions about sexual morality. One can only imagine the repercussions this lovely film would have if it were shown in high-school biology classes in the United States today.

The Vampire, the best-known Painlevé film (at least in this country), makes its politics more specific and more overt. During the German occupation of France, Painlevé was a persona non grata for a variety of reasons (including the help he gave refugees from Fascism to obtain work visas and French citizenship), and spent those years in hiding. Soon after the German occupation of France, he escaped to Spain underwater by using the diving gear he had invented. Just before the war, Painlevé had seen, for the first time, the Brazilian vampire bat *(Desmodus rotundus),* and had begun work on what would become *The Vampire.* His interest in the creature and the film seems to have been closely related to his hatred of Nazism: the bat, which could be a scourge to its animal and human neighbors, was, like the Nazis, a "brown pest." Near the end of *The Vampire,* Painlevé reveals "the salute of the vampire": "When I was finishing the film, I noticed how the vampire bat extends its wing before going to sleep. I thought it looked like the Nazi 'Heil-Hitler' salute."[21] In this instance, the bat is used overtly as a political metaphor in a way that is not particularly characteristic of Painlevé's work—though, as usual, the film is good science.

Throughout his career, Painlevé was primarily committed to the creation of first-rate science films and the development of audiences for these and other forms of cinema that might energize and inform the public. Soon after the war, he became president of the French Federation of Ciné-Clubs, and continued to promote the use of cinema as a way of popularizing science through his work with the Institute of Scientific Cinema (which he started in 1930) and by helping to found the International Association of Science Films. He was also among the first science filmmakers to work with television and, in time, would experiment with new video techniques. While for Disney the nature film was one small part in the construction of an empire, for Painlevé, filmmaking always remained a means of democratizing scientific research and of using cinema to work across theoretical and cultural distinctions to share information about our remarkably complex, sometimes terrifying, but always wondrous world.

[. . .]

The Natural World as Parallel Universe: *A Divided World* (1948) and *Microcosmos* (1996)

One of the problems with the failure of academic film studies to seriously explore the nature film is that even landmarks in the genre have gotten lost, sometimes in instances when such a loss was easily avoidable. A particularly good example is Swedish director Arne Sucksdorff's remarkable short, *A Divided World.* During the postwar explosion of the film society movement in the United States, the Sucksdorff film was celebrated. It was shown at Cinema 16, accompanied by program notes written by distinguished critic Arthur Knight. During the following decades, when libraries were buying 16mm films, many acquired *A Divided World.* In recent years, however, as many academics have abandoned 16mm, these collections have been disbanded, and many of what were considered film classics a generation ago are no longer available to audiences. This seems particularly the case with nature films, including *A Divided World,* which is no longer in distribution in the United States.[22]

A Divided World begins with an organist playing a Bach fantasia as we see shots of a marsh and a snowy forest lit by a full moon. A small church, cemetery, and several houses in a small village are visible; then the camera slowly moves back into the snow-covered forest, where we see the eyes of a distant owl. The music becomes subdued and the night cries of animals and birds become audible. A tiny white weasel is eating the carcass of a bird, but runs and hides from a fox that eats what remains. A white rabbit is seen running through the woods (the church is seen in the distance at one point) as wind blows through the trees, making eerie shadows on the snow. The eyes of the owl are again seen in the distance. The owl then flies across the woods and confronts the fox, which has apparently killed the rabbit. While the weasel watches, staying carefully out of reach, the owl and fox battle over the carcass. The owl flies off with the carcass, and the fox is seen nursing an injured paw. At the end of the film, Arthur Knight suggested in his program notes, "when the camera turns back to the snug little house on the edge of the forest, civilization takes on new meanings. The music of Bach suggests the sublimation of primitive instincts through art and man's creation."[23]

Much of the impact of *A Divided World* comes from Sucksdorff's recognition that the two parts of our "divided world" are in very close proximity, that indeed they exist in virtually the same place and time. In *A Divided World,* one world is visually the background of the other and vice versa, and the Bach fantasia and the sounds of nature interweave throughout the film. While the action in *A Divided World* is reminiscent of the Disney True-Life Adventures the impact of the film is very different from these other films, in large part because of Sucksdorff's way of combining reality and fantasy.

It is a fundamental trope of the nature film that long shots of real landscapes are used to cover up the fact that the close shots of animal or insect life are fabricated within carefully controlled environments.[24] While the kinds of events we see are certainly part of the real existence of the creatures depicted, the particular depictions are constructed, either by setting up a situation that would be impractical to wait for or by creatively editing events. Both methods are used in *A Divided World.*

However, while the animals and actions in *A Divided World* are clearly real—and, as in most nature films, are made reasonably convincing through the careful control of mini-environments and creative editing—the scintillating, gorgeously lit long shots of farm and woods *and* the close-ups of the animals (all of which are beautiful specimens, seemingly unmarked by life in the wild) create an aura of fantasy. As a result, the film seems more a parable than an exercise in stark realism. The houses and church appear to be models. No people are ever visible, though smoke is coming out of the chimney during the final shot of the farmhouse. This is a fairy-tale town. Ultimately, the two levels of

Sucksdorff's divided world re-contextualize each other, each making the other seem less solid, less complete, less "real." The ambiguity of the film is confirmed by what is perhaps the most obvious deviation from the conventional nature film in *A Divided World*: Sucksdorff's refusal of direct commentary or explanation. There is neither text nor narration, and the result is a sense that both human nature and non-human nature are beautiful and powerful mysteries.

A related approach is evident in the remarkable French feature *Microcosmos, Le peuple de l'herbe (The People of the Grass)*, by Claude Nuridsany and Marie Pérennou. In making *Microcosmos,* Nuridsany and Pérennou were at great pains to combine science and art as a means of avoiding some of the implications of more conventional nature films. According to Pérennou, "We try to engage the imagination of the spectator. We tell the story of this world as if it were an opera, not simple biology. We are right in the middle of art and science; we put these two fields together—people have a tendency to separate them."[25] As is true in *A Divided World* (and in some of the Painlevé films as well), in *Microcosmos* the focus is not on a distant, exotic, vanishing "Last Great Place," but on dimensions of the everyday world we normally ignore: in this case the life of insects in a meadow during the summer.[26] Like Sucksdorff, Nuridsany and Pérennou do not pretend to explain what they show us, but rather, confront us with the essential mystery, beauty, and wonder of our natural surroundings.

In general, the tendency of most nature documentaries since the Disney True-Life Adventures has been to rely on narration to provide one or another form of general context for the various life forms depicted. In most cases this is not scientific commentary, but a kind of emotional contextualization. The Disney films promote a kind of amused, nuclear-family-oriented detachment, whereas the many nature films produced by National Geographic for television use a more "masculine" approach that works to create a sense of the nitty-gritty reality of the cycle of predation, mating, and death. The National Geographic approach can cause the creatures depicted to seem the enemies of civilized human life. See for example, *Sonoran Desert, A Violent Eden* (1997, part of the National Geographic series *World's Last Great Places*), which can create a sense that the remarkable environment of the Sonoran Desert is to be avoided, or at least that the suburbanization of the expanding population of Arizona is probably a good thing. In *Microcosmos* Nuridsany and Pérennou carefully avoid the traditional reliance on narration. *Microcosmos* uses only two brief passages of narration during its 80 minutes (both spoken by Kristin Scott Thomas, in the English version of the film; and by Jacques Perrin in the French version). Each is an attempt to provide a mood unusual for a nature film.

During the précis, we move from airplane shots of cloudscapes down to a helicopter shot of a meadow and then *into* the meadow grass via microscopic cinematography that makes the grass stems look like tree trunks. We hear the first of the two passages of narration, read as if they were poetry:

> A meadow in early morning,
> somewhere on earth.
> Hidden here is a world as vast as
> our own,
> Where the weeds are impenetrable
> jungles,
> The stones are mountains,
> And even the smallest pond becomes
> an ocean.
> Time passes differently here.
> An hour is like a day;
> A day is like a season;
> And the passing of a season is a
> lifetime.
> But to observe this world, we must
> fall silent now
> and listen to its murmurs.

And the filmmakers do fall silent, until nearly the end of the film.

Nuridsany and Pérennou's decision to back away from words and to allow what they show us to speak for itself reflects their confidence in both their subject matter and their cinematic skills in communicating what they feel about the world they are depicting. For Nuridsany and Pérennou, the natural world is an awesome—not fearful—place. As Pérennou explains, "Insects are so often portrayed as little robots who are always killing each other, like [in] science fiction movies. To us they are like mythological creatures, creatures of great beauty."[27] This attitude is evident in the choices of both narrator and narration. Scott Thomas's soft-spoken voice is a far cry from the usual authoritative male voice-of-god narrator, as is the language of the brief bits of narration, which are poetically evocative.

Of course, in *Microcosmos,* as in most nature films, music and sound effects function as indirect forms of narration. In general, Nuridsany and Pérennou use various combinations of sound effects (including what I presume are insect sounds recorded and played back at various speeds) with one of several forms of music (the sound design of the film is by Laurent Quaglio; the original music by Bruno Coulais). At times, it is not entirely clear whether a sound *is* a sound effect or a musical imitation of insect sounds; at others, imagery is accompanied by orchestral, sometimes operatic music. The mood created by the sound effects and music depends on the particular subject matter, but the filmmakers are at great pains to avoid using music that might confirm conventional clichés about insects being creepy and dirty.

Microcosmos offers a considerable variety of insect life encountered during a typical summer day, which begins with early morning and ends, after an evening rainstorm, with night.[28] Imagery of insects (and in one instance, a pheasant) grounded in fifteen years of research and three years of shooting (in some cases with equipment designed by the filmmakers) is presented at appropriate moments during the daily cycle. It is, of course, one of the inherent properties of theatrical cinema that the combination of camera and projector magnifies whatever is shot, and in this particular instance, cinematic magnification powerfully amplifies the stunning micro-photography by Nuridsany, Pérennou, Hugues Ryffel, and Thierry Machado. What is most notable about *Microcosmos,* however, is that the directors chose to focus not on exotic creatures we are relatively unacquainted with, but on astonishing traits of common insects, many of which are usually considered as pests.

One of the early sequences in the film follows a ladybug crawling on a stem where ants are tending to a colony of aphids. The ants repel the ladybug, which goes on its way, and we watch as the ants harvest the honeydew the aphids are producing.[29] The clarity of this imagery needs no narration, allowing us to confront the astonishing spectacle of one insect species domesticating another, protecting it, and caring tenderly for it. In another of the film's most remarkable sequences, two snails are apparently having sex. They are filmed in gorgeous, extended, glistening visuals that are accompanied by operatic music. The visual beauty and the operatic track seem perfectly matched. The film's final sequence powerfully confirms the filmmakers' tendency to invest the mundane with deep significance: after the second passage of narration, an insect—most viewers, I would guess, are not clear at first what insect this might be—emerges from water and undergoes several astonishing and beautiful transformations to the accompaniment of orchestral music. At the climax of the passage, we realize that the amazing process we've witnessed was the growth of a common mosquito.

While visual beauty is an aspect of many nature films (the True-Life Adventures are full of beautiful shots), in *Microcosmos* the filmmakers are at considerable pains to confirm their respect for the insect world by consistently creating lovely visual compositions and using a sumptuous palette of color. But often it is the mythical dimension of "the people of the grass" that seems to determine the directors' decision to include the images they choose. The sequence of a dung beetle pushing its ball along the ground, only to have it get stuck on a thorn, and then struggling to free the ball until it can once again continue on its way is positively Sisyphusian; the pheasant that attacks the ant colony, seen sometimes from inside the anthill, is reminiscent of many mythological giants from the Cyclops to King Kong; and the emergence of the mosquito at the end of the film evokes, as Pérennou has indicated, the mythological Venus, "rising out of the water."[30] Indeed, it is this mythological character of the world of insect life that justifies the loving attention the filmmakers dedicated to the film. Like some of Painlevé's films, *Microcosmos* is as much interested in what we can learn *from* the activities that take place in its "underworld" as it is in what we can learn *about* them.

The implication of the National Geographic series title "World's Last Great Places" is that the subjects of these films are among the few remaining "edenic" wilderness environments on earth—"edenic" meaning, apparently, not interfered with by humanity. And yet, to maintain what is essentially a fantasy, director Sean Morris needed to go to great lengths to hide the human presence in the Sonoran desert (some of *Sonoran Desert* was shot on the grounds of the Desert Museum, now Arizona's second biggest tourist attraction, drawing nearly half a million visitors each year). Nuridsany and Pérennou, on the other hand, do not participate in the kind of romantic fantasy promoted by Morris and National Geographic. They are interested in using cinema to rediscover the complexity of the real life that surrounds us, to alert us to an astonishing world, "Beyond anything we could imagine/And yet almost beneath our notice," as they explain in the narration that leads into the final sequence of *Microcosmos*. The life forms they reveal to us have clearly adapted to life as successfully as we have, and precisely in a "neighborhood" they share with human beings. The message here is not one of fear and disgust, but one of empathy, respect, and appreciation.

One final conjecture . . . In her video *The Head of a Pin* (2004), independent film/videomaker Su Friedrich intercuts between wide shots documenting a vacation near the Delaware River in northern New Jersey (Friedrich and several others are staying in a small cabin and walk to the river to enjoy swimming and picnicking) and in-close shots of a spider subduing and wrapping a wasp that has gotten caught in its web.[31] During the shots of the spider and mayfly, the vacationers discuss the strange, grisly spectacle. At one point, they admit to each other that "what we know about Nature" would fit "on the head of a pin." Near the end of the video, the final in-close shot of the spider and the now entangled wasp concludes when the camera pulls back and up, revealing that this tiny saga of predation has been occurring underneath the kitchen table in the cabin. As in *A Divided World,* we see that what can seem to be two different worlds are simply two aspects of the same space; but whereas Sucksdorff emphasizes the differences between two mysterious realms, Friedrich's concluding gesture suggests that there is a relationship between what happens below the table and what occurs on top of it: both spiders and humans live by means of the periodic exploitation of other life forms. Intelligence lies in recognizing the intricate relationships between what may at first seem separate worlds.

In the present context, *The Head of a Pin* can serve as a metaphor for the gap that has formed between the humanities and the sciences in the current American academic environment. While educators generally recognize that anything like a sensible liberal arts education requires experiences with both the sciences and the humanities, the tendency for many faculty and students is to see one of these areas as primary and the other as, for all practical purposes, a strange, hidden world. This gap has produced one of the more remarkable paradoxes of modern intellectual life: the seemingly contradictory nature of recent conclusions/discoveries in the humanities and in the sciences.

The major conclusion of many scholars working across the humanities during recent decades has been that the categories that earlier generations assumed were biological givens—gender, race, sexual preference, even individual identity itself—are in fact social constructions. Our ways of understanding the world around us and of coming to terms with one another are not biologically intrinsic to us—not *essential* dimensions of us—but rather the social fabrications of postmodern capitalism. On the other hand, one of the most remarkable conclusions of many scholars working in the sciences during recent decades is that our DNA charts our physical being from the moment of conception. This DNA mapping is so distinct for each of us that anyone with the right tools to read it can distinguish each human individual from every other, and various classes of humans from each other, on the basis of even the tiniest molecule of the human body, living or dead. In other words, however much our socialization constructs predictable, conventional, often problematic patterns of action and thought, there *is* an essential identity within each of us.

Of course, I recognize that I am oversimplifying very complex issues, but I cannot help but wonder whether the tendency on the part of the first generation of academic film teachers and scholars to ignore the history of cinema devoted to scientific exploration and explanation might be, at least in part, a reflection of a repressed fear of confronting those dimensions of the physical world around us that might frustrate our desire for an unambiguous, stable political consciousness, and for definitive theoretical solutions to complex social questions. Obviously, the humanities and the sciences need each other more than they sometimes realize, and the wide world of cinema, including the long history of films devoted to depictions of the natural world, remains one of those dimensions of culture that may yet help us come to terms with this interdependence.

NOTES

1. Amos Vogel on programming science films, in Scott MacDonald, "An Interview with Amos Vogel," *Cinema 16: Documents Toward a History of the Film Society* (Philadelphia, PA: Temple University Press, 2002), 49.
2. In this particular context, I prefer "nature film" to "wildlife film" because "wildlife film" has come to refer primarily to films about relatively large, terrestrial animals, whereas "nature film" more comfortably includes the lives of insects and sea organisms, as well.
3. There is also Oliver Gaycken's " 'A Drama Unites Them in a Fight to the Death': Some Remarks on the Flourishing of a Cinema of Scientific Vernacularization in France, 1909–1914," *Historical Journal of Film, Radio and Television*, vol. 22, no. 3 (August 2002): 353–74. Gaycken's discussion of early French scientific films produced by the Éclair, Pathé, and Gaumont studios, especially the Éclair series called "Scientia," is very useful. Gaycken discusses the distinction between films made in the service of scientific experimentation and films of "scientific vernacularization": that is, films that attempted to make scientific investigations and ideas available to a more general audience; and he examines a number of films involving insects and animals doing battle with one another in ways that are early instances of some of the trends discussed in this essay.
4. Lewis Jacobs' seminal anthology *The Documentary Tradition: From* Nanook *to* Woodstock (New York: Hopkinson and Blake, 1971) includes Arthur Knight's brief discussion of Arne Sucksdorff, "Sweden's Arne Sucksdorff," which mentions *Struggle for Survival* (1944), Sucksdorff's study of bird life on a Baltic Island; and Bosley Crowther's review, "Cousteau's *The Silent World* (1956)." Erik Barnouw's *Documentary: A History of the Non-Fiction Film* (New York: Oxford University Press, 1993) devotes a single paragraph to the nature film (210–12), in which the early Disney True-Life Adventures and Jacques-Yves Cousteau's film work are mentioned. But none of the recent anthologies focusing on documentary so much as mentions this dimension of documentary history.

Derek Bousé's first chapter includes an extensive consideration of the ways in which wildlife films correspond and fail to correspond to conventional understandings of documentary. In general, Bousé sees the wildlife film as a genre separate from what we usually call documentary. See Derek Bousé, *Wildlife Films* (Philadelphia, PA: University of Pennsylvania Press, 2000). I, however, consider the films I discuss here documentaries; for me, Jean Painlevé's definition has been particularly useful: a documentary is "any film that documents real phenomena or their honest and justified reconstruction in order to consciously increase human knowledge through rational or emotional means and to expose problems and offer solutions from an economic, social, or cultural point of view." Painlevé, in "Castration du documentaire," *Cahiers du cinéma* (March 1951); reprinted in Andy Masaki Bellows, et al., eds., *Science Is Fiction: The Films of Jean Painlevé* (San Francisco, CA: Brico Press, 2000), 39.

5. Bill Nichols, *Introduction to Documentary* (Bloomington, IN: Indiana University Press, 2001), 85.
6. I'm sure Nichols would agree that the films I discuss in this essay *are* more fully documentary than the strictly scientific use of cinema to collect data, which is his focus in the lines I've quoted. Nevertheless, the position he enunciates does, I think, confirm the broad tendency not to take the nature film seriously *as cinema*. If I have stretched Nichols' position beyond what is fair, I apologize to him.
7. Both Gregg Mitman and Bousé focus primarily on American wildlife films, and both tend to exclude films that focus on insects and sea organisms.
8. Gaycken, 368.
9. Mitman provides a useful overview of the evolution of the "bring 'em back alive film" in *Reel Nature* (Cambridge, MA: Harvard University Press, 1999), chapters 2 and 3.
10. The nature film was also an early staple of the ciné-club movement that swept Europe and the United Kingdom in the 1920s and 1930s. For example, at its third public presentation, December 20, 1925, the London Film Society began the "*Film Society* Bionomica Series" focusing on animal and insect life. Throughout the Film Society's 14-year run, nature films were regularly part of diverse programs that also included avantgarde works, revived classics, instructional films, animations, documentaries of all sorts, and narrative entertainments from around the world. See the London Film Society's *The Film Society Programs, 1925–1939* (New York: Arno Press, 1972).
11. Dorsky, in Scott MacDonald, "Sacred Speed: An Interview with Nathaniel Dorsky," *Film Quarterly*, vol. 54, no. 4 (Summer 2001): 2–11. Dorsky's *Hours for Jerome* (shot in the late 1960s and edited in 1982) seems particularly indebted to the True-Life Adventures. Dorsky's film takes the viewer through a year spent in New York City and at a lakeside retreat in northern New Jersey. He doesn't particularly focus on wildlife but does create a sense of the seasonal cycle (as represented by weather, plant life, and human activity) as an event worth contemplating in cinema.
12. Mitman, 111–14.
13. Algar, in an interview with Gregg Mitman, in Mitman, 119.
14. Bousé suggests that wildlife films may "entail an ever greater potential [than Hollywood features] for naturalizing ideological values—for example, by 'finding' in nature the predominance of the nuclear family, or the values of hard work, industry, and deferred gratification. Indeed, because wildlife films are about nature, there may be an ever greater commitment than in Hollywood films to making things appear natural" (Bousé, 18).
15. Brigitte Berg explains that when Painlevé's early research film, *The Stickleback's Egg: From Fertilization to Hatching (L'Oeuf d'épinoche: De la fecundation à l'éclosion,* 1927), was screened for scientists at the Academie des Sciences in 1928, it was met with skepticism and outrage: "One scientist, infuriated, stormed out, declaring: 'Cinema is not to be taken seriously!' " Brigitte Berg, "Contradictory Forces: Jean Painlevé, 1902–1989," in Bellows, 17.
16. Berg,25.
17. Painlevé's "Ten Commandments" were written in 1948 for a program called "Poets of the Documentary," and are reprinted in Bellows, 159. Commandment Four—"You will seek reality without aestheticism or ideological apparatus"—suggests that what Painlevé means by "convictions" in his second commandment is not *political* convictions in the contemporary sense, but convictions that develop from an exploration of natural reality from an unbiased position.
18. Painlevé's contribution to *Surréalisme* was a bit of prose that may well be coherent biology, but reads like Surrealist fantasy. The piece begins, "The plasmodium of the Myxomycetes is so sweet; the eyeless *Prorhynchus* has the dull color of the born-blind, and its proboscis stuffed with zoochlorellae solicits the oxygen of the *Frontoniella antypyretica*; he carries his pharynx in a rosette, a locomotive requirement, horned, stupid, and not at all calcareous." The entire contribution is included in Bellows, 117.
19. Several of Painlevé's films are available on a DVD from Les Documents Cinématographiques (lesdocs.com): the title is *Jean Painlevé, Compilation no. 1* (it includes eight films: *Les Amours de la pieuvre, Oursins* (*Sea Urchins*, 1954), *Comment naissent des méduses* (*How Some Jellyfish Are Born*, 1960), *Hyas et stenorinques* (*Hyas and Stenorhynchus*, 1929), *L'Hippocampe, Cristaux liquides* (*Liquid Crystals*, 1978), *Acéra, ou le bal des scorciéres*, and *Histoires des crevettes.*
20. Berg, 23.
21. Ibid.,33.
22. I have a decent 16mm print of *A Divided World* only because a public library in northern Minnesota gave away its collection of 16mm

films. The original film is in 35mm, prints of which are sometimes available through the Swedish Film Institute in New York City (212-583-2584). Over the years I have often presented "Cinema 16 shows" at colleges, universities, and other organizations interested in film history, and the nature films that Cinema 16 audiences saw and admired have consistently been the hardest to locate.

23. Quoted in MacDonald, *Cinema 16*, 144.
24. As Gaycken explains, even in the earliest nature films, the movement from long shot of real environment to close-up of fabricated environment "is deployed in order to enhance the believability of the ethological fiction that the observations are of animals in their natural habitats." He describes a number of such instances, pointing out that match-on-action shots are the primary tool for accomplishing this illusion (364).
25. Pérennou, in an interview with Charles Wright, in www.bostonphoenix.com/archives/1996/documents/00443388htm.
26. Of course, sometimes Painlevé did choose to focus on exotic creatures—*The Vampire*, for instance—but, at least in the films I've seen, he usually chose to explore the lives of organisms that most of us would normally consider beneath our notice.
27. Pérennou interview.
28. Because narrative development, especially controllable narrative development leading to climax, is difficult to find, or even to orchestrate, in nature films, it is common for longer nature films to include either fires or dramatic rainstorms, or both—often just where a commercial dramatic feature would present its climax.
29. Aphids suck the sugars produced by plants, but cannot digest all of what they imbibe. They release some of it through their anuses in the form of liquid "honeydew" that is eaten by ants.
30. Pérennou interview.
31. I've not been able to determine whether the insect is a wasp *(Bracónidae* or *Ichneumónidae)* or a stem sawfly *(Cèphidae)*. Thanks to Dr. William H. Gotwald, Jr., Professor of Biology at Utica College for his assistance in narrowing down the possibilities.

113

AMY VILLAREJO

BUS 174 AND THE LIVING PRESENT (2006)

José Padilha's 2002 film *Bus 174* brings the resources of vigilance and clarity to the medium of television. Focusing on the hijacking of a bus in Rio de Janeiro on June 12, 2000 (Valentine's Day in Brazil), *Bus 174* sets into motion an analysis of the "incident" or "situation" as it was seen widely on live television in order to understand its constellation of rage, fear, poverty, and despair: all among the elements cut or occluded from television's frame. This is a film that makes a fierce argument against Anglo-American strains of individualism in documentary cinema (exemplified in subsequent years by the bad and the good, both Morgan Spurlock's indulgent *Supersize Me* [2004] and Jonathan Caouette's riveting *Tarnation* [2003]) and an argument in favor of a form capable of complicated social understanding. I therefore understand the film as a type of pedagogy: an essay on the future of cinema and on the limits of representation.

In what follows I put the film into conversation with the work of Jacques Derrida, whose passing in 2004 sent me to a book of his that television scholar Lynn Spigel had, in print at least, discouraged me from reading. *Echographies of Television,* more or less a series of transcripts of filmed interviews between Bernard Stiegler and Jacques Derrida, despite Spigel's warning about its discussion of the "waning of the TV object," helped me to think about the effects of television liveness alongside a number of themes that preoccupied Derrida in his writings over the past decade or so: justice (versus law or right), the archive, hospitality, democracy to come, and so on.[1] I think his insights from those interviews about media and "on film," as it were, can guide a reading of *Bus 174,* a film that might be seen to invoke a number of these themes, if obliquely. Since Derrida's work on and around "visuality" remains, as Spigel rightly points out, largely untested in the domain of film and media studies, we have in *Bus 174* an opportunity to explore this nexus. We inherit a beginning from Derrida, an archive (what Akira Lippit calls a "virtual archive on the subjects of visibility and invisibility") to build upon.[2]

Bus 174 investigates the production of *hyper*visibility. On that June day cameras swarmed into the Jardim Botânico neighborhood, where a public city bus had come to a stop after a hijacker's robbery attempt. The bus remained there for what would eventually total four and a half hours. Vivo (live) television feeds, date-stamped and time-coded, showed several different angles of the stationary bus from a relative long shot, while camera operators from newspapers and television approached the bus from virtually every possible trajectory on the ground. Glare from the windows of the bus prevented unmediated access to the events involving the hostages unfolding within. Racking their focus in order to frame events through partially opened windows, the television camera operators, later lodged directly adjacent to the bus, trained their lenses nonetheless on every part of the bus's anatomy: the number and destination on its front banner, the door (through which all transactions would take place), the driver's seat and steering wheel, the seats row by row. Amidst the crowds of the initially unsecured scene, the cameras offered complete spatial coverage and consistent orientation according to the broadcast ideals of transparency, reportage, and information. Throughout the bus-passenger hostage crisis the people of Brazil stopped to watch what was importantly a national drama, one that earned the highest television ratings of the year.

The film is aware of the borders and contours of the nation-state, contradictorily represented as a tourist oasis (the beaches of Copacabana) and as a coagulated *favela* (slum). It begins, in fact, with a beautiful (majestic, awe-inspiring) aerial shot of Rio that ultimately cedes to lower altitude visuals of the slums out of which come the street kids who speak the film's first words (an index of the esteem or care in which Padilha holds them). *Bus 174* is a story, from its very first moment, about Brazil and particularly its dense cities that breed *invisibility*, about kids who come from somewhere but are going nowhere, about streets filled with homeless and penniless kids everywhere. "It's a cold floor," we hear over images of those streets. "Can I talk about my dreams?" If these words travel in global circuits, and they do immediately by way of television itself as well as via DVD and other formats, *Bus 174* remains vigilant about its national location as it probes the failed state institutions (law, social service, penal, educational, media) that can provide no justice for its young citizens such as the hijacker, Sandro Nasciemento. The street as nation as locus of mediatized violence: this is the film's opening gesture, one it continues through the motif of aerials that anchor our vision to those *socially and nationally marked* streets. By contrast to the U.S. media's use of aerials both to foreground the power of the cameras to perform surveillance and to render space generic, Padilha rewrites the geography of Rio in insistently social terms.

In order to mount a critique of its own conditions of possibility, then, *Bus 174* draws upon the resources of documentary. How to make sense of this televised drama of the hijacker and the hostages? Its *mise-en-scène* and its actors, especially its protagonist? Its frame and its out-of-frame, its context, its iterability (possibility of repetition with a difference)? What of such drama can be represented, and what of its violence remains stubbornly unrepresentable? What of this event makes it timely, "newsworthy" of being selected from the "noninfinite mass of events" of its time or of its moment?[3] These are the questions Padilha raises, and it behooves us to note that he poses them largely through conventional documentary filmic strategies, including talking head interviews and an expository treatment of the story's main constituents (the police, the hijacker, the hostages, and so on). His most startling innovation comes in his treatment of the televisual material, an element João Luis Viera tells me is important to much Brazilian cinema after Hector Babenco's *Pixote* (1981).[4]

Padilha frames television, then, as a national medium, but he also draws attention to its mediatized effects and functions beyond or beside it. First, Padilha foregrounds how television acts as a witness, one that shapes what it incessantly records, and, second, how television functions as a conduit that also codifies performances of power. To the extent that his film (here meant as an interrogation of media effects) answers the televisual image, it seeks to make visible a prior dramatization that television acts as though it records. In other words, the life of Sandro Nasciemento, all of that which led him to that bus and into the situation constituted as an event, cannot enter the televisual frame. It is a life marked by the trauma of witnessing his mother's murder as she was butchered in front of him at the age of six. It is a life spent on the streets, narcotized by addiction and hardened by the experience of prison. The "reality," what Derrida might have called the "artifactuality," of his situation on bus 174 is that of an actor with only one role to play: a man who will be dead. This begs the question, How do we mine the effect of liveness to understand this occluded drama of death within the living present?

> We should never forget that this "live" is not an absolute "live" but only a live effect [*un effet de direct*], an allegation of live. Whatever the apparent immediacy of the transmission or broadcast, it negotiates with choices, with framing, with selectivity.
>
> —Bernard Stiegler and Jacques Derrida, *Echographies of Television*

Deconstructing Liveness

Derrida repeats what television scholars have known since Jane Feuer's essay, "The Concept of Live Television: Ontology as Ideology," noticed it in 1983.[5] Recall that Feuer's essay argues that the less that television is a live medium in the sense of an equivalence between the time of an event and the time of its transmission (and now, with the capacity for "time shifting" via TiVo and DVD recorders, the time of its reception), the more television seems to insist upon the *ideology* of liveness (the immediate, the direct, the spontaneous, the true). A circuit of meanings therefore lodges in the idea of the live, conflating an ideological claim for lack of mediation with a denial of death with a boastful sense of a technical feat of presence. Or, to put it slightly differently, the "live" both describes the actuality of a convergence between global capital and digital technology *and* the ideological effect of that convergence, which is to mystify the conditions of its own emergence and hegemony. Much television scholarship on the topic of liveness has subsequently been devoted to Derrida's descriptions "ad infinitum" of the interventions through which the live is produced as an effect.[6] Chief among these interventions is the mere declaration that it is so, whether through time coding, announcements from anchors on location, or graphic assertions.[7]

Bus 174 advances a different relationship to televisual liveness than ideology critique. Sandro Nasciemento, the film insists over and over again, is but one among many; *Bus 174* is not a film about an individual who became a protagonist but about the mediated and mediatized effects of social invisibility and anonymity multiplied a thousandfold. To speak about those effects, however, is never to lose sight of his singularity as well as his loss.

One touchtone for that multiplication is the massacre at Candelábria Church in downtown Rio, where police killed seven street children (who first approached their car anticipating nighttime soup). Sandro was one of the sixty-two children sleeping at the church that evening who survived the assault, and he invokes this prior "incident" and its ghosts to his national audience as he waves his gun on bus 174: "Brazil, check this out. I was at Candelábria. This is serious shit. My little friends were murdered by cowards."

The social worker Yvonne Bezerra de Mello, herself a mediatized construction, asks on-screen, as though it had been the stuff of dreams or films, "Who could imagine that there'd be a massacre downtown?" Downtown, where business and tourism mingled in the shadow of a Catholic church, seemed an impossible location for police to slaughter children? She summarizes the fate of the sixty-two survivors: thirty-two were subsequently murdered, several disappeared, and the remaining group survives precariously, marked with the distress of having witnessed the massacre and having survived continuing violence at the hands of Brazil's police.

But the incident on the bus is not the same event as Candelábria, just as the multiplication of deaths does not liquidate the specificity of each:

> The question—or the demand—of the phantom is the question and the demand of the future and of justice as well. We confuse the analogous with the identical: "Exactly the same thing is repeating itself, exactly the same thing." No, a phantom's return is, each time, another different return, on a different stage, in new conditions to which we must always pay the closest attention if we don't want to say or do just anything.[8]

To recognize Sandro's psychobiography is to grant the specificity of his experience, including the trauma of his mother's murder, which he incessantly repeats, but it is also to locate him within a wider social world upon which *Bus 174* dwells in order to refuse the personalization of social antagonisms. "The same way [glue addiction] fucks him up, it fucks up lots of other kids," Coelho, a former street kid, explains. "Many of them are just like him." Former and current street children populate *Bus 174* in intimate and proximate interviews, reminding the viewer of two things: first, that the film's construction of the idea of the multitude takes place at the level of the production *process* as much as at the level of its meaning and, second, that the living and the dead populate this "live" moment.

This movie is also a morgue. The "return on a different stage," then, requires a type of paying attention to the phantoms even as they are conjured away through mediation. How to restore the dignity of singularity to those who have been rendered marginal and anonymous? How to recognize the event as wholly other?

Many street kids will have died since their images were captured, just as Fernando Ramos Da Silva, star of Babenco's *Pixote,* was murdered after his only leading role. In the end, this is *and* isn't a movie. Its living present is accessible through the image of the dead. "You think that this is a movie?" Sandro yells from the bus. "This ain't no fuckin' movie!" "This ain't no action movie. This is serious shit." Sandro's moment on the bus fuses contradictory positions together regarding the politics of visibility. If he appears, becomes the protagonist, renders visible the lives of the street kids who long for social recognition (as the sociologist interviewed for the film alleges), that gesture is doubly illusory. "All those people around the bus were worried about us," recollects one of the hostages. "Not about him. It was him against everybody." If the lenses trained upon his toweled head seemed to guarantee his life, the moment they could no longer access the action he would be suffocated, as he is at the end of the ordeal at the hands of the incompetent and aggressive police. And if the movie that is *Bus 174* presents Sandro in the living present, the film nonetheless "bears death within itself and divides itself between its life and its afterlife, without which there would be no image, no recording."

Yvonne Bezerra de Mello insists that the incident is *not* a movie for a different reason: "If he were really that violent, he wouldn't only have shot the hostages but the people around the bus. People would have died like in American films." That is, if Sandro were a character in a Hollywood film, he would be the pathologized criminal of North American fantasies rather than the frightened street kid with no options, no recognition, no future. Here the counterlogic to visibility obtains: Sandro cannot be rendered visible within the image repertoires of dominant media. To do so would only be to repeat the gesture of the television footage in its claims to transparency, spontaneity, direct access.

Within these binds there is no easy answer, no set of filmic or media strategies to counterbalance the social effects of globalization and neoliberalism or to demystify, as Jacqui Alexander puts it, "the state's will to represent itself as disinterested, neutered, or otherwise benign."[9] Part of his agenda embraces radical cinematic traditions that seek to defamiliarize those institutions that collude in the society of control, from *Hour of the Furnaces* (Octavio Getino and Fernando Solanas, 1968) to *Performing the Border* (Ursula Biemann, 1999). In his serious treatment of the live television feed, however, Padilha treads upon new ground in the denaturalization of the mediatized spaces that are themselves effects of the same rhythms of neoliberalism and globalization. The gift he offers is a multilayered vision of a future to come, democracy to come, justice. Its vehicle is a vigilant and clear assessment of the living present.

NOTES

1. Lynn Spigel, "TV's Next Season?" *Cinema Journal* 45, no. 1 (Fall 2005): 85.
2. Akira Lippit, "The Derrida That I Love," *Grey Room* 20 (Summer 2005): 85.
3. Bernard Stiegler and Jacques Derrida, *Echographies of Television*, trans. Jennifer Bajorek (Cambridge: Polity Press, 2002).
4. Personal conversation, Vancouver, B.C., March 2006.
5. Jane Feuer, "The Concept of Live Television: Ontology as Ideology," in *Regarding Television: Critical Approaches: An Anthology*, ed. E. Ann Kaplan (Frederick, Md.: University Presses of America, 1983).
6. See Jerome Bourdon, "Live Television Is Still Alive," *Media, Culture & Society* 22, no. 5: 531–56; Sean Cubitt, *Timeshift* (London: Routledge, 1991); John Ellis, *Seeing Things* (London: IB Tauris, 2000); as well as the discussion in performance studies inaugurated by Peggy Phelan in *Unmarked: The Politics of Performance* (London: Routledge, 1993) and continued in Philip Auslander, *Liveness: Performance in a Mediatized Culture* (London: Routledge, 1999).
7. See *Reality Squared: Televisual Discourse on the Real*, ed. James Friedman (New Brunswick, N.J.: Rutgers University Press, 2002).
8. Derrida in Stiegler and Derrida, *Echographies*, 24.
9. M. Jacqui Alexander, *Pedagogies of Crossing: Meditations on Feminism, Sexual Politics, Memory, and the Sacred* (Durham, N.C.: Duke University Press, 2005), 23.

BARBARA KLINGER

CAVE OF FORGOTTEN DREAMS

Meditations on 3D (2012)

By mid-summer 2011, having earned more than $5 million in domestic box-office receipts in the United States, Werner Herzog's *Cave of Forgotten Dreams* had become a major success in the world of independently produced documentaries. The film also received largely positive, even ecstatic, reviews. Many critics and bloggers were awestruck by the glimpses the film afforded of the oldest known art in the world. Created at least 32,000 years ago, the Chauvet Cave paintings in the south of France feature impressively well-preserved drawings of late Paleolithic Age horses, bison, rhinoceroses, panthers, lions, and more. Herzog, the director of other documentaries shot in extraordinary places, such as Antarctica in *Encounters at the End of the World* (2007), had managed to gain access to an otherwise restricted space, closed to the public and to all but a small number of specialists since its discovery in 1994.

Along with exhibiting excitement about the subject matter, favorable reviews hailed *Cave of Forgotten Dreams* as one of the few films to use the contemporary rebirth of 3D filmmaking in an artistic manner. Even those who typically object to 3D as a gimmick (such as critic Roger Ebert) argued that Herzog's documentary justifiably employed this technology. A rough consensus emerged that *Cave* not only had to be seen in 3D to be truly appreciated, but that it was one of the best 3D films yet to appear.

At first glance, we can discern the factors that contributed to the "must-see-in-3D" status of *Cave of Forgotten Dreams.* The film earned some immediate credibility as an arthouse documentary made by a renowned German filmmaker and released during a summer season otherwise rife with 3D blockbusters, including *Thor, Pirates of the Caribbean: On Stranger Tides,* and *Harry Potter and the Deathly Hallows 2.* While Herzog's film was shown in commercial theater chains in 2D and 3D, it was also screened at the few U.S. arthouses with 3D capabilities (such as the IFC Center in New York City and the place where I first saw the film, the IU Cinema in Bloomington, Indiana), enhancing its boutique aura. Moreover, *Cave* not only focused on a real-life marvel rather than a CGI-manufactured landscape, it was shot in 3D. By comparison, most 3D live-action films last summer were converted in post-production and thus considered as "fake 3D." Herzog enhanced *Cave's* 3D credentials when he asserted that 3D digital cameras were necessary to truly render the paintings as they cascade across the cave walls' uneven surfaces. The protrusions and recesses required a technology that could capture the dimensionality of the paintings and the experience of seeing them in their habitat. Identifying style as dictated by subject matter and environment, Herzog distinguished *Cave* as an organic deployment of the technology, offering a clear rationale for its use. Given his remarks in interviews that he was only persuaded to use 3D upon seeing the cave, the film emerged more emphatically as a special case.

Together these factors characterize *Cave* as "indie" counter-programming that was produced in 3D out of creative necessity. The film appears as an authentic, naturalistic, and legitimate use of the technology—especially as opposed to "fake 3D" blockbusters that appear to exploit the technology as a cash cow in the construction of artificial worlds. However, *Cave*'s relationship to 3D is more paradoxical and interesting than such contrasts suggest. In fact, Herzog's film is as much about 3D as it is about its archaeological site.

The film's core premises offer a provocative test for this technology. Herzog uses ultramodern cameras to shoot the oldest known art in the world, while deploying 3D's ability to promote a sense of depth and expansiveness in the context of often extremely cramped quarters. In the course of this test *Cave* meditates, through its style and themes, on issues central to 3D cinema: the relationship between natural space and spectacle, realism and fantasy, art and science, and, ultimately, old and new media. Herzog's customary iconoclasm, aimed at challenging documentary cinema's association with sobriety and truth by introducing elements of the fantastic, is on full view (notably in the scene featuring an allegedly irradiated albino crocodile). Yet, this iconoclasm materializes more subtly in the blurring of boundaries between these seemingly opposed categories. As boundaries are crossed, *Cave* becomes more closely associated with the phantasms of contemporary 3D extravaganzas than initial appearances would suggest. At the same time, the film's musings distinguish it as an ambitiously self-reflexive take on 3D and image-making more broadly.

Nature, Spectacle, and Style

As *Cave* opens, Herzog dramatizes 3D's ability to render spatial depth and sheer expanse. The film begins with a forward tracking shot, in deep focus, of a field near the cave. The camera movement is continuous but it is neither smooth nor invisible. With extravagant motions, the camera travels from just above ground level to over the treetops until it reveals the Ardeche River and natural bridge, the Pont d'Arc, a landscape near the Chauvet Cave. This breathtaking shot is achieved by Skybot, an innovative remote-controlled aerial device with attached camera that, in a single take, mimics tracking, crane, and helicopter shots. The film's second scene uses the same apparatus to show the mountain pathway travelled by the Chauvet Cave's original discoverers. As the prelude unfurls, the audience is treated to more deep focus in the darkened cave interior where light issues from a lamp held by a figure in the background. When the lamp is moved, the rest of the cave is momentarily illuminated, showing stalactites and stalagmites along its shimmering calcite surfaces. Composer Ernst Reijseger's choral score accompanies these opening shots and, as it does throughout the film, unambiguously indicates the sacrality of this space—a common trope of Herzog's landscape documentaries (see Eric Ames, "Herzog, Landscape, and Documentary," *Cinema Journal,* winter 2009, 61–62).

In only a few moments, Herzog has signaled a theme and an aesthetic. Space and spatial dimensionality are among his key concerns. The film will continue to alternate between exterior vistas and the cave's claustrophobic interiors as visual counterpoints, while presenting both as spaciously as possible through deep focus and traveling shots. In either case, as we shall see, the stylistic choices of deep-focus cinematography (which presents foreground, middle ground, and background in focus) and a dynamically mobile camera help to wed spectacular natural phenomena to the spectacle of space. Spectacle—the dazzling, awe-inspiring nature of the image—is pointedly produced by a synergy between subject matter, visual style, and film music.

In its ability to clearly display multiple planes of action, deep focus maximizes the potentialities of 3D as a technology and an experience. The mobile camera also heightens the illusion of 3D. When it tracks in or out, or traces space in other ways, it explicitly limns dimensionality. Camera movements that call attention to their own visibility better accentuate the viewer's awareness of the recession or progression of space or of its sheer magnitude. The film's vertiginous aerial shots, moving us into and out of the vast environment surrounding the cave, most vividly invest in the spatial effects of camera mobility. But Herzog's commitment to a conspicuously active camera also extends to handheld shooting. While his camera is not always on the move, the restricted circumstances of filming in the cave (Herzog and a skeleton crew had to maneuver on a two-foot walkway) and the desire to make the most of 3D, encourage handheld traveling and panning shots. These techniques provide the vicarious experience of cave exploration as the crew makes its way into the cave's interior. When Herzog and crew film the paintings, the camera and the light from handheld panels trace the walls' contours, bringing out the undulating surfaces that give the pictured animals additional dimensionality and life. The importance of the "restless" camera to the subject matter and the 3D experience is evident even in the film's presentation of a digital map of the cave. The map could be presented as a static model. Instead, as the black-and-white digitized image appears, the camera elegantly rushes through and around it, displaying the minute details of the cave's oblong shape. Through such methods, *Cave* opens closed spaces to expansive view.

Because of their ability to convey dimensionality, deep focus and a roving camera are gold standards of 3D filmmaking, of achieving "3Dness." Herzog employs these techniques more consistently than most live-action 3D filmmakers, who often default to shallow focus in dialogue scenes (where only the front plane of action is crystal clear) to privilege narrative elements and to exploit the star charisma of actors. *Cave* portrays comparable scenes—"talking heads" interviews with scientists and scholars (among them, archaeologists, paleontologists, geologists, and art historians)—through deep focus, using it even in such ordinary moments. While Herzog as documentarian opts for longer takes over the rapid editing schemes of today's narrative films, the penetrating, swooping, operatic camera is de rigueur in 2D and 3D blockbusters. This is particularly true in scenes that present magnificent set pieces—for example, the exterior establishing shots of *Thor's* Hall of Asgard or *Harry Potter*'s Hogwarts under siege. Granting such differences, in its use of deep focus and dynamic camera, *Cave* joins a family of 3D films more overtly invested in spectacle and links tendencies in both documentary and fiction cinemas.

The interplay between naturalistic space and spectacle with respect to *Cave*'s stylistic repertoire has more extensive foundations and implications. Deep focus, dynamically mobile camera, aerial shots, sustained takes, and interviews—and the nature documentary itself as genre—have multiple legacies. Some of these elements are linked to cinematic realism. In his writing on Orson Welles, André Bazin famously identified deep focus and long takes as defining cinema's ability to preserve the space and time in front of the camera. As the handheld camera appears to give spontaneous, unmediated access to its subjects, it too has long been related to a realist aesthetic. Herzog's film draws on these associations to give us the sense that we are there in the Chauvet Cave. Upon closer inspection, though, we can see that *Cave*'s 3D effects exploit the double impact of realism and spectacle that such shooting styles have always engendered. Well before 3D deployed deep focus and a volatile camera, these techniques were affiliated with cinematic spectacle. *Citizen Kane*'s (1941) deep-focus moments or *Touch of Evil*'s (1958) legendary opening crane shot and long take convey the majesty and exhilaration of highly self-conscious presentations of space. Similarly, the handheld camera's unstable image calls attention to itself and to how subject and space appear.

The aerial shot is more obviously related to spectacle. Because of its impressive flexibility as an "all-in-one" mobile technology, *Cave*'s Skybot both alludes to and surpasses the crane, helicopter, and airplane shots that have been mainstays of filming aloft. As I have mentioned, dazzling aerial shots are conventions of contemporary 2D and 3D films; they are also key elements of IMAX nature documentaries. The early IMAX film, *To Fly* (1976), makes explicit just how central aerial photography is to providing a sensational optic onto the world and a roller-coaster-like ride for audiences. IMAX film titles further indicate that natural wonders are inherently sites of history and adventure that will be revealed as such by a daringly exploratory camera. *Grand Canyon: The Hidden Secrets* (1984), *Into the Deep 3D* (1994), *Everest* (1998), *Journey into Amazing Caves* (2001), and James Cameron's pre-*Avatar* (2009) *Aliens of the Deep 3D* (2005) are among IMAX documentaries that offer a heady combination of pedagogical instruction/history, vicarious adventure, and tourism—an adrenaline rush based on camera-induced kinesis, and worlds otherwise often difficult to see. While *Cave of Forgotten Dreams* features only a few aerial scenes, it shares this pervasive combination of fact and sensation. Producers and exhibitors of nature documentaries, such as IMAX, the Discovery Channel, and the History Channel (part of History Films, one of *Cave*'s production companies), bank on this convergence. *Cave* is rooted in such contemporary trends of documentary filmmaking. They, in turn, date back to cinema's earliest years, when the actualities of the Lumière brothers depended on the eye-catching novelty of cinema as a new technology (see Tom Gunning, "The Cinema of Attraction," in *Film and Theory*, ed. Robert Stam and Toby Miller, Blackwell Publishing, 2000). Herzog's use of 3D explicitly reminds us that there is no naturalism without spectacle and that this spectacle and its pleasures have long derived from the techniques and technologies on display.

Science, Art, and Fantasy

The related tension between realism and fantasy materializes explicitly, among other places, in Herzog's discussions of science and art. Without science, of course, nothing could be known about the paintings. Conversely, without the scientists' own creative activities, this knowledge could not proceed beyond brute fact. Herzog's interviews with the scientists, while showcasing their knowledge, often emphasize this latter point; he shows the scientists drawing, diagramming, and acting out the past as a kind of theater (as when Director of the Chauvet Cave Research Project, Jean-Michel Geneste, demonstrates how Paleolithic peoples used spears). Scientists, it turns out, are also storytellers. To make sense of this distant and therefore abstract past, they must generate stories about the painters and their times. Pursuing the artistic dimensions of scientific practice, Herzog poses questions to the scientists designed to bring out the presence of imagination, fantasy, and even obsession in their experiences of the cave. For example, the site so vividly invades archaeologist Julien Monney's dreams that he must end his visits. When Monney mentions that he was once a circus performer, Herzog asks if he was a lion tamer—a humorous aside that momentarily suggests the coexistence in this person of death-defying performer and scientist.

As this exchange intimates, Herzog considers the scientists in *Cave,* as he did those in *Encounters at the End of the World,* as fellow questers in extraordinary circumstances. They too must abide by the French government's rules of restricted access to the cave, designed to conserve its fragile environment. Hence, in an era when science and art seem antipathetic, Herzog demonstrates their close affiliation. *Cave* subtly portrays a romance between science and art and the fluid ways in which one depends on the other. Since 3D films tend to expose the relation between technology/science and art that subtends all filmmaking, Herzog's exploration of the intersection between the two reflects on his own enterprise as well.

In his narration, Herzog provides a genealogy of the arts that defines their evolution as driven, in part, by a desire to better approximate reality (again, at least initially, recalling Bazin). Herzog remarks that the crews' lights on the cave walls must have similar effects to the Paleolithic painters' torchlights. Both sources provide the visibility necessary for producing images; both also seem to animate these images. The Paleolithic torches are, then, antecedents to the flickering effects of animation and cinema as they reproduce movement. In fact, several of the beasts have been drawn with double the number of legs, indicating that the cave painters sought a graphic means of suggesting movement. Herzog describes this early desire to capture movement as "a kind of proto-cinema": through the play of light and shadow and proliferating legs, the impulses behind prehistoric image-making forecast cinema.

More broadly, Herzog contends that figuration lies at the heart of the arts—both prehistoric and modern. In *Cave,* he asks whether the birth of the modern soul began with the urge to represent the world through creative means. As testimony to this, the film is a virtual compendium of types of figuration that reproduce or enshrine aspects of the world. Besides the cave drawings that portray prehistoric animals and a female figure, Herzog's camera shows skeletal remains, footprints, and the wall scratches of cave bears; a painter's palm prints; cave "sculptures" in the form of stalagmites and stalactites; ancient museum sculptures; a spear; a flute, and so on. Contemporary acts of figuration include the scientists' drawings of the cave, the laser-scanned map, and the 3D digital camera as it appears in the frame and records its subject matter.

However, as the Chauvet Cave inevitably invokes Plato's Cave, Herzog rejects Plato's definition of these shadows as deceptive phantoms. It is their mysteries, rather than their realities, that are compelling. (Herzog's surprise cut to Fred Astaire's "Shadow Dance" from *Swing Time* [1936], wherein the shadows assume a life of their own, suggests where the director's fascinations lie.) Of the Paleolithic painters, Herzog inquires, "Do they dream, do they cry at night, what are their hopes, what are their families?" No matter what its commitments to verisimilitude, art fuels speculation about subjectivity and the phantasmagoric that no amount of factfinding or replication of the real can fully address. As we have seen, Herzog is equally attentive to the fantastical elements of science, showing us how its investigation of the past is not so different from his own: each attempt to re-present the past through technologies animated by the imagination.

The film's 3D qualities play no small part in blurring the boundaries between the binaries that course through the film. Because it adds a missing dimension to cinema that ostensibly brings it closer to verisimilitude—but only through an illusion of that dimension—3D is already a technology that defies easy categorization. At one level, 3D's inherent illusionism influences the film's overall canvas. Whether we are aloft or entering the cave via a moving camera, *Cave*'s evocative 3D cinematography tends to turn everything into spectacle: the cave's interiors, paintings, interviewees, landscapes, and the filmmakers themselves. Like the Chauvet Cave's shimmering calcite deposits, even interviewees in talking-head segments are radiant, insofar as 3D creates an aura around its objects. While critics complain about the diorama effect in converted films (in which characters or elements in the foreground are inadequately integrated into the space), a degree of spatial inconsistency in "true" 3D conveys a related sense of unreality. *Cave* thus produces a visual spectacle associated with 3D more generally through the technology's spectral effects.

At another level, *Cave*'s complication of simple distinctions between its binary themes creates an equally potent editorial. The tension that runs through such distinctions informs the film's pleasures and impact. Ultimately, though, the synergies between luminous 3D, devotional music, arresting cinematic techniques, and depictions of science and art as inflamed by the imagination, suggest once again that the tendency toward the sensational and the mythological assumes precedence. The cave becomes a fantasy-scape after all which, while lacking big-budget CGI, invokes a kingdom as spectacular as those presented in 3D blockbusters. In the film, then, Herzog need not explicitly describe the cave as "an enchanted world of the imaginary" or, in interviews, as a "fairy tale universe" ("Herzog Doc Brings Prehistoric Paintings to Life," www.npr.org). He has already indicated, through multiple means, the elusive and enigmatic inner life that defines this place of forgotten dreams.

New Media and Self-Reflexivity

In keeping with *Cave*'s interplay of paradoxes, the very characteristics that indicate its membership in a family of 3D films also point to its especially noteworthy status in this cinematic milieu. Through the gaze of its 3D camera on Paleolithic-era paintings and modes of figuration from the past, and through its employment of established elements of cinematic style, *Cave* shows time and again how intimately and intricately new media are wedded to the old. The film is one of the most vivid recent confirmations we have—along with Martin Scorsese's 3D *Hugo* (2011), a film that revisits the life and work of film pioneer Georges Méliès—of Jay David Bolter and Richard Gruisin's contention in *Remediation* (MIT Press, 2000) about new media: that they inevitably repurpose older media, functioning "in a constant dialectic" with what came before. The uniqueness of a new media text lies not in its "radical break" from tradition, but in its "particular strategies" of appropriating existing media (50).

Herzog's 3D experiment earns a unique status by virtue of its extensive and thoughtful self-reflexivity. Through the couplets that animate its aesthetic enterprise, *Cave* explicitly confronts matters essential to understanding 3D as a contemporary mode of expression and experience. It meditates impressively upon issues that are continually negotiated in 3D filmmaking today: its competing capacities to enhance cinema's verisimilitude and tendency toward spectacle; its use in both documentaries and fantasy-oriented films; its complicated existence as a scientific, technological, and artistic instrument; and its dependence for subject matter and style on interactions with old media and their conventions.

Given that 3D is still very much a work in progress in terms of technical refinement, cinema aesthetics, and audience reception, Herzog's testing of the most expansive of technologies in a confined space creates another dimension of reflection. Of his own arthouse venture, dance film *Pina* (2011), fellow German director Wim Wenders has remarked that, "3D really thrives on space—the 3D camera loves infinity, the horizon" ("Wim Wenders Explores New Dimensions With 'Pina,'" www.hollywoodreporter.com). If this is true, then Herzog's film plays a fascinating game with the 3D optic, as *Cave* advances on and recedes dramatically from this horizon, exploring what can be seen, what is difficult to see, and what remains beyond technology's ability to reveal.

PERMISSIONS ACKNOWLEDGMENTS

Altman, Rick. "From Lecturer's Prop to Industrial Product: The Early History of Travel Films." In *Virtual Voyages: Cinema and Travel*, edited by Jeffery Ruoff, 61–76. Durham, NC: Duke University Press, 2006. Republished by permission of Duke University Press.

The Washington Post. 1905. "Burton Holmes Pleases a Large Audience at the Columbia." November 14.

Whissel, Kristen. "Placing Audiences on the Scene of History: Modern Warfare and the Battle Reenactment at the Turn of the Century." In *Picturing American Modernity: Traffic, Technology, and the Silent Cinema*, 63–116. Durham, NC: Duke University Press, 2008. Republished by permission of Duke University Press.

Vaughan, Dai. "Let There Be Lumière." In *For Documentary: Twelve Essays*, 1–8. Berkeley: University of California Press, 1999. Republished by permission of University of California Press.

Matuszewski, Boleslas. "A New Source of History." *Film History* 7, no. 3 (Autumn 1995): 322–324. Translated by Laura U. Marks and Diane Koszarski. Originally published as "Une nouvelle source de l'histoire (création d'un dépôt cinématographie historique)," *Le Figaro*, March 25, 1898. Republished by permission of Indiana University Press.

Gunning, Tom. "Before Documentary: Early Nonfiction Films and the 'View' Aesthetic." In *Uncharted Territory: Essays on Early Nonfiction Films*, edited by Daan Hertogs and Nico de Klerk, 9–24. Amsterdam: Nederlands Filmmuseum, 1997. Republished by permission of the author.

[Curtis, Edward S., et al.]. "The Continental Film Company." 1912. In *Edward S. Curtis in the Land of the War Canoes: A Pioneer Cinematographer in the Pacific Northwest*, edited by Bill Holm and George Irving Quimby, 113–14. Seattle: University of Washington Press, 1980.

Bush, W. Stephen. 1914. Review of *In The Land of the Head Hunters*. *The Moving Picture World*. December 19.

Russell, Catherine. "Playing Primitive." In *Experimental Ethnography: The Work of Film in the Age of Video*, 98–115. Durham, NC: Duke Univeristy Press, 1999. Republished by permission of Duke Universty Press.

"Movies of Eskimo Life Win Much Appreciation." In *Robert Flaherty: Photographer/Filmmaker: The Inuit 1910–1922*, edited by Jo-Anne Birnie Danzker, 64. Vancouver: The Vancouver Art Gallery, 1979. Originally published in *The Globe* (Toronto), March 31, 1915.

The New York Times. 1922. Unsigned review of *Nanook of the North*. *The Screen*. June 12.

Grierson, John [The Moviegoer, pseud.]. 1926. "Flaherty's Poetic *Moana*." *New York Sun*, February 8.

Grierson, John. "Flaherty." In *Grierson on Documentary*, edited by Forsyth Hardy, 139–144. London: Faber and Faber, 1966. Originally published in two parts, in *Artwork* 7, no. 27 (Autumn 1931) and *Cinema Quarterly* 1, no. 1 (Autumn 1932). Republished by permission of Faber and Faber Ltd. and the John Grierson Archive, University of Stirling.

Naficy, Hamid. "Lured by the East: Ethnographic and Expedition Films about Nomadic Tribes; The Case of *Grass*." In *Virtual Voyages: Cinema and Travel*, edited by Jeffery Ruoff, 117–38. Durham, NC: Duke University Press, 2006. Republished by permission of Duke University Press.

Balázs, Béla. "Compulsive Cameramen." Translated by Russell Stockman. *October* 115 (Winter 2006): 51–52. Originally published in *Der Tag*, March 22, 1925. Republished by permission of Russell Stockman.

New York Tribune. 1916. "New Films Make War Seem More Personal." October 21.

Reeves, Nicholas. "Cinema, Spectatorship, and Propaganda: *Battle of the Somme* (1916) and Its Contemporary Audience." *Historical Journal of Film, Radio and Television* 17, no. 1 (1997): 5–28. Republished by permission of Taylor & Francis Ltd, on behalf of IAMHIST & Taylor & Francis.

Parker, Robert Allerton. "The Art of the Camera: An Experimental 'Movie.'" *Arts and Decoration* 15 (October 1921): 369, 414–15.

Kracauer, Siegfried. "Montage." In *From Caligari to Hitler: A Psychological History of the German Film* (Princeton, NJ: Princeton University Press, 1947), 181–88. Republished by permission of Princeton University Press.

Michelson, Annette. "*The Man with the Movie Camera*: From Magician to Epistemologist." *Artforum* (March 1972): 60–72. Republished by permission of *Artforum*.

Feldman, Seth. "Cinema Weekly and Cinema Truth: Dziga Vertov and the Leninist Proportion." *Sight and Sound* 43, no. 1 (Winter 1973–74): 34–37. Republished by permission of the British Film Institute.

Vertov, Dziga. "WE: Variant of a Manifesto." In *Kino-Eye: The Writings of Dziga Vertov*, edited by Annette Michelson and translated by Kevin O'Brien. Berkeley: University of California Press, 1984, 5–9. Originally published in *Kinofot* 1, 1922. Republished by permission of University of California Press.

Leyda, Jay. "Bridge." In *Films Beget Films: A Study of the Compilation Film*, 22–28. 1964. New York: Hill and Wang, 1971. Republished by permission of FSG Books and the estate of Jay Leyda.

Yampolsky, Mikhail. "Reality at Second Hand." Translated by Derek Spring. *Historical Journal of Film, Radio and Television* 11, no. 2 (1991): 161–72. Republished by permission of Taylor & Francis Ltd., on behalf of IAMHIST & Taylor & Francis.

Ivens, Joris. "The Making of *Rain*." In *The Camera and I*, 34–40. New York/Berlin: International Publishers/Seven Seas Books, 1969. Republished by permission of International Publishers.

Ivens, Joris. "Reflections on the Avant-Garde Documentary." Translated by Richard Abel. In *French Film Theory and Criticism: 1907–1939; Volume II: 1929–1939*, 78–80. Edited by Richard Abel. Princeton, NJ: Princeton University Press, 1988. Originally published as "Quelques réflections sur les documentaires d'avant-garde," *La revue des vivants* 10 (1931): 518–20. Republished by permission of Richard Abel and Princeton University Press.

Conley, Tom. "Documentary Surrealism: On *Land Without Bread*." *Dada/Surrealism* 15 (1986): 176–98. Republished by permission of Tom Conley.

Grierson, John. "The Documentary Producer." *Cinema Quarterly* 2, no. 1 (Autumn 1933): 7–9. Reprinted by permission of The Museum of Modern Art.

Grierson, John. "First Principles of Documentary." In *Grierson on Documentary*, 145–56. Edited by Forsyth Hardy. London: Faber and Faber, 1966. Originally published in three parts, in *Cinema Quarterly* 1, no. 2 (Winter 1932), 1, no. 3 (Spring 1933), and 2, no. 3 (Spring 1934). Republished by permission of Faber and Faber Ltd. and the John Grierson Archive, University of Stirling.

Ferguson, Otis. "Home Truths from Abroad." In *The Film Criticism of Otis Ferguson*, 206–08. Edited by Robert Wilson. Philadelphia: Temple University Press, 1971. Originally published in *The New Republic*, December 15, 1937.

Wolfe, Charles. "Straight Shots and Crooked Plots: Social Documentary and the Avant-Garde in the 1930s." Revised version. Originally published in *Lovers of Cinema: The First American Film Avant-Garde 1919–1945*, edited by Jan-Christopher Horak, 234–66. Madison: University of Wisconsin Press, 1995. Republished by permission of University of Wisconsin Press.

Brody, Samuel. "The Revolutionary Film: Problem of Form." *New Theatre*, February 1934.

Hurwitz, Leo T. "The Revolutionary Film—Next Step." *New Theatre*, May 1934.

Steiner, Ralph, and Leo T. Hurwitz. "A New Approach to Filmmaking." *New Theatre*, September 1935.

Van Dyke, Willard. Letter from Knoxville, Tennessee. Originally published in "Letters from *The River*," *Film Comment* 3, no. 2 (Spring 1965): 38–60. Republished by permission of *Film Comment*.

Steiner, Ralph. Letter to Jay Leyda, October 9, 1935. Leyda Papers. Tamiment Library, New York University. Republished by the permission of the estate of Jay Leyda.

McManus, John T. 1937. "Down to Earth in Spain." *The New York Times*, July 25. Republished by permission of *The New York Times*.

Wolfe, Charles. "Historicizing the 'Voice of God': The Place of Voice-Over Commentary in Classical Documentary." *Film History* 9, no. 2 (1997): 149–67. Republished by permission of Indiana University Press.

Neale, Steve. "*Triumph of the Will*: Notes on Documentary and Spectacle." *Screen* 20, no. 1 (Spring 1979): 63–86.

Griffith, Richard. "Films at the Fair." *Films* 1, no. 1 (November 1939): 61–75.

Agee, James. Review of Iwo Jima newsreels. Films. *The Nation*, March 24, 1945. Republished by permission of *The Nation*.

Agee, James. Review of *San Pietro*. Films. *The Nation*, May 26, 1945. Republished by permission of *The Nation*.

Cripps, Thomas, and David Culbert. "*The Negro Soldier* (1944): Film Propaganda in Black and White." *American Quarterly* 31, no. 5 (Winter 1979): 616–40. © 1979 Trustees of the University of Pennsylvania. Republished by permission of The Johns Hopkins University Press.

Bazin, André. "On *Why We Fight*: History, Documentation, and the Newsreel." In *Bazin at Work: Major Essays and Reviews from the Forties and Fifties*, edited by Bert Cardullo and translated by Alain Piette and Bert Cardullo, 187–92. New York and London: Routledge, 1997. First published in French in *Esprit* 14, no. 123 (June 1946). Republished by permission of Taylor & Francis Group, LLC.

Leach, Jim. "The Poetics of Propaganda: Humphrey Jennings and *Listen to Britain*." In *Documenting the Documentary: Close Readings of Documentary Film and Video*, edited by Barry Keith Grant and

Jeannette Sloniowski, 154–170. Detroit: Wayne State University Press, 1998. Republished by permission of Wayne State University Press.

Stoney, George C. "Documentary in the United States in the Immediate Post-World War II Years." Originally published as "Appendix. Documentary in the United States in the Immediate Post-World War II Years: A Supplement to Chapter 11," in Jack C. Ellis, *The Documentary Idea: A Critical History of English-Language Documentary Film and Video*, 302. Englewood Cliffs, NJ: Prentice Hall, 1989. Republished by permission of Pearson Education, Inc.

Druick, Zoë. "Documenting Citizenship: Reexamining the 1950s National Film Board Films about Citizenship." *Canadian Journal of Film Studies* 9, no. 1 (Spring 2000): 55–79. Republished by the permission of *Canadian Journal of Film Studies.*

Roy, Srirupa. "Moving Pictures: The Films Division of India and the Visual Practices of the Nation-State." In *Beyond Belief: India and the Politics of Postcolonial Nationalism*, 32–65. Durham, NC: Duke University Press, 2007. Republished by permission of Duke University Press.

Horne, Jennifer. "Experiments in Propaganda: Reintroducing James Blue's Colombian Trilogy." *The Moving Image* 9, no. 1 (Spring 2009): 183–200. Republished by permission of University of Minnesota Press.

Watkins, Peter, with James Blue and Michael Gill. "Peter Watkins Discusses His Suppressed Nuclear Film *The War Game.*" *Film Comment* 3, no. 4 (Fall 1965): 14–19. Republished by permission of *Film Comment.*

Painlevé, Jean. "The Castration of Documentary." In *Science Is Fiction: The Films of Jean Painlevé*, edited by Andy Masaki Bellows and Marina McDougall with Brigitte Berg, and translated by Jeanine Herman, 148–56. San Francisco: Brico Press, 2000. Originally published in French as "La Castration du documentaire," in *Cahiers du cinéma* 21 (March 1953). Republished with permission by Brico Press and Birgitte Berg.

Cocteau, Jean. "On *Blood of the Beasts.*" Translated by Tami Williams. Originally published in French in *Cahiers du Cinéma* 149 (November 1963).

Anderson, Lindsay. "Free Cinema." *Universities & Left Review* 1, no. 2 (Summer 1957): 51–52. Republished by permission of the Lindsay Anderson Archive, University of Stirling.

Whiteside, Tom. "The One-Ton Pencil." *The New Yorker*, February 17, 1962. Republished by permission of *The New Yorker.*

Morin, Edgar. "Chronicle of a Film." Translated by Anny Ewing and Steven Feld. *Studies in Visual Communication* 11, no. 1 (Winter 1985): 4–29. Originally published in French in in *Chronique d'un été* (Paris: Interspectacles, Domaine Cinéma, 1962). Republished by permission of Edgar Morin.

Rosenbaum, Jonathan. "Radical Humanism and the Coexistence of Film and Poetry in *The House is Black.*" *Goodbye Cinema, Hello Cinephilia: Film Culture in Transition*, 260–65. Chicago: University of Chicago Press, 2010. Republished by permission of The University of Chicago Press.

Rouch, Jean, with Dan Georgakas, Udayan Gupta, and Judy Janda. "The Politics of Visual Anthropology." In *Ciné-Ethnography: Jean Rouch*, edited by and translated by Steven Feld, 210–25. Minneapolis: University of Minnesota Press, 2003. Originally published in *Cineaste* 8, no. 4 (1978). Republished by permission of *Cineaste.*

Leacock, Ricky. "For an Uncontrolled Cinema." *Film Culture* 22/23 (Summer 1961): 23–25.

Elder, Bruce. "On the Candid-Eye Movement." In *Canadian Film Reader*, edited by Seth Feldman and Joyce Nelson, 86–93. Toronto: Peter Martin Associates, 1977.

Mekas, Jonas. "To Mayor Lindsay/On Film Journalism and Newsreels." In *Movie Journal: The Rise of a New American Cinema, 1959–1971*, 235–36. New York: Macmillan, 1972. Originally published as "To Mayor Lindsay/On Film Journalism and Newreels," Movie Journal, *The Village Voice*, April 21, 1966.

Hall, Jeanne. "Realism as a Style in Cinema Verite: A Critical Analysis of *Primary.*" *Cinema Journal* 30, no. 4 (Summer 1991): 24–50. Republished by permission of University of Texas Press.

Mead, Margaret. "As Significant as the Invention of Drama or the Novel." *TV Guide*, January 6, 1973.

Stam, Robert. "*Hour of the Furnaces* and the Two Avant Gardes." *Millennium Film Journal* 7/8/9 (Fall–Winter 1980–1981): 151–64. Republished by permission of Robert Stam.

Fraga, Jorge, Estrella Pantin, and Julio Garcia Espinosa. "Toward a Definition of the Didactic Documentary: A Paper Presented to the First National Congress of Education and Culture." *Latin American Filmmakers and the Third Cinema*, edited by and translated by Zuzana Pick, 199–207. Ottawa: Carleton University Press, 1978. Republished by permission of Zuzana Pick.

Fruchter, Norm, Marilyn Buck, Karen Ross, and Robert Kramer. "Newsreel." *Film Quarterly* 21, no. 2 (Winter 1968–1969): 43–48. Republished by permission of University of California Press.

Wiseman, Frederick, with Alan Westin. "'You Start Off With a Bromide': Conversation with Film Maker Frederick Wiseman," in *The Civil Liberties Review* 1, no. 2 (Winter–Spring 1974): 56–67. Republished by the permission of the ACLU.

MacDougall, David. "Beyond Observational Cinema." In *Transcultural Cinema*, edited by Lucien Taylor, 125–39. Princeton: Princeton University Press, 1998. 125–39. Revised and expanded from original publication in *Principles of Visual Anthropology*, edited by Paul Hockings (The Hague: Mouton De Gruyter, 1975). Republished by permission of De Gruyter.

Kael, Pauline. "Beyond Pirandello." The Current Cinema. *The New Yorker*, December 19, 1970. Republished by permission of Curtis Brown, Ltd. on behalf of the estate of Pauline Kael.

Bowser, Pearl. "Pioneers of Black Documentary Film." In *Struggles for Representation: African American Documentary Film and Video*, edited by Phyllis R. Klotman and Janet K. Cutler, 1–33. Bloomington: Indiana University Press, 1999. Republished by permission of Indiana University Press.

Chanan, Michael. "Rediscovering Documentary: Cultural Context and Intentionality." In *The Social Documentary in Latin America*, edited by Julianne Burton, 31–47. Pittsburgh: University of Pittsburgh Press, 1990. Republished by permission of University of Pittsburgh Press.

Alvarez, Santiago, with *Cineaste* editors. "'5 Frames Are 5 Frames, Not 6, But 5': An Interview with Santiago Alvarez." *Cineaste* 6, no. 4 (Spring 1975): 16–21. Republished by permission of *Cineaste*.

Nornes, Abé Mark. "The Postwar Documentary Trace: Groping in the Dark." Revised version. Originally published in *Positions* 10, no. 1 (Spring 2002): 39–77. Republished by permission of Duke University Press.

de Antonio, Emile, with Tanya Neufeld. "An Interview with Emile de Antonio." In *Emile de Antonio: A Reader*, edited by Douglas Kellner and Dan Streible, 102–12. Minneapolis: University of Minnesota Press, 2000. Originally published in *Artforum* 11, no. 7 (March 1973). Republished by permission of *Artforum*.

Michelson, Annette. "Reply to de Antonio." *Artforum* 11, no. 7 (March 1973): 83. Republished by permission of *Artforum*.

Nichols, Bill. "The Voice of Documentary." *Film Quarterly* 36, no. 3 (Spring 1983): 17–30. Republished by permission of University of California Press.

MacBean, James Roy. "*Two Laws* from Australia, One White, One Black: The Recent Past and the Challenging Future of Ethnographic Film." *Film Quarterly* 36, no. 3 (Winter 1983): 30–43. Reprinted by permission of University of California Press.

Atwell, Lee. Review of *Word is Out*. Originally published as review of *Word is Out* and *Gay U.S.A.*, in *Film Quarterly* 32, no. 2 (Winter 1978–79): 50–57. Reprinted by permission of University of California Press.

Lesage, Julia. "The Political Aesthetics of the Feminist Documentary Film." *Quarterly Review of Film Studies* 3, no. 4 (Fall 1978): 507–23. Republished by permission of Taylor and Francis Group, LLC.

Kaplan, E. Ann. "Theories and Strategies of the Feminist Documentary." *Millennium Film Journal* 12 (Fall-Winter 1982–1983): 44–67. Republished by permission of Elizabeth Kaplan.

Godmilow, Jill. "Paying Dues: A Personal Experience with Theatrical Distribution." Revised version. Originally published in *16mm Distribution*. Compiled by Judith Trojan and Nadine Covert, 91–95. New York: Educational Film Library Association, 1977. Republished by permission of Jill Godmilow.

Fusco, Coco. "A Black Avant-Garde? Notes on Black Audio Film Collective and Sankofa." In *Young, British, and Black: The Work of Sankofa and Black Audio Film Collective*, 7–22. Buffalo: Hallwalls/Contemporary Arts Center, 1988. Republished by permission of Coco Fusco.

Greyson, John. "Strategic Compromises: AIDS and Alternative Video Practices." In *Reimaging America: The Arts of Social Change*, edited by Mark O'Brien and Craig Little, 60–74. Philadelphia: New Society Publishers, 1990. Republished by permission of John Greyson.

Sklar, Robert. "Documentary: Artifice in the Service of Truth." *Reviews in American History* 3, no. 3 (September 1975): 299–304. Republished by permission of The Johns Hopkins University Press.

Strand, Chick. "Notes on Ethnographic Film by a Film Artist." *Wide Angle* 2, no. 3 (Spring 1978): 44–51. Republished by permission of *Wide Angle*.

Mekas, Jonas. "The Diary Film (A Lecture on *Reminiscences of a Journey to Lithuania*)." In *The Avant-Garde Film: A Reader of Theory and Criticism*, edited by P. Adams Sitney, 190–98. New York: NYU Press, 1978. Republished by permission of P. Adams Sitney.

Renov, Michael. "Toward a Poetics of Documentary." In *Theorizing Documentary*, edited by Michael Renov, 12–36. New York: Routledge, 1993. Republished by permission of Taylor and Francis Group, LLC.

Trinh T. Minh-ha. "Mechanical Eye, Electronic Ear and the Lure of Authenticity." *Wide Angle* 6, no. 2 (Summer 1984): 58–63. Republished by permission of *Wide Angle*.

Winston, Brian. "The Tradition of the Victim in Griersonian Documentary." Revised version. Originally published in *Image Ethics: The Moral Rights of Subjects in Photographs, Film, and Television*, edited by Larry Gross, John Stuart Katz, and Jay Ruby, 34–57. New York: Oxford University Press, 1988.

Hoberman, J. "*Shoah*: The Being of Nothingness." In *Vulgar Modernism: Writing on Movies and Other Media*, 218–222. Philadelphia: Temple University Press, 1991. Republished by permission of J. Hoberman.

Lanzmann, Claude, with Marc Chevrie and Hervé Le Roux. "Site and Speech: An Interview with Claude Lanzmann about *Shoah*." In *Claude Lanzmann's* Shoah: *Key Essays*, edited and translated by Stuart Liebman, 37–49. New York: Oxford University Press, 2007. Originally published as "Le lieu et la parole: Entretien avec Claude Lanzmann réalisé par Marc Chevrie et Hervé Le Roux," in *Cahiers du cinéma* 374 (July–August 1985).

Williams, Linda. "Mirrors without Memories: Truth, History, and the New Documentary." *Film Quarterly* 46, no. 3 (Spring 1993): 9–21. Republished by permission of University of California Press.

Morris, Errol, with Peter Bates. "Truth Not Guaranteed: An Interview with Errol Morris." *Cineaste* 17, no. 1 (1989): 16–17. Republished by permission of *Cineaste*.

Moore, Michael, with Harlan Jacobson. "Michael & Me." *Film Comment* 25, no. 6 (Nov–Dec 1989): 16–26. Republished by permission of Harlan Jacobson.

Waugh, Thomas. "'Acting to Play Oneself': Notes on Performance in Documentary." In *Making Visible the Invisible: An Anthology of Original Essays on Film Acting*, edited by Carole Zucker, 64–91. Metuchen, NJ: The Scarecrow Press, 1990. Republished by permission of The Scarecrow Press.

Harper, Phillip Brian. "Marlon Riggs: The Subjective Position of Documentary Video." *Art Journal* 54, no. 4 (Winter 1995): 69–72. Republished by permission of Phillip Brian Harper.

Rabinowitz, Paula. "Melodrama/Male Drama: The Sentimental Contract of American Labor Films." In *Black & White & Noir: America's Pulp Modernism*, 121–141. New York: Columbia University Press, 2002. Republished by permission of Columbia University Press.

Orgeron, Marsha, and Devin Orgeron. "Familial Pursuits, Editorial Acts: Documentaries after the Age of Home Video." *The Velvet Light Trap* 60 (Fall 2007): 47–62. Republished by permission of University of Texas Press.

Sobchack, Vivian. "Inscribing Ethical Space: 10 Propositions on Death, Representation, and Documentary." *Quarterly Review of Film Studies* 9, no. 4 (Fall 1984): 283–300. Republished by permission of Taylor and Francis Group, LLC.

Arthur, Paul. "Jargons of Authenticity (Three American Moments)." In *Theorizing Documentary*, edited by Michael Renov, 108–34. New York: Routledge, 1993. Republished by permission of Taylor and Francis Group, LLC.

Farocki, Harun, and Jill Godmilow, with Jennifer Horne and Jonathan Kahana. "A Perfect Replica: An Interview with Harun Farocki and Jill Godmilow." Translated by Anne Bilek. *Afterimage* 26, no. 3 (November–December 1998): 12–14. Republished by permission of *Afterimage*.

Gabara, Rachel. "Mixing Impossible Genres: David Achkar and African Autobiographical Documentary." Revised version. Originally published in *New Literary History* 34, no. 2 (Spring 2003): 331–52. Republished by permission of The Johns Hopkins University Press.

Teno, Jean-Marie. "Writing on Walls: The Future of African Documentary Cinema." In *Through African Eyes: Conversations with the Directors, Vol. 2*, edited by Mahen Bonetti and Morgan Seag, 89–92. New York: African Film Festival, 2011.

Berry, Chris. "Getting Real: Chinese Documentary, Chinese Postsocialism." In *The Urban Generation: Chinese Cinema and Society at the Turn of the Twenty-first Century*, 115–34. Durham, NC: Duke University Press, 2007. Republished by permission of Duke University Press.

Wu Wenguang. "DV: Individual Filmmaking." Translated by Cathryn Clayton. *Cinema Journal* 36, no. 1 (Fall 2006): 136–140. Republished by permission of University of Texas Press.

Porton, Richard. "Weapon of Mass Instruction: Michael Moore's *Fahrenheit 9/11*." *Cineaste* 29, no. 4 (Fall 2004): 3–7. Republished by permission of *Cineaste*.

MacDonald, Scott. "Up Close and Political: Three Short Ruminations on Ideology in the Nature Film." Revised version. Originally published in *Film Quarterly* 59, no. 3 (Spring 2006): 4–21. Republished by the permission of University of California Press.

Villarejo, Amy. "*Bus 174* and the Living Present." *Cinema Journal* 46, no. 1 (Fall 2006): 115–20. Republished by the permission of University of Texas Press.

Klinger, Barbara. "*Cave of Forgotten Dreams*: Meditations on 3D." *Film Quarterly* 65, no. 3 (Spring 2012): 38–43. Republished by permission of University of California Press.

INDEX

Printed in the USA
CPSIA information can be obtained
at www.ICGtesting.com
BVHW020720310723
668012BV00004B/11